A MATTER OF FACT

Editor-in-Chief

C. Edward Wall

Managing Editor

Mary K. Hashman

Associate Editor

Jennifer C. O'Haver

Assistant Editors

Marian E. Haggard
Stephanie J. Matthews
M. Kramer Stefl

Editorial Assistant

Malara P. Bragg

Cover Design

Heather Rae

Production

Annette Ferguson
Gloria A. Thompson

Acknowledgements

Special thanks are extended to
Congressman Sander Levin (D-Michigan) and
Eastern Michigan University Library
for providing access to U.S. Congressional hearings.

A MATTER OF FACT

Statements Containing Statistics on Current Social, Economic, and Political Issues

20

January–June 1994

Pierian Press
1994

ISBN 0-87650-333-4

The Pierian Press
P.O. Box 1808
Ann Arbor, MI 48106
(800) 678-2435
fax (313) 434-6409

INTRODUCTION

The full-text abstracts in *A Matter of Fact* encompass statistical statements related to current social, economic, political, health, and environmental public policy issues.

- Approximately 25 percent of the abstracts come from congressional hearings, where expert witnesses attempt to influence the perspectives of senators and representatives.

- Another 15 percent come from the *Congressional Record*, reflecting the statements of senators and representatives, which are constructed to influence colleagues or address the concerns of constituents back home.

- The remaining abstracts reflect the editorial content of sources designed to inform and influence the general public and/or special interest groups, who, in turn, elect public policy makers to support their values and objectives.

A Matter of Fact is designed for use on three levels:

- First, *A Matter of Fact* contains interesting information about the world and the human condition. Many people may benefit from browsing through the abstracts to gain a statistical perspective of the issues facing the United States and the world.

- Second, *A Matter of Fact* functions as a handy, current source of statistics and facts, much like an almanac. However, unlike an almanac or other statistical sources, *A Matter of Fact* presents the facts and statistics that have been selected by writers and speakers to influence others, in their own words. Writers of papers and speeches seeking brief, pertinent statements may wish to consult specific subject headings to find appropriate information (and arguments).

- Third, and most importantly, *A Matter of Fact*, as an abstracting service, helps users locate sources containing the information they seek. The substantive, full-text statistical abstracts indicate the kind of related information likely to be found in the sources from which the abstracts come. *A Matter of Fact* entries always cite the source from which an abstract is derived. Furthermore, if a statement included in a congressional hearing, periodical, or newspaper article is based on a book or recent study, the editors cite that book or study also. Thus, *A Matter of Fact* acts as a bibliography as well as a primary resource of facts. (Readers should note that, occasionally, the focus of a particular entry may not match the primary focus of its source article. This can be determined in most cases by comparing the title of the article to the content of the abstract.)

Content

This volume of *A Matter of Fact* provides abstracts from the *Congressional Record*, congressional hearings, and over 200 newspapers and periodicals published and/or received during 1994. The statistical abstracts contained in *A Matter of Fact* generally reflect topics and subjects of high current, public policy interest.

The content of *A Matter of Fact* is governed by public policy issues facing the federal government, as well as by news coverage and recent scholarship. The abstracts reflect the social, economic, political, health, and environmental issues of the day.

Arrangement

Entries are grouped under Library of Congress subject headings, which are alphabetized as follows: 1) headings with no punctuation, 2) headings with subtopics set off by hyphens, and 3) inverted headings with commas. For example:

Education
Education--Aims and Objectives
Education--Statistics
Education, Higher

Cross-References

Two types of cross-references are included in this volume. The first type includes cross-references to abstracts contained in this volume. The second type is a cross-reference to abstracts that appear in volume seventeen of *A Matter of Fact*. The latter cross-reference consists of the code "(v19)" following a subject heading. It is the policy of *A Matter of Fact* to provide cross-references to the most recent published volume.

Errors

The editors have encountered statistics and statements that may contain errors. Some abstracts contradict one another—for example, in volume one of *A Matter of Fact* conflicting dates were given for the construction of the first nuclear bomb and for the delivery dates of B-52 bombers. The editors have not resolved these discrepancies; however, the publication date of each article sometimes explains seemingly contradictory statements. The editors recognize that the content of *A Matter of Fact* is no more accurate than the sources cited.

Readers should use these statements with care and with critical skepticism, verifying facts and figures in alternative sources whenever possible (*A Matter of Fact* facilitates this cross-verification by frequently presenting two or more entries on the same subject from different sources) and checking the dates of sources to find which are the most current. Because the editors of *A Matter of Fact* abstract statements as they are presented in their original sources, *A Matter of Fact* both encourages and aids critical reading and critical thinking, skills we should develop and apply to all sources at all times. Statistical statements are, obviously, only as accurate as the methods used to compile the statistics and subsequently interpret them. (Readers will have recognized the problem, for example, when hearing news agencies of two warring nations both claiming victory in a particular battle.) The editors of *A Matter of Fact* recommend that readers consult the sources cited for each entry in order to establish the original context as well as the perspectives of the author(s) and publication.

Sources

The newspapers and journals monitored for this volume represent, for the most part, major sources generally available in libraries. When initial publications were selected for this service, consideration was given to the accessibility of those sources. Increasingly, less-accessible sources will be introduced to *A Matter of Fact*, with the recognition that the substantive abstracts can be used to gain perspectives of hard-to-locate sources, even when those sources can't be consulted directly. Nevertheless, the core of this publication—and one of its strengths—is the coverage of many sources that are readily available.

Abbreviations

The editors use standard abbreviations for countries. Acronyms and initialisms for government agencies and corporations are described in the entry when needed. The following abbreviations are used in the source citations:

Approp.	Appropriation(s)	Dir.	Director	Org.	Organization(s)
Assoc.	Association	GPO	Government Printing Office	Rep.	Representative
Dept.	Department			Sen.	Senator

A MATTER OF FACT

(please print or type)

SUBJECT HEADINGS____

ABSTRACT____

____

____

____

____

____

____

____

____

____

____

____

____

____

____

(page number)

____

Author(s)

____

Title of Article

____

Journal Title

____

Volume Number Issue Number Date

____

Page Number(s) Contributor's Name

Use this form to submit entries for possible inclusion in *A Matter of Fact*. Please send the original source document with this abstract, to: The Editors, *A Matter of Fact*, Box 1808, Ann Arbor, MI 48106. Please consult the introduction to this volume for further information on submitting entries.

How to Use *A Matter of Fact*

- **Quickly locate facts on current topics.**

See also this subject in volume 19 of *AMOF*

For example:

Subject

Cross-references

Facts

TOBACCO INDUSTRY--U.S. (v19)

see also ADVERTISING--TOBACCO INDUSTRY--U.S.

"Pension systems, retirement funds, and universities across the [U.S.]...have been profiting from tobacco stock for years. A 1990 study by divestment activists Dr. Gregory Connolly details some $21 billion worth of tobacco stock held by state pension funds, insurance companies, investment funds, banks, college endowments, and academic retirement funds as of December 1987. The state of Texas alone holds nearly $400 million in tobacco stock, including $250 million in its Teacher Retirement System. Connolly, head of the Massachusetts Office for Non-Smoking and Health, has also uncovered $7 billion worth of tobacco stock held by 37 state retirement funds. The California system contains some $500 million in tobacco investments--even though the state is considered a leader in anti-smoking initiatives." (p11-12)

Root, Jay. "The Fight to Switch." Southern Exposure v21 n3, Fall 1993. p11-14.(ISSN0146-809X).

- **Easily locate sources of further information.**

For example:

Sources

TRAFFIC CONGESTION--U.S. (v19)

"Americans lose 1.25 billion hours a year in traffic congestion. The Union of Concerned Scientists estimate that two billion gallons of gasoline are wasted each year in traffic tie-ups. Currently, congestion costs the American economy between $10 billion and $30 billion per year. This figure could reach $50 billion a year in 2005 when highway congestion will triple as forecasted by the General Accounting Office. Traffic congestion imposes direct costs upon individuals by increasing personal travel time and vehicle operating costs in terms of fuel and motor oil consumption. For example, the California Chamber of Commerce estimated that traffic delays and rough roads cost motorists $135 per year in lost time and another $97 in fuel and maintenance costs. The Texas Transportation Institute estimated the 1986 per capita cost of congestion (user cost and additional fuel cost) at $330 without the added cost of higher insurance premiums associated with more congestion-related accidents, and $440 per capita including the insurance adjustments." (p829-830)

Mellott, Paul C., Jr. (Executive V.P., H.B. Mellott Estate Inc.). U.S. House. Committee on Appropriations. "Department of Transportation and Related Agencies Approp. for 1994 (Part 7A)." Hearing, Washington, D.C.: GPO 1993. (ISBN0160411033). (Y4.Ap6/1:T68/4/994/pt.7A).

Periodicals Covered by *A Matter of Fact*, Volume Twenty

AARP Bulletin
1909 K St., N.W.
Washington, D.C. 20049

AARP Highlights
1909 K St., N.W.
Washington, D.C. 20049

ABA Journal
American Bar Association
750 N. Lake Shore Dr.
Chicago, IL 60611

ACLU News
1663 Mission St., 4th Fl.
San Francisco, CA 94103

AFL-CIO News
815 Sixteenth St., N.W.
Washington, D.C. 20006

APF Reporter
1001 Pennsylvania Ave., N.W., Ste. 1250
Washington, D.C. 20004

ASH Smoking and Health Review
Action on Smoking and Health (ASH)
2013 H St., N.W.
Washington, D.C. 20006

Abya Yala News: Journal of the South and Meso American Indian Information Center
SAIIC
P.O. Box 28703
Oakland, CA 94604

Access
American Forum for Global Education
120 Wall St., Ste. 2600
New York, NY 10005

Acres, U.S.A.
10008 E. 60th Terrace
Kansas City, MO 64133

Adolescence
Libra Publishers, Inc.
4901 Morena Blvd., Ste. 207
San Diego, CA 92117

Africa Recovery Briefing Paper
Africa Recovery Pamphlets
Africa Recovery Update
UN Africa Recovery
DPI Rm. S0931
United Nations
New York, NY 10017

Africa Today
Africa Today Associates
University of Denver
Graduate School of International Studies
Denver, CO 80208

African Farmer
1 Madison Ave.
New York, NY 10038

Agricultural Outlook
U.S. Dept. of Agriculture
1301 New York Ave., N.W.
Washington, D.C. 20005-4789

Agricultural Research
U.S. Dept. of Agriculture--Rm. 318-A
Federal Building
Hyattsville, MD 20782

Allied Industrial Worker
Allied Industrial Workers of America
AFL-CIO
P.O. Box 343913
Milwaukee, WI 53234

Alternative Agriculture News
Henry A. Wallace Institute for Alternative Agriculture
9200 Edmonston Rd.
Greenbelt, MD 20700

America
America Press, Inc.
106 West 56th St.
New York, NY 10019

American Demographics
108 N. Cayuga St.
Ithaca, NY 14850

American Educator
American Federation of Teachers
555 New Jersey Ave., N.W.
Washington, D.C. 20001

American Journal of Alternative Agriculture
Henry A. Wallace Institute for Alternative Agriculture
9200 Edmonston Rd.
Greenbelt, MD 20700

American Journal of Economics and Sociology
5 East 44th St.
New York, NY 10017

American Journal of Psychology
University of Illinois Press
54 E. Gregory Dr.
Champaign, IL 61820

American Rehabilitation
Mary E. Switzer Bldg., Rm. 3212
330 C St., S.W.
Washington, D.C. 20202

American Spectator
2020 N. 14th St., Ste. 750
Arlington, VA 22216

Amicus Journal
40 West 20 St.
New York, NY 10011

Anglican Digest
SPEAK
100 Skyline Dr.
Eureka Springs, AR 72632-9705

Animals
350 S. Huntington Ave.
Boston, MA 02130

Ann Arbor News
340 E. Huron
Ann Arbor, MI 48104

Appalachia
Appalachian Regional Commission
1666 Connecticut Ave., N.W.
Washington, D.C. 20235

Aramco World
Aramco Services Company
9009 West Loop South
Houston, TX 77096

Arctic
Arctic Institute of North America
MLT 11th Floor
University of Calgary
2500 University Dr., N.W.
Calgary, Alberta T2N IN4 Canada

Audubon Activist
Audubon Society
700 Broadway
New York, NY 10003

Barricada Internacional
Barricada USA-G
P.O. Box 410150
San Francisco, CA 94141

BioScience
American Institute of Biological Sciences
1401 Wilson Blvd.
Arlington, VA 22209

Blue Goose Flyer
10824 Fox Hunt Lane
Potomac, MD 20854-1553

Boston Review
Boston Critic, Inc.
33 Harrison Ave.
Boston, MA 02111

Bulletin of the American Society for Information Science
8720 Georgia Ave., Ste. 501
Silver Spring, MD 20910-3602

Business Week
McGraw-Hill Publications Co.
1221 Ave. of the Americas
New York, NY 10020

CEP Research Report
Council on Economic Priorities
30 Irving Place
New York, NY 10003

Carrying Capacity Network Clearinghouse Bulletin
Carrying Capacity Network
1325 G St., N.W., #1003
Washington, D.C. 20005

Catholic World
Paulist Press
997 Macarthur Blvd.
Mahwah, NJ 07430

Center Focus
3700 13th St., N.E.
Washington, D.C. 20017

Center for Rural Affairs Newsletter
P.O. Box 405
Walthill, NE 68067

Change
Heldref Publications
4000 Albemarle St., N.W.
Washington, D.C. 20016

Christian Century
Christian Century Foundation
407 S. Dearborn St.
Chicago, IL 60605

The Christian Science Monitor
Christian Science Publishing Society
One Norway St.
Boston, MA 02115

Clean-Water Action News
Clean Water Action
1320 18th St., N.W., #300
Washington, D.C. 20036

Clearing House
Heldref Publications
4000 Albemarle St., N.W.
Washington, D.C. 20016

Climate Alert
324 4th St., N.E.
Washington, D.C. 20016

Commentary
American Jewish Committee
165 East 56th St.
New York, NY 10022

Common Cause
2030 M St., N.W.
Washington, D.C. 20036

Communication Education
Speech Communication Association
5105 Backlick Rd.
Annandale, VA 22003

Community Mental Health Journal
Human Sciences Press, Inc.
233 Spring St.
New York, NY 10013-1578

Community Service Newsletter
P.O. Box 243
Yellow Springs, OH 45387

Congressional Budget Office
Second and D Streets, S.W.
Washington, D.C. 20515

Congressional Hearings from the following committees:

- Aging
- Agriculture
- Appropriations
- Armed Services
- Banking, Finance, and Urban Affairs
- Budget
- Children, Youth, and Families
- Commerce, Science, and Transportation
- Education and Labor
- Energy and Commerce
- Foreign Affairs
- Governmental Affairs
- Interior and Insular Affairs
- Judiciary
- Labor and Human Resources
- Public Works and Transportation
- Science and Technology
- Ways and Means

Congressional Quarterly Weekly Report
1414 22nd St., N.W.
Washington, D.C. 20037

Congressional Record
Government Printing Office
Washington, D.C. 20402

Contemporary Review
Contemporary Review Co., Ltd.
61 Carey St.
London WC2 2JG
England

Corporate Detroit
Business Journal Publishing Co.
26111 Evergreen Rd., Ste. 303
Southfield, MI 48076

Cuba Update
124 W. 23rd St.
New York, NY 10011

Cultural Survival Quarterly
53-A Church St.
Cambridge, MA 02138

Currents in Theology and Mission
Lutheran School of Theology
1100 East 55th St.
Chicago, IL 60615

Customs Today
U.S. Customs Service
Rm. 2146
Washington, D.C. 20229

Defense 94
American Forces Information Service
1735 N. Lynn St., Rm. 210
Arlington, VA 22209-2086

Defense Monitor
Center for Defense Information
1500 Massachusetts Ave., N.W.
Washington, D.C. 20005

Demography
Population Association of America
1429 Duke St.
Alexandria, VA 22314-3402

Detroit News and Free Press
615 W. Lafayette
Detroit, MI 48231

Dimensions: A Journal of Holocaust Studies
823 UN Plaza
New York, NY 10017

Dispute Resolution Journal
American Arbitration Association
140 W. 51 St.
New York, NY 10020

Dollars & Sense
Economic Affairs Bureau, Inc.
38 Union Square, Rm. 14
Somerville, MA 02143

E Magazine
P.O. Box 6667
Syracuse, NY 13217

EDF Letter
257 Park Ave. S.
New York, NY 10010

Earth First!
P.O. Box 5176
Missoula, MT 59806

Earth Island Journal
300 Broadway #28
San Francisco, CA 94133

Earth News
P.O. Box 1620
Agoura Hills, CA 91376

Economic Newsletter
Comerica
Renaissance Center
Detroit, MI 48243

Economics and Business Education
1a Keymer Rd.
Hassocks
West Sussex BN6 8AD
England

Economist
Economist Newspaper Ltd.
25 St. James's St.
London SW1A 1HG
England

Engineer
U.S. Army Engineer School
Fort Leonard Wood, MO 65473-6650

Engineer Update
CEPA-C
Washington, D.C. 20314-1000

Environment Action Magazine
6930 Carroll Ave., #600
Tacoma Park, MD 20912

Environmental Forum
Environmental Law Institute
1616 P St., N.W.
Washington, D.C. 20036

Europe
Delegation of the Commission of the European Communities
2100 M St., N.W., Ste. 707
Washington, D.C. 20037

EXTRA!
130 W. 25th St., 8th Fl.
New York, NY 10001

FAIR Immigration Report
Federation for American Immigration Reform
1424 16th St., N.W., Rm. 701
Washington, D.C. 20036

Families in Society
11700 W. Lake Park Dr.
Milwaukee, WI 53224

Family Day Care Bulletin
725 15th St., N.W.
Washington, D.C. 20005

Federal Election Commission Record
Federal Election Commission
999 E Street, N.W.
Washington, D.C. 20463

Federal Probation
Probation Division
Administrative Office of the U.S. Courts
Washington, D.C. 20544

Foodlines
1875 Connecticut Ave., N.W.
Washington, D.C. 20009

FoodReview
Rm. 228 USDA
1301 New York Ave., N.W.
Washington, D.C. 20005-4789

Ford Foundation Report
Ford Foundation
320 East 43rd St.
New York, NY 10017

Foreign Policy
Carnegie Endowment for International Peace
2400 N St., N.W.
Washington, D.C. 20037-1153

Foremanship
Dartnell Corp.
4660 Ravenswood Ave.
Chicago, IL 60640

Free Inquiry
P.O. Box 5
Buffalo, NY 14215-0005

Freedom Today
35 Westminster Bridge Rd.
London SE1 7JB
England

Frontier
Share Out Strength (SOS)
1511 K St., N.W., Ste. 940
Washington, D.C. 20005

The Furrow
P.O. Box 663
Moline, IL 61265-0663

geneWATCH
19 Garden St.
Cambridge, MA 02138

Government Union Review
Public Services Research Foundation
1761 Business Center Dr., Ste. 230
Reston, VA 22090-5333

Groundwater Newsletter
6800 Jericho Tpke.
Syosset, NY 11791

Guild Practitioner
P.O. Box 673
Berkeley, CA 94701

Harper's
Harper's Magazine Company
2 Park Ave.
New York, NY 10016

Health Advocate
2639 S. LaCienega Blvd.
Los Angeles, CA 90034

Health Letter
Public Citizen Health Research Group
2000 P St., N.W.
Washington, D.C. 20036

Healthline
830 Menlo Ave., Ste. 100
Menlo Park, CA 94025

High Country News
P.O. Box 1090
Paonia, CO 81428

Human Quest
Churchman Co.
1074-23rd Ave., N.
St. Petersburg, FL 33704

Humanist
American Humanist Association
7 Harwood Dr., P.O. Box 1188
Amherst, NY 14226-7188

Hydrogen Today
219 S. Siesta Lane, #101
Tempe, AZ 85281

IBF News
4887 Columbia Dr., S.
Seattle, WA 98108-1919

IDB
Inter-American Development Bank
1300 New York Ave., N.W.
Washington, D.C. 20577

IPM Practitioner
P.O. Box 7414
Berkeley, CA 94707

Imprint
National Student Nurses' Association, Inc.
555 W. 57th St.
New York, NY 10019

Inner Voice
P.O. Box 11615
Eugene, OK 97440

Insight
3600 New York Ave., N.E.
Washington, D.C. 20002

Intergovernmental Perspective
U.S. Advisory Commission on Intergovernmental Relations
Washington, D.C. 20575

International Environmental Affairs
17 1/2 Lebanon
Hanover, NH 03755

International Labour Review
ILO Publications
International Labour Office
CH-1211 Geneva 22
Switzerland

International Permaculture Solutions Journal
7781 Lenox St.
Jacksonville, FL 32221

Journal of Agricultural Economics Research
U.S. Dept. of Agriculture
1301 New York Avenue, N.W.
Washington, D.C. 20005-4789

Journal of Business and Psychology
Human Sciences Press, Inc.
233 Spring St.
New York, NY 10013-1578

Journal of Education for Business
Heldref Publications
4000 Albemarle St., N.W.
Washington, D.C. 20016

Journal of Health Politics, Policy and Law
Duke University Press
401 N. Buchanan Blvd.
Box 90660
College Station
Durham, NC 27708-0660

Journal of Pesticide Reform
P.O. Box 1393
Eugene, OR 97440

Journal of Political Economy
University of Chicago Press
5720 S. Woodlawn Ave.
Chicago, IL 60637

Journal of Soil and Water Conservation
Soil and Water Conservation Society
7515 N.E. Ankeny Rd.
Ankeny, IA 50021-9764

Journal of Third World Studies
P.O. Box 1232
Americus, GA 31709

Journal of Travel Research
Business Research Division
University of Colorado
Boulder, CO 80309-0420

Journal of the U.S. Army Medical Department
Commander, Hq., 7th Medical Command
APO NY 09102-3304

Kerr Center for Sustainable Agriculture Newsletter
P.O. Box 588, Hwy 271S
Poteau, OK 74953-0588

Lamp
Exxon Corporation
P.O. Box 101
Florham Park, NJ 07932

Land Report
2440 E. Water Well Rd.
Salina, KS 67401

Land Stewardship Newsletter
The Land Stewardship Project
14758 Ostlund Trail North
Marine, MN 55047

Lies of Our Times
145 W. 4th St.
New York, NY 10012

Look Japan
Look Japan Ltd.
2-2 Kanda-Ogawamachi
Chiyoda-ku, Tokyo 101
Japan

Maritime Newsletter
Room 510
815 16th Street, N.W.
Washington, D.C. 20006

Middle East Policy
Middle East Policy Council
1730 M St., N.W., Ste. 512
Washington, D.C. 20036

Mother Jones
Foundation for National Progress
1663 Mission St., 2nd Floor
San Francisco, CA 94103

NASSP Bulletin
National Association of Secondary School Principals
1904 Association Dr.
Reston, VA 22091

NATO Review
Atlantic Council of the United States
1616 H St., N.W.
Washington, D.C. 20006

NSTA Reports!
National Science Teachers
Association
1742 Connecticut Ave., N.W.
Washington, D.C. 20009

National Forum
Honor Society of Phi Kappa Phi
P.O. Box 16000
Louisiana State University
Baton Rouge, LA 70893

National Prison Project Journal
ACLU Foundation
1875 Connecticut Ave., N.W., #410
Washington, D.C. 20009

National Research Council News
Office of News and Public
Information
2101 Constitution Ave., N.W.
Washington, D.C. 20418

National Review
National Review, Inc.
150 East 35th St.
New York, NY 10016

Naval Aviation News
Building 159E, Rm. 512
Washington Navy Yard Annex
Washington, D.C. 20374-1595

Neighborhood Works
2125 W. North Ave.
Chicago, IL 60647

Network Connection
806 Rhode Island Ave., N.E.
Washington, D.C. 20018

Networker
Alliance for the Wild Rockies
P.O. Box 8731
Missoula, MT 59807

New Directions for Women
New Directions for Women, Inc.
108 West Palisade Ave.
Englewood, NJ 07631

New Leader
American Labor Conference on
International Affairs, Inc.
275 Seventh Ave.
New York, NY 10001

New Left Review
6 Meard St.
London, England W1V 3HR

New Outlook
Hashkafah Hadashah
Tel Aviv
Israel

New Patriot
202 S. State St., #1420
Chicago, IL 60604

New Republic
1220 19th St., N.W.
Washington, D.C. 20036

New York Review of Books
250 West 57th St.
New York, NY 10107

NewsNotes
Maryknoll Fathers and Brothers
Justice and Peace Office
P.O. Box 29132
Washington, D.C. 20017

Newsweek
Newsweek, Inc.
444 Madison Ave.
New York, NY 10022

Nonviolent Activist
War Registers League
339 Lafayette St.
New York, NY 10012

Northwest Conservation
c/o Greater Ecosystem Alliance
P.O. Box 2813
Belsingham, WA 98227

Nuclear Resister
P.O. Box 43383
Tucson, AZ 85733

Nucleus
Union of Concerned Scientists
26 Church St.
Cambridge, MA 02238

Observer
Catholic Diocese of Rockford
921 W. State St.
Rockford, IL 61102

Oil Progress
Caltex Petroleum Corporation
P.O. Box 619500
Dallas, TX 75261-9500

Outdoor America
Izaak Walton League of America
1401 Wilson Blvd.
Arlington, VA 22209-2318

Pacific Affairs
University of British Columbia
Vancouver, B.C. V6T 1W5
Canada

Panoscope (PS)
1717 Massachusetts Ave., N.W.,
#301
Washington, D.C. 20036-2001

People's Medical Society Newsletter
People's Medical Society, Inc.
462 Walnut St.
Allentown, PA 18102

People's Tribune
P.O. Box 3524
Chicago, IL 60654

Perspectives in Health Promotion
and Aging
National Eldercare Institute on
Health Promotion
AARP
601 E St., N.W., 5th floor-B
Washington, D.C. 20049

Photovoltaic Insider's Report
1011 W. Colorado Blvd.
Dallas, TX 75208

Planning
American Planning Association
1313 E. 60th St.
Chicago, IL 60637

Population and Development Review
Population Council
One Dag Hammarskjold Plaza
New York, NY 10017

Population Bulletin
Population Reference Bureau
1875 Connecticut Ave., N.W., #520
Washington, D.C. 20009

Population Today
Population Reference Bureau
1875 Connecticut Ave., N.W., #520
Washington, D.C. 20009

Positive Alternatives
Center for Economic Conversion
222 View St., Ste. C
Mountain View, CA 94041-1344

Prairie Journal
PrairieFire Rural Action
550 11th St.
Des Monies, IA 50309

Proceedings
U.S. Naval Institute
2062 Generals Highway
Annapolis, MD 21401

Program & Legislative Action Bulletin
Women's International League for Peace and Freedom (WILPF)
U.S. Section Office
1213 Race St.
Philadelphia, PA 19107-1691

Progressive Review
1739 Connecticut Ave., N.W.
Washington, D.C. 20009

ProLife News
Alliance for Life Canada
B1-90 Garry St.
Winnipeg, Manitoba R3C 4H1
Canada

Propaganda Review
Media Alliance
Bldg. D, Fort Mason Ctr.
San Francisco, CA 94123

Protecting Children
American Humane Association
63 Inverness Dr., East
Englewood, CO 80112-5117

Public Power
American Public Power Association
2301 M St., N.W.
Washington, D.C. 20037

Quadrant
Quadrant Magazine Co. Ltd.
115 Clarence St.
Sydney 2000
Australia

Quarterly Journal of Speech
Speech Communication Association
5105 Backlick Rd.
Annandale, VA 22003

Rain
P.O. Box 30097
Eugene, OR 97403-1097

Raise the Stakes
Planet Drum Foundation
P.O. Box 31251
San Francisco, CA 94131

Reading Today
International Reading Association, Inc.
800 Barksdale Rd.
P.O. Box 8139
Newark, DE 19714-8139

Reason
Reason Foundation
3415 Sepulveda Blvd., Ste. 400
Los Angeles, CA 90034

Responsive Philanthropy
National Committee for Responsive Philanthropy
2001 S St., N.W., Ste. 620
Washington, D.C. 20009

Review for Religious
Missouri Province Educational Institute
3601 Lindell Blvd.
St. Louis, MO 63108

Rocky Mountain Institute Newsletter
Rocky Mountain Institute
1739 Snowmass Creek Rd.
Old Snowmass, CO 81654-9199

Rollin' Times
Michigan Paralyzed Veterans of America
30406 Ford Rd.
Garden City, MI 48135-1899

Science and Public Policy
Beech Tree Publishing
10 Watford Close
Guildford, Surrey GU1 2EP
England

Shelter Sense
Humane Society of the US
2100 L St., N.W.
Washington, D.C. 20037

Sierra
Sierra Club
730 Polk St.
San Francisco, CA 94109

Skeptical Inquirer
Committee for the Scientific Investigation of Claims of the Paranormal
3025 Palo Alto Dr., N.E.
Albuquerque, NM 87111

Social Forces
05 Manning Hall
University of North Carolina
Chapel Hill, NC 27599-3355

Social Justice Review
3835 Westminster Pl.
St. Louis, MO 63108

Solar Industry Journal
777 N. Capitol St., N.E., #805
Washington, D.C. 20002

Solar Today
United States Section of the International Solar Energy Society
2400 Central Ave., #G-1
Boulder, CO 80301

Southern Exposure
Institute for Southern Studies
P.O. Box 531
Durham, NC 27702

Statistical Bulletin
Metropolitan Life Insurance Company
428 E. Preston St.
Baltimore, MD 21202

Student Press Law Center Report
Student Press Law Center
1735 Eye St., N.W., Ste. 504
Washington, D.C. 20006

Studies in Conflict and Terrorism
Taylor & Francis Ltd.
4 John St.
London WC1N 2ET
England

Studies in Family Planning
Population Council
One Dag Hammarskjold Plaza
New York, NY 10017

Surviving Together
Institute for Soviet American Relations
1601 Connecticut Ave., N.W., #301
Washington, D.C. 20009

Tennessee Farm and Home Science
University of Tennessee Agricultural Experiment Station
P.O. Box 1071
Knoxville, TN 37901-1071

Tobacco Alert
World Health Organization
1211 Geneva 27
Switzerland

Tobacco-Free Youth Reporter
STAT--Stop Teenage Addiction to Tobacco
121 Lyman St., Ste. 210
Springfield, MA 01103

Toward Freedom
Toward Freedom, Inc.
209 College St.
Burlington, VT 05401

Transition
Oxford University Press
200 Madison Ave.
New York, NY 10016

Turning the Tide
P.O. Box 1990
Burbank, CA 91507

UN Chronicle
United Nations
Rm. DC1-530
New York, NY 10017

U.S. Dept. of Agriculture Publications
Economic Research Service
1301 New York Ave., N.W.
Washington, D.C. 20005-4789

U.S. News & World Report
2400 N Street, N.W.
Washington, D.C. 20037-1196

Union Democracy Review
Association for Union Democracy
500 State St.
Brooklyn, NY 11217

United States Institute of Peace Journal
United States Institute of Peace
1550 M St., N.W., Ste. 700
Washington, D.C. 20005-1708

University of Michigan News and Information Services
412 Maynard
Ann Arbor, MI 48109-1399

Urban Review
Human Sciences Press
233 Spring St.
New York, NY 10013-1578

Veterans for Peace Journal
P.O. Box 3881
Portland, ME 04104

Vital Signs
International Physicians for the Prevention of Nuclear War
126 Rigers St.
Cambridge, MA 02142-1096

WHO Press, WHO Features
World Health Organization
Office of Information
1211 Geneva 27
Switzerland

Wastelines
Environmental Action Foundation
6930 Carroll Ave., #600
Tacoma Park, MD 20912

Wild Earth
Cenozoic Society, Inc.
P.O. Box 492
Canton, NY 13617

Wilderness
The Wilderness Society
900 17th St., N.W.
Washington, D.C. 20006-2596

Wildlife Conservation
Wilderness Conservation Park/ Bronx Zoo
Bronx, NY 10460

Window on the World
Unitarian Universalist, UN Office
777 UN Plaza, #7D
New York, NY 10017

Women and Recovery
Need to Know Press
P.O. Box 161775
Cupertino, CA 95016

WorldAIDS
The Panos Institute
9 White Lion St.
London, England N1 9PD

World Federalist News
c/o WFM, U.N. Office
777 UN Plaza, 12th Fl.
New York, NY 10017

World Health
World Health Organization
Avenue Appia
1211 Geneva 27
Switzerland

World of Work
Bureau of Public Information
International Labor Organization
1828 L St., N.W., Ste. 801
Washington, D.C. 20036

World Watch
Worldwatch Institute
1776 Massachusetts Ave., N.W.
Washington, D.C. 20036

ABANDONED CHILDREN--U.S. (v19)

ABDUCTION--U.S.--CHILDREN

"The most recent Department of Justice national annual estimates taken in 1988 [in the U.S.] indicate that there were 114,600 attempted abductions of children by nonfamily members, 450,700 runaways, and 438,200 children who were lost, injured or otherwise missing. These statistics do not paint the whole picture of child victimization since they do not scratch the surface of child abuse and molestation. An FBI Law Enforcement Bulletin reports that 'like rape, child molestation is one of the most underreported crimes, only one to ten percent are ever disclosed.'" (pS1751)

DeConcini, Dennis (Sen.-Ariz.). "Child Safety Educational Programs," Congressional Record (23 Feb 1994). Daily ed. pS1751-1752. (ISSN0363-7239).

ABIDJAN (COTE D'IVOIRE)

see HIV INFECTIONS--ABIDJAN (COTE D'IVOIRE)

ABORTION--BELGIUM (v19)

ABORTION--CANADA (v19)

"In 1969, only one in 50 pregnancies in Canada ended in abortion. But that year the federal government effectively ended the criminal prohibition against it. Then Dr. Henry Morgentaler opened the first of his chain of free-standing abortion clinics. And in 1988 the Supreme Court struck down Canada's abortion law altogether. The result was inevitable. According to a Statistics Canada report released two weeks ago, Canadian women had nearly 1.5 million abortions between 1970 and 1991, and the country's abortion rate had risen to one for every four live births, the highest in Canada's history." (p5)

McGovern, Celeste. "The Abortion Business Boom." ProLife News v18 n7, Aug 1993. p5.

"There were 95,059 abortions performed on Canadian women (in 1991), almost nine times the 11,152 recorded in 1970. The average Canadian woman seeking an abortion in 1991 was single, 23 years old, had never been pregnant before and was 10 weeks pregnant at the time of her abortion, Statscan reported. Canada's abortion clinics have benefitted most from the abortion boom. In 1989 they performed only 7,059, less than 10% of the national total. That tripled in 1990 to 20,236. And it rose another 15% in 1991 to 23,343, almost a quarter of all performed." (p5)

McGovern, Celeste. "The Abortion Business Boom." ProLife News v18 n7, Aug 1993. p5.

According to Statistics Canada, in 1991 "95,059 Canadian children...died by abortion. Abortion is by far our major cause of death. More than twice as many Canadians die by abortion than from our next biggest killer cardiovascular disease-- strokes and heart attacks. Since the floodgates were opened 25 years ago this August, the total score for the abortionists is a million and a half missing Canadians; more than the populations of Manitoba and Prince Edward Island combined. In 1969 only one in 50 pregnancies in Canada ended in abortion; it is now one in five." (p3)

Lamont, Mary. "A Million and a Half Missing Children." ProLife News v19 n2, Feb 1994. p3,6.

ABORTION--CANADA--PUBLIC OPINION

"In its pro-abortion propaganda for the '93 federal election, CARAL [Canadian Abortion Rights Action League] kept repeating the same line, 'We know the Canadian population is 79% pro-choice.'...However, the latest Gallup Poll (August 2, 1993) shows that 66% of Canadians oppose abortion on demand (3% are undecided). This poll found that 10% of Canadians oppose abortion under any circumstances. Most Canadians would allow abortion if it were the only way to save the mother's life or if the pregnancy were caused by rape or incest. A majority would also accept aborting a baby with a serious defect." (p10)

Lamont, Mary. "Speaking of the Big-Lie Technique...." ProLife News v19 n1, Jan 1994. p10.

ABORTION--CHILE (v19)

ABORTION--CUBA (v19)

ABORTION--ESTONIA

"Both because it is legal and because generally it is not highly stigmatized by the population, abortion is very common in Estonia. In 1990, 1,107 abortions were performed per 1,000 live births. In comparison, in the United States in 1987, 289 abortions were performed per 1,000 live births (Henshaw 1991). In Estonia, few abortions are performed outside medical facilities. Although there are no plans to make abortion illegal, Estonian officials are concerned about the high level of abortion because of its high costs and its possible consequences, such as secondary female sterility. The crude abortion rate has declined in Estonia in recent years. In 1980 it was 96.7; in 1985, 91.4; in 1990, 77.0. Similarly, the abortion ratio (abortions per 1000 live births) declined from 1,628 in 1980, to 1,475 in 1985, to 1,107 in 1990 (USSR, Goskomstat 1990)." (p116-117)

Anderson, Barbara A./others. "The Validity of Survey Responses on Abortion: Evidence from Estonia." Demography v31 n1, Feb 1994. p115-132. (ISSN0070-3370).

ABORTION--GREAT BRITAIN

"The latest Gallup Poll taken in Britain (conducted in March 1993 and published in April) showed that 38% of British men favoured abortion on demand; only 24% of women did so. It is worth noting that a Gallup Poll taken five years ago (1988) found 29% of British men supporting abortion on demand and 26% of women. Mrs. Grace Kirkham, spokesperson for BRITISH VICTIMS OF ABORTION, a support group of aborted women, discussed this shift during the press conference held at the House of Commons to announce the Gallup Poll results. She said, 'Women are the ones who suffer the consequences of (abortion); so it is not surprising that increasingly they oppose abortion on demand, as they come to realize this.'" (p6)

"Men More Pro-Abortion than Women." ProLife News v19 n1, Jan 1994. p6.

ABORTION--HISPANIC AMERICANS

"Not only do we [Latinas] have abortions, but we have them at a higher rate than other ethnic groups. The abortion rate for Latinas is 42.6 per thousand, compared to 26.6 per thousand for non-Latinas. (See Henshaw, S. & Silverman, J., THE CHARACTERISTICS IN PRIOR CONTRACEPTIVE USE OF UNITED STATES ABORTION PATIENTS, 20 Fam. Planning Perspectives Journal, Jul-Aug 1988, at 158)." (p4)

Alvarez, Luz. "The Latina Reproductive Rights Movement." Guild Practitioner v50 n1, Win 1993. p4-8. (ISSN0017-5390).

ABORTION--LATIN AMERICA--MORTALITY (v19)

ABORTION--MORTALITY (v19)

ABORTION--PERU (v19)

ABORTION--ROMANIA (v19)

ABORTION--U.S. (v19)

"Of the 1.5 million abortions performed annually in the United States, only a few hundred are Medicaid-funded to save the life of the mother. The addition of rape and incest means 'we'll be talking, at most, 2,000 abortions a year,' says Roger Evans, legal counsel for the Planned Parenthood Federation of America." According to Kate Michelman, executive director of the National Abortion Rights Action League, "The law for Medicaid requires states to pay for all medically necessary procedures for the poor...until 1981, that included abortions. The so-called Hyde amendment of 1981 ruled out federal money for abortions, except to save a mother's life." (p7)

Feldmann, Linda. "National: Abortion Edict Fuels Concern."

The Christian Science Monitor v86 n24, 29 Dec 1993. p7. (ISSN0882-7729).

ABORTION--U.S.--PUBLIC OPINION (v19)

ABORTION--U.S.--YOUTH (v19)

ABORTION SERVICES--U.S.--CRIMES AGAINST (v19)

"From 1977 to March 1994, more than 1,587 acts of violence against reproductive health providers were reported in the United States, including 37 bombings, 87 arsons, 175 death threats, 91 assaults, 2 kidnapings, 345 clinic invasions, and 1 murder. From January 1992 to date, 79 chemical attacks were reported in 17 States as well, with damages totaling $560,000. And in a nationwide survey in 1993, 50 percent of the clinics responding reported...extreme violence--with 25 percent of those clinics having experienced physical invasions or chemical attacks in 1993 alone." (pH1501)

Morella, Constance A. (Rep.-Md.). "Providing for Consideration of S.636...and Motion to Substitute H.R.796," Congressional Record (17 Mar 1994). Daily ed. pH1498-1507. (ISSN0363-7239).

ABUSE OF ANIMALS

see ANIMAL WELFARE

ABUSE OF CHILDREN

see CHILD ABUSE

ABUSED AGED--U.S.

"Elder abuse is a very serious problem in the United States. It is estimated that up to ten percent of all elders (those over 65) suffer some form of abuse, making it almost as common a problem as child abuse. Elder abuse may also be a growing problem. By the year 2000, 13.1% of the population will be 65 years of age or older, with the oldest (those over 85) the fastest growing percentage of the population. These individuals are often the least able to care for themselves, and so most vulnerable to abuse." (p59)

Peirce, Ann Griswold. "Elder Abuse." Imprint v41 n2, Feb-Mar 1994. p59-60. (ISSN0019-3038).

ABUSED CHILDREN--U.S. (v19)

ABUSED WOMEN--U.S. (v19)

"Helton et al interviewed 290 pregnant women in both private and public prenatal clinics. Of these women, 8% reported abuse during the pregnancy and 15% were abused prior to the pregnancy. Abuse did not vary by ethnicity. Gelles reported pregnant women have a 28.3% chance of experiencing minor violence, a 60.6% greater risk of encountering abusive violence, and a 35.6% overall risk of being involved in a violent episode. McFarlane et al have shown that one in six pregnant women are at risk for abuse." (p57)

Greenberg, E. M. "Violence against Women: Implications for Nursing Practice." Imprint v41 n2, Feb-Mar 1994. p56-58. (ISSN0019-3038).

ACADEMIC DEGREES

see DEGREES, ACADEMIC

ACADIANA (LA)--ECONOMIC CONDITIONS

"When Louisiana's thriving oil and gas market went belly up in the 1980s, with oil dropping to less than $15 a barrel from $30-plus in under two years, few regions were hit as hard as Cajun country [or Acadiana], where much oil was drilled. For many, jobs and fortunes were lost....While the national average for per-capita income stood above $18,600 in 1990, in Cajun country it averaged just over $10,000. At the same time, Acadiana median house values improved only marginally from the 1980s--from $47,000 to $53,000. Nationally, the value jumped from $47,000 to more than $84,000. The region's growth rate is also troubling, up 2.6 percent from the 1980s, compared with a national-average hike of nearly 10 percent." (p7)

Boulard, Garry. "Windows on America: Louisiana Cajuns Celebrate Bid to Promote Their Culture." The Christian Science Monitor v86 n23, 28 Dec 1993. p7. (ISSN0882-7729).

ACCIDENTS

see also AIR TRAVEL--ACCIDENTS--U.S.; BICYCLES--U.S.--ACCIDENTS AND INJURIES; BOATS AND BOATING--U.S.--ACCIDENTS AND INJURIES; CHEMICALS--MEXICO--ACCIDENTS; CHILDREN'S ACCIDENTS--U.S.; CYCLING--U.S.--ACCIDENTS AND INJURIES; DRINKING AND TRAFFIC ACCIDENTS--U.S.; FIREARMS--U.S.--ACCIDENTS; FIRES; HAZARDOUS SUBSTANCES--U.S.--TRANSPORTATION--ACCIDENTS; NUCLEAR REACTORS--U.S.--ACCIDENTS; PIPELINES--U.S.--ACCIDENTS; RAILROADS--U.S.--ACCIDENTS; TOYS--U.S.--ACCIDENTS--MORTALITY; TRAFFIC ACCIDENTS--MICHIGAN; TRAFFIC ACCIDENTS--MISSOURI--YOUTH; TRAFFIC ACCIDENTS--U.S.; TRUCKS--U.S.--ACCIDENTS

ACCIDENTS--U.S. (v19)

ACCIDENTS--U.S.--MORTALITY (v19)

"According to the National Safety Council, 94,500 people died in accidents in 1989. The risk of driving a car, flying, bike riding, eating too much fat and cholesterol, getting salmonella infections or other food-borne diseases is certainly far greater than a one-in-a-million risk. Indeed, the risk to a Member of the House of Representatives dying in a plane crash is 1 in 1,000." (p5)

Bliley, Thomas J., Jr. (Rep.-Va.). U.S. House. Committee on Energy and Commerce/U.S. Senate. Committee on Labor and Human Resources. "Safety of Pesticides in Food." Hearing, 21 Sep 1993. Washington, D.C.: GPO, 1994. (ISBN0160434912). (Y4.En2/3:103-55).

ACCOUNTANTS--U.S. (v19)

"The 1992 edition of 'The Supply of Accounting Graduates and the Demand for Public Accounting Recruits' of the American Institute of Certified Public Accountants (AICPA) reported that the number of accounting graduates recruited by public accounting firms has mirrored the condition of the economy in recent years. Whereas the supply of new graduates increased by 2% in 1990-91, the number of new recruits declined 14% from 1989 levels. Firms lowered their recruiting by another 14% in 1991-92, with 1992-93 figures expected to rise by only 4%." (p136)

Cook, Ellen D./Finch, Beth. "Qualities Employers Seek in New Accounting Employees." Journal of Education for Business v69 n3, Jan-Feb 1994. p136-139. (ISSN0883-2323).

ACQUAINTANCE RAPE--U.S. (v19)

ACQUIRED IMMUNE DEFICIENCY SYNDROME

see AIDS (DISEASE)

ACTIONS AND DEFENSES--GERMANY--JAPAN (v19)

ACTIONS AND DEFENSES--TEXAS

"Punitive damage awards 'carpet-bomb' the economy of Texas instead of striking surgically at wrongdoers, according to a study by the Texas Public Policy Foundation (TPPF)....Texas is one of the most popular places for plaintiffs to sue businesses because juries here tend to award huge sums....The study found that punitive damage claims are on the rise. For the five-year periods ending in 1986 and 1992, such cases increased from 21 percent of all civil cases to 30 percent in Houston and from 33 percent to 43 percent in Dallas. Damage awards have soared, the study found. For the three-year periods ending in 1981 and 1992, the average award rose from $280,000 to $2.1 million in Houston. For Dallas, the figures were $59,000 and $1.1 million." (p9)

Pendleton, Scott. "Economy: Punitive Damages Awards Get Harsh Criticism by Texas Body." The Christian Science Monitor v86 n108, 28 Apr 1994. p9. (ISSN0882-7729).

ACTIONS AND DEFENSES--U.S. (v19)

"Traditionally, the product-liability field has been the most fertile for multiple cases. But these days, much of the piling on comes from shareholder suits. A review of cases conducted by SECURITIES CLASS ACTION ALERT, a newsletter based in Cresskill, N.J., found that shareholder class actions filed in [U.S.] federal court have increased by 57% in the past four years, while the number of companies sued has risen only 4.6%. 'It's a typical scenario for four, five, or more class actions to be filed simultaneously, all concerning the same stock-price drop,' suggests Jonathan C. Dickey, a defense lawyer in Palo Alto, Calif." (p112)

Himelstein, Linda. "Legal Affairs: Litigation: Monkey See, Monkey Sue." Business Week n3347, 7 Feb 1994. p112,114. (ISSN0007-7135).

The Association of Trial Lawyers of America's "opponents say the current civil justice system is costly, inefficient and unfair to both plaintiffs and defendants. [Professor Lester] Brickman estimates that $30 billion to $40 billion in annual health care costs are 'created by lawyers' who send their personal injury clients to physicians and chiropractors again and again for the purpose of inflating the victim's medical expenses and thus the size of the awards--and the lawyer's fees. Injury victims often wait years for their cases to move through the legal system and then receive no more than 30 percent of their legal settlements or awards, he says, while trial lawyers earn $14 to $15 billion a year in contingent fees from personal injury cases." (p15-16)

Kemper, Vicki. "Lawyers on Trial." Common Cause Magazine v19 n3, Fall 1993. p14-20. (ISSN0271-9592).

ADC PROGRAMS

see AID TO FAMILIES WITH DEPENDENT CHILDREN PROGRAMS

ADDICTION TO DRUGS

see DRUG ABUSE

ADMINISTRATION OF CRIMINAL JUSTICE

see CRIMINAL JUSTICE, ADMINISTRATION OF

ADOPTION--U.S. (v19)

ADVERTISING

see also COUPONS (RETAIL TRADE)

ADVERTISING--ALCOHOLIC BEVERAGES--U.S.

"American teenages drink more than 1 billion bottles and cans of beer every year. Although the beer industry insists that its commercials don't influence teenager drinkers, new research suggests that alcohol ads can have a far-reaching--and far from benign--influence on young people....Joel Grube, a scientist and the author of two studies published last week in the AMERICAN JOURNAL OF PUBLIC HEALTH, tallied 685 alcohol commercials--mostly for beer--airing during 122 sporting events on television. That averages more than five ads per event. Only three of those ads, Mr. Grube reports, urged moderation in drinking. The rest used lively music and fun-filled scenes to sell their product. No wonder the 10-year-olds in Grube's survey couldn't recall any public service ads warning about the dangers of alcohol." (p18)

"Editorials: Alcohol and the Soft Sell." The Christian Science Monitor v86 n59, 17 Feb 1994. p18. (ISSN0882-7729).

ADVERTISING--CIGARETTE INDUSTRY--CALIFORNIA--YOUTH

"The following numbers apply to experiences and/or behaviors of students in grades 8,10 and 12 from four rural (primarily Latino) communities in central California: 52% had heard of Camel Cash; 47% had heard of Marlboro Adventure Team; 30% had a copy of Camel Catalog; 25% had a copy of the Marlboro Adv. Team catalog; 20% had saved coupons to get a promo item; 14% had saved Camel cash; 12% had saved Marlboro Miles; 15% had received mail from a tobacco company; 45% has a friend who owns a promo item." (p10)

"Tobacco Tactics: Survey Results: Promotional Items Reach Their Goal." Tobacco-Free Youth Reporter v5 n3, Fall 1993. p10.

ADVERTISING--CIGARETTE INDUSTRY--GREAT BRITAIN

"Ministers [in Great Britain] are worried about cigarette advertising....Their target is to cut smoking by children under 16 years, who cannot legally buy cigarettes, by a third by 1995. But smoking among those 11-15-year-olds who own up to it has remained static at 10% since 1990. The government, to the annoyance of the anti-smoking lobby, has for years blocked European Union moves to ban advertising outright....Tobacco firms claim that they advertise not to expand demand for cigarettes, but merely to maintain their market share against other brands. This sounds like a bogus argument. And yet there may be some truth to it. Advertising has failed abysmally to halt smoking's decline. In 1972 46% of all British adults were smokers, compared with around 30% today." (p60)

"Britain: Tobacco Adverts: Fuming." Economist v330 n7849, 5 Feb 1994. p60-61. (ISSN0013-0613).

ADVERTISING--CIGARETTE INDUSTRY--U.S.

The "campaigns of old Joe Camel are all part of over $10 million a day, $4 billion a year, that tobacco companies put into pushing their product. And you and I are helping to subsidize them because it is all tax deductible. At a time when the Government is spending $114 million a year to stop people from smoking, the American taxpayers are providing a $1 billion-a-year subsidy to promote smoking, especially among young people." (pS1798)

Harkin, Tom (Sen.-Iowa). "Tobacco and Children," Congressional Record (24 Feb 1994). Daily ed. pS1797-1798. (ISSN0363-7239).

ADVERTISING--CIGARETTE INDUSTRY--U.S.--WOMEN

"Many cigarette ads target young women. These ads contain carefully designed themes highlighting 'Thinness and femininity.' The slogan for Virginia Slims emphasizes women's liberation and active participation in society. 'You've come a long way, baby,' should be changed to, 'You've come the wrong way, baby,' for lung cancer now has surpassed breast cancer as a leading cause of death in women. In 1968, when Virginia Slims were first introduced, less than 8 percent of teenage girls smoked. In 6 years, that figure jumped...[to] 15 percent." (pH1129)

Morella, Constance A. (Rep.-Md.). "Improving America's Schools Act of 1994," Congressional Record (9 Mar 1994). Daily ed. pH1123-1134. (ISSN0363-7239).

Dr. John Pierce, a researcher at the University of California, "found that in 1967, when advertising aimed at women first began, smoking initiation rates jumped for teen girls. Between 1967 and 1973 there was a 110% increase in smoking initiation among 12 year olds, a 55% increase among 13 year olds, a 70% increase among 14 year olds, a 75% increase among 15 year olds, a 55% increase among 16 year olds and a 35% increase among 17 year olds--but no increase in initiation rates among young males." (p14)

"Advertising Linked to Increased Youth Smoking." Tobacco-Free Youth Reporter v6 n1, Spr 1994. p1,14.

ADVERTISING--CIGARETTE INDUSTRY--U.S.--YOUTH

"In a recent study published in the Journal of the American Medical Association, more 6-year-old kids can identify old Joe Camel than adults. In fact, just as many kids can recognize old Joe Camel as they can Mickey Mouse. And his name recognition has really paid off. In the 3 years since the introduction of old Joe, sales of Camel cigarettes to children under 18 went from $6 million to $476 million per year....What old Joe Camel says is this. You smoke cigarettes, you get C notes, and you get 2 C notes on each pack of new Special Lights, and with these C notes of course you can buy all kinds of gifts....If you have 175 C notes, you can get a fish and game club camouflaged thermos....That means you only have to smoke 3,500 Camel cigarettes and then you can get that. At around $1.90 a pack, that is $332.50 for the thermos. It looks like a GI Joe thermos....For a cigarette lighter you have to smoke 400 cigarettes." (pS1797)

Harkin, Tom (Sen.-Iowa). "Tobacco and Children," Congressional Record (24 Feb 1994). Daily ed. pS1797-1798. (ISSN0363-7239).

ADVERTISING--CIGARETTE INDUSTRY--U.S.--YOUTH--PUBLIC OPINION

"An ADVERTISING AGE/Gallup Organization Poll (Feb. 21, 1994) shows that 68% of Americans believe cigarette ads influence children and teens to smoke. Moreover, 66% of the respondents believe that some ads are specifically designed to appeal to young people. Half of the smokers polled believe that the United States government should restrict cigarette advertising--53% want a total ban, while 15% want further restrictions. Interest in a total ad ban appears to have been growing since 1991." (p1,14)

"Advertising Linked to Increased Youth Smoking." Tobacco-Free Youth Reporter v6 n1, Spr 1994. p1,14.

ADVERTISING--FOOD--U.S. (v19)

ADVERTISING--JAPAN (v19)

ADVERTISING--LAWYERS--U.S.

"The legal profession's internal conflict over advertising is reflected in the results of a Gallup poll conducted in November 1993 for the ABA JOURNAL....The poll produced these somewhat conflicting findings: Of the 400 ABA [or American Bar Association] members responding to the random telephone poll, 61 percent said their firms engage in some form of advertising....Of the respondents whose firms advertise, 87 percent said they expected to advertise as much or more in the future as they do now. A whopping 87 percent of the respondents said they believe advertising has a negative effect on the image of the legal profession, compared to 3 percent who said it has a positive effect." (p68)

Podgers, James. "Image Problem." ABA Journal v80, Feb 1994. p66-68,70,72. (ISSN0747-0088).

ADVERTISING--RUSSIA

"According to Bruce Macdonald, director general of BBDO Marketing in Moscow, the average ad budget for a foreign company in Russia for 1993 was $400,000--four times what it was the year before. And in 1994, the average budget should double, to $800,000. Those sums, small by Western standards, pack a wallop in Russia, where a minute of television time costs just $12,000. The experience of Mars Inc. shows the effectiveness of these techniques. According to a Gallup UK poll in late 1992, only 5% of Russians surveyed could come up with the name Snickers when asked to list familiar candy bars. One year later, after Mars blitzed the airwaves with commercials featuring the Rolling Stones' '(I Can't Get No) Satisfaction,' 82% could name Snickers." (p40)

Kranz, Patricia. "Top of the News: In Moscow, the Attack of the Killer Brands." Business Week n3353, 10 Jan 1994. p40. (ISSN0007-7135).

ADVERTISING--TOBACCO INDUSTRY--U.S.

"When the tobacco companies agreed to warning labels on cigarette packs in 1965, Congress preempted states from any further restriction on tobacco advertising relating to public health....this preemption convinced a Washington State legislator to withdraw a bill banning outdoor advertising for alcohol, tobacco, or firearms within 1,000 feet of school grounds. However, Seattle recently passed legislation banning all outdoor advertising within 500 feet of a school. This type of ban irritates the Outdoor Advertising Association of America, Inc. (OAAA), a trade group, which complains about the First Amendment implications of banning the advertising of a legal product. In a prior 1986 congressional attempt to restrict outdoor tobacco advertising, the industry complained that it could not afford to lose the business. However, tobacco's share of outdoor advertising is steadily declining. According to the OAAA, tobacco represented only 8 percent of all outdoor expenditures last year, down from 40.3 percent in 1979." (p2)

Scherer, Ron. "National: Anti-Tobacco Activists Make Gains, Arguing the Need to Protect Youths." The Christian Science Monitor v86 n63, 24 Feb 1994. p2. (ISSN0882-7729).

ADVERTISING--TOBACCO INDUSTRY--U.S.--PUBLIC OPINION

"In March [1993], the Coalition on Smoking OR Health asked the Gallup Organization to conduct a survey to gauge public opinion on the issues of tobacco excise taxes and federal regulation of tobacco products. Results highly support pro-health efforts. Key findings include: 75% of adults favor restricting cigarette advertising that appeals to children. 53% percent of adults believe all tobacco advertising should be banned. Nearly 70% of adults believe that the FDA should regulate tobacco products in a way similar to the way drugs are regulated....67% of adults favor a $2 a pack tax on cigarettes. 62% of adults believe that increasing the cigarette tax would discourage young people from starting to smoke." (p4)

"National News: Coalition Survey Reveals Broad Public Support for Tobacco Control." Tobacco-Free Youth Reporter v5 n2, Sum 1993. p4.

ADVERTISING--U.S. (v19)

"The cultivation of needs is a mammoth global enterprise. For four decades, advertising has been one of the world's fastest-growing industries. In the U.S., ad expenditures rose from about $200 per capita in 1950 to almost $500 in 1990, while total global advertising expenditures rose from an estimated $39 billion in 1950 to a whopping $247 billion in 1988, growing far more rapidly than economic output. Marketers increasingly target the young. One specialist told THE WALL STREET JOURNAL, 'Even two-year-olds are concerned about their brand of clothes, and by the age of six are full-out consumers.' The children's market in the U.S. is so valuable--over $75 billion in 1990--that our companies spent $500 million marketing to it in 1990, five times more than a decade earlier." (p30)

Durning, Alan Thein. "American Excess--Are We Shopping Our Planet to Death?" E Magazine v4 n1, Feb 1993. p26-31. (ISSN1046-8021).

ADVERTISING--U.S.--PERIODICALS

"Advertising promotes consumerism, but it also uses lots of paper. Ads pack the daily mail--14 billion catalogs plus 38 billion other pieces of junk mail clog the post each year in the U.S. They fill periodicals: a typical American newspaper is 65 percent advertising, up from 40 percent half a century ago. Every year, Canada cuts 17,000 hectares of its primeval forests--an area the size of the District of Columbia--just to provide American dailies with newsprint for ads. As Colleen McCrory, one of a growing cadre of Canadians trying to protect their forests, says, 'Basically, we're turning the whole nation into pulp.'" (p30)

Durning, Alan Thein. "American Excess--Are We Shopping Our Planet to Death?" E Magazine v4 n1, Feb 1993. p26-31. (ISSN1046-8021).

ADVERTISING--U.S.--POLITICS AND GOVERNMENT (v19)

ADVERTISING, DIRECT-MAIL--U.S.

"Over 42 percent of...[people in the U.S.] want less mail, the Postal Service knows, and 2.5 million people have now joined the

Direct Marketing Association's (DMA) Mail Preference Service to purge their names from most mailing lists. We may answer only one or two letters in 100. The others, most likely, go directly into the garbage. In 1990, we got 3.8 million tons of bulk mail and recycled only 200,000 tons of it." (p32)

Nixon, Will. "Are We Burying Ourselves in Junk Mail?" E Magazine v4 n6, Dec 1993. p30-33,36-37. (ISSN1046-8021).

ADVERTISING, MAGAZINE--CIGARETTE INDUSTRY--U.S.

"According to Elizabeth Whelan, president of the American Council on Science and Health, the one thing most women's magazines have in common, is practically no coverage of the dangers of smoking. 'All told, the 48 magazines I read contained more than 200 cigarette ads,' Whelan writes in a recent WASHINGTON TIMES op-ed piece.'" (p10) "The fastest growing group of American smokers are women under age 23, and in 1990, lung cancer surpassed breast cancer as the leading killer of women. According to Whelan, COSMOPOLITAN fretted about allergic reactions to costume jewelry, the causes of claustrophobia, and a dubious link between lung cancer and radiation from excessive chest x-rays. But not one of the periodicals included articles on the hazards of smoking, and none mentioned it as a leading cause of female death. Only MIRABELLA published full length articles on the hazards of smoking, and during the four months reviewed, hadn't carried a single cigarette ad." (p22)

"Women's Magazines Eat Their Own." Tobacco-Free Youth Reporter v5 n3, Fall 1993. p10,22.

AERONAUTICS--SAFETY MEASURES

see also AIR TRAFFIC CONTROL

AERONAUTICS--U.S.--SAFETY MEASURES

"If airlines are required to install cabin water spray systems for smoke and fire suppression in all their aircraft, the operational costs--in terms of extra fuel consumed alone--will be excessive. Aircraft would be required to carry between 325 and 3600 additional pounds of equipment and water for the entire duration of every trip. Even more troubling is the fact that if any cabin water spray system malfunctions, and the on-board water is sprayed or dumped into the aircraft cabin, the result is an almost assured loss of on-board control systems and the possible loss of the aircraft. Hopefully this proposal will be relegated--sooner rather than later--to the 'bad ideas' file at the FAA [Federal Aviation Administration]. In an industry which has removed olives and lettuce leaves to save costs, and reduced fuel burn by eliminating the weight of ash trays, the operational costs of this system amount to as many as 20 additional passengers being carried with no additional revenue; and that's after spending $11.6 billion for the system to begin with." (p503)

Merlis, Edward A. (Senior V.P., Air Transportation Assoc. of America). U.S. House. Committee on Appropriations. "Department of Transportation and Related Agencies Approp. for 1994 (Part 8)." Hearing, Washington, D.C.: GPO, 1993. (ISBN0160410657). (Y4.Ap6/1:T68/4/994/pt.8).

AERONAUTICS, COMMERCIAL--U.S.

see also AIRLINES--U.S.

"Commercial aviation in the U.S. is self-supporting through the elaborate and expensive system of 'user fees' we pay. The 10% federal ticket tax; PFCs; airport rental charges and concession fees; airport landing fees; state/local jet fuel taxes; and the myriad other federal, state, and local taxes we pay all combine to make us a 'pay as we go' system. The train sellers say 'aviation' is subsidized....'Aviation' in all its forms and manifestations, with the exception of commercial aviation, is subsidized. Those F-16's and corporate jets take up airspace too. But, according to the most comprehensive study on the subject yet done, domestic commercial airlines pay 111.2% of our share of the fully allocated federal cost of the nation's airport and airway system. And this calculation was done before the ticket tax was increased by 25% in 1990 and before Congress authorized airports to levy passenger facility charges. That's why the Congressional Budget Office said in its 1985 report that while intercity rail received a net federal subsidy of 23 cents per passenger mile ($56.81 in subsidy per passenger for a Dallas-Houston trip) commercial aviation got a negative 0.2 cents per mile because 'user fee payments to the federal government exceeded federal spending.'" (p246-247)

Kelleher, Herbert D. (Chairman, President, CEO, SouthWest Airlines Co.). U.S. House. Committee on Appropriations. "Department of Transportation and Related Agencies Approp. for 1994 (Part 8)." Hearing, Washington, D.C.: GPO, 1993. (ISBN0160410657). (Y4.Ap6/1:T68/4/994/pt.8).

AEROSPACE INDUSTRIES--CALIFORNIA (v19)

AEROSPACE INDUSTRIES--CHINA--U.S. (v19)

AEROSPACE INDUSTRIES--U.S.

see also AIRCRAFT INDUSTRY--U.S.

"The United States aerospace industry badly needs refueling. After a dismal 1993--aviation sales dropped 10 percent, exports fell 18 percent, and employment declined by an estimated 14 percent....According to the AIA [the Aerospace Industries Association] aerospace employment (including the military aircraft sector) has fallen by one-third (422,000 jobs) since its peak in 1989....Aerospace exports play a major offsetting role in the US trade balance. While the US experienced a merchandise trade deficit of $84.3 billion in 1992, aerospace exports were more than $45 billion." (p8)

Popiel, Leslie Albrecht. "Economy: Aircraft Producers Expect to Make $5.5 Billion Profit." The Christian Science Monitor v86 n39, 20 Jan 1994. p8. (ISSN0882-7729).

AFDC PROGRAMS

see AID TO FAMILIES WITH DEPENDENT CHILDREN PROGRAMS

AFRICA

see also AGRICULTURE--AFRICA; AIDS (DISEASE)--AFRICA; CHOLERA--AFRICA; DEBTS, EXTERNAL--AFRICA; DEFORESTATION--AFRICA; DENTAL CARE--AFRICA; DROUGHTS--AFRICA; ECONOMIC ASSISTANCE, JAPANESE--AFRICA; ECONOMIC ASSISTANCE--AFRICA; EDUCATION--AFRICA; EXPORTS--AFRICA; FOOD RELIEF--AFRICA; HIV INFECTIONS--AFRICA; INVESTMENTS, FOREIGN--AFRICA; JAPAN--COMMERCE--AFRICA; LABOR SUPPLY--AFRICA--WOMEN; LOANS--AFRICA; MALARIA--AFRICA; MASS MEDIA--AFRICA; MORTALITY--AFRICA; POOR--AFRICA; TOURIST TRADE--AFRICA; WATER-SUPPLY--AFRICA

AFRICA--COMMERCE--U.S. (v19)

AFRICA--ECONOMIC CONDITIONS (v19)

"So far during the 1990s, African economies have grown by a mere 1.5 per cent a year--worse than during the 'lost decade' of the 1980s....Last year saw a modest upturn, but only from 1992's appalling 0.7 per cent. Even then, North African economies grew by only 0.1 per cent in 1993, while Central Africa 'stagnated,' ECA [Economic Commission for Africa] figures show." (p12) "Ethiopia enjoyed growth of over 9 per cent in 1993, Uganda 7 per cent and Mozambique 5.6 per cent, convincing demonstration of the benefits of peace,...[ECA Executive Secretary Layashi] Yaker pointed out. But the expected persistence of low oil prices will restrain Africa's overall growth figures and export revenues, while conflict and political turmoil still threaten many parts of the continent." (p13)

Laishley, Roy. "Africa's Debt Burden Continues to Grow." Africa Recovery v7 n3-4, Dec 1993-Mar 1994. p12-14.

"UNCTAD's [the United Nations Conference on Trade and Development's] 1992 'Least Developed Countries' report warns that per capita incomes will again fall in 1993 in many of Africa's poorest countries, despite a modest rise in growth rates. After annual negative growth of gross domestic product (GDP) in 1991 and 1992, African LDCs are expected to grow by only 1.6 per cent in 1993, well below population growth rates of some 3 per cent. Thirty-two out of the 46 countries of sub-Saharan Africa are included in the list of 47 LDCs. While a small group has recently shown faster growth, largely as a result of strong and stable government commitment to economic reforms, 'there are many LDCs where the development process has come to a virtual standstill,' says UNCTAD Secretary-General Kenneth Dadzie. On the positive side, exports from Malawi, Mauritania and Uganda have risen by some 5 per cent, while Gambia has diversified trade by producing basic consumer and intermediate goods. Botswana and Lesotho, like 12 other African LDCs, have had faster growth due to strong export performance in diamonds and manufacturing respectively." (p12)

Ogan, Amma. "Least-Developed Need More Resources." Africa Recovery v7 n1, Jun 1993. p12.

"Recent statistics from the UN Economic Commission for Africa and UNDP [United Nations Development Programme] indicate that if living standards are to rise in the 1990s African economies will have to grow by 4-6% a year. Current growth rates and projections, as well as policies imposed by World Bank/IMF, indicate that this is unlikely to happen. What Africa needs is to rely on its heritage, traditions and resources to evolve political and socio-economic systems that meet the needs of Africans instead of the needs of industrialized countries. Economically, African countries need development strategies that fit their circumstances and place the continent's 600 million people at the center of development efforts....Strategies advocating exports of primary commodities, whose prices are generated by Western-based cartels, have not benefitted the majority of citizens. An African perspective is severely lacking in projects pursued by African governments during the past 30 years. African peoples' knowledge of traditional methods of production can, if effectively harnessed, contribute greatly toward the development of the continent, but donors and African governments need to address the needs of African peoples as a central concern." (p2)

Maoulidi, Moumie. "Africa Can Teach." Window on the World v24 n3-4, May-Jun 1993. p2.

AFRICA--ECONOMIC CONDITIONS--SOCIAL CONDITIONS (v19)

AFRICA--EMIGRATION AND IMMIGRATION (v19)

AFRICA--ENVIRONMENTAL ASPECTS (v19)

AFRICA--POPULATION (v19)

"Africa still has the highest population growth rate--2.9 percent a year--of any continent, enough to double the population in 24 years, according to the Population Reference Bureau in Washington." (p4)

Press, Robert M. "Kenya Shows Dramatic Drop in Fertility Rate." The Christian Science Monitor v86 n78, 17 Mar 1994. p1,4. (ISSN0882-7729).

AFRICA--PUBLIC OPINION

"Stereotypes and myths about Africa still abound in American published materials and in the media. Some of these distortions are obvious to discerning readers, others are more difficult to detect. These stereotypes and myths contribute to the 'Tarzan' image of Africa that many of our students develop about the continent and retain throughout their lives....Myths about the continent are numerous and should be challenged. For instance, what few large animals there are don't live in the 'jungle' but on the savannas--the grasslands--which make up about 40 percent of the continent's area. The 'jungle' on the other hand comprises only about five percent of the continent's land and in any case should be called 'rain forest.' Africa is not uniformly hot. Highland areas have a mild year-round climate and even at many lower elevations the temperatures seldom rise above the mid-eighties." (p1-2)

Corby, Richard. "Understanding Contemporary Africa." ACCESS n121, Jan-Feb 1994. p1-2.

AFRICA--SOCIAL CONDITIONS (v19)

In Africa, "The death rate of children under 5 has been halved since 1960, and life expectancy in Africa has risen to 54 years, an increase of 13 years since 1960. However, Africa's life expectancy still lags 20 years behind that of the industrialized world. Children in Africa die at 10 times the rate of industrialized countries. The current under-five-years-of-age mortality rate of 180 per 1,000 live births is half that of 1960....Two thirds of African countries have immunized 75% of their children against six major childhood diseases. Oral rehydration counters 60% of the cases of diarrhoeal dehydration....40 African countries have programs to counter iodine deficiency. 18 African countries are implementing the 'Bamako Initiative,' a system of community-run primary health care programs. However, half of all Africans still have no access to basic health care. Of the 6.5 million HIV-infected Africans, 750,000 are children. About 29 million African children (one-quarter of those under five) are underweight. Although food production and household incomes fell sharply in the mid-80s, increase in malnutrition was less pronounced than might be expected. Still, malnutrition affects about 30% of African children. Today, approximately 18 million Africans are at risk of malnutrition and starvation from famine and drought." (p14)

"Day of the African Child June 16, 1993: Facts, Achievements and Challenges." Window on the World v24 n3-4, May-Jun 1993. 14.

The "predominant view of Africa as a continent in perpetual crisis has reinforced the mistaken belief that the solution to African problems lies in the importation of outside skills and resources rather than in the abilities of African citizens. It has also obscured substantial gains achieved by African countries since independence. As former Tanzanian President Julius Nyere once remarked, 'We were under the British and Germans for nearly 80 years but when we gained independence, 85% of our people were illiterate. We had only two university-qualified engineers and 12 doctors. Now 30 years later, although we still don't have enough doctors, we have thousands, although we do not have enough engineers, we have thousands. We still have education problems but 90% of adults are literate.'" (p2)

Maoulidi, Moumie. "Africa Can Teach." Window on the World v24 n3-4, May-Jun 1993. p2.

AFRICA--STUDY AND TEACHING--U.S.

"Nearly 12% of the U.S. population is of African descent, and yet, very few Americans know about Africa and its various peoples and cultures. For a long time, the study of Africa in the schools has been relegated to the background. Where it is done, it is only done haphazardly. Inaccurate information--full of distortions, omissions of important issues, periods of history, cultural themes, as well as blatant and sophisticated stereotypes about the peoples and cultures of Africa--is still perpetuated in the way ideas and facts are presented in educational materials and the public media." (p3)

Farouk, Mohammed K. "Africa: Continent of the 21st Century." ACCESS n121, Jan-Feb 1994. p3.

AFRICA, NORTH--COMMERCE--MIDDLE EAST (v19)

AFRICA, NORTH--MIDDLE EAST--ECONOMIC CONDITIONS (v19)

AFRICA, NORTH--MIDDLE EAST--POPULATION (v19)

AFRICA, SUB-SAHARAN

see also ECONOMIC ASSISTANCE, JAPANESE--AFRICA, SUB-SAHARAN; INVESTMENTS, FOREIGN--AFRICA, SUB-SAHARAN

AFRICA, SUB-SAHARAN--HEALTH AND HYGIENE

"While sub-Saharan Africa is the only world region where malnutrition rates have not fallen over the last 15 years, 15 countries have managed to bring their rates below 15 per cent of children under-5, which is much better than the average for all developing countries. Another area of progress is the rise from 32 to 47 per cent of African families with access to safe drinking water, and even in Zambia, one of the poorest countries, maternal mortality has been lowered to some 150 deaths per 100,000 births." (p10)

Ogan, Amma. "Struggle for Child Health in Africa." Africa Recovery v7 n3-4, Dec 1993-Mar 1994. p10-11.

AFRICA, SUB-SAHARAN--SOCIAL CONDITIONS

"The winds of change are blowing across Sub-Saharan Africa, a diverse region of 47 countries stretching from the rolling savannas south of the Sahara desert to the coastal mountains and valleys of the Cape....over 70 percent of the people in Sub-Saharan Africa still lack basic civil liberties and human rights. Moreover, the region faces what amounts to a humanitarian crisis as a combination of drought, civil conflict, and economic decline threaten nearly 60 million of the region's 550 million people. Millions more, possibly a quarter of the total population, are poverty-stricken." (p41)

Hitchcock, Robert K. "State of the Peoples: Sub-Saharan Africa: Environment, Politics, and Development." Cultural Survival Quarterly v17 n3, Fall 1993. p41-43. (ISSN0740-3291).

AFRO-AMERICAN AGED

"A vast disparity exists between black males and black females older than 65 who are married and living with their spouse. Nearly 92% of black male elderly persons 65-74 and 86.4% of those 75 years of age and older live with their spouses. However, for black females in the same age groups, only 12.4% and 5.2%, respectively, are married and living with a spouse (U.S. Bureau of the Census, 1989). Therefore, male spouses are rarely available to perform caregiving functions for a female partner." (p87)

Luckey, Irene. "African American Elders: The Support Network of Generational Kin." Families in Society v75 n2, Feb 1994. p82-89. (ISSN1044-3894).

AFRO-AMERICAN CHILDREN--SOCIAL CONDITIONS

A University of Michigan study found that "Depression peaks in African American boys about age 9-10 and then falls off, but then academic failure kicks in. At ages 15-16, girls chart a similar course....Boys, ages 4-11, were reported to cheat, tell lies, and be disobedient at home and at school more often than girls. Girls were more likely to cling to adults. Adolescent boys were more likely than adolescent girls to have difficulty sitting still and concentrating. They also were more worried than girls. Adolescent girls, however, were more often depressed. Also, anti-social behavior among girls rose precipitously around ages 13-14, peaked at 15, and then declined." (p3)

News release. "Barbarin." University of Michigan News and Information Services 25 Jan 1994. p1-3.

AFRO-AMERICAN COLLEGE STUDENTS

"Among 18- to 24-year-old [U.S.] high school graduates, the percentage of black males who enrolled in college dropped about five points from 1990 to 1992, while the percentage of African-American women increased about six points over two years." (p4)

"College-Completion Rates." Education Week v13 n27, 30 Mar 1994. p4. (ISSN0277-4232).

AFRO-AMERICAN CRIMINALS (v19)

AFRO-AMERICAN FAMILIES

"Child care is particularly necessary for Black families because of the family composition of many African Americans. In 1992, only 36 percent of Black children under the age of 18 lived with their mother and father compared with 67 percent in 1960. For Whites the percentages were 77.4 percent in 1992 and 91 percent in 1960. In addition to the large number of single parents, child care is important for African American families because of the significant number of young children who need care. The Black population is younger than the White population. Based upon 1992 data, a third of the Black population was under 18 compared to one-quarter of the White population under 18 years of age. Although the trend is for Black and White women to have fewer children than they had more than 30 years ago, according to the Bureau of Census, 'Black women in each age group have somewhat higher average numbers of children ever born than comparable Whites.'" (p138)

Tollett, Erica E. (Senior Public Policy Analyst, National Black Child Devel. Inst.). U.S. House. Committee on Ways and Means. "Historical Trends in Poverty and Family Income." Hearing, 26 Oct 1993. Washington, D.C.: GPO, 1994. (ISBN0160435765). (Y4.W36:103-42).

AFRO-AMERICAN FARMERS

"Black-operated farms averaged just $14,500 in farm sales in 1987, compared with $65,200 for all U.S. farms. Almost half had less than $2,500 in farm product sales. Black-operated farms were also small in acreage, averaging only 115 acres--about one-fourth the national average of 462 acres. Nearly half had fewer than 50 acres. Half of the loss of 10,296 black-operated farms between 1982 and 1987 was in the size classes with less than $2,500 in farm product sales and fewer than 50 acres." (p27)

U.S. Dept. of Agriculture/Kalbacher, Judy/Rhoades, Doug. "Rural Development: Profiling Black Farmers in the U.S." Agricultural Outlook Dec 1993. p25-29.

"Both the number and proportion of black farmers have declined steadily since 1920, when the number of black farm operators peaked at 926,000, and one out of every seven U.S. farmers was black. Although the total number of U.S. farms also dropped, black-operated farms declined at a faster rate. By 1987, only 23,000 black-operated farms remained--and only 1 in every 100 farmers was black. Black farmers ran only 1 percent of U.S. farms, operated less than 1 percent of the farmland, and generated less than 1 percent of farm product sales reported in 1987, according to the most recently available Census of Agriculture data." (p25)

U.S. Dept. of Agriculture/Kalbacher, Judy/Rhoades, Doug. "Rural Development: Profiling Black Farmers in the U.S." Agricultural Outlook Dec 1993. p25-29.

"The average age of black farm operators in 1987 was about 58, compared with an average of 52 for all farmers. Black farmers 65 years and older outnumbered those under age 35 by almost 6 to 1, but this ratio was less than 2 to 1 for all farmers. The ratio of old to young black operators had increased since 1982, when it was 5 to 1." (p28)

U.S. Dept. of Agriculture/Kalbacher, Judy/Rhoades, Doug. "Rural Development: Profiling Black Farmers in the U.S." Agricultural Outlook Dec 1993. p25-29.

"Black farmers...[in the U.S.] have been especially hard hit by the farm crisis of the 1980s. Black-owned farms are generally a fourth the size of the national average, and 79 percent sell less than $10,000 of agricultural products a year. What's more, black farmers have always had a tougher time than whites getting federal loans, making it hard to get through a bad season. As a result, blacks have been losing land at a rate two and a half times that of whites. When black farmowners were at their peak in 1920, they numbered almost a million. By 1982, only 33,000 remained." (p18)

Bates, Eric. "Rural Life and Land: Plowing Up a Storm." Southern Exposure v21 n1-2, Spr-Sum 1993. p17-18,20. (ISSN0146-809X).

AFRO-AMERICAN FARMERS--CALIFORNIA--FLORIDA

"California and Florida, while not among the leaders in number of black-operated farms, nevertheless ranked fifth and sixth in agricultural sales from these farms in 1987. While most of California's 309 black-operated farms were small--73 percent had fewer than 50 acres and 72 percent had sales of less than $10,000--a small number had very high product sales. These high-value enterprises pushed average sales of the state's black-operated farms up to $75,900--higher than the national average of $65,200 for all farms and $14,500 for all black-operated farms....Most of Florida's 708 black-operated farms were also small--62 percent had fewer than 50 acres and 78 percent had less than $10,000 in product sales. Florida's black-operated farms averaged $29,300 in farm product sales, more than double the average for black-operated farms nationally." (p26)

U.S. Dept. of Agriculture/Kalbacher, Judy/Rhoades, Doug. "Rural Development: Profiling Black Farmers in the U.S." Agricultural Outlook Dec 1993. p25-29.

AFRO-AMERICAN PRISONERS

"Young black American males who experience education and employment problems are at exceptionally high risk of arrest and imprisonment as well as criminal victimization. One in every three arrests and one in every two incarcerations in the United States involves a black American. Three in every four black American prison inmates have less than 12 years of schooling.... An increasing awareness and fear of crime has resulted in an escalation in the use of imprisonment. In little more than a decade, between 1974 and 1986, commitments to state prisons increased nationally nearly 2-1/2 times. During this period, the rate of incarceration for blacks was more than six times the rate for whites. At current rates of growth, as many as one million Americans may be in prison by the year two thousand. On average, it costs about $15,000 a year to incarcerate an individual. The United States is a world leader in investment in imprisonment." (p60)

Hagan, John (Member, Panel on High Risk Youth). U.S. House. Committee on Ways and Means. "Children and Families at Risk in Deteriorating Communities." Hearing, 7 Dec 1993. Washington, D.C.: GPO, 1994. (ISBN0160436567). (Y4.W36:103-43).

"The justice system is most troubling in its impact on minorities, particularly on African Americans. As Jerome Miller, the head of the National Center on Institutions and Alternatives, recently reported, 42 percent of black men in Washington, DC, between the ages of eighteen and thirty-five are either in prison or on probation or parole, out on bail, or being sought on an arrest warrant. For black men in Baltimore, the comparable figure is 57 percent. Nationwide, blacks make up 48 percent of prison inmates, as against 12 percent of the population. The disparity is even more flagrant if one looks, as did Michael Tonry, professor of law at the University of Minnesota, at rates of confinement per 100,000. For whites, it is 289, for blacks, 1,860. The likelihood of being in prison or in jail is seven times higher for black Americans than for whites." (p34-35)

Rothman, David J. "The Crime of Punishment." New York Review of Books v41 n4, 17 Feb 1994. p34-38. (ISSN0028-7504).

AFRO-AMERICAN SOLDIERS (v19)

"Since the early 1970s, the [U.S.] armed forces' affirmative-action practices have markedly advanced blacks (women, too) in one of America's most segregated institutions. Studies by Northwestern University sociologist Charles Moskos reveal that while barely 2 percent of officers were black in the 1970s, by the end of the 1980s some 12 percent of armed forces' officers were black (7,000), which includes 7 percent of generals and 11 percent of colonels. In the 1970s, only 5 percent of non-commissioned officers were black, but by the end of the 1980s there were 85,000 black noncommissioned officers (24 percent of master sergeants and 31 percent of sergeant major rank)." (p13)

Kilson, Martin. "Anatomy of Black Conservatism." Transition v3 n1, 1993. p4-19. (ISSN0041-1191).

AFRO-AMERICAN UNIVERSITIES AND COLLEGES

"Although they only represent 3 percent of all U.S. institutions of higher learning, historically black colleges and universities graduate 33 percent of all African-Americans with bachelor's degrees and 43 percent of all African-Americans who go on to earn their Ph.D.'s....In 1990-91...the average tuition and fees charged by private historically black colleges and universities was $4,657--less than half the $9,351 average charged by private colleges nationwide....A study conducted by the United Negro College Fund (UNCF) found that 90 percent of students at private historically black colleges and universities require financial aid compared with 65 percent of private college students nationally. The study also found that nearly one-half of these students come from families earning under $25,000." (pS3694)

Moseley-Braun, Carol (Sen.-Ill.). "Statements on Introduced Bills and Joint Resolutions," Congressional Record (24 Mar 1994). Daily ed. pS3685-3745. (ISSN0363-7239).

"The Reference Library of Black America (Ploski & Williams 1990) lists more than 120 HBCUs [historically black colleges and universities]. The large majority of these institutions are located in the southern states. As recently as 1964, 51% of all black college students attended HBCUs. Today HBCUs only enroll about 16% of the more than one million black college students. Significantly, these institutions continue to provide at least 30% of the bachelor's degrees awarded to African Americans. Just as significantly, HBCUs employ more than two-thirds of blacks teaching in southern colleges and universities (THE ECONOMIST 1987). This may be related to the fact that the majority of black faculty are no longer employed in the South. Not an insignificant number of white faculty also is employed at HBCUs." (p886)

Hudgins, John L. "The Segmentation of Southern Sociology? Social Research at Historically Black Colleges and Universities." Social Forces v72 n3, Mar 1994. p885-893. (ISSN0037-7732).

AFRO-AMERICAN WOMEN--EMPLOYMENT

"In 1990, the U.S. Department of Labor reported an annual unemployment rate of 11.9 percent for African American women, ages 25 to 34. This figure is more than twice that of African American women in the 45 to 54- year age range. Young African American women face the greatest difficulty in finding employment due to discrimination. In short, corporations are using women, but they are not providing for them. With basic benefits, women can do the job, according to Transit Women United. The number of working mothers has increased fivefold in forty years. Statistics show that most pregnant women work full time, and are back at work within six months after giving birth. Working women, like those of Transit Women United, insist they will not be driven out of the work force. Currently, 57 percent of all women hold jobs. And, in 1987, women made up 50 percent of all African Americans employed." (p29)

Hilliard, Patricia. "Metro: Hero Rides Discrimination Out on a Rail." New Directions for Women v22 n1, Jan-Feb 1993. p29. (ISSN0160-1075).

AFRO-AMERICAN WOMEN HEADS OF HOUSEHOLDS

"Consider there is a race/gender dimension to financial hardship such that single black women heads of households are now symbols of that condition and of the distaff side of the underclass (Wilson, 1978, 1987, 1990). Approximately 74 percent of all poor black families are headed by such women. In fact, they are singularly largely responsible for the poorest population in the country--minor black children. Further, some one-third to one-half of them are welfare recipients (Edelman, 1991). In recent years, a relatively small number of black women described by the preceding traits have been drawn to their local urban, nonelite university by a federal government program designed to reduce national social welfare rolls (Megerian, 1984; Te Boekhorst, 1986). Yet, while the support has been provided to encourage them to obtain education and independence from public assistance, comparable support is not provided for buying time-saving materials and services that promote maximal educational development and productivity." (p202-203)

Arnold, Faye W. "'Time Is Not on Our Side'...Black American Women Students' Achievement in the Urban Nonelite University." Urban Review v25 n3, Sep 1993. p199-220. (ISSN0042-0972).

AFRO-AMERICAN YOUTH--SOCIAL CONDITIONS--PUBLIC OPINION

"Polls surely show that African-Americans place great emphasis on moral values related to family, personal responsibility, fairness and hard work. Take, for example, the results of a study conducted of black youth, that most bitterly complained-about segment of black America. In a 1991 study by Peter D. Hart Research Associates for People for the American Way, an overwhelming (87 percent) majority of young blacks called family 'extremely important.' Rated as No. 2 among values the young blacks believed Americans care about was 'fair treatment for all' (86 percent); third was 'belief in God' (85 percent); and fourth was 'emphasis on self-reliance and taking responsibility for yourself' (84 percent)." (p23)

Williams, Linda Faye. "Symposium: Black Leadership Shows Voter Savvy." Insight v10 n10, 7 Mar 1994. p23-25. (ISSN1051-4880).

AFRO-AMERICANS (v19)

see also AIDS (DISEASE)--AFRO-AMERICANS--HISPANIC AMERICANS; CABLE TELEVISION--AFRO-AMERICANS; CAREGIVERS--AFRO-AMERICANS; HOMICIDE--AFRO-AMERICANS; HOUSEHOLDS--AFRO-AMERICANS; INCOME--AFRO-AMERICANS; LOANS--AFRO-AMERICANS; MIGRATION, INTERNAL--AFRO-AMERICANS; POOR--AFRO-AMERICANS; VIOLENCE--AFRO-AMERICANS--HISPANIC AMERICANS--MORTALITY; WAGES--AFRO-AMERICANS

"Urban America continues to be segregated along racial lines. Apartheid-type housing and urban development policies limit mobility, reduce neighborhood options, and diminish job opportunities for millions of Americans. This is especially the case for African Americans who live in central cities. In 1990, more than 57% of African Americans lived in central cities, the highest concentration of any racial and ethnic group. Even affluent African American families--those with household incomes of $50,000 or more--are more likely to live in central cities than their white counterparts. For example, 56% of affluent African Americans live in central cities, and 40% live in the suburbs. Only 25% of affluent whites live in central cities and 61% live in the suburbs." (p35)

Bullard, Robert D. "Urban Habitat Program: Residential Apartheid in Urban America." Earth Island Journal v8 n4, Fall 1993. p35-36. (ISSN1041-0406).

AFRO-AMERICANS--ECONOMIC CONDITIONS (v19)

"Before the close of the 1990s, homelessness will envelop millions more of our fellow citizens who are currently unemployed. Millions of people, whether they realize it or not, stand but a paycheck or two away from the same fate. Many of the homeless draw paychecks but the paychecks are inadequate to pay for a room, to say nothing of an apartment or house. Black families, whether with a male or a female head of the household, are overrepresented among the urban poor. The Black poverty rate in 1984 was 33.8 percent, higher than any year since 1968. Today it is even higher. The number of female-headed families living below the poverty level is dramatically higher than in 1970. The number of female-headed homes is increasing in white, black and Hispanic families." (p8)

Carter, Arleen. "Baltimore Homeless Poet and NOC Member Speaks Out on...the Tragedy of Homelessness." People's Tribune v20 n44, 1 Nov 1993. p8.

AFRO-AMERICANS--EMPLOYMENT (v19)

AFRO-AMERICANS--HEALTH AND HYGIENE (v19)

AFRO-AMERICANS--POLITICAL ACTIVITY (v19)

"The numbers speak for themselves. Before the Voting Rights Act was enacted in 1965, there were four African Americans in the House of Representatives. After the 1970 redistricting, the number tripled to 13. Following the 1980 redistricting, the number of African Americans grew to 19. In the last Congress, the 102d, there were 27 African Americans. With the 1990 redistricting, there are 39, the highest number in this body's history. I must note, however, that at 39, African Americans, who constitute almost 15 percent of the Nation's population, are only 9 percent of total representatives." (pH1878)

Collins, Barbara-Rose (Rep.-Mich.). "1965 Voting Rights Act under Attack," Congressional Record (22 Mar 1994). Daily ed. pH1870-1879. (ISSN0363-7239).

"With voter-registration numbers showing blacks at almost 60 percent and whites at about 40 percent, New Orleans has elected black mayors over white competitors in four consecutive elections, going back to 1978 when the elder [Earnest] Morial won an upset victory." (p10)

Boulard, Garry. "National: New Orleans Chooses Its Mayor." The Christian Science Monitor v86 n48, 2 Feb 1994. p10. (ISSN0882-7729).

AFRO-AMERICANS--POPULATION (v19)

AFRO-AMERICANS--PUBLIC OPINION (v19)

AFRO-AMERICANS--SOCIAL CONDITIONS (v19)

AFRO-AMERICANS--SOCIAL CONDITIONS--PUBLIC OPINION

"According to Voter Research and Surveys exit polls, the issues that mattered most to blacks in 1992 were the economy and jobs (48 percent) and health care (30 percent), not family values (11 percent) or abortion (5 percent). The black issue agenda shifted early this year to crime (24 percent), unemployment (17 percent) and drugs (12 percent), according to CBS/NEW YORK TIMES polls, and so too did the focus of traditional black leaders--as witnessed by the number who participated in [Mr. Jesse] Jackson's Rainbow Coalition Summit on Violence in early January." (p24)

Williams, Linda Faye. "Symposium: Black Leadership Shows Voter Savvy." Insight v10 n10, 7 Mar 1994. p23-25. (ISSN1051-4880).

"It...is true that blacks lean toward conservatism on many issues. In 1982, Charles Hamilton, writing for the Urban League's STATE OF BLACK AMERICA reported that in 1980 76 percent of blacks believed courts were not dealing harshly enough with criminals. Forty-one percent favored the death penalty for murder and 80 percent believed homosexuality was wrong. On the other hand, the data on reproductive rights are unclear given the substantial impact of changes in question wording. (For example, exit polls in 1992 reported that 68 percent of blacks wanted abortion to be 'always legal' or 'almost always legal.' Yet many polls also find blacks holding conservative opinions on abortion and other issues such as school prayer and the role of women in society." (p23-24)

Williams, Linda Faye. "Symposium: Black Leadership Shows Voter Savvy." Insight v10 n10, 7 Mar 1994. p23-25. (ISSN1051-4880).

AGED (v19)

see also ABUSED AGED--U.S.; AFRO-AMERICAN AGED; CAMPAIGN FUNDS--U.S.--AGED; CAREGIVERS--AFRO-AMERICAN AGED; COMPUTERS--U.S.--AGED; LABOR SUPPLY--AGED; MINORITY AGED--U.S.; POOR--U.S.--AGED; SOCIAL SECURITY--U.S.--AGED--ECONOMIC CONDITIONS; TRAFFIC ACCIDENTS--U.S.--AGED; VOLUNTARISM--U.S.--AGED

AGED--CANADA

"The age structure of our population is changing dramatically. For the past 100,000 years, people aged 65 and over have made up less than 1% of the total world population (SCIENTIFIC AMERICAN, April 1993). In Canada those 65 and older now make up 12% of our population. The ratio will rise much faster after the baby-boom generation hits retirement age, around the year 2010. Demographers predict that the elderly will then make up about 25% of the population, because the baby-boom generation are not replacing themselves." (p6)

Lamont, Mary. "A Million and a Half Missing Children." ProLife News v19 n2, Feb 1994. p3,6.

AGED--CANADA--GERMANY--GREAT BRITAIN--JAPAN--U.S. (v19)

AGED--CARE--GERMANY (v19)

AGED--CARE--MALAYSIA

"The majority of the older Asian population, approximately three-quarters, reside with their adult children (Martin 1989)....In many non-Western countries, such as Malaysia and Singapore, there is considerable debate over how much government (versus family) support should be provided for the care of the older population. In contrast to the United States, whose government provides substantial transfers to the elderly through Social Security and Medicare, some non-Western countries are trying to reinforce family support networks. Malaysia...provides adult children with some economic motivators in the form of tax incentives to help support and to live with their parents. Since 1979, adult children who live with their parents have received a tax rebate of M$1,000 (approximately US $400). In 1991 tax amendments were introduced such that adult children can claim a M$1,000 tax deduction for medical expenses incurred for their parents and a M$3,000 deduction for the purchase of any necessary basic supporting equipment for disabled parents (J.K.C. Kiet, head of Inland Revenue Tax Department, Sarawak, Malaysia, personal communication, January, 1993)." (p95-96)

DaVanzo, Julie/Chan, Angelique. "Living Arrangments of Older Malaysians: Who Coresides with Their Adult Children?" Demography v31 n1, Feb 1994. p95-113. (ISSN0070-3370).

AGED--CARE--U.S. (v19)

"Most elderly people who live on their own don't need help with washing, dressing, doing housework, or preparing meals. Fewer than half of noninstitutionalized people aged 85 and older (45 percent) need help with at least one of these everyday activities, according to a 1990 Census Bureau report. Among those in their late 60s, only 9 percent need help with at least one of these activities. Yet the number of older Americans who do need assistance is large and growing. A 1993 report from the National Association for Home Care estimates that the current elderly population needing assistance ranges from 9 to 11 million." (p41)

Braus, Patricia. "When Mom Needs Help." American Demographics v16 n3, Mar 1994. p38-41,44-45. (ISSN0163-4089).

AGED--EUROPE (v19)

"Across Western Europe, savvy companies are realizing they must prepare for an age wave about to transform their markets. In the next quarter century, the 50-plus crowd will mushroom from 120 million to 165 million--triple the general growth rate--as the baby boom generation approaches retirement age....According to one trade group, the European Travel Commission, Europeans 55 and older made more than 200 million holiday trips of varying lengths last year--20% of the total travel market and growing. In Britain, research by pub operator Whitbread PLC indicates that Britons over 50 own 75% of the wealth and spend 21% more than the national average. Studies in Italy and France show similar trends. And even though European governments must soon reform their overloaded pension systems, these older citizens should still be the wealthiest generation in European history." (p92A)

Osten, Patrick/Nayeri, Farah. "International Economics: Europe: The Old World Gets Older." Business Week n3355, 24 Jan 1994. p92A,92D. (ISSN0007-7135).

AGED--FLORIDA--ECONOMIC CONDITIONS (v19)

AGED--HEALTH AND HYGIENE--U.S. (v19)

AGED--HOSPITAL CARE--WISCONSIN (v19)

AGED--JAPAN (v19)

AGED--MORTALITY

"For 22 countries, rich and poor...[the ECONOMIST] examined over 30 indicators which sum up the economic, social, cultural and political aspects of life." (p39) "People like to be healthy, as well as wealthy and wise. The Japanese get the prize for longevity, living for an average of 79 years. The average Indian lives for 60 years. Russia's life expectancy (69 years) is no higher than China's, even though its income per head is four times bigger. Yet, bizarrely, Russia (equal with Italy) has more doctors per head than any other country in our sample: it has twice as many doctors as America and three times as many as Britain." (p40)

"Where to Live: Nirvana by Numbers." Economist v329 n7843, 25 Dec 1993. p39-42. (ISSN0013-0613).

AGED--NICARAGUA

"According to the Nicaraguan Statistics and Census Bureau, there are some 126,000 senior citizens, of which 71,300 are women. Obviously, these figures omit those old people who...wander the streets of the capital without any protection or care, or those who live in cave-like dwellings, like the ruins of old Managua: the ones who really know misery. Social and humanitarian programs for the aged, run by the Nicaraguan Social Security and Welfare Institute (Inssbi) or religious organizations, scarcely scratch the surface of this immense problem." (p23)

Duarte, Vilma. "Real Lives: Senior Citizens: Abandoned at the End of the Road." Barricada Internacional v13 n366, Oct 1993. p22-23. (ISSN1013-9567).

AGED--POPULATION (v19)

"In 1900 there were 10-17 million people age 65 or older, constituting less than 1 percent of the world's population. In 1992 there were about 342 million people 65 or older, making up 6.2 percent of the population. By the year 2050 people over 65 will number at least 2.5 billion--about one-fifth of the world's projected population." (p83)

Maller, Allen S. "The Modern Development of Messianic Prophecy." Review for Religious v53 n1, Jan-Feb 1994. p82-88. (ISSN0034-639X).

AGED--TAXATION--U.S. (v19)

AGED--U.S. (v19)

"Social Security benefits and government spending on the health of the elderly total 7% of gross national product and 30% of federal spending in the U.S., up from only 20% of federal spending in 1970....Even though persons over age 60 constitute only about 12% of the U.S. population, they absorb some 40% of spending on medical care....It's easier for a country to be generous to its senior citizens when they are a small fraction of the population, but that is not the case in industrialized countries, where a declining birth rate has combined with increasing life expectancy to raise the proportion of the population that is over 60. In the U.S., this proportion was under 10% in 1960; it is projected to rise to 20% by 2020." (p20)

Becker, Gary S. "Economic Viewpoint: Cut the Graybeards a Smaller Slice of the Pie." Business Week n3364, 28 Mar 1994. p20. (ISSN0007-7135).

"Within U.S. metro areas, concentration of the older population ranges from a low of about 4 percent (for Anchorage, Alaska) to 32 percent (for Sarasota, Florida). The ten most concentrated metros in 1990 are all in Florida, and all are more than 18 percent elderly. These metro areas include Sarasota, Bradenton, Fort Myers/Cape Coral, West Palm Beach/Boca Raton/Delray Beach, Fort Pierce, Daytona Beach, Naples, Ocala, Tampa/St. Petersburg/Clearwater, and Lakeland/Winter Haven." (p7)

Frey, William H. "Demographic Perspective: U.S. Elderly Population Becoming More Concentrated." Population Today v21 n4, Apr 1993. p6-7. (ISSN0749-2448).

AGED--U.S.--ECONOMIC CONDITIONS (v19)

AGED--U.S.--POPULATION (v19)

AGED, ABUSED

see ABUSED AGED

AGED WOMEN--U.S.--ECONOMIC CONDITIONS (v19)

AGRICHEMICALS

see AGRICULTURAL CHEMICALS

AGRICULTURAL BIOTECHNOLOGY

"Chemical and pharmaceutical companies are stepping up their purchase of seed companies. Shell Co. of Netherlands and England has control over 70 seed firms in the United Kingdom, Spain, Netherlands, Japan, West Germany and the United States. Ciba-Geigy of Switzerland had control over 31 seed companies in the United States and Canada, while Sandoz (a Swiss Chemical firm) has control over 36 seed companies. This consolidation of seed companies with chemical companies breeds a conflict of interest which has the propensity of working against farmers. It is clear that the new biotechnologies are not aimed at making farmers in rural areas develop self-supporting and sustainable agricultural systems. If external control of the agricultural production processes dominated the Green Revolution in the past, the new biorevolution in agriculture will similarly be characterized by new and stronger forms of dominance and manipulation." (p4)

"Humanity at the Crossroad of Biotechnology." International Permaculture Solutions Journal v1 n2. p3-4. (ISSN1046-8366).

AGRICULTURAL CHEMICALS

see also FERTILIZERS; FUNGICIDES; PESTICIDES

AGRICULTURAL CHEMICALS--U.S. (v19)

AGRICULTURAL CHEMICALS--U.S.--PUBLIC OPINION

According to the study entitled "What Americans Think about Agrichemicals--A Nationwide Survey on Health, Environment, and Public Policy," "A majority of Americans polled recently by Public Voice for Food & Health Policy are looking for food grown with fewer chemicals, and stronger government policies to reduce agrichemical use. According to that poll, 92% feel it is very important for farmers to switch to production methods that rely less on chemicals and more on natural alternatives; 65% believe it is very important for the federal government to have stronger policies to reduce the use of agrichemicals in food production. Some 71% of those polled said they are very concerned about the impact of agricultural chemicals on water quality, and 68% said they are very concerned about the health effects on young children. There was strong support from those polled for consumers to have a right to know about chemicals used in food production, with nearly 80% strongly favoring laws requiring clear labeling of chemicals and pesticides used to grow a food product." (p1)

"Widespread Public Concern over Chemical Use, Poll Finds." Alternative Agriculture News v11 n5, May 1993. p1. (ISSN8755-4941).

"To examine the policy positions of agricultural interest groups...[Curtis E. Beus and Riley E. Dunlap] studied the members of six interest groups and a representative sample of farmers from Washington State." (p99) "While most alternative agriculturalists (from 76% to 87%) agree that farmers should not receive subsidies unless they adopt an adequate agrichemical compliance plan, we did not expect such large proportions of farmers and conventional agriculturalists to agree with this policy position. The AAA [Pacific Northwest Aerial Applicators' Alliance] is the only exception, splitting almost evenly (48% disagreeing and 44% agreeing). Almost half (46%) of the agricultural chemical dealers agree that farmers should have an adequate agrichemical compliance program before they receive any subsidies, with only 18% disagreeing and 36% undecided. Similarly, the Farm Bureau officers also favor agrichemical compliance programs by almost a 2 to 1 margin. The statewide farmer sample expressed even stronger agreement (64% agreeing and 20% disagreeing). This is particularly puzzling because...the conventional agriculturalists agree that regulations on agricultural chemicals should not be strengthened." (104)

Beus, Curtis E./Dunlap, Riley E. "Agricultural Policy Debates: Examining the Alternative and Conventional Perspectives." American Journal of Alternative Agriculture v8 n3, 1993. p98-106. (ISSN0889-1893).

"A national poll taken in May [1993] by Public Voice for Food & Health Policy found a majority of Americans are looking for food grown with fewer chemicals and support stronger government policies to reduce agrichemical use. According to that poll, 92 percent feel it is very important for farmers to switch to production methods that rely less on chemicals and more on natural alternatives. At the same time, a recent survey of certified pesticide applicators in Minnesota--most of whom are farmers--found 30 percent reported they have stopped using a pesticide in the past few years due to concerns of possible health effects. Two percent said they always or usually experience a symptom of pesticide poisoning when handling pesticides. However, the survey, conducted by the University of Minnesota's Extension Service, also found 75 percent of the 3,300 applicators consider their own health risks to be relatively low." (p14)

"Panel Finds Pesticide Residues Put Kids at Risk, Federal Standards Too Low." Land Stewardship Letter v11 n3, Sum 1993. p14.

AGRICULTURAL CROPS

see CROPS

AGRICULTURAL EDUCATION--ARGENTINA

"Three new schools for future farmers were recently inaugurated in Argentina's province of Santa Fe....Some 80 students are enrolled in each school for a standard offering of secondary-level agricultural courses. An additional 25-30 nonmatriculating students per school take courses in such areas as mechanics, soybean cultivation and machinery maintenance." (p8)

"The Bank in Action: Argentina: Staying Down on the Farm." IDB v21 n1-2, Jan-Feb 1994. p8.

AGRICULTURAL INCOME

see FARM INCOME

AGRICULTURAL LAWS AND LEGISLATION--IOWA--PUBLIC OPINION

"A poll of 570 Iowa farmers' opinions about farm policy, published in the [DES MOINES REGISTER]...found that 25% favor expanding the Conservation Reserve program; 56% want it kept as is; 15% want it reduced; and 4% were not sure. Just 11% want the 'swampbuster' rules for wetlands expanded; 34% want them kept as is; 47% want them reduced; and 8% were not sure. The poll also found that 39% of those surveyed felt that environmental groups have a great deal of influence on shaping farm policy; 46% felt they had some influence; 14% felt they had not much influence; and 1% were not sure. Asked 'to what extent current U.S. farm policy emphasizes protecting the environment,' 33% said too much; 15%, too little; 50%, about right; and 2% were not sure." (p1)

"DES MOINES REGISTER Asks: Who Shapes U.S. Farm Policy?" Alternative Agriculture News v12 n3, Mar 1994. p1. (ISSN8755-4941).

AGRICULTURAL LAWS AND LEGISLATION--U.S. (v19)

AGRICULTURAL PESTS--CALIFORNIA

"According to Ed Show (Driscoll Strawberry Assoc., Watsonville, CA 95077), predatory mites are a major biological control success story in strawberries (see IPMP 11(5): 1-7)....Predatory mites such as 'Phytoseiulus persimilis' may be used on as many as 15,000 of the 25,000 acres of California strawberries. Strawberries are the 10th most valuable California crop, worth about $433 million last year....In 1986, California strawberry growers used 3 million 'P. persimilis' costing $15 per thousand. By 1990, growers used 300 million 'P. persimilis' costing $7.50 per thousand. By 1993, costs dropped to $4.50-$6.75 per thousand. Surveys in 1993 by Driscoll and the California Strawberry Advisory Board (CSAB) of 45 growers representing all the state's production districts indicated that 60-75% of strawberry growers used 'P. persimilis' for spider mite biocontrol." (p13)

Grossman, Joel. "Conference Notes: Entomological Society of America's 1993 Annual Meeting--Part 2." IPM Practitioner v16 n3, Mar 1994. p13-15. (ISSN0738-968X).

AGRICULTURAL PESTS--U.S.

"About 100 years ago, when boll weevils first crossed the Rio Grande River, they used Texas cotton as their first 'highway' across the South....Today, boll weevils cost the U.S. cotton industry more than $300 million a year, according to the National Cotton Council. A substantial part of the cost is for insecticides." (p4)

Suszkiw, Jan/De Quattro, Jim. "Evicting the Boll Weevil." Agricultural Research v42 n3, Mar 1994. p4-10. (ISSN0002-161X).

AGRICULTURAL PRODUCTIVITY--AFRICA, SUB-SAHARAN (v19)

AGRICULTURAL PRODUCTIVITY--CHINA (v19)

AGRICULTURAL PRODUCTIVITY--U.S.

"Corn production [in the U.S.] could reach 8.9 billion bushels, up 37% from 1993, and the soybean harvest could jump 17%. Wheat production should remain steady, with exports unchanged from 1993's 99.4 million metric tons. Cotton production should rise slightly, to 16.3 billion bales. As for meats, broiler production should rise 4% with prices remaining stable; beef production and pricing should remain unchanged; and a 2% decline in hog output should lead to slightly higher prices. The outlook for dairies depends on how quickly farmers turn to the genetically engineered growth hormone BST, which increases milk production up to 15% per cow. The dairy herd has shrunk 3% since 1990, and BST use will probably remain relatively low this year." (p88)

Greising, David. "Natural Resources: Agriculture: Knee-High by July." Business Week n3353, 10 Jan 1994. p88. (ISSN0007-7135).

AGRICULTURAL RESEARCH

see AGRICULTURE--RESEARCH

AGRICULTURAL SUBSIDIES (v19)

AGRICULTURAL SUBSIDIES--CANADA--U.S.

"When we had the United States-Canada Free-Trade Agreement before the Congress, our farmers were literally sold out by then Trade Ambassador Yeutter and by the administration. We had zero durum wheat shipped into our country at that point from Canada. Do you know what it is now? Twenty percent of domestic consumption--all of it--is coming in unfairly subsidized. None of it is trade with which we can compete--50 cents a bushel subsidy just on the subsidized Canadian railroad alone....It is fundamentally unfair trade. It has sucked hundreds of millions of dollars out of the pockets of our farmers. It has cost us an extra $600 million in added farm program payments, said the USDA, according to their own testimony." (pS2336)

Dorgan, Byron L. (Sen.-N.Dak.). "Trade," Congressional Record (3 Mar 1994). Daily ed. pS2335-2336. (ISSN0363-7239).

AGRICULTURAL SUBSIDIES--EUROPEAN ECONOMIC COMMUNITY (v19)

AGRICULTURAL SUBSIDIES--EUROPEAN ECONOMIC COMMUNITY--U.S. (v19)

AGRICULTURE (v19)

see also ANIMAL INDUSTRY; AQUACULTURE; FARMERS; FARMS; FORESTS AND FORESTRY; LIVESTOCK

AGRICULTURE--AFRICA

An "underexplored issue [in U.S. media coverage] is the economic causes of famine--in particular, the way the U.S. and international agencies like the IMF [International Monetary Fund] pressure underdeveloped countries to shift agriculture from local subsistence to export crops. To take a non-Somali example, Zimbabwe cut corn planting from 895,000 acres to 245,000 acres because U.S. AID encouraged them to grow, of all things, high-grade tobacco. The IMF told Zimbabwe that its Grain Marketing Board had to be run to make a profit, so it sold much of the grain it was storing. The result is that Zimbabwe, which used to be the breadbasket of Southern Africa, now faces major famine (SOUTHERN AFRICA PERSPECTIVES, '92 #2). While news accounts stress the aid Western nations give to Africa, the amount of money taken from Africa in the form of profits and income on loans (an average of $22 billion a year) is greater than all Western aid to Africa ($10 billion a year). This disparity has contributed to Africa's debt burden, which now stands at $235 billion (IMF WORLD ECONOMIC OUTLOOK, 10/92). These structural economic problems are seldom addressed as part of the cause of Africa's chronic hunger." (p12)

Naureckas, Jim. "The Somalia Intervention: Tragedy Made Simple." EXTRA! v6 n2, Mar 1993. p10-13. (ISSN0895-2310).

AGRICULTURE--ASIA--U.S.

"Asia is the fastest growing economic region in the world and the largest regional market for U.S. agricultural exports--accounting for over $16 billion or nearly 40 percent of U.S. exports in fiscal 1993. East Asia takes close to 90 percent of these exports." (p12)

U.S. Dept. of Agriculture/Moos, Eugene. "World Agriculture & Trade: U.S. Ag Exports Steady in FY '94." Agricultural Outlook Jan-Feb 1994. p10-13.

AGRICULTURE--BELIZE (v19)

AGRICULTURE--BRAZIL--U.S.

"Brazil's imports of U.S. agricultural commodities reached $230 million in fiscal 1993, up 60 percent. U.S. exports gained because of changes in import tariffs, and greater demand for soybeans, cotton, wheat, and high-valued vegetable, fruit, and nut products. In a temporary move to fight inflation, Brazil reduced import tariffs at midyear for some agricultural products. This contributed to larger imports of processed fruits, vegetables, and nuts. Wheat exports through EEP [Export Enhancement Program] boosted U.S. shipments nearly 600 percent in fiscal 1993." (p16) "Although the 1992/93 Brazilian harvest was generally good for most crops, a severe and prolonged drought in northeast Brazil may have affected the regional import demand for wheat, soybeans and feed grains. Despite ample supplies of these commodities in Brazil's south-central region, the United States often has some freight and price advantages in supplying the northeastern area." (p17)

U.S. Dept. of Agriculture. "Regional Highlights: Brazil." Outlook for U.S. Agricultural Exports 30 Nov 1993. p16-17.

AGRICULTURE--CALIFORNIA

"California led the Nation with $18.2 billion in cash receipts from all commodities [for 1992]. California's five top commodities in sales--dairy products, greenhouse and nursery products, grapes, cattle, and cotton--accounted for 47 percent of the State's cash receipts. California led the Nation in crop sales with $13.2 billion, and was the top producing State for six commodities: greenhouse and nursery products, cotton, eggs, hay, grapes, and lettuce. The State ranked fourth in livestock commodity receipts at $5.1 billion." (piv)

U.S. Dept. of Agriculture. "State Financial Summary, 1992: Highlights." Economic Indicators of the Farm Sector Jan 1994. piv-vi.

AGRICULTURE--CHINA (v19)

AGRICULTURE--CHINA--U.S.

"Henry A. Wallace always harbored a concern for developing a durable agriculture. He frequently called attention to the importance of maintaining soil fertility. He was particularly concerned about the precarious food situation of the world's populous nations such as India and China. Repeatedly he expressed dismay that more than 100 million acres of farm land in China had been seriously damaged by erosion, and he looked for remedies within Chinese agriculture (such as the practice of returning nutrients to the soil) and remedies also through the application of new technologies. Wallace worried that the United States, with resources plentiful for its modest population, was becoming reckless in the use of them. 'Destructive as (the Chinese) may have been,' he said, 'we in the United States, during the past mere 150 years, have handled our land in a way that indicates even more destructive possibilities' (Wallace, 1934, p. 239)." (p3)

Hadwiger, Don F. "Henry A. Wallace, Champion of a Durable Agriculture." American Journal of Alternative Agriculture v8 n1, 1993. p2-3. (ISSN0889-1893).

"U.S. agricultural exports to China in fiscal 1993 declined to $320 million, 54 percent below 1992. The sharp decrease in exports stems primarily from a 50-percent reduction in shipments of wheat to 2.1 million tons, and cotton exports that plummeted from 172,245 tons in 1992 to 160 tons in 1993." (p11)

U.S. Dept. of Agriculture. "Regional Highlights: China." Outlook for U.S. Agricultural Exports 30 Nov 1993. p11-12.

AGRICULTURE--COMMONWEALTH OF INDEPENDENT STATES (v19)

AGRICULTURE--CUBA

"On September 15, the Communist Party Political Bureau announced sweeping changes in the organization of...[Cuba's] agriculture--including the sugar industry, which accounts for 80% of the island's exports. Until now, state farms and some 180 agro-industrial complexes (CAI's) have cultivated 82% of Cuba's arable lands; while cooperatives held ten percent and individual private farmers eight percent. The big change is coming in the state sector, and will be completed, according to Sugar Industry Minister Nelson Torres, in time for the November startup of the 1993-94 sugar harvest. Under the new scheme, salaried agricultural workers become members of a new kind of cooperative: they farm government lands, but own the crop they harvest. This differs from the traditional cooperative (CPA), where private farmers pooled their plots for common land ownership." (p9)

Reed, Gail. "Dateline Havana: New Economic Reforms: Can They Work?" Cuba Update n6, Nov-Dec 1993. p9-10. (ISSN0196-0830).

AGRICULTURE--ECONOMIC ASPECTS--U.S. (v19)

AGRICULTURE--EMPLOYMENT--U.S. (v19)

AGRICULTURE--EUROPE

"Agriculture contributed in 1987 about 2 percent to the gross national product (GNP) in Belgium, West Germany, and the United Kingdom. In France, Italy, Spain, Denmark, and the Netherlands, it was about 4 percent. In Greece it was more than 15 percent. Correspondingly, agriculture's share in the total labor force varies between 2 percent in the United Kingdom to 5 percent in EC countries other than Ireland, Portugal, and Greece--where it ranges from 15 to 27 percent. Thirty years ago, these figures were about triple what they are now. Figures related to the degree of mechanization, application of agrochemicals, yields, number, and size of farms typically were about one-third of what they are now. In the production of most agricultural goods, the EC [European Community] as a whole has achieved complete self-sufficiency, even though considerable differences exist among member states....The amount of arable land in production ranges from 20 percent in Ireland (with about 80 percent of that given over to pasture land) to more than 90 percent in Denmark. Most EC countries show figures of about 50 percent. Forests account for less than 10 percent of the total country size in Ireland and the United Kingdom, and for about 30 percent in West Germany, the Netherlands, France, Spain, and Portugal." (p80)

Conrad, Jobst. "Agriculture and the Environment in Western Europe." International Environmental Affairs v5 n2, Spr 1993. p79-94. (ISSN1041-4665).

AGRICULTURE--EUROPE--U.S. (v19)

AGRICULTURE--EUROPE, EASTERN (v19)

AGRICULTURE--FRANCE (v19)

AGRICULTURE--IDAHO

"For the past two years, IDA [Idaho Department of Agriculture] has held an organic growers conference about farming sustainably. According to Jim Boatman, IDA organic certification coordinator, the conferences have gone exceedingly well. He said he sees more interest in sustainable agriculture as time goes by. At the birth of the certification program, 11 growers participated who were cultivating 756 acres. By 1992, the number of certified growers reached 38 and the total area of land increased to 8,700 acres. The size of operations range from a one-fifth acre market garden to a 4,000 acre dryland wheat farm." (p8)

Flocchini, Jim. "Organic Agriculture: A Growth Industry in Idaho." Journal of Pesticide Reform v13 n1, Spr 1993. p8-9. (ISSN0893-357X).

AGRICULTURE--KAZAKHSTAN (v19)

AGRICULTURE--KYRGYZSTAN

"Kyrgyzstan is a landlocked, largely mountainous republic with an economy that is heavily dependent on its land resources. In recent years agriculture has accounted for about 40 percent of net material product and 35 percent of employment, yet only seven percent of Krygyzstan's land is arable....The inefficient and unsustainable use of the collectively farmed land contrasted sharply with the 'private plots' farmed by individual households living on the collective or state farm. Although technically owned by the state, these plots were given for long-term use to individuals to grow crops and raise animals for household consumption....Statistics show that although the plots constituted less than five percent of agricultural land, they produced more than 25 percent of Kyrgyzstan's agricultural production. Field interviews done in Kyrgyzstan indicated that farmworkers rarely used chemical fertilizers on their private plots. Rather, they depended on organic fertilizers which, although requiring much more labor, were known to maintain soil fertility over the long-term." (p48)

Hanstad, Tim. "Sustainable Agriculture: Protecting Kyrgystan's Land Resources." Surviving Together v12 n1, Spr 1994. p48-49. (ISSN0859-6286).

AGRICULTURE--LAW AND LEGISLATION

see AGRICULTURAL LAWS AND LEGISLATION

AGRICULTURE--MEXICO

"The government drive for farm specialization, the need for peasants to earn off-farm income, and population growth, have all contributed to the decline of traditional peasant practices that sustained the resource base [in Mexico] for centuries. Fallow periods have grown shorter. Intercropping of corn, beans and squash have given way to mono-cropping and off-farm employment. The result has been declining productivity, increased poverty, and erosion. Fifty percent of Mexico's land surface is affected by erosion, and each year 371,000 acres reach the point where they are unusable for crop production. This too, contributes to rural depopulation." (pSR3)

"Special Report: Sustainable Rural Development in North America and the North American Free Trade Agreement." Center for Rural Affairs Newsletter Apr 1993. pSR1-4.

AGRICULTURE--MEXICO--U.S. (v19)

AGRICULTURE--NEW ZEALAND (v19)

AGRICULTURE--OHIO (v19)

AGRICULTURE--PUERTO RICO

"The period of 1970 to the present has been marked by Puerto Rico's regional integration into the U.S. economy, during which time the insular agrarian sector has not recovered from the decline suffered in previous decades. During most of this period, there has been a decline in the agrarian sector's contribution to the island's gross national product, net income, and domestic income. Although the monetary value of agricultural production has increased somewhat (due largely to inflation), the overall volume of production has not increased substantially, and there has been little change in the real value of production. Furthermore, the agrarian sector's generation of employment, measured in both absolute terms and in terms of its percentage of total employment, has declined. Finally, food imports have increased slightly when measured as a percentage of total food consumption expenditures. During fiscal year 1991-92, only 35.7% of the food products consumed on the island was grown and processed in Puerto Rico." (p308)

Collo, Martin J. "Capital Imports and Endogenous Productive Capacity: A Proposal for Agrarian Development in Puerto Rico." Journal of Third World Studies v10 n1, Spr 1993. p306-326. (ISSN8755-3449).

AGRICULTURE--RESEARCH--U.S.

"Millions of dollars have been spent to develop a bovine growth hormone that promises to increase milk production up to 25% per cow, even though milk is in surplus in our society and the competition resulting from use of this expensive purchased drug would drive thousands of smaller dairy farmers out of business. On the other hand, relatively little research investment has gone into new techniques of rotational grazing that promise to save dairy farmers 25% in feed costs--reducing off-farm inputs, increasing farmers' profits, and stabilizing production. The biases of the agriculture research establishment are clear." (p12)

Austin, Dick. "New Roots for Agriculture." Land Report n46, Spr 1993. p11-13.

AGRICULTURE--RUSSIA (v19)

AGRICULTURE--SOUTH DAKOTA

"In 1992, South Dakota's agricultural exports totaled nearly $900 million. Many of these exports are going to our foreign neighbors to the north and south. As much as 65 percent of South Dakota's wheat production is exported overseas. Maintaining and expanding foreign market opportunities are vital to the economic growth of South Dakota farmers and ranchers." (pS16923)

Pressler, Larry (Sen.-S.Dak.). "Managed Competition Works," Congressional Record (22 Nov 1993). Daily ed. pS16921-16924. (ISSN0363-7239).

AGRICULTURE--TEXAS

"While Texas ranked second overall in cash receipts, with $11.6 billion in sales [for 1992], it was first in livestock receipts ($7.5 billion) and fifth in crop receipts ($4.1 billion). Texas was also the leading producer of cattle and calves and grain sorghum." (piv)

U.S. Dept. of Agriculture. "State Financial Summary, 1992: Highlights." Economic Indicators of the Farm Sector Jan 1994. piv-vi.

AGRICULTURE--U.S. (v19)

"Agriculture no longer dominates rural America. In 1890, 24.8 million Americans (42.3 percent of the total population) lived on farms. By 1990, only 3.9 million (1.5 percent) lived on farms. Agriculture is no longer the major source of employment in rural America, and it is no longer the major source of income for the majority of farmers." (p23)

U.S. Dept. of Agriculture/Stauber, Karl N. "Rural Development: The Diversity of Rural America." Agricultural Outlook Jan-Feb 1994. p23-24.

"Production agriculture is a fragile business. The elements, floods and droughts, pests and disease have more to say about how successful we are than anything we can humanly do. The use of new and developing technologies has allowed agriculture to cut the use of chemicals 20 percent since 1982, to cut soil erosion 90 percent on 36.5 million acres of conservation reserve program, to develop renewable and environmentally friendly products such as ethanol, soy ink, corn deicers, plastics from corn starch, high value oils, and the list goes on. In agriculture, every day is Earth Day. There is a way we Americans can destroy this food machine. We can regulate, prevent the use of technologies, and do away with the infrastructure to develop new technologies. Since only 4.6 million Americans live on our farms and ranches--only 2 percent of our total population--...they are easily overlooked and outvoted in national policy debates. The U.S. population has increased 10 percent in the last decade but farm population has declined 12 percent." (pS16701)

Burns, Conrad R. (Sen.-Mont.). "Farm-City Week," Congressional Record (20 Nov 1993). Daily ed. pS16700-16701. (ISSN0363-7239).

"A key factor affecting [U.S.] farmers' net farm income in 1992 was the weather, which was, for the most part, extremely favorable with adequate rain and an absence of seasonal high temperatures in summer and early fall. These below-average temperatures eliminated the heat stress that often inhibits production of fall crops and livestock. Corn yields jumped to a record-shattering 131 bushels per acre, and yields were high for all crops harvested in both summer and fall. Corn and soybeans had record-setting harvests in 1992, boosting cash receipts for crops to an all-time high. (The combination of cash receipts and inventory change reflects annual value of the sector's commodity production.) Corn and soybean prices declined in the second half of the year as the size of the harvest became apparent, but held up surprisingly well because of favorable demand conditions. Milk production was up 2 percent in 1992 as output per cow more than offset a decline in the number of dairy cows. The mild temperature conditions in late summer and early fall that contributed to the record harvest of fall crops also reduced the heat stress on cows mitigating the seasonal decline in the yearly milk production cycle." (piv)

U.S. Dept. of Agriculture. "State Financial Summary, 1992: Highlights." Economic Indicators of the Farm Sector Jan 1994. piv-vi.

"U.S. agricultural exports dropped $320 million to $42.6 billion in 1993, but were still the third highest ever. In 1981, exports totaled $43.3 billion and last year, $42.9 billion. Exports declined because of a $1.1-billion drop in bulk commodities to $18.2 billion. High-value product exports partially offset the decline in bulk commodities by growing nearly $800 million to $24.4 billion." (p2)

U.S. Dept. of Agriculture/Greene, Joel. "Agricultural Exports Decline in 1993." Foreign Agricultural Trade of the United States Jan-Feb 1994. p2.

"U.S. agricultural exports totaled nearly $42.6 billion in fiscal year (FY) 1993, rising to the second highest level since 1981's $43.8 billion. Exports gained only $160 million from last year as larger exports of high-value products (HVP) offset a decline in bulk exports. Japan was again the leading destination for U.S. exports, followed by the European Community (EC), Canada, and Mexico. The export volume of bulk commodities rose nearly 3 million tons to 111 million tons. However, lower prices for feed grains and cotton, and sharply reduced cotton shipments, decreased the value of bulk exports by more than $680 million to $18.5 billion. Japan imported nearly 24 million tons of bulk commodities (70 percent feed grains), and the EC took nearly 11 million tons (75 percent soybeans). The greatest change was the sharp decline in shipments to the former Soviet Union (FSU), dropping from over 16 million tons to under 10 million tons in FY 1993." (p2)

U.S. Dept. of Agriculture/Greene, Joel. "Exports Rose Slightly in FY 1993." Foreign Agricultural Trade of the United States Nov-Dec 1993. p2-3.

"While land goes out of agriculture, that which remains is farmed more intensively. National Inter Regional Agricultural Projection model anticipates reduction in pasture and less productive fragile lands in agriculture with continued increases in irrigated cropland up from 19 million acres in 1945 to 47 million acres in 1987, capturing about 30 percent of profits in food production....Fewer farmers does not mean fewer people working in agriculture as the food system responds to lifestyle changes associated with a developed society. Today's consumers, who capture about three-fourths of the benefit of increased farm productivity, consume more packages and services than did an earlier generation. Real cost of food has dropped from 25 percent of per capita income to 15 percent in the past twenty years...." (p290)

Libby, Lawrence W. "The Natural Resource Limits of U.S. Agriculture." Journal of Soil and Water Conservation v48 n4, Jul-Aug 1993. p289-294. (ISSN0022-4561).

"Only 1 percent of the research projects operated by USDA's in-house research agency contribute to advancing the sustainability of agriculture, according to a recent project review in which LSP [Land Stewardship Project] participated. In April, five panels, each composed of ARS [or Agricultural Research Service], university, agribusiness, nonprofit and farmer representatives, assessed 1,177 Agricultural Research Service projects using criteria drawn from Congress' definition of sustainable agriculture (e.g. integrated farming systems conserving resources and enhancing environmental quality and economic viability). The panels found only 21 projects fully qualified as sustainable agriculture research. Their share of ARS's research budget--$6.7 million--is less than 1 percent. Nearly a third of the projects were found to 'contribute to sustainability.'" (p8)

"LSP Participates in Study: USDA's Research Adds Little to Sustainability, Assessment Finds." Land Stewardship Letter v11 n3, Sum 1993. p8.

"Fiscal 1993 EEP [Export Enhancement Program] sales of eggs, wheat, and wheat flour were significantly higher than fiscal 1992 sales. Fiscal 1993 wheat sales of 21.6 million tons were up 9 percent from fiscal 1992. Fiscal 1993 wheat flour sales almost tripled 1992 sales. Egg sales in 1993 were almost double 1992 sales. Fiscal 1993 EEP bonuses of $967 million are less than $1 million less than fiscal 1992 bonuses. Wheat EEP bonuses represented 80 percent of total EEP bonuses. High-value products accounted for 14 percent of total EEP bonuses in 1993. When subsidies for the Dairy Export Incentive Program, Sunflowerseed Oil Assistance Program, and Cottonseed Oil Assistance Program are added to the EEP bonuses, high-value and value-added products accounted for 28 percent of total bonuses for price competition programs ($1.2 billion)." (p19)

U.S. Dept. of Agriculture. "U.S. Agricultural Export Programs: The Export Enhancement Program." Outlook for U.S. Agricultural Exports 30 Nov 1993. p19-20.

"Calendar 1993 [U.S.] exports were valued at $42.6 billion, 1 percent less than 1992. Vegetable and vegetable product exports rose 14 percent to $3.3 billion in 1993. Fruit and preparations were steady at $2.3 billion. Beef fell slightly, ending at $2 billion and tobacco leaf plummeted 14 percent due to large global stocks. Poultry meat exports continued to rise, ending at $1.1 billion. Soybean meal fell to $1.1 billion as world prices sank." (p1)

U.S. Dept. of Agriculture. "Exports Drop." U.S. Agricultural Trade Update 18 Feb 1994. p1.

"The October U.S. agricultural trade surplus rose 38 percent to $1.8 billion from September 1993. Exports increased 20 percent and imports were up 9 percent for a net gain of $482 million. The cumulative calendar year surplus through October is 4 percent below 1992 at $14.1 billion...." (p1)

U.S. Dept. of Agriculture. "Trade Surplus Up." U.S. Agricultural Trade Update 21 Dec 1993. p1.

AGRICULTURE--U.S.--ENERGY CONSUMPTION (v19)

AGRICULTURE--U.S.--FORECASTING (v19)

AID TO FAMILIES WITH DEPENDENT CHILDREN PROGRAMS--U.S. (v19)

"The recent growth in the number of people on welfare is alarming. Between 1979 and 1989, about 7 million children were in the AFDC [or Aid to Families with Dependent Children] Program at any given time. But between 1989 and 1993, the number of children receiving AFDC increased by about 30 percent to 9.3 million children. Today 14 million people--5 million families--receive AFDC assistance. And the numbers alone don't tell the worst part of the story. An increasing percentage of those entering the system are never-married mothers at greatest risk of long-term welfare dependency. Between 1983 and 1992, families headed by unwed mothers accounted for about four-fifths of the growth in people on welfare, and at least 40 percent of never-married mothers receiving AFDC remain in the system for 10 years or more." (pS2967)

Lieberman, Joseph F. (Sen.-Conn.). "Statements on Introduced Bills and Joint Resolutions," Congressional Record (15 Mar 1994). Daily ed. pS2963-2979. (ISSN0363-7239).

"In the year ending in September 1991, 8.5 million children drew their sustenance from the Aid to Families with Dependent Children (AFDC) program. Their monthly grants are 42 percent lower than they were in real-dollar values in 1972. Even that triumph failed to warm the chill of the official heart; and in 1992 Michigan reduced its monthly AFDC grant for a family of three from $526 to $459." (p33)

Kempton, Murray. "A New Year's Wish." New York Review of Books v41 n3, 3 Feb 1994. p33. (ISSN0028-7504).

AIDS (DISEASE) (v19)

"At least 4,621 AIDS cases have been documented since 1984 in which there is no HIV. About one-third of these, 1,691, were recorded in the U.S.; 475 were recorded in Europe and 2,555 in Africa. Since Africa uses only the clinical, rather than the HIV-based AIDS definition, most of these cases were observed there." (p28)

Duesberg, Peter H. "Symposium: Results Fall Short for HIV Theory." Insight v10 n7, 14 Feb 1994. p27-29. (ISSN1051-4880).

"The government currently is spending $6 billion annually for AIDS research and treatment, according to the U.S. Public Health Service. Yet despite spending more than $22 billion since 1982, and despite a staggering 75,000 scientific papers written during the last decade, a cure for AIDS remains as elusive as ever. It now appears likely that AIDS researchers have made a terrible mistake in blaming HIV, the so-called AIDS virus, for causing AIDS." (p27)

Duesberg, Peter H. "Symposium: Results Fall Short for HIV Theory." Insight v10 n7, 14 Feb 1994. p27-29. (ISSN1051-4880).

"Since the pandemic [of AIDS] began, WHO [World Health Organization] estimates that over 14 million adults and 1 million children have been infected with HIV. Less than one fifth of these have gone on to develop AIDS, and fewer still have died of their infection. The worst is yet to come in terms of disease, death and related suffering. The cumulative number of AIDS cases is expected to quadruple by the year 2000." (p1)

News release. "World Health Organization to Administer New U.N. Programme on AIDS." WHO Press 21 Jan 1994. p1-2.

"With well over 5000 new infections every day, time is of the essence in the fight against AIDS. More than 14 million men, women and children are now estimated to have been infected with HIV, the virus which causes AIDS. Without urgent action the number could reach 40 million by the end of the century." (p1)

News release. "World AIDS Day 1993--'Time to Act.'" WHO Press 29 Nov 1993. p1-2.

"The World Health Organization (WHO) estimates that during the 1990s between 10 and 15 million children around the world will lose a mother, father, or both parents to AIDS. Among the most wretched of these orphans will be those--a small minority--born to HIV-infected mothers who are themselves infected. The chance of a woman with HIV/AIDS passing the virus on to her child is about 30%. Such children are sickly from birth. One in four dies before his or her first birthday, and less than one in five survives past the age of five....Of the 10 to 15 million orphans expected by the turn of the century, 90% will be in sub-Saharan Africa, where the pandemic is most advanced. But it is only a matter of time before parts of Asia and Latin America--where HIV is spreading at an explosive rate--face the same social problems as Africa. Thailand, for example, expects to have some two million motherless children by the year 2010." (p5)

Armstrong, Sue. "WorldAIDS Briefing: The Lost Generation." WorldAIDS n26, Mar 1993. p5-8. (ISSN0954-6510).

AIDS (DISEASE)--AFRICA (v19)

"According to the World Health Organization (WHO), the UN's lead agency in the fight against AIDS, an estimated 8 million adult Africans are afflicted by HIV, the virus that leads to AIDS, out of a global figure of some 14 million adults. Ms. Dorothy Blake, Deputy Director of WHO's Global Programme on AIDS told the Abidjan symposium that by 2000, Africa--which presently accounts for 12 per cent of the world's population--could account for 80 per cent of HIV cases worldwide. 'And yet there is still complacency and denial among leaders at all levels,' she said. Added to this, Ms. Blake warned, 'tuberculosis is spreading, and threatening to take off as a separate epidemic.' Some 60 per cent of HIV patients also contract TB, a highly infectious disease. Combined with the acute pressure on health budgets, gains made over the last 10-20 years in combating the killer disease could now be reversed, WHO recently warned. Over 170 million people, a third of Africa's population, have latent TB infection, estimates suggest." (p27)

"Leadership Needed for AIDS Fight." Africa Recovery v7 n1, Jun 1993. p27.

"Another international conference on AIDS was held in Morocco in December, attended as usual by hundreds of scientific experts as well as by government leaders. The message proclaimed there by World Health Organization officials was reported widely in the American media: African HIV infections were up 1.5 million in 1993 and now total 10 million; there may be as many as 1.75 million Africans dying of AIDS, although only 264,000 cases have actually been reported; women and youths are particularly at risk for infection." (p24)

Johnson, Phillip E. "Symposium: AIDS and the Dog That Didn't Bark." Insight v10 n7, 14 Feb 1994. p24-26. (ISSN1051-4880).

"Some 6.5 million Africans, including 750,000 children, are infected with the AIDS virus, according to the World Health Organization. AIDS is having a 'catastrophically costly' impact on the economy of Africa because it kills people in their productive years, the World Bank says." (p2)

Press, Robert M. "International: Challenges for 1994: Peacekeeping, Droughts Dominate Africa's Agenda." The Christian Science Monitor v86 n28, 4 Jan 1994. p2. (ISSN0882-7729).

"To date, sub-Saharan Africa is one of the world's regions most affected by AIDS; up to mid-1993, WHO [World Health Organization] estimates that more than eight million adult infections have occurred there. In 1990, UNICEF forecast that between 3.1 and 5.5 million children would shortly be orphaned in ten East and Central African countries alone." (p8) "Women are being overwhelmed with having to provide care for chronically ill husbands and brothers. When women fall ill, now at a ratio of 6 women to 5 men in Africa, they are usually cared for by their mothers, sisters or children." (p9)

Kalibala, Samuel/Anderson, Sandra. "AIDS in Africa: A Family Disease." World Health n6, Nov-Dec 1993. p8-10. (ISSN0043-8502).

"In Uganda's Rakai district, where the country's earliest AIDS cases were reported, a 1989 survey found there were 25,000 orphans--12% of the population--under the age of 15. While civil war has played a part, AIDS is the main culprit for the unusually high proportion of parentless children in the district. In 1991, Kagera--Tanzania's worst affected region--was thought to have about 30,000 orphans in a population of 1.4 million." (p5)

Armstrong, Sue. "WorldAIDS Briefing: The Lost Generation." WorldAIDS n26, Mar 1993. p5-8. (ISSN0954-6510).

AIDS (DISEASE)--AFRICA--COSTS

"African health budgets would be overwhelmed by the combined demand of AIDS patients and TB victims. According to papers presented at...[a symposium hosted by the African Development Bank (ADB) on May 11], the direct cost of treating some 90 per cent of expected AIDS patients alone will amount to some $2.2 bn by 1995. This compares to an estimated entire expenditure on health in Africa of some $2.7 bn in 1992. This does not include the cost treating for TB, nor for the indirect costs related to prevention campaigns or for the care of AIDS-related orphans, the numbers of whom could reach 10-15 million by 2000." (p27)

"Leadership Needed for AIDS Fight." Africa Recovery v7 n1, Jun 1993. p27.

"The new scourge of AIDS could cause 8.5 million premature deaths in sub-Saharan Africa by 2000, the [World] Bank says, with falling trends in child mortality already being reversed in some high-prevalence areas. The 10 worst affected African countries may be losing about 0.6 per cent in annual per capita income growth due to lost productivity and costly treatments, and while some one in 40 sub-Saharan adults--one in three in some cities--is now HIV-positive, total spending on AIDS prevention in the sub-region was only $90 mn in 1992. The Bank blames the prevalence of disease and disability in Africa as much on poor resource allocation as on lack of funds. It argues that the cost of disease and disability could be cut by a quarter to a third if African countries spent less on urban hospitals and more on basic health care for the rural poor. Often, 20 per cent of the health budget goes to one central hospital, generally catering to the more affluent, and the Bank argues that health subsidies mostly benefit middle and upper-income groups." (p14-15)

Collins, Carole. "Bank Links Health to Economic Growth." Africa Recovery v7 n2, Oct 1993. p14-15.

"The direct cost of AIDS treatment in Africa is enormous, even though it is not comparable to that in the western world: US$ 32 000 in the United States, as against $393 in sub-Saharan Africa per patient for one year. According to the World Bank, public expenditures on health in sub-Saharan Africa currently range from $1 to $30 per capita. However, most countries spend $5 or less per person." (p9)

Kalibala, Samuel/Anderson, Sandra. "AIDS in Africa: A Family Disease." World Health n6, Nov-Dec 1993. p8-10. (ISSN0043-8502).

AIDS (DISEASE)--AFRICA, SUB-SAHARAN (v19)

AIDS (DISEASE)--AFRO-AMERICANS--HISPANIC AMERICANS

"A study entitled 'AIDS-Related Knowledge, Perceptions and Behaviors among Improverished Minority Women', printed in the January 1993 issue of AMERICAN JOURNAL OF PUBLIC HEALTH, suggests the need for culturally sensitive AIDS prevention programs based on race and levels of acculturation for Latinas and African-American women....High risk behavior was common among all participants in varying degrees. Intravenous drug use was reported by 25% of the high acculturated Latinas as compared with less than 10% of the low acculturated Latinas and African-American women participants. Nonintravenous drugs were used by over 50% of the African-American women and 17% of the high acculturated Latinas but by less than 1% of the low-acculturated Latinas." (p13)

"HIV/AIDS Watch: Minority Women and AIDS." Health Advocate n175, Win 1993. p13.

AIDS (DISEASE)--CUBA

"As of April, a total of 903 people had tested HIV-positive [in Cuba]: of these, 801 are living. They are treated in sanatoriums throughout the island--a controversial policy which was adopted when AIDS was first detected in Cuba. Some have charged that the mandatory sanatorial care violates the rights of AIDS patients. Cuban health authorities argue that the incidence of AIDS has been kept low in Cuba, thanks in part to this policy, and that life is prolonged by the special medical attention guaranteed in the sanatoriums. About 13 million tests have been carried out to date in Cuba; with an overall seropositive rate of .007. Rates for 1991 and 1992 remained stable at .009--an important indicator, given Cuba's economic crunch. The Ministry of Public Health (MINSAP) estimates that sanatorial care costs $14,000 annually per person (an estimate in pesos, but a good share of which MINSAP says is actually U.S. dollars). That figure climbs to $24,000 annually, once a patient is hospitalized." (p28)

Reed, Gail. "Dateline Havana: AIDS Update." Cuba Update n3-4, Summer 1993. p28. (ISSN0196-0830).

AIDS (DISEASE)--EDUCATION--CANADA (v19)

AIDS (DISEASE)--EDUCATION--TANZANIA

According to a study on Tanzanian AIDS related knowledge, "Ignorance and misinformation about AIDS are still rife....15% of respondents believed AIDS is a punishment from God and cannot be prevented; 10-12% think AIDS can be contracted by touching the body or wearing the clothes of a person who died of AIDS; 25% believe AIDS can be transmitted through mosquito and other insect bites; and 20% say the disease only affects prostitutes, barmaids and long-distance truckers." (p4)

Ndejembi, Edna. "Ignorance and AIDS Myths 'Rife'." WorldAIDS n30, Nov 1993. p4. (ISSN0954-6510).

AIDS (DISEASE)--EDUCATION--U.S. (v19)

AIDS (DISEASE)--FORMER SOVIET REPUBLICS

According to Murray Feshbach, "There is a complete lack of clarity in reporting the difference between AIDS and HIV [in the former Soviet Union]. The official number of around 50 to 70 full-blown AIDS, and 580 or so HIV infected individuals is undoubtedly too low. The real numbers are closer to 2,000-5,000 with full-blown AIDS and 10,000-20,000 who are HIV infected. Why does the government not tell the truth about the numbers? If you know the truth you have to spend $100,000 a year per patient. That means you have to budget it and the budget does not have that money." (p42)

Feshbach, Murray. "An American Demographer's View." Surviving Together v11 n3, Fall 1993. p42. (ISSN0859-6286).

AIDS (DISEASE)--HISPANIC AMERICANS

"The prevalence of HIV infection and new AIDS cases among Hispanics is increasing dramatically. In California, the proportion of Hispanics among newly diagnosed AIDS patients increased from 7 percent in 1982 to 18 percent in 1991. Recent focus groups explored norms and beliefs of Hispanic men: single and married, heterosexual and homosexual, native-born and immigrant. Factual knowledge about AIDS and HIV was moderately high in the test groups, but condom use was sporadic." (p8)

"News Clips: AIDS-Related Beliefs among California's Hispanic Men." Population Today v21 n11, Nov 1993. p8. (ISSN0749-2448).

AIDS (DISEASE)--HONDURAS

"Over 75,000 Hondurans are believed to be infected with the [HIV] virus, another 1,500 AIDS cases have been reported, and over 500 Hondurans have died from the disease. Little medical care is available and medication to fight the disease is too expensive for most who have been infected. The lack of public education has led to widespread fear of the disease and of those who have been infected. Employers fire workers who have tested positive and many have been thrown out of their homes by their families....a February 1992 [SAN FRANCISCO] CHRONICLE article...attributed the spread of AIDS to members of the Honduran merchant marines and one gay Honduran orthodontist who frequently visited San Francisco....[It is also possible] that the thousands of US soldiers stationed in Honduras during the 1980s are connected with the spread of AIDS. Known to frequent local brothels (which proliferate near US bases) and even to trade food for sex with starving locals, there is reason to believe that US soldiers are largely responsible for the spread of AIDS in Honduras. The incubation period for the disease would certainly seem to coincide." (p56)

Johnson, Barbara/others. "Whatever Happened to Central America?" Propaganda Review n10, Sum 1993. p10-13,53-56.

AIDS (DISEASE)--HOUSING--U.S.

"Affordable housing is a major problem for many of the 26,000 people in Chicago who have tested positive for the Human Immunodeficiency Virus (HIV). HUD does not recognize HIV or AIDS as a priority for placement in Section 8 housing. If people with AIDS do qualify for Section 8 housing, they are then placed on a four-year waiting list! Officials at the Centers for Disease Control estimate that 15 percent of homeless people in the United States are HIV positive. Workers at homeless shelters in Chicago claim the actual figure is 30-40 percent. One-third to one-half of all people with AIDS are homeless or in imminent danger of becoming homeless. At any given time, 30 percent of all people with AIDS in hospitals are living there because no other residential programs are available." (p8)

"World AIDS Day Dec. 1: Homeless People with AIDS to Protest against HUD." People's Tribune v20 n49, 6 Dec 1993. p8.

AIDS (DISEASE)--INDIA

"After China, India has the largest population of first peoples. Nearly 70 million people--7% of India's total population--live in the subcontinent in 200 tribal groups. India is poised on the brink of a severe AIDS epidemic and its tribal peoples have--in some cases--already encountered HIV and AIDS. The Naga people of India's north-east frontier have the second highest HIV seroprevalence rate in India....A recent survey by India's National AIDS Control Organisation discovered that a third of injecting drug users in Nagaland were HIV positive, and that HIV seroprevalence--at 90.40 cases per thousand--was almost 13 times the national average." (p8)

McKenna, Neil. "Briefing: A Disaster Waiting to Happen: India." WorldAIDS n27, May 1993. p5-9. (ISSN0954-6510).

"An estimated two million truck drivers drive a million trucks on India's highways every day. The nature of their work keeps truckers away from their families for 20 days a month on average. Most of the drivers are young men, aged between 20 and 35, and may have sex with several commercial sex workers at various rest points along the highway where prostitution is common. Many of these prostitutes are HIV positive....Studies about the prevalence of HIV among truck drivers are few and far between. SPYM [Society for Promotion of Youth and Masses] is carrying out a large survey to update a 1990 study of 300 truckers which found half of them had a past history of STD infection, and 14% of them had an active STD at the time." (p11)

"AidsWatch: India: Hitching a Ride." WorldAIDS n31, Jan 1994. p11. (ISSN0954-6510).

AIDS (DISEASE)--INDIANS OF NORTH AMERICA--CANADA

"Statistics on HIV and AIDS among Canadian Indians is scarce. A 1990 study of 1,694 homeless people in Vancouver suggested that HIV infection in Indians was 50% higher than in non-Indians. The first major study on AIDS and Canadian Indians was published earlier this year. Carried out in Ontario by Professor Ted Myers of the University of Toronto, the study found that 45% of Canadian Indians had not heard of AIDS, and few took precautions when having sex." (p9)

McKenna, Neil. "Briefing: A Disaster Waiting to Happen: Canada." WorldAIDS n27, May 1993. p5-9. (ISSN0954-6510).

AIDS (DISEASE)--JAPAN (v19)

AIDS (DISEASE)--KENYA (v19)

"Children orphaned by AIDS or abandoned by HIV positive mothers are a growing problem in Kenya. Since 1984, Dr Elizabeth Ngugi of the University of Nairobi, has been studying 1,500 prostitutes in the city's Pumwani slums. Over 200 of these women since died of AIDS, leaving orphans behind. To date, an estimated 11,500 Kenyan children have lost either one or both parents to AIDS and UNICEF predicts Kenya will have 300,000 AIDS orphans by 1998." (p7)

Munyakho, Dorothy. "We Are Referred to as the AIDS Children." WorldAIDS n26, Mar 1993. p7. (ISSN0954-6510).

AIDS (DISEASE)--NEW YORK (STATE)--PRISONERS

"Advocates and families of prisoners with HIV/AIDS were hopeful when New York passed its medical parole law in April 1992, despite the limitations incorporated within the law....Three hundred and ten prisoners died during 1992 in the New York State correctional system--210 of AIDS. The Correctional Association of New York estimates that an average of 18 prisoners die of AIDS each month in the New York system. According to New York DOCS [Department of Correctional Services] statistics, 234 medical parole applications have been received. Of that number, only nine have been approved for release. Don't look for these figures to change anytime soon, since DOCS has estimated that only 25 prisoners will be released this year under the new law." (p18)

Walker, Jackie. "The National Prison Project AIDS Update." National Prison Project Journal v8 n3, Jul 1993. p18.

AIDS (DISEASE)--NORTH AMERICA--SOUTH AMERICA (v19)

AIDS (DISEASE)--PERU

"While homosexual men still represent a significant percentage of Peru's HIV and AIDS cases--85% of sexually transmitted cases are among gay and bisexual men--in the past four years a large number of new cases have been registered among heterosexuals, especially women. In 1987 the ratio of AIDS cases among men and women was approximately 15 to 1. Today, the male to female ratio is 7 to 1." (p10)

Chauvin, Lucien. "'Pink Plague' Changes Course." WorldAIDS n26, Mar 1993. p10. (ISSN0954-6510).

AIDS (DISEASE)--RUSSIA (v19)

AIDS (DISEASE)--SOUTH AFRICA

"With AIDS reaching this country some five years later than neighbouring countries such as Zimbabwe and Malawi, South Africa had a chance to prevent an epidemic of similarly devastating proportions. But too little money has been thrown at the problem. The budget for the government AIDS programme was R5.4 million (approximately US$1.5 million) in 1991/92--a figure which rose to only R20.9 million (US$6.2 million) in the last financial year." (p1)

Armstrong, Sue. "Apartheid's AIDS Legacy." WorldAIDS n32, Mar 1994. p1. (ISSN0954-6510).

AIDS (DISEASE)--SRI LANKA

"Nearly 400,000 tourists visited Sri Lanka last year, 50,000 of them British. The probable increase of high risk sexual contacts between tourists and Sri Lankan youths is something that worries the government's health department. To date, there have only been 22 cases of AIDS and 65 people have tested HIV positive. But Dr Gamini Jayakuru, the Sri Lankan government's chief venereologist, says there are around 200,000 cases of sexually transmitted diseases each year. Dr Jayakuru estimates that as many as 2,500 Sri Lankans are HIV positive. In a population of 17 million, this figure may seem small, but it represents an increase of 300% in just over a year. The parallels with nearby Thailand--where HIV spread with explosive ferocity--are both obvious and ominous." (p9)

West, Julian. "Selling Cheap Sex and Seashells." WorldAIDS

n26, Mar 1993. p9. (ISSN0954-6510).

AIDS (DISEASE)--THAILAND

"Anxious about damage to tourism, the Chatichai administration...refused to acknowledge the AIDS epidemic [in Thailand]. As many as half a million Thais are now HIV-positive, and by the year 2000, unless government programs are effective, the number will rise to somewhere between two and four million, half of them women. Half of Thai men don't use condoms, and 95 percent of those over twenty-one have slept with a prostitute. Surveys of brothels show an overall HIV infection rate of 22 percent, rising as high as 72 percent in Chiang Mai, the largest city in the North. With a per-capita public-health expenditure of twenty-five dollars, the Thai government says it can only treat four hundred AIDS patients a year." (p47)

Sesser, Stan. "The Course of Corruption." Mother Jones v18 n3, May-Jun 1993. p44-47,67-70,72,74-76. (ISSN0362-8841).

"Thailand already has the most serious AIDS epidemic in Asia. Now there is evidence that HIV has taken root among Thailand's 554,000 tribal peoples. According to Thai government statistics, over 75% of first peoples in the country have received no education. Most are landless and denied Thai citizenship. Many are unable to speak the Thai language. There is a high birth rate, very high unemployment, and drug addiction is common." (p7-8)

McKenna, Neil. "Briefing: A Disaster Waiting to Happen: Thailand." WorldAIDS n27, May 1993. p5-9. (ISSN0954-6510).

AIDS (DISEASE)--U.S. (v19)

"Americans over 50 may want to pay more attention to the AIDS problem. Of the 339,000 Americans infected with the AIDS virus, more than 10 percent are over 50 years old....Last September, the Centers for Disease Control and Prevention reported that more than 34,000 people over 50 had full-blown AIDS (acquired immunodeficiency syndrome), more than double the 16,608 cases in January 1991." (p5)

Baker, Beth/Crowley, Susan L. "AIDS Crisis Reaches Those 50 Plus." AARP Bulletin v35 n2, Feb 1994. p5,8. (ISSN1044-1123).

"Since acquired immune deficiency syndrome (AIDS) was identified in June of 1981, 339,250 cases had been reported through September 1993. Of those individuals, over 204,000 (60 percent) have died (Centers for Disease Control 1993). Individuals 20-29 years of age now account for 20 percent of all cases reported....between September 1992 and September 1993, the number of AIDS cases in adolescents and adults under age 25 reported to the Centers for Disease Control and Prevention (CDC) increased dramatically; the percentage increases were, for males, 20-24 years old--125 percent; females, 20-24 years old--150 percent; males, 13-19 years old--223 percent; and females, 13-19 years old--188 percent (Centers for Disease Control 1993)." (p229)

Robenstine, Clark. "HIV/AIDS Education for Adolescents: School Policy and Practice." Clearing House v67 n4, Mar-Apr 1994. p229-232. (ISSN0009-8655).

AIDS (DISEASE)--U.S.--COSTS (v19)

"The human toll of AIDS in the early 1980s confronted society with a major public health crisis. The severity and rising incidence of the illness also engendered fears that its economic impact, particularly on the health care system, could be overwhelming. When researchers from the Centers for Disease Control (CDC) (Hardy et al. 1986) published the first cost study of AIDS-related care, apprehension increased further. The CDC report estimated that charges for inpatient medical care from diagnosis to death for the first 10,000 persons in the United States reported to have AIDS were $147,000 per case, among the highest costs ever estimated for treatment of a specific illness. However, the CDC study findings (which appeared in January 1986) have never been replicated. Empirical studies published since then have consistently produced much lower estimates of the cost of AIDS care...but the first of these findings did not appear in print until December 1986 (Scitovsky et al. 1986; Seage et al. 1986), almost a year after Hardy et al. published their findings. During nearly all of 1986, key AIDS-related health policies then being formulated were influenced by the belief that, on average, an AIDS patients' hospital costs were $147,000." (p70)

Green, Jesse/others. "The $147,000 Misunderstanding: Repercussions of Overestimating the Cost of AIDS." Journal of Health Politics, Policy and Law v19 n1, Spr 1994. p69-90.

AIDS (DISEASE)--U.S.--HEMOPHILIACS (v19)

"In the early 1980's before proper screening for AIDS was available, 50 percent of hemophiliacs [in the U.S.]--some of whom can be exposed to blood products gleaned from as many as 100,000 donors of blood in a single year--were infected. In most cases, it was years before these victims discovered their plight, and as a result more than 10 percent of their wives and some yet-unborn babies were also unknowingly infected. Today, Americans are told that such a devastating lapse could not recur because technology and awareness has improved to the point that the blood supply is completely safe. Understandably, hemophiliac victims, their families, and those members of the community who have not been infected have a hard time trusting this fact." (pH1868)

Goss, Porter J. (Rep.-Fla.). "Ten Thousand Will Die," Congressional Record (22 Mar 1994). Daily ed. pH1867-1868. (ISSN0363-7239).

AIDS (DISEASE)--U.S.--MINORITIES (v19)

AIDS (DISEASE)--U.S.--MINORITY WOMEN (v19)

AIDS (DISEASE)--U.S.--MORTALITY

"Estimated AIDS deaths [in the U.S.] rose from 29,860 to 33,590 between 1991 and 1992. Although 60 percent of the HIV infected deaths were for white males, compared with 27 percent for black males, the age-adjusted death rate from AIDS was highest for black men. Black women, however, had the largest increase in age-adjusted death rate from AIDS between 1991 and 1992. Of all U.S. AIDS deaths in 1992, 8 percent were to black females." (p4)

"U.S. Reaches Its Highest-Ever Levels for Life Expectancy." Population Today v21 n12, Dec 1993. p4. (ISSN0749-2448).

AIDS (DISEASE)--U.S.--PRISONERS

"For prisoners with HIV/AIDS the lack of a comprehensive discharge plan can be a blueprint for failure. In some cases prisoners with HIV/AIDS unable to find treatment and services on the outside recidivate in order to receive medical care. California Department of Corrections' statistics for 1992 showed a recidivism rate of 70% for prisoners with HIV/AIDS compared to 52% for HIV-negative prisoners." (p18)

Walker, Jackie. "AIDS Update: Prisoners with HIV/AIDS Need Services after Discharge." National Prison Project Journal v9 n2, Spr 1994. p18.

AIDS (DISEASE)--U.S.--WOMEN (v19)

AIDS (DISEASE)--WOMEN (v19)

"Women--specifically women of color--are the fastest growing HIV-positive group. In 1990, women accounted for 25 percent of HIV infections worldwide. Today they constitute 40 percent of all AIDS cases. And by the year 2000, women are expected to constitute the majority of people with AIDS (AIDS IN THE WORLD 1992, ed. Mann, Tantola and Netter). In large part, the rise in AIDS among women has to do with the little reported fact that women are 10 times more at risk of HIV transmission through heterosexual sex with an infected partner (now the primary mode of transmission) than men (Gena Corea, THE INVISIBLE EPIDEMIC: THE STORY OF WOMEN AND AIDS)....All around the world women who work in the sex industry are at a high risk of contracting AIDS.

A study conducted in northern Thailand, for example, found that 70 percent of all prostitutes who had worked at least one year in brothels were HIV positive. The majority of articles in the U.S. press on women with AIDS allude to the prevalence of HIV among prostitutes. But in almost every instance the emphasis is on the potential for sex workers to spread the disease, rather than catch it." (p10)

Devitt, Tiffany. "Women & AIDS: Scant Coverage of a Growing Epidemic." EXTRA! v6 n5, Jul-Aug 1993. p10-11. (ISSN0895-2310).

AIDS (DISEASE)--YOUTH

"At least 100 million children--a population larger than Mexico's--live and work in the streets of cities across the world. Most of them are young teenagers aged between 11 and 14." (p6) "For streetchildren, survival is a constant struggle. Many earn a miserable living selling gum or cigarettes, shining shoes, washing cars or doing odd labouring jobs. Others scavenge on rubbish tips, steal, deal drugs or sell their bodies--sometimes just for a meal or a bed for the night. In the Philippines, an estimated 30% of Manila's 50,000 to 75,000 streetchildren are involved in prostitution....In Brazil...an estimated 8.5% of streetchildren are infected with HIV....A small-scale study in Guatemala reported that 95% of a group of streetgirls had experienced sexual abuse, 34% of them from strangers. Only about 20% of streetchildren are girls, but it varies greatly from country to country....The proportion of girls on the street is increasing in Africa with the impact of AIDS. 'Four years ago, in Lusaka,' adds [Peter] Dalglish, 'the average age of the streetchildren was 14, and 95% of them were male. Today, the average age has dropped to 10, and about 25% are female.'" (p7)

Zavriew, Laurence/McKenna, Neil. "Briefing: On the Brink." WorldAIDS n31, Jan 1994. p6-9. (ISSN0954-6510).

AIDS (DISEASE)--ZIMBABWE

"Zimbabwe is thought to have one of Africa's highest rates of HIV infection. It is hard to know for sure, because health services and statistics are rudimentary. Last year another 30,000 new cases of AIDS were reported. That is twice the entire total for 1987-92; even so, government officials estimate that the actual total for 1993 was 90,000. Extrapolating from periodic blood tests of selected groups, officials estimate that nearly 600,000 Zimbabweans are HIV-positive, out of a population of 10.5m." (p47-48)

"International: AIDS in Zimbabwe: No Myth." Economist v330 n7855, 19 Mar 1994. p47-48,51. (ISSN0013-0613).

AIDS (DISEASE)--ZIMBABWE--MORTALITY

"In Zimbabwe, HIV is mainly transmitted by heterosexuals. Among those worst affected are town-dwelling middle managers in their 30s and 40s. This is a well-off and generally healthy population, except for the prevalence of HIV. Mortality statistics prove something strange is happening. Before 1985, employed men aged 40-44 died at a stable yearly rate of about 3.6 per thousand, according to figures compiled by a leading life-insurance company. By 1990 the figure was 4.3 per thousand; in 1992 it reached 7.5 per thousand." (p48)

"International: AIDS in Zimbabwe: No Myth." Economist v330 n7855, 19 Mar 1994. p47-48,51. (ISSN0013-0613).

AIDS (DISEASE) IN ADOLESCENCE--U.S. (v19)

AIDS (DISEASE) IN CHILDREN--U.S.

"HIV disproportionately affects low-income African-Americans and Latinos. Fifty-four percent of the reported children with AIDS are African-American, although only 14 percent of the nation's children are African-American. In addition, 24 percent of the children with AIDS are Latino, although only 11 percent of the United States are Latino....If the incidence of AIDS continues to increase, within the next 10 years AIDS may become the fifth leading cause of death among children of all ages in the United States. Equally dire are the projections of the number of children that will be orphaned as a result of the HIV-AIDS epidemic--24,6000 under age 13, and 21,000 between the ages of 13 and 17 by 1995. With the current trends, the total number of children orphaned by AIDS is estimated to reach over 85,000 by the year 2000." (pE416)

Serrano, Jose E. (Rep.-N.Y.). "Introduction of a House Resolution to Name the Week...'Pediatric and Adolescent AIDS Awareness Week,'" Congressional Record (11 Mar 1994). Daily ed. pE416. (ISSN0363-7239).

"As of October 1993, 1,412 cases of AIDS were reported among adolescents. Although this number is low and represents only 0.4% of all AIDS cases in the United States, it is very probable that many young adults with AIDS were infected as teens (Centers for Disease Control, 1993, October). Twenty-five percent of infected adolescents acquired HIV through gay sexual activity and another 4% through gay sexual activity and the use of intravenous drugs (Centers for Disease Control, 1993, February; Remafedi, 1988)." (p165)

Dempsey, Cleta L. "Health and Social Issues of Gay, Lesbian, and Bisexual Adolescents." Families in Society v75 n3, Mar 1994. p160-167. (ISSN1044-3894).

According to the Centers for Disease Control and the NCLR AGENDA SUPPLEMENT "Of all populations, children are the least able to avoid HIV infection and are developing AIDS. The CDC reports that there are more than 4,700 children with full-blown AIDS in the U.S. & an estimated 20,000 who are HIV-infected. Minority children represent the majority of pediatric AIDS cases. HIV infection in newborns has been rising on an average of 38% a year. Women and children are the fastest growing population in the AIDS pandemic. An estimated 150,000 women in the U.S. are HIV infected; women of all ages are becoming infected at a rate four times faster than men....Hispanic women are being infected at a higher rate than White women, are younger, and have a 58.7% higher birth rate than non-Hispanic women. 100,000 adolescents are HIV infected; 20% of all AIDS cases are acquired during adolescence. Hispanic children account for more than 24% of the reported pediatric AIDS cases, although they comprise only 13% of the nation's children. Between 1988 and 1993, reported pediatric AIDS cases for White children decreased by 15.8%, but increased 4% for Blacks and 6.6% for Hispanics." (p5)

"Facts about Children Infected with HIV." Family Day Care Bulletin Feb 1994. p5.

AIR--POLLUTION (v19)

AIR--POLLUTION--CHINA

"China...derives three-quarters of its energy supply from coal-burning. And most of China's coal is of the high-sulphur variety, while the country's rate of conversion of coal to energy is only 30 percent, compared to 70 percent for the developed world. As a result of these factors, parts of China are choking on poisonous air." (p17)

Hanson, Eric. "Asia: With Wealth Comes Filth." Toward Freedom v43 n1, Feb 1994. p17,20. (ISSN0048-9898).

AIR--POLLUTION--LAW AND LEGISLATION--U.S.

"State governments, not the federal Environmental Protection Agency, have the primary responsibility for reducing air pollution. Yet states are behind on their 1992 obligations to implement specific control measures required by the Clean Air Act, and they have not completed their 1993 plans to achieve a mandatory 15 percent reduction in pollution. And states with serious ozone smog or carbon monoxide violations have until November 1994 to finalize clean air plans to bring air quality into the healthy range. In many areas, this will require curbs on pollution two to three times greater than the initial 15 percent reduction." (p8)

"Editorials: Pulp Nonfiction." Amicus Journal v15 n4, Win 1994. p8. (ISSN0276-7201).

AIR--POLLUTION--U.S. (v19)

see also AUTOMOBILES--U.S.--POLLUTION CONTROL DEVICES

"The transportation sector [in the U.S.] accounts for a substantial portion of emissions that contribute to ground-level pollution and climate change. Transportation accounts for 30-50% of all ozone-forming emissions and approximately one third of the greenhouse gases emitted nationwide. Emission trends from this sector are profoundly affected by the amount Americans choose to drive. In the past, increasingly stringent standards for emissions of hydrocarbons, nitrogen oxides, and carbon monoxide from motor vehicles and motor vehicle fuels have been able to overcome the impact of increasing travel on levels of health-threatening criteria air pollutants. However, over the past ten years, overall average fuel economy of the new passenger fleet has remained constant but vehicle miles traveled has steadily increased, resulting in an increase in fuel consumption and carbon dioxide emissions." (p20)

Sussman, Robert (Deputy Admin., U.S. Environmental Protection Agency). U.S. House. Committee on Energy and Commerce. "Global Climate Change and Air Pollutants." Hearing, 4 Aug 1993. Washington, D.C.: GPO, 1994. (ISBN0160440661). (Y4.En2/3:103-71).

AIR FARES

see AIRLINES--RATES

AIR TRAFFIC CONTROL

"The global market for air traffic control systems is growing at a rate of 10% annually. Currently about $7 billion per year, the ATC market is expected to reach more than $14 billion by 2002. It is already a fiercely competitive business, particularly since it is dominated by firms seeking to broaden their non-defense work. The capabilities, credibility and competitiveness of American firms in this arena will be strongly affected by the degree to which the United States Air Traffic Control System reflects technical leadership and demonstrates the benefits of advanced technology." (p814)

John, Richard R. (Director, John A. Volpe Nat. Trans. Systems Center). U.S. House. Committee on Appropriations. "Department of Transportation and Related Agencies Approp. for 1994 (Part 6)." Hearing, Washington, D.C.: GPO, 1993. (ISBN0160410746). (Y4.Ap6/1:T68/4/994/pt.6).

"At the heart of...[the air traffic control] system are the computers and communications that take in radar and other data, process it, and display it on console screens. These screens are the window through which the controller receives most of the information needed to assure the safe and efficient movement of traffic through the region of his or her responsibility. Much of the system is quite old, with the result that maintenance requirements and costs are increasing rapidly. The system is inflexible, and overall functionality is limited by the computer and display technology, much of which was installed in the 1970's and embodies technology dating from the 1950's and 1960's. The 1200 controller consoles at the 20 enroute centers now experience approximately 12,000 failures of components every year--an average of one failure every five weeks for each unit." (p804)

John, Richard R. (Director, John A. Volpe Nat. Trans. Systems Center). U.S. House. Committee on Appropriations. "Department of Transportation and Related Agnecies Approp. for 1994 (Part 6)." Hearing, Washington, D.C.: GPO, 1993. (ISBN0160410746). (Y4.Ap6/1:T68/4/994/pt.6).

AIR TRAFFIC CONTROL--U.S.

"Since the air traffic controllers' strike, U.S. aviation has bounced along with delays averaging 900 to 1100 per day....It is only recently that there has been a measurable decline, 770 per day for 1992, but that achievement is tempered by the decline in departures during this recent period of traffic stagnation. What will happen when the economy improves? We fear, without appropriate efforts being put into reducing the systemic causes of air traffic control delays, delays will bounce right back up again to the 900-1100 or even greater range once the industry recovers. When it comes to enhancing the economic condition of the airline industry, improvements in air traffic control can have the greatest immediate payback. Elimination of current ATC delays would result in the elimination of an estimated $2 billion in annual airline losses." (p497)

Merlis, Edward A. (Senior V.P., Air Transportation Assoc. of America). U.S. House. Committee on Appropriations. "Department of Transportation and Related Agencies Approp. for 1994 (Part 8)." Hearing, Washington, D.C.: GPO, 1993. (ISBN0160410657). (Y4.Ap6/1:T68/4/994/pt.8).

AIR TRAVEL--ACCIDENTS--U.S.

"During the 1983 through 1988 period, there was a downward trend in general aviation accidents [in the U.S.], including alcohol-involved general aviation accidents fatal to the pilot. Further, the data show that the percent of conclusive toxicological tests that were alcohol positive for fatally injured general aviation pilots decreased from about 10 percent (corresponding to about 47 accidents per year) in the mid-1970's to about 6 percent (about 17 accidents per year) in the late 1980s. However, data on the general aviation pilots fatally injured in alcohol-involved accidents show evidence of high blood alcohol concentrations (BAC). The mean BAC of the alcohol-positive pilots was 0.15 percent, nearly four times the 0.04 percent BAC offense level established by current Federal Aviation Regulations. The data also show evidence of certificate violations (pertaining to biennial flight review, medical certificates, and airman certificates), and flying experience. Tests for drugs other than alcohol in fatal general aviation accidents were not sufficiently frequent during the 1983 through 1988 period to support any conclusions regarding drug involvement in general aviation accidents. There were a total of 35 drug-involved fatal-to-the-pilot general aviation accidents identified during the period 1983 through 1988." (p177-178)

U.S. House. Committee on Appropriations. "Department of Transportation and Related Agencies Approp. for 1994 (Part 6)." Hearing, Washington, D.C.: GPO, 1993. (ISBN0160410746). (Y4.Ap6/1:T68/4/994/pt.6).

AIR TRAVEL--CHINA (v19)

AIR TRAVEL--U.S. (v19)

"A safe and efficient national airspace system, capable of meeting the demand for air service, is fundamental to the economic stability of the airlines and the aviation industry. Our latest aviation forecasts predict that, over the next decade, the number of passengers using U.S. commercial air services will increase from an average of 1.3 million a day to nearly 2 million. We further predict that a 25 percent increase in air carrier operations will be needed to meet this demand. Today, the top 100 of the nation's busiest airports account for 95 percent of all air carrier passengers and 92 percent of all air carrier operations. Such concentration leads inevitably to delays. The problem lies in the limited capacity of airports to accommodate aircraft on the ground, the limited capacity of the air traffic management system to accommodate aircraft in the air, and the difficulties in integrating the two. Compounding the problem is mounting public concern over noise, congestion, and pollution created by urban airports." (p362-363)

Del Balzo, Joseph M. (Acting Administrator, Federal Aviation Administration). U.S. House. Committee on Appropriations.

"Department of Transportation and Related Agencies Approp. for 1994 (Part 6)." Hearing, Washington, D.C.: GPO, 1993. (ISBN0160410746). (Y4.Ap6/1:T68:4/994/pt.6).

"The FAA [Federal Aviation Association]...makes long term forecasts of industry trends and uses their forecast to determine their personnel and facilities requirements. Prior to this recession (1988) they were forecasting long-term rates of growth for domestic travel that would average 4.8 percent. In their 1993 forecast, that estimate was reduced to 3.9 percent. While this seems a significant reduction, their forecast for international travel increased from 5.1 percent in 1988 to 6.6 percent in 1993. Overall, their long-term forecast for the growth rate in passenger travel is roughly the same today as before the recession. However, while it was expected that the number of passengers would reach 800 million by the year 2000, it is now expected that the airlines will not reach that level until sometime after 2005. The airlines view this period of slow growth as an opportunity for the FAA to make some real progress in reducing the level of air traffic control delays and to build a system that will be ready to respond to the resumption in growth that we all expect." (p577)

U.S. House. Committee on Appropriations. "Department of Transportation and Related Agencies Approp. for 1994 (Part 8)." Hearing, Washington, D.C.: GPO, 1993. (ISBN0160410657). (Y4.Ap6/1:T68/4/994/pt.8).

AIRCRAFT CARRIERS--U.S. (v19)

AIRCRAFT INDUSTRY--U.S. (v19)

"The general aviation industry [in the U.S] has experienced a dramatic decline in production since 1978. In that year, the industry produced 18,000 aircraft, of which 17,000 were piston-engine aircraft. Last year, the industry manufactured only 900 aircraft, including only 555 piston-engine aircraft. According to the General Aviation Manufacturers Association (GAMA), a major reason for the dramatic decline in the light aircraft industry is the application of the doctrine of strict liability in product liability cases arising out of aircraft accidents. GAMA statistics indicate that claim and defense costs for light aircraft airframe and component manufacturers have risen from $24 million in 1976 to $210 million in 1986. The three largest manufacturers of piston-engine aircraft are virtually out of that line of business. By 1986, Cessna, which has been the largest manufacturer of piston-engine models, had dropped completely out of that business. Last year, Beech manufactured only 18 percent of the piston aircraft they made in 1978, and Piper's production of piston aircraft has dropped to 2 percent of the 1978 level. Piper has been in bankruptcy since 1991." (pS3007)

Danforth, John C. (Sen.-Mo.). "General Aviation Revitalization Act of 1994," Congressional Record (16 Mar 1994). Daily ed. pS3006-3009. (ISSN0363-7239).

AIRLINES (v19)

AIRLINES--ASIA

"Aviation activity is growing faster in Asia-Pacific than anywhere else in the world. Asia-Pacific airlines currently account for about 20% of the world market and should capture 25% by year 2000. Both ICAO [International Civil Aviation Organization] and FAA [Federal Aviation Administration] studies project that the international passenger growth rate in Asia-Pacific will average twice the growth rate of anywhere else in the next few years. This region is a vital market for U.S. aviation firms, with U.S. manufactured aircraft comprising about 75% of total air carrier fleets in Asia-Pacific. Japan Airlines and All Nippon Airways are the largest purchasers of Boeing 747s and 767s, respectively. U.S. aerospace exports to Pacific rim almost doubled from 1985 to 1990, rising from $5.8 to over $10 billion. About 20% of commercial jet orders projected by 2005 are destined for the Asia-Pacific region. Finally, Asia-Pacific nations will likely spend nearly $300 billion on air travel infrastructure in the 1990s." (p659)

U.S. House. Committee on Appropriations. "Department of Transportation and Related Agencies Approp. for 1994 (Part 6)." Hearing, Washington, D.C.: GPO, 1993. (ISBN0160410746). (Y4.Ap6/1:T68/4/994/pt.6).

AIRLINES--ECONOMIC CONDITIONS

"Over the past decade, several large airlines have developed serious problems that weaken their financial positions. Chief among these problems are the high levels of debt some airlines have incurred to finance leveraged buy-outs and expansion plans and the operating and marketing practices that raise the costs of competing with the dominant airlines in a market. The five major airlines in financial trouble in 1990--America West, Continental, Eastern, Pan Am, and TWA--all experienced substantial increases in their debt ratios (i.e., long-term debt as a percentage of total capitalization) during the 1980s. All of those airlines had average debt ratios over 80 percent. In contrast, the other six major airlines all held their debt ratios under 65 percent, and most of them held their average debt ratios under 50 percent in 1985-89." (p430)

Mead, Kenneth M. (Director, Trans. Issues Resources, Community, and Economic Dev. Division). U.S. House. Committee on Appropriations. "Department of Transportation and Related Agencies Approp. for 1994 (Part 8)." Hearing, Washington, D.C.: GPO, 1993. (ISBN0160410657). (Y4.Ap6/1:T68/4/994/pt.8).

AIRLINES--EUROPE--U.S. (v19)

AIRLINES--FRANCE (v19)

AIRLINES--JAPAN

"JAL, ANA, and JAS [the three largest airlines in Japan] were extremely profitable during the boom at the end of the 1980s, but when business conditions turned down in the latter half of 1991, so did their results. Fiscal 1992 was dismal all around. JAL and JAS posted current losses of Y53.8 billion ($506 million) and Y4.8 billion ($45 million) respectively; ANA was still in the black, but its profits had plummeted by almost a third in the space of a year. This year, all three are forecasting red ink, and unless their restructuring programs are successful, the losses will be large indeed." (p18)

Yamauchi, Hirotaka. "Strategic Restructuring: Airlines: Flying Low." Look Japan v39 n453, Dec 1993. p18-19. (ISSN0456-5339).

"There are 10 Japanese airlines: seven run scheduled air passenger services; two are charter airlines; and one is a freight carrier. The Big Three in the industry are Japan Airlines (JAL), All Nippon Airways (ANA), and Japan Air System (JAS): together they service roughly 91% of the passengers on both domestic and international routes, with ANA claiming about 45% of the domestic market and JAL about 75% of the international market. The other airlines are for the most part their subsidiaries. The domestic air transport market, with about 70 million passengers annually (55 billion revenue-passenger kilometers), is one-sixth (one-tenth) the size of the US market. On international routes, Japan's airlines carry about 101 million passengers a year, about one-quarter what US carriers do." (p18)

Yamauchi, Hirotaka. "Strategic Restructuring: Airlines: Flying Low." Look Japan v39 n453, Dec 1993. p18-19. (ISSN0456-5339).

AIRLINES--TAXATION--U.S. (v19)

"Like others in the industry, NWA [Northwest Airlines] has suffered in excess of $1.68 billion in after-tax losses over the past three years (and $1.48 billion over the past five years). In spite of our losses, we have continued to pay enormous sums of excise taxes and fees to the federal treasury....A review of NWA's recent financial results discloses the following staggering economic facts: Between 1990 and 1992, our domestic operating revenues rose 3.86%, but our federal transportation excise tax payments increased 42.02%. During this same 3 year period, our after-tax losses totalled some $1.68 billion, but we actually paid $1.04 billion in federal transportation excise taxes. Over the five years from 1988-92, NWA's losses were $1.48 billion, but NWA paid $1.55 billion in transportation excise taxes to the federal government." (p534-535)

Seiden, Elliott M. (V.P., Law and Government Affairs, Northwest Airlines). U.S. House. Committee on Appropriations. "Department of Transportation and Related Agencies Approp. for 1994 (Part 8)." Hearing, Washington, D.C.: GPO, 1993. (ISBN0160410657). (Y4.Ap6/1:T68/4/994/pt.8).

"The airlines have estimated the cost of the proposed BTU tax to be $1.1 to $2.1 billion annually. The lower number is based on the assumption that the tax pass-thru would result in an 8 cents per gallon increase in the price of jet fuel. The American Petroleum Institute, however, contends that refiners, for competitive reasons, will not be able to pass through the full cost of the tax to their customers who purchase bunker fuel since many of these customers would be able to switch to coal or natural gas which are taxed at a lower rate. The American Petroleum Institute estimates that the refiners will pass these costs on to those customers who have no substitute fuel available or whose demand is inelastic. They estimate that the impact on jet fuel will raise the price an additional two to seven cents bringing the total tax increase on jet fuel to 10 to 15 cents per gallon. In 1992, the airlines consumed 11.76 billion gallons in domestic service and purchased another 2.05 billion gallons in this country for international service bringing total purchases in the U.S. to 13.81 billion gallons. At 10 cents per gallon the added cost to the industry would be $1.4 billion. At 15 cents per gallon the added cost to the industry would be $2.1 billion." (p579)

U.S. House. Committee on Appropriations. "Department of Transportation and Related Agencies Approp. for 1994 (Part 8)." Hearing, Washington, D.C.: GPO, 1993. (ISBN0160410657). (Y4.Ap6/1:T68/4/994/pt.8).

AIRLINES--U.S.

"Since deregulation, the number of passengers using the domestic aviation system has exploded. As a result of the vast increases in passengers, 23 airports [in the U.S.] currently suffer 20,000 hours of delay or more per year. If nothing further is done to increase system capacity, the FAA forecasts that the number of airports with 20,000 hours or more of delay per year will increase to 36 in less than 10 years--a daunting increase. This results in billions of dollars per year of delay costs and lost productivity throughout the system." (p953)

Howard, George (President, ACI-NA). U.S. House. Committee on Appropriations. "Department of Transportation and Related Agencies Approp. for 1994 (Part 7A)." Hearing, Washington, D.C.: GPO, 1993. (ISBN0160411033). (Y4.Ap6/1:T68/4/994/pt.7A).

"The airline industry and its users already have a disproportionately high tax burden--fees, excise taxes, property taxes, alternative minimum taxes, etc. Since the airline industry is the core of the immense travel and tourism business, which employs an estimated 8.8 million--more than 7.2% of all the jobs in the United States--the United States will not have an improved economy without a healthy airline industry. Therefore, it is only reasonable to ask that certain tax issues particularly adverse to the airlines be mitigated. Because of the impact of travel and tourism on the economy, and since it generates a $9.4 billion surplus in the nation's trade balance, imposition of major new taxes--including the BTU tax--may disproportionately impact the nation's economic recovery." (p593)

U.S. House. Committee on Appropriations. "Department of Transportation and Related Agencies Approp. for 1994 (Part 8)." Hearing, Washington, D.C.: GPO, 1993. (ISBN0160410657). (Y4.Ap6/1:T68/4/994/pt.8).

"The international aviation industry, like the domestic industry, has been changing. The international market is expected to grow about twice as fast as the domestic market through the year 2000. Thus, the major U.S. airlines have begun to focus greater attention on expanding their international operations. Between 1987 and 1991 the proportion of major U.S. airlines' systemwide revenue passenger miles represented by international operations grew about 22 percent, and international operations now account for about 26 percent operations....For the three largest major airlines, the growth in international operations has been dramatic, with international revenue passenger miles more than doubling between 1987 and 1991." (p440-441)

Mead, Kenneth M. (Director, Trans. Issues Resources, Community, and Economic Dev. Division). U.S. House. Committee on Appropriations. "Department of Transportation and Related Agencies Approp. for 1994 (Part 8)." Hearing, Washington, D.C.: GPO, 1993. (ISBN0160410657). (Y4.Ap6/1:T68/4/994/pt.8).

"The National Transportation Safety Board, an organization we created to look into accidents, and in this case aircraft accidents, reported that in 203 accidents which resulted in litigation against the Beech Aircraft Co. between 1983 and 1986, design or manufacturing error was not a cause of any of the accidents. Yet the average cost of each one of those lawsuits to the manufacturer was $530,000--$530,000 multiplied by 203 lawsuits--in which the expert outside board determined that manufacturing and design defects were not the cause of the accident." (pS2441)

Gorton, Slade (Sen.-Wash.). "National Competitiveness Act," Congressional Record (8 Mar 1994). Daily ed. pS2438-2452. (ISSN0363-7239).

AIRLINES--U.S.--DEREGULATION (v19)

AIRLINES--U.S.--ECONOMIC CONDITIONS

"Reduced income and employment in any one sector of the economy will have repercussions on other sectors--the magnitude of the impact depending on the interstitial relationships among effected industries. The impact is called the 'multiplier effect'....Obviously such effects go both ways and downturns in one sector have effects on related industries. The Bureau of Economic Analysis in the Department of Commerce calculates input-output tables for the nation's economic activity. The Bureau of Labor Statistics updates these tables and calculates industry specific employment multipliers. According to a BLS analyst, the multiplier for airline employment is 1.02--that is, for every job gained or lost in the airline industry just over 1 additional job is lost in other industries related to the airline industry. Industry claims that 2 or 3 jobs are lost in other travel-related industries for each job lost in the airline industry are not necessarily wrong, however. The multiplier relates to the loss of other jobs directly as a result of the lost job in the airline industry. The loss of jobs in the travel industry might be coincidental to the lost airline jobs. Each was caused by the same set of factors (weak economy, etc.), but only one of the 2 or 3 other jobs lost can be traced directly to the reduced airline employee." (p472)

U.S. House. Committee on Appropriations. "Department of Transportation and Related Agencies Approp. for 1994 (Part

8)." Hearing, Washington, D.C.: GPO, 1993. (ISBN0160410657). (Y4.Ap6/1:T68/4/994/pt.8).

"The Big Three [airlines] (American, United and Delta) account for 58 percent of the traffic and, except for a small profit recorded by United in 1990, all three have reported losses in each of the past three years. However, removing the losses associated with FAS 106 (a federal accounting standard that requires that airlines' financial records more accurately reflect the expected costs of benefits offered to retirees), the Big Three lost $2.27 billion of the $7.91 billion lost by the industry between 1990 and 1992. Thus, the carriers with 58 percent of the market experienced 29 percent of the losses. Our concern is that a sufficient number of airlines survive to ensure that the benefits to the travelling public from the competition spawned by deregulation continue." (p485)

U.S. House. Committee on Appropriations. "Department of Transportation and Related Agencies Approp. for 1994 (Part 8)." Hearing, Washington, D.C.: GPO, 1993. (ISBN0160410657). (Y4.Ap6/1:T68/4/994/pt.8).

"The deregulation of the American airline industry began in the mid 1970s and was designed to inaugurate a free market in passenger air transport....Surprisingly, however, the industry has been in continuous crisis with the firms remaining after the shakeout making very large losses. In total, they have lost about $8 billion over the past three years. This is a sum so large that it actually exceeds the total profits of the industry as a whole throughout its entire history. And losses are expected to continue in 1993 at about $700 million. American, for example, lost $935 million in 1992, and Delta $565 million. In the industry, the consequences of these losses are severe: Delta laid off 600 pilots in early 1993 (abandoning a 36 year old policy of no lay-offs), retired 21 jets and cancelled orders from Boeing." (p190)

Romer, Stephen. "Barriers to Exit: Chapter 11 Bankruptcy and the U.S. Passenger Airline Industry." Economics and Business Education v1 n4, Win 1993. p190-191.

AIRLINES--U.S.--RATES

"Both GAO [United States General Accounting Office] and the Department of Transportation (DOT) have found that [U.S.] consumers pay higher fares when flying from airports where there is little competition. In our analysis of 1988 fares, we found that fares for flights from concentrated airports were about 20 percent higher than for trips of similar lengths from other airports....DOT reported that fares at a group of eight airports dominated by one airline were about 19 percent higher than average fares in 1988. A recently released DOT study of 1991 fares showed no change in this premium. While most routes continue to be served by several competitors, if the industry continues to consolidate, the decrease in competition could lead to higher fares." (p429)

Mead, Kenneth M. (Director, Trans. Issues Resources, Community, and Economic Dev. Division). U.S. House. Committee on Appropriations. "Department of Transportation and Related Agencies Approp. for 1994 (Part 8)." Hearing, Washington, D.C.: GPO, 1993. (ISBN0160410657). (Y4.Ap6/1:T68/4/994/pt.8).

"TWA's 1992 actions are a good example of fare cuts which are damaging to the industry. All told, TWA initiated 35 fare cuts, offering an average discount of 32%. On average, these fare cuts were available for only 5.9 days. Even this average selling period is somewhat overstated, since only 3 of 35 sales were available for more than 3 days. Northwest's actions were also harmful. They initiated four fare cuts for 1992, with an average discount of 41% and average duration of 7.3 days. In 1993 America West has been responsible for half of all fare cuts. Their strategy has been to continually roll-over their Winter Sale special. This effectively produced a semi-permanent sale, which to date has lasted four months. Northwest has initiated the remaining 1993 fare cuts. On average, Northwest's fare actions have discounted travel by 35% and have been available to consumers for only 4.8 days. Reaffirming our results, Aviation Forecasting & Economics (AF&E) has stated in a recent study that the primary cause for the decline in industry yields, the amount a passenger pays to fly one mile, are pricing practices resulting from insolvent carriers' needs for cash. In fact, AF&E states that these pricing policies actually begin years before a carrier files for bankruptcy." (p584)

U.S. House. Committee on Appropriations. "Department of Transportation and Related Agencies Approp. for 1994 (Part 8)." Hearing, Washington, D.C.: GPO, 1993. (ISBN0160410657). (Y4.Ap6/1:T68/4/994/pt.8).

AIRPLANES--SAFETY MEASURES

see AERONAUTICS--U.S.--SAFETY MEASURES

AIRPORTS--ORLANDO (FLA)

"Orlando International Airport has experienced unprecedented growth in the past eleven years, and is ranked the 18th busiest airport in the...[U.S.]. In 1992, domestic passenger traffic increased by 13.3%, and international traffic increased 27.5%. During this same period, more than 21.1 million passengers used the airport as compared to only 6 million in 1981....In 1992, the Orlando International Airport generated a $5.4 billion economic impact in Central Florida. Approximately 10,500 jobs are directly associated with the airport. International and domestic tourists contributed $2.4 billion to the Orlando metropolitan economy. As the world's most popular tourist destination, Central Florida substantially attracts foreign currency to assist in the balance of trade. According to an independent Peat Marwick study, within the next five years, total passenger traffic is expected to increase by 61% and international activities will increase 148%. In 1998 nearly 30 million passengers are expected to use Orlando International Airport." (p132)

U.S. House. Committee on Appropriations. "Department of Transportation and Related Agencies Approp. for 1994 (Part 7A)." Hearing, Washington, D.C.: GPO, 1993. (ISBN0160411033). (Y4.Ap6/1:T68/4/994/pt.7A).

AIRPORTS--TEXAS

"Today, our 1960's-vintage control system is in danger of being overwhelmed by the increased air traffic (D/FW [Dallas/Fort Worth] Airport is served by 17 airlines flying to a total of 200 cities both in the United States and abroad). Our skies are so crowded that FAA air traffic controllers sometimes have as many as 56 airplanes, in train 7 miles apart, strung out over 350 miles and four states, all queued up for entry into the Dallas/Fort Worth area. In addition to D/FW Airport, the FAA serves an astonishing total of 131 other airports in the Dallas-Fort Worth area. While many of these are small landing strips, there are a number of very busy satellite airports including Addison, Alliance, Redbird, Meacham, Love, Dallas Naval Air Station, and Carswell Air Force Base. All of these airports will benefit from the Metroplex Plan as well." (p310)

Frost, Martin (Rep.-Tex.)/others. U.S. House. Committee on Appropriations. "Department of Transportation and Related Agencies Approp. for 1994 (Part 7A)." Hearing, Washington, D.C.: GPO, 1993. (ISBN0160411033). (Y4.Ap6/1:T68/4/994/pt.7A).

AIRPORTS--U.S.

"Miami International Airport (MIA) is the world's tenth busiest airport in total passenger traffic. On a national scale, our airport is second busiest in terms of international passengers and cargo. The Dade County System of Airports, and particularly MIA, is one of Dade County's primary economic catalysts and continues to experience significant growth under the direction of the Metro-Dade Aviation Department. Nearly 27 million passengers and over one million tons of cargo travelled through MIA during 1992. The aviation industry has a tremendous impact on our community, as one in five of us derives our livelihood from aviation-related activities, accounting for an annual payroll of $1.4 billion. Aviation's total local economic impact amounts to over $9 billion." (p578)

Penelas, Alexander (Chairman, Community Affairs Committee, Metro-Dade County, FL). U.S. House. Committee on Appropriations. "Department of Transportation and Related Agencies Approp. for 1994 (Part 7A)." Hearing, Washington, D.C.: GPO, 1993. (ISBN0160411033). (Y4.Ap6/1:T68/4/994/pt.7A).

"Gold plating is perhaps not the correct word, but has become a euphemism for wasteful spending. A few examples: National Airport's new terminal, for which the airlines agreed to a 25 percent construction contingency is being designed to cost $50 million more than the budget, prior to turning the first spade of dirt. The entire modernization program to date is $125 million over budget. By the Authority's own admission, they are out to build a monument. At JFK airport, the Port Authority spent $21 million on the construction of a baggage tunnel which sits unfinished and unused. The Port Authority also built a $56 million parking garage, which cost an average of $39,000 per space, nearly four times the industry average for such construction. That garage remains a tremendously under-used facility in the middle of the airport's circular roadway system. New Denver Airport will cost $2.3 billion for an airport with the same number of runways and fewer gates than the existing facility. This airport is being built over the strong objections of the carriers, who supported a less expensive solution to the delay problems in Denver--a new runway at Stapleton." (p574)

U.S. House. Committee on Appropriations. "Department of Transportation and Related Agencies Approp. for 1994 (Part 8)." Hearing, Washington, D.C.: GPO, 1993. (ISBN0160410657). (Y4.Ap6/1:T68/4/994/pt.8).

AIRPORTS--U.S.--COSTS

"Airport costs constitute approximately 4 percent of airline operating costs. PFCs [Passenger Facility Charges] at any given airport may account for 1 percent of airlines costs. So, to begin with, we are looking at a very small percentage of airline costs. Further, these costs vary significantly when examined airport by airport. For example, Minneapolis has airport costs, excluding their PFC, of $2.96 per passenger. Detroit, again exclusive of their PFC, is $3.54. Chicago O'Hare is $11.72 per passenger, and Chicago has applied to collect PFCs. So the 'playing field' of airport costs is not level to begin with. We expect any disparate impacts which can be attributed to PFCs are negligible and will disappear within a few years. 19 of the 28 large hub airports in the country either have PFCs approved of [or] are in the application process. We fully expect that virtually all airports, both hubs and destination airports, will eventually seek PFC revenue to fund major airport expansion programs....Nearly 100 locations are currently authorized to collect PFCs, providing revenue in excess of $6.4 billion, over an average collection period of 8 years. The total amount originally requested in these applications was $14.6 billion. Of this amount, FAA has approved $6.4 billion; disapproved $1.8 billion; and deferred decision on $141 million." (p563)

U.S. House. Committee on Appropriations. "Department of Transportation and Related Agencies Approp. for 1994 (Part 6)." Hearing, Washington, D.C.: GPO, 1993. (ISBN0160410746). (Y4.Ap6/1:T68:4/994/pt.6).

ALABAMA

see HAZARDOUS WASTE SITES--ALABAMA

ALASKA

see also FISHERIES--ALASKA; GRIZZLY BEAR--ALASKA; LOGGING--ALASKA; PETROLEUM RESERVES--ALASKA

ALASKA--ECONOMIC CONDITIONS (v19)

ALASKA--FUEL CONSUMPTION (v19)

ALASKA--POLITICS AND GOVERNMENT

"For two decades Alaska's 550,000 residents have sat gratefully at a groaning board of goodies, all courtesy of an oil industry that finances 85% of the state's budget. They pay neither a sales tax nor a state income tax. One recent survey showed that Alaskans are the least-taxed members of the Union. Not only that; each resident also receives an annual cheque from the state of $900 or more. In all, Alaska's state government spends over four times as much on each of its pampered residents as any other state. Such a party. Such a hangover. State legislators who convened in Juneau...now face a two-year budget deficit of $1.2 billion or more. Oil prices have plunged since hitting $32 a barrel in September 1990, and now stand at barely $10 a barrel. That sharply diminishes the amount the state can skim off in royalties and taxes." (p33)

"American Survey: Alaska's Budget: Now, the Diet." Economist v330 n7848, 29 Jan 1994. p33. (ISSN0013-0613).

ALBANIA

see also PRIVATIZATION--ALBANIA; UNEMPLOYMENT--ALBANIA

ALBANIA--POPULATION

"Today if you look at the Albanian nation of seven million people in the Balkans, only 3.5 million are in Albania and there is another 3.5 million on the borders of Albania--2 million in Kosova, 1 million in Macedonia, 100,000 in Montenegro and another 100,000 in Presheva, Bujanovc and Medvegje." (pE737)

DioGuardi, Joe. "The Albanian Perspective on Peace in the Balkans," Congressional Record (21 Apr 1994). Daily ed. pE737-738. (ISSN0363-7239).

ALCOHOL--U.S. (v19)

ALCOHOLIC BEVERAGES

see also ADVERTISING--ALCOHOLIC BEVERAGES

ALCOHOLIC BEVERAGES--RUSSIA

"Russians have not stopped drinking vodka: every year they spend some $10 billion on the stuff, knocking back some 4.5 billion bottles--or about 15 litres (3 1/3 gallons) for each man, woman and child." (p68)

"Business: Rasputin is Alive and Bottled." Economist v331 n7858, 9 Apr 1994. p68. (ISSN0013-0613).

ALCOHOLIC BEVERAGES--TAXATION--FRANCE--GREAT BRITAIN

"Since the European Union's single market officially came into being in January 1993, Britain's drinks trade claims to have lost more than 1 billion [pounds sterling] ($1.5 billion) in sales. People have poured across the English Channel to buy their booze in France, where excise duties are much lower. France levies 99 [pence] less on a bottle of wine than Britain. For champagne, the saving is 1.57 [pounds sterling]; and for a pint of beer, 25 [pence]. Since the pre-tax prices of champagne and lager are also lower in France, total savings can be bigger still--up to 60 [pounds sterling] on a case of bubbly and 10 [pounds sterling] on six litres of some beers." (p56)

"Britain: Cross-Channel Booze: Glug Glug." Economist v331 n7860, 23 Apr 1994. p56,61. (ISSN0013-0613).

ALCOHOLIC BEVERAGES--TAXATION--GREAT BRITAIN--U.S. (v19)

ALCOHOLISM

see also FETAL ALCOHOL SYNDROME--U.S.; WOMEN--

U.S.--ALCOHOL USE; YOUTH--U.S.--ALCOHOL USE

ALCOHOLISM--JAPAN (v19)

"'Japanese society is very tolerant of drunks,' comments [Dr. Nobuhiko] Ishii. 'We sell beer and whiskey in vending machines, merchants sell liquor to kids 'for their parents,' and drunks are forgiven because, after all, they are drunk.' He adds that if intoxication were seen as a public nuisance, alcoholics would have a better chance of being diagnosed sooner. Satoru Saito, a psychiatrist and author of several books on alcoholism, agrees: 'Alcoholics have to be pretty far gone--with liver problems and other serious diseases--before they or anyone else recognizes that there is a problem.' The government equates the number of alcoholics with the number of people being treated for alcoholism as inpatients in psychiatric wards, and reports a total of 18,000 for 1992. Saito puts the number at about 3.5 million, and several times that if alcohol abusers (a category that includes many people who will eventually become alcoholic) are included. Even doctors, who are supposed to be trained to recognize diseases, are generally ignorant when it comes to alcoholism." (p33)

Saphir, Ann/Mineshige, Miyuki. "Body and Soul: Alcoholism: Walk on By." Look Japan v39 n452, Nov 1993. p32-35. (ISSN0456-5339).

ALCOHOLISM--NEW MEXICO

"The roads in America's west are long and lonely, running for miles through spectacular mountains, plains and deserts. And policemen are few. Small wonder, then, that an agreeable companion for western journeys is often a bottle of liquor or a six-pack of beer; small wonder, too, that the drunk-driving rates in western states have long been the highest in the country. New Mexico, one of the worst offenders...is the one that has made the most dramatic effort to improve. Until last year, the state had the worst drunken-driving rate in the country. In America at large, the chance of being involved in an alcohol-related traffic crash at some time during your life is about 40%; in New Mexico, it is more than twice that. It is part of New Mexico's wider weakness for the bottle. Its rates of fetal alcohol syndrome and cirrhosis of the liver also run at more than twice the national average. The alcoholism rate is more than three times as high." (p30)

"American Survey: Drinking and Driving: Six-Pack Highway." Economist v331 n7858, 9 Apr 1994. p30. (ISSN0013-0613).

ALCOHOLISM--U.S. (v19)

ALCOHOLISM AND TRAFFIC ACCIDENTS

see DRINKING AND TRAFFIC ACCIDENTS

ALFALFA INDUSTRY--U.S.

"In 1993/94, alfalfa hay was harvested on 24.3 million acres [in the U.S.], up slightly from 24.2 million a year ago. Alfalfa's share of total hay acres barely declined to 40 percent. Alfalfa yields for 1993/94 rose to 3.46 tons per acre, up from 3.30 tons for last year's crop." (p11)

U.S. Dept. of Agriculture. "Hay Supplies Decline in 1993/94; Quality Questioned." Feed Situation and Outlook Report Nov 1993. p11-12.

ALGERIA--ECONOMIC CONDITIONS

"Muslim terrorists [in Algeria]...have murdered two dozen foreigners since September and vow to kill others who don't leave. There's a chance that this wave of terror may mark the worst point in Algeria's two-year-old struggle between a repressive, army-backed regime and Islamic fundamentalists seeking an Iranian-style government....Popular support for the fundamentalists stems less from religious zeal than from a sick economy with 30% unemployment--the result of a corrupt, one-party socialist system. Algeria is oil-rich, but falling prices mean petroleum income is down--to $10 billion in 1993, from $12 billion in 1992. And 90% of oil revenues go to service the country's foreign debt of more than $26 billion." (p55)

Toy, Stewart/Hoots, Charles. "International Outlook: Algeria: A Storm Gathering on the Mediterranean." Business Week n3353, 10 Jan 1994. p55. (ISSN0007-7135).

"One obstacle [to ending economic problems] is beyond Algeria's control: world oil prices. Oil and gas account for more than 90% of exports. Last year they were expected, at one time, to bring in $12 billion, around a quarter of GDP [gross domestic product]. The outcome was probably $10 billion-11 billion. With prices now still lower, this year's total could be no better--and merely servicing foreign debt costs $9 billion. No wonder the government headed by Redha Malek has been talking for months to the IMF [International Monetary Fund], and is now seeking to reschedule the $7 billion a year or so of capital repayment that make up the bulk of the debt burden." (p46)

"International: Algeria: The Economy Too." Economist v330 n7846, 15 Jan 1994. p46,48. (ISSN0013-0613).

Algeria's $26 billion foreign debt "costs the country $9 billion a year in interest payments. At the same time, the country's income (which is derived largely from oil-based products) has suffered from a worldwide price slump. The country loses $500 million for every dollar drop in world oil prices, and prices are now the lowest since the Persian Gulf war. This year's receipts barely covered the interest payments, leaving the government with little to pay for vital imports." (p16)

Barraclough, Colin. "Algeria Lurches toward Civil War." Insight v10 n6, 7 Feb 1994. p14-17. (ISSN1051-4880).

"For 30 years, the government [in Algeria] consistently neglected the agricultural sector despite its potential as a spur to the country's development. Bad management simultaneously hastened the flight of villagers from the countryside, impoverishing farming areas and swelling the cities with people who could find neither homes nor jobs. The government now spends $3 billion a year to import wheat from the United States while many of Algeria's own farms go untended. Following the expulsion of the French, the country's self-proclaimed liberators imposed restrictions that succeeded in gagging healthy criticism and in driving away many of Algeria's intellectuals. Population control programs have proven an utter failure, with the number of Algerians increasing from nine million in 1962 to some 26 million today. The nation is now drowning amidst a foreign debt of $26 billion, the equivalent of $1000 for every Algerian. Critical housing and transportation needs are going unmet, while educational programs are being cut in a country where three out of four people are under 30 years of age." (p20)

Aziz, Barbara Nimri. "North Africa: Algeria: From Liberation to Terrorism in 30 Years." Toward Freedom v43 n1, Feb 1994. p19-20. (ISSN0048-9898).

ALGERIA--HISTORY--CIVIL WAR (v19)

ALGERIA--POPULATION

"Most of the antigovernment feeling [in Algeria] stems from a growing underclass of disaffected Arabic speakers--largely young males--who feel rejected by mainstream society. A knowledge of French still is required for most decent jobs, yet Algeria's young learn only Arabic. Two-thirds of the country's population is under the age of 26 and half of those are unemployed. And with one of the world's highest growth rates doubling the population every 23 years, the housing shortage is critical." (p16)

Barraclough, Colin. "Algeria Lurches toward Civil War." Insight v10 n6, 7 Feb 1994. p14-17. (ISSN1051-4880).

ALGERIA--SOCIAL CONDITIONS

"Algeria has had a modest rate of increase in its GNP [gross national product] per capita, of 2.1 percent per year, to an estimated $2,060 in 1990. Its life expectancy is in the mid-60s and its IMR [infant mortality rate] is about 74. The rate of natural increase has decreased slightly, from 3.1 percent in 1960-65 to 2.7 percent in 1985-90. The crude death rate was cut in half during this period, and the crude birth rate declined by 15 points from 50 to 35. The TFR [total fertility rate] is still high, although it declined by almost two children per woman from 7.38 to 5.43 from 1960-65 to 1985-90. Literacy remains at the low level of 57 percent for males and 45 percent for females. Major gains have been achieved in primary plus secondary school enrollment both for males and females during the past three decades, with female enrollment ratios at 72 percent in 1990. Algeria's family planning efforts have been weak, but they improved from a score of 25 in 1982 to 46 in 1989. Contraceptive prevalence was 35.5 percent in 1986-87, the date of the latest national sample survey." (p87)

Mauldin, W. Parker/Ross, John A. "Prospects and Programs for Fertility Reduction, 1990-2015." Studies in Family Planning v25 n2, Mar-Apr 1994. p77-95. (ISSN0039-3665).

ALIENS--U.S. (v19)

ALIENS, ILLEGAL

see also CRIME--LOS ANGELES (CALIF)--ALIENS, ILLEGAL

ALIENS, ILLEGAL--CALIFORNIA (v19)

"It is estimated that 1,000,000 illegal immigrants and their children live in Los Angeles. Gov. Pete Wilson estimates that medical, K-12 educational, and law enforcement costs for California's illegal immigrants total nearly $2 billion annually, and that figure is rising. Currently, two-thirds of all the babies born in Los Angeles County public hospitals are born to undocumented immigrants." (pH10499)

Harman, Jane (Rep.-Calif.). "Immigration Policy," Congressional Record (21 Nov 1993). Daily ed. pH10499-10500. (ISSN0363-7239).

"Characteristics of the illegal alien population of San Diego County: 220,000 illegal aliens reside in the County, accounting for 7.9 percent of the total population. There are 13,310 illegal alien students in County public schools. Illegal aliens account for 22 percent of all felony arrests in San Diego....Illegal aliens in San Diego remit $179 million to their home countries." (p3)

"San Diego Ups Estimated County Cost for Illegal Immigration to $244 Million Annually." FAIR Immigration Report v13 n10, Dec 1993. p3.

"South of Orange County at the Mexican frontier, the U.S. Border Patrol makes the conservative estimate that each day 2,700 people enter America illegally. Most are Mexican nationals, coming to what Chicano activists call 'Aztlan,' the area from Texas to California, lands taken during the Mexican-American War." (p24)

Maharidge, Dale. "Can We All Get Along?" Mother Jones v18 n6, Nov-Dec 1993. p20-27. (ISSN0362-8841).

"The number of foreigners entering the US reached 1.1 million last year, the highest since 1907, and nearly 10 million have arrived over the past decade. Forty percent have come to California. Now that the state is mired in recession, and budget cuts are being forced at state, city and county levels, voters have become highly sensitive to footing welfare bills, the competition for too few jobs, additional strain on schools caused by non-English-speaking students, and a surge in hate crimes against foreigners....a November 1993 study by Rice University sociologist Don Huddle is drawing attention. The study argues the 7.4 million legal and illegal immigrants who have settled in California since 1970 cost taxpayers $18 billion more than they paid in taxes." (p3)

Wood, Daniel B. "In Immigration, Lawmakers See Source of California's Problems." The Christian Science Monitor v86 n59, 17 Feb 1994. p3. (ISSN0882-7729).

ALIENS, ILLEGAL--CALIFORNIA--COSTS

"In San Diego County, one of the country's areas hardest hit by illegal immigration, illegal aliens pay $59.7 million annually in local and state taxes. These same immigrants, though, use $244.2 million in public services each year, according to a report released by two San Diego State University professors in October last year." (p2)

"Costs Prove 'Borderless World' Advocates Wrong." FAIR Immigration Report v16 n2, Feb 1994. p2.

ALIENS, ILLEGAL--CALIFORNIA--ILLINOIS

"America's largest states, led by California and Florida, are up in arms over the soaring costs of illegal immigration.... Governor [Pete] Wilson says the costs have gone wild. For example, in just four years, California's price tag for free medical care to indigent illegal aliens has risen 18-fold to more than $800 million....California...has an estimated 1 million illegal residents. Even some states far from the border, such as Illinois, find their costs expanding for services to illegal immigrants. In Illinois, such services currently cost $177 million a year. An aide to Governor Edgar says that includes $48 million for medical care, $77 million for education (K-12), and well over $40 million for prisons to house criminal aliens....Migration from Mexico--legal and illegal--has given Chicago the second largest Hispanic population in the US." (p3)

Dillin, John. "Big States Want US to Pay Costs of Illegal Aliens." The Christian Science Monitor v86 n49, 3 Feb 1994. p3. (ISSN0882-7729).

ALIENS, ILLEGAL--FLORIDA

"According to Florida's governor, Lawton Chiles, immigration already accounts for 95% of the state's population growth over the past decade. More than 20% of schoolchildren in Dade County, which includes Miami, are illegal immigrants, and in the past three years Miami's main public hospital has accumulated a bill of $154m for treatment given to 'aliens'. In all, Florida is demanding $1 billion for education, health and other costs incurred by around 345,000 illegal immigrants." (p31)

"American Survey: All Right, Just This Once." Economist v331 n7861, 30 Apr 1994. p31. (ISSN0013-0613).

"Florida taxpayers spent an estimated $180 million last fiscal year to educate illegal aliens, according to a study released...by Gov. Lawton Chiles. The study found that education, by far, was the most expensive of the programs serving illegal aliens, which cost the state and local governments a total of about $884 million in 1993. The state spent an estimated $2.5 billion on services for both legal and illegal immigrants, the report says. In addition to education, those services include health care, law enforcement, and public infrastructure. There are about 345,000 undocumented immigrants and about one million other foreign-born noncitizens living in Florida." (p4)

"News Roundup: States: Education for Fla.'s Illegal Aliens Estimated to Cost $180 Million." Education Week v13 n27, 30 Mar 1994. p4. (ISSN0277-4232).

ALIENS, ILLEGAL--FLORIDA--COSTS

"In the criminal justice system, the problem has changed dramatically in the past 14 years. In 1980, the supervision cost--probation and parole--of criminal aliens in Florida totaled about $86,000 for 245 offenders. By 1993, this cost--which comes entirely from State revenues--increased to $6.8 million to cover nearly 5,100 aliens. In 1988, the cost of incarcerating 1,288 other aliens--non-Mariel Cubans--was nearly $13.8 million. By 1993 it was $27.7 million for 2,042 prisoners--now $15,500 a year per prisoner. During this period, Florida spent $130.7 million from its general revenues. The Federal

Government provided Florida with nothing. Since 1988, Florida has spent nearly $52.6 million to incarcerate Mariel Cubans. The Federal contribution was $11.4 million, or 18 percent." (pH2522)

Thurman, Karen L. (Rep.-Fla.). "Violent Crime Control and Law Enforcement Act of 1994," Congressional Record (20 Apr 1994). Daily ed. pH2518-2539. (ISSN0363-7239).

ALIENS, ILLEGAL--JAPAN (v19)

ALIENS, ILLEGAL--LOS ANGELES (CALIF) (v19)

ALIENS, ILLEGAL--NEW YORK (NY)

"The network of Chinese gangs in New York...amass great fortunes by trafficking in human cargo. Just last week, the press reported that these New York gangs are now smuggling Chinese nationals into this country through Virginia. These gang lords amass great fortunes by charging $30,000 per immigrant--or $6 to $9 million per ship--and then enslaving their human cargoes in lives of narcotics, gambling, and prostitution. Despite the best efforts of Federal and local law enforcement officials, we are not winning the war against these gangs because very simply, our laws are incredibly weak. The average sentence for slave trading is 18 months; the maximum fine is $5,000--not a bad cost of doing business when the profit is up to $9 million per cargo." (pH2241)

King, Peter T. (Rep.-N.Y.). "Providing for Further Consideration of H.R. 4092, Violent Crime Control and Law Enforcement Act of 1994," Congressional Record (13 Apr 1994). Daily ed. pH2233-2247. (ISSN0363-7239).

ALIENS, ILLEGAL--TAXATION--U.S. (v19)

ALIENS, ILLEGAL--U.S. (v19)

"During the past decade, nearly 9 million people have immigrated legally into...[the U.S.]--a population greater than most States. Unfortunately, millions more have chosen to enter the United States illegally, without our consent. The Immigration and Naturalization Service, for example, estimates that more than 3,000 people attempt to illegally cross the California-Mexico border each night. Nearly 60 percent of them succeed. In 1986, the apprehension of illegal undocumented aliens reached an all-time high of 1.8 million. And in 1992, the number of apprehensions was still staggering--more than 1 million. Of course, illegal immigration has a disproportionate impact on certain areas of the country. In California, for example, there are an estimated 1.3 million illegal aliens, and more than half of these illegals live in a single county--the county of Los Angeles. Not surprisingly, a staggering 10 percent of the 1992 budget of Los Angeles County was spent on providing services to illegal aliens. The Governor of Florida, another State heavily impacted by immigration, has even threatened to sue the Federal Government for reimbursement of the cost of providing services to immigrants, both legal and illegal." (pS2293)

Dole, Bob (Sen.-Kans.). "Statements on Introduced Bills and Joint Resolutions," Congressional Record (2 Mar 1994). Daily ed. pS2288-2302. (ISSN0363-7239).

"Illegal aliens constitute one out of four people that are inmates in our Federal prisons. Each one of those inmates costs about $85,000 a year that the taxpayers have to pay for....There were 1,064 illegal aliens in the Los Angeles riots that did billions of dollars worth of damage....Two-thirds of the births in Los Angeles County last year or 37,000 births were illegal alien births, and the AFDC [or Aid to Families with Dependent Children] payments per month...[are] $26 million just to take care of those children and take care of their families. That did not include other forms of health care, education, or anything else." (pH1018)

Burton, Dan (Rep.-Ind.). "Improving America's Schools Act of 1994," Congressional Record (3 Mar 1994). Daily ed. pH1006-1051. (ISSN0363-7239).

"Although the Immigration and Naturalization Service (INS) once claimed that the number of illegal entrants [in the U.S.] was between 8 and 12 million, research by Census Bureau and academic demographers in the 1980s put the figure closer to three million--about how many eventually sought legalization under the 1986 Immigration Reform and Control Act. Recent INS reports of over one million arrests of undocumented aliens per year are invalid, since multiple arrests of repeat border crossers inflate those numbers greatly. In contrast, the Census Bureau estimates that an average of about 200,000 have been entering annually so far in the 1990s." (p9)

Defreitas, Gregory. "Fear of Foreigners: Immigrants as Scapegoats for Domestic Woes." Dollars and Sense n191, Jan-Feb 1994. p8-9,33-35.

ALIENS, ILLEGAL--U.S.--COSTS (v19)

ALL TERRAIN VEHICLES--U.S.

"Many desert conservationists, while critical of the behavior of many mining companies in the desert, agree that the worst impact is caused by armies of off-road vehicles (ORVs). In the mid-1970s there was a boom in sales of ORVs, such as motocross motorbikes and all-terrain cycles with balloon tires. Since that time, on any holiday weekend, up to 40,000 ORV users head to the desert from nearby urban areas....Already, the impact on wildlife has been devastating. Moderate ORV use in some areas caused a 60 percent loss of animal life, according to a study conducted in 1977 by the U.S. Department of Fish and Wildlife." (p51)

Watson, Hari. "Defending the Desert." Earth News v4 n2, Mar-Apr 1993. p45-48. (ISSN1068-9400).

ALLIGATORS--FLORIDA (v19)

ALTERNATIVE MEDICINE--U.S. (v19)

"A survey published this January in the NEW ENGLAND JOURNAL OF MEDICINE found that more Americans visited their alternative healthcare practitioner than their primary care physician, such as a family doctor or a specialist in internal medicine. Thirty-four percent of the 1,539 adults questioned in 1990 said they had used at least one unconventional therapy that year. Others had averaged 19 visits. According to the researchers, this finding suggests that Americans visited their unconventional therapists 425 million times that year, as compared to the 388 million visits they paid their primary care physicians combined. The majority of those surveyed went to the alternative practitioners for back problems, anxiety, headaches and cancer. The therapies most often used were relaxation techniques, chiropractic and massage. Hypnosis, homeopathy and acupuncture ranked among the least often used. Almost 90 percent of those who went did so without consulting their doctor. The price people paid for these visits came to a total of $10.3 billion in out-of-pocket expenses that year. Most of those who sought unconventional therapies were college educated whites, aged 25-49, with incomes above $35,000. Many of them lived in the Western United States." (p41)

Haase, Carolin. "Emerging from the Closet." Earth News v4 n3, May-Jun 1993. p41-43. (ISSN1068-9400).

"Medical alternatives received a media spotlight when the NEW ENGLAND JOURNAL OF MEDICINE (1/28/93) reported that 34 percent of Americans used some type of alternative therapy in 1990. Few media outlets noted that these numbers were inflated by the inclusion of people who attended self-help groups and diet centers. Still, in one year, some 25 percent of Americans (more than 60 million people) sought the care of a chiropractor, acupuncturist, homeopath or other alternative practitioner. This survey was published at a time when news media were focused on alternative medicine for several reasons: the development of the Office of Alternative Medicine within the National Institutes of Health, Bill Moyers' 'Healing and the Mind' series on PBS (2/22-24/93), and the premiere of the movie LORENZO'S OIL. While news consumers have benefitted from a wider discussion of unconventional therapies, much of the coverage has reflected biases against alternative medicine on the part of journalists and their sources in the medical establishment." (p11)

Ullman, Dana. "Reporting on Alternative Medicine: Journalists, HEAL Thyselves." EXTRA! v6 n5, Jul-Aug 1993. 11-12. (ISSN0895-2310).

ALTERNATIVE MINIMUM TAX--U.S. (v19)

ALUMINUM INDUSTRY AND TRADE--U.S. (v19)

"Forty-three percent of the aluminum made in this country is manufactured in the Northwest; in turn, the aluminum industry is the single largest user of electricity in the region. It consumes more than one-fifth of the region's power--but pays reduced electricity rates....the Northwest aluminum industry today employs about 8,000 workers at middle-class wages and generates about $2.5 billion a year in revenues....Six years ago, the price of aluminum shot above $1.10 a pound. At that time, the Soviet Union exported 200,000 metric tons of aluminum annually. Today the price hovers around 50 cents a pound, while exports from the former Soviet Union exceed 1.6 million tons." (p12)

Koberstein, Paul. "Northwest Is Asked to Give." High Country News v26 n2, 27 Feb 1994. p12-13. (ISSN0191-5657).

ALZHEIMER'S DISEASE--U.S. (v19)

ALZHEIMER'S DISEASE--U.S.--COSTS (v19)

AMERICAN COLLEGE NEWSPAPERS (v19)

AMERICAN ECONOMIC ASSISTANCE

see ECONOMIC ASSISTANCE, AMERICAN

AMERICAN NEWSPAPERS (v19)

AMERICAN NEWSPAPERS--WOMEN (v19)

AMERICAN PROPERTY--CUBA

"On June 15 Cuban officials made what was widely interpreted as a gesture of peace to the United States by announcing that they are willing to negotiate reparations for U.S. properties confiscated by the state in the 1960s....According to the U.S. State Department, 5,911 North Americans lost a total of $1.8 billion in property during the Cuban Revolution, a figure that has escalated with inflation and interest to between $5 billion and $6 billion. State Department spokesmen responded to Cuba's announcement by saying that if the Cubans are serious, they should make a solid offer through the proper diplomatic channels." (p2)

"News Update: Cuba Offers Repayment for Nationalized U.S. Holdings." Cuba Update n3-4, Summer 1993. p2. (ISSN0196-0830).

AMMUNITION--TAXATION--U.S. (v19)

AMPHETAMINES--POLAND (v19)

AMUSEMENT PARKS--U.S. (v19)

"Outdoor theme parks and amusement arcades in America currently generate revenues of $6 billion and $5.3 billion a year respectively, compared with the film industry's annual box-office take of $5.2 billion. Over the past decade, the number of amusement parks in America has increased by a third, to more than 600. With more than 140m visitors a year, attendances at the top 40 theme parks in the country have more than doubled over the past decade. Meanwhile, the amount Americans spend on going to the cinema has slipped from 4.2% of the money they spent on recreation a decade ago to 1.6% today." (p74)

"Business: Theme Parks: Feeling the Future." Economist v330 n7851, 19 Feb 1994. p74,79. (ISSN0013-0613).

"With more than 200 million paid attendees each year since 1985, amusement parks in the United States represent a lucrative consumer market. This strong consumer demand has resulted in the development of many new parks, saturating the U.S. market. Given industry estimates that a minimum of one million patrons is necessary for economic viability, no regions of such size are unserved (Duffy 1984)." (p51)

Thach, Sharon V./Axinn, Catherine N. "Patron Assessments of Amusement Park Attributes." Journal of Travel Research v32 n3, Win 1994. p51-60. (ISSN0047-2875).

AMUSEMENTS

"For 22 countries, rich and poor...[the ECONOMIST] examined over 30 indicators which sum up the economic, social, cultural and political aspects of life." (p39) "America has the most televisions, with 815 for every 1,000 people. At the other extreme, China has only 31 for every 1,000. Among the big seven industrial countries, France has the fewest (406 per 1,000). On the other hand, it has the most cinemas: 89 for every 1m people, almost twice as many as Germany. The best place for film buffs is Russia (580 cinemas per 1m people) and Sweden (135), but they should give the Bahamas (3) and Japan (15) a miss. In contrast, newspapers thrive in Japan: 587 newspapers for every 1,000 people are sold daily. Only Hong Kong has a higher ratio of sales. At the other extreme, newspaper circulation in Italy is a mere 107 per 1,000, and in India only 28." (p40)

"Where to Live: Nirvana by Numbers." Economist v329 n7843, 25 Dec 1993. p39-42. (ISSN0013-0613).

AMUSEMENTS--EUROPE--U.S.

"Last year, U.S. audiovisual exports to the European Community (with films, TV and videotapes accounting for about one-third each) amounted to roughly $4 billion. They have much more than doubled in the past ten years and dwarf shipments in the opposite direction, estimated at around $250 million....Out of the total film revenue earned within the E.C., nearly three-quarters now goes to American companies, the proportion ranging from about 60 percent in France to 90 percent in Britain....Americans want [to] remove...film subsidies and quotas for television....France has a National Center of Cinematography, which levies a tax on cinema tickets (11 percent), TV revenue (5.5 percent) and videotapes (2 percent). From this it raises nearly $80 million a year, which it plows back into the trade, notably through credits to filmmakers as an advance on their future earnings. About a third of French films get such credits, which provide for a substantial portion of their budgets....The TV quota system...stipulates that...a majority of the programs shown on each TV station must originate within the E.C. (Actually, the proportion is not supposed to fall below the level of 1988, which was 60 percent.) The French have made an additional stipulation: At least 40 percent of the programs must be produced in a Francophone country." (p54-55)

Singer, Daniel. "Letter from Europe: GATT & the Shape of Our Dreams." Nation v258 n2, 17 Jan 1994. p54-55. (ISSN0027-8378).

AMUSEMENTS--U.S.

"Americans spent about $340 billion on entertainment and recreation in 1993. That compares with $270 billion in spending--public and private--on elementary and secondary education. In 1980, those figures were roughly equal. It's not necessarily a crime that America spends more on fun than on educating its children. Years of well-intentioned failure tell us that dollars don't automatically translate into scholars. But it's a sure sign of how our priorities have changed. One more sign: The rise in entertainment spending has coincided with a dramatic decline in personal savings. In 1980, Americans saved an average of 7.9% of their disposable personal income. In 1993, they saved just 4%." (p66)

Landler, Mark. "Cover Story: Are We Having Fun Yet? Maybe Too Much." Business Week n3362, 14 Mar 1994. p66. (ISSN0007-7135).

"Using data from the Bureau of Labor Statistics, BUSINESS WEEK calculates that the entertainment and recreation industries added 200,000 workers in 1993--a stunning 12% of all net new employment. That's more workers than were hired last year by the health-care industry, the preeminent job creator of the 1980s....Consider that over the last 10 years, entertainment and recreation have claimed a steadily increasing share of consumer spending....Or that since 1991, consumers have boosted their outlays on entertainment and recreation by some 13%, adjusted for inflation--more than twice the growth rate of overall consumer spending." (p59)

Mandel, Michael J. "Cover Story: The Entertainment Economy." Business Week n3362, 14 Mar 1994. p58-64. (ISSN0007-7135).

AMUSEMENTS--U.S.--SINGLE PEOPLE (v19)

AMYOTROPHIC LATERAL SCLEROSIS--TREATMENT--U.S. (v19)

ANABOLIC STEROIDS--U.S.--YOUTH (v19)

"While anabolic-androgenic steroids have been used since the early 1950s to enhance athletic performance, the incidence of use appears to have increased considerably in recent years (Buckley et al., 1988; Duda, 1988; Johnson, Jay, Shoup, & Rickert, 1989; Nightingale, 1986; Office of The Inspector General (OIG), 1990; Tierney & McLain, 1990; Windsor & Dumitru, 1989; Yesalis et al., 1989). Particularly disturbing is the increased frequency of their use among adolescents. Although there are no definitive national statistics, the estimated incidence of use by adolescents in the United States ranges from 6.6% of male 12th grade students (Buckley et al., 1988; Johnson et al., 1989; OIG, 1990) to 11.1% of male 11th grade students (Johnson, 1990). It has been estimated that at least 700,000 high school students use anabolic steroids (Tierney & McLain, 1990) and that at least two thirds begin use by 16 years of age (Johnson, 1990; OIG, 1990; OIG, 1990; Yesalis et al., 1989)....Recent literature clearly shows that adolescent users believe that steroids produce the physical effects they desire, and approximately 86% of those cited in the 1990 study of the OIG have no plans to stop using steroids. Nearly all the adolescent users interviewed in the OIG report (93%) stated that starting steroid use was a good decision (1990)." (p81-82)

Burnett, Kent F./Kleiman, Mark E. "Psychological Characteristics of Adolescent Steroid Users." Adolescence v29 n113, Spr 1994. p81-89. (ISSN0001-8449).

ANCHORAGE (ALASKA)--EMPLOYMENT--WOMEN (v19)

ANGOLA

see also MINES (MILITARY EXPLOSIVES)--ANGOLA

ANGOLA--HISTORY--CIVIL WAR, 1975-

"Angola has become one of the worst wars in the world, according to UN officials now trying to bring peace and increased relief to the country. The UN Secretary-General's Special Representative Alioune Blondin Beye, returning from an early-October tour of areas until recently cut-off for up to 10 months by heavy fighting between government forces and those of opposition Uniao Nacional para a Independencia Total de Angola (UNITA), said earlier figures of 1,000 deaths a day must 'be considered conservative.' Some estimates put the daily death toll during fighting in 1992-93 as high as 2,000, comparable to or even more than in Bosnia or Somalia." (p1)

Hecht, David. "UN Battles to Bring Relief to War-Torn Angola." Africa Recovery Jan 1994. p1-6.

"Estimates of the total number of dead in Kuito in the last 10 months range from 18,000 to 35,000, or around 20 per cent of the population. Of survivors, many are injured, and there is the continuing threat of mass starvation. Angola's Foreign Minister Venancio de Moura says many people ate 'human flesh to survive,' and WFP's [World Food Programme's] Robert Sanchez, who travelled with the first relief flight on 16 October,described an 'apocalypse' with people having to drink from the river next to 'dead bodies in the water.' The situation in Kuito has been repeated across much of Angola. Its resumed military activity in 1992/93 led to UNITA [Uniao Nacional para a Independencia Total de Angola] occupying up to 75 per cent of the country. UNITA has been laying siege to three of Angola's 18 provincial capitals, and is holding four others. This includes Huambo, Angola's second largest city, which was occupied by UNITA in March." (p3)

Hecht, David. "UN Battles to Bring Relief to War-Torn Angola." Africa Recovery Jan 1994. p1-6.

"More Angolans have died from November 1992 to November 1993 than in all the previous sixteen years of civil war in that country according to UN Secretary General Boutros Boutros-Ghali. Out of a country of some 12 million people, up to 3 million require food or emergency assistance, UN agencies and non-governmental organizations estimate, but that figure does not include an incalculable number of children and adults who are sick and injured as a result of the renewed fighting and drought." (p7)

"Angola: Civil War Continues to Rage." NewsNotes v19 n2, Mar-Apr 1994. p7. (ISSN1064-1556).

ANIMAL GENETIC ENGINEERING

"Although serious questions about its safety remain unanswered, the Food and Drug Administration has approved synthetic Bovine Growth Hormone (BGH), the genetically-engineered drug designed to increase milk production in dairy cows. Farmers, consumer advocates, environmentalists and labor groups reacted angrily to last November's decision, calling BGH 'crack for cows.'...Injecting cows with BGH can raise milk yields by an average of 10 to 25 percent. This artificially increased production puts the cows under extreme stress. In this weakened state, cows are more susceptible to infectious diseases, particularly mastitis, an infection of the udder. In addition to animal cruelty concerns, the higher rates of disease in BGH-injected cows have negative implications for human health. Increased cases of infectious diseases in BGH-injected cows leads to increased antibiotic use. Traces of these antibiotics end up in the milk, and pose human health hazards." (p10)

McGoodwin, Wendy. "Agribusiness: FDA Approves BGH, Coalition Promises Boycott." geneWATCH v9 n3-4, Jan 1994. p10.

ANIMAL INDUSTRY

see also CATTLE TRADE; DAIRY PRODUCTS INDUSTRY; LIVESTOCK; POULTRY INDUSTRY

"Around the world, wildlife is under siege. Each year, trade in wildlife generates an estimated $5 to $8 billion--$2 to $3 billion of it illegal. With monetary stakes this high, the peddling of contraband animals--dead or alive--has been likened to the underworld traffic in drugs. Recently, both worlds combined when Florida customs inspectors confiscated 223 boa constrictors. Eighty pounds of cocaine had been stuffed into condoms and inserted through the snakes' rectums, which were then sewn shut. Internal injuries or heat killed all the snakes." (p12)

Sleeper, Barbara. "Scotland Yard for Wildlife." Animals v126 n5, Sep-Oct 1993. p12-15. (ISSN0030-6835).

ANIMAL INDUSTRY--COMMONWEALTH OF INDEPENDENT STATES (v19)

ANIMAL INDUSTRY--TAIPEI (TAIWAN)

"In Taipei alone are hundreds of 'apothecaries'--essentially small folk medicine pharmacies--that stock and sell rhino horn from Africa, tiger bone from India and bear gall from the United States. In all of Taiwan, an island nation of 20 million only one and a half times the size of Vermont, there are nearly 14,000 such pharmacies. Of 135 pharmacies recently surveyed in Taipei by Earthtrust, stocks of tiger bone were found in two out of every three. A study released last year by TRAFFIC

International estimated that 77% of Taiwan's apothecaries--10,500 shops--stock rhino horn." (p10)

LaBudde, Samuel. "Unmade in Taiwan: Endangered Species Project Sheds Light on the Black Hole of the Illegal Wildlife Trade." Earth First! v14 n2, 21 Dec 1993. p10-11.

ANIMAL INDUSTRY--TAIWAN

"Economics play a critical role in endangered species trade. Taiwan has the 12th highest per capita income in the world and over $85 billion...in foreign currency reserves. In 1990 Taiwan exported $23.3 billion in goods to the United States, its largest trading partner. Much of this newly acquired wealth--provided by American consumers--ultimately funds poaching and smuggling operations around the world....TAIWAN TRADE TRENDS magazine cited one Taiwanese brewery as importing almost half a ton of tiger bone--representing about 150 tigers--to make 100,000 bottles of tiger bone wine in one year. One famous restaurant outside of Taipei serves tiger penis soup, considered a powerful aphrodisiac, for $320 per bowl." (p3-4)

"Endangered Species Project Alert: Taiwan Is the End of the Line for Endangered Species." Earth Island Journal v8 n3, Sum 1993. p44(1-8). (ISSN1041-0406).

ANIMAL INDUSTRY--U.S. (v19)

"The animal business these days is almost completely dominated by a handful of large enterprises. Hardly any independent producers are left....Today, of the more than 2 million farms in the U.S., about 50,000 families and their integrators or corporations dominate the animal business, with their domination increasing all the time." (p161)

Bergland, Bob. "Concluding Remarks." American Journal of Alternative Agriculture v8 n4, Fall 1994. p160-161. (ISSN0889-1893).

"The United States plays a large role in wildlife trafficking, and is a major consumer of wildlife products--up to one fifth of the estimated worldwide trade of $5 to $8 billion. Of that total, between $2 and $3 billion is illegal. Perhaps, then, it is fitting that the world's first forensics lab for crimes against animals is located in this country." (p34)

Kane, Karen. "To Catch a Poacher." ZOOLIFE v4 n2, Spr 1993. p32-40. (ISSN1046-4565).

ANIMAL INDUSTRY--UTAH (v19)

ANIMAL WELFARE--U.S.

"As a public service last year, agents of the Federal Animal Damage Control program destroyed more than 2.2 million wild animals, only slightly fewer than they had dispatched the previous year. Though 71 percent of the 1992 casualties were blackbirds, grackles, and European starlings guilty of eating farmers' grain or behaving as pests in urban areas, hundreds of thousands of other wild creatures were eliminated, among them coyotes, foxes, mountain lions, and wolves....Although it now operates nationwide, ADC is most entrenched in the West, where far and away its most well-funded and controversial function is its continuing war on allegedly troublesome predators that attack livestock, especially coyotes accused of killing sheep. (According to the USDA's latest data, close to half a million sheep and lambs in the United States are taken by predators each year, nearly 60 percent of them by coyotes in western states. These figures, however, are reported to the government by sheep growers, and are likely to be highly inflated.) By the 1970s, with ADC's help, the largest predators--grizzlies, mountain lions, wolves--had been wiped out in most of their natural range." (p70,72)

Schueler, Donald G. "Contract Killers." Sierra v78 n6, Nov-Dec 1993. p70-76,97. (ISSN0161-7362).

ANIMAL WELFARE--U.S.--SOCIETIES, ETC.

"According to HSUS [Humane Society of the United States] estimates, as many as 25 percent of the estimated 12 million animals who enter shelters each year are purebred. That means that up to 3 million purebred animals enter shelters each year, representing not only dogs registered by the Animal Kennel Club (AKC)--the largest registry of purebred dogs in the United States--but also animals from other registries and unregisterable purebreds. Despite help from breed-rescue groups, thousands upon thousands of unwanted purebreds must still be euthanized for want of a home." (p3)

Miller, Julie E. "Purebreds and Pet Overpopulation: The Case for a Breeding Moratorium." Shelter Sense v16 n8, Sep 1993. p3-12. (ISSN0734-3078).

"In 1991, King County (Washington) Animal Control kennel worker Shelby Russel tracked purebreds in the county shelter for four months as that county's spray/neuter ordinance was being considered. Russel found that the lowest percentage of purebreds on a given day was 17 percent and the highest over 50 percent. Shelters in surrounding areas had similar statistics--purebreds averaging 25 to 30 percent of dogs entering the shelters." (p3) "In 1990, an estimated 6,000 purebred dogs were euthanized in Seattle-area shelters. 'Almost 40 percent of the dogs at our humane society who need new homes are purebreds,' said Mary Eno, representing the Montgomery County Humane Society, in her testimony in support of breeding legislation (now passed)." (p4)

Miller, Julie E. "Purebreds and Pet Overpopulation: The Case for a Breeding Moratorium." Shelter Sense v16 n8, Sep 1993. p3-12. (ISSN0734-3078).

"National estimates indicate that 50 percent of animals entering shelters are stray, and an average of only 15 percent of stray dogs and 3 percent of stray cats ever make it back to their owners. In addition, every shelter [in the U.S.] has countless lost-pet reports that just don't match up with the animals waiting in the kennel." (p8)

Fekety, Sally. "Animal Care and Control Agencies Play Vital Role in Deterring Pet Theft." Shelter Sense v17 n2, Feb 1994. p8-9,12. (ISSN0734-3078).

"The public, [animal] shelter board members, and even shelter management put more emphasis on adoption numbers than on compliance statistics. Under constant pressure from the public, and wanting to place as many healthy animals as possible, shelters [in the U.S.] do everything they can to increase adoptions. An adoption rate of more than 35 percent is considered something to be proud of, higher than the national average. But shelters are less apt to quote--or even know--their own sterilization compliance percentages for those adoptions. Estimates from shelters are frightening--often around 60-70 percent. Shelters with a compliance rate around 80 percent may even brag about it. But take a look at the other part of that statistic. An 80 percent compliance rate actually means that 20 percent of the animals you place are not sterilized. They remain animals capable of reproduction." (p3-4)

Rindy, Kate. "Looking in the Mirror: Reflections of a Former Shelter Director." Shelter Sense v16 n10, Nov 1993. p3-4. (ISSN0734-3078).

ANIMALS--AMERICAN SAMOA

"In American Samoa, where the growth rate is 3.7 percent per year, population increases correlate directly with the depletion of wildlife resources through deforestation, habitat degradation for construction, and the toxicity of aquatic organisms from heavy metals. Since 1986, wildlife resources in American Samoa have fallen 90 percent due to tropical storms and surges in human population. In both Samoas, population pressures have led to the degradation of coral reef biosystems and of the quality and supply of ground water." (p37)

Sinavaina, Caroline G. "Samoa." Cultural Survival Quarterly

v17 n3, Fall 1993. p37-40. (ISSN0740-3291).

ANIMALS--ANATOMY

"Although the element calcium is functionally concerned in the coagulation of blood, regulation of excretions from the bowels, and with proper nerve and muscle functioning--approximately 99.4% of the total calcium found in the body is stored in the bones and teeth of...[ruminant animals]. On the other hand, it is found that of the total amount of phosphorus found in the body,...only 70% is stored in bones and teeth. The remaining 30% of the phosphorus is widely distributed in the body, where it participates in practically all of the vital functions that concern the growth development and proper functioning of the animal." (p28)

Ozolins, Rudolf. "Nutrition Program for Beef and Dairy Herds." Acres, U.S.A. Feb 1994. p28-29.

ANIMALS--FOOD

"Cats cannot be vegetarians. Ideally, their diets should consist of 60 percent raw meat (with a little raw organic egg), 25 percent vegetables, and 15 percent grains and other carbohydrates. Dogs, on the other hand, can do well on vegetable proteins from beans, lentils, tofu or soaked nuts, but Dr. Pitcairn [author of DR. PITCAIRN'S COMPLETE GUIDE TO NATURAL HEALTH FOR DOGS AND CATS] also suggests raw organic eggs, cottage cheese and fish. Such high protein foods should make up only 30 percent of a dog's diet, with vegetable and grains each comprising 35 percent." (p48)

Frazier, Anitra/Eckroate, Norma. "Consumer News: The Natural Pet." E Magazine v4 n3, May-Jun 1993. p48-51. (ISSN1046-8021).

ANIMALS--GENETIC ENGINEERING

see ANIMAL GENETIC ENGINEERING

ANIMALS--U.S.--MORTALITY

"In the past few months, the animal-protection community has seen some heated discussion about the number of pets euthanized annually in U.S. animal shelters. One organization put the figure at 12.1 million animals; another stated the statistic was closer to 5 million. Over the years, estimates of animals put to death have fluctuated. But a large majority of experts believes the figure hasn't dropped below the tens of millions range for the past 30 years. What is the actual number of animals killed in our country's shelters? No one, at present, has an accurate count. Because animal sheltering and animal control are not federally regulated services and no single entity tracks data on domestic-animal populations, obtaining valid information is difficult, if not impossible. Most statistics have been extrapolated from data obtained through voluntary reporting by animal agencies. But relying on this data to provide statistics is risky." (p32)

Armstrong, Martha. "MSPCA Viewpoint: Statistics, Truth, and Action." Animals v127 n1, Jan-Feb 1994. p32. (ISSN0030-6835).

ANIMALS--VENEZUELA

"Crossing the heart of Venezuela from the Orinoco Delta in the east to the Andes in the west is a vast grassland prairie known as the Llanos. Representing about one-third of the total area of Venezuela, this region has some of the most spectacular wildlife in South America, including 33 species of mammals, more than 254 species of birds, 27 amphibians, 47 reptiles, and 350 species of fish. The soils are poor and support little vegetation other than grasses, except along the many rivers and streams where forests form dense thickets. Traditionally used as grazing land, the Llanos is sparsely populated, which in part contributes to the great abundance of wildlife." (p6)

Goodwin, Mary Lou. "Audubon at Work: Venezuela Group: Protectors of the Llanos." Audubon Activist v8 n2, Oct 1993. p6. (ISSN0898-915X).

ANTI-POVERTY PROGRAMS

see ECONOMIC ASSISTANCE, DOMESTIC

ANTISEMITISM--EUROPE--SOVIET UNION--U.S. (v19)

ANTISEMITISM--GERMANY--PUBLIC OPINION (v19)

ANTISEMITISM--SLOVAKIA--PUBLIC OPINION (v19)

ANTISEMITISM--U.S.

"The Anti-Defamation League's 1993 survey indicates that the number and severity of anti-Semitic hate crimes has worsened nationwide. There were 1,867 incidents reported to the ADL from 44 States and the District of Columbia in 1993 alone. This represents an overall increase of 8 percent from 1992, and constitutes the second highest total in the audit's 15-year history....For the third year, the number of anti-Semitic acts against individuals outnumber the incidents of vandalism against institutions and other property. The number of reported incidents of assault, threat, and harassment totaled 1,079. This represents a 23-percent increase from 1992." (pS2662)

Simon, Paul (Sen.-Ill.). "Commending the Anti-Defamation League for Their Efforts to Combat Hate Crimes," Congressional Record (9 Mar 1994). Daily ed. pS2662. (ISSN0363-7239).

ANTS--U.S.

"A 21-year study of nearly 1 million ants in the Gainesville [Florida] area confirms that imported fire ants are continuing to spread [throughout the U.S.], displacing native ant species and causing a large number of other ecological problems....[Solenopsis] invicta was found in 65 of 100 traps in 1992, compared to only 1 trap when the study began in 1972, says entomologist Daniel P. Wojcik. The study was the first to gauge the impact of the pest in an area that has not received large-scale insecticide treatments. In the study, scientists collected 990,079 ant specimens--representing 55 ant species--in 100 roadside traps containing meat or honey-based baits." (p9)

Adams, Sean. "Fighting the Fire Ant." Agricultural Research v42 n1, Jan 1994. p4-9. (ISSN0002-161X).

APPELLATE PROCEDURE--U.S. (v19)

APPLE INDUSTRY--JAPAN (v19)

APPLE INDUSTRY--U.S. (v19)

APPRENTICES--GERMANY

"In Germany, 70% of the future workforce is engaged in structured apprenticeships while in high school--apprenticeships that connect classroom learning to applied work tasks, and open doors to high-skill, high-wage future employment opportunities. And as we learned from visits to and from representatives of the German dual-system, there is much more flexibility to change 'tracks', and indeed it is increasingly common to see the apprenticeship, university, and technical college pathways blending together more than is commonly believed by critics in this country. Our U.S. system is neither revamping curriculum to reflect new workplace demands, nor building in opportunities for students to marry applied learning to traditional study of theoretical or 'academic' disciplines." (p10)

Austin, John (President, Flint Roundtable)/Donohue, Bill (President, Genesee Area Focus Council). U.S. House. Committee on Education and Labor. "Hearing on School-to-Work Transition." Hearing, 15 Jul 1993. Washington, D.C.: GPO, 1994. (ISBN0160440858). (Y4.Ed8/1:103-42).

APPRENTICES--GERMANY--U.S. (v19)

APPRENTICES--U.S. (v19)

AQUACULTURE (v19)

"As the price of fish climbs and biotechnology develops, the most valuable fish will increasingly be farmed. Aquaculture yielded more than 12m tonnes in 1990, and is growing by more than 10% a year. Fin-fish make up almost 70% of the total; shellfish, a quarter; and shrimp about 6%. But intensive fish farming tends to damage coastlines. And, though the technology is developing rapidly, the FAO [Food and Agriculture Organization] doubts whether farmed fish will account for more than 12% of world fish consumption by the end of the century." (p21-22)

"Fish: The Tragedy of the Oceans." Economist v330 n7855, 19 Mar 1994. p21-22,24. (ISSN0013-0613).

AQUACULTURE--ENVIRONMENTAL ASPECTS (v19)

ARAB AMERICANS--ECONOMIC CONDITIONS

"Among the ten metros with the most Arab Americans, median Arab-American household income in 1990 ranged from $32,300 in the Detroit metropolitan area to $53,600 in Washington, D.C. Median household income for all Arab-American households in 1990 stood at $39,100, compared with the U.S. average of $30,100." (p26)

El-Badry, Samia. "The Arab-American Market." American Demographics v16 n1, Jan 1994. p22-27,30. (ISSN0163-4089).

ARAB AMERICANS--EMPLOYMENT

"Sixty percent of Arab Americans work as executives, professionals, salespeople, administrative support, or service personnel, compared with 66 percent of the general American population. Arab Americans are more likely than average to work in sales and less likely to work in most other broad occupational categories, particularly administrative support and service jobs. Although many large companies are laying people off, Arab Americans may be better able to survive a changing economy. They are more likely than average to be entrepreneurs or self-employed (12 percent versus 7 percent)." (p26)

El-Badry, Samia. "The Arab-American Market." American Demographics v16 n1, Jan 1994. p22-27,30. (ISSN0163-4089).

ARABS--PALESTINE

see PALESTINIAN ARABS

ARBITRATION, INDUSTRIAL--U.S. (v19)

ARBITRATION AND AWARD--U.S.

"Business use of ADR [or Alternative Dispute Resolution] has grown tremendously in recent years. For example, in 1991 the AAA [or American Arbitration Association] handled 60,000 ADR cases. In the international commercial setting, the growth in ADR has been just as dramatic. Between 1987 and 1992 the AAA nearly doubled its international commercial arbitration caseload, from 106 to 204 cases. The ICC has handled 7,500 international arbitrations since it was founded in 1923. Of the number, 3,500 have taken place in the last 10 years. In fact, ADR is now the most used method of international commercial dispute resolution." (p69)

Murphy, Betty Southard. "ADR's Impact: On International Commerce." Dispute Resolution Journal v48 n4, Dec 1993. p54-63.

ARGENTINA

see also AGRICULTURAL EDUCATION--ARGENTINA; INFLATION (FINANCE)--ARGENTINA--BRAZIL

ARGENTINA--ECONOMIC CONDITIONS (v19)

"The halo over Argentina's President Carlos Menem is dimming. After three years of privatisations, tariff cuts and budget-pruning, the view from on high is bright. The budget is balanced. Inflation has fallen from four digits to under 10%. The economy has grown by 8% a year since 1991. Billions of investment dollars have poured in. Yet down on the ground there is a growing murmur: nice economic miracle, shame about the social cost. Although Mr Menem has increased social spending, the macroeconomic figures conceal considerable hardship. Hundreds of thousands of jobs have gone as the federal government and privatised industries have slimmed, and as private-sector firms have buckled before foreign competition. Over 2m people, 18% of the workforce, are unemployed or under-employed. Less than half of these receive income support, which can be as low as $120 month, and does not go on for more than a year." (p38-39)

"International: Argentina: The Other Side of the Halo." Economist v330 n7850, 12 Feb 1994. p38-39. (ISSN0013-0613).

ARGENTINA--SOCIAL CONDITIONS

"During the past few years, renewed growth in Latin America has produced a steady flow of U.S. press reports touting that region's economic 'revival.' Attention has focused on three major countries, Venezuela, Mexico, and Argentina, all of which are said to be in the throes of 'economic miracles' produced by 'free-market' policies....Meanwhile, the social costs of the Argentine miracle have been extremely high. With [President Carlos] Menem's government greatly reducing health-care spending, there has been a major increase in diseases such as tuberculosis, malaria, and leprosy. The infant mortality rate has reached 26 of every 1,000 live births, almost three times the rate in Cuba. Unemployment, pushed upward by massive public sector firings, now stands at 10 percent--and nearly 25 percent for those under 21." (p9)

Silverstein, Ken. "Latin 'Miracles': Two Down, One to Go." Lies of Our Times v5 n3, Mar 1994. p9-10. (ISSN1046-7912).

"For fertility decline, Argentina is a country stalled in time, and there is no assurance that this will change within the next few decades. Its TFR [total fertily rate] stayed very close to 3.0 from 1950-55 to 1985-90, and its crude birth rate has fallen by only 2 births per 1,000 population, from 25 in 1950-55 to 23 in 1985-90. Its rate of natural increase has decreased gradually, from 1.63 percent in the earlier period to 1.27 percent in 1985-90. Literacy has been at 95 percent or above during this period, and primary plus secondary school enrollment ratios have increased, from 73 percent in 1960 to 96 percent in 1990. Female literacy and enrollment ratios are slightly higher than those of males. Life expectancy at birth is 70 years, and the infant mortality rate is in the low 30s. However, Argentina's economy has been stagnant throughout this period, although its GNP [gross national product] per capita is relatively high at $2,555." (p85)

Mauldin, W. Parker/Ross, John A. "Prospects and Programs for Fertility Reduction, 1990-2015." Studies in Family Planning v25 n2, Mar-Apr 1994. p77-95. (ISSN0039-3665).

ARGIDENE (v19)

ARIZONA

see CANCER--ARIZONA

ARIZONA--ECONOMIC CONDITIONS (v19)

ARMAMENTS

see MILITARY WEAPONS

ARMAMENTS INDUSTRIES

see DEFENSE INDUSTRIES

ARMED FORCES

see also BRAZIL--U.S.--ARMED FORCES--APPROPRIATIONS AND EXPENDITURES; CUBA--ARMED FORCES; FRANCE--ARMED FORCES--APPROPRIATIONS AND EXPENDITURES; GREAT BRITAIN--ARMED FORCES--APPROPRIATIONS AND EXPENDITURES; MALAYSIA--ARMED FORCES--APPROPRIATIONS AND EXPENDITURES; MIDDLE EAST--ARMED FORCES; RUSSIA--ARMED FORCES; U.S.--ARMED FORCES; UNITED NATIONS--ARMED FORCES--CANADA

ARMED FORCES--APPROPRIATIONS AND EXPENDITURES (v19)

"A new cooperative security system should involve not only reliance on multilateral peacekeeping and peacemaking, but also cutbacks to nonoffensive conventional defenses and a ban on production and trade of weapon systems essential for cross-border aggression. These changes, though economically disruptive in the short term, offer tremendous benefits over the longer run. With a strategy of nonoffensive defense and multilateral peacekeeping, the world could cut military spending from $850 billion per year to around $250 billion, while steadily strengthening support for the norm of nonviolent conflict resolution. By replacing reliance on nuclear weapons to deter conventional war, an effective collective security system would aid immeasurably in stopping the spread of nuclear weapons. Moreover, eventually, when it is clear to all that nuclear weapons play no role in the outbreak or outcome of conventional war, people may come to view nuclear arms like chemical and biological weapons--as instruments of mass destruction which can be abolished because their use is simply unthinkable." (p21)

Forsbert, Randall. "After the Cold War: Looking for Common Ground." Boston Review v18 n3-4, Jun-Aug 1993. p21. (ISSN0734-2306).

"A 1990 UNDP [United Nations Development Programme] report notes that between 1965-1990, military expenditure in developing countries multiplied by seven times while spending in industrialized countries doubled. UNDP's '1992 Human Development Report,' however, states that between 1987 and 1992, industrial countries reduced their military spending from $838 to $762 billion and developing countries reduced their spending from $155 to $123 billion during the period 1984-1990. Moreover, a recent WORLDWATCH INSTITUTE publication, 'Vital Signs 1992,' notes that 'between 1990-1991, the number of strategic offensive warheads in the world's nuclear arsenal has been reduced from 23,700 to 19,165.' The publication also mentions that 'the number of nuclear tests has declined...France has suspended its testing for one year' and 'Russia is observing a unilateral one year testing moratorium.' Although these trends are in line with recommendations made by the Secretary-General in a report entitled 'New Dimensions in Arms Regulation and Disarmament in the Post-Cold War Era', they cannot be interpreted as a commitment by nations to spend less on arms and more on human beings." (p1)

Maoulidi, Moumie. "Disarmament and Development." Window on the World v24 n1, Jan 1993. p1-2.

United Nations Development Programme's "'1990 Special Report' explores the relationship between disarmament and development and observes that 'money that could be used for human development often goes to military budgets, even in the poorest countries.' Studies conducted by the STOCKHOLM INTERNATIONAL PEACE RESEARCH INSTITUTE also assert that, although developing countries account for only 15% of the total world military expenditures, a high proportion of their gross domestic product is spent on the military. In his report to the General Assembly during Disarmament Week in October 1992, the Secretary-General stated: 'while governments are spending an average of $36,000 per year per member of the armed forces, 30 times more than they invest in the education of each enrolled child, a 1990 World Bank report reveals that an increase of only one year in average years of education may lead to a 3% rise in gross domestic product.' To invest in human development, governments will obviously have to reorganize existing priorities and reorient efforts towards improving social services." (p2)

Maoulidi, Moumie. "Disarmament and Development." Window on the World v24 n1, Jan 1993. p1-2.

ARMENIA

see also GENOCIDE--ARMENIA

ARMENIA--ECONOMIC CONDITIONS

"The average salary in Armenia today is 10,000-15,000 rubles. Pensions are even smaller. Only a few can afford a propane tank in the kitchen; it costs more than 100,000 rubles. Others make do with a kerosene lamp (one liter of kerosene--four hours' worth--is 550 rubles), candles, or alcohol burners. The most reliable source of warmth, however, is still wood. According to modest estimates, 800,000 trees were chopped down last winter. People in the northern regions that suffered the earthquake in 1988 are in the most difficult position. About 300,000 people are living in temporary shelters because fewer than half of the buildings that were destroyed have been rebuilt." (p28)

Isaryan, Drastamat. "Armenia: Until There Are No More Trees." Bulletin of the Atomic Scientists v50 n1, Jan-Feb 1994. p28-31. (ISSN0096-3402).

"Armenia now has, perhaps, the world's most aptly named currency: the drama....In two months, the drama's exchange rate with the U.S. dollar has gone from 14 to 1 to 77 to 1....Sometimes inflation doesn't even matter. Bus fare has quadrupled, for example, but there are no buses running, for lack of gasoline and diesel fuel. When the price of natural gas tripled, it was another piece of theoretical news: it's been two years since most of Yerevan's [the capital of Armenia] apartments have been supplied with gas for heating and cooking....Winter days in Yerevan (where 1.5 million people or a third of the country's population lives) end with a de facto 5 p.m. curfew because there is no electricity to light the streets or houses (candles and batteries are so precious they should be sold in jewelry stores)....The three main sources of energy in Armenia (nuclear, hydro and oil/gas) are failing. The country's two nuclear reactors were shut down in 1989, following an earthquake that killed 25,000 people and left half a million homeless." (p16) "To the list of disasters facing his country [Mr. Sepuh] Tashjian [minister of energy] added deforestation: in 1993, 1.5 million trees were chopped down." (p17)

Husarska, Anna. "Yerevan Postcard: Tinder Box." New Republic v210 n6, 7 Feb 1994. p16-17. (ISSN0028-6583).

ARMORED VEHICLE INDUSTRY--U.S. (v19)

ARSON--U.S. (v19)

ARTIFICIAL SATELLITES IN TELECOMMUNICATION--CHINA (v19)

"Trade in commercial launches with the People's Republic of China (PRC) is currently governed by the 1989 U.S.-PRC Memorandum of Agreement Regarding International Trade in Commercial Launch Services (MOA). The MOA allows PRC launch providers a total of nine launches for international customers during the term of the agreement, which expires December 31, 1994. The MOA also requires that PRC providers offer prices, terms, and conditions for launches that are 'on a par' with those prevailing in the international market for commercial launch services. At the present time, PRC launch providers have conducted three launches of communications satellites for international customers, and are expected to launch an additional satellite before the end of the agreement. Each of these satellites was manufactured by the Hughes Aircraft Co. of the U.S. In addition, the PRC is currently scheduled to launch three U.S.-built satellites for international customers after 1994. In general, PRC providers win 5 to 10 percent of available launches in the international market for commercial launch services." (p547)

Collins, Katherine E. (Acting Asst. Sec. for Budget and Programs). U.S. House. Committee on Appropriations. "Department of Transportation and Related Agencies Approp. for 1994 (Part 3)." Hearing, Washington, D.C.: GPO, 1993. (ISBN0160410649). (Y4.Ap6/1:T68/4/994/pt.3).

ARTS--NEW YORK (NY)--FINANCE (v19)

ARTS--U.S.

"Several million adults [in the U.S.] describe themselves as artists by avocation, far more than the number who describe art as their occupation. About one-quarter of adults say they do some needlework at least once a year, and about 4.5 million had their sewing displayed in public. About 8 percent of adults took part in modern, folk, or tap dancing, with 2.2 million dancing in a performance. In general, the proportions of amateur artists held steady between 1982 and 1992, but there were downturns. The proportion doing needlework declined from 32 percent to 25 percent, and those who do pottery, metal, leather, or other crafts declined from 12 percent to 8 percent. Only 40 percent of Americans have ever taken music lessons, down from 47 percent in 1982. Only 18 percent have taken classes in the visual arts, down from 24 percent. But the proportion who have taken an art appreciation class actually increased, from 20 percent to 23 percent." (p10)

Robinson, John. "Business Reports: Trends: The Arts Hold Steady in Hard Times." American Demographics v16 n2, Feb 1994. p9-10. (ISSN0163-4089).

ARTS--U.S.--FINANCE (v19)

ARTS AUDIENCES--U.S.

"The proportion of adults [in the U.S.] who go to an art museum or gallery at least once a year has increased from 22 percent in 1982 to 27 percent in 1992, according to surveys conducted by the Census Bureau for the National Endowment for the Arts. That's an increase of more than 12 million visitors a year. The proportion of adults who attend an arts and crafts fair at least once a year increased from 39 percent to 41 percent, or 7 million new browsers. The proportion who attend nonmusical stage plays increased from 12 percent to 14 percent, or 5.6 million new seats filled....The proportion of adults who go to historic sites at least once a year declined from 39 percent to 35 percent, and the proportion who attend musicals or operettas declined from 19 percent to 17 percent. There was also a 3 percentage point decline in those who read novels, short stories, poetry, and plays. Overall, more than 41 percent of American adults attended an arts event in 1992 (defined as a performance of jazz or classical music, operas, musicals, plays, or ballets, plus art museums and galleries). In surveys conducted in 1982 and 1985, that proportion held steady at 39 percent." (p9)

Robinson, John. "Business Reports: Trends: The Arts Hold Steady in Hard Times." American Demographics v16 n2, Feb 1994. p9-10. (ISSN0163-4089).

ASBESTOS--U.S.

"More than 100,000 asbestos lawsuits are pending, and at least that many new suits could still be filed. Forty to 60 percent of suits are filed by people who do not have an asbestos-related disease. These suits clog court dockets, and many of these claimants actually recover money in 'batch settlements,' reducing funds available for ill claimants. Asbestos litigation drove 18 corporations into bankruptcy, and dozens more face enormous liability exposure. More than $7 billion has already been spent on asbestos claims, of which 60 percent has gone to lawyer fees and legal costs." (p13)

Andrews, James H. "Mass Remedies for Mass Torts." The Christian Science Monitor v86 n61, 22 Feb 1994. p13. (ISSN0882-7729).

ASIA

see also AGRICULTURE--ASIA--U.S.; AIRLINES--ASIA; CHINESE--ASIA; ELEPHANTS--ASIA; ENERGY CONSUMPTION--ASIA; HARBORS--ASIA; HIV INFECTIONS--ASIA; INVESTMENTS, FOREIGN--ASIA; U.S.--COMMERCE--ASIA

ASIA--COMMERCE (v19)

"Between 1986 and 1992, the share of Asia's exports sold to the U.S. dropped from 30 to 22 percent, and the U.S. share of exports from Asia's NIE's [newly industrialized economies of Hong Kong, Korea, Singapore, and Taiwan] dropped from 40 to 26 percent. The diversion of Asia's exports away from the U.S. towards itself consequently boosted intra-regional exports to 37 percent of Asia's total, displacing Canada and the U.S. as the largest regional market for Asian exports....The share of Japan's imports from Asia also declined. Despite the yen's appreciation against other Asian currencies after the mid-1980's, the share of Asia's exports shipped to Japan steadily declined from 15 percent in 1986 to 12 percent in 1992....the NIE's...watched their share shrink from 10 to 9 percent." (p23)

U.S. Dept. of Agriculture/Jerardo, Alberto. "World Agriculture & Trade: Trade within Asia Is Expanding." Agricultural Outlook Dec 1993. p22-25.

"Since 1986, inter-Asian trade, excluding Japan, has averaged 25 percent annual growth, faster than in any other part of the world. By 1992, inter-Asian trade accounted for 36 percent of the region's total trade with the world, in contrast to 25 percent in 1986. Both imports and exports with the EC [European Community], Asia's third-largest trading partner, have declined compared with Asian trade since 1986." (p22)

U.S. Dept. of Agriculture/Jerardo, Alberto. "World Agriculture & Trade: Trade within Asia Is Expanding." Agricultural Outlook Dec 1993. p22-25.

ASIA--ECONOMIC CONDITIONS (v19)

"The dynamic Pacific market has experienced remarkable growth over the last decade. Even with Japan's disappointing economic performance and the slower than hoped United States recovery in 1992, the weighted average growth rate for the region rose to 3.3 percent, from 2.6 percent in 1991. In large part, this is due to the growing economic diversity of the region, most notably, the emergence of multiple and diverse growth centers particularly in the ASEAN and China markets. This growth level is expected to increase to 4.2 percent in 1993, according to the Pacific Economic Cooperation Council, and to accelerate in 1994, in large part facilitated by growth in international trade." (pS16527)

Johnston, J. Bennett (Sen.-La.). "Seattle Asia Pacific Economic Cooperation Leaders Meeting," Congressional Record (19 Nov 1993). Daily ed. pS16527-16528. (ISSN0363-7239).

"The rapid progress of developing nations, particularly in Asia, lies in striking contrast to the economic stagnation of industrialized Western countries. These developing nations have expanded trade within the Asian region, and are now in a position to achieve economic growth unaided. The traditional Asian trading patterns will continue to develop, and forecasters predict that, by the year 2000, moderately advanced economies will have established an economic community of some 100 million people with a per capita GNP [gross national product] of more than US$5,000 (Japan's per capita GNP is around $15,000). In years to come, Japanese industries, especially labor-intensive assembly operations, will increasingly shift their production bases to the Asian region, with the twin aims of accessing the Asian market and lowering production costs. Japan will also continue to transfer high-value-added processes and development to the region." (p15)

Sano, Tadakatsu. "Economy Feature: Leading the Way: The World's Pacesetter." Look Japan v39 n451, Oct 1993. p15. (ISSN0456-5339).

"With factories sprouting, exports booming and governments turning more progressive, Asia's emerging countries look like the world's best moneymaking opportunities into the next century. Those who grab a piece of China, Malaysia, Singapore, South Korea, Thailand or even Vietnam could participate in one of history's great economic booms--if they hang in for at least three to five years. [China's] economy is estimated to have grown by 13 percent in 1993, for the second year in a row--despite the Chinese government's go-slow efforts to reduce inflation and curb speculation. Early bettors on Asia have won big. Hong Kong's stock market, rich with companies doing business in China, has gained 80 percent in 1993 as money from around the globe flooded in. Thai stocks have earned dollar investors 77 percent, Indonesian stocks 83 percent and Malaysian stocks 88 percent, according to Morgan Stanley Capital International." (p76)

Kaye, Steven D./Egan, Jack. "Predictions: Is Asia Still the Best Place to Invest?" U.S. News & World Report v115 n25, 27 Dec 1993. p76. (ISSN0041-5537).

ASIA--POPULATION (v19)

ASIA, SOUTHEASTERN

see COASTS--ASIA, SOUTHEASTERN

ASIA, SOUTHEASTERN--COMMERCE--INDONESIA (v19)

ASIAN AMERICANS (v19)

U.S. census data from 1990 "shows that the Asian, Pacific Islander category grew by 108 percent to nearly 7.3 million. Within that category, Chinese, Filipinos and Japanese still rank as the largest Asian groups, with Japanese having an increase of over 20 percent. Additionally, Immigration and Naturalization Service figures confirm that of the nearly 21 million short term visitors (those on 6-month visas) in 1992, the largest number, almost 4 million, came from Japan." (p4)

Wojtan, Linda S. "Resources for Teaching about Japan." Access n119, Oct-Nov 1993. p4,15-16.

"The Asian American population is the fastest growing of any minority group in the United States, and the number of Asians in this country has more than doubled over the past 10 years, Charles Lee says. According to the 1990 census, there are about 7.3 million Asian and Pacific Islanders living in this country." (p31)

Shaffer, Gwen. "Asian Americans Organize for Justice." Environmental Action v25 n4, Win 1994. p30-33. (ISSN0013-922X).

ASIAN AMERICANS--CALIFORNIA--SOCIAL CONDITIONS (v19)

ASIAN AMERICANS--POPULATION (v19)

"The Korean community in the United States has been growing at an incredible rate over the past two decades, mainly through the influx of new immigrants as an outcome of the Immigration Act of 1965. The new act became effective in 1968 allowing as many as 20,000 to 30,000 Koreans to enter the U.S. annually (Kim, 1980). The 1990 Census data shows that there are 815,447 Koreans in the United States, which represents an increase of nearly 130 percent since 1980 (U.S. Bureau of Census, 1990). Approximately 30 percent of this population are concentrated in the Los Angeles area earning this city the name of the Korean Capital in the United States." (p17-18)

Yamamoto, Joe/others. "Psychiatric Disorders among Elderly Koreans in the United States." Community Mental Health Journal v30 n1, Feb 1994. p17-27. (ISSN0010-3853).

"The elderly Asian population is the fastest growing age group among Asian Americans. The elderly comprised 6.6 percent of the total Asian population in 1980, and 10.3 percent will be age 65 and over by the end of the century (Ong, 1989)....More than 95 percent of the Korean elderly in the United States are and will continue to be foreign-born." (p18)

Yamamoto, Joe/others. "Psychiatric Disorders among Elderly Koreans in the United States." Community Mental Health Journal v30 n1, Feb 1994. p17-27. (ISSN0010-3853).

ASIAN STUDENTS--U.S. (v19)

ASPEN (COLO)

see ENERGY CONSUMPTION--ASPEN (COLO); HOUSING--ASPEN (COLO)

ASPHALT-RUBBER--U.S.

"Many states [in the U.S.] have experimented with crumb rubber in hot mix asphalt, some have met with success and others have met with failure. In a recent survey conducted by the Maryland Environmental Service (in which 41 states responded), it was noted that over 490 miles of state highways (nationwide) have been paved with crumb rubber modified asphalt. Of the states responding, the reported cost per ton for conventional hot mix asphalt was $20 to $40, and the cost per ton of crumb rubber modified hot mix asphalt was $50 to $70. Only 13 percent of the states considered the crumb rubber projects to be cost-effective at this time." (p837)

Welke, Robert A. (Chief Engineer, Deputy Director, Bureau of Highways). U.S. House. Committee on Appropriations. "Department of Transportation and Related Agencies Approp. for 1994 (Part 8)." Hearing, Washington, D.C.: GPO, 1993. (ISBN0160410657). (Y4.Ap6/1:T68/4/994/pt.8).

"There have been over 150 reports and papers relating to asphalt rubber that show that it extends the life of pavement. In the City of Phoenix alone, the 20-Year Asphalt Rubber Report shows surfaces that have been used for over 21 years with no maintenance. Normal conventional pavement requires maintenance every 3 to 5 years. In a TRB [or Transportation Research Board] Report from California, the Ravendale Study showed that asphalt rubber of 1-1/2" thickness had outlasted 4" of conventional pavement and was still performing, even though the conventional pavement had to be replaced. The FAA [Federal Aviation Administration] Report...showed that asphalt rubber would last as much as 17 times longer than conventional pavement." (p977)

Jacobson, Carl C. (President, International Surfacing Inc.). U.S. House. Committee on Appropriations. "Department of Transportation and Related Agencies Approp. for 1994 (Part 8)." Hearing, Washington, D.C.: GPO, 1993. (ISBN0160410657). (Y4.Ap6/1:T68/4/994/pt.8).

ASSOCIATIONS, INSTITUTIONS, ETC.

see also ANIMAL WELFARE--SOCIETIES; CHARITIES; NONPROFIT ORGANIZATIONS

ASSOCIATIONS, INSTITUTIONS, ETC.--U.S.

"We have been called, accurately, a nation of joiners. Seven out of 10 adult Americans belong to at least one association. Four out of 10 belong to four or more. The 9,300 associations in the American Society of Association Executives have more than 287 million memberships in their organizations. But there are more than 100,000 associations nationwide--probably one for every industry, profession, philanthropy, cause or point of view--representing millions of Americans of varying economic and educational levels and cultures. They are the very fabric of America." (p33)

Taylor, R. William. "Fair Comment: Congress Sets a High Price on Free Speech." Insight v10 n7, 14 Feb 1994. p33. (ISSN1051-4880).

ASTHMA--U.S. (v19)

ASTHMA IN CHILDREN (v19)

ASYLUM, RIGHT OF--EUROPE (v19)

ASYLUM, RIGHT OF--GERMANY (v19)

AT&T

see ENVIRONMENTAL POLICY--AT&T

ATHEROSCLEROSIS--U.S.

"A recent study published in August 1993 by THE JOURNAL OF AMERICAN COLLEGE OF CARDIOLOGY, shows that young Americans have a high prevalence of coronary atherosclerosis. Autopsies after the Korean War showed that 77% of young American soldiers had some degree of coronary atherosclerosis. To determine whether atherosclerosis is declining as a result of lower average cholesterol levels, researchers examined at autopsy, 111 victims of noncardiac trauma, each 14 to 35 years (average age, 26). The subjects were 86% male and 86% white, and an estimated 68% were smokers. However, only an estimated 5% had a serum cholesterol over 200 mg/dl. Autopsies found signs of atherosclerosis in 78% of the subjects, including 21% who had lesions with more than 50% stenosis. Fully 5% had significant stenoses of the left main coronary artery. Subjects with and without severe atherosclerosis had similar demographic characteristics." (p33)

McDonagh, E. W. "Clinic: Atherosclerosis Prevention." Acres, U.S.A. Dec 1993. p33.

ATHLETES, COLLEGE

see COLLEGE ATHLETES

ATHLETES, COMMUNITY COLLEGE

see COMMUNITY COLLEGE ATHLETES

ATLANTA (GA) (v19)

see also OLYMPIC GAMES (1996: ATLANTA, GEORGIA)

ATLANTA (GA)--POPULATION (v19)

"When a metro area is growing rapidly, its percentage change will tend to fall over time as the population base increases. Atlanta, for example, had an average annual percentage change of 2.8 from 1980 to 1990, but from 1990 to 1991, the growth rate was 2.4 percent....This slower growth can be accounted for, in part, because Atlanta grew from over 2.2 million in 1980 to almost 3.0 million in 1990, greatly increasing the base. Nonetheless, Atlanta added 72,770 new residents between 1990 and 1991, more than the annual increase of the 1980s of 72,670." (p5)

Gober, Patricia/Haub, Carl. "U.S. Migration: South Retains Its Magnetism; Midwest Rallies." Population Today v22 n1, Jan 1994. p4-5. (ISSN0749-2448).

ATMOSPHERIC CARBON DIOXIDE (v19)

"Road transport is the biggest single emitter of CO2 in the world (estimated at 20-25%). The share from motor vehicles has risen to about 14%. The megacities of the world, especially the rapidly expanding ones of Asia and South America, are contributing a rising portion. The growth rate in CO2 emissions from motor vehicles in the developing world--increasing at about 3.5 percent a year--now accounts for about 45 percent of global growth in vehicle releases." (p4)

Wilson, Nancy C. "U.S. Electric Vehicle Controversy May Have Global Implications." Climate Alert v6 n6, Nov-Dec 1993. p1,4-6.

"The UN Intergovernmental Panel on Climate Change (IPCC)--the major force behind last year's Rio summit--contends that immediate reductions of over 60 percent in 'greenhouse emissions from human activities' are needed just to stabilize CO2 concentrations at today's levels. Other observers put the figure at closer to 80 percent. The impact of such numbers is difficult to fathom. According to the Department of Energy, for the U.S. alone, even a 20-percent reduction in CO2 emissions by the year 2000--the goal President Clinton has committed us to achieving--would require a carbon tax forcing the price of electricity to double, oil prices to triple, and the cost of coal to quintuple. Since the U.S. emits only 30 percent of the earth's greenhouse gases, stabilizing CO2 emissions worldwide would require much more draconian measures still: it would require a fundamental restructuring of the global economy." (p25)

Salmon, Jeffrey. "Greenhouse Anxiety." Commentary v96 n1, Jul 1993. p25-28. (ISSN0010-2601).

"Many Great Plains soils have declined in soil organic carbon (organic matter) content and nutrient supplying capacity since they were initially cultivated. Numerous studies have shown that tillage reduces soil organic carbon and nitrogen contents by 30 to 70 percent in as little as 20 years (Bauer and Black, 1981; Bowman et al., 1990). Current estimates (CAST, 1992) suggest that cultivated cropland soils in the United States lose about six billion pounds of carbon per year. Another 78 billion pounds of carbon are emitted annually from agricultural fossil fuel use and the manufacture of nitrogen fertilizers. These figures indicate that agricultural activities release significant amounts of carbon dioxide to the atmosphere every year. Atmospheric carbon dioxide levels have been steadily increasing for the past 75 years and are expected to double by the middle of the next century. A doubling of carbon dioxide levels could increase global temperatures by 5...[degrees] to 15...[degrees Fahrenheit] and have dramatic effects on agriculture (Adams et al., 1990). Therefore, the agricultural industry should actively look for ways to decrease carbon dioxide emissions." (p1)

Gebhart, Dick. "Some Agricultural Activities Are Related to Carbon Dioxide Emissions." Kerr Center for Sustainable Agriculture Newsletter v19 n8, Nov-Dec 1993. p1.

"Fossil fuels release around 5.4 units of carbon in the form of CO2. Land-use changes release about 1.6 units. About 3.2 units remain in the air, while 2 units go into the sea. But 1.8 units are unaccounted for. Geochemists now think this 'missing' carbon is absorbed on land, especially by northern forests." (p14)

Cowen, Robert C. "Science & Technology: Picture This: A Living, Breathing Earth." The Christian Science Monitor v86 n38, 19 Jan 1994. p14. (ISSN0882-7729).

ATMOSPHERIC CARBON DIOXIDE--U.S.

"Carbon dioxide emissions are the single largest cause of global warming, and the concentrations have increased dramatically during the past 100 years. The United States is a major culprit, contributing nearly 25 percent of all atmospheric CO2 (Union of Concerned Scientists, 1990). The global cash register is now ringing up the price of American affluence and nearly two centuries of industrialization. The costs will be borne for generations to come....Electricity is responsible for 33 percent of the CO2 emissions from fossil fuels in the United States (Renew America, 1988). The average household consumes about 7,000 kilowatt hours (kWh) per year at a cost of $600." (p3)

Elliott, Luke. "CO2--You Can Make a Difference." Kerr Center for Sustainable Agriculture Newsletter v20 n2, Mar-Apr 1994. p3-4.

ATMOSPHERIC OZONE (v19)

ATMOSPHERIC OZONE--REDUCTION

"Scientists have not yet established a quantitative relation between amounts of ozone-depleting chemicals in the atmosphere and degree of ozone depletion on a global basis. One can make a crude guess that annual average depletion over mid-latitude regions such as the U.S. will double, from the current 4-5% depletion to 8-10%, by the year 2000. This guess implies a potential increase of 13% or more in levels of damaging ultraviolet radiation, which would lead to a significant rise in skin cancer rates and ecological effects over the long term." (p4)

Oppenheimer, Michael. "EDF Column: Clearing Up the Confusion about Ozone Depletion." EDF News v24 n5, Sep 1993. p4.

"The floods of 1993 may be nothing compared to the floods of 2023. In 1989, the EPA released the results of a two-year, $2.5 million study that predicted a doubling of CO2 and methane gases over the next 40 years. The report warned that the resulting 2-5 C increase in global temperatures could raise sea levels as much as two meters (6.6 feet). The Intergovernmental Panel on Climate Change (IPCC), a UN-affiliated group of the world's leading climatologists, has predicted that, over the next 30 years, unchecked CO2 emissions will trigger a sea-level rise that could swamp Hong Kong, Venice, Rio de Janeiro and the Nile Delta. Meanwhile, IPCC Secretary 'Ram' Sundararaman predicts that, as a result of global heating, '20 to 30 percent of our ecosystems--as we know them today--will change.' One computer model forecasts the death of 40 percent of the planet's boreal forests. Members of the Canadian House of Commons' Standing Committee on the Environment have concluded that 'the entire boreal forest will cease to exist in our lifetime' due to global heating." (p26)

Smith, Gar. "The Greenhouse-Gas/Ozone-Hole Connection." Earth Island Journal v9 n1, Win 1993-94. p26. (ISSN1041-0406).

"UCLA physicist Alfred Wong wants to stabilize stratospheric chlorine levels by using negative ions. Fifteen huge solar-powered ion-generators suspended over Antarctica and 15 more in the Arctic will do the trick, Wong said. The half-mile square, helium-suspended platforms would produce DC currents to provide a continuous flow of electrons and negative ions. The removed chlorine would combine with sodium on the electrodes to form salt, which would be dropped into the ocean. Wong recently won plaudits for his proposal from international scientists attending an ozone conference in Italy. Meanwhile, he has $1 million in equipment and 20 people working on the project. Wong claims that his plan would cost 'less than a 747.'" (p16)

Strachan, Don. "Techno-Fixing the Ozone Layer." Earth Island Journal v8 n3, Sum 1993. p16. (ISSN1041-0406).

"While ozone levels normally increase above the Arctic between mid-February and early-March, NASA researcher Joe Waters found that ozone actually 'decreased by 0.7 percent per day' during the same period in 1992-3. On April 23, the SAN FRANCISCO CHRONICLE reported that last winter's ozone levels over the Northern Hemisphere dropped 'to the lowest levels ever recorded.' In February, record lows were registered over Sweden, Finland, Norway, Canada and Japan, as ozone concentrations dropped to levels previously found only over Antarctica. NASA reported that ozone levels above the equator last winter were 2-3 percent lower than ever before. Over much of Central Asia, Western Europe and the western US, ozone levels were down 10-20 percent. NASA's James Gleason observed that 'global ozone levels are still way below normal and they have not recovered.'" (p17)

Smith, Gar. "Ozone Down; Radiation Up." Earth Island Journal v8 n3, Sum 1993. p17. (ISSN1041-0406).

"A paper published in NATURE by Joe Farman of the British Antarctic Survey in May 1985 presented data showing a 40 percent depletion over Antarctica in October levels of total column ozone from 1957 to 1984. Farman had delayed publication of his article for nearly two years to verify his findings, given their challenge to the then-existing understanding of the science. Farman's observations caused turmoil in the scientific community because its members did not have a theory to explain the unexpectedly large depletions discovered at Antarctica. A reanalysis of readings from the National Aeronautics and Space Administration's (NASA) Nimbus 7 satellite, presented in August of the same year, confirmed the extent of the depletion for the years 1979 to 1983." (p26)

Maxwell, James H./Weiner, Sanford L. "Green Consciousness or Dollar Diplomacy? The British Response to the Threat of Ozone Depletion." International Environmental Affairs v5 n1, Win 1993. p19-41. (ISSN1041-4665).

"Already scientists have discovered holes over both poles and a 50 percent thinning of the tattered Antarctic ozone layer. Below these swathes of unshielded sky researchers have measured unprecedented levels of ultraviolet (UV-B) light, which many say have caused a 12 percent decrease in the reproductive rate of Antarctic phyloplankton--phyloplankton being the basis of the aquatic food chain. The prognosis for these delicate life forms is getting worse. It has been discovered that UV-B solar radiation penetrates as deep as 100 feet below the surface of the sea. Bad news for small organisms in Antarctica and any other life form that can't, as Ronald Reagan once suggested, 'wear sunscreen and a baseball hat.'" (p22-23)

Parenti, Christian. "NASA's Assault on the Ozone Layer." Lies of Our Times Sep 1993. p22-23. (ISSN1046-7912).

"The National Toxics Campaign, which obtains much of its information from the National Aeronautics and Space Administration (NASA) itself, reports that three shuttle launches release as much ozone-destroying chlorine into the atmosphere as the single large industrial producer of chlorofluorocarbons (CFCs) generates in a year. The annual output of DuPont's West Virginia facility is 800,000 pounds of CFCs, which contain 450,000 pounds of chlorine. Each shuttle launch deposits 150,000 pounds of chlorine into the stratosphere, according to NASA. NASA now averages about nine shuttle flights a year, making it the single largest destroyer of ozone in the U.S." (p22)

Parenti, Christian. "NASA's Assault on the Ozone Layer." Lies of Our Times Sep 1993. p22-23. (ISSN1046-7912).

"The ozone hole's depth and size has increased since researchers at the British Halley Bay base first discovered it in the mid-1980s. In recent years, between 30 and 50 percent of springtime ozone over Antarctica has disappeared, scientists say. But this year, more than 60 percent of the ozone was destroyed over an area larger than Europe." (p11)

Walters, David C. "Science on Ice: Antarctica Lab Researches Effects of the Ozone Hole." The Christian Science Monitor v86 n24, 29 Dec 1993. p11,14. (ISSN0882-7729).

According to James Teeri, "'In 1983, the ozone hole over the Antarctic was the size of the United States. In 1993, it was three times the size of the United States. Furthermore, if the release of CFCs [chlorofluorocarbons] ceased instantly, it would still take nearly 100 years for the ozone to recover.' While ozone depletion seems to be greatest in the Southern Hemisphere, recent studies in Canada suggest that ozone layers may be thinning in the Northern Hemisphere as well." (p2)

News release. "UV-B." University of Michigan News and Information Services 28 Feb 1994. p1-2.

ATMOSPHERIC OZONE--U.S. (v19)

ATOMIC ENERGY

see NUCLEAR ENERGY

ATOMIC POWER

see NUCLEAR ENERGY

ATOMIC WEAPONS

see NUCLEAR WEAPONS

ATRIAL FIBRILLATION--U.S. (v19)

ATTENDANCE, CHURCH

see CHURCH ATTENDANCE

ATTITUDES

see U.S.--POPULATION--ATTITUDES

ATTORNEYS

see LAWYERS

AUDIENCES, ARTS

see ARTS AUDIENCES

AUJESZKY'S DISEASE IN SWINE--U.S.--COSTS (v19)

AUSTRALIA

see also DIAMOND INDUSTRY AND TRADE--AUSTRALIA; ECONOMIC FORECASTING--AUSTRALIA; IMMIGRANTS--AUSTRALIA--CANADA--GREAT BRITAIN--U.S.; KANGAROOS--AUSTRALIA; MEDICAL CARE--AUSTRALIA--U.S.; MONEY--AUSTRALIA; TOURIST TRADE--AUSTRALIA; UNEMPLOYMENT--AUSTRALIA--GREAT BRITAIN; WOOL INDUSTRY--AUSTRALIA

AUSTRALIA--ECONOMIC CONDITIONS

"The Australian dollar has been flexing its muscle. Its rise to US 70 cents, analysts say, reflects increasing confidence here and abroad in the Australian economy....The Reserve Bank of Australia, after cutting interest rates 15 times since 1990, from 18 percent to 4.75 percent, said the renewed strength of the Australian dollar was 'lessening any case for further easing in policy.'...Although Australia's economy officially has been in recovery for the last nine quarters, the 11 percent unemployment rate has fallen little from its peak. Companies have put more money into plant upgrades than into creating new jobs. But the unemployment rate is expected to drop to just over 10 percent later this year and to around 9 percent later next year." (p9)

Foster, Catherine. "Economy: Economy Down Under: Foreign Investment, Commodity Price Rise Give Australia a Boost." The Christian Science Monitor v86 n43, 26 Jan 1994. p9. (ISSN0882-7729).

AUSTRALIA--EMPLOYMENT (v19)

AUSTRALIA--POPULATION

"Ever since the seventies, almost all Western countries have seen a shift in the age profile of their populations. If we take the age bracket 15-64 as the limit of normal availability for work, the percentage of the OECD [Organization for Economic Cooperation and Development] population aged 15-64 increased from 62.9% in 1966 to 66.7% in 1989. In Australia, the percentage aged 15-64 rose from 61.2% in 1966 to 66.9% in 1989. Most of this increase actually took place (in Australia) between 1970 (61.9%) and 1988 (66.8%). Since 1989 there has been little increase. The reason for this age shift, in Australia and everywhere else, is a decline in the birth rate. In Australia, the birth rate per thousand of population declined from around 21 in the late sixties to around 16 in the middle seventies. Since then, it has fallen more slowly to around 15." (p58)

Munford, Michael. "Unemployment and the Problem of Work." Quadrant v38 n1-2, Jan-Feb 1994. p56-60. (ISSN0033-5010).

AUTOMATED TELLERS--U.S. (v19)

AUTOMOBILE INDUSTRY AND TRADE (v19)

"By 1998, predicts DRI/McGraw-Hill in a new Asia study, auto markets in South Korea, Taiwan, and Thailand combined will rival Britain or France. The contrast with the industrial world is stark. Western Europe's car market slumped 15% last year, while Japan's sank 6%. Even the rebounding U.S. market grew only 8%, vs. 12% in the developing world. Auto sales in those 167 countries will grow 44%, to 11.3 million by 1998, predicts DRI/McGraw-Hill, nearly doubling the growth rate in the markets of the industrial world, which are 2.5 times as large but saturated." (p50)

Treece, James B./others. "International Business: Autos: New Worlds to Conquer." Business Week n3360, 28 Feb 1994. p50-52. (ISSN0007-7135).

"The global population of motor vehicles now stands at 500 million; if linear trends continue it could reach 1.1 billion by 2025." (p4) "Since 1950 auto manufacturing has shifted from the U.S., Germany and the U.K. to Asia, especially Japan, and present production is divided fairly evenly among the U.S., Japan and Western Europe. As of 1988, 14 manufacturers accounted for 80 percent of the 48 million cars produced: three American manufacturers, six Japanese, two German, two French and one Italian, counting by company rather than where the vehicles were manufactured or assembled." (p6)

Wilson, Nancy C. "U.S. Electric Vehicle Controversy May Have Global Implications." Climate Alert v6 n6, Nov-Dec 1993. p1,4-6.

AUTOMOBILE INDUSTRY AND TRADE--BRAZIL (v19)

AUTOMOBILE INDUSTRY AND TRADE--CHINA (v19)

AUTOMOBILE INDUSTRY AND TRADE--EMPLOYMENT--U.S. (v19)

"About half the autoworkers at the Big Three will retire over the next five years, forcing the automakers to hire huge numbers of new workers for the first time in two decades, experts say. University of Michigan auto researcher Sean McAlinden says the Big Three will need to hire up to 200,000 hourly workers by the end of the decade to replace retiring employees. Roughly 90,000 of those jobs will be in Michigan. 'We've been calling it the great turnover,' McAlinden said. 'This is a rate of attrition that hasn't been matched in the auto industry since the Great Depression.'" (p1 secD) "The average Big Three hourly worker is 47 years old and has 22 years of seniority....Big Three hourly employees, under a United Auto Workers contract, can retire after 30 years." (p5 secD)

Haglund, Rick. "Retirements Mean Big 3 Will Be Hiring." Ann Arbor News 1 May 1994. p1,5 secD.

AUTOMOBILE INDUSTRY AND TRADE--EUROPE (v19)

AUTOMOBILE INDUSTRY AND TRADE--EUROPE--JAPAN (v19)

AUTOMOBILE INDUSTRY AND TRADE--GREAT BRITAIN

"Thirty years ago the idea of a Britain without a car industry would have been as unthinkable as a France without wine or a Japan without radios. Now Germany's BMW has bought 80% of Rover, the last-remaining big British-owned car company, for 800m [pounds sterling] ($1.2 billion); the other 20% is owned by Japan's Honda. Some Britons see the sale as one more blow to the country's industrial manhood." (p14)

"Leaders: Too Late for Champions." Economist v330 n7849, 5 Feb 1994. p14. (ISSN0013-0613).

AUTOMOBILE INDUSTRY AND TRADE--JAPAN--U.S. (v19)

"In the United States last year, Japanese and European manufacturers held 35% of the U.S. passenger car market, 30% held by Japan alone. In Japan, however, imports from all countries, Europe, America and Asia, represent about 3% of the market." (p47)

Collins, Stephen J. (Director of Economics and Int. Affairs, American Automobile Manufacturers Assoc.). U.S. Senate. Committee on Finance. "United States-Japan Trade Negotiations." Hearing, 8 Nov 1993. Washington, D.C.: GPO, 1994. (ISBN0160435625). (Y4.F49:S.hrg.103-399).

"The following developments highlight some of the dramatic changes that have taken place during the last several years with respect to automotive trade between the United States and Japan: Japanese vehicle exports to the U.S. have dropped by almost half since FY86, a decline of more than 1.6 million units. U.S. production of motor vehicles by Nissan and other Japanese-owned American manufacturers has more than doubled since FY86 to 1.689 million units in FY92. The number of American suppliers doing business with Japanese-owned American manufacturers and their Japanese parent companies has risen from fewer than 300 in FY86 to nearly 1200 in FY92. Sales by these suppliers have grown from less than $2.5 billion to $13.62 billion during the same period." (p92)

U.S. Senate. Committee on Finance. "United States-Japan Trade Negotiations." Hearing, 8 Nov 1993. Washington, D.C.: GPO, 1994. (ISBN0160435625). (Y4.F49:S.hrg.103-399).

"The trade deficit in...[the motor vehicle and parts] sector has...not shown signs of real improvement. Indeed it has deteriorated further in 1993. During the first half of 1993, the U.S. automotive trade deficit with Japan was 5.6 percent greater than during the same period in the previous year, reaching approximately $32.2 billion dollars on an annual basis. Auto and auto parts have been the major portion of the bilateral trade deficit for many years. The bilateral automotive trade deficit has accounted for more than 50 percent of our total trade deficit with Japan for each of the last eight years. In 1993, it accounts for 60 percent of the total bilateral trade deficit." (p50)

Hauser, Timothy J. (Acting Under Secretary of Commerce for International Trade). U.S. Senate. Committee on Finance. "United States-Japan Trade Negotiations." Hearing, 8 Nov 1993. Washington, D.C.: GPO, 1994. (ISBN0160435625). (Y4.F49:S.hrg.103-399).

"In 1993, for the second straight year...[the Japanese] share of the U.S. market for cars and light trucks fell--this time to 23.2%, off 2.6 points since 1991....Indeed, only one Japanese auto maker--Nissan--gained market share last year. By contrast, Honda's U.S. sales fell 6.8%, and its share dropped 0.8 points, to 5.2%. Toyota's share dropped a half-point, to 7.5%. This year and next, researcher AutoPacific Inc. predicts, Japanese carmakers' collective share will continue to hover around 23%." (p32)

Armstrong, Larry/others. "Top of the News: Autos: Trying to Rev Up." Business Week i3355, 24 Jan 1994. p32-33. (ISSN0007-7135).

"Truck sales are on a roll. Despite bitter cold across much of the country and California's earthquake, U.S. sales of light trucks stormed ahead 24% in January, to 416,828 vehicles, easily outpacing a 7.8% rise in car sales....Partly because of their weak truck lineups, Japanese companies' share of the U.S. light-vehicle market slipped to 23.2% in 1993 from 24.5% in 1992 and likely will slide further this year. Until recently, though, only Chrysler really went after truck buyers tooth and nail. Trucks made up 59% of Chrysler's vehicle sales in 1993, vs. 47% for Ford Motor Co. and 38% for General Motors Corp. Overall, truck sales have expanded from 33% of the U.S. market in 1989 to 39% last year...." (p46)

Treece, James B./Kerwin, Kathleen. "Top of the News: Detroit: Highballing It into Trucks." Business Week n3361, 7 Mar 1994. p46. (ISSN0007-7135).

"A report commissioned by the US and Japanese governments confirms some of US automakers' complaints. The study finds that US cars sell for approximately 40 percent more in Japan than in the US. Only 40 percent of Japanese dealers handle imports (including US vehicles manufactured in Japan), compared with 94 percent of American dealers. The report also finds that 45 percent of Japanese consumers would consider buying an import." (p8)

Popiel, Leslie Albrecht. "Economy: The US Sees Need for Fairer Auto Export Policy to Japan." The Christian Science Monitor v86 n54, 10 Feb 1994. p8. (ISSN0882-7729).

AUTOMOBILE INDUSTRY AND TRADE--MEXICO (v19)

AUTOMOBILE INDUSTRY AND TRADE--MEXICO--U.S. (v19)

AUTOMOBILE INDUSTRY AND TRADE--MICHIGAN

"'The auto industry is like a gold mine that took 70 years to play out,' said [University of Michigan economist Paul] Courant, noting that the state once had 400,000 auto manufacturing jobs--high paying jobs that kept Michigan's per-capita income significantly above the national average until 1980. With the boom in auto sales promising to keep auto employment from dropping below 260,000 and with a steady growth in non-manufacturing private employment 'and not just flipping hamburgers,' he said the state's per-capita income should climb back up to the national average later this year or in 1995." (p1 secC)

Cain, Stephen. "Local: Auto Surge Boosting State Economy--to Average, Says U-M Prof." Ann Arbor News 21 Jan 1994. p1 secC.

AUTOMOBILE INDUSTRY AND TRADE--U.S. (v19)

"During 1990 and 1991 in the United States, vehicle production declined by 2 million units and employment in the sector dropped by 71,000 jobs. The big three lost $12.1 billion dollars during this period. Nevertheless, the U.S. market remained open. Indeed the Japanese increased their market share in the United States during the last recession." (p51)

Hauser, Timothy J. (Acting Under Secretary of Commerce for International Trade). U.S. Senate. Committee on Finance. "United States-Japan Trade Negotiations." Hearing, 8 Nov 1993. Washington, D.C.: GPO, 1994. (ISBN0160435625). (Y4.F49:S.hrg.103-399).

"The motor vehicle and parts industries are a large and important segment of the U.S. economy. Estimated total employment in automotive and allied industries is 6 million persons, or 6 percent of non-farm employment in the U.S. economy. Estimated manufacturing employment in automotive and allied industries is 1 million persons, equal to approximately 7 percent of total manufacturing employment in the United States. In 1992, auto industry production represented close to 6 percent of the GDP [gross domestic product]." (p50)

Hauser, Timothy J. (Acting Under Secretary of Commerce for International Trade). U.S. Senate. Committee on Finance. "United States-Japan Trade Negotiations." Hearing, 8 Nov 1993. Washington, D.C.: GPO, 1994. (ISBN0160435625). (Y4.F49:S.hrg.103-399).

"A University of Michigan forecast...said North American carmakers must develop technology that continues to boost fuel economy, reduce emissions, add more safety features and use more recyclable materials....Highlights of the U-M forecast include: In the next decade, the cost of regular unleaded gasoline is expected to rise to $1.75 per gallon in 1993 dollars. Federal Corporate Average Fuel Economy standards for passenger cars are projected to increase from 27.5 miles per gallon to 32 mpg in the next decade--with 45 mpg for a five-passenger car possible by the year 2020. Although only about 20 percent of North American-produced passenger cars presently have antilock brake systems, by 2003 nearly all are expected to be equipped with them because of consumer demand and lower costs. Driver-side air bags, currently installed in about half of North American-produced passenger cars and 10 percent of light trucks, essentially should become standard features in the next 10 years, according to the authors." (p6 secB)

"Business: Automotive Challenges." Ann Arbor News 11 Jan 1994. p6 secB.

"Donald Hilty, chief economist at Chrysler Corp., and Martin Zimmerman, his counterpart at Ford Motor Co., said...sales of cars and trucks in the United States could far surpass the record of 16.3 million units set in 1986. Hilty said sales are likely to hit 17.3 million units in 1997. He spoke at a Society of Automotive Analysts meeting, held in conjunction with the media days preceding the Jan. 8 opening of the North American International Auto Show at Cobo Hall. Automakers today are expected to report 1993 sales of around 14.2 million units. That is up from 1992's 13.1 million units and 1991's 12.5 million." (p1 secA)

Haglund, Rick. "Record Auto Sales Will Boost State, Experts Say." Ann Arbor News 4 Jan 1994. p1 secA.

"The average car now costs about $18,500, half the median U.S. family income, up from $11,450, or 44% of income, in 1984, according to the American Automobile Manufacturers Assn. Leasing helps ease the shock by adjusting terms to keep monthly payments low. That's why leasing has boomed to 25% of overall car sales, and to 77% for some luxury models, such as Jaguar....Trucks accounted for 38% of all light-vehicle sales last year, up from 21% in 1980, and the trend shows no signs of slowing. In addition, the North American Free Trade Agreement is expected to increase sales to Mexico, the fastest-growing auto market in North America." (p71)

Kerwin, Kathleen. "Manufacturing: Autos: Value Will Keep Detroit Moving." Business Week n3353, 10 Jan 1994. p71. (ISSN0007-7135).

Auto industry executives in the U.S. "expect to sell about 14.8 million cars and light trucks [in 1994], up 6%--a good, if not booming, year. First-quarter U.S. car production may rise 15% from 1993. Light-truck output will jump 18%, according to WARD'S AUTOMOTIVE REPORTS. Consumer confidence is still a concern for carmakers, as 1993's seesaw market showed: Sales perked up in spring, flattened in summer, then surged in the fall. For the year, they rose 8.5%, half of normal for an economic rebound. But Detroit is getting more of those buyers. Ford Motor Co. and Chrysler Corp. gained 2.5 points of market share. Beleaguered General Motors Corp. lost nearly a point as it slashed unprofitable sales to rental-car companies. Even so, the Big Three have added 3.4 points since 1991, to 73.8%, and may hit 75% this year....The soaring yen, up 13% against the dollar last year, forced the Japanese to raise prices again, by 3% to 4% for 1994 models. The Big Three held their increases to an average 2%. That gives them a price advantage of $3,100 per car, up from $2,500 last spring, says Salomon Brothers Inc. analyst John V. Kirnan. With U.S. car quality rivaling that of Japan, consumers are harder-pressed to justify buying an import." (p71)

Kerwin, Kathleen. "Manufacturing: Autos: Value Will Keep Detroit Moving." Business Week n3353, 10 Jan 1994. p71. (ISSN0007-7135).

"The Office of Technology Assessment compared the cost of making cars for the U.S. market. They counted in not just wages but health benefits, productivity, transport costs, and other factors. They found that when Ford wants to sell a car in the United States, it costs $8,770 to make it here and $9,180 to make it in Mexico. Thus, for every car Ford makes in Mexico and sells here, Ford loses $410 in profits." (pS16625)

Baucus, Max (Sen.-Mont.). "Morning Business," Congressional Record (20 Nov 1993). Daily ed. pS16622-16633. (ISSN0363-7239).

The automobile industry "accounts for about 4% of America's GDP [gross domestic product]. Vehicle sales have been rising briskly, but something more fundamental is at work. Chrysler has introduced five basic chassis designs since 1992, compared with three in the previous 20 years. Ford and General Motors have both reduced the number of chassis platforms they use, but are turning out new models at an unprecedented pace. Ford has a dozen or so scheduled for the next two years--three times the rate of a decade ago. General Motors has 12 coming out this year alone. This year Detroit's share of the American market may climb back to 75%, against just over 70% in 1991." (p65)

"Business: Ready to Take on the World." Economist v330 n7846, 15 Jan 1994. p65-66. (ISSN0013-0613).

"The U.S. has a large appetite for natural resources. Increasing consumption is so important that, in the words of author Alan Durning, 'It is the primary goal of national economic policy.' But with high levels of consumption come resource depletion and pollution, both nationally and globally. As an example, consider the automobile. Americans own more cars per person than any other country in the world--190 million total. We have paved over more than 58,000 square miles of land--an area larger than the state of Iowa--covering productive soils and increasing polluted storm water runoff into streams, lakes and rivers. To build each car, we use on average 2,200 pounds of metals and roughly 220 pounds of plastic, according to Durning. The production of metals and petroleum-based plastics rank second and fifth respectively among U.S. industries in energy use. To run our vehicles, we import more than half our oil, increasing our trade deficit and impacting the environments of petroleum-producing countries. Fueled largely by this foreign oil, we drive more than 2 trillion miles total every year--twice the 1970 average--diminishing gains in pollution control and fuel efficiency we have made in the last 20 years." (p20)

Hren, Ben/Bartolomeo, Nick. "Special Report: Carrying Capacity Project: Consumption: Compounding the Problem." Outdoor America v59 n1, Win 1994. p15-22.

"Automobile manufacturing...creates many jobs because productive hourly workers in the industry tend to be better paid than their counterparts in other sectors. In 1992, for example, the average hourly earnings for production workers in the auto business was $15.46, compared with an economywide average of $10.58. This means that an auto worker's family has more money to spend and, thus, can more easily stimulate demand and growth." (p52)

Collins, Sara. "Business: Driving Hard into the Future." U.S. News & World Report v115 n24, 20 Dec 1993. p50-52. (ISSN0041-5537).

"With [U.S.] consumers responding to low interest rates, attractive leasing deals and a sense that the job market is improving, domestic car and light truck sales climbed to a 13 million annual rate in November. Moreover, the appreciation of the yen against the dollar and higher quality, better designed vehicles are leading consumers to buy American. As a result, the Big Three's domestic market share recently increased to 73 percent, up from 70 percent in 1991....Employment in the motor vehicle industry declined by 94,300 jobs between 1985 and 1991....A study by the University of Michigan's Office for the Study of Automotive Transportation found that replacing Japanese imports with 500,000 domestically produced vehicles annually would add 119,094 jobs to the economy by 1995; yet only 15,336 of these positions would be added to auto factory payrolls. Nearly 104,000 jobs would be produced outside the auto industry--in 25 different sectors, ranging from primary metals manufacturing to trucking." (p51)

Collins, Sara. "Business: Driving Hard into the Future." U.S. News & World Report v115 n24, 20 Dec 1993. p50-52. (ISSN0041-5537).

AUTOMOBILE PARKING--EMPLOYMENT--U.S. (v19)

AUTOMOBILE THEFT--U.S. (v19)

AUTOMOBILE TRAVEL--U.S.

"In the November 1992 issue of the American Academy of Arts and Sciences BULLETIN, Elmer Johnson, a former director of General Motors, stated, 'The private motor vehicle now accounts for over 95 percent of all person-miles of surface travel in the country.' Moreover, 'about two-thirds of passenger-vehicle miles in the United States are driven in urban areas,' which are home to almost 80 percent of the population. If we add to these statistics the fact that more than 75 percent of U.S. households have two or more private vehicles, compared with about 7 percent in 1950, we begin to see the magnitude of our continuing love affair with the automobile." (p32)

"Research Update: National Renewable Energy Laboratory: Gearing Up for Hybrid Vehicles." Solar Industry Journal v4 n1, 1993. p31-32.

AUTOMOBILE TRAVEL--WASHINGTON (STATE)

"The fundamental enabling element in the current transport system in most of the world is a 'laissez-faire' policy towards the public supplying of roads to meet the increasing demand of private automobiles. For example, in Washington State, USA, in the twenty years from 1970 to 1990, the population grew 34%, the number of registered vehicles grew by 76%, the number of person trips increased 85% and the total vehicle miles travelled shot-up by 123%. (Growth Management Clearinghouse, Univ. of Washington) These, not atypical figures, show that the number of trips and distances travelled has increased much faster than the rate of population growth. The government's response has been to build more roads to make it easier for more people to drive more. Congestion has not been reduced and pollution continues to poison the area." (p1)

"Transport & Development: Sustainable Access." IBF News n2, 1993. p1-2.

AUTOMOBILES

"The greatest weakness of a battery car is its battery. The Energizer Bunny aside, batteries are an inefficient way to store energy; they don't 'keep going and going.' In fact, there's as much energy in 10 lb. of gasoline as in 1000 lb. of batteries. In practice, this means that battery cars can go only about 75 miles between recharges. Since about 90% of U.S. cars are driven less than 60 miles a day, that is not a fatal flaw. The larger question is, How many people will pay roughly $20,000 for what is not a do-everything car, but a second car, most useful for commuting and tooling around town--particularly once they learn they'll need to replace its $2,000 battery bank every 30,000 miles? So far, the jury is out." (p5)

"Electric Vehicles: Battery Cars & Supercars." Rocky Mountain Institute Newsletter v10 n1, Spr 1994. p5.

AUTOMOBILES--CALIFORNIA--FUEL SYSTEMS (v19)

AUTOMOBILES--MOTORS--EXHAUST GAS--CALIFORNIA (v19)

AUTOMOBILES--PRICES--U.S. (v19)

"Many consumers can't afford today's wheels. In 1993, the average price of a car was $18,100, a 69% jump in 10 years, according to the National Automobile Dealers Assn. Family earnings, meanwhile, have lagged behind. Based on median household income, consumers now spend about 26 weeks of wages on a new car, up from 22 a decade ago. In the 1980s, carmakers cut payments by extending loans to five years, but that backfired: Consumers often tired of their cars in two or three years, only to find they owed more than the cars were worth." (p94)

Woodruff, David/others. "Cover Story: Leasing Fever." Business Week n3357, 7 Feb 1994. p92-96. (ISSN0007-7135).

AUTOMOBILES--TAXATION--U.S.

"Under section 4064 of the [tax] code, a tax is imposed if an automobile's fuel economy performance falls below the Environmental Protection Agency's (EPA) fuel economy ratings for that automobile's model type. The tax, which is imposed upon the sale or initial lease of the vehicle by a manufacturer, ranges from $1,000 to $7,000....In 1986 Congress amended the gas guzzler tax to exempt small manufacturers, generally manufacturers of fewer than 10,000 vehicles annually, who lengthen existing automobiles into limousines....Regrettably ...the coachbuilder's exemption was repealed with the enactment of the luxury tax on automobiles in the Revenue Reconciliation Act of 1990....The repeal of the coachbuilder's exemption in 1990 has had a devastating effect on coachbuilders and operators. Jobs have been lost and costs to operators have increased dramatically. During 1988 and 1989, prior to the repeal of the exemption, there were approximately 35 coachbuilders who lengthened 8,000 to 9,000 cars annually. Today, only 12 coachbuilders remain and less than 1,400 vehicles annually are lengthened. These vehicles bear an average tax of $2,000 per automobile--the economic burden of which is directly borne by the operator." (pE98)

Jefferson, William J. (Rep.-La.). "Coachbuilder's Exemption Act of 1994," Congressional Record (3 Feb 1994). Daily ed. pE98. (ISSN0363-7239).

AUTOMOBILES--U.S.--AGE

"As the percentage of vehicles on the road that are at least six years old has continued to climb from 53% in 1989 to 58% last year, the number of vehicles being junked has jumped to record levels....Economist William Wilson of Detroit's Comerica Bank notes that more than 77 million vehicles were sold from 1984 through 1988. Since 73% of all vehicles are junked by their 10th year, he predicts that scrappage will rise steadily, topping 14.7 million vehicles by 1998." (p20)

Koretz, Gene. "Economic Trends: What's Good for Scrap Is Good for Detroit." Business Week n3357, 7 Feb 1994. p20. (ISSN0007-7135).

AUTOMOBILES--U.S.--BUMPERS

"Bumpers on cars go largely unnoticed; that is, until consumers need them. Low-speed vehicle collisions occur frequently. In fact, 20 percent of all insurance claims for automobile damage are the result of parking lot collisions. The 20-percent figure does not include the bumps that cars experience in driveways, at stop lights, or at stop signs. Many of these collisions go unreported since they are below insurance deductibles. Unfortunately, today's bumpers are failing to protect vehicles in low-speed collisions, and consumers, without any information on bumper performance, are left with large repair bills. Even though 67 percent of car buyers surveyed are concerned with the capacity of bumpers to prevent damage in these low-speed collisions, in 47 States they are unable to obtain relevant information on bumper performance." (pS1474)

Danforth, John C. (Sen.-Mo.). "Statements on Introduced Bills and Joint Resolutions," Congressional Record (10 Feb 1994). Daily ed. pS1457-1487. (ISSN0363-7239).

AUTOMOBILES--U.S.--COST OF OPERATION

"A short readable report, 'The Going Rate: What It Really Costs To Drive' by the World Resources Institute concludes that motorized travel in the U.S. is heavily subsidized....Gas taxes and other user fees covered only 60 percent of the US$33.3 billion governments spent on building, improving and repairing roads in 1989. The rest of the money came from taxpayers (property taxes--also indirectly paid by renters through their rent) and other non-user sources. An estimated US$68 billion not covered by user fees is spent each year on such services as highway patrols, traffic management, parking enforcement, traffic accident response teams, police work on auto accidents and thefts, and routine street maintenance. The costs of vehicular air pollution are hard to pin down because they include such elusive damages as illness, premature death, and reduced crop yield; but even at the low estimate of US$10 billion a year, they are substantial--and all of them are borne by society at large. Since motorists use about half of the U.S.'s imported oil, up to half the cost of maintaining a U.S. military presence in the middle east--or US$50 billion a year--could be considered part of the cost of driving--not paid for by user fees." (p1)

"Transport Economics: Who Pays?" IBF News n1, 1993. p1.

AUTOMOBILES--U.S.--CRASHWORTHINESS

The National Highway Traffic Safety Administration "issued an Interim Evaluation Report on the effectiveness of occupant protection in June 1992, based on data available as of May 1992. This report showed that the fatality risk of occupants in cars equipped with air bags plus manual belts (at 1991 use rates) is 23 percent lower than in 'baseline' cars with manual belts at 1983 use rates. Based on limited data, the report also estimates that an occupant protected by the air bag plus manual belts has 68-77 percent lower risk of moderate-to-serious injury than an unrestrained occupant. By the end of 1991, air bags (in combination with safety belts) had saved an estimated 300 lives [in the U.S.] and prevented 15,000 moderate-to-critical injuries. The agency estimates that if all passenger cars on the road were equipped with air bags and safety belts (at 1991 use rates), there would only be 2,840 fewer fatalities per year than if cars were equipped only with safety belts." (p208-209)

Smolkin, Howard (Acting Administrator, National Highway Traffic Safety Admin.). U.S. House. Committee on Appropriations. "Department of Transportation and Related Agencies Approp. for 1994 (Part 4)." Hearing, Washington, D.C.: GPO, 1993. (ISBN0160410738). (Y4.Ap6/1:T68/4/994/pt.4).

AUTOMOBILES--U.S.--FUEL SYSTEMS (v19)

"The Department of Energy's record to date on alternative fuels is not inspiring. Program strategy and leadership responsibility appear to be fragmented with the Department. The results have been detrimental to development efforts. For example, despite recommendations from western states as far back as 1988, DOE, until recently, has neglected the need to coordinate vehicle purchases between the federal government and the states. As a result, the General Accounting Office found DOE's progress in purchasing alternative fueled vehicles 'has been slower than anticipated' and the average incremental vehicle cost has been much higher than expected, $8,300 versus $2,500 per vehicle....Part of the reason for this higher than expected cost was an insufficient order of vehicles to interest original equipment manufacturers. DOE has also provided little help to states and fleet operators who must adopt policies and invest resources to make alternative fuels a reality." (p2751)

Anderson, Richard M. (Utah Dir. of Energy, Director, Chairman, Western Interstate Energy Board). U.S. House. Committee on Appropriations. "Department of Transportation and Related Agencies Approp. for 1994 (Part 7B)." Hearing, Washington, D.C.: GPO, 1993. (ISBN0160411041). (Y4.Ap6/1:T68/4/994/pt.7B).

"Carbon fibers have the potential to improve safety and fuel consumption in regular automobiles, if only they were cheaper--carbon versions are often as much as 25 times the cost of steel alloys. If all of the metal in a Y2 million ($19,000) car were switched to carbon fibers, the price tag, according to some estimates, would jump to about Y50 million ($480,000). The key to bringing down costs will be to seek out larger and better markets. Up until about 1989, the world carbon fiber market was posting steady growth in excess of 10% (in 1989 world demand was more than 10 times that of 1979), but coming into the 1990s, growth slowed sharply to 5% in 1990 and only 2% in 1991. In 1992, world demand was 6,335 tons, exactly the same as the year before. The biggest reason for this is the end of the Cold War. Military aircraft and spacecraft accounted for about 40% of demand, and as defense contracts dry up, European manufacturers are cutting production or pulling out altogether. In the end, the market will probably be dominated by the Japanese companies Toray, Toho Rayon, and Mitsubishi Rayon, and by the American company Hercules. Toray, Toho Rayon, Mitsubishi Rayon and their foreign subsidiaries control about 60% of the market already." (p29)

"Sports and Science: Carbon Fibers: Material Blessings." Look Japan v39 n452, Nov 1993. p28-29. (ISSN0456-5339).

AUTOMOBILES--U.S.--POLLUTION CONTROL DEVICES

"A Chevy Cavalier (2 liter) gets about 30 miles per gallon (a top performer in its class and above the overall fleet average for all makes) and is estimated to emit 39.4 tons of carbon dioxide (CO2) over its useful life (120,000 miles). A single mature tree can absorb 13 pounds of CO2 per year from the atmosphere. Assuming that the useful life of the Cavalier is 13.9 years how many mature trees does it take to absorb the emissions of one Cavalier? If each tree takes a 20'x20' (6mx6m) area, how many acres of forest are required for each Cavalier? (There are 43,560 square feet in an acre.) A BMW 750/850 (5L) emits twice as much CO2. How large a forest does a BMW require? If a city has an average 5 Cavaliers and 5 BMW's per acre of developed land, how many acres of forest does the city need for each acre of developed land?" (p3)

"IBF Math Department: Math Quiz." IBF News n1, 1993. p3.

AUTOMOBILES--U.S.--SAFETY APPLIANCES

"Nationally, child safety seats are used only 60 percent of the time by children ages 0-3 years old, according to Col. Michael D. Robinson, director of the Michigan State Police. Robinson says that percentage drops to 39.3 for children between 4 and 15. During 1992, 61 children ages 1-15 were killed and another 7,301 injured in automobile crashes on Michigan roads, according to a study done by the National Highway Traffic Safety Administration." (p1 secC)

Chadiha, Jeffri. "State Police Stress Buckling Up Kids." Ann Arbor News 15 Feb 1994. p1 secC.

"Consumers are spending hundreds of millions of dollars in extra repair costs and higher insurance premiums because of the extra damage incurred in low-speed accidents. In IIHS's [Insurance Institute for Highway Safety's] latest series of 5-mile-per-hour crash tests, all of the nine 1993 midsize four-door models tested sustained more than $1,000 in damage; five sustained more than $3,000 in damage....a survey conducted in 1992 by the Insurance Research Council found that almost 70 percent of respondents said cars should have bumpers that provide protection in low-speed collisions and over 80 percent said they would choose protective bumpers over stylish bumpers." (pE745)

Beilenson, Anthony C. (Rep.-Calif.). "Return to Stronger 5 MPH Bumper Standard," Congressional Record (21 Apr 1994). Daily ed. pE745. (ISSN0363-7239).

AUTOMOBILES--U.S.--SEAT BELTS

"Based on the Fatal Accident Reporting System data, safety belt use [in the U.S.] saved the lives of an estimated 29,568 occupants in the front seats of light passenger vehicles (that is, in passenger cars, light trucks, passenger vans, and sport utility vehicles) in all types of crashes during the nine years from 1983 to 1991. Rollovers account for about 30 percent of occupant fatalities, and safety belts are especially effective in preventing fatality in rollovers. It is estimated that 9,600 of the lives that were saved by belt use from 1983 to 1991 were in rollover crashes." (p261)

Boehly, William A. (Associate Administrator for Enforcement, National Highway Traffic Safety Admin.). U.S. House. Committee on Appropriations. "Department of Transportation and Related Agencies Approp. for 1994 (Part 4)." Hearing, Washington, D.C.: GPO, 1993. (ISBN0160410738). (Y4.Ap6/1:T68/4/994/pt.4).

"The importance of [safety] belt use cannot be over emphasized, especially now with the high volume availability of inflatable restraints, or airbags. In the model years 1988-91 alone, over 6.5 million driver-side airbag equipped cars...have come onto our roads and highways....In the next 3-5 years driver-passenger front airbag systems will cover the new car fleet....A similar plan is in place for MPV's [multipurpose vehicles], vans and light trucks. Airbags, already available on some 1992 models, are slated for the entire fleet by 1998. During the 1980's, the sales of these vehicles increased dramatically (up 39%), as did the number of miles they traveled (up 60%). As a result the number of fatalities associated with these vehicles also increased, even though the fatality rate declined from 2.6 to 1.8 (per 100 million light truck vehicle miles travelled). In 1991, light truck occupant fatalities showed a decrease over 1990. Nonetheless, just installing the system is not enough for full protection--in order for it to work as designed, the occupant must keep in place when the airbag deploys. This can only be assured if safety belts are also properly worn." (p2316-2317)

Hanna, Tom (President, American Automobile Manufacturers Association). U.S. House. Committee on Appropriations. "Department of Transportation and Related Agencies Approp. for 1994 (Part 7B)." Hearing, Washington, D.C.: GPO, 1993. (ISBN0160411041). (Y4.Ap6/1:T68/4/994/pt.7B).

AUTOMOBILES--U.S.--SEAT BELTS--LAW AND LEGISLATION

"Massachusetts now joins 45 states that require drivers to buckle up. The Bay State's new seat-belt law, which went into effect Feb. 1, mandates a $25 fine for drivers and passengers 16 years of age or older that haven't fastened safety belts. Now, four states remain that do not have safety-belt laws: New Hampshire, Maine, South Dakota, and Kentucky....The new law provides for a 5 percent reduction in bodily insurance premiums if 50 percent of Bay State drivers buckle up within a year. Seat-belt use in the state has been only 32 percent; the national rate is 66 percent." (p10)

Ross, Elizabeth. "National: From the States: Bay State Passes Seat-Belt Law." The Christian Science Monitor v86 n48, 2 Feb 1994. p10. (ISSN0882-7729).

AUTOMOBILES--U.S.--SIZES

"NHTSA [National Highway Traffic Safety Administration] estimates that the average model year (MY) 1992 [U.S.] car weighed over 200 pounds more than the average MY 1988 car (average equivalent test weights of 3,307 pounds and 3,100 pounds, respectively). There also has been a shift towards more mid-size and large cars, although the average interior volume of new cars has changed very little (108 cubic feet in MY 1992, versus 107 cubic feet in MY 1988 and 109 cubic feet in MY 1987). The average MY 1992 light truck weighed 282 pounds more than the average MY 1988 light trucks, and 372 pounds more than the average MY 1987 light truck (average equivalent test weights of 4,169, 3,887, and 3,797 pounds respectively). The average horsepower/weight ratio for cars has risen 33 percent since MY 1981; for light trucks, this ratio has risen 26 percent since MY 1984 (the earliest year for which we have this data). This does not mean, however, that vehicle performance necessarily has increased by these amounts; with the increased use of 4-valve-per-cylinder engines (particularly for passenger cars) that develop their peak of power at higher engine speeds, horsepower/weight ratios need to increase to maintain low-engine-speed performance." (p286)

Boehly, William A. (Associate Administrator for Enforcement, National Highway Traffic Safety Admin.). U.S. House. Committee on Appropriations. "Department of Transportation and Related Agencies Approp. for 1994 (Part 4)." Hearing, Washington, D.C.: GPO, 1993. (ISBN0160410738). (Y4.Ap6/1:T68/4/994/pt.4).

AUTOMOBILES--U.S.--SIZES--SAFETY MEASURES

"Recent analyses on the effect of car size on fatality and injury risk lead to the following conclusions. During model years 1970-1982, passenger cars became substantially smaller in the U.S. The median curb weight of new cars involved in fatal crashes decreased by about 1,000 pounds (from 3,700 to 2,00 pounds). NHTSA [National Highway Traffic Safety Administration] estimates that the reduction of the average weight of new cars from 3,700 to 2,700 pounds (or the associated reductions in car length and width) resulted in increases of nearly 2,000 fatalities and 20,000 serious injuries per year. Car size has a larger effect on fatality risk in rollover crashes than in other crash modes, not because small cars are less crashworthy in rollovers, but because they are more rollover prone." (p191)

Smolkin, Howard (Acting Administrator, National Highway Traffic Safety Admin.). U.S. House. Committee on Appropriations. "Department of Transportation and Related Agencies Approp. for 1994 (Part 4)." Hearing, Washington, D.C.: GPO, 1993. (ISBN0160410738). (Y4.Ap6/1:T68/4/994/pt.4).

AUTOMOBILES--U.S.--WEIGHT

"'The past decade has seen exceptional activity in the development of lightweight automotive materials,' said forecast authors Brett C. Smith, a researcher with the Office for the Study of Automotive Transportation at the U-M Transportation Research Institute, and Michael V. DiBernardo, a retired General Motors Corp. executive....Smith and DiBernardo said the use of lightweight materials--aluminum, plastics, magnesium and powdered metals--will increase by as much as 20 percent over the next decade in cars and light trucks. Car makers will use about 10-15 percent less steel and cast iron over the next decade, they projected....Consumers don't want to see their vehicles become any smaller, they wrote, so manufacturers are turning to lighter materials for weight and fuel savings, despite their higher costs....The report projects the weight of an average passenger car will decrease 8 percent by 2003." (p6 secB)

Grantham, Russell. "Cars to Become Lighter, Utilize Recycled Goods." Ann Arbor News 8 Feb 1994. p6 secB.

AUTOMOBILES, ELECTRIC (v19)

AUTOMOBILES, RENTAL--U.S.

"Nearly one in every four new cars [in the U.S.] is leased, according to the National Automobile Dealers Association (NADA) in McLean, Va. 'There's a change in the (consumer) mind-set,' says Ted Orme of NADA. In the past, 'the idea of renting without gaining any equity was foreign.' Leasing has nearly doubled in the past two to three years, Mr. Orme says, as car manufacturers have begun to promote leases rather than rebates and other buyer incentives. In 1992, Americans leased 1.7 million new vehicles, up 20 percent from 1991, NADA reports." (p10)

Popiel, Leslie Albrecht. "Economy: For Drivers with Expensive Taste, Better Lease Than Buy." The Christian Science Monitor v86 n10, 9 Dec 1993. p10. (ISSN0882-7729).

AUTOMOBILES, SOLAR

see SOLAR CARS

AVIATION

see AERONAUTICS

AVIATION INDUSTRY

see AIRLINES

AWARDS AND ARBITRATION

see ARBITRATION AND AWARD

AZERBAIJAN

see also ECONOMIC ASSISTANCE, AMERICAN--AZERBAIJAN

AZERBAIJAN--COMMERCE--RUSSIA (v19)

AZERBAIJAN--SOCIAL CONDITIONS

"One can understand the ominous choice Azerbaijan faces between preserving human life and sustaining the ecological life of the country by examining the following facts. Nearly 50 percent of its rivers are contaminated by DDT at levels 35 times higher than the other former republics....Grain harvests have been reduced to less than 75 percent of normal levels through intentional burning of crops and displacement of rural populations. The subsistence level of 1.35 metric tons of imported cereal required to feed the population, stands at only half this level. The livestock population has been reduced over 35 percent as veterinary supplies dwindle and indiscriminate killings continue....Over 110,000 homes, schools, hospitals, pharmacies and medical relief centers have been destroyed....The relatively young population (more than 50 percent are under 24) is expected to suffer from rising rates of cancer, reproductive disorders, developmental disorders and other pesticide and heavy metal related illnesses due to severe water and land contamination....Complications from respiratory infections contribute directly to 55 percent of infant deaths." (p33-34)

Cox, Nermin Sultanova. "Challenges of Sovereignty: A Call for More US Aid to Azerbaijan." Surviving Together v12 n1, Spr 1994. p33-35. (ISSN0859-6286).

AZT (DRUG) (v19)

B-1 BOMBER (v19)

BABY BOOM GENERATION--U.S. (v19)

BABY BOOM GENERATION--U.S.--ECONOMIC CONDITIONS (v19)

BACKACHE--U.S.

"Of the 80 million Americans who suffer from chronic back pain each year, 4 out of 5 cases could have been prevented. Back problems are the most common work injury today, usually striking people between the ages of 20 and 50. According to THE POWER OF PAIN by Shirly Kraus, 100 million Americans are either permanently disabled or are less productive due to back pain. And those who work lose about 5 work days per year, a productivity loss of $55 billion." (pE67)

Traficant, James A., Jr. (Rep.-Ohio). "Health Care Reform," Congressional Record (2 Feb 1994). Daily ed. pE67-68. (ISSN0363-7239).

BAIKAL, LAKE (RUSSIA)

see also BIOLOGICAL DIVERSITY--BAIKAL, LAKE (RUSSIA); COPPER MINES AND MINING--BAIKAL, LAKE (RUSSIA)

BAIKAL, LAKE (RUSSIA)--ENVIRONMENTAL ASPECTS

"Environmentalists in the United States, in collaboration with former Soviets, are working to develop economically sustainable agriculture and tourism enterprises in Siberia's vast Lake Baikal region....With a 20-million-year unbroken evolutionary history, Baikal is one of the most biologically rich lakes on Earth. Over a mile deep, it contains 20 percent of the world's fresh water and supports over 1,200 species of plants and animals, including the 'nerpa,' the world's only freshwater seal." (p27) "Containing 26 percent of the world's remaining forests, the fate of the Baikal area is ultimately a global issue." (p29)

Goodstein, Carol. "Polluted Waters Run Deep." E Magazine v4 n3, May-Jun 1993. p27-29. (ISSN1046-8021).

BALANCE OF TRADE--CANADA (v19)

BALANCE OF TRADE--CHINA (v19)

"Trade between China and Central Asia has boomed since the collapse of the Soviet Union in 1991, particularly with potentially oil-rich Kazakhstan. In 1990 Kazakhstan's imports from China were not quite 4% of its total exports. By 1992 the proportion was nearly 44%. Trade has slowed since mid-1993, partly because Kazakhstan ditched the rouble and introduced its own currency." (p35)

"Asia: China and Central Asia: On the Silk Road." Economist v331 n7860, 23 Apr 1994. p35. (ISSN0013-0613).

"Since 1978, imports have usually grown more rapidly than exports with the result that China has run a trade deficit in every year except four (1982, 1983, 1990 and 1991). Since 1989, the government has devalued the currency by 43 per cent in the effort to boost exports. In the face of chronic budget and foreign trade deficits, the government has come to rely more and more on foreign loans to finance key infrastructure, industrial and raw materials projects. Consequently, whereas China was virtually debt free in 1978, by the late eighties the government was heavily in debt to foreign bankers. China's foreign debt grew by 38 per cent per year between 1984 and 1988, when it hit $35 billion. By the end of 1991 China's foreign debt totalled $60.6 billion (though this has been offset to a great extent by China's steadily rising foreign exchange earnings, reserves of which totalled $45 billion in 1991 compared with around $7 billion in the early eighties)." (p70)

Smith, Richard. "The Chinese Road to Capitalism." New Left Review n199, May-Jun 1993. p55-99. (ISSN0028-6060).

BALANCE OF TRADE--CHINA--U.S. (v19)

BALANCE OF TRADE--EUROPEAN ECONOMIC COMMUNITY--JAPAN (v19)

BALANCE OF TRADE--JAPAN--U.S. (v19)

"Since 1982, the U.S. trade deficit with Japan has grown from $17.1 billion to $48.7 billion in 1992. And, in the first five months of this year, our trade deficit with Japan has continued to grow from $18.8 billion last year to $22.5 billion this year. Japan accounts for 58% of the overall U.S. trade deficit. Japan ranks second only to Canada as the largest U.S. export market. Major U.S. exports to Japan include agricultural exports such as corn and meat; crude materials such as wood; and U.S.-produced aircraft. The United States also imports more from Japan than from all but one other country. Major Japanese imports into the U.S. include cars, consumer electronics, telecommunications equipment, and computers." (p12)

U.S. House. Committee on Energy and Commerce. "Telecommunications Trade." Hearing, 3 Aug 1993. Washington, D.C.: GPO, 1994. (ISBN0160435919). (Y4.En2/3:103-60).

"In 1965, nearly 30 years ago...[the U.S.] began recording trade deficits with Japan. Japan rebuilt its economy after World War II, using economic policies directed at high production and exports, but freezing out virtually all imports not needed for its own factories. After some years those policies started to take their toll in United States-Japan trade, and in 1965 we saw the balance tip against the United States: a $359 million deficit....The merchandise trade deficit was $1.1 billion in the final year of the Johnson administration. It was $4.1 billion at the end of President Nixon's first term, and $5.5 billion when President Ford left the White House. It was $10.1 billion in the last year of the Carter administration. By the 1980's, the disparity between an accessible United States market, on the one hand, and a trade sanctuary in Japan on the other, had become economically intolerable. President Reagan responded to Japan's violation of a trade agreement on semiconductors, and he imposed some sanctions. But, the deficit in President Reagan's last year had climbed to $52 billion." (pS2999)

Dorgan, Byron L. (Sen.-N.Dak.). "The Balance of Trade," Congressional Record (16 Mar 1994). Daily ed. pS2997-3000. (ISSN0363-7239).

"The most visible symbol of the United States-Japan relationship is our merchandise trade deficit, now over $59 billion. Our current account deficit, which takes into account our surplus in service trade, is only around $12 billion smaller. To understand what can work to reduce the bilateral trade balance, we must first understand what will not work. Quantitative measures will not eliminate the bilateral trade imbalance....studies...indicate that removing every single Japanese barrier would reduce the merchandise trade deficit by less than 20 percent. For example, a comprehensive study by the Institute for International Economics concludes that Japanese market access barriers are limiting American merchandise exports by only about $9 to $18 billion, or less than the increase in that deficit since 1990. This is significant, of course, and argues for effective policies to open Japanese markets. But it pales in comparison with the magnitude of the overall problem." (pS3378)

Bradley, Bill (Sen.-N.J.). "United States-Japan Relations: A Strategic Framework," Congressional Record (22 Mar 1994). Daily ed. pS3378-3397. (ISSN0363-7239).

BALANCE OF TRADE--MEXICO--U.S. (v19)

"Even with current trade barriers, Mexico has become the third largest export market for the United States. From a deficit of nearly $6 billion in 1986, the United States has gone to a surplus of over $5 billion based on $40 billion in export business in 1992. More than 70 percent of all Mexican imports come from the United States. Today, Mexicans purchase more American imports per person than do the Europeans and Japanese." (p206)

U.S. House. Committee on Energy and Commerce. "NAFTA: Energy Provisions and Environmental Implications." Hearing, 22 Sep 1993. Washington, D.C.: GPO, 1994. (ISBN0160440459). (Y4.En2/3:103:70).

"Starting in 1986, Mexico, recognizing that its economic policies had been disastrous, began to lower trade and investment barriers. The results have been dramatic for the United States: From 1987 to 1992, we transformed a $5.7 billion trade deficit with Mexico into a $5.4 billion trade surplus. U.S. exports to Mexico increased from $12.4 billion in 1986 to $40.6 billion in 1992, with increases coming across the board from computers to services to agriculture. Mexico has become our third leading export market; it is our second largest market for manufactured exports ($34.5 billion) and third largest market for agricultural products ($3.7 billion). 84 percent of this growth has been exports for Mexican consumption. 400,000 U.S. jobs related to exports to Mexico were created." (p23)

Yerxa, Rufus (Deputy U.S. Trade Rep.). U.S. House. Committee on Energy and Commerce. "NAFTA: Energy Provisions and Environmental Implications." Hearing, 22 Sep 1993. Washington, D.C.: GPO, 1994. (ISBN0160440459). (Y4.En2/3:103/70).

"Maquila-related exports account for a declining share of total U.S. exports to Mexico, based on Commission staff estimates....Their share declined from 32 percent in 1987, the year in which Mexico sharply cut its tariffs, to 21 percent in 1992, when U.S. exports to Mexico totaled $39.6 billion. While exports to the maquila sector rose by 93 percent during 1987-92, to $8.7 billion, exports for consumption in Mexico rose by a much higher 224 percent, to $30.9 billion....Thus, the net bilateral trade balance with Mexico improved markedly, shifting from a U.S. deficit of $5.72 billion in 1987 to a U.S. surplus of $5.67 billion in 1992." (p94-95)

Newquist, Don (Chair, U.S. International Trade Commission). U.S. House. Committee on Energy and Commerce. "Telecommunications Trade." Hearing, 3 Aug 1993. Washington, D.C.: GPO, 1994. (ISBN0160435919). (Y4.En2/3:103-60).

BALANCE OF TRADE--RUSSIA

"Although oil production [in Russia] fell by 12% in 1993, to 353m tonnes, oil exports increased by 21%, to 80m tonnes. Exports of gas also increased. These commodities accounted for the bulk of Russia's trade surplus, which Goskomstat, the official collector of statistics, recorded at $15.9 billion for 1993. This does not include Russia's $5 billion trade surplus with the former republics of the Soviet Union. Nor does it include the bulk of foreign trade conducted by private individuals: Goskomstat began to collect data on private trade only at the end of 1993." (p68)

"Business: Russian Industry: Carry on Comrade." Economist v330 n7846, 15 Jan 1994. p67-68. (ISSN0013-0613).

"The debate over aid for Russia has always assumed that financial support will be temporary and that the eventual health of the economies of all the former Soviet republics will depend on their successful integration into the global economic system. In short, their future depends on trade. In December 1993, the European Union became the first Western institution to sign a comprehensive and far-reaching trade cooperation agreement with Russia. Building on the original 1989 trade agreement with the former Soviet Union, where 83 percent of EU imports from Russia have entered duty-free, the new agreement aims to free the trade even further, and pledges the EU to promote full Russian membership in the GATT [General Agreement on Tariffs and Trade] world trade agreement....But the process of freeing the trade has until recently taken place against a background of declining trade figures. Russian exports collapsed from $81 billion in 1990 to $56.5 billion in 1991, and although the full figures for 1992 and 1993 have not been collated (and for 1992 are very unreliable), they fell even further, probably to around $40 billion in 1992. Russian imports also slumped from $83 billion to $44.7 billion between 1990 and 1991." (p9)

Walker, Martin. "Trade: The Key to Russia's Future." Europe n333, Feb 1994. p9. (ISSN0191-4545).

BALANCE OF TRADE--U.S. (v19)

"The U.S. has experienced ever increasing trade deficits with its trading partners over the last decade. The U.S. cumulative trade deficit since 1980 is more than $1.1 trillion dollars. In 1992, our trade deficit with Japan was $49 billion, up 14 percent from 1991, and our 1992 trade deficit with China was $18 billion, up 44 percent from 1991. The U.S. is again experiencing record deficits with Japan. Our trade deficit with Japan for March 1993 was $5.3 billion, an increase of 27 percent over the previous month. These trade deficits are largely due to the unfair trade practices of our competitors, resulting in closed markets for U.S. exports." (p52)

Riegle, Donald W., Jr. (Sen.-Mich.). U.S. Senate. Committee on Finance. "Renewing 'Super 301.'" Hearing, 14 Jun 1993. Washington, D.C.: GPO, 1994. (ISBN016043372X). (Y4.F49:S.hrg.103-332).

The U.S. "trade deficit is growing not shrinking, particularly our trade deficit with Japan. In 1991, $43.44 billion of our total trade deficit was with one nation--Japan. In 1992, the U.S. trade deficit with Japan grew to $49.4 billion." (p40)

Levin, Carl (Sen.-Mich.). U.S. Senate. Committee on Finance. "Renewing 'Super 301.'" Hearing, 14 Jun 1993. Washington, D.C.: GPO, 1993. (ISBN016043372X). (Y4.F49:S.hrg.103-332).

"The U.S. foreign trade deficit widened to $109 billion in the first 11 months of 1993--43 percent more than the $76 billion shortfall in the same 11 months of 1992. According to Commerce Department data, merchandise imports surged 10 percent to $531 billion from January through November while exports inched up 3 percent to $422 billion. At that pace, the total 1993 trade gap is expected to exceed $120 billion, the worst showing in several years. The 1992 trade deficit totaled $84.5 billion. Imports of manufactured goods accounted for most of the deepening trade deficit. Before seasonal adjustment, the influx of factory-made goods amounted to $439 billion over the 11-month period, compared with $332 billion in exports. The bottom line was a $107 billion imbalance....The U.S. trade position in North America continued to deteriorate during 1993 as the overall deficit ballooned to $8.4 billion from $2 billion in the 1992 period. The imbalance with Canada widened to $9.9 billion, while the U.S. surplus with Mexico shrank from $4.8 to $1.5 billion." (p6)

"Trade Deficit Widens to $109 Billion." AFL-CIO News v39 n3, 31 Jan 1994. p6. (ISSN0001-1185).

"The United States was battered with a $115.8 billion foreign trade deficit last year, the worst imbalance since 1988. The deficit surged 37 percent above the 1992 shortfall of $84.5 billion. The Commerce Department reported that imports of merchandised goods jumped by $48 billion to a record $581 billion, while exports edged up $17 billion to $465 billion, also a new high. More than half of the 1993 shortfall came in transactions with Japan, as the U.S. bilateral trade gap soared to a record $59.3 billion. Japan shipped $107.3 billion worth of goods to U.S. markets, but limited imports from the United States to $47.9 billion." (p14)

Oravec, John R. "Economy: Trade Deficit Surges 37 Percent in 1993." AFL-CIO News v39 n6, 7 Mar 1994. p14. (ISSN0001-1185).

"In 1983 the value of all crops [in the U.S.] was $67.2 billion. The trade imbalance was $67.1 billion, a near wash. But the trade imbalance has continued to climb, and farm values have either lagged or remained the same. Trade imbalances ran $112.5 in 1984; $122.2 billion in 1985; $145.1 billion in 1986; $159.6 billion in 1987; $127.0 billion in 1988; $115.7 billion in 1989; $108.9 billion in 1990, etc." (p22)

"Newsletter." Acres, U.S.A. v24 n3, Mar 1994. p22-23.

According to the MIT study "Made In America--Regaining The Productive Edge" by Michael L. Dertouzos, Richard K. Lester, Robert M. Solow, and the MIT Commission on Industrial

Productivity "In 1987 the total value of manufactured goods purchased in the United States was about $1 trillion, nearly 20 times the volume of services exported. Moreover, the long-term trend in the United States is toward increased demand for manufactured goods. Between [the] 1960s and 1986 total spending on manufactured goods other than food and fuel in the United States increased threefold in real terms. In short, it is unreasonable to expect that the United States could achieve a trade surplus in services large enough to satisfy its huge appetite for manufactured goods, if all such goods had to be imported." (pS2683)

Hollings, Ernest F. (Sen.-S.C.). "National Competitiveness Act," Congressional Record (10 Mar 1994). Daily ed. pS2675-2700. (ISSN0363-7239).

"Research and development expenditure in developed countries has grown faster than gross domestic product, but competition is increasing and the US is losing its leadership in areas like microelectronics. Between 1980 and 1986 the US had a high technology trade deficit of US$ 5,000 million with Mexico, Brazil, South Korea, Taiwan, Hong Kong and Singapore." (p6)

Hormenku-Ajei, Tetteh. "GATT: Copyrighting Knowledge." Panoscope n38, Jan 1994. p6. (ISSN0951-8819).

BALD EAGLE--U.S.

"Driven to near-extinction by widespread use of the pesticide DDT in the 1960s, eagles have come back in nearly every Western state except Nevada. Bald eagle populations exceeded 950 nesting pairs last year in the seven-state Pacific recovery region, a dramatic rise from 285 pairs in 1980. Nationwide, bald eagles have vaulted from a low count of 417 nesting pairs in 1963, to nearly 3,747 pairs in 1992. That's nearly a 10-fold increase in about 30 years." (p1)

Stuebner, Stephen. "Eagles Make a Comeback." High Country News v25 n16, 6 Sep 1993. p1,10-12. (ISSN0191-5657).

"Jim Frazier, a professor of fisheries and wildlife science at Virginia Polytechnical Institute, says that bald eagles are generally 'nowhere near as adaptable' to man or urban settings as other wild critters. Frazier has studied bald eagles for more than a decade around the perimeter of Chesapeake Bay, where 250 pairs reside close to thousands of homes and people. He's found that eagles do not like being around people continuously....In the West, the eagles' refuge often consists of public lands and public waters. In Chesapeake Bay, the eagles may lose 70 percent of their habitat by the year 2020 to housing and other developments on private land, Frazier says. He isn't sure that the Endangered Species Act has enough strength to preclude development from destroying eagle habitat on private land, an issue looming in the West." (p12)

Stuebner, Stephen. "Eagles Make a Comeback." High Country News v25 n16, 6 Sep 1993. p1,10-12. (ISSN0191-5657).

BANGLADESH

see also CHILDREN--EMPLOYMENT--BANGLADESH; FERTILITY, HUMAN--BANGLADESH; IRRIGATION--BANGLADESH; RICKSHAW MEN--BANGLADESH

BANGLADESH--ECONOMIC CONDITIONS

"Today, Bangladesh is still a predominantly agricultural country: Some 80 percent of its people live in farming villages and the country's few industries are jute mills, small manufacturing concerns and clothing factories owned by multinational corporations. The ordinary people of Bangladesh--about 90 percent of the population--live below what even they consider to be the poverty line." (p33)

Kirkpatrick, Joanna/Bubriski, Kevin. "Transports of Delight." Aramco World v45 n1, Jan-Feb 1994. p33-35. (ISSN1044-1891).

BANK ACCOUNTS--U.S.--COSTS (v19)

BANKRUPTCY--U.S. (v19)

"For the reporting period in 1993, there were a total of 918,734 bankruptcy filings. This represents a slight decrease in 1993 over the number of bankruptcy filings reported in 1992, but even with a decrease the filings in 1993 are still more than double the number of case filings of any year prior to 1985. In fact, the annual reported filings during 1990-93 have been about twice the annual average for the entire 1980's. Over the past 8 years filings nationwide have increased by 152 percent. Filings have doubled during this period in 37 of the 50 States and in Puerto Rico and the District of Columbia. In fact, in 13 States the bankruptcy filings have increased by a staggering 200 percent since 1985. To give you an idea of the volume of cases, we can look to the average number of new cases a bankruptcy judge handles at any given time. In 1993 the average number of cases filed per judge was 2,818. In 1985 the average number of cases filed per judge was only 1,571. This increase is nearly a double increase with only an approximate 41 percent growth of new bankruptcy judgeships since 1983 to handle this caseload." (pS4504)

Heflin, Howell (Sen.-Ala.). "Conclusion of Morning Business," Congressional Record (20 Apr 1994). Daily ed. pS4504-4520. (ISSN0363-7239).

BANKS AND BANKING

"For a quarter of a century banks have invested heavily in information technology. America's commercial banks spent more than $20 billion on computer paraphernalia in 1993 alone. Since much of the activity of a bank, such as the processing of transactions and payments, lends itself to automation, this has created impressive leaps in productivity...and big job losses. More than 300,000 American banking jobs have disappeared since 1984. In a recent survey of European banks conducted by Arthur Andersen for the Economist Intelligence Unit (our sister company) 80% of those questioned said they expected to see a continuing decline in the number of people employed in banking and in the capital markets. The report forecast that up to 250,000 jobs could be lost in the industry in Europe in the coming five to seven years." (p25)

"International Banking Survey: For Our Next Trick...." Economist v331 n7861, 30 Apr 1994. p62(25,27-28,31-32). (ISSN0013-0613).

BANKS AND BANKING--ARIZONA (v19)

BANKS AND BANKING--CALIFORNIA (v19)

BANKS AND BANKING--CANADA (v19)

BANKS AND BANKING--IDAHO (v19)

BANKS AND BANKING--INDONESIA (v19)

BANKS AND BANKING--JAPAN--U.S. (v19)

BANKS AND BANKING--KOREA (SOUTH) (v19)

BANKS AND BANKING--MEXICO (v19)

"Only two years ago investors queued up to buy Mexico's 18 commercial banks in privatisations that netted $12.4 billion for the government of President Carlos Salinas. With NAFTA [North American Free Trade Agreement] around the corner, buyers expected Mexico's economy to boom; on average, they paid 3.2 times book value for its banks. They are now a chastened lot. Commercial bank deposits have grown by more than two-thirds in real terms since 1991. Yet as the economy turned sharply down last year (output shrank by 1.2% in the third quarter of 1993), banks found themselves on the end of an exploding chain of dubious debt. The ratio of overdue loans to total loans climbed from 4.1% in December 1991 to 7.5% in September 1993." (p79-80)

"Finance: Mexican Banks: On Their Toes." Economist v330 n7848, 29 Jan 1994. p79-80. (ISSN0013-0613).

BANKS AND BANKING--NEVADA (v19)

BANKS AND BANKING--OREGON (v19)

BANKS AND BANKING--PAKISTAN (v19)
BANKS AND BANKING--SWITZERLAND--U.S. (v19)
BANKS AND BANKING--TAIWAN (v19)
BANKS AND BANKING--U.S. (v19)

"The [U.S. banking] industry will have to overcome stiff challenges to excel again this year. The downside of low interest rates is starting to show, for example. Falling rates lift bank profits by cutting borrowing costs while increasing the value of a bank's investment securities. But stable rates reduce borrower's payments on new loans and gains on bond investments, key sources of bank revenue. The effects started showing up in last year's third quarter. Banks earned $11.45 billion, up 35% from a year earlier, and even though the number of S&Ls [savings & loans] fell 8%, to 1,719, thrift operating earnings rose a smidgen, to $1.26 billion. Still, bank net interest margins--the profitability of loans and investments--fell nearly a quarter of a point in the first nine months of 1993, to 4.45%. Profit margins declined for thrifts as well." (p103)

Holland, Kelley. "Finance: Banking: Another Year in 'Bank Heaven?'" Business Week n3353, 10 Jan 1994. p103. (ISSN0007-7135).

"In their fervor to squeeze every last dollar out of S&L [Savings and Loan] and bank professionals, the RTC [Resolution Trust Corporation] and the FDIC [Federal Deposit Insurance Corporation] are spending an inordinate amount of time and money pursuing marginal cases in which the culpability of the defendants is highly questionable. Faced with an enormous pool of potential individuals to sue, the RTC and the FDIC have contracted most of the legal work to outside counsel. The RTC and the FDIC employ over 2,400 law firms, paying them over $504 million in 1992 alone. The current caseload is over 60,000 lawsuits. These law firms have little incentive to reduce taxpayer costs and every incentive to bill thousands of hours in the pursuit of former directors and officers, regardless of their culpability. Defending these suits is a costly, demeaning, and time consuming enterprise. Many defendants have agreed to settlements in order to avoid bankruptcy." (pE3030)

McCollum, Bill (Rep.-Fla.). "Lending Enhancement through Necessary Due Process Act--Director and Officer Bill." Congressional Record (22 Nov 1993). Daily ed. pE3030. (ISSN0363-7239).

"The General Accounting Office found that 90 percent of the banks that failed in 1987 were in States that allowed only unit banks or limited branching. The GAO noted that 'when a bank's assets are not geographically diversified, the quality of its balance sheet can be severally affected by fluctuations in the local economy.' Interstate branching will permit banks to diversify their loan portfolio, thus making our banking system less vulnerable to downturns in any particular community or region. The Congressional Budget Office also found that nationwide interstate banking will enable banks to increase geographic and industry diversification, thereby reducing the probability of bank failure and lead to a healthier and more stable banking system." (pS4766)

D'Amato, Alfonse (Sen.-N.Y.). "Interstate Banking and Branching Act of 1994," Congressional Record (25 Apr 1994). Daily ed. pS4764-4770. (ISSN0363-7239).

"In 1993, foreign banks operating in the United States controlled $872 billion in banking assets....Foreign banks controlled an additional $329 billion in off-shore assets. Ninety percent of these assets were booked in the Cayman Islands, and most of the remainder were booked in the Bahamas. The Federal Reserve has just begun calculating these off-shore assets, presenting a more accurate picture of the reach and influence of foreign banking operations in this country. Together, these totals show that foreign banks in 1993 held a staggering $1.5 trillion in U.S. loans and securities out of a total U.S. market of $3.9 trillion. This means foreign banks controlled 30.5 percent of U.S. bank assets in 1993. Forty-two percent of all business loans in the United States last year were made by foreign bank-owned entities. Foreign banks held more than $200 billion in commercial and industrial loans for each of the last 3 years, compared to $85 billion 10 years ago. Foreign banks held an additional $70 billion in commercial real estate loans last year as well." (pS4812)

Ford, Wendell H. (Sen.-Ky.). "GATT Treaty Concerns," Congressional Record (26 Apr 1994). Daily ed. pS4798-4827. (ISSN0363-7239).

"Most of those who care agree that bank supervision in America needs radical surgery. More than 70% of commercial bank assets are held by organisations that are supervised by at least two federal agencies; almost half attract the attention of three or four. Banks devote on average about 14% of their non-interest expenses to complying with rules." (p88)

"Finance: American Bank Regulation: Four into One Can Go." Economist v330 n7853, 5 Mar 1994. p88,91. (ISSN0013-0613).

"In February [1993], the General Accounting Office completed a study of fifty-eight randomly selected bank and thrift examinations to see if, in fact, regulators were unduly hassling banks. What they found was just the opposite. The GAO reported that: in 94 percent of the cases, regulators engaged in 'less than adequate' examinations; in 70 percent of the cases, regulators' examination of the banks' loan quality was slipshod and seriously lacking; and, in general, the regulators' review of bank-holding companies was too cursory to ensure that the banks' owners were not milking their own banks." (p56,58)

Pizzo, Stephen. "The Banker's Hour." Mother Jones v18 n3, May-Jun 1993. p56,58. (ISSN0362-8841).

"As the United States has become the largest debtor nation in the world over the past decade, household and business debt have also soared to record levels. Consumer credit alone is now a $4 trillion business. To cash in on the debt frenzy and evade regulations that govern the nation's 11,300 commercial banks, a diverse range of new businesses have started performing banking functions. According to a study conducted for the Economic Policy Institute, a Washington-based think tank, banks currently guarantee 90 percent--$112 billion--of the commercial paper sold by the 15 largest finance companies. Westinghouse, for example, draws on a $6 billion line of credit issued by 49 banks. This leaves the banks in what the study calls 'a classic Catch-22 position.' If the finance companies prosper, they will lure more borrowers away from banks. If they continue to run into financial trouble--as several have done in the past year--the banks will inherit the risk." (p21)

Bates, Eric. "Banking on Debt." Southern Exposure v21 n3, Fall 1993. p21. (ISSN0146-809X).

"United States banks are ringing in the new year on a heady note: Profits in 1993 reached an all-time industry high of $32.6 billion--even without adding the still-unknown figures for the quarter just ended....One key measure of profitability, return on assets, was more than 1.2 percent last year. This is twice the average attained during the 1980-91 period. In the Midwest, currently the healthiest region, the figure recently reached 1.53 percent. The assets of the banks and savings-and-loan associations on the FDIC's 'problem' list have fallen to $379 billion, half of their 1991 peak and less than 10 percent of total industry assets." (p11)

Trumbull, Mark. "Economy: Profitable Year Gives Banks Short Breather." The Christian Science Monitor v86 n30, 6 Jan 1994. p11. (ISSN0882-7729).

BANKS AND BANKING--U.S.--SERVICE CHARGES (v19)

"Banks [in the U.S.] not only shut off credit to poor consumers, they also make it expensive to maintain a checking account. According to a survey of 300 large banks by the Consumer Federation of America and the U.S. Public Interest Research Group, the average annual cost of a regular checking account hit $184 this year--up 18.5 percent since 1990, nearly double the rate of inflation. Such price hikes have left many consumers unable to afford a bank account. According to the Federal Reserve, the portion of American families without an account has increased from 9 percent to 14 percent in the past 15 years." (p20)

Hudson, Mike. "SE Special Section: The Poverty Industry." Southern Exposure v21 n3, Fall 1993. p16-18,20-26. (ISSN0146-809X).

BANKS AND BANKING, FOREIGN--U.S.

"According to recent Federal Reserve Board data there are presently over 300 foreign banking organizations from 62 different countries operating banking facilities in the United States. Of the almost 700 different types of facilities, only 93 are subsidiaries, while 378 are branches and 211 agencies. These latter two types of facilities from which foreign banks do most of their business in this country are exempt from FDIC insurance, HMDA requirements, CRA provisions, etc.--thus giving such foreign bank offices a distinct advantage in loan pricing. Foreign banks are not small players in the U.S. market. They now account for a 42 percent share of all business loans being made in the United States. This foreign share of our banking market is larger than the foreign banking share of most other major financial markets in the world." (pS4815)

Cassady, Ballard W., Jr. (Exec. Vice President, Kentucky Bankers Assoc.). "GATT Treaty Concerns," Congressional Record (26 Apr 1994). Daily ed. pS4798-4827. (ISSN0363-7239).

BARLEY INDUSTRY--U.S. (v19)

BARNEY (FICTITIOUS CHARACTER) (v19)

BASEBALL--U.S.

"Soaring payrolls notwithstanding, baseball ownership continues to be a profitable enterprise, with franchise values rising year after year. The Seattle Mariners, for example, who were bought for $13.1 million in 1981, were recently sold for more than $100 million. And just last month, the Baltimore Orioles were sold for $173 million, the highest price ever paid for a professional sports team and over $100 million more than the team fetched only four years ago. When the National League announced that it would expand to allow two new franchises for the 1993 season, competition for ownership was fierce despite the $95-million initiation fee." (p61)

Lefkowitz, Jay P. "Books in Review: The Baseball Business." Commentary v96 n3, Sep 1993. p61-62,64. (ISSN0010-2601).

BASEBALL PLAYERS--U.S.--TOBACCO USE

"Baseball's ban on all tobacco products in the minor league went into effect on June 15th [1993], affecting more than 6,000 players, managers, coaches, umpires and other uniformed personnel. Players are banned from smoking and chewing tobacco at minor league stadiums for health reasons, baseball officials said....Under policy terms, use of tobacco products of any kind is not permitted in any team area, including ballparks, buses and planes. Violators are subject to fines of $100 to $300 and game ejections....Travis Baptist of the Class AA Minor League KNOXVILLE SMOKIES (how ironic) was one of the first players caught breaking the rule. He was ejected from a game on June 20th for chewing tobacco in the dugout, and drew an automatic fine of $300." (p5)

"National News: Minor League Bans Tobacco Use." Tobacco-Free Youth Reporter v5 n2, Sum 1993. p5.

BATTERIES--U.S.

"In 1992 Americans used approximately 4 billion dry cell batteries each year. While dry cell batteries account for less than one-tenth of 1 percent of the 180 million tons of garbage we generate each year, dry cell batteries have been significant sources of mercury, cadmium and lead in our solid waste stream. According to the 'Report on Dry Cell Batteries in New York State,' mercury batteries accounted for 85 percent of the mercury, and rechargeable batteries accounted for 68 percent of the cadmium in New York's solid waste." (pS3230)

Lautenberg, Frank R. (Sen.-N.J.). "Statements on Introduced Bills and Joint Resolutions," Congressional Record (17 Mar 1994). Daily ed. pS3208-3256. (ISSN0363-7239).

"Americans buy about 4 billion batteries a year, and throw out 2.5 billion of them. Household batteries make up a relatively small proportion of the waste stream by volume, but they are a significant source of contaminants; more than 80 percent of the mercury in the waste stream, for instance, can be traced to discarded batteries. When buried in landfills, battery casings will eventually corrode, and heavy metals may leach into groundwater. Burning batteries is no better, and maybe worse: if they are incinerated, the toxics are released into the atmosphere, and the incinerator ash becomes contaminated and thus harder to dispose of safely. Incineration is the major cause of environmental mercury contamination." (p42)

Lecard, Marc. "Hearth & Home: Recharge It." Sierra v78 n6, Nov-Dec 1993. p42,44. (ISSN0161-7362).

BEARS

see also GRIZZLY BEAR

BEARS--BRITISH COLUMBIA

"The growing traffic in bear parts, often for the Asian market, is responsible for highly organized, systematic poaching of both grizzly and black bears. Galls are used for a variety of 'medicines.' Genitals, paws and bones are used for aphrodisiacs, paws for soup, teeth and claws for jewelry, and heads and hides as display 'trophies.' In March, 1992, the North American black bear was officially listed in Appendix II of the Convention on International Trade in Endangered Species (upgraded from Appendix III) as a result of the incredible pressure on bears for this heinous trade. In [British Columbia] at least 100 black bears and 15 grizzlies are known to have been poached in 1991 for their body parts. The real figure is certainly much higher. Recently the B.C. government approved a ban on the commercial trade of bear galls, paws or genitalia separated from the carcass or hide. As of February 1, 1993, possession, trafficking, import or export of these parts is illegal in B.C." (p8)

Batycki, Candace. "Reports from the Field: Biting the Bullet for Grizzly Survival in B.C." Northwest Conservation Sum 1993. p7-8.

BEEF INDUSTRY--EUROPEAN ECONOMIC COMMUNITY (v19)

BEEF INDUSTRY--MEXICO--U.S.

"During the first three quarters of 1993, U.S. beef exports to Mexico were down 37 percent from a year earlier and cattle exports down 69 percent. The reductions were the result of tariff rates of 15 to 25 percent imposed by Mexico in 1992." (p10)

U.S. Dept. of Agriculture/Collins, Keith. "Commodity Overview: Agriculture in 1994: Backdrop & Outlook." Agricultural Outlook Jan-Feb 1994. p7-10.

BEEF INDUSTRY--U.S. (v19)

"Beef production in January 1994 will be nearly 8 percent above the weather-abated levels of a year earlier. Cattle slaughter is up about 4.5 percent and dressed commercial weights are 20 pounds heavier than a year earlier. Choice fed steers in Nebraska are trading near $73 per cwt [hundredweight], down about $6 from January 1993. First-quarter beef production is expected to average nearly 7 percent above a year earlier. Cattle slaughter may increase 4 percent, with slaughter weights averaging more than 20 pounds above a year earlier." (p1-2)

U.S. Dept. of Agriculture. "Beef Production to Increase." Livestock, Dairy and Poultry Situation and Outlook 25 Jan 1994. p1-2.

BEER--GREAT BRITAIN (v19)

BEER--U.S. (v19)

BEES

"Of the more than 20,000 known bee species, only six are honey bees (genus Apis). The rest are pollen bees, also called solitary or wild bees. There are about 3,500 kinds of pollen bees in North America. A good example of the mix of honey and pollen bees in a typical natural habitat is illustrated in a 3-year study that [Suzanne] Batra and a cooperator at Georgetown University are conducting in the Fernow Experimental Forest in West Virginia. In 1991--the first year of the study--they randomly trapped 1,701 pollen bees, but only 34 honey bees. They found similar mixes during 1992 and 1993." (p9)

Adams, Sean/Senft, Dennis. "The Busiest of Bees." Agricultural Research v42 n2, Feb 1994. p9-12. (ISSN0002-161X).

BEES--TEXAS (v19)

BEET SUGAR INDUSTRY--EUROPEAN ECONOMIC COMMUNITY--U.S. (v19)

BEHAVIOR, CONSUMER

see CONSUMER BEHAVIOR

BELARUS

see also DEFENSE INDUSTRIES--BELARUS; ENERGY CONSUMPTION--BELARUS

BELARUS--ECONOMIC CONDITIONS

"Belarus's economy is essentially closed to the non-Commonwealth world. About 60 percent of the country's production is exported to the states of the former Soviet Union, and only 4 percent is exported to other nations." (p37)

Tiurina, Tatiana. "Belarus: Neutrality, Maybe." Bulletin of the Atomic Scientists v50 n1, Jan-Feb 1994. p36-40. (ISSN0096-3402).

"Belarus, the fifth most populous former Soviet republic, was the industrial powerhouse of the western Soviet Union before its collapse. But current indicators show a rapid decline in the country, whose capital was chosen to be the seat of the Commonwealth of Independent States in 1991. Industrial production fell by 12 percent last year, no full-scale privatization program has yet been adopted, and prices have been liberalized only gradually. Inflation reached 40 percent in August, and heavy agricultural subsidies are planned for 1994. Also, the country of 10 million is still suffering the effects of the 1986 Chernobyl disaster, when 70 percent of the fallout landed in Belarus. And opinion polls conducted in December revealed that 73 percent of Belarussians believe their lives worsened in the past year." (p2)

Sloane, Wendy. "International: Clinton Visit Is 'Reward' for Belarus." The Christian Science Monitor v86 n36, 14 Jan 1994. p2. (ISSN0882-7729).

BELGIUM

see CELLULAR RADIO--BELGIUM; FIREARMS--BELGIUM

BELIZE--ECONOMIC CONDITIONS (v19)

BENEFITS, EMPLOYEE

see EMPLOYEE FRINGE BENEFITS

BENEFITS, FRINGE

see EMPLOYEE FRINGE BENEFITS

BETTING

see GAMBLING

BEVERAGE CONTAINERS--GERMANY--GREAT BRITAIN--RECYCLING

"Great Britain still refills nearly 100% of its milk bottles, including small glass bottles for school children. Reuse in England has not been limited to beverage containers. The Body Shop, a UK-based natural cosmetics company with stores worldwide, dispenses its shampoos and conditioners in returnable deposit containers. In Germany 72% of all carbonated beverages must be sold in refillable bottles. Enacted in 1991, this law will increase the percentage each year so that by the year 2000, 81% of Germany's beverages will be packaged in refillables. Both Coca-cola and Pepsi have been successful in Germany marketing their soft drinks in refillable 1.5 liter polyethylene terephthalate (PET) bottles. These bottles are made from the same material as 2 liter bottles in the United States, except a bit thicker to withstand the washing. The PET bottle can hold together for about 25 refillings, fewer than glass bottles, and many fewer than its plastic cousin Lexan." (p29)

Figenshau, Chris. "Refillables." Rain v14 n3, Spr 1993. p24-29.

BEVERAGE CONTAINERS--U.S.--RECYCLING (v19)

"Castle Creamery in Hayward, California still uses special thick glass milk bottles, for which they require a $1 deposit. The return rate is about 97% on the half-gallon bottles, but only 80-85% on the traditional quart bottles, since many people keep them for nostalgia's sake. One advantage glass has over plastic bottles is flavor--heavily reused plastic bottles retain flavors and odors, and superhigh temperature sterilization would melt the bottle. Plastics eventually stink. Since glass is a superior barrier the product lasts longer and tastes better. Castle creamery containers last on average 30 trips, but at the end of their lives they can be made into a bottle again. Worn-out plastic bottles cannot easily be made into another container, so they are chopped up and used as various fillers. The plastics industry coined the oxymoron 'linear recycling' to label the limits of their reprocessing." (p26)

Figenshau, Chris. "Refillables." Rain v14 n3, Spr 1993. p24-29.

"In 1960, only 4% of all beer and soft drinks came in non-returnable containers. Seven years later that figure rose to 33%. In 1978 it jumped to 80% and by 1986, 90% of all beer and soda containers were thrown away. According to the National Solid Waste Management Association, between the years 1958 and 1976 US per capita consumption of bottles, cans, boxes, wrappers and other packaging increased by 63%. In 1990 packaging accounted for some 30% of the municipal solid waste stream." (p24)

Figenshau, Chris. "Refillables." Rain v14 n3, Spr 1993. p24-29.

"Why break a container down and send it through an energy-intensive process of melting, purifying and re-molding when the same container could simply be washed and re-used? A study by the Franklin Associates found that use of a refillable glass bottle consumed as much as eight times less energy than any other container, including recycled containers. An EPA survey concluded that savings from refillable containers ranged from 60 cents to $2.00 per case for beer, and from 3.5 to 5 cents per container for soft drinks. Refilling is clearly cheaper and more efficient than immediate recycling or disposal. Deposit legislation is helping the refillable bottle make a comeback. In 1990 refillable bottles made up over 16% of packaged beer sales in the nine states requiring a minimum 5 cent deposit on beer and soda containers, compared to less than 4% in non-deposit states." (p24)

Figenshau, Chris. "Refillables." Rain v14 n3, Spr 1993. p24-29.

"Stewart's, Inc., a dairy in Saratoga County [New York], has always used refillable containers for the milk sold in its 191 retail stores and, since the 1970s, has sold soda in refillables as well....'The real selling point here' argues Karen O'Donnell of GE Plastics, 'is the cost savings for the dairy.' She cites a cost of only .3 cents per container when the little bottles make 100 trips, as opposed to the 2 cents per container the dairy paid for paperboard containers. 'Refillables make sense,' agrees Bill Dake, President of Stewart's. 'Recycling is not always feasible; it's getting harder and harder to find markets for the materials. Reuse is easy and makes economic sense,' he adds." (p2)

"The Return of Refillables." Wastelines v4 n3, Mar 1993. p2.

BICYCLE COMMUTING

"Is America ready for bicycle commuting? Only one in sixty Americans (2.8 million people) rides a bike to work. But if better facilities were available, the numbers would change to one in five, according to a 1992 poll done by BICYCLING MAGAZINE. Still, those figures pale in comparison to countries like the Netherlands, China, Cuba, Denmark, Sweden, and Finland where the use of bicycles is more widespread. In Helsinki, Finland, the percentage of people who cycle regularly to work, even during the long, snowy winter days, exceeds 15 percent. The federal government appears ready to put the brakes on the number of one-person, toxin-belching cars roaming the roadways. With the pending Employer Trip Reduction Program, companies with 100 or more employees must increase their average passenger occupancy per vehicle by 25 percent between 6 a.m. and 10 a.m. or be liable for fines of as much as $25,000 a day." (p13)

Pirro, Joe F. "Trends: Two-Wheel Highway." Amicus Journal v16 n1, Spr 1994. p11-13. (ISSN0276-7201).

BICYCLE COMMUTING--U.S. (v19)

BICYCLES--CALIFORNIA--FLORIDA--ACCIDENTS AND INJURIES--MORTALITY (v19)

BICYCLES--CANADA (v19)

BICYCLES--NETHERLANDS (v19)

BICYCLES--U.S. (v19)

BICYCLES--U.S.--ACCIDENTS AND INJURIES (v19)

"Head injury is the leading cause of death and disability for children and young adults in the United States. More young children die from bicycle injuries than from poisoning, falls, or firearm injuries. Approximately 400 to 500 children die each year from bicycle injuries, with head injury being the most common cause. Three-fourths of bicycle injury deaths are due to head injury and two-thirds of bicycle injury-related hospitalizations are due to head injury. Wearing a helmet when bicycling reduces head injury risk by 85 percent. In Minnesota in 1992 there were 1,343 crashes that involved a motor vehicle and a bicycle. Eleven bicyclists were killed; 1,249 were injured." (pS4784)

Durenberger, Dave (Sen.-Minn.). "'Headsmart: Helmets First for Safety'," Congressional Record (25 Apr 1994). Daily ed. pS4784-4785. (ISSN0363-7239).

BICYCLES--U.S.--ACCIDENTS AND INJURIES--MORTALITY (v19)

BICYCLING

see CYCLING

BILINGUALISM--U.S.

"The National Association for Bilingual Education estimates that U.S. school districts currently need roughly 175,000 more certified bilingual teachers than are available to serve some 3.5 million limited-English-proficient students. A 1993 study done for the U.S. Education Department estimated that at least 35,000 certified bilingual teachers were teaching across the country, although department officials say that estimate is too low." (p5)

Schnaiberg, Lynn. "'Homegrown' Bilingual-Ed. Teachers Take Root." Education Week v13 n26, 23 Mar 1994. p5. (ISSN0277-4232).

BIOLOGICAL DIVERSITY

"No other animal species five kilograms or larger with partly carnivorous habitats has ever come remotely close to present-day humanity in sheer biomass (dry weight of protoplasm). The effects of this profligacy on the environment are staggering. We are co-opting somewhere between 20 percent and 40 percent of the sun's energy fixed by photosynthesis, which means that humans are taking over the area where plants are grown, replacing vegetation with human structures and wasteland. So, we've already greatly diminished the capacity of natural ecosystems to sustain us, and along with this, we are extinguishing the diversity of the world at an accelerating rate. At the present time, I estimate that extinction in the rain forests due to reduction in habitat alone (never mind the components of loss due to the introduction of exotic organisms and partial disturbance of the forests) is in the range of about .5 percent of species annually. Furthermore, the human species has become a geophysical force, as most people are now aware. We are not only reducing the remainder of life in bulk and variety rapidly, we are also altering the very composition of the atmosphere in ways that destroy the protective ozone layer and very probably is warming the Earth's climate with potentially catastrophic effects." (p30)

Wilson, Edward O. "On Biodiversity." Free Inquiry v13 n2, Spr 1993. p28-31. (ISSN0272-0701).

"An array of problems confronts scientists attempting to evaluate...[the] rates of loss of biodiversity. First, we simply don't know how much diversity there is. Estimates of the total number of species worldwide range from 5 million to 30 million or even 100 million, and there may be billions of genetically distinct populations. Second, no one knows how many species and populations of all kinds of organisms disappear each year, although rising rates of extinction in groups as diverse as North American fishes and Hawaiian birds have been abundantly documented. But it is not difficult to ascertain that the overall loss of biodiversity is accelerating. After all, it is not necessary to have counted and named each grain of sand on a beach, and recorded which have been washed away, to observe that the beach is rapidly eroding." (p66)

Ehrlich, Paul R. "Bioessay: Is the Extinction Crisis Real?" Wildlife Conservation v96 n5, Sep-Oct 1993. p66-67. (ISSN1048-4949).

BIOLOGICAL DIVERSITY--BAIKAL, LAKE (RUSSIA)

"The natural world of Baikal beckons. It is a lake of superlatives--the deepest and oldest on the planet. Of the 2,635 identified species and sub-species in Baikal, approximately 70 percent are found nowhere else. Both the quantity and quality of the water are unique, to a large degree as a result of the activity of these endemic organisms which compose over 90 percent of the Lake's biomass. Baikal is an invaluable treasure chest of the Earth's genetic wealth. Its pure, transparent waters are oxygen-rich throughout. It has a magnificent capacity for cleansing the more than 60 cubic meters of water a year that enter from more than 300 tributaries." (p41)

"Views from Ecologists of the Lake Baikal Region: Baikal, Unseen Dangers." Surviving Together v11 n4, Win 1993. p41. (ISSN0859-6286).

BIOLOGICAL DIVERSITY--COSTA RICA

"Costa Rica is well-known throughout the world for its efforts at conserving its rich biodiversity. Because of its attraction to people around the world, Costa Rica has not been short of help: In just the last four years, the country has attracted $36 million in foreign assistance for conservation, and traded $75 million in debt-for-nature swaps whereby natural areas are set aside in exchange for having a portion of their foreign debt forgiven. In 1987, the Central American country received the largest amount of U.S. funding for conservation from both the American government and private donors. Of the total $37.5 million Americans gave that year to conserve nature around the world, Costa Rica received $5.7 million." (p47)

Rogers, Adam. "Earth Travels." Earth News v4 n2, Mar-Apr 1993. p45-48. (ISSN1068-9400).

BIOLOGICAL DIVERSITY--COSTA RICA--U.S.

"Merck and Company Inc., a leading U.S. pharmaceutical company, has established a partnership with the National Biodiversity Institute (INBio) of Costa Rica. INBio has launched a decade-long research initiative to document the rain forest's fauna and flora, the largest biological project undertaken by any tropical country. Merck will provide INBio with $1 million and a $140,000 donation of equipment. In exchange, INBio will provide Merck with a certain number of plant, insect, and other specimens each year, engaging in a practice known as bio-prospecting. In exchange, Merck will receive the exclusive rights to screen these samples for medicinal properties. Should Merck develop a drug from one of the samples, INBio will receive royalties from the sale of the drug. The program helps to ensure that the tropical rainforests of Costa Rica are not destroyed, while fostering the local scientific community. INBio contributes 10 percent of its budget and 50 percent of its royalties to conserving national parks in Costa Rica." (p5)

"Case Study: Merck's Investment in Biodiversity." CEP Research Report Oct 1993. p5. (ISSN0898-4328).

BIOLOGICAL DIVERSITY--NEW JERSEY

"Over 11,338 species of birds, mammals, plants, reptiles, amphibians, fish and invertebrates call...[the Pinelands National Reserve] home and today at least 578 of those are either endangered or threatened (not counting the invertebrates--no one's sure about them)....In the Pines, 299 species of birds have been identified, 163 of which are local breeders. All of these identified species are classified by the state of New Jersey as either endangered or threatened, with two species, the bald eagle and peregrine falcon, listed as endangered by the federal government....The total number of amphibians and reptiles in the Pinelands is unusually large for an area with a northern climate. Fifty-nine species, including 18 varieties of snakes, 15 frogs and toads, 12 turtles and 11 species of salamanders have been identified in the New Jersey Pinelands. Nine of these have been listed as either threatened or endangered by the state, the most famous being the Pine Barrens treefrog." (p10)

Semcer, Bart. "New Jersey Pinelands: Nation's First National Reserve Needs Help." Earth First! v14 n3, 2 Feb 1994. p10.

BIOMASS ENERGY--DEVELOPING COUNTRIES (v19)

BIOTECHNOLOGY--U.S. (v19)

BIOTECHNOLOGY, AGRICULTURAL

see AGRICULTURAL BIOTECHNOLOGY; GENETIC ENGINEERING

BIOTECHNOLOGY INDUSTRIES

see also GENETIC ENGINEERING

"According to Ernst & Young, the biotechnology industry lost $3.6 billion last year. It is not unusual for a biotechnology company to spend $350 million...and 8 to 12 years to get a new product to market. Most biotechnology companies are small--75 percent have fewer than 50 employees--and more than 50 percent of their costs are for research and development....Initial public offerings for stock in biotechnology companies have fallen dramatically just this year. In 1991-92, IPO's for biotechnology stocks averaged about $100 to $150 million per month. In 1992-93, fear of Federal regulation of launch prices had dropped IPO's to $20 to $30 million per month. And where have these struggling companies gone to find capital?...To Japan. According to David Hale of Gensia, hundreds of companies are going to Japan for capital, and giving away large shares of their companies in return. Mr. Hale says that if price controls are instituted in the United States, 'Japan will be a world biotechnology power in 15 years.'" (pS16538)

Gregg, Judd (Sen.-N.H.). "Statement on Health Care Reform, Quality and Innovation," Congressional Record (19 Nov 1993). Daily ed. pS16537-16539. (ISSN0363-7239).

BIOTECHNOLOGY INDUSTRIES--EUROPE--U.S.

"According to Steve Burrill, a biotechnology buff, in the year to June 1993 drug firms formed around 100 strategic alliances with small biotech firms to tap into their know-how--twice as many as in the previous year. Research successes have fuelled a huge expansion of the biotechnology industry. In 1993 Mr Burrill counted 1,300 biotech firms in America, 200 in Britain, and 400 elsewhere in Europe. Mr Burrill reckons that by 2010 biotechnology firms' sales will have grown ten-fold compared with 1993, to some $100 billion. Because of the long lead-times involved, products began to trickle out of biotech R&D [Research and Development] laboratories only about five years ago. Two drugs already have sales in excess of $1 billion a year, because they are so good at what they do: Amgen's EPO, which prevents anaemia during kidney dialysis, and its Neupogen, which decreases the incidence of infection in cancer patients undergoing chemotherapy." (p13-14)

"Survey: The Future of Medicine: Engineering Health." Economist v330 n7855, 19 Mar 1994. p66(13-15). (ISSN0013-0613).

BIOTECHNOLOGY INDUSTRIES--U.S. (v19)

"The fiercely competitive biotechnology industry [in the U.S.] is ever on the lookout for first-rate researchers and ways to keep research costs down. A 1986 study of industry support for biotechnology research reported that 'per current dollar invested, university labs over the past five years have generated 4.2 times as many patent applications as company laboratories.' Such a record goes a long way toward explaining corporate interest in sponsoring university research." (p6)

Griffith, Katherine. "In Our Universities: Private Interests and Public Responsibilities." geneWATCH v9 n1-2, Aug 1993. p6-8.

BIRD WATCHERS--U.S.

"More than 51 million Americans are bird watchers, according to a 1991 survey conducted by the Census Bureau for the Fish and Wildlife Service. Many wildlife enthusiasts are content to watch birds in their backyard or in a nearby park. But nearly 25 million bird watchers report traveling a mile or more in hopes of seeing a loon, a titmouse, or a hawk. Eight million cross state lines in their search for more species." (p4)

Waldrop, Judith. "Seasons: For the Birds." American Demographics v16 n1, Jan 1994. p4. (ISSN0163-4089).

BIRDS

"As the planet's human population swells and spreads over once-wild areas, some 70 percent of the world's 9,600 bird species are responding with declines, and 1,000 species are threatened with extinction in the near future, according to a recent report by BirdLife International, a Cambridge, England-based conservation group that charts habitat and species loss. The phenomenon of disappearing birds has not only alarmed ornithologists, but has caused apprehension among botanists, foresters, farmers, agronomists, and ecologists. What is alarming, beyond the direct losses taking place, is that birds, unlike many other life forms, are particularly good indicators of the health of other species--and of whole ecosystems." (p10-

11)

Youth, Howard. "Flying into Trouble." World Watch v7 n1, Jan 1994. p10-19. (ISSN0896-0615).

"Since the 1600s, some 150 bird species have been lost, including North America's passenger pigeon--one of the world's most abundant birds (more than 3 billion) until the second decade of this century, when deforestation and overhunting wiped it out. Some of the most recent losses include the Atitlan grebe in Guatemala in 1987, the imperial woodpecker of Mexico (last seen in 1958), and possibly the Bachman's warbler (last seen in 1981), a small yellow and black bird that bred in southeastern U.S. swamp forest and wintered in Cuba's evergreen forest before it was converted to sugarcane fields. The pace of bird extinctions--along with those of other animals and plants--appears likely to accelerate rapidly. Many scientists predict that humanity is about to cause the greatest wave of plant and animal extinctions since the die-off of the dinosaurs 65 million years ago, and many of the first victims will be birds." (p18)

Youth, Howard. "Flying into Trouble." World Watch v7 n1, Jan 1994. p10-19. (ISSN0896-0615).

"Today, introduced species continue to devastate bird populations. A study in Britain, for example, found that the country's domestic cats had killed 20 million birds. A survey conducted in the Australian state of Victoria, similarly, estimated that the 500,000 cats in Victoria kill 13 million small animals a year, including members of 67 native bird species. Accidentally introduced animals can be just as devastating. The brown tree snake, for example, arrived on the Pacific island of Guam around the early 1950s in cargo shipments from Australia, New Guinea or the Solomon Islands. By 1986, the snake had eaten four of the island's five endemic bird species into extinction (one, the Guam rail, was extinct in the wild but has been bred in captivity and rereleased on a nearby--snake-free--island; the other three are extinct). The island's small mammals and reptiles have also suffered; Guam had never had a predator that ate serpents, so the snakes have proliferated." (p17)

Youth, Howard. "Flying into Trouble." World Watch v7 n1, Jan 1994. p10-19. (ISSN0896-0615).

BIRDS--NORTHWEST, PACIFIC

"Ornithologist Brian Sharp, after an extensive analysis of breeding bird surveys in Oregon and Washington, recently concluded that of the 16 [songbird] species studied, the populations of 4 species increased, while the remainder significantly declined, including the familiar northern oriole (formerly the Baltimore oriole), the barn swallow, and the olive-sided, willow, and Hammond flycatchers. Populations of the eastern kingbird and turkey vulture also have plummeted. Sharp points out, however, that what is happening in the Pacific Northwest does not necessarily reflect what's happening to western birds in general. In the Pacific Northwest, Sharp determined that 'thirty percent of the declining species live in old-growth forests, the others in riparian habitat. The decline might be occurring on the summer breeding grounds rather than in the tropics, where they winter.' Various species may be declining for different reasons. While the old-growth species may be suffering from loss of habitat, turkey vultures may be falling victim to poisons used to kill rodents." (p22)

Walters, Mark Jerome. "The Songbird Connection." Animals v126 n14, Jul-Aug 1993. p22-25. (ISSN0030-6835).

BIRDS--TEXAS (v19)

BIRDS--U.S.

"The pesticide DDT had a nearly catastrophic impact on many birds' reproductive success. The peregrine falcon disappeared as a nesting species in the Eastern U.S.; the bald eagle declined to a few hundred breeding pairs in the lower 48 states; and the East Coast range of the brown pelican contracted to the far Southeast. Osprey, although they were never listed as endangered, were reduced by 80% to 90% in the Northeast. EDF's [Environmental Defense Fund's] success in securing a nationwide ban on DDT made possible the ongoing recovery of all these species. Today, the peregrine falcon is again breeding in the East; there are more than 3,000 bald eagle nesting pairs in the lower 48 states; and the Atlantic Coast brown pelican has been taken off the endangered list. Osprey in the Northeast now number three times what they did in 1970." (p7)

"EDF's 25-Year Campaign on Behalf of Endangered Wildlife." EDF Letter v24 n2, Mar 1993. p7. (ISSN0163-2566).

"In 1989--now referred to as the 'pivotal year'--three things happened that together forced neotropical migrants into the spotlight: an international symposium at the Manomet Bird Observatory that revealed disturbing and corroborating data about neotropical migrants; the publishing of John Terborgh's powerful book, WHERE HAVE ALL THE BIRDS GONE? and the completed analyses of data collected through the Breeding Bird Survey (BBS), a roadside survey of U.S. and Canadian birds conducted by the USFWS [U.S. Fish and Wildlife Service]. The three events reached the same conclusion: populations of the birds were declining. Specifically, the BBS results showed that in eastern North America, populations of 71 percent of neotropical migrant species dropped between 1978 and 1987. Bay-breasted and Tennessee warblers, for instance, decreased an average of 16 percent and 12 percent per year, respectively, during the decade. The cerulean warbler experienced an average 2.5 percent drop per year since 1966." (p18)

Merriman, Kristin. "Sounds of Silence." Outdoor America v58 n2, Spr 1993. p17-19,30.

"According to the United States Fish and Wildlife Service, 70 percent of all neotropical bird species that summer in the Eastern United States have declined over the past decade. (Between 300 and 400 species of neotropical migrants spend the winter in Central and South America, Mexico, and the Caribbean then head north to the US and Canada.) The number of cerulean warblers has been dropping about 3 percent a year; olive-sided flycatchers, nearly 4 percent a year; yellow-billed cuckoos, 1.5 percent a year. Rose-breasted grosbeaks have declined by more than 40 percent overall; blackpoll warblers by 60 percent." (p10)

Knickerbocker, Brad. "Habitat: Stopping the Flight to Extinction." The Christian Science Monitor v86 n57, 15 Feb 1994. p10-11. (ISSN0882-7729).

BIRDS--U.S.--HABITAT

"Reporting last summer on the decline in native grassland birds, the U.S. Fish and Wildlife Service noted the impact of plowing: 'In North Dakota, for example, less than 25 percent of the native prairie remains. In Iowa, where 30 million acres of tall-grass prairie are estimated to have existed at the beginning of the 19th century, only a small fraction remains in isolated tracts scattered throughout the state." (p10)

Knickerbocker, Brad. "Habitat: Stopping the Flight to Extinction." The Christian Science Monitor v86 n57, 15 Feb 1994. p10-11. (ISSN0882-7729).

BIRTH

see CHILDBIRTH

BIRTH CONTROL (v19)

see also ABORTION; CONTRACEPTION

"For Jayne Lyons, a public health specialist who has lived and worked for international agencies in Guatemala for 15 years, family planning means making contraception choices accessible, but 'it also means availability of oral-rehydration supplies (diarrhea is one of the leading causes of infant death in developing nations), an emphasis on breast-feeding, and building latrines.' It implies informing women of the facts: that infant mortality doubles when mothers are under 18, and babies born three or more years apart have a 50-percent-better chance at survival. 'Birth spacing saves people's lives,' she says. 'It's not a liberation issue.'" (p65)

McConahay, Mary Jo. "Seven Children...Four Alive." Sierra v78 n6, Nov-Dec 1993. p62-69,98-101. (ISSN0161-7362).

BIRTH CONTROL--DEVELOPING COUNTRIES (v19)

BIRTH CONTROL--HEALTH ASPECTS (v19)

BIRTH CONTROL--JAMAICA

"Over 66 percent of married Jamaican women ages 15 to 44 uses some form of birth control, according to the 1993 Jamaica Contraceptive Prevalence Survey. This is a significant increase from the 55 percent who used contraception in 1989 and the 46 percent in 1975-76. The largest portion of women rely on the pill (23.7 percent), followed by condoms (17.9 percent) and female sterilization (12.1 percent). Although use of both the pill and female sterilization increased since 1989, condom use about doubled since 1989." (p8)

"News Clips: Contraceptive Use in Jamaica." Population Today v22 n1, Jan 1994. p8. (ISSN0749-2448).

BIRTH CONTROL--NEW HAMPSHIRE

"The New Hampshire Family Planning Program, a program of the Division of Public Health Services, currently serves over 16,000 women annually for comprehensive medical, social and educational services. Of the women served, 74% fall within 150% of the CSA poverty guidelines; 19% are 17 years of age or younger. Based on program data for the last six months, 100% of all adolescents received counseling prior to any medical services being provided. At this session, teens were helped to explore the realities of the decisions they were making, and were urged to discuss them with their parents. A recent national study indicated that 25% of teens seeking family planning services would not have enrolled in clinics if parental notification was necessary. The New Hampshire experience indicates that this percentage may be low. However, using the more conservative figure, at least 770 teens would not have obtained family planning services last year, and increased their risks of an unplanned pregnancy." (pS903)

Helms, Edgar, Jr. "Good News on the Deficit Front," Congressional Record (4 Feb 1994). Daily ed. pS891-905. (ISSN0363-7239).

BIRTH CONTROL--U.S.

"In 1956, when the first large trial of the pill was carried out, women formed 32% of the American workforce, and earned around a fifth of its total income. Now, the figures are 46% and well over a third. And even though time has taken some of the shine off it, with evidence that early versions affected blood pressure and may have caused breast cancer, the pill is still the preferred method of contraception for more than 90m women worldwide." (p48)

"Modern Wonders: The Equaliser." Economist v329 n7843, 25 Dec 1993. p47-48. (ISSN0013-0613).

BIRTH WEIGHT, LOW--HAITI

"According to AID's [a relief agency] December 1993 'Monitoring Report,' low birth weights in Port-au-Prince rose from 11.4 percent of all live births in 1992 to 13.6 percent last year. In the north, the number more than doubled." (p16)

James, David. "Embargo Forces Haiti's Last Gasp." Insight v10 n12, 21 Mar 1994. p14-17. (ISSN1051-4880).

BIRTH WEIGHT, LOW--U.S. (v19)

BISON--CANADA

"In 1800, Canada's wood bison population was estimated at 168,000. By 1940, the herd was believed to be extinct. Not until 1957 did local hunters discover 200 of these bison in a remote area of northern Alberta, about 180 miles north of Fort McMurry. Today, Canada's wood bison population is about 2,300." (p14)

"Panorama." Lamp v75 n4, Win 1994. p13-16. (ISSN0023-7418).

BISON, AMERICAN--U.S.

"When cattlemen, railwaymen, hunters and the United States Army had finished slaughtering the bison they called buffalo at the end of the last century, fewer than 1,000 remained. From this nadir, the buffalo population is rebounding. Today there are 150,000 buffaloes on ranches, in reserves and on Indian lands. And the numbers are growing. The reason for this resurgence is simple: buffalo meat is catching on. It has more protein, fewer calories, less cholesterol and less fat than beef or chicken; it tastes almost the same as beef, but a little sweeter. And because it is lean, buffalo meat cooks faster than beef and requires lower cooking temperatures. Even the National Heart Association has endorsed it....Demand for buffalo meat is now out-stripping supply. Only 12,000 buffaloes of the ideal age--between 18 and 24 months old--are available each year for slaughter. (By contrast, 125,000 head of cattle are slaughtered daily to supply consumer demand.) At January's annual National Stock Show in Denver the average buffalo sold for $2,000, up from $1,600 a year ago. There are now 55 buffalo ranches in Colorado and nearly 1,000 nationwide. Raising buffalo is cheaper than raising cattle. Feed costs are minimal. A buffalo eats 30lb of grass a day, grazes all year round and will eat snow for water--which a cow will not do." (p30-31)

"American Survey: Buffalo-Ranching: Back to the Frontier." Economist v331 n7861, 30 Apr 1994. p30-31. (ISSN0013-0613).

BLACK BEAR--LOUISIANA (v19)

BLACK MARKET--GREAT BRITAIN (v19)

BLIND--EDUCATION--U.S.

"According to goal five of the recently enacted Goals 2000: Educate American Act: 'By the year 2000, every American will be literate.' Yet, nearly half of all blind elementary and secondary level students cannot read Braille or print. In fact, the numbers of the blind who can read at all are declining. In 1968, out of 19,902 blind students enrolled in elementary and secondary education, 40 percent read Braille, 45 percent read large type or regular print, and 4 percent read both. In January, 1993, out of 50,204 blind students, fewer than 9 percent could read Braille, 27 percent could read print, and 40 percent could not read at all. In other words, while there are 40,000 more blind children in school today, only 30 percent can read--a far cry from 95 percent in 1968. These figures reflect the shocking magnitude of the literacy crisis among the visually impaired in our Nation today." (pE665)

Traficant, James A., Jr. (Rep.-Ohio). "Blind Are Unable to Read Braille Today," Congressional Record (15 Apr 1994). Daily ed. pE665-666. (ISSN0363-7239).

BLIND--U.S.--BOOKS AND READING--STUDY AND TEACHING

"In 1968 [in the U.S.], there were 20,000 blind students in our secondary and elementary schools, 40 percent of those blind students could read Braille, 45 percent could read large print, large type; 4 percent could read both. It is now 1994. There are 50,000 blind students in our elementary and secondary schools. Only 9 percent can read Braille. Only 27 percent can read large type. And 40 percent of all of our blind students cannot read at all." (pH816)

Traficant, James A., Jr. (Rep.-Ohio). "Improving America's Schools Act of 1994," Congressional Record (24 Feb 1994). Daily ed. pH798-857. (ISSN0363-7239).

BLOOD

"In 1993, WHO [World Health Organization] estimated that 91

million units of blood--one unit is 450 ml--were collected worldwide, nearly 65 million of these in industrialised countries and the rest in the developing world. Another WHO estimate suggests that most industrialised countries have about 50 units of blood for every 1,000 people, compared with 2.2 units for every 1,000 in the developing world." (p7)
Brown, Phyllida. "Briefing: A Question of Life and Death." WorldAIDS n32, Mar 1994. p6-9. (ISSN0954-6510).

BLOOD--NAIROBI
"Throughout the 1980s, the Nairobi Blood Centre received on average over 4,000 units of blood a year. In the 1990s, it's been a very different story: only 1,500 donors turned up in 1991, and barely 1,000 in 1992." (p8)
Kweyuh, Pamphil. "Briefing: Disappearing Donors." WorldAIDS n32, Mar 1994. p8. (ISSN0954-6510).

BLOOD--U.S.
"Every year about 12 million units of blood are collected in the United States. About half of the donations occur at Red Cross blood banks and the remainder at other community blood centers or hospitals....The first level of precautions seeks to eliminate high risk donors by encouraging those whose blood may pose a health hazard to exclude themselves, and by evaluating their behavioral and medical history as a basis for deferral. The second safeguard entails constant updating of a list of unsuitable donors and checking donors' names against the list to prevent use of their blood. The third consists of testing the blood for such bloodborne agents as HIV, hepatitis, and syphilis. The fourth safeguard enforced by FDA [Food and Drug Administration] is a quarantine of all donated blood until tests and other control procedures establish its safety. Last, the blood collection centers are obligated to investigate incidents, audit their systems, and correct deficiencies." (p24)
Kessler, David A. (Commissioner, Food and Drug Admin.). U.S. House. Committee on Energy and Commerce. "Blood Supply Safety." Hearing, 28 Jul 1993. Washington, D.C.: GPO, 1993. (ISBN0160432081). (Y4.En2/3:103-42).

"One of FDA's [Food and Drug Administration's] biggest challenges in enforcing blood bank requirements has been to get the American Red Cross, which is responsible for 50 percent of the blood supply, into compliance without interrupting the Nation's blood supply and without unnecessarily alarming the public." (p21)
Kessler, David A. (Commissioner, Food and Drug Admin.). U.S. House. Committee on Energy and Commerce. "Blood Supply Safety." Hearing, 28 Jul 1993. Washington, D.C.: GPO, 1993. (ISBN0160432081). (Y4.En2/3:103-42).

"The American Association of Blood Banks estimates the following: 13 million units of whole blood are collected each year. 20 million transfusions of blood and blood components are given to 4 million patients each year. A unit of whole blood can be split into components such as plasma, red blood cells and platelets. 11.6 million units are whole blood and red blood cells. 6.4 million units are platelets. 2.0 million units are plasma." (p67)
Mande, Jerold R. (Acting Assoc. Commissioner, Legislative Affairs, U.S. Dept. of Health and Human Services). U.S. House. Committee on Energy and Commerce. "Blood Supply Safety." Hearing, 28 Jul 1993. Washington, D.C.: GPO, 1993. (ISBN0160432081). (Y4.En2/3:103-42).

Twelve million units of blood are donated in the U.S. each year. "The risk for HIV disease is anywhere between one in 30,000 and one in 225,000. That's because of the window period. That translates into somewhere between 90 and 460 cases...the order of risk of over 12 million donations." (p33-34)
Kessler, David A. (Commissioner, Food and Drug Admin.). U.S. House. Committee on Energy and Commerce. "Blood Supply Safety." Hearing, 28 Jul 1993. Washington, D.C.: GPO, 1993. (ISBN0160432081). (Y4.En2/3:103-42).

BLOOD--U.S.--INFANTS--TRANSFUSION (v19)
BLOOD--U.S.--TRANSFUSION (v19)
BLOOD--U.S.--TRANSFUSION--COMPLICATIONS (v19)
"One in 30,000 (the actual figure is 1:38,000) was the first published estimate for the risk of HIV infection from screened blood. (Ward, JW, Holmberg SD, Allen JR, et al. Transmission of human immunodeficiency virus (HIV) by blood transfusions screened as negative for HIV antibody. NEW ENGLAND JOURNAL OF MEDICINE 1988; 318:473-8.) This estimate was obtained as a theoretical 'worst case' calculation. One in 225,000 is the most current estimate of risk of contracting HIV from transfusion. (Petersen, L.R., Satten G., Dodd, R.Y., et al. Current Estimates of the Infectious Window Period and Risk of HIV Infection from Seronegative Blood Donations. In Program and Abstracts of the Fifth National Forum on AIDS, Hepatitis, and Other Blood Borne Diseases, Atlanta, March 30, 1992. Princeton, N.J.: Symedco, 1992:37.)" (p63-64)
Mande, Jerold R. (Acting Assoc. Commissioner, Legislative Affairs, U.S. Dept. of Health and Human Services). U.S. House. Committee on Energy and Commerce. "Blood Supply Safety." Hearing, 28 Jul 1993. Washington, D.C.: GPO, 1993. (ISBN0160432081). (Y4.En2/3:103-42).

"The risk of post transfusion hepatitis [in the U.S.] was determined to be 3 per 10,000 units transfused or 1 per 3,300 units transfused in a study published by Donahue, J.G., Munoz, A., Ness, P.M., et al. NEW ENGLAND JOURNAL OF MEDICINE, 1992; 327:369-73. Roger Dodd published a commentary stating that, since the Donahue study was concluded, the risk decreased further due to implementation of newer, more sensitive tests for antibodies to HCV." (p64)
Mande, Jerold R. (Acting Assoc. Commissioner, Legislative Affairs, U.S. Dept. of Health and Human Services). U.S. House. Committee on Energy and Commerce. "Blood Supply Safety." Hearing, 28 Jul 1993. Washington, D.C.: GPO, 1993. (ISBN0160432081). (Y4.En2/3:103-42).

BLOOD DONORS
see HIV INFECTIONS--BLOOD DONORS

BLUE COLLAR WORKERS--U.S.
"A study of prime-time television dramas by the International Association of Machinists and Aerospace Workers (IAM) found that working people are consistently underrepresented and portrayed in negative, marginal, and patronizing ways. There are many times more prostitutes, pimps, government officials, secret agents, doctors, butlers, police, military personnel, and private detectives than there are production-line workers. Other studies find that blue collar and service workers compose 60 percent of the US work force but only 10 percent of the television characters, usually waiters, bartenders, and store clerks. Even prime-time shows in recent years have been about law enforcement, national security, and private investigation of crime, in that order." (p32)
Parenti, Michael. "Blue Collar Blues." Propaganda Review n10, Sum 1993. p32-34.

BLUE WHALE (v19)
BLUES (MUSIC)--U.S. (v19)
BOATS AND BOATING--U.S.--ACCIDENTS AND INJURIES
"A sobering statistic is that nearly 1,000 people die in boating accidents every year nationwide. Ninety percent drown and more than 50 percent of the deaths involve alcohol, according to the U.S. Coast Guard. Another staggering fact is that more than 80 percent of those who die in boating accidents aren't wearing life jackets....Besides alcohol, not knowing the rules of the road is a major cause of accidents. U.S. Coast Guard Statistics

for 1992 show that 8,206 boats were involved in accidents nationwide. Of that, 4,353 collided with another boat." (p1 secC)

Meyerson, Howard. "Venture Outdoors: Think Summer, Boats, Safety." Ann Arbor News 12 Mar 1994. p1 secC.

BODY IMAGE--U.S.--YOUTH (v19)

BOGOTA (COLOMBIA)

see HOMELESS PERSONS--BOGOTA (COLOMBIA); TRAFFIC CONGESTION--BOGOTA (COLOMBIA)

BOLIVIA

see also COCAINE INDUSTRY--BOLIVIA; COCAINE INDUSTRY--BOLIVIA--COLOMBIA--PERU; RADIO STATIONS--BOLIVIA

BOLIVIA--ECONOMIC CONDITIONS (v19)

"The extreme levels of poverty in the rural regions of Peru are considered one of the conditions that led to the development of the Maoist Shining Path guerilla group. According to the United Nations, Bolivia has the poorest rural population in the world, with a per capita income of US$250 a year. Although most Bolivians have traditionally lived in rural areas, last year's population and housing census revealed that 57.5% of the country's 6.4 million inhabitants now live in cities." (p32)

"Latin American Focus: Bolivia: Will Extreme Poverty Lead to Political Violence?" Barricada Internacional v13 n363, Jul 1993. p32-33. (ISSN1013-9567).

BOMBINGS--U.S. (v19)

"During calendar year 1991, there were 2,490 reported bombings or attempted bombings [in the U.S.], which caused 27 deaths, 246 injuries, and in excess of $6.3 million in property damage. In addition, more than 8 tons of explosives were reported stolen in 127 separate incidents. ATF's [Bureau of Alchohol, Tobacco and Firearms'] investigative efforts and those of other law enforcement agencies resulted in the recovery of 5 tons of stolen explosives. During FY 1992, the Bureau initiated a total of 2,299 investigations in our Law Enforcement Explosives Program and recommended 928 defendants for prosecution." (p671)

U.S. House. Committee on Appropriations. "Treasury, Postal Service...Approp. for Fiscal Year 1994 (Part 1)." Hearing, Washington, D.C.: GPO, 1993. (Y4.Ap6/1:T71/994/pt.1).

BOND FUNDS--U.S.

"From 1989 through 1993, taxable bond funds racked up average annual total returns of 10.5% and tax-free funds 9.6%...." (p91)

Laderman, Jeffrey M. "Mutual Fund Scoreboard: How the Bond Funds Stack Up." Business Week n3359, 21 Feb 1994. p91-92. (ISSN0007-7135).

BONDS

see also COMMODITY-BACKED FUNDS; DEBTS, PUBLIC; JUNK BONDS; MUNICIPAL BONDS; STOCKS

BONDS--ISRAEL--U.S. (v19)

BONDS--U.S.

"Last year, state and local governments and agencies issued approximately $280 billion of bonds [in the U.S.]. Backed as they often are by the taxpayer, they are considered among the safest of investments. And for the investors the interest is tax-exempt....As of the third quarter of this year there have been $180 billion in negotiated bond deals awarded nationwide, and only $41 billion in competitive deals, according to statistics compiled by THE BOND BUYER. Public finance specialists are quick to say that the complicated, idiosyncratic nature of many bond issues makes them better candidates for a negotiated deal, which offers more flexibility than a straightforward competitive bidding process." (p33)

Lutterbeck, Deborah. "The Bond Merchants." Common Cause Magazine v19 n4, Win 1993. p30-34. (ISSN0271-9592).

BONDS, MUNICIPAL

see MUNICIPAL BONDS

BONE MARROW--TRANSPLANTATION (v19)

BONE MARROW--TRANSPLANTATION--U.S.

"As of April 30, 1993, the NMDP [National Marrow Donor Program] registry [in the U.S.] contains 866,431 donors, of which 132,929 are minorities. To date, the program has facilitated 1,766 unrelated donor transplants; they occur currently at a rate of about 53 per month. Recruitment of minority donors has continued to increase; more than 50,000 have been added in the past year. The number of minority patients receiving transplants has also continued to increase; more than 50 minority patients were transplanted in the past year, an increase of nearly 10 percent over the previous 12 months....Currently, the chances of finding a matched donor and having a transplant are 40 to 45 percent for nonminorities and 15 to 20 percent for African-Americans. It is also clear that more Asian Americans and Hispanics will be needed than are presently available." (p215-216)

Lenfant, Claude (Dir., National Heart, Lung, and Blood Inst., NIH). U.S. House. Committee on Energy and Commerce. "Organ Transplant and Bone Marrow Donor Reauthorization." Hearing, 22 Apr 1993. Washington, D.C.: GPO, 1994. (ISBN0160434653). (Y4.En2/3:103-54).

"Over 866,000 volunteer donors [in the U.S.] have been listed by the National [Bone Marrow] Registry since its founding. Of this total, approximately 15 percent or 133,000 are minority donors. More needs to be accomplished....Less than 2 percent of African-American patients needing bone marrow transplants are able to identify suitable donors." (p179-180)

Waxman, Henry A. (Sen.-Calif.). U.S. House. Committee on Energy and Commerce. "Organ Transplant and Bone Marrow Donor Reauthorization." Hearing, 22 Apr 1993. Washington, D.C.: GPO, 1994. (ISBN0160434653). (Y4.En2/3:103-54).

"The National Heart, Lung and Blood Institute (NHLBI) of the National Institutes of Health [in the U.S.] administers the National Marrow Donor Program (NMDP). NMDP provides a vital resource for many patients in need of a bone marrow transplant. Its registry now lists about 700,000 volunteer marrow donors, an increase of 270,000 over a year ago. Minority donors, the subject of intensive recruitment efforts, now total 100,000, more than double the number listed last year. There has also been a corresponding increase in the number of transplants involving minority patients." (p31)

Harmon, Robert G. (Administrator, Health Resources and Services Admin.). U.S. House. Committee on Energy and Commerce. "Organ Transplant and Bone Marrow Donor Reauthorization." Hearing, 22 Apr 1993. Washington, D.C.: GPO, 1993. (ISBN0160434653). (Y4.En2/3:103-54).

"The National Marrow Donor program was established [in the U.S.] in 1989. It is administered under a Federal contract by the National Heart, Lung and Blood Institute of the NIH [National Institutes of Health]. Currently, the program is funded by appropriations under the Public Health Service Act and from an appropriation to the Department of the Navy. Federal funds for fiscal year 1993 totaled $36.4 million. In addition, the Registry receives over $24 million annually from private donations and patient fees. Bone marrow transplants are an accepted mode of therapy for an increasing number of life-threatening diseases such as leukemia, aplastic anemia, and certain cancers. Last year about 600 bone marrow transplants were carried out at bone marrow transplant centers throughout the United States." (p179)

Waxman, Henry A. (Sen.-Calif.). U.S. House. Committee on Energy and Commerce. "Organ Transplant and Bone Marrow Donor Reauthorization." Hearing, 22 Apr 1993. Washington, D.C.: GPO, 1994. (ISBN0160434653). (Y4.En2/3:103-54).

"The ultimate success of bone marrow transplantation [in the

U.S.] rests in the ability to match patients with donors. Like blood transfusions, these bone marrow donor matches must be perfect. But unlike blood transfusions, perfect matches are extremely rare. In some cases, matches can be found within the patient's family, but only about 35 percent of the time. The remaining 65 percent of the patients are forced to find a bone marrow donor through the existing registries of potential bone marrow donors or through donor drives. Such drives involve recruiting hundreds of members of the patient's community who are willing to undergo a simple blood test to see if they are a compatible match. The odds of a patient finding a bone marrow donor are 1:20,000; this is a median statistic and certain groups of patients, such as minorities, have a much lesser chance of finding a donor....An increase in the number of donors of a particular ethnic heritage increases the chance of successful searches for patients of that ethnicity, as well as a certain percentage of patients in general. The fact that less than 2 percent of African-American patients, and less than 12 percent of other minority populations identify donors further emphasizes the need for increased minority recruitment." (p229)

Anderson, Nancy (Dir., American Bone Marrow Donor Registry). U.S. House. Committee on Energy and Commerce. "Organ Transplant and Bone Marrow Donor Reauthorization." Hearing, 22 Apr 1993. Washington, D.C.: GPO, 1994. (ISBN0160434653). (Y4.En2/3:103-54).

"To date, the American [Bone Marrow Donor] Registry has successfully recruited over 43,000 donors--39 percent of which are minorities--and established agreements with European registries that allow immediate access to over 600,000 donors worldwide. The minority populations within the American Registry donor pool consist of 17.8 percent African-American, 10.5 percent Asian, 6 percent Hispanic, 7 percent Greek, and 2.3 percent other minorities. The ethnic diversity in the American Registry has been successfully accomplished without any Federal assistance. An unfair burden is placed on minorities to recruit a higher percentage of their population. Financial assistance will be required to achieve equitable representation in the marrow donor pool, so critical to the minority patient." (p228)

Anderson, Nancy (Dir., American Bone Marrow Donor Registry). U.S. House. Committee on Energy and Commerce. "Organ Transplant and Bone Marrow Donor Reauthorization." Hearing, 22 Apr 1993. Washington, D.C.: GPO, 1994. (ISBN0160434653). (Y4.En2/3:103-54).

The National Marrow Donor Program "has facilitated 1,766 unrelated donor transplants. Twenty years ago, such progress in the science of transplantation and the quality of life [of] transplant patients would have been unthinkable. However, it is clear that the pace of science has exceeded the awareness of the American people about the importance of organ donations, particularly bone marrow donations. Currently, the chances of finding a matched donor and having a transplant are about 40 percent for non-minorities and 15 percent for African-Americans." (p180-181)

Waxman, Henry A. (Sen.-Calif.). U.S. House. Committee on Energy and Commerce. "Organ Transplant and Bone Marrow Donor Reauthorization." Hearing, 22 Apr 1993. Washington, D.C.: GPO, 1994. (ISBN0160434653). (Y4.En2/3:103-54).

BOOBY TRAPS (MILITARY SCIENCE)

see MINES (MILITARY EXPLOSIVES)

BOOKKEEPERS

see ACCOUNTANTS

BOOKS AND READING--U.S.--FATHERS (v19)

BORDER PATROLS--MEXICO--U.S. (v19)

BOSNIA

see MILITARY WEAPONS--BOSNIA--SERBIA

BOSNIA AND HERCEGOVINA--HISTORY--CIVIL WAR (v19)

BOTSWANA--ECONOMIC CONDITIONS (v19)

BOTTLED WATER--GREAT BRITAIN (v19)

BOTTLED WATER--JAPAN

"The popularity of bottled water has been growing steadily since the mineral-water fad of 1989. According to statistics from the Japan Mineral Water Association, 175,348kl of mineral water were consumed in Japan in 1990, 270,686kl in 1991, and over 345,594kl in 1992. In comparison, consumption of all kinds of juice fell slightly, from 2.4 million kiloliters in 1991 to 2.2 million in 1992....Over 200 mineral-water brands, both domestic and imported, are currently sold in Japan, feeding a market worth Y50 billion ($450 million) annually." (p46)

Sasaki, Yukie. "Facts of Life: Bottled Water: Surging Water." Look Japan v39 n456, Mar 1994. p46. (ISSN0456-5339).

BOTTLED WATER--U.S. (v19)

BOWLING--U.S.

"Nearly 50 million Americans aged 6 and older bowled at least once in 1992, according to the Billiard & Bowling Institute of America. The average bowler hits the lanes 16 times a year. But growth in the market is slow. Between 1987 and 1992, the total number of bowlers increased less than 4 percent, while the number of frequent participants who bowl 25 times or more a year declined 15 percent, to 9 million. Demographic data show that bowlers are headed in two directions: male and upscale. The number of women bowlers did not grow between 1987 and 1992, but the number of men grew 7 percent. Today, 53 percent of bowlers are men. During the same period, the number of players with annual household incomes of less than $25,000 fell 19 percent, while the number with incomes of $50,000 or more jumped 52 percent. High-income bowlers are now 28 percent of the market, about equal to their share of all households (27 percent)." (p4)

Waldrop, Judith. "Seasons: The Perfect Game." American Demographics v16 n2, Feb 1994. p4. (ISSN0163-4089).

BRAND NAME PRODUCTS--CANADA--GREAT BRITAIN--U.S.

"Sales of own-label goods continue to rise, pushing branded goods from the shelves, especially if they are not leaders in their category. In Britain, own-label takes 36% of the grocery market. In America, where own-label brands still have a cheaper image, sales of own-label goods at supermarkets rose from 22% of their total grocery sales in 1990 to 23.5% last year. By 2000, the figure will be 27%, according to a study by J.P. Morgan, a New York bank. Even mighty Coca-Cola is not immune. In the past three years, Cott Corporation, which bottles private-label colas, has grabbed about 20% of the cola market in Canada and 2% of America's. Coca-Cola's Canadian operation lost C$143m ($111m) in the year to January and closed half of its 16 plants." (p67)

"Business: Death of the Brand Manager." Economist v331 n7858, 9 Apr 1994. p67-68. (ISSN0013-0613).

BRAZIL

see also AGRICULTURE--BRAZIL--U.S.; CHILDREN--BRAZIL--SOCIAL CONDITIONS; DEFORESTATION--BRAZIL; DEVELOPING COUNTRIES--BRAZIL--THAILAND; FORCED LABOR--BRAZIL; GOLD INDUSTRY--BRAZIL; HIV INFECTIONS--BRAZIL--PRISONERS; HUNGER--BRAZIL; INDIGENOUS PEOPLES--BRAZIL; INFLATION (FINANCE)--ARGENTINA--BRAZIL; INFLATION (FINANCE)--BRAZIL--GERMANY--JAPAN; LOCAL TRANSIT--BRAZIL; LOGGING--BRAZIL; VIOLENCE--BRAZIL--WOMEN; WATER--FLUORIDATION--BRAZIL; WEAPONS INDUSTRY--BRAZIL

BRAZIL--ECONOMIC CONDITIONS (v19)

BRAZIL--POPULATION (v19)

BRAZIL--U.S.--ARMED FORCES--APPROPRIATIONS AND EXPENDITURES

"Official data indicates that National Defence and Security absorbed less than 1% of the Brazilian R&D [research and development] public budget....Previous research by the author has shown that military R&D expenditure represents approximately 20% of the total public budget. This research also evaluated the economic significance of the Brazilian arms sector. Its production has been estimated as less than 0.2% of GNP (gross national product)....In the USA the share of military R&D in total public expenditure on R&D can be taken as 40%. The share of arms production in GNP is 4%. Hence, the US ratio between the two indicators is 10:1." (p392)

Dagnino, Renato. "Brazilian S&T: To the Barracks or into the Labs? Military Programmes and Brazilian S&T Policy." Science and Public Policy v20 n6, Dec 1993. p389-395.

BREAST--CANCER (v19)

"In 1993, 182,000 women in the U.S. alone will be diagnosed with breast cancer, and 46,000 will die. Globally, all industrialized countries except Japan are witnessing alarmingly high death rates from this disease. The top 10 worst countries, as reported in the World Health Statistics Annual, 1984-1988, are: England/Wales, Malta, Denmark, Scotland, Luxembourg, the Netherlands, Belgium, Northern Ireland, Switzerland and Ireland. Countries with the lowest death rates include Ecuador, Japan, Mauritius, Suriname and Hong Kong. Other examples: Israel ranks 14th, the U.S. 15th, the former Soviet Union 41st, and Japan 47th. (The lower the ranking the higher the death rates.)" (p11)

Soffa, Virginia. "Sounding the Alarm on Breast Cancer." Toward Freedom v42 n2, Mar 1993. p11. (ISSN0048-9898).

BREAST--CANCER--CANADA

"Breast cancer rates in Canada are among the highest in the world. Each year over 16,000 Canadian women are diagnosed with it. That is 30 percent of all new cancer cases. Breast cancer killed 5,400 Canadian women in 1993, raising the death toll to more than 65,000 within the last 13 years." (p4)

LeBow, Barbara. "CAUTION: If You Choose Abortion, You Could Be Choosing Breast Cancer." ProLife News v19 n3, Mar 1994. p4-5.

BREAST--CANCER--GREAT BRITAIN (v19)

BREAST--CANCER--MORTALITY (v19)

BREAST--CANCER--U.S. (v19)

"Research...suggests the risk of breast cancer may be linked to a woman's lifetime exposure to reproductive hormones. Whatever the cause, Dr. Christine Watt, medical director of mammography services at St. John Hospital and Medical Center, is concerned that too many women believe myths that could lead to personal disaster. Some of the myths are: 'If a mammogram detects cancer, it's too late'; 'Mammograms cause more tumors than they detect'; 'Young women don't need to examine their breasts.'...Screening mammography is the key to early detection--and the only way to identify breast cancer before it can be felt. If found and treated early, the five year survival rate is more than 90 percent." According to Christine Watt, "A 1991 estimate said that one out of nine women will develop breast cancer in her lifetime.'" (p24)

"Health: The Battle against Breast Cancer." Corporate Detroit v11 n1, Jan 1994. p24.

"In 1992, estimates are that 180,000 women will develop breast cancer, and 46,000 will die from it....Cancer is the leading cause of death among women ages 35-54, with about a third of these due to breast cancer." (p17) "There is evidence that mammography screening reduces breast cancer deaths in women age 50 or older. However, Dr. Rosalie Bertell, (Director of the International Institute of Concern for Public Health...and well known critic of the nuclear establishment) raises serious questions about mammography screening. In a paper entitled, 'Comments on Ontario Mammography Program'...Bertell criticized a breast cancer screening program planned by the Ontario Health Minister in 1989. Bertell argued that the program, which would potentially screen 300,000 women, was a plan to 'reduce breast cancer death by increasing breast cancer incidence.'...Bertell's critique of mammography is supported by a recent multi-million dollar Canadian study of 90,000 women that looked at cancer rates between 1980 and 1988. The study has yet to be released, but preliminary results showed that for women aged 40 to 49, mammograms have no benefits and may indeed harm them: 44 deaths were found in the group that received mammograms and 29 in the control group." (p23)

Arditti, Rita/Schreiber, Tatiana. "Killing Us Quietly." New Directions for Women v22 n1, Jan-Feb 1993. p17-18,23-25. (ISSN0160-1075).

"In the last few years, questions have...arisen about the possible biological effects of electromagnetic fields. Studies looking at EMF and childhood leukemia are inconclusive, but two studies on telephone company and electrical workers have raised the possibility of a connection between EMF exposure and breast cancer in males. Genevieve Matanoski of Johns Hopkins University studied breast cancer rates in male New York Telephone employees between 1976 to 1980, and observed a dose-response relationship to cancer. There were two cases of breast cancer, a very high number for such a small group. Breast cancer in men is rare; in the U.S. the annual incidence is 1 in 100,000, as compared to 110 in 100,000 for women." (p23)

Arditti, Rita/Schreiber, Tatiana. "Killing Us Quietly." New Directions for Women v22 n1, Jan-Feb 1993. p17-18,23-25. (ISSN0160-1075).

"The breast cancer rate for lesbians is two to three times that of heterosexual women, according to a recent report by the National Cancer Institute. Epidemiologist Suzanne Haynes says that lesbians have a one-in-three lifetime risk of getting breast cancer. Suzanne came up with those projections after comparing the results of a number of different studies. She noted that 45% of lesbians don't have regular gynecological checkups including breast exams and mammograms. The fact that 70% of lesbians have not had children before the age of thirty creates another risk factor....Furthermore, there's the possibility that...higher levels of body fat also predispose lesbians to breast cancer." (p9)

"Illness: News & Facts: Breast Cancer Risk Higher for Lesbians?" Women & Recovery Fall 1993. p9.

BREAST--CANCER--U.S.--MORTALITY (v19)

BREAST FEEDING--EMPLOYMENT--U.S.

"According to the National Center for Health Statistics in Hyattsville, Md., more than 50 percent of adult women [in the U.S.] work outside the home, and 80 percent will become pregnant during their working lives. As the number of women entering the work force continues to increase, some advocates are moving the issue of breast-feeding out of the supply room and into the boardroom....[Rona] Cohen is the national manager of Sanvita, a unique program that helps companies set up lactation programs. Sanvita was launched in 1992 by Medela Inc., a breast-pump manufacturer in McHenry, Ill. Of the 50 percent of mothers who breast-feed their babies, only 12 percent are employed, according to Sanvita. Many women stop breast-feeding after they return to work, Cohen says, anticipating obstacles....According to Sanvita, companies with a lactation program reduced health-care costs by 35.7 percent and absenteeism by 27.3 percent. The program helps companies reduce their turnover rate and enhances employee morale, Cohen says." (p9)

Coolidge, Shelley Donald. "Economy: Women in the Workplace: Sanvita Program Promotes Breast-Feeding by Mothers." The Christian Science Monitor v86 n66, 1 Mar 1994. p9. (ISSN0882-7729).

BREAST FEEDING--U.S. (v19)

BRITISH COLUMBIA

see BEARS--BRITISH COLUMBIA; DEFORESTATION--BRITISH COLUMBIA; FORESTS AND FORESTRY--BRITISH COLUMBIA; GRIZZLY BEAR--BRITISH COLUMBIA; WOLVES--BRITISH COLUMBIA

BROKERS--JAPAN--U.S. (v19)

BRUCELLOSIS (v19)

BUDGET--U.S. (v19)

BUDGET--U.S.--STATES

"Despite years of budget cuts and tax hikes, state and local governments are still in financial turmoil. In 1985 these governments had a combined budget surplus of $56.1 billion, equaling 12 per cent of total state and local spending. By 1992 that cushion had shrunk to $15.5 billion, equaling less than 2 per cent of spending." (p15)

Rubenstein, Ed. "Right Data: Dire States?" National Review v46 n1, 24 Jan 1994. p15. (ISSN0028-0038).

BUDGET DEFICITS--CHINA (v19)

BUDGET DEFICITS--EUROPE--U.S. (v19)

BUDGET DEFICITS--FRANCE

"Unlike Britain during its recession, France has managed to reduce its yawning budget gap. The total public deficit (including the social-security fund) had more than tripled between 1989 and 1991 and seemed set to reach nearly 6% of GDP [gross domestic product] in 1992. But by raising taxes, cutting spending and reducing health-care benefits, the government brought the deficit down from a forecast FFr333 billion last year to FFr317 billion. It plans to cut it back to FFr300 billion (4.2% of GDP) this year, with the aim of getting it down to 2.5% of GDP by 1997." (p50)

"Europe: Edouard Balladur and the Triumph of Politics." Economist v330 n7849, 5 Feb 1994. p49-50. (ISSN0013-0613).

BUDGET DEFICITS--ITALY (v19)

BUDGET DEFICITS--JAPAN--U.S.

"In the 1980s economists lost sleep fretting about the effects of the American government's profligacy, yet the OECD [Organization for Economic Cooperation and Development] now reckons that America's general-government budget deficit (central, state and local government plus social-security funds) will fall to 2.7% of GDP [gross domestic product] this year, from a peak of 4.5% in 1992, and narrow further to 2.1% next year....Japan, which had a budget surplus of 3% of GDP in 1991, is expected to have a deficit of about 3% once this week's tax cuts take effect. Japan's Ministry of Finance uses such figures as proof that it has done more than enough to boost its economy. But this is misleading. America's economy is now growing strongly, which helps to trim its deficit; Japan's is in a slump. Adjust the budget balances for the cycle, and America is running a 'structural' deficit of 2-3% of GDP, while Japan's structural position is still in surplus....In other words, Japan's fiscal policy is not as loose as it seems." (p73)

"Business: Balancing the Government's Books." Economist v330 n7850, 12 Feb 1994. p73. (ISSN0013-0613).

BUDGET DEFICITS--NIGERIA

"Lavish [Nigerian] government spending in 1993--including more building in [the capital] Abuja and the painstaking conduct of a presidential election that was then declared void--piled up a budget deficit estimated at 75 billion naira ($3.75 billion at the then rate of 20 to the dollar). This was more than 2 1/2 times the projected deficit, and 15% of GDP [gross domestic product]." (p44)

"International: Nigeria: Cleaned Out, but Not Up." Economist v330 n7844, 8 Jan 1994. p43-44. (ISSN0013-0613).

BUDGET DEFICITS--SAUDI ARABIA

"Arms dealers fear the flu when Saudi Arabia sneezes. The kingdom is strapped for cash, after ten years or so of governmental over-spending and borrowing. Though oil revenues are still not as low as in the mid-1980s, the Saudis cannot shrug off an oil price that has tumbled by 30% in less than a year. Saudi figures put the 1993 budget deficit at about $7 1/2 billion, roughly 6 1/2% of GDP [gross domestic product]; and on past form it will be surprising if it does not turn out to be much bigger. The 1994 budget is supposed to bring the deficit down to little more than $1 billion, thanks to sharp cuts--around 20%--in spending." (p45)

"International: Saudi Arabia: Pressured Reform." Economist v330 n7846, 15 Jan 1994. p45-46. (ISSN0013-0613).

BUDGET DEFICITS--U.S. (v19)

The U.S. budget deficit "is now $4.2 trillion and the yearly interest costs have reached $300 billion a year. The deficit for fiscal 1993 has been estimated at $325 billion, but that does not include the $100 billion the government annually takes from the trust funds, especially the Social Security and Medicare surpluses. That makes the true deficit $425 billion." (p101)

Gross, Martin L. (Author of "The Government Racket: Washington Waste from A to Z."). U.S. Senate. Committee on Governmental Affairs. "Improving Government Organization and Performance." Hearing, 11 Mar 1993. Washington, D.C.: GPO, 1994. (ISBN0160435838). (Y4.G74/9:S.hrg.103-401).

"Even assuming that all the projected revenues appear and spending cuts occur as projected, the gross Federal debt [in the U.S.] increases by 35 percent to over $6 trillion in 1999. From 1995 to 1999, Federal outlays will increase by almost $340 billion, and the deficit is expected to begin rising in 1997 unless we take further action. The Congressional Budget Office projects that net interest on the debt alone will be over $200 billion for 1994. This is almost 80 percent of what we will spend on all domestic discretionary programs." (pH1383)

Lazio, Rick (Rep.-N.Y.). "Balanced Budget Constitutional Amendment," Congressional Record (16 Mar 1994). Daily ed. pH1373-1414. (ISSN0363-7239).

"In the fall of 1990, [the U.S.] Congress completed an arduous effort to come to grips with the deficit, cutting approximately $500 billion over 5 years, only to see the deficit rise in the next fiscal year. Last summer, Congress enacted legislation the administration argued would reduce the deficit by a similar amount--roughly half a trillion dollars--during the 1994-98 period. Even taking such claimed savings into account, OMB [Office of Management and Budget] estimates the national debt will reach $5.953 trillion by the end of fiscal year 1998, more than five times the level of just 16 years earlier, and an increase of $1.277 trillion during the 4 fiscal years beginning this October. Although the Congressional Budget Office anticipates relatively flat deficits in the $166 to $182 billion range during fiscal years 1995 through 1998, steep increases thereafter are projected even with the steps Congress has taken to date to address the deficit." (pH1361)

Fish, Hamilton, Jr. (Rep.-N.Y.). "Balanced Budget Constitutional Amendment," Congressional Record (16 Mar 1994). Daily ed. pH1358-1372. (ISSN0363-7239).

"The most devastating and alarming impact the deficit has had on...[the U.S.] economy is its effect on economic growth and job creation. The New York Federal Reserve Bank says that from 1979 to 1989, we lost 5 percent growth in the GNP [gross national product] and national income because of the deficit. The CBO [Congressional Budget Office] says that for every percentage that is lost on the GNP, we lose 650,000 jobs. That means as a result of our recurring deficits, we will lose approximately 3.75 million jobs. We can hardly afford that, given the fact that we are having a low job growth rate compared to historical levels of the past." (pH1367)

Snowe, Olympia J. (Rep.-Maine). "Balanced Budget Constitutional Amendment," Congressional Record (16 Mar 1994). Daily ed. pH1358-1372. (ISSN0363-7239).

"In April 1993, the Office of Management and Budget was predicting a budget deficit for fiscal year 1994 of $305 billion. The current OMB estimate, after the passage of the Deficit Reduction Act, is $236 billion, and the current Congressional Budget Office estimate is $228 billion....In April 1993, we were predicting for fiscal year 1995 a deficit of $302 billion. We are now anticipating, because of the Deficit Reduction Act that we passed, a deficit of $177 billion by OMB estimates and $179 billion by CBO estimates, a very dramatic reduction. In April 1993, we were predicting for 1996 a deficit of $298 billion. Because of the Deficit Reduction Act we passed and the expanding economy, that is now predicted to be between $178 billion and $180 billion, well over a $100-billion reduction; well over a one-third reduction in the so-called deficit. The same is true for 1997 and for 1998." (pS3407)

Sasser, Jim (Sen.-Tenn.). "Congressional Budget Concurrent Resolution," Congressional Record (22 Mar 1994). Daily ed. pS3403-3415. (ISSN0363-7239).

"In terms of spending, as a result of the reconciliation package overall spending [in the U.S.] will average 22.5% of GDP [gross domestic product] over the next five years, compared to 23.3% for the Bush and Reagan years combined. The average of discretionary spending as a percentage of GDP will be 7.8%, while under Bush it was 9.2% and under Reagan it was 10.2%. Another important measure is the deficit as a percentage of GDP. Since 1989, this percentage has been growing steadily from 2.9% in that year to 4% in 1990, 4.8% in 1991, and 4.9% in 1992. Due to the President's deficit reduction package this percentage will drop significantly. In 1993, the deficit as a percentage of GDP is estimated to be 4.3% and is projected to drop in each of the next five years and reach a low of 2.5% in 1998. In other words, rather than continuing the upward trend the deficit has been going along, the deficit as a percentage of GDP will be sliced in half over the next five years. Although this trend is often overlooked, I believe it is essential if one is to appreciate the magnitude of the efforts being taken currently to reign in the deficit and provide economic growth." (pH10742)

Unsoeld, Jolene (Rep.-Wash.). "Government Reform and Savings Act of 1993." Congressional Record (22 Nov 1993). Daily ed. pH10729-10893. (ISSN0363-7239).

"Just a few months ago...[the U.S.] Congress enacted the largest tax increase in American history and at the same time in the name of deficit reduction...Congress also passed the largest deficit spending increase in American history. The numbers make it quite clear, fiscal 1993, just ended, the numbers are in: Congress spent $1.4 trillion last year....Under the Clinton budget enacted by this Congress, next year's spending will rise to $1.5 trillion, a whopping increase; $1.6 trillion will be the spending called for by the budget we pass in 1996, and $1.8 trillion in 1998, collectively the largest 5-year increase in deficit spending in American history, all in the name of deficit spending." (pH10729)

Cox, Christopher (Rep.-Calif.). "Government Reform and Savings Act of 1993." Congressional Record (22 Nov 1993). Daily ed. pH10729-10893. (ISSN0363-7239).

"If 1980 interest rates returned this year and replaced currently projected interest rates on Treasury securities, that one change alone would: More than double the fiscal year 1999 deficit; almost double total deficit spending over the next 5 years; and almost double net interest spending in fiscal year 1999....How large would these increases in interest costs really be? By FY 1999, just the increase above baseline interest payments would be equal to: 46 percent of all discretionary spending in the budget resolution; 62 percent of Social Security; 91 percent of all means-tested entitlements; 95 percent of Medicare; 98 percent of defense spending in the budget resolution; 167 percent of Medicaid; 280 percent of total federal civilian and military retirement; and 525 percent of the Education and Training function in the budget resolution." (pS3613)

Craig, Larry E. (Sen.-Idaho). "Congressional Budget Concurrent Resolution," Congressional Record (24 Mar 1994). Daily ed. pS3599-3615. (ISSN0363-7239).

"Last year, CBO [U.S. Congressional Budget Office] projected a fiscal year 1995 deficit of $284 billion. One year later, CBO reestimated the fiscal year 1995 deficit at $171 billion, a decrease of $113 billion. But a quick look at how this was achieved will show that the serious job of making tough choices and cutting spending hardly is happening at all. According to CBO, the drop in the deficit comes from new taxes and user fees of $46 billion; technical reestimates, $45 billion; technical improvement, $15 billion; spending cuts, $5 billion; debt service, $2 billion. The point is, out of a $113 billion drop in the deficit, only $5 billion of that is a result of the actions taken to cut Federal spending." (pS3588)

Mack, Connie (Sen.-Fla.). "Congressional Budget Concurrent Resolution," Congressional Record (24 Mar 1994). Daily ed. pS3586-3599. (ISSN0363-7239).

"In 1981, President Carter submitted a budget to Congress of a $34 billion deficit. Congress when it got through with that budget, gave us a deficit of $79 billion, a full $44 billion more than what the President had recommended. In fiscal 1982, President Carter submitted a budget recommending the deficit of $46 billion, but Congress ended up appropriating, taxing to a deficit of $128 billion. In 1983, President Reagan submitted a budget recommending the deficit of $107 billion, but a reluctant Congress gave him a deficit of almost twice that much, $208 billion. In 1984, President Reagan recommended a deficit of $203 billion, and it came in a little bit less in actual terms, a remarkable achievement primarily attributed to the remarkable turnaround." (pS3889)

Brown, Hank (Sen.-Colo.). "Ron Speed," Congressional Record (25 Mar 1994). Daily ed. pS3885-3892. (ISSN0363-7239).

"The Federal Government has been operating at a deficit since 1961. Since then, the problem has grown worse, culminating in the huge budget deficits over the past decade. In fiscal year 1989, the deficit was $152.5 billion. The President's budget request for fiscal year 1995 projects a deficit of $165.1 billion compared to the $234.7 billion recorded for fiscal year 1994....However, we must recognize that although it is below the fiscal year 1994 deficit total, the Congressional Budget Office estimates that the deficit will be above $200 billion by 1999 unless prompt action is taken. Further, it is important to understand that our Nation's debt continues to increase. Under President Clinton's budget proposal the Nation's debt is projected to increase from $4.6 trillion in fiscal year 1994 to $6.27 trillion by fiscal year 1999." (pS2003)

Specter, Arlen (Sen.-Pa.). "Balanced Budget Amendment," Congressional Record (28 Feb 1994). Daily ed. pS1964-2015. (ISSN0363-7239).

"As recently as 1976, the last year of President Ford's administration, the total amount of net interest payments by the Federal Government was $26.7 billion. This year, we will pay an interest on the national debt of $212.8 billion....75 percent of that $212.8 billion has been accumulated in the last 13 years. We have been on a deficit frenzy, a collapse of fiscal responsibility in the last 13 years, the likes of which this Nation has never experienced. That frenzy has placed a straitjacket on our future generations." (pS1217)

Graham, Bob (Sen.-Fla.). "Emergency Supplemental Appropriations Act for Fiscal Year 1994," Congressional Record (9 Feb 1994). Daily ed. pS1201-1229. (ISSN0363-7239).

"Last year Congress enacted a comprehensive economic recovery plan designed to reduce the Federal budget deficit and lay the groundwork for economic growth. Today, we see the fruits of that difficult effort. There is a new vigor in the economy and the prospects are strong for long-term sustained growth. In 1993, 1.6 million private-sector jobs were created--more than the previous 4 years combined. Solid economic advances were recorded across the board. A year ago, the deficit for 1995 was projected at $302 billion. Today, the forecast is for $176 billion. In fact, from 1994 through 1998, there is a 40 percent drop in the projected deficit numbers. Measured as a percentage of Gross Domestic Product, the 1996 deficit falls to 2.3 percent--the lowest share since 1979." (pS1243)

Sasser, Jim (Sen.-Tenn.). "Unanimous Consent Agreement," Congressional Record (9 Feb 1994). Daily ed. pS1229-1251. (ISSN0363-7239).

"The influence of the Jeffersonian philosophy is illustrated in the fact that...in February of 1885, in the immediate aftermath of the Civil War--the total debt that the...[U.S.] had accumulated over the first almost century since the adoption of the Constitution, was $1.6 billion, most of which had been accumulated during the Civil War. That $1.6 billion is about what we have added to the national debt since we convened here 2 days ago. It took 100 years to do what we are now doing in approximately every 48 hours." (pS1219)

Graham, Bob (Sen.-Fla.). "Emergency Supplemental Appropriations Act for Fiscal Year 1994," Congressional Record (9 Feb 1994). Daily ed. pS1201-1229. (ISSN0363-7239).

"America no longer needs to rely on foreigners to finance its budget deficit, for during the 1990s the deficit has fallen and domestic savings have become available. Edward Hyman, chairman of New York-based International Strategy and Investment, says that borrowing by government, companies and consumers rose by more than $900 billion a year in the mid-1980s. In 1993, however, it increased by only $575 billion. Meanwhile, their saving has risen from $600 billion a year in the mid-1980s to around $800 billion last year, resulting in net saving of about $225 billion....Mr Hyman reckons that underlying inflation will be 2% this year, which means that a 30-year bond offers a respectable real yield of 4.5%." (p74)

"Finance: Debunking the Yellow Peril." Economist v330 n7852, 26 Feb 1994. p74. (ISSN0013-0613).

"At the beginning of fiscal 1994, the gross national debt stood at $4.4 trillion, and was projected to grow an additional $311 billion this year. Net interest on the national debt reached $198 billion last year, making it the third largest program in the budget--after Social Security and defense. And Congress isn't even close to controlling the problem. The projected budget deficit for fiscal 1994 is $253 billion, not including the costs of the Clinton health plan, which Harvard economist Martin Feldstein says could increase deficits as much as $120 billion per year." (p31)

Hewitt, Paul. "Fair Comment: Entitlements for the Elderly Drive Deficits." Insight v10 n6, 7 Feb 1994. p31. (ISSN1051-4880).

"President Clinton's budget plan adopted by Congress will increase the total national debt--now $4.3 trillion--by another $1 trillion in five years. This is because the 'deficit reduction' in the plan doesn't eliminate annual budget deficits; the 'reduction' only means they won't be as big as they would have been without the planned spending cuts and tax increases. But even the inadequate $496 billion savings Clinton hopes for may prove difficult to achieve. It assumes economic growth rates over the next five years that the economy isn't close to reaching currently. If the economy grows just 1% less than the administration projects each of those five years, the entire budget savings will disappear due to lower tax revenues and higher expenditures for social benefits than now anticipated." (p1)

Chapman, Jonathan. "Clinton Continues His Betrayal!" New Patriot v6 n5, Sep-Oct 1993. p1.

"True, last year's budget deal was designed to save $500 billion over the next five years (with the 'savings' calculated as reductions from a sharply rising projection of deficits), and it is projected to reduce the annual deficit from 4.0 percent of the Gross Domestic Product (GDP) in 1993 to 2.2 percent in 1998. Seen from a different angle, however, the prospect for the deficit during the 1990s doesn't look so bright. Even with the recent improvement, the money borrowed by the US Treasury to finance our deficits will still siphon off nearly half of all net savings made by US businesses and households--a far greater share of savings than deficits typically consume in any other industrial nation." (p39)

Peterson, Peter G. "Entitlement Reform: The Way to Eliminate the Deficit." New York Review of Books v41 n7, 7 Apr 1994. p39-47. (ISSN0028-7504).

"A year ago, it seemed likely that the record-high 1992 [U.S. budget] deficit of $290 billion would be eclipsed in 1993, with deficits in succeeding years near or above that level. Instead, the 1993 deficit came in at $255 billion, and the combination of OBRA-93 [Omnibus Budget Reconciliation Act of 1993] and continued economic growth keeps currently projected deficits well below $300 billion through the end of the century....As a percentage of GDP [gross domestic product], deficits dip to 2.2 percent (compared with the 1984-1993 average of 4.2 percent) before beginning to climb slowly in 1999." (pxvi)

U.S. Congressional Budget Office. "Summary." The Economic and Budget Outlook: Fiscal Years 1995-1999 Jan 1994. Washington, D.C.: GPO, 1994.

BUDGET DEFICITS--U.S.--FORECASTING

President "Clinton's budget for fiscal 1995 will project a deficit of roughly $178 billion--a dramatic improvement over the $230 billion shortfall that administration economists predicted just one year ago. Clinton will propose freezing or cutting budgets at 10 of 14 cabinet agencies and eliminating perhaps 115 separate federal programs. But he wants to redeploy the savings to federal 'investments,' such as Head Start and worker training, rather than pressing for deeper deficit reduction....In its widely watched annual economic forecast, the Congressional Budget Office said last month that the federal deficit came in at $255 billion last year--fully $55 billion less than the agency predicted just one year ago--and will continue shrinking gradually until 1996. The yield on a 10-year Treasury note averaged just 5.9 percent in 1993, compared with the 6.7 percent forecast by CBO one year ago, and consumer inflation moderated to 2.7 percent, down from the 3 percent that CBO had predicted." (p39)

Hage, David. "Business: Like a Rolling Stone." U.S. News & World Report v116 n6, 14 Feb 1994. p38-40. (ISSN0041-5537).

BUFFALO

see BISON

BUILDING INDUSTRY
see CONSTRUCTION INDUSTRY
BUILDING MATERIALS--U.S.--COSTS (v19)
BULGARIA. NAVY
"The Bulgarian Navy is in the process of reform....Presently, professionals make up 56% of the Navy; in the future, 65% of our sailors will be professionals....We have decommissioned 36 surface combatants--including two frigates, two submarines, and six fast torpedo boats. In the future, the Navy will have approximately 52 combat units--including 2 or 3 frigates, 8 corvettes, 2 or 3 submarines, 10 fast missile boats, and a number of minesweepers and minelayers." (p42)
Velkov, Ventseslav. "The Commanders Respond." Proceedings v120 n3, Mar 1994. p34-43. (ISSN0041-798X).
BULIMIA--U.S. (v19)
BULLDOZERS
"Komatsu, Ltd. (Komatsu Seisakusho), was incorporated in 1921 to carry on the work of a parent company founded in 1884. Komatsu produced Japan's first tractor in 1931 and built the country's first bulldozer in 1943. Now the world's second-largest diversified construction-machine builder, with 26,000 employees, bulldozers remain Komatsu's main product. The corporation exports machinery to more than 150 countries. Net sales in 1981 were Y567.4 billion ($2.6 billion at 1981 rates). In 1992, Standard & Poor's set Komatsu Ltd.'s net sales at Y919.7 billion ($8.5 billion at 1993 rates). In 1988, Komatsu merged with Dresser Industries, Inc., a $4.5 billion Dallas-based firm, to take the number two position in the $10 billion US earth-moving industry." (p18)
Smith, Gar. "Green War Profiteers." Earth Island Journal v8 n4, Fall 1993. p18-19. (ISSN1041-0406).
"Six billion dollars of Caterpillar's 1990 revenue came from overseas sales. The company boasts a global network of 215 independent dealers and more than 1200 stores and branches in 150 countries. Caterpillar employs more than 50,000 people worldwide and maintains 15 factories outside the US (in Brazil, the UK, Australia, France, Belgium, Italy, Indonesia and Mexico). Caterpillar's 22 domestic factories employ 18,500 workers and account for $3.4 billion in exports. In 1990, 'Cat' added nearly $2 billion to the US trade balance." (p18)
Smith, Gar. "Green War Profiteers." Earth Island Journal v8 n4, Fall 1993. p18-19. (ISSN1041-0406).
BUMPERS, AUTOMOBILE
see AUTOMOBILES--BUMPERS
BURGLARY--U.S.
"The latest [U.S.] victimization survey estimates that robbers strike 1.2 million times each year, injuring their prey a third of the time. Unlike most other violent crimes like murder, rape and assault, in which the assailant more often than not knows the victim, an estimated 84 percent of robberies are committed by strangers. Still, the national robbery rate has declined since a peak in 1981, and most encounters do not end in violence: One in 20 cases results in both serious injury and lost property." (p27)
Gest, Ted/others. "U.S. News: Violence in America." U.S. News & World Report v116 n2, 17 Jan 1994. p22-24,26-27,30,32-33. (ISSN0041-5537).
BURUNDI--HISTORY--CIVIL WAR
"Rivers clogged by bodies with their hands bound, locked rooms crowded with the charred corpses of schoolboys, homes left eerily empty. These are some of the nightmarish images of life in Burundi since the October 21 assassination of newly elected President Melchior Ndadaye. The roads, observers say, are lined with armed camps of soldiers and civilians; burning villages illuminate the night. Estimates of the death toll far exceed those of the 1972 military rampage that left 150,000 civilians dead in two weeks and made close to a million people refugees....After more than two months of killing, no one denies that the conflict has degenerated into violence between enclaves of the two largest tribal groups, Hutus and Tutsis. Ndadaye was the country's first president from the Hutu tribe--85 percent of Burundi's 5.6 million citizens--and its only democratically elected leader. The minority Tutsis had ruled Burundi since independence from Belgium in 1962....More threatened than either ethnic group by Ndadaye was the military, which is over 90 percent Tutsi but, more significant, had seen its power waning after a civilian congress replaced the military ruling committee as Burundi's legislative body in 1988." (p41)
Sharlett, Jeff. "Burundi Bleeds." Nation v258 n2, 17 Jan 1994. p41. (ISSN0027-8378).
BUS DRIVERS--DRUG TESTING--U.S.
Regulations for drug and alcohol testing of school bus drivers were published in the FEDERAL REGISTER on February 15, 1994. "The trade journal SCHOOL BUS FLEET surveyed about 140 school-bus contractors [in the U.S.] in 1992 and found that 54 percent used pre-employment drug testing, 46 percent had random drug tests, and 49 percent tested drivers after accidents....A separate 1992 SCHOOL BUS FLEET survey of 100 school districts found that 58 percent had implemented pre-employment drug testing, but only 9 percent used random testing, and only 15 percent tested drivers after accidents." (p8)
Schmidt, Peter. "Rules Mandate Drug Testing for Bus Drivers." Education Week v13 n22, 23 Feb 1994. p1,8. (ISSN0277-4232).
BUS LINES--U.S.
"Greyhound dominates the provision of regular route intercity bus service. GAO recently reported that, as of December 1991, Greyhound represented about 75 percent of intercity bus revenues and 43 percent of passengers. It served about 2,700 of the 5,690 locations then receiving bus service, and another 600 or so communities in 20 states were served by the 73 local transit providers participating in Greyhound's Rural Connection Program, which is now called its Rural Van Service." (p241)
McDonald, Gail C. (Chair, Interstate Commerce Commission). U.S. House. Committee on Appropriations. "Department of Transportation and Related Agencies Approp. for 1994 (Part 5)." Hearing, Washington, D.C.: GPO, 1993. (ISBN0160410509). (Y4.Ap6/1:T68/4/994/pt.5).
"Regular route bus service has long represented a small, declining, and relatively unprofitable share of intercity passenger travel [in the U.S.]. Shrinking rural populations, increased competition from air and (heavily subsidized) rail transportation, and increased car ownership have led to continuing losses in bus ridership and to reductions in bus service. Over 16,000 locations received bus service in 1968, over 14,000 in 1977, and 11,280 in 1982. The General Accounting Office recently reported the number of locations receiving bus service had fallen to about 5,700 in 1991, and to only 5,160 by January 1993. Most of the lost service has been in rural areas." (p240)
McDonald, Gail C. (Chair, Interstate Commerce Commission). U.S. House. Committee on Appropriations. "Department of Transportation and Related Agencies Approp. for 1994 (Part 5)." Hearing, Washington, D.C.: GPO, 1993. (ISBN0160410509). (Y4.Ap6/1:T68/4/994/pt.5).
BUSINESS AND GOVERNMENT
see INDUSTRY AND STATE
BUSINESS CORPORATIONS
see CORPORATIONS
BUSINESS EDUCATION--U.S.
"At business schools from Wharton to Berkeley, a new kind of MBA is emerging: one with dirty--and sometimes wet--hands. By

combining courses from engineering, computer science, and business schools into one curriculum, some of America's top universities are producing corporate triathletes. These are managers made to order for the new horizontal corporation--people who not only understand the basics of marketing, accounting, and finance but also have a feel for computers and the other technologies that help companies deliver their products or services. Call them techno-MBAs. Right now, they number only about 3,000 of the 75,000 MBAs who graduate each year. But corporate recruiters are gobbling them up at such a rate that B-schools are rapidly adding computer and engineering courses to their core curriculums. 'We're dissolving the boundaries between marketing and manufacturing,' says James I. Cash, chairman of Harvard University's MBA program. Actually, engineers have long pursued MBAs--traditionally making up 15% to 25% of most B-school classes." (p71) "At Texas, where 25% of 400 new MBAs left school last spring without a job, the 25 graduates of the B-school's Informational Systems Management program averaged 3.5 offers each, most of them in the $50,000 range." (p72)

Baker, Stephen/McWilliams, Gary. "Science & Technology: Education: Now Comes the Corporate Triathlete." Business Week n3356, 31 Jan 1994. p71-72. (ISSN0007-7135).

"Over the past 5 years, the U.S. public has become increasingly aware of the importance of international trade because of the break-up of the Soviet Union and the subsequent attempts of their republics to convert to free-market economies. Furthermore, the political debates about the North American Free Trade Agreement (NAFTA) have further sensitized U.S. citizens to the increasing importance of global trade. Any college student graduating today who has not been exposed to international perspectives has been miseducated. It is even more so for a student majoring in business. In a recent comprehensive survey of 374 U.S. business schools conducted by the American Assembly of Collegiate Schools of Business (AACSB), nearly 80% reported that they were without a clearly defined approach to international education. Only 13% of these business schools' faculty had advanced expertise, and more than half had little or no international experience at all (NEWSLINE, 1993, p. 10)." (p199-200)

Ahmed, Zafar V./Krohn, Franklin B. "The Symbiosis of Liberal Arts and International Business." Journal of Education for Business v69 n4, Mar-Apr 1994. p199-203. (ISSN0883-2323).

BUSINESS ENTERPRISES--CALIFORNIA (v19)

BUSINESS ENTERPRISES--CHILE (v19)

BUSINESS ENTERPRISES--HUNGARY (v19)

BUSINESS ENTERPRISES--INDONESIA (v19)

BUSINESS ENTERPRISES--ISRAEL

"Israel's is a small economy, designed by socialists and cut off from neighbors. It is therefore highly centralised, and still highly taxed. The government owns about 150 companies, some 80 of which it deems to be 'business-oriented'. The public sector is large: in 1991 state-owned firms produced nearly a fifth of GDP [gross domestic product] and a similar proportion of exports. Ever since the stabilisation plan, successive governments have been committed, on paper, to a programme of privatisation. More than 20 companies are considered near-term candidates for sale. But progress has been excruciatingly slow." (p15)

"Survey: Israel: Milk and Honey." Economist v330 n7847, 22 Jan 1994. p58(15-16,19). (ISSN0013-0613).

BUSINESS ENTERPRISES--JAPAN--U.S.

"According to a September 1992 JETRO (Japan External Trade Organization) survey, employment of US locals at Japanese manufacturing plants far exceeds 400,000....There are Japanese factories in Puerto Rico and all US states except North Dakota. These Japanese manufacturers in the US helped develop the US export market. Japanese companies that exported their products from the US abroad increased to 66.4% from 61.8% in the previous year. More than 40% of Japanese manufacturers in the US exported to Japan. Localization of Japanese plants in the US has been accelerating. 63.5% of companies now have a local-procurement ratio (of equipment and parts) of over 70%, and show a steady annual increase. The number of Japanese personnel per factory has accordingly decreased every year: 8.4 persons in 1990, 6.9 in 1991, and 6.2 in 1992, promoting a transfer of power to local staff." (p5)

Nishimura, Kunio. "Cover Story: Japan and US States: Let's Get Closer." Look Japan v39 n454, Jan 1994. p4-7. (ISSN0456-5339).

BUSINESS ENTERPRISES--MICHIGAN (v19)

BUSINESS ENTERPRISES--MINNESOTA--PENNSYLVANIA--WISCONSIN (v19)

BUSINESS ENTERPRISES--SOUTH AFRICA

"Entrenched by 40 years of apartheid law, the white 14% of South Africa's population owns almost 90% of the country's land and probably 90% of formal businesses. Run a finger down a register of the 100 biggest companies and you will find only 40 black directors among them. Publicly listed companies produce roughly half of South Africa's GDP [gross domestic product], which was $114 billion last year; almost 90% of those listed companies are in turn controlled by just six groups, a centralisation encouraged by political and economic isolation." (p19)

"Business in South Africa." Economist v329 n7842, 18 Dec 1993. p19-21. (ISSN0013-0613).

Roland Pearson Jr. "is executive director of Ebony Development Alternatives Ltd. (EDA), a brand-new firm based in Johannesburg. EDA is an enterprise development corporation; it specializes in helping new black-owned businesses gain access to management and planning services, as well as bank financing....Although whites make up only 13 percent of the total population, they control most business activity, as well as 55 percent of the nation's wealth. White-controlled national holding companies, for example, comprise about 1 percent of the total number of business entities in South Africa, yet account for 80 percent of all trading activity on the Johannesburg Stock Exchange....About 42 percent of the black population is younger than age 14, compared with only 25 percent of the white population. And the population growth rate for blacks is 2.85 percent, compared with 0.8 percent for whites. 'Black unemployment already runs around 40 percent; underemployment is estimated at 50 percent,' Pearson says. According to the South African Reserve Bank, the South African economy now produces only seven jobs for every 100 new job seekers." (p10)

Halverson, Guy. "Economy: US Consultant Aims to Boost Black-Held Firms in S. Africa." The Christian Science Monitor v86 n58, 16 Feb 1994. p10. (ISSN0882-7729).

BUSINESS ENTERPRISES--TAXATION--U.S. (v19)

BUSINESS ENTERPRISES--TEXAS (v19)

BUSINESS ENTERPRISES--U.S. (v19)

"In 1991, the number of small businesses [in the U.S.] with fewer than 10 employees grew 0.6 percent over the year before. Those with 10 to 100 workers declined 0.2 percent, and those with more than 100 workers declined 1.7 percent, according to the Census Bureau's '1991 County Business Patterns.' This may be a reversal of recent trends. Between 1987 and 1990, large businesses grew three times faster than smaller firms....Big business isn't gone yet. Firms with fewer than 10 employees represent three-quarters of the more than 6 million businesses in the report, but they employ only 15 percent of the nation's 93 million workers. Companies with 100 employees or more are just 2 percent of businesses but 44 percent of workers." (p15)

Dunn, William. "Business Reports: Markets: Small Business Takes a Licking and Keeps on Growing." American Demographics v16 n1, Jan 1994. p14-15. (ISSN0163-4089).

BUSINESS ENTERPRISES--U.S.--FINANCE (v19)

BUSINESS ENTERPRISES, FOREIGN--JAPAN (v19)

BUSINESS ENTERPRISES, FOREIGN--U.S.

"Foreign-owned U.S. companies contribute substantially to the productivity of the U.S. economy. According to a recent Bureau of Labor Statistics study, over 1.7 million U.S. manufacturing jobs had been created with foreign equity by 1989, nearly 1 in every 11 manufacturing jobs." (p87)

U.S. Senate. Committee on Finance. "United States-Japan Trade Negotiations." Hearing, 8 Nov 1993. Washington, D.C.: GPO, 1994. (ISBN0160435625). (Y4.F49:S.hrg.103-399).

BUSINESS ETHICS--U.S.

"It is no secret that businesses and the people who manage them have received low marks for their ethical decisions and behavior through the years. There have been many major events and issues to encourage the formation of negative opinions. Consider the Bhopal tragedy in India, the Alaskan oil spill, the asbestos crises, insider security trading scandals, gas tank controversies with two major automobile builders, and leveraged buyouts and hostile takeovers with subsequent layoffs and downsizing, just to mention a few....In most studies done to identify the level of trust the general population has in big business, less than one third of the participants showed that they have a high level of confidence in the ethical performance of big business." (p145) "Most students and graduates agree that business ethics should be taught in universities. In one study of business graduates who had been out of school for a few years, 92% agreed that business instructors should emphasize ethics in their courses. The same 92% believed that business professors' actions are one of the most important factors influencing the students' development of ethical values. Only 1% of the recent graduates, however, believed that their instruction in ethics had been excellent (David, Anderson, & Lawrimore, 1990)." (p146)

Stevens, Robert E./others. "Evaluations of Ethical Situations by University Faculty: A Comparative Study." Journal of Education for Business v69 n3, Jan-Feb 1994. p145-148. (ISSN0883-2323).

BUSINESS INTELLIGENCE--U.S. (v19)

BUSINESSMEN--JAPAN (v19)

BUSINESSWOMEN

see WOMEN IN BUSINESS

BUTTER TRADE--EUROPEAN ECONOMIC COMMUNITY (v19)

BUTTERFLIES

"Every day in craft factories in Taiwan, hundreds of workers pull the wings off butterflies supplied by collectors, glue them to paper bodies, and stick on pig-bristle antennae. The real bodies (perhaps some 50 million a year) become pig feed, and the new creations end up as part of Taiwan's low-quality, high-volume market for ornamental novelties such as table coasters, serving trays, and plastic toilet seats. Meanwhile, in Papua New Guinea, where insect conservation is part of the national constitution, butterfly farmers carefully cultivate perfect specimens to supply a low-volume trade to museums, entomologists, private collectors, and students. The world's butterfly numbers are shrinking. But collectors are not the easy scapegoats you might think, and farming is not the final word in butterfly conservation." (p60)

Hay, Deborah. "Net Losses." Wildlife Conservation v96 n5, Sep-Oct 1993. p60. (ISSN1048-4949).

CABLE TELEVISION--AFRO-AMERICANS

"When NABOB [National Association of Black Owned Broadcasters] was founded in 1976, African Americans owned approximately 30 radio stations, and only one television station. This represented substantially less than 1% of the stations then operating in the U.S. Today, African Americans own approximately 182 radio stations and 20 commercial television stations and one cable programming network. Despite the increase over 1976 numbers, minority ownership represents under 2% of all stations operating today. Television is clearly the most powerful medium which has ever existed for shaping ideas, views, public opinion, and self image. For African Americans this medium has always been one which has created and continues to create negative stereotypes." (p54)

Sutton, Pierre M. (Chair, National Association of Black Owned Broadcasters, Inc.). U.S. House. Committee on Energy and Commerce. "Cable Television Rates." Hearing, 28 Sep 1993. Washington, D.C.: GPO, 1994. (ISBN0160440238). (Y4.En2/3:103-69).

CABLE TELEVISION--EUROPE (v19)

CABLE TELEVISION--U.S.

"Many cable operators demanded that local governments grant them a monopoly and bar all competitors from offering cable services in the franchise area. The result was that more than 99 percent of Americans have only one choice of cable operator today. The 1992 Cable Act made that illegal....Clearly, competition is a better solution than regulation to the existence of monopolies. But, as...virtually every cable subscriber in America knows, until competition takes hold, consumers need protection....Let us review briefly what was happening to consumers who had only one cable operator in their own hometown: In reports conducted by the General Accounting Office in 1989, 1990 and 1991...cable price increases were, on average, three times the rate of inflation. In the three years following deregulation in 1986, 80 percent of subscribers for both the basic tier and the most popular tier of service, received increases of more than 20 percent. Almost half of subscribers to both of these services received increases of more than 40 percent. Inflation during this period, as measured by the Consumer Price Index, was approximately 4.5 percent per year....The GAO again reported...that in the period between December of 1989 to April of 1991 more than 66 percent of subscribers to basic services received an increase above 10 percent." (p1-2)

Markey, Edward J. (Rep.-Mass.). U.S. House. Committee on Energy and Commerce. "Cable Television Rates." Hearing, 28 Sep 1993. Washington, D.C.: GPO, 1994. (ISBN0160440238). (Y4.En2/3:103-69).

"Over the years, many studies were completed in an effort to document the difference between prices for competitive and noncompetitive systems. A Consumers' Research study of 52 separate markets in 1990 found that in areas where only one cable company existed, fewer channels were provided on average (33 vs. 40) and the cost per channel was 33 percent higher (52 cents per channel vs. 35 cents per channel) than in areas with competition. The Wireless Cable Association reported that cable rates in the 110 localities where microwave distribution systems existed were an average of 30 percent lower than in areas where cable companies were monopolies. Finally, an August 1991 Department of Justice study found that up to 50 percent of cable's basic rate increases since deregulation reflect monopoly power to charge above-competitive prices and were not reasonable." (p5)

U.S. House. Committee on Energy and Commerce. "Cable Television Rates." Hearing, 28 Sep 1993. Washington, D.C.: GPO, 1994. (ISBN0160440238). (Y4.En2/3:103-69).

"America's cable TV customers should have an extra $3 billion jingling in their pockets after the latest action by the Federal Communications Commission. The FCC, responding to pressure from the public and Congress, voted 3-to-0 to reduce cable television rates by an average of 7 percent. That comes atop a 10 percent cut ordered last year. Chairman Reed Hundt claimed the FCC action would bring about one of the largest savings for consumers in the history of regulation. The commission's action was a delicate balancing act. The nation's 57 million cable customers have endured significant price increases in recent years. But the industry insists it needs the higher rates to pay for rapid expansion and greater services....The National Cable Television Association claims its operating companies have already lost $2 billion since the first FCC pricing regulation went into effect in September 1993. A study by the FCC found that its first order cut the average monthly bill for cable TV from $25.61 to $24.11, a drop of 5.9 percent. Those figures do not include premium services like HBO and Showtime, which are not regulated." (p3)

Dillin, John. "National: FCC Reins In Cable TV Rates." The Christian Science Monitor v86 n63, 24 Feb 1994. p3. (ISSN0882-7729).

CALI (COLOMBIA)--INDUSTRIES

"Cali...[is the] capital of the fertile Cauca Valley in western Colombia. Its local cartel has in recent years taken over world domination of the cocaine trade. Experts say the Cali cartel supplies 80% of drugs flowing into the United States, and largely controls a growing trade to Europe--via a Sicilian Mafia network in Venezuela--that is now put at 300 tonnes a year....With 1.6m people, Cali is Colombia's third city, and booming. Nowhere has benefited more from the government's economic opening up. Cali is only two hours from the port of Buenaventura on the Pacific coast, the fastest way to Asia and many South American markets. Beside the old sugar, fruit and coffee industries, some 40 multinational firms operate in the area. Cali accounts for 40% of Colombia's industrial output and is home to 17 of the country's leading 100 companies." (p58)

"International: Colombia: Cali High." Economist v329 n7843, 25 Dec 1993. p58. (ISSN0013-0613).

CALIFORNIA

see also ADVERTISING--CIGARETTE INDUSTRY--CALIFORNIA--YOUTH; AFRO-AMERICAN FARMERS--CALIFORNIA--FLORIDA; AGRICULTURAL PESTS--CALIFORNIA; AGRICULTURE--CALIFORNIA; ALIENS, ILLEGAL--CALIFORNIA; CIGARETTE HABIT--CALIFORNIA; CIVIL SERVICE--CALIFORNIA; COMPUTER INDUSTRY--CALIFORNIA; CRIMINALS--CALIFORNIA; EARTHQUAKES--CALIFORNIA; EDUCATION--CALIFORNIA; ENDANGERED SPECIES--CALIFORNIA; ENERGY CONSUMPTION--CALIFORNIA; ENVIRONMENTAL PROTECTION--CALIFORNIA; FIREARMS--CALIFORNIA; FIRES--CALIFORNIA; HOSPITALS--CALIFORNIA; HOUSING--CALIFORNIA; IMMIGRANTS--CALIFORNIA; INFRASTRUCTURE (ECONOMICS)--CALIFORNIA; MEDICAL CARE--CALIFORNIA; MEDICINE--RESEARCH--CALIFORNIA; MIGRATION, INTERNAL--CALIFORNIA; NATIONAL PARKS AND RESERVES--CALIFORNIA; NUCLEAR POWER PLANTS--CALIFORNIA; PEDIATRIC TOXICOLOGY--CALIFORNIA; PRISONS--CALIFIORNIA; PUBLIC WELFARE--CALIFORNIA; TRANSPORTATION--CALIFORNIA; UNEMPLOYMENT--CALIFORNIA; WATER-SUPPLY--CALIFORNIA; WETLANDS--CALIFORNIA; WILDLIFE CONSERVATION--CALIFORNIA

CALIFORNIA--COMMERCE (v19)

CALIFORNIA--COMMERCE--MEXICO (v19)

CALIFORNIA--ECONOMIC CONDITIONS (v19)

"Southern California is one area where community and business interests together are jumping information hurdles (see Action Alert, p. 5) to make conversion happen. The region has lost 250,000 defense jobs since 1987, and 71,000 in the aerospace sector alone since 1989. With these lay-offs of skilled workers, many large manufacturing facilities have been idled. With no conversion programs in place until recently, the state's economy has been devastated. Over the next several years, further defense reductions could cost the state an additional 420,000 jobs and $85 billion in personal income." (p4)

"TRP Goals Are Too Narrow and the Funding Too Little to Really Make a Difference for Calstart." CEP Research Report Aug 1993. p4. (ISSN0898-4328).

"If California were a country, local politicians like to point out, it would have the seventh largest economy in the world. But that economy may not be eternally resilient. The seven-year drought in the Central Valley cost farmers roughly $1.7 billion. The three days of rioting in 1992 cost 57 lives and $1 billion in destroyed property. Last summer brush fires devoured nearly 1,000 homes in some of the richest enclaves in America. All the while the re-engineering of America's post-cold war economy drained California of 202,000 aerospace jobs, plunging the state into the country's most stubborn recession and lifting unemployment up near 10%. During his three years in office, Governor Wilson has issued 27 declarations of emergency covering 56 of the state's 58 counties." (p34-35)

Gibbs, Nancy. "California: Aftershock." Time v143 n5, 31 Jan 1994. p26-37. (ISSN0040-781X).

CALIFORNIA--EMPLOYMENT (v19)

"In both the United States and Canada, we have lost jobs. Over 1.5 million people have lost manufacturing jobs in the United States and are forced into low paying service jobs or unemployment. Watsonville, once the nation's 'frozen food capitol,' has lost 2,000 food processing jobs, or about half of the work force that existed in 1979 when there were seven frozen food plants in the community. It is said that Dean Foods, the owner of one of the last Watsonville plants, Shaw Frozen Foods, is looking for a location in Mexico. In California, more than half of the frozen food firms have gone to Mexico in the last decade, as have 16,000 jobs. Now more than 40% of the frozen vegetables that we eat are imported, almost all from the US firms in Mexico." (p6)

Brough, Maria. "North American Free Trade Agreement: Guess Who Pays?" Program & Legislative Action Apr-May 1993. p6-7.

CALIFORNIA--EMPLOYMENT--MANUFACTURES (v19)

CALIFORNIA--MANUFACTURES (v19)

CALIFORNIA--PENNSYLVANIA--POPULATION (v19)

CALIFORNIA--POLITICS AND GOVERNMENT (v19)

"Even though whites in California are a fast-shrinking majority, they enjoy a virtual electoral apartheid. Whites are now less than 55 percent of California's population (down from 67 percent in 1980), Latinos 27 percent, Asians less than 10 percent, blacks 7 percent. But in the 1992 presidential election, 82 percent of the voters were white, 7 percent Latino, 3 percent Asian, and 6 percent black, according to a LOS ANGELES TIMES survey. Ethnic leaders say the low turnout is due largely to the view in Mexico and most Asian nations that government is corrupt, even dangerous, and something to be shunned. Many Latinos and Asians are culturally separate enough to believe that the same is true here. And, politicians also have not courted their votes." (p22)

Maharidge, Dale. "Can We All Get Along?" Mother Jones v18 n6, Nov-Dec 1993. p20-27. (ISSN0362-8841).

CALIFORNIA--POPULATION (v19)

"California is the fastest growing state in the U.S. Although the country's population as a whole increased by 10 percent during the past decade, California's grew by an explosive 30 percent....Fueling this rapid growth is a fertility rate of 2.5 children per family and a large immigrant population. About 40 percent of legal immigrants and an estimated 50 percent of illegal immigrants settle in California. All told, 800,000 more people are added to the state's population each year." (p17)

Hren, Ben/Bartolomeo, Nick. "Special Report: Carrying Capacity Project: After the Rush." Outdoor America v59 n1, Win 1994. p15-22.

"While [California's] population as a whole has grown only 4.9 percent since 1990, the number of preschoolers has jumped 14.4 percent--the second highest rate in the country (behind Nevada). Some 9.1 percent of the state's population is below five years of age, the third highest proportion in the country. Utah, the highest, has 9.7 percent." (p1) "Though births in California peaked in 1992, they continue at a rate of about 600,000 a year--creating a city the size of Boston annually. New births have accounted for most of the 2.8 million new infants and toddlers to arrive in the state since 1990." (p24)

Armstrong, Scott. "Classroom Alert: Baby Boomlet Has California State Officials Scrambling." The Christian Science Monitor v86 n80, 21 Mar 1994. p1,24. (ISSN0882-7729).

CAMBODIA

see also FORESTS AND FORESTRY--CAMBODIA; LOGGING--CAMBODIA; MINES (MILITARY EXPLOSIVES)--CAMBODIA; UNITED NATIONS--CAMBODIA; WEAPONS--CAMBODIA

CAMBODIA--ECONOMIC CONDITIONS

"Rebuilding the war-torn, mismanaged and corrupt Cambodian economy remains a distant dream. The influx of 22,000 peacekeepers and billions of UN dollars bloated the economy to unnatural levels and political in-fighting between Cambodian factions blocked development aid until after the elections. Agriculture is still held hostage by the millions of mines lacing the countryside. UNTAC's [United Nations Transitional Authority in Cambodia's] demining program is an utter flop: More than $10 million has been spent to remove only about 9000 mines, fewer than are now being laid by the still warring Khmer Rouge and government troops." (p17)

Coburn, Judith. "Good Intentions Gone Awry: The U.N. Leaves Cambodia." APF Reporter v16 n2, 1994. p15-20. (ISSN0913-4562).

CAMPAIGN FUNDS--U.S.

"The overall amount of campaign finances reported to and regulated by the [Federal Election] Commission continues to increase. The total disbursements for Federal candidates in 1992, the last Presidential election cycle, are expected to finally total about $1.75 billion. Because most of the growth from 1990 to 1992 was in the congressional elections area, we are projecting at least $1.75 billion in federal campaign finance activity reportable to the FEC for the 1994 cycle. This would represent approximately a 60% increase from 1990." (p620-621)

Potter, Trevor (Vice Chairman, Federal Election Committee). U.S. House. Committee on Appropriations. "Treasury, Postal Service, and General Government Approp. for Fiscal Year 1994 (Part 4)." Hearing, Washington, D.C.: GPO, 1993. (ISBN0160407702). (Y4.Ap6/1:T71/994/pt.4).

CAMPAIGN FUNDS--U.S.--AGED

"Retiree contributors gave $8.1 million to GOP candidates and $5.9 million to Democrats, a 58-42 percent ratio. For all contributors of all ages, the ratio was reversed; Democrats got 56 percent of the funds, Republicans 44 percent." (p6)

Lewis, Robert. "Money Votes." AARP Bulletin v35 n1, Jan 1994. p6. (ISSN1044-1123).

CAMPAIGN FUNDS--U.S. CONGRESS (v19)

CANADA

see ABORTION--CANADA; AGED--CANADA; AGRICULTURAL SUBSIDIES--CANADA--U.S.; AIDS (DISEASE)--INDIANS OF NORTH AMERICA--CANADA; BISON--CANADA; BRAND NAME PRODUCTS--CANADA--GREAT BRITAIN--U.S.; BREAST--CANCER--CANADA; CIGARETTE INDUSTRY--CANADA; CIGARETTE TAX--CANADA; DEBTS, PUBLIC--CANADA; DOG INDUSTRY--CANADA--U.S.; EXPORTS--CANADA; HOCKEY--CANADA; IMMIGRANTS-AUSTRALIA--CANADA--GREAT BRITAIN--U.S.; INFLATION (FINANCE)--CANADA; LOBBYING--CANADA; MEDICAL CARE--CANADA; MUTUAL FUNDS--CANADA; NATURAL RESOURCES--CANADA--MEXICO--U.S.; NORTH AMERICAN FREE TRADE AGREEMENT--CANADA; RAIN FORESTS--CANADA; RECYCLING (WASTE, ETC.)--CANADA; SELF-EMPLOYED--CANADA--GREAT BRITAIN; SEXUAL HARASSMENT--CANADA--U.S.; TRADE-UNIONS--CANADA--U.S.--WOMEN; UNITED NATIONS--ARMED FORCES--CANADA; VOTING--CANADA--U.S.; WHEAT TRADE--CANADA; YOUTH--CANADA--U.S.

CANADA--COMMERCE--MEXICO (v19)

CANADA--COMMERCE--U.S. (v19)

CANADA--ECONOMIC CONDITIONS (v19)

CANADA--EMIGRATION AND IMMIGRATION (v19)

CANADA--EMPLOYMENT (v19)

CANADA--MANUFACTURES (v19)

CANADA--RELIGION (v19)

CANCER (v19)

see also BREAST--CANCER; LUNGS--CANCER--U.S.; MELANOMA; RESPIRATORY ORGANS--CANCER--U.S.

"In sub-Saharan Africa, with the exception of South Africa, there are fewer than 75 cancer specialists for a population of more than 300 million. Morphine is an essential drug in pain control, but there are at least 50 countries where the drug is not available. Twenty-seven of these countries are in Africa, and nine in the Americas. In developing countries, eight or nine out of every ten patients with incurable cancer do not receive efficient palliative care. At least 80 per cent of these patients are already incurable by the time their disease is diagnosed, but little effort and money is spent on their terminal care." (p1)

News release. "WHO Urges Better Palliative Care for the Terminally Ill." WHO Press 8 Feb 1994. p1.

CANCER--ARIZONA

"Right now there is a cancer cluster in Nogales, AZ. The specific cause is unknown at this time, but evidence points to chemical and heavy metal contaminants used in Mexican factories that flow down Nogales Wash from Mexico into Arizona. Mexico does not pretreat its industrial waste and the existing facility is unable to handle the amount of inflow. Citizens of Nogales are facing a cancer epidemic. A study by the University of Arizona Cancer Center found that Nogales has 4.8 times the expected average of mylow-ma (myeloma) cases, 1.6 times the leukemia cases and 4.5 times the lupus cases--the highest rate of lupus in the world. The exact cause of lupus is unknown, but one of the probable causes is exposure to toxic chemicals." (pS502)

DeConcini, Dennis (Sen.-Ariz.). "Foreign Relations Authorization Act," Congressional Record (1 Feb 1994). Daily ed. pS492-520. (ISSN0363-7239).

CANCER--FLORIDA (v19)

CANCER--JAPAN--MORTALITY

"As a potential cause of early death, cancer is public enemy number one. Its suppression is of paramount importance to all humankind. In Japan, cancer research has been subsidized since 1963 by the Ministry of Health and Welfare (MHW) and the Ministry of Education (MOE), but despite the amount of time and money spent and the remarkable advances made, the rate of death from cancer in Japan has continued to rise: in 1950 the rate was

77.4 per 100,000 population: in 1991 it was 181.7, with 223,727 people dying from the disease that year. Since 1981, cancer has been the leading cause of death in Japan." (p28)

Terada, Masaaki. "Sci-Tech Feature: Cancer: Research Intensifies." Look Japan v39 n455, Feb 1994. p28-29. (ISSN0456-5339).

CANCER--SCANDINAVIA

"Among men aged 35-74 the age-adjusted death rate [from malignant neoplasms] in Iceland rose by 29.0 percent, from 205.6 per 100,000 in 1980 to 265.2 per 100,000 in 1990." In Sweden and Norway, "death rates of 221.6 and 258.1 per 100,000 were recorded, respectively." In Finland, "the death rate declined by over 13 percent...." (p7)

Kranczer, Stanley. "International Cancer Mortality Comparisons." Statistical Bulletin v75 n1, Jan-Mar 1994. p2-10. (ISSN0790-8334).

CANCER--U.S. (v19)

"A National Cancer Institute (NCI) study found that [U.S.] farmers exposed to herbicides had a six times greater risk than nonfarmers of contracting one type of cancer. Another, just-released study found a link between breast cancer in women and elevated levels of DDE, a metabolite of the pesticide DDT, in their fat tissue. Research also indicates that children in homes where household and garden pesticides are used are seven times as likely to develop childhood leukemia." (p173-174)

Meyerhoff, Albert H. (Senior Attorney, Natural Resources Defense Council). U.S. House. Committee on Energy and Commerce/U.S. Senate. Committee on Labor and Human Resources. "Safety of Pesticides in Food." Hearing, 21 Sep 1993. Washington, D.C.: GPO, 1994. (ISBN0160434912). (Y4.En2/3:103-55).

"This year, more than 500,000 Americans will die from cancer. A million more will find that they have this pernicious disease. Meanwhile, the incidence of many forms of cancer is on the rise. Breast cancer in American women is epidemic, striking one in eight. Childhood cancer has increased 9.8 percent, just since 1950. In the same time period, the incidence of other forms of cancer has also increased, including bladder cancer (up 55.7 percent), testicular cancer (up 115 percent), skin cancer (up 321 percent), kidney cancer (up 109.4 percent) and non-Hodgkins lymphoma (up 158.6 percent). All new cancer cases combined have risen by 44.3 percent. New cancer cases, excluding lung cancer, have risen 29.9 percent." (p166)

Meyerhoff, Albert H. (Senior Attorney, Natural Resources Defense Council). U.S. House. Committee on Energy and Commerce/U.S. Senate. Committee on Labor and Human Resources. "Safety of Pesticides in Food." Hearing, 21 Sep 1993. Washington, D.C.: GPO, 1994. (ISBN0160434912). (Y4.En2/3:103-55).

"Regardless of the press and political 'stamp of approval' AIDS receives, the greatest malady on the face of the earth is cancer. Nearly 50% of the obituary notices in any area of 100,000 or more cite an age of 66 or less. Often, cancer is the killer. Almost all of these people are dying suddenly with no history of illness, or as a consequence of short term illness such as heart attacks, pneumonia, pulmonary dysfunction, and so on." (p19)

Walters, Charles. "Stray Carbon." Acres, U.S.A. Aug 1993. p18-19,39.

"It is estimated that more than 1 million new cases of cancer will have been diagnosed in the United States in 1993. Over 500,000 Americans died of cancer in 1991, with associated costs of $104 billion." (p2)

Frazao, Betsy. "Health Linked to Nutrition: The High Costs of Poor Diets." Food Review v17 n1, Jan-Apr 1994. p2-3.

"Cancer [in the U.S.] is currently the second leading cause of death; it is estimated that by the year 2000 it will become the primary cause of death. It is now more than two decades since the National Cancer Act was signed, yet the treatments offered to cancer patients are the same as those offered fifty years ago: surgery, radiation and chemotherapy (or slash, burn and poison, as they are called bitterly by both patients and increasingly disappointed professionals)....Extensive evidence exists to indicate that cancer is an environmental disease. Even the most conservative scientists agree that approximately 80 percent of all cancers are in some way related to environmental factors (Richard Doll and Richard Peto, The Causes of Cancer: Quantitative Estimates of Avoidable Risks of Cancer in the United States Today)....under current EPA regulations as many as 60 cancer-causing pesticides can legally be used in the most commonly eaten foods. Some of these foods are allowed to contain 20 or more carcinogens, making it impossible to measure how much of the substances a person actually consumes ('Presumed Innocent: a Report on 69 cancer-causing pesticides allowed in our foods,' by Rick Hind, and Jim Back, U.S. Public Interest Research Group, September 1990)." (p17)

Arditti, Rita/Schreiber, Tatiana. "Killing Us Quietly." New Directions for Women v22 n1, Jan-Feb 1993. p17-18,23-25. (ISSN0160-1075).

CANCER--U.S.--MORTALITY (v19)

"Examination of the age-adjusted mortality rates from cancer among [U.S.] men reveals that those for whites plateaued in the mid-1970s while those for all other races, after exhibiting indications of a sustained decline during the 1980s, again turned upward in 1989. In 1991 the cancer death rate for nonwhite men was 207.4 per 100,000 compared with 159.5 per 100,000 for white men; in sharp contrast, the rates among women were 121.2 and 111.2 per 100,000, respectively." (p4)

Kranczer, Stanley. "International Cancer Mortality Comparisons." Statistical Bulletin v75 n1, Jan-Mar 1994. p2-10. (ISSN0790-8334).

"In the United States the death rate from all cancers was 125.4 per 100,000 in 1950, slowly rose to 129.9 in 1970, to 132.8 in 1980, and to 135.0 per 100,000 in 1990. However, it is encouraging to note that the age-adjusted mortality rate declined to 134.5 per 100,000 in 1991 and is estimated to fall to 133.2 in 1992. Notwithstanding the recent encouraging, although small, decreases in age-adjusted rates, the absolute number of deaths from the nation's second leading cause of mortality continues to climb. In 1991, the last year for which final data are available, there were 514,657 cancer deaths, up from 505,322 in 1990; these compared to 422,702 deaths in 1980 and 335,558 in 1970. Moreover, deaths from cancer have been rising more rapidly than total deaths. As a result, mortality from cancer as a proportion of deaths from all causes jumped from 17.5 percent in 1970 to 21.2 percent in 1980, 23.5 percent in 1990 and 23.7 percent in 1991." (p2)

Kranczer, Stanley. "International Cancer Mortality Comparisons." Statistical Bulletin v75 n1, Jan-Mar 1994. p2-10. (ISSN0790-8334).

CANCER--U.S.--WOMEN (v19)

CAPITAL GAINS TAX--U.S. (v19)

CAPITAL INVESTMENTS--U.S. (v19)

CAPITAL INVESTMENTS--VIETNAM

In Vietnam, "capital is coming in from foreigners attracted by a prospective new Asian 'tiger'; inflows of foreign capital for large industrial and infrastructure projects have totalled about $2 billion since 1988, reckons ANZ Grindlays Bank. Vietnamese who live abroad are doing their bit to help. Their remittances amounted to about $600m in 1992, and may have risen to $1 billion in 1993." (p94)

"Finance: The Smile on the Tiger's Face." Economist v330

n7855, 19 Mar 1994. p94. (ISSN0013-0613).

CAPITAL PUNISHMENT--CHINA (v19)

CAPITAL PUNISHMENT--U.S. (v19)

"In 1933, there was an effort to assassinate President Franklin D. Roosevelt and the assassin missed and he killed Mayor Cermak of Chicago who was standing next to the President....The assassin was tried, and less than 35 days after the assassination, the assassin was given the death penalty and he was executed so that people in America who had seen the horror of Mayor Cermak being killed could remember, 35 days later, why the man was being executed....in Georgia...we had a man executed for a terrible murder, a man executed after a long period of appeals. That murder occurred 16 years ago....It took 192 times as long...because of all the appeals the criminal defense lawyers have built into the system over the years....For 40 years the Democrats have run the House, it has gotten harder and harder to have an effective death penalty...." (pH2245)

Gingrich, Newt (Rep.-Ga.). "Providing for Further Consideration of H.R. 4092, Violent Crime Control and Law Enforcement Act of 1994," Congressional Record (13 Apr 1994). Daily ed. pH2233-2247. (ISSN0363-7239).

"Between 1930 and 1990, roughly 4,000 persons were executed in the United States, 53 percent of whom were black. During these years, African-Americans made up roughly 12 percent of the country, indicating they are executed in extreme disproportion to their representation in society. A 1990 GAO [General Accounting Office] report confirms prior findings that a convicted perpetrator of a capital crime is much more likely to receive the death penalty if the victim is white and much less likely to receive the death penalty if the victim is black. Since 1976, 87 percent of those executed had white victims while only 11 percent had black victims. Besides race, the death penalty discriminates against the poor. According to the U.S. Bureau of Justice Statistics, roughly 90 percent of those on death row could not afford to hire an attorney." (pH2326)

Kopetski, Michael J. (Rep.-Oreg.). "Violent Crime Control and Law Enforcement Act of 1994," Congressional Record (14 Apr 1994). Daily ed. pH2322-2343. (ISSN0363-7239).

"Since 1988, 33 of the 37 federal death penalty defendants have been African-Americans. In the current administration...all of the defendants the Attorney General has approved for the death penalty have been African-American. The General Accounting Office, Congress' own investigative arm, has concluded in its study that racism definitely affects the use of the death penalty in the United States. Further studies have found undeniably that in an alarming 82 percent of the time, the race of the victim influences whether or not the defendant is sentenced to death." (pH2532)

Collins, Cardiss (Rep.-Ill.). "Violent Crime Control and Law Enforcement Act of 1994," Congressional Record (20 Apr 1994). Daily ed. pH2518-2539. (ISSN0363-7239).

"In 1972, when the Supreme Court declared capital punishment as then arbitrarily administered unconstitutional, virtually all of the 700 persons on death row were penniless and half were black. Half of the 3,859 people executed in the U.S. between 1930 and 1972 were black, though blacks constituted 10% of the population. The situation is not largely different today. The percentage of those executed who are black is still disproportionately high. The nonwhite population currently under sentence of death constitutes about 42% of the total number. The poor continue to fare badly. A fairly recent survey of 236 death row inmates in Texas revealed that 60 could not pursue appeals in federal courts for lack of legal representation." (p151)

DeCelles, Charles. "The American Bishops and Capital Punishment." Social Justice Review v84 n9-10, Sep-Oct 1993. p149-153.

CAPITAL PUNISHMENT--U.S.--PUBLIC OPINION (v19)

CAPITAL PUNISHMENT--U.S.--RELIGIOUS ASPECTS--CATHOLIC CHURCH

"Convinced that the Gospel has a social side, the American [Catholic] bishops in recent times have taken stands on numerous crucial but controversial social issues with ethical dimensions. The bishops realize that their positions will be severely criticized, even ridiculed. Nevertheless, they speak out with admirable courage. In 1974 they voted 108-68 to oppose capital punishment. Since then collectively they have maintained their stand without wavering. In 1980 they issued a declaration statement of opposition. From that year forward some eleven state conferences of bishops have spoken out against state sanctioned executions, including those of California, Florida (two occasions), Georgia, Kentucky, Massachusetts, Mississippi, Ohio, Oklahoma, Pennsylvania, Tenessee and Missouri." (p149-150)

DeCelles, Charles. "The American Bishops and Capital Punishment." Social Justice Review v84 n9-10, Sep-Oct 1993. p149-153.

CAR

see AUTOMOBILE

CARBARYL

"Carbaryl (1-naphthyl methyl carbamate...) is one of the three most commonly used insecticides in the United States with an estimated annual use of between 10 and 15 million pounds....It is a broadspectrum insecticide and is registered for use on more than 100 different crops, animals, ornamental plants, and indoor areas. Carbaryl is also sometimes used as a chemical thinning agent for apples....It has been registered in the U.S. since 1958. Previously manufactured by Union Carbide, the primary U.S. manufacturer is now Rhone Poulenc Agricultural Company; many of its carbaryl-containing products are marketed under the brand name Sevin." (p31)

Cox, Caroline. "Carbaryl." Journal of Pesticide Reform v13 n1, Spr 1993. p31-36. (ISSN0893-357X).

CARBARYL--TOXICOLOGY

"Carbaryl's acute oral LD50 (the dose that causes death in 50 percent of a population of test animals) in rats is 255 milligrams per kilogram (mg/kg) of body weight. Extrapolated to the weight of an average 70 kilogram (154 pound) human who is assumed to be as sensitive to carbaryl as are rats, this means that a dose of about 18 grams or two-thirds of an ounce would be fatal. Lower doses of carbaryl over a longer period of time cause a variety of adverse effects. In humans, ingestion of 0.13 mg/kg/day (less than a thousandth of the LD50) caused abdominal cramps and a decrease in the ability of the kidneys to resorb amino acids. In rats, decreases in weight and body temperature occurred following single injections of doses of less than one-twentieth of the LD50. Similar doses given for two years caused kidney abnormalities in rats as well as dogs. In addition, drinking water contaminated with 10 parts per million (ppm) of carbaryl caused liver pathologies and reduced blood clotting activity in rats and single sublethal doses in rabbits reduced their heart rate and caused changes in their electrocardiograms." (p31-32)

Cox, Caroline. "Carbaryl." Journal of Pesticide Reform v13 n1, Spr 1993. p31-36. (ISSN0893-357X).

CARBON

"It is being estimated that...[there] are approximately 41,000 petagrams, meaning 10 [to the 15th power] grams, of circulating carbon on planet earth. The ocean sink is believed to contain 38,000 petagrams, the atmosphere 750 petagrams, and terrestrial ecosystems approximately 2,100 petagrams of carbon. Living plants manage some 550 petagrams of carbon and soils account for about 1,500 petagrams. If there is valid meaning to this arithmetic, it is simply that soils provide us with the largest, non-fossil reservoir of carbon. The net loss of carbon from plants and soils combined is being calculated at 1 petagram....100 to 120 petagrams of carbon are fixed annually by plants through the agency of photosynthesis. Respiration in turn releases some 40 to 60 petagrams, and decomposition of organic matter, soil carbon included, set up a release of 50 to 60 petagrams. In theory the carbon oxidized by both processes ought to balance the carbon amount fixed by photosynthesis....In our time [however], land use changes, killer agriculture and...wind and water...have upset nature's requirements. Consequently there is a shortfall between oxidation of plant and soil carbon and the fix that photosynthesis can account for. Thus the oft-cited conclusion that there is in fact a 3 petagram annual increase in atmospheric carbon dioxide." (p19)

Walters, Charles. "Stray Carbon." Acres, U.S.A. Aug 1993. p18-19,39.

CARBON DIOXIDE (v19)

see also ATMOSPHERIC CARBON DIOXIDE; GREENHOUSE EFFECT, ATMOSPHERIC

"Every year the U.S. population grows by 2.6 million. Assume that each extra person generates the average U.S. carbon dioxide output of 20 tons. Then the carbon dioxide increase due to population growth in the United States is 52 million tons a year. Do the same sum for other countries or regions, and the results are shocking. India grows by 17 million people a year, but it adds only an extra 13 million tons of CO2--a quarter of the U.S. total. China's extra 17 million people add just under 37 million tons. Overall, population growth in the two biggest countries on earth has at present less impact on the global climate than that of the United States." (p20)

Harrison, Paul. "The United States: Booming with Buyers--and Babies, Too." Amicus Journal v15 n45, Win 1994. p20-21. (ISSN0276-7201).

CARBON DIOXIDE--TEXAS

"Texas Utilities (TU), serving one-third of the Texas population, is projected to have a greater increase in carbon dioxide emissions this decade than any other major investor-owned electric utility company except ComEd, and the fourth largest increase in the industry on a percentage basis. CEP [the Council on Economic Priorities] estimates that TU's plants released 134 billion pounds of CO2 in 1990, and projects that they will release 152 billion pounds of CO2 in the year 2000. TU plans to build several coal- and natural-gas fired plants to accommodate 80 percent of its future growth. Only 20 percent of its anticipated growth will be met through conservation, efficiency and other forms of demand-side management." (p5)

Scott, Ken/Moulton, Sean. "America's Least Wanted: The 1993 Campaign for Cleaner Corporations (C3)." CEP Research Report Nov-Dec 1993. p1-5. (ISSN0898-4328).

CARBON DIOXIDE--U.S.

"Acknowledging the link between industrial pollution and global climate change, President Clinton called on the nation's electric power companies to reduce their output of global warming gases. A first step is to hold carbon dioxide (CO2) emissions in the year 2000 to their 1990 levels. Commonwealth Edison (ComEd), Texas Utilities (TU) and 60 other companies endorsed Clinton's 'Climate Challenge.' Yet, ComEd projects its CO2 emissions will increase almost 50 percent from 1990 to 2000 through increased use of existing fossil-fuel plants--an increase larger than any other investor-owned electric utility. TU plans to build several plants this decade that could boost its CO2 emissions by an additional 18 billion pounds in the year 2000." (p1)

Scott, Ken/Moulton, Sean. "America's Least Wanted: The 1993 Campaign for Cleaner Corporations (C3)." CEP Research Report Nov-Dec 1993. p1-5. (ISSN0898-4328).

"ComEd, an electric utility serving Chicago and northeastern Illinois, has the worst overall performance in terms of air emissions among the 24 largest investor-owned electric utilities and has paid the third largest amount of fines for its nuclear power plants. ComEd projects that its CO2 emissions in the year 2000 will be 63.2 billion pounds, 47.5 percent greater than estimated 1990 emissions of 42.8 billion pounds. Both in actual and percentage terms, this increase is greater than that of any other electric utility. ComEd emitted 30 percent more oxides of nitrogen (NOx, an air pollutant that contributes to urban smog and 'acid rain') per unit of electricity generated than the industry average in 1991 (the most recent year for which figures are available). ComEd emitted 20 percent more sulfur dioxide (SO2) per megawatt-hour than the industry average. SO2 emissions are the primary contributor to acid rain." (p1-2)

Scott, Ken/Moulton, Sean. "America's Least Wanted: The 1993 Campaign for Cleaner Corporations (C3)." CEP Research Report Nov-Dec 1993. p1-5. (ISSN0898-4328).

"The amount of CO2 and methane in the atmosphere have exponentially increased over natural processes of biomass decay. This build-up of CO2 correlates to additions from the combustion of some 25 billion barrels of oil each year. Nature's green plants have been stimulated but they have not been able to utilize the extra carbon dioxide since about 1900. The atmosphere has been changed by burning so much fuel and now contains 25% more carbon dioxide and 100% more methane than at any time in the last 160 thousand years. This is proven by testing arctic snow cores." (p17)

McAlister, Roy/McAlister, Sara. "Making Fuel from Wastes." Hydrogen Today v4 n2, 1993. p17.

CARCINOMA

see CANCER

CARDIOVASCULAR SYSTEM--DISEASES--U.S. (v19)

see also HEART--DISEASE--U.S.

"Cardiovascular diseases in the United States rank as the leading cause of limitation of physical activity, of hospital bed use and of Social Security disability. In 1991 (the latest year for which final data are available), CVD was the first-listed diagnosis for an estimated 5,338,000 U.S. patients discharged from nonfederal short-stay hospitals. (This number climbed to some 21.4 million, however, when all-listed CVD diagnoses are included.) The rate for first-listed CVD diagnosis was 213.1 per 10,000 population in 1991, with the rate for men estimated at 224.4 per 10,000 population and for women, 202.3. CVD accounted for 17.2 percent of all first-listed diagnosis conditions in 1991, and these patients had an average length of stay of 7.3 days." (p12-13)

Mushinski, Margaret. "1992 Hospital Charges for Two Major Surgical Procedures for Cardiovascular Diseases." Statistical Bulletin v75 n1, Jan-Mar 1994. p12-20. (ISSN0790-8334).

CARDIOVASCULAR SYSTEM--DISEASES--U.S.--MORTALITY

"Cardiovascular diseases (CVDs) remain the leading cause of death in the United States despite declining mortality rates since the mid-1960s. In 1992 an estimated 915,360 American deaths were due to major cardiovascular diseases, producing a provisional mortality rate of 358.8 per 100,000 population--about 1 percent lower than the rate in 1991. CVD deaths account for more than two out of every five U.S. deaths and estimates further indicate that one in every four Americans suffer from some form of cardiovascular disease." (p12)

Mushinski, Margaret. "1992 Hospital Charges for Two Major Surgical Procedures for Cardiovascular Diseases." Statistical Bulletin v75 n1, Jan-Mar 1994. p12-20.

(ISSN0790-8334).

CARDIOVASCULAR SYSTEM--DISEASES--U.S.--WOMEN

"Cardiovascular diseases, including heart attack and stroke, remain the No. 1 killer of American females. Heart disease kills 240,000 American women every year, while stroke claims another 88,000, according to...[the American Heart] association." (pE672)

Schroeder, Patricia (Rep.-Colo.). "Women and Heart Disease: A History of Inequity," Congressional Record (15 Apr 1994). Daily ed. pE672-673. (ISSN0363-7239).

CAREGIVERS--AFRO-AMERICAN AGED

"Social supports in the informal network of African American elders play a vital role in maintaining the elderly in the community. The functioning of the support network and identification of key players can have an important impact on the effectiveness of formal interventions." (p82) "Older African Americans' choice of helper differs from the configuration put forth by the substitution principle, although a serial progression does exist. Chatters and colleagues (1986) used a national probability sample of 581 African Americans 55 years of age and older to identify patterns of choice for a helper in the informal support network. They reported that the kin most frequently chosen as helpers were daughters (41.5%), sons (37.2%), and spouses (32.8%). Sisters (28.7%), brothers (20%), and friends (19.6%) were the other preferred helpers. Unmarried persons were more likely to choose sister, friend, and neighbor; children, if present, were selected as informal helpers over siblings and friends (Chatters et al., 1986)." (p84)

Luckey, Irene. "African American Elders: The Support Network of Generational Kin." Families in Society v75 n2, Feb 1994. p82-89. (ISSN1044-3894).

CAREGIVERS--U.S. (v19)

"About one-third of all caregivers are special needs. Even so, the old are far more likely to need such services. Only 3 percent of adult women under age 65 need assistance with at least one daily living activity, compared with 30 percent of those aged 75 and older." (p41,44)

Braus, Patricia. "When Mom Needs Help." American Demographics v16 n3, Mar 1994. p38-41,44-46. (ISSN0163-4089).

"Most families provide home care so their relatives can keep living independently. Fueling this trend is a decrease in the proportion of adult children who invite aging parents to live with them. In 1991, 5 percent of people aged 75 and older lived with an adult child householder, down from 8 percent in 1970." (p40-41)

Braus, Patricia. "When Mom Needs Help." American Demographics v16 n3, Mar 1994. p38-41,44-46. (ISSN0163-4089).

"Single women spend more time helping aged parents than do married people or single men, according to the 1992 Health and Retirement study, conducted by Thomas Juster, an economist at the Institute for Social Research at the University of Michigan. Single women who gave care helped an average of about 24 hours per week. Single men, on the other hand, were more likely to help elderly parents by living with them in the parent's home. Long seen as society's nurturers, many women still bear the brunt of caregiving even if they work full-time jobs. A 1993 study by the Families and Work Institute in New York City measured how full-time workers provide care to the elderly. It found that women who provide direct care to an elderly relative spend an average of 14 hours a week on caregiving activities, including bathing and feeding. Men who give care spend an average of 7.5 hours on these tasks. The gender gap is smaller for indirect care, such as paying bills and shopping. Men spend 4 hours a week on these tasks, compared with nearly 6 hours for women." (p41)

Braus, Patricia. "When Mom Needs Help." American Demographics v16 n3, Mar 1994. p38-41,44-46. (ISSN0163-4089).

CAREGIVERS--U.S.--EMPLOYEES

"The availability of paid home care is critical to employers, because these services relieve workers of caregiving duties. Still, workers who care for an older relative inevitably face conflicts between work and home. A study conducted for the American Association of Retired Persons in 1989 found that 12 percent of adult caregivers had left the work force to take care of someone....A 1984 survey of 69 members of the New York Business Group on Health found that two-thirds to three-fourths of employer respondents reported excessive absenteeism, lateness, and use of unscheduled time off among individual caregivers. In addition, two-thirds of employers reported that caregivers made excessive use of the telephone for personal reasons." (p45-46)

Braus, Patricia. "When Mom Needs Help." American Demographics v16 n3, Mar 1994. p38-41,44-46. (ISSN0163-4089).

"The bottom line for employers is that 20 to 30 percent of American workers care for older relatives, says Dana Zackin, research analyst for The Conference Board in New York City. This proportion is expected to grow as the age of the average American worker increases, adds Sally Coberly, director of the Institute on Aging, Work and Health for the Washington Business Group on Health." (p41)

Braus, Patricia. "When Mom Needs Help." American Demographics v16 n3, Mar 1994. p38-41,44-46. (ISSN0163-4089).

CAREGIVERS--U.S.--PUBLIC OPINION

"Attitudes about home care...vary by age. In an August 1993 Gallup-HEALTH magazine poll of 601 people, 90 percent of those aged 18 to 29 would consider asking their parents to move in with them if their parents could not live alone. Among those aged 50 and older, however, only 72 percent would consider such a move. The results suggest the changing perspective that age and experience bring, says Sheridan Warrick, managing editor of HEALTH. 'People in the 50-plus group have already had experience caring for an aging parent. The 18-to-29-year-olds have a more idealistic outlook, because their parents are younger.' In other words, they haven't had to truly face the issue. The results could also suggest a shift in the way younger people view home care today, compared with their middle-aged parents' perspective." (p44)

Braus, Patricia. "When Mom Needs Help." American Demographics v16 n3, Mar 1994. p38-41,44-46. (ISSN0163-4089).

CARIBBEAN AREA--LATIN AMERICA--ECONOMIC CONDITIONS

"The countries of Latin America and the Caribbean have proved it: virtue pays. The structural economic reforms that they introduced in the 1980s were painful, but new figures from the UN's Economic Commission for Latin America and the Caribbean (ECLAC) show the reward: an estimated regional GDP [gross domestic product] growth of 3.2% for 1993. 'The phase of moderate expansion in most economies, with relative price stability and a copious inflow of capital, is continuing for the third consecutive year.' Not so rapidly, though, nor everywhere. Forget big Brazil's 4.5% growth, and the rest of the region averages 2.6%, far below its 5% a year in the previous two years....Argentina, Chile, Costa Rica and Panama, all recorded lower growth than last year but nonetheless 'hovered quite satisfactorily at about 6%'. After a dismal

1992, Peru reached 6.5%...." (p60)
"International: Latin America: Doing Well." Economist v329 n7843, 25 Dec 1993. p60. (ISSN0013-0613).

CARIBOU--WOLVES--ALASKA (v19)

CASH MANAGEMENT--U.S. (v19)

CASINOS--CZECHOSLOVAKIA (v19)

CASPIAN SEA

see also OIL SPILLS--CASPIAN SEA; WATER--POLLUTION--CASPIAN SEA--VOLGA RIVER

"An inexplicable rise in the level of the Caspian is alarming Russia, Iran, and the three other states along its shores. In the past 15 years this salty landlocked sea has risen by some 2.1 metres (nearly seven feet), flooding villages, factories and farmland. It is continuing to rise by 15 centimeters a year. Scientists at the Caspian Research Centre in Baku, the capital of Azerbaijan, believe the sea could rise by over five metres by 2010....The sea has gone up and down inexplicably in the past. It fell consistently between the late 1920s and the 1970s. By 1977 it had dropped to almost 30 metres below sea level--its lowest point for five centuries....Russian and Iranian environment organisations reckon that the current rise has so far inundated 32,000 square km (12,360 square miles) of land." (p52)
"Europe: The Caspian Also Rises." Economist v331 n7860, 23 Apr 1994. p52. (ISSN0013-0613).

CASPIAN SEA--ENVIRONMENTAL ASPECTS

"Oil and gas drilling has been a key contributor to the unexpected and enormously disruptive rise in the level of the Caspian Sea, according to Caspian specialist Dr Boris Golubov....for 150 years, the water level fell steadily, but since 1978 the Sea has risen 2.2 metres and shows no signs of stopping. Another one-metre rise, expected within five years, will wreck more than 60 villages and 53 towns, which are already flood-prone. In 1988, the town of Kaspiysky was flooded when a storm drove waves 30-35 kilometres inland. There may be worse to come, because the Caspian is known for storm waves of up to four metres." (p11)
Speranskaya, Olga. "Eastern Europe: Caspian Oil on Troubled Waters." Panoscope n37, Oct 1993. p11. (ISSN0951-8819).

CASSAVA (v19)

CATARACT

"Prolonged exposure of the eyes [to ultraviolet radiation] may lead to the development of cancer of conjunctiva and cataracts. Half of the world's 35 million blind people lost their eyesight because of cataract. It is believed that the disease may be triggered off by shorter wavelength UV in as many as 3.5 million people, or 20% of the global figure of cataract sufferers. In the so-called 'cataract belt', geographical areas near the equator, the condition strikes individuals in the prime of life, between 35 and 45 years of age. On the contrary, in Europe and North America it is a disease of the elderly. In the tropical regions, which lack the sharp seasonal variations of northern latitudes, UV radiation is much more intense." (p2)
News release. "Ultraviolet Radiation Can Seriously Damage Your Health." WHO Press 17 Dec 1993. p1-2.

CATARACT--U.S. (v19)

CATASTROPHES

see DISASTERS

CATHOLIC CHURCH

see also CAPITAL PUNISHMENT--U.S.--RELIGIOUS ASPECTS--CATHOLIC CHURCH
see also NUNS

CATHOLIC CHURCH--FRANCE

"Four out of five French people describe themselves as Catholics, but less than 10% go to mass regularly and only 6% go to confession even once a year. That is perhaps just as well, since there is a chronic shortage of priests. Only around 25,000 parish priests remain, two-thirds of them over 60. Thanks to a big recruiting drive over the past few years, just over 100 new priests are ordained each year. But this is a tenth of the number 40 years ago." (p64)
"Europe: The Spirit, Yes--Priests, No." Economist v329 n7843, 25 Dec 1993. p64. (ISSN0013-0613).

CATHOLIC SCHOOLS--NEW YORK (STATE) (v19)

CATHOLIC SCHOOLS--U.S.

"Catholic schools provide a strong foundation on which students can develop solid moral values and achieve academic excellence. One need only look to recent reports, which show that Catholic students excel in reading, science, and mathematics. In addition, 83 percent of Catholic high school graduates go on to college and realize the merits of Catholic education. Catholic schools provide spiritual guidance and nurturing to their students, and by offering solid academic instruction, they equip their pupils with the educational and social tools necessary for successful lives. With parochial school enrollment increasing nationwide--Catholic schools continue to enroll more than 50 percent of all private school students and educate over 2.5 million students overall--there is clear evidence of the enduring quality of Catholic education. Parochial education is increasing its presence in urban areas and serves diverse populations. The percentage of minorities in Catholic schools has more than doubled since 1970 and continues to increase." (pE56)
Roemer, Tim (Rep.-Ind.). "Catholic Schools Week," Congressional Record (1 Feb 1994). Daily ed. pE56. (ISSN0363-7239).

"While demanding reading lists and renewed emphasis on homework are reappearing in many public schools, Catholic educators have been surprised by the new interest in their brand of education....Enrollment has grown moderately since 1990, with a nationwide increase of 17,000 students in 1991 and 1992, fueled in part by a rise in the U.S. birthrate....But almost all Catholic schools continue to operate under tight financial circumstances. According to [Catholic University's John J.] Convey, 'a good elementary school,' with a gymnasium and cafeteria, costs $5 million to $6 million. And the days are gone when the chruch could rely on nuns and priests to teach students. About 88 percent of teachers at Catholic schools are salaried laypeople....The church offers some aid to Catholic schools, but it is more likely to pressure local parishes to make up shortfalls, notes St. Angela Merici's Kelly. Part of the problem, which Kelly pointed out in the Catholic magazine COMMONWEAL, is that Catholics tithe low (an average of 1.1 percent of their salaries) compared with other religious groups (2.1 percent for mainline Protestants and almost 10 percent for Mormons)." (p14)
Goode, Stephen. "The Renaissance of the Catholic School." Insight v10 n13, 28 Mar 1994. p12-15. (ISSN1051-4880).

CATHOLICS--U.S. (v19)

see also VOTING--U.S.--CATHOLICS

"Catholics [in the U.S.] are far more likely to live in metropolitan areas than in rural areas and small towns. The National Survey of Religious Identification discovered that 84.5 percent of Catholics live in metropolitan areas, making them the most urban group except for Jews. There has been a shift from the cities to the suburbs, however. A generation ago, cities were Catholic strongholds; today, the suburbs hold the bulk of the Catholic population, while inner cities are much more likely to be black and Protestant. Catholics are also younger than Protestants or Jews, the survey found. The Catholic median age is 40.1 compared to 44 for both Protestants and Jews. This survey also found that only 66 percent of Hispanic Americans are

Catholic, a decline that is continuing as a result of fundamentalist Protestant proselytism. (Protestants are up from 18 percent to 25 percent among Hispanics.) About 9 percent of blacks are Catholic, a slight increase since 1960." (p17)

Menedez, Albert J. "The Political Power of the Catholic Church: American Catholics: A Social and Political Portrait." Humanist v53 n5, Sep-Oct 1993. p17-20. (ISSN0018-7399).

"In the U.S., only Catholics are a large enough group to investigate the scope of a specific religious authority with survey data. The evidence clearly shows a substantially narrowing scope for Catholic religious authority over Catholic individuals. The percentage of Catholics who agreed that it is 'certainly true that Jesus handed over leadership of his church to Peter and the popes' dropped from 70% in 1963 to 42% in 1973. By 1990, only 12% of U.S. Catholics accepted the Church's ban on artificial contraception (Christiano 1992). Research reviewed by Kalmijn (1991) finds largely nonexistent differences between Protestants and Catholics with respect to family-size preferences, marital fertility, and birth control practices. As Christiano (1992) put it, there is 'loyalty, but not obedience'...among U.S. Catholics. To rephrase, there is religion, but there is little effective religious authority." (p768-769)

Chaves, Mark. "Secularization as Declining Religious Authority." Social Forces v72 n3, Mar 1994. p749-774. (ISSN0037-7732).

CATHOLICS--U.S.--ATTITUDES (v19)

CATS

"Among the concerns about declawing are the medical risks and possible complications. There is little dispute that hospitalization, anesthesia, and surgery are stressful and that there is some risk in any surgical procedure. There is also agreement that complications--shattered bone, hemorrhage, infection, deformed nail regrowth--usually result from inadequate surgical technique. The frequency of these outcomes has not been documented, but veterinarian Gary Landsberg surveyed practitioners in Ontario, Canada, and extrapolated from their responses that approximately 1 out of 6,000 declawed cats was likely to have long-term physical problems." (p27)

Ginsberg, Susan. "Cats, Claws and Conflict." Animals v126 n14, Jul-Aug 1993. p26-29. (ISSN0030-6835).

CATTLE

see also GRAZING

CATTLE--SOUTH AMERICA (v19)

CATTLE--U.S. (v19)

CATTLE TRADE--U.S.

"There were about 99 million head of cattle and calves in the United States in 1990....This is down from 102 million head in 1987 and 132 million head in 1975....About 84 million of these cattle and calves are grown for beef production....About 28 million head of cattle were fattened on grain and concentrates in the United States in 1987...of which 64 percent were concentrated in the Great Plains area compared to 58 percent in 1982." (p115)

Eghball, Bahman/Power, J. F. "Beef Cattle Feedlot Manure Management." Journal of Soil and Water Conservation v49 n2, Mar-Apr 1994. p113-122. (ISSN0022-4561).

CD-ROM--U.S.

"Optical disks called CD-ROMs are spinning in a growing number of computers. Sales of CD-ROM drives more than tripled last year from 1992. Sales are expected to rise again this year by 50 percent. As a result, software companies are rushing to develop new programs for the technology....A major reason for the growth: the dramatic drop in prices for CD-ROM drives. A few years ago, they cost nearly $1,000. Today, they are as low as $199." (p6)

Belsie, Laurent. "Economy: CD-ROM Growth Leaps in 1993: More to Come." The Christian Science Monitor v86 n27, 3 Jan 1994. p6. (ISSN0882-7729).

CELLULAR RADIO--BELGIUM

"Belgium has long had one of Europe's worst cellular networks, which is why only 0.6% of Belgians (compared with 3.1% of Britons) own cellphones. But on January 1st Belgium launched a high-tech cellular network called GSM (Global System for Mobiles). And a new digital age dawned for Belgacom, the state telecoms monopoly. Or so Bessel Kok, Belgacom's managing director, hopes....When Mr Kok took over, the 50,000-strong waiting list for a telephone stretched to a year. Today the list is down to 9,000, and 80% of customers are connected in 20 working days." (p68)

"Business: A New Line for Belgacom." Economist v330 n7844, 8 Jan 1994. p68. (ISSN0013-0613).

CELLULAR RADIO--U.S. (v19)

CENTRAL AMERICA

see DEFORESTATION--CENTRAL AMERICA--SOUTH AMERICA--U.S.

CEREALS, PREPARED--PRICES--U.S. (v19)

"Consumers have a right to be agitated when a box containing 14 cents' worth of raw ingredients costs $2.20. New York State Attorney General Robert Abrams, for one, is so bent out of shape about it that he's gone to court to stop the No. 3 cereal maker from gobbling up No. 6. Pointing out that the price of all food eaten at home has risen 37 percent in the past eight years while the price of RTE [ready-to-eat] cereals has increased 71 percent, Abrams says, 'These soaring price increases, far out of line with other food products, are a clear result of an over-concentrated industry....The last thing this industry needs is less competition.'" (p33)

Baldwin, Deborah. "The Cornflake Cartel." Common Cause Magazine v19 n2, Sum 1993. p32-36. (ISSN0271-9592).

CEREALS, PREPARED--U.S.

"In 1970 government researchers concluded that a mere four companies dominated 90 percent of the [U.S.] cereal market, up from 68 percent in 1940. Such 'shared monopolies,' critics charged, opened the door for a subtle kind of price fixing based on the notion that if no one cuts prices, no one gets hurt. Economists at the Federal Trade Commission (FTC) also maintained that by dividing the market into smaller and smaller fragments and then flooding them with new brands, the cereal kingpins had crowded out smaller contenders. To help pay for all this, the FTC figured, the public was spending an extra 20 to 25 percent--or $150 to $250 million a year--for what was basically a group of heavily advertised boxed grains with funny names." (p32)

Baldwin, Deborah. "The Cornflake Cartel." Common Cause Magazine v19 n2, Sum 1993. p32-36. (ISSN0271-9592).

"Today cereal moguls Kellogg and General Mills control nearly two-thirds of the $8-billion-a-year domestic cereal market, with Kellogg holding about 38 percent and General Mills about one-fourth. To protect their market shares--which are worth some $80 million per percentage point--each spends heavily on marketing. Kellogg, for example, spent $100 million in one quarter alone in 1991, according to FOOD BUSINESS magazine (and increased its sales 11.4 percent). Scrambling to hold onto smaller but still-lucrative shares of the market are companies No. 3,4,5 and 6 (Kraft General Foods/Post, Quaker, Ralston Purina and Nabisco)." (p34)

Baldwin, Deborah. "The Cornflake Cartel." Common Cause Magazine v19 n2, Sum 1993. p32-36. (ISSN0271-9592).

CEREBROVASCULAR DISEASE--U.S.

"Strokes affect over 500,000 people each year. In 1991, over 143,000 died of stroke. Some 3 million Americans suffer from stroke-related disabilities, at an annual cost of more than $18 billion." (p2)

Frazao, Betsy. "Health Linked to Nutrition: The High Costs of Poor Diets." Food Review v17 n1, Jan-Apr 1994. p2-3.

"Although stroke rates nationwide have declined dramatically in the 20th century, strokes are still the third largest killer in the...[U.S.]. Ten of the 12 states with the highest death rates from strokes are in the South, with South Carolina ranking first. 'The places of high stroke mortality have been in the old Black Belt, farmer, plantation-economy areas,' says Steve Wing, an epidemiologist at the University of North Carolina in Chapel Hill. The coastal plain long experienced the highest stroke rates, but with coastal development, higher rates have shifted westward to farmland in the Mississippi and Ohio River valleys. The factors that cause strokes are closely intertwined with elements of Southern culture, from tobacco and fatback to race and poverty. Smoking, for example, is highest among Southern men." (p64)

Kerr, Mary Lee. "Still the South: The Stroke Belt." Southern Exposure v21 n4, Win 1993. p64. (ISSN0146-809X).

CESAREAN SECTION--U.S. (v19)

CHARITABLE USES, TRUSTS, AND FOUNDATIONS--U.S.

"Making money is big business for some of the nation's major foundations. At the Ford Foundation, which funds poverty, education and health programs around the world, 15 staff members are responsible for managing more than $6 billion in assets. These staff members work with more than 50 million shares in about 100 companies. Ford's investment efforts have paid off. In 10 years, the foundation's assets have more than doubled. And they have grown by nearly three times the consumer inflation rate. Perhaps Ford reflects its priorities in its salaries. Next to officers and directors, the three highest paid employees are those responsible for making sure Ford's assets continue to multiply, in charge of fixed-income investments, equity investments and special investments. The Ford Foundation received no gifts in 1990, its tax return shows. But the foundation earned $314 million in interest on savings and dividends that year and paid out $237 million in grants." (p13)

"$163 Billion: As Foundations' Assets Grow Questions Arise about Payout." Responsive Philanthropy Sum 1993. p1,12-14.

CHAGAS' DISEASE--LATIN AMERICA

"Some 90 million people, about a quarter of the total population of Latin America, are exposed to the risk of infection with Chagas disease. In the southern part of South America (known from its shape as the 'southern cone' in Spanish) over 54 million people are at risk, representing 31% of the population. The risk is particularly high in countries such as Paraguay, where 43% of the population is exposed, and Bolivia, where the proportion is 35% according to a study by the Pan American Health Organization. This Andean country is the one where the highest proportion of the population is infected, namely 22%. In the rest of Latin America the risk is highest in Venezuela and Guatemala, at two-thirds and one-half of the population respectively." (p1)

News release. "Chagas Disease in Retreat in the Southern Part of Latin America." WHO Press 8 Mar 1993. p1-2.

CHAMPAGNE (WINE) (v19)

CHARITABLE USES, TRUSTS, AND FOUNDATIONS

"Even though grantmakers must now give away at least 5% of their assets annually, many foundations actually give far less because of legal loopholes. The 203 wealthiest foundations in the 1993 FOUNDATION DIRECTORY on average spent only 3.8% of their assets on grants to nonprofits. Had they actually distributed 5% of their assets as grants, an additional $1.1 billion would have gone to needy organizations." (p10)

Eisenberg, Pablo. "5% Is Not Enough." Responsive Philanthropy Win 1994. p10.

"The wealthiest foundations pay out a smaller percentage of assets in actual grants than do smaller foundations. The 203 largest foundations of all types listed in the Foundation Center's 1993 FOUNDATION DIRECTORY have assets totaling $94 billion. Yet they paid out only $3.6 billion in actual grants. This represents only a 3.8% payout. Had they actually paid out 5% directly in grants, these foundations would have donated $4.7 billion. In contrast, the 5,922 foundations with $50 million or less in assets ($43 billion in total assets) paid out $4.0 billion in grants. This represents 9.3% of assets, far more than the 5% legal requirement, and far more than the 3.8% the largest foundations donate in grants." (p12)

"$163 Billion: As Foundations' Assets Grow Questions Arise about Payout." Responsive Philanthropy Sum 1993. p1,12.-14.

CHARITABLE USES, TRUSTS, AND FOUNDATIONS--U.S.

"The...33,000 tax-exempt foundations [in the U.S.] control property, cash, and investments worth at least $163 billion. The 10 largest foundations account for 20% of all foundation assets. And foundations' wealth is rapidly increasing. Their current $163 billion worth of assets represents more than a fivefold increase since 1975 when foundation assets totalled just $30 billion, according to the Foundation Center, an organization that maintains records on foundations and serves as a resource for grant applicants. Even after adjusting for inflation, foundations' assets have more than doubled since 1975." (p1)

"$163 Billion: As Foundations' Assets Grow Questions Arise about Payout." Responsive Philanthropy Sum 1993. p1,12-14.

CHARITIES

see also FOOD RELIEF

CHARITIES--U.S.

"The church has long been a significant provider of social services in [the U.S.]...and elsewhere. Although some of the funds for these services come from other sources--including the United Way, private foundations, and the Catholic people--many services are largely funded by the government. In 1989, Catholic Charities USA, for example, received 54.5 percent ($756 million) of its $1.4 billion budget from local, state, and federal government grants and contracts; in 1991, government support had risen to $1.16 billion, or 62.9 percent of the organization's funding." (p21-22)

Shannon, Denise. "The Political Power of the Catholic Church: The Bishops Lobby." Humanist v53 n5, Sep-Oct 1993. p21-23. (ISSN0018-7399).

CHECK CASHING SERVICES--U.S. (v19)

CHECKS--U.S. (v19)

CHEESE INDUSTRY--EUROPEAN ECONOMIC COMMUNITY (v19)

CHEMICAL INDUSTRY--INSPECTION (v19)

CHEMICAL INDUSTRY--U.S. (v19)

see also DYE INDUSTRY--U.S.; PESTICIDES INDUSTRY--U.S.; SOLVENTS INDUSTRY--U.S.

"Sales of chemicals [in the U.S.] may rise only 5% this year, to about $327.6 billion, according to a survey of 107 producers by the Chemical Manufacturers Assn. (CMA). But cost-cutting could boost profits 10%, to $23.1 billion, recouping last year's 10% decline....Even though new products are crucial, the industry isn't exempting research from its cost-cutting drive. After rising an estimated 4.3%, to about $14.5 billion last year, R&D [research and development] spending may grow just 3% this year, according to the CMA. Industry heavyweights, after overexpanding in the late 1980s, also plan to remain stingy with capital outlays, which may rise little more than 2.5%, after a paltry 1.8% increase last year, to $23.4 billion. The industry will be able to make do: In 1993, its plants ran at 81.2% of capacity, only a half-point higher than 1992 and well below the 86.8% peak in 1988. This year, utilization may hit only 82%--held down by the effects of recent capacity additions in the Middle East and Asia." (p76)

Weber, Joseph. "Manufacturing: Chemicals: Lean, Mean, and...Healthier?" Business Week n3353, 10 Jan 1994. p76. (ISSN0007-7135).

CHEMICAL WEAPONS--U.S. (v19)

CHEMICALS

see also AGRICULTURAL CHEMICALS

"Close to 10 million natural and man-made chemical substances have been identified to date and at least 1,000 new substances are added to the list each year. The present annual production of chemicals is over 400 million tons. Approximately 100,000 substances are produced in significant industrial quantities. Facing this, most of the world's economically active population--up to three thousand million to date--is exposed in one way or another to possibly toxic chemicals, agricultural workers being probably more at risk than others because of exposure to pesticides and herbicides." (p4)

Obadia, Isaac. "Dossier: Chemicals: Benefits and Dangers." World of Work n7, Mar 1994. p4-5. (ISSN1020-0029).

CHEMICALS--MEXICO--ACCIDENTS

"Of the world's 55 most serious chemical accidents on record--and they include those of Seveso, Bhopal, and Chernobyl--nine (more than 15%) have occurred in Mexico. The current rate of chemical accidents in this country is one major accident every 18 months and many smaller ones occur frequently at industrial facilities or during the transport of hazardous chemicals. This is far higher than for any other country, regardless of its stage of development. The results of such accidents are human suffering and financial loss, as well as long-term problems. For example, after the Guadalajara gasoline explosion in April 1992, which caused 202 deaths, 15% of all the demonstrations staged in the city the following year were directly related to the accident. The costs, including rebuilding and compensation, are well over US$ 200 million so far." (p9)

Albert, Lilia A. "Accident-Prone Mexico." World Health n5, Sep-Oct 1993. p9-10. (ISSN0043-8502).

CHEMICALS--PHYSIOLOGICAL EFFECT (v19)

CHERNOBYL NUCLEAR ACCIDENT, CHERNOBYL', UKRAINE, 1986 (v19)

"The Chernobyl disaster has affected Belarus financially and emotionally. The republic was declared an ecological disaster area, and the zones of radioactive contamination from the nuclear explosion coincided with pre-existing areas of high chemical contamination. The greatest concentrations of contamination are in the Polesie region, formerly the 'greenest' area of Belarus, considered to be the country's 'lungs.' Radiation contaminated 23 percent of the republic's land--home to 3,678 settlements, villages, and towns--and 20 percent of the population. In the fertile Gomel region, farming and food processing were stopped, and 6 percent of its people had to be evacuated to other regions to try to find other ways of making a living. In the Mogilev region, nearly a third of the population lives on contaminated land." (p39-40)

Tiurina, Tatiana. "Belarus: Neutrality, Maybe." Bulletin of the Atomic Scientists v50 n1, Jan-Feb 1994. p36-40. (ISSN0096-3402).

"The [Belarus] government's health programs cannot keep up with treatment for diseases appearing in people exposed to the radiation. The 1992 statistics are not comforting. Only 60 percent of 815,000 people who were exposed to Chernobyl radiation have had even minimal medical care. (But 80 percent of exposed children have had some medical treatment.)...In 115 of 118 regions in Belarus, the child mortality rate is alarmingly high. In the Gomel, Mogilev, Novopolotsk, and Minsk regions, unfavorable environmental factors are said to contribute to 15-20 percent of all illnesses. The average life span is declining, especially for males; it is 66 years in Belarus, 70 in Europe. It is difficult to anticipate other long-term effects, but according to the Department of Psychiatry of the Minsk Medical Institute, every year 25,000 psychological illnesses are diagnosed. There are 144,350 people registered at psychiatric hospitals--and in reality there may be five times as many. There are 2,000 suicides yearly, the majority among young people of working age. This is a very large number for Belarussians, who were considered to be emotionally stable." (p40)

Tiurina, Tatiana. "Belarus: Neutrality, Maybe." Bulletin of the Atomic Scientists v50 n1, Jan-Feb 1994. p36-40. (ISSN0096-3402).

"Official Soviet estimates of immediate deaths from the 1986 [Chernobyl] meltdown ranged between 31 and 250. Some Ukrainian authorities, however, claim that several thousand people have already lost their lives. Most estimates of deaths from radiation-induced cancer over the long term range between 2,500 and 39,000 (although some significantly higher numbers have also been suggested). Two thousand villages were abandoned, 180,000 people resettled, and more than 15,000 square miles of land contaminated. Ominously, the hastily erected concrete 'sarcophagus' encasing the burned-out reactor is now showing signs of failure; its collapse could release huge amounts of heavily contaminated radioactive dust into the atmosphere, and could cause additional radiation injuries and deaths. Incredibly, it could all happen again. In the Commonwealth of Independent States and Eastern Europe, 15 Chernobyl-style RBMK reactors continue to operate, as well as 10 other older Soviet-designed plants. None were built with safety systems that meet Western standards." (p81)

Greenberg, Phillip A. "Dreams Die Hard." Sierra v78 n6, Nov-Dec 1993. p78-85,102-103. (ISSN0161-7362).

CHERNOBYL NUCLEAR ACCIDENT, CHERNOBYL', UKRAINE, 1986--HEALTH ASPECTS

"The state of oral health was the least of the worries of the population who found themselves in a radioactive zone after the Chernobyl nuclear power station disaster in 1986. The first teams of dentists from the Minsk Medical Institute who arrived at strictly controlled areas of Belarus several days after the accident had no evidence of any specific oral health problems among the population....There was an obvious deterioration in the oral health status of the surveyed population. The latest data showed moderate to high levels of periodontal disease, and an increasing proportion of oral mucosal diseases. The average number of decayed, missing, or filled (DMF) teeth varied from 4.6 in 15-year-old children to 19.6 in the over-65-year-old age group....The prevalence of gingivitis and/or periodontitis, which was almost 100% in teenagers and the adult population, coincided with the lack of regular oral hygiene practices. The most frequent complaint was gum bleeding and dryness of the mouth. The latter condition was observed in 12% of 18-year-olds, 29% in the 35-44 age group, and 86% in 65-year-olds, compared with 3%, 20%, and 33% respectively in similar age groups surveyed in non-contaminated regions of the country. About 17% of the surveyed population had some abnormality or oral mucosa lesions compared with 10% in noncontaminated areas." (p24-25)

Leous, P. A. "Chernobyl 'Fall-Out' on Oral Health." World Health n1, Jan-Feb 1994. p24-25. (ISSN0043-8502).

CHIAPAS (MEXICO)

see also COFFEE INDUSTRY--CHIAPAS (MEXICO);

FORESTS AND FORESTRY--CHIAPAS (MEXICO)

"Chiapas has a total area of some 7.5 million hectares (18.5 million acres). It is Mexico's eighth-largest state, divided into 111 municipalities, organized for looting purposes into nine economic regions. Forty percent of the nation's plant varieties, 36 percent of its mammals, 34 percent of its reptiles and amphibians, 66 percent of the bird species, 20 percent of the freshwater fish and 80 percent of the butterfly species are found in Chiapas. Seven percent of the total national precipitation falls in Chiapas. But its greatest wealth is the 35 million people of Chiapas, of whom two-thirds live and die in rural communities. Half of them do not have potable water and two-thirds have no sewage." (p30)

Marcos, Subcommandante. "Defending the Commons: A Reality Tour of the Heart of Chiapas." Earth Island Journal v9 n2, Spr 1994. p30-31. (ISSN1041-0406).

CHIAPAS (MEXICO)--POPULATION

"One-and-a-half million people in Chiapas have no medical services at their disposal. There are two clinics for every 10,000 inhabitants, five times less than the national average. There are three hospital beds for every 10,000 Chiapans--one-third the ratio of the rest of Mexico. There is one operating room per 100,000 inhabitants--half the number in the rest of Mexico, and five doctors and four nurses per 10,000 people--half the national average. Fifty-four percent of the Chiapan population suffers from malnutrition. In the highlands and forests this portion increases to 80 percent. A peasant's average diet consists of coffee, corn, tortillas and beans." (p31)

Marcos, Subcommandante. "Defending the Commons: A Reality Tour of the Heart of Chiapas." Earth Island Journal v9 n2, Spr 1994. p30-31. (ISSN1041-0406).

CHIAPAS (MEXICO)--SOCIAL CONDITIONS

Chiapas is "a large state in southern Mexico with 3.5 million people, more than a million of whom are indigenous and live in the Selva Lacandona mountain region....During the '80s, 150,000 people died in Chiapas from curable illnesses, according to local humanitarian organizations. About 70% of the population are temporary agricultural workers, earning under minimum wage, who must cope with a lack of water, infrastructure and health centers. Malnutrition, afflicting 33% of the population, is the most common cause of death in the state, which is also plagued with the highest illiteracy rate in the country (30%). In addition, according to government figures, 35% of the 16,302 communities do not have electricity and 80% of the houses have dirt floors." (p27-28)

Selser, Gabriela. "International: Mexico: The End of a Myth?" Barricada Internacional n370, Feb 1994. p27-29. (ISSN1013-9567).

"Chiapas is Mexico's deep south, where the PRI's [Institutional Revolutionary Party's] rule has traditionally been at its most corrupt and feudal. Geographically and socially, this is part of Central America, where guerrilla wars abounded in the 1980s. On most indicators, it ranks as Mexico's poorest state, and its large Mayan population is both poor and ill-used. In Ococingo, for example, illiteracy exceeds 45%. Four houses out of five there have earth floors and no drains." (p41-42)

"International: Mexico's Second-Class Citizens Say Enough Is Enough." Economist v330 n7844, 8 Jan 1994. p41-42. (ISSN0013-0613).

CHICAGO (ILL)

see also CORPORATIONS--CHICAGO (ILL)--ECONOMIC CONDITIONS; FILLS (EARTHWORK)--CHICAGO (ILL); FIREARMS--CHICAGO (ILL); GANGS--CHICAGO (ILL); HIGH SCHOOL DROPOUTS--CHICAGO (ILL); POLLUTION--CHICAGO (ILL)--HEALTH AND HYGIENE; PUBLIC HOUSING--CHICAGO (ILL); RECYCLING (WASTE, ETC.)--CHICAGO (ILL); REFUSE AND REFUSE DISPOSAL--CHICAGO (ILL); WOMEN--CHICAGO (ILL)--SOCIAL CONDITIONS

CHICAGO (ILL)--ECONOMIC CONDITIONS (v19)

"A 1990 study determined that a worker [in Chicago] needed to earn $10/hour in order to stay off public aid and meet the basic needs for a family of three. In 1992, six percent of Chicagoans had gone hungry in the past year, and 26 percent had fallen behind on either housing or utility bills in the past two years. Chicago's employment level dropped 3 percent between 1979 and 1989, but the number employed in manufacturing jobs, which traditionally pay better than non-manufacturing jobs for low-skilled workers, dropped by 35 percent. In 1990, 10.7 percent of Chicago's labor force was unemployed." (p17)

Bardoe, Cheryl. "Chicago's Sustainability Indicators." Neighborhood Works v16 n5, Oct-Nov 1993. p16-20.

CHICKEN INDUSTRY--U.S. (v19)

CHICKENPOX--U.S. (v19)

CHILD ABUSE

see also CHILD MOLESTING

CHILD ABUSE--NEW YORK (NY) (v19)

CHILD ABUSE--U.S. (v19)

According to a report entitled "Understanding Child Abuse and Neglect" by the U.S. National Academy of Science, "In 1990, case reports involving over 2 million children were made to social service agencies [in the U.S.]. About 2,000 child deaths (ages 0-17) due to abuse or neglect were recorded annually between 1979 and 1988, and an additional 160,000 cases resulted in serious injury in 1990 alone. There is insufficient knowledge about the nature of child abuse and neglect to formulate public policy." (p112)

Orme, Thomas W. (American Council on Science and Health). U.S. House. Committee on Science, Space, and Technology. "Risk Assessment Research." Hearing, 16 Nov 1993. Washington, D.C.: GPO, 1994. (ISBN016043615X). (Y4.Sci2:103/85).

"The national extent of child abuse and neglect has grown to shocking epidemic proportions--more than 2,500,000 reports of child abuse and neglect are made each year. Many abused children are victimized in their homes, but there is a large and growing number of children being victimized outside the home." (pS16777)

Biden, Joseph R., Jr. (Sen.-Del.). "Statements on Introduced Bills and Joint Resolutions," Congressional Record (20 Nov 1993). Daily ed. pS16719-16785. (ISSN0363-7239).

"Between 1976 and 1992, the number of reports of child abuse and neglect nationwide increased from an estimated 669,000 to 2,936,000, an increase of 339 percent (statistics from American Humane Association, 1976 and National Committee for the Prevention of Child Abuse, 1992). Use of substitute care as a service to respond to substantiated reports has also risen. At the end of FY 1990, there were 407,000 children in substitute care in the United States, a 45.4 percent increase in the number of children in care over the FY 1986 figure of 280,000 children nationwide (American Public Welfare Association, VCIS Research Notes No.5, November, 1991). What has been most concerning about these numbers is that resources to respond to child maltreatment have not increased at a commensurate pace. Moreover, at the federal level, funding has focused largely on out-of-home care, with a patchwork of funds available for other services. In 1993, for example, states received $2.5 billion for foster care, but only $295 million for child welfare services." (p7)

Winterfeld, Amy Perintz. "New Developments in Funding Family Preservation and Support Services." Protecting Children v10 n1, 1993. p7-8.

"Too many of America's families are hard pressed by economic stress and the lack of the community support they need to properly care for their children. As a consequence, reports of abused and neglected children increase each year. The U.S. Advisory Board on Child Abuse and Neglect has called this predicament 'a national emergency.' In 1991, 2.7 million children were reported as victims of child maltreatment. Between 1985 and 1991, child abuse reports increased 40 percent nationwide. There continues to be, year to year, an over-representation of ethnic minority children and families in the child welfare system. Child maltreatment is related to many social problems....Child abuse fatalities remain high--almost four children die each day in the United States as a result of maltreatment. In 1991, an estimated 1,383 children died from abuse or neglect; the number of child abuse fatalities rose by 54 percent between 1985 and 1991. By providing more prevention services to children and families, we can prevent child abuse and neglect from happening and avoid the costs of child maltreatment." (p5)

"Child Abuse and Neglect: A Challenge to the Nation." Protecting Children v9 n4, 1993. p5-7.

"Courts across the United States...face a deluge of new cases. Some 2,936,000 children were abused in the United States in 1992, an increase of 53 percent since 1985. That means that 45 out of every 1,000 US children were mistreated, according to the National Committee to Prevent Child Abuse. In Illinois, the number of abused and neglected children jumped 33 percent to 43,138 from 1985 to 1992, according to the Illinois Department of Children and Family Services (DCFS)." (p4)

Tyson, James L. "National: Illinois Helps Judges Faced with Surge of Child Abuse." The Christian Science Monitor v86 n42, 25 Jan 1994. p4. (ISSN0882-7729).

CHILD ABUSE--U.S.--CRIMINALS (v19)

CHILD ABUSE--U.S.--MORTALITY

Death rates of children as a result of abuse and neglect vary in different states and regions of the U.S. According to researchers from the Centers for Disease Control and Prevention and the University of Missouri, the ranges of death rates per 100,000 children was 5.4 to 11.5 in the South, 5.2 to 11.2 in the West, 4.6 to 9.8 in the North-Central states, and 4.3 to 8.2 in the Northeast. (p4)

"News Roundup: Child-Abuse Deaths." Education Week v13 n21, 16 Feb 1994. p4. (ISSN0277-4232).

CHILD CARE (v19)

CHILD CARE--GREAT BRITAIN (v19)

CHILD CARE--JAPAN--U.S. (v19)

CHILD CARE--RUSSIA

"As Russia struggles to accommodate itself to the realities of life after socialism, economic hardship and political chaos are exacerbating social dislocation. With the old social safety net in disarray, St. Petersburg is struggling to adapt to the exigencies of the present. (St. Petersburg alone has an estimated 12,000-15,000 runaways and homeless youth.) The traditional state child care system can no longer handle the demand placed upon it. Serving approximately 4,000 youth, the system consists of baby homes, orphanages and several institutions for the disabled. At the age of 16, most of the children in the system are left on their own. Those unable to take care of themselves remain institutionalized. Only a lucky few are ever adopted." (p37)

Groark, Christina/others. "Civil Society: Opening the Door to Youth in St. Petersburg." Surviving Together v11 n2, Sum 1993. p37-38. (ISSN0859-6286).

CHILD CARE--U.S.

"Today, about 6 million preschool children are in a day care program for some or all of their day. By 1995, at least 8 million preschoolers will be in day care." (pS16777)

Biden, Joseph R., Jr. (Sen.-Del.). "Statements on Introduced Bills and Joint Resolutions," Congressional Record (20 Nov 1993). Daily ed. pS16719-16785. (ISSN0363-7239).

"Many states [in the U.S.] use federal child-care aid to pay for informal arrangements that 'are falling far short of providing basic health and safety protections' for young children, a new report from the Children's Defense Fund warns....The study found that: 25 states do not require smaller family child-care providers to submit to inspections; 24 do not require those providers to receive first-aid or any other training in health and safety; 21 do not require child immunizations in small family-care homes; Only 19 require criminal background checks or child-abuse registry checks for workers in exempt settings; and More than one in five states do not consistently set health and safety standards for children in informal settings under the welfare measures, or offer less protections than they extend to children whose care is funded by block-grant programs." (p3)

Cohen, Deborah L. "Publicly Funded Informal Child Care Poorly Regulated, C.D.F. Finds." Education Week v13 n26, 23 Mar 1994. p3. (ISSN0277-4232).

"There are more than 23 million American children under 6, and an estimated 9 million need full-time care--yet only about 5 million licensed-day-care slots are available. Michelle Seligson of the School-Age Child Care Project at Wellesley College in Massachusetts estimates that as many as 10 million children need care before or after school--with slots for just 1.5 to 3 million." (p27)

Creighton, Linda L. "U.S. News: Kids Taking Care of Kids." U.S. News & World Report v115 n24, 20 Dec 1993. p26-27,30-33. (ISSN0041-5537).

CHILD CARE--U.S.--FATHERS (v19)

CHILD CARE WORKERS--MARYLAND

"In 1991, the Maryland Committee conducted a random sample statewide salary and benefits survey. While family day care providers ranked slightly higher than [day care] center aides in wage ($10,753 vs $10,400 per year), they were less than senior staff or teachers ($13,229) or directors ($19,094). When comparing these wages to other positions in the education field, all are incredibly low and demeaning! In the area of benefits, only 2.4% of family day care providers had health insurance paid through their business, while 11.3% of center employees had fully paid insurance and 21.4% had it partially paid. For vacation and sick days, 27.4% of family day care providers had paid vacation and 23.9% had paid sick days. However, in contrast, 73.2% of center staff had paid vacation and 63.9% had paid sick days." (p5)

"Child Care Costs." Family Day Care Bulletin Jun 1993. p5.

CHILD MOLESTING--U.S. (v19)

"The prevalence of childhood sexual abuse in the United States is very high. The National Center on Child Abuse and Neglect estimates the number of child sexual abuse victims to be more than 200,000 per year. Incidence studies report a wide prevalence range for sexual victimization (from 6 to 62%) but generally the rate of 30% for females and 15% for males has been presented consistently in the literature." (p50)

Grant, Christine A. "Incest: The Hidden Abuse." Imprint v41 n2, Feb-Mar 1994. p50-53. (ISSN0019-3038).

CHILD NEGLECT

see CHILD ABUSE

CHILD SNATCHING BY PARENTS

see KIDNAPPING, PARENTAL

CHILD SUPPORT--GREAT BRITAIN

"More than two-thirds of absent fathers [in Great Britain] make no contribution at all to their children's upkeep. Those that do, pay an average of only 25 [pounds sterling] ($37) a week. The result is that 1m out of 1.3m lone mothers with children are now living on state benefits." (p62)

"Britain: Child Support: Dad's Army." Economist v331 n7858, 9 Apr 1994. p62. (ISSN0013-0613).

CHILD SUPPORT--U.S. (v19)

"The first step toward getting children the support they are owed is federalizing child support collection. By having the IRS maintain a national registry of child support orders, and using wage withholding to collect support, that $34 billion gap will close. Today, States use over $500 million a year in Federal dollars to collect child support--resulting in confusion, duplication, and failing collection rates which range as low as 11.9 percent. Further, 33 percent of child support cases are interstate. Since it is difficult for States to enforce child support across State lines, less than $1 for every $10 owed to interstate child support is collected." (pH2571-2572)

Woolsey, Lynn C. (Rep.-Calif.). "Welfare Reform," Congressional Record (20 Apr 1994). Daily ed. pH2568-2577. (ISSN0363-7239).

"We have known for some time now that...[the U.S.] child support system needs a major overhaul. The Child Support Amendments of 1984 and the Family Support Act of 1988 made modest improvements. For every 100 child support cases in 1983, there were 15 in which there was a collection. In 1990, there were 18. Out of 100, 15 to 18 is a step in the right direction, but we clearly have a long, long way to go." (pS3463)

Dodd, Christopher J. (Sen.-Conn.). "Submission of Concurrent and Senate Resolutions," Congressional Record (22 Mar 1994). Daily ed. pS3446-3466. (ISSN0363-7239).

One in four U.S. "children live in a single-parent household. Most of us know how difficult it is to make ends meet with a two-income family. It does not take much imagination to envision how hard it must be for a single parent trying to juggle a job and family. One of the most startling statistics is that only half the single parents have sought out and obtained child support orders. That means that 50 percent of the single mothers either have been unable to track down the father or have not pursued or are unaware of their legal rights. Of the parents who have sought out and obtained child support, only half receive the full amount they are entitled to. In other words, 50 percent of the mothers don't even have child support orders and of the 50 percent that do, only half of them are getting what their children are entitled to. Approximately 25 percent of the single parents who have child support orders actually receive nothing at all. These are the worst offenders--the so-called dead beat dads." (pS2509)

Bryan, Richard H. (Sen.-Nev.). "Statements on Introduced Bills and Joint Resolutions," Congressional Record (8 Mar 1994). Daily ed. pS2475-2509. (ISSN0363-7239).

"Rising rates of divorce, single parenthood, and desertion have produced what is being called a 'dad deficit' of enormous proportions. Last year biological fathers were absent in an estimated 35 percent of households with children. Beyond the lack of emotional support these numbers suggest, there exists a lack of financial support. In 1989, $5 billion in court-ordered child support went unpaid, pushing countless children and their mothers below the poverty line. Although unpaid child support is not the only factor, 1 in 5 American children lives in poverty." (p22)

"Moral Issues of Our Times: Reaffirming the Family." The Christian Science Monitor v86 n48, 2 Feb 1994. p22. (ISSN0882-7729).

CHILD WELFARE

see also CHILD ABUSE; CHILD SUPPORT; FOSTER HOME CARE

CHILD WELFARE--MICHIGAN

A study by researchers at the University of Michigan School of Social Work's Center for the Study of Youth Policy "shows that the median length of time in the child welfare system is about 459 days (15.3 months) for children from Wayne County, compared with 237 days (7.9 months) for children from the rest of Michigan. Overall, the median stay is 294 days (9.8 months). The median length of stay is the point at which half of the children move from foster care to a permanent living arrangement, such as a return home or placement with a relative, legal guardian or in an adoptive home....According to the report, the median length of stay in the child welfare system for African American children is 348 days, compared with 272 days for Caucasian youth. Moreover, an even larger difference was found between African American youth in Wayne County (480 days) compared with African American children in the rest of the state (187 days)." (p1-2)

News release. "Child Welfare." University of Michigan News and Information Services 2 Feb 1994. p1-3.

CHILDBIRTH (v19)

"In parts of the United States and Canada as many as 50 percent of babies are born by Cesarean section, with a national average of 25 percent (one in four). This reflects a 400 percent increase in 20 years. In parts of Brazil and southern Italy, the percentage of Cesarean sections can be as high as 90 percent. In Greece around 70 percent of the births are chemically induced. Even in Great Britain, where we pride ourselves on being a pioneering nation in the move toward natural childbirth, we have the highest intervention rate in Europe, and about 85 percent of our first-time mothers are given some form of interventive help to give birth. Only one percent of British mothers give birth in their own homes, where conditions are most conducive to physiological childbirth. By contrast, Holland has 35 percent of home births and the best birth statistics of any industrialized nation." (p8)

Balaskas, Janet. "Agony & Ecstasy: Reclaiming the Power of Childbirth." New Directions for Women v22 n4, Jul-Aug 1993. p8. (ISSN0160-1075).

CHILDBIRTH--COMPLICATIONS (v19)

CHILDBIRTH--DEVELOPING COUNTRIES

"Making a basic package of prenatal, delivery and postpartum care available to 80% of the developing world's women and newborn babies would cost US$ 4 to $9 per capita, and would reduce the burden of pregnancy-related mortality and ill-health by two-thirds. This is a small price to pay considering that the total health expenditure per person in developing countries in 1990 was estimated at $41 per annum." (p31)

"WHO on....Making Motherhood Safer." World Health n5, Sep-Oct 1993. p30-31. (ISSN0043-8502).

CHILDBIRTH--KENYA (v19)

CHILDBIRTH--MORTALITY (v19)

CHILDBIRTH--NIGERIA--MORTALITY (v19)

CHILDBIRTH--U.S.

"Births in the U.S. surpassed 4 million each year between 1954 and 1964, during the second and much larger wave of the baby boom. In similar style, the baby boomlet that began in the late 1970s gained momentum throughout the 1980s, reaching its peak with 4.2 million births in 1990. Births then fell 1 percent in 1991 and a little less than 1 percent in 1992. In the first half of 1993, births were down 2 percent from the first half of 1992. If that trend continued in the second half, the 1993 total would come in at just under 4 million." (p16-17)

Crispell, Diane. "Business Reports: Generations: The Baby Boomlet May End with a Blizzard." American Demographics v16 n3, Mar 1994. p16-17. (ISSN0163-4089).

CHILDLESSNESS--U.S. (v19)

CHILDREN

see also ABDUCTION--U.S.--CHILDREN; AFRO-AMERICAN CHILDREN--SOCIAL CONDITIONS; AID TO FAMILIES WITH DEPENDENT CHILDREN PROGRAM; YOUTHS--U.S.; AIDS (DISEASE) IN CHILDREN--U.S.; DIARRHEA IN CHILDREN--DEVELOPING COUNTRIES--MORTALITY; ECONOMIC ASSISTANCE, AMERICAN--DEVELOPING COUNTRIES--CHILDREN; FIREARMS--U.S.--CHILDREN--MORTALITY; HOMELESS CHILDREN; IMMUNIZATION OF CHILDREN; INFANTS; LATCHKEY CHILDREN--U.S.; NONNUTRITIVE SWEETENERS--U.S.--CHILDREN; PASSIVE SMOKING IN CHILDREN--U.S.; POOR CHILDREN; SCHOOL CHILDREN; SEX OF CHILDREN, PARENTAL PREFERENCES FOR; VIOLENCE IN TELEVISION--U.S.--CHILDREN; VIOLENCE--U.S.--CHILDREN; VITAMIN A DEFICIENCY IN CHILDREN; WOMEN, INFANTS, AND CHILDREN PROGRAM

CHILDREN--BRAZIL--SOCIAL CONDITIONS (v19)

"Almost 10,000 children have been killed since 1991 [in Brazil], 31 per cent are due to traffic accidents, no doubt involving the little lime-sellers, and there is hope for stiffer penalties for careless drivers; 90 per cent of those under five are murdered by parents or relatives. In 1993, two children per day were killed in Rio de Janeiro. Eighty per cent of street children use drugs, mostly shoemaker's glue which is a sedative to hunger." (p192)

Hillman, Elizabeth. "Some Hope for Brazil's Abandoned Children." Contemporary Review v264 n1539, Apr 1994. p190-196. (ISSN0010-7565).

CHILDREN--CARE

see CHILD CARE

CHILDREN--CUBA--MORTALITY

"Children born in Cuba have a better chance of surviving the early years of life than those born anywhere else in the Central America and Caribbean region, according to THE PROGRESS OF NATIONS, a new publication released on September 22 by UNICEF, the United Nations Children's Fund....For every 1,000 Cuban children born alive in 1991 only 12 die before their fifth birthday (the same rate as Israel), the best child survival rate in Central America and the Caribbean (which averages 48) and just below the average of 11 for industrialized countries. The significance of the Cuban statistic can readily be seen by comparing it with a few other countries: Mexico, 36; Chile, 20; India, 126; Kuwait, 17; Mozambique, 292." (p17)

"Cuba/International: UNICEF Lauds Cuba's Program for Children." Cuba Update n6, Nov-Dec 1993. p17-18. (ISSN0196-0830).

CHILDREN--EMPLOYMENT (v19)

CHILDREN--EMPLOYMENT--BANGLADESH

"Bangladesh is one country where there is widespread use of child labor in the garment industry. Local human rights groups estimate conservatively that 20% of the 700,000 workers in the garment industry are under the age of 15. Children are considered more desirable as employees because they are paid less than adults, are less likely to try to organize a union or otherwise complain about working conditions, and won't get pregnant and seek leave time. Most child workers are children of adult workers in the same factory. Children are usually at the low end of the pay scale, earning only $7 per month; adult workers are paid little more, often earning only $8-$12 per month." (p14)

"Bangladesh: Threatened U.S. Sanctions for Child Labor." NewsNotes v18 n4, Jul-Aug 1993. p14. (ISSN1064-1556).

CHILDREN--EMPLOYMENT--INDIA--NEPAL--PAKISTAN (v19)

CHILDREN--EMPLOYMENT--U.S. (v19)

CHILDREN--FLORIDA--SOCIAL CONDITIONS (v19)

CHILDREN--HAITI--SOCIAL CONDITIONS (v19)

CHILDREN--HEALTH AND HYGIENE (v19)

CHILDREN--HEALTH AND HYGIENE--AFRICA (v19)

CHILDREN--HEALTH AND HYGIENE--U.S. (v19)

"Almost 60 percent of the deaths in the United States are attributable to cardiovascular disease and cancer. Unfortunately, American children are increasingly engaging in the three behaviors that contribute to these diseases: tobacco use, improper diet, and insufficient exercise. For instance, 40 percent of American children aged 5 to 8 are obese, inactive, or have elevated blood pressure or cholesterol--all risk factors associated with cardiovascular disease. These problems are particularly marked in inner-city areas, where children are often exposed to other factors that threaten their health--crime, drugs, and inadequate access to health care. Almost half of our elementary school students have tried smoking--the No. 1 preventable cause of death in the United States. What is particularly alarming is that children--especially girls--are smoking at younger and younger ages. Tobacco addiction is increasingly a 'teen onset' disease: 90 percent of all smokers start before they are 21, 60 percent before they are 14, and 22 percent before they are 9...." (pS647)

Kennedy, Edward M. (Sen.-Mass.). "Goals 2000: Educate America Act," Congressional Record (2 Feb 1994). Daily ed. pS634-653. (ISSN0363-7239).

CHILDREN--IRAQ--MORTALITY

"After visiting Iraq in May 1991, a team of public health experts organized by Harvard University predicted that about 170,000 infants would die in 1991 alone of hunger or of treatable ailments such as dysentery and typhoid fever. Another investigation conducted in October 1991 by an international Study Team, consisting of 35 researchers from 13 countries, concluded that Iraq's child mortality rate had more than quadrupled since the end of the war. The major reason for the increase was diarrheal illness. About 1 million Iraqi children under the age of 5 (29 percent) were found perilously malnourished, and many of them exhibited signs of severe psychological trauma as a result of the relentless bombing. According to figures published by Iraq's Ministry of Health, about 3,000 children die each month because of malnutrition and lack of proper medical care. International relief organizations say the figures are not unrealistic." (p8)

Almaney, Adnan J. "Who Speaks for the Iraqui Children?" New Patroit v6 n4, Jul-Aug 1993. p8.

CHILDREN--MICHIGAN--SOCIAL CONDITIONS (v19)

"Children who enroll in high-quality preschool programs are less likely to turn to crime as they grow up, according to a study by the High/Scope Educational Research Foundation. The study, which followed a group of 123 people in Michigan from childhood through age 27, found those who were in a good preschool program were much more likely to end up owning a home than to be arrested for breaking into one....Young African-American children born into poverty were chosen for the study in the early 1960s. Half were enrolled in a high-quality preschool program that stressed active learning and developed the students' decision-making skills. The other half comprised the control group. When the subjects were re-evaluated at age 27, one of the most striking differences was in criminal activity: 35 percent of the control group had been arrested five or more times, compared to 7 percent of those enrolled in the program." (p1,13 secA)

Stergianis, Susanna. "Study: Good Preschool May Prevent Criminals." Ann Arbor News 23 Apr 1994. p1,13 secA.

"Nearly 281,000 children in Michigan are living in troubled

neighborhoods--their lives torn apart by poverty and crime, a national survey reported today. The Kids Count Data Book, compiled annually by the Anne E. Casey Foundation, ranked Michigan near last in the percentage of children living in distressed communities. Only three states had poorer rankings....About four million of the nation's 63 million children are growing up in ailing neighborhoods, the report found. Eighty percent of children at-risk are from black or Hispanic families. Nearly half of all children living in severely distressed areas live in just six states: Michigan, California, Illinois, New York, Ohio and Texas." (p6 secA)

"State Ranking Dismal for Poor Kids." Ann Arbor News 25 Apr 1994. p6 secA.

CHILDREN--MORTALITY (v19)

CHILDREN--NUTRITION

"More than 30% of the world's under-five-year-old children--about 192 million in all--are still malnourished and underweight. Over two-thirds (80%) of these children live in Asia--especially southern Asia--15% in Africa, and 5% in Latin America....Iodine deficiency disorders (IDD), the greatest worldwide cause of preventable brain damage in infants and young children, is currently a significant public health problem in 118 countries: 1571 million people live in iodine-deficient environments and are therefore at risk of IDD, while 655 million people actually have goitre....More than a quarter of a million children are estimated to go blind every year due to a deficiency of vitamin A, and some 14 million currently exhibit signs of clinical xerophthalmia ranging from dryness to severe ulceration." (p1) "Iron deficiency in early childhood is associated with higher mortality and impairment of cognitive development. A 1985 WHO [World Health Organization] global assessment of anaemia indicated that 51% of under-five-year-old children in developing countries were anaemic." (p2)

News release. "WHO Report on Infant and Young Child Nutrition: Global Problems and Promising Developments." WHO Press 18 Jan 1994. p1-3.

CHILDREN--RUSSIA--ECONOMIC CONDITIONS (v19)

CHILDREN--SOCIAL CONDITIONS (v19)

CHILDREN--TEXAS--SOCIAL CONDITIONS

"Over 4 million Texans are hungry, and 1.2 million of those are children under 12. Moreover, almost 25 percent of Texas children live in poverty--higher than the national average--and children of poor families frequently do not receive adequate nutrition. Numerous studies link improper nutrition in childhood with reduced cognitive abilities. And government programs providing food assistance are often insufficient. The average food stamp benefit in Texas is just $67 a month, and only 60 percent of those eligible for the food stamp program are enrolled....Residents of low-income urban areas pay 10-30 percent more for their food and spend an average of $400-$1000 annually just on transportation to buy food. Convenience markets and 'mini-marts' in gasoline stations fill a certain gap in food marketing, and are extremely profitable in low-income areas, but generally have even higher prices and offer an even more limited selection of fresh staples and produce. Because of lack of access to other shopping, some people do their weekly grocery shopping at these convenience marts." (p30)

Katcher, Jennifer. "Promoting Sustainable Agriculture and Reducing Hunger: Progress from the Lone Star State." Land Report i48, Fall 1993. p30-31.

CHILDREN--U.S. (v19)

CHILDREN--U.S.--SAFETY MEASURES--PUBLIC OPINION (v19)

CHILDREN--U.S.--SOCIAL CONDITIONS (v19)

"In virtually every critical area of child development and healthy maturation, family poverty creates huge roadblocks to individual accomplishment, future economic self-sufficiency, and national progress....Every 12 seconds of the school day, an American child drops out (380,000 a year). Every 13 seconds, an American child is reported abused or neglected (2.7 million a year). Every 26 seconds, an American child runs away from home (1.2 million a year)....Every 9 minutes, an American child is arrested for a drug offense. Every 40 minutes, an American child is arrested for drunk driving....Every 3 hours, a child is murdered." (p177)

Weill, James D. (General Counsel, Children's Defense Fund). U.S. Congress. Joint Economic Committee. "The 1993 Economic Report of the President." Hearing, 27 Jan 1993. Washington, D.C.: GPO, 1994. (ISBN0160440300). (Y4.Ec:Ec7/2/993/pt.1).

According to a Fact Sheet prepared by the Select Committee on Children, Youth, and Families of the U.S. House of Representatives, and cited in an article written by Daniel Patrick Moynihan, "Between 1970 and 1991, the value of AFDC (Aid to Families with Dependent Children) benefits decreased by 41 percent. In spite of proven success of Head Start, only 28 percent of eligible children are being served. As of 1990, more than $18 billion in child support went uncollected. At the same time, the poverty rate among single-parent families with children under 18 was 44 percent. Between 1980 and 1990, the rate of growth in the total federal budget was four times greater than the rate of growth in children's programs." (p15)

Moynihan, Daniel Patrick. "Defining Deviancy Down." American Educator v17 n4, Win 1993-94. p10,12-18. (ISSN0148-432X).

"Every 5 seconds of the school day [in the U.S.], a student drops out of public school. Every 30 seconds, a baby is born into poverty. Every 34 seconds, a baby is born to a mother who did not graduate from high school. Every 2 minutes, a baby is born at low birth weight. Every 2 minutes, a baby is born to a mother who had late or no prenatal care. Every 4 minutes, a child is arrested for an alcohol-related crime. Every 5 minutes a child is arrested for a violent crime. Every 7 minutes, a child is arrested for a drug crime. Every 2 hours, a child is murdered. Every 4 hours in the United States of America, a child commits suicide. And every 9 hours, a child or young adult under 25 dies from HIV." (pS3820)

Wellstone, Paul D. (Sen.-Minn.). "The State of America's Children," Congressional Record (25 Mar 1994). Daily ed. pS3820. (ISSN0363-7239).

President Clinton's initiative for reform in education, the Goals 2000: Educate America Act, includes the vision that by the year 2000 all children in America will start school ready to learn. "Entering the schoolhouse at age 5 is not, for a significant number of young children, an innoculation against the ravages of a life of deprivation....Examine these current realities of childhood in America: Over 1,000 cocaine babies are born each year. Eighteen percent of children between the ages of 1 and 4 have not seen a doctor for routine health care. A hundred thousand children a year die as a direct result of poverty. The number of homeless children on a given night is about 100,000--there could be as many as two million each year. The percentage of American households with TV sets exceeds the percentage of children who have been vaccinated against polio. The number of learning-disabled children has increased by 40 percent in the last two years--to two million children. Since 1975, children have been poorer than any age group in our society." (p34)

Tirozzi, Gerald N. "School Readiness: An Inextricable Link to Achieving All the Education Goals." Education Week v13 n28, 6 Apr 1994. p34. (ISSN0277-4232).

"Children in the United States are deprived unbelievably. According to a UNICEF report, the U.S. child poverty rate is more than double that of other major industrial countries. In comparing child health worldwide, only children in the United States and Britain are worse off now than they were in 1970. One in five American children live below the poverty level and suffer health problems because of it. The report said that children in the USA who grow up without a father 'more than doubled from 1960 to the end of the 1980s.' It also noted that 'by far the highest murder rate for young people--with nine of ten killings of youths in the industrialized world--takes place in the U.S.' Tufts University's Center on Poverty, Hunger and Nutrition has estimated that 'hunger afflicts about 12-million American children, most pronounced in the South.' A national survey of the U.S. Department of Health and Human Services found that 22,000 infants were abandoned in 1991 in the nation's hospitals." (p5)

"Editorials: This 190th Milestone a Challenge to Creativity." Human Quest v208 n1, Jan-Feb 1994. p5. (ISSN0897-8786).

"Children are now the poorest age group in America. In 1991, more than one in five--14.3 million children--was poor; 4 million more than in 1979. Poverty is the single most important factor causing most children to not do well in school. Also in 1991, nearly 13 million American children--2 million more than in 1980--lived in single-parent families. Twenty percent of all children are not covered by private or public health insurance. One of every six babies born in the United States has a teenage mother." (p9)

Payzant, Thomas W./Gardner, Maruta. "Toward a New Kind of Leadership: Changing Roles and Responsibilities in a Restructuring School District." NASSP Bulletin v78 n560, Mar 1994. p8-17. (ISSN0192-6365).

CHILDREN--WASHINGTON (STATE)--SOCIAL CONDITIONS

"How serious is the need for welfare reform? In 1987 the Washington State Legislature directed the Washington State Institute for Public Policy to answer that question via a five-year study of those in Washington State who received or who are at risk of receiving government assistance....Of the children living in public assistance households: 82 percent had mothers who were not currently married; 55 percent lived in households with only one adult; 25 percent of children 6 to 12 years old and 36 percent of children 13 to 18 years old, had repeated a grade in school; and 21 percent of children 13 to 18 years old had been suspended or expelled from school." (pS16667)

Gorton, Slade (Sen.-Wash.). "The Need for Welfare Reform," Congressional Record (20 Nov 1993). Daily ed. pS16667-16668. (ISSN0363-7239).

CHILDREN, DEAF--U.S. (v19)

CHILDREN, POOR

see POOR CHILDREN

CHILDREN AS CONSUMERS

"According to Teenage Research Unlimited of Northbrook, Illinois, and author James McNeal (KIDS AS CUSTOMERS, 1992), children [in the U.S.] between the ages of 3 and 17 spend an estimated $40 billion each year on direct purchases. Even more significantly, their collective influence on annual family purchases represents approximately $295 billion annually. Little wonder that advertisers are racing to reach this lucrative market. With kids averaging 21 to 26 hours a week--or roughly a day--in front of the television, and spending equivalent hours in school, the two best places for advertisers to target a captive youth audience are television and the classroom." (p27)

Sleeper, Barbara. "The Battle for the Child's Mind." Animals v126 n6, Nov-Dec 1993. p24-28. (ISSN0030-6835).

CHILDREN AS CONSUMERS--U.S. (v19)

CHILDREN OF MINORITIES--U.S.--SOCIAL CONDITIONS

"Children from racial minorities are the most rapidly increasing group in the U.S. population; by the year 2010, one of every four children will be a child of color (Chan, 1990). These children are also the largest at-risk group for disabilities associated with poverty. Lack of maternal prenatal care, poor prenatal nutrition, and inadequate health care for poor children themselves (Edmunds, Marinson, & Goldberg, 1990; Schorr, 1989) all contribute to risk of disability. A disproportionate number of low-income African American and Hispanic infants are born at risk for prenatal exposure to HIV and/or to crack cocaine; both factors are associated with increased risk of developmental delay. It is estimated that within three to five years, HIV will be the primary infectious cause of developmental delay in children (Dokecki, Baumeister, & Kupstas, 1989)." (p3-4)

Rounds, Kathleen A./others. "Practice with Culturally Diverse Families of Young Children with Disabilities." Families in Society v75 n1, Jan 1994. p3-15. (ISSN1044-3894).

CHILDREN'S ACCIDENTS--U.S. (v19)

According to a report entitled "Emergency Medical Services for Children" by the U.S. National Academy of Science, "21,000 children and young people under the age of 20 died from injuries [in the U.S.] in 1988. Nearly 21,000 more deaths occurred because of illness and other disorders (excluding congenital anomalies and birth related conditions) that required emergency intervention. Thousands more children were hospitalized and millions were treated in emergency departments. Despite the number of childhood medical emergencies, many emergency departments of hospitals are poorly prepared to handle the emergency needs of children. The number of deaths and permanent disabilities which children suffer as a result of medical emergencies can be reduced by improvements in hospital emergency care for children." (p110-111)

Orme, Thomas W. (American Council on Science and Health). U.S. House. Committee on Science, Space, and Technology. "Risk Assessment Research." Hearing, 16 Nov 1993. Washington, D.C.: GPO, 1994. (ISBN016043615X). (Y4.Sci2:103/85).

CHILDREN'S ACCIDENTS--U.S.--MORTALITY (v19)

CHILE

see also CONTRACEPTION--CHILE; EXPORTS--CHILE; PENSIONS--CHILE; PETROLEUM INDUSTRY AND TRADE--CHILE

CHILE--ECONOMIC CONDITIONS (v19)

"In December, Eduardo Frei, candidate of the ruling Christian Democratic Party, easily won the election with 55 percent of the vote. Mr. Frei's victory represents the first democratic transition between governments in more than 20 years. Chileans voted to continue current government policies. News on the economic front has been outstanding: The economy has grown an average of 6 percent a year since 1985. Unemployment is running between 4 percent and 5 percent. The inflation rate plummeted from 505 percent in 1974 to about 12 percent in 1993. Economists are forecasting a 9 percent inflation rate for 1994. Exports, about 12 percent of gross domestic product 20 years ago, now run at about 35 percent of GDP [gross domestic product]. Total investment in Chile last year was an impressive 27 percent of GDP." (p6)

Walters, David C. "Economy: Good News in Chile: Economy Is Growing, Unemployment Down." The Christian Science Monitor v86 n48, 2 Feb 1994. p6. (ISSN0882-7729).

CHINA

see also AGRICULTURE--CHINA--U.S.; AIR--POLLUTION--CHINA; ARTIFICIAL SATELLITES IN TELECOMMUNICATION--CHINA--U.S.; BALANCE OF TRADE--CHINA; COMMUNIST PARTIES--CHINA;

COPYRIGHT INFRINGEMENT--CHINA; DAMS--CHINA; DEFENSE INDUSTRIES--CHINA; DENTAL CARE--CHINA; ECONOMIC FORECASTING--CHINA; ELECTRIC POWER--CHINA; ENERGY CONSUMPTION--CHINA; FERTILITY, HUMAN--CHINA; FOSSIL FUELS--CHINA--FORMER SOVIET REPUBLICS; FUJIAN (CHINA)--ECONOMIC CONDITIONS; GREENHOUSE EFFECT, ATMOSPHERIC--CHINA; GUANGDONG (CHINA)--ECONOMIC CONDITIONS; INDUSTRY AND STATE--CHINA; INVESTMENTS, FOREIGN--CHINA--HONG KONG; LEAD--TOXICOLOGY--CHINA; MIGRATION, INTERNAL--CHINA; MOTOR VEHICLES--CHINA--THAILAND; PETROLEUM INDUSTRY AND TRADE--CHINA; SEX RATIO--CHINA; SHANGHAI (CHINA)--ECONOMIC CONDITIONS; SMOKING--CHINA; TOURIST TRADE--CHINA; UNEMPLOYMENT--CHINA; WATER-POWER--CHINA; WATER-SUPPLY--CHINA; WOMEN--CHINA

CHINA--COMMERCE (v19)

CHINA--COMMERCE--U.S. (v19)

"Every year since 1989, when pro-democracy demonstrators were crushed in Beijing, America has threatened to end China's trade privileges unless there were big improvements in human rights for the Chinese. Every year China has kept its status as a most-favoured nation (MFN) by making minimal concessions on rights....According to the World Bank, the removal of MFN could slash Chinese exports to America by 96%....China exported $7.2 billion-worth of textiles to America last year, but the Americans say it trans-shipped nearly $2 billion-worth more to sidestep quota regulations." (p34)

"Asia: China: Wolf or Sheep?" Economist v330 n7847, 22 Jan 1994. p34. (ISSN0013-0613).

"China is now America's 13th-largest export market, buying $8.8 billion of U.S. goods last year, up 18.2 percent from 1992." (p67)

Lawrence, Susan V. "On China: Stumbling into a Dead End." U.S. News & World Report v116 n16, 25 Apr 1994. p67. (ISSN0041-5537).

CHINA--ECONOMIC CONDITIONS (v19)

"China's economy...in 1993 grew at a dizzying pace of 13%--for the second straight year. Inflation is on the rise, with prices in the largest cities climbing more than 20% annually. Subsidies to money-losing state enterprises, relics of the Stalinist economy, are bleeding the center dry. And decentralization has created a crisis between Beijing and the provinces. In the midst of an economic boom, Beijing's revenues are falling, as provincial leaders grab an ever expanding share of taxes for themselves and help local companies evade Beijing's collectors....In a draft of its annual human-rights report, the [U.S.] State Dept. blasted China for lack of progress, endangering renewal of its most-favored-nation trade (MFN) status. Making matters worse, while Beijing had an overall deficit of $12 billion in 1993, its surplus with the U.S. is $23 billion and growing. That puts it second to Japan in the size of its imbalance with Washington." (p42-43)

Barnathan, Joyce/others. "International Business: China: Birth of a New Economy." Business Week n3356, 31 Jan 1994. p42-44,48. (ISSN0007-7135).

"Inflation...remains the biggest worry for China: the urban inflation rate hit 21.9% in November, and panic-buying in coastal provinces in December drove up local prices of grains and staple foods by 30%. The national economy grew by 13% in 1993; the government seems committed to more high-speed growth, and to be gambling that foreign-exchange and other financial reforms will help rather than hinder the fight against inflation." (p74)

"Finance: China's Financial Reforms: Then There Was Yuan." Economist v330 n7844, 8 Jan 1994. p73-74. (ISSN0013-0613).

"The last time the monetary reins were yanked back in China was in 1988. The economy was then growing at a rate of 11%, the consumer price index (CPI) at 20.7%. By 1990, however, stiff monetary control had slowed CPI growth to 1.3%. Credit was eased, and the economic growth rate surged to 12.8% in 1992 and 13.9% in 1993. In the process, the inflation rate jumped to 21.6% and a large deficit was posted on the trade balance." (p18)

Ueda, Kazuo. "Viewpoints: China: Dragon Gone Bullish." Look Japan v39 n454, Jan 1994. p18. (ISSN0456-5339).

"China's industrial takeoff has created huge markets for both imports (growing close to 30 percent a year) and investments by outside companies forming subsidiaries and joint ventures. Foreign direct investment soared to $30 billion in new commitments last year....China's trade account went from a small surplus in 1992 to negative $12 billion last year, and likely a worse figure this year....Living costs rose by more than 15 percent in 1993, versus 6 percent inflation in 1992. Money-supply growth, near a 50 percent annual rate, must be held down to prevent a scramble for hard currencies and gold." (p9)

Trumbull, Mark. "Economy: China Spurs Asia Economies but Challenges Still Remain." The Christian Science Monitor v86 n63, 24 Feb 1994. p9. (ISSN0882-7729).

"China's economy...is expanding at an annual rate of more than 10 percent. This means that each year China generates the equivalent of a new market the size of Argentina. Officially, China's per capita gross domestic product stands at $400. But using new World Bank calculations based on purchasing power parity, China's production per person is actually between $1000 and $2000. That makes the Chinese economy the third-biggest in the world." (p17)

Hanson, Eric. "Asia: With Wealth Comes Filth." Toward Freedom v43 n1, Feb 1994. p17,20. (ISSN0048-9898).

CHINA--EMPLOYMENT (v19)

"Whereas China's total rural labour force grew from 306 million to 401 million between 1979 and 1988, the proportion of those employed in farming and related fields grew by just 14 per cent while non-farm employment in village and township industries doubled (from 17 to 34 million), employment in construction increased sixfold (from 2 to 15 million), employment in transportation surged more than sevenfold (from 800,000 to 6 million), and employment in trade and marketing shot up more than twelvefold (from 500,000 to nearly 7 million). In all, more than 70 million peasants transferred out of agriculture and into non-farm employment during the first decade of reform." (p69)

Smith, Richard. "The Chinese Road to Capitalism." New Left Review n199, May-Jun 1993. p55-99. (ISSN0028-6060).

"According to the Chinese government, 128,000 Chinese workers were sent under government-negotiated contracts to other countries in 1992, mostly to Hong Kong, Macau and the former Soviet Union where many were employed by Chinese construction companies. In addition to earning foreign currency, exporting labor enables China to provide jobs for its large and growing unemployed workforce. Rural unemployment in China is now estimated to be about 100 million, but it will reach 300 million by the year 2000. Although workers from China and elsewhere had entered Taiwan illegally for years, it was only in 1991, because of a severe labor shortage, that Taiwan's government allocated about 15,000 work visas for foreign workers." (p18)

"Asian Migrant Workers Face Exploitation." NewsNotes v19 n1, Jan-Feb 1994. p17-18. (ISSN1064-1556).

CHINA--INDIA--ECONOMIC CONDITIONS (v19)

"Over the past decade, there has been no serious contest between Asia's two giants. China started its market reforms in 1978, and has since been haring along. India, after small spurts of reform in the early and middle years of the 1980s, started again in earnest only in 1991. Its GDP [gross domestic product] growth has been lumbering behind at an average of 3.1% a year since then (compared with China's average over the same period of 10.9%). Still, as all children know, the tortoise won in the end. As the economic and political risks in China become ever more evident, India's steadiness is looking increasingly attractive to investors....The flow of foreign money into India demonstrates investors' new interest. Some $1 billion poured into Indian stockmarkets in 1993, most of it in the second half of the year. In January, Morgan Stanley launched the first Indian mutual fund: hoping for $100m, it pulled in $300m within three days. New foreign direct investment, into factories rather than equities, reached $900m last year, compared with $200m in 1992. Of course, China is in a different league: in 1993, it attracted $15 billion-worth of direct investment." (p17)

"Leaders: India in a Hurry." Economist v330 n7853, 5 Mar 1994. p17. (ISSN0013-0613).

CHINA--INDIA--U.S.--ECONOMIC CONDITIONS (v19)

CHINA--POPULATION (v19)

"China is struggling with the reality that they already have about 11 people per half an acre....They are the fastest growing population on the face of this planet. They are one-quarter of the world's population, 1.2 billion people. In fact, if you want to talk about problems, China, just to keep up with the current rate of population, has to create something like 2 million jobs a year." The U.S. needs "to be much more engaged with China, and in fact with the rest of the world, on this question of population growth. It is not insignificant. You look at a country like Haiti where already it has enormous turmoil. Haiti is a country of 7 million people. In the next 18 years it is going to become a country of 14 million people, and it already cannot sustain the 7 million that it has. You can go from country to country around the world and find this replicated." (pS328)

Kerry, John F. (Sen.-Mass.). "Foreign Relations Authorization Act," Congressional Record (28 Jan 1994). Daily ed. pS327-354. (ISSN0363-7239).

CHINA--RURAL CONDITIONS (v19)

CHINA--SOCIAL CONDITIONS

"China's State Statistical Bureau reports retail prices in the first two months of this year were 20 percent higher than they were in the same period a year ago. The Public Security Ministry says violent crime rose 52.6 percent during the first 11 months of 1993. In China's traditional industrial centers, millions of workers are idle, particularly in the energy, power, chemicals, metals and machine-building sectors. Some are receiving minimal stipends, others no pay at all. Real farm incomes continue to shrink, with the costs of fertilizers, hybrid seeds and other necessities rising much faster than crop prices. So many farmers are on the move in search of work that at least two provinces, Hunan and Sichuan, have placed restrictions on farmers' use of trains and buses." (p67)

Lawrence, Susan V. "On China: Stumbling into a Dead End." U.S. News & World Report v116 n16, 25 Apr 1994. p67. (ISSN0041-5537).

CHINESE--ASIA (v19)

"In Indonesia, where Chinese account for only 4 percent of the population, they control 20 of the 25 biggest business groups. Although only about 10 percent of the population in Thailand, they own 90 percent of commercial and manufacturing capital and half of the banking capital in the country." (p11)

Tefft, Sheila. "Overseas Chinese Face Suspicion in Native and Adopted Lands." The Christian Science Monitor v86 n82, 23 Mar 1994. p11-14. (ISSN0882-7729).

CHINESE--HONG KONG--INDONESIA--PHILIPPINES (v19)

CHLORINE--U.S.

"Chlorine and chlorinated compounds are used to meet the most essential and vital needs of modern society, and are found in 85 percent of all medicines, 96 percent of all crop-protection chemicals, all vinyl plastics, and thousands of other products. They save U.S. consumers more than $90 billion annually--$1,440 for every family of four--versus alternative products or processes, with no guarantee that the alternatives would enhance human health or the environment. Furthermore, according to the Chemical Manufacturers Association, 1.3 million U.S. jobs depend on the chlorine industry and almost 40 percent of all U.S. jobs and income depend in some way on chlorine and the products of the chlorine industry." (pH180)

DeLay, Tom (Rep.-Tex.). "Providing for Consideration of H.R. 3425, Department of Environmental Protection Act," Congressional Record (2 Feb 1994). Daily ed. pH171-183. (ISSN0363-7239).

"Most people first associate chlorine with their drinking water, although only about five percent of the 12 million tons of chlorine produced each year in the U.S. ends up in water treatment. About 30 percent goes into making chlorinated organic chemicals for industry, including a wide range of solvents, such as the perchloroethylene used by dry cleaners. About 15 percent goes into bleaching of wood pulp to make paper, and another 12 percent into inorganic chemcials, like hydrochloric acid. But as these uses have tapered off, due to health and environmental pressures, the fastest growing use of chlorine has been in making polyvinyl chloride (PVC), often known simply as vinyl, which consumes 30 percent of chlorine. As long as companies produce alkali by electrolysis, creating chlorine as a leftover, they will want products like PVC to absorb this element." (p28)

Moberg, David. "Sunset for Chlorine?" E Magazine v4 n4, Jul-Aug 1993. p26-31. (ISSN1046-8021).

CHLOROFLUOROCARBONS

"Population growth played only a minor role in creating the ozone hole. The main blame lay with rising consumption and technology change. Between 1940 and 1980, world chlorofluorocarbon (CFC) emissions grew at more than 15 percent a year. Almost all of this was in developed countries, where population grew at less than 1 percent a year. So population growth accounted for less than 7 percent (one-fifteenth) of increased CFC emissions. (p18,21)

Harrison, Paul. "Sex and the Single Planet." Amicus Journal v15 n45, Win 1994. p16-18,21-23,26. (ISSN0276-7201).

CHOLERA (v19)

CHOLERA--AFRICA

"This year alone, there have been 25 193 cases of cholera reported in Malawi, over 12 000 cases in Mozambique. Large outbreaks have been reported also in Zimbabwe and Zambia. However, there are fears that due to inadequate reporting systems and poor communications, these officially--reported figures do not always reflect the situation accurately. Up to 40% of cholera patients may die in the early stages of an epidemic, before the diagnosis is firmly established and appropriate drug supplies are obtained. The fatality rate typically drops as efforts are organized to deal with the epidemic but Africa continues to have a high overall rate, with as many as 5% of cases succumbing to this disease. Rapid rehydration of patients, including oral rehydration therapy as soon as a patient can drink, can reduce the death toll to less than one per cent." (p2)

News release. "WHO Steps Up Fight against Cholera and Dysentery in Southern Africa." WHO Press 2 Dec 1993. p1-2.

CHOLERA--AFRICA--LATIN AMERICA

"During 1993, a total of 72,500 cholera cases were recorded in Sub-Saharan Africa where the disease is considered endemic. Approximately 3% of these cases proved fatal. In Latin America, more than 200 000 cases were recorded over the same period with a death rate of 1%." (p2)

News release. "WHO Calls for New International Partnership on Water and Sanitation in Africa." WHO Press 21 Mar 1994. p1-2.

CHOLERA--LATIN AMERICA (v19)

CHRISTIAN SCIENTISTS--MEDICAL CARE

"A recent study examined more than 7,000 testimonies of physical healings published in 'The Christian Science Journal' and the 'Christian Science Sentinel' from 1969-1988. Over that period, 2,451 healings of children were recorded, 640 of which involved conditions that were medically diagnosed. Many diagnoses involved X-rays or were confirmed by second opinions by specialists or other physicians. At least 88 cases were pronounced life-threatening by the examining doctor or doctors....Reasonable persons understand that there is no such thing today as a flawless system of care for adults or children. And they agree it would be irresponsible to outlaw an entire system because of a few losses. No one, for instance, would prohibit traditional Western medicine even though U.S. government data show that 975 Michigan children from four days through 15 years died under its treatment in 1985, which was an average year. Likewise, reasonable persons would not outlaw Christian Science because of a few losses that are not remotely representative of its overall excellent record. The fact is that there is no objective evidence that Christian Science children are more at risk than children who receive medical treatment. In fact, they may be less at risk." (p8 secA)

Schlaff, Barbara. "Christian Science Seeks to Do What Is Best for Children." Ann Arbor News 25 Feb 1994. p8 secA.

CHROMIUM COMPOUNDS--DISEASES--U.S. (v19)

CHURCH ATTENDANCE--U.S.

"Catholics [in the U.S.] have reduced their giving to the church from 2 percent of their income a quarter century ago to 1 percent today (Protestant giving has remained steady at about 2 percent). This has resulted in the loss of billions of dollars to church coffers. Weekly attendance has also fallen, from 75 to 80 percent before the Council to 50 percent today. Most of the decline occurred from 1965 to 1975 and then leveled off; but instead of rebounding, as it has among evangelical Protestants, Catholic church attendance continues to inch downward. (Church attendance remains a significant factor in predicting individual opinion on many social and political issues for both Catholics and Protestants. Weekly attendance is highly correlated with more conservative political and social attitudes.) There has also been an enormous decline in parochial school attendance, from 5.5 million students in 1965 to about 2.5 million today. Increasing assimilation and a preference for public education are major factors affecting the reduction in Catholic attendance at church-related schools." (p18)

Menedez, Albert J. "The Political Power of the Catholic Church: American Catholics: A Social and Political Portrait." Humanist v53 n5, Sep-Oct 1993. p17-20. (ISSN0018-7399).

"Ironically, in light of the frequent complaint from American pulpits that the nation has lost its spiritual moorings, the United States appears to be more religious today than it was at its founding. In their 1992 study, 'The Churching of America: 1776-1990,' religion sociologists Roger Finke of Purdue University and Rodney Stark of the University of Washington traced the dramatic growth in church membership over the past 200 years--from 17 percent of the U.S. population in 1776 to over 62 percent in 1980. The latest figures show 68 percent of Americans are members of a church or synagogue." (p50)

Sheler, Jeffery L. "Cover Story: Spiritual America." U.S. News & World Report v116 n13, 4 Apr 1994. p48-54,56-59. (ISSN0041-5537).

CHURCHES--CHARITABLE CONTRIBUTIONS--U.S.

"U.S. Christians are gradually giving smaller and smaller portions of their income to their churches, says a new study analyzing church finances since 1968....The report, 'The State of Church Giving Through 1991,' was released in late December by Empty Tomb, a nonprofit Christian research and service organization in Champaign, Ill. It was co- written by John and Sylvia Ronsvalle and funded by a grant from the Lilly Endowment, a major U.S. contributor to religious research....Empty Tomb did not include the Catholic Church in its study. But it did include 38 denominations with a combined membership of 41 million....The report measured the yearly giving levels of members of selected denominations over a 24-year period from 1968 to 1991 inclusive....After adjusting for inflation by converting all figures into their equivalent in 1987 constant dollars, the study found that total contributions of members to their church rose about 18 percent in real value--from the equivalent of $304 a year per full or confirmed member in 1968 to $359 a year per full or confirmed member in 1991. However, average disposable income per capita in the U.S. went up 40 percent in constant 1987 dollars over that period--so the 18 percent increase in total contributions represented a decline in giving as a percentage of disposable income." (p4)

"Study of Christians Shows U.S. Church Giving in Gradual Decline." Observer v54 n4, 28 Jan 1994. p4. (ISSN0029-7712).

CHURCHES--MOSCOW (RUSSIA) (v19)

CIGARETTE HABIT

"In Japan, consumption [of cigarettes] used to be falling, but is now growing by 3% a year. Fourteen per cent of women are current smokers. In Argentina, the use of tobacco was rising by 2.4% in the 1960s. Since the penetration of the tobacco multinationals, it has been increasing annually by 6.4%....In developing countries as diverse as Malaysia, Mauritius, the Philippines and Tunisia, almost 50% of men smoke on average compared with about 25-30% in Australia, Canada and the United States of America." (p8)

"Section 1: Worldwide Trends in Smoking: The Tobacco Industry: Strategies and Prospects." Tobacco Alert 1994 (Special Issue). p6-8.

CIGARETTE HABIT--AFRO-AMERICANS (v19)

CIGARETTE HABIT--CALIFORNIA

"Since 1988, when Californians voted under Proposition 99 to slap a 25-cent tobacco tax on every packet of cigarettes, smokers have dropped from 30% to 19% of the state's adult population. Los Angeles, San Francisco and more than 100 other cities and counties within the state have banned smoking in restaurants. A new bill has been working its way through the legislature in Sacramento that would ban smoking in the workplace and in public buildings throughout California." (p31)

"American Survey: California Ballots: Smokescreen." Economist v331 n7860, 23 Apr 1994. p28,31. (ISSN0013-0613).

CIGARETTE HABIT--JAPAN (v19)

CIGARETTE HABIT--U.S. (v19)

"Between 1983 and 1992 the proportion of adults smoking cigarettes declined from 30% to 24%--a 20% reduction. This information, from a Louis Harris poll that has been conducted every year since 1983, confirms other studies documenting the continued slide in adult smoking rates. Tragically, smoking by children and teenagers has not been following the same downward course. Throughout the 1980's, teen smoking stayed at a stubborn plateau despite all efforts to bring them down. Since about 1988, the number of young people smoking cigarettes has begun to increase." (p1)

"Teen Smoking Rates Increase." Tobacco-Free Youth Reporter v5 n1, Spr 1993. p1,21.

CIGARETTE HABIT--U.S.--ARMED FORCES (v19)

CIGARETTE HABIT--U.S.--YOUTH (v19)

"Although it is now illegal in all States to sell cigarettes to minors, research shows that vending machines offer easy access for children to obtain this deadly product. While cigarette manufacturers use cartoon characters and beautiful people to make smoking appear attractive, wholesome, and sexy, Congress has a responsibility to prevent minors from obtaining cigarettes in Federal buildings. We have the responsibility to make it more difficult for minors to obtain products that if used as directed will kill them. Over 90 percent of smokers start smoking in adolescence or childhood, and they continue to smoke throughout their adult lives. Each day, more than 3,000 children and adolescents start smoking and collectively smoke nearly 1 billion packs of cigarettes per year. In addition, reliable studies indicate that tobacco use is a gateway to other, more harmful drugs." (pE162)

Visclosky, Peter J. (Rep.-Ind.). "Prohibition of Cigarette Sales to Minors in Federal Buildings and Lands Act," Congressional Record (10 Feb 1994). Daily ed. pE162. (ISSN0363-7239).

"High school students who smoke their first full cigarette during childhood will smoke more often and in greater amounts than those who smoke their first full cigarette during adolescence, according to a study released in the March 17th issue of JAMA. By analyzing data on 11,248 adolescents from the 1990 Youth Risk Behavior Survey, researchers found that teens who experimented with smoking at or before age 12 were more likely to be regular smokers than those who tried cigarettes later....The peak age for smoking initiation seems to fall between 13 and 14 years of age (when nearly 25% of students smoke their first cigarette), and declines after age 16. Yet, current smoking prevention strategies generally target these same teens, who have already tried smoking and may already be addicted." (p17)

"Research: Start Prevention/Cessation Earlier, Study Suggests." Tobacco-Free Youth Reporter v5 n3, Fall 1993. p17.

"Drug use among American young people has been making a clear comeback in the past two years. That is the conclusion of University of Michigan research scientists Lloyd Johnston, Patrick O'Malley, and Jerald Bachman, all at the University's Institute for Social Research." (p1) "The rate of daily smoking rose significantly in all three grade levels in 1993--from 7 percent to 8 percent among eighth-graders, from 12 percent to 14 percent among 10th-graders, and from 17 percent to 19 percent among 12th-graders." (p4) "While perceptions of the dangers associated with smoking have, if anything, risen slightly over the past two years, still nearly half (47 percent) of the eighth-graders do not believe that there is a great risk associated with pack-a-day smoking. Among seniors, more than 30 percent still do not believe there is great risk." (p5)

News release. "Drug Survey." University of Michigan News and Information Services 27 Jan 1994. p1-6.

CIGARETTE HABIT--U.S.--YOUTH--PUBLIC OPINION

"A comprehensive study of youth smoking by the Institute for Social Research at the University of Michigan for the U.S. Department of Health and Human Services found that cigarette smoking prevalence did not significantly change among 8th, 10th, and 12-graders in 1992. The report...[is entitled] 'Smoking, Drinking, and Illicit Drug Use Among American Secondary School Students, College Students and Young Adults, 1975-1991, Vol. I, Secondary School Students,' U.S. Department of Health and Human Services, 1992....The proportion of high school seniors who believe there is 'great risk' of physical harm caused by a pack-a-day habit is just 69%--an increase of just 5% from 1980. Only 60 percent of tenth graders and 50% of eighth graders perceive a 'great risk.' Cigarettes have been tried by 44 percent of eighth graders and 14 percent say they smoked in the prior month. Only 53 percent say they think there is a great risk associated with being a pack-a-day smoker. Regular use of smokeless tobacco is viewed as entailing 'great risk' by only 35% of eighth graders." (p17)

"Research: Addiction Keeps Teen Smoking Rates Up." Tobacco-Free Youth Reporter v5 n3, Fall 1993. p17.

CIGARETTE INDUSTRY

see also ADVERTISING--CIGARETTE INDUSTRY; ADVERTISING, MAGAZINE--CIGARETTE INDUSTRY

CIGARETTE INDUSTRY--CANADA (v19)

"Last year Canadians bought around 30 billion cigarettes legally. The Canadian Tobacco Manufacturers' Council estimates that about 30% of all cigarettes sold in Canada are now contraband. In Quebec the figure may be as high as 65-70%....The Canadian police estimate that they intercept only 5-10% of the illicit trade, much of which is channelled through Indian reserves that straddle the border. The boom in smuggling demonstrates that it is not as easy to tax cigarettes as punitively as politicians and health lobbyists commonly assume. The ten provinces and the federal government tax tobacco to the hilt. In Quebec, taxes make up about 75% of the retail price of a packet. The result is that 25 cigarettes sell for C$6.45 ($4.90) in Montreal. Just 60 miles (97 kilometres) away, in Plattsburgh, New York, the same packet costs $3.69." (p68)

"Business: Smoke Smuggling." Economist v330 n7846, 15 Jan 1994. p68. (ISSN0013-0613).

"Nearly all the smuggled cigarettes [in Canada] are made by three companies in Quebec, then exported to subsidiaries in New York state. Middlemen buy them there, then truck them to the Mohawk Indian reserve of Akwesasne, which bestrides the St Lawrence river on Ontario's border with the United States. Via another Mohawk reserve they reach Montreal, where they sell for $20 a carton; the above-board price is about $45, three-quarters of it provincial and federal taxes. Quebec lost more than $600m in revenues last year as a result of this trade. Fortunes are being made by Mohawk operators and networks in Montreal and Toronto, while many small shops that relied on legal sales face disaster....The companies saw home sales shrink as taxes were increased fivefold during the 1980s. But their exports to the United States jumped from $39m in 1990 to more than $500m last year." (p43,46)

"International: Canada: Smoke Rings." Economist v330 n7849, 5 Feb 1994. p43,46. (ISSN0013-0613).

"Curiously, while there has been no big rise in US smoking of imported cigarettes, Canadian cigarette exports to the US have shot through the roof. According to Statistics Canada, the value of tobacco exports to the US in the first 11 months of 1993 was C$500 million, compared with C$39.3 million in 1990. Law enforcement officials estimate up to 90 percent of Canadian cigarette exports to the US are smuggled back to Canada." (p2)

Clayton, Mark. "International: The Smoke of Canadian Politics." The Christian Science Monitor v86 n51, 7 Feb 1994. p2. (ISSN0882-7729).

"Less than 60 miles from Ottawa, with its beehive of clean-cut civil servants, is a stretch of the United States-Canadian border police call 'smugglers' alley.' There, where the Akwesasne Mohawk Indian reservation straddles the St. Lawrence

River that forms the border, snowmobiles and small trucks can be seen in broad daylight hauling loads of cigarettes from the US to Canada. Up to C$1 million (US$750,000) worth crosses daily through the reservation, police estimate....Heavy provincial and federal taxes on cigarettes account for up to 75 percent of the retail price of a pack of cigarettes in Canada. A carton (10 packs) of cigarettes legally sold in Ontario or Quebec costs around C$48. A smuggled carton may sell for C$28 in Toronto or C$18 in Montreal." (p2)

Clayton, Mark. "International: The Smoke of Canadian Politics." The Christian Science Monitor v86 n51, 7 Feb 1994. p2. (ISSN0882-7729).

CIGARETTE INDUSTRY--COLOMBIA (v19)

CIGARETTE INDUSTRY--HONDURAS (v19)

CIGARETTE TAX--CANADA

"Canada has long taxed cigarettes heavily as a matter of policy to reduce smoking. Studies have shown higher prices discourage youth from smoking. The Non-Smokers Rights Association says a 50 percent cut in cigarette prices would mean a 14-36 percent jump in smoking, with 350,000 more teenagers lighting up simply because they can afford it. But health consequences are not the only problem. Cutting cigarette taxes poses a financial problem for...[Prime Minister Jean] Chretien and the 10 provincial premiers, all of whom are hard pressed to reduce huge budget deficits. Cigarette taxes raked in about C$3.2 billion last year for the federal government and C$3 billion for provinces, reports the federal agency Statistics Canada." (p2)

Clayton, Mark. "International: The Smoke of Canadian Politics." The Christian Science Monitor v86 n51, 7 Feb 1994. p2. (ISSN0882-7729).

"According to Jeffrey E. Harris, an economics professor at M.I.T. and a physician, even with a $2 per pack tax, smoking rates would not drop off steeply enough to hurt revenues. 'The best way to try to predict the impact of a major tax increase on cigarettes is to look at Canada, where cigarette taxes and prices have been rising faster than ours,' said Harris in a June 4, 1993 interview with the WALL STREET JOURNAL. 'Between 1984 and 1992, the average price of cigarettes in Canada rose 114 percent over the inflation rate, but cigarette consumption dropped by only 27 percent.' Based on Canada's record, Harris projects that a $2 increase would reduce U.S. sales by 25 percent, and by subtracting lost income taxes, calculates that the $2 hike would add $28 billion annually to the U.S. Treasury." (p5)

"National News: Support the Tax--NOW!" Tobacco-Free Youth Reporter v5 n2, Sum 1993. p5.

CIGARETTE TAX--FLORIDA

"The Florida Coalition on Smoking OR Health has filed legislation for the 1993 session to raise the Florida tobacco tax by $1.00/pack. The Coalition includes the Florida divisions of the American Cancer Society, the American Heart Association, and the American Lung Association. The Coalition estimates that smoking-attributable economic costs for tobacco-related mortality and morbidity in Florida are in excess of $2.5 billion a year. The proposed tax is intended to alleviate this burden on the state's taxpayers." (p8)

"State News: Florida Groups Propose New Tobacco Tax of $1.00/Pack." Tobacco-Free Youth Reporter v5 n1, Spr 1993. p8-9.

CIGARETTE TAX--MASSACHUSETTS

The Massachusetts tobacco tax "generates about $10 to $12 million per month and is expected to produce about $180 to $200 million in the first 18 months. Both Governor William Weld, in his annual budget, and the legislature made clear that they wanted to divert a substantial amount of the revenues for purposes other than toabacco control. Clearly, tobacco industry lobbyists were pressing hard for such diversions. As a result, the Coalition for a Healthy Future developed its own detailed budget, calling for appropriations of about $96 million for tobacco control programs in the first 18 months, and asking that the remaining approximately $90 million be kept in reserve in the Health Protection Fund, created by the tobacco tax revenues, for expenditure in future years." (p11)

"State News: MA Tobacco Tax Funds $96 Million for Tobacco Control." Tobacco-Free Youth Reporter v5 n2, Sum 1993. p1,11.

CIGARETTE TAX--U.S.

According to "the U.S. Department of Labor, Congressional Budget Office, and Congressional Research Service, it is estimated that a 75 cent increase in the cigarette tax would increase the Consumer Price Index (CPI) by 0.7 percent, and thus, increase Federal Government COLA payments by $3 to $4 billion the first year. The cost to State and local governments would be equally significant. The Government should not increase Government payments to individuals as a result of rising prices for a product that may be harmful, and is not used by most of those individuals having their benefits increased. It is estimated that 12 percent of retirees use tobacco. But the fact is that cigarettes and alcohol continue to be a substantial factor in the market basket of goods that makes up the CPI used to calculate cost-of-living-adjustments (COLA's)." (pH169)

Smith, Nick (Rep.-Mich.). "Legislation Regarding Changing the Computation of CPI," Congressional Record (2 Feb 1994). Daily ed. pH168-169. (ISSN0363-7239).

"Fourteen States and the District of Columbia raised taxes in 1993 [on cigarettes] an average of about 10.8 cents a pack of 20. The weighted average state tax on cigarettes was 29 cents per pack of 20 in July. Rates currently average from 2.5 cents in Virginia to 65 cents in the District of Columbia. Many cities and other local governments also tax cigarettes, and four-fifths of the states now impose sales taxes on cigarettes. The Federal excise tax rose 4 cents to 24 cents per pack in January. The Administration's proposed health care reform Health Security Act would increase Federal excise taxes 75 cents to 99 cents per pack of 20." (p4)

U.S. Dept. of Agriculture. "Tobacco Products." Tobacco Situation and Outlook Yearbook Dec 1993. p4-5.

"New and proposed tobacco taxes, coming on top of years of price increases by the tobacco industry to increase their profits, have begun to price the premium brands out of the reach of some consumers--including youth, the most price-sensitive group. The tobacco industry quickly noticed the need for a lower-priced cigarette, so they introduced 'discount' brands, such as Basic and Cambridge, which usually sell for under $1.00/pack. In 1982, discount brands accounted for just 1% of cigarette sales. Today, discount brands have 36% share of the market--cutting directly into premium brand sales. Marlboro saw its market share drop from 24.3% last year to 22.2% this year. Fearing further loss of market share, Philip Morris announced that it will drop its average price of Marlboro's by about $0.40/pack. RJR quickly followed suit and said it would match this cut for its Camel and Winston brands. This could put the price below $2.00 a pack. These price decreases are clearly intended to entice youth to smoke the premium brands and not to switch once they have started. Prior to the price cuts, Philip Morris made an average profit of $0.55 a pack on Marlboro's, but only $0.05/pack on its discount brands. Thus, even with a $0.40 price cut, Philip Morris still makes three times the profit on Marlboro versus its discount brands." (p11)

"Federal & State Taxes Prompt Cig Price Cuts: Youth Targeted." Tobacco-Free Youth Reporter v5 n1, Spr 1993. p1,11.

CIGARETTES--PRICES--U.S. (v19)

CIRCULATORY SYSTEM

see CARDIOVASCULAR SYSTEM

CIRCUMCISION

"Female genital mutilation (FGM), or female circumcision as it is politely called, is best known as a cultural practice in some countries of Africa and the Middle East. Although about 80 million women have been victims of the painful, dangerous procedure, it remains shrouded in myth and secrecy. But with the emigration of people from countries where FGM is widely practiced, an increasing number of Western social workers, teachers and doctors have been forced to confront the problem in their own countries. It is estimated that 10,000 girls are at risk in both Britain and Canada, and 20,000 in France." (p7)

Langenegger, Stefani. "Mutilation in Suburbia: When an Appalling Tradition Moves In Next Door." Toward Freedom v42 n2, Mar 1993. p7,23. (ISSN0048-9898).

CITIES AND TOWNS

see also URBANIZATION

CITIES AND TOWNS--POPULATION

"If the UN had not revised its map of Tokyo, it would probably have named Sao Paulo, Brazil, as the largest city in the world, with 19 million people. Rio de Janeiro may be the best known city in Brazil, but Sao Paulo, with 19 million people, is truly a demographic giant. Only two countries have more than one city in the urban top ten: China, with Shanghai and Beijing and the United States with New York and Los Angeles. India had two cities in 1990's top ten list (Bombay and Calcutta), but only Bombay remains in the top ten in the latest series. New York will lose its third position to Mexico City by 2010, when the UN projections show Mexico City rising to 18 million. New York is projected to be only 17.2 million in that year." (p2)

Haub, Carl. "Tokyo Now Recognized as World's Largest City." Population Today v21 n3, Mar 1993. p1-2. (ISSN0749-2448).

CITIES AND TOWNS--U.S. (v19)

CITIES AND TOWNS--U.S.--BUDGETS (v19)

CIVIL SERVICE--CALIFORNIA

"Despite continued problems with illegal immigration and labor exploitation, the staff at the Department of Labor dedicated to investigating labor law violations has plummeted over the last decade from 1,100 employees in 1980, down to 817 in 1993. The regional office in San Francisco, which has the job of covering violations throughout California--the destination for over half of the illegal immigrants in the United States--is only equipped with 89 investigators. Subsequently, as of July 1993, they faced a backlog of over 1,300 cases in the California area. It is amazing that there are only 16 employees struggling with the task of investigating labor law violations in the large five county Los Angeles area." (pS3956)

Boxer, Barbara (Sen.-Calif.). "Statements on Introduced Bills and Joint Resolutions," Congressional Record (25 Mar 1994). Daily ed. pS3954-3985. (ISSN0363-7239).

CIVIL SERVICE--DISMISSAL OF--U.S. (v19)

CIVIL SERVICE--JAPAN

"Moving the government out of Tokyo was first suggested as a way of overcoming the problems caused by the centralization of people, goods, money, and information in Japan's capital." (p12) "The Prime Minister's group tried to estimate the size of the new capital. The first item to be calculated was the number of people involved: 6,400 for the legislature (Diet members, secretaries, administrative staff), 1,110 for the judiciary (the Supreme Court and its training facilities and library), and 46,800 for the executive branch (central government agencies and related institutions). Moreover, another 30,000 or so from the headquarters of government-run companies, prefectural liaison offices, foreign embassies, international institutions, and political party offices would have to move. Finally, an estimated 20,000 come from private-sector companies, yielding a total working population of about 100,000 for the new capital. Assuming two dependants per worker, the total direct population shift would be about 300,000. Factoring in another 300,000 or so from workers from support industries and their families gives a potential population shift of about 600,000 people." (p13)

Morino, Yoshinori. "Essay: Decentralization: Get Out of Tokyo!" Look Japan v39 n455, Feb 1994. p12-14. (ISSN0456-5339).

CIVIL SERVICE--U.S. (v19)

"We now have 2.26 million Federal employees [in the U.S.], not counting the Post Office or the military. FDR's so-called 'big government' had 625,000 employees. The population has doubled, which should give us 1.3 employees. But today the Defense Department alone has almost 1 million civilian employees, or four times as many per serviceman as in World War II. The Department of Agriculture has 60,000 people serving farmers--three times as many as under FDR even though we have only one-third as many farmers. By the year 2040, following that progression, there will be one D of A employee for every full time farmer. The Forest Service had 4,000 people under FDR, and now has 35,000 employees even though our forests are no larger. The Federal bureaucracy is top heavy in management. There are 237,000 official 'managers' and 116,000 upper-level specialists who would be called executives in the commercial world. This makes one executive for every five workers, an excessive ratio, especially today as private firms are drastically downsizing management." (p102)

Gross, Martin L. (Author of "The Government Racket: Washington Waste from A to Z."). U.S. Senate. Committee on Governmental Affairs. "Improving Government Organization and Performance." Hearing, 11 Mar 1993. Washington, D.C.: GPO, 1994. (ISBN0160435838). (Y4.G74/9:S.hrg.103-401).

"A recent GAO [General Accounting Office] survey of the views of Senate-confirmed presidential appointees (Report B-251275, December 28, 1992) found that 62.5% of respondents believe that orientation to ethical guidelines is of very great importance, 31.3% believe it very important. When asked to rate the adequacy of the orientations they had received, 97.7% stated that the subject was covered and 67.5% believed it to be Very Adequate and 27.5% Generally Adequate." (p379)

Potts, Stephen D. (Director, U.S. Office of Government Ethics). U.S. House. Committee on Appropriations. "Treasury, Postal Service, and General Government Approp. for Fiscal Year 1994 (Part 4)." Hearing, Washington, D.C.: GPO, 1993. (ISBN0160407702). (Y4.Ap6/1:T71/994/pt.4).

"The Office of Management and Budget assigned Executive Branch non-postal, non-military agencies an aggregate work year ceiling of 1,187,260 for FY 1992 (as updated in the President's FY 1993 Budget). OMB has revised this figure down by 7,611 to 1,179,649 due mainly to 6,475 fewer work years for Federal Deposit Insurance Corporation (including the Resolution Trust Corporation). Through September 1992, non-postal, non-military agencies have used 1,169,626 work years--10,023 fewer work years than the projected year-end ceiling of 1,179,649 work years. While 100% of the ceiling year has elapsed, the rate of work year usage overall was 99.2% for the non-postal, non-military agencies. In its response to natural disasters, the Federal Emergency Management Agency has used 118% of its allocated work years." (p764)

Lattimore, Patricia Watkins (Acting Director, Office of Personnel Management). U.S. House. Committee on Appropriations. "Treasury, Postal Service, and General Government Approp. for Fiscal Year 1994 (Part 4)." Hearing, Washington, D.C.: GPO, 1993. (ISBN0160407702).

(Y4.Ap6/1:T71/994/pt.4).

"Since 1979, appropriations for the entire [U.S.] legislative branch have actually declined by 1.7 percent after adjusting for infation (AFI). In contrast, funding for the executive branch has increased by 30 percent (AFI) during this time period....during the Reagan-Bush years civilian executive branch employment grew at an alarming rate--from 2.8 million in 1981 to a high point of over 3.06 million in 1987. This increase under Republican administrations represented the addition of approximately 250,000 workers to the Federal pay roll....It is no wonder President Clinton wants to reduce the executive branch by a quarter million workers. He inherited a lot of left-over fat to trim....in contrast...both the legislative branch in general, and the House and Senate in particular, remained static in terms of employees from 1981 to 1993. Committee investigative employees have actually decreased by 2.47 percent, from 1,013 in 1983, to 988 as of January of 1994." (pH1816)

Frost, Martin (Rep.-Tex.). "Providing Amounts for Expenses of Investigations and Studies by Certain Standing Committees," Congressional Record (22 Mar 1994). Daily ed. pH1814-1824. (ISSN0363-7239).

The U.S. "Congress has increased spending for its own budget at double the inflation rate. We talk about health care. We have the same runaway increase in expenditures in our own legislative branch. In 10 years, the Consumer Price Index has risen 44 percent, the legislative branch 95 percent. The legislative branch staff has approximately 38,000 workers, which is larger than the combined legislative staff of Canada, Great Britain, Germany, and France. Canada has the second largest legislative staff with only 4,000 employees." (pS3593)

Coverdell, Paul (Rep.-Ga.). "Congressional Budget Concurrent Resolution," Congressional Record (24 Mar 1994). Daily ed. pS3586-3599. (ISSN0363-7239).

"According to the Center for the Study of American Business, the number of federal regulatory personnel hit 127,841 in 1993, the highest number of bureaucrats ever to administer regulatory programs. Clinton's budget for 1994 calls for an increase to a record 128,615 government bureaucrats." (p30)

Kasten, Robert W., Jr. "Fair Comment: Moderation in Regulation Will Help Economy Grow." Insight v10 n7, 14 Feb 1994. p30-31. (ISSN1051-4880).

"Non-Hispanic whites, who make up 75 percent of the population, received 76 percent of the [presidential] appointments made in 1993. African Americans, who make up 14 percent of the population, received 14 percent of the appointments. Hispanics, who make up 9.5 percent of the population, received 6 percent of the appointments. Asian Americans received 3 percent of the appointments, the same as their share of the population. Native Americans received 0.6 percent, also the same as their share of the population. The gender split was close to half: 54 percent men, 46 percent women." (p3)

Riche, Martha Farnsworth. "The Riche Report: Clinton's Appointments: They Do 'Look Like America.'" Population Today v22 n3, Mar 1994. p3. (ISSN0749-2448).

"Clinton appointed and nominated unprecedented numbers and percentages of women and minorities, although the Senate has yet to confirm two-fifths of his nominees. He named 11 women out of 28 judges (39 percent) and seven minorities out of 28 judges (25 percent). He nominated 18 female lawyers out of 48 (37 percent) and 13 minority attorneys out of 48 (27 percent). These figures eclipse Mr. Reagan's record and substantially surpass those of Mr. Bush and Mr. Carter." (p23)

Tobias, Carl. "Opinion/Essays: Keeping the Covenant on the Federal Courts." The Christian Science Monitor v86 n56, 14 Feb 1994. p23. (ISSN0882-7729).

CIVIL SERVICE--U.S.--ECONOMIC CONDITIONS

"Commerce Department data show that [U.S.] federal employees earn, on average, far more than private employees. In 1991, the average full-time federal employee received 20 percent more in wages than the average full-time private employee. Commerce data indicate an even greater federal employee advantage when fringe benefits are included. In 1991, the total average compensation for federal civilian employees, including employer-paid fringe benefits, was $46,200. Average private employee compensation was $31,800, which means that federal civilian employees were paid 45 percent more than private sector employees. Moreover, federal civilian employee compensation is also considerably above that of state and local government workers, whose compensation was $35,100. While the compensation of state and local government employees exceeds that of private employees by 16 percent, the average state and local government employee gets $11,100 less in compensation than the average federal civilian employee." (p25)

Cox, Wendell. "Symposium: Federal Workers Benefit Heavily." Insight v10 n3, 17 Jan 1994. p25-27. (ISSN1051-4880).

"In 1993, Hay and Associates Consulting Co. conducted a study commissioned by the Senior Executives Association comparing the compensation of senior executive service positions with that of comparable private sector positions. Preliminary results from that study show that for 90 percent of the senior executive positions with the biggest 'jobsize' (determined by job content points used to rate the positions against private sector executive jobs), average total cash compensation, including bonuses, was only 79 percent of the average industrial total cash compensation for private sector jobs of the same difficulty. It would take a 27 percent increase of total senior executive service compensation to achieve comparability overall. For some of the most senior career executive jobs--bureau directors, deputy assistant secretaries of major bureaus and so on--the gap widened to as much as 96 percent." (p24)

Shaw, G. Jerry. "Symposium: Wage Gap Cured with Locality Pay." Insight v10 n3, 17 Jan 1994. p22-24. (ISSN1051-4880).

CIVIL SERVICE--U.S.--WOMEN (v19)

CLONING--PUBLIC OPINION (v19)

CLOTHING TRADE--LEGAL STATUS, LAWS, ETC.--CALIFORNIA (v19)

COAL

"After four decades of nearly uninterrupted growth, world use of coal is no longer growing. It fell 1.4 percent during 1990 and 1991, and preliminary data from 1992 show it falling another 0.3 percent, to 2.18 billion tons (oil equivalent). Economic contraction in Russia and Eastern Europe and a more modest recession elsewhere primarily caused the drop....New pollution control technologies can help alleviate some of these problems, but not coal's threat to the global climate. Coal contains 80 percent more carbon per unit of energy than natural gas, and 30 percent more than oil. Burning it released 2.4 billion tons of carbon into the atmosphere in 1990, and trapping the carbon that coal releases would be expensive, probably prohibitively so. Some governments are addressing this issue by levying carbon taxes that make coal more expensive and discourage its use." (p40)

Flavin, Christopher/Kane, Hal. "Vital Signs: Coal Use Levels Off." World Watch v6 n6, Nov-Dec 1993. p40. (ISSN0896-0615).

COAL MINES AND MINING--U.S.

"Appalachia delivers more than 70 percent of the coal consumed in the United States and provides 15 percent of the nation's energy. Last March, the President's Council on Environmental Quality reported that Appalachian coal is generally 'of a high quality and in demand for steam electric plants, coke and gas plants, and exports.' (Fifteen percent of the region's coal--about $675,000,000 worth--is exported annually to Canada and Japan.) But the report says that at current rates of production, there are enough reserves to last for several hundred years....In five major coal-producing counties of northeast Tennessee, nine corporations, all but one controlled from the outside, own 34 percent of the land surface and approximately 85 percent of the coal wealth. In 11 major coal-producing counties of east Kentucky, 31 individuals and corporations control 80 percent of the coal wealth. In 14 major coal-producing counties of West Virginia, containing over half of the state's coal reserves, 25 landowners control 49 percent of the land area. Ten companies control 31 percent of the land. While more than 1,000 coal companies operated in West Virginina in 1966, 75 percent of the tonnage produced came from the 25 largest firms." (p16)

Gaventa, John. "Property Is Theft." Southern Exposure v21 n1-2, Spr-Sum 1993. p16. (ISSN0146-809X).

COAL TRADE--MEXICO (v19)

COAL TRADE--RUSSIA (v19)

COAL TRADE--U.S. (v19)

"In 1992, the United States was the second largest coal exporter worldwide exporting 102 million short tons to more than 40 countries including Canada. This contributes more than $4.2 billion in terms of value to the positive side of the trade balance. Coal exports are the third largest commodity, after wheat and corn exported from the United States. In terms of volume, coal is the largest commodity exported. Australia, Canada, South Africa and Colombia are major U.S. competitors. Typically, about 10 percent of the coal produced in the United States is exported. More than 20,000 direct coal mining jobs are dependent upon the export of U.S. coal. This activity accounts for an additional 140,000 jobs in U.S. companies supporting the production of coal for export." (p205)

U.S. House. Committee on Energy and Commerce. "NAFTA: Energy Provisions and Environmental Implications." Hearing, 22 Sep 1993. Washington, D.C.: GPO, 1994. (ISBN0160440459). (Y4.En2/3:103:70).

COAST CHANGES--U.S. (v19)

COASTS

"The coastal zone, extending from the beginning of the coastal plain to the end of the continental shelf, accounts for only 8 percent of the world's surface area, but hosts 26 percent of the earth's primary (plant) productivity, the world's major spawning and nursery grounds, and one of the earth's most diverse ecosystems, the coral reefs....Not all coastal habitat is highly productive; about half of the world's 440,000 kilometers of coastline are lined by cliffs and ice, and another 20 percent are beaches, which have relatively low biological activity." (p22)

Weber, Peter. "It Comes Down to the Coasts." World Watch v7 n2, Mar-Apr 1994. p20-29. (ISSN0896-0615).

COASTS--ASIA, SOUTHEASTERN

"Few areas of the world are as dependent on their coastal resources as are the nations of Southeast Asia. Indonesia, Singapore, and the Philippines are completely surrounded by water, whereas Malaysia and Thailand have about 8,000 kilometers of coastline between them. These five countries' coastal areas, the adjacent waters, and their marine life sustain millions of people. One recent estimate suggests that, of the approximately 300 million people who live in these five countries, as many as three-quarters live in coastal areas. Furthermore, of all the animal protein consumed by the region's people, 60 percent is derived from the sea." (p51)

Tobin, Richard J./White, Alan T. "Coastal Resources Management and Sustainable Development: A Southeast Asian Perspective." International Environmental Affairs v5 n1, Win 1993. p50-65. (ISSN1041-4665).

COASTS--U.S. (v19)

"Since many Americans want to live as close to the water as possible, coastal areas are now among the most heavily developed regions in the U.S. About half of the nation's construction between 1970 and 1989 took place in coastal counties, according to a 1992 National Oceanic and Atmospheric Administration report. About 700,000 new homes and 620,000 commercial and industrial buildings are built in coastal counties each year--hard structures in soft places that, by nature's design, are perpetually moving." (p19)

Tibbetts, John. "Currents: On Shifting Sands." E Magazine v4 n4, Jul-Aug 1993. p19-21. (ISSN1046-8021).

COCAINE HABIT--U.S. (v19)

"In 1986, during the fervor of the war on drugs [in the U.S.] and with a lack of substantive information about a new type of cocaine substance, crack, Congress enacted penalties for crack cocaine that have proven to be unwarranted, unjust and do not achieve the goal of removing big-time dealers. Powder and crack cocaine were treated as two entirely different substances. The threshold for the powder cocaine 5-year mandatory minimum was set at 500 grams. The threshold for the crack cocaine mandatory minimum was set at 5 grams, a weight equivalent to 2 pennies. In addition, simple possession of 5 grams of crack cocaine, but not powder cocaine, can trigger the mandatory minimum....The bottom line is that poor people are the ones that use crack cocaine and mostly minorities. It is interesting that about 95 percent of those that are charged with crack cocaine violations are black and other minorities." (pH2594)

Hughes, William J. (Rep.-N.J.). "Violent Crime Control and Law Enforcement Act of 1994," Congressional Record (21 Apr 1994). Daily ed. pH2593-2596. (ISSN0363-7239).

"In the United States, recreational drug use has increased during the last decade at about the same rate as AIDS. For example, cocaine consumption increased 200-fold from 1980 to 1990, based on the fact that the amount of cocaine seized by authorities increased from 500 kilograms in 1980 to 100,000 kilograms in 1990. During the same period, cocaine-related hospital emergencies increased 24-fold from 3,296 cases in 1981 to 80,355 cases in 1990." (p29)

Duesberg, Peter H. "Symposium: Results Fall Short for HIV Theory." Insight v10 n7, 14 Feb 1994. p27-29. (ISSN1051-4880).

COCAINE INDUSTRY--BOLIVIA

"Though the United Nations, the U.S. Agency for International Development (USAID) and other national and international groups have tried unsuccessfully for twenty years to develop alternative crops for Bolivian farmers, one out of every five Bolivians makes his or her livelihood from the coca and cocaine trade. The trade accounts for well over 50 percent of Bolivia's GNP [gross national product], with revenues totaling several billion dollars a year--more than any of the country's other exports, including tin....Meanwhile, the cocaine trade is causing extensive damage to an already fragile forest ecosystem. Coca-paste producers have been dumping kerosene and sulfuric acid--used to convert the raw leaves--directly into the rivers and streams of the Amazon river network. The League for the Defense of the Environment, Bolivia's most respected environmental group, estimated in 1990 that coca-paste production releases up to 38,000 tons of toxic waste into the rivers each year." (p3)

Clarke, Virginia. "Briefly Noted: Bolivian Coca Growers Take On the United Nations." Cultural Survival Quarterly v17 n3, Fall 1993. p3-4. (ISSN0740-3291).

COCAINE INDUSTRY--BOLIVIA--COLOMBIA--PERU

"The countries of Colombia, Peru and Bolivia have been most affected by the cocaine industry. In Colombia, powerful cartels dominate the drug trade and wield considerable economic, social and political influence. The combination of a powerful military, drug cartels, paramilitary groups and a guerrilla movement has led to profound systemic violence. Peru has been in a spiralling crisis for over 10 years. Both the government and the Maoist-inspired guerrila movement, Shining Path, have created a flood of human rights abuses. Impoverished migrants, who have flocked to the semi-tropical eastern slopes of the Andes, now grow 60% of the world's coca. U.S. insistence that the military attack the coca growing regions has pushed coca farmers to seek protection from Shining Path, thus exacerbating the civil war. Bolivia, economically the poorest of the three, produces 40% of the world's coca. Some 40,000 indigenous families, forced by increased parcelization of land off small highland plots, grow coca. Organized into peasant unions, they are demanding viable economic alternatives before agreeing to U.S. programs pushing crop eradication." (p6)

"Andean Information Network." NewsNotes v18 n4, Jul-Aug 1993. p6-7. (ISSN1064-1556).

COCAINE INDUSTRY--JAPAN

"A US drug-control officer posted in Japan said, 'The growth in the Japanese cocaine market has been incredible.' According to the monthly secret reports on smuggling from South America that he receives, cocaine use is spreading in Japan very rapidly. 'Cocaine is easily available to anyone, from high-school students to homemakers. The number of cocaine users in Japan is officially estimated at 150,000 to 160,000, but I believe the actual number is probably larger by several factors of ten,' he said." (p46)

Matsumoto, Mina. "Facts of Life: Cocaine: White Lines." Look Japan v39 n455, Feb 1994. p46. (ISSN0456-5339).

COCAINE INDUSTRY--NICARAGUA

"The Colombians are...making strenuous efforts to develop a local market [for cocaine] in Nicaragua....Erwin Areas, a spokesman for the...El Patriarca Foundation, Nicaragua's only addict rehabilitation group, reports that 'there has been a generalized offensive aimed at promoting cocaine consumption in schools and places of nighttime entertainment.' According to El Patriarca's statistics, cocaine use leaped 100 percent in each of the last two years, leaving 40,000 Nicaraguans now addicted. Deaths from drug overdosing have also risen steeply, from 27 in 1991 to 60 in 1993. Though efforts to map the drug problem focus on the capital, the spread of hard drugs has had its greatest effects on Nicaragua's sparsely populated Atlantic Coast, an area inhabited in large part by Miskito Indians and blacks. Here, the police and Army presence is minimal and unemployment rates reach 80 percent." (p2)

Dye, David R. "International: Nicaraguan Cocaine Bust Reveals New Cartel Route." The Christian Science Monitor v86 n43, 26 Jan 1994. p2. (ISSN0882-7729).

COCAINE INDUSTRY--PERU (v19)

COCAINE INDUSTRY--U.S.

"Rather than categorizing our significant efforts to date as being unsuccessful, I would say that the Nation's Drug Interdiction Strategy is maturing. In fact, it has begun to produce increasing results. These results are evident in the unprecedented degree of interagency and international cooperation which, a few years ago, would have been considered unachievable. Last year alone, the combined international counternarcotics effort interdicted 338 metric tons of cocaine; US law enforcement agencies seized 139 tons of the total, while other nations seized 199 metric tons. Shiprider agreements, boarding agreements, joint prosecutions, and strengthening political will in some key source and transit countries all point to success as the process matures. OPBAT, a joint international counternarcotics operation between the US and Bahamian governments is a model in international cooperation and effectiveness. OPBAT has responded to 100 percent of known smuggling events in progress during FY93. In addition, intelligence efforts, detection technology/reporting, and interdiction response form a truly impressive system. Ultimately, we will create a coalition of cooperative nations, throughout the Western Hemisphere, that effectively deny traffickers access to any safe haven or supporting infrastructure." (p886-887)

Kime, J. William (Commandant, U.S. Coast Guard). U.S. House. Committee on Appropriations. "Department of Transportation and Related Agencies Approp. for 1994 (Part 3)." Hearing, Washington, D.C.: GPO, 1993. (ISBN0160410649). (Y4.Ap6/1:T68/4/994/pt.3).

"Studies have shown that the massive amounts of funding supplied for drug interdiction beginning in the late 1980s have had no appreciable effect on either the availability or price of listed drugs nationwide. Some reports have estimated that if even 50 percent of the cocaine shipped to the United States were confiscated, it would only result in a 3-percent increase in the street price. In a September 1991 report, the GAO [General Accounting Office] stated the interdiction may raise operating costs but it is doubtful whether it would raise costs to the extent that it would affect trafficking operations." (p817)

U.S. House. Committee on Appropriations. "Department of Transportation and Related Agencies Approp. for 1994 (Part 3)." Hearing, Washington, D.C.: GPO, 1993. (ISBN0160410649). (Y4.Ap6/1:T68/4/994/pt.3).

COCOA TRADE--COFFEE INDUSTRY--BRAZIL--U.S. (v19)

COFFEE INDUSTRY

"At an average of 3.4 cups per day, Americans are the world's top coffee drinkers, but that doesn't mean beans if you don't know what you're buying. And, with the growing demand for greener, healthier products, how does that cup of joe stack up? For one thing, coffee trees, which thrive on plantations mainly in Mexico, Central and South America, Indonesia, and Africa, are the third most heavily sprayed crop in the world, next to cotton and tobacco. 'More than 70 percent of the world's coffee is sprayed with synthetic chemicals,'--including malathion and DDT, long banned in the U.S., says Karen Cebreros of Elan International, a San Diego, California-based coffee importer and exporter. However, coffee beans are protectively isolated inside a cherry-like fruit, and the 400-degree coffee roasting process effectively breaks down the toxic chemicals. So, although the sprays don't directly affect consumer health, they do 'pose a threat to growers' health, besides being an overall hazard to the ecosystem,' notes Paul Katzeff, CEO of Fort Bragg, California's Thanksgiving Coffee Company, whose motto is: 'Not just a cup, but a just cup.'" (p40)

Lane, Hilary. "Food & Health: Coffees with Conscience: Choices for the Caffeinated Environmentalist." E Magazine v5 n1, Feb 1994. p40,42. (ISSN1046-8021).

COFFEE INDUSTRY--CHIAPAS (MEXICO)

"Thirty-five percent of the coffee produced in Mexico comes from [Chiapas]....Fifty-three percent of the harvest is exported, principally to the US and Europe. More than 100,000 tons of coffee leave the state....In 1988, a kilo (2.2 pounds) of pergamino coffee sold abroad for 8000 pesos ($2.57); the Chiapan producers were paid 2500 pesos ($.80) or less." (p30)

Marcos, Subcommandante. "Defending the Commons: A Reality Tour of the Heart of Chiapas." Earth Island Journal v9 n2, Spr 1994. p30-31. (ISSN1041-0406).

COFFEE INDUSTRY--UGANDA

In Uganda, "coffee production has been falling recently, largely due to old trees in need of replacement, and exports may reach only 2.4 mn bags in 1995/96, compared to 2.04 mn in 1992/93. With prices forecast to average only $0.95 a kilo in 1995/96, projected coffee earnings of $136.8 mn will be less than half the 1980s average." (p17-18)

Laishley, Roy. "Uganda: Turning Growth into Prosperity." Africa Recovery v7 n2, Oct 1993. p16-21.

COHO SALMON--U.S.

"The coho salmon, long a staple of the...[Pacific Northwest] fishing industry, is extinct in 55 percent of its historic range in the region and declining elsewhere. In California alone, the coho salmon run has declined from more than 200,000 to fewer than 5,000 since the 1940s. As a result, there hasn't been a commercial coho salmon fishing season off the California coast for five years." (p2)

Engelmeyer, Paul. "The Rivers Run All Too Slowly." Audubon Activist Jan-Feb 1994. p2-3. (ISSN0898-915X).

"California: Historic population of coho ranged between 200,000 and 500,000 in the 1940s. Today, 1,500 to 5,000 adult fish return, less than 1 percent of their number during World War II. Oregon coast: Wild coho runs exceeded 1.3 million fish a century ago, and were perhaps much higher before white settlers arrived in the mid-19th century. Today, wild coho runs on the northern Oregon coasts may be as low as 10,000 fish, and are almost extinct in southern coastal streams such as the Pistol. Columbia River:...The historic run may have exceeded 1.2 million fish. By 1940, landings of coho declined to nearly 10 percent of the 1890 peak. Today, the wild coho may be extinct in the Columbia. All that remain, according to a recent ruling by the National Marine Fisheries Service, are coho of hatchery origin. Washington coast and Puget Sound:...In Puget Sound, the average annual catch declined by 43 percent from the turn of the century to the mid-1970s. Among 54 coho stocks outside the Columbia basin, the state of Washington lists 17 as critical or depressed." (p10-11)

Koberstein, Paul. "The Decline and Fall of Salmon." High Country News v25 n21, 15 Nov 1993. p1,10-11. (ISSN0191-5657).

COINING, ILLICIT

see COUNTERFEITS AND COUNTERFEITING

COINS--U.S.

"Fiscal Year 1992...saw the Mint produce coins to commemorate the 1992 Olympic Games, the 1992 Christopher Columbus Quincentenary, and the 1992 White House 200th Anniversary. The Olympic Coin Program raised approximately $9 million in surcharges for the United States Olympic Committee to support the training of American athletes for the games. To date, sales of the Christopher Columbus coins have generated over $7 million in surcharges. These surcharges will be paid to the Christopher Columbus Fellowship Foundation and used to award fellowships to outstanding individuals to encourage new discoveries in all fields of endeavor for the benefit of mankind. The White House Coin Program resulted in a sell-out of the 500,000 coins that were legislatively authorized. Surcharges of $5 million were raised to support the White House Collection of fine art and historic furnishings, and for the maintenance of the historic public rooms at the White House. Operating profits for the Mint's recurring annual numismatic and bullion programs as well as residual profits for the three commemorative programs amounted to approximately $25 million for the year." (p153)

Ryder, David J. (Director, U.S. Mint, U.S. Dept. of the Treasury). U.S. House. Committee on Appropriations. "Treasury, Postal Service...Approp. for Fiscal Year 1994 (Part 1)." Hearing, Washington, D.C.: GPO, 1993. (Y4.Ap6/1:T71/994/pt.1).

COLLEGE ATHLETES--FLORIDA

"In 1990-91, 70% of the students who participated in athletics at Florida public universities were male. Participation rates for women ranged from a low of 23% to a high of 40%. The number of women athletes in the State University System increased by 4% between 1988-89 and 1990-91 while male athletes increased by 18% during the same years." (p137)

Benda, Nancy (Director, Equal Education Opportunity Program, Florida Dept. of Education). U.S. House. Committee on Energy and Commerce. "Intercollegiate Sports." Hearing, 23 Jun 1993. Washington, D.C.: GPO, 1994. (ISBN0160435307). (Y4.En2/3:103-58).

COLLEGE ATHLETES--U.S. (v19)

COLLEGE ATHLETES--U.S.--WOMEN (v19)

COLLEGE COSTS--U.S. (v19)

see also STUDENT LOAN FUNDS--U.S.

"A college graduate [in the U.S.] can expect to earn an average of $26,772 a year. For high school graduates, the average is only $12,924. Clearly, a college degree will eventually pay for itself--but parents usually have to pay for it first. The vast majority of parents with college-bound children (83 percent) say they are worried about how they will pay the bill, according to a 1993 survey for Northwestern National Life Insurance Company. In 1992-93, the average cost of a year at a public university for an in-state student was $6,000, and the average cost at a private university was $15,100, according to the National Center for Education Statistics....average tuition costs...continue to rise about 10 percent a year. Financial aid will cover some of the cost, but not all of it, and not for everyone. Only half of all students receive some combination of federal, state, private, or school-based financial aid. The total package averages $5,040 a year per student." (p20-21)

Sandor, Gabrielle. "Business Reports: Education: College Pays Off, but Who's Going to Pay for It?" American Demographics v16 n2, Feb 1994. p20-22. (ISSN0163-4089).

"The highest-income households are not much more likely than the moderately affluent to buy something--but when they buy, they spend a lot more on it. For example, 11 percent of households with incomes of $70,000 or more paid college tuition in 1992, compared with 9 percent of those with incomes of $50,000 to $69,999. But the average expenditure among those who had this cost was $7,000 for the most affluent, compared with less than $3,000 for the moderately affluent. These wealthiest parents may have children attending more expensive schools, and they may foot more of the bill." (p13)

Crispell, Diane. "Business Reports: Households: The Very Rich Are Sort of Different." American Demographics v16 n3, Mar 1994. p11-13. (ISSN0163-4089).

"America spends more per student on higher education than any other country in the world--$13,000 per year as against $6,000-$7,000 for 24 advanced-industrial nations." (p22)

Stelzer, Irwin M. "Commentary: What Health-Care Crisis?" Commentary v97 n2, Feb 1994. p19-24. (ISSN0010-2601).

"Tuition for the 1993-1994 academic year rose seven percent over last year's figures for public four-year colleges and universities and eight percent since last year for public two-year colleges, according to Peterson's Annual Higher Education Survey. The average costs (tuition and fees) for a four-year public school in 1993-1994 was $2,532; for two-year public schools, $1,557....Average costs for private four-year institutions averaged $9,559 this year; for private two-year institutions, $5,746....Applications to two- and four-year colleges rose an average eight percent between 1988 and 1992. The highest percentage increase over the last five years--21 percent--occurred among two-year colleges; applications to four-year institutions increased about four percent over these five years. In addition, education is the second most popular major at four-year institutions; business is the first." (p15)

"NewsBits." NSTA Reports! Dec 1993-Jan 1994. p14-15,39.

The American Council on Education "reported in 1989 that in the previous two years the number of students choosing colleges on the basis of low tuition increased from 23.4 to 27.75 percent, those having to live closer to home rose from 19.8 to 21.3 percent, and those whose plans were dictated by financial aid offers rose from 25.2 to 27.8 percent. From 1989 to 1992 the percentage of students from the middle class (from families earning $40,000 to $70,000 in 1989) enrolling in the top twenty-five institutions dropped from 39 percent to 31 percent, and the percentage from the bottom 10 percent by income (from families earning less than $30,000) has dropped slightly from 13 percent to 12.4 percent, while the percentage of students from the top 5 percent of U.S. households by income (those earning over $100,000) increased from 31 percent to 37 percent. Forced out of the elite public and private institutions, students from the middle classes have swamped the state and community college system. Last year, community college enrollment increased 8 percent to 5,334,000." (p83)

Spear, Bruce. "Multiculturalism Inc." Transition v3 n3, 1993. p72-86. (ISSN0041-1191).

COLLEGE DEGREES

see DEGREES, ACADEMIC

COLLEGE ENTRANCE ACHIEVEMENT TESTS--U.S. (v19)

COLLEGE GRADUATES--EMPLOYMENT--U.S. (v19)

"Despite widespread corporate layoffs, top-tier B-schools [in the U.S.] are reporting increases in on-campus interviews and job offers. 'A lot of companies that held back MBA hiring have holes in their management lineup, and they're playing catchup,' says Maury Hanigan, a New York-based staffing consultant....At Stanford University, companies have conducted 9,200 interviews so far, up from 8,000 last year and only 4,000 in 1990. The University of Texas at Austin's B-school boasted 3,280 interviews last fall, up from 2,200. Offers at Northwestern University's Kellogg School are up 8% over last year. 'The days of the multiple job offers are back,' says Karen O. Dowd of the University of Virginia's Darden School." (p146)

Bongiorno, Lori. "The Corporation: Business Schools: The Selling of a B-School Grad, 1994." Business Week n3364, 28 Mar 1994. p146-147. (ISSN0007-7135).

U.S. "college graduates typically enter the labour force around $10,000 in debt, from loans taken out to pay soaring tuition bills. The job market they encounter is one in which 22% of employed Americans are either part-time or temporary workers, the highest proportion ever; indeed, employment with temp agencies accounted for 15% of the new jobs created last year and 26% the year before. Since 1989 median full-time earnings for workers aged 20 to 24 have fallen, in real terms, by 7%." (p27)

"American Survey: Generation X-onomics." Economist v330 n7855, 19 Mar 1994. p27-28. (ISSN0013-0613).

COLLEGE INTEGRATION--U.S.

"A University of Michigan study...paints the first national portrait of social integration on college campuses....The study was presented...at the annual meeting of the American Educational Research Association by Sylvia Hurtado, assistant professor of education at the U-M School of Education's Center for the Study of Higher and Postsecondary Education. The study is based on a nationally representative sample of 6,000 college students at 390 schools, who were surveyed in 1987 and followed up 1991....About 69 percent of Asian American students and 78 percent of Mexican Americans reported frequently dining with someone of a different racial or ethnic group, with 60 percent and 72 percent, respectively, reporting they often studied with someone of a different group. About 55 percent of the African American students said they frequently dined with members of other groups, and 49 percent said they frequently studied with members of other groups. Only 21 percent of white students frequently dined and only about 15 percent frequently studied with someone from a different group. About 42 percent of Asian American students reported that they frequently dated someone outside their own racial or ethnic group, compared with about 24 percent of Mexican Americans, 13 percent of African Americans and 4 percent of whites." (p1-2)

News release. "Hurtado." University of Michigan News and Information Services 31 Mar 1994. p1-3.

COLLEGE SPORTS--FINANCE (v19)

COLLEGE SPORTS--U.S.--ORGANIZATION AND ADMINISTRATION (v19)

COLLEGE STUDENTS

see also AFRO-AMERICAN COLLEGE STUDENTS

COLLEGE STUDENTS--EUROPE (v19)

COLLEGE STUDENTS--U.S. (v19)

"Based on the College Board's study of the mainstreaming of adults on American campuses, the large majority of adult students enrolled in credit programs come through the College's front door and are well integrated into the regular programs and units of the college. This is certainly true of the 1200 or so two-year community colleges, but it is increasingly evident in the four-year institutions as well, such as the California State University System, where roughly 45% of its more than 350,000 students are above the age of 25. Adult students and traditional age students are looking more alike than different. While many adults have taken on the characteristics of traditional age students, such as study during the day (close to one half of them) as well as during the evenings, studying full-time (about 25% of them) as well as part time, studying on campus (close to 90%) more often than studying off campus, studying for degrees (about 60%) as well as taking single courses, and studying for credit, as well as for noncredit." (p5,16)

Aslanian, Carol. "Trends in Adult Learning." New Horizons for Learning v14 n3, Spr 1993. p5,16.

"WASHINGTON POST'S Paul Blustein...views American higher education's internationalization as 'the flip side of the much-lamented decline in American manufacturing,' and...argues that the significant increase in foreign students attending American universities--from 92,000 in 1980 to 435,000 in 1990--should be interpreted as 'a sign of the high value foreigners place on American university degrees.'...William Raspberry notes that during the period that the number of foreign students receiving Ph.D.'s has doubled, the number of black American men receiving them has dropped by half; moreover, while only 13.8 percent of the foreigners supported themselves, a full 60 percent of African-Americans worked and had to borrow money to make their way through school." (p80-81)

Spear, Bruce. "Multiculturalism Inc." Transition v3 n3, 1993. p72-86. (ISSN0041-1191).

COLLEGE STUDENTS--U.S.--ALCOHOL USE (v19)

COLLEGE STUDENTS--U.S.--ATTITUDES (v19)

COLLEGE STUDENTS--U.S.--DRUG USE (v19)

COLLEGE STUDENTS--U.S.--ECONOMIC CONDITIONS (v19)

COLLEGE STUDENTS--U.S.--SEXUAL BEHAVIOR (v19)

COLLEGE TEACHERS--SALARIES, ETC.--U.S.

"The faculty salary report released...by the American Association of University Professors shows the average salary for faculty members at public universities is $47,780 this year, compared to $53,280 at private institutions....The University of Michigan is the state's most generous public university, paying full professors an average of $77,700 this year. Full compensation for professors, which includes salary and benefits, averaged $95,500 for the 1993-94 school year....U-M faculty members may be getting top dollar in Michigan, for example, but they lag behind Harvard University in Massachusetts and other private, research schools. The average salary for a full professor at Harvard this year is $100,900. The average compensation package is valued at $123,600....Nationwide, over the past 10 years salaries increased by 62.6 percent at public institutions while they increased by 72.5 percent at private schools. The annual increase for this year was 3.1 percent in the public sector and 3.6 percent among private colleges." (p4 secC)

Kellogg, Sarah. "Public, Private College Pay Gap Persists." Ann Arbor News 19 Apr 1994. p4 secC.

COLLEGE TEACHERS--U.S. (v19)

COLLEGES AND UNIVERSITIES

see AFRO-AMERICAN UNIVERSITIES AND COLLEGES; CRIME--U.S.--COLLEGES AND UNIVERSITIES

COLOMBIA

see also CALI (COLOMBIA)--INDUSTRIES; COCAINE INDUSTRY--BOLIVIA--COLOMBIA--PERU; CRIME--COLOMBIA; HOMELESS PERSONS--BOGOTA (COLOMBIA); INDIGENOUS PEOPLES--EL CHOCO (COLOMBIA); MURDER--COLOMBIA--U.S.; TRAFFIC CONGESTION--BOGOTA (COLOMBIA); VIOLENCE--COLOMBIA

COLOMBIA--ECONOMIC CONDITIONS (v19)

In Colombia, "inflation has averaged 24% a year over the past two decades. But over the same period (and helped by recycled drug money) real GDP [gross domestic product] has grown at an average annual rate of 4.4%. And Colombia never stopped servicing its foreign debt. But officials in Colombia, as elsewhere in the region, have tended towards paternalism and heavy regulation, especially in financial matters. This began to change with the launch, in 1990, of a reform programme called 'apertura,' or opening....Foreign exchange transactions have largely been freed. Tariffs on goods have been reduced from an average of 44% in 1989 to 12% in 1992, according to J.P. Morgan, an American bank." (p74)

"Finance: Colombia's Financial Markets: Opening at Last." Economist v329 n7842, 18 Dec 1993. p74-75. (ISSN0013-0613).

COLOMBIA--MEXICO--SOCIAL CONDITIONS

"Life expectancy at birth has increased by 12 years in Colombia and Mexico during the past three decades and is approaching 70 years. Income per capita is $700 in Colombia and more than $950 in Mexico. Growth in income has been above 2 percent per year in both countries. Literacy is high at 87 percent, and primary plus secondary school enrollment is about 80 percent. Fertility has fallen dramatically in each of these countries, decreasing by 3.15 births in Mexico and 3.86 in Colombia. Contraceptive prevalence is 66 percent in Colombia and 53 percent in Mexico. Unless there is a sharp attenuation of the rates of decline in fertility, each of these countries will reach replacement fertility by the end of this century." (p83-84)

Mauldin, W. Parker/Ross, John A. "Prospects and Programs for Fertility Reduction, 1990-2015." Studies in Family Planning v25 n2, Mar-Apr 1994. p77-95. (ISSN0039-3665).

COLON (ANATOMY)--CANCER--U.S.--EXAMINATION (v19)

COLORADO

see FORESTS AND FORESTRY--COLORADO--SPORTS; RANCHES--COLORADO

COLORADO RIVER (COLO.-MEXICO) (v19)

COMFORT, STANDARD OF

see COST AND STANDARD OF LIVING

COMMERCE (v19)

see also ASIA--COMMERCE; CHINA--COMMERCE--U.S.; EUROPEAN ECONOMIC COMMUNITY--COMMERCE--ENVIRONMENTAL ASPECTS; EUROPEAN ECONOMIC COMMUNITY--U.S.--COMMERCE; IOWA--COMMERCE--MEXICO; ISRAEL--COMMERCE; JAPAN--COMMERCE; U.S.--COMMERCE

"The evolution of a North American trading bloc...is not likely to diminish support in the region for the multilateral trading system. All three countries regard their bilateral and/or trilateral trade agreements as complementing but not supplanting their multilateral trade relations. Unlike the EC [European Community], intra-North American trade (combined exports and imports) accounted for only 37 percent of North America's world trade in 1989, compared to EC's 59 percent. At the same time, North America's inter-regional trade is much more diversified than the EC trade--about 19 percent with the EC and 28 percent with East Asia, whereas the EC's trade with East Asia and North America was limited to only 7.5 percent and 9.0 percent respectively....the non-North American markets (especially those of East Asia) are too important for these countries (the United States in particular) to turn aggressively inward in their trade policy in the near future. NAFTA [North American Free Trade Agreement] is essentially a U.S.-initiated defensive strategy against the ongoing process of Europe 1992 on the one hand and the emergence of Japan as an economic superpower on the other. The move towards NAFTA, if anything, is a second-best alternative to the multilateral trading system in the event that the Uruguay Round of the GATT falters." (p363)

Park, Jong H. "Emerging Trading Blocs and Trade Policy Options for Third World LDCs." Journal of Third World Studies v10 n1, Spr 1993. p358-385. (ISSN8755-3449).

"From 1981 to 1991, total world trade increased in real terms by 48%. During the same period, total trade among the core economies of the Common Market (Germany, France, Italy, Great Britain) increased by almost 60%. Yet for Japan, as for all the rest of East Asia, trade virtually doubled, and for the powerhouse economies of Singapore, Hong Kong, Korea and Taiwan, total trade today is fourfold larger than it was just a decade ago." (p30)

Courtis, Kenneth S. "Foreign Voices: Good Trade." Look Japan v39 n455, Feb 1994. p30-31. (ISSN0456-5339).

"One explanation for the increase in world trade since 1950 is the decline in the cost of transporting goods. This relationship is usually measured by examining the ratio of the value of cargo traded plus transportation and insurance costs--or Costs in Full (CIF)--to the cost of the cargo before adding insurance and transportation--or Free on Board (FOB). For the world as a whole, the CIF/FOB ratio fell by 36 percent between 1950 and 1990. The Boeing Corporation has estimated that the real price of passenger air transport fell 58 percent between 1960 and 1990. Transportation costs among the industrial countries are relatively low because of the shorter distances goods need to travel. The ratio of transportation costs to total costs for Germany, which trades mostly with other EEC [European Economic Community] members, is only 1.03, while the ratio for Japan, which is relatively far from its trading partners, is 1.09....The decline over time in the CIF/FOB ratio was sharper for the developed countries, which dominated the increase in world trade." (p27-28)

Bloom, David E./Brender, Adi. "Labor and the Emerging World Economy." Population Bulletin v48 n2, Oct 1993. p2-39. (ISSN0032-468X).

"According to the World Bank, in 1987, the US--controlling just 23 per cent of world production--took almost half the manufactured exports of the Third World--mostly from the so-called Asian tigers. By comparison, Japan, with about half the level of US GNP [gross national product], took only 12 per cent of developing country exports. The EU [European Union], with a greater world GNP share than the US, took just 29 per cent." (p48)

Teese, Colin. "Australia after Uruguay, and the Crisis in International Trade." Quadrant v38 n3, Mar 1994. p45-51. (ISSN0033-5010).

COMMERCIAL AERONAUTICS

see AERONAUTICS, COMMERCIAL

COMMERCIAL FISHING

see FISHERIES

COMMERCIAL LOANS--U.S. (v19)

COMMERCIAL LOANS--VIETNAM (v19)

COMMERCIAL PRODUCTS--U.S. (v19)

COMMODITY-BACKED FUNDS

"The 514 futures funds and commodity pools tracked by industry newsletter MANAGED ACCOUNT REPORTS posted an average 12% gain through October, the latest date for which results are available. Fund managers cashed in on volatility in the currency markets, the steady decline in interest rates, and a sizable drop in energy prices. This year's results are down from the industry's 1987 return of 46.9% but better than the 11.5% loss posted in 1986, the worst performance since MAR began tabulating results in 1979." (p122)

Greising, David. "Commodity Funds: The Investment Spectrum: Taking Some of the Fear Out of Futures." Business Week i3352, 27 Dec 1993. p122,124-125. (ISSN0007-7135).

COMMONWEALTH OF INDEPENDENT STATES

see ECONOMIC ASSISTANCE, EUROPEAN--COMMONWEALTH OF INDEPENDENT STATES; ECONOMIC ASSISTANCE--COMMONWEALTH OF INDEPENDENT STATES; EUROPEAN ECONOMIC COMMUNITY--U.S.--COMMERCE--COMMONWEALTH OF INDEPENDENT STATES

COMMUNICABLE DISEASES (v19)

COMMUNICABLE DISEASES--RUSSIA (v19)

COMMUNICATION SATELLITES

see ARTIFICIAL SATELLITES IN TELECOMMUNICATION

COMMUNICATION SYSTEMS, COMPUTER

see COMPUTER NETWORKS

COMMUNIST PARTIES--CHINA

The Communist Party in China "announced it had accepted 1.76m new members in 1992, bringing the total to more than 52m, about 5% of the population. Of the new members, it said 45.9% were peasants and fishermen, 16.5% were technical workers, and 13.9% were students and academic researchers. More than two-thirds were under 35, and more than two-thirds had been educated beyond high school. Some 100,000 people are thought to have resigned from the party after the pro-democracy demonstrators were crushed in Tiananmen Square in 1989, but now the party appears again to be in the ascendant. Amazingly, given the social changes, the party can still afford to pick and choose. In 1992 only one in 12 of the nearly 13m people who applied was accepted--that was 2m more than had applied in 1991." (p44)

"Asia: China: How Now, Chairman Mao?" Economist v329 n7843, 25 Dec 1993. p44. (ISSN0013-0613).

COMMUNITY ASSOCIATIONS--U.S. (v19)

COMMUNITY COLLEGE ATHLETES--FLORIDA

"In 1991-92, 62% of the Florida community college athletes were male and 38% were female. Of the 146 athletic teams offered in community colleges, 67 (46%) were women's teams and 79 (54%) were men's teams. Data were collected in the Study Commission survey on financial support from booster clubs. The colleges reported a total of $276,795 in booster club contributions in athletics programs in Florida community colleges. Of that total, 22% went to women's teams." (p136)

Benda, Nancy (Director, Equal Education Opportunity Program, Florida Dept. of Education). U.S. House. Committee on Energy and Commerce. "Intercollegiate Sports." Hearing, 23 Jun 1993. Washington, D.C.: GPO, 1994. (ISBN0160435307). (Y4.En2/3:103-58).

COMMUNITY COLLEGE STUDENTS--U.S. (v19)

COMMUNITY COLLEGES--U.S. (v19)

COMMUTING

see also BICYCLE COMMUTING

COMMUTING--LOS ANGELES (CALIF)

"For five years, Commuter Transportation Services (CTS) has conducted surveys of commuter attitudes and behaviors." The CTS survey "shows that the number of Los Angeles commuters who shared a ride three or more days a week declined between 1991 and 1992, from 1.5 million to 1.4 million out of an estimated total of 6.6 million workers in the five-county region....The 1993 survey reports that both the length and distance of the average Los Angeles commute is shorter. The average distance Los Angelinos cover is 30 miles round trip, down 3 miles from the year before. The average commuter spent 69 minutes on the road, 7 minutes less than the year before." (p18-19)

Nichols, Paula. "Business Reports: Transportation: Los Angeles without Traffic Jams? It Could Happen." American Demographics v16 n2, Feb 1994. p18-19. (ISSN0163-4089).

In the 1993 Commuter Transportation Services survey, Los Angeles "Commuters cite convenience and flexibility as the primary factor for choosing a mode of transportation. One-fifth of commuters make a stop on the way to work to drop a child at day care or school, buy gas, or get something to eat. Women are almost three times as likely as men to say they need to have a vehicle to drop off children at school or day care. Men, on the other hand, are twice as likely as women to stop for gas or a bite to eat on their way to work. Nearly three in ten commuters make a stop on the way home, usually to shop or pick up a child." (p19)

Nichols, Paula. "Business Reports: Transportation: Los Angeles without Traffic Jams? It Could Happen." American Demographics v16 n2, Feb 1994. p18-19. (ISSN0163-4089).

Los Angeles' "grand experiment in altering its driving habits in the wake of the earthquake is producing important changes but not the fundamental shifts in transportation patterns that some had hoped for." (p1) "About 20,000 riders are now taking Metrolink trains a day--double the number before the earthquake. Immediately after the temblor, ridership on one line increased more than 20-fold. Long term, rail officials say they will be 'happy' if they retain a 10 percent increase in ridership. The city's nascent subway system, of which only 4.4 miles have been completed downtown so far, has seen a jump from 14,000 riders to 17,000....Bus use is up 8 percent--or about 80,000 riders a day--out of a total of 1.2 million passengers....Calls coming into a local hotline that matches riders have gone up from 286 a day to over 400. An estimated 16 percent of Los Angeles' commuters carpool--the highest rate of any major US city. Still, that means more than 80 percent drive to work alone, and, given the congestion and pollution that habit creates, the attempts to reinvent the region's transportation system will go on." (p4)

Armstrong, Scott. "Angelenos Can't Shake Auto Habits Even after Earthquake." The Christian Science Monitor v86 n59, 17 Feb 1994. p1,4. (ISSN0882-7729).

COMMUTING--MILWAUKEE (WIS)

Job-Ride, a van service launched in 1989 by the Wisconsin Department of Transportation to carry inner-city residents to jobs in the suburbs "serves Milwaukee residents who are unemployed, underemployed, or receiving some form of public assistance. Over 90 percent of Job-Ride passengers are African American and about 60 percent are male. In its first year, the program received funding from two sources. It got $100,000 from federal oil overcharge restitution funds and another $100,000 from the state's general purpose revenue funds. Since 1990, 80 percent of the program's expenses (now over $500,000 per year) are met by the oil overcharge restitution funds--allocated to each state from the national petroleum violation escrow account. The remainder is provided by United Way, private donations, employer contributions, and fares." (p18)

Nelson, Toya M. "Planning Practice: Wisconsin Picks Up the Tab." Planning v59 n12, Dec 1993. p18-19. (ISSN0001-2610).

COMMUTING--PHILADELPHIA (PA)

"As in other metropolitan areas, decentralization has had an impact on the Philadelphia region. In 1990, only 10 percent of all work trips were traditional suburb-to-city commutes, while 46 percent were within one suburban county and 15 percent were from one county to another. City-to-suburb commuters now represent about four percent of all SEPTA [or Southeastern Pennsylvania Transportation Authority] riders, and 13 of its bus routes (including the 200 Series) and the Norris-town high speed rail line carry mostly reverse commuters." (p21)

Bickel, Richard. "Planning Practice: Philadelphia Links Bus and Rail." Planning v59 n12, Dec 1993. p21-22. (ISSN0001-2610).

COMMUTING--SYDNEY (AUSTRALIA) (v19)

COMMUTING--U.S. (v19)

"The National Personal Transportation Survey points out that the number of people departing for work [in the U.S.] before 6 a.m. has risen from 6.9 million workers in 1985 to 8.2 million in 1989 and from 17.6 million to 18.7 million workers in the 6 a.m. to 7 a.m. travel period. However, the resulting changes in market share are minimal. The share of the market departing for work before 6 a.m. increased by only 1 percent over the four year period and the percentage of people commuting during the traditional peak hours of 6 to 9 a.m. has remained unchanged at 70 percent. The congestion facing over two-thirds of workers during the peak commuting period increases the attractiveness of transit and the lengthening of the peak periods of travel improves the economics of transit. Transit providers will need to be flexible in serving patrons at untraditional travel times." (p69)

Pena, Federico (Secretary of Transportation). U.S. House. Committee on Appropriations. "Department of Transportation and Related Agencies Approp. for 1994 (Part 3)." Hearing, Washington, D.C.: GPO, 1993. (ISBN0160410649). (Y4.Ap6/1:T68/4/994/pt.3).

COMPACT DISC INDUSTRY--U.S. (v19)

COMPACT DISK READ-ONLY MEMORY

see CD-ROM

COMPANIES

see BUSINESS ENTERPRISES

COMPOST--GERMANY--U.S.

"The last few years have at least established composting as a rising green industry, especially in the most populous regions of the developed world. In the United States, as recently as 1988, the Environmental Protection Agency (EPA) listed the percentage of yard waste composted in the entire country as 'negligible.' The EPA's 1992 report, though, reveals a healthy 12 percent composting rate. Eight years ago, only 5,000 Germans had their organic wastes collected separately; by 1995, the ranks are expected to swell to 12 million. 'Rot,' says [composting consultant Clark] Gregory, 'is hot.'" (p36-37)

Sachs, Aaron. "Trends: Composting: Dirty Riches." World Watch v6 n4, Jul-Aug 1993. p36-38. (ISSN0896-0615).

COMPOST--U.S. (v19)

COMPUTER CRIMES--U.S.

"The incidence of hacker attacks [in the U.S.] increased from 339,000 hacker attacks on workplace computers in 1989 to 684,000 hacker attacks on workplace computers in 1991. The total monetary damage due to hacker attacks likewise increased from approximately $75 million in 1989 to nearly $160 million in 1991. Analysis of study results shows that without the aggressive use of computer security policies, the incidence of hacker attacks--as well as monetary damage due to these attacks--would be much higher." (p253)

Carlson, Cynthia E. (Vice President, USA Research, Inc.). U.S. House. Committee on Energy and Commerce. "Telecommunications Network Security." Hearing, 29 Apr 1993. Washington, D.C.: GPO, 1994. (ISBN0160434130). (Y4.En2/3:103-53).

COMPUTER GAMES--U.S. (v19)

COMPUTER INDUSTRY

"American industry has invested heavily in technology. Last year, for example, spending on durable equipment like computers soared 16.2 percent. As a result, 34.5 percent of the U.S. work force had PCs in 1993, compared with 14.6 percent in Germany and 9 percent in Japan." (p58) "The United States has always led the world in computers--and that is so now more than at any time in the past. U.S. computer hardware workers are 5 percent more productive than those in Japan and 11 percent more productive than their German rivals." (p60)

Collins, Sara. "Business: America Cranks It Up." U.S. News & World Report v116 n12, 28 Mar 1994. p57-58,60. (ISSN0041-5537).

COMPUTER INDUSTRY--CALIFORNIA

"U.S. export controls are necessary to contain the spread of weapons and to prevent terrorists from obtaining technology that could threaten this Nation's security. We can all agree on that. But, at the same time, these controls should not unnecessarily undermine highly competitive and growing California industries, such as our computer and computer equipment makers. Over 280,000 Californians are employed by businesses that make computers, software and other computer equipment. Nationwide, these companies exported over $52.8 billion in goods last year. To promote economic growth and job creation in California, we must support, not inhibit, this growing, export-oriented sector." (pS664)

Boxer, Barbara (Sen.-Calif.). "Statements on Introduced Bills and Joint Resolutions," Congressional Record (2 Feb 1994). Daily ed. pS659-669. (ISSN0363-7239).

COMPUTER INDUSTRY--JAPAN

"Take a look at Fujitsu, the top company in the Japanese computer industry. In fiscal 1992, it posted a current loss of Y8.7 billion ($82 million), compared to a current profit of Y40 billion ($380 million) in fiscal 1991. This was the company's first current loss since it went public in 1949, and the major reason for it was a Y56 billion ($530 million) decline in sales of computer products, which make up 73% of its total business....Based on volume, supercomputer orders are down 41%, mainframes 26%, and 'office computers' (small business systems) 10%. In contrast to the declines for big, mainframe-class machines, personal computer sales were down only 2% and sales of UNIX workstations were actually up 40%." (p14) Fujitsu's "domestic sales were down 4.9% this year while exports were up 6.6%. Most of the export gains were from compact magnetic disk drives, which have been popular with computer users in the US. Similar trends are seen at Toshiba, which was the only one of the Japanese 'big ten' to post sales growth last year, albeit by only 0.6%. Toshiba's domestic sales were down 5.5%, but exports, mainly of personal computers, soared 35.8%, enabling the company to barely keep its head above water." (p15)

Nanohiko. "Industrial Restructuring: Computers: Downsizing, Bit by Bit." Look Japan v39 n452, Nov 1993. p14-15. (ISSN0456-5339).

COMPUTER INDUSTRY--RESEARCH--U.S. (v19)
COMPUTER INDUSTRY--U.S. (v19)

"A new generation of ultrafast PCs based on Intel Corp.'s Pentium microprocessor--and forthcoming IBM and Apple Computer Inc. models based on the PowerPC chip--is making corporate customers think twice about workstations. While workstation sales growth in 1993 slowed to 6.3%, to $10.3 billion...the huge PC market grew by 10.8%, to $69.8 billion, says market researcher International Data Corp. A lot of that growth came from the red-hot home-computer market. But, increasingly, top-end PCs are squeezing workstation makers. Data-quest Inc. predicts that some 20% of the Pentium PCs sold this year will be used for workstation applications." (p69)

Hof, Robert D./others. "Information Processing: Computers: Workstations Have Their Work Cut Out." Business Week n3356, 31 Jan 1994. p69-70. (ISSN0007-7135).

"Last year [1993], mainframe sales [in the U.S.] fell 9%, on top of a 1% decline in 1992, according to International Data Corp. Sales of minicomputers priced at $1 million and up are shrinking by 20% annually." (p92)

McWilliams, Gary/Hof, Robert D. "Information Processing: Computers: They Can't Wait to Serve You." Business Week i3355, 24 Jan 1994. p92. (ISSN0007-7135).

"Sales of PCs and workstations will reach $42.8 billion in 1994, or 58.4% of all U.S. computer hardware sales, according to market researcher International Data Corp. That's up from 56.6% in 1993, and 50.2% five years ago. Mainframe and minicomputer sales, at $23.1 billion, will constitute less than 20% of the total, while the remaining $7.4 billion will be spent on data-communications equipment....There is still a big question concerning just when this year the newest PCs will start selling, since so many 486 PCs were purchased in 1993. Lower prices, powerful new software, and pent-up demand all drove sales far higher last year than anyone expected--a total of 14.8 million units in the U.S., up 25.8% from 1992, says IDC. Indeed, the biggest headache in 1993 for both manufacturers and customers was frustratingly big backlogs. Now, with backlogs whittled down, IDC expects PC sales to grow around 10% in 1994, to 16.28 million units." (p81)

Arnst, Catherine. "High Technology: Computers: The End of the End for 'Big Iron.'" Business Week i3353, 10 Jan 1994. p81. (ISSN0007-7135).

"Some 5 million multimedia PCs are in use in the U.S., according to the newsletter MULTIMEDIA BUSINESS REPORT, which predicts an additional 4.5 million such machines will be bought in 1994. That's creating a boon for the upstart software makers that have been pioneering edutainment. In 1992, retail sales of home learning programs spurted 47%, to $147 million, according to the Software Publishers Assn. (SPA). Sales in 1994 will approach $250 million, estimates San Francisco brokerage Volpe, Welty & Co., which forecasts that by the end of the decade, parents will be spending $1 billion a year on software for at-home learning." (p81)

Armstrong, Larry/others. "Special Report: The Learning Revolution." Business Week n3360, 28 Feb 1994. p80-86,88. (ISSN0007-7135).

COMPUTER LITERACY--U.S.

"Women and men view computers differently, according to a recent poll by Logitech of Fremont, California. And women who work with desktop computers outnumber men by more than two to one....Among office-PC users, more women than men think that computers are fun, says Logitech. More women would use a PC even if their jobs did not require it. Women are also more likely to say that computers have made their jobs easier, and they are more concerned than men are about learning to use a computer. Yet 77 percent of women who use office PCs rarely read any computer magazine or technical articles, compared with 56 percent of men." (p18)

Kaplan, Rachel. "Business Reports: Markets: The Gender Gap at the PC Keyboard." American Demographics v16 n1, Jan 1994. p18. (ISSN0163-4089).

COMPUTER NETWORKS--U.S.

"The Internet, begun in 1969, was originally an experimental computer network organized and financed by the Department of Defense (ARPAnet). It was made available to facilitate the research of a small number of scientists, engineers, and researchers. The National Science Foundation (NSF) also contributed funds. In this period, commercial usage of the network was prohibited. Over time, the number of users of Internet multiplied greatly, although it remains mostly a university and research tool. Currently, however, it is estimated that there are more than 15 million users, mostly in the United States but also in 134 other countries, among which are increasing numbers of commercial enterprises. In early 1993, more than half of the registered networks were private businesses." (p20)

Schiller, Herbert I. "Electronic Highway to Where?" National Forum v74 n2, Spr 1994. p19-21. (ISSN0162-1831).

COMPUTER SOFTWARE INDUSTRY

"Worldwide sales of packaged software will climb 12.1%, to $80.3 billion, topping 1993's 11.5% increase, predicts International Data Corp. Those gains should hold, too, for U.S. producers, which own 75% of the world market. But the story this year will be the battle in personal computer software. Competition that was merely torrid in 1993 will become cutthroat in 1994." (p82)

Brandt, Richard. "High Technology: Software: Software Will Play Hardball Again." Business Week i3353, 10 Jan 1994. p82. (ISSN0007-7135).

"After two years in which the cost of personal computers has fallen by more than half, the price of the applications software used in those PCs--spreadsheets, word processors, databases and the like--is being dragged down too. In 1993 alone the price of applications software probably fell by around a quarter in America and by more than a third in Europe. Such software accounts for some $20 billion of the world's $60 billion off-the-shelf software market, and remains, in unit sales, the fastest-growing part of the industry. Now an all-out price war looks inevitable....Sales and marketing costs, which in the late 1980s were little more than research-and-development expenses, have soared. According to Datamonitor, an industry consultancy, expenditure on sales and marketing has now risen to about 40% of big software companies' annual revenues, while R&D [research & development] has languished at around 14%--not enough, according to some insiders, to support the industry's ambitious long-term product plans. Spending on sales and marketing may hit 50% of revenues at some software firms in 1994." (p63)

"Business: The Softening of Software." Economist v330 n7844, 8 Jan 1994. p63-64. (ISSN0013-0613).

COMPUTER SOFTWARE INDUSTRY--JAPAN--U.S. (v19)

"In contrast with other U.S. industries which have faced roadblocks in doing business in Japan, the U.S. software industry has achieved considerable success in penetrating the Japanese marketplace. At present, an estimated 55% of the market for personal computer (prepackaged) software in Japan is held by U.S. software companies. While this is lower than the 75% market share U.S. software companies hold worldwide, it is nonetheless substantial for Japan." (p55)

Holleyman, Robert (President, Business Software Alliance). U.S. Senate. Committee on Finance. "United States-Japan Trade Negotiations." Hearing, 8 Nov 1993. Washington, D.C.: GPO, 1994. (ISBN0160435635). (Y4.F49:S.hrg.103-399).

COMPUTER SOFTWARE INDUSTRY--U.S. (v19)

"The computer software industry is one of the nation's greatest business success stories. For the period 1982 to 1992, the software industry grew by 269% in real terms, while the remainder of the U.S. economy grew by about 30%. Larger than all but five manufacturing industries, the core software industry (prepackaged software, custom programming and computer integrated design) accounts for $36.7 billion in value added to the U.S. economy." (p55)

Holleyman, Robert (President, Business Software Alliance). U.S. Senate. Committee on Finance. "United States-Japan Trade Negotiations." Hearing, 8 Nov 1993. Washington, D.C.: GPO, 1994. (ISBN0160435625). (Y4.F49:S.hrg.103-339).

"Microsoft is...[the U.S.'s] leading software exporter. In 1993, Microsoft sold more than $2 billion worth of software outside the United States. That is more than 55 percent of its total revenue. Microsoft markets products in 27 different languages, and its products are available in virtually every country. The Department of Commerce estimates that U.S. companies sell three-quarters of the world's prepackaged software and earn half their revenues from foreign sales. Oddly enough, however, the Federal Government still does not specifically track software export data; those numbers are lumped together into a larger category. Despite this very strong world leadership, U.S. software companies face significant problems in the overseas markets. The most blatant problem is piracy....Piracy is most rampant abroad, where it occurs on a mass level. It costs U.S. companies an estimated $10 billion in lost foreign revenues." (pH481)

McDermott, Jim (Rep.-Wash.). "Tribute to Microsoft," Congressional Record (10 Feb 1994). Daily ed. pH479-482. (ISSN0363-7239).

COMPUTER VIRUSES--U.S.

"By far, three viruses were most commonly reported to infect DOS PCs in 1989, 1990, and 1991: Jerusalem B (with decreasing reports over time), Stoned (with increasing reports over time), and Joshi (with increasing reports over time). Approximately 15 to 20 other virus types were reported significantly less frequently, including Friday the 13th and Michelangelo (the latter was reported only in 1991). It is important to note that 40% of respondents who had infected DOS PCs during 1989, 37% of respondents who had infected DOS PCs during 1990, and 30% of respondents who had infected DOS PCs during 1991 did not know the name of the virus(es) that infected the DOS PCs overseen. Three viruses were most commonly reported to infect Macintoshes in 1989, 1990, and 1991: nVIR, WDEF, and Scores. Approximately 8 to 10 other virus types were reported significantly less frequently, including Mosaic and CDEF. It is important to note that 16% of the respondents who had infected Macintoshes during 1989, 24% of respondents who had infected Macintoshes during 1990, and 24% of respondents who had infected Macintoshes during 1991 did not know the name of the virus(es) that had infected the Macintoshes overseen." (p258)

Carlson, Cynthia E. (Vice President, USA Research, Inc.). U.S. House. Committee on Energy and Commerce. "Telecommunications Network Security." Hearing, 29 Apr 1993. Washington, D.C.: GPO, 1994. (ISBN0160434130). (Y4.En2/3:103-53).

"In December 1991, USA Research conducted a survey of 5000 computer managers designed to document (1) the actual damage that computer viruses have caused in the U.S. and (2) effective technologies employed by computer users to fight computer viruses." (p254) "For DOS PCs, survey results show that the portion of respondents reporting one or more virus-infected DOS PCs during 1989, 1990, and 1991 increased significantly each year: 7% in 1989, 19% in 1990, and 31% in 1991....For Macintoshes, survey results show that the portion of respondents reporting one or more virus-infected Macintoshes during 1989, 1990, and 1991 peaked in 1990: 11% in 1989, 19% in 1990, and 19% in 1991....During 1991, the infection rate for DOS PCs peaked at 2.9 infections or re-infections per 100 computers across the U.S. Based on an epidemic penetration model, the DOS PC virus risk is estimated to be 1.0 infections or re-infections per 100 computers in 1992 and is projected to be 0.1 infections or re-infections per 100 computers in 1993. During 1990, the infection rate for Macintoshes peaked at 10.1 infections or re-infections per 100 computers across the U.S. Based on an epidemic penetration model, the Macintosh virus risk is estimated to be 1.7 infections or re-infections per 100 computers in 1992 and is projected to be 0.3 infections per 100 computers in 1993." (p255)

Carlson, Cynthia E. (Vice President, USA Research, Inc.). U.S. House. Committee on Energy and Commerce. "Telecommunications Network Security." Hearing, 29 Apr 1993. Washington, D.C.: GPO, 1994. (ISBN0160434130). (Y4.En2/3:103-53).

"In December 1991, USA Research conducted a survey of 5000 computer managers designed to document (1) the actual damage that computer viruses have caused in the U.S. and (2) effective technologies employed by computer users and managers to fight computer viruses." (p254) "Among all respondents, 63% reported using anti-virus software to prevent virus infections, the most common method, 41% of all respondents employed computer access policies as a virus prevention technique. Other virus infection prevention techniques include the use of other utility software (9%), the use of write-protect floppy tabs (19%), the use of file encryption (4%), the use of isolated or off-network computers (20%), and the use of anti-virus hardware (1%). 20% of all respondents reported doing nothing to prevent virus infections." (p259)

Carlson, Cynthia E. (Vice President, USA Research, Inc.). U.S. House. Committee on Energy and Commerce. "Telecommunications Network Security." Hearing, 29 Apr 1993. Washington, D.C.: GPO, 1994. (ISBN0160434130). (Y4.En2/3:103-53).

"United States PC users spent approximately 75 Million dollars because of computer viruses during 1990. This figure climbed to over 267 Million dollars because of computer viruses during 1991, and $350 Million during 1992. The total virus costs for the first three and one half years of this decade already exceed one Billion dollars in the United States alone. If the virus growth trends continue, even considering the reduction of the computer virus population during the Michelangelo time frame and a reduced growth rate after that time, then costs related to computer viruses during 1993 will still exceed 670 Million dollars. In 1994, the costs will exceed 1.3 Billion dollars." (p225)

Tippett, Peter S. (Dir., Security and Enterprise Products, Symantec Corp.). U.S. House. Committee on Energy and Commerce. "Telecommunications Network Security." Hearing, 29 Apr 1993. Washington, D.C.: GPO, 1994. (ISBN0160434130). (Y4.En2/3:103-53).

"Using conservative data and assumptions, the average organization [in the U.S.] with 1000 personal computers will spend $176,000 on computer viruses this year (1993) and over a quarter of a Million dollars during 1994. Computer viruses cost personal computer users in the United States more than one Billion dollars so far this decade. Viruses will cost U.S. citizens almost 700 Million dollars during 1993 alone and will exceed 1.3 Billion dollars during 1994." (p218)

Tippett, Peter S. (Dir., Security and Enterprise Products, Symantec Corp.). U.S. House. Committee on Energy and

Commerce. "Telecommunications Network Security." Hearing, 29 Apr 1993. Washington, D.C.: GPO, 1994. (ISBN0160434130). (Y4.En2/3:103-53).

"When analysis is performed to estimate the number of virus infections or re-infections for all workplace computers in the U.S., the following picture emerges: During 1991, the number of virus infections for DOS PCs across the U.S. peaked at 1.064 million infections or re-infections. Based on an epidemic penetration model, 0.466 million DOS PC infections or re-infections are estimated to occur in 1992, and 51,438 DOS PC infections or re-infections are projected to occur in 1993. During 1990, the number of virus infections for Macintoshes across the U.S. peaked at 0.275 million infections or re-infections. Based on an epidemic penetration model, 0.114 million Macintosh infections or re-infections are estimated to occur in 1992, and 24,601 Macintosh infections or re-infections are projected to occur in 1993." (p256)

Carlson, Cynthia E. (Vice President, USA Research, Inc.). U.S. House. Committee on Energy and Commerce. "Telecommunications Network Security." Hearing, 29 Apr 1993. Washington, D.C.: GPO, 1994. (ISBN0160434130). (Y4.En2/3:103-53).

COMPUTERS--RECYCLING

"Computers are a lot like fashion: Nobody wants yesterday's models. And in the computer industry at least, the leftovers are piling up at an alarming rate. By 2005, more personal computers (PCs) will be in landfills than in operation, according to projections from a two-year-old study by students at Carnegie Mellon University in Pittsburgh. The PCs would fill a hole an acre wide and 3.5 miles deep. That is not counting bulkier mainframe and mini-computers. Can anything be done? The United States is taking a few promising stabs at recyclable computers. But so far, Germany has the lead. This year, the German government is expected to pass legislation requiring manufacturers to take back their durable and sophisticated consumer goods. By one estimate, computers represent nearly 8 percent of the 1.5 million metric tons of electrical and electronic scrap that the nation will have to reprocess each year." (p6)

Belsie, Laurent. "Economy: US Looks at Germany's Example in Recycling Computers." The Christian Science Monitor v86 n41, 24 Jan 1994. p6. (ISSN0882-7729).

COMPUTERS--U.S. (v19)

"The...[U.S.] increasing reliance on computers means it is vulnerable to electronic glitches. Computer gremlins hassle shoppers. In a 1992 study of three retail chains in California, UCLA researchers found that bar-code scanners rang up the wrong price in 5 percent to 12 percent of the sales, usually overcharging. They also upset car dealers. Chrysler Corporation recalled all its 1995 Neons...because a water leak in the computer system could cause the engine to stall. They are sometimes lethal. On July 3, 1988, the USS Vincennes misidentified and shot down an Iranian airliner, killing 290 people, in part because of computer problems. More often, they're just costly. In 1985, a software problem caused the Bank of New York to run up a $32 billion overdraft. The problem left several of the bank's customers in the lurch, not to mention the $5 million the bank had to shell out in interest charges....Computers are always becoming all fouled up, says Mr. [Peter] Neumann, author of an upcoming book on the subject. The record stretches from space satellites that disappear to hospital machines with faulty software that have given patients huge doses of radiation with sometimes fatal results." (p10)

Belsie, Laurent. "Economy: As Computers Proliferate, So Does Potential for Bugs." The Christian Science Monitor v86 n58, 16 Feb 1994. p10. (ISSN0882-7729).

COMPUTERS--U.S.--AGED

"According to a 1989 Census Bureau report, computers hum in 15 percent of all American households. More recently, SeniorNet statisticians found computers in 9 percent of all households headed by someone age 60 to 69. More than 11,000 people pay $25 a year to participate in SeniorNet, a telecommunications network offered for older computer users through America Online. Half of them are women....Marketing and sociology surveys indicate that more than 50 percent of consumers older than 50 are interested in trying new technologies and products. Twenty-seven percent of a large 70-plus focus group studied by sociologist Daniel Yankelovich demonstrated 'a strong need' to keep up with the latest developments in technology." (p1,2 secE)

Foote, Jennifer. "Connection: Older Adults Are Plugged into Computer Age." Ann Arbor News 17 Jan 1994. p1,2 secE.

COMPUTERS--U.S.--CRYPTOGRAPHY (v19)

COMPUTERS--U.S.--ENERGY CONSUMPTION (v19)

"According to the EPA, office equipment is the fastest growing electricity load in the commercial sector, and computer systems alone are believed to account for 5 percent of commercial electricity consumption. That amounts to an estimated 70 billion kilowatt-hours a year, which in turn produces roughly 54 million tons of carbon dioxide (the major greenhouse gas), 377,000 tons of sulfur dioxide, and 202,000 tons of nitrogen oxides, the latter two gases being the major cause of acid rain. The typical computer draws 75 watts of electricity when not in use, which the EPA estimates to be the vast majority of the time--including nights and weekends, when 30 to 40 percent of computers are left running." (p3)

Naar, Jon. "Computer Makers See Gold in Environmental Equipment." Audubon Activist v8 n3, Nov 1993. p3. (ISSN0898-915X).

COMPUTERS--U.S.--PUBLIC OPINION (v19)

"According to the 1992 poll sponsored by Equifax and conducted by Louis Harris Associates and Alan Westin, more than three-quarters of the American public believe that computers have improved the quality of life in our society, while at the same time two-thirds of Americans believe that the use of computers in the private sector should be regulated to preserve privacy." (p65)

Reidenberg, Joel R. (Assoc. Professor of Law, the Fordham University School of Law, New York City). U.S. House. Committee on Energy and Commerce. "Telecommunications Network Security." Hearing, 29 Apr 1993. Washington, D.C.: GPO, 1994. (ISBN0160434130). (Y4.En2/3:103-53).

CONCESSIONS (AMUSEMENTS, ETC.)--U.S.--POLITICS AND GOVERNMENT

"Compared to the management of concessionaires at [U.S.] state parks, the Federal Government is literally giving the store away. According to a 1988 GAO [General Accounting Office] report States receive an average concession fee of 12 percent of gross sales. This is in sharp contrast to the 2.6 percent the Federal government received from its concessions 1992. Even if the Federal Government were simply to collect from concessionaires what States collect on average, we could collect an additional $60 million--or about 3 1/2 times what the Park Service is currently receiving from its concession operations." (pS3326)

Cohen, William S. (Sen.-Maine). "National Park Service Concessions Policy Reform Act of 1994," Congressional Record (21 Mar 1994). Daily ed. pS3311-3328. (ISSN0363-7239).

"While visitors to National Parks are paying high prices to concessionaires for their hotdogs, sodas, and parking, the Federal Government often gets little or nothing. For example, visitors to Alaska's Denali National Park spent on average about $17 per person on concessions--$16.72. At the same time the

Government collected less than 14 cents from that $17 sale for the concessionaire's use of Federal buildings and the exclusive right to peddle its goods and services to the 504,000 people who visit Denali every year. At the Grand Canyon, the concessionaire who runs the luxury hotel, charging between $102 and $252 a night, took in more than $63 million but paid the Government a mere $1,250 a month in rent and a $1.7 million franchise fee. The same concessionaire took in almost $5.3 million in sales from its operations at California's Death Valley National Monument and Arizona's Petrified Forest National Park. However, the Government's share was less than $125,000 or 2.3 percent." (pS3326)

Cohen, William S. (Sen.-Maine). "National Park Service Concessions Policy Reform Act of 1994," Congressional Record (21 Mar 1994). Daily ed. pS3311-3328. (ISSN0363-7239).

CONCRETE ROADS

see ROADS, CONCRETE

CONGO (BRAZZAVILLE)

see also GOVERNMENT SPENDING POLICY--CONGO (BRAZZAVILLE); INDUSTRY AND STATE--CONGO (BRAZZAVILLE); PETROLEUM INDUSTRY AND TRADE--CONGO (BRAZZAVILLE)

CONGO (BRAZZAVILLE)--SOCIAL CONDITIONS

"Congo is highly urbanized by African standards, with some 61 percent of its 2 million people living in cities over 5000; half the population lives in Congo's two largest cities, Brazzaville and Pointe Noire. The former government's agricultural, investment and monetary policies unintentionally encouraged this trend towards urbanization, which is apparently continuing. Secondly, Congo's well-developed education system has brought literacy to about 62 percent of the people, making it one of Africa's most literate societies. Meanwhile, Brazzaville's Marien Ngouabi University produces hundreds of graduates each year, a disproportionate number of whom are trained in social science or the humanities rather than in technical fields. While these social features serve to dampen ethnic conflict and its negative features, they also lend a sophistication to Congolese society that makes governing there tricky." (p53)

Clark, John F. "Socio-Political Change in the Republic of Congo: Political Dilemmas of Economic Reform." Journal of Third World Studies v10 n1, Spr 1993. p52-77. (ISSN8755-3449).

CONJUGAL VIOLENCE--LONDON (ENGLAND)

"Combatting violence against women was the objective behind a high-profile campaign launched in January by the Association of London Authorities, a consortium of the Labor-controlled boroughs in London. Domestic violence accounts for 25 percent of all reported crime in the city: 100,000 women a year seek medical treatment for injuries sustained from current or previous partners; 50 percent of all murders of women are committed by these same men; 40 percent of homeless women have fled from such violence. Surveys show that 71 percent of young boys expect they will use violence against women in their future relationships, and that 60 percent of men admit they would respond with violence against their partners in certain situations." (p11)

Henry, Margaret. "Domestic Violence: The Original Vicious Cycle." Toward Freedom v43 n2, Mar 1994. p11. (ISSN0048-9898).

CONJUGAL VIOLENCE--PENNSYLVANIA (v19)

CONJUGAL VIOLENCE--U.S. (v19)

"The Super Bowl is one of the most widely viewed television events every year. Unfortunately, many women's shelters report that Super Bowl Sunday is also one of the worst days of the year for violence against women in the home....For too many households, the violence of football's most-watched game is not confined to the TV screen. The Super Bowl brings together many activities that may 'trigger' a man predisposed to battering: intense viewing of sanctioned violence, heavy drinking, betting....Domestic violence is not limited to Super Bowl Sunday. According to the FBI, a battering incident occurs every 18 seconds in the U.S., and 30 percent of female homicide victims are killed by their husbands or boyfriends. In October 1992, the Senate Judiciary Committee found that at least 1.1 million assaults against women in the home were reported in 1991. By some estimates, as many as 3 million more such crimes go unreported each year." (p7)

"Super Bowl Sunday: A Wake-Up Call on Domestic Violence." EXTRA! v6 n2, Mar 1993. p7. (ISSN0895-2310).

CONJUGAL VIOLENCE--WEST VIRGINIA (v19)

CONNECTICUT--COMMERCE--MEXICO (v19)

CONNECTICUT--ECONOMIC CONDITIONS (v19)

CONSERVATION OF ENERGY RESOURCES

see ENERGY CONSERVATION

CONSERVATION OF NATURAL RESOURCES

see also ENERGY CONSERVATION; NATIONAL PARKS AND RESERVES; RECYCLING (WASTE, ETC.); WILDLIFE CONSERVATION

CONSERVATION OF NATURAL RESOURCES--OREGON

"Jim Britell has watched the log trucks roll by his home on the southern Oregon coast....He's seen clearcuts grow on the hillsides near his home town of Port Orford. And he's noticed another intrusion: dirt, once held fast by roots, washing down the bare canyon walls, then carried away in the swift currents of steams fed by the rain-soaked coastal mountains. This dirt can be deadly to salmon and trout. Baby salmon smother when silt covers the gravel in which they are born. After they emerge, silt robs them of deep holes they need for feeding and hiding from predators. Britell, an officer with the local Audubon Society chapter, noticed one more thing: salmon runs were disappearing everywhere on the West Coast, undermining a cornerstone of the region's culture and ravaging local economies. The coho salmon, a smaller sibling of the chinook, has been particularly devastated in Oregon. Its demise has cost fishing communities well over $100 million a year....Until the last two or three years, state and federal agencies denied any connection between timber operations and the coho's decline. The government's solution has been to reduce ocean harvests, which has put people out of work without bringing back the fish." (p1)

Koberstein, Paul. "The Decline and Fall of Salmon." High Country News v25 n21, 15 Nov 1993. p1,10-11. (ISSN0191-5657).

CONSERVATION TILLAGE--U.S.

"Conservation tillage, either no-till, ridge-till or mulch-till has been used on approximately an additional 9 million acres a year for the last two years [in the U.S.], according to the 1993 national crop residue management survey by the Conservation Technology Information Center. Conservation tillage leaves 30 percent or more of the residues from previous crops on the ground after planting. The survey found that conservation tillage accounted for more than 97 million acres, or nearly 35 percent of total cropland acres planted in 1993. Almost 39 percent, or nearly 108 million acres, is being clean tilled, leaving little or no residue." (p2)

"Use of Conservation Tillage on the Increase, Survey Finds." Alternative Agriculture News v11 n12, Dec 1993. p2. (ISSN8755-4941).

CONSOLIDATION AND MERGER OF CORPORATIONS--U.S. (v19)

CONSTRUCTION INDUSTRY--JAPAN--U.S. (v19)

CONSTRUCTION INDUSTRY--U.S. (v19)

CONSTRUCTION INDUSTRY--U.S.--ENERGY CONSUMPTION

"According to studies, the [U.S.] construction industry uses 54 percent of the energy we expend as a nation, not just in heating and cooling but in 'embodied energy,' the energy used to extract, manufacture, and transport materials. Making portland cement contributes 8 percent of the carbon dioxide that adds to global warming worldwide. Cutting forests for timber adds carbon to the atmosphere as well as removing forests' capacity to absorb carbon dioxide. Plastics, aluminum, and other materials used in construction often squander virgin materials and cause pollution in their manufacture. Construction waste takes up about one-third of today's landfills. Clearing land for construction is destructive to habitats and is soil-eroding. Changing our architectural forms and building practices is key to solving a lot of interrelated problems at once--saving energy, materials, precious land, and habitat." (p7)

"Editorial: Draw It. Build It. Show Sustain 'Ability.'" Amicus Journal v15 n2, Sum 1993. p7. (ISSN0276-7201).

CONSTRUCTION INDUSTRY--UTAH (v19)

CONSTRUCTION INDUSTRY--WASHINGTON (STATE) (v19)

CONSTRUCTION WORKERS--U.S.--MORTALITY

"In 1970, construction workers constituted 4% of the total [U.S.] workforce and accounted for 15% of the total fatalities. Today, construction workers constitute 5.5% of the workforce and account for 25% of the fatalities. Meanwhile, between 1973 and 1986, the lost workday injury rate in construction industry increased 13.3 percent. This is the largest increase in injury rates of all major industry divisions. American construction workers fare very poorly compared to their counterparts in countries in Europe. Data of the International Labour Organization (ILO) show that the U.S. could save 1,426 lives per year if it had the same fatality rate as the United Kingdom (39 versus 15 fatalities per 100,000 workers). The U.S. rate was more than twice as high as the rates of Greece, Finland and New Zealand." (p142)

Georgine, Robert A. (President, Building and Construction Trades Dept., AFL-CIO). U.S. House. Committee on Education and Labor. "Hearings on H.R. 1280, Comprehensive Occupational Safety and Health Reform Act." Hearing, 28 Apr 1993. Washington, D.C.: GPO, 1994. (ISBN0160434033). (Y4.Ed8/1:103-35).

CONSUMER BEHAVIOR--DETROIT (MICH) (v19)

CONSUMER BEHAVIOR--MEXICO

"Those who support NAFTA [North American Free Trade Agreement] see a burgeoning Mexican marketplace for United States goods. They argue that a growing Mexican economy and eager Mexican consumers will snap up United States goods. The truth is that Mexican consumers never see most United States exports because they are largely capital equipment and assembly parts. Only 15 percent of exports to Mexico were finished consumer goods. Mexican consumers pay an average of $50-a-year on American consumer goods versus the $450 which is cited by the administration. Mexican consumers simply do not have the purchasing power to buy American-made products." (pS16618)

Sasser, Jim (Sen.-Tenn.). "North American Free-Trade Agreement Implementation Act," Congressional Record (20 Nov 1993). Daily ed. pS16602-16622. (ISSN0363-7239).

CONSUMER BEHAVIOR--U.S. (v19)

"Consumer spending has...been strengthened by improved consumer wealth and liquidity. In the 1980's, consumer debt increased at an annual rate of 10 percent as individuals borrowed to support a high level of consumption relative to current disposable income. In response to a more uncertain economic outlook in the early 1990's, consumers increased their overall liquidity by increasing their savings rate and their holdings of financial assets. During the economic recovery period from the second quarter of 1991 through the second quarter of 1993, consumer debt grew at an annual rate of only 3.5 percent while consumer financial assets rose 7.8 percent. The improved consumer financial position and a slowly improving job market reduced the need to save because of uncertainty and increased overall consumer confidence and spending." (p12)

"General Economy: Economic Growth Slowly Accelerated in Second-Half 1993." U.S. Dept. of Agriculture: Economic Research Service Dec 1993. p12-13.

CONSUMER BEHAVIOR--U.S.--SINGLE PEOPLE (v19)

CONSUMER PRICE INDEXES--U.S. (v19)

CONSUMPTION (ECONOMICS)--GERMANY--NETHERLANDS--U.S.

"Given plenty of time and pressure, conspicuous consumption of all types might decline as have smoking in the US and ivory sales worldwide." (p10) "The best targets are the parts of our consumption that are wasted or unwanted in the first place. Germans drive 6,200 kilometers a year, mostly going places they would not need to drive to if livable neighborhoods were closer to work, a variety of local merchants were closer to home, and public transit were easier and faster. The Dutch would rather never see most of the 78 kilograms of packaging they have to carry out with the trash each year. Americans feel the same way about the 37 percent of the mail they receive that consists of unsolicited sales pitches. Each day, the United States turns over 23 square kilometers of rural land to new housing developments, 'industrial parks,' and commercial strips that would mostly be unnecessary if Americans insisted on well-planned land use inside city limits." (p10-11)

Durning, Alan. "Choosing Sufficiency over Excess." Surviving Together v11 n4, Win 1993. p8-11. (ISSN0859-6286).

CONSUMPTION (ECONOMICS)--U.S.

"Population growth isn't the only reason for overstressed global resources. Many countries with slow growth have a huge impact on the environment. By age 75, the typical American will have produced 52 tons of garbage, consumed 10 million gallons of water, and used 5 times the energy of a child born in the developing world, says, [Werner] Fornos [president of the Population Institute in Washington, D.C.]." (p23)

Waldrop, Judith. "Business Reports: International: This Is Not a Doomsday Scenario." American Demographics v16 n3, Mar 1994. p22-23. (ISSN0163-4089).

CONTRACEPTION (v19)

see also BIRTH CONTROL; STERILIZATION (BIRTH CONTROL)

"In the early 1970s, surveys of men in sub-Saharan Africa showed consistently that more than half fervently disapproved of birth control. In the 1990s, though, outright rejection of contraception is rare even in this region. Approval ratings are still low in some countries, such as Mali, where only 17 percent of men aged 20 to 55 support family planning; but in Burundi, for instance, male approval has soared to 94 percent. In 10 other recent Third World surveys cited in a paper written by Cynthia Green for WHO [World Health Organization], countries reported contraceptive approval rates among men of between 56 percent and 96 percent." (p16)

Sachs, Aaron. "Men, Sex, and Parenthood in an Overpopulating World." World Watch v7 n2, Mar-Apr 1994. p12-19. (ISSN0896-0615).

CONTRACEPTION--AFRICA (v19)

CONTRACEPTION--BRAZIL (v19)

CONTRACEPTION--CHILE (v19)

"Surveys conducted in 1989 and 1990 by the Chilean family planning association APROFA reveal previously unrecognized high contraceptive prevalence rates for Chilean women. In the capital and its suburbs, 57 percent of women ages 15 to 44 regularly used contraception. Forty-five percent of the women surveyed were not married and 58 percent were 'poor' or 'very poor' making the contraceptive use rates more remarkable." (p8)

"News Clips: High Contraceptive Use in Chile." Population Today v21 n4, Apr 1993. p8. (ISSN0749-2448).

CONTRACEPTION--CHINA (v19)

CONTRACEPTION--DEVELOPING COUNTRIES (v19)

"World contraceptive use has reached an all time high, due mainly to increased use in developing countries. In 1965-1970, only 9 percent of married couples in developing countries used contraceptives. By 1985-1990, married couple contraceptive use in LDCs [least developed countries] had increased to 50 percent. The proportion of users is expected to increase to 59 percent by the year 2000. Additionally, the average fertility rate in the developing world has dropped from 6.1 children per women to 3.9 in the past two decades." (p8)

"News Clips: More LDC Couples Using Contraceptives." Population Today v21 n1, Jan 1993. p8. (ISSN0749-2448).

"A 1992 study by Population Action International (then called the Population Crisis Committee) found 22 countries in which men and women still have no access, in effect, to birth control information or services. The contraceptive prevalence rate--or percentage of married women of reproductive age (15 to 49) using birth control--has surpassed 50 percent in a few countries in Latin America and Asia, but in sub-Saharan Africa, for example, it averages only 14 percent." (p16)

Sachs, Aaron. "Men, Sex, and Parenthood in an Overpopulating World." World Watch v7 n2, Mar-Apr 1994. p12-19. (ISSN0896-0615).

CONTRACEPTION--GAMBIA

"Despite enthusiastic contraceptive campaigns launched by various agencies, the 1990 Gambian national contraceptive prevalence survey indicates that many women know about contraceptives, but very few use them. In fact, only 11 percent of all women and 12 percent of married women reported using any form of contraception, and only 6 percent of all women and 7 percent of married women were using Western contraceptives (Republic of The Gambia, 1993: 69). In a rural area 200 kilometers from Banjul, the capital, our 1992 survey found an even lower percentage. Just 9.3 percent of non-sterile women answered 'yes' to the question, 'Are you currently using any method to avoid pregnancy?' and only 5.4 percent were using Western contraception. Even the latter appeared to be trying contraceptives briefly but then stopping, perhaps claiming objections from religion or husbands." (p84)

Bledsoe, Caroline H./others. "Constructing Natural Fertility: The Use of Western Contraceptive Technologies in Rural Gambia." Population and Development Review v20 n1, Mar 1994. p81-113. (ISSN0098-7921).

CONTRACEPTION--IRELAND--PUBLIC OPINION

According to Rosemary Mahoney, author of WHOREDOM IN KIMMAGE, "women's demands have contributed to a changing climate in Irish society. In 1992, the 'nays' prevailed in a referendum on permitting abortion under extreme circumstances. But in the same election 62 percent of voters agreed that women should be allowed to travel abroad for an abortion, and 60 percent supported the right to distribute abortion information within the Irish Republic. Furthermore, the number of women in the 140-member Irish parliament increased from 13 to 20. Recent polls also show that most Irish people now favor some form of legal divorce. Ireland's birthrate, though still the highest in Europe, is declining; more people than ever are using contraception, and one in 10 births occurs out of wedlock. Since Ireland's best-known bishop, Eamonn Casey, was found in 1992 to have fathered a child, the moral authority of the Catholic Church has been undermined." (p8)

Polston, Pamela. "Ireland: Women Give Birth to a New Ireland." Toward Freedom v43 n1, Feb 1994. p8. (ISSN0048-9898).

CONTRACEPTION--MALAYSIA

"Over half (56 percent) of all married women in Peninsular Malaysia were using contraception in 1988, and more than one-third (36 percent) were using a modern method, according to the Malaysian Family Life Survey II. This is a substantial increase from the previous survey just four years earlier, when 51 percent were using some form of contraception and 30 percent were using modern methods." (p8)

"News Clips: Contraceptive Use Up in Malaysia." Population Today v21 n4, Apr 1993. p8. (ISSN0749-2448).

CONTRACEPTION--NICARAGUA

"In spite of the Catholic church's edict and the husband's traditional authority on the matter, 53.3% of Nicaraguan women use contraceptives. And two-thirds of the women who do not have access to contraceptives want to use them. Women prefer the so-called 'modern' methods to the 'natural' methods favored by the Catholic church. Thirty-nine percent use the pill, 16% use an IUD, 13.9% resort to sterilization and 9.2% use condoms. These figures reveal a fundamental change. An earlier report, based on findings from 1988 and 1989, showed that only 23% of women used family planning methods." (p25)

"Periscope: Women Use Contraceptives without Permission." Barricada Internacional v14 n369, Jan 1994. p25. (ISSN1013-9567).

CONTRACEPTIVES (v19)

CONTRACEPTIVES--BELGIUM (v19)

CONTRACEPTIVES--SWITZERLAND (v19)

CONVENTION FACILITIES--U.S.

"Between hotel bills, restaurant meals, cab fares, car rentals, and entertainment expenses, one attendee in Boston spends an average of $1,150 while at a convention, according to the accounting firm Price Waterhouse. Multiplied by hundreds or thousands of people, and adding the costs of exhibitors, one convention can mean millions of dollars flowing into a local economy. As a result, cities and states are falling over themselves to build convention centers. Three dozen cities have opened or expanded centers in the past few years, and at least 17 more are under construction, including Los Angeles, Seattle, San Diego, St. Louis, Dallas, Philadelphia, Providence, and Atlantic City. The Trade Show Bureau says that between 1980 and 1987 the number of convention facilities grew 37%, while exhibition space rose 60%. Among cities that own centers but are considering building larger ones are Baltimore, Washington D.C., Milwaukee, New Orleans, Toronto, and Boston. The Bureau recently projected that exhibition space would grow 36% by 1995." (p12)

Breslow, Marc. "Fool's Gold: Cities Bet Their Budgets on Risky Convention Centers." Dollars and Sense n192, Mar-Apr 1994. p12-15.

COOPERATIVE SOCIETIES--SPAIN

"In 1956, in a 1,000 year old city named Mondragon nestled in the mountains of Spain's northern Basque country, five engineers established a cooperative gas stove manufacturing enterprise. By 1959 the cooperative had 200 worker-owners and its example had inspired the formation of three other industrial cooperatives. By 1965 the Mondragon Group had expanded to include not only several dozen more manufacturing firms, but its own bank, university R&D [research and development] center, social security fund and supermarket. Today the Group consists of 170 cooperatives, 90 of which are industrial. The number of worker-owners is over 21,000. Mondragon boasts Spain's largest manufacturer of refrigerators and machine tools and the only Spanish R&D center invited to be a member of the European R&D consortium. Bank deposits are over 3 billion dollars; social security fund assets are over one billion. Industrial sales in 1990 were $2.6 billion, 25 percent of which were to foreign markets. Mondragon, now a prosperous city of 30,000, is still the heart of this unique experiment. About 40% of the city's labor force works in cooperatives." (p1)

Morris, David. "Mondragon: The Cooperative Alternative Meets Free Trade." Progressive Review n317, May 1993. p1-2.

COPPER MINES AND MINING--BAIKAL, LAKE (RUSSIA)

"In the scramble to rescue the ailing Russian economy, international mining concerns were invited to submit tenders to exploit a massive copper deposit--though the mines may devastate a range of mountains, demolish a rich taiga forest and pollute Lake Baikal, which holds 20% of the world's fresh water and is home to at least 1,500 species found nowhere else....The untapped copper deposit in eastern Siberia's Udokan Mountains is one of the largest in the world, with a potential capacity of 20 million tonnes. The mines, quarries, tunnels, associated ore mills, power station, roads and possibly a new town for miners would all be situated in the catchment area for Lake Baikal, deep in the taiga forest. Local nomadic peoples would also be under threat, as they depend on the area's natural resources for hunting and fishing. The winning bid for the tender, announced in January [1993], was a Russian-foreign joint venture called the Udokan Mining Company. The US$1 billion project should revitalise the underloaded Baikal-Amur Mainline (BAM) railway, which runs along the north end of Lake Baikal. Local officials hope the scheme will bring hard currency, jobs and better living conditions to their hard-pressed region." (p20)

Podobed, Sergey. "Focus: Mining: New Threat Looms over Lake Baikal." Panoscope i35, Apr 1993. p20-21. (ISSN0951-8819).

COPYRIGHT--U.S.

"The copyright industries are the brightest of our domestic industries. American motion pictures, records, and computer programs are sought throughout the world. Over 5.5 million workers are employed by the copyright industries, or about 4.8 percent of the U.S. workforce. Economists estimate that in 1992, foreign sales of copyrighted works were almost $40 billion dollars, an increase of 9 percent over 1991." (pH10311)

Brooks, Jack (Rep.-Tex.). "Copyright Reform Act of 1993," Congressional Record (20 Nov 1993). Daily ed. pH10308-10312. (ISSN0363-7239).

COPYRIGHT--UNAUTHORIZED REPRODUCTION OF VIDEO RECORDINGS (v19)

COPYRIGHT INFRINGEMENT (v19)

"The U.S. video game industry is being severely injured by the foreign manufacture of counterfeit video games, particularly in China and Taiwan....Counterfeiting caused losses of $2.5 to $3 billion in 1993 to Nintendo of America, Inc., Redmond, WA, a leading video game company located in...[Washington], to the over 170 independent U.S. companies, which create and sell Nintendo video games, and to the more than 300 companies, such as a movie studio that license properties for use in Nintendo video games." (pS4917)

Gorton, Slade (Sen.-Wash.). "Counterfeit Video Games," Congressional Record (26 Apr 1994). Daily ed. pS4917. (ISSN0363-7239).

COPYRIGHT INFRINGEMENT--CHINA

"Today, 26 pirate CD factories are operating in China, with a production capacity of 50 million CD's a year. They are not only causing American artists to lose money--and it's a lot of money, $827 million last year, more than double the estimate of $415 million in losses for 1992--but are beginning to compete with our legitimate industries in other Asian markets and even Latin America." (pS4747)

Baucus, Max (Sen.-Mont.). "'Special 301' Trade Law," Congressional Record (21 Apr 1994). Daily ed. pS4747-4748. (ISSN0363-7239).

"The shopkeeper should beware. On April 20th police raided 400 music stores in five southern Chinese cities and seized more than 50,000 pirated CDs. Officials in Beijing also promised there would be a crackdown on producers and gave local governments until the end of May to report all unauthorised CD pressing plants....Nicholas Garnett, director-general of the International Federation of the Phonographic Industry, says that at least 25 CD plants have opened in China. Together they have the potential to make about 75m CDs a year, some 70m more than the estimated annual number of CDs sold in China. Mr Garnett fears that many of these plants have been getting ready to export a torrent of counterfeit discs, with Hong Kong as the worldwide dispatch point." (p70)

"Business: Digital Banditry in China." Economist v331 n7860, 23 Apr 1994. p70. (ISSN0013-0613).

COPYRIGHT INFRINGEMENT--EUROPE--U.S. (v19)

COPYRIGHT INFRINGEMENT--U.S. (v19)

"The piracy of U.S. patents and copyrights by foreign countries costs our companies $15 to 17 billion each year. That means over 300,000 American jobs are put at risk every year by foreign pirates. Pharmaceutical companies like Pfizer lose $5 billion or more each and every year, jeopardizing at least 100,000 American jobs. America's strongest asset in this competitive world is its ingenuity and its...[creativity]. From the pencil-making machine to the microchip, U.S. inventors have created millions of groundbreaking products over the years. But products like these are being stolen every day by countries that have no respect for the rights of the inventor. From the scientists who invent the products to the men and women who make and ship them, American workers are being ripped off by foreign pirates." (pE695)

Gejdenson, Sam (Rep.-Conn.). "Piracy of U.S. Patents and Copyrights Costs Our Companies Billions," Congressional Record (18 Apr 1994). Daily ed. pE695-696. (ISSN0363-7239).

CORN INDUSTRY--CHINA (v19)

CORN INDUSTRY--MEXICO

"Corn is Mexico's major crop, and accounts for close to half its total cropland. Corn is the principal crop of over 2.4 million farmers (46 percent of all agricultural producers). It is grown in all 33 Mexican states on farms ranging from small subsistence plots in the southeast to large commercial farms in the central and northwest regions. About two-thirds of the corn area is farmed under the ejido system of land tenure (collective farming). Almost 90 percent of corn producers in this system cultivate subsistence farms--containing 5 or less hectares." (p20)

U.S. Dept. of Agriculture/Valdes, Constanza/others. "World Agriculture & Trade: Mexico to Curtail Farmers' Price Subsidies." Agricultural Outlook Dec 1993. p19-22.

"Corn is more than a commodity in Mexico--it is the staple of the Mexican diet and the heart of the rural economy. Overwhelmingly, corn is used as a human food. Over 30,000 small businesses mill corn flour and/or make tortillas. Corn is the most important farm crop and rural employer, grown on 43 percent of all arable land in Mexico and employing one out of every three rural workers. It is both a market crop and a subsistence crop. About 40 percent of the crop is consumed by people on the farm where it is produced, and nearly two thirds of those farmers who raise corn also buy corn for their own consumption. Another one-third of the crop is purchased by the government at a guaranteed price for distribution at lower prices to consumers....The policy of Mexican President [Carlos] Salinas is to reduce domestic corn and bean production, in part because it is cheaper to import basic grains from the U.S. NAFTA [North American Free Trade Agreement] will fulfill this policy by phasing out import restrictions on corn and beans over a 15-year period. The United States currently supplies over 80 percent of Mexico's corn imports. On average, about 82% of U.S. corn exports to Mexico are made under Commodity Credit Corporation concessional sales offering long repayment terms at low interest rates." (pSR2)

"Special Report: Sustainable Rural Development in North America and the North American Free Trade Agreement." Center for Rural Affairs Newsletter Apr 1993. pSR1-4.

CORN INDUSTRY--U.S. (v19)

U.S. "Corn exports rose to 42 million tons, but a 10-percent decline in export price reduced its value to $4.3 billion, 8 percent below the previous year. Shipments to Mexico, the EC [European Community], and the FSU [former Soviet Union] declined in 1993, but were offset by gains to Japan, Algeria, Egypt, and Canada." (p2)

U.S. Dept. of Agriculture/Greene, Joel. "Exports Rose Slightly in FY 1993." Foreign Agricultural Trade of the United States Nov-Dec 1993. p2-3.

CORN INDUSTRY--ZIMBABWE

"Encouraged by a substantially higher price for their maize, small-scale farmers in Zimbabwe's communal areas produced 60 per cent of the crop's marketed output in 1993, according to Gary Magadzire, president of the Zimbabwe Farmers Union (ZFU). This marked an enormous increase from 1980, the year of Zimbabwe's independence, when they and other African smallholders accounted for only one-tenth of the maize sold on the market, which was then dominated by the large-scale, mostly white, commercial growers. The ZFU--representing farmers in the densely populated communal areas, small-scale commercial growers and those resettled since independence--has been crucial in reducing the dominance of the Commercial Farmers Union (CFU), which represents 5,000 growers. The ZFU expects to increase its membership of 170,000 to 400,000 by the end of 1994." (p12)

Amanor-Wilks, Dede. "Getting Cash into Rural Hands: Zimbabwe's Maize Farmers Conquering the Market." African Farmer n10, Jan 1994. p12-13.

CORPORATE DEBT--U.S. (v19)

CORPORATIONS

see also COOPERATIVE SOCIETIES

"The United Nations, the GATT [General Agreement on Tariffs and Trade], and the World Bank are increasingly seen as inadequate to address the challenges posed by the 1990s. But the large corporation is on the rise with 37,000 companies accounting for one-quarter of the combined gross national product of all of the countries of the world. Transnational corporations (TNCs) have become the powerhouses of the global economic system. The $36 billion annual TNC investment in developing countries affects economic growth, employment practices, technology transfer, and the environment. Because such significant resources are at the disposal of TNCs, there is increasing recognition that with global influence comes global responsibility. Levi Straus, Merck, Ford and others have developed benchmark initiatives." (p1)

Leipziger, Deborah. "The Transnational Corporation: Global Influence, Global Responsibility." CEP Research Report Oct 1993. p1-5. (ISSN0898-4328).

"We need only ask what these [following] corporations are doing with their own technology, how they are restructuring, how they are increasing productivity and enhancing their human capital. The answers, in the case of IBM, AT&T, Kodak, Ameritech, BellSouth, Time Warner, Philips Electronics, Apple, Xerox, and most other high-tech firms, is that 'restructuring' means massive 'retrenchment,' or 'downsizing'--made possible, in part, by global telecommunications and technological innovation. Under intense competition, IBM has desperately reduced its workforce by over 25% since 1986, by 40,000 in 1992 alone--despite its highly touted no layoff policy--resulting in what has been called a 'psychological reign of terror' throughout the company. Philips Electronics has laid off 45,000 workers since 1990; Kodak has cut 20,000 workers, a third of its local workforce, in the last decade; AT&T and the Baby Bells have been undergoing equally massive downsizing; and Apple and Xerox have recently undergone sizable though less severe cuts in management ranks." (p11)

Noble, Douglas D. "The Regime of Technology in Education." Holistic Education Review v6 n2, Sum 1993. p4-13. (ISSN0898-0926).

CORPORATIONS--CHICAGO (ILL)--ECONOMIC CONDITIONS

"During the past year: USX (formerly U.S. Steel...) closed down the South Works in Chicago. At its peak, South Works employed 20,000 workers; the closing put the last 690 remaining workers out of work. In the same business, Inland Steel plans to cut 3,500 workers, one-quarter of its total work force. Oscar Meyer (the meat processor) closed its Chicago plant. Amoco cut 8,500 employees, including 1,100 in the Chicago area. In October, Schwinn Bicycle filed for Chapter 11. Sears Roebuck plans to close one hundred or so of its stores, as part of the process of cutting more than 48,000 jobs nationwide. And IBM is planning to cut 25,000 jobs....The Fortune 500 have not added a single net job to the workforce in over 10 years. The nicest thing we can say about them is that most of them still provide health insurance for most of their permanent full-time employees. Which may in fact account for their having added no net jobs to the economy in over 10 years." (p9)

Neudel, Marian H. "Boycotting the Misfortune 500." New Patriot v6 n2, Mar-Apr 1993. p9.

CORPORATIONS--JAPAN (v19)

CORPORATIONS--KOREA (SOUTH)--FINANCE

"The sales of South Korea's top 30 conglomerates equal almost 70% of the country's annual GDP [gross domestic product] (though there is double-counting). The firms are staggeringly indebted: in 1990 their debt was 3.6 times their equity. Two-thirds are still owned privately....by 1995, conglomerates must cut the value of their loan guarantees to twice their equity, down from four times last year. To comply, big firms will have to replace loan finance with equity....Foreign investors, having bid up most of the world's emerging markets, are happy to pay premium prices for South Korean paper. For bonds that can be converted into equity, the difference is still bigger. Convertible bonds carry coupons of 9% at home, compared with 1.5% in Europe, according to the Seoul office of Jardine Fleming, a stockbroking firm. By cutting the cost of capital, foreign equity-linked issues would improve South Korean companies' competitiveness considerably." (p102)

"Finance: South Korean Finance: Hastening Slowly." Economist v329 n7843, 25 Dec 1993. p102. (ISSN0013-0613).

CORPORATIONS--TAXATION--U.S. (v19)

CORPORATIONS--U.S. (v19)

CORPORATIONS--U.S.--ECONOMIC CONDITIONS (v19)

CORPORATIONS, AMERICAN--MEXICO (v19)

CORPORATIONS, FOREIGN--GREAT BRITAIN (v19)

CORPORATIONS, FOREIGN--U.S. (v19)

COSMETICS INDUSTRY--U.S. (v19)

COST AND STANDARD OF LIVING

see also FOOD CONSUMPTION; FOOD PRICES

COST AND STANDARD OF LIVING--ASIA (v19)
COST AND STANDARD OF LIVING--CHINA (v19)
COST AND STANDARD OF LIVING--HUNGARY--PUBLIC OPINION (v19)
COST AND STANDARD OF LIVING--JORDAN (v19)
COST AND STANDARD OF LIVING--U.S. (v19)
COST AND STANDARD OF LIVING--U.S.--PUBLIC OPINION (v19)

"According to opinion surveys a rising share of adults doubt that the next generation will be 'better off' than they are....this attitude shift is especially marked among the young. A new Roper poll shows that, among eighteen-to-twenty-nine-year-olds of both sexes, the number of those who think they have a 'very good' chance of achieving 'the good life' has declined from 41 to 21 percent over the last fifteen years." (p40)

Peterson, Peter G. "Entitlement Reform: The Way to Eliminate the Deficit." New York Review of Books v41 n7, 7 Apr 1994. p39-47. (ISSN0028-7504).

COSTA RICA

see also BIOLOGICAL DIVERSITY--COSTA RICA; INCOME DISTRIBUTION--COSTA RICA

COSTA RICA--ECONOMIC CONDITIONS (v19)

"On the surface, Costa Rica's economy is booming. Never mind that San Jose, the capital of what was once called the Switzerland of Central America, is a car-crammed and increasingly smog-ridden city. Costa Rica is riding a $400 million wave of tourist investment....Costa Rica...sells on world markets a wide variety of agricultural produce and simple manufactured goods, many of them produced in duty-free zones within Costa Rica. One question, however, is whether the 6 to 7 percent growth of the last two years can be sustained. Noting that outgoing President Rafael Calderon is leaving behind record high reserves and a tiny government deficit, economist Ronulfo Jimenez with the governing Social Christian Unity Party argues that 'if current policies are adhered to, the economy can grow 5 to 6 percent over the next four years.' Carlos Manuel Castillo, also an economist and president of the National Liberation Party which won a national election Feb. 6, disagrees....Mr. Castillo is pointing to the immediate problem which will confront president-elect Jose Maria Figueres when he takes office May 8--Costa Rica's massive trade deficit. If tourist income and 'nontraditional' exports are booming, imports are rising even more rapidly; to the point of creating an $800 million deficit--7.8 percent of national output--in 1993." (p11)

Dye, David. "Economy: Costa Rica's Economy Bears Fruit of Ten Years of 'Structural Adjustment.'" The Christian Science Monitor v86 n62, 23 Feb 1994. p11. (ISSN0882-7729).

COSTS

see AIDS (DISEASE)--AFRICA--COSTS; AIDS (DISEASE)--U.S.--COSTS; AIRPORTS--U.S.--COSTS; ALIENS, ILLEGAL--CALIFORNIA--COSTS; ALIENS, ILLEGAL--FLORIDA--COSTS; COLLEGE COSTS; CRIME PREVENTION--U.S.--COSTS; EDUCATION--U.S.--COSTS; FIREARMS--U.S.--ACCIDENTS--COSTS; HOSPITALS--U.S.--ADMINISTRATION--COSTS; IRELAND--HISTORY--CIVIL WAR--COSTS; LABOR COSTS--GERMANY; MENTAL ILLNESS--U.S.--COSTS; MINES (MILITARY EXPLOSIVES)--COSTS; NUCLEAR ENERGY--U.S.--COSTS; NUCLEAR POWER PLANTS--U.S.--COSTS; PARKING LOTS--U.S.--COSTS; PESTICIDES--COSTS; PESTICIDES--U.S.--COSTS; PRENATAL CARE--U.S.--COSTS; PRISONERS--MICHIGAN--COSTS; PRISONS--U.S.--COSTS; SMOKING--U.S.--COSTS; SPACE STATIONS--COSTS; SUBSTANCE ABUSE--U.S.--COSTS; TRAFFIC ACCIDENTS--U.S.--COSTS; TRANSPORTATION--COSTS

COTTON TRADE--CHINA (v19)
COTTON TRADE--NORTH CAROLINA (v19)
COTTON TRADE--U.S. (v19)

"Cotton continues to account for more than three-fourths of fiber use [in the U.S.] on the cotton system. Cotton's share has remained above 75 percent for over a year now, and in October reached 76 percent, the largest since January 1993. Although cotton's share has continued stable, the number of spindles in place has declined approximately 600,000, or 6 percent, since October 1992. Despite this decrease, the percentage of active spindles devoted to 100 percent cotton remains near 42 percent." (p1)

U.S. Dept. of Agriculture. "Consumption Down Marginally." Cotton and Wool Update 10 Dec 1993. p1.

"In 1993, [U.S.] cotton producers planted 13.3 million and 190,000 acres of upland and American-Pima (ELS) cotton, respectively. Upland planted acreage was up 2 percent from 1992, and harvested area, at 12.6 million, was 16 percent above last season. A major factor influencing the lower acreage abandonment this season occurred in Texas. Texas harvested 91 percent of planted acreage this season, compared with only 65 percent in 1992. ELS plantings were down 28 percent from 1992 and harvested acreage was estimated at 188,900, a 27 percent decline from last year." (p1)

"The 1993 Cotton Crop in Review." Cotton and Wool Update 13 Jan 1994. p1.

"On December 22, [1993], the U.S. Commerce Department reported preliminary November cotton mill consumption at 833,000 bales, down from 864,000 in October but above November 1992's 825,000 bales. Domestic mills used 37,900 bales per day, compared with 41,100 in October and 39,300 during November 1992. On a seasonally adjusted annual rate (SAAR) basis, the November estimate fell below 10 million bales and is the lowest since September 1992." (p1)

"Consumption Moves Lower." Cotton and Wool Update 13 Jan 1994. p1.

"Trade in cotton textiles followed a similar pattern as total fibers. Cotton textile exports reached a record 958 million pounds in 1993 compared with 845 million in 1992. However, cotton textile imports rose 12 percent to a high of 3.6 billion pounds. Despite rising textile exports and continued strong domestic mill use, the cotton textile trade deficit has expanded to a record 2.6 billion pounds or about 5.5 million bale equivalents. Total domestic cotton consumption in 1993 rose to nearly 7.6 billion pounds. U.S. per capita cotton consumption increased to 29.3 pounds, 5 percent above 1992 and the largest since 1951. Net cotton textile imports accounted for almost 35 percent of domestic consumption in 1993." (p2)

U.S. Dept. of Agriculture. "Record Textile Trade in 1993." Cotton and Wool Update 11 Mar 1994. p2.

U.S. "Cotton exports dropped to 1.1 million tons, the smallest shipments since 1986. Large global stocks and reduced import demand because of declining textile industries in the EC [European Community], Japan, Taiwan, and Korea slowed U.S. exports. But U.S. exports benefited from increased import demand in Mexico, Brazil, and Colombia, where textile industries were expanding." (p2)

U.S. Dept. of Agriculture/Greene, Joel. "Exports Rose Slightly in FY 1993." Foreign Agricultural Trade of the United States Nov-Dec 1993. p2-3.

COTTONSEED--U.S.

"Despite slightly larger cotton plantings [in the U.S.] in 1993/94, 13.4 million acres versus 13.2 million in 1992/93, and much larger harvested area, 12.8 million acres versus 11.1 million in 1992-93, low yields are holding cottonseed production near last year's level. Cottonseed production in 1993/94 is placed at 6.27 million short tons, up only 0.7 percent from the previous season. The modest use in production belies a 1.6-million-acre increase in harvested area and is attributed to a low 980-pound-per-acre yield, 12 percent below 1992/93's 1,118-pound yield." (p8)

U.S. Dept. of Agriculture. "Outlook for Other Oil Crops." Oil Crops Situation and Outlook Report Jan 1994. p8-9.

COUNTERFEITS AND COUNTERFEITING--GREAT BRITAIN--U.S.

"In Britain, best guesses suggest that about 17m [pounds sterling]-worth ($25m-worth) of counterfeit notes are circulating today--by value, far less than 1% of the total notes in issue. In America in 1992 a mere $17m of counterfeit notes were apprehended by banks and a further $87m seized by the Treasury's secret service before it hit the streets. These amounts are indeed almost an irrelevance--the Federal Reserve handled $265 billion-worth of notes in 1992. There are thought to be some 50 billion banknotes circulating worldwide." (p101)

"Finance: Counterfeiting: Plastic Is Beautiful." Economist v329 n7843, 25 Dec 1993. p101. (ISSN0013-0613).

COUNTERFEITS AND COUNTERFEITING--U.S.

"New counterfeit deterrent features were incorporated into the currency design beginning in 1991 with the printing of the $100 denomination note. The new features have also been introduced into the $50, $20, and $10 denominations and the $5 denomination will be converted to the new design format in FY 1994. The features include a denominated security thread and microprinting around the portrait. The security thread consists of a clear polyester thread imprinted with the denomination vertically embedded in the currency paper. The thread is inconspicuous in reflected light, which copiers use, but visible in transmitted light (when held to a light). The microprinting consists of the words 'United States of America' which are printed repeatedly around the portrait on the face of the note. This microprinting is too small for most copiers to replicate." (p30)

Daly, Peter H. (Director, Bureau of Engraving and Printing, U.S. Dept. of the Treasury). U.S. House. Committee on Appropriations. "Treasury, Postal Service...Approp. for Fiscal Year 1994 (Part 1)." Hearing, Washington, D.C.: GPO, 1993. (Y4.Ap6/1:T71/994/pt.1).

COUNTRY MUSIC--U.S. (v19)

COUPONS (RETAIL TRADE)--U.S. (v19)

"According to NCH Promotional Services, Inc., a coupon clearinghouse outside of Chicago, some 300 billion coupons were distributed in 1993, but only 7 billion coupons were redeemed (2 percent). Distribution was doubling about every five years since 1980. But last year, distribution declined for the first time since 1970--mainly because of changes in manufacturers' promotional strategies. Coupon value has continued to rise, however; the average coupon value has gone from 15 cents in the early 1970s, to 27 cents in 1982, to 59 cents in 1993." (p13)

Conover, Kirsten A. "Snip a Little Here, Save a Lot There." The Christian Science Monitor v86 n59, 17 Feb 1994. p13. (ISSN0882-7729).

COURT CALENDARS--U.S.

"The Administrative Office of the U.S. Courts recently reported that in 1993, the number of criminal cases filed by Federal prosecutors decreased by over 3 percent. This was the first decrease in 10 years. The Administrative Office attributes this overall decrease in criminal filings to the Clinton Justice Department's significant reduction in drug prosecutions. Drug prosecutions in 1993 decreased by 7 percent--or 902 cases." (pS3636)

Hatch, Orrin G. (Sen.-Utah). "Congressional Budget Concurrent Resolution," Congressional Record (24 Mar 1994). Daily ed. pS3631-3659. (ISSN0363-7239).

COURTHOUSES--U.S.

"In buildings added to GSA's [General Service Administration's] owned inventory in the 10 years from 1983 to 1992, GSA has added 9,940,963 occupiable square feet. Of that amount 484,864 square feet, or 4.9 percent of the total, is currently assigned to the U.S. Courts. During that same time period a total of 63,076,687 occupiable square feet was acquired in leased buildings new to the inventory. Of that amount, 2,015,480 square feet, or 3.2 percent of the total, is currently occupied by the U.S. Courts. The total amount of space assigned to the U.S. Courts increased from 10,485,000 square feet in fiscal year 1982 to 15,907,000 in fiscal year 1993, a 5,422,000 square feet increase. Most of this growth occurred in buildings which have been in GSA's inventory for over 10 years. There are currently 20 new construction projects under way, 11 of which contain Courts and Courts related activities." (p58)

Thacker, Gerald P. (Commissioner, Public Buildings Service). U.S. House. Committee on Appropriations. "Treasury, Postal Service, and General Government Approp. for Fiscal Year 1994 (Part 5)." Hearing, Washington, D.C.: GPO, 1993. (ISBN0160410053). (Y4.Ap6/1:T71/994/pt.5).

"The vast majority of the [U.S.] Federal construction projects managed by the GSA are Federal courthouses....In 1991, Congress appropriated over $564 million for 13 new court construction projects, which represented 42 percent of the total appropriated to the General Services Administration for new construction. The FY 1994 appropriation for GSA building projects included funding for 16 new Federal courthouses amounting to $781 million or about 84 percent of the $943 million appropriated last year for new building construction. This year, the President is asking for an additional $1 billion to construct 11 new Federal courthouses." (pS3641)

Cohen, William S. (Sen.-Maine). "Congressional Budget Concurrent Resolution," Congressional Record (24 Mar 1994). Daily ed. pS3631-3659. (ISSN0363-7239).

COURTHOUSES--U.S.--COSTS (v19)

COURTS

see also JUDGES

COURTS--U.S.

"In 1991, the total number of state court filings [in the U.S.] reached 93 million. Of that, only 12 million were criminal filings, with traffic and ordinance filings leading the list at 60 million. Civil filings were 19 million and juvenile filings, at 2 million, rounded out the list. Between 1984 and 1991, the total civil filings increased by 33 percent. Criminal filings increased 24 percent and juvenile filings went up 34 percent. During the same seven-year period, the population increased only 7 percent." (p8)

Ide, R. William, III. "President's Message: It's Time to Work Together." ABA Journal v80, Feb 1994. p8. (ISSN0747-0088).

COURTS--U.S.--CRIME AGAINST (v19)

CREDIT--U.S. (v19)

CREDIT CARD FRAUD--U.S.

"Credit-card fraud is growing rapidly, alarming consumers and often putting big holes in their credit records. Experts estimate card fraud in the U.S. ran close to $1 billion in 1993, up from $864 billion in 1992. Increasingly sophisticated scamsters are coming up with a bewildering variety of ploys to rip off card holders and card issuers. As soon as Visa, MasterCard, and the issuing banks tackle one type of fraud, the bad guys come up with something new....Some of the worst abuses these days involve counterfeit cards. MasterCard's losses from counterfeiting reached at least $113 million of its total $395 million in worldwide fraud losses in 1993. Visa International's counterfeit losses were roughly $160 million. According to

CREDIT CARD NEWS, an industry newsletter, U.S. losses from credit-card fraud in 1992 were more than 18% of issuers' profits from merchant fees and interest paid by card holders." (p68)

Holland, Kelley. "Finance: Stalking the Credit-Card Scamsters." Business Week n3354, 17 Jan 1994. p68-69. (ISSN0007-7135).

CREDIT CARDS--CANADA (v19)

CREDIT CARDS--U.S. (v19)

CREDIT UNIONS--U.S.

"Over the past three years (Dec. 1989-Dec. 1992), federally insured credit unions' assets have increased by $74.4 billion or 40 percent. Total savings for the same period have grown $65 billion or 39 percent. Total savings have increased approximately 13 percent per annum. Approximately 5 percent in total asset and savings growth during this time may be attributed to the significant conversion of privately insured state-chartered credit unions to federal share insurance. At year-end 1992, the 12,653 federally insured credit unions represented over 95 percent of all credit unions. Federally insured credit unions have $258.4 billion in assets and hold $233 billion in savings." (p487)

Jepsen, Roger W. (Chairman, National Credit Union Administration). U.S. House. Committee on Appropriations. "Depts. of Veterans Affairs and Housing and Urban Development...Approp. for 1994 (Part 4)." Hearing, Washington, D.C.: GPO, 1993. (ISBN016040911X). (Y4.Ap6/1:V64/4/994/pt.4).

CRIME (v19)

see also COMPUTER CRIMES; CRIMINAL JUSTICE, ADMINISTRATION OF; DRUG ABUSE AND CRIME; FIREARMS--GERMANY--CRIME; FIREARMS--GREAT BRITAIN--CRIME; FIREARMS--GREECE--CRIME; FIREARMS--U.S.--CRIME; HATE CRIMES; JUVENILE DELINQUENCY; RURAL CRIMES; SEX CRIMES; VIOLENT CRIMES

CRIME--COLOMBIA

"The past three years have brought Colombia (population 32m) 90,000 murders, counting in killings by guerrillas, drug traffickers and jealous husbands alike. Newspapers report some 700 political killings so far in 1993." (p58)

"International: Styled for a Way of Life." Economist v329 n7843, 25 Dec 1993. p58. (ISSN0013-0613).

CRIME--FLORIDA (v19)

CRIME--FRANCE--U.S. (v19)

CRIME--GERMANY

"Since 1991, there have been 4,761 officially recorded criminal acts by extreme Rightists in Germany as a whole, resulting in 26 deaths, 1,738 injuries--mostly among foreigners or those suspected of being foreigners--and flagrant property damage. Anti-Nazi demonstrations and graffiti are common too. Indeed, newspapers and television programs are flooded with lengthy debates on the meaning of it all." (p8)

Oppenheimer, Paul. "Unresolved Conflicts: Nurturing the New Germany." New Leader v76 n14, 13 Dec 1993. p7-10. (ISSN0028-6044).

CRIME--GREAT BRITAIN (v19)

CRIME--GREAT BRITAIN--SAFETY MEASURES

"Neighborhood Watch schemes themselves, which aim to educate communities in crime prevention, are not provably successful. Since the idea came to Britain from America in the 1980s, 115,000 schemes involving over 5m households have been set up. But there is no firm evidence that they reduce crime. Trevor Bennett, a lecturer in criminology at Cambridge University, studied four areas, two with schemes, two without. He found that crime rose slower in the two areas without a scheme." (p62)

"Britain: Crime: Watch Out." Economist v330 n7847, 22 Jan 1994. p62. (ISSN0013-0613).

CRIME--LONDON (ENGLAND) (v19)

CRIME--LOS ANGELES (CALIF)--ALIENS, ILLEGAL

"The impact of convicted criminal aliens on Los Angeles County was documented in two studies conducted in 1990 and 1992 by the countywide Criminal Justice Coordination Committee in conjunction with the County Sheriff and the Immigration and Naturalization Service (INS). Those reports estimated that 19 percent of the inmates in Los Angeles County jails were foreign born and 11 percent were deportable aliens. They found that over 23,000 deportable aliens go through the Los Angeles County justice system each year....The [1992] study found that 40 percent of the 1,875 deportable aliens who were released from the county jail in May 1990 were re-arrested an average of two times in the following 12 months. Only 339 of the 1,875--less than one-fifth--of those deportable aliens had no previous or subsequent arrests. The other 1,536 had been arrested an average of seven times, for a combined total of 10,989 arrests, since they arrived in the United States." (pH2527)

Beilenson, Anthony C. (Rep.-Calif.). "Violent Crime Control and Law Enforcement Act of 1994," Congressional Record (20 Apr 1994). Daily ed. pH2518-2539. (ISSN0363-7239).

CRIME--MICHIGAN

"Michigan residents rank crime and drugs as their biggest worries by almost a 2-1 margin, according to a survey done late last year by EPIC-MRA, a Lansing-based polling company....Ironically, even as concern over crime is growing, the crime rate has decreased over the last 10 years in Michigan. Michigan State Police reports show the number of serious crimes reported in the state in 1992 was off 12.8 percent from the total reported in 1982. Washtenaw County reported a 5.6 percent decrease over that 10-year span." (p1 secA)

Chadiha, Jeffri. "Crime Falling, but Fear Growing." Ann Arbor News 1 Mar 1994. p1,10 secA.

CRIME--NEW YORK (NY) (v19)

"In New York City public housing alone, in 1991, there were: 200 homicides, 336 rapes, 4,451 assaults, 3,961 robberies, 151 arsons, and 2,538 weapons offenses....Only yesterday, Mayor Sharon Pratt Kelly stated during a radio interview that approximately 80 percent of all crimes committed in the District of Columbia were in or near public housing. Statistics for other cities around the Nation are similar." (pE583)

Lazio, Rick (Rep.-N.Y.). "The Neighborhood Crime Fighters Housing Assistance Act," Congressional Record (24 Mar 1994). Daily ed. pE583. (ISSN0363-7239).

"Homicides in New York City are down for the third year in a row. But that is small consolation to citizens who have come to believe that virtually anyone, anywhere, is likely to become a victim....poor people in bad neighborhoods are most likely to be victims of violent crimes. Twelve of New York's seventy-five police precincts, for example, account for 44 percent of total homicides, and the twelve are located in the most depressed sections of East Brooklyn, Harlem, and the South Bronx." (p36)

Rothman, David J. "The Crime of Punishment." New York Review of Books v41 n4, 17 Feb 1994. p34-38. (ISSN0028-7504).

CRIME--NEW YORK (NY)--WASHINGTON (D.C.)

"A study by a Miami consulting firm of transit-system crime in 1988-90 in several cities (Washington, Miami, San Francisco, Cleveland, Atlanta and Los Angeles) found Washington the safest. Last year Washington had no reported cases of metro rape; in the first ten months of 1993 the New York subway had 18 rapes and eight murders. True, Washington's system is far smaller--carrying some 250,000 people a day, compared with New York's 3.2m--but its safety record is nonetheless enviable, and has survived its extension into some of the area's worst crime-spots, such as Anacostia....the strategy of New York's transit police is now much the same as Washington's. Crime rates on the New York subway have fallen by about a third over the past three years. Yet Washington cannot afford to become complacent...The number of robberies on the transit system (buses as well as trains) was up by a quarter last year compared with 1992." (p31-32)

"American Survey: Washington Metro: Safe as Trains?" Economist v330 n7844, 8 Jan 1994. p31-32. (ISSN0013-0613).

CRIME--NICARAGUA

"The police recorded 43,000 crimes [in Nicaragua] last year at an average of 118 per day. These included assaults, kidnappings, street robberies and burglaries....Comandante [Fernando] Caldera feels that the rise of delinquency has its roots in the grave economic situation facing the Nicaraguan people at this moment. A police report shows that 76% of those arrested for various offences were underemployed or out of work. Only 1% were employed and another 1% were studying. An amazing 88% of those detained in 1993 were first-time offenders, reflecting the desperate situation of the typical citizen in this country, according to Caldera. It is impossible to view police attempts to safeguard Nicaraguan citizens independently from the economic crisis. They have an annual budget of about US$17 million when they actually need about $24.5 million to carry out their work effectively." (p19)

"Trying to Keep the Boat Afloat." Barricada Internacional n371, Mar 1994. p19-21. (ISSN1013-9567).

CRIME--RUSSIA (v19)

"It is above all episodes of violent crime that arouse Russian ire and disgust. The daily landscape is littered with such acts. Some of them are spectacular, like the recent kidnapping of schoolchildren in Rostov-on-Don (there are ten to fifteen hostage-takings a month in Russia) and the separate murders, apparently mafia hits, of two leading businesspeople on December 2 (there were thirty-eight such assassinations in 1993). Burglaries of flats, car thefts, muggings and vandalism on the 'elektrichka' commuter train, which ferries into Moscow those too poor to afford a car, no longer even raise an eyebrow. More than 2.5 million crimes were registered in Russia in 1993, 70 percent of them acts of larceny." (p80) "According to press reports, the murder rate in Russia (11 per 100,000) is now higher than that of the United States, which, with its rate of 9 per 100,000, has long been the most violent of the developed democracies." (p81)

Bernstein, Jonas. "Russia Watch (I): Bardak Shadows." American Spectator v72 n2, Feb 1994. p80-81. (ISSN0148-8414).

"Russia's communists exploit their country's home-grown crime wave as an argument for slowing down reform. Vladimir Zhirinovsky exploits it as a reason for returning Russia to authoritarianism. Certainly, the crime wave is connected to the failures of reform. Rules, where they exist, are vague. Public servants are underpaid, demoralised and hungry for bribes. Weapons are sold by disillusioned and unpaid soldiers and ex-soldiers....In a report prepared for President Boris Yeltsin, the Analytical Centre for Social and Economic Policies claims that three-quarters of private enterprises are forced to pay 10-20% of their earnings to criminal gangs; 150 such gangs, it says, control some 40,000 private and state-run companies, including most of the country's 1,800 commercial banks....Resisting extortionists' threats is risky; the interior ministry reported the murders in 1993 of 94 people described as entrepreneurs....Army stockpiles deliver gangsters their weapons, from machineguns to hand grenades. The defence ministry reported 6,430 cases of theft of weapons from military depots in 1993, and 3,923 cases in 1992. The interior ministry records two attacks involving explosives every day, almost one-third of them against 'entrepreneurs'." (p57)

"Europe: Crime in Russia: The High Price of Freeing Markets." Economist v330 n7851, 19 Feb 1994. p57-58. (ISSN0013-0613).

"Americans worried about drugs and violence wring their hands over a supposed crime wave; in Russia, it's more like a tsunami. Last year in Moscow, police recorded more than 5,000 murders and 20,000 incidents of violent crime. That represents a 36 percent increase over the year before--and that's just the crimes the police know about....In some quarters of Moscow, residents say gunfire is a nightly occurrence. Nearly every banker in the city has been approached by one of Moscow's eight big criminal groups. Banking, in fact, ranks as one of the most dangerous jobs in Russia today. Last year, 10 bankers in Moscow were murdered; across Russia, the number was 30." (p43)

Duffy, Brian/Trimble, Jeff. "World Report: The Wise Guys of Russia." U.S. News & World Report v116 n9, 7 Mar 1994. p41-43,45-47. (ISSN0041-5537).

CRIME--U.S. (v19)

"Reports of robberies and aggravated assaults at the nation's largest colleges rose during 1992, according to a survey by THE CHRONICLE OF HIGHER EDUCATION, a Washington-based higher education journal....THE CHRONICLE polled two-year and four-year colleges with enrollments of 5,000 or more students. Nearly 745 schools from across the country responded. The survey found that: Reported robberies rose 12 percent, climbing from 1,210 in 1991 to 1,353 in 1992; Reported aggravated assaults increased from 3,141 to 3,224 between 1991 and 1992; Drug arrests jumped 46 percent, shooting up from 2,301 in 1991 to 3,350 in 1992; Weapons-related arrests climbed 16 percent, rising from 1,142 to 1,322. Motor-vehicle thefts rose from 7,159 to 7,350; and Liquor-law arrests inched up from 14,474 to 14,544." (p4 secA)

"Crime Dropping at U-M While Rising on Other U.S. Campuses." Ann Arbor News 30 Jan 1994. p4 secA.

"Despite massive infusions of money, federal prisons have a design capacity of about 40,000. Every year federal judges sentence 45,000 defendants, mostly in drug prosecutions that are crowding civil cases off the dockets. Meanwhile violent crime in the United States is at a historic high, increasing 45 percent between 1982 and 1991. State and local agencies made 1.1 million drug arrests in 1991. One out of 46 adults is behind bars or on probation or parole." (p13)

Overby, Peter. "It Ain't Necessarily So." Common Cause Magazine v19 n4, Win 1993. p11-13. (ISSN0271-9592).

"Claims that criminal cases are taking up a disproportionate amount of Federal filings are not supported by the facts. According to the Administrative Office of U.S. Courts, the criminal caseload per judge is nearly 50 percent below that of 1972. The number of criminal cases reached a 40-year peak in 1972 and, despite all of the cries from the defense bar, the number of criminal cases filed in 1992 was actually 14 percent below the 1972 figures. There were fewer criminal cases in Federal courts in 1992 than there were in 1972 even though the number of authorized judges is now 62 percent higher than in 1972." (pS458)

Hatch, Orrin G. (Sen.-Utah). "The Need to Retain the Anti-Gang Provision of the Crime Bill," Congressional Record (1 Feb 1994). Daily ed. pS457-458. (ISSN0363-7239).

"Although opinion polls show that Americans are increasingly worried about crime, the curious thing is that over the past couple of years Americans appear to have been committing fewer crimes. The violent crime rate dropped by 3% in the first half of last year compared with the same period in 1992. Down in south Florida, the Metro-Dade police department reports that there were 39% fewer robberies of tourists last year than in 1992. Yet in one area of crime the figures and the fears tally ominously: more and more youngsters are breaking the law, and they are doing so more and more violently....The murder arrest rate for juveniles has nearly doubled over the past ten years. The arrest rate for violent crime is some five times higher among black youths than among whites (the arrest rate for murder rose for young blacks by 145% in the 1980s), though recently juvenile white crime has been increasing fastest. With the number of Americans aged from 14 to 17 expected to rise by about a fifth over the next ten years, matters look likely to get worse." (p25)

"American Survey: After Dark." Economist v330 n7853, 5 Mar 1994. p25-26. (ISSN0013-0613).

"The problem [in U.S. society] is a growing class of criminals and inadequate support for law enforcement across the country. Thirty percent of murders, 25 percent of rapes and 40 percent of robberies are committed by people out on bail, probation or parole. There are those who lament that we lock up more of our people than any other industrialized nation, but when 24 million people a year are victims of serious crime, we ought to be jailing more criminals." (p30)

du Pont, Pete. "Fair Comment: Gun Control Is a Substitute for Solutions." Insight v9 n52, 27 Dec 1993. p29-30. (ISSN1051-4880).

"Despite the popular faith in prisons, rates of imprisonment cannot be closely correlated with rates of crime. The number of people in prisons and jails [in the U.S.] between 1980 and 1991 doubled and did so at a steady rate. But the overall crime rate followed a very jagged pattern--down from 1980 to 1984, then up between 1985 and 1991, then down again in 1992 and 1993." (p38)

Rothman, David J. "The Crime of Punishment." New York Review of Books v41 n4, 17 Feb 1994. p34-38. (ISSN0028-7504).

"The BJS [Bureau of Justice Statistics] report on its National Crime Victimization Survey estimates that 34.7 million crimes were attempted or completed in 1991. About 6.4 million were violent personal crimes such as rape, robbery, and assaults. Another 12.5 million were personal crimes of theft. An additional 15.8 million household crimes, such as burglary and motor vehicle theft, occurred. Crime levels peaked in the United States in 1981 and since then have dropped overall--about 21 percent less for personal crimes of theft and 17 percent less for household crimes. However, the number of violent crimes in 1991 had not diminished significantly from the number reported a decade ago for 1981." (p4)

Kalish, Susan. "Who Are Crime's Victims?" Population Today v21 n3, Mar 1993. p4. (ISSN0749-2448).

During 1991, "In every personal crime category, males [in the U.S.] experienced considerably higher rates of victimization....The overall rate for males was 105 per 1,000 population; for females, 80 per 1,000. Males were more than two and one-half times as likely as females to experience an aggravated assault (12 versus 4 per 1,000). Rates are calculated per 1,000 persons age 12 or older. Blacks were generally more likely than whites or persons of other races (such as Asians or Native Americans), to be victims of violent crime. In 1991, there were 14 robberies for every 1,000 black persons, 4 robberies for every 1,000 whites, and 7 for other races." (p4)

Kalish, Susan. "Who Are Crime's Victims?" Population Today v21 n3, Mar 1993. p4. (ISSN0749-2448).

"Washington is awash with bad ideas about how to deal with crime. Not since the depths of the Nixon administration has such a mindless spirit of retribution flourished....Prison construction is now America's major public housing program. Nearly a quarter of black men between 20 and 29 are in jail or on parole or probation....The WASHINGTON POST reported that in 1992 there were only 240 rape, murder, manslaughter, attempted murder and aggravated assault convictions in federal courts....The major source of prison overcrowding is draconian and pointless drug laws. According to former Attorney General Philip Heymann, 21% of all federal prisoners are low-level, non-violent drug offenders." (p1)

"Crime Rampage!" Progressive Review n323, Mar 1994. p1-2.

"Rape has risen steadily from 22 reported incidents per 100,000 people in 1972 to 42 in 1992....The FBI reports 188 aggravated assaults per 100,000 inhabitants in 1972 compared with 441 in '92....Among all people aged 12 to 15, the crime rate is 36 percent higher than it was in 1973, [Stuart Smith, a BJS spokesman] says. For 16- to 19-year-olds, the increase is 27 percent. Among people 35 years of age and older, on the other hand, the crime rate is down significantly." (p4)

Henderson, Keith. "Numbers on Crime Reveal a Different Picture from the 'Crisis' That Many Politicians Paint." The Christian Science Monitor v86 n52, 8 Feb 1994. p1,4. (ISSN0882-7729).

"According to the FBI's Uniform Crime Reports (UCR) Index, major crimes rose only 4 percent between 1979 and 1989. The UCR Index includes attempted and completed homicide, forcible rape, robbery, aggravated assault, burglary, larceny-theft and motor vehicle theft....according to the U.S. Department of Justice's National Crime Survey (NCS)...the reported number of crime victimizations actually decreased nearly 27 percent in 1979-89." (p1)

News release. "Crime." University of Michigan News and Information Services 18 Jan 1994. p1-2.

CRIME--U.S.--COLLEGES AND UNIVERSITIES

"As a tidal wave of newspaper thefts washes over college campuses from California to Maryland, many administrators and campus police are doing nothing to prevent thousands of papers from being swept away. In many of the 29 incidents reported to the Student Press Law Center in 1993, no one has been caught. When the thieves do confess, the university has sometimes let them off scot-free. That trend is beginning to turn around, however. At Duke University a student was recently placed on disciplinary probation for trashing copies of a conservative campus paper. And two Pennsylvania State University students charged with criminal theft agreed to enter a rehabilitation program to avoid prosecution." (p28)

"College Censorship: A Crime Wave." Student Press Law Center Report v15 n1, Win 1993-94. p28-30.

CRIME--U.S.--FINANCE (v19)

CRIME--U.S.--PUBLIC OPINION (v19)

CRIME--U.S.--YOUTH (v19)

CRIME--VENEZUELA

"Crime is at an all time high [in Venezuela]. Media reports describe Caracas as Latin America's most dangerous city, with 72 homicides a week, one bank hold-up every two days, and four killings per day in the city's jails. The nation's prison system is disastrous. According to the government, 26,276 inmates are jammed into facilities designed for 15,550, where conditions are described as inhuman. The explosive situation was underscored with the January 4th massacre of 105 inmates at the Sabaneta prison in Maracaibo." (p13)

"Venezuela: A Daunting Task." NewsNotes v19 n2, Mar-Apr 1994. p12-13. (ISSN1064-1556).

CRIME--WASHINGTON

"Even though some crime rates are down, the fear of crime--especially random, senseless violence--is destroying the quality of life for millions of Americans. In Washington State, the percent of homicides in which the victim was killed by a stranger increased from 12 percent to 28 percent from 1984 to 1992. We used to think of crime as a problem of the inner cities, and it still is among the greatest problems in urban areas. The congressional district...[Mike Kriedler represents] is almost entirely suburban. But in one community of 20,000 people, there were 1,500 violent crimes last year--a rate three and a half times New York City's. Suburban schools are installing metal detectors. Driveby shootings can happen anywhere. Children are killing children." (pH1913)

Kreidler, Mike (Rep.-Wash.). "Violent Crime Control and Law Enforcement Act of 1994," Congressional Record (23 Mar 1994). Daily ed. pH1905-1937. (ISSN0363-7239).

CRIME AND DRUG ABUSE

see DRUG ABUSE AND CRIME

CRIME PREVENTION--GREAT BRITAIN (v19)

CRIME PREVENTION--U.S.--COSTS

"Comparing costs and benefits of tax money spent to combat crime is instructive." (p35) "In 1993, the only year for which there are federal statistics, the FBI used just 13 agents and eight support employees to investigate some 290 carjackings nationwide. That cost taxpayers $1.5 million. The picture is pretty much the same for most other federal police agencies. Over the past five years, the budget for the Drug Enforcement Administration increased about 37 percent, from $535 million in 1989 to $731 million this year. Over this same period--while street prices for drugs and other evidence indicated that drug trafficking remained steady or even increased--DEA arrests decreased. By far the most complex issue of costs and benefits of crime spending involves federal prosecutors. Today some 4,000 government lawyers work in 94 U.S. attorneys' offices around the country. The budget for federal prosecutors increased nearly 29 percent over the past five years, from $628 million in 1989 to $808 million this year. During this same period, the number of criminal cases filed by federal prosecutors decreased by 12 percent." (p36)

Johnson, Constance. "U.S. News: Law and Disorder." U.S. News & World Report v116 n12, 28 Mar 1994. p35-36,37. (ISSN0041-5537).

CRIMEA--POPULATION

"Like Bosnia, Crimea has two large malcontented minorities. Of its 2.5m people, 620,000 are ethnic Ukrainians who, if Crimea were to secede from Ukraine, might well seek to secede from Crimea. Another 250,000 are Crimean Tatars whose forefathers were exiled from the peninsula by Stalin and who have been trickling back since the mid-1980s. They have not been made welcome. Most live in shanty-towns on odd patches of wasteland. The Tatar unemployment rate is said to be 70%." (p49)

"Europe: Heavy Brigades." Economist v330 n7844, 8 Jan 1994. p48-49. (ISSN0013-0613).

CRIMES, VIOLENT

see VIOLENT CRIMES

CRIMINAL JUSTICE, ADMINISTRATION OF

see also LAW ENFORCEMENT; POLICE; PRISONS

CRIMINAL JUSTICE, ADMINISTRATION OF--GREAT BRITAIN (v19)

CRIMINAL JUSTICE, ADMINISTRATION OF--MARYLAND

"In 1989, of the total number (52,785) of new parole and probation cases in Maryland, only 11,329 involved orders for monetary payments (fines, court costs, and restitution). Of these 11,329, only 6,125 cases included orders for restitution to victims. Restitution was ordered by the courts in only eleven percent (11%) of the total cases: The actual amount of restitution ultimately collected by the Division of Parole and Probation for 1989 was a relatively small percent of the total ordered. Thus current restitution orders too frequently neither impact the offender or benefit the victim. Clearly, since only twenty-one percent...of the total number of Maryland parole and probation cases in 1989 were ordered to pay fines, the use of the fine as a punitive sanction must be expanded." (p95)

U.S. House. Committee on Ways and Means. "To Bar Social Security Benefit Payments...by Court Order." Hearing, 21 Sep 1993. Washington, D.C.: GPO, 1994. (ISBN0160435315). (Y4.W36:103-41).

CRIMINAL JUSTICE, ADMINISTRATION OF--PHILADELPHIA (PA)

"The criminals across the Nation are winning the war on crime. They have learned that if they refuse to reappear for trial, the local law enforcement does not have the facilities to go after them. Criminals rarely, if ever, report for trial. In Philadelphia, of all the defendants released under the prison cap, 47 percent fail to appear in court. What this means is that over a period of 6 years, from 1988 to 1994, over 230,000 cases remained unprosecutable due to prisoners refusing to appear in court. In one city, 230,000 criminal acts went unanswered and close to 230,000 victims did not receive justice." (pH2525)

Borski, Robert A. (Rep.-Pa.). "Violent Crime Control and Law Enforcement Act of 1994," Congressional Record (20 Apr 1994). Daily ed. pH2518-2539. (ISSN0363-7239).

CRIMINAL JUSTICE, ADMINISTRATION OF--U.S. (v19)

"The Administrative Office of the U.S. Courts recently reported that in 1993, the number of criminal cases filed by Federal prosecutors decreased by over 3 percent. This was the first decrease in 10 years. The Administrative office attributes this overall decrease in criminal filings to the Clinton Justice Department's significant reduction in drug prosecutions. Drug prosecutions in 1993 decreased by 7 percent, or 902 cases." (pS4051)

Hatch, Orrin G. (Sen.-Utah). "Crime," Congressional Record (11 Apr 1994). Daily ed. pS4050-4051. (ISSN0363-7239).

"According to the Federal Bureau of Investigation (FBI), 81 percent of the assaults on law enforcement officers in the United States during 1992 were committed with personal weapons, such as hands, fists, and feet. Our current prison system provides convicted felons, many of whom are already prone to violence, the chance to significantly increase their strength and their bulk--thus making future acts of violence even more likely....According to a 1991 survey, 54 percent of inmates convicted of violent crimes used no weapon other than their own body when they committed their offenses. Thus, by building a better thug, we are actually providing the weapon used in many violent crimes. Finally, of the 50,000 violent criminals put on probation during 1992, over 9,000 were rearrested for a violent crime within 3 years in the same state." (pH2524)

Pryce, Deborah (Rep.-Ohio). "Violent Crime Control and Law Enforcement Act of 1994," Congressional Record (20 Apr 1994). Daily ed. pH2518-2539. (ISSN0363-7239).

"As of January 31, 1994, 224 offenders [in the U.S.] have participated in day reporting. The program has a success rate of 84 percent, and only one client has been rearrested while in the program. The new arrest was for a non-violent misdemeanor offense. Over $136,000 in supervision fees were collected from clients to help offset the cost of the center. A study of the clients that successfully finished the day reporting center program showed that 8 percent of them were rearrested after completing the program. The amount of time between completing the program and rearrest averaged 7.5 months, with the shortest period being 1 month and the longest, 17 months. Of the seven reoffenders, four were arrested for new misdemeanors and three were accused of committing felony offenses. None of the seven were first-time offenders when accepted to the day reporting center and they had an average 7.2 prior arrests. Six of the seven committed the same offense for which they were in the day reporting center program." (p11-12)

Diggs, David W./Pieper, Stephen L. "Using Day Reporting

Centers as an Alternative to Jail." Federal Probation v58 n1, Mar 1994. p9-12. (ISSN0014-9128).

"In mid-1987, there were 826 offenders [in the U.S.] on monitoring devices. As of February 1989, the number had grown to 6,490 nationwide....When electronic monitoring was used for pretrial offenders in the Federal system during fiscal year 1989, only 9 cases out of 168 failed to appear for a failure rate of 5.4 percent. This compares to a 2.8 percent failure for all other offenders; however, those placed on electronic monitoring were presumably perceived as presenting a greater risk of flight or danger to the community. The rearrest rates for the electronic monitoring cases were 3.6 percent for felonies and 2.4 percent for misdemeanors compared to the national rates of 1.9 percent and 1.0 percent for unmonitored cases. Once again, the issue of greater risk may be the variable that resulted in the increased rearrest rates." (p50-51)

Rackmill, Stephen J. "An Analysis of Home Confinement as a Sanction." Federal Probation v58 n1, Mar 1994. p45-52. (ISSN0014-9128).

CRIMINAL JUSTICE, ADMINISTRATION OF--U.S.--PUBLIC OPINION (v19)

CRIMINALS

see also GANGS; JUVENILE DELINQUENTS

CRIMINALS--CALIFORNIA

"The Department of Corrections already consumes 7 percent of...[California's] $40 billion general fund budget. According to Craig Brown, undersecretary for Youth and Adult Corrections, there are 277,000 Californians in and out of prison with one or more felony 'strikes.' Of those, as many as 40,000 have two prior serious or violent felonies." (p4)

Wood, Daniel B. "Californians Wonder Whether a 'Three Strikes' Anticrime Law Is Worth Price." The Christian Science Monitor v86 n68, 3 Mar 1994. p1,4. (ISSN0882-7729).

CRIMINALS--GREAT BRITAIN (v19)

CRIMINALS--U.S. (v19)

"Of the 13 million arrests police make [in the U.S.] in a year, less than 2 percent result in a prison sentence. Less than one in six murders a year results in incarceration. It has gotten so bad that the expected punishment for committing a serious crime now averages about 22 months. The problem is too many of these criminals are serving their time on our streets and not a prison cell....Texas, right now, has nearly 420,000 convicts on either probation or parole, after serving an average of only 2.4 years--21 percent--of their prison sentences. Experts predict that a criminal serving only 4 years of a 10-year sentence will commit approximately 70 more crimes during his unserved time. Those are sobering figures, especially when two-thirds of the violent crime is committed by repeat offenders who have at least five previous arrests. In Texas, for example, nearly half--47 percent--of violent crimes are committed by repeat offenders." (pE8)

Andrews, Michael A. (Rep.-Tex.). "Abolish Parole for Violent and Repeat Offenders," Congressional Record (25 Jan 1994). Daily ed. pE8. (ISSN0363-7239).

"At the national level where they represent only about 12 percent of the United States population, blacks formed about 29 percent of all arrestees in 1991 (United States Department of Justice, 1991)....In 1991, there were 13.5 robberies for every 1,000 blacks, 4.4 robberies for every 1,000 whites, and 7.4 for every 1,000 persons in other racial categories (Bureau of Justice Statistics, 1991, p. 6)." (p57)

Arthur, John A. "Correctional Ideology of Black Correctional Officers." Federal Probation v58 n1, Mar 1994. p57-66. (ISSN0014-9128).

"Citing figures from a 1982 Rand study [in the U.S.], supporters of regional prisons note that a typical career robber commits 41 to 61 crimes per year. Auto thieves each steal an average of 76 to 100 cars annually. Burglars break into 76 to 118 homes and businesses a year. On average, every career criminal costs society $400,000 or more per year in lost property, hospital bills, lost wages, and other damages." (p4)

Dillin, John. "Cries against Crime Lead to Proposal for Regional Prisons." The Christian Science Monitor v86 n57, 15 Feb 1994. p1,4. (ISSN0882-7729).

"The social cost of letting career predators go every few years is enormous. According to a recent study, rapists and child molesters are arrested once for every 30 offenses they commit. So even if every arrest results in conviction, an average of 30 new victims will be created before each serial sex criminal goes back to jail for a while....Under a predator law, testimony on the continuing danger of people...could be introduced as evidence. And so could comments by predators that they intend to strike again after release. In cases of gruesome sexual assault in New Jersey and Minnesota, for instance, officials scrambled for ways to keep offenders off the streets after hearing of their plans to attack again. Despite fears that authorities would overpredict dangerousness, after four years only 16 men are being held under the law, seven are awaiting trial and one was released. The legislation has been upheld by the state Supreme Court. No doubt it will one day wend its way to the U.S. Supreme Court. But for now, it seems to be working as intended. Predator laws are probably the wave of the future. There are probably only a few thousand highly dangerous sex criminals in the country. These laws are a way to keep them out of circulation." (p19)

Leo, John. "On Society: Dealing with Career Predators." U.S. News & World Report v116 n14, 11 Apr 1994. p19. (ISSN0041-5537).

CRIMINALS--U.S.--ALIENS (v19)

CRIMINALS--U.S.--COSTS (v19)

CRIMINALS--U.S.--DRUG USE (v19)

CROATIA--WARS--SERBIA

"The 1991 war between Croatia and Serbia, which killed 10,000 people, has paused but never ended. A December 1991 peace plan and 13,000 United Nations troops have not stopped the struggle between the Croatian government and the Croatian Serbs who have seized 25 to 30 percent of Croatia's territory and declared independence." (p68)

Zimmerman, Tim. "Predictions: Will Conflict in the Balkans Spread?" U.S. News & World Report v115 n25, 27 Dec 1993. p68. (ISSN0041-5537).

CROP LOSSES (v19)

CROP LOSSES--U.S. (v19)

CROP PESTS

see AGRICULTURAL PESTS

CROPS--POSTHARVEST LOSSES--U.S.

"Postharvest disease control is necessary for two reasons: losses are unacceptably large without protection, and some pathogens of food can also cause human disease when the food is eaten. Despite fungicide use, postharvest losses amount to about 10 to 30% of the total yield of crops in the U.S. Conservative estimates for the U.S. alone 'indicate that under present conditions, the food wasted and lost during the post-harvest period could provide basic nutritional requirements for almost 200 million people' (Moline 1984). Estimates of postharvest losses of fresh fruit and vegetables in the U.S. range from 12 to 23% (Cappellini and Ceponis 1984; Wilson and Pusey 1985). Without refrigeration or other treatment, losses can reach 50%, which is the case in many underdeveloped countries (Coursey 1983). After picking, another 5 to 21 days are needed to place fresh produce in the hands of consumers. Loss occurs at every step of postharvest processing all the way to retail sales and the home refrigerator." (p2)

Quarles, William. "Update: Biological Control of Postharvest Fruit Disease." IPM Practitioner v15 n5-6, May-Jun 1993. p1-11. (ISSN0738-968X).

CRUELTY TO ANIMALS

see ANIMAL WELFARE

CRUISE SHIPS (v19)

CUBA

see also AGRICULTURE--CUBA; AIDS (DISEASE)--CUBA; AMERICAN PROPERTY--CUBA; CHILDREN--CUBA--MORTALITY; DOLLAR, AMERICAN--CUBA; FERTILITY, HUMAN--CUBA; INFANTS--CUBA--MORTALITY; INVESTMENTS, FOREIGN--CUBA; NEUROPATHY--CUBA; PETROLEUM INDUSTRY AND TRADE--CUBA; SCHOOLS--CUBA; SUGAR TRADE--CUBA; VISA--CUBA--U.S.

CUBA--ARMED FORCES

"There are no longer any Russian troops in Cuba. Russian support personnel have left the support base at Cienfuegos. No Russian navy ships have called on Cuba in the last 2 to 3 years. Cuba is reducing its standing army of 180,000 by 30 to 40 percent. All Cuban troops have been withdrawn from Angola. Cuba provides no support to other socialist nations nor support or encouragement to insurgents threatening governments friendly to the U.S." (p3)

"Cuba: A Policy of U.S. Engagement." Defense Monitor v23 n1, 1994. p2-4. (ISSN0195-6450).

CUBA--ECONOMIC CONDITIONS (v19)

"Cuba, caught in the double bind of being abandoned by the former Soviet Union and having to contend with a [U.S.] blockade more stringent than ever, is riddled with shortages that affect the lives of all Cubans in the most dramatic ways." According to President Fidel Castro, the USSR "constituted a formidable point of support to resist not only the blockade, but also the innumerable imperialist aggressions.' Its fall was a determining factor in the path the Cuban economy would have to take. In 1989 Cuba received imports valued at $8,139 million, and three years later imports amounted to no more than $2,236 million. This brutal reduction occurred between 1991 and 1992, the year in which the sugar harvest declined to 4,280,000 tons, almost three million tons less than the preceding harvest. 'This year,' the president emphasized, 'we have $450 million less from sugar alone and we expect imports to amount to approximately $1,719 million.' To these problems we must add natural disasters such as the one now known as 'the storm of the century' that caused the Cuban economy losses amounting to one billion dollars." (p4)

Gonzales, Reynaldo. "A Bed of Nails: The Dollar in Cuba." Cuba Update Supplement Sep 1993. p3-6.

Cuba's president Fidel "Castro points out that, with the collapse of the USSR and the eastern European socialist bloc, Cuba's imports dropped from $8,139 million in 1989 to $2,236 in 1992. In regard to sugar alone, Cuba's main export product, the harvest fell from 7,030,000 tons in the 1991-92 season to 4,280,000 in the 1992-93 season. 'It is true that we hadn't planned on seven million tons this year,' Castro said, referring to the crop damage caused by the March storm now being referred to in Cuba as 'The Storm of the Century.' 'We were already suffering the consequences of a deficit in fertilizer and other problems, but we were hoping for a harvest of a little over six million tons. However, this year and under such difficult conditions we received approximately $450 million less, in a situation in which our imports have been reduced practically to 25 percent of their previous level.'" (p1)

Rose, William. "Fidel Castro Confronts the Dollar Issue." Cuba Update Supplement Sep 1993. p1-2.

CUSTOMER SERVICE--EMPLOYMENT--U.S. (v19)

CUSTOMS ADMINISTRATION AND TOURISTS--U.S.

"Customs is constantly putting out fires because it lacks the resources needed to bring each of its many functions to an acceptable level of performance. Customs inspectional force of 8,000 is approximately the size of a big city police force, yet is spread among more than 300 ports of entry. Customs depends on a mere 4,200 workers to process some 10 million trade entries a year while enforcing tariffs, quotas, intellectual property rights, and collecting nearly $20 billion in revenue. NTEU [National Treasury Employees Union] continues to believe that providing Customs with sizeable resource increments each year for the next several years--to be allocated to areas of greatest need--is a cost-effective way to enable the Service to put its principal functions on a sound footing. GAO [General Accounting Office] portrays Customs as a 'high-risk' agency with a tremendous gap between promise and performance. GAO found that Customs' Automated Commercial System processed more than 7 million entries in 1991 and detected only 43,000 or 16 percent of an estimated 265,000 violations of U.S. trade law. The potential revenue loss from these undetected violations amounts to hundreds of millions of dollars." (p1542)

Tobias, Robert M. (National President, National Treasury Employees Union). U.S. House. Committee on Appropriations. "Treasury, Postal Service...Approp. for Fiscal Year 1994 (Part 1)." Hearing, Washington, D.C.: GPO, 1993. (Y4.Ap6/1:T71/994/pt.1).

CYCLING

see also BICYCLE COMMUTING

CYCLING--CANADA--ACCIDENTS AND INJURIES (v19)

CYCLING--DENMARK--JAPAN--NETHERLANDS

"Secure bike storage at public transit stations dramatically increases the number of people who can conveniently use each station. This can be seen both in Japan, where all train stations have huge, well-used bicycle parking lots, and in Holland, where all 351 train stations have bicycle parking, some of which are guarded....One of Holland's 'new towns' (Houton) improves bicycling safety by paving bike lanes with slightly elevated, purple asphalt to keep cars off the bikeways. Eighty percent of the people use bikes for daily transportation. In Amsterdam (Holland's largest city), a March 1992 popular vote closed the city center to auto traffic. It was sensible to ban cars, given the city's dense mix of businesses and residences. Housing near businesses help car-free areas survive. Holland also administers an 'excessive driving tax'. Denmark has a 200% sales tax on all car purchases and a $1000/year automobile registration fee which helps fund public transit and bicycle facilities." (p48)

Janes, Danielle. "The Bike Column." Rain v14 n3, Spr 1993. p48-52.

CYCLING--U.S.--ACCIDENTS AND INJURIES (v19)

"Bicycle related death and injuries are...a very serious problem. Between 1984 and 1988, 2,985 bicyclists in the United States died from head injuries and 905,752 suffered head injuries that required treatment in hospital emergency rooms. Eighty-five percent of all head injuries suffered by bicyclists could be prevented by using bicycle helmets." (pS16889)

Gorton, Slade (Sen.-Wash.). "Child Safety Protection Act," Congressional Record (20 Nov 1993). Daily ed. pS16885-16892. (ISSN0363-7239).

"The Consumer Product Safety Commission (CPSC) estimates that bicycle-related deaths and injuries cost society $7.6 billion annually. The statistics regarding children are even more compelling. The CDC [Centers for Disease Control] study found that 41 percent of head injury deaths and 76 percent of total head injuries occurred among children under age 15. According to the National Head Injury Foundation, the cost of supporting a child who has suffered a severe head injury, on average, is $4.5 million over that individual's lifetime....A 1989 study published in the NEW ENGLAND JOURNAL OF MEDICINE found that use of a bicycle helmet reduces the risk of all head injuries by 85 percent and injuries to the brain by 90 percent. According to the CDC study, universal use of bicycle helmets would have prevented 2,600 deaths and 757,000 injuries between 1984 and 1988. Unfortunately, few riders wear helmets. In the case of children cyclists, it is a tragic fact that only 5 percent of these vulnerable riders wear helmets, according to the American Academy of Pediatrics." (pS16890)

Danforth, John C. (Sen.-Mo.). "Child Safety Protection Act," Congressional Record (20 Nov 1993). Daily ed. pS16885-16892. (ISSN0363-7239).

CYPRUS--HISTORY--CYPRUS CRISIS, 1974- (v19)

CZECHOSLOVAKIA--ECONOMIC CONDITIONS (v19)

DAIRY FARMS--U.S.

"In 1985, Congress pulled the floor out from under dairy prices, letting the government-supported 'target price' fall from $12.10 per 100 pounds of milk to $10.10 today. In 1990, Congress turned back an effort to raise the milk price again. And between 1986 and 1992, annual federal payments to dairy farmers plummeted from $2.3 billion to $300 million." (p52)

Hage, David. "Business: Weeding Out Waste." U.S. News & World Report v116 n1, 10 Jan 1994. p51-53. (ISSN0041-5537).

DAIRY PRODUCTS INDUSTRY--MEXICO--U.S.

"The United States exported $160 million of dairy products to Mexico in 1992, about one-fourth of which was nonfat dry milk. The United States imported less than $1 million of dairy products from Mexico in 1992. Mexico is the world's largest importer of milk powders. The United States shipped an annual average of more than 40,000 metric tons of U.S. nonfat dry milk between 1980 and 1990, about 20 percent of U.S. powder exports and 25 percent of Mexico's imports. U.S. exports of other dairy products to Mexico have been relatively small, but exports have been growing in recent years--especially yogurt, ice cream, cheese, and fluid milk." (p10)

U.S. Dept. of Agriculture. "In Focus: NAFTA." Dairy Situation and Outlook Report Dec 1993. p8-10.

DAIRY PRODUCTS INDUSTRY--PRICES--U.S.

"The CPI [Consumer Price Index] for dairy products rose only 0.7 percent last year. Retail prices for fresh milk and cream rose slightly (1.3 percent) in 1993, while prices for manufactured dairy products (except ice cream) declined. Cheese prices declined 0.1 percent, and butter prices fell 6.1 percent. Lackluster demand in the dairy market is indicative of the sluggish 1993 general economy. Slow movement of dairy products in 1993 brought a buildup of inventories of some processed products which, in turn, led to lower prices." (p39)

Parlett, Ralph. "News of Food Prices: Food Prices Rose Moderately for the Third Consecutive Year." Food Review v17 n1, Jan-Apr 1994. p36-39.

DAIRYING--AUSTRALIA (v19)

DAIRYING--EUROPEAN ECONOMIC COMMUNITY (v19)

DAIRYING--MEXICO--U.S. (v19)

DAIRYING--THAILAND (v19)

DAIRYING--U.S. (v19)

DALMATIAN DOG--U.S.

"Over the last two years, largely due to the re-release of Disney's 101 DALMATIANS, the spotted canines have experienced rising popularity [in the U.S.]. 'In 1992, the Dalmatian cemented its claim to the title of America's fad breed,'" according to John Mandeville of the American Kennel Club (AKC). "According to AKC's 1992 registration statistics, Dalmatian registrations increased by 28.8 percent last year. 'Dalmatian litter registrations, in percentage terms, were the fastest increasing of any of the top-ranked breeds in 1992.'" (p10)

Miller, Julie E. "Purebreds and Pet Overpopulation: The Case for a Breeding Moratorium." Shelter Sense v16 n8, Sep 1993. p3-12. (ISSN0734-3078).

DAMS--CHINA

"China has begun seeking international funds to finance the Three Gorges Dam, which will cost at least $11 billion and take eighteen years to build. The mile-long, 600-foot-high colossus will require 11.3 million tons of cement and 1.83 million tons of steel. An assortment of environmental groups around the world, including the International Rivers Network, Friends of the Earth, Probe International of Canada, the Center for Marine Conservation, Defenders of Wildlife, the Worldwide Fund for Nature in Hong Kong, and the Asian Pacific Peoples' Network in Malaysia, have joined forces with several Chinese environmental and dissident groups to stop the dam. They are pressuring the World Bank--the leading financier of mega-dams such as Itaipu in Brazil--not to fund this one." (p9-10)

Magagnini, Stephen. "International Notebook: Taming the Dragon." Amicus Journal v15 n2, Sum 1993. p9-12. (ISSN0276-7201).

The Three Gorges Dam, which is to be built in China, "is expected to generate a record 17.7 million kilowatts a year, or 84 billion kilowatt-hours. 'Maybe many people now have money to buy televisions and refrigerators, but electricity is very expensive and usage is limited to 60 kilowatt hours every month,' says Frank Zhou, an engineer from Wuxi, near Shanghai. (The average Sacramento, California home uses 750 kilowatt-hours a month.)...An even more crucial function of the dam than power generation, says Tang [Zhangjin], will be flood control. 'The most important reason for the dam is to prevent flooding downstream,' he says. In 1931, monster floods submerged more than 35,000 square miles in the Yangtze Basin, killing 140,000 people and leaving as many as 40 million others homeless. Killer floods in 1935 and 1954 took another 175,000 lives. 'Today, so much silt has been deposited on the bottom that the river bed has risen,' says Tang. 'A 100-year-flood would do unimaginable damage.'" (p10-11)

Magagnini, Stephen. "International Notebook: Taming the Dragon." Amicus Journal v15 n2, Sum 1993. p9-12. (ISSN0276-7201).

"The Three Gorges project has been described as the most important construction in China since the building of the Great Wall. The environmental impacts of the dam--which will soar to 607 feet, stretch for 1.2 miles along the river, and create a lake 350 miles long--will be enormous. While not the world's largest dam, it will generate almost 18,000 megawatts, easily the highest electrical output of any dam in the world." (p6)

Walters, Mark Jerome. "Animals in Peril: Who Speaks for the Baiji?" Animals v126 n6, Nov-Dec 1993. p6. (ISSN0030-6835).

DANCE COMPANIES--U.S. (v19)

DATA NETWORKS, COMPUTER

see COMPUTER NETWORKS

DEATH, MERCY

see EUTHANASIA

DEATH PENALTY

see CAPITAL PUNISHMENT

DEBT

see also BANKRUPTCY

DEBT--AFRICA

"Africa's debt rose sharply during the 1980s, when the prices of its commodity exports began a long and steep decline. By 1992, the continent's total debt of some $290 billion was about two and a half times greater than in 1980, while Sub-Saharan Africa's debt had more than tripled. To service this debt, Africa paid over $26 bn to its creditors in 1991. Africa's debt is about a fifth of the developing world's total debt, but this is a burden far heavier than that faced by any other region because of the relatively small size of African economies. The continent's debt is equivalent to 90 per cent of its gross national product (GNP), and for Sub-Saharan Africa, it is 110 per cent of GNP." (p1-2)

"African Debt Crisis: A Continuing Impediment to Development." United Nations Department of Public Information 1993. p1-6.

"The lack of significant debt relief has meant that Africa's debt servicing continued to soar throughout the 1980s, growing five-fold between 1983 and 1990 and accounting for 30 per cent of the continent's export earnings--themselves hard-hit by commodity price declines. This is an extraordinary burden for the world's poorest continent. Africa spends four times more on debt servicing than it does for all the health services it provides to its 600 million people. It is not surprising, therefore, that a single African country, Mozambique, loses more children to malnutrition and easily preventable or curable diseases than do all the struggling countries of the former Soviet Union. Indeed, less than one-third of Africa's debt service bill would fund the additional annual costs of programmes required to meet the key social-sector goals set by the World Summit for Children in 1990." (p2-3)

"African Debt Crisis: A Continuing Impediment to Development." United Nations Department of Public Information 1993. p1-6.

DEBT--AFRICA--LATIN AMERICA

"In sub-Saharan Africa debt is now the equivalent of 106 per cent of gross domestic product (GDP)--compared to 37.4 per cent in Latin America, another debt-affected area. In many countries, such as Mozambique, Somalia, United Republic of Tanzania, Guinea-Bissau and Mauritania, external debt is higher than GDP. In these circumstances--given low world prices for most export commodities--it is not surprising that debt servicing schedules become impossible. Arrears pile debt upon debt. The burden increases." (p2)

Boutros-Ghali, Boutros. "New Concepts for Development Action in Africa." United Nations Department of Public Information n1359, Mar 1993. p1-6.

DEBT--U.S. (v19)

DEBTS, EXTERNAL--AFRICA

"Official creditors--IFIs [International Financial Institutions] as well as governments--account for some 65 per cent of Africa's overall debt stock, with the remainder owed to private and short-term creditors. This heavy reliance on official lending--unique to Africa--was accentuated during the course of the 1980s by the steady contraction in commercial bank lending to Africa. Even so, Africa owes over $70 billion to private creditors, and servicing this debt costs Africa over $14 billion a year. With the sharp decline in new lending by banks, the private sector in recent years has been taking out far more than it puts into Africa, to the tune of a net outflow of almost $30 billion for the 1983-90 period." (p5)

"African Debt Crisis: A Continuing Impediment to Development." United Nations Department of Public Information 1993. p1-6.

"The World Bank's implicit acceptance of policy failures in Africa lends weight to a recent report by Oxfam, the UK-based international charity, which said both World Bank and IMF [International Monetary Fund] policies for Africa needed to be reviewed. But while Oxfam has called for a Marshall Plan-type aid to Africa, critics point out that such a package 'can only lead Africa to perpetual and perennial indebtedness to the world's lending institutions.' With a total external debt of $288 billion, Africa spends four times more paying interest on debt than on health for its people. Compared with other regions, Africa's debt appears manageable, but relative to the size of its economics, the debt is far beyond the continent's ability to repay." (p5)

Tafirenyika, Masimba. "Center Focus: World Bank Overhauls Its Africa Strategy." Center Focus n113, Sep 1993. p4-5.

DEBTS, EXTERNAL--AFRICA--LATIN AMERICA

"Although Latin American debt has received more attention because of its size, Sub-Saharan African debt is more extreme with debt levels at 75 percent of GDP [gross domestic product] compared to 47 percent of GDP in Latin America. For all LDCs [less-developed countries], debt service payments have resulted in an almost annual 5 percent transfer of income to creditor nations since 1982--without any decline in debt-to-export ratios, even though new capital inflows have been almost nil." (p66)

Tucker, Michael. "A Proposed Debt-for-Nature Swap in Madagascar and the Larger Problem of LDC Debt." International Environmental Affairs v6 n1, Win 1994. p59-68. (ISSN1041-4665).

DEBTS, EXTERNAL--AFRICA, SUB-SAHARAN (v19)

DEBTS, EXTERNAL--CARIBBEAN AREA--LATIN AMERICA

Markets in Latin America and the Caribbean were not "worried by a modest rise of 4% in the region's foreign debt, to $487 billion. For a start, dollar interest rates are much lower than in the 1980s; interest payments, as a proportion of exports of goods and services, fell to 17% in 1993 from 19%." (p60)

"International: Latin America: Doing Well." Economist v329 n7843, 25 Dec 1993. p60. (ISSN0013-0613).

DEBTS, EXTERNAL--DEVELOPING COUNTRIES (v19)

DEBTS, EXTERNAL--IRAQ

"When the international community, led by the United States, imposed sanctions against Iraq following its invasion of Kuwait in August 1990, Iraq had approximately $1.9 billion in outstanding obligations that were guaranteed under the CCC [Commodity Credit Corporation] program. Of that amount, $340 million was owed to BNL [Banca Nazionale del Lavoro]-Atlanta. Significantly, of the $1.9 billion in total outstanding obligations, only $392 million was attributable to action taken by the Bush administration, as only $392 million of the approximately $500 million in credit guarantees that the Bush administration had authorized had actually been extended for commodities shipped before the imposition of sanctions." (p111-112)

Juster, Kenneth I. "The Myth of Iraqgate." Foreign Policy n94, Spr 1994. p105-119. (ISSN0015-7228).

DEBTS, EXTERNAL--ISRAEL (v19)

DEBTS, EXTERNAL--JAPAN

"In 1986 Japan's households had debts worth 92% of their annual post-tax incomes. The American figure was similar. By the end of the decade Japan's ratio had jumped to 116%, while America's had risen only slightly. Japan's debt binge aggravated the subsequent bust: according to some estimates, the burden of repaying debt has cut consumer demand by 2% or so since 1990. The newest numbers on household finances relate to December 1992. These show that private debt had fallen to 109% of disposable incomes--a decline far sharper than America or Britain achieved at similar points in their recessions. In 1992 Japan's housewives (husbands leave money matters to their wives) paid off a net Y1 trillion of debt, producing the first fall in the stock of household debt ever recorded." (p35)

"Asia: The Good News from Japan." Economist v330 n7848, 29 Jan 1994. p35-36. (ISSN0013-0613).

DEBTS, EXTERNAL--MADAGASCAR

"Although there have been several instances of debt forgiveness by western countries, including $750 million by French President Francois Mitterand, Madagascar still has an external debt of $3.5 billion. The size of the debt is overwhelming for an economy with a total gross national product of only $2.283 billion. A negative trade balance has further worsened the situation. By the end of 1991, foreign reserves had dwindled to $113 million." (p62-63)

Tucker, Michael. "A Proposed Debt-for-Nature Swap in Madagascar and the Larger Problem of LDC Debt." International Environmental Affairs v6 n1, Win 1994. p59-68. (ISSN1041-4665).

DEBTS, EXTERNAL--MOROCCO (v19)

DEBTS, EXTERNAL--MOZAMBIQUE

"At $4.7 bn in 1991, Mozambique's debt is more than four times the country's GDP [gross domestic product], the highest ratio in Africa. Scheduled debt servicing obligations in 1992 of over $500 mn, if actually paid, would have been equivalent to 133 per cent of export earnings." (p16)

Harsch, Ernest/Laishley, Roy. "UN Mobilizes for Peace: Mozambique: Out of the Ruins of War." Africa Recovery Briefing Paper n8, May 1993. p1-20.

DEBTS, EXTERNAL--U.S. (v19)

DEBTS, PUBLIC--CANADA

"Canada's federal debt now rests above the C$500 billion mark. Almost C$40 billion of the C$160 billion Canadian budget is spent paying interest on the nation's debt, [Finance Minister Paul] Martin reported." (p9)

Clayton, Mark. "Economy: Canadian Budget Reform: Liberal Government Vows to Cut Deficit, Create Jobs." The Christian Science Monitor v86 n63, 24 Feb 1994. p9. (ISSN0882-7729).

DEBTS, PUBLIC--TAIWAN (v19)

DEBTS, PUBLIC--U.S. (v19)

"Of the gross federal debt, 75 percent or $3.0 trillion was held by the public in 1992. The amount held by foreigners is extremely difficult to measure because, even after establishing adequate definitions of foreign ownership...tracking the purchase and sale of a particular issue of debt throughout the world becomes a virtually insurmountable task. The latest Economic Report of the President reports that as of September 1992, it was estimated that about 18 percent of outstanding Federal debt...was held by foreigners. This was roughly unchanged from September of 1990." (p620)

U.S. House. Committee on Appropriations. "Treasury, Postal Service, and General Government Approp. for Fiscal Year 1994 (Part 3)." Hearing, Washington, D.C.: GPO, 1993. (Y4.Ap6/1:T71/994/pt.3).

"It has been said, 'Blessed are the young, for they shall inherit the national debt.' Today, every child born in America inherits $17,000 in public debt. Today, the total Federal income tax collected each year from west of the Mississippi River does not even cover the interest paid on our debt burden. Today, the Federal Government spends $3 for every $2 it collects. This is the destructive legacy of a Congress without courage. Our budget deficit represents a failure to lead, and that failure is felt in every city, in every community, on every farm, and in every family." (pS1380)

Coats, Dan (Sen.-Ind.). "Reduction in Spending on Federal Buildings," Congressional Record (10 Feb 1994). Daily ed. pS1350-1419. (ISSN0363-7239).

"A national debt of over $4.5 trillion is slowly but surely killing businesses and individuals by soaking up capital that could be used to create jobs and wealth for Americans. Our national debt is now over $18,000 for each man, woman, and child in this country....In 1975 it was only $2,500. A year ago it was $1,300 less. In just 1 year we have gone up 1,300 more dollars for every man, woman, and child in America, to be in debt." (pS1591)

Hatch, Orrin G. (Sen.-Utah). "Balanced Budget Amendment," Congressional Record (22 Feb 1994). Daily ed. pS1590-1609. (ISSN0363-7239).

"One of the most pernicious effects of the enormous deficit beast is the interest cost required to feed it. Interest on the Federal debt in 1993 amounted to nearly $293 billion. That is more than total Federal revenues in 1975. Interest alone is more than all revenues that came to the Government in 1975. Last year's interest costs took 26 percent of all Federal revenues and 57 percent of all individual income tax revenues....OMB [Office of Management and Budget] projects that interest on the debt will rise substantially over the next 5 years....It will pass the $300 billion mark in 1995 and reach $373 billion in 1999. CBO's [Congressional Budget Office's] estimates are even higher, with $311 billion in interest in 1995 and $382 billion in 1999." (pS1702)

Hatch, Orrin G. (Sen.-Utah). "Balanced Budget Amendment," Congressional Record (23 Feb 1994). Daily ed. pS1695-1734. (ISSN0363-7239).

"As the debt [in the U.S.] stands now a child or young adult on average can expect to pay well over $100,000 in extra taxes to cover interest payments on the debt during his or her lifetime. Each year that we run a $200 billion deficit, another $8,000 is added to that figure. Over the last 20 years, the net annual interest payment has risen from $14 billion in 1970 to over $180 billion in 1990, money which could have gone to vital domestic programs or to pay off the Federal debt....too much of Government spending is needed to pay off past debts instead of investing in our future." (pS1809)

DeConcini, Dennis (Sen.-Ariz.). "The Balanced Budget Amendment," Congressional Record (24 Feb 1994). Daily ed. pS1807-1810. (ISSN0363-7239).

"In 1980,...interest on the debt [in the U.S.] was $75 billion. In 1983 that number had increased 400 percent, to $295 billion. By 1996, interest on the debt is expected to exceed Social Security payments as the single largest Government expense in the budget of this Government. And right now, every single day, our Government is spending...$800 million on interest payments alone." (pS1809)

DeConcini, Dennis (Sen.-Ariz.). "The Balanced Budget Amendment," Congressional Record (24 Feb 1994). Daily ed. pS1807-1810. (ISSN0363-7239).

"The [U.S.] Federal Government now spends over $200 billion annually just to pay interest on its $4 trillion debt. If current policies continue, the CBO [Congressional Budget Office] estimates that net interest payments will reach $334 billion by the year 2004. To put spending on interest into perspective, this year the Federal Government will spend only $43 billion more on domestic discretionary spending than it will on interest and the debt; $244 billion in discretionary spending to $201 billion in net interest." (pS1831)

Feinstein, Dianne (Sen.-Calif.). "Balanced Budget Amendment," Congressional Record (24 Feb 1994). Daily ed. pS1826-1834. (ISSN0363-7239).

"The gross interest on the debt today exceeds $290 billion [in the U.S.], a figure higher than the entire Federal budget just 20 years ago. To make these figures more understandable: We now spend more than $800 million a day in interest on the debt....Interest payments as a percentage of the budget have doubled just since 1970 from 7 to 14 percent. In addition, nearly 20 percent of our interest payments are sent overseas to foreign investors. In 1993, the treasury sent $41 billion overseas in interest payments. The numbers don't stop there. Do most of my colleagues realize that the Government has spent more than it has taken in for 55 of the last 63 years? Or that we last had a balanced budget in 1969?" (pS2014)

D'Amato, Alfonse (Sen.-N.Y.). "Balanced Budget Amendment," Congressional Record (28 Feb 1994). Daily ed. pS1964-2015. (ISSN0363-7239).

"The most serious threat to Social Security [in the U.S.] is our $4.7 trillion national debt. Net interest on the debt now consumes 16 percent of the Federal budget. If the debt remains unchecked by the year 2015 interest on the debt will devour more than 10 percent of the gross domestic product. This is equal to about 40 percent of anticipated Federal spending. This interest obligation will begin to crowd out Social Security while the continued buildup of debt will impair the ability of future taxpayers to refund moneys borrowed from the trust fund." (pS1963)

DeConcini, Dennis (Sen.-Ariz.). "Balanced Budget Amendment," Congressional Record (28 Feb 1994). Daily ed. pS1959-1963. (ISSN0363-7239).

"By 1982, the national debt had climbed past $1 trillion. It passed $2 trillion in 1986; $3 trillion in 1990; $4 trillion in 1992. Today, the nation's IOUs total $4.7 trillion, or $18,000 for every man, woman, and child in America. It could reach $6.3 trillion by 1999, the White House estimates." (p6)

Dillin, John. "National: Balanced Budget Showdown." The Christian Science Monitor v86 n65, 28 Feb 1994. p6. (ISSN0882-7729).

DEBTS, PUBLIC--UGANDA

"Government of Uganda figures show the stock of debt moving from $2.6 bn in June 1993 to $3.2 bn by June 1996, mainly due to rising arrears. This is despite a $280 mn--48 per cent--reduction in arrears in 1992/93. Annual debt payments are expected to be some 47-49 per cent of what are high projections for export earnings. If export growth is more modest, the debt burden will remain as heavy as it is now. 'The next two-three years look very bleak,' comments a senior official." (p3,26)

Laishley, Roy. "Creditors Consider Improved Debt Relief." Africa Recovery v7 n2, Oct 1993. p3,26.

DEER--MICHIGAN--ACCIDENTS (v19)

DEFENSE INDUSTRIES (v19)

see also MILITARY WEAPONS; WEAPONS INDUSTRY

DEFENSE INDUSTRIES--BELARUS

"Belarus's military-industrial complex represents 55 percent of the government's budget and employs approximately 250,000 people; 40,000-60,000 workers may lose their jobs as these industries are converted to non-defense production. After the former Soviet Union and Belarus ended their cooperative arms production ventures, the volume of orders for Belarus's defense industries plummeted. In 1992-1993, the government did not purchase technology or weapons, and the possibility of exporting weapons components went down to zero. Although Belarus's own military equipment is becoming obsolete, the republic cannot afford to pay world prices for armaments or military technology." (p37)

Tiurina, Tatiana. "Belarus: Neutrality, Maybe." Bulletin of the Atomic Scientists v50 n1, Jan-Feb 1994. p36-40. (ISSN0096-3402).

DEFENSE INDUSTRIES--CALIFORNIA (v19)

DEFENSE INDUSTRIES--CHINA

China's "defense sector portrays itself as successfully converting to civilian products. China claims 70 percent of military enterprises have converted, although Western analysts estimate the figure to be closer to 40 percent. According to government figures, the more than 1,000 large- and medium-sized defense enterprises have increased civilian output by 20 percent annually since being ordered to convert 15 years ago. Civilian products such as motorcycles, sewing machines, cameras, televisions, and refrigerators are said to account for 65 percent of defense-sector production....Although defense production once accounted for 10 percent of China's gross national output, two-thirds of the defense industry is either barely getting by or hampered by heavy debt, Western and Chinese analysts say. The fading cold war and a rapidly changing economy have left China with hundreds of useless factories and too many defense workers." (p4)

Tefft, Sheila. "A Closer Look: China's Military Grapples with Conversion." The Christian Science Monitor v86 n51, 7 Feb 1994. p4. (ISSN0882-7729).

DEFENSE INDUSTRIES--EMPLOYMENT--U.S.

"Before defense downsizing started, there were about six million people involved either directly or indirectly in defense employment. Various studies conclude that close to 1.5 million of those jobs, 25% of all defense jobs, will disappear by 1996. Significantly, almost 50% of those let go will be professionals who are among the most highly-skilled and highly-educated people in the U.S. From trained technicians and administrators, to engineers and nontechnical professionals, to managers and executives, they have skills that can help solve today's problems, from transportation infrastructure to the environment....The good news is that there are jobs opening up for defense people; companies that can most use the skills of defense people are hiring. Small to mid-sized technology companies project hiring close to 5 percent additional employees next year. These companies can lead a coming recovery and are key to rebuilding our nation's research and development capability." (p4)

Souveroff, V. W. "Focus: Defense Professionals: A Valuable Asset Slipping Away?" Positive Alternatives v3 n2, Win 1993. p4-5. (ISSN1065-0075).

A congresional study, "released by Rep. John Conyers (D-MI), Chairman of the House Government Operations Committee, counters arguments by defense contractors and their advocates that economic conversion means a net loss of jobs. The report shows that shifting $3 billion from defense to state and local governments would create about 23,600 new jobs in certain economic sectors and eliminate 11,500 in others, for a net gain of about 12,000 jobs. This is due to the fact that the defense economy is less labor-intensive, and relies more on imports, than work done by state and local governments. Increased in magnitude, $30 billion in converted federal funds would provide 121,000 more jobs than are now generated by defense spending." (p3)

"Congressional Study: Peace Pays." Positive Alternatives v3 n3, Spr 1993. p3. (ISSN1065-0075).

DEFENSE INDUSTRIES--SLOVAKIA

"In the 1950s and '60s, the Slovakia region was rapidly industrialized to meet military needs of the Warsaw Pact and emerged as one of the world's most important arms producers. In the 1980s, Czechoslovakia was the world's 10th-largest arms exporter. Two-thirds of Czechoslovakia's military production came from Slovakia's factories, which supplied tanks, armored cars, howitzers, heavy artillery, and ammunition to Warsaw Pact armies. When Czechoslovakia's Velvet Revolution overthrew the communist regime in 1988, military production represented nearly 60 percent of total industrial production in Slovakia. The sector provided employment to more than 100,000 people in Slovakia, whose population totals only 5 million. It also generated more than one-seventh of Slovakia's exports, according to Peter Stanck of the Institute of Economy in Bratislava, the capital of Slovakia. 'You can imagine the problems that followed when (then Czechoslovak President Vaclav) Havel decided to cease all military production in the country overnight'...[Milos] Lelovsky [head of the Economic Ministry's policy department] says. The result was 40,000 jobs lost in 1988-92. Unemployment has reached nearly 25 percent in Martin, Dubnica, and other areas with major military employers." (p10)

Woodard, Colin. "To Keep Jobs, Slovakia Revives Arms Production." The Christian Science Monitor v86 n69, 4 Mar 1994. p10. (ISSN0882-7729).

DEFENSE INDUSTRIES--SOUTHERN STATES

In the U.S. "Except for the Far West, the South, more than any other region, has built its economy on the military dollar. In 1968, one in 14 breadwinners in the South was directly on the Pentagon's payroll or on the payroll of a private supplier of military goods and services. That compares with one in 20 for the rest of the nation. Regionally, it means if you counted all the South's gigantic textile, apparel, and synthetics industries, you'd still have to add 200,000 workers to reach the number of people in defense-related jobs. That's a lot of people--over 1,600,000--and figuring in their families and the people who live by servicing them, that is even more votes for continued military spending." (p7)

Hall, Bob/Hughes, Chip. "War and Peace: Southern Militarism." Southern Exposure v21 n1-2, Spr-Sum 1993. p7-8. (ISSN0146-809X).

DEFENSE INDUSTRIES--U.S. (v19)

"As for [U.S.] military bases, some 100 around the country are in various stages of the conversion planning process, with another round of closings expected in 1995. In its survey of 97 bases that have already been shut down and completely converted since 1961, the office of Economic Adjustment (the Defense Department agency charged with assisting base closure) found that 171,000 new jobs have more than replaced the 87,557 Defense Department civilian jobs the bases used to provide....Many individual defense firms are also working to convert significant portions of their business to civilian activities....A May 1991 study by the Winbridge Group found that more than three-quarters of the senior executives at 148 defense firms were planning commercialization over the next five years. According to a 1992 report from the CEC [Center for Economic Conversion], 77 defense dependent firms were described in newspaper accounts to be already actively engaged in converting or planning to convert defense technology, materials, or products into civilian business opportunities. And in 1993, when the Clinton administration made about $456 million available through the Technology Reinvestment Program to firms planning 'dual use' products and technologies, it received nearly 3,000 proposals." (p11-12)

Strong, Susan C. "The Business of Peace." Boston Review v19 n2, Apr-May 1994. p11-13. (ISSN0734-2306).

"The [defense] industry may cut 100,000 more jobs on top of 600,000 so far....Washington will cut arms outlays 11% this year, to $62 billion--39% below the 1987 peak of $101 billion. In 1993, industry cost-cutters raced ahead of the Pentagon, slashing jobs--especially in managerial and engineering ranks--faster than revenues tailed off. As productivity soared, the companies reaped the rewards....Starting in 1990, [McDonnell Douglas Corp.]...pared 40% of its work force. Combined with aggressive debt reduction, that helped operating profits soar last year, from $346 million to an estimated $940 million, and the company's stock price more than doubled. Overall, net profit margins for 22 major aerospace companies rose 17% in 1993, to $7.2 billion, estimates analyst Howard Rubel of Goldman, Sachs & Co....Unlike in other downturns, arms makers can't count on much relief from foreign military sales or commercial aerospace. As domestic sales plummet, exports are becoming a larger piece of total defense business. Even so aerospace exports fell 15% in 1993, to $6.9 billion, and should stay flat in 1994, according to the Aerospace Industries Assn." (p72)

Schine, Eric. "Manufacturing: Defense: Cuts Won't Cut It Anymore." Business Week n3353, 10 Jan 1994. p72. (ISSN0007-7135).

A survey conducted by the Economic Roundtable of Los Angeles of 60 top aerospace firms and smaller subcontractors in southern California "examines how such firms are adapting to defense cutbacks and conversion. One conclusion: The five-county area with America's largest concentration of aerospace firms has grown more reliant on military spending since the cold war ended more than two years ago. Because of recession, a drop in passenger aircraft orders, and military contractors' reluctance to convert to commercial work, the region's dependence on defense spending increased from 59 percent in 1991 to 65 percent in 1993, the survey found....The 60 firms lost a total of 150,000 jobs between 1988 and 1993, as national defense spending dropped from $140 billion in 1987 to about $105 billion in 1993, according to the roundtable. That includes a drop from $12 billion to $6 billion in Los Angeles county alone." (p8)

Wood, Daniel B. "Economy: Defense Firms Are Learning 'Real World.'" The Christian Science Monitor v86 n59, 17 Feb 1994. p8. (ISSN0882-7729).

DEFICITS, BUDGET

see BUDGET DEFICITS

DEFORESTATION (v19)

DEFORESTATION--AFRICA

"The demand for land is critical in developing countries. Estimates show that over the last 50 years, 650,000 square kilometers of once productive land in the extreme southern part of Sahara have been transformed into a desert. Today, more than one-third of Africa is threatened by desertification. Scientists estimate that climate changes due to deforestation occur after 250,000 square kilometers of land have been cleared of trees. Yet in Africa, the total area of land already cleared of trees exceeds that number by far." (p5)

Khisa, Joseph W. "Population Threatens Environment." Community Service Newsletter v41 n5, Sep-Oct 1993. p4-5.

DEFORESTATION--BRAZIL

"Brazil was the world's eighth-leading pulp exporter in 1992, with more than five million tons. According to Greenpeace, an estimated 885,000 hectares (2.19 million acres) have been planted with eucalyptus; 169,300 hectares (418,170 acres) of which are in Bahia. The group estimates that 40 percent of Brazilian pulp is produced for export, principally to Europe (38 percent), North America (30 percent) and Japan (15 percent). SOS Mata Atlantica director Joao Paulo Capobianco called Veracruz's destruction of Atlantic Forest 'the worst devastation ever seen.' Preliminary results of an SOS satellite-data study show that 92,300 hectares (227,240 acres) of Atlantic Forest were destroyed in Bahia between 1985 and 1990--an area larger than that lost in the states of Rio de Janeiro and Sao Paulo combined. 'What is happening in southern Bahia is ecocide,' Capobianco said. 'It has one of the highest rates of deforestation on the Atlantic coast.'" (p17)

Lowe, Justin. "A Paradise Pulped for Profit." Earth Island Journal v8 n4, Fall 1993. p17. (ISSN1041-0406).

"The Mata Atlantica, or Atlantic Forest, once stretched along 2500 miles of coast--from northeastern Brazil to northern Argentina--covering more than one million square kilometers (400,000 square miles), or 12 percent of Brazil. Today, only an estimated two-to-eight percent of that forest is left. The remainder has been cut for timber, cattle pasture and to make way for the settlement of 70 percent of the Brazilian population in coastal regions." (p17)

Lowe, Justin. "A Paradise Pulped for Profit." Earth Island Journal v8 n4, Fall 1993. p17. (ISSN1041-0406).

DEFORESTATION--BRITISH COLUMBIA

"British Columbia (BC), the western most province in Canada, contains 50% of North America's remaining temperate rainforest, and contains more wildlife species than any other province in Canada. BC has been dubbed 'Brazil of the North' by international media, and with good reason. The rate of logging in BC has increased traumatically: the volume of wood cut in 1990 was 3 times the volume cut in 1960. According to the Federal Government of Canada: 'The annual area logged is approximately 1000 sq.mi/year in B.C....At this rate, in 16 years all the commercial coastal old-growth will be gone, except the minuscule amount that is protected in parks.' And as of 1990, the number of jobs per volume cut in BC had fallen to half of what it was in 1960." (p19)

"Stop Destroying Native Lands." Earth First! v13 n7, 1 Aug 1993. p19.

DEFORESTATION--CENTRAL AMERICA--SOUTH AMERICA--U.S.

"Some 42 million acres of tropical forests are lost each year (an area about the size of Washington State). More than half of all temperate rain forests (the kind found along the Pacific coast of North America) are gone. The United States is losing some quarter-million acres of wetlands a year. (Ninety-five percent of California's Central Valley wetlands along the Pacific flyway have disappeared over the past century.)" (p10)

Knickerbocker, Brad. "Habitat: Stopping the Flight to Extinction." The Christian Science Monitor v86 n57, 15 Feb 1994. p10-11. (ISSN0882-7729).

DEFORESTATION--ENGLAND

"Less than 1% of England's land is ancient woodland; land that is constantly under threat. 'Ancient, semi-natural woodland' is the nearest we have in England to virgin forest. It is land that has never been clearcut, however it has been grazed by cows and sheep. Few woods are more than 100 acres, and of that most are small isolated pockets. England is the second most deforested part of Europe, with only some 5% forest and woodland cover remaining. So, as small as it seems, any land must be defended as a vital biological bank--an ecosystem, not to mention being the nearest we have left to 'wilderness.'" (p6)

"British Road Wars." Earth First! v14 n4, 20 Mar 1994. p6.

DEFORESTATION--GREAT BRITAIN

"The UK is one of the most deforested parts of Europe, with only an estimated five percent of its forest and woodland cover remaining. According to ENGLISH NATURE, less than one percent of the nation's land is ancient woodland and this is constantly under threat. Nearly all woods in the UK are small, isolated and surrounded by cleared agricultural land or urban development. Few woods are more than 100 acres; most are 10 acres or less. An area of 1000 acres is considered extremely large." (p25)

"Defending the Commons: Road Resisters Declare: 'Long Live Wanstonia!'" Earth Island Journal v9 n2, Spr 1994. p25. (ISSN1041-0406).

DEFORESTATION--GUATEMALA

"Every day, trucks loaded with mahogany make their way across the Guatemalan border towards Mexico. They take with them small pieces of the Peten forest, formerly the heart of the Mayan empire. Satellite photographs show that over one-third of this tropical forest has disappeared in the last two decades. At this rate, only 11% of the Peten will remain by 1998, said Antonio Saravia, director of the governmental National Council on Protected Areas (Conap)." (p27)

"Latin American Focus: Guatemala: Logging Destroys Mayan Tropical Forest." Barricada Internacional v13 n366, Oct 1993. p27. (ISSN1013-9567).

DEFORESTATION--MADAGASCAR

"At the local level, links between growing population densities and land degradation are becoming clearer in some cases. Take the case of Madagascar. Madagascar's forests have been reduced to a narrowing strip along the eastern escarpment. Of the original forest cover of 27.6 million acres, only 18.8 million acres remained in 1950. Today this has been halved to 9.4 million acres--which means that habitat for the island's unique wildlife has been halved in just forty years. Every year some 3 percent of the remaining forest is cleared, almost all of that to provide land for populations expanding at 3.2 percent a year." (p16)

Harrison, Paul. "Sex and the Single Planet." Amicus Journal v15 n45, Win 1994. p16-18,21-23,26. (ISSN0276-7201).

DEFORESTATION--MALAYSIA

"Malaysia is the world's biggest exporter of tropical timber, and it accounts for more than 10 percent of the country's export earnings. According to the World Bank, trees are being felled on the Malaysian island of Borneo at four times the sustainable rate. Indonesia is also being accused of over-cutting. Malaysian officials respond that 58 percent of the country's land is under tree cover and that their goal is to maintain a 50 percent cover indefinitely. Many Malaysians are also angry that the West is getting involved in what they regard as an internal matter." (p20)

Hanson, Eric. "Asia: With Wealth Comes Filth." Toward Freedom v43 n1, Feb 1994. p17,20. (ISSN0048-9898).

DEFORESTATION--U.S.

"On the west side of the Cascade Mountains, where more than 80 inches of rainfall a year creates huge trees, the northern spotted owl has provoked a national debate over the surviving ancient forests. To the east, in the rain shadow of the Cascades, only 20 inches of precipitation falls each year. Nevertheless, these forests too are in an ecological crisis and could soon be at the center of yet another national controversy. Dying trees mark the forests in eastern Oregon and Washington, and scientists call the 14 million acres of east side forests an ecosystem unraveling. The Forest Service estimates 6 million of those acres suffer from nearly a decade of drought and bug infestation as well as historic over-cutting and fire suppression. The result is a huge buildup of dry wood that could fuel catastrophic wildfires. Bruce Dunn, a forester for R.Y. Timber Inc., in Joseph, Ore., told the OREGONIAN the buildup of fuels could create a fire 'that makes Yellowstone look like a marshmallow roast.' Fires burned 45 percent of Yellowstone National Park in 1988 (HCN, 8/15/88)." (p10)

Peterson, Greg. "Another Chunk of Northwest Forest Prepares to Blow Up." High Country News v25 n13, 26 Jul 1993. p10. (ISSN0191-5657).

DEGREES, ACADEMIC--U.S.

"American universities conferred 35,996 undergraduate degrees in sociology in 1973--a high--compared with 14,393 in 1991, notes [Irving Louis] Horowitz....Is sociology really as bad off as its critics claim? Probably not. More than 2,000 sociology departments continue to carry on across the country, for better or worse." (p16-17)

Goode, Stephen. "Lamenting the Left's Lock on Sociology." Insight v10 n7, 14 Feb 1994. p14-17. (ISSN1051-4880).

DENMARK

see also CYCLING--DENMARK--JAPAN--NETHERLANDS; ENERGY CONSERVATION--DENMARK--NETHERLANDS; FIREARMS--DENMARK

DENMARK--ECONOMIC CONDITIONS (v19)

DENMARK--POLITICS AND GOVERNMENT

"After two referenda about the Maastricht Treaty, the political scene in Denmark is about to go back to normal. Or as normal as it can get after almost all our professional politicians cheated the voters into accepting the European Union created by the Maastricht Treaty. Will the next Danish general election be affected by the fact that in 1992 50% of Danish voters and, in 1993, 43% rejected their elected politicians' recommendations to vote yes to the European Union? The political system in Denmark is different from the British. We are a much smaller country, with five million inhabitants, and the voting system is based on a form of proportional representation. At present we have eight political parties in the Danish parliament, the Folketing. A party achieves parliamentary representation with 2% of the national vote....To be able to stand for parliament nationwide, a new party has to collect approximately 18,500 signatures; this represents 1/175th part of all votes cast at the last general election. Parties already represented in the Folketing do not need to collect any signatures to stand again." (p10)

Nielsen, Henrik Overgaard. "Danish Politics after Maastricht." Freedom Today v18 n6, Dec 1993. p10.

DENTAL CARE

A "technique...has been developed...called Atraumatic Restorative Treatment (ART), and is based on cleaning the hole in the tooth by removing soft tooth material using a small hand instrument and, after cleaning is completed, filling the cavity with glass-ionomer cement. This filling material sticks to the tooth surfaces and makes the tooth stronger than can be done by any other type of filling material. Cotton pellets are used to clean the cavities in teeth, and cotton rolls to control the saliva and keep the teeth dry during treatment. If the patient complains of pain during cleaning, a local anaesthetic can be administered. A head lamp powered by a small portable battery provides lighting. Researchers from the Netherlands, Thailand, and Zimbabwe are carrying out a three-year field trial on the cost-effectiveness of the ART technique in a village community in Thailand....After one month, only two children remembered having had pain after treatment, whereas 97% of the children and adults were pleased with the treatment they received. Clinically, 86% of the fillings on the chewing surfaces, where the decay was mainly located, were judged successful after two years. In the 13-year-olds and over, the success-rate was higher (91%) than in the 6- to 12-year-olds (83%)." (p17)

Frencken, Jo/Makoni, Fiona. "A Treatment Technique for Tooth Decay in Deprived Communities." World Health n1, Jan-Feb 1994. p15-17. (ISSN0043-8502).

DENTAL CARE--AFRICA

"During the seventh international conference on dental research, held in Harare in December 1992, Dr S. Thrope of the WHO [World Health Organization] Oral Health Programme in Brazzaville stated that more than 90% of tooth decay in Africa goes untreated. If we look at the oral health situation prevailing amongst 15-year-olds in Zimbabwe, we see that they have on average 1.5 decayed teeth. Of all those decayed teeth only 7% have been treated. The untreated teeth are just left to decay further until they hurt and have to be removed. This shows the great discrepancy which exists between the presence of disease (tooth decay) and its possible treatment (fillings)." (p15)

Frencken, Jo/Makoni, Fiona. "A Treatment Technique for Tooth Decay in Deprived Communities." World Health n1, Jan-Feb 1994. p15-17. (ISSN0043-8502).

DENTAL CARE--CHINA

"A massive national campaign called 'Love Your Teeth Day' has been celebrated [in China] on 20 September each year. This campaign started in the municipalities and capitals of provinces and cities, and has gradually spread to the rural areas year by year since 1989." (p13) "The findings from a four-year study of Love Your Teeth Day indicated that the activities which started in 1989 in three municipalities, 26 capitals of provinces and some large cities had by 1992 spread to most cities in the urban sector to about 300 counties in the rural sector. Some 14 000 oral health personnel and health workers participated as providers of information in 1989, but this total increased to 40 000 in 1992. As a result, oral health knowledge--assessed at 37% in 1989--rose to 76.2% in 1992." (p14)

You, Bian Jin. "Love Your Teeth Day." World Health n1, Jan-Feb 1994. p13-14. (ISSN0043-8502).

"The Chinese government recently integrated Health for All firmly within the state plan for social and economic development in the near future....In a population of about 1200 million, of whom nearly 900 million live in the rural areas, this system covers 790 million people or 66% of the total. With the assistance of the WHO Collaborating Centre for Research and Training in Preventive Dentistry in Beijing, a first rural community care model for oral health was developed in 1984 in Yuncheng. Since 1988, when the Ministry of Public Health established the Chinese National Committee for Oral Health (CNCORH), a further three models have been started." (p13) "The results show a remarkable improvement in oral health status....The percentage of people with caries fell from 49.8% (1986) to 38.7% (1990), the average number of decayed, missing and filled teeth dropped from 0.97 to 0.67, and the fillings rate increased from 0.1% to 11.7% at 12 years of age. The percentage of people who regularly brush their teeth increased to 67.4% in 1990 compared with 13.5% in 1984 in Yuncheng, and reached levels of more than 80% in other target areas. Data from Yuncheng also indicated that the percentage of people with healthy gums increased from 1% to 37%, gingivitis dropped from 99% to 63%, and calculus decreased from 85% to 43% at 15 years of age." (p14)

Bian Jin You. "Love Your Teeth Day." World Health n1, Jan-Feb 1994. p13-14. (ISSN0043-8502).

DENTAL CARE--INDIA

"Most people living in rural areas of India cannot afford the money to buy a toothbrush and fluoride toothpaste, which for a family of four would mean an expenditure of 60 rupees (US$ 2) per month. This difficulty came to the fore when a demonstration module for primary prevention of oral diseases in rural India was being prepared, involving 120 000 people who had no access to any professional oral health care. As application of fluoride to the teeth every day in low concentrations has been so effective in preventing dental caries, a cheap and easy-to-use method was devised as an alternative through rinsing with soluble sodium fluroide tablets. These tablets are known by the name of 'fluoriwash'; they contain 10 mg of sodium fluoride (4.4 mg of fluoride), and are available in packets of 30 tablets. One tablet, when dissolved in five teaspoonfuls (25 ml) of cold, clean water in a plastic cup, makes a fluoride solution with a concentration of 0.04% sodium fluoride. The cost of one packet was Rs 1.25 five years ago and Rs 4 (US$ 0.12) today. This pack is sufficient for a family of four (two adults and two children) to do a daily fluoride mouth rinse for a full month; the cost proved to be easily affordable by rural people." (p18-19)

Tewari, Amrit. "A Family Care Programme in India." World Health n1, Jan-Feb 1994. p18-19. (ISSN0043-8502).

DENTAL CARE--MALI

"A study in Mali in 1990 showed that, according to WHO's [World Health Organization's] recommended criteria, 90% of children aged 12 have poor oral hygiene--allowing caries and other oral diseases to develop unchallenged. The scarcity of hospital structures and qualified personnel as well as the high cost of curative treatment means that they have almost no access to the care they need. In view of this situation, a programme was started by International Odontological Aid, a Paris-based agency, in collaboration with the Ministry of Health of Mali....The object of the programme was to teach daily hygiene to children while giving preference to traditional methods, such as using special sticks as toothbrushes....Evaluation of the results shows that in the course of the school year 1992-93 some 3000 schoolchildren aged between seven and twelve have benefited from this preventive action. In addition, about 5000 children who are not yet at school have learnt about oral hygiene from the older ones. An even more telling result is that 1100 children have gone for dental checkups at the Mopti hospital as a consequence of these awareness sessions." (p12)

Abellard, Jacques. "Oral Health in Mali's Schools." World Health n1, Jan-Feb 1994. p12. (ISSN0043-8502).

DENTAL CARIES

"Until 1980 dental caries severely affected most of the population in the developed countries where levels as high as twelve teeth were found to be decayed in children aged between 12 and 15. But since 1980, it has been controlled in most Western countries--e.g., Denmark, Netherlands, Norway, Sweden, United Kingdom and the United States--and also in some others--Australia, Hong Kong, New Zealand, and Singapore--where the distribution of decayed teeth has been brought down to as low as one to two per 12-year-old child. This is mainly due to the appropriate use of fluorides and oral hygiene measures, especially brushing with fluoridated toothpaste. In developing countries such as Bangladesh, India, Nepal, and Sri Lanka, the incidence of dental caries used to be comparatively low, but now has been found to be on the increase....In the rural areas of most of these countries, the dentist to population ratio may be as low as 1:300 000." (p18)

Tewari, Amrit. "A Family Care Programme in India." World Health n1, Jan-Feb 1994. p18-19. (ISSN0043-8502).

DENTAL CARIES--THAILAND

"The WHO [World Health Organization] Global Data Bank shows that dental caries in developing countries has been increasing over the past 20 years. Caries on the pits and fissures of the teeth accounts for up to 90% of all caries cases in these countries. The use of pit and fissure sealants has proved to be a highly effective means of preventing and arresting this type of caries. It can be highly recommended for any Third World community where there is a high prevalence of occlusal caries, with little smooth surface caries, limited access to and use of dental care, and low social and economic status." (p5) "A national oral health survey in Thailand in 1989 indicated that 12-year-old children had an average of 1.5 decayed, extracted and filled teeth, and 77% of these teeth needed restorative care on occlusal pits and fissures. So a project was started to treat primary schoolchildren in Bangkok--a typical example of a city in a developing country experiencing ever greater caries prevalence....The study demonstrated that schoolteachers given...brief training could apply the treatment just as well as the dentist. Although only a small percentage of the sealant remained in position when the children's teeth were checked six months later, a significant reduction in caries was observed after two years, particularly among the younger age group." (p6)

Songpaisan, Yupin. "Teeth Sealing in Thailand." World Health n1, Jan-Feb 1994. p5-6. (ISSN0043-8502).

DEPARTMENT STORES--GREAT BRITAIN

"Department stores were once the kings of the British high street, the retail palaces where the rich and not-so-rich bought everything from socks to stereos to sports gear. But in the 1980s the rise of specialist retailers selling such items as clothes, furniture or electrical appliances, some of them operating from big, out-of-town sites, hit department stores badly. The latters' numbers fell from 652 in 1983 to 525 in 1992, according to Verdict, a retail analyst." (p72)

"Business: British Department Stores: House for Sale." Economist v330 n7853, 5 Mar 1994. p72,77. (ISSN0013-0613).

DEPARTMENT STORES--JAPAN

"Because of the high costs they incur, profit margins at Japan's department stores are only about 24%, roughly half those of department stores in the US. This low-profit structure also means a high break-even point--over 90% in most cases. In 1993, this profit structure virtually collapsed. The ratio of operating profits to sales plunged to 0.7%; current profits to sales, 0.8%. In other words, department stores made virtually no money at all last year." (p14-15)

Azukizawa, Yukiteru. "Strategic Restructuring: Department Stores: Shop Lifting." Look Japan v39 n456, Mar 1994. p14-15. (ISSN0456-5339).

"The general recession has hit department stores [in Japan] hard, as not only individual consumers but also corporate customers scaled down their purchases. Year-on-year sales (sales per month compared to the same month a year earlier) had declined for the 19th straight month to Y615 billion ($5.8 billion) in September 1993, according to the Japan Department Stores Association. Sales in Japan's six largest cities (Tokyo, Osaka, Yokohama, Kyoto, Kobe, Nagoya) dropped by 8.4% from the previous year; sales in other areas fell an average of 4.4%. The total decline in September 1993 from September 1992 was 6.4%." (p42)

Mann, Elisa Akiko/Amemiya, Keiko. "Culture: Department Stores: A World in Themselves." Look Japan v39 n454, Jan 1994. p40-42. (ISSN0456-5339).

DEPLETION OF ATMOSPHERIC OZONE

see ATMOSPHERIC OZONE--REDUCTION

DEPOSIT INSURANCE--U.S.

"Deposit insurance contributed little to the [U.S. federal government] spending totals before the late 1980s, as premiums paid by financial institutions and other income to the deposit insurance funds (such as interest and proceeds from liquidations of assets) roughly equaled the costs of covering failed institutions. This pattern held fairly true even in the early 1980s, when savings and loan institutions--then hamstrung by restrictions on their investments and on the interest they could pay to depositors--faced big losses. But choices made in the wake of that first crisis to relax regulation and to postpone shutdowns of troubled institutions proved to be costly. Deposit insurance outlays shot up to a record $66 billion in 1991....They skidded to $3 billion in 1992, and the agencies actually recorded negative outlays (that is, net receipts) of $28 billion in 1993, indicating that their income from liquidations and other sources far exceeded their disbursements." (p43)

U.S. Congressional Budget Office. "The Budget Outlook." The Economic and Budget Outlook: Fiscal Years 1995-1999 Jan 1994. Washington, D.C.: GPO, 1994.

DESERTS--AFRICA (v19)

DETROIT (MICH)

see also FISH AS FOOD--CONTAMINATION--DETROIT (MICH)--PUBLIC OPINION

DETROIT (MICH)--ECONOMIC CONDITIONS (v19)

DETROIT (MICH)--EMPLOYMENT

"From 1970 to 1980, the percentage of jobs occupied by those who had less than a high school degree dropped from 37.3% to 21.2% in Detroit. Meanwhile, the combined percentage of jobs occupied by those who had had at least some higher education and those who had graduated from college increased from 25.9% in 1970 to 46.1% in 1980. Though not completely conclusive, these data suggest that employment gains were greater in those jobs that required some advanced training and education. In sum, the local economy of Detroit has transformed dramatically. Jobs that require high skills and advanced training and education are rising just as the dropout rates are increasing and achievement test scores are falling. Thus, the future for thousands of Detroiters is bleak and distressing. For employers in Detroit's burgeoning service industries, the 'mismatch' between their laborforce needs and the labor force the local population is making available could bring about a labor shortage. For leaders in Detroit, the structural transformation has meant putting in place policies to deal with the dilemma. Detroit's leaders have turned to the idea of a school compact in an effort to enhance their city's human capital." (p107-108)

Orr, Marion. "Urban Regimes and School Compacts: The Development of the Detroit Compact." Urban Review v25 n2, Jun 1993. p105-122. (ISSN0042-0972).

DETROIT (MICH)--POPULATION (v19)

DEVELOPING COUNTRIES

see also CHILDBIRTH--DEVELOPING COUNTRIES; CONTRACEPTION--DEVELOPING COUNTRIES; DIARRHEA IN CHILDREN--DEVELOPING COUNTRIES--MORTALITY; ECONOMIC ASSISTANCE, AMERICAN--DEVELOPING COUNTRIES--CHILDREN; ELECTRIC POWER PRODUCTION--DEVELOPING COUNTRIES; ENERGY CONSUMPTION--DEVELOPING COUNTRIES; HUNGER--DEVELOPING COUNTRIES; LOANS--DEVELOPING COUNTRIES; PESTICIDES--DEVELOPING COUNTRIES; SCHISTOSOMA--DEVELOPING COUNTRIES; TECHNOLOGY--DEVELOPING COUNTRIES; WATER-SUPPLY--DEVELOPING COUNTRIES; WEAPONS INDUSTRY--DEVELOPING COUNTRIES

DEVELOPING COUNTRIES--BRAZIL--THAILAND

"In country after country, gaps between the enclosing rich and the enclosed poor continue to grow, with devastating social and environmental consequences. In Brazil, the site of an early development 'miracle,' nine million households are landless while 82 million acres of farmland lie idle. In Thailand, one of the shining development success stories of the 1970s and 1980s, the share of national income of the wealthiest fifth of the population increased from 49 percent in 1975 to almost 55 percent in 1986, while the share of the poorest 20 percent (which includes thousands of forest colonizers) dropped from 6.1 percent to 4.6 percent." (p35)

"Defending the Commons: The Enclosure of the Commons." Earth Island Journal v9 n2, Spr 1994. p33-35. (ISSN1041-0406).

DEVELOPING COUNTRIES--ECONOMIC CONDITIONS (v19)

DEVELOPING COUNTRIES--ENVIRONMENTAL ASPECTS (v19)

DEVELOPING COUNTRIES--HEALTH AND HYGIENE

"Developing countries made impressive gains...[between 1950 and 1990], with life expectancy rising from 40 to 63 years and under-five mortality falling by almost two-thirds. However, the [World] Bank points out that child deaths are still 10 times, and maternal mortality 30 times higher than in established market economies (EMEs). The disparities are even more striking when the $800 bn annual health spending for 250 million Americans is compared to the $170 bn for 4.1 billion people in developing countries. The Bank uses a new statistical indicator--disability-adjusted life years (DALYs), or that portion of an average, healthy life lost through disability or premature death--to measure the 'global burden of disease' (GBD). Sub-Saharan Africa has the world's highest GBD per 1,000 people, 70 per cent more than in India, twice as high as...in the Middle East and almost five times higher than in EMEs. Communicable diseases account for 71 per cent of Africa's GBD compared to 42 per cent in Latin America and 10 per cent in EMEs." (p14)

Collins, Carole. "Bank Links Health to Economic Growth." Africa Recovery v7 n2, Oct 1993. p14-15.

DEVELOPING COUNTRIES--MANUFACTURES (v19)

DEVELOPING COUNTRIES--POPULATION (v19)

"From 1950 to 1990, population in the developing world grew at historically unprecedented rates, more than doubling to reach 4.1 billion. By 2025, population in the developing world is projected to exceed 7 billion (World Bank, 1993a). Even those skeptical about the destructive power of the population bomb should be convinced that the political, economic, and environmental landscape of the next century will be greatly affected by the speed of the demographic transition in developing countries. Policies that can accelerate (or delay) this transition have been the focus of countless debates since 1798, when Malthus warned that the 'power of population' would someday overwhelm the planet. Since mortality rates have fallen and are continuing to fall rapidly almost worldwide, differences in fertility are the dominant determinant of the evolution of population in the developing world. Since there are large variations in fertility rates across countries (e.g., total fertility rates of 6.5 births per woman in Kenya and 6.3 in Syria versus 3.0 in Indonesia and 2.8 in Argentina), and large changes in fertility over time, it is reasonable to expect social scientists to be able to reach a consensus on the primary determinants of fertility." (p1)

Pritchett, Lant H. "Desired Fertility and the Impact of Population Policies." Population and Development Review v20 n1, Mar 1994. p1-55. (ISSN0098-7921).

DEVELOPING COUNTRIES--SOCIAL CONDITIONS (v19)

DIABETES (v19)

DIABETES--RESEARCH--U.S. (v19)

DIABETES--U.S. (v19)

"Diabetes is the fourth leading cause of death by disease in the United States, taking the lives of more than 160,000 people annually, and it should be noted it affects in greater numbers the elderly, native American, Hispanic, and African-American communities. In sum, it costs nearly $92 billion annually to fight this disease. One way the impact of diabetes-related compliations can be diminished is through the stabilization of blood glucose levels, and in order to accomplish this stabilization and prevent complications, people with insulin-treated diabetes require four or more injections of insulin every day as well as frequent testing of blood-sugar levels." (pH2577)

Furse, Elizabeth (Rep.-Oreg.). "Welfare Reform in Relation to Immigrants," Congressional Record (20 Apr 1994). Daily ed. pH2577-2580. (ISSN0363-7239).

DIAMOND INDUSTRY AND TRADE--AUSTRALIA

"Australia produces 40 percent of the world's diamonds, most of them industrial cutting diamonds. A high proportion come from Argyle Diamonds, the largest diamond mine in the world, in terms of carats. Argyle, owned by CRA Ltd., had a record production year in 1993 of 41 million carats....Diamond production...[in Australia] is forecast to reach a record 43 million carats in 1993-94. Export earnings from diamonds are forecast to increase 20 percent in 1993-94, to around $600 million (Australian; US$426 million), according to the Australian Bureau of Agriculture Resource Economics." (p7)

Foster, Catherine. "Australian Diamonds Lead Market Uptick." The Christian Science Monitor v86 n48, 2 Feb 1994. p7. (ISSN0882-7729).

DIAPER INDUSTRY--AUSTRALIA--SWEDEN--U.S. (v19)

DIARRHEA--DEVELOPING COUNTRIES--MORTALITY (v19)

DIARRHEA--TREATMENT--DEVELOPING COUNTRIES (v19)

DIARRHEA IN CHILDREN--DEVELOPING COUNTRIES--MORTALITY

"Every year in the developing world, about 3.2 million children under five years die from conditions related to diarrhoea. Most of these deaths are due to dehydration and malnutrition, and therefore millions of young lives could be saved if only mothers knew how to give their children appropriate home care. The three basic rules of home care for diarrhoea are: 1) to give the child more fluids than usual to prevent dehydration, 2) to give the child plenty of food to prevent undernutrition, and 3) to take the child to a health worker if there is no improvement in three days or if danger signs appear....Unfortunately, surveys of home care practices for diarrhoea conducted by Ministries of Health in collaboration with WHO [World Health Organization] show that few mothers are following the three basic rules. For example, a household survey in 1991 in Pakistan found that only about one in three mothers (29%) said they offered more fluids than usual to their children during a diarrhoeal episode, and only 40% said they continued feeding the child, while 70% reported using drugs to treat their child. In many countries, mothers use oral rehydration salts but do not prepare them correctly and do not give them in sufficient quantities." (p14)

Hirnschall, Gottfried/Hudelson, Patricia. "Diarrhoea--Scourge of Children." World Health n6, Nov-Dec 1993. p14-15. (ISSN0043-8502).

DIESEL FUELS INDUSTRY--RUSSIA (v19)

DIET--JAPAN (v19)

DIET--MORTALITY

"By 1992, more than 100 major reports from 36 countries throughout the world had reviewed the research evidence, and had come to the same conclusions: Six of the 10 leading causes of death are related to diets too high in calories, fat, saturated fat, cholesterol, salt, or alcohol, and too low in fiber." (p15)

U.S. Dept. of Agriculture/Nestle, Marion. "Food & Nutrition: Nutrients & Health: Making the Connection." Agricultural Outlook Jan-Feb 1994. p15-17.

DIET--U.S. (v19)

"Although the proportion of the population [in the U.S.] classified as overweight increased considerably since 1977-78, calorie levels fell slightly for most groups in the same period. The average caloric intake in 1989-90 was 1,763, compared with 1,826 in 1977-78. Men ate more than women--2,119 calories compared with 1,492 calories in 1989-90. But, on average, men also have higher energy requirements than women." (p10)

Tippett, Katherine S./Goldman, Joseph D. "Health Linked to Nutrition: Diets More Healthful, but Still Fall Short of Dietary Guidelines." Food Review v17 n1, Jan-Apr 1994. p8-14.

"Of the 10 leading causes of death in the United States, 4--including the top 3--are associated with dietary excesses: coronary heart disease, some types of cancer, stroke, and noninsulin-dependent diabetes mellitus (also called type II diabetes, or adult-onset diabetes)....Together, these conditions account for nearly two-thirds of the deaths occurring each year in the United States." (p2)

Frazao, Betsy. "Health Linked to Nutrition: The High Costs of Poor Diets." Food Review v17 n1, Jan-Apr 1994. p2-3.

DIETARY SUPPLEMENTS--U.S. (v19)

DIPHTHERIA

"While Eurasia makes up one-third of the European population, it accounted for 95 percent of all registered cases of diphtheria by September 1992. In 1990, Russia experienced the highest incidence rate of diphtheria in the USSR at 0.82 cases per 100,000, the largest outbreak occurring in Moscow. For the same year, Ukraine reported 0.21 cases per 100,000, but in 1991 that ratio increased to 2.1 per 100,000. In Belarus, Tajikistan, Armenia, Georgia and Kazakhstan, the number of diphtheria cases reported per 100,000 was 0.2, 0.22, 0.2, 0.18 and 0.17 respectively. The total number of reported cases of diphtheria in the US in 1990 was four, while the number of reported cases in Moscow alone by mid-1992 reached 438 (including 66 children). This approximates the total number of cases in Moscow during all of 1991." (p60)

Watson, Amanda. "Health: Primary Immunization in Eurasia." Surviving Together v11 n2, Sum 1993. p59-61. (ISSN0859-6286).

DIPHTHERIA--RUSSIA (v19)

"Fears of HIV infection have led to a severe diphtheria epidemic in Russia, which has killed more than a hundred people in the past year. These are the first recorded deaths from diphtheria since 1965 in the former Soviet Union, where the disease had been virtually eradicated. Nearly 6,000 cases have been detected and 129 people have died--77 in Moscow alone--a situation described as 'catastrophic' by many medical specialists." (p4)

Podobed, Sergey. "Science: HIV Fears Fuel Diphtheria." WorldAIDS n31, Jan 1994. p4. (ISSN0954-6510).

DIPHTHERIA--VACCINATION (v19)

DIPLOMATIC AND CONSULAR SERVICE--HISPANIC AMERICANS

"Whereas Hispanic-Americans are America's fastest growing ethnic group and in 1990 made up 9 percent of the American population, they made up only 4.2 percent of Foreign Service Officers in fiscal year 1993. This figure is no improvement over 1992 in percentage terms, and a drop of three officers in absolute terms. It is also only a small increase over the 1985-91 average of 3.8 percent. At the senior executive level, there are only 10 Hispanic men, including 2 ambassadors, and no Hispanic women." (pS349)

Bradley, Bill (Sen.-N.J.). "Foreign Relations Authorization Act," Congressional Record (28 Jan 1994). Daily ed. pS327-354. (ISSN0363-7239).

DIRECT-MAIL ADVERTISING

see ADVERTISING, DIRECT-MAIL

DIRECT MARKETING--U.S. (v19)

DISABLED

see HANDICAPPED

DISARMAMENT--UKRAINE

"Ukrainian leaders continue to insist that they will not honor their commitment to disarm the 176 long-range strategic missiles that are aimed at American soil until they receive security guarantees from the United States, other Western powers and the current Russian government--as well as more than $3 billion in direct aid from the United States for the dismantling of the weapons. (In December, Ukraine agreed to deactivate 17 of its SS-24 missiles in an effort to get Russia to cancel its $750 billion energy debt.)" (p34)

Goldstein, Edward. "Fair Comment: Time May Be Ukraine's First Enemy." Insight v10 n5, 31 Jan 1994. p34. (ISSN1051-4880).

DISASTER RELIEF--U.S.

see also FOOD RELIEF--U.S.

"Since 1988, the Congress has enacted six major disaster relief supplementals providing for 17 plus billion dollars for Federal disaster assistance. Today we are recommending $10 billion to be added to the deficit....we appropriated almost $1 billion in 1980 for the Mount St. Helen's disaster. So here we are in this kind of a circumstance not able to predict natural disasters and yet under obligation to respond to natural disasters. But we have to find a better funding mechanism and policy to carry out that responsibility." (pS1180)

Hatfield, Mark O. (Sen.-Oreg.). "Emergency Supplemental Appropriations Act for Fiscal Year 1994," Congressional Record (9 Feb 1994). Daily ed. pS1169-1186. (ISSN0363-7239).

"Since 1989, Congress has spent some $17 billion in emergency relief. In 1993, there was $5.1 billion for the Midwest flood; in 1992, $5.4 billion for Hurricane Andrew. Then we had other disasters...at that time. In 1991, we had $943 million for Hurricane Bob; 1990, $2.6 billion for another California earthquake; 1989, $2.8 billion for Hurricane Hugo. Emergency spending adds to the deficit. It simply has to because it is not budgeted, and there is no identifiable way to pay for it other than a supplemental. We know that the House has just passed an $8.6 billion relief bill. It is my understanding that they have only paid for $2.6 billion." (pS1237)

Murkowski, Frank H. (Sen.-Alaska). "Unanimous Consent Agreement," Congressional Record (9 Feb 1994). Daily ed. pS1229-1251. (ISSN0363-7239).

DISASTERS (v19)

see also EARTHQUAKES; FIRES

"The United Nations and the International Red Cross report that the annual number of disasters--events whose losses overwhelmed the restorative capacity of the affected area, requiring assistance from outside the region or from foreign countries--increased from three at the beginning of the century to about 20 today. Skyrocketing losses are a relatively new phenomenon. From 1966-87 no losses from catastrophes topped $1 billion. From 1987-1992, there were 15 catastrophes whose insured losses exceeded $1 billion, 10 of them windstorms, accounting for 86 percent of the $53 billion losses. The insured loss from the 1960s to the 1980s increased 4.8 times." (p4)

Wilson, Nancy C. "Surge of Hurricanes and Floods Perturb Insurance Industry." Climate Alert v6 n4, Jul-Aug 1993. p1,4-7.

"The burden of climate and weather-related catastrophes does not fall equally on both industrialized and developing countries." According to Irving Mintzer in his book CONFRONTING CLIMATE CHANGE, "'During a recent 20-year period, natural disaster resulted in 2.8 million deaths and adversely affected over 820 million people....Costs...were not evenly distributed or equally important to the affected economies.' Winds of 140 mph in Hurricane Andrew resulted in the loss of 20 lives; in the cyclone in Bangladesh one year earlier, winds of the same strength resulted in the death of 138,000 people. Hong Kong lost 10,000 people, many of them living in boats, in typhoons in 1906 and 1937. The population has now grown, living standards are higher and many fewer people live in boats. The risk of loss of life from future typhoons has been reduced, but of property damage has greatly increased. While 1989 losses of $7.6 billion (more than half from Hurricane Hugo) represented less than 0.1 percent of U.S. GNP [gross national product], 1982-83 losses in Bolivia, Ecuador and Peru from El Nino were nearly 100 times as large, almost 10 percent of GNP, costing the three Latin American countries the equivalent of nearly half their annual tax revenues for those years." (p7)

Wilson, Nancy C. "Surge of Hurricanes and Floods Perturb Insurance Industry." Climate Alert v6 n4, Jul-Aug 1993. p1,4-7.

DISCOUNT HOUSES (RETAIL TRADE)--U.S. (v19)

DISCRIMINATION IN EDUCATION--U.S.

Research on gender bias in the classroom conducted by Myra and David Sadker and others demonstrates that gender bias begins at an early age. "Calling out in class, for example, is an 'open invitation for male dominance,' the Sadkers write. Their research shows that boys call out eight times more often than girls do. In more than 100 classrooms the Sadkers studied, they found boys received more of four reactions from teachers: praise, correction, help, criticism--'all reactions that foster student achievement,' they write. 'Girls received the more superficial "O.K." reaction,' the Sadkers continue, 'the one that packs far less educational punch.' Male dominance continues on the playground, the Sadkers note. In a 'typical' schoolyard, they write, the area where boys play is 10 times larger than the play area for girls. 'Girls huddle along the sidelines, on the fringe....Recess becomes a spectator sport.'...In 1989 elementary school textbooks in mathematics, language arts, and history, the Sadkers discovered that mentions of boys outnumbered those of girls two to one or three to one. In one 631-page textbook covering the history of the world, only seven pages related to women." (p25)

Lawton, Millicent. "Girls Will--and Should--Be Girls." Education Week v13 n27, 30 Mar 1994. p24-27. (ISSN0277-4232).

DISCRIMINATION IN EMPLOYMENT--JAPAN

"Until about ten years ago, women were seldom treated as an important part of the male-dominated Japanese work force. Typically their work was confined to serving tea and making photocopies, and even women university graduates were rarely hired for work other than 'ippanshoku' (ordinary work). For all women in the work force, there was little hope of promotion. Since the enactment of the Equal Employment Opportunity Law in 1986, however, the situation has been improving. An increasing number of companies are hiring women for the same jobs, at the same pay, and under the same conditions as men. Many women are now classed as 'sogoshoku' (comprehensive work) employees, and more can realistically aspire to climb the corporate ladder and become managers. In its 1993 White Paper on Women Labor, the Ministry of Labor reports that 19.74 million women were hired in 1992, up 2.9% from 1991. The percentage of women in the work force has also been rising annually, from 36.8% in 1989 to 38.6% in 1993." (p37)

Sasaki, Yukie. "Facts of Life: Women in the Work Force: Still Searching for Status." Look Japan v40 n457, Apr 1994. p37. (ISSN0456-5339).

DISCRIMINATION IN EMPLOYMENT--U.S. (v19)

"There is considerable evidence to show that [U.S.] Federal employees who have filed complaints are not receiving their due process....many agencies put little effort into their investigations, move so slowly that the complaints become moot, and even if discrimination is found, rarely impose meaningful sanctions. Between 1988 and 1990, for instance, 1,682 cases yielded findings of discrimination, yet discipline was recommended in only seven, and on only two occasions was the punishment more severe than sensitivity training." (p51)

Akaka, Daniel K. (Sen.-Hawaii). U.S. Senate. Committee on Governmental Affairs. "The Federal Employee Fairness Act--S. 404." Hearing, 26 May 1993. Washington, D.C.: GPO, 1994. (ISBN016044019X). (Y4.G74/9:S.hrg.103-471).

"The Americans with Disabilities Act (ADA) opened the door for disabled workers to enter the workforce, but that door remains inadvertently blocked in companies that don't know how to make reasonable accommodations, a key provision of the law. The ADA specifies that employers are obliged to reasonably accommodate the 'known physical or mental limitations of an otherwise qualified applicant or employee with a disability' unless the company suffers undue hardship. Most accommodations are quite easy to make and are inexpensive, says D.J. Hendricks, assistant project manager at the Job Accommodation Network (JAN). JAN is a free and confidential call-in consulting service established by the President's Committee on Employment of People with Disabilities. 'Many...accommodations are made for less than $500, and the average cost is around $1,000,' Hendricks says. A survey her organization conducted backs up this claim: Nineteen percent of the survey respondents incurred no cost to make accommodations; 50 percent stated a cost between $1 and $500; and 84 percent said that accommodations cost less than $1,500." (p1)

Segall, Linda. "Unblocking Doors for the Disabled." Foremanship 31 Jan 1994. p1.

DISCRIMINATION IN EMPLOYMENT--U.S.--IMMIGRANTS (v19)

DISCRIMINATION IN HOUSING--U.S.

A comparison of census data from 1980 and 1990 shows that housing patterns in U.S. cities have slowly become more racially integrated. According to a study by the University of Michigan's population-studies center, out of 232 large cities compared, 194 had declining proportions of whites and blacks living apart, continuing a trend that began in the 1970's. "The least segregated areas tend to be in the South, which has countywide governments that serve to limit the development of racially isolated suburbs, and the West, where the presence of other minority groups appears to have buffered blacks from white intolerance, the researchers say....'Where there is a history of racial antagonism, a ring of white suburbs surrounding a black central city, and little new housing construction, segregation is likely to persist, despite more liberal white attitudes and government policies,' the researchers say." (p4)

"News Roundup: National: Housing Segregation Declining in U.S. Cities, Study Shows." Education Week v13 n23, 2 Mar 1994. p4. (ISSN0277-4232).

DISCRIMINATION IN MORTGAGE LOANS--U.S.

"As appalling as it was, the latest annual report on mortgage lending shocked few observers when the Clinton Administration's top regulators unveiled it before the Senate Banking Committee in early November. In keeping with past patterns, black mortgage applicants were turned down more than twice as often as whites in 1992. Indeed, the most closely watched single number indicated that things were getting worse rather than better: The ratio of the black denial rate to the white denial rate rose from 2.16 in 1991 to 2.26 in 1992. What was different this year was the response to the statistics. Instead of denying the obvious as they have in the past, government officials acknowledged that discrimination is 'alive and well in America,' as Housing Secretary Henry Cisneros put it." (p16)

Campen, Jim. "Lending Insights: Hard Proof That Banks Discriminate." Dollars and Sense n191, Jan-Feb 1994. p16-19,36-37.

"The ATLANTA JOURNAL-CONSTITUTION'S Pulitzer Prize-winning series 'The Color of Money' (May 1988) compared stable, middle-income neighborhoods that were at least 80% white to those that were at least 80% nonwhite. It found that between 1984 and 1986, Atlanta banks and savings & loans (S&Ls) made 4.5 times as many loans per 1,000 single-family structures in white neighborhoods as in comparable black neighborhoods. In city after city, studies documented similarly dramatic racial disparities in mortgage lending. Between 1981 and 1987 in Boston, for instance, banks made 2.9 times as many mortgage loans per 1,000 housing units in low-income white neighborhoods as in minority neighborhoods with similar incomes. In Detroit, the ratio of the mortgage lending rate (loans per 1,000 homes) in middle-income white neighborhoods to that in middle-income black neighborhoods rose every year between 1981 and 1986, reaching 3.14 to 1 in 1986. Similar patterns appeared in Chicago, Los Angeles, Milwaukee, and New York as well as in 14 cities observed by the Center for Community Change. A survey of 23 studies by Professor Anne Shlay of Temple University showed that all 23 found a negative impact of race on conventional mortgage lending." (p17)

Campen, Jim. "Lending Insights: Hard Proof That Banks Discriminate." Dollars and Sense n191, Jan-Feb 1994. p16-19,36-37.

DISCRIMINATION IN SPORTS--U.S.

"Twenty-one years ago, [the U.S.] Congress passed Title IX of the Education Amendments Act to put an end to sex discrimination in education, including sports....We know that our Nation's colleges and universities continue to provide men with more than twice the funding of women in categories ranging from scholarships, recruitment, and operating expenses. Despite the fact that women represent about 50 percent of the enrollment on campuses, participation rates are one-third or less at most schools." (p1)

Collins, Cardiss (Rep.-Ill.). U.S. House. Committee on Energy and Commerce. "Intercollegiate Sports." Hearing, 23 Jun 1993. Washington, D.C.: GPO, 1994. (ISBN0160435307). (Y4.En2/3:103-58).

DISEASES (v19)

DISEASES--FORMER SOVIET REPUBLICS (v19)

DISEASES--MORTALITY (v19)

DIVERSITY, BIOLOGICAL

see BIOLOGICAL DIVERSITY

DIVORCE--U.S. (v19)

DIVORCE--U.S.--MARINE CORPS

"Marriage rates are decreasing among civilians, but Marines are marrying in ever-increasing numbers. In 1980, for example, 33% of all Marines were married. Five years later, that number had increased to 44.4%. Today, some 48.6% of Marines are married. Because the number of Marines marrying between the ages of 17 and 21 is steadily increasing, it is not surprising that the number of divorces also is growing. The United States has the highest divorce rate in the world. That rate peaked in the early 1980s with 22.6 divorces per 1,000 couples. Since then, the annual rate has decreased slightly and has remained fairly constant throughout the 1990s at around 21 per 1,000. While it is difficult to compare civilian and Marine Corps divorce rates directly, it is noteworthy that there were 51 divorces or separations per 1,000 married Marines in 1980. That number increased to 63 divorces or separations per 1,000 in 1992. It is easy to understand why the Marine Corps is concerned about this escalating problem. In 1980, there were 3,477 divorces in a force of 188,474 Marines. By 1992 there were 6,134 divorces in a force of 188,023. Using 1980 figures as a base line, this represents an increase of 2,657 divorces, or 76.8%." (p77-78)

Gomulka, Eugene T. "Balancing Corps & Marriage." Proceedings v119 n12, Dec 1993. p77-80. (ISSN0041-798X).

DIVORCE--U.S.--PSYCHOLOGICAL ASPECTS (v19)

DOCTOR OF PHILOSOPHY DEGREE--U.S.--MINORITIES (v19)

DOG, DALMATIAN

see DALMATIAN DOG

DOG INDUSTRY--CANADA--U.S.

"Last year, Canadian businesses purchased approximately 20,000 dogs, totaling about $4 million, from U.S. distributors. Because of what is perceived as a limited supply of Canadian-bred dogs--breeders in Canada have less pressure to mass-produce because they generally sell directly to owners--and because imported dogs are cheaper than native pups. Canadian pet stores have been a major market for U.S. pet distributors. Although American exporters claim that 96% of the dogs going into Canada are completely healthy, the number of reported incidents of puppies becoming ill immediately after purchase from Canadian pet stores has increased." (p13)

"Shelter Shorts: Canadian Government Reconsiders Trade in U.S. Puppies." Shelter Sense v16 n5, May 1993. p13. (ISSN0734-3078).

DOLLAR, AMERICAN--CUBA

"In his annual July 26th speech, the Cuban President [Fidel Castro] said there were no 'magic formulas' to pull the economy out of its tailspin. And he noted that the leadership was ready to make 'concessions' to save 'the achievements of socialism,' and guarantee 'the right' to continue along the socialist path.

He identified bringing in more hard currency as a 'vital necessity' for the country. One immediate way to do that, of course, was to legalize the dollar. Cuban economists have estimated that there are from $100 to $300 million floating around the island, as a result of the increased volume of tourism, clandestine family remittances, and various other sources. Legalized family remittances--although nominally limited in the United States by blockade--could bring in as much as $500 million a year, and perhaps more. Cubans will have the option of spending the hard currency at special stores, and for the time being at least, will also be able to purchase goods in the tourist shops and diplo-markets." (p2)

Reed, Gail. "Behind the Dollar Dilemma." Cuba Update Supplement Sep 1993. p2-3.

DOLLAR, AMERICAN--VALUATION (v19)

DOMESTIC VIOLENCE

see CONJUGAL VIOLENCE; FAMILY VIOLENCE

DOMESTICS--U.S.

"Twenty-two percent of top-income households bought housekeeping services in 1992, compared with 10 percent of the next highest income group and fewer than 5 percent of households with incomes below $50,000." (p13)

Crispell, Diane. "Business Reports: Households: The Very Rich Are Sort of Different." American Demographics v16 n3, Mar 1994. p11-13. (ISSN0163-4089).

DOMINICAN REPUBLIC--ECONOMIC CONDITIONS

"From 100% in 1990, inflation [in the Dominican Republic] fell to 4% in 1991, 7% in 1992 and about 3% last year. Output, which slumped in 1990 by 5% and slid another 1% in 1991, rose 7% in 1992 and 2% last year." (p48,50)

"International: Dominican Republic: Old Man in No Hurry." Economist v330 n7848, 29 Jan 1994. p48,50. (ISSN0013-0613).

DONATION OF ORGANS, TISSUES, ETC.--U.S.

"Every year more than 10,000 tissue donors supply approximately 500,000 pieces of tissue for transplantation in the United States. Approximately 400 tissue banks are operating in our country procuring, processing, storing, and/or distributing this tissue. These figures are approximate because no one really knows how many tissue banks are operating. There is currently no Federal oversight and only a handful of States require such tissue banks to register." (pS16452)

Simon, Paul (Sen.-Ill.). "Statements on Introduced Bills and Joint Resolutions," Congressional Record (19 Nov 1993). Daily ed. pS16433-16501. (ISSN0363-7239).

DONATIONS

see CHARITABLE USES, TRUSTS, AND FOUNDATIONS

DOWN'S SYNDROME (v19)

DOWN'S SYNDROME--GREAT BRITAIN

"In Britain, a child born to a 38-year-old has one chance in 150 of being born with Down's. By the age of 42 the risk is one in 40. But the risks seem to come, not from the inability of ageing reproductive equipment to cope with pregnancy, but from faults in the way in which eggs are produced. Down's syndrome is caused by an extra chromosome....In 19 Down's cases out of 20 the extra chromosome comes with the egg rather than the sperm." (p78)

"Science and Technology: Embryology: Not Too Late." Economist v330 n7844, 8 Jan 1994. p78-79. (ISSN0013-0613).

DRAFT--SOVIET UNION (v19)

DRAWBACKS--U.S. (v19)

DRIED FOODS--NUTRITION

"Drying a fish or vegetable in the sun can double or even triple its nutritional value. Take the 'daikon' (giant radish), for example. It's a pretty big root, so it's usually cut into thin slices before being set out to dry--but what a difference drying makes! A sliver of sun-dried daikon has 15 times as much calcium and 10 times as much iron, vitamin B1, and vitamin B2 as a raw piece. Drying a sweet potato in the sun can double its calcium and vitamin B1 content. Dried fish and vegetables almost make the winter worth waiting for." (p25)

Nagayama, Hisao. "The Naked Kitchen: Himono." Look Japan v39 n455, Feb 1994. p24-25. (ISSN0456-5339).

DRINKING AND TRAFFIC ACCIDENTS--U.S. (v19)

"In 1988, 20.5 percent of the 10,411 15-20 year old drivers [in the U.S.] involved in fatal crashes had blood alcohol concentrations (BAC) of 0.10 or greater, compared to 30.8 percent of the 35,010 drivers 21-44 years old. In 1991, 19.8 percent of the 8,207 15-20 year old drivers had a BAC of 0.10 or greater, compared to 30.4 percent of the 30,344 drivers 21-44 years old. The estimates for the years 1989 and 1990 are comparable for drivers under age 21 (19.2 percent and 20.9 percent, respectively). These figures do not indicate increases in alcohol involvement in fatal crashes among drivers under age 21." (p160)

U.S. House. Committee on Appropriations. "Department of Transportation and Related Agencies Approp. for 1994 (Part 4)." Hearing, Washington, D.C.: GPO, 1993. (ISBN0160410738). (Y4.Ap6/1:T68/4/994/pt.4).

The High Risk Drivers Act "focuses on...high risk drivers who are disproportionately represented in the crash rates. Drivers with repeated traffic violations and/or crashes in a given period are several times more likely than the general population of drivers to have subsequent accidents. Repeat drunk driving offenders are over-represented in crashes. 1992 figures supplied by Mothers Against Drunk Drivers (MADD) estimate that 17,699 people were killed in the United States in alcohol-related traffic accidents and 1.2 million suffered injuries in crashes where police or medical personnel reported a presence of alcohol." (pS16879)

Danforth, John C. (Sen.-Mo.). "High Risk Drivers Act of 1993," Congressional Record (20 Nov 1993). Daily ed. pS16875-16879. (ISSN0363-7239).

DRINKING AND TRAFFIC ACCIDENTS--U.S.--MORTALITY (v19)

DRINKING AND TRAFFIC ACCIDENTS--U.S.--YOUTH--MORTALITY (v19)

DRINKING WATER, BOTTLED

see BOTTLED WATER

DROUGHTS--AFRICA

"In 1992-93 Southern Africa was hit by the worst drought in a century. Yet, the threat of disastrous famine and countless deaths did not materialize thanks to remarkable collaboration between the region and the international community. Thirty per cent of the region's 121 million people were affected by the drought in 1992. Over 20 million of the most vulnerable people in the 10 nations that make up the Southern Africa Development Community (SADC) were at risk of starvation or disease, and at least 1 million in South Africa. When seasonal rains failed in late 1991 and early 1992, harvests dropped 30 to 80 per cent below normal across the region, a steeper fall than in the Horn of Africa in 1984-85. Zimbabwe's total 1992 cereal production dropped over 70 per cent below the previous five years' average. Namibia, almost self-sufficient in food the year before, lost 80 per cent of its maize harvest. Large numbers of livestock and wildlife, a source of emergency food in times of crisis, died of starvation or thirst." (p1)

Collins, Carole. "Famine Defeated." Africa Recovery Briefing Paper n9, Aug 1993. p1-12.

DRUG ABUSE

see also EMPLOYEES--U.S.--DRUG USE; YOUTH--U.S.--DRUG USE

DRUG ABUSE--COMMONWEALTH OF INDEPENDENT STATES (v19)

DRUG ABUSE--POLAND (v19)

DRUG ABUSE--RUSSIA

"Russia has become a corridor for drugs from both the Golden Triangle and Central Asia. We now find that IV drug use is growing dramatically. In Moscow, the official figure for drug addicts is 2,000. The internal security agency estimates 60,000 to 80,000. Therefore, the potential for the spread of AIDS is much greater. Child prostitution is much worse than imaginable because no one wants to believe it exists. It is being practiced in Scandinavia by Russian girls aged 10 and older. It will probably bring an explosion in HIV carriers and then further penetrate the population. The estimate of the number of homosexuals,...conservatively estimated at 50,000 several years ago, is probably much larger than estimated." (p42)

Feshbach, Murray. "An American Demographer's View." Surviving Together v11 n3, Fall 1993. p42. (ISSN0859-6286).

DRUG ABUSE--TREATMENT--U.S.

"Law enforcement absorbs 70 cents of every dollar spent in the drug war. But the war, after a generation in the trenches and at least $100 billion spent since 1981, does not go well. As many experts suggest, we should place more emphasis on the demand side: better education, more rehabilitation. Drug treatment for inmates, a captive audience if there ever was one, should be accelerated; only 2 in 10 inmates get treatment even though nearly 1 million of America's 1.4 million prisoners have dependency problems." (p80)

Ruby, Michael. "Editorial: Should Drugs Be Legalized?" U.S. News & World Report v115 n24, 20 Dec 1993. p80. (ISSN0041-5537).

DRUG ABUSE--U.S. (v19)

"It is estimated that in 1988, 14.5 million Americans were using drugs on a current basis. By 1991 that number had dropped by about 13 percent and continues its downward trend. During that same period, the number of adolescent drug users fell about 27 percent. Other statistics are encouraging. Occasional cocaine use is down 22 percent for all users. Adolescent cocaine use dropped an impressive 63 percent and is still falling." (p27)

U.S. House. Committee on Appropriations. "Treasury, Postal Service, and General Government Approp. for Fiscal Year 1994 (Part 3)." Hearing, Washington, D.C.: GPO, 1993. (Y4.Ap6/1:T71/994/pt.3).

"Few Americans favor legalization [of drugs]--only 14 percent, according to a 1993 Gallup Poll. Fewer than 5 percent who are age 12 or older say they use marijuana, according to a 1991 survey by the U.S. Substance Abuse and Mental Health Services Administration, and fewer than 1 percent say they use cocaine. People from ages 17 to 25 tend to use drugs more often than others, and within this group, fewer than 1 percent say they have ever tried heroin. Despite such hopeful statistics, drugs remain a major concern for well over 75 percent of parents, says Gallup." (p7)

Sileo, Chi Chi. "Is It Time to Just Say No to the War on Drugs?" Insight v10 n6, 7 Feb 1994. p6-12. (ISSN1051-4880).

"One of the great untold success stories of recent years is the effect of a huge, coordinated media campaign on the use of illegal drugs. Between 1985 and 1992, the number of Americans who regularly used drugs declined 50 percent, from 23 million to 11.4 million. Drug use among blacks is down 58 percent. Many factors contributed to the decline, including the sudden death of basketball star Len Bias in 1986. But public-service ads created and placed by the Partnership for a Drug-Free America clearly made a huge difference, not so much for the roughly 6 million hard-core drug users as for young recreational users influenced by definitions of what's cool." (p23)

Alter, Jonathan. "National Affairs: Between the Lines: The Power to Change What's 'Cool.'" Newsweek v123 n3, 17 Jan 1994. p23. (ISSN0028-9604).

"The National Council on Crime and Delinquency reports that cocaine has 860,000 weekly users and the death toll attributed directly to cocaine is 547 deaths per week. Heroin weekly users number around 900,000, the weekly deaths are unknown. Marijuana has 6.6 million weekly users which is 3.3 percent of the adult population. There are no known deaths attributed solely to marijuana use. Alcohol claims 47.3 million weekly users which is 23.9 percent of the adult population and 96,000 weekly deaths are attributed to alcohol use. Tobacco is used by 46.8 million per week or 19.2% of the adult population. Tobacco deaths per week are about 390,000. The report says that the casual cocaine users declined, but it also says that the daily cocaine users increased by about 44,000 from 1988 to 1990. Nearly 12.9 million people (6.4% of the population age 12 and older) use illicit drugs at least once a month." (p26)

Watson, Douglas D. "Drug Warfare." Social Justice Review v85 n1-2, Jan-Feb 1994. p25-27.

"The September 6, 1990, issue of the USA TODAY states the following facts. Cocaine users who used the drug once a week in 1985 averaged out to 5.3%, in 1988 the percentage almost doubled to 10.5%. Men arrested in the first three months of 1990 in Philadelphia and San Diego revealed by blood tests that 80% were on drugs at the time of arrest. The state of Nevada has an average of 24.9 drug addicts per 1,000 people. New York has 24.5 addicts per 1,000. The District of Columbia has 40.5 addicts per 1,000." (p26) "In the May 10, 1990, issue of USA TODAY, it was reported that the state of New York has 434,000 cocaine addicts. Washington, DC, has a per capita rating of 32.9 cocaine addicts per 1,000. South Dakota has the fewest hard-core cocaine addicts--800. One out of every five people arrested for any crime is a hard core cocaine addict. Homeless people are 5 times more likely to be cocaine addicts than the general population." (p27)

Watson, Douglas D. "Drug Warfare." Social Justice Review v85 n1-2, Jan-Feb 1994. p25-27.

DRUG ABUSE--U.S.--PUBLIC OPINION

"The National Institute on Drug Abuse estimates that cocaine use in America has dropped by 45% since 1988. The estimate was derived...by telephoning 9,250 households and asking the residents if they used drugs. Twenty percent of the interviewed refused to give any answer. The homeless were not contacted. People have to be skeptical of negative responses about an illegal activity. While most Americans polled see drugs as a declining issue, 58% of the young (ages 16-24) Americans view drugs as the number one problem facing today's youth....Forty percent of the people under age 45 say that they personally knew a cocaine dealer. A 1989 national survey showed that 64% of the American people thought that the drug problem was the most serious issue facing the country. In 1990, the drug problem was viewed as the most serious issue facing the country by only 10% of the people." (p26)

Watson, Douglas D. "Drug Warfare." Social Justice Review v85 n1-2, Jan-Feb 1994. p25-27.

DRUG ABUSE--U.S.--WOMEN (v19)

DRUG ABUSE AND CRIME--SOUTHERN STATES

"Every Southern state [in the U.S.] ranked below the national average for drug programs in 1988, spending less than $8.60 per capita. Texas has the stingiest record. With the third highest crime rate in the nation, the Lone Star state spends $175.13 per capita to put criminals behind bars. Yet it spends only $1.47 to prevent drug abuse and treat addicts. Paying for punishment while skimping on prevention means that Southern states are turning drug users away from treatment centers and packing them into overcrowded prisons. Georgia imprisoned 4,924 people for drug crimes last year--six times more than a decade ago. That same year, the city of Atlanta turned away 4,000 people seeking treatment for drug and alcohol addiction." (p56)

Bates, Eric. "Crime and Punishment: War and Peace." Southern Exposure v21 n1-2, Spr-Sum 1993. p55-56. (ISSN0146-809X).

DRUG ABUSE AND CRIME--U.S. (v19)

"From 1991-1992, the [U.S.] Federal government spent $61.4 billion on drug interdiction, drug abuse prevention and treatment, prosecution of offenders, and other aspects of controlling illegal drugs. The amount has grown from $4.7 billion in 1988 to 12 billion in 1993--an almost three-fold increase. Despite this increase, there is conflicting evidence on any change in illegal drug usage patterns." (p27)

Hoyer, Steny H. (Rep.-Md.). U.S. House. Committee on Appropriations. "Treasury, Postal Service, and General Government Approp. for Fiscal Year 1994 (Part 3)." Hearing, Washington, D.C.: GPO, 1993. (Y4.Ap6/1:T71/994/pt.3).

In the U.S., "Substance abuse...is associated with 52 percent of rapes, 49 percent of murders, 62 percent of assaults and half of all spousal abuse cases and traffic fatalities. In fact, 75 to 80 percent of U.S. prison inmates are abusers of drugs or alcohol, with half of them under the influence when they committed their crimes. Of the nearly 600,000 prisoners needing treatment, a scant 15 percent are getting it, according to a 1991 report by the U.S. General Accounting Office (GAO). The same applies to those on parole." (p6)

Baker, Beth. "No Sacred Cows: Drug Treatment on Demand." Common Cause Magazine v19 n4, Win 1993. p5-6. (ISSN0271-9592).

"Most of the violent crime committed in...[the U.S.] today is caused by people who traffick in drugs. Forty-eight percent of all men arrested for homicide test positive for using drugs at the time of the arrest. Illegal drug use is the cause of half of family violence....And most of this violence is directed against women and children. And what about the effect of illegal drugs on young children? The fact is that 30 percent of all child abuse cases...[are] caused by parents using illegal drugs. And even worse, infants in this country are now suffering under the pain and violence of the drug pushers....Eleven percent of all newborn babies in America are already drug addicted. What is going to happen when that gets up to 20 percent? What is this country coming to when 1 out of 9 babies are already addicted at the time of their birth?" (pH2534-2535)

Solomon, Gerald B. H. (Rep.-N.Y.). "Violent Crime Control and Law Enforcement Act of 1994," Congressional Record (20 Apr 1994). Daily ed. pH2518-2539. (ISSN0363-7239).

"Drug users frequently resort to robberies, burglaries, shoplifting, embezzlement, fraud, and prostitution in order to raise enough money to buy drugs sold at prohibition-inflated prices. Twenty-six percent of prison inmates [in the U.S.] convicted of property offenses reported in a 1991 survey that they committed the offense for which they were incarcerated to get money to buy drugs. This was true for 30% of the burglars and 31% of those convicted of larceny." (p1)

Sterling, Eric. "Why Dr. Elders Was Right: Drugs and Public Health." Progressive Review n321, Jan 1994. p1-4.

"From 1980 to 1989, the arrest rate for drug offenses [in the U.S.] increased by more than 111 percent compared with 19 percent increase for the seven UCR [FBI's Uniform Crime Reports] index crimes....In 1982, 2 percent of all murders were drug related but by 1989 7.4 percent were drug-related." (p2)

News release. "Crime." University of Michigan News and Information Services 18 Jan 1994. p1-2.

DRUG ABUSE IN PREGNANCY--U.S. (v19)

"Recent statistics compiled by the American Civil Liberties Union's Reproductive Freedom Project suggest that as many as 167 women in 24 states have been arrested because of their behavior during pregnancy. Often times these cases are not reported. The negative baggage that comes with being a bad mother is so ingrained, a woman's guilt is assumed without protest. As a result, women are punished for escaping the pain and violence of their lives through alcohol or drugs and for having the ability to reproduce. Furthermore, a disproportionate number of prosecutions have been brought against minority women in states like Florida where there are few residential rehabilitation facilities for pregnant addicts. Sexist and racist attitudes are blamed by many activists for this trend that persists despite evidence that substance-abuse problems are prevalent regardless of gender or ethnicity." (p7)

Monica, Andrea Della. "Poor, Pregnant & Prosecuted." New Directions for Women v22 n3, May-Jun 1993. p7. (ISSN0160-1075).

DRUG ENFORCEMENT

see NARCOTICS, CONTROL OF

DRUG INDUSTRY

see PHARMACEUTICAL INDUSTRY

DRUG TESTING

see BUS DRIVERS--DRUG TESTING--U.S.

DRUG TESTING--U.S. (v19)

DRUG TRAFFIC

see also COCAINE INDUSTRY

DRUG TRAFFIC--AFGHANISTAN--PAKISTAN (v19)

DRUG TRAFFIC--EUROPE, EASTERN (v19)

DRUG TRAFFIC--NICARAGUA

"The crime rate in drug-related activities has...sky-rocketed [in Nicaragua]. This fact is reflected in the following figures: in 1992, some 500 drug-related crimes were registered. In 1993, this number almost doubled to 965 cases. Similarly, 430 people connected to the drug trade were arrested in 1992, but in 1993, there were 1,517 arrests, a 253% rise. During these two years, a total of 250 kilograms of cocaine was confiscated, but so far in 1994 (January and the first part of February), 540 kilograms have been seized." (p22)

"Drug Trafficking and Consumption: Spreading Out of Control." Barricada Internacional n371, Mar 1994. p22. (ISSN1013-9567).

DRUG TRAFFIC--PANAMA--U.S.

"At the State Department, allegations linking [Panamanian] President Endara to money laundering are well known. In fact, the cocaine flow from Panama to the US has increased under Endara. Between January and October 20, 1991, 250 murders and 17,000 crimes in Panama were reported, 80 percent of which were drug-related. An agent of the DEA [U.S. Drug Enforcement Administration] in Panama City left the country after receiving a series of death threats. Over 250 charges of corruption have been filed against police officers since August 1990, including claims of armed robbery and murder. One poll shows 70 percent of Panamanians distrust the police. Another poll shows 72 percent think corruption in government is out of control. The violent crime rate has tripled under Endara." (p12)

Johnson, Barbara/others. "Whatever Happened to Central America?" Propaganda Review n10, Sum 1993. p10-13,53-56.

DRUG TRAFFIC--POLAND

"Poland...now provides Western Europe with its highest-quality illegal drugs, including 20 percent of the amphetamines confiscated in 1991, up from 6 percent in the late 1980s. Poland may also be the biggest transshipment point for narcotics from Central America, Afghanistan, and the Southeast Asian golden triangle, though 'drug trafficking has also increased sharply throughout the region,' Raymond Bonner reports. Costa Rica's Ambassador to Poland was arrested at the Warsaw airport with almost $1 million worth of pure heroin, and 'a staggering 1.2 tons of cocaine was seized in St. Petersburg,' from Colombia, where cartels are hiring Polish couriers to smuggle cocaine to the West." (p17)

Chomsky, Noam. "Letter from Lexington: New World Discipline." Lies of Our Times v5 n3, Mar 1994. p15-18. (ISSN1046-7912).

DRUG TRAFFIC--SYRIA (v19)

DRUG TRAFFIC--THAILAND (v19)

DRUG TRAFFIC--TURKEY (v19)

DRUG TRAFFIC--U.S.

"In response to the growing use of containers to smuggle drugs into this country during the 1980's, [U.S.] Customs created a system for tracking containers and their examinations. In FY 1992, the total number of sea containers that arrived at our seaports was over 3,860,000. Of that total, 44,388 full and empty sea containers arrived from cocaine source and transit countries. Within this group, Customs examined 13 percent of the full containers and 25 percent of the empty ones for narcotics....Detecting drugs in containers is not simply a matter of numbers. In past years, Customs has searched many more containers for drugs than in FY 1992. However, we discovered and seized twice as much cocaine from containers last year (85,000 lbs.) than in any prior year. More containers are not searched because Customs has learned to focus its resources on shipments that have some level of risk. The vast majority of cargo entering the U.S. is legitimate, even cargo from cocaine source countries. We have developed practices and systems to analyze the commercial data available from ships' manifests and commercial entries to target suspect shipments." (p1174)

Lane, Michael H. (Acting Commissioner, U.S. Customs Service). U.S. House. Committee on Appropriations. "Treasury, Postal Service...Approp. for Fiscal Year 1994 (Part 1)." Hearing, Washington, D.C.: GPO, 1993. (Y4.Ap6/1:T71/994/pt.1).

"In 1990, over 1.5 billion dollars' worth of marijuana and cocaine was seized by the INS [Immigration and Naturalization Service], U.S. Customs, and the DEA [U.S. Drug Enforcement Administration]." (pH10499)

Harman, Jane (Rep.-Calif.). "Immigration Policy," Congressional Record (21 Nov 1993). Daily ed. pH10499-10500. (ISSN0363-7239).

DRUGS (v19)

DRUGS--PRICES--U.S. (v19)

DRUGS--PRICES--U.S.--AGED (v19)

DRUGS--U.S. (v19)

DRUGS, PRESCRIPTION--U.S.--AGED (v19)

DRUNKEN DRIVERS

see DRINKING AND TRAFFIC ACCIDENTS

DRUNKENNESS

see ALCOHOLISM

DWELLINGS--NORTHEASTERN STATES--HEATING AND VENTILATION (v19)

DYE INDUSTRY--U.S.

"During the past decade, the number of U.S. dye manufacturers has diminished until only eight remain, of which only two are totally U.S.-owned. As the major domestic dyes manufacturers ceased operations, the domestic sources for intermediates needed to make dyes also disappeared. Foreign manufacturers have been quick to fill this void in the U.S. dye market. Today, over 50 percent of the dyes sold in the United States, and a much higher share of the dye intermediates, are imported. They come primarily from Europe, but increasingly from less developed countries, such as India. As foreign-based dye manufacturers become more dominant in the industry, the remaining U.S.-based dye manufacturers are struggling to compete and survive." (pS16457)

Wofford, Harris (Sen.-Pa.). "Statements on Introduced Bills and Joint Resolutions," Congressional Record (19 Nov 1993). Daily ed. pS16433-16501. (ISSN0363-7239).

EAR--INFECTIONS--U.S. (v19)

EARTHQUAKES--CALIFORNIA

"In the Loma Prieta Earthquake of 1989, both the Cypress Viaduct and the San Francisco Bay Bridge suffered severe damage. In fact, two-thirds of the 63 people who died in that earthquake perished when the viaduct collapsed. As a result of the Northridge Earthquake, 12 bridges were damaged, including the collapse of the Interstate 5 and Golden Gate Freeway Bridges, which severely disrupted the major north-south artery for the Los Angeles basin. There are 24,000 bridges in...California. More than 9,770 of these were constructed before the higher earthquake building code. The State Department of Transportation has determined that about 1,500 bridges will need seismic retrofit and of these, about 300 are not otherwise structurally deficient. California needs over $1.5 billion to correct seismic deficiencies on its bridges yet while it receives about $127 million a year from the Highway Bridge Rehabilitation and Repair Program, it cannot spend any of these funds on those 300 bridges because of the current interpretation of the law." (pH918)

Mineta, Norman Y. (Rep.-Calif.). "Permitting Use of Funds for Seismic Retrofit of Bridges," Congressional Record (2 Mar 1994). Daily ed. pH917-919. (ISSN0363-7239).

"In the early hours of January 17th people throughout the Los Angeles basin were shaken out of their beds by a shock measuring 6.6 on the Richter scale, with its centre under the suburb of Northridge, 20 miles north-west of the heart of the city....Caltrans, the California transport department, reckons the Santa Monica freeway will be out of service for no more than a year. Sceptics expect it to be at least two years, if San Francisco is any guide: there are still diversions around the Nimitz double-decker freeway in Oakland, which collapsed and killed 43 people when a Richter 7.1 earthquake hit the San Francisco area in 1989....Preliminary estimates put the whole bill at anything up to $30 billion. That would be more than the cost of the 1989 San Francisco earthquake; in fact, it would make this disaster the country's most expensive, even exceeding the $17 billion-worth of damage caused by Hurricane Andrew in 1992. Monday's earthquake seems to have been of an especially lethal sort. The Richter 7.5 shock which in 1992 hit the small community of Landers, 100 miles east of Los Angeles, was much stronger and yet killed only one person and caused no vast damage." (p23)

"American Survey: It Hit Like an Upper-Cut." Economist v330 n7847, 22 Jan 1994. p23. (ISSN0013-0613).

EARTHQUAKES--CALIFORNIA--ECONOMIC CONDITIONS

"For 30 terrifying seconds, the earth shook as hard as anyone could remember. When it stopped, virtually all of Los Angeles' 3 million residents were left in darkness....The earthquake that hit L.A.'s Northridge section on Jan. 17, the most powerful to shake the region in decades, leveled scores of buildings and killed dozens of residents....On top of all the human drama and misery, economically, the quake's timing couldn't have been worse. After a three-year slump, California's economy was bottoming out. Its unemployment rate fell to 8.7% in December from 9.8% in October, and the pace of job losses at California-based aerospace contractors had slowed by 42% in the last half of 1993 from the first half. Retail sales and home buying were up, as was tourism. A revival in California, which accounts for about 12% of gross domestic product, would have boosted the national economy. Now, crippled highways, damaged homes, and lost business will delay any California rebound. Early estimates put the structural damage around L.A. well above the $7 billion in damage sustained during the 1989 San Francisco earthquake--perhaps as high as $30 billion." (p26)

Schine, Eric/others. "Top of the News: Disasters: Golden Heartbreak." Business Week n3356, 31 Jan 1994. p26-27. (ISSN0007-7135).

EARTHQUAKES--LOS ANGELES (CALIF)

"The 6.6-Richter scale earthquake that devastated parts of the Los Angeles region on January 17, impacted an area the size of Cleveland." (pS7) "The initial earthquake left 20,000 to 25,000 homeless. To date 57 have died and 7,500 have been injured. The first day there were 70 structure fires. About 25,000 structures have been damaged, 11,000 are uninhabitable. Initially, electric power was lost to more than 1.4 million customers, with damages to two electric generating plants and severe damage to two substations. Fifty-seven percent of the electric generating power of the Los Angeles Department of Water and Power was down, affecting 800,000 customers. About 20,000 water customers were without service. A water aqueduct was broken in San Fernando Valley, with five major breaks in the area's water system. About 20,000 natural gas customers were without service. The Los Angeles Unified School System shut down, sending 800,000 students home; 150 schools are damaged." (pS8)

Boxer, Barbara (Sen.-Calif.). "The Southern California Earthquake of 1994," Congressional Record (25 Jan 1994). Daily ed. pS7-9. (ISSN0363-7239).

"After the earthquake [in Los Angeles on January 17, 1994], 20,000 people were sleeping in 70 local parks. Thousands more were sleeping in emergency shelters. Uncounted numbers huddled under blankets outside their ruined apartments. Regardless of their nationality, renters told the same story: landlords ordered them to evacuate, refused to refund their unused rent money and called the cops to clear them out. Meanwhile, Willie Williams, chief of the Los Angeles Police Department, threatened to crack down on the 'looters' he expected to appear 'like in the riots of 1992.'...The 'wave of looting' never came--except for the looting done by the capitalists. One company charged people $1,000 for four sheets of plywood worth $100. An ARCO station raised prices 140 percent, breaking a disaster rights law. Police left the ARCO station after the raise was scaled back somewhat. They did not arrest the landlords holding on to people's money or the contractors whose shoddy work murdered 16 people in one building alone." (p2)

Teixeira, Steve. "The Earthquake: Another Crisis Shows Who Rules L.A." People's Tribune v21 n5, 31 Jan 1994. p2.

"The quake that ripped and roared through the Los Angeles basin...[on January 17, 1994] left stunning devastation: more than 50 dead, 5,900 injured, 20,000 homeless, at least six major freeways buckled, countless businesses closed and workers idled." (p26)

Roberts, Steven V./others. "Special Report: Breaking Point." U.S. News & World Report v116 n4, 31 Jan 1994. p26-32,36. (ISSN0041-5537).

EARTHQUAKES--UTAH (v19)

EAST TIMOR (INDONESIA)--MORTALITY

"Establishing the true death toll in East Timor since Indonesia invaded in 1975 is difficult. Amnesty International gives a figure of 200,000 dead. The government admits to 30,000--made up of 5,000 killed by fighting and 25,000 by hunger." (p41)

"Asia: What Is the Big Fuss?" Economist v331 n7860, 23 Apr 1994. p41. (ISSN0013-0613).

ECONOMIC ASSISTANCE (v19)

"UN agencies, while retaining their priority concern for Africa, are also feeling the effect of increased competition for funds. In its 1992-96 programme cycle, UN Development Programme funds are 25-30 per cent down on the previous five-year period, a fact which drew strong protest from African delegates to its June Governing Council. The UN High Commissioner for Refugees and UNICEF both report pressures on their funding, despite renewed US commitment for the latter. Overall, bilateral aid remains stable, with its share of OECD [Organization for Economic Cooperation and Development] gross national product (GNP) in 1992 at 0.33 per cent, according to the OECD's Development Assistance Committee. Denmark and Sweden have joined Norway in committing more than 1 per cent of their GNP to aid. Finnish aid, however, has slipped below the UN target of 0.7 per cent, following a near 24 per cent cut in real aid. In total, eight of DAC's 21 members showed a decline in real aid flows in 1992, including Japan, which competes with the US as the world's largest aid donor....Recently, a US Congress committee made a $50 mn cut in the $800 mn request from the Clinton Administration which would have kept funding stable in nominal terms for the US' main African aid arm." (p25)

Laishley, Roy. "Africa Faces Crisis over Aid as World Bank Lending Falls." Africa Recovery v7 n2, Oct 1993. p1,24-25.

The United Nations Development Programme's 'Human Development Report' "criticizes past patterns of aid-giving based on political or geo-strategic reasons rather than on people's needs. It notes that El Salvador, with 5 million people and an annual per capita income of $1,000, receives more US assistance than Bangladesh, with 116 million people and a per capita income of only $210. Calling for new forms of international cooperation, the report repeats the suggestion that at least 20 per cent of both official development assistance (ODA) and government budgets be allocated to human priority areas like health and basic education (against the present 6.5 per cent). It also urges that ODA allocations be based on levels of poverty. Only a quarter of global ODA goes to the 10 countries with three-quarters of the world's poor." (p5)

Collins, Carole. "Growth Not Benefiting People: UNDP." Africa Recovery v7 n1, Jun 1993. p4-5.

"The West might argue that it has already shown great generosity toward its former enemies: One recent United Nations study counts more than $210 billion in aid to the East from the West since 1989. But the overwhelming majority of that--$170 billion--represents Bonn's ongoing effort to integrate the 16 million citizens of the former East Germany. The remaining $40 billion--most of it selective debt relief or (largely unused) trade credits--has been spread unevenly among the 400 million other inhabitants of the postcommunist world." (p53)

Parker, Richard. "Clintonomics for the East." Foreign Policy n94, Spr 1994. p53-68. (ISSN0015-7228).

"It is imperative that aid flows be used for productive purposes, particularly the development of human, physical and institutional infrastructure. At the present time, only a small fraction of official development assistance (ODA) flows are used for human development, widely recognized as a crucial ingredient of development. It has been estimated that in 1988-1989, only 7 per cent of bilateral ODA and less than 10 per cent of multilateral ODA was directed to programmes in the 'human priority areas' (basic education, primary health care, supply of safe water, sanitation, family planning and nutrition)." (p8)

Boutros-Ghali, Boutros. "Overcoming the Crisis in Development Cooperation." United Nations Department of Public Information n1359, Mar 1993. p8-12.

ECONOMIC ASSISTANCE--AFRICA (v19)

"Financial flows to Africa fell by 14 per cent in 1991 and by an even greater magnitude in 1992, said UN Secretary-General Boutros Boutros-Ghali in a special, October 1993 report....In current dollars, net financial flows to Africa fell from $22.2 bn in 1990 to $18.4 bn in 1992. This means that in constant 1985 dollars, net resource flows were only $14.7 bn in 1992, even lower than the $15.8 bn received in 1985....However, sub-Saharan Africa did not fare as badly. In 1992, its net resource flows were $14.2 bn (in 1985 dollars), down from $14.6 bn in 1990, but still significantly higher than the $9.6 bn level of 1985....But overall aid flows, while still higher than in the mid-1980s, also fell sharply in 1992. In current dollars, official development assistance (ODA) to Africa went from a 1990 peak of $19.7 bn to $18.3 bn in 1991 and plunged by 33 per cent in 1992 to just $12.1 bn, a far cry from the NADAF-recommended target of $30 bn a year. For sub-Saharan Africa, ODA in 1992 fell by 22 per cent from 1991, though the latest figures from the Organization for Economic Cooperation and Development show a slight upward trend for 1992...." (p37)

"Improved Financial Flows Vital to Africa." Africa Recovery v7 n3-4, Dec 1993-Mar 1994. p37,40.

"In current dollars, net financial resource flows to Africa declined to $18.4 bn in 1992 from $22.2 in 1990. When measured in constant 1985 dollars, this meant that Africa obtained resource flows of just $14.7 bn in 1992, below the $15.8 bn received in 1985, the year before the start of the UN Programme of Action for African Economic Recovery and Development, the New Agenda's predecessor. When allowance is made for repayments of capital, interest and profits, net transfers of aid, loans and foreign investment to Africa, in real terms, declined from $10.4 bn in 1990 to $5.3 in 1992...." (p6)

"First Report on the New Agenda for Africa: Decline in Financial Flows to Africa Must Be Reversed." Africa Recovery Dec 1993. p5-7.

"Reflecting a trend in multilateral aid of rising lending for health, the [World] Bank currently provides $350 mn a year for health, four times its 1987 level, and expects to become the largest single external source of health funding for developing countries by 1995. But the share of health in total donor aid fell from 7 to 6 per cent in the 1980s, apparently minor, but with dramatic effect on many African countries. Foreign aid provides a fifth of Africa's health spending and over 50 per cent in Burundi, Chad, Guinea-Bissau, Mozambique and Tanzania. In a few countries, such as Mozambique, it also finances over 90 per cent of capital spending for health. Alongside declining donor aid, Africa's total health spending fell in the 1980s to an average of less than 4 per cent of public spending, and under 2 per cent of gross domestic product." (p14)

Collins, Carole. "Bank Links Health to Economic Growth." Africa Recovery v7 n2, Oct 1993. p14-15.

ECONOMIC ASSISTANCE--ASIA (v19)

ECONOMIC ASSISTANCE--COMMONWEALTH OF INDEPENDENT STATES

"Since 1989, the USSR and its successor, the Commonwealth of Independent States, have received a grand total of $94.4 billion in aid from the West. Almost two thirds of this ($60.5 billion) has been provided by EU [European Union] nations, and more than two thirds of that from Germany--a fact which Germany and the EU point to with pride whenever the question of more money is raised. The US, by contrast, has provided just under $12 billion. At the Vancouver Summit with Russian President Boris Yeltsin in April 1993, President Clinton said he was 'proud to announce' that the US would provide an extra $1.6 billion for the fiscal year that ended in October 1993 and a further $2.5 billion for the fiscal year ending in October 1994. As of January 1994, only two thirds of the 1992-93 money had been disbursed and less than $500 million, or 20 percent, of the 1993-94 money. Of the $2.5 billion Mr. Clinton promised, Congress has so far authorized only $1.6 billion." (p6)

Walker, Martin. "Russia: Financing Russia's Future." Europe n333, Feb 1994. p6-8. (ISSN0191-4545).

ECONOMIC ASSISTANCE--DEVELOPING COUNTRIES (v19)

ECONOMIC ASSISTANCE--FORMER SOVIET REPUBLICS (v19)

ECONOMIC ASSISTANCE--RUSSIA

"The West's efforts to help economic reform [in Russia] have been badly handled. In 1992 America announced $24 billion in aid; some $15 billion arrived. Promises inflated in 1993: the Group of Seven big industrial countries offered $43 billion, including $15 billion of debt relief; the debt relief came, but only $5 billion with it. Given Russia's failure to meet its own commitments on economic reform, this holding back was quite defensible. But the West's leaders had already taken the credit for the full measure of their promised generosity, as though the aid would come with no strings attached. Many of Russia's reformers feel betrayed, and the idea that the West can be relied on to finance economic reform has been discredited." (p16)

"Leaders: Russia in Need." Economist v330 n7846, 15 Jan 1994. p16-17. (ISSN0013-0613).

"The International Monetary Fund was expected to provide [Russia with] $13 billion for currency stabilization, for conversion of industrial plants from defense to civilian production, for sectoral investment, and for a social safety net. But the IMF condition that Russia reduce its inflation rate to 10 percent a month by the autumn of 1993 and to 2 percent a month by the end of 1994 has never been met. In January 1994, Russian inflation was still running at 18 percent a month. Accordingly, the IMF has only paid out $1 billion in 1992 and another $1.5 billion in 1993 and has been cast--not altogether fairly--as the harsh and miserly banker by the Russian government and Western critics alike." (p7)

Walker, Martin. "Russia: Financing Russia's Future." Europe n333, Feb 1994. p6-8. (ISSN0191-4545).

ECONOMIC ASSISTANCE--U.S. (v19)

ECONOMIC ASSISTANCE, AMERICAN (v19)

"The Clinton administration...has proposed the biggest overhaul of foreign aid since 1961. Overall, aid is to be cut by about 10 percent, but the cuts will fall unevenly....Among the losers will be Central America, a key ideological battleground during the Reagan years, and Cold War allies such as Pakistan, which during the 1980s played host to Afghan rebels fighting the Soviet puppet regime in Kabul. Aid to Pakistan has dropped from $565 million in 1990 to $4.2 million now. Another Cold War ally, Turkey, whose support proved crucial during the Persian Gulf war, has been cut to $128 million, only about one-sixth of the total it received in 1991." (p6-7)

Bering-Jensen, Henrik. "Foreign Aid: From Waste to Investment." Insight v10 n5, 31 Jan 1994. p6-10. (ISSN1051-4880).

ECONOMIC ASSISTANCE, AMERICAN--AZERBAIJAN

"Gross Domestic Product has fallen 20 percent, while the devaluation of the local currency, the 'manat,' at rates of up to 75 percent monthly, has used up Azerbaijan's hard currency supply....During Fiscal Year 1992-93, US grant assistance to the NIS [Newly Independent States] totaled nearly $2.32 billion. This aid was intended to privatize markets, support humanitarian needs, facilitate environmental restoration and the adoption of environmentally sound policies and technologies, as well as improving the health of women and children. Despite the fact that over one-third of its territory has been rendered unproductive through large-scale burning and chemical treatments applied by invading Armenian forces, Azerbaijan was the only NIS republic denied US funding. Therefore, it will not benefit from other direct programs such as the Peace Corps, EPA studies, Food for Peace, etc. The fact that programs of nongovernmental groups such as the Red Cross are delivering humanitarian aid to Azerbaijan with US government funding illustrates the contradictory nature of the policy." (p35)

Cox, Nermin Sultanova. "Challenges of Sovereignty: A Call for More US Aid to Azerbaijan." Surviving Together v12 n1, Spr 1994. p33-35. (ISSN0859-6286).

ECONOMIC ASSISTANCE, AMERICAN--DEVELOPING COUNTRIES--CHILDREN

"Since 1985, AID [or Agency for International Development] has funded child survival programs to the tune of $1.56 billion, including immunization, diarrheic disease control and nutrition programs. In 1985, 190 African children under 5 years of age died for every 1,000 live births. By 1992, the figure had dropped to 171. In Asia during the same period, the figure dropped from 136 to 120. In Latin America, the figure fell from 71 to 50, and in the Near East, from 140 to 75." (p9)

Bering-Jensen, Henrik. "Foreign Aid: From Waste to Investment." Insight v10 n5, 31 Jan 1994. p6-10. (ISSN1051-4880).

ECONOMIC ASSISTANCE, AMERICAN--EGYPT--ISRAEL (v19)

ECONOMIC ASSISTANCE, AMERICAN--INDONESIA

"In 1975, Indonesia invaded East Timor. Human rights monitors estimate that more than 200,000 people, one-third of the pre-invasion population, have died as a result of the invasion and the ensuing occupation....Since the 1975 invasion, the U.S. has provided Indonesia with hundreds of millions of dollars in economic and military assistance. In 1992, over objections from the Bush Administration, Congress cut off $2.3 million in military training funds to Indonesia for fiscal year 1993 in protest to its repressive policies and human rights violations in East Timor. This was the first time Congress had taken punitive action against Indonesia on the issue of East Timor. Yet this represents only a small portion of total U.S. aid. Last year, Indonesia purchased $110 million worth of U.S. weaponry and received U.S. economic aid totaling $93 million in grants and loans." (p13)

"East Timor: Sale of U.S. Jets to Indonesia Opposed." NewsNotes v18 n4, Jul-Aug 1993. p13. (ISSN1064-1556).

ECONOMIC ASSISTANCE, AMERICAN--KURDS

"The sincerity of the concern for the Kurds is demonstrated by what happened as public attention waned. They are subject to Iraqi embargo in addition to the sanctions against Iraq. The West refuses to provide the piddling sums required to satisfy their basic needs and keep them from Saddam's hideous embrace. The UN Department of Humanitarian Affairs prepared a 1/2 billion dollar relief and rehabilitation program for Kurds, Shiites, and poverty-stricken Sunnis in central Iraq. The Clinton Administration--'haunted by the pictures of Kurdish women and children cut down by poison gas,' the President assured the UN--offered $15 million, 'money left over from contributions to a previous UN program in northern Iraq,' the director of Middle East Watch reports." (p7)

Chomsky, Noam. "On Intervention: 'Humanitarian Intervention.'" Boston Review v18 n6, Dec-Jan 1993-94. p3-7. (ISSN0734-2306).

ECONOMIC ASSISTANCE, AMERICAN--MIDDLE EAST (v19)

ECONOMIC ASSISTANCE, AMERICAN--RUSSIA

"No aid money goes to the Russian Government. The vast bulk--over 75 percent of our Russian aid package--goes directly to the private sector. It never reaches the hands of Russian Government officials. It is aimed at building a private sector in the Russian economy and bringing thousands of young Russians to the United States in exchange programs or cleaning up the environment or feeding the old, poor, and vulnerable sectors of the population. It is aimed at training farmers, economists, bankers, business men and women, and the thousand and one other things necessary to overcome the 70 years of communism. The remaining aid, less than 25 percent, is used to provide technical assistance in building effective, workable democratic institutions at the Russian federal governmental level. None of that aid goes directly to the Russian Government. It is provided primarily to U.S. companies and individuals with special expertise, who are contracted by the Agency for International Development." (pS1799)

Leahy, Patrick J. (Sen.-Vt.). "Russian Aid," Congressional Record (24 Feb 1994). Daily ed. pS1798-1799. (ISSN0363-7239).

ECONOMIC ASSISTANCE, AMERICAN--TURKEY (v19)

ECONOMIC ASSISTANCE, AMERICAN--UKRAINE (v19)

ECONOMIC ASSISTANCE, DOMESTIC--U.S.

"More than 50 percent of all [U.S.] federal statutes preempting state and local authority enacted in...204-year history have been enacted only in the past 24 years. Federal mandates on state and local governments have reached unprecedented levels as well, often requiring state and local governments to raise taxes and cut services at the same time. Contrary to conventional wisdom, federal regulation of state and local governments did not decrease during the 1980s. Both regulation and conditions of aid increased during the decade. Federal aid to state and local governments dropped from 26.5% of state-local outlays in 1978 to 20.5% in 1990 and from 17.0% of federal outlays in 1978 to 11.5% in 1991. Federal aid has shifted dramatically from human and capital investment to current service consumption. Federal aid to state and local governments that is dedicated to payments to individuals has increased from 31.8 percent of all grant funding in 1978 to an estimated 64.7% this year. Yet, the number of grant programs leaped from 404 in 1984 to 557 in 1991. However, categorical grants accounted for 89.4% of all federal aid outlays in 1991. Moreover, the median grant obligation was only $4.2 million." (p5)

Hawkins, Robert B., Jr. (Chairman, U.S. Advisory Comm. on Intergovernmental Relations). U.S. House. Committee on Appropriations. "Treasury, Postal Service, and General Government Approp. for Fiscal Year 1994 (Part 4)." Hearing, Washington, D.C.: GPO, 1993. (ISBN0160407702). (Y4.Ap6/1:T71/994/pt.4).

ECONOMIC ASSISTANCE, EUROPEAN--COMMONWEALTH OF INDEPENDENT STATES

"In the period 1990 to 1992, the EU [European Union] provided 73 percent of the total of 72 billion ecus [European currency units] ($81 billion) of grants and credits committed to the former USSR states. This total combines the contributions of the 12 member states and the EU's own operations." (p14)

Emerson, Michael. "Russia: EU Ambassador to Russia Michael Emerson." Europe n333, Feb 1994. p14-15. (ISSN0191-4545).

ECONOMIC ASSISTANCE, GERMAN--SOVIET UNION (v19)

ECONOMIC ASSISTANCE, JAPANESE (v19)

ECONOMIC ASSISTANCE, JAPANESE--AFRICA

"Some 60 per cent of Japan's aid goes to Asia, but Africa's share has been rising. From some $268 mn in 1982, Japan's support to Africa rose to over $1 bn in 1989. After falling back in 1990, partially as a result of negotiations over debt relief, Japan's aid to Africa again rose in 1991 to over $900 mn. In 1990-91, Japan was the fourth largest source of bilateral aid to Africa after the US, France and Germany. For countries such as Ghana and Nigeria it was the largest donor. Japan is also the second largest contributor to the International Development Association, the biggest source of concessional funds for Africa, and is the largest contributor to the African Development Fund." (p11)

Collins, Carole. "Tokyo Conference Seeks Higher Priority for African Development." Africa Recovery v7 n2, Oct 1993. p1,10-

11.

ECONOMIC ASSISTANCE, JAPANESE--AFRICA, SUB-SAHARAN

"Japan provided 10 per cent of total ODA [official development aid] to sub-Saharan Africa in 1992, with an allocation to all Africa of $859 mn, making Japan the fourth largest donor to the region. But this was some $50 mn down on 1991, and was part of 9.9 per cent fall (in yen terms; 4.4 per cent in dollar terms) in total Japanese ODA disbursements. While Japan overtook the US in 1991 as the world's largest aid donor and consolidated this position with total ODA of $11.51 bn in 1992, this ranked Japan 15th among major donors as a percentage of GNP [gross national product]; the US ranked 20th out of the 21 countries in the Organization for Economic Cooperation and Development." (p34)

Swinnerton, R. C. F. "Japan Raises Its Profile in Africa." Africa Recovery v7 n3-4, Dec 1993-Mar 1994. p34-35.

ECONOMIC ASSISTANCE, JAPANESE--BURMA (v19)

ECONOMIC ASSISTANCE, JAPANESE--VIETNAM

"Japan's economic assistance to Vietnam, frozen in 1978, was reestablished in November 1992 with a Y45.5 billion loan ($420 million). In 1993, a group of countries led by Japan and France agreed to repay Vietnam's debt to international financial institutions such as the World Bank and the International Monetary Fund (IMF). These institutions then resumed lending to Vietnam in October 1993." (p3)

Tsuboi, Yoshiharu. "Japanese Perspective: Vietnam: Plan for Vietnam." Look Japan v39 n456, Mar 1994. p3. (ISSN0456-5339).

ECONOMIC ASSISTANCE, TURKISH--ASIA (CENTRAL)--AZERBAIJAN (v19)

ECONOMIC ASSISTANCE, TURKISH--SOVIET UNION (v19)

ECONOMIC FORECASTING (v19)

"DRI, the largest economic forecasting company in the U.S., was asked to study the effect of the Uruguay Round on U.S. jobs--or how GDP [gross domestic product] gains would be captured in terms of job increases, productivity increases, and real wage increases." (p10) "DRI then found that, for the U.S., after ten years: there would be net employment increases of 1.4 million jobs; the average productivity increase for labor would be slightly over 2 percent; the real wage gain would be 1.6 percent. And, looking out three years after that: net employment would increase by 2 million additional jobs; average productivity and real wage gains would approach 3 percent." (p11)

U.S. House. Committee on Energy and Commerce. "Telecommunications Trade." Hearing, 3 Aug 1993. Washington, D.C.: GPO, 1994. (ISBN0160435919). (Y4.En2/3:103-60).

Economies in Korea, Taiwan, and Malaysia "should grow 5.5%, 6.0%, and 8.0%, respectively, after inflation, according to the Organization for Economic Cooperation & Development. After China's move to cool down its red-hot economy, growth in Asia outside Japan will slow slightly--to a still-torrid 6.9%, figures Merrill Lynch & Co. economist William P. Sterling. And he forecasts that Latin America will grow 4.5% this year, vs. 3.7% in 1993. Even recession-battered Europe, U.S. industry's chief foreign market, will fare better in 1994. 'The worst is over for the major industrialized (European) economies,' says Lehman Brothers Inc. Chief Economist Allen Sinai. He forecasts European growth of 1.2% in 1994 and double that in 1995." (p62)

Ellis, James E. "Industry Outlook: Introduction: Why Overseas? 'Cause That's Where the Sales Are." Business Week n3353, 10 Jan 1994. p62-63. (ISSN0007-7135).

The Organisation for Economic Cooperation and Development "now predicts that average growth in its member countries will speed up to 2.1% in 1994 and 2.7% in 1995, after average growth of only 1.2% in each of the past three years. Some countries will fare better than others. A solid, if unspectacular, recovery is already under way in the United States, Canada, Britain, Australia and New Zealand--the countries that dipped into recession first. All five are tipped to grow by around 3% or more in both 1994 and 1995....A year ago the OECD forecast that Japan would grow by 2.3% in 1993 and by 3.1% in 1994....Japan's GDP [gross domestic product] now seems to have shrunk by 0.5% in 1993, and its 1994 forecast has been shaved to 0.5%. Even the 2.3% growth predicted for 1995 looks sluggish by Japan's usual standards of 4-5% a year. The good news is that the OECD reckons that 19 of its 24 member countries will have inflation rates (measured by the consumer-expenditure deflator) of 3% or below by 1995. The exceptions are Britain, Greece, Ireland, Portugal and Turkey. The bad news is that unemployment in the rich industrial economies will remain stuck at almost 8.5% of the labour force over the next two years. The average jobless rate in Europe will rise to 11.5%." (p92)

"Business: Economics Focus: The Richer, the Slower." Economist v329 n7843, 25 Dec 1993. p92. (ISSN0013-0613).

The International Monetary Fund "forecasts that the world economy will grow by 3.0% this year (its fastest since 1989), and 3.7% in 1995. Developing countries will lead the way, with average growth of almost 6% this year and next. The rich industrial economies are expected to expand by a more modest 2.4% in 1994 and 2.6% in 1995....Last September the IMF expected growth of 2.6% in America in 1994. It is now forecasting a heady 3.9%....Japan...is now expected to grow by only 0.7% this year, down from the 2.0% pencilled in last September and an embarrassing 3.5% forecast a year ago. Western Germany is tipped to see growth of only 0.5% for the year as a whole." (p71)

"Business: Infuriatingly Misleading Forecasts." Economist v331 n7860, 23 Apr 1994. p71. (ISSN0013-0613).

ECONOMIC FORECASTING--ASIA (v19)

ECONOMIC FORECASTING--AUSTRALIA

"The seers, looking at forecasts of economic growth, lower inflation and more jobs, reckon that at last Australia's prospects are good. Or, as Ralph Willis, the treasurer (finance minister), prefers to put it, they show the 'best conjuncture of economic fundamentals for 30 years'....Mr Willis says growth in the financial year to June will be 3.5%, instead of the 2.75% previously predicted; and that inflation will be 2% instead of the 3.5% predicted. Short-term interest rates have come down to a respectable 4.6%." (p36)

"Asia: Australia: Turning Point." Economist v330 n7850, 12 Feb 1994. p36. (ISSN0013-0613).

ECONOMIC FORECASTING--BANGKOK (THAILAND) (v19)

ECONOMIC FORECASTING--CANADA--U.S. (v19)

ECONOMIC FORECASTING--CHINA

"China's economy is the fastest growing large economy in the world. The International Monetary Fund already ranks China as the third largest economy in the world, behind the U.S. and Japan. Predictions are that the Chinese economy will grow between 13 and 14 percent this year despite stringent efforts to rein it in and cool it down. This is after a 12 percent growth rate last year. No end is in sight. Economists around the world expect China's economy to continue growing at least 6 to 8 percent annually for the next 10 years. In contrast, growth rates for industralized countries, including the United States, are predicted to remain at only 2 to 3 percent for at least the next five years. This means that China could overtake the U.S. as the world's largest economy within the next decade." (pE491)

Franklin, Barbara Hackman (Former U.S. Secretary of Commerce). "China: The Emerging Economic Colossus," Congressional Record (21 Mar 1994). Daily ed. pE491-493.

(ISSN0363-7239).

ECONOMIC FORECASTING--EUROPE

"Although the depth of the [unemployment] problem varies from country to country, all of Europe is suffering. With more than 20 million people out of work, a projected 12 percent jobless rate this year, and a barely perceptible 1.3 percent gross domestic product (GDP) growth rate forecast for 1994, the future looks bleak for new jobs....Germany, which represents more than 30 percent of the EU's [European Union's] GDP, is where Europe's job picture is painted....The Netherlands and Belgium, for example, have inextricable financial and trade links with Germany. The European Commission forecasts 0.8 percent growth for Germany this year. Joblessness reached 9 percent at the end of 1993, and will be a drag on the economy for many years to come, private economists say." (p6)

Kaslow, Amy. "Economy: Group's Biggest Challenge Is Finding Common Ground." The Christian Science Monitor v86 n46, 31 Jan 1994. p6. (ISSN0882-7729).

ECONOMIC FORECASTING--EUROPEAN ECONOMIC COMMUNITY

"French Economics Minister Edmond Alphandery has said repeatedly that the government's projection of 1.4 percent growth next year was 'prudent.' That upbeat prediction compares with a recessionary performance of minus 1 percent projected for this year amid a consensus among most private economists that the French economy will remain stagnant next year. For the European Union as a whole, economists predict around 1.3 percent growth in 1994, compared to a contraction of 0.4 percent this year." (p8)

Krause, Axel. "Member Country Report: France: France Confronts Profound Change." Europe n332, Dec-Jan 1993-94. p6-8. (ISSN0191-4545).

ECONOMIC FORECASTING--EUROPEAN ECONOMIC COMMUNITY--JAPAN--U.S. (v19)

ECONOMIC FORECASTING--FRANCE (v19)

ECONOMIC FORECASTING--GERMANY (v19)

ECONOMIC FORECASTING--INDIA

"The forecast for economic growth [in India] in 1993-94 remains unimpressive. The government's finances are therefore out of kilter. The budget deficit, which shrank for two years, is now growing again. In 1992-93 it was 5.7% of GDP [gross domestic product]; the target for this fiscal year is 4.7%, but the figure is likely to be above 6%. Inflation, which seemed to be under control, is now rising again....Interest rates are likely to come down, as part of the slow process of reforming the state-owned banking system. High interest rates for business currently subsidise cheap money for the government. The government has gone some way towards getting rid of that distortion, and the minimum commercial lending rate came down in three steps in 1993 from 18% to 15%." (p35)

"Asia: Rao's New-Year Resolution." Economist v330 n7844, 8 Jan 1994. p35-36. (ISSN0013-0613).

ECONOMIC FORECASTING--IRELAND

"Ireland's outlook for 1994 presented in the budget is for economic growth of between 4 and 5 percent; accelerated exports; significant recovery in investment reflecting lower interest rates; consumer spending up by 4 percent; continued moderate inflation of less than 3 percent; a further strong surplus on the current account of the balance of payments; Exchequer borrowing of under 3 percent; and a moderate reduction in the debt/GNP [gross national product] ratio which is still too high at around 100 percent. The jobs target is disappointingly modest. With unemployment above 290,000, the net fall predicted for 1994 is only 5,000 although it is hoped to create about 25,000 new jobs. The problem is the increasing number of young people coming on the jobs market as a result of the 'baby boom' of the 1970s, a trend which will last until the end of the century." (p15)

Carroll, Joe. "Member Country Report: Ireland: High Hopes." Europe n335, Apr 1994. p12-13,15. (ISSN0191-4545).

ECONOMIC FORECASTING--JAPAN

Japan's "GDP [gross domestic product] is now expected to shrink by about 0.5% in 1993, and to grow by 0.5% at most in 1994. That might not sound bad by western standards, but post-1945 Japan has not before experienced even two consecutive years with growth of less than 3%. If the forecasts are right, Japan will have had four such years by 1995." (p18)

"Leaders: Remade in Japan." Economist v329 n7842, 18 Dec 1993. p18. (ISSN0013-0613).

"The Japanese economy is still hurting: Unemployment is rising and consumer spending, exports and corporate profits are falling. As a result, 1994 promises to be rough for Japan. Even with the recently reported 0.5 percent growth in third-quarter gross domestic product, the nation's economy is likely to expand by a mere 1 percentage point next year. Japanese unemployment--still low by American standards--is becoming more troublesome. Analysts now predict that Japan's jobless rate will rise from 2.7 percent to over 3 percent, with a million or more excess workers idling on the payrolls of big companies. And if the economy continues to struggle, Japanese corporations may be forced to take a harder line in cutting jobs, pushing unemployment toward 4 percent." (p71)

Butler, Steven. "Predictions: Will Japan Inc. Boom Again in '94?" U.S. News & World Report v115 n25, 27 Dec 1993. p71. (ISSN0041-5537).

ECONOMIC FORECASTING--KOREA (SOUTH) (v19)

ECONOMIC FORECASTING--MEXICO (v19)

ECONOMIC FORECASTING--NEW ZEALAND

"Underlying inflation [in New Zealand] (excluding forestry products and home-mortgage payments) is likely to be 1.3% this year. On December 1st the Reserve Bank of New Zealand (the central bank) reduced its inflation prediction for 1994 from 1.4% to 0.8%. Low inflation is combined with relatively strong real growth. The Reserve Bank predicts that GDP [gross domestic product] will increase by 2.6% this year and by 2.8% next year. Its guess looks conservative: most economists expect output to grow by 4% in 1994. Unemployment, the main cause of the National Party's poor showing in November, also shows signs of abating. In early 1992 it was running at 11%; now it is 9% and employment has increased by 3%." (p76)

"Finance: Market Focus: Southward, Look, the P/E Ratios Are Low." Economist v329 n7842, 18 Dec 1993. p76. (ISSN0013-0613).

ECONOMIC FORECASTING--NORTHWEST, PACIFIC

"The Northwest, which in the last few years has outperformed the national economy, is seeing its job growth slow down....Although all five states [Idaho, Alaska, Montana, Oregon and Washington] have had job-creation rates above the United States average since 1992, next year 'Washington and Alaska are likely to be below the national average,' the economists conclude in their newly released 'Northwest Portrait,' an annual economic survey. A similar conclusion was reached by Western Blue Chip economists, who recently revised their consensus forecast downward to only a 0.8-percent job-growth rate next year....'Idaho is the bright spot in the Pacific Northwest,' [economist] Dr. Mitchell says. Aided by the success of high-tech companies, Idaho promises to repeat its roughly 3-percent job growth of this year, he forecasts....Oregon, with about 3 million people, is another positive story, with employment growth likely to hit 2.3 percent next year, up from 2 percent in 1993, Mitchell says....Employment growth next year promises to be about 1 percent for Montana--based mostly in services and tourism--and 1.5 percent in Alaska." (p11)

Trumbull, Mark. "Economy: A Formerly Booming Northwest Faces a Dimmer Forecast on Jobs." The Christian Science Monitor v86 n10, 9 Dec 1993. p11. (ISSN0882-7729).

ECONOMIC FORECASTING--TEXAS

Economist Ray Perryman "forecasts US real gross domestic product at 3.1 percent this year. Texas will fare slightly better at 3.2 percent. Employment will grow 2 percent in the US and 2.1 percent in Texas. By 2020, Perryman forecasts 141 percent job growth in medical services and 134 percent in business services in Texas. Employment will more than double in engineering services, legal services, and air transportation, he says. Farming will lose 27 percent of its jobs, railroads 23 percent, textile manufacturing 22 percent, mililtary 19 percent, apparel manufacturing 17 percent, and pipelines 11 percent, he predicts." (p11)

Pendleton, Scott. "Economy: As Texas Economy Expands, State Pins Future on Educating Youth." The Christian Science Monitor v86 n50, 4 Feb 1994. p11. (ISSN0882-7729).

ECONOMIC FORECASTING--U.S. (v19)

"According to the monthly survey of the National Federation of Independent Business, its small-business optimism index surged higher in November, erasing virtually all of its decline since last January....NFIB economist William C. Dunkelberg notes that some 17% of respondents now expect the economy to improve over the next six months, nearly double the 9% low hit in August. And 12% think it's a good time to expand, the highest November reading since 1989. Moreover, 34% reported higher sales during the past three months, compared with 23% reporting declines." (p28)

Koretz, Gene. "Economic Trends: A Little Glow of Optimism from the Small Fry." Business Week n3352, 27 Dec 1993. p28. (ISSN0007-7135).

"As the U.S. recovery broadens and the North American Free Trade Agreement spurs sales into Mexico and Canada, industry revenue should rise 5.9%, a touch more than in 1993, and profits should be up nearly 6%, predicts the National Association of Wholesaler-Distributors. Gross profit margins will resemble 1993's 21.1%." (p96)

Melcher, Richard A. "Services: Wholesaling: Cut Out the Middleman? Never." Business Week n3353, 10 Jan 1994. p96. (ISSN0007-7135).

"In a BUSINESS WEEK/Harris Executive Poll, 80% of respondents said they were at least somewhat optimistic in their outlook for the U.S. economy in 1994....Says C. E. Bryant Jr., president of Continental Conveyor & Equipment Co. in Winfield, Ala.: 'The economy in general is slowly improving. But I don't think it will be a boom year by any means....some economists believe inflation could fall well below the consensus expectation of 3% for 1994. Worldwide supplies of commodities are ample, international competition for jobs is fierce, and global industrial over-capacity is substantial. If the recent drop in crude-oil prices holds in 1994, that could trim about 0.5% from consumer price inflation. With productivity growth up from its abysmal 1%-a-year trend of the 1970s and 1980s, the economy can grow faster than before without triggering inflation. And the Fed [Federal Reserve] will probably raise short-term rates by a modest 0.25% to 0.5% sometime in 1994 just to reassure the markets of its inflation-fighting credentials." (p60-61)

Farrell, Christopher/others. "Industry Outlook: Introduction: It Won't Take Your Breath Away, But...." Business Week n3353, 10 Jan 1994. p60-63,66. (ISSN0007-7135).

According to BUSINESS WEEK, the U.S. economy is expected "to grow a moderate but healthy 3.2% in 1994, without the growth swoon that marred 1993's performance in the first half. We look for inflation of 2.7%, essentially unchanged from 1993. The yield curve will flatten, as the Federal Reserve makes a couple of small hikes in short-term rates and as tame inflation keeps long-term rates down. And we expect unemployment to dip below 6%, although that excludes the impact of government revisions, due in February, which will shift the rate up slightly." (p68)

Cooper, James C./Madigan, Kathleen. "Business Outlook: At Last, the Recovery Is Coming of Age." Business Week n3352, 27 Dec 1993. p68-69,72. (ISSN0007-7135).

"Under the Clinton budget, the Federal debt will grow from $4.6 trillion in fiscal year 1994 to nearly $6.3 trillion in fiscal year 1999, an increase of $1.7 trillion over 5 years. Additionally, the deficit will increase from $176 billion in fiscal year 1995 to $201 billion in fiscal year 1999. The $176.1 billion deficit, which is the lowest the deficit has been since the mid-1980's, reflects three factors which had nothing to do with President Clinton's policies. The country does not have to spend $27 billion for the savings and loan cleanup process, $25 billion for reduced Medicare costs, or $20 billion due to economic growth. Moreover, the Congressional Budget Office (CBO) now estimates the deficit will exceed $365 billion by the year 2004. It is painfully obvious that Federal spending is not being controlled." (pH1189-1190)

Goodling, William F. (Rep.-Pa.). "Concurrent Resolution on the Budget--Fiscal Year 1995," Congressional Record (10 Mar 1994). Daily ed. pH1170-1242. (ISSN0363-7239).

"By including agricultural trade under world trade rules for the first time ever, the Uruguay round is projected to: Increase U.S. agricultural exports from $1.6 to $4.7 billion by year 2000 and from $4.7 to $8.7 billion by 2005, with grain and animal products accounting for 75 percent of the increase. Increase net farm sector income by as much as $1.3 billion in 2000 and by as much as $2.5 billion in 2005. This could help to reduce Government spending on agricultural subsidies by roughly the same amount." (pH2567)

Bereuter, Doug (Rep.-Nebr.). "Including Agricultural Trade under World Trade Rules," Congressional Record (20 Apr 1994). Daily ed. pH2567-2568. (ISSN0363-7239).

"In 1994, [the U.S.] will borrow $62 billion from the Social Security trust fund. By the end of the century we will be borrowing $100 billion a year. In the year 2010 we will borrow over $200 billion. In the year 2015 the total amount borrowed from the Social Security trust fund will reach $4.4 trillion. In the year 2016, just 22 years from now, we will have to pay out more from the Social Security trust fund than it receives in taxes. At that time less than 2 workers will support each beneficiary. In 1950, this ratio was 16 to 1." (pS3830)

Nunn, Sam (Sen.-Ga.). "Congressional Budget Concurrent Resolution," Congressional Record (25 Mar 1994). Daily ed. pS3820-3842. (ISSN0363-7239).

"For all of 1994, the federal government is predicting 3-percent growth in GDP [gross domestic product]. In Michigan, where the economic recovery so far has been ahead of national improvements, economists are more optimistic. David Littmann, senior economist for Detroit-based Comerica Bank, said he expects the U.S. economy to grow by 3.5 percent this year. Michigan should do much better, with 5.5 percent growth, he said....David Sowerby, chief economist for Beacon Investment Co. in Ann Arbor, said he expects national economic growth of 3.5 percent to 4 percent." (p2 secE)

Hyatt, James C. "Business: Progress Is Easy as 1-2-3 Buzzwords." Detroit Free Press 2 Mar 1994. p1-2 secE.

"'We expect 1994 to be a much stronger year than 1993,' says David Wyss, an economist with DRI/McGraw-Hill, an economics consulting firm in Lexington, Mass. US economic growth 'should reach a tad over 3 percent in 1994, a little stronger' than the growth rate of about 2.8 percent for 1993, Mr. Wyss says....A strong economy, of course, means cash flow for corporate America. Fundamentals are in place for positive corporate earnings results for many US corporations this year, according to analysis by Richard Rippe, chief economist for Prudential Securities Inc. Operating profits for US corporations could rise as much as 18 percent in 1994, he says, up from around 12 percent in 1993." (p6)

Halverson, Guy. "Economy: Market Watch: Stock Watchers Like the Looks of 1994." The Christian Science Monitor v86 n27, 3 Jan 1994. p6. (ISSN0882-7729).

The Congressional Budget Office "forecasts that real GDP [gross domestic product] will grow at an annual rate of nearly 3 percent through calendar year 1995 [in the U.S.]....The combination of moderate economic growth and an increasing number of people actively looking for work will result in a gradual decline in the unemployment rate--from the 6.4 percent reported for December 1993 to 6.0 percent at the end of 1995. The persistence of excess domestic capacity and weak demand from sluggish economies elsewhere in the world will dampen inflationary pressures. The consumer price index is expected to grow at a rate of around 3 percent a year through 1995. But as the expansion continues, the Federal Reserve is likely to allow interest rates to rise in order to ensure that inflation does not heat up. CBO forecasts that the rate on three-month Treasury bills will increase from 3.1 percent at the end of 1993 to 4.5 percent at the end of 1995. It also expects that long-term rates will rise slightly over that same period." (pxiii,xv)

U.S. Congressional Budget Office. "Summary." The Economic and Budget Outlook: Fiscal Years 1995-1999 Jan 1994. Washington, D.C.: GPO, 1994.

"To illustrate the impact of shrinking deficits on economic performance, U.S. NEWS asked the WEFA Group, a Pennsylvania-based forecasting firm, to simulate the effects of additional deficit reduction. WEFA did not assume that Congress would enact new taxes or bigger spending cuts, but it did assume that inflation will remain at about 2.5 percent annually for the next four years instead of rising above 3 percent as the economy expands....The WEFA simulation shows dramatic payoffs from that sort of price restraint. With low inflation curbing federal outlays, the budget deficit shrinks to $110.5 billion in 1997, almost 14 percent less than it would be if inflation rebounded. The reduction in federal credit demands releases funds for business investment and consumer borrowing, triggering a growth spurt that adds $26.1 billion to national economic output by 1997 and leaving gross domestic product 0.5 percentage points higher than it would have been with bigger federal deficits. Consumers get an extra $17.3 billion of disposable income from an expanding economy, auto sales climb an extra 150,000 units to reach almost 10.5 million because of higher incomes and lower financing costs, and employers create an additional 380,000 jobs by 1997." (p39)

Hage, David. "Business: Like a Rolling Stone." U.S. News & World Report v116 n6, 14 Feb 1994. p38-40. (ISSN0041-5537).

ECONOMIC HISTORY (v19)

ECONOMIC INDICATORS

"For 22 countries, rich and poor...[the ECONOMIST] examined over 30 indicators which sum up the economic, social, cultural and political aspects of life....If all you want is affluence, then America is the country of your dreams, with a GDP [gross domestic product] per head of $22,130, followed closely by Switzerland. At the other extreme the average Indian has an income of only $1,150 (all figures for 1991, converted at purchasing-power parities). Many rich countries, however, have sluggish growth compared with the newly industrialising countries. A faster-growing, poorer economy may offer greater opportunities to get rich quick. For example, China and South Korea have both grown by an average of more than 9% a year over the past decade--more than three times as fast as America. The exception is Hong Kong, which has both a high average income of $18,520 (well ahead of Britain's $16,340) and one of the fastest growth rates." (p39)

"Where to Live: Nirvana by Numbers." Economist v329 n7843, 25 Dec 1993. p39-42. (ISSN0013-0613).

EDUCATION

see also AGRICULTURAL EDUCATION--ARGENTINA; AIDS (DISEASE)--EDUCATION--TANZANIA; BLIND--EDUCATION--U.S.; BUSINESS EDUCATION--U.S.; DISCRIMINATION IN EDUCATION--U.S.; ENVIRONMENTAL EDUCATION--U.S.; FEDERAL AID TO EDUCATION--U.S.; HEARING IMPAIRED--EDUCATION--U.S.; HISPANIC AMERICANS--EDUCATION; INDIANS OF NORTH AMERICA --EDUCATION; LIFE EXPECTANCY--EDUCATION--U.S.; LITERACY; MOVING, HOUSEHOLD--EDUCATION --U.S.; NIGER--EDUCATION; OCCUPATIONAL TRAINING; POOR--EDUCATION--U.S.; RELIGIOUS EDUCATION--FRANCE; SEGREGATION IN EDUCATION--U.S.; TEACHERS; U.S.--ARMED FORCES--EDUCATION; VOCATIONAL EDUCATION--U.S.; WOMEN--EDUCATION (HIGHER)--U.S.; WOMEN--EDUCATION--U.S.

A survey of 112 countries shows that female citizens in the United States receive 12.4 years of schooling, a higher level than women in any other country. But girls "lag significantly behind boys in education opportunities in 50 countries," and the U.S. falls short in the proportion of girls who attend secondary schools. "In France and Canada, 100 and 107 out of 100 girls of secondary school age respectively, attend school. The figures exceed 100 because of underage or overage girls who attend secondary school." In the U.S., 91 out of 100 girls attend secondary school. These numbers probably reflect "the impact of high rates of teenage pregnancy," according to Sally Ethelston of Population Action International which conducted the study titled "Closing the Gender Gap: Educating Girls." (p4)

"News Roundup: Secondary School Gap." Education Week v13 n21, 16 Feb 1994. p4. (ISSN0277-4232).

"The result for countries with a large gender gap in schooling is high infant-mortality rates and higher family size, according to a study on the education of girls released...by Population Action International (PAI), a research and advocacy organization. Only access to birth control has a greater impact on family size than education. In the 112 countries for which data were available, which account for 95 percent of the world's population, 76 million more boys than girls are attending school, the study found....When less well-off countries have decided to put their resources into education, a decline in the educational gender gap has been observed. Cuba, Mongolia, Uruguay, and the Philippines all scored well in PAI's ranking system for countries' educational gender gaps. The worst ranking went to Chad, where the average adult woman has less than one month of education. France, where the average is 11 years, holds the highest ranking. PAI estimates that $6.5 billion would need to be spent in the 50 countries identified as having a significant gender gap." (p8)

Feldmann, Linda. "Washington Watch: Study Finds Boys Attend School More Than Girls." The Christian Science Monitor v86 n46, 31 Jan 1994. p8. (ISSN0882-7729).

EDUCATION--AFRICA (v19)

"Enrolment levels have risen in several countries and not every statistic on Africa is bleak: in some countries children can expect nearly as many years of schooling as children in industrialized countries. A child in Botswana or Tunisia will get 10 or 10.3 years of schooling, which is comparable to...Ireland's 12.6 or Japan's 13.3 years. Still, drop-out rates are more significant than enrolment levels. UNESCO [United Nations Educational, Scientific and Cultural Organization] points out that in the poorest countries, the average number of years a child spends in school is well below the four years it considers the minimum needed to attain literacy and basic life skills. In Niger, for example, a 5 year-old boy may spend just 2.1 years in school; in Burkina Faso 2.4; in Guinea 2.7, and in Djibouti 3.4 years. The situation is even worse for girls, and conditions are similar in a dozen other countries." (p23)

Noonan, Patricia. "Continuing Crisis in African Education." Africa Recovery v7 n3-4, Dec 1993-Mar 1994. p23.

EDUCATION--CALIFORNIA--FINANCE (v19)

"According to demographer Leon Bouvier, author of 50 MILLION CALIFORNIANS?, in order to adequately accommodate the number of school-age children being added to California's population each day, the state must build 22 classrooms every 24 hours. Spending per student is now down to its lowest level ever in California, with the state ranking 41st in the nation, even though California's taxpayers spend $900 million more each year just to cover enrollment growth. The state now spends 53% of its budget on education, and yet the state had a deficit last year of $11 billion....California is growing by one million people per year, with half the growth a result of foreign immigration. It would appear as if California's financial crisis and its educational system are inextricably intertwined, and that as population grows beyond the ability of any state budget to pay for it, quality of education is only one of many social services which will continue to decline." (p2)

"500 Million Americans by 2050?" Carrying Capacity Network Clearinghouse Bulletin v3 n2, Mar 1993. 1-2,7. (ISSN1066-5404).

"In California we spend about $4,200 per year to keep a child in school. We spend $32,000 to keep a youth the same age locked up in a youth facility if he or she has committed a crime. When we consider that 80 percent of all the prisoners in our jails and prisons are school dropouts, it becomes very, very easy to understand why we want to have programs like Head Start, and then have the transition programs once the child is no longer in Head Start but has moved on to school." (pH1012)

Becerra, Xavier (Rep.-Calif.). "Improving America's Schools Act of 1994," Congressional Record (3 Mar 1994). Daily ed. pH1006-1051. (ISSN0363-7239).

EDUCATION--CALIFORNIA--PUBLIC OPINION (v19)

EDUCATION--CANADA--MEXICO--U.S. (v19)

EDUCATION--DEVELOPING COUNTRIES--FINANCE (v19)

EDUCATION--EUROPE (v19)

EDUCATION--FINANCE (v19)

EDUCATION--FRANCE (v19)

EDUCATION--GREAT BRITAIN (v19)

EDUCATION--HEALTH ASPECTS--U.S. (v19)

EDUCATION--HISPANIC AMERICANS

"In 1991, the five million Latino students enrolled in U.S. public schools represented nearly 12 percent of the total student population and the Latino numbers were growing quickly. Meanwhile, Latino teachers comprised less than 4 percent of the teaching force. To create faculties that would reflect the Latino proportions of their student bodies would require about 200,000 new Latino teachers." (p29)

Suro, Roberto. "A Voice to Be Heard." Lamp v75 n4, Win 1994. p25-30. (ISSN0023-7418).

EDUCATION--ILLINOIS--FINANCE

"In 1990, the owner of a $100,000 home in a prosperous community [in Illinois] paid $2,103 in local property taxes. This community spent an average of $10,085 on its public school students. On the other hand, the owner of a $100,000 home in a low- and moderate-income community paid $4,139, almost twice as much, even though that community was able to spend only $3,483 on each of their public schools students--less than one-third of the money the more prosperous community was spending. In 1992, 57 percent of voters in Illinois voted to address the problems created by our system's reliance on local property taxes by directing the State to increase its share of public education funding." (pS4565)

Moseley-Braun, Carol (Sen.-Ill.). "Statements on Introduced Bills and Joint Resolutions," Congressional Record (20 Apr 1994). Daily ed. pS4554-4574. (ISSN0363-7239).

EDUCATION--ISRAEL

"Data compiled by Sammy Smooha of Haifa University shows that only 16% of oriental Jews born in Israel have received higher education, compared with 56% of their Ashkenazic counterparts. The orientals are half as likely to become professionals, managers or technicians. They inhabit poorer neighbourhoods, have more menial jobs and produce bigger families." (p10)

"Survey: Israel: Clay in the Potters Hand." Economist v330 n7847, 22 Jan 1994. p58(9-10). (ISSN0013-0613).

EDUCATION--JAPAN (v19)

"According to the Ministry of Education, 96.2% of youngsters [in Japan] entered high schools in 1993, and 34.5% of youngsters entered colleges or universities. Such figures point to the 'white-collarization' of the Japanese work force. The Ministry of Labor reports that at the end of 1992, Japan had a deficit of 1.74 million skilled laborers. Of these vacancies, approximately 600,000 were in the manufacturing industry, 400,000 in construction. Japanese industry relied on automation to help." (p24)

Yonemoto, Kanji. "Sci-Tech Feature: Robots in Japan: Lending a Hand." Look Japan v40 n457, Apr 1994. p24-25. (ISSN0456-5339).

EDUCATION--JAPAN--WOMEN (v19)

EDUCATION--KENYA

"Kenya's national state has placed great emphasis on education as a vehicle for development (Republic of Kenya 1989). In fact, education beyond the primary level is a strong determinant of social mobility by increasing income and enhancing quality of life (Court 1984). As a consequence, government leaders have long admonished citizens to promote education as a development tool and, in fact, the country has realized a dramatic increase in education since independence. The number of secondary schools at independence in 1963 was only 151, whereas the number for 1987 had reached 2,485 (Republic of Kenya 1989). The percentage of secondary-school aged children enrolled in school has increased from 4% in 1965 to 23% in 1987 (2% to 19% for females). The percentage of primary-school aged children enrolled in school has increased from 54% to 96% during the same time period (40% to 93% for females) (World Bank 1990:234)." (p352)

Bradshaw, York W. "State Limitations, Self-Help Secondary Schooling, and Development in Kenya." Social Forces v72 n2, Dec 1993. p347-378. (ISSN0037-7732).

EDUCATION--KOLA PENINSULA (RUSSIA)

"The educational level in the Kola Peninsula [in northern Russia] is high: in 1987 the number of specialists with advanced and technical education amounted to 160 000, or one-third of all workers and employees, including 62 000 people with a higher university degree. This number increased by a factor of 2.65 between 1970 and 1987; however, at many state enterprises up to

40% of these specialists did not work according to their profession, which speaks of their ineffective use (Lazarev and Korchak, 1991). Ninety percent of the Kola region's population has at least a secondary level education, and this figure is above 99% for those aged 20-39. The Kola region contains 252 full-time schools, 21 evening schools, 27 vocational schools, 10 special secondary schools, and 2 institutions of higher learning." (p8)

Luzin, Gennady P./others. "The Kola Peninsula: Geography, History and Resources." Arctic v47 n1, Mar 1994. p1-15. (ISSN0004-0843).

EDUCATION--KOSOVO

"In June 1990, Serbia's legislature revoked Kosovo's autonomy; and the Kosovo Assembly responded in July by declaring Kosovo an independent republic within the Yugoslav federation. In September Serbia adopted a new constitution placing all government activities in Vojvodina under the direct control of Belgrade and abolishing all the locally controlled institutions in Kosovo, including the provincial assembly, the courts, and the police....By the end of 1991, virtually every Albanian doctor, teacher, university professor, judge, and court employee had either been dismissed from state employment or had resigned in sympathy with those who lost their jobs--some 73,000 persons were put out of work....To replace the schools from which Albanian teachers were fired, Kosovars have organized classes in private homes. The Association of Albanian Teachers and officials of the suspended pedagogical Administration of Kosovo claim that 274,280 pupils attended primary school classes and 63,340 attended secondary school classes during the 1992-1993 school year, figures that are comparable to the attendance at Albanian language schools before the dismissals." (p27)

Neier, Aryeh. "Kosovo Survives!" New York Review of Books v41 n3, 3 Feb 1994. p26-28. (ISSN0028-7504).

EDUCATION--MICHIGAN (v19)

EDUCATION--MICHIGAN--FINANCE (v19)

The old school finance system in Michigan "has created gross inequities among school districts. Students who live in districts that have high property values, and thus high tax bases, fare well while students in poorer districts do not. Schools that have a mere $3,000 to spend per student cannot possibly offer the educational opportunities offered by districts that can spend $8,000 to $10,000 per student. The inequities in the old system were apparent in 1993 rankings by GOVERNING magazine: Michigan led 12 Midwest states in school spending, but was 10th in state spending for education and dead last in high school graduation rate. Compared to all 50 states, Michigan was 14th in school spending, 46th in state spending for schools and 34th in graduation rate." (p8 secA)

"Opinion: Editorials: State of State." Ann Arbor News 19 Jan 1994. p8 secA.

Michigan's governor and legislature "abolished the two-thirds of local property taxes that go towards the schools--$6.9 billion out of an education budget of just over $9 billion....Under the old system school-boards, subject to voter approval, were responsible for fixing the rate of the property tax. As a result, some districts have been spending as little as $3,000 per child, others as much as $10,000. Under the terms of the new deal each school will receive from the state between $4,200 and $6,500 per student; the disparity will be reduced over time....The new legislation requires voters to choose between two different versions of tax reform, both of which would reimpose some property taxes. If they vote in favour of a ballot proposal in March, the state sales tax will rise from 4% to 6%. The state income tax would then drop from 4.6% to 4.4%; property taxes would be cut by about five-sixths on average; a property-transfer tax of 2% would be imposed; and the cigarette tax would rise from 25 cents to 75 cents a packet. If voters reject the ballot proposal...another set of taxes, intended to bring in the same amount of revenue, will take effect. Income tax will rise to 6%; property taxes will be cut by two-thirds; the property-transfer tax will be 1%; business taxes will rise; and cigarette taxes will rise to 40 cents a packet." (p26,31)

"American Survey: Michigan's Schools: First Lessons in Equity." Economist v330 n7844, 8 Jan 1994. p26,31. (ISSN0013-0613).

"The Michigan legislature eliminated the property tax as the main source of education funding for its 3,286 schools. That meant a loss of nearly $7 billion or 62 percent of the money used to educate Michigan's 1.6 million schoolchildren." (p11)

Walters, Laurel Shaper. "Cover Story: States Seek Fairer School Funding." The Christian Science Monitor v86 n85, 28 Mar 1994. p11-13. (ISSN0882-7729).

EDUCATION--MOZAMBIQUE

"The extent of reconstruction needs, the more immediate demands of on-going emergency programmes and the sheer complexity of the political process are severely overstretching...[Mozambique's] limited managerial and technical capacity. Few Mozambicans had been able to obtain any professional training under colonial rule. And despite some initial gains in the immediate years after independence, the disruptions of war and the diversion of resources and personnel to defence hampered efforts to overcome the shortage. Only 3,000 Mozambicans are university graduates and fully a third of senior civil servants have just primary education." (p19)

Harsch, Ernest/Laishley, Roy. "UN Mobilizes for Peace: Mozambique: Out of the Ruins of War." Africa Recovery Briefing Paper n8, May 1993. p1-20.

EDUCATION--NEW YORK (NY)--FINANCE (v19)

EDUCATION--NICARAGUA

In Nicaragua, "the 1993 school year was characterized by low grades and a high drop-out rate. According to Ministry of Education (MED) figures compiled before the end of the school year in December, only 48% of students passed all their first semester subjects. The MED estimates that only 60% of all students will pass the year. Spanish, math, physics and chemistry are causing the greatest problems. For the most part, only students from private urban schools or those with outside subsidies received grades over 80%." (p13)

"News Briefs: Society: Low Grades in 1993." Barricada Internacional v14 n369, Jan 1994. p13. (ISSN1013-9567).

EDUCATION--PENNSYLVANIA (v19)

EDUCATION--PORTUGAL (v19)

EDUCATION--RESEARCH--U.S.--FINANCE

"In 1977 a National Research Council report, 'Fundamental Research and the Process of Education,' recommended that the [U.S.] federal government 'increase...the proportion of the federal investment in education research and development designated for fundamental research' and that NIE [National Institute of Education] 'take immediate steps to implement a policy of strong support for fundamental research relevant to education.' Support for basic research at NIE increased substantially for a few years after the report's publication (Timpane, 1982). During the early years of the 1980s, the entire Department of Education invested about 11 percent of its R&D [research & development] budget on basic research; since 1986 it has spent only about 2 percent (National Science Foundation, 1991)." (p28)

Porter, Andrew C./Ball, G. Carl (National Academy of Sciences' Committee on the Federal Role in Education Research). U.S. House. Committee on Education and Labor. "Hearing on H.R. 856, the Educational Research...Excellence Act." Hearing, 27 May 1993. Washington, D.C.: GPO, 1993.

(ISBN016043338X). (Y4.Ed8/1:103-33).

"Telling evidence of the low status of education research is the very small portion of federal education funding that goes to research--just $350 million of $64.1 billion in fiscal 1991. In comparison, the federal government spends 3 times as much for space research and development, and 30 times as much for research related to health. Policy makers are not alone in their general low regard for research as an integral part of a robust system of education: teachers commonly indicate that they do not use research and do not see its connection to what they do on a daily basis in the classroom (Louis et al., 1984)." (p18-19)

Porter, Andrew C./Ball, G. Carl (National Academy of Sciences' Committee on the Federal Role in Education Research). U.S. House. Committee on Education and Labor. "Hearing on H.R. 856, the Educational Research...Excellence Act." Hearing, 27 May 1993. Washington, D.C.: GPO, 1993. (ISBN016043338X). (Y4.Ed8/1:103-33).

EDUCATION--SINGAPORE (v19)

EDUCATION--SOUTHERN STATES (v19)

EDUCATION--U.S. (v19)

"While there has actually been an increase in the percent of young people with a high school education since 1970 [in the U.S.], even in central cities, there has been a growing concentration of the least educated in poor neighborhoods. Whereas in 1970, only 1 in 16 adults with less than a high school education lived in an area of extreme poverty, by 1990 1 in 6 lived in one [of] the cities' extremely poor areas. Joblessness among these young high school dropouts was about 80 percent in 1990." (p12)

Bane, Mary Jo (Asst. Secretary, Children and Families, U.S. Dept. of Health and Human Services). U.S. House. Committee on Ways and Means. "Children and Families at Risk in Deteriorating Communities." Hearing, 7 Dec 1993. Washington, D.C.: GPO, 1994. (ISBN1060436567). (Y4.W36:103-43).

"Nearly 25% of all U.S. workers have college degrees, and over 85% high school diplomas, but we now face a high school drop out rate of 29%. That's 700,000 kids a year...and an equal number who do graduate, have skills at or below the 6th grade level. The Business Roundtable, a group of 200 U.S. CEOs, reported in 1989 that: 'as many as 60% of high school graduates are not prepared for entry-level jobs.' And for every 100 children who enter the ninth grade, only five will graduate from college eight years later. Less than one will have a technical degree." (p693-694)

Houghton, J. R. U.S. House. Committee on Appropriations. "Depts. of Veterans Affairs and Housing and Urban Development...Approp. for 1994 (Part 4)." Hearing, Washington, D.C.: GPO, 1993. (ISBN016040911X). (Y4.Ap6/1:V64/4/994/pt.4).

"Poverty is the biggest risk factor to a child's educational success. In the last two decades, the percentage of children living in poverty has increased by 48 percent. The Department of Commerce announced yesterday that this figure has gone up for the third consecutive year. It now stands at 22 percent. Saddest of all is the fact that poverty rates are highest among the youngest children. Of children under the age of six, almost 25 percent live in poverty. There are other risk factors as well: language, family status, drugs, and many others. Most of them are increasing, as well." (pS3497)

Jeffords, James M. (Sen.-Vt.). "Congressional Budget Concurrent Resolution," Congressional Record (23 Mar 1994). Daily ed. pS3477-3502. (ISSN0363-7239).

"The U.S. Department of Education, in 'The Condition of Education, 1993,' reports trends in proficiency in science, math, reading, and writing of 9-, 13-, and 17-year-old students. All measures for all groups were unchanged or worse over the last two decades, except for a small improvement in math for 9- and 13-year-olds, and in reading for 17-year-olds....the data indicates that, when measured in traditional ways, our students are about as good as they were 20 years ago. The alarming aspect of this becomes evident when our students are compared with those of our international competitors. A recent test of students from 11 industrialized nations reported in the 'National Assessment of Educational Progress,' put our 13-year-old students last in mathematics and next-to-last in science. The test results indicated our 13-year-old students were approximately 2 years behind students in Taiwan." (pS3496-3497)

Jeffords, James M. (Sen.-Vt.). "Congressional Budget Concurrent Resolution," Congressional Record (23 Mar 1994). Daily ed. pS3477-3502. (ISSN0363-7239).

"Our educational system is enormous and diverse. Over 60 million people--almost one out of every four Americans--is enrolled in school at the elementary, secondary, or postsecondary level. Another 3.7 million people are employed as elementary and secondary teachers and faculty of colleges and universities, and 4 million more work in the administrative, professional, and support staff functions. In addition, thousands of everyday citizens participate in State and local school boards governing over 15,000 school districts and 110,000 schools." (pS760)

Roth, William V., Jr. (Sen.-Del.). "Reaffirmation of the Role of State and Local Governments in Education," Congressional Record (3 Feb 1994). Daily ed. pS760. (ISSN0363-7239).

"Data collected in a 13-year study of...early [childhood] development by the Harvard University preschool project, indicate that language, curiosity, social skills, and cognitive intelligence, lay the foundation for learning. The study further shows that, with few exceptions, the development of these skills in a 6-year-old can be predicted at age 3. An official who headed several departments in the Mobile, AL, County Public School System, told a group of State legislatures and business persons: We weep when we see the conditions some of the 4- and 5-year-old children are in when they come to us. They don't understand simple directions, are afraid of adults and other children, and have low receptive and expressive language. They are simply not ready either for kindergarten or first grade." (pS920)

Heflin, Howell (Sen.-Ala.). "GOALS 2000: Educate America Act," Congressional Record (4 Feb 1994). Daily ed. pS910-932. (ISSN0363-7239).

"It is estimated that 30 percent of 16- to 24-year-olds nationwide lack the skills necessary for entry level employment....The United States lags way behind our competitors in Europe and Asia in preparing young people--especially those who choose not to go to college--for the world of work. Germany and Japan have developed extensive, integrated youth education and job training programs to succeed in the high-technology global economy of the 21st century. As a former college president, I think it is critical for us to open the doors of opportunity to college to every young person through grants and loans....But it is wrong that this country spends $55 on college aid for every dollar we spend on opportunities for those who do not go to college, especially when such a small percent of today's high school freshmen will graduate from both high school and college. That is penny-wise and dollar-foolish." (pS1022)

Wofford, Harris (Sen.-Pa.). "The Shooting of Patrolman Steven Shaw," Congressional Record (7 Feb 1994). Daily ed. pS1019-1024. (ISSN0363-7239).

"Only 27 percent of public school kindergarten teachers assume that all children will be ready for 1st grade after kindergarten, and 70 percent would hesitate to promote those who are not ready, a survey of teachers shows. The National Center for Education Statistics 1993 survey of 1,448 kindergarten teachers shows that most believe readiness cannot be pushed but that it can be enhanced by activities such as reading to children. An N.C.E.S. brief comparing parents' and teachers' views, however, shows that parents are more likely to define readiness as knowing numbers and letters and paying attention." (p6)

Cohen, Deborah L. "Early Years." Education Week v13 n21, 16 Feb 1994. p6. (ISSN0277-4232).

"The proportion of Americans who have finished high school or who have earned at least a bachelor's degree has reached record levels, according to the U.S. Census Bureau. In 1993, 80.2 percent of people 25 and older had finished high school, and 21.9 percent had earned a bachelor's degree. The Census report attributes the higher education levels to population shifts, with the proportion of younger, more educated people getting larger as the pool of older, less educated people shrinks. In 1993, among people ages 35 to 44, nearly 87 percent had finished high school, compared with about 52 percent of people 75 and older." (p4)

"News Roundup: National: Education Record." Education Week v13 n25, 16 Mar 1994. p4. (ISSN0277-4232).

A study of the Channel One news program which is broadcast in classrooms for 12 minutes daily shows that students at "exemplary" schools, where teachers make good use of the program's content, performed 5 percent better on current events tests than students at schools where the program was not broadcast. Students were tested twice in 1993 on news from the previous three to six months. (p12)

Walsh, Mark. "Channel One Impact on Performance Found to Be 'Moderate.'" Education Week v13 n20, 9 Feb 1994. p12. (ISSN0277-4232).

In Philadelphia 22 neighborhood high schools have been reorganizing into 110 charters, each having several hundred students and emphasizing a particular instructional approach. A study of the reforms by the Center for Assessment and Policy Development says the charters "have an independent effect on student performance", apart from other factors that affect student achievement. "Students enrolled in three or more major courses within their charters were 11 percent more likely to be promoted to the next grade than were other students. Charter students were 7 percent more likely, after controlling for demographic differences and prior school experience, to be promoted than were those not in charters." (p10)

Bradley, Ann. "Student-Achievement Gains Seen in Phila. Charter Schools." Education Week v13 n28, 6 Apr 1994. p10. (ISSN0277-4232).

"Sandia National Laboratories, headquartered in Albuquerque, New Mexico, is one of the nation's largest scientific and engineering laboratories. Operated for the U.S. Department of Energy, it conducts scientific research for the U.S. government....The New Initiatives Department of Sandia's Strategic Studies Center undertook a wide-ranging analysis of secondary-school education systems....The participants told a Congressional subcommittee on July 18, 1991: 'The study is producing interesting results.'" (p27) For example, "About three in five (57%) U.S. youths attempt postsecondary studies. This is roughly the high-school graduation rate of the early 1950s. Moreover, they say, this rate is about twice that of Japanese students. Approximately one in four persons in the 25- to 29-year-old age group has completed at least a four-year college degree. This rate is nearly the same as the U.S. high school graduation rate of the 1930s. The percentage of 22-year-olds obtaining bachelor's degrees in the natural sciences and engineering was rather stable from 1960 to 1980, at nearly 4 percent....From 1977 to 1987, the total number of bachelor's degrees awarded to U.S. citizens in math, computer science, physical science, and engineering rose more than 75 percent, from roughly 90,000 degrees in 1977 to 155,000 in 1987." (p30)

Frazier, Kendrick. "Special Report: 'Perspectives on Education in America': Sandia Study Challenges Misconceptions." Skeptical Inquirer v18 n1, Fall 1993. p26-31. (ISSN0194-6730).

EDUCATION--U.S.--COSTS

"Approximately $400 billion of Federal spending [in the U.S.] is for programs--welfare, unemployment, crime, health care, housing and training--that were created to assist low-income individuals. These programs would be highly sensitive to increased literacy and higher education attainment. If we could reach the goals set out in Goals 2000, we would expect major savings in these programs. If one assumes the savings amounted to 30 percent, that would translate to a reduction in annual Federal spending of $120 billion. If we do nothing, spending will probably get worse. There would be a savings at the State level. A comparable estimate would be $150 billion, of which we might be able to save $45 billion. So the cost to the States right now for their programs of this nature is $150 billion, with potential savings of one-third. That certainly would justify the expenditure of greater amounts of money in our educational programs." (pS930)

Jeffords, James M. (Sen.-Vt.). "GOALS 2000: Educate America Act," Congressional Record (4 Feb 1994). Daily ed. pS910-932. (ISSN0363-7239).

EDUCATION--U.S.--DATA PROCESSING

"'Computers in American Schools,' an international assessment of educational technology recently released by the C.C.S.S.O. [Council of Chief State School Officers], notes that only 35 percent of U.S. high schools reported using an external computer network, and only 16 percent of those schools reported using such an external network daily or weekly. Network use, the report adds, is primarily for electronic mail, rather than for accessing on-line information services." (p33)

West, Peter. "The Last Mile." Education Week v13 n23, 2 Mar 1994. p31-34. (ISSN0277-4232).

"According to the SPA [the Software Publishers Association], of the 17,000 school districts in the US, small districts spend an average of $48,000 on technology, medium-sized districts spend $192,900, and large districts 968,000. Federal spending on technology in schools is less than 1 percent of the total US federal fiscal year 1993 budget." (p9)

Thomas, Andrea. "Economy: School Courses Weave in Software." The Christian Science Monitor v86 n26, 31 Dec 1993. p9. (ISSN0882-7729).

EDUCATION--U.S.--FINANCE (v19)

"In a recent survey of State educational agencies, the Education Writers Association found that...education infrastructure needs [in the U.S.] are about $125 billion; $84 billion for new construction and $41 billion for maintenance and repairs. In fact, the EWA survey also reported that, while 42 percent of our Nation's school facilities are in good condition, 33 percent are only adequate, and 25 percent are shoddy places for learning. More specifically, this survey found that 61 percent of our Nation's inadequate school facilities needed major repairs; 43 percent were obsolete; 42 percent were environmentally hazardous; 25 percent were overcrowded; and 13 percent were structurally unsound. Other studies have shown that our Nation's education infrastructure is falling apart in both rural and urban school districts alike." (pS4565)

Moseley-Braun, Carol (Sen.-Ill.). "Statements on Introduced Bills and Joint Resolutions," Congressional Record (20 Apr

1994). Daily ed. pS4554-4574. (ISSN0363-7239).

"In her research at Georgetown University, Maureen Edwards found that students in poor school facilities can be expected to fall 5.5 percentage points below those at schools in fair condition and 11 percentage points below those in schools in excellent condition. And so the learning environment is directly related to educational performance in school." (pS4566)

Moseley-Braun, Carol (Sen.-Ill.). "Statements on Introduced Bills and Joint Resolutions," Congressional Record (20 Apr 1994). Daily ed. pS4554-4574. (ISSN0363-7239).

"While increased funding for education clearly cannot by itself solve the systemic problems associated with poverty, it is a 'sine qua non' for placing low-income children on a more equal footing with their more advantaged peers....The fact is that the amount spent on the education of children in affluent schools is often two to three times higher than in low-income schools. For example, the 100 poorest districts in Texas spend an average of about $3,000 per student, while the 100 wealthiest districts spend an average of about $7,200. Illinois school districts spend between $2,400 and $8,300 per student." (p44)

Rotberg, Iris C. "Separate and Unequal." Education Week v13 n24, 9 Mar 1994. p44. (ISSN0277-4232).

"There is no systemic link between spending and student performance, says a study conducted by Emily Feistritzer of the National Center for Education Information (NCEI) and released by the American Legislative Exchange Council (ALEC) and Empower America. 'Report Card on American Education: A State-by-State Analysis 1972-1973 to 1992-1993' is the first extensive state-by-state compendium of education indicators since the annual 'State Education Performance Chart,' which the Department of Education stopped publishing in 1990....The report found that even though education spending has risen 62 percent (in constant U.S. dollars) over the last 20 years, from $52 billion in total public school expenditures in 1972-1973 to $253 billion in 1992-1993, there has been no significant improvement in student performance....Utah, for example, ranked last on the amount spent on each student in 1992-1993 ($3,128), 49th in per-capita income, and 45th in average teacher salary ($26,997). However, Utah had the second-highest increase in student enrollment over the past 20 years and ranked in the top 10 on standardized test scores and 14th in graduation rates." (p5)

"Higher Spending May Not Raise Performance." NSTA Reports! Dec 1993-Jan 1994. p5,45.

"In 1972, more than 50 percent of education funds came from local sources, with the state providing 41 percent and 8 percent coming from federal sources. Today, the national average is 46 percent from local sources, 47 percent from state sources, and 7 percent from federal sources." (p13)

Walters, Laurel Shaper. "Cover Story: States Seek Fairer School Funding." The Christian Science Monitor v86 n85, 28 Mar 1994. p11-13. (ISSN0882-7729).

EDUCATION--U.S.--MINORITIES

Almost one in three students in public schools belongs to a minority group. "Yet, only 8 percent of teachers are African-American and only 3 percent are Latino. Demand for faculty members of color is at its highest point, and the supply cannot even begin to meet the demand....According to a National Research Council report, a total of 24,721 Ph.D.'s were awarded to Americans in 1991. Of this number, African-Americans received 933, Hispanics 708, and Native Americans 128." (p38)

Wise, Kelly/Perez-Torres, Rafael. "Needed: More Teachers of Color." Education Week v13 n21, 16 Feb 1994. p38. (ISSN0277-4232).

"About 90 percent of both Asians and non-Hispanic whites graduate from high school, but Asians are more likely than whites to complete four or more years of college. Among the high school graduating class of 1980, for example, 45 percent of Asian-American students had enrolled in a four-year college by the following fall, compared with 32 percent of non-Hispanic whites, 28 percent of blacks, 17 percent of Hispanics, and 15 percent of American Indians. The educational success of Asians and Pacific Islanders may be best exemplified by the share who continue beyond a four-year college degree. Almost one out of seven (14 percent) Asians and Pacific Islanders age 25 or older have a graduate or professional degree--almost twice the percentage for whites (8 percent) and three to four times the rates for other minorities." (p29-30)

O'Hare, William P. "America's Minorities--The Demographics of Diversity." Population Bulletin v47 n4, Dec 1992. p2-47. (ISSN0032-468X).

EDUCATION--U.S.--PARENT PARTICIPATION (v19)

EDUCATION--U.S.--PUBLIC OPINION

"Children need more inspiration, not more pressure from parents and teachers, said 59 percent of U.S. registered voters surveyed recently by the American Association of School Administrators (AASA). Fifty-seven percent of voters said they support tougher standards for teachers and students and say they will put up with even more homework for children. Twenty-six percent said teachers and parents should be tougher on kids; 12 percent said teachers and parents should be both tougher and more inspirational, and three percent fell into the 'neither/don't know' category. Most (87 percent) said they favor training teachers to help them make learning more interesting to students. At the same time, 90 percent said students need more discipline in class, while 87 percent said standards for student performance should be raised. When talking about the problems schools face, 25 percent of voters cited lack of parental involvement as a problem, followed by drugs and violence (17 percent); crowded classrooms (16 percent); low standards (13 percent); lack of money (10 percent); administration (nine percent); and poor teaching (five percent)." (p14)

"NewsBits." NSTA Reports! Dec 1993-Jan 1994. p14-15,39.

EDUCATION--VIETNAM

"Vietnam qualifies as a Third World nation by virtue of its poor infrastructure, low wages and lack of capital improvements. But there is more to consider. For one thing, the Vietnamese are well-educated, with a 90 percent literacy rate. More than 7,000 Vietnamese have earned doctoral degrees, and 1,500 Vietnamese graduate from college every year. English is the prevalent second language." (p36)

Pirozzolo, Dick. "Fair Comment: Time to Lift U.S. Embargo on Vietnam." Insight v10 n8, 21 Feb 1994. p36. (ISSN1051-4880).

EDUCATION, BUSINESS

see BUSINESS EDUCATION

EDUCATION, HIGHER

see also COLLEGE INTEGRATION; WOMEN--EDUCATION (HIGHER)

EDUCATION, HIGHER--GERMANY (v19)

EDUCATION, HIGHER--GERMANY--JAPAN--U.S. (v19)

EDUCATION, HIGHER--GREAT BRITAIN (v19)

"Wherever the market, and especially the notion of linking funding to performance, has been tried, it has led to howls of protest from academics who regard it as an affront to their dignity as self-governing professionals and a waste of their time as high-powered brain-workers. For all that, it has produced dramatic results. Thanks to a vigorous use of penalties against departments with low submission rates, for instance, the proportion of British phD students completing their theses within four years has soared from 25% in 1980 to 69% today." (p74)

"Universities: Towers of Babble." Economist v329 n7843, 25

Dec 1993. p72-74. (ISSN0013-0613).

EDUCATION, HIGHER--JAPAN--U.S. (v19)

EDUCATION, HIGHER--MICHIGAN

In Michigan, "the state's contribution to higher education has increased slightly over the last two decades when measured as a percentage of the state's general fund. In 1970-71, 15.6 percent of the general fund went to colleges and universities; in 1993-94 and in the proposed 1994-95 budget, 16.2 percent goes to higher education. During that period, student enrollment in all state institutions have remained about the same--ranging roughly from about 200,000 to 215,000." (p8 secA)

"Opinion: Editorial: Tuition." Ann Arbor News 25 Jan 1994. p8 secA.

EDUCATION, HIGHER--NAMIBIA

"Currently in Namibia, which has been independent and multiracial since 21 March 1990, the ratio of white to black university graduates is 500:1. Whites and expatriates continue to dominate medium and top managerial positions in practically all business sectors. The government of Namibia is very much aware of these imbalances, which are the legacy of a political system which, for decades, systematically favored the white minority in education and hiring. Access to training and certain professions were even off-limits to black Namibians." (p28)

Goodson, Rodger. "Social Partners: The Long Road to Equality in Southern Africa." World of Work n7, Mar 1994. p28-29. (ISSN1020-0029).

EDUCATION, HIGHER--NICARAGUA

"Despite government financial support--estimated at $80.5 million for 1993--for the elementary, secondary and tertiary levels of the national education system [in Nicaragua], in the three public universities the basic administrative, technical, teaching and academic needs could not be met by the meager $25 million budget allocated. The UCA [Central American University] is a private university run by Jesuit priests and open to the general public. According to Maria Antonieta D'Leon, coordinator of the department of student development, only 700 of the 3,017 students applying for the first time to get into the UCA were accepted, thus 2,317 students were rejected. Of the thirteen undergraduate programs, law and business administration receive the most applicants, while humanities and librarianship are among the least popular fields. In addition, in 1992 the Russian translation program was terminated due to a lack of demand." (p15-16)

Duarte, Vilma. "Education: University Crisis." Barricada Internacional v13 n364, Aug 1993. p15-17. (ISSN1013-9567).

EDUCATION, HIGHER--U.S. (v19)

"About half of America's young people do not go on to college; 75 percent do not earn a college degree. And yet today's typical high school education is geared toward the college-bound student and not the vast majority who go directly into the workforce. Unless all students, including gifted and talented, have the skills to produce quality goods and services in a technologically-oriented and fast changing consumer marketplace, America will not prosper in the global economy." (p25)

Kaltenmark, Sharon (Director of Guidance, George C. Marshall High School, Fairfax, VA). U.S. House. Committee on Education and Labor. "Hearing on School-to-Work Transition." Hearing, 15 Jul 1993. Washington, D.C.: GPO, 1994. (ISBN0160440858). (Y4.Ed8/1:103-42).

"Attendance at M.B.A. forums, where prospective students can gather information on dozens of programs...has surged. Last fall, a record 3,287 potential applicants converged on New York--a 27 percent jump over 1992. Several schools ran out of catalogs and had to print thousands more. Employer recruiting--a key measure of B-school health--also is on the upswing. Some 18 percent more companies turned up this year at Duke University's Fuqua School of Business, and many sent line managers, not personnel staffers. Carnegie Mellon University's Graduate School of Industrial Administration is seeing a 10-percent increase in recruiters. 'We're almost back to where we were in the mid-1980s,' says Columbia Business School Dean Meyer Feldberg--with some students getting four or five offers....Admittedly, with fewer managerial berths to fill, corporations have grown choosier. A recent survey by Pennsylvania State University's Smeal College of Business Administration found that 56 percent of major U.S. firms planned to hire a smaller number of M.B.A.'s this year....Significantly, almost 75 percent of the chief executives and other ranking managers who responded to the Penn State survey said they would advise their own children that an M.B.A. is worth the investment." (p76)

Lord, Mary. "Graduate Schools: Business: The M.B.A. Hard Sell." U.S. News & World Report v116 n11, 21 Mar 1994. p75-76,79. (ISSN0041-5537).

EDUCATION, HIGHER--U.S.--FINANCE (v19)

EDUCATION, HIGHER--U.S.--MINORITIES

"Between 1982 and 1992 the number of people earning doctoral degrees increased 6 percent, but the number earned by black men dropped 20 percent. The largest number of doctoral degrees earned by members of minority groups is in education, but even in that field minority doctorates were down to 29 percent in 1992, compared to 40 percent in 1982." (p4)

"News Roundup: Minority Doctorates." Education Week v13 n19, 2 Feb 1994. p4. (ISSN0277-4232).

EDUCATION, HIGHER--U.S.--PUBLIC OPINION

A survey of [U.S.] college freshmen reports that the largest proportion ever--65 percent--plan to seek advanced degrees. In the 1970s fewer than half of all freshmen had such plans. In addition, more women than men want advanced degrees. Thirty-nine percent of women want masters degrees compared with 37.3 percent of men, and 27.3 percent of women want doctoral degrees, compared with 25.8 percent of men. This is a dramatic change from 1967, when "men were three times more likely than women to want to pursue a doctoral, medical or law degree--26.7 percent compared with 8.5 percent." (p5)

Lawton, Millicent. "More Students Aspiring to Advanced Degrees." Education Week v13 n19, 2 Feb 1994. p5. (ISSN0277-4232).

EDUCATION, PRESCHOOL--U.S. (v19)

EDUCATION, RELIGIOUS

see RELIGIOUS EDUCATION

EDUCATIONAL TESTS AND MEASUREMENTS

"Over the past 20 years [in the U.S.], we have seen SAT scores decline by 35 points, even though the amount of money spent per pupil on primary and secondary school students has increased 47 percent. After 1983, when the Carnegie Foundation published 'A Nation At Risk,' States and the Congress were spurred to implement a number of major reforms, including reducing class sizes, increasing teacher pay and professional development opportunities, placing increased emphasis on math and science, and the like. Despite 10 years of reform, our education system still struggles. Our kids rank next to last in the world among industrialized nations on proficiency in science. Only Spain, Slovenia, and Jordan score lower in math than United States students. Our kids take fewer foreign languages, and test scores have shown little or modest improvement. These trends are particularly disturbing as we enter a period of global competition." (pS918)

Bond, Christopher S. (Sen-Mo.). "GOALS 2000: Educate America Act," Congressional Record (4 Feb 1994). Daily ed. pS910-932. (ISSN0363-7239).

EDUCATIONAL TESTS AND MEASUREMENTS--U.S.

"The Congressionally mandated NAEP [National Assessment of Educational Progress] program has tested national samples of students in certain academic subjects for 20 years. The program became more prominent, however, after it was expanded in 1988 to permit state-by-state comparisons of student achievement. Some states complained that the results cast them in an unfair light. They pointed out that the program simply scores and ranks states without considering differences among them that could influence those results. California's 4th, 8th, and 12th graders, for example, scored at the bottom among states on the latest NAEP reading assessment. But, at 22 percent, the proportion of disadvantaged California children taking the assessment was almost 2 1/2 times that of the nation as a whole. Moreover, 21 percent of the state's schoolchildren are not native speakers of English." (p18)

Viadero, Debra. "Proposal to Adjust NAEP Scores for Diversity Mulled." Education Week v13 n24, 9 Mar 1994. p1,18. (ISSN0277-4232).

The number of [U.S.] states having mandated student assessment programs is up to 46 in 1992, from 29 in 1980. (p4)

"News Roundup: Student Assessment Mandates Now in 46 States, Survey Finds." Education Week v13 n19, 2 Feb 1994. p4. (ISSN0277-4232).

While 70 percent of statewide tests of schoolchildren are multiple choice tests, alternatives are being used in some states. "According to a survey by the Educational Testing Service, 12 percent of statewide tests require students to provide writing samples. Eighteen states are developing short-answer questions for their assessments, and 22 states are working with longer, open-ended questions. In addition, individual-performance assessments are being used in 14 states, and nine states are using portfolios of student work or learning records to evaluate students." (p5)

Viadero, Debra. "Testing." Education Week v13 n17, 19 Jan 1994. p5. (ISSN0277-4232).

EGG TRADE--EUROPEAN ECONOMIC COMMUNITY (v19)

EGG TRADE--MEXICO--U.S. (v19)

EGG TRADE--U.S.

"In the last 12 years, 80 percent of U.S. egg producers have been driven out of business. About 30 agribusiness corporations now produce most of our eggs, with just one person tending every 50,000 hens. Diseases and infections resulting from close confinement are remedied with hormones and antibiotics. Hens are also fed and sprayed with insecticides to control pests. Such practices translate into food safety concerns. Salmonella is an increasing public health threat. Although the Centers for Disease Control estimate that less than 10 percent of salmonella cases are reported, from 1985 to 1991, some 12,916 salmonella illnesses and 49 deaths were reported, with 77 percent caused by eggs." (p44)

Bria, Rosemarie Dorothy. "Food & Health: Brave New Egg Farm." E Magazine v4 n4, Jul-Aug 1993. p44,46. (ISSN1046-8021).

EGYPT

see also LABOR SUPPLY--EGYPT--FRANCE; MILITARY ASSISTANCE, AMERICAN--EGYPT; WATER-SUPPLY--EGYPT--SUDAN

EGYPT--ECONOMIC CONDITIONS

"The Subcommittee on Europe and the Middle East of the House Foreign Affairs Committee has recently received reports from the U.S. Agency for International Development on the economic situation in Egypt and Israel--the top two recipients of U.S. foreign assistance....Participation in the Gulf War has proved to be a financial boon for Egypt. Due to debt forgiveness and its own reforms, Egypt's financial position has greatly improved....As a result, Egypt's economy has stabilized. Though an expected drop in real GDP [gross domestic product] for 1991/92 did not materialize, the economy is stagnant. We estimate real GDP grew at the annual rate of 2.8 percent in 1991/92 and only 1.5 percent in 1992/93. Various revenue measures and greater control of expenditures have cut the budget deficit to 4.7 percent of GDP in 1992/93. Egypt achieved a positive current account balance (excluding transfers) in 1991/92 for the first time in ten years, although the current account balance is now expected to be slightly negative in 1992/93. Foreign reserves are now quite healthy, over $15 billion dollars (equivalent to over a year of imports). With the latest debt reduction, Egypt's outstanding debt will amount to less than $35 billion." (pE470)

Hamilton, Lee H. (Rep.-Ind.). "Aid Reports on Egypt and Israel," Congressional Record (17 Mar 1994). Daily ed. pE470-472. (ISSN0363-7239).

EGYPT--SOCIAL CONDITIONS

"Egypt has had rapid economic growth, with GNP [gross national product] per capita increasing at an annual rate of 4.1 percent from 1965-1990. Life expectancy increased by 12 years during approximately the same period, and was estimated to be 59 years in the 1985-90 period. The infant mortality rate is still moderately high at 65, but this represents a decrease of 110 points and more than 60 percent from 175 deaths for 1960-65. Adult literacy remains at a low level, 48 percent in 1990, and only 34 percent for females. Primary plus secondary school enrollment ratios have increased appreciably during the past 25 years; they were 81 percent for females and 90 percent for both sexes in 1990....Contraceptive prevalence increased slowly from 25 percent in 1974-75 to 30 percent in 1984, and then more rapidly to 37 percent in 1988-89 and to 47 percent in 1992." (p85-86)

Mauldin, W. Parker/Ross, John A. "Prospects and Programs for Fertility Reduction, 1990-2015." Studies in Family Planning v25 n2, Mar-Apr 1994. p77-95. (ISSN0039-3665).

ELDERLY PERSONS

see AGED

ELECTIONS--FINANCE

see CAMPAIGN FUNDS

ELECTRIC AUTOMOBILES

see AUTOMOBILES, ELECTRIC

ELECTRIC LIGHTING, FLUORESCENT

see FLUORESCENT LIGHTING

ELECTRIC POWER--CHINA

"Only 67% of households in China were connected to the mains electricity supply by 1992, low even by Asian standards (82% of Indian homes are electrified)....Last year China boosted investment in its power industry by a fifth to about 50 billion yuan ($8.7 billion). The Hong Kong branch of Japan's Nomura Research Institute says that, even so, China's growth in generation capacity...is unable to keep pace with economic growth. To cope with demand, Nomura calculates that China must increase generating capacity by more than 20,000 MW each year. Yet China's domestic manufacturers can only produce 12,000 MW of power stations a year." (p82)

"Business: Electricity in China: Power Surge." Economist v330 n7855, 19 Mar 1994. p81-82. (ISSN0013-0613).

ELECTRIC POWER--U.S. (v19)

ELECTRIC POWER CONSUMPTION--CHINA (v19)

ELECTRIC POWER CONSUMPTION--INDIA

"The biggest consumers of electrical energy in the Third World are in the industrial sector and are still not part of any energy-efficiency campaign, be it World Bank or IIEC [International Institute of Energy Conservation] inspired. In India, for example, it has been calculated that most industries wallow in energy waste, pay far too little for the energy they use, and generally consume 20 to 30 times the energy used in developed countries to produce equivalent products. However, a large number of these industrial plants were relocated to the Third World, often with World Bank assistance, after completing their life spans in the advanced economies. Naturally they reflect the energy efficiencies operating at the time they were installed in their country of origin. Du Pont, for instance, has been attempting to relocate a plant of 1938 vintage--which manufactures a synthetic fibre used in airplane tyres--from Richmond, Virginia, to Goa in India." (p28)

Alvares, Claude. "In My View: The World Bank's '1% Solution.'" Panoscope n35, Apr 1993. p28. (ISSN0951-8819).

ELECTRIC POWER CONSUMPTION--MEXICO

"Mexican planners estimate that, over the next 10 to 15 years, projected growth rates of about 7 percent annually in electricity demand could require nearly doubling current generating capacity of 28,000 megawatts (MW). The Mexican government liberalized its laws regarding foreign investment in the electricity generating sector in order to help meet its expected growth in domestic demand." (p58)

White, William (Deputy Secretary of Energy, U.S. Dept. of Energy). U.S. House. Committee on Energy and Commerce. "NAFTA: Energy Provisions and Environmental Implications." Hearing, 22 Sep 1993. Washington, D.C.: GPO, 1994. (ISBN0160440459). (Y4.En2/3:103/70).

ELECTRIC POWER CONSUMPTION--U.S.

"An examination of the distribution expenses of 294 large public power distribution utilities and 868 rural electric distribution borrowers--largely cooperatives--shows that in 1991 distribution expenses account for approximately 2 percent of the difference in retail rates between these sectors. (Rural distribution systems are utilities with outstanding loans from the U.S. Rural Electrification Administration, a federal agency housed within the Department of Agriculture.) The average retail rate for these co-ops was 6.91 cents per kilowatt-hour versus 5.90 cents per kilowatt-hour for the 294 public systems, or 17 percent higher." (p42)

Kelly, John/Hipps, Kaylyn. "Distribution Expenses: A 2 Percent Difference." Public Power v52 n1, Jan-Feb 1994. p42-43. (ISSN0033-3654).

"Over the past two decades [in the U.S.], the gross domestic product and the consumption of electricity have proceeded in tandem, both rising about 70 percent. Yet total energy use has risen only 20 percent. Electricity has replaced direct burning of fuels in every sector of the economy. The result is a wholesale change in energy use patterns. In 1970, the U.S. economy spent $150 billion on fuels but only $88 billion on electricity. By 1990, these figures had reversed, with electricity expenditures rising to $180 billion while expenditures on the direct use of fuels fell to $112 billion." (p26)

Richardson, Alan. "Industry Trends That Are Changing Our World." Public Power v52 n2, Mar-Apr 1994. p26-31. (ISSN0033-3654).

"Many of the first regulator-ordered efforts to reduce demand [of electricity] were conservative, low-budget affairs. One mid-1970s PG&E [Pacific Gas and Electric Company] brochure reminded customers to turn off televisions and lights when not using them, and to avoid overcooking foods, 'especially vegetables.' But in the past few years, spending on DSM [demand-side management] in the United States has boomed, from an estimated $900 million in 1989 to $2.3 billion in 1992. The West Coast, Wisconsin, and the Northeast, where populations and economies have expanded rapidly and new power plants have been controversial, account for most of this total." (p26)

Roodman, David Malin. "Power Brokers: Managing Demand for Electricity." World Watch v6 n6, Nov-Dec 1993. p22-29. (ISSN0896-0615).

ELECTRIC POWER PLANTS

see also GEOTHERMAL POWER PLANTS

ELECTRIC POWER PLANTS--ENVIRONMENTAL ASPECTS--U.S.

"Coal-fired power plants generate most of the electricity produced in the American Southwest. Some 7000 megawatts (MW) of this power originates from four giant generating stations located near the Grand Canyon, the Colorado River and in the northwestern corner of New Mexico....Regional studies have demonstrated that visibility has decreased about 50 percent since the plants were built during the '60s and '70s. This is not surprising, since a number of the units presently lack scrubbers and other common air-pollution mitigation equipment. The New Mexico Game and Fish Department reports that mercury deposition in lakes and streams in New Mexico has also increased 5 percent per year possibly as a result of pollution from coal-fired power plants. Acid rain levels in the region are the worst west of the Mississippi." (p20)

Bensinger, Charles. "Solar Thermal Repowering of Coal-Fired Power Plants." Solar Today v7 n6, Nov-Dec 1993. p20-22. (ISSN1042-0630).

ELECTRIC POWER PRODUCTION--CANADA--MEXICO--U.S. (v19)

ELECTRIC POWER PRODUCTION--DEVELOPING COUNTRIES

"George Soros, an American investment manager, joined forces with the financial arm of General Electric to form a $2.5 billion fund to invest in power projects in the developing world. Its initial focus will be on China, India, Indonesia and Mexico....After almost two years of talking, an agreement has been signed to construct Paiton, a $2.3 billion coal-fired power plant in East Java. Indonesia's biggest private power station will add 1,220 megawatts to the country's 9,700MW grid. Paiton, which is now looking for financing, will be built by an international consortium that includes General Electric, Japan's Mitsui and America's Mission Energy....Other governments are also looking out both for contractors to build power plants and for the money to pay for them. Malaysia, which has current installed capacity of 5,500MW, reckons it will need 12,000MW by 2000. The Chinese hope to add 15,000MW of capacity every year for the next decade, while the Indians are talking about needing 6,000MW a year over the next five years. Enron, a fast-growing American energy company, is due soon to start work on the world's largest gas-fired plant, costing some $2.8 billion, at Dabhol in India, with a 20-year contract to supply electricity to the Maharashtra State Electricity Board." (p66)

"Business: Infrastructure in Asia: The Trillion-Dollar Dream." Economist v330 n7852, 26 Feb 1994. p66. (ISSN0013-0613).

ELECTRIC POWER PRODUCTION--ENVIRONMENTAL ASPECTS

"Assuming a 20% capacity factor for PV [photovoltaic] and average emissions factors from electric-power generation using today's mix of power plants, it is estimated that for each 1,000 megawatts of PV generating capacity, approximately 1.1 million metric tons of carbon-dioxide emissions would be avoided each year. The EPA has calculated that if all U.S. residences were fully equipped with rooftop PV generators to produce daytime electricity, the resulting decrease in CO2 emissions would exceed 170 million metric tons per year." (p25-26)

Kern, Ed/Polansky, Anne. "Cover Story: How Many Rooftop PV Systems Does It Take to Save the Planet?" Solar Industry Journal v4 n4, 1993. p18-22,24-27.

ELECTRIC UTILITIES--U.S.

Utility demand, "which grew by more than 3% annually from 1985 to 1988, rose an anemic 1% in 1993, estimates Daniel Scotto, an analyst at Donaldson, Lufkin & Jenrette Securities Corp. His 1994 forecast: 1.5%. Cheap fuel and excess capacity have led to brutal wholesale pricing. Even in the high-cost Northeast, some utilities are signing 10-year contracts for 4...[cents] a kilowatt-hour, well below the region's 6...[cents] to 7...[cents] average generating cost. Stir in tightfisted regulators, and the industry's return on equity may average just 10% in 1994, down from a peak of 13.8% in 1984." (p100)

Maremont, Marie. "Services: Utilities: Danger: Competition Dead Ahead." Business Week n3353, 10 Jan 1994. p100. (ISSN0007-7135).

"General managers of local publicly owned electric utilities earned an average salary of $58,545 and a median salary of $54,059 as of June 1, 1993, according to data collected by the American Public Power Association and published in its 1993 'Survey of Management Salaries in Local Publicly Owned Electric Utilities.' APPA collected data on 16 managerial occupations for public power systems with annual electric revenues of $10 million or more and on nine managerial occupations from utilities with electric revenues less than $10 million. Data are based on responses of 823 local public power systems. Of the respondents, 54 percent are utilities with less than $5 million in annual electric revenues and 81 percent had revenues below $20 million. Only 8 percent of respondents had revenues of $50 million or more and 4 percent had revenues of $100 million or more." (p22)

Choate, Scott. "Management Salaries." Public Power v52 n1, Jan-Feb 1994. p22. (ISSN0033-3654).

"In the 1986 to 1991 time period, the nation's cooperative electric systems have exhibited stronger growth in both customers and sales than have publicly owned systems. According to data collected by the U.S. Department of Energy's Energy Information Administration, the number of ultimate customers served by cooperatives rose from 10.4 million in 1986 to 11.7 million in 1991, an increase of 12.7 percent. In comparison, the number of customers served by publicly owned systems grew from 14.1 million to 15.3 million over the same time period, an increase of 8.5 percent. Similarly, cooperatives' sales to ultimate customers rose by 23.3 percent, from 166 million megawatt-hours in 1986 to 205 million megawatt-hours in 1991, while publicly owned utilities' sales to ultimate customers rose by 17.3 percent, from 335 million megawatt-hours in 1986 to 393 million megawatt-hours in 1991." (p18)

Moody, Diane. "Co-op Growth Record Does Not Square with Battle Cry of Shrinking Customer Base." Public Power v52 n1, Jan-Feb 1994. p18. (ISSN0033-3654).

"Molten carbonate fuel cells have 50 to 60 percent fuel-to-electricity efficiency, compared with 35 to 40 percent for conventional steam and internal combustion engines, according to EPRI [Electric Power Research Institute]. Because they function at a higher temperature, they also can operate with existing systems for cogeneration power, where the steam and hot water by-products can be used both in industrial processes and for heating and air conditioning. Unlike conventional power plants, the system is built at a manufacturing facility as small pre-fabricated modules and then shipped to the site. When assembled, a two-MW plant is about the size of a tennis court and can power 1,000 homes. During the MCFC process, natural gas is fed into the fuel cell chamber where its fuel energy is converted into electricity. The electric current is converted for home use and the leftover stream of air, water and carbon dioxide are exhausted. Because the natural gas is not burned, but reacts electrochemically like a battery, there are no measurable nitrogen or sulfur oxide by-products to affect air quality. Carbon dioxide emissions are about 50 percent less than coal-burning plants and 10 to 30 percent lower than other natural gas-fired plants." (p44-45)

Hobart, Stacey. "Innovations: The Commercialization of a Fuel Cell." Public Power v52 n1, Jan-Feb 1994. p44-45. (ISSN0033-3654).

"Residential customers of [U.S.] investor-owned utilities paid average rates that were 33 percent above those paid by customers of publicly owned systems during 1991, while residential customers of cooperative systems paid average rates that were 17 percent above those paid by customers of publicly owned systems. Public power customers paid an average of 6.4 cents per kilowatt-hour for residential electric service, compared to 8.5 cents per kilowatt-hour paid by residential customers of investor-owned utilities, and 7.5 cents per kilowatt-hour paid by residential customers of cooperative systems....Commercial customers of investor-owned systems paid 18 percent more for electricity than public power customers in 1991, and commercial customers of cooperative systems paid 11 percent more than public power customers. Public power commercial customers paid an average of 6.5 cents per kWh, compared to 7.7 cents per kWh paid by commercial customers of investor-owned utilities, and 7.2 cents per kWh paid by commercial customers of cooperative systems." (p14)

Moody, Diane. "Public Power Costs Less." Public Power v52 n1, Jan-Feb 1994. p14-15. (ISSN0033-3654).

"The increasing size, complexity, and cost of T&D [transmission and distribution] systems are...a concern for many [U.S.] utility executives who must assure their customers that the utility is doing all it can to deliver power economically as well as efficiently and reliably. In the past, the cost of T&D has been a fraction of the cost of power generation. But that has changed to the point where some utilities are spending $1.50 to distribute power for every $1.00 they spend producing it, according to PG&E's [Pacific Gas & Electric Company's] Joseph Iannucci. Last year alone, utilities invested nearly $16 billion in T&D equipment....Many utilities are reluctant to order new plants, in the face of uncertainties about future electricity demand. Even as the number of customers increases, the demand for electricity has shrunk to an average increase of less than 2% annually in the last few years, down from nearly 8% per year in the 1960s, according to EPRI [Electric Power Research Institute]." (p38)

Pitchford, Paula. "Research Update: National Renewable Energy Laboratory: NREL Helps to Envision the Utilities of the Future." Solar Industry Journal v4 n3, 1993. p36,38-39.

ELECTRIC VEHICLES

"EVs [electronic vehicles] suffer from three main drawbacks that have prevented them from penetrating the market: they have a lower range than gasoline-powered vehicles; recharging the batteries takes a lot longer than filling a tank of gas; and EVs cost much more than comparable gasoline-powered vehicles. For example, a Geo Metro EV conversion has a range of about 50 miles, a top speed of 65 mph, takes 8 hours to fully recharge its batteries, and sells for about $20,000; a conventional Geo Metro sells for about $7000. The GM Impact has a range of about 120 miles, a top speed of 75 mph, and is projected to cost $25,000--at least $10,000 more than a comparable gasoline car." (p2-3)

Hwang, Roland J. "All Charged Up." Nucleus v15 n3, Fall 1993. p1-3,12. (ISSN0888-5729).

"One very promising alternative to battery powered electric vehicles (BPEV) is the fuel cell electric vehicle (FCEV) powered by hydrogen. The fuel cell is a remarkable electro-chemical device. Some have said that the fuel cell may do for energy and transportation in the 21st century what the transistor did for electronics in this century. A fuel cell produces electricity quietly without any moving parts, as long as the cell is supplied with hydrogen and oxygen (or air). Fuel cell efficiencies can be over 50 percent, compared to the 30 to 35 percent efficiency typical of today's steam powered electrical generators, and well above the 15 percent efficiency of the gasoline powered internal combustion engine (ICE)." (p12)

Thomas, C. E. 'Sandy'. "Solar Hydrogen: A Sustainable Energy Option." Solar Today v7 n5, Sept-Oct 1993. p11-13. (ISSN1042-0630).

ELECTRIC VEHICLES--U.S. (v19)

"California's Clean Air Act of 1990 mandates that by 1998, two percent of the vehicles manufactured for sale in California must emit no pollutants. By 2003, 10 percent must be zero emission. According to...[Stan Skokan, president of the San Francisco Bay Area chapter of the Electric Auto Assoc.], 18 other states have recently adopted the same clean air rules as California, putting new pressure on automakers to clean up their acts. One of the most influential policies nurturing the EV [electric vehicle] industry is the Energy Policy Act of 1992. The 'EPAct' offers a 10 percent tax credit--up to $4,000--for owners of electric vehicles. Additionally, EPA [Environmental Protection Agency] made $50 million available for electric and electric hybrid vehicle demonstrations throughout the next nine years. $40 million has been earmarked for electric vehicle infrastructure development between 1993 and 1997." (p4)

Grennan, Heather. "Focus: Green Wheels." Positive Alternatives v4 n1, Fall 1993. p4-5. (ISSN1065-0075).

ELECTROMAGNETIC FIELDS--U.S.

"The wiring in your home and office puts out EMFs [electromagnetic fields]. Your toaster, refrigerator, coffee maker, television, VCR, CD player, bathroom fan, and electric razor put out EMFs. Your hair dryer, electric blanket, and computer put out EMFs. And the 642,000 miles of overhead transmission lines that swing merrily across the country put out EMFs. Fields from appliances range from .5 mG for a refrigerator (nearly too small to measure) to 20,000 mG for some can openers and hair dryers--although at a distance of three feet most are well below 2 mG. EMFs from power lines, however, can remain strong to a distance of 100 feet or more." (p30)

Dana, Amy/Turner, Tom. "Currents of Controversy." Amicus Journal v15 n2, Sum 1993. p29-32. (ISSN0276-7201).

ELECTRONIC INDUSTRIES

see also COMPUTER INDUSTRY; SEMICONDUCTOR INDUSTRY

ELECTRONIC INDUSTRIES--JAPAN--U.S.

"One of the more important facts about...[the U.S. electronics] industry is that over 470 U.S. electronics firms have offices, people and representation in Japan. This is an industry which has committed significant resources to compete for Japan's lucrative markets. These are not companies that can be criticized for inadequate efforts to sell in Japan. The overall bilateral trade deficit with Japan is concentrated in two sectors--autos and electronics, with electronics representing about 45% of the deficit. This deficit in electronics has increased despite the appreciation of the yen. It rose 12% in 1992 alone, reaching $22.3 billion. Furthermore, the deficit continues to deteriorate despite as many as 20 bilateral trade agreements focused in the electronics sector." (p59)

Saldich, Robert J. (Chair, Board of the American Electronics Assoc.). U.S. Senate. Committee on Finance. "United States-Japan Trade Negotiations." Hearing, 8 Nov 1993. Washington, D.C.: GPO, 1994. (ISBN0160435625). (Y4.F49:S.hrg.103-399).

ELECTRONIC INDUSTRIES--U.S.

"Electronics is the nation's largest manufacturing sector with approximately 2.3 million American workers employed directly in the industry. Worldwide sales of electronics firms now total over $400 billion per year. Moreover, as the tool builder for the rest of the economy, the U.S. electronics industry certainly would rank very high, if not number one in strategic importance for the economic well being of the U.S." (p58)

Saldich, Robert J. (Chair, Board of the American Electronics Assoc.). U.S. Senate. Committee on Finance. "United States-Japan Trade Negotiations." Hearing, 8 Nov 1993. Washington, D.C.: GPO, 1994. (ISBN0160435625). (Y4.F49:S.hrg.103-399).

"Eighty-one percent of American households now have microwave ovens, according to Roper. Sixty-eight percent own VCRs, 32 percent have Nintendo or other electronic TV games, 21 percent own compact disc players, 20 percent own home computers, 15 percent have video cameras, and 11 percent have video-disc players. You are most likely to find these techno-toys and products in baby-boomer households headed by people aged 30 to 44. Households headed by people aged 60 and older are least likely to contain electronic goodies. It's no surprise that income is a major factor in ownership of electronic items. Only 10 percent of households with incomes under $15,000 own a home computer, compared with 41 percent of households with incomes of $50,000 or more. Married-couple households with both spouses working are also more likely to own a variety of electronic items, including home computers, than are those with one earner." (p42)

Mitchell, Susan. "Technophiles and Technophobes." American Demographics v16 n2, Feb 1994. p36-40,42. (ISSN0163-4089).

"Roper Starch Worldwide of New York City asked people if they had heard of 15 new or emerging home-electronics products. Only four products were familiar to at least half of the general public--car phones, fax machines, lap-top computers, and laser discs. It's hard to build consumer demand for products the public doesn't even know exist. Awareness is just the first step, because people do not always stampede to buy the things they do know about. Only 10 percent of Americans who are familiar with car phones want to buy one in the next year or two. Just 7 percent want a lap-top computer, 5 percent want a fax machine, and 3 percent want a laser disc." (p40) "Roper finds that only 20 percent of households headed by people aged 18 to 29 own a home computer, compared with 28 percent of those headed by 30-to-44-year-olds." (p42)

Mitchell, Susan. "Technophiles and Technophobes." American Demographics v16 n2, Feb 1994. p36-40,42. (ISSN0163-4089).

ELECTRONIC SURVEILLANCE--U.S. (v19)

ELEPHANTS--ASIA

"Although Asian elephants are still numerous and are a familiar sight as domestic animals in the southeastern portion of the country, they have suffered relentless poaching. Moreover, their populations are dangerously fragmented. It is estimated that only 60 animals remain in the wilds of Nepal, while the population in China has plunged to 500. India probably has 20,000 elephants, but at least 5,000 of these have no satisfactory habitat: The hungry elephants raid farms, killing scores of villagers each year. Mudumulai is one of a handful of places that harbor a viable population. Asian elephants are forest creatures that range widely sometimes occurring at altitudes as high as 12,000 feet; they are extremely difficult to count. In most countries the numbers are unknown. About 10,000 Asian elephants, perhaps a third of Earth's population, are working animals. They may include half of the world's female adults, as females are preferred to the more aggressive males. Only a minority are permitted to breed: When they are pregnant or have youngsters at their heels, they do less work." (p9)

Tudge, Colin. "Conservation Hotline: A Pachyderm Paradox."

Wildlife Conservation v96 n5, Sep-Oct 1993. p8-9. (ISSN1048-4949).

ELEPHANTS--FOOD

"Every day [at the Los Angeles Zoo], each adult African elephant eats 100 pounds of hay, 50 pounds of carrots, 8 pounds of apples, 8 pounds of bananas, 4 pounds of onions, and 10 pounds of vitamins the size of wine bottle corks (containing vitamin E, calcium, copper, and zinc)....On the African plains, elephants eat a simpler diet consisting mostly of the acacia tree, which they knock over to get at its tasty roots and leaves. This huge animal also has an enormous thirst. Elephants guzzle approximately 25 gallons of water on a typical day and as much as 40 gallons on a hot one. Although all this food and drink seems like quite a heavy meal, it's surprisingly light on the wallet--only $16.30 at the Los Angeles Zoo, less than many people spend on one trip to a restaurant." (p19)

Luiso, John. "Animal Fare: Entrees Elephantine." ZOOLIFE v4 n2, Spr 1993. p19. (ISSN1046-4565).

ELEVATORS--U.S.--SAFETY MEASURES (v19)

ELM--U.S. (v19)

EMBASSIES

see DIPLOMATIC AND CONSULAR SERVICE

EMBASSY BUILDINGS--U.S. (v19)

EMIGRATION AND IMMIGRATION (v19)

see also ISRAEL--FORMER SOVIET REPUBLICS--EMIGRATION AND IMMIGRATION; U.S.--EMIGRATION AND IMMIGRATION

"When you see a potential immigrant on television, our whole heritage [in the U.S.] says that we must make room for him or her; but I increasingly question whether we should or can. Of the 160 countries that belong to the United Nations, only three take any appreciable number of legal immigrants. The United States takes about one million a year, Canada takes about 150,000 per year, and Australia takes about 125,000. So, perhaps, 1.25 million people in a total pool of three billion people are lucky enough to come to one of the immigrant-receiving countries. Yet that pool increases by about 80 million people a year (90 percent of the 90 million people the global population increases by every year are born in less-developed countries). The maximum amount of 'good' that the immigrant-receiving countries can do to alleviate the pressures on those countries where people want to migrate is infinitesimally small--less than 0.05 percent." (p14)

Lamm, Richard D. "Saint Martin of Tours and the New World of Public Policy." Humanist v53 n5, Sep-Oct 1993. p13-15. (ISSN0018-7399).

"In the early 1990s, an estimated 100 million people live outside their nations of citizenship. Although this number may increase as the result of further political and economic changes in the 1990s, it still constitutes less than 2 percent of the world's population. On a global scale, population movement across borders is a relatively limited phenomenon and most often involves moving from one developing country to another. In the late 1980s, about 44 percent of the world's migrants were in sub-Saharan Africa and another 8 percent were Afghani war refugees in Pakistan and Iran. Migrants from the developing to industrial countries constitute only a modest proportion of the world stock of migrants." (p21)

Bloom, David E./Brender, Adi. "Labor and the Emerging World Economy." Population Bulletin v48 n2, Oct 1993. p2-39. (ISSN0032-468X).

"The 100 million people 'living outside their countries of birth or citizenship' include 36 million people in Asia, the Middle East, and North Africa; 10 million in sub-Saharan Africa; 6 million in Latin America and the Caribbean; over 23 million in Eastern and Western Europe; 4 million in Oceania (including Australia and New Zealand); and over 20 million in the United States and Canada....These figures include refugees as well as temporary and permanent migrants. At the beginning of 1993, there were about 19 million people designated as refugees by the U.N. and perhaps again as many 'forced migrants in refugee-like situations.'" (p1-2)

Kalish, Susan. "International Migration: New Findings on Magnitude, Importance." Population Today v22 n3, Mar 1994. p1-2. (ISSN0749-2448).

"Under the 1990 Immigration Act, the United States is expected to admit between 800,000 and 1 million immigrants each year in the 1990s. Canada expects about 250,000 annually, and Australia less than 150,000." (p2)

Kalish, Susan. "International Migration: New Findings on Magnitude, Importance." Population Today v22 n3, Mar 1994. p1-2. (ISSN0749-2448).

EMIGRATION AND IMMIGRATION LAW--U.S. (v19)

EMPLOYEE FRINGE BENEFITS

see also SOCIAL SECURITY

"In the private sector, [U.S.] employer-paid fringe benefits raise total labor costs by nearly 20 percent. Among federal employees, employer-paid fringe benefits add considerably more--nearly 35 percent, according to the Commerce Department. The average federal civilian employee received $6,400 more in fringe benefits than the average private sector employee in 1991, an advantage enhanced by the tax-free nature of such benefits....Federal employees put in fewer hours, primarily because they have far more generous vacation and holiday allowances. The average federal government employee has 13 more paid vacation and holidays annually than the average private employee, an extra 108 hours of paid time off. For each five days of paid time off for private employees, federal employees receive eight. Over the course of a career, federal employees receive nearly 1 1/2 years (78 weeks) more in paid vacation and holidays than the average private employee." (p26)

Cox, Wendell. "Symposium: Federal Workers Benefit Heavily." Insight v10 n3, 17 Jan 1994. p25-27. (ISSN1051-4880).

EMPLOYEE FRINGE BENEFITS--EUROPE--CIVIL SERVICE

"In the typical [European] parliamentary session a quarter or more of the members will be absent, even though, in addition to salaries equal to those of their national counterparts, they also receive some wallet-packing perks: a secretarial allowance of 7,468 ecus [European currency units], ($8,433) a month; office expenses of 2,732 ecus a month; and travel allowances that run at 0.73 ecus (83 cents) per kilometre for the first 800 and 0.37 ecus for each extra kilometre." (p53)

"Europe: European Enlargement: May Be Delayed." Economist v331 n7860, 23 Apr 1994. p52-53. (ISSN0013-0613).

EMPLOYEE FRINGE BENEFITS--GERMANY (v19)

"In Germany, employers are required by law to provide at least three weeks of paid vacation, but nearly everyone gets four to six weeks. [Gerald] Canning explains that the typical German family goes on one skiing holiday and one 'holiday in the sun' each year--to the Canary Islands, for instance, or Mallorca. 'I also get approximately 1000 marks (roughly $650) of holiday money, which is paid in June and July,' Canning tells me. 'This is on top of the regular pay--it's quite usual here. And, on top of that,' he adds, 'people here are generally paid 13 months of salary rather than 12.'" (p7)

McClure, Laura. "Welfare State: Europeans Still Have It Better Than Americans." Toward Freedom v42 n6, Oct 1993. p7. (ISSN0048-9898).

EMPLOYEE FRINGE BENEFITS--U.S. (v19)

"Health insurance [in the U.S.] has grown to become by far the most costly fringe benefit that employers provide. In 1992, employers' contributions for group health insurance made up 6.0 percent of total compensation, up from 5.1 percent just three years earlier. By comparison, employers' contributions to pensions and profit-sharing plans constituted 1.5 percent of payroll in 1992, and all other benefits totaled 1.4 percent." (p24)

U.S. Congressional Budget Office. "How the Tax Exclusion Affects the Health Insurance Market." The Tax Treatment of Employment-Based Health Insurance Mar 1994. Washington, D.C.: GPO, 1994.

"According to the U.S. Bureau of Labor Statistics, the average small business [in the U.S.] provides a worker with 7.6 days of paid vacation per year (and that's not until one year of employment has been completed). Only after 10 years on the job does vacation time increase to an average of 13.5 days. Mid-size companies don't do much better, offering an average of 9.1 days of paid vacation after a workers' first year." (p7)

McClure, Laura. "Welfare State: Europeans Still Have It Better Than Americans." Toward Freedom v42 n6, Oct 1993. p7. (ISSN0048-9898).

EMPLOYEES

see also BLUE COLLAR WORKERS; DOMESTICS; FORCED LABOR; MIGRANT LABOR

EMPLOYEES--EDUCATION--U.S. (v19)

EMPLOYEES--JAPAN (v19)

EMPLOYEES--TRAINING OF--U.S. (v19)

"The need for upgrading the skills of...workers [in the U.S] should not be underestimated. A study by the Competitiveness Policy Council found that approximately 40 percent of business executives say they cannot modernize their equipment due to worker skill deficiencies. In addition to promoting the implementation of new technologies, skills upgrading has been documented to result in a host of other positive outcomes including increased productivity, quality improvements, and decreased job related injuries. In fact, studies of work force development programs show employers' return on investment for every dollar spent on job training is at a rate of $3. The benefits to the employees are equally impressive. Employees who receive formal skill upgrading enjoy earnings advantages of 25 percent or more over those with no such training. They also benefit from increased job security and mobility in the event they do lose their job. Unfortunately, not enough of this type of training is being provided. It is estimated that nationally, only about 7 percent of the work force is receiving formal training. Recent statistics have found of the roughly 2 million workers who are losing their jobs, nearly one quarter lack the skills being demanded in the U.S. economy." (pE668)

Gunderson, Steve (Rep.-Wis.). "Work Force Skills and Development Loan Bill," Congressional Record (15 Apr 1994). Daily ed. pE668. (ISSN0363-7239).

"In 1992 the number of employees receiving formal, budgeted training grew by nearly 4 million people to a total of over 41 million. On average, each engaged in learning for over 30 hours annually, or for about the same amount of time a college undergraduate would attend class over one and a half weeks. If this new employee pool were housed at a university, 17 new universities the size of Harvard would have to be built just to handle a single year's growth in corporate education. By way of comparison, NO new universities were built in 1991/1992 for traditional-age students. In fact, all of the dozen religious and specialized four-year institutions built in the two decades of the 70s and 80s would have handled barely 1% of the new corporate entrants in the single year of 1992." (p12)

Botkin, Jim. "InterClass: A Corporate Learning and Education Consortium." New Horizons for Learning v14 n3, Spr 1993. p12-13.

"In the corporate world, most people believe that during stringent financial times, training budgets are among the first to be cut. Prior to the mid-1980s, the facts verify this to be so. The facts after 1987, however, tell another story. Even during the recession of 1991/92, training budgets either increased, or at least were not cut any more deeply than business budgets in general. Employee education, it seems, is being seen as ever more crucial to competitive advantage in a knowledge economy. A good example of the phenomenal growth in corporate education is Arthur Andersen, the $5 billion accounting and consulting firm. Its 150 acre campus training center near Chicago teaches 4,000 new employees a year. The $157 million spent on training each year equates to an average of $7,200 per professional, or 6.5% of their time and 6.5% of the firm's revenues." (p12)

Botkin, Jim. "InterClass: A Corporate Learning and Education Consortium." New Horizons for Learning v14 n3, Spr 1993. p12-13.

EMPLOYEES--U.S.

"'The gap between our educational system and the society's needs is widening,' said Willard R. Daggett, director of the International Center for Leadership in Education and a noted education reformist. He said...that the workforce in 1950 consisted of 60 percent unskilled workers, with the professional/managerial and skilled groups each accounting for 20 percent. In 1992, 65 percent of American workers were skilled workers, managers and professionals, with 35 percent unskilled. By the year 2000, only 15 percent of jobs will be held by unskilled workers, with 85 percent requiring professional skills and training." (p1,3 secB)

Pyen, Chong W. "Local: Schools on Wrong Path?" Ann Arbor News 12 Jan 1994. p1,3 secB.

EMPLOYEES--U.S.--DRUG USE (v19)

"According to some government studies, two-thirds of drug users [in the U.S.] are currently employed, and 44 percent admit selling drugs to coworkers." (p10)

Coolidge, Shelley Donald. "Economy: Drugs in the Workplace: Firms Find Effective Way to Detect Drug Use: Hair." The Christian Science Monitor v86 n62, 23 Feb 1994. p10. (ISSN0882-7729).

EMPLOYER-SUPPORTED DAY CARE--U.S. (v19)

EMPLOYMENT

see AFRO-AMERICAN WOMEN--EMPLOYMENT; ARAB AMERICANS--EMPLOYMENT; AUTOMOBILE INDUSTRY AND TRADE--EMPLOYMENT--U.S.; BREAST FEEDING--EMPLOYMENT--U.S.; CALIFORNIA--EMPLOYMENT; CHILDREN--EMPLOYMENT--BANGLADESH; CHINA--EMPLOYMENT; COLLEGE GRADUATES--EMPLOYMENT--U.S.; DEFENSE INDUSTRIES--EMPLOYMENT--U.S.; DETROIT (MICH)--EMPLOYMENT; DISCRIMINATION IN EMPLOYMENT; EUROPE--JAPAN--U.S.--EMPLOYMENT; EXPORT PROCESSING ZONES--EMPLOYMENT; EXPORTS--EMPLOYMENT--U.S.; FORESTS AND FORESTRY--EMPLOYMENT--OREGON; FRANCE--EMPLOYMENT; GAZA STRIP--WEST BANK--EMPLOYMENT; GERMANY--EMPLOYMENT; GREAT BRITAIN--U.S.--EMPLOYMENT; HANDICAPPED--EMPLOYMENT--U.S.; HIGH SCHOOL DROPOUTS--EMPLOYMENT--U.S.; HISPANIC AMERICANS--EMPLOYMENT; IMMIGRANTS--EMPLOYMENT--U.S.; INSURANCE, HEALTH--EMPLOYMENT--U.S.; JAPAN--EMPLOYMENT; KOLA PENINSULA (RUSSIA)--EMPLOYMENT; LOS ANGELES (CALIF)--EMPLOYMENT; MINES AND MINERAL RESOURCES--EMPLOYMENT--U.S.; MINORITIES--EMPLOYMENT--GREAT BRITAIN; NEW YORK (NY)--EMPLOYMENT; PART-TIME EMPLOYMENT--U.S.; PHILADELPHIA (PA)--EMPLOYMENT; POSTAL SERVICE--

EMPLOYMENT--U.S.; PRISONERS--EMPLOYMENT--U.S.; SINGLE MOTHERS--EMPLOYMENT--POLAND; SWEDEN--EMPLOYMENT; TEMPORARY EMPLOYMENT--U.S.; TRUCKING--EMPLOYMENT--U.S.; TURKEY--EMPLOYMENT; U.S.--EMPLOYMENT; UNEMPLOYMENT; WOMEN--EMPLOYMENT; YOUTH--EMPLOYMENT; ZAMBIA--EMPLOYMENT

EMPLOYMENT, PART-TIME

see PART-TIME EMPLOYMENT

EMPLOYMENT, TEMPORARY

see TEMPORARY EMPLOYMENT

EMPLOYMENT DISCRIMINATION

see DISCRIMINATION IN EMPLOYMENT

ENDANGERED SPECIES

see also WILDLIFE CONSERVATION

ENDANGERED SPECIES--AFRICA--ASIA (v19)

ENDANGERED SPECIES--CALIFORNIA

"The 4,200 square miles of the San Diego region encompass a wide variety of habitats--coastal, scrub, grassland, forest, and desert. Those habitats are home to 24 plant and animal species that are listed or proposed for listing as endangered by the federal or state governments. Some 300 species are considered 'sensitive.' The endangered species list includes the least Bell's vireo, the California least tern, California orcutt grass, and San Diego button celery. The California gnatcatcher was listed as threatened last spring. Candidates for listing include the saltmarsh skipper and the San Diego barrel cactus." (p25)

Fairbanks, Janet/Toma, Lan Xu. "Room to Roam." Planning v60 n1, Jan 1994. p24-26. (ISSN0001-2610).

ENDANGERED SPECIES--U.S. (v19)

"Approximately one-fourth of all the recovery plans aimed at bringing back plants under the Endangered Species Act include some form of reintroduction, say Falk and Peggy Olwell, manager of CPC's [Center for Plant Conservation's] conservation programs....Despite their popularity, reintroductions are not 100% successful. Of 45 reintroduction projects in California in the past decade, 4 were completely successful, 15 partly successful, and 10 failed, where success is defined as the ability of the population to survive and reproduce. It is too soon to tell for the rest. In a 1991 British Nature Conservancy Council study of 144 plant reintroduction attempts, only 22% were deemed successful. More than half had appeared to have failed." (p66)

Allen, William H. "Reintroduction of Endangered Plants." BioScience v44 n2, Feb 1994. p65-68. (ISSN0006-3568).

"The...report, 'What Exactly Is an Endangered Species?,' by Wilcove and fellow EDF [Environmental Defense Fund] staffers Margaret McMillan and Keith Winston,...concludes that listing declining species sooner could significantly improve their chances of recovery--and at lower cost. From 1985 to 1991, the median population of an endangered species at the time of its listing was only about 1,000 for animals and less than 120 for plants. Such tiny populations are at high risk of extinction, according to most experts, and are difficult to protect. Critics of the [Endangered Species] Act argue that it protects too many species and that the endangered list has grown in recent years because many subspecies and regional populations of more widespread species--rather than full species--have been added. But EDF found that about 80% of the animals and plants listed from 1985 to 1991 were full species, 18% were subspecies, and only 2% were populations." (p3)

"Law Gives Many Species a New Lease on Life." EDF Letter v24 n4, Jul 1993. p3. (ISSN0163-2566).

"Conservation biologists developed the concept of Minimum Viable Populations (or MVPs) to establish population recovery goals and to develop conservation plans. In general, a minimum viable population has at least a 95 percent chance of surviving for 100 years or more. Conservation biologists develop computer models incorporating species specific life history information and make projections to determine the number of individuals needed to meet this goal. For non-isolated, rapidly reproducing species, the MVP may be around 500 individuals. Estimates for other species may be much higher (at least several thousand) due to naturally low population densities, low reproduction, increased isolation resulting from habitat fragmentation and a number of other factors. In order to accurately estimate MVPs, a great deal of species specific information is needed. Such information is currently not available for most species, and thus, even among those listed as threatened and endangered, relatively few have reliable MVP estimates." (p17)

Snetsinger, Susan. "Conservation Biology: Where the Rubber Meets the Road." Northwest Conservation Fall 1993. p17.

"The U.S. Fish and Wildlife Service has the responsibility of securing protection for endangered plant and animal species, a process known as 'listing.' According to a 1990 Inspector General's report, bureaucratic delays caused the extinction of species before federal protection could be granted. By the U.S. Fish and Wildlife Service's own admission, between 1980 and 1990, 34 species perished while awaiting listing under the ESA. The Inspector General's report estimated that there may be as many as 3,600 species in immediate need of ESA protection." (p9)

Henkel, William B. "Reports from the Field: Lawsuit Brings Victory for Endangered Species." Northwest Conservation Win 1993. p9.

ENDOWED CHARITIES

see CHARITABLE USES, TRUSTS, AND FOUNDATIONS

ENERGY

see FORCE AND ENERGY

ENERGY, NUCLEAR

see NUCLEAR ENERGY

ENERGY ASSISTANCE FOR THE POOR

see POOR--ENERGY ASSISTANCE

ENERGY CONSERVATION

"Around the globe, DSM's [demand-side management's] potential remains largely untapped. Efficiency could cut total energy investments 40 percent in developing countries over the next 30 years--saving at least $1.5 trillion--and 50 percent in industrialized nations (another $700 billion), according to the Lawrence Berkeley Laboratory in Berkeley, California. But demand-side management is more than a way to save money. After all the greater cost of energy use lies in the risk of dependence on nonrenewable resources and the insidious dangers of fossil fuel pollution, from mercury poisoning to global warming (electricity production alone accounts for a quarter of world carbon dioxide emissions)." (p29)

Roodman, David Malin. "Power Brokers: Managing Demand for Electricity." World Watch v6 n6, Nov-Dec 1993. p22-29. (ISSN0896-0615).

ENERGY CONSERVATION--DENMARK--NETHERLANDS

Both the Netherlands and Denmark "are supporting the aggressive growth of cogeneration, an efficient technology that simultaneously generates electricity and heat. A standard fossil fuel power plant discards huge amounts of heat (usually all but 33 percent of the heat energy released in combustion), pumping it into the air as steam, or into a nearby river as hot water, disrupting downstream ecosystems. At the same time, thousands of people in the region will buy additional energy to heat homes, offices, and factories. A cogenerating plant eliminates this tremendous waste by supplying its leftover heat to nearby factories, or to whole neighborhoods via underground pipes. If half the heat is put to good use, the overall efficiency of cogeneration doubles to a typical 66 percent. If most of the heat can be used, 90 percent efficiency is possible." (p7)

Roodman, David Malin. "Pioneering Greenhouse Policy." World Watch v6 n4, Jul-Aug 1993. p7-8. (ISSN0896-0615).

ENERGY CONSERVATION--U.S. (v19)

"Colorado's largest electric utility is asking its customers to donate money to fund development of renewable energy. Public Service Company of Colorado wants customers to pay an additional $1-to-$3 a month to fund experimental windmills and solar electric panels. Already 2,000 people have pledged $50,000, and the company expects to raise almost $2 million a year....Public Service supplies three-quarters of the state's electricity, 98 percent of which comes from coal-fired power plants. The company's most recent 20-year plan estimates that 70 percent of its new power resources will come from natural-gas power plants, 25 percent from energy-efficient projects and only 5 percent from renewable power." (p6)

"Hotline: Begging for Windmills." High Country News v25 n22, 29 Nov 1993. p6. (ISSN0191-5657).

ENERGY CONSERVATION--U.S.--PUBLIC OPINION

"According to the U.S. Department of Energy, water heating currently accounts for 12 percent of residential energy use, and this percentage is rising. Eleven states have 9 [cents]/kWh (or higher) electric rates, and these are climbing as well. The 1993 book ENERGY MANAGEMENT & CONSERVATION, released by the National Conference of State Legislatures, states that 'Despite the Persian Gulf crises, energy issues played only a minor role in the 1990 elections. However, there is a growing realization at the state level that energy is both scarce and expensive...as state budget constraints increase, energy efficiency and conservation are expected to increase in importance in 1992 and beyond.' The book also outlines the results of a 1991 survey of priority issues for state legislatures, in which over 60 percent of the respondents identified incentives for alternative energy as one of the top five priorities, and 30 percent of the responding states indicate that incentives for alternative power are the number one priority. Yet, except for some minor activities by state legislatures in 1992 and 1993, renewable energy received little attention." (p3)

Sklar, Scott. "Executive Director's Report: Bittersweet Opportunities: Realities vs. 'Photo Ops.'" Solar Industry Journal v4 n2, 1993. p3,39.

ENERGY CONSUMPTION (v19)

see also ELECTRIC POWER CONSUMPTION

"A widely held view in the one-third world (OTW) of economically developed countries is that the major threat to the environment comes from the overpopulated two-thirds world (TTW) of the poorer countries....But the TTW may see it differently. [Malcolm] Edmunds states '...it is pressure from increasing demands that are placing the world's natural systems in jeopardy.' This seems to suggest that the increase in population is the most important factor, whereas seen from a TTW view, it is the increasing demands of the OTW that is the major cause. With the average person in the United States consuming 40 times the energy of the average Indian, the effective U.S. population would be equivalent to ten billion Indians." (p1)

Pabaney, Aziz. "People vs. the World: A View from Another Window." Community Service Newsletter v42 n1, Jan-Feb 1994. p1-3.

"Indeed, the worldwide consumption of energy resources has grown even faster than the population, with an estimated 20-25% increase in total energy use versus an 8% increase in population since 1985. Consumption patterns are not equal throughout the world. The industrialized countries account for only 25% of the world's population but consume 75% of all energy, 85% of all wood products, and 72% of all steel, according to United Nations statistics." (p4)

"EDF Column: Population and Consumption Are Interlocking Issues." EDF Letter v24 n4, Jul 1993. p4. (ISSN0163-2566).

ENERGY CONSUMPTION--ASIA

"According to the World Bank, the bill for electrifying Asia under a 'business as usual' scenario will be staggering--more than $500 billion during this decade. The ecological price will be measured in dramatic increases of greenhouse gas emissions and nuclear waste. In short, it is neither economically possible nor environmentally prudent for Asia to follow the West's bad example....More efficient lights, motors, windows, and appliances can sharply reduce the number of new power plants needed, while dramatically increasing the amount of capital left over. Two examples of efficiency's leverage: A $7.5 million compact-fluorescent lamp factory saves as much electricity as a $1 billion power plant makes. While consuming 140 times less capital, the factory also avoids the power plant's fuel cost and pollution. A $10 million 'superglass' factory making windows that block heat but pass light can produce more comfort than the air conditioners run by $2 billion worth of generating stations. Over 30 years, a single glass factory's output would save $12.25 billion in power investment." (p4)

"The Dragon Stirs: Negawatts in Asia." Rocky Mountain Institute Newsletter v9 n1, Spr 1993. p4-5.

ENERGY CONSUMPTION--ASPEN (COLO)

"Aspen [Colorado] has one mansion that is 55,000 square feet, bigger than a football field. But most Valley residents live in modest-sized homes, apartments, and trailer parks. Here, as elsewhere, high energy bills hurt elderly and low-income residents the most. In our frosty climate, heating a poorly insulated mobile home can cost $500 a month. Today, typical Valley homes use about $1 worth of energy per year per square foot. But the best-designed new homes--those that incorporate high-performance windows, superinsulation, and passive solar heat--use between 5-10 [cents] worth. Reducing energy waste is not just a way to save money. It also strengthens the local economy. Energy dollars saved by residents, businesses, and schools circulate here, instead of being siphoned off for imported fuels and electricity. Saving energy also reduces pollution--important when the average U.S. household produces 25,000 pounds of carbon dioxide annually." (p7)

"Energy Efficiency in the Roaring Fork Valley." Rocky Mountain Institute Newsletter v9 n3, Fall-Win 1993. p7.

ENERGY CONSUMPTION--BELARUS

"Traditionally, Russia supplied 95 percent of the [Belarus] republic's oil and synthetic rubber; all of its natural and liquefied gas, cellulose, and aluminum; 78 percent of its rolled steel; and 50 percent of its brass, copper, and sodium bicarbonate. In 1992, Russia began to charge the other Commonwealth states world market prices....Oil prices increased to 30 times the artificial 1991 price, an increase that affected all areas of Belarus's economy. By mid-1993, the Belarussian consumer was paying 45,000 rubles a ton for Russian oil (two and a half to three times the price in Russia) and 15,600 rubles per thousand cubic meters of natural gas (more than three times the price in Russia). When Belarussian consumers were unable to pay, Russia temporarily stopped the supply and sewage system services increased 10-15 times, the cost of heat increased 30 times, and apartment rents quadrupled. Fewer and fewer goods are available to the Belarussian shopper, and the minimum monthly salary in Belarus is $4." (p38)

Tiurina, Tatiana. "Belarus: Neutrality, Maybe." Bulletin of the Atomic Scientists v50 n1, Jan-Feb 1994. p36-40. (ISSN0096-3402).

ENERGY CONSUMPTION--CALIFORNIA

"California imports electricity...from plants built and proposed around the Mountain West. In 1987, California consumed 190.3 billion kwh, but generated only 130.3. In 1988, consumption was 200.6 and generation only 126. The trend is clear--California consumes more and generates less for itself every year. California's strict air-quality regulations, energetic environmental activists, and affluent, well-connected 'not in my back yard' protesters mean that the new power comes from coal-fired plants in the Four Corners region and Nevada--facilities that can't legally be placed in California. Although Southern California Edison, which supplies 11 million people, is currently stressing efficiency rather than added generation, further demands will most likely be met from plants in the new L.A. hinterland, which now extends as far eastward as Colorado." (p11)

Quillen, Ed. "Now That Denver Has Abdicated...." High Country News v25 n9, 3 May 1993. p1,6-15. (ISSN0191-5657).

ENERGY CONSUMPTION--CHINA

"The core of China's emission reduction strategy is increased efficiency. China has tremendous potential for improvement, especially in the power generation and industrial sector. The nation uses energy at 30 percent efficiency as compared with Japan at 57 percent and the U.S. at 51 percent. Less than one-fourth of the billion tons of coal which are mined annually are converted to electricity, a relatively clean and convenient usage, although this percentage is expected to rise to 35 percent of total coal produced by 2000. Other inefficiencies exist in coal delivery: one-third of the nation's railway freight capacity is used just to transport coal. In 1989, railway freight charges were estimated to constitute about 80 percent of the cost of coal delivered to the power sector." (p5)

Wilson, Nancy C. "China Faces Hard Energy Choices: Booming Economy, Soaring Emissions." Climate Alert v6 n3, May-Jun 1993. p1,4-7.

ENERGY CONSUMPTION--DEVELOPING COUNTRIES (v19)

"In the next several decades, the growth in world energy demand will be greatest in the developing world, due to the combination of rapid population growth, industrialization, and urbanization. The World Bank estimates that over the next decade, developing countries will require $100 billion annually or a total of more than one trillion dollars in capital investments to address the explosive growth in their energy needs. Despite $60 billion in energy investments annually, more than half the developing world's population, roughly two billion people, remain without basic electric service....If solar and other renewable energy technology suppliers were to capture even 10% of the developing world's projected annual energy investment, this would represent more than $10 billion in technology sales per year for the next decade!" (p23)

"Cover Story: Breaking Down Market Barriers in the Developing World." Solar Industry Journal v4 n2, 1993. p22-32.

ENERGY CONSUMPTION--SOVIET UNION--U.S.

"Experts estimate that between 75 and 80 percent of energy use in a building or home can be cut with a comprehensive, integrated energy system. One-quarter of energy worldwide is spent on buildings, and where there is big spending, there is potential for big savings. Before the breakup of the Soviet Union, the share of energy consumed by buildings there was estimated at 20 percent, and the most recent figure for Eastern European and developing countries is 28 percent. In Western Europe, buildings consume about 33 percent, and in the United States, with its climate-controlled, high-tech office space, buildings eat up 36 percent of the U.S. energy budget--which is the largest in the world. Cutting building energy use by 75 percent in the United States would reduce annual energy bills by more than $130 billion, and eliminate the release of millions of tons of pollutants into the atmosphere." (p36)

Scholand, Michael. "Building for the Future." World Watch v6 n6, Nov-Dec 1993. p36-38. (ISSN0896-0615).

ENERGY CONSUMPTION--U.S. (v19)

"Industrial nations, with 22 percent of the world's population, consume 70 percent of the world's energy, 75 percent of its metals, 85 percent of its wood, and 60 percent of its food." (p9)

Jacobson, Jodi L. "Perspective: Population Mythology." Amicus Journal v16 n1, Spr 1994. p9-10. (ISSN0276-7201).

"The cost of residential energy use [in the U.S.] has increased steadily and is projected by the Department of Energy to continue to increase. In 1973, the average price for home energy was $7.88/mmbtu. In 1979, it was $11.46. In 1992, it was $12.33." (pH2745)

Sharp, Philip R. (Rep.-Ind.). "Providing for Concurrence with S.1636, Marine Mammal Protection Act Amendments of 1994," Congressional Record (26 Apr 1994). Daily ed. pH2714-2751. (ISSN0363-7239).

"Continuing efficiency will sharply restrain growth in U.S. energy consumption to the year 2010, according to the Energy Information Administration's ANNUAL ENERGY OUTLOOK 1994 --WITH PROJECTIONS TO 2010 (DOE/EIA-0383-94)....The publication...shows net oil imports rising to 60 percent of consumption by 2010, up from 38 percent in 1992. Petroleum consumption is expected to climb to over 21 million barrels per day in 2010, from 17 million barrels per day in 1992. People will continue to drive more, the forecast notes, and new car efficiency gains will not be as rapid as in the 1980's." (p10)

"Building Efficiency, New Appliances Slow Demand for Energy." DOE This Month v17 n2, Feb 1994. p10. (ISSN1057-5782).

"While America spent 10 percent of its gross national product to buy energy in 1989, Germany and Japan spent 5 percent. In the international marketplace, therefore, goods from the U.S. are at a 5 percent cost disadvantage solely due to the inefficient use of energy. In the future, as energy prices rise due to resource depletion, U.S. competitiveness will diminish further....Some improvements in energy efficiency were started during the oil price shocks of the 1970s, and these changes have brought about a 28 percent reduction in energy use since 1973. In dollar terms, these efficiency gains have saved $150 billion per year in avoided energy costs. Despite these large savings, there is much more to be gained through further advances in efficiency, with the benefits accruing to the nation's economy and the world's environmental quality." (p33)

Grant, William. "Power to Spare." Outdoor America v58 n1, Win 1993. p31-33.

"Since OPEC (Organization of Petroleum Exporting Countries) Price Shock I in 1973, natural gas consumption [in the U.S.] has dropped 25 percent and petroleum consumption has plunged 73 percent. However, since 1986 gas use has stabilized. In 1992 gas accounted for 9.6 percent of electric generation, while petroleum had fallen to 3.2 percent. Including transportation to the power plants, electric utility expenditures for gas and oil were $6.0 billion and $2.2 billion, respectively. In the 1970s, nuclear electric output in the United States more than tripled. In the 1980s it doubled, and now accounts for 22 percent of electric generation. However, because of the intense political opposition of the past 20 years, growth of the nuclear industry has ground to a stop. The number of operating plants peaked at 112 in 1990, and fell back to 110 in 1992." (p46-47)

Nadler, Arnold. "Oil Prices: What to Expect and Why It Matters." Public Power v52 n1, Jan-Feb 1994. p46-48,50,52-

54,56. (ISSN0033-3654).
"In 1992, the U.S. imported 46 percent of its oil, adding more than $55 billion to the U.S. trade deficit. U.S. annual energy consumption accounts for 20 percent of the world's annual energy use, and that energy use costs individuals and businesses more than $475 billion per year. At the same time, our country subsidizes conventional energy from $7 billion to $25 billion per year, and appears to be resistant to change. As a result of these status quo policies and practices, the U.S. is still the world's largest debtor nation, the largest carbon producer, and ranks high in per capita and GDP [gross domestic product] energy use. Aside from narrowing the jobs base in the U.S., these policies inherently make U.S. goods less competitive." (p3)
Sklar, Scott. "Executive Director's Report: A Time to Lay Down the Operating Principles for Sustained Economic Growth." Solar Industry Journal v4 n1, 1993. p3.
"Water heating is an important energy end-use [in the U.S.], consuming 2 to 3 quads annually of primary energy. Nationally, approximately 8 percent of the energy used in residential and commercial buildings is used to heat water. While the majority (54 percent) of water heating in U.S. households is provided with natural gas, electric water heating represents a significant and growing market share. At present, 35 percent of U.S. households use electricity to heat water, and almost half of all new water heaters sold are electric." (p20)
Carlisle, Nancy/Christensen, Craig. "Solar Domestic Hot Water." Solar Today v7 n2, Mar-Apr 1993. p19-22. (ISSN1042-0630).

ENERGY DEVELOPMENT--U.S. (v19)
"The Department of Transportation has been working with the Department of Energy (DOE) for a number of years in alternative fuels research and development. The Department's Federal Transit Administration is leading the Alternative Fuels Bus Demonstration program, which has the objective of helping State and local agencies in test programs, in urban settings, of buses capable of operating on alcohol or natural gas fuels. Over 400 alternative fuel buses are in the program, throughout the U.S. Several transit authorities, including those in Phoenix, Denver, Los Angeles, and New York City, are providing detailed operating, maintenance and emissions data. Data generated from all methanol, ethanol, CNG and LNG transit buses are being transmitted to DOE's Alternative Fuels Data Center for use in performance evaluations." (p140)
Pena, Federico (Secretary of Transportation). U.S. House. Committee on Appropriations. "Department of Transportation and Related Agencies Approp. for 1994 (Part 3)." Hearing, Washington, D.C.: GPO, 1993. (ISBN0160410649). (Y4.Ap6/1:T68/4/994/pt.3).
"Coal liquefaction, the process of turning hard coal into liquid synthetic oil, is returning to the energy limelight after its invention about a decade ago, THE WALL STREET JOURNAL reports....When liquefaction becomes economically viable, it should decrease dependence on oil producers and importers. The current price of liquefaction is about $30 a barrel, which is $10 more a barrel than the going market rate of oil. But an economic liquefaction process could bring the price of synthetic oil down to about $25 a barrel by 2005. With competitive pricing, liquefaction could eventually account for about 13 percent of the nation's 15 million barrels per day oil usage, estimates Jack Siegel of the [U.S.] Department of Energy." (p2)
Segall, Linda. "Coal, Tires Contribute to Energy Alternatives." Foremanship 31 Jan 1994. p2.
"When UCS [the Union of Concerned Scientists] studied the biomass potential in the Midwest for our report 'Powering the Midwest: Renewable Electricity for the Economy and the Environment (1993),' we concluded that nearly 1.5 percent of the Midwest's energy demand could be met using wood and municipal solid waste sources alone (crop residues are currently too expensive to collect and utilize)." (p8) "Perennial energy crops could also be grown on cropland that would otherwise be idle. With their soil-holding capability, perennial grasses might make a good cover on land that is currently out of crop production because of extremely high soil-loss rates. In 'Powering the Midwest,' we estimated that the potential exists to provide over 20 percent of the region's energy needs by growing trees and perennial grasses on land not used for growing food crops--which would also provide important economic benefits for the region." (p9)
Denzler, Eric. "Green Energy." Nucleus v15 n3, Fall 1993. p7-9. (ISSN0888-5729).

ENGLAND
see CONJUGAL VIOLENCE--LONDON (ENGLAND); DEFORESTATION--ENGLAND

ENGLISH LANGUAGE--U.S.--PUBLIC OPINION (v19)

ENTERPRISE ZONES--U.S. (v19)

ENTERTAINMENTS
see AMUSEMENTS

ENTITLEMENT SPENDING--EUROPE (v19)

ENTITLEMENT SPENDING--U.S. (v19)
"Programs designed specifically for low-income Americans--food stamps, Aid to Families with Dependent Children and Medicaid--form only the tip of the entitlement pyramid....non-means-tested programs account for 79 percent of entitlement spending and consume 41 percent of the annual federal budget. Three of them alone consumed nearly $500 billion last year: Social Security cost $300 billion, with 40 million beneficiaries; Medicare cost $116 billion, with 35.5 million beneficiaries; and federal civil service and military retirement benefits cost $68 billion, with 3.3 million beneficiaries." (p34)
Feulner, Edwin. "Fair Comment: Who's Entitled to Our Cash?" Insight v10 n1, 3 Jan 1993. p32,34. (ISSN1051-4880).
"In 1993, entitlements amounted to $761 billion, or 54 percent of all federal spending, with 40 percent of the total going to Social Security, 8 percent to federal pensions, and 29 percent to Medicare and Medicaid. And this doesn't include $150 billion more in consumption benefits dispensed through the tax code--so-called tax expenditures--such as the deduction for home mortgage interest and the exclusion from employees' taxable income of health care paid for by employers." (p42)
Peterson, Peter G. "Entitlement Reform: The Way to Eliminate the Deficit." New York Review of Books v41 n7, 7 Apr 1994. p39-47. (ISSN0028-7504).

ENVIRONMENTAL ASPECTS
see BAIKAL, LAKE (RUSSIA)--ENVIRONMENTAL ASPECTS; CASPIAN SEA--ENVIRONMENTAL ASPECTS; ELECTRIC POWER PRODUCTION--ENVIRONMENTAL ASPECTS; ELECTRIC POWER-PLANTS--ENVIRONMENTAL ASPECTS--U.S.; EUROPEAN ECONOMIC COMMUNITY--COMMERCE--ENVIRONMENTAL ASPECTS; FISHERIES--ENVIRONMENTAL ASPECTS; GOLF COURSES--U.S.--ENVIRONMENTAL ASPECTS; IRAQ-KUWAIT CRISIS, 1990-1991--ENVIRONMENTAL ASPECTS; LAWNS--U.S.--ENVIRONMENTAL ASPECTS; MILITARY WEAPONS--ENVIRONMENTAL ASPECTS; MINES AND MINERAL RESOURCES--ENVIRONMENTAL ASPECTS; MOTION PICTURE INDUSTRY--U.S.--ENVIRONMENTAL ASPECTS; OFFSHORE ASSEMBLY INDUSTRY--ENVIRONMENTAL ASPECTS--MEXICO; PESTICIDES--ENVIRONMENTAL ASPECTS--U.S.; PETROLEUM REFINERIES--ENVIRONMENTAL ASPECTS; POPULATION--ENVIRONMENTAL ASPECTS; U.S.--ENVIRONMENTAL ASPECTS

ENVIRONMENTAL CONSUMERISM
see GREEN MARKETING

ENVIRONMENTAL EDUCATION--U.S.

According to Jon Miller, director of the Northern Illinois University Public Opinion Laboratory, "'Only about 1 in 18 U.S. adults knows enough about the vocabulary and methodology of science to function effectively as a citizen and consumer when faced with decisions about scientific topics such as nuclear power, acid rain, or health.'...In February [1993], Miller presented a paper to the American Association for the Advancement of Science on a poll by his laboratory that focused exclusively on what might be called environmental literacy....In his study, only 15 percent of the public understood what causes acid rain and only 25 percent could state the causes of ozone depletion. Miller constructed an Index of Environmental Knowledge based on the number of correct answers to these and five other basic questions about environmental science. On this seven-point scale, the average score was a dismal 2.3. Fully 35 percent got none or one right. Only 20 percent answered four or more of the questions correctly." (p10)

Dujack, Stephen R. "Notes & Comment: Environmental Illiteracy." Environmental Forum v10 n2, Mar-Apr 1993. p10-11. (ISSN0731-5732).

ENVIRONMENTAL LAW--U.S.
see also AIR--POLLUTION--LAW AND LEGISLATION--U.S.; REFUSE AND REFUSE DISPOSAL--LAW AND LEGISLATION--U.S.

A study released in October 1992 by the investment firm of Smith Barney, Harris Upham "predicts that an average annual revenue increase due to the [Clean Air] Act's implementation should range from $2.3 billion to $5.8 billion during 1996 to 2000. This translates into about 15,000 to 25,000 full-time equivalent jobs annually through 1995, and an average of 20,000 to 40,000 full-time equivalent jobs during 1996 to 2000." (p4)

"Conservation USA: Wall Street Study Details Job Benefits of Clean Air Rules." Outdoor America v58 n2, Spr 1993. p4.

ENVIRONMENTAL POLICY
see also POLLUTION

"A year has passed since the world's leaders convened in the 'Greatest Conference in the History of Humanity' to reevaluate humankind's relationship with the Earth and discuss ways to heal the planet's numerous environmental sores. Since then, the population of Earth increased by at least 90 million; 51 million more cars, trucks and buses were built to burn more fossil fuels and add to the problem of global warming; an estimated 4 million barrels of crude oil spilled into the world's oceans; 65,700 square miles of forest disappeared; 547,500 metric tons of chlorofluorocarbons leaked from refrigerators, air conditioners, aerosol spray cans and industry, further worsening the hole in the protective ozone layer; more than 14 million people, mostly children, died from starvation; and more than 40,000 species of plants, animals and other living organisms disappeared forever....Despite the acknowledged fact that many of these problems could be solved with money, in the year since the Earth Summit, more than $1 trillion was spent on the world's military." (p32)

Rogers, Adam. "Progress on the Road from Rio." Earth News v4 n3, May-Jun 1993. p32-34. (ISSN1068-9400).

ENVIRONMENTAL POLICY--AT&T

"AT&T's electronics manufacturing operations once depended on ozone-depleting CFCs--chemicals they used as solvents and cleaning agents. But when the Montreal Protocol on ozone depleting substances was signed, AT&T pledged to reduce its CFC use by 50 percent by the end of 1991 and eliminate it entirely by the end of 1994, six years ahead of the international treaty's deadline. It was the first U.S. manufacturer to set such ambitious goals." (p24) AT&T was "using some 2.5 million pounds annually at a cost of about $.75 to $.80 a pound. Because of the federal tax on the chemical, which is now $2.68 per pound, and the otherwise rising price, the total cost is about $8.00 a pound and is expected to increase by 25 percent per year." (p25)

"Forum Profile: AT&T's David Chittick." Environmental Forum v10 n3, May-Jun 1993. p24-29. (ISSN0731-5732).

ENVIRONMENTAL POLICY--U.S. (v19)

ENVIRONMENTAL PROTECTION
see also CONSERVATION OF NATURAL RESOURCES

ENVIRONMENTAL PROTECTION--CALIFORNIA

"With the passing of the Clean Air Act in 1990, tougher emissions standards for all modes of transportation will be required by 1995. In Southern California for example, the 9th Circuit Court of Appeals recently ordered the federal EPA to draw up a clean air plan for the greater Los Angeles area. That may mean emissions caps for all modes of transportation including rail and aviation. A direct result could be a limit on airline take-off and landings at Los Angeles International Airport. Passenger rail, which has been determined to be 50% more fuel efficient than air travel, could compete for air passenger traffic between...cities if a clean burning locomotive is available. Turbine engines by nature are much more clean burning than diesels. Studies have shown that in a typical 250 mile corridor, turbine powered locomotives emit only 17% of the exhaust emissions of a standard diesel locomotive, and 25% of the exhaust emissions of a fossil fuel power plant which could provide the power for an electric train. Turbines have the capability to run on alternative fuels such as natural gas, methanol, and ethanol. This can reduce emissions even further." (p405)

Nichols, Dennis B. (President, CEO, Turbomeca Engine Corp.). U.S. House. Committee on Appropriations. "Department of Transportation and Related Agencies Approp. for 1994 (Part 8)." Hearing, Washington, D.C.: GPO, 1993. (ISBN0160410657). (Y4.Ap6/1:T68/4/994/pt.8).

"The California Environmental Protection Agency is actively promoting its Green Lights program, which encourages corporations, governments, and others to install energy-efficient lighting, dramatically reducing energy consumption while delivering the same or better illumination. After only one year of operation, the Cal/EPA Green Lights partnership--the first state agreement established under the federal EPA Green Lights program--has 29 corporate and government partners, representing over 175 million square feet of office and facility space, with potential energy savings exceeding 765 million kilowatt-hours annually--enough to provide the power needs of more than 23,000 homes. In addition, California has retrofitted 18.7 million square feet in state-owned facilities, representing 14.8 percent of its total square footage and a savings of 27.9 million kWh of electricity annually. This translates into 4 percent of the total electric bill for California's state office buildings--and large reductions in greenhouse gases and other air pollutants." (p23)

Edgerton, Lynne. "Acting Locally." Environmental Forum v10 n2, Mar-Apr 1993. p22-27. (ISSN0731-5732).

ENVIRONMENTAL PROTECTION--MEXICO (v19)

ENVIRONMENTAL PROTECTION--OHIO--COSTS (v19)

ENVIRONMENTAL PROTECTION--U.S. (v19)

"The CRP [Conservation Reserve Program], created in the 1985 Farm Bill, paid farmers to plant grass on highly erodible land and leave it idle for ten years. Over 36 million acres were enrolled in the CRP....The nearly $17 billion spent on the CRP has produced significant short term benefits. It provided income support for farmers and reduced surpluses by eliminating production on the two-thirds of the CRP land that was enrolled in farm programs. Soil erosion was reduced by an average 19 tons per acre per year. Water quality in some areas improved from reduced sediment, less fertilizer and pesticide pollution, and 2,500 miles of grass filterstrips along waterways. Wildlife benefited from more habitat and wetlands. But critics of the CRP say the United States Department of Agriculture (USDA) was more interested in signing up acres than in protecting the most highly erodible land, and did not use the most cost-effective bidding process to select parcels. The rate of erosion reductions decreased each year--from 28 tons/ac/yr in 1986 to 14 tons/ac/yr in 1990." (p3)

"CRP, 1985-1992, Rest in Peace." Center for Rural Affairs Newsletter Aug 1993. p3-4.

"Membership of many green groups peaked in the last years of the Reagan administration, and is now falling....Several groups are running deficits. At federal level, a budget-conscious America is tightening its belt. The Environmental Protection Agency (EPA) calculates that it costs consumers $115 billion a year, or 2.1% of GNP [gross national product] to comply with its regulations: twice as much as in Japan. By the end of the decade it will be 2.8%. Yet many important laws have already been passed, and Americans wonder whether more can be afforded. In 1988 a Lou Harris poll found that 97% of Americans believed more should be done to protect the environment. That number dropped to 82% in 1993." (p27)

"American Survey: Environmental Groups: As Green Turns to Brown." Economist v330 n7853, 5 Mar 1994. p27-28. (ISSN0013-0613).

"The vital signs of any political movement are measured in dollars, donors and staff. The top 10 environmental organizations have combined budgets in excess of $500 million. That sounds impressive, but the indicators are pointing downward. For almost all the major environmental groups, contributions are flat or falling, recruitment of new members is off and donors are drifting away....As many green groups flirt with red ink, cost-cutting measures are on the rise. The National Wildlife Federation, which saw revenues fall $77 million in 1991, dismissed 56 employees that year and left another 54 positions unfilled. It also eliminated its book and school programs. Greenpeace U.S.A. temporarily reduced its direct mail appeals from 5 million pieces per month to 500,000, fired 20 staff members, left about 30 positions vacant and closed its offices in Boston and Fort Lauderdale, Fla. The Sierra Club ran a deficit of more than $1 million in 1990, according to the New York-based National Charities Information Bureau, and pruned excess staff. Funding was flat for 1991, the bureau reported. The Wilderness Society also cut its staff and the National Resources Defense Council held employee raises to an average of 1 percent." (p8)

Miniter, Richard. "Are the Greens Losing Their Grip?" Insight v9 n52, 27 Dec 1993. p6-12. (ISSN1051-4880).

"Even with protective legislation, we still destroy 300,000 acres of wetlands every year. So far, more than half of [the U.S.]...original wetlands have been drained or filled in. Our best conservation efforts may only be able to restore waterfowl populations to a fraction of their historic numbers. In 1988, 15 years after the passage of the Endangered Species Act, there were 500 plant and animal species listed as endangered. Five years later, that number has increased to more than 700." (p16)

Hren, Ben/Bartolomeo, Nick. "Specialty Report: Carrying Capacity Project: Conservation Is in Trouble." Outdoor America v59 n1, Win 1994. p15-22.

ENVIRONMENTAL PROTECTION--U.S.--PUBLIC OPINION

"'Close to 10 percent of corporate environmental health and safety officers now report directly to their companies' chief executive officers, supporting the notion that the environmental affairs function is increasing in rank and responsibility. According to (a survey sponsored by E. Bruce Harrison Company), another quarter of those executives surveyed said that their companies' environmental affairs functions report directly to the general counsel or vice president, operations levels or higher. In addition, 86 percent of the executives polled said that environmental issues affect all aspects of their businesses, ranging from planning to public relations, and manufacturing to marketing. Ninety-six percent of those responding have personnel in place for managing environmental issues and related risks. And two-thirds of those use a combination of internal staff, cross function committees, and outside consultants to effectively manage their environmental protection and communication efforts.'" (p13)

Harrison, E. Bruce. "Environmental Management Moves Up." Environmental Forum v10 n5, Sep-Oct 1993. p13. (ISSN0731-5732).

ENVIRONMENTAL SCIENCES--U.S. (v19)

EQUAL EMPLOYMENT OPPORTUNITY COMMISSION (v19)

ERITREA

see FOOD SUPPLY--ERITREA

ERITREANS (v19)

EROSION--U.S.

see also SOIL EROSION--U.S.

"The available national baselines are the 1977 and 1982 Natural Resource Inventories (NRI). They were used by Ken Cook and others to define the magnitude and distribution of the erosion problem before Congress. The 1982 NRI identified total erosion on cropland at almost 3.1 billion tons per year, almost all of it on cultivated cropland. ASCS [or Agricultural Stabilization and Conservation Service] estimates that CRP [Conservation Reserve Program] reduces total erosion nationwide by about 685 million tons. On a per acre basis, erosion has dropped from more than 20 tons per acre to less than two tons on participating acres, according to the same data series. But participating acres do not precisely mirror the national pattern of erosion. Some areas with high erosion rates have high participation rates, but other areas with high erosion rates do not. The pattern of participation appears to correlate more closely with relationships between local land values and rental rates, and annual rental rates paid to CRP participants." (p256)

Zinn, Jeffrey. "How Are Soil Erosion Control Programs Working?" Journal of Soil and Water Conservation v48 n4, Jul-Aug 1993. p254-259. (ISSN0022-4561).

ESTONIA

see also ABORTION--ESTONIA; FARMS--ESTONIA

"In Estonia, Russians almost outnumber ethnic Estonians in the capital, Tallinn. Overall, about 60% of the country is Estonian-speaking, and 40% Russian-speaking (though not all these last are ethnic Russians). Russia reacted to a recent Estonian law that set language and other requirements for citizenship by threatening an oil blockade and taking the issue to the CSCE [Conference on Security and Co-operation in Europe]. The CSCE and the Council of Europe recommended revisions to the law." (p20)

"Minorities: That Other Europe." Economist v329 n7843, 25 Dec 1993. p17-18,20. (ISSN0013-0613).

ETHICS, BUSINESS

see BUSINESS ETHICS

ETHIOPIA

see also FOOD SUPPLY--ETHIOPIA; MIGRATION, INTERNAL--ETHIOPIA

ETHIOPIA--POLITICS AND GOVERNMENT

"Ethiopia is one of the poorest countries in the world. 27

million people, over half of its population, live in poverty. After thirty years of conflict, post-war reconstruction challenges are immense. The composition of and conditions which donors--which have been supportive of the government generally--place on outside aid will be critical in the Ethiopian people's quest for democratic development and governance. Over eighty ethnic groups, more than 130 political organizations, and a history of divide-and-rule leadership have made democratic governance in Ethiopia a real tight-wire act." (p5)

Prendergast, John. "Fostering Democratic Development. " Center Focus n119, Jan 1994. p5-6.

ETHNOLOGY

see also INDIGENOUS PEOPLE; LANGUAGE AND LANGUAGES

ETHNOLOGY--FORMER SOVIET REPUBLICS

"There are significant Russian minorities in various former republics. In Kazakhstan, 38% of the population is Russian and 40% is Kazakh. The third and fourth largest groups are other Slavs, at 7%, and ethnic Germans, at 6%. In Kyrgyzstan, 21% of the population is Russian, 13% is Uzbek, and 52% is Kyrgyz. There is a similar proportion of Russians to native populations in the Baltic states (e.g., in Latvia, Russians make up 34% of the total population of that nation). There is also a significant Russian minority in the Ukraine and, to a lesser extent, in Belarus." (p6)

Shultz, Richard H., Jr./Schmauder, J. Marlow. "Emerging Regional Conflicts and U.S. Interests: Challenges and Responses in the 1990s." Studies in Conflict and Terrorism v17 n1, Jan-Mar 1994. p1-22. (ISSN1057-610X).

ETHNOLOGY--ISLANDS OF THE PACIFIC

"Due to colonial neglect and historical isolation, the Pacific Islands, home to the world's most diverse range of indigenous cultures, continue to sustain many ancestral life-ways. Fewer than 6.5 million in all, the peoples of Oceania possess a vast repository of cultural traditions and ecological adaptations. Papua New Guinea alone is home to one-third of the world's languages--about 780 distinct vernaculars. Oceania thus has the most to lose, culturally speaking, from the pressures of global political and economic change." (p32)

White, Geoffrey M./Lindstrom, Lamount. "State of the Peoples: Oceania: Islands, Land, People." Cultural Survival Quarterly v17 n3, Fall 1993. p32-34. (ISSN0740-3291).

ETHNOLOGY--KAZAKHSTAN (v19)

"Three centuries of colonization and in-migration have made the Kazakhs a minority in their own territory. Europeans comprise over half of the population (Russians, 38 percent)--while Kazakhs make up only 40 percent. Ethnic Germans, forced from their farms along the Volga River by Stalin in the 1930s, make up almost 6 percent. Today, differential fertility and Russian out-migration favor growth of the Kazakh population. Surveys show that the majority of Muslims of the former USSR prefer to have four or more children, while Russian women prefer only two. Currently, Kazakh women average 3.6 lifetime births per woman. Family planning services are limited, with heavy reliance on abortion. Women in Kazakhstan typically average two to three abortions in their lifetimes." (p11)

De Sherbinin, Alex. "Spotlight: Kazakhstan." Population Today v21 n11, Nov 1993. p11. (ISSN0749-2448).

ETHNOLOGY--LOS ANGELES (CALIF) (v19)

ETHNOLOGY--NICARAGUA

"Since the defeat of Nicaragua's Sandinista government in 1990, Nicaragua's Atlantic Coast region has been inundated with proposals from U.S. and other foreign companies trying to dispose of toxic wastes there." (p6) "The Atlantic Coast is an especially vulnerable target for such ventures because the region is in severe financial crisis, with a 60 percent unemployment rate. There is also an unresolved autonomy question that makes government accountability highly elusive. The Atlantic Coast peoples have historically considered themselves separate from the rest of the country. When the Sandinistas came to power in 1979, they initially tried to involve these peoples in the social and political transformations then sweeping Nicaragua. In an effort to maintain their autonomy, many Miskitos joined the United States-backed armed struggle against the Sandinistas. By the end of 1984, however, the coastal peoples had entered negotiations with the Nicaraguan government, and signed an autonomy agreement in 1987." (p7)

Wilcox, Meg. "Briefly Noted: Miskito Activists Draw the Line on Toxic Wastes." Cultural Survival Quarterly v17 n3, Fall 1993. p6-7. (ISSN0740-3291).

ETHNOLOGY--ROMANIA (v19)

ETHNOLOGY--SARAWAK (MALAYSIA)

"Sarawak encompasses roughly 38 percent of Malaysian territory. Among some 27 distinct ethnic groups in the state, the Melanau and Malay comprise one-fifth of the population of 1.2 million; another 30 percent of the people are Chinese or recent immigrants from Southeast Asia. Close to half the population is Dayak, a term that refers to more than a dozen indigenous peoples, including the Iban, Bidayuh, Kenyah, Kayan, Kedayan, Murut, Punan, Bisayah, Kelabit, and Penan. The Penan, in northeastern Sarawak, number about 7,600, of whom 25 percent are settled. The remainder are semi-settled or nomadic and depend on the rain forest for most of their needs. Of an estimated 100,000 indigenous peoples who roamed the forests of Sarawak at the turn of this century, only the nomadic Penan remain." (p15)

Davis, Wade. "State of the Peoples: Societies in Danger: Death of a People: Logging in the Penan Homeland." Cultural Survival Quarterly v17 n3, Fall 1993. p15-20. (ISSN0740-3291).

ETHNOLOGY--U.S.

"Ninety-four percent of Americans were listed as either black or white in reports from the 1990 [United States Census] survey. That year had fifteen different racial classifications: white, black, Indian, Aleut, ten variations of Asian/Pacific Islander and, for the first time, a new box labeled 'other.' But federal statistics cannot account for 'other,' so the 10 million people who checked that box were divvied up proportionally among the other categories. That may soon change. Over the past six months, mixed-race activists--light brown, yellow/white and black/yellow--have been lobbying the Census Bureau for recognition through a separate box labeled 'multiracial.' There are already an estimated 1 million children of mixed-race marriages, and they are fast multiplying, as these marriages have quadrupled in the last twenty years to reach 1.2 million, or 2.2 percent of all marriages. The movement is spreading. At dozens of universities across the country, from Brown to the University of California-San Francisco, groups of mixed-race students are demanding recognition on application forms and in curricula." (p12)

Rosin, Hanna. "Boxed In." New Republic v210 n1, 3 Jan 1994. p12,14. (ISSN0028-6583).

EUROPE

see also AGED--EUROPE; AGRICULTURE--EUROPE; AMUSEMENTS--EUROPE--U.S.; BIOTECHNOLOGY INDUSTRIES--EUROPE--U.S.; ECONOMIC ASSISTANCE, EUROPEAN --COMMONWEALTH OF INDEPENDENT STATES; ECONOMIC FORECASTING--EUROPE; EMPLOYEE FRINGE BENEFITS--EUROPE--CIVIL SERVICE; FIREARMS--EUROPE--JAPAN--U.S.; FISHERIES--EUROPE--U.S.; GOLF COURSES--EUROPE; GRAIN TRADE--EUROPE--RUSSIA; INFLATION (FINANCE)--EUROPE;

INFRASTRUCTURE (ECONOMICS)--EUROPE; INVESTMENTS, AMERICAN--EUROPE; MEDICAL CARE, COST OF--EUROPE--U.S.; MOTION PICTURE INDUSTRY--EUROPE--U.S.; NUCLEAR POWER PLANTS--EUROPE; PATENTS--EUROPE--JAPAN--U.S.; POLIOMYELITIS--EUROPE; RABIES--EUROPE; REFUGEES, YUGOSLAVIAN--EUROPE; STOCK PRICE INDEXES--EUROPE; TELEVISION BROADCASTING--EUROPE; TELEVISION PROGRAMS--LAW AND LEGISLATION--EUROPE; TRANSPORTATION--EUROPE--U.S.; U.S.--ARMED FORCES--EUROPE; UNEMPLOYMENT--EUROPE; WOLVES--EUROPE

EUROPE--EMPLOYMENT (v19)

EUROPE--INDUSTRIES

"Europe's car giants are equipped to make up to 3.5m cars more than they can sell each year; its steel firms use 72% of their capacity; its airlines are only two-thirds full. Regardless of who owns them, companies such as Air France, Fiat or Daimler Benz will have to cut costs and shed staff." (p14)

"Leaders: Too Late for Champions." Economist v330 n7849, 5 Feb 1994. p14. (ISSN0013-0613).

EUROPE--JAPAN--U.S.--EMPLOYMENT

"The proportion of working-age Americans with jobs jumped from 62% in 1972 to 71% in 1992. Japan's employment rate rose from 70% to 74%. In most EU [European Union] countries, however, it is broadly the same or slightly lower than 20 years ago. The proportion of Europeans with jobs is also lower than in America or Japan. In France, only 59% of 15-64-year-olds have jobs." (p74)

"Schools Brief: Labour Pains." Economist v330 n7850, 12 Feb 1994. p74-75. (ISSN0013-0613).

EUROPE--MORTALITY (v19)

EUROPE--U.S.--ECONOMIC CONDITIONS (v19)

"Today's world economy is in recession. Germany and Japan are both recording near 0% growth. France, healthiest of European economies, has kept its inflation down and cleaned up most of its distortions by shutting down inefficient state-run industries and privatizing others. Still, France suffers 11% unemployment. While US GDP [gross domestic product] is beginning to expand again, the unemployment and underemployment figures are relatively unaffected. Most distressing for the future health of the US economy is the federal debt, which now exceeds $4 trillion, with interest payments consuming nearly 20% of the federal expenditures." (p2)

Griesgraber, Jo Marie. "Bretton Woods: After 50 Years, Time for a New World Vision." Center Focus n119, Jan 1994. p1-3.

EUROPE, EASTERN

see also PENSIONS--EUROPE, EASTERN; PRIVATIZATION--EUROPE, EASTERN; UNEMPLOYMENT--EUROPE, EASTERN--WOMEN; WOMEN IN POLITICS--EUROPE, EASTERN

EUROPE, EASTERN--POLITICS AND GOVERNMENT--PUBLIC OPINION

"According to Eurobarometer '93, a study conducted by the Gallup and Pentor polling firms, 71 per cent of East Europeans believe their economies worsened in 1992, and 60 per cent said their own lives were worse; only 17 per cent saw signs of improvement. Even in the more advanced states, public discontent with the post-communist world is rife--39 per cent of Poles now say they were better off under the old regime, while slightly more than half think democracy 'is here to stay.' Two-thirds of Hungarians think their country is 'headed in the wrong direction,' while only 18 per cent think things are better under the current system; 53 per cent say things were better under 'goulash communism.'" (p62)

Parker, Richard. "Clintonomics for the East." Foreign Policy n94, Spr 1994. p53-68. (ISSN0015-7228).

EUROPEAN ECONOMIC COMMUNITY (v19)

see also ECONOMIC FORECASTING--EUROPEAN ECONOMIC COMMUNITY; EXPORTS--EUROPEAN ECONOMIC COMMUNITY; JAPAN--COMMERCE--EUROPEAN ECONOMIC COMMUNITY

EUROPEAN ECONOMIC COMMUNITY--COMMERCE (v19)

EUROPEAN ECONOMIC COMMUNITY--COMMERCE--ENVIRONMENTAL ASPECTS

"In November 1989, the European Commission published a study of the environmental effects of the implementation of the Common Internal Market in 1992....The task force explored a wide range of effects, the most significant of which was the increase in transportation that would result from greater trade. The task force concluded that the Common Internal Market would increase interstate truck transport in the EC [European Community] between 30 and 50 percent. According to the task force, 'the growth impact of the Internal Market is likely to cause atmospheric emissions of SO2 and NOx to increase respectively by 8-9% and 12-14% by 2010.'" (p136)

Blackwelder, Brent (Vice President for Policy, Friends of the Earth). U.S. House. Committee on Energy and Commerce. "NAFTA: Energy Provisions and Environmental Implications." Hearing, 22 Sep 1993. Washington, D.C.: GPO, 1994. (ISBN0160440459). (Y4.En2/3:103:70).

EUROPEAN ECONOMIC COMMUNITY--COMMERCE--U.S. (v19)

EUROPEAN ECONOMIC COMMUNITY--ECONOMIC CONDITIONS--POPULATION (v19)

EUROPEAN ECONOMIC COMMUNITY--JAPAN--U.S.--EMPLOYMENT (v19)

EUROPEAN ECONOMIC COMMUNITY--MANUFACTURES (v19)

EUROPEAN ECONOMIC COMMUNITY--U.S.--COMMERCE--COMMONWEALTH OF INDEPENDENT STATES

"If the private, rather than the public sector, and trade, rather than aid, is the way to help Russia, then...the figures suggest that the Europeans are playing the lead role, thanks in part to Europe's traditional imports of Russian energy and natural gas. European Union countries imported $9.75 billion from Russia in 1992, or 20 times more than the US imports. And while the CIS [Commonwealth of Independent States]...had a joint $2.9 billion trade deficit with the US, they enjoyed a trade surplus of $4.7 billion (an increase of over 60 percent in four years) with the European Union." (p8)

Walker, Martin. "Russia: Financing Russia's Future." Europe n333, Feb 1994. p6-8. (ISSN0191-4545).

EUROPEAN ECONOMIC COMMUNITY--U.S.--COMMERCE--RUSSIA

"What trade Russia enjoyed with the West (and the bulk of Russian trade is still with other former Soviet republics) is dominated by the European Union. EU exports to Russia are five times higher than those of the US, and the EU imports 20 times more from Russia than the US. And what new growth Russian trade has begun to enjoy has been with the EU. By the last quarter of 1992 and the first quarter of 1993 (the latest official figures available), imports from Russia more than doubled to an average $3.5 billion a quarter, while exports showed a similar jump to around $2.5 billion a quarter, reflecting the then European Community's expanded trade credits. Since 1992, the EU has provided a total of $44.5 billion in export credits and loan guarantees to Russia, or 66 percent of the total for the G7 countries. (The US, by contrast, has provided $6.8 billion, or around 10 percent of the G7 total.)" (p9)

Walker, Martin. "Trade: The Key to Russia's Future." Europe n333, Feb 1994. p9. (ISSN0191-4545).

EUROPEAN ECONOMIC COMMUNITY--U.S.--EMPLOYMENT (v19)

EUTHANASIA

"According to the Remmelink Commission, there were 2,300 cases of voluntary euthanasia (1.8% of all deaths) and 400 assisted suicides (0.3%) in 1990....In addition, the Dutch government Remmelink Commission found 1,030 cases of a toxic agent directly given to induce death without the patient's consent. There also were 8,100 cases of morphine overdose of which 61% (5,000 cases) were given without patient consent and 8,750 cases in which treatment was withdrawn or withheld without consent in all instances....Of 22,500 deaths due to withdrawal of life support, 63% (14,175 patients) were denied medical treatment without their consent and 12% (1,701 patients) were mentally competent but not consulted." (p6)

LeBow, Barbara. "What Happens When Euthanasia Is Tolerated or Permitted?" ProLife News v19 n3, Mar 1994. p6-8.

EUTHANASIA--MICHIGAN--PUBLIC OPINION

Wayne County Prosecutor John O'Hair is "...promoting a law that would make...[Michigan] the first to allow a physician to help end a life, as long as the patient is in the last few months of life and is competent to make such a choice. In a U.S. NEWS poll, respondents seem to agree: Fifty-four percent of Americans favor letting doctors assist in suicides, while 40 percent are opposed." (p90)

Shapiro, Joseph P. "Face-Offs: When Can Someone Assist in a Suicide?" U.S. News & World Report v115 n25, 27 Dec 1993. p90. (ISSN0041-5537).

EUTHANASIA--U.S.--PUBLIC OPINION

"For many, the public dialogue over death and dying [in the U.S.] has become badly distorted. That is clear when a how-to-kill-yourself guide that weighs the relative merits of cyanide vs. car exhaust sells a half-million copies and a quirky pathologist becomes an icon of compassion for helping 20 frightened people end their lives. Too often, death is viewed as inevitably painful, suicide is seen as an act of logic and courage and euthanasia is treated as a civil right. But a growing number of doctors and bioethicists are challenging these attitudes. They say...that medical and social service breakthroughs can take the pain and financial ruin out of most deaths." (p31,34) In a study, Dr. John Bach of the New Jersey Medical School, "asked 600 ventilator-dependent adults with debilitating neuro-muscular conditions whether they were satisfied with their 'life as a whole,' and fully 82 percent responded positively....One new survey found that 42 percent of all patients with metastatic cancer who had pain were undermedicated....Still, only 31 percent of dying patients even need a painkiller the day before they die, according to another study....Nearly 100 percent of cancer pain is controllable, specialists say, although pain research for AIDS and other chronic illnesses remains less advanced." (p35)

Shapiro, Joseph P./Bowermaster, David. "Cover Story: Death on Trial." U.S. News & World Report v116 n16, 25 Apr 1994. p31,34-36,38-39. (ISSN0041-5537).

"Polls show it is the young and healthy--not the old and sick, as is widely assumed--who clamor for a right to die. One Harvard study showed that 79 percent of those ages 18 to 34 believe a physician should be allowed to give lethal injections to the terminally ill, but only 53 percent of older Americans agree. Says Dr. Judith Ahronheim of New York's Mount Sinai Hospital: 'When my patients get sick or very old, they have a different view: They want to live.' Others who are devalued by society or who lack access to health care also express suspicion of euthanasia. The DETROIT FREE PRESS, for example, found that only 22 percent of blacks in Michigan said they envision choosing assisted suicide, compared with 53 percent of whites." (p39)

Shapiro, Joseph P./Bowermaster, David. "Cover Story: Death on Trial." U.S. News & World Report v116 n16, 25 Apr 1994. p31,34-36,38-39. (ISSN0041-5537).

EVERGLADES NATIONAL PARK (FLA) (v19)

EVOLUTION--U.S.--PUBLIC OPINION

"Biologist Michael Zimmerman of Oberlin College has surveyed members of Congress, the Ohio legislature, newspaper editors, school board presidents, and biology teachers, finding that significant numbers of each group--up to 30 percent--do not believe in evolution. Science writer Lys Ann Shore finds this disturbing. 'If public officials believe the earth was created in 4004 B.C., they're likely to dismiss any concern about a worldwide temperature increase of a few degrees, because after the cataclysmic events of Noah's flood, a mere rise in temperature seems insignificant." (p11)

Dujack, Stephen R. "Notes & Comment: Environmental Illiteracy." Environmental Forum v10 n2, Mar-Apr 1993. p10-11. (ISSN0731-5732).

EXECUTIVES

see also WOMEN EXECUTIVES

EXECUTIVES--EDUCATION--U.S. (v19)

EXECUTIVES--JAPAN--U.S. (v19)

EXECUTIVES--SALARIES, ETC.--U.S. (v19)

"Up until 1980, pretty much, we had a social compact in this country that lasted for 200 years where, in effect, the chief executive or the highest paid employee of the company never received more than 40 times the income of the lowest paid employee in the company. We have broken that compact. Now how do we get that compact or some form of it back into a range that makes sense? Paying corporate executives $50, $75 or $100 million a year certainly will not lead to good ends for American business no matter how good that particular executive is." (p31)

Tisch, Laurence A. (Chair, CBS, Inc.). U.S. House. Committee on Energy and Commerce. "Corporate Governance." Hearing, 21 Apr 1993. Washington, D.C.: GPO, 1994. (ISBN0160434750). (Y4.En2/3:103-56).

"When BUSINESSWEEK reports that the average CEO of a big U.S. company averaged a 56 percent increase in their income last year, so that they're each making a record $3.8 million in total pay--that's the average--something has gone wrong in our country if it does not match up with the overall economic performance of the company as a whole." (p30)

Markey, Edward J. (Rep.-Mass.). U.S. House. Committee on Energy and Commerce. "Corporate Governance." Hearing, 21 Apr 1993. Washington, D.C.: GPO, 1994. (ISBN0160434750). (Y4.EN2/3:103-56).

EXECUTIVES--U.S. (v19)

EXECUTIVES, WOMEN

see WOMEN EXECUTIVES

EXERCISE--GREAT BRITAIN--U.S.

"A study in the July 24, 1993 BRITISH MEDICAL JOURNAL...found that exercise may help prevent stroke. Researchers, who compared the exercise habits of patients who have and have not had strokes, found that those who had undertaken regular vigorous exercise between the ages of 15 and 55 were 80 percent less likely to have a stroke than those who did not exercise. But while long-term vigorous exercise offered the most protection, researchers found that walking, too, reduced the risks. Patients who had recently engaged in a walking routine were 68 percent less likely to have a stroke than nonexercisers. A CDC [Centers for Disease Control and Prevention] report published in the Oct. 6, 1993 JOURNAL OF THE AMERICAN MEDICAL ASSOCIATION found that the risk for coronary heart disease (CHD) is 1.9 percent higher for physically inactive people, a level they say is comparable to the risks associated with high blood pressure and high cholesterol levels." (p8)

"Exercise Lite." People's Medical Society Newsletter v13 n1, Feb 1994. p8. (ISSN0736-4873).

EXERCISE FOR WOMEN--U.S.

"Working women [in the U.S.] are working out. Almost half exercise at least once a week, according to a 1992 survey of white-collar women developed by the Women's Sports Foundation (WSF) and WORKING WOMAN magazine. Three in ten white-collar women work out at least three times a week. Nonwhite women are much less likely than white women to work out. Among women who get any exercise, whites are almost twice as likely as other women to participate 'every day' or 'almost every day' (16 percent versus 9 percent). There are two reasons for the difference, according to Marjorie Snyder, research coordinator for the study: money and access to athletic facilities....Eighty-five percent of working women who exercised, walk. Bicycling and aerobics follow, with more than six in ten participating. Swimming ranks fourth overall, capturing half of those who exercised. Bowling was the favorite athletic activity, with one-third of working women who exercised at all participating. Second place for athletic activities went to tennis and other racquet sports." (p12)

Bosanko, Deborah. "Business Reports: Sports: Why Do Working Women Work Out?" American Demographics v16 n2, Feb 1994. p12-13. (ISSN0163-4089).

A 1992 survey of white-collar women in the U.S. by the Women's Sports Foundation and WORKING WOMAN magazine found that "About four in ten working women who exercised...see business benefits to working out. Nonwhite women are significantly more likely than average to believe that involvement in sports will help them in the workplace. Fifty-two percent of minority women who exercised believe it will give them 'access to decision-making outside the office,' versus 37 percent of white women. And while 39 percent of white women believe working out helps with 'being accepted by co-workers,' 51 percent of blacks, Asians, and Hispanics cite this benefit." (p12)

Bosanko, Deborah. "Business Reports: Sports: Why Do Working Women Work Out?" American Demographics v16 n2, Feb 1994. p12-13. (ISSN0163-4089).

EXPORT MARKETING--EUROPE--U.S. (v19)

EXPORT PROCESSING ZONES

"Export processing zones now number more than 200 around the world, in some 60 countries, nearly all of which are developing countries. These zones welcome multinationals from the electronics, textile, garment and leather industries, and other 'assembly line' operations. Foreign investment in these zones is high and the enterprises which operate in them export the major portion of their products, which sometimes represents a significant percentage of national exports. For example, in Mauritius in 1992, 89 per cent of workers in manufacturing industries worked in EPZs and produced 83 per cent of all textile and garment exports. These zones grew spectacularly during the mid-eighties. The number of EPZ wage-earners is estimated to have risen from 50,000 in 1970, to 1.3 million in 1986." (p18)

Cabado, Fabienne. "Panorama: Free Zones: A Risky Wager." World of Work n7, Mar 1994. p18-20. (ISSN1020-0029).

EXPORT PROCESSING ZONES--EMPLOYMENT

"China leads all countries with EPZs [export processing zones] and employs more than two million workers in free zones. It is followed by Mexico where employment in the EPZs grew by 7 per cent between the end of 1989 and September 1990, bringing the number of wage-earners in these zones to nearly 500,000, or 20 per cent of total employment in the manufacturing sector. In the Dominican Republic, which holds third place, the figures almost quadrupled between 1986 and 1992, increasing from 36,000 to more than 142,000, or 90 per cent of employment in the manufacturing sector....Between 1986 and 1990, the number of workers employed in Tunisian EPZs grew from 40,000 to 91,000 and the numbers in India grew from 17,000 to 30,000. In the case of Mauritius, some 90,200 people were employed in EPZs in 1990, and some firms even had to recruit foreign workers, although in 1992, the total number of wage-earners in the zones dropped slightly, to 89,950. It should be noted that the EPZ workforce is made up primarily of young women: 48 per cent in India, 65 per cent in Mauritius, 74 per cent in the Philippines and 79 per cent in El Salvador." (p18-19)

Cabado, Fabienne. "Panorama: Free Zones: A Risky Wager." World of Work n7, Mar 1994. p18-20. (ISSN1020-0029).

EXPORTS

"The industrial economies accounted for a major share of world exports during the past four decades. They maintained a 61 to 71 percent share between 1950 and 1989....Among the industrial nations, Japan's share of world trade increased sevenfold between 1950 and 1989, and reached 9 percent by 1989. Over the same period, the U.S. share decreased from 17 to 12 percent, while the EEC [European Economic Community] share rose from 27 to 37 percent of world exports. The developing countries' share of world trade declined in the 1950s, a consequence of decreasing demand for primary goods--such as agricultural and mineral products--that constituted the vast majority of their exports....Since 1960, the developing-country share in world trade has remained fairly stable after accounting for changes in oil prices. Yet, the six major developing-country exporters of manufacturing goods increased their share of world exports from 4 percent in 1960 to 10 percent in 1989, while the share of all other developing countries decreased from 18 percent to 12 percent." (p28)

Bloom, David E./Brender, Adi. "Labor and the Emerging World Economy." Population Bulletin v48 n2, Oct 1993. p2-39. (ISSN0032-468X).

EXPORTS--AFRICA

"Africa's share in world trade has declined steadily, and according to General Agreement on Tariffs and Trade statistics accounted for only 2.6 per cent of world merchandise trade in 1992. World prices for agricultural exports crucial to Africa have been spiralling downward: by 1992, real export prices of coffee and cocoa had fallen 69 per cent from the start of the 1980s, while the price for palm oil had fallen 49 per cent and for sisal and cotton by 47 per cent." (p40)

"Delay for Africa's Commodity Diversification Fund." Africa Recovery v7 n3-4, Dec 1993-Mar 1994. p39-40.

"African exports...[have fallen] from an average of over $90 bn in the early 1980s to $80 bn in 1990, with a further drop in 1992 to $70.8 bn, according to latest figures from the UN Economic Commission for Africa (ECA). The economies of African exporters of cocoa, coffee and tea grew by only 0.1 per cent in 1992, while African mineral exporters suffered a 3.2 per cent fall. The ECA's African export index shows that average commodity prices were down 1.3 per cent in 1992 while non-oil commodities were down 14.3 per cent. The World Bank's aggregate index for real prices of non-oil commodities in 1992 was at its lowest level since the index was started in 1948." (p13)

"Producers Act to Boost Prices." Africa Recovery v7 n2, Oct 1993. p13.

"Commodity prices posted a clear upturn in 1993, the first since 1988. The World Bank's index of 33 commodities, excluding oil, ended the year at 94.3 (1990 = 100) from a 1992 average of 93, not enough to raise real prices, but still welcome after previous years failed to bring predicted upturns. Eight of Africa's 13 major export commodities monitored by AFRICA RECOVERY had average prices higher in 1993 than in 1992, though still lower than in 1990." (p46)

"Rare Good News for African Export Commodities." Africa Recovery v7 n3-4, Dec 1993-Mar 1994. p46.

EXPORTS--CANADA

"Last year, Canada exported $169.5 billion (Canadian; US$ 124 billion) in goods and services. Fully $113.6 billion (67 percent) went to the US, according to Statistics Canada, a government agency. But Japan, South Korea, China, and Taiwan absorbed 35 percent of all of the rest of Canada's exports." (p9)

Clayton, Mark. "Economy: Canada Resolutely Builds Trade Ties with China." The Christian Science Monitor v86 n84, 25 Mar 1994. p9. (ISSN0882-7729).

EXPORTS--CANADA--U.S.

"U.S. exports to Canada in FY 1993 increased 8 percent to $5.2 billion, the largest percentage gain of any major destination. Canada was the leading market for U.S. HVP [high-value products] exports for the third consecutive year, rising 6 percent to $4.9 billion. Vegetable exports, including fresh and highly processed, increased 12 percent to $1.2 billion. There were smaller gains in animal products, but beef exports declined 5 percent to $346 million as Canada purchased more beef from Australia and New Zealand." (p2)

U.S. Dept. of Agriculture/Greene, Joel. "Exports Rose Slightly in FY 1993." Foreign Agricultural Trade of the United States Nov-Dec 1993. p2-3.

EXPORTS--CHILE

"Jorge Marshall, Chile's economy minister, reported that while the total number of new companies created between 1990 and 1992 was up 9.2 percent, the number of new firms that were formed to participate in export activities was up 32 percent in the same period. The nation's exports have expanded from $3 billion in 1984 to $10 billion in 1992. The export boom has helped Chile cut its external debt from 131 percent of GDP [gross domestic product] in 1984 to 50 percent last year. Interest payments on this debt accounted for 35 percent of exports last year, compared with 338 percent in the 1980s." (p6)

Walters, David C. "Economy: Good News in Chile: Economy Is Growing, Unemployment Down." The Christian Science Monitor v86 n48, 2 Feb 1994. p6. (ISSN0882-7729).

EXPORTS--CHINA (v19)

EXPORTS--EMPLOYMENT--U.S. (v19)

"From 1983 to 1989, export jobs in the United States went from 3.8 to 6 million. In...New Jersey, they went from 133,000 to 199,000 in just 6 years. Exports are one of the few forces that are creating jobs. Moreover, export jobs earn 12 to 17 percent more than other jobs." (pS16697)

Bradley, Bill (Sen.-N.J.). "North American Free-Trade Agreement," Congressional Record (20 Nov 1993). Daily ed. pS16678-16700. (ISSN0363-7239).

EXPORTS--EUROPE (v19)

EXPORTS--EUROPEAN ECONOMIC COMMUNITY--U.S.

U.S. "Exports to the EC [European Community] declined to $7 billion, 2 percent below the previous year. The EC was the third largest market for U.S. HVP [high-value products] commodities, but the value of HVP exports declined 4 percent to $4.1 billion, causing most of the decline in U.S. exports to the EC. Fruit, nuts, and vegetables, which accounted for about one-quarter of U.S. HVP exports to the EC, declined 5 percent despite a rise in primarily highly processed vegetable exports. Fruit and nut exports were 15 percent and 11 percent below the previous year." (p2)

U.S. Dept. of Agriculture/Greene, Joel. "Exports Rose Slightly in FY 1993." Foreign Agricultural Trade of the United States Nov-Dec 1993. p2-3.

"U.S. exports to the European Community (EC) were $7 billion in fiscal 1993, over $100 million less than the previous year, as U.S. export growth was slowed by a weak EC economy, an unfavorable exchange rate, and lower commodity prices that offset volume gains in oilseeds." (p6)

U.S. Dept. of Agriculture. "Regional Highlights: European Community." Outlook for U.S. Agricultural Exports 30 Nov 1993. p6-8.

EXPORTS--IRAN (v19)

EXPORTS--JAPAN--U.S.

"U.S. exports to Japan were nearly $8.5 billion, making Japan the leading destination for the fifth consecutive year. Japan was the second leading market for HVP [high-value products] exports, which rose 7 percent to $4.8 billion. Beef and pork accounted for nearly one-third of HVP exports. U.S. beef exports gained 18 percent to $1.2 billion on shipments of 230,000 tons, and pork increased 20 percent to $330 million. Beef exports benefited from a further tariff reduction and the yen's strength relative to the dollar. There were also gains in feeds and fodders, up 12 percent to $500 million, and vegetables, up 13 percent to $446 million." (p2)

U.S. Dept. of Agriculture/Greene, Joel. "Exports Rose Slightly in FY 1993." Foreign Agricultural Trade of the United States Nov-Dec 1993. p2-3.

EXPORTS--LATIN AMERICA (v19)

EXPORTS--MEXICO--U.S.

"Although U.S. exports of $3.7 billion to Mexico were down slightly compared with the previous year, HVP [high-value products] exports gained 4 percent to almost $2.4 billion. Tariffs on beef imports, imposed in November 1992, reduced U.S. beef exports almost 40 percent to $137 million, constraining HVP growth in 1993. Poultry and dairy exports each expanded nearly 30 percent to $220 million and $245 million, respectively. Fruit exports expanded 28 percent to $100 million on increased deciduous fruit shipments, and vegetable exports rose 19 percent to over $180 million from gains in fresh vegetables. Vegetable oil exports, primarily soybean and sunflowerseed, rose nearly 100 percent to $138 million." (p3)

U.S. Dept. of Agriculture/Greene, Joel. "Exports Rose Slightly in FY 1993." Foreign Agricultural Trade of the United States Nov-Dec 1993. p2-3.

EXPORTS--OREGON (v19)

EXPORTS--RUSSIA (v19)

EXPORTS--U.S. (v19)

"The importance of an open, expanding world economy to our economic well-being [in the U.S.] has grown enormously over the past decades: Since the mid-1980s, over half of our growth in income and almost all our growth in manufacturing jobs has resulted from export growth. Exports as a share of GDP [gross domestic product] have increased from about 4 percent in 1959 to just under 11 percent today. Export-related jobs pay 17 percent more, on average, than other jobs, 10 percent more in the manufacturing sector, and 20 percent more in services." (p47)

Altman, Roger (Deputy Secretary of the Treasury, Washington, DC). U.S. Senate. Committee on Finance. "United States-Japan Trade Policy." Hearing, 22 Jul 1993. Washington, D.C.: GPO, 1994. (ISBN0160434092). (Y4.F49:S.hrg.103-354).

"In the 1995 budget, Clinton will ask Congress for an additional $5 million to $10 million for Commerce's Foreign Commercial Service to be used to train embassy personnel to help business make overseas contacts and gain access to bidding on foreign contracts. Business, while pleasantly surprised at all these initiatives, isn't yet rejoicing. E. Martin Duggan, executive director of the Small Business Exporters Assn., notes that the Administration is mostly rejiggering existing funds, not pouring in new money. The U.S. spends $5 billion a year in direct aid to promote exports, but Duggan contends it's not spent properly: About 80% of the money in the 1995 budget will go to agriculture, which accounts for only 10% of exports....most trade experts and economists say that one way or another, exports will be the U.S.'s engine of growth. Merchandise exports as a percentage of American output grew from 5.5% in 1986 to 7.5% in 1992 and are heading higher. With the dollar weak and productivity gains high, U.S. companies are showing that they can compete." (p67)

Harbrecht, Douglas/Hof, Robert D. "Government: Trade: Greasing the Skids for Exports." Business Week n3356, 31 Jan 1994. p66-67. (ISSN0007-7135).

"The share of America's exports that goes to Europe has fallen from 31% to 26% over the past 20 years, while the share going to Asia has risen from 20% to 30%." (p21)

"America and Europe: A Ghost at the Feast." Economist v330 n7851, 19 Feb 1994. p21-22,24. (ISSN0013-0613).

U.S. "HVP [high-value products] exports increased almost $850 million, surpassing $24 billion in FY 1993, and countered the decline in bulk exports. HVP exports had averaged about 10 percent of annual growth since 1985, but slowed to 4 percent in 1993 as sluggish world economic conditions hampered expansion. Despite slowed growth, HVP gains bolstered exports to Japan and Canada, and maintained exports to Mexico. U.S. vegetable exports increased over $400 million to $3.2 billion, leading HVP growth. There were also gains in dairy, poultry, and feeds and fodders that maintained HVP growth in FY 1993." (p2)

U.S. Dept. of Agriculture/Greene, Joel. "Exports Rose Slightly in FY 1993." Foreign Agricultural Trade of the United States Nov-Dec 1993. p2-3.

EXPORTS--U.S.--POLITICS AND GOVERNMENT (v19)

EXPORTS--WASHINGTON (STATE) (v19)

EYE--DISEASES AND DEFECTS--CUBA (v19)

FAIR TRADE COMMISSION--JAPAN (v19)

FAIRFAX COUNTY (VA)--POPULATION

"Fairfax County is the largest local government in Virginia with more than 850,000 residents, making us equivalent in size to the 11th largest city in the United States. The County encompasses some 400 square miles. We have 51 miles of interstate, 151 miles of primary roads, 2,270 miles of secondary roads, 6 Metrorail stations on two lines, the Virginia Railway Express serving two commuter rail routes of 20 and 30 mile lengths, and 99 Metrobus routes augmented by our Fairfax Connector system. Transportation remains at the top of the list of concerns on the minds of Northern Virginians. We face significant challenges over the next decade as we endeavor to ease traffic gridlock and achieve a balanced mix of road and transit facilities. The 1990 Census data indicates that currently more than half of the County's residents work within the County, nearly 75 percent work in Virginia, and only 20 percent work in D.C." (p99)

Davis, Tom (Chairman, Fairfax County, Virginia Board of Supervisors). U.S. House. Committee on Appropriations. "Department of Transportation and Related Agencies Approp. for 1994 (Part 7A)." Hearing, Washington, D.C.: GPO, 1993. (ISBN0160411033). (Y4.Ap6/1:T68/4/994/pt.7A).

FALKLAND ISLANDS--ECONOMIC CONDITIONS (v19)

FAMILY

see also AFRO-AMERICAN FAMILIES; CHILDREN; DIVORCE; HOUSEHOLDS; SINGLE-PARENT FAMILY

FAMILY--MICHIGAN (v19)

FAMILY--U.S. (v19)

"In 1970, in 40 percent of [U.S.] families both husband and wife worked. By 1990, the percentage had increased to 60. Women began to marry later: 62.5 percent of women in their early twenties were already married in 1975, but only 38.5 percent in 1990. Birth rates fell. There were more divorces: for every 1,000 who were married in 1970 there were only 47 who were divorced, while in 1990 there were 152. Seventy percent of households in 1970 included a married couple; twenty years later the percentage had dropped to 56." (p9)

Lemann, Nicholas. "Mysteries of the Middle Class." New York Review of Books v41 n3, 3 Feb 1994. p9-13. (ISSN0028-7504).

"Half of all marriages [in the U.S.] now end in divorce. Three quarters of married women with children 6 to 17 were in the labor force in 1992, as were nearly three fifths of those with children under 6. Yet even if we wanted to go back to the days when women rarely worked outside the home, it is no longer an economic possibility for most families." (p47)

Adler, Jerry. "Lifestyle: Kids Growing Up Scared." Newsweek v123 n2, 10 Jan 1994. p43-49. (ISSN0028-9604).

FAMILY--U.S.--ECONOMIC CONDITIONS (v19)

FAMILY--U.S.--PUBLIC OPINION (v19)

FAMILY CAREGIVERS

see CAREGIVERS

FAMILY PLANNING

see BIRTH CONTROL

FAMILY SERVICES--U.S. (v19)

FAMILY SIZE

see also BIRTH CONTROL

FAMILY SIZE--RUSSIA

According to demographer Valentina V. Bodrova of the All-Russian Center for Study of Public Opinion (VCIOM), "When Russians were asked in 1992 how many children they expected to have, the answers averaged to about one child per family 1.3 children)....But when asked how many children they wanted, the answers averaged closer to two (1.96 children). The ideal family size fell somewhere in the middle (1.53 children).... Muslims in the [1991 and 1992 VCIOM] survey had considerably higher reproductive expectations than the norm. When asked the ideal number of children, the 1992 answers averaged almost four children per family (3.87 children). The number considered desirable was only a bit smaller at 3.74 children. And, Muslims expected to have on average three children (3.33 children)....In this and other studies, Russian women with higher education have a higher desired number of children (1.92 children in 1992) than do women with a secondary education (1.69 children)." (p5)

Kalish, Susan. "Russians Want More Children Than They Are Having." Population Today v21 n12, Dec 1993. p5. (ISSN0749-2448).

FAMILY SIZE--U.S. (v19)

FAMILY VIOLENCE

see also CHILD ABUSE; CONJUGAL VIOLENCE

FAMILY VIOLENCE--U.S. (v19)

"According to the National Coalition Against Domestic Violence, the number of programs (including shelters) for battered women in the US increased from 1,500 in 1991 to 2,027 in 1993." (p2)

Holmstrom, David. "National: Programs Aim to Help Men Who Batter Women." The Christian Science Monitor v86 n33, 11 Jan 1994. p2. (ISSN0882-7729).

FAMILY VIOLENCE--U.S.--ECONOMIC CONDITIONS (v19)

FAMILY VIOLENCE--U.S.--MINORITIES (v19)

FAMINE RELIEF

see FOOD RELIEF

FARM EQUIPMENT--U.S. (v19)

FARM INCOME--AUSTRALIA (v19)

FARM INCOME--EUROPEAN ECONOMIC COMMUNITY (v19)

FARM INCOME--ILLINOIS

"Dale Lattz, a University of Illinois farm-management specialist, says there's potential for wringing far more profit from many existing crop and livestock operations. Lattz points to figures from the Illinois Farm Business Farm Management Association for 1992. He says the top 25 percent of Illinois corn and soybean growers who farmed 340 to 799 acres earned $120 more per acre than the bottom 25 percent of farmers. 'The top

25 percent generated net income of about $90 per acre while the bottom 25 percent lost $30 per acre,' he adds." (p10)

McGill, Steve. "Expand without More Land?" Furrow v99 n4, Mar-Apr 1994. p10-13. (ISSN0016-3112).

FARM INCOME--U.S.

"In 1986, farmers' net cash income was about $48 billion, government outlays were a record $26 billion, and farm exports stood at $26 billion. Contrast this with the situation 6 years later, with net cash income at nearly $57 billion, Federal outlays down to $10 billion, and farm exports over $42 billion. Moreover, the U.S. economy simply cannot grow rapidly enough to absorb the output from the steady rise in farm productivity. The expansion of export markets is critical to U.S. agriculture....exports currently account for about 20 percent of farm output, and one out of every three acres of cropland." (p2-3)

U.S. Dept. of Agriculture/Espy, Mike. "Agricultural Economy: U.S. Agriculture: New Priorities." Agricultural Outlook Jan-Feb 1994. p2-4.

"Despite hardships, farms [in the U.S.] tallied near-record income of $59 billion in 1993, and they should earn about the same this year. If Mother Nature behaves, prices of farm commodities should rise only slightly, so food costs should edge up just 2% or so. Considering last year's natural disasters, the farm economy is surprisingly healthy. Raging waters covered nearly 8 million acres temporarily, and crop losses reached $5 billion. But the damage was concentrated in a relatively narrow band along the Mississippi and Missouri rivers. And even inundated farms emerged with up to 90% of normal income, the Agriculture Dept. figures, if they took full advantage of $2.5 billion in federal flood-relief payments, crop subsidies, and a harvest-time jump in commodity prices....the financial health of most American farmers should be strong. Their debt-to-asset ratio, which has dropped from a high of 23% during the mid-1980s farm crisis to 16% now, is expected to remain steady. That's good news for farm-equipment dealers, who reversed a two-year slide by selling 56,900 tractors and 8,200 combines last year." (p88)

Greising, David. "Natural Resources: Agriculture: Knee-High by July." Business Week n3353, 10 Jan 1994. p88. (ISSN0007-7135).

U.S. "net farm income [for 1992] was $48.6 billion, up from $40 billion. This measure of the farm sector's net value of production is the net farm product. Corn, as both the Nation's most important crop and the one most sensitive to weather conditions, serves as a barometer of production for the entire agricultural sector. Thus, when the corn harvest is a recordbreaker, net farm income can be expected to follow suit. The six leading States in net farm income were California ($4.8 billion), Texas ($3.5 billion), Florida ($2.8 billion), Nebraska ($2.7 billion), Iowa ($2.5 billion), and North Carolina ($2.5 billion). Production expenses incurred in producing the net farm income were $149.1 billion, down less than 1-percent. The leading States in production expenses were California ($14.8 billion), Texas ($10.8 billion), Iowa ($9.6 billion), Illinois ($7.6 billion), and Nebraska ($7.3 billion). There were no changes in the composition or the ranking of the top nine states from a year earlier. Returns to operators, which differ from net farm income by the amount of net rent to operator dwellings as a result of excluding all income and expenses related to operator dwellings in the farm sector, were up 21.8 percent in 1992 to $47.4 billion." (piv)

U.S. Dept. of Agriculture. "State Financial Summary, 1992: Highlights." Economic Indicators of the Farm Sector Jan 1994. piv-vi.

"For 40 years farmers have been guided by a U.S. agricultural policy, and advances in science and technology, that has rewarded production over other societal values. Over this period, improved farming practices have boosted agricultural productivity per work hour at twice the rate of that for manufacturing. Now we have less excess productive capacity, a decline in export of our agricultural products along with degraded ecosystems and impaired surface and groundwaters. The last two farm bills have recognized and promoted an increasing role for conservation in the way we handle our agricultural business. It is logical to expect this trend to continue and increase with the 1995 farm bill. Public interest and investment in American agriculture is substantial. Net farm income last year was approximately $40 billion, $20 billion of which was public monies--$17 billion in farm payments/price supports and $3 billion in services from state and federal agencies. This presents a powerful tool with which to shape farming practices in a more environmentally sound manner." (p265-266)

Wayland, Robert. "What Progress in Improving Water Quality?" Journal of Soil and Water Conservation v48 n4, Jul-Aug 1993. p261-266. (ISSN0022-4561).

"Average sales of agricultural products on metro farms (at $61,200) are 15 percent greater than for nonmetro farms [in the U.S.]....This result is heavily influenced by the large number of residential farms that average less than $3,000 of sales per farm. The metro average disguises the relatively large amount of sales from business-oriented farms in metro areas, whose average sales ($128,900) are more than double the metro average. Business-oriented farms in metro areas have more than 42 percent larger sales than business-oriented farms in nonmetro areas." (p24-25)

Barnard, Charles H./Heimlich, Ralph E. "Special Article: Agricultural Adaptation to Urban Influence in U.S. Metro Counties." U.S. Dept. of Agriculture: Economic Research Service Dec 1993. p22-30.

FARM PRODUCE--EUROPEAN ECONOMIC COMMUNITY (v19)

FARM PRODUCE--MEXICO--U.S. (v19)

FARM SUBSIDIES

see AGRICULTURAL SUBSIDIES

FARMERS--FRANCE (v19)

FARMERS--HEALTH AND HYGIENE--U.S.

"According to the Centers for Disease Control, agriculture is the second most dangerous occupation in the United States. Yet farmworkers are rarely offered or seldom able to afford health insurance. (Farmworkers are not covered by workers compensation of any kind in 14 states.) A UCLA study found that a startling 65% of all California farmworkers are uninsured. This is well above national estimates of the uninsured population as a whole." (p88-89)

Schneider, Cynthia G. (Staff Attorney, Migrant Legal Action Program). U.S. House. Committee on Energy and Commerce. "Medicaid Managed Care in California." Hearing, 20 Apr 1993. Washington, D.C.: GPO, 1994. (ISBN0160434122). (Y4.En2/3:103-52).

FARMERS--TAXATION--U.S. (v19)

FARMERS--U.S.

see also RANCHERS--U.S.; TUBERCULOSIS--U.S.--FARMERS

"What happens to the young people [of the U.S.]--the coming generation--who are denied a future on the land in the home where they were children? It doesn't matter. Fewer than one-fourth of them remain on the farm after their schooling is completed. By age 16, an estimated one-fifth have already departed and are in a core-center city from which they will never return. For an estimated 55% of this group, there is nothing left if they did return home. The farm is an

acquisition and the family is gone to some urban hub." (p13)
Wills, Harold E. "Farmers of the Future? A Point of No Return." Acres, U.S.A. v24 n1, Jan 1994. p13.
"Individuals and families comprise 85 percent of farm landlords [in the U.S.] (the census designation for a landowner who rents out land is a landlord). Among this group of landlords, 40 percent are women, 31 percent are men, and 29 percent are joint owners. The remaining 15 percent of owners are nonfamily partnerships, corporations, or other forms of organization. A typical landlord is also most likely: a nonfarmer (9 out of 10), white (98 out of 100), 60 years or older (2 out of 3), and owner of less than 180 acres (2 out of 3). About 36 percent of landlords live on their farmland, while 44 percent live in a city, town, or urban area. Another 19 percent live on another farm or elsewhere in a rural area. Only 2 percent of landlords are nonfamily corporations, holding 7 percent of landlord-owned farmland." (p4)
U.S. Dept. of Agriculture/Wunderlich, Gene. "Agricultural Economy: U.S. Farmland Ownership: A Century of Change." Agricultural Outlook Dec 1993. p3-5.
"In an indication of the further diminishing of the...[U.S.] farm population, the USDA and the Census Bureau have announced plans to drop the government's survey of farm residents. Farm residents now represent just 1.9% of the national population, or 4.6 million, compared with 40% at the turn of the century; nearly a third of farm managers and 86% of farm workers live away from the farm. In addition, many family farms have been sold and consolidated. All those factors would make a survey of farm residents an inaccurate measure of the characteristics of agricultural life, according to published reports. The Census Bureau will attempt to count agricultural workers and managers through other ongoing surveys." (p2)
"Census Bureau Drops Survey of Farm Residents." Alternative Agriculture News v11 n12, Nov 1993. p2. (ISSN8755-4941).
"We are rapidly running out of farmers. In 1990, according to the U.S. Census, there was a farm population of less than 4 million. This was down from more than 30 million in 1940--a decline of more than 26 million in fifty years, an average of more than half a million a year, or nearly 1,500 a day. In the decade from 1980 to 1990, 1,746,320 people left the farm--a decline of 31 percent. Under present circumstances, the only reasonable expectation is that our farm population will decline further by the year 2000. The tragedy of this decline is not just in its numbers; it is also in the fact that these farming people, assuming we will ever recognize our need to replace them, cannot be replaced anything like so quickly or easily as they were dispensed with. Contrary to popular assumption, good farmers are not in any simple way part of the 'labor force.' Good farmers, like good musicians, must be raised to their trade." (p32)
Berry, Wendell. "Free Trade and the Environment." Amicus Journal v15 n3, Fall 1993. p31-34. (ISSN0276-7201).

FARMING
see AGRICULTURE

FARMS
see also DAIRY FARMS; RANCHES

FARMS--ESTONIA
In Estonia "Collective farms typically consist of 200-cow units compared to the small, subsistence family farms (which generally had less than five cows), that they replaced. The 25,000-acre Vaike Maarja farm, which was selected as the model for the first comprehensive privatization, had seven 200-cow units and employed 1,200 people. The farm, one of the largest and most successful collectives, also had a slaughterhouse, pig and poultry production, a cheese plant and a potato farm. In the US a 200-cow farm would be run by about five people, and they would grow all the crops as well. US production is about 900,000 pounds of milk per worker. In Estonia, it is 195,000 pounds." (p34)
MacKillop, John. "Diary of the Estonian Dairy Industry." Surviving Together v11 n3, Fall 1993. p34-35. (ISSN0859-6286).

FARMS--EUROPEAN ECONOMIC COMMUNITY (v19)
FARMS--GERMANY (EAST) (v19)
FARMS--KAZAKHSTAN (v19)
FARMS--RUSSIA (v19)
"Private plots provide the majority of basic food items for Russian families. As might be expected, women supply most of the labor while male contributions are limited to repair work, yard cleaning and biannual soil treatment. Women bear the major responsibility for day-to-day upkeep of the plot and care of livestock. In fact, a survey in western Siberia showed that women contribute nearly 23 hours a week toward their plots, while men work less than 12 hours. In the Novosibirsk region, women provide 70 percent of the total time spent on private plots. For 33 percent of rural women, work on private plots is their most time-consuming activity because of the lack of small-scale mechanization. On these plots, people work for themselves and as a result, their work is several times more productive than work performed on collective farms. However, because private farmers usually replace chemicals (both for health and economic reasons) with crop rotation and organic fertilizers, their farming is much more labor-intensive. These measures make their produce healthier and more popular at local markets, but they do require extra work." (p29)
Mirovitskaya, Natalia. "Women: The Double Burden Weighs Heavier on Rural Russian Women." Surviving Together v11 n3, Fall 1993. p27-30. (ISSN0859-6286).

FARMS--U.S. (v19)
"About 41 percent of U.S. farmers now rent all or part of their farms. These farmers control--through ownership or lease--67 percent of the land in farms and produce over 60 percent of the value of agricultural sales." (p4)
U.S. Dept. of Agriculture/Wunderlich, Gene. "Agricultural Economy: U.S. Farmland Ownership: A Century of Change." Agricultural Outlook Dec 1993. p3-5.
"After 45 years, the Census Bureau has ended its series of reports on the resident farm population. RESIDENTS OF FARMS AND RURAL AREAS: 1991 marks the end of the government's efforts to collect data on people who live on farms. The number of farm residents declined from 31 million in 1940 to fewer than 5 million in 1991. The discontinuation of the count is not so much due to these dwindling numbers, however, but to the fact that farm residence no longer tells us much about farmers. In 1940, 90 percent of farm operators lived on farms, as did most farm laborers, says Calvin Beale, senior demographer at the U.S. Department of Agriculture. Today, only one-third of farmers live on farms....More than half (53 percent) of employed farm residents work in nonagricultural industries. Seventy-three percent of employed women who live on farms do not work in farming." (p21-22)
Dortch, Shannon. "Business Reports: Trends: Farewell to the Farm Report." American Demographics v16 n3, Mar 1994. p21-22. (ISSN0163-4089).
"We've lost 350,000 farms in the U.S. since 1980. Nebraska has 9,000 fewer farmers, a loss of 14 percent, equal to the national average. With farm loss comes rural population loss. Eighty four of Nebraska's 93 counties lost population between 1980 and 1990. There was nothing inevitable about this depopulation of farm communities. It was a product of U.S. agricultural policy, including farm programs that support economic concentration in agriculture by rewarding specialized production of a few export

crops and by providing the largest rewards to the largest farmers. In 1987, for example, nearly 60 percent of all payments went to cash grain producers and the top 26 percent of all farms received 58 percent of the benefits." (pSR3)

"Special Report: Sustainable Rural Development in North America and the North American Free Trade Agreement." Center for Rural Affairs Newsletter Apr 1993. pSR1-4.

"Farms in metropolitan areas are an increasingly important component of U.S. agriculture....They make up 30 percent of all farms and control 36 percent of farm assets. Seventeen percent of farmland is located in metro areas, roughly proportional to the total land in metro areas. Again, residential farms blur the contributions of more productive, business-oriented farms. Residential farms account for 46 percent of U.S. farms, but contribute only 2 percent to aggregate U.S. sales of agricultural products....Within metro areas, residential farms account for 54 percent of farms, control 30 percent of farm sector assets and equity and 13 percent of the land operated....Business-oriented farms account for 46 percent of metro farms, 57 percent of nonmetro farms, and 54 percent of U.S. farms....They control assets and equity twice their numbers and size and have 4 times larger farm sales. Business-oriented farms produce returns 6 to 10 times greater than their proportional numbers or acreage." (p29)

Barnard, Charles H./Heimlich, Ralph E. "Special Article: Agricultural Adaptation to Urban Influence in U.S. Metro Counties." U.S. Dept. of Agriculture: Economic Research Service Dec 1993. p22-30.

"In the late 1930's, farm productivity began to increase after stagnating since 1900....Growing productivity led to farm consolidation, declining farm numbers, and excess capacity in agriculture....Farmers and farm laborers left farming, encouraged by higher nonfarm wages. By 1990, only 2.7 percent of U.S. employment was in production agriculture, compared with 12.2 percent in 1950 and 24 percent in 1935. Not surprisingly, the number of areas economically dependent on farming also declined. Over 2,000 counties (of a U.S. total of 3,070) were farming-dependent in 1950, relying on farming for at least 20 percent of their total earnings....By 1986, the number had dropped to 521." (p14)

Hoppe, Robert A. "Special Article: Farm Business and Household Characteristics Vary by County Type." U.S. Dept. of Agriculture: Economic Research Service Dec 1993. p14-21.

"Metropolitan Statistical Areas (MSAs) defined by the Bureau of the Census now contain 16 percent of U.S. land area and 75 percent of U.S. population (Bureau of the Census). Metro areas also contain nearly one-third of all U.S. farms (1991), farms that produce a similar proportion of the value of U.S. agricultural production." (p22) "More than 627,000 farms are located in metro areas, accounting for 30 percent of the 2.1 million U.S. farms, and producing 33 percent of crop and livestock sales." (p23)

Barnard, Charles H./Heimlich, Ralph E. "Special Article: Agricultural Adaptation to Urban Influence in U.S. Metro Counties." U.S. Dept. of Agriculture: Economic Research Service Dec 1993. p22-30.

FARMS--U.S.--ECONOMIC CONDITIONS (v19)

FARMS--U.S.--LOCATION

Fifty-eight "percent of the total U.S. agricultural production comes from counties that are in or adjacent to major cities; 30 percent for the counties that the Census Bureau classifies as metropolitan, those containing sizable cities; and another 28 percent from the counties right next door. The concentration of agriculture around cities is even more pronounced in some of the nation's most strategic farming areas. In...California, for example, 93 percent of all farm production, measured by gross sales, comes from these so-called urban fringe counties. That so much of the nation's production is in this high conflict area should be of concern to us all." (p288)

Grossi, Ralph E. "A Green Evolution: Retooling Agricultural Policy for Greater Sustainability." Journal of Soil and Water Conservation v48 n4, Jul-Aug 1993. p285-288. (ISSN0022-4561).

FAST FOOD RESTAURANTS--U.S. (v19)

FATHERS--U.S. (v19)

FEDERAL AID TO BIRTH CONTROL--U.S. (v19)

FEDERAL AID TO COMMUNITY HEALTH SERVICES--U.S. (v19)

FEDERAL AID TO EDUCATION--U.S. (v19)

"Education in the United States exists on a vast scale with annual budgets of $240 billion for just the K-12 component and more than $375 billion for the total education enterprise--encompassing higher education, industrial education, and supporting organizations. Both the scale and the decentralized character of education make the imposition of central solutions impossible. If schools in the United States are going to get better, it will require the combined effort and commitment of all concerned--parents, teachers, administrators, and government officials. The challenge for federal and state policy makers is to create conditions that will make education reform more likely--to help schools and communities equip themselves with the tools of reform." (p17-18)

Porter, Andrew C./Ball, G. Carl (National Academy of Sciences' Committee on the Federal Role in Education Research). U.S. House. Committee on Education and Labor. "Hearing on H.R. 856, the Educational Research...Excellence Act." Hearing, 27 May 1993. Washington, D.C.: GPO, 1993. (ISBN016043338X). (Y4.Ed8/1:103-33).

FEDERAL AID TO EDUCATION--U.S.--PRISONERS (v19)

FEDERAL AID TO MEDICAL RESEARCH--U.S. (v19)

"Today, federally supported research on Alzhemier's disease totals $300 million [in the U.S.], yet it is estimated that $90 billion is expended annually on care. Federally supported research on diabetes totals $290 million, yet it is estimated that $25 billion is expended annually on care. Federally supported research on mental health totals $613 million, yet it is estimated that $130 billion is expended annually on care." (pS2042)

Hatfield, Mark O. (Sen.-Oreg.). "Amendments Submitted," Congressional Record (28 Feb 1994). Daily ed. pS2037-2043. (ISSN0363-7239).

FEDERAL AID TO MEDICAL RESEARCH--U.S.--PUBLIC OPINION

"A recent Harris poll has shown that Americans strongly support health research and are willing to put their money behind their words. The poll asked Americans which type of scientific research they favored--66 percent favored medical research. Environmental research followed at 18 percent, energy research at 6 percent, and defense finished at 4 percent. At the moment, about 3 cents out of each health care dollar spent in the United States goes to medical research. Of those surveyed, the value suggested was at least 10 cents per dollar. Even more encouraging is that if assured that the funds would be spent for medical research, 74 percent of Americans are willing to spend $1 more per week in taxes, 75 percent are willing to spend $1 more per prescription drug, and 77 percent are willing to spend $1 more per week in insurance premiums." (pS2043)

Hatfield, Mark O. (Sen.-Oreg.). "Amendments Submitted," Congressional Record (28 Feb 1994). Daily ed. pS2037-2043. (ISSN0363-7239).

FEDERAL AID TO TRANSPORTATION--U.S. (v19)

FEDERAL RESERVE BANKS--EMPLOYEES

"The Fed's [Federal Reserve's] seven-member Board of Governors is all white and includes just one woman, Susan M. Phillips. Of the next 30 top jobs, all are held by white males except for the director of maintenance services, a black man. At the regional Federal Reserve banks, all 12 presidents and 98 of the 111 vice-presidents are white men....The Fed has little turnover, and nearly all promotions are from within....Working conditions are good, and the pay is great--top staff get $162,000, more than members of Congress or the Cabinet. Nonetheless, women and minorities are slowly working their way up through the ranks. At the Fed's Washington headquarters, 28% of the second-tier staff jobs are held by women and 14% by minorities....The 12 regional banks have made better progress. Three women are first vice-presidents of regional banks, putting them next in line to become presidents....The Fed also boasts that 25% of the 812 regional bank officers below the rank of vice-president are women and that 10% are minorities." (p42)

Ullmann, Owen. "Top of the News: Diversity: Is the Fed Facing a Political Correction?" Business Week n3353, 10 Jan 1994. p42. (ISSN0007-7135).

FERTILITY, HUMAN (v19)

FERTILITY, HUMAN--BANGLADESH

"In Bangladesh--one of the world's largest and most densely populated countries--average family size has dropped since the 1970s from about seven births per women to 4.9 births in 1991. This means that Bangladeshi couples are averaging two children fewer than two decades ago. Two in five couples are using some form of contraception (up from 8 percent in 1975). Over half use modern reversible methods, such as the pill. Bangladesh is the only one of the world's 20 poorest countries to show a significant sustained fertility decline since the 1970s." (p5)

Kalish, Susan. "Culturally Sensitive Family Planning: Bangladesh Story Suggests It Can Reduce Family Size." Population Today v22 n2, Feb 1994. p5. (ISSN0749-2448).

FERTILITY, HUMAN--CHINA

"Women in China average just over two children. The TFR (total fertility rate, or average lifetime births per woman) was 2.2 in 1992. This is substantially below the average TFR for the world (3.3) or for other developing countries (4.4 children per woman). The TFR in China fell by half during the 1970s, from 5.8 in 1970 to 2.2 by 1980. It has fluctuated somewhat since then, remaining within a range of more than two but less than three children. This dramatic decline slowed population growth in the country. At 1960 fertility levels, China would have reached 1.1 billion people by the mid-1970s; because of the fertility drop, it did not do so until 1989, according to H. Yuan Tien, of Ohio State University." (p5)

Kalish, Susan. "In China, the Peak Childbearing Years Have Peaked." Population Today v21 n1, Jan 1993. p5. (ISSN0749-2448).

FERTILITY, HUMAN--CUBA

THE PROGRESS OF NATIONS, a publication released by UNICEF, "uses the average number of births per woman (total fertility rate) as a vital indicator of the transition to smaller families and stable populations, and of the well-being of mothers and children. Family planning helped to more than halve Cuba's birth rate from 4.2 children in 1960 to 1.9 in 1991, giving the country one of the lowest fertility rates in the developing world. Cuba's fertility level is almost half the regional and global averages of 3.5 and 3.4 respectively...a few comparative figures dramatically illustrate Cuba's progress: the United States, 2; Costa Rica, 3.2; Guatemala, 5.5; Australia, 1.9; Bolivia, 4.7; Somalia, 7." (p17)

"Cuba/International: UNICEF Lauds Cuba's Program for Children." Cuba Update n6, Nov-Dec 1993. p17-18. (ISSN0196-0830).

FERTILITY, HUMAN--DEVELOPING COUNTRIES (v19)

FERTILITY, HUMAN--FRANCE

"After a stable rate during much of the 1980s that averaged about 1.8 children per French woman, the rate in 1992 dropped to 1.73. New statistics released by the National Institute of Statistics and Economic Studies (INSEE) show that the rate in 1993 dropped to 1.65. That rate, well below the 2.1 required for long-term population stability, is still above Spain's 1.23, Italy's 1.26, Germany's 1.3, and Belgium's 1.56. France's population is still growing--by about 300,000 last year, to 57.8 million--and will continue to grow until the end of the decade...[Guy] Desplanques says." (p7)

LaFranchi, Howard. "French Families Grow Smaller, and Government Asks Why." The Christian Science Monitor v86 n57, 15 Feb 1994. p7. (ISSN0882-7729).

FERTILITY, HUMAN--GERMANY

"In the May issue of EUROPE-ASIA STUDIES, Nicholas Eberstadt, a demographer with the American Enterprise Institute in Washington, remarks: 'Eastern Germany's adults appear to have come as close to a temporary suspension of child-bearing as any large population in the human experience.' In 1992, he says, the birth rate was 55% lower than it had been in 1989, and still declining: in the first five months of 1993, eastern Germany had fewer than 5.1 births per thousand people--over 60% fewer than in the same period of 1989, and less than half the (famously low) rate in western Germany. The fall was steepest in births to married women, and to women aged between 25 and 34." (p54)

"Europe: Eastern Germany: Living and Dying, in a Barren Land." Economist v331 n7860, 23 Apr 1994. p54. (ISSN0013-0613).

FERTILITY, HUMAN--GERMANY (EAST)

"During the decade before the end of East German Communism, aggregate fertility levels were relatively stable. Between 1980 and 1988, for example, the annual number of live births in the German Democratic Republic (GDR) ranged between 216,000 and 245,000; crude birth rates per thousand residents fluctuated, gradually declining from 14.6 at the beginning of the decade to 12.9 in 1988....Patterns changed drastically after 1989. In the two years between 1989 and 1991, the number of live births reported in Eastern Germany fell by over 91,000, or about 46 percent. The downslide continued thereafter. By 1992, births amounted to a mere 44 percent of the 1989 total, and birth rates were 53 percent lower than they had been three years earlier. Data through early 1993 suggest that fertility levels in Eastern Germany had not yet stabilized. In the first five months of 1993, Eastern Germany's total number of live births was down by more than 60 percent from the same period in 1989; whereas the region's annualized crude birth rate had been 13.3 per thousand for January-May 1989, it was under 5.1 per thousand in January-May 1993." (p137-138)

Eberstadt, Nicholas. "Demographic Shocks after Communism: Eastern Germany, 1989-93." Population and Development Review v20 n1, Mar 1994. p137-152. (ISSN0098-7921).

FERTILITY, HUMAN--INDONESIA

"Indonesia's fertility decline has been one of the most striking demographic transitions in modern history. Total fertility rates (TFR) declined 22% over 11 years, from 5.6 in 1970 to 4.1 in 1980, and declined another 23% in the next five years alone, from 4.1 to 3.2 (Biro Pusat Statistik 1989). Historically, most of this decline has been attributed to two proximate determinants: a dramatic rise in contraceptive prevalence and an increase in age of marriage (Adioetomo, Kitting, and Taufik 1990; Hull and Hatmadji 1990). The proportion of women using contraception increased from 27% in 1980 to 47% in 1987 (Biro Pusat Statistik 1989). In addition, the mean age of marriage rose from 19.3 in 1971 to 21.1 in 1985 (Hull and Hatmadji 1990). Two important institutional factors are often cited for the changes in these proximate determinants: 1) a strong government commitment, both political and financial, to limiting population growth through family planning, and 2) expansion of women's economic welfare and opportunities (Hull and Hatmadji 1990; Hull and Hull 1987; McNicoll and Singarimbun 1983; World Bank 1990a)." (p36)

Gertler, Paul J./Molyneaux, John W. "How Economic Development and Family Planning Programs Combined to Reduce Indonesian Fertility." Demography v31 n1, Feb 1994. p33-63. (ISSN0070-3370).

FERTILITY, HUMAN--ITALY

"Italy has the distinction of having one of the lowest fertility rates in the world. Italian women average 1.3 children in their lifetimes, and the rate of natural increase is a very slight 0.1 percent per year. Italy's population almost doubled in the century between 1861 and 1961. It grew 2.1 percent over the past decade. Unlike some other low-fertility countries, Italy's low fertility has not been a recent occurrence....With Italy's low birth rate, 85 percent of population growth in Italy today is due to immigration. But even so, net immigration is extremely low--fewer than 16,000 people entered Italy in 1989." (p11)

Kalish, Susan. "Spotlight: Italy." Population Today v21 n4, Apr 1993. p11. (ISSN0749-2448).

FERTILITY, HUMAN--JAPAN

"Japan's total fertility rate (TFR) fell by more than half between 1947 and 1957, from 4.54 to 2.04 births per woman....Between 1957 and 1973, it remained close to the replacement level of about two births per woman, except for a dip in 1966 during the Year of the Fire Horse, traditionally considered an unlucky year in which to give birth to a girl (Hodge and Ogawa, 1991). In 1973 the TFR resumed its downward trend, falling from 2.14 to 1.50 births per woman by 1992. After 1973, annual births fell even more steeply than the TFR because of changes in population age structure that affected annual births but not the TFR. The number of births in 1992 was 42 percent smaller than in 1973....The public and even the government, however, paid little attention to this new development until 1989, when the TFR reached an all-time low of 1.57. At that time Japan's low fertility burst into public consciousness when the media coined the phrase '1.57 shock,' a term that received wide publicity both in Japan and elsewhere (e.g., U.S. NEWS & WORLD REPORT, 1990). By 1992 the TFR had declined even further, to 1.53." (p703)

Ogawa, Naohiro/Retherford, Robert D. "The Resumption of Fertility Decline in Japan: 1973-92." Population and Development Review v19 n4, Dec 1993. p703-741. (ISSN0098-7921).

FERTILITY, HUMAN--KENYA

"Fertility is declining in Kenya which, with a population of 28 million, is one of the largest countries in Africa. According to the 1993 Kenya Demographic and Health Survey (DHS), the country's total fertility rate (TFR, or average lifetime births per woman) for the three-year period prior to the survey was 5.4 children per woman, significantly lower than the TFR of 6.7 children for the five-year period preceding the 1989 fertility survey. The 20 percent decline in just over four years is one of the swiftest ever recorded, according to the report. The family planning program began in 1967." (p8)

"News Clips: Kenya Fertility Update." Population Today v21 n12, Dec 1993. p8. (ISSN0749-2448).

"Final results of a nationwide survey by the Kenyan government, to be released soon, are expected to confirm preliminary results showing a 20 percent decline in fertility rates between 1988 and 1993, according to Kenyan and United States officials here. Such a decline means there has been a drop in the average lifetime births of a Kenyan woman from 6.7 to 5.4. 'Should this trend continue, it would mean about 70 million fewer people in Kenya by the year 2025, to feed, educate, and employ,' says Gary Newton, chief of the Office of Population and Health of the United States Agency for International Development (USAID), the major donor to family planning in Kenya over the past 20 years." (p1)

Press, Robert M. "Kenya Shows Dramatic Drop in Fertility Rate." The Christian Science Monitor v86 n78, 17 Mar 1994. p1,4. (ISSN0882-7729).

FERTILITY, HUMAN--LATIN AMERICA (v19)

"Latin America (Mexico, Central and South America, and the Caribbean) has seen not only substantial societal change and modernization, but family planning programs have succeeded in lowering fertility rates through educational campaigns and extension of services into underserved areas. Over the past thirty years the regional TFR (total fertility rate or average lifetime births per woman) has been cut in half, from 5.9 to 3.0. In countries with populations over 10 million, the TFR is now 3.1 in Brazil, 3.8 in Mexico, 2.9 in Colombia, 4.0 in Peru, 3.6 in Venezuela, 2.7 in Chile, 1.9 in Cuba, and 3.8 in Ecuador....Change is not universal, however. Some of the poorer countries in Central America (Guatemala, Honduras, and Nicaragua) and the Caribbean (Haiti) still have TFRs of 5 or more." (p6)

de Sherbinin, Alex. "Demographic Perspective: Latin America: How a Region Surprised the Experts." Population Today v21 n2, Feb 1993. p6-7,9. (ISSN0749-2448).

FERTILITY, HUMAN--MIDDLE EAST

"Women in the Middle East have, on average, one of the highest levels of childbearing in the world. The total fertility rate (TFR, or average births in a woman's lifetime) for the region is close to five children. The 1991/1992 Yemen Demographic and Health Survey showed that women in rural Yemen average more than eight children in their lifetimes--one of the highest fertility rates in the world. In contrast, Cyprus has a TFR of 2.4 and Jewish women in Israel average 2.7 children in their lifetimes." (p3)

Roudi, Nazy. "Population Policies Vary in Middle East." Population Today v21 n4, Apr 1993. p3,10. (ISSN0749-2448).

FERTILITY, HUMAN--RUSSIA (v19)

"In Russia, the total fertility rate (TFR), or average lifetime births per woman, plummeted from 2.12 in 1988 to 1.55 in 1992, according to recent official data. In this period, the birth rate fell for every age group of Russian women except for teenagers....With a 1992 crude birth rate of 10.7 births per 1,000 population and a death rate of 12.2, Russia experienced a natural decrease of 1.5 people per 1,000 population in 1992. This was one of the fastest rates of natural decrease (more deaths than births) in the world that year." (p1)

Haub, Carl. "Russia's New Revolution: A Demographic Baby Bust." Population Today v22 n4, Apr 1994. p1-2. (ISSN0749-2448).

FERTILITY, HUMAN--SOUTH AFRICA (v19)

FERTILITY, HUMAN--SPAIN

"At the current fertility rate, Spanish women will average only 1.23 births in their lifetimes. The average age at first birth is increasing, from 28.2 in 1980, to 28.5 in 1985, and 28.6 in 1989. Fertility in Spain has been steadily decreasing since the 1970s. Between 1981 and 1990, Spain's population showed the smallest intercensal increase of the century (3.2 percent). Natural increase (births minus deaths) was only 0.1 percent per year in 1993....Nineteen percent of Spain's population is below age 15, while 14 percent is age 65 or older....The most recent contraceptive-use survey showed that in 1985, 59 percent of married women were using some form of contraception and 38 percent were using modern methods." (p7)

Hershey, Sharon. "Spotlight: Spain." Population Today v22 n3, Mar 1994. p7. (ISSN0749-2448).

FERTILITY, HUMAN--SUDAN

"Sudan, the largest country in Africa, is characterized by a stable high level of fertility and a high, but slightly declining, level of mortality. As a result, the rate of population growth has remained high, and although maternal and child mortality rates have declined, they are still high by international standards. All statistical sources but one give the total marital fertility rate in Sudan as stable at about 6.5 births per woman since the mid-1950s. The 1989 Demographic and Health Survey (SDHS) figure of 5.0 seems to be an underestimate when compared with the other international and national estimates...." (p366)

Swar-Eldahab, Amna M. "Constraints on Effective Family Planning in Urban Sudan." Studies in Family Planning v24 n6, Nov-Dec 1993. p366-374. (ISSN0039-3665).

FERTILITY, HUMAN--THAILAND

"If we want to bring population growth rates down rapidly, we must learn from the real success stories like Thailand. In the early 1960s, the average Thai woman was having 6.4 children. Today she is having only 2.2. This represents a drop of 3.5 percent per year--as speedy as the fastest change in technology." (p26)

Harrison, Paul. "Sex and the Single Planet." Amicus Journal v15 n45, Win 1994. p16-18,21-23,26. (ISSN0276-7201).

FERTILITY, HUMAN--U.S. (v19)

"Immigration accounted for most of the growth of the minority population [in the U.S.] in the 1980s. Immigration contributed about half of the growth among Hispanics and nearly three-fourths of the growth among Asians. Higher fertility among minorities compared to non-Hispanic whites was the other major cause of minority growth. Non-Hispanic white women average just under two children in their lifetime (1.9 children). Black women average 2.5 children, Asians 2.3, American Indians 2.9, and Hispanics 2.7 children. In 1989, minorities accounted for about one-third (35 percent) of the 4 million births in the United States." (p2)

O'Hare, William P. "Diversity Trend: More Minorities Looking Less Alike." Population Today v21 n4, Apr 1993. p1-2. (ISSN0749-2448).

"U.S. pregnancies kept growing through the 1980s, increasing from 5.9 million in 1980 to 6.3 million in 1988, a gain of 7 percent. The number of pregnancies increased, according to NCHS [National Center for Health Statistics] because the number of women in their childbearing years continued to grow: from 48.7 million women ages 15 to 44 in 1976, to 52.8 million in 1980, to 58.1 million in 1988. Unless desired family size increases radically in the next few years, the number should drop in the future as smaller cohorts of women replace baby boomers in the prime childbearing years....The most likely ages for pregnancy are 18 to 29. In 1988, the rate was 185 pregnancies per 1,000 women ages 20 to 24 years (nearly one in five) and almost as high for women ages 25 to 29 (167 pregnancies per 1,000). In contrast, the pregnancy rate for women ages 30 to 34 was 110 per 1,000, or about one in ten." (p3)

Kalish, Susan. "Pregnancy Rates Fall while Number Rise." Population Today v21 n3, Mar 1993. p3. (ISSN0749-2448).

FERTILIZATION IN VITRO--MICHIGAN

"In vitro fertilization [is]...the combining of a mature egg and sperm in the laboratory, to be implanted in the woman for a natural development and birth....Not everybody gets pregnant with in vitro fertilization." Dr. Maria Hayes, "one of the first physicians to perform in vitro in Michigan, says that 25 percent will get pregnant per attempt. Most people, she says, are under a misconception about multiple births; the vast majority who receive treatment--70 percent--have one child; 25 percent have two and only about five percent have three or more babies. 'In the last five years we have had 6 triples and 3 quads.'" (p24)

Grant, John. "Health: Strong Medicine." Corporate Detroit v11 n1, Jan 1994. p23-24,26,28.

FERTILIZERS (v19)

"Although there was little new land to plow from mid-century onward, the world's farmers were able to achieve the largest expansion of food output in history by dramatically raising land productivity. The engine of growth was fertilizer use, which increased ninefold in three decades--from 14 million tons in 1950 to 126 million tons in 1984--before starting to slow...." (p20)

Brown, Lester R. "A Decade of Discontinuity." World Watch v6 n4, Jul-Aug 1993. p19-26. (ISSN0896-0615).

FERTILIZERS--RUSSIA (v19)

FERTILIZERS--U.S. (v19)

"Most of the increase in grain yields during the post-World War II era can be credited to fertilizers. The use of fertilizers climbed from 14 million tons annually to a peak of 146 million tons in 1989. But since 1984, the increase in grain production per ton of fertilizer applied has dropped sharply." (p10)

Knickerbocker, Brad. "Economy: The Balance between Food and People Has Become Threatened." The Christian Science Monitor v86 n37, 18 Jan 1994. p10. (ISSN0882-7729).

FETAL ALCOHOL SYNDROME--U.S.

"Fetal Alcohol Syndrome (FAS) is...[the] primary known cause of mental retardation [in the U.S.], and it is completely preventable. According to a report issued last summer by the Centers for Disease Control and Prevention, the number of reported FAS cases has tripled over the past decade. The CDC reports that in 1992, nearly 4 infants--possibly more--out of every 10,000 births were born with FAS, suffering irreversible physical and mental harm. In 1979, the first year CDC collected information on the incidence of Fetal Alcohol Syndrome, it estimated the number of reported FAS cases at only one per 10,000 births. Adding to the extent of the problem are estimates which indicate that each year 10,000 to 12,000 infants are born with lesser, though still serious, alcohol-related birth defects known as fetal alcohol effects (FAE)." (pS668-669)

Bingaman, Jeff (Sen.-N.Mex). "Statements on Introduced Bills and Joint Resolutions," Congressional Record (2 Feb 1994). Daily ed. pS659-669. (ISSN0363-7239).

"The Office for Substance Abuse Prevention estimates that as many as 66 percent of all women drink while they are pregnant, endangering their infants' health and putting them at risk of being born with FAS [fetal alcohol syndrome] or FAE [fetal alcohol effect]. The National Council on Alcoholism and Drug Dependence reports that the number of women who believe it is safe to consume up to three drinks per day while they are pregnant may be as high as one-third....There are approximately 5,000 children born each year in the United States with FAS. It is estimated that the incidence of FAS is as high as 1 per 100 in some Native American communities. The Centers for Disease Control and Prevention estimate that the life-time cost of treating an individual with FAS is almost $1.4 million. The total cost in terms of health care and social services to treat all Americans with FAS is close to $1.6 billion each year. This is an extraordinary and unnecessary expense, given the fact that FAS is 100-percent preventable." (pS666)

Daschle, Thomas A. (Sen.-S.Dak.). "Statements on Introduced Bills and Joint Resolutions," Congressional Record (2 Feb

1994). Daily ed. pS659-669. (ISSN0363-7239).

FETAL ALCOHOL SYNDROME--U.S.--COSTS (v19)

FILLS (EARTHWORK)--CHICAGO (ILL)

"In 1990, active landfills in Cook County reported a total remaining capacity of 50,312,130 tons. At the rate of solid waste generation projected by the City of Chicago, Chicago's waste could exhaust available landfill space by the year 2002. (Numbers exclude landfill capacity being...built downstate.)" (p19)

Bardoe, Cheryl. "Chicago's Sustainability Indicators." Neighborhood Works v16 n5, Oct-Nov 1993. p16-20.

FILLS (EARTHWORK)--U.S. (v19)

"Organic materials not only remain intact inside landfills, they make up a larger portion of the fill than expected. At excavations in Florida, Illinois, and Arizona, the Garbage Project found ten-to fifteen-year old garbage that still contained 32.5, 50.6, and 66.5 percent organics, respectively. A California landfill yielded twenty-five year old garbage that was 40 percent organic, and a forty-year old sample from Arizona was 49 percent organic. In the oxygen-poor atmosphere of the landfills' depths, the microbes that consume organics--or natural carbon-based materials--cannot survive, so these artifacts of modern life become mummified." (p38)

Hanson, Beth. "Pass the Humus." Amicus Journal v15 n3, Fall 1993. p38-42. (ISSN0276-7201).

FILLS (EARTHWORK)--U.S.--MINORITIES (v19)

FINANCE

see CORPORATIONS--KOREA (SOUTH)--FINANCE; EDUCATION--ILLINOIS--FINANCE; EDUCATION--MICHIGAN--FINANCE; EDUCATION--RESEARCH--U.S.--FINANCE; EDUCATION--U.S.--FINANCE; HEALTH FACILITIES--U.S.--FINANCE; HOUSING--U.S.--FINANCE; INFLATION (FINANCE); PUBLIC TELEVISION--U.S.--FINANCE

FINANCIAL SERVICES INDUSTRY--LUXEMBOURG (v19)

FINLAND--ECONOMIC CONDITIONS (v19)

"Largely because of the collapse of trade with the old Soviet Union, the economy [in Finland] is in a dreadful state, with unemployment at 20%, a cumulative fall in GDP [gross domestic product] of 14% between 1990 and 1993, and a decline in GDP per person (measured in American dollars) of no less than 40% in the same period. People are understandably ready for change. Relations with Russia and the country's application to join the EU [European Union] are the central issues." (p49)

"Europe: Enter, Pursued by a Bear?" Economist v330 n7844, 8 Jan 1994. p49. (ISSN0013-0613).

FIRE FIGHTERS--U.S. (v19)

FIREARMS--BELGIUM

"Prior to 1989 Begium had very lax gun control laws. The law passed that year tightened the control considerably--at least on paper....The new law has had a marked effect on the legal arms trade in Belgium. Sales of rifles, for example, have decreased from 6,000 a year to 500. Sales of handguns, however, have actually gone up from 6,000 to 7,000 per year. Sales of hunting guns, which only need to be declared and do not require a permit, have gone up by 17 percent over the past two years. Altogether there are some 465,000 guns legally owned in Belgium--a substantial number for a country whose population is 10 million." (p41)

Leonard, Dick. "Capitals: Brussels: Few Armed Robberies." Europe n335, Apr 1994. p41-42. (ISSN0191-4545).

FIREARMS--CALIFORNIA (v19)

"Last year, Californians went out and bought themselves 665,000 firearms--22% more than in 1992. The figures may have been inflated by fears of more riots like those in Los Angeles; even so, the number of handguns bought each year has doubled over the past decade." (p29)

"American Survey: Crime in California: Three Strikes, You're Out." Economist v330 n7846, 15 Jan 1994. p29,32. (ISSN0013-0613).

FIREARMS--CANADA--U.S.--MORTALITY (v19)

FIREARMS--CHICAGO (ILL) (v19)

"Weapons seizures in public housing facilities have increased dramatically since 1990 in Chicago. Last year alone, housing authority and Chicago police confiscated over 1100 firearms from inside Chicago housing projects, a 22 percent increase from the nearly 900 seizures in 1990. Equally as disturbing are some recent statistics on the incidence of gun shots. Authorities estimate that during one weekend late last month, there were over 300 reports of shots fired at one Chicago Housing Authority property, the Robert Taylor Homes." (pE690)

Durbin, Richard J. (Rep.-Ill.). "Gun-Free Public Housing Zones Act of 1994," Congressional Record (18 Apr 1994). Daily ed. pE690-691. (ISSN0363-7239).

FIREARMS--CRIME (v19)

FIREARMS--DENMARK

"Only about 40,000 Danes, fewer than one out of 100, have a license to possess firearms. This reflects the fact that Denmark has restrictive gun laws, but also the country does not have a gun lobby like the US's National Rifle Association. Furthermore, over the past five years the number of licenses issued has dropped by a fifth, despite the absence of a corresponding increase in crime and violence." (p37-38)

Fallesen, Leif Beck. "Capitals: Copenhagen: Guns Not Part of Culture." Europe n335, Apr 1994. p37-38. (ISSN0191-4545).

FIREARMS--EUROPE--JAPAN--U.S.

"The romantic...love affair with the gun is something Americans should try to dump....It is a deadly addiction. When you compare what guns are doing in our society to what the absence of guns in other industrialized societies means, then you can see. Less than 100 people in Great Britain 2 years ago died from gunshot wounds or were killed with guns. Less than 50 people in Japan. Shockingly small numbers in Italy and Germany. While we had numbers like 14,000 people killed with guns, there were less than 100 killed in Great Britain. When you look at the two societies, you have to say something about the civilization factor. We may be civilized in many many ways, but when it comes to guns, we are an uncivilized nation. We are a savage nation. And we have to come to grips with that, because that is destroying our children." (pH69)

Owens, Major R. (Rep.-N.Y.). "Comments on the State of the Union Address," Congressional Record (26 Jan 1994). Daily ed. pH67-73. (ISSN0363-7239).

"According to the latest US statistics, every year 8.7 people are murdered per 100,000 of the American population. In the UK, where gun control is thought to be much stricter, the figure is 9.1 murders. Compare this with 1.1 murders in Japan, 4 in Germany and 5 in France. The area that does appear to correlate well with a widespread availability of guns is robbery. The US reports a robbery rate of 233, which is much higher than the 94.6 reported for Germany. None of these figures compares at all with Japan's mere 1.3 (Keizai Koho Center, Japan 1993: An International Comparison)." (p3)

Sato, Kinko. "Japanese Perspective: Gun Control: Where the Peace Religion Fails." Look Japan v39 n452, Nov 1993. p3. (ISSN0456-5339).

FIREARMS--FRANCE

"With an arsenal of approximately 40 million privately owned firearms for a population of 57 million, it is easy to get the impression that the French are all armed to the teeth and in need of tight controls. But gun ownership is concentrated among hunters, marksmen, and collectors, who usually own several weapons each and do not make a habit of using them for self-defense. There is remarkably little gun violence: in 1989, for example, only 56 deaths were attributed to firearms, and the numbers are holding fairly constant. Hunters are the most visible group of gun owners. With 1.65 million of them holding a valid hunting permit, France has more people chasing fur and feathers than any other country in Europe. Deaths from hunting accidents number around 20 a year and are dropping all the time, but then so is the number of new hunters, by about 4,000 a year." (p42)

Laushway, Ester. "Capitals: Paris: Guns Part of Liberty and History." Europe n335, Apr 1994. p42. (ISSN0191-4545).

FIREARMS--GERMANY--CRIME

"In Germany, there is a national registration and licensing system for handgun owners, but few criminals get their guns from ordinary shops. In 1992 the gun law was violated in more than 19,000 cases. The statistical data for 1993 has not yet been completed, but experts speak of a dramatic increase in the illegal arms trade in handguns and assault weapons....Homicide rates also rose considerably. In 1991 there were 962 murders; in 1992 they increased by 16.7 percent to 1,123. From January 1993 to September 1993 the homicide rates rose by 19 percent." (p39-40)

Gluckert, Wanda Menke. "Capitals: Berlin: Gun Violence Rises." Europe n335, Apr 1994. p39-40. (ISSN0191-4545).

FIREARMS--GREAT BRITAIN---CRIME

"Offenses involving firearms in the UK increased by 50 percent between 1988 and 1991, to more than 5,000 a year. Police believe the use of weapons, especially by drug dealers, is growing at an unprecedented rate. However, it is essential to place this in context. In the US, 16,000 people died from gunshot wounds in 1990, the vast majority in robberies; in the same year only 55 people died in armed robberies in the UK." (p38)

Lennon, David. "Capitals: London: No Right to Bear Arms." Europe n335, Apr 1994. p38. (ISSN0191-4545).

FIREARMS--GREAT BRITAIN--U.S.

"By British standards, criminals are on a shooting spree. The number of armed robberies went up 127% between 1982 and 1992....Around 4% of violent crimes in Britain involve guns, compared with around 15% in America. An American is still roughly 70 times more likely to be killed with a gun than a Briton." The firearm regulations in Great Britain "are among the strictest in Western Europe. Anyone who wants to own a gun legally needs the permission of a chief constable. Self-defence is not considered a good reason for applying. Only vermin controllers, gun-sport addicts and gun collectors are likely to be awarded a certificate. The police vet applicants and often insist that they buy a secure gun cabinet, or even a burglar alarm. The bother of renewing certificates appears to have deterred many. Since 1988 the number of certificates has fallen by 20%....Few licensed guns end up in the hands of violent criminals. Many of the 700 or so guns stolen each year are collectors', rather than murderers', items. Senior police officers estimate that only 5% of the firearms used in crimes were originally licensed." (p69)

"Britain: Guns: Firing Up." Economist v330 n7856, 26 Mar 1994. p69. (ISSN0013-0613).

FIREARMS--GREECE--CRIME

"Gun violence has become a problem in Greece over the past 10 years, with the growth of armed crime in cities often directed against banks. The number of armed robberies rose from 1,519 in 1982 to 50,626 in 1992. However, deaths from shootings remain low, at just under 200 in 1992--the latest year for which figures are available." (p41)

Hope, Kerin. "Capitals: Athens: Few Gun Homicides." Europe n335, Apr 1994. p41. (ISSN0191-4545).

FIREARMS--ITALY

"Authorities don't release the official numbers for security reasons, but unofficial estimates peg the figure at 120,000 privately owned guns in Italy. The largest category, ironically, is doctors, who own 30 percent of the guns, followed by lawyers (25 percent), goldsmiths and jewelers (20 percent), bank couriers (10 percent), and journalists (5 percent)." (p40)

d'Aquino, Niccolo. "Capitals: Rome: Guns Becoming Status Symbols." Europe n335, Apr 1994. p40-41. (ISSN0191-4545).

FIREARMS--LAW AND LEGISLATION--CALIFORNIA (v19)

FIREARMS--LAW AND LEGISLATION--DELAWARE (v19)

FIREARMS--LAW AND LEGISLATION--MARYLAND (v19)

FIREARMS--LAW AND LEGISLATION--U.S. (v19)

"Every ten seconds a gun is made in America; every nine seconds one is imported, adding over 6m guns annually to the estimated 212m already in private circulation, nearly one per citizen. The country's 1,200 gun makers, most of them tiny firms, pay $150 for their three-yearly federal permits and are subject to a single initial inspection by the Bureau of Alcohol, Tobacco and Firearms (ATF). Unless the guns they make are fully automatic (in other words, machine-guns), they are subject to virtually no federal restrictions. Manufacturers of ammunition, even of hollow-point rounds, banned under the Geneva Convention for use in warfare, are also virtually unregulated: they pay $10 a year for a manufacturing licence plus 10% federal excise tax." (p23)

"Guns in America: Home on the Range." Economist v330 n7856, 26 Mar 1994. p23-24,28. (ISSN0013-0613).

"Having bought their guns, Americans cannot use them with entire freedom. They may generally display them, and pull the trigger, only in their home or place of business. To be caught in possession of a gun somewhere else is an offence, but not a serious one; arrest usually leads to probation. Thirty-five states have concealed-weapons laws, whereby for around $200 a gun owner can get a permit to carry his weapon under a coat or in the glove-compartment of his car. In Oregon, for example, 80,000 people have such permits. This number, which may seem large, represents a fraction of the state's gun-owning population." (p24)

"Guns in America: Home on the Range." Economist v330 n7856, 26 Mar 1994. p23-24,28. (ISSN0013-0613).

FIREARMS--LAW AND LEGISLATION--U.S.--PUBLIC OPINION (v19)

"Clinton now believes that gun control is a political winner, and recent polls seem to support him. An April 1993 Harris poll showed 89 percent of Americans supporting passage of the Brady Bill 'to require a waiting period for the purchase of handguns so that the authorities can check who is buying a handgun.' Harris found 82 percent of Americans supporting a proposal that all handguns be registered by the federal government....Asked a stand-alone question on guns, the public has always overwhelmingly supported gun control. The hitch is that people who 'support gun control' in polls seldom vote on the issue; gun owners often do. In October 1988...Gallup released a poll showing 91 percent...supported a federal waiting period for gun purchases....Frank Luntz, pollster for the Perot and Giuliani campaigns, showed that 88 percent...believe a citizen has the right to own a gun, 78 percent oppose a gun ban, and 83 percent believe citizens have a right to self-defense. More importantly, asked whether new gun control measures or 'stricter penalties for criminals and reduced parole' would best fight crime, 75 percent of Americans favor tougher sentences and only 20 percent favor more gun control. Forty-six percent of Americans believe the Brady Bill will 'not reduce gun-related crimes significantly,' against only 33 percent who believe it will." (p78)

Norquist, Grover G. "Politics: Democrats Misfire on Guns." American Spectator v72 n2, Feb 1994. p78-80. (ISSN0148-8414).

"Fully 80% of Americans (including about 60% of the 3.3m members of the NRA [National Rifle Association]) now favour some sort of restrictions on guns; fewer than 30% support a ban. Most Americans want controls, but most also doubt that controls will reduce crime overall. The connection between guns and crime rates is still considered controversial. The present wave of gun proliferation started with the arrival of crack cocaine in the 1980s. But though the number of violent crimes involving guns rose by 55% between 1987 and 1992, such incidents still account for less than 15% of all violent crime." (p24,28)

"Guns in America: Home on the Range." Economist v330 n7856, 26 Mar 1994. p23-24,28. (ISSN0013-0613).

FIREARMS--LOS ANGELES (CALIF) (v19)

FIREARMS--LOS ANGELES (CALIF)--MORTALITY (v19)

FIREARMS--MORTALITY (v19)

FIREARMS--NEW YORK (NY)

"Last year, the New York City Housing Authority Police Department listed 1063 firearms seized and over 1,500 reports of gunfire in public housing facilities. The housing authority also reported 135 gun-related deaths." (pE690)

Durbin, Richard J. (Rep.-Ill.). "Gun-Free Public Housing Zones Act of 1994," Congressional Record (18 Apr 1994). Daily ed. pE690-691. (ISSN0363-7239).

FIREARMS--NEW YORK (NY)--YOUTH

"According to THE NEW YORK TIMES, arrests on gun charges of children ages 7 to 15 in New York City increased 75% between 1987 and 1990." (p94-95)

U.S. Senate. Committee on the Judiciary. "Children and Gun Violence." Hearing, 9 Jun 1993. Washington, D.C.: GPO, 1994. (ISBN0160439280). (Y4.J89/2:S.hrg.103-393).

FIREARMS--SPAIN

"Of the almost 3 million rifles, shotguns, and pistols registered in Spain, some 2.8 million belong to hunters, with the next highest number in the hands of target shooters, followed by private security staff, collectors, and finally private citizens who need the guns for personal protection." (p39)

Jones, Benjamin. "Capitals: Madrid: Second Look at Gun Laws." Europe n335, Apr 1994. p39. (ISSN0191-4545).

FIREARMS--U.S. (v19)

"The U.S. gun business is an industry in structural decline. Pummeled by a combination of outdated technology and foreign competition, the industry has slashed production of pistols, rifles, revolvers, and shotguns in the U.S. by nearly a third since 1989, to a little more than 3 million units in 1992....The violent-crime rate fell by 3% in the first half of this year and rose only 1% in 1992--the slowest rate of increase in five years, according to the Federal Bureau of Investigation. That statistic may do as much as anything to drive whatever growth is left out of the nation's gun industry." (p34-35)

Smart, Tim/others. "Top of the News: Public Policy: Ready, Aim...." Business Week n3352, 27 Dec 1993. p34-35. (ISSN0007-7135).

"Urban Americans endure a level of daily violence practically unknown outside of actual war. Consider: There are more than 67 million handguns and 200 million guns overall in circulation in the U.S. Each year, handguns kill 23,000 people--64 a day. Each day, criminals wielding guns rape 33 women, rob 575 people, and assault 1,100 more. All this puts the U.S. homicide rate at 21.9 per 100,000 people per year. By contrast, the rate in Canada is just 2.9 and in Japan, 0.5." (p16)

Magnusson, Paul. "Books: Cry, the Trigger-Happy Country." Business Week n3362, 14 Mar 1994. p16-17. (ISSN0007-7135).

"In 1986, of the guns traced to crimes [in the U.S.], 5.5 percent were assault guns. In 1989, that number nearly doubled--of the guns traced to crimes, 10.5 percent were assault guns. In 1993, although assault weapons were only one-half percent of all privately owned American guns, they accounted for 9.7 percent of guns traced to crimes." (pH2256)

Cardin, Benjamin L. (Rep.-Md.). "Support Urged for Legislation to Ban Semiautomatic Assault Weapons," Congressional Record (14 Apr 1994). Daily ed. pH2256. (ISSN0363-7239).

"Of the 212m firearms in circulation [in the U.S.], about 67m are handguns. Three-quarters of the handguns produced in America are now semi-automatic pistols (that is, pistols carrying up to 12 rounds, where a bullet is expelled with each squeeze of the trigger), which until the 1980s were used mainly by soldiers. Handguns now figure in about 60% of firearms homicides. By contrast, semi-automatic rifles account for a mere 1% of homicides; there are around 3m in circulation. Opponents of semi-automatic rifles, which are widely used in hunting, say they can easily be converted for fully automatic fire, so that one squeeze of the trigger produces a stream of bullets. This makes them into machine-guns, banned by federal law. Their defenders say that conversion is difficult, needing a machine-tool shop and a supply of scarce or restricted parts." (p24)

"Guns in America: Home on the Range." Economist v330 n7856, 26 Mar 1994. p23-24,28. (ISSN0013-0613).

"Prohibition of gun ownership [doesn't] work. In 1977 the District of Columbia stopped issuing permits for handgun purchases; in the 16 years since, the homicide rate has tripled, to 75.2 for each 100,000 residents. The U.S. average is 9.3. Waiting periods such as those in the Brady bill are ineffective as well. The 1992 FBI Uniform Crime Reports show that states and cities with waiting periods and other firearm purchase restrictions have higher overall rates of violent crime than those that do not....California has had a waiting period requirement since 1923 and has regularly increased its length--from one day to three in 1955, to five days in 1965 and to 15 days in 1975. But as a study has revealed, while waiting periods were increasing so were murder rates, from two per 100,000 in 1952 to 10 by 1975." (p30)

du Pont, Pete. "Fair Comment: Gun Control Is a Substitute for Solutions." Insight v9 n52, 27 Dec 1993. p29-30. (ISSN1051-4880).

"It's the [U.S.] gun industry's biggest boom these days: firearms from the ex-communist bloc and China, sold cheaply. Imports from Russia have just started to pick up in the last six months, but they're moving fast; Chinese firearms have already flooded the American market. In 1992 the United States imported 97,000 Chinese firearms (mostly copies of Soviet models); in 1993 it imported about 900,000, nearly a tenfold increase. Prices for an SKS rifle have gone as low as $70; a comparable American rifle would cost at least $600. But lately demand has risen so fast that prices for old commie firearms have doubled or even tripled. Suppliers can't keep up....The Chinese sold 55 million rounds of ammo in the United States in 1992, at a retail cost of about 10 cents a round, less than a third of its American equivalents....According to the ATF [the Bureau of Alcohol, Tobacco and Firearms], in 1991 the United States made more than three times as many rifles as it imported; in 1992 it made about half as many rifles as it imported." (p31)

Bogert, Caroll. "Comrades Do a Booming Business." Newsweek v123 n4, 24 Jan 1994. p31. (ISSN0028-9604).

"From 1989 to 1992, the number of handguns in the US increased by 5 million. The ATF [Bureau of Alcohol, Tobacco, and Firearms] now estimates there are 212 million guns in the US, a third of them handguns. And while the gun population continues to grow, another 7.5 million guns change hands every year." (p3)

Bryce, Robert. "National: Seems a Lot of People Got Guns for Christmas." The Christian Science Monitor v86 n31, 7 Jan 1994. p3. (ISSN0882-7729).

"The rising wave of violence worldwide involving individuals and groups who use firearms once again turns the public attention to the question of indiscriminate killing, free access to guns, and the growing tendency to use them....The statistics of gunshot deaths and damage are staggering: Over the past two years, firearms have killed 60,000 Americans, more than the number of American soldiers killed in Vietnam. US Department of Justice statistics show that, every 24 hours, handgun-wielding assailants rape 33 women, rob 575 people, and assault another 1,116." (p18)

Oren, Itzhak. "Opinion/Essays: Weapons Need Not Kill to Enforce the Law." The Christian Science Monitor v86 n59, 17 Feb 1994. p18. (ISSN0882-7729).

FIREARMS--U.S.--ACCIDENTS (v19)

"Currently in the United States, about 1,400 to 1,500 people are killed each year from accidental firearms shootings, and thousands more are injured. In 1988 alone, 277 children under age 15 were...[killed] by accidental shootings....Although there is no information on the actual number of nonfatal injuries from firearm accidents nationwide, it is reasonable to infer that the number of accidental injuries is substantial and far exceeds the number of fatalities. GAO [General Accounting Office] examined data on accidental shootings in 10 cities and found that in 1988 and 1989, these areas had a ratio of more than 100 injuries for each death. That means if 1,400 people are killed each year from accidental shootings, about 140,000 people are injured from accidental shootings." (pS1473)

Metzenbaum, Howard M. (Sen.-Ohio). "Statements on Introduced Bills and Joint Resolutions," Congressional Record (10 Feb 1994). Daily ed. pS1457-1487. (ISSN0363-7239).

FIREARMS--U.S.--ACCIDENTS--COSTS

"The high rate of gun-related violence is wreaking havoc with our health care system. Every 14 minutes someone in the United States dies from a gunshot. The total lifetime costs associated with firearm deaths and injuries were over $20 billion in 1990. We spend an estimated $3 billion a year treating firearm injuries, and 80 percent of the cost of hospitalization for these injuries is paid by public funds. Although handguns and assault weapons cost the Government millions of dollars in health care each year, the dealers and consumers of these firearms do not pay their fair share. Instead, the American public must foot the bill." (pS59)

Bradley, Bill (Sen.-N.J.). "Statements on Introduced Bills and Joint Resolutions," Congressional Record (25 Jan 1994). Daily ed. pS55-61. (ISSN0363-7239).

FIREARMS--U.S.--ACCIDENTS--PREVENTION

The General Accounting Office "estimated that 31 percent of accidental deaths caused by firearms might be prevented by the addition of two simple devices: a child-proof safety device that prevents the trigger from accidentally being engaged by young children and a device that indicates whether a gun is loaded. So about 1 out of every 3 deaths from accidental shootings could be prevented by these safety features. A device that prevents a gun from firing when the magazine has been removed would further reduce accidental shootings that result when children or others do not realize that a bullet may be in the chamber after the magazine has been removed." (pS1473)

Metzenbaum, Howard M. (Sen.-Ohio). "Statements on Introduced Bills and Joint Resolutions," Congressional Record (10 Feb 1994). Daily ed. pS1457-1487. (ISSN0363-7239).

FIREARMS--U.S.--CHILDREN--MORTALITY

"Gun violence takes the life of a child every 2 hours--that is a classroom-full every 2 days. Murder is now the third leading cause of death [in the U.S.] for elementary and middle school children--ages 5 to 14. Between 1979 and 1991, nearly 50,000 children were killed by guns--that is the same number of American battle casualties in the Vietnam war. The number of 10- to 17-year-olds who used guns to commit murder skyrocketed 79 percent during the 1980's. Given current trends, more than half the persons arrested for homicide will soon be under the age of 21." (pS2024)

Metzenbaum, Howard M. (Sen.-Ohio). "Statements on Introduced Bills and Joint Resolutions," Congressional Record (28 Feb 1994). Daily ed. pS2023-2035. (ISSN0363-7239).

"A 'classroomful' of children die in gun-related incidents every two days [in the U.S.], according to a Children's Defense Fund report." Homicide is the third-leading cause of death for elementary and middle school children. "Between 1979 and 1991, nearly 50,000 children under age 19 were killed by guns....The number of juveniles arrested for murder and manslaughter climbed 93 percent from 1982 to 1991, while the number of adults arrested for the same crimes rose only 11 percent." (p7)

Portner, Jessica. "Homicide Is Now Third-Leading Cause of Death for Youngsters, C.D.F. Says." Education Week v13 n19, 2 Feb 1994. p7. (ISSN0277-4232).

FIREARMS--U.S.--COSTS (v19)

FIREARMS--U.S.--CRIME (v19)

"According to a Justice Department survey, about 27% of felons buy their guns over the counter like anyone else; 31% get them from family and friends, most of whom will also have bought them routinely in a store; and 42% obtain them 'by other means'--predominantly theft--from legal dealers or private owners. Almost every gun that ends up in the illegal street network starts its active life in the hands of a licensed dealer. He may be careful; but the system will fail him. These days dealers are busier than ever. Sales rose by an estimated 10-20% in 1993, as people rushed to buy in advance of more federal regulations." (p24)

"Guns in America: Home on the Range." Economist v330 n7856, 26 Mar 1994. p23-24,28. (ISSN0013-0613).

"While the statistics leave no doubt that America is a far more violent place than Europe, Japan or Australia, (the FBI reports 13,220 handgun murders in 1992) the debate about why this is so and what to do about it is intense....Whatever its causes and notwithstanding the fact that the FBI recently reported that overall US violent crime actually declined in the last decade, American violence and particularly handgun violence is, at least for the moment, seen as the major problem confronting the nation. Whether the five day waiting period required by the Brady Law which went into effect February 28, will have any impact in the continuing increase in handguns' share of crime, which rose from 9.2 percent of all violent crimes in 1979 to 12.7 in 1992, what is sure is that the debate in the US will continue." (p36-37)

Bassman, Robert. "Capitals: Letter from America." Europe n335, Apr 1994. p36-37. (ISSN0191-4545).

FIREARMS--U.S.--CRIMINALS (v19)

FIREARMS--U.S.--MINORITIES (v19)

FIREARMS--U.S.--MORTALITY (v19)

"Every year, more than 24,000 Americans, 65 a day, are killed with handguns, in homicides, by committing suicide, and by unintentional injuries. Handguns account for only one-third of all firearms, but are responsible for two-thirds of all firearm-related deaths. Handguns are used in about 80 percent of all firearm murders. Ninety-five percent of the people injured by a handgun each year require emergency care or hospitalization. Of these, 68 percent require overnight care and 32 percent require a hospital stay of 8 days or more. In 1991, the United States led the developed world with 14,373 gun murders, as compared to 186 gun murders in Canada, 76 in Australia, 60 in England, and 74 in Japan. One difference between the United States and the other countries cited is that the other countries all have much stricter gun control laws." (pS2033)

Bradley, Bill (Sen.-N.J.). "Statements on Introduced Bills and Joint Resolutions," Congressional Record (28 Feb 1994). Daily ed. pS2023-2035. (ISSN0363-7239).

"Since 1968, more than 300,000 Americans have been murdered by guns. In 1992, more than 35,000 people were killed by gunfire. Today, only cars cause more fatal injuries than guns, and guns are expected to take the lead very soon. And we cannot even begin to count the number of nonfatal injuries from guns. From 1987 to 1992, the rate of murders committed with handguns increased 52 percent, while the murder rate committed with all weapons other than handguns has actually declined. In 1990, 10 people were killed in Australia by handguns, 22 in Great Britain, and 68 in Canada. In the United States, that figure was 10,567. Handgun homicides have now reached 13,000 a year." (pS2024)

Metzenbaum, Howard M. (Sen.-Ohio). "Statements on Introduced Bills and Joint Resolutions," Congressional Record (28 Feb 1994). Daily ed. pS2023-2035. (ISSN0363-7239).

"For historical and political reasons, firearms are explicitly excluded from the Consumer Product Safety Act. Firearms injuries are therefore not tallied officially. At a rough estimate, about 38,000 Americans die each year of gunshot wounds, almost as many as are killed on the roads. Fewer than half of these deaths are homicides. Together, accidents and suicides account for 54% of firearms deaths. Among 15-24-year-olds, deaths by gunshot went up by 40% between 1985 and 1991." (p24)

"Guns in America: Home on the Range." Economist v330 n7856, 26 Mar 1994. p23-24,28. (ISSN0013-0613).

FIREARMS--U.S.--YOUTH (v19)

"Last year, roughly 15,000 Americans, including 3,000 juveniles, were murdered by firearms....According to a Harris poll...one in five Americans know a child shot by another child, and 77 percent of the respondents feel that young people's safety is endangered by so many guns. Additional States tell an even more alarming story about how gun-related violence envelopes our young people. The National School Safety Center estimates that more than...100,000 students carry a gun to school every day. The leading cause of death for both black and white teenage boys in America is gunshot wounds." (p1-2)

Kohl, Herbert (Sen.-Wis.). U.S. Senate. Committee on the Judiciary. "Children and Gun Violence." Hearing, 9 Jun 1993. Washington, D.C.: GPO, 1994. (ISBN0160439280). (Y4.J89/2:S.hrg.103-393).

A U.S. "survey found that 59 percent of the students surveyed nationwide said guns were easily obtainable, while 35 percent said it would take them less than 60 minutes to get one. The survey also found that more than one in five (22 percent) students claimed they carried a weapon to school during the last school year (survey conducted by the Louis Harris Corporation, prepared for the Harvard School of Public Health, July 1993). These findings are consistent with the findings of the Centers for Disease Control and Prevention (CDC) which reported that nearly 20 percent of all students in grades 9-12 said they had carried a weapon at least once during the 30 days preceding the survey. Male students (31.5 percent) were much more likely than female students (8.1 percent) to report having carried a weapon (CDC's 1990-1991 youth risk behavior surveillance system)." (p14)

Kunin, Madeleine M. (Deputy Secretary, U.S. Dept. of Education). U.S. Senate. Committee on Labor and Human Resources. "Recess from Violence: Making Our Schools Safe." Hearing, 23 Sep 1993. Washington, D.C.: GPO, 1993. (ISBN0160433096). (Y4.L11/4:S.hrg.103-313).

"Between 1987 and 1991, juvenile arrests for murder rose more than 85 percent. In 1992, 3,355 youths under the age of 18 were arrested for murder, including 55 13-year-olds, 166 14-year-olds and 393 15-year-olds. The 1980s witnessed a 79 percent increase in the number of juveniles who commit murders with guns. And most frightening, it is estimated that 135,000 students now carry guns to school every day." (p46)

Moseley-Braun, Carol. "At Issue: Juvenile Justice: Yes: Send a Message to Young Criminals." ABA Journal v80, Mar 1994. p46. (ISSN0747-0088).

"The U.S. Department of Justice reports that, between 1987 and 1991, juvenile arrests for weapons violations rose by 62 percent. Black youths under the age of eighteen are the group most frequently involved in violence. In 1991 they were arrested for weapons-law violations at a rate triple that for white youths, and they were murdered at a rate six times that for whites." (p2) "Roughly one in ten teenagers between the ages of ten and nineteen has fired a gun at someone or been shot at, and about two in five say they know someone who has been killed or wounded by gunfire. This is the finding of a 1993 survey of a representative sample of 2,508 students at ninety-six public and private elementary, middle, and senior high schools, conducted by Louis Harris for Harvard University's School of Public Health. Harris reports that 60 percent of the youths said they could get a handgun; one-fifth claimed they could do so within an hour, and more than a third said they could do so within a day." (p3)

"Saving Youth from Violence." Carnegie Quarterly v39 n1, Win 1994. p1-5.

"The Centers for Disease Control has estimated that nearly 1 in 5 [U.S.] students carries a weapon--a knife, a firearm, or a club--to school. Roughly 130,000 students, it is estimated, bring a gun to school every day; the overwhelming majority not to inflict violence on one of their classmates but to protect themselves from the violence they anticipate from some of the students or someone outside of the school. The National Crime Survey has estimated that nearly 3 million crimes occur on or near school campuses each year. A recent national survey in USA WEEKEND found that 37 percent of students said they do not feel safe at school any longer, and 63 percent said they would learn more if they felt safer." (pS716)

Dodd, Christopher J. (Sen.-Conn.). "Goals 2000: Educate America Act," Congressional Record (3 Feb 1994). Daily ed. pS699-720. (ISSN0363-7239).

"A series of studies done in 1992 by the American Medical Association disclosed that 6 percent of high school students own handguns, and one-third of those have fired the gun at someone. In New York City, between 1987 and 1990, arrests on gun charges for children between the ages of 7 and 15 increased by 75 percent." (p4)

Holmstrom, David. "From the States: Violent Crime Is Down--But Not in Public Schools." The Christian Science Monitor v86 n35, 13 Jan 1994. p4. (ISSN0882-7729).

FIREARMS--U.S.--YOUTH--MORTALITY (v19)

"Beyond the fact that violent crime is being committed more and more by kids is the reality that their victims are also increasingly younger as well. Furthermore, the witnesses to these crimes of violence are disproportionately young themselves. The cumulative impact that this circle of terror has on our youth is still unknown, but certainly no one can doubt that it is and will be pervasive for some time to come.

The anecdotal evidence from our officers appears to be substantiated by a recent (1991) U.S. Department of Justice study on crime in America. In that study, it was found that of all individuals arrested for murder nationwide, slightly over 30 percent were under the age of 21. Of that 30 percent grouping, at least half were under the age of 18. What police on the streets are seeing is nothing short of a national epidemic of violence involving firearms perpetrated by kids, against kids, and in front of kids. What is especially tragic is that this collection of perpetrators, victims, and witnesses are all increasingly younger in age--no longer are we talking strictly about the 16 to 21 year old age bracket. Our officers report that they are dealing with children in middle schools or just barely into high school." (p23)

Stokes, Dewey R. (National President, Fraternal Order of Police). U.S. Senate. Committee on the Judiciary. "Children and Gun Violence." Hearing, 9 Jun 1993. Washington, D.C.: GPO, 1994. (ISBN0160439280). (Y4.J89/2:S.hrg.103-393).

"Gun violence takes the life of a child every 2 hours--that's a classroom-full every 2 days. Murder is now the 3rd leading cause of death for elementary and middle school children--ages 5 to 14. Between 1979 and 1991, nearly 50,000 children were killed by guns--that's the same number of American battle casualties in the Vietnam war. The number of 10- to 17-year-olds who used guns to commit murder skyrocketed 79 percent during the 1980's. Given current trends, more than half the persons arrested for homicide will soon be under the age of 21." (pS2173)

Metzenbaum, Howard M. (Sen.-Ohio). "Statements on Introduced Bills and Joint Resolutions," Congressional Record (1 Mar 1994). Daily ed. pS2169-2183. (ISSN0363-7239).

"Perhaps the most horrifying aspect of gun-related violence is its impact on children. Firearms are the second leading cause of death for the young, second only to automobile crashes. Every day in America, 12 children are killed with guns. In 1988, for the first time, the firearm death rate for teenagers exceeded the death rate from natural causes. And this trend has continued. In 1990, there were nearly 40 percent more deaths by firearms among 15- to 19-year-olds than from natural causes. Firearms kill more teenagers than cancer, heart disease, and all other natural causes combined. Among young people 15 to 24 years old, one in four deaths are by firearms. The statistics among black teenage males are even more shocking; 3 out of 5 deaths in this age group--60 percent--result from a firearm injury." (pS16413)

Kennedy, Edward M. (Sen.-Mass.). "Brady Handgun Violence Prevention Act," Congressional Record (19 Nov 1993). Daily ed. pS16413-16417. (ISSN0363-7239).

FIREARMS INDUSTRY AND TRADE--MICHIGAN

"There's one federally licensed gun dealer for every 631 residents in Michigan, making it the gun-buying capital of the nation's largest states. With 14,724 dealers for 9.3 million people--that's 158 dealers per 100,000 residents--it's much easier to find a gun dealer than a toy store in the state. According to 1987 U.S. Census Bureau data, there are 347 hobby, toy and game stores in Michigan. Rural states such as Montana and North Dakota have higher concentrations of gun dealers, according to the Bureau of Alcohol, Tobacco and Firearms (ATF), the branch of the U.S. Treasury department that issues federal firearms licenses. But among states with more than 3 million residents, Michigan is tops in the ratio of gun dealers to residents, ATF records show." (p1 secA) "All other large states have fewer gun dealers than Michigan. New Jersey, which ranks ninth in population just behind Michigan, has the lowest percentage of dealers in the nation, with 22 dealers per 100,000 residents. The state has rough gun laws. Nationwide, there are 284,000 licensed dealers, or 114 per 100,000 residents, according to the ATF." (p10 secA)

Magner, Michael/Stewart, Will. "Sellers of Guns Flourish." Ann Arbor News 23 Jan 1994. p1,10 secA.

FIREARMS INDUSTRY AND TRADE--U.S. (v19)

"Of the 284,000 gun dealers, about 20,000 have proper stores; just over half of these are pawnbrokers. The rest sell guns out of car boots, over the kitchen table, or at gun shows and flea markets. They do not buy solely from manufacturers. Until January this year, federal law-enforcement agencies also sold off their surplus weapons--some 60,000 handguns and rifles, including the quasi-military 9mm automatic pistols so popular with young bloods....In 1993, the ATF [Bureau of Alcohol, Tobacco and Firearms] visited 400 dealers. Only 26% had storefronts; more than half maintained no stock of firearms; 34% were found in violation of firearms regulations. About 12% surrendered their licences during the inspection. Some of these dealers had had their licences withheld by their states; but under present law the ATF cannot use this as a reason to withhold a federal licence." (p23)

"Guns in America: Home on the Range." Economist v330 n7856, 26 Mar 1994. p23-24,28. (ISSN0013-0613).

FIREARMS INDUSTRY AND TRADE--WEST VIRGINIA (v19)

FIRES

see also FOREST FIRES

FIRES--CALIFORNIA

"Southern California...has evolved with fire as an integral landscape component. Couple this fact with a history of fire suppression and the blazes that raged through the southland the last week of October come as no surprise. The fires, 25 in all, burned over 173,000 acres in six counties, fueled by hot, dry Santa Ana winds. Roughly 24,000 acres were coastal sage scrub and mixed sage scrub/grassland. The remaining acreage was chaparral and houses. Over 300 endangered California gnatcatchers representing 6% of the total population are thought to have perished in the fires, along with 800 coastal cactus wrens (17% of the nation's population)." (p5)

Beneville, Craig. "Fire in Southern California's Endangered Ecosystems." Earth First! v14 n2, 21 Dec 1993. p5,9.

FIRES--U.S. (v19)

"For years the [Consumer Product Safety] Commission has been working to address the tremendous losses associated with electrical fires [in the U.S.] involving consumer products in residences. In 1990, there were an estimated 150,000 residential structural electrical fires resulting in 770 deaths and 6400 injuries. Property damage related to electrical fires is at least [$]500 million annually. Projects focusing on fires with electrical heating equipment and electrical appliances have resulted in upgraded safety standards that are expected to make significant progress in reducing injuries and deaths. However, nearly 30% of the electrical fire problem in residences relates to the electrical distribution system (i.e., the installed wiring, receptacles, light fixtures, electrical cords, circuit breakers, fuses, switches, etc.). In 1990, 42,000 electrical distribution system fires accounted for 1,370 injuries, 410 deaths, and $568 million in property losses. Past Commission studies show that fires occur at the highest rates among dwellings over 40 years old, and that inadequate electrical systems and consumer actions to modify or accommodate those systems were involved in over 2/3 of the fires studied." (p815)

Dawson, Carol G. (Commissioner, U.S. Consumer Product Safety Commission). U.S. House. Committee on Appropriations. "Depts. of Veterans Affairs and Housing and Urban Development...Approp. for 1994 (Part 4)." Hearing, Washington, D.C.: GPO, 1993. (ISBN016040911X). (Y4.Ap6/1:V64/4/994/pt.4).

FIRES--U.S.--MORTALITY

"Cigarette-related fires [in the U.S.] are the leading cause of fire deaths....in 1990 alone, there were 44,000 cigarette-related fires that resulted in 1,200 deaths and 3,360 injuries....These fires take a considerable toll on society. A recent study concluded that the direct cost of cigarette-ignited fire deaths, injuries, and property damage was $4 billion a year." (pH651)

Moakley, John Joseph (Rep.-Mass.). "Fire Safe Cigarette Act of 1994," Congressional Record (23 Feb 1994). Daily ed. pH651-652. (ISSN0363-7239).

FISH AND GAME LICENSES--FALKLAND ISLANDS (v19)

FISH AS FOOD

"Between 1950 and 1989, the global catch [of seafood] expanded from 22 million tons to 100 million tons. The per capita seafood supply increased from 9 to 19 kilograms during this period. Since 1989, the catch has actually declined slightly, totalling an estimated 97 million tons in 1992....United Nations marine biologists believe that the oceans have reached their limit and may not be able to sustain a yield of more than 100 million tons per year." (p23)

Brown, Lester R. "A Decade of Discontinuity." World Watch v6 n4, Jul-Aug 1993. p19-26. (ISSN0896-0615).

FISH AS FOOD--CONTAMINATION--DETROIT (MICH)--PUBLIC OPINION

"In the first major effort to find out what Detroit-area anglers eat and what government tells them about health risks, Clean Water Fund's Southeast Michigan coordinator, Lawton Jackson, surveyed 300 men and women along the banks of the Detroit River last summer and fall." (p1) "Of the anglers surveyed, 98% said they eat the fish or pass it along for eating by family and friends. The anglers reported that young people, children under 18, and women are heavy consumers of sportfish they catch. But 38% of the anglers said they have no concern about eating the fish, despite the advisory. And many more know little about the specific advice offered in the advisory. Over 90% of the people surveyed are African-Americans." (p3)

"Minority Anglers at Risk." Clean Water Action News v20 n1, 1993. p1,3.

FISH AS FOOD--CONTAMINATION--U.S.

"Among states where fish have been tested [for mercury contamination], Michigan, Minnesota, Wisconsin and Florida are suffering from the most serious problems. All 2,000 lakes in Minnesota's Superior National Forest are subject to official mercury advisories, and mercury concentrations in Minnesota fish are rising at a rate of 3-5% per year. Minnesota's lakes are visited by 3.5 million vacationers each year, at least one third of whom fish, catching 35 million pounds of walleye, northern pike, bass and other species. In much of the Florida Everglades, large game fish have mercury levels 50% higher than the level at which federal rules require fish to be removed from the market, and largemouth bass have been found with over four times the federal standard. Fish-eating animals in the area are already suffering the impacts: the last known female panther in the Everglades died in 1991 with high levels of mercury in her body." (p1)

"Mercury Warning: The Fish You Catch May Be Unsafe to Eat." Clean Water Action News v20 n1, 1993. p1,3.

"The Environmental Protection Agency (EPA) has consistently understated the human health risks of eating fish from U.S. inland waters, an EDF [Environmental Defense Fund] analysis shows. EDF found that EPA misled the public by releasing a national survey that selectively cited only 46 locations where fish presented a health risk, even though EPA's own database contains over 4,000 listings of state health bans and advisories from all over the country, involving millions of acres of U.S. lakes and streams. EPA's listings include 30 states and territories with warnings for PCB's, 29 for heavy metals, 26 for pesticides, and 23 for dioxin. Many listings are for long-lasting old pollutants, such as DDT (which EDF helped ban 20 years ago). Others are from newly increased sources, such as mercury, which began from industrial pollution in the 1950's but is now increasing as a result of emissions at coal-burning power plants and incinerators." (p1)

"EPA Underestimates Risks of Fish in Americans' Diet." EDF Letter v24 n2, Mar 1993. p1,3. (ISSN0163-2566).

FISH AS FOOD--U.S. (v19)

FISHERIES (v19)

"Spurred by new advances in fishing and navigational technology, expanding global markets, and a growing international appetite for seafood, the world fish catch has increased more than fourfold during the past forty years. The marine catch peaked at 86 million tons in 1989 and has declined steadily since then. The problem has reached the point at which most fish populations that occur in international waters are either 'fully exploited,' 'over exploited,' or depleted, according to the United Nations Food and Agriculture Organization (FAO)....But the race to catch fish continues. Between 1970 and 1989, the capacity of the international fishing fleet nearly doubled, from 13.5 million to 25.5 million gross tons. The number of large vessels fishing the world's oceans jumped from 585,000 to 1.2 million during the same two decades, reports the FAO." (p28-29)

Pollack, Susan. "No More Fish Stories." Amicus Journal v16 n1, Spr 1994. p28-31. (ISSN0276-7201).

"As fishing techniques have become ever more efficient, the catch of unwanted fish has increased dramatically. Billions of pounds of this 'by-catch' are tossed dead and dying back into the sea each year because the fish are too big, too small, not the target species, or because it is illegal to keep them....The U.N. Food and Agriculture Organization estimates that by-catch accounts for 20 percent of the world's total annual catch. In the Gulf of Mexico alone, shrimpers annually kill 20 million juvenile red snappers, about 80 percent of the new generation. For every pound of shrimp taken from the Gulf and the Atlantic Ocean, an average of 10 pounds of fish are tossed overboard." (p2)

England, Marilyn. "Teaching TEDs to Release Fish." Audubon Activist Jan-Feb 1994. p2. (ISSN0898-915X).

"After growing ever since records began, the world's marine fish catch peaked in 1989 at 86m tonnes. Since then it has declined. Without firm action, it will fall further; and the more fishermen try to catch, the faster it will fall....Since 1950 the world's fish catch has increased almost five-fold, mostly because fishermen have turned to new seas, many of them around poorer countries, and new species. But though the catch is larger, the fish themselves are getting smaller. In the past decade most of the rich world's fisheries have been exploited to the point of near exhaustion. As stocks are fished out, species previously ignored get caught, as do small fry of the big species: fishermen in the North Sea now bring home whiting that they would have sneered at 20 years ago, and their catches are as small as they were in the 1970s...." (p13)

"March 19th 1994: The Catch about Fish." Economist v330 n7855, 19 Mar 1994. p13-14. (ISSN0013-0613).

"The world's [fishing] fleets say they operate at a loss: $22 billion in 1989, not counting capital expenditure or profit from unreported illicit catches. Almost all the 200 fisheries monitored by the FAO [Food and Agriculture Organization] are fully exploited. One in three is depleted or heavily over-exploited, almost all in the developed countries....Although fishermen still catch relatively few of the 15,000 species of fish extant, most of the remainder are expensive to catch, unappetising, or both....The rich countries' fleets have outstripped their fishing grounds' capacities by such a long way that Iceland and the European Union could cut their fleets by 40%, Norway by two-thirds, and all three would still catch as much fish as they do today." (p21)

"Fish: The Tragedy of the Oceans." Economist v330 n7855, 19 Mar 1994. p21-22,24. (ISSN0013-0613).

"Worldwide, overfishing wastes $15 billion-30 billion a year, according to the UN's Food and Agriculture Organisation--the annual GDP [gross domestic product] of, say, Bangladesh or Belorussia. Economic waste apart, overfishing has non-economic costs. The environmental damage that it does is hidden beneath the surface, where changes in the size of fish populations can alter entire ecosystems....Do not blame fishermen for overfishing....Blame instead those who have power over the fleets, and who have taken the sea into their custody: governments. Only 10% or so of the world's catch swims in international waters. The rest is caught within 200 nautical miles of some country's shore, in water some government claims sovereignty over....Indeed, many governments are going out of their way to exacerbate the problem. Japan, Norway and the former Soviet Union, among others, have poured money into the fishing industry. The European Union increased fishing support from $80m in 1983 to $580m in 1990. A fifth of that went to build new boats or to improve old ones." (p13)

"March 19th 1994: The Catch about Fish." Economist v330 n7855, 19 Mar 1994. p13-14. (ISSN0013-0613).

"As high-tech factory boats and traditional fishers alike have extracted larger and larger proportions of the biomass from coastal waters, whole ecosystems have begun to break down. In the Shetland Islands, Arctic terns, puffins, and other nesting birds failed to breed in the mid- and late 1980s, apparently due to overfishing of the sand eel, a small shoaling fish caught for fish meal and oil. The birds normally feed young sand eels to their chicks, but the fish's population declined with the commercial catch, which peaked at 56,000 tons in 1982 and then plunged to 4,800 tons in 1988. In a similar disaster, off the coast of Peru, guano birds abandoned their young when the Peruvian anchovy fishery collapsed. In Kenya, researchers found that heavy fishing of triggerfish on coral reefs allowed the proliferation of rock-boring sea urchins, which were endangering the entire ecosystem." (p26)

Weber, Peter. "It Comes Down to the Coasts." World Watch v7 n2, Mar-Apr 1994. p20-29. (ISSN0896-0615).

FISHERIES--ALASKA (v19)

"Roughly 60 percent of the fish caught in the U.S. waters...are caught off Alaska....In terms of harvesting fisheries, the problem in Alaska is not necessarily the gear being used but the way the gear is being used. Virtually all the gear in use in the fisheries of the North Pacific could be used more cleanly. In 1993, some trawl fisheries discarded over half of the target species for economic reasons. Those fish were either too big or too small to be processed by the facilities on board. Some hook and line fisheries discarded 30 percent of the fish they caught. In 1993, fishermen off Alaska discarded 693 million pounds of groundfish, 14 million pounds of halibut, 19 million crab, and 372,000 salmon." (pS4349)

Stevens, Ted (Sen.-Alaska). "Statements on Introduced Bills and Joint Resolutions," Congressional Record (14 Apr 1994). Daily ed. pS4334-4350. (ISSN0363-7239).

FISHERIES--ENVIRONMENTAL ASPECTS

"Overfishing is not the only threat to the world's fisheries, although it is the most severe. Development and pollution are also reducing stocks. According to Paul Brouha, director of the American Fisheries Society, 11m-15m salmon once spawned in the Columbia river system. Now there are only 3m, of which 2.75m come from hatcheries. So much of the river system has been dammed that only 250,000 salmon can find their way back to old spawning grounds. According to a recent study, three-quarters of the American catch comprises species that depend upon estuaries (often as a habitat for juveniles, which can safely feed in the shallows). But estuaries are themselves vulnerable. Almost a third of the world's 5.5 billion people live within 60 kilometres of the sea, polluting inshore waters with effluent from industry and farmland." (p21)

"Fish: The Tragedy of the Oceans." Economist v330 n7855, 19 Mar 1994. p21-22,24. (ISSN0013-0613).

FISHERIES--EUROPE--U.S.

"Overfishing is waste on a grand scale. American fishery managers estimate that the United States' catch is almost half as valuable as it could be if fish stocks in federal waters were allowed to recover. The EU [European Union] said that its waters could, if properly regulated, yield a further $2.5 billion-worth of fish a year. The FAO [Food and Agriculture Organization] has estimated the annual loss worldwide at $15 billion-30 billion." (p22)

"Fish: The Tragedy of the Oceans." Economist v330 n7855, 19 Mar 1994. p21-22,24. (ISSN0013-0613).

FISHERIES--FRANCE

"Over the last 20 years, out of total fish sales [in France], the share of fish sold in shops and street markets--generally supplied by national fishermen--has tumbled from almost three-quarters to about one-half. The big supermarkets' share of sales has gone from about 13 percent to 42 percent." (p9)

LaFranchi, Howard. "Economic Reports: Angry French Fishermen Trash Supermarket Fish." The Christian Science Monitor v86 n53, 9 Feb 1994. p9. (ISSN0882-7729).

FISHERIES--NEW ENGLAND

"New England fishermen, struggling with an already depleted fish supply, have been dealt yet another blow with the issuance of stiff conservation rules. The restrictions imposed by the Commerce Department...come in the midst of a battle to restore overfished New England waters....The goal is to halve ground fishing over five to seven years. Restrictions include limits on the number of fishing days by about 10 percent each year, a moratorium on new groundfishing permits, and a 500-pound limit on haddock landings per boat trip....Federal officials and environmentalists say the restrictions are necessary. In fact, the limits may not even begin to curb the problem, says Douglas Hall, assistant commerce secretary for oceans and atmosphere. He says the haddock population is so depleted that it is now considered commercially extinct in the Gulf of Maine....Indeed, groundfish harvests have plummeted in recent years. Landings of cod, haddock, and yellowtail flounder dropped 30 percent from 1991 to 1992, and initial figures show another 28 percent to 30 percent drop from 1992 to 1993, according to the National Marine Fisheries Service." (p10)

Ross, Elizabeth. "New England: Fishermen Say New Restrictions Will Force Them to Scale Back." The Christian Science Monitor v86 n51, 7 Feb 1994. p10. (ISSN0882-7729).

FISHERIES--NORTHWEST, PACIFIC (v19)

FISHERIES--NOVA SCOTIA (v19)

FISHERIES--THAILAND

"In the Gulf of Thailand in the early 1960s...only a few hundred trawlers could be counted and the catch rate was about 300 kilograms of seafood per hour. Two decades later, the number of trawlers had increased to 10,000--and as a group they were far more efficient, too--the catch rate had declined to 50 kg/hour. Philippine fishermen have experienced a similar decline, and Daniel Pauly reports that a 'clear pattern of overcapitalization and overfishing has emerged....Effort in the fisheries sector as a whole is two to three times in excess of optimum exploitation rates.'" (p51)

Tobin, Richard J./White, Alan T. "Coastal Resources Management and Sustainable Development: A Southeast Asian Perspective." International Environmental Affairs v5 n1, Win 1993. p50-65. (ISSN1041-4665).

FISHERIES--U.S. (v19)

"As overfishing and pollution deplete natural fish populations, the aquaculture industry is booming. The annual production of 'farmed' seafood--such as catfish, salmon, trout, redfish, sturgeon, carp, oysters and crayfish--has grown over 300 percent in the U.S. since 1980. Half of the 500 million pounds of shrimp imported each year--and about 12 percent of the fish eaten by Americans today--are raised on fish farms. Aquaculture solves some environmental health problems, but can also create new ones. Since the aquatic environment can be more carefully monitored and controlled, there are fewer problems with contaminants. Pesticides in farmed catfish are generally far lower than in wild catfish, for example." (p40)

Lefferts, Lisa Y. "Too Many Risks in the Sea." E Magazine v4 n1, Feb 1993. p36-41. (ISSN1046-8021).

"American fisheries are in serious trouble. In many U.S. waters, fish populations are collapsing from overfishing. New England groundfish, for example--cod, haddock, flounder, and hake--have declined more than 50% since 1977. Many other populations, including Atlantic bluefin tuna, Gulf of Mexico king mackerel, and some Pacific salmon stocks, have suffered similar crashes. Overharvesting has cost the U.S. fishing industry about $1 billion a year and tens of thousands of jobs--14,000 in New England alone--according to the National Marine Fisheries Service and the National Coalition for Marine Conservation." (p8)

"EDF Is Advocating Reforms to Reduce Overfishing." EDF Letter v25 n1, Jan 1994. p8. (ISSN0163-2566).

"Bit by bit, the United States government is taking steps to preserve the US fishing industry. To families whose livelihoods rely directly or indirectly on harvesting the sea, the steps may appear to carry a 'burn the village to save it' logic. But without tighter restrictions on commercial and even some sport fishing, the stocks that have sustained the industry for generations may be irretrievably lost. A number of factors have contributed to declining stocks. But the single largest factor has been overfishing. The annual catch of 'groundfish,' such as cod, haddock, and flounder, has plunged from about 200,000 tons in 1980 to just under 50,000 tons in 1992. The Chinook salmon catch on the West Coast has fallen from about 3 million fish in 1986 to less than a million in 1992." (p18)

"Editorials: Difficult Chantey to Sing." The Christian Science Monitor v86 n73, 10 Mar 1994. p18. (ISSN0882-7729).

FISHES

"Ninety percent of all salt water fish, the bulk of the world catch, are taken from continental shelves, estuaries, and coastal rivers, which receive fertilizing nutrients washed from the land. But these are the very locales where burgeoning humanity has imposed negative impacts of one kind or another. Consider these few instances....Throughout the United States, millions of fish eggs, larvae, and fish are withdrawn every day in the cooling water used by power plants and killed. (Power plants annually kill one trillion fish at all life stages on the Atlantic Coast alone, according a study by the Hudson Riverkeeper Fund.) The population of adult striped bass in the San Francisco Bay-Delta ecosystem, the largest estuary on the Pacific Coast of the Americas, fell by 70 percent between 1972 and 1991, from 1.8 million to 682,000, as the result of diversion of fresh water for irrigation. The runs of adult salmon and steelhead on the Columbia River, once the greatest salmon river in the world, have declined from a historic high of 16 million fish to 1.5 million in 1992. The reason: dam after dam after dam." (p22)

Boyle, Robert H. "The Cost of Caviar." Amicus Journal v16 n1, Spr 1994. p22-28. (ISSN0276-7201).

"Fish currently are the main source of protein for many coastal regions of Asia and Africa and account for 16 percent of the animal protein consumed worldwide. Yet the world catch of seafood has continued to decline since reaching a peak of 86 million tons in 1989. Those numbers are likely to keep falling unless the nations of the world can better manage fish populations, says [Carl] Safina [director of Audubon's Living Oceans Program]. But he adds that conservationists and others have begun to awaken in recent years to the need for greater marine protection and sustainable use of the seas." (p5)

Cusick, Steve. "A Chance for the Fishes." Audubon Activist Jan-Feb 1994. p1,4-5. (ISSN0898-915X).

FISHES--SAN FRANCISCO (CALIF)

"Since 1969, winter-run chinook salmon have declined [in the San Francisco Bay Delta] from 118,000 spawning fish to 341 in 1993. Delta smelt have declined 90 percent in 10 years, and striped bass are also down 90 percent, from the 3-million-to-5-million level of the 1970s." (p12)

Wood, Daniel B. "Points of the Compass: Clock Starts Ticking on California's Water Wars." The Christian Science Monitor v86 n29, 5 Jan 1994. p12-13. (ISSN0882-7729).

FISHING--U.S.

"Fishing can be as relaxing or strenuous as one chooses, so it appeals to all ages. The share of people [in the U.S.] who fish ranges from 20 percent to 23 percent among age groups under 45. But even among those aged 65 and older, almost one in ten still fishes occasionally....It's easier to get to the animals if you live near them. One-quarter of adults living outside of metropolitan areas go fishing, compared with 14 percent of those in metropolitan areas of 1 million or more." (p36)

Crispell, Diane. "Targeting Hunters." American Demographics v16 n1, Jan 1994. p34-38,40. (ISSN0163-4089).

FLIGHT ATTENDANTS--EMPLOYMENT--U.S. (v19)

FLOOD CONTROL--MISSISSIPPI RIVER

"Floodplain management is still being conducted on a segment-by-segment, structure-by-structure basis that does not consider how flood control efforts operate in concert. On the Upper Mississippi, flood control structures may be federal, nonfederal governmental, or private. At present, 275 federal levees in the region--those built by the Corps with federal funds to federal specifications, and more than 1,000 private and nonfederal levees, most of which were either overtopped or ruptured during recent floods--straitjacket the Mississippi. Most of private and nonfederal levees are built and maintained by levee or drainage districts to widely differing specifications and regulations. Many are completely unregulated. The lack of coordination explains why, despite spending $25 billion on flood control nationally, per capita flood damage is more than twice as costly as it was before these programs were instituted." (p4)

"Mississippi River Sends a Powerful Message." Community Service Newsletter v42 n1, Jan-Feb 1994. p3-5.

FLOOD CONTROL--U.S. (v19)

FLOODS--KANSAS (v19)

FLOODS--LAS VEGAS (NEV) (v19)

FLOODS--U.S. (v19)

FLORICULTURE--COLOMBIA (v19)

FLORIDA

see AFRO-AMERICAN FARMERS--CALIFORNIA--FLORIDA; ALIENS, ILLEGAL--FLORIDA; CIGARETTE TAX--FLORIDA; COLLEGE ATHLETES--FLORIDA; COMMUNITY COLLEGE ATHLETES--FLORIDA; REFUGEES, HAITIAN--

FLORIDA; SOLAR ENERGY--FLORIDA; TOURIST TRADE--FLORIDA

FLORIDA--ECONOMIC CONDITIONS (v19)

FLORIDA--EMPLOYMENT (v19)

FLORIDA--POPULATION (v19)

FLUORESCENT LIGHTING

"Dramatic monetary and environmental savings accrue from the lower wattage and longer life span. Every 15-watt compact fluorescent saves nearly $40 in electric and lamp replacement costs when used instead of a 60-watt incandescent. Although compact fluorescents are expensive ($12 to $30 apiece), they will save enough energy to pay for themselves while returning a net savings of at least $25 per lamp. Each one will also save close to a quarter ton of coal, as much as 1,000 pounds of carbon dioxide, and significant amounts of sulphur dioxide emissions." (p2)

Elliott, Luke. "Compact Fluorescents, Lighting the Way to Savings." Kerr Center for Sustainable Agriculture Newsletter v19 n8, Nov-Dec 1993. p2-3.

FOOD

see also ANIMAL FOOD; DRIED FOOD; ELEPHANTS--FOOD; FISH AS FOOD; PESTICIDE RESIDUES IN FOOD; SCHOOL CHILDREN--FOOD

FOOD--LABELING--U.S. (v19)

FOOD--U.S. (v19)

FOOD CONSUMPTION

"With about one-quarter of the world's total population, the rich countries consume almost three-quarters of all the food produced. The average North American consumes 2888 pounds of grain yearly, mostly in the form of meats, milk, eggs, and alcoholic beverages. In the U.S., almost half of all harvested cropland is sown in feed crops and animals ultimately eat about four-fifths of the grain. The average Asian, on the other hand, eats less than 488 pounds of grain per year, mostly in original form. Still, we find 36 of the world's 40 most impoverished countries actually exporting food to the United States." (p96)

Kline, Gary. "Food as a Human Right." Journal of Third World Studies v10 n1, Spr 1993. p92-107. (ISSN8755-3449).

FOOD HABITS--U.S.

"Americans say they prefer home-cooked meals. Even if money were no object, 71 percent say they would eat most dinners at home, according to Roper. Yet 56 percent say they ate dinner at a restaurant or fast-food place sometime during the last week. And another 28 percent ate out sometime during the last month. On some occasions, dinner at a restaurant isn't a treat--it's a time-saving device. Young adults eat out more than older Americans. Only 45 percent of those aged 60 and older have eaten out during the last week, compared with 66 percent of adults under age 30. Affluent Americans are the most likely to eat out: 70 percent of adults with annual household incomes of $50,000 or more went out to dinner during the last week. For most Americans (59 percent), dinner away from home means a full-service restaurant. The only exception is for adults under age 30; a slight majority (52 percent) of this group say their last dinner out was at a fast-food place. Elderly, affluent, and college-educated adults are most likely to choose a full-service restaurant." (p16)

Waldrop, Judith. "Business Reports: Food: Most Restaurant Meals Are Bought on Impulse." American Demographics v16 n2, Feb 1994. p16-17. (ISSN0163-4089).

FOOD HABITS--U.S.--SINGLE PEOPLE (v19)

FOOD INDUSTRY AND TRADE

see also DAIRY PRODUCTS INDUSTRY; GROCERY TRADE; MEAT INDUSTRY AND TRADE

"The share of consumers' budget allocated to food differs widely throughout the Western Hemisphere....While the United States and Canada devoted 13 and 11 percent, respectively, of all private spending to food, Latin America spent an average of 33 percent. These differences are to be expected, given the wide gaps in per capita incomes. According to the World Bank, U.S. and Canadian incomes were above $20,000 (U.S. dollars) per person in 1990, while average Latin American income was US$2,180--about one-tenth that of the United States, and below the world average of US$4,200." (p41)

Stuart, Miriam. "Food Consumption Throughout the Western Hemisphere:...Latin America's Food Expenditures and Consumption." Food Review v17 n1, Jan-Apr 1994. p40-45.

FOOD INDUSTRY AND TRADE--ASIA--JAPAN (v19)

FOOD INDUSTRY AND TRADE--EMPLOYMENT--U.S. (v19)

FOOD INDUSTRY AND TRADE--IOWA

"Although Iowa ranks second in U.S. agricultural production, only 2.6 percent of the nation's food-processing jobs can be found in the state....a recent study by economists at Iowa State University found that if the state could increase its pork production, Iowa could add 7,500 jobs." (p60)

Cohen, Warren. "Business: Cities Try to Bring Home the Bacon." U.S. News & World Report v116 n4, 31 Jan 1994. p59-60. (ISSN0041-5537).

FOOD INDUSTRY AND TRADE--LATIN AMERICA--U.S.

"Virtually all major Latin American countries have less meat and vegetable oil available per capita than do U.S. consumers. In 1990, vegetable oil available for consumption in the United States was 23 kilograms per capita, over twice that of Latin America's average of 9.5 kilograms. U.S. meat supplies were 115 kilograms per person in 1990, compared with an average of 35 kilograms in Latin America--only 30 percent of the U.S. level. Vegetable oil supplies would have to increase by 5 million metric tons per year, and meat supplies would have to increase by 31 million metric tons to bring Latin America up to the 1990 U.S. levels. In addition, food supplies would have to grow at the same rate as the Latin American population, about 2 percent per year, to maintain these higher per capita consumption levels." (p45)

Stuart, Miriam. "Food Consumption Throughout the Western Hemisphere:...Latin America's Food Expenditures and Consumption." Food Review v17 n1, Jan-Apr 1994. p40-45.

FOOD INDUSTRY AND TRADE--MEXICO--U.S. (v19)

FOOD INDUSTRY AND TRADE--RUSSIA

"Contrary to Western predictions, the trend toward privatization in Russian agriculture still has not solved the national food problem. For almost half the farms in Russia, the average profitability indices have been negative. Changes in the structure of the labor force have reduced the output of kolkhozes and state farms. For instance, total agricultural production dropped by eight percent in 1992, while the production of the most valuable products (meat, eggs and milk) decreased by 10-13 percent. The diet of an average Russian citizen is now characterized by a 25 percent shortage of complete proteins, a 30 percent shortage of vitamins A and B, and a 50 percent shortage of vitamin C. Thus, social processes in the countryside in general, and their gender dimension in particular, exasperate health problems for the whole nation." (p30)

Mirovitskaya, Natalia. "Women: The Double Burden Weighs Heavier on Rural Russian Women." Surviving Together v11 n3, Fall 1993. p27-30. (ISSN0859-6286).

FOOD INDUSTRY AND TRADE--U.S. (v19)

U.S. "Fruit, nut, and vegetable exports grew by 7 percent to $7.2 billion, however, growth was primarily in vegetables. Fruit and fruit juice exports increased slightly over 1 percent to $2.8 billion, and nuts rose 4 percent to $1.2 billion. Vegetable exports soared by 14 percent to $3.3 billion. Fresh vegetables rose 9 percent on large gains in broccoli, cabbage, celery, garlic, lettuce, and onions. The strongest gains were in exports of highly processed vegetables, rising 22 percent to $1.5 billion. This group of vegetables has been the fastest growing over the past several years, and the expansion is spread among all markets. Exports of tropical products (coffee, cocoa, chocolate, tea, and spices) rose 25 percent to over $700 million. Chocolate and preparations exports led with over $335 million from $244 million in 1992. The largest gain in chocolate was to the FSU [former Soviet Union] as imports from the United States jumped to over $75 million from $2 million in 1992." (p2)

U.S. Dept. of Agriculture/Greene, Joel. "Agricultural Exports Decline in 1993." Foreign Agricultural Trade of the United States Jan-Feb 1994. p2.

"In March, the Dinkins Administration proposed the first city law [in New York] that would require genetically engineered foods to be displayed separately and identified by a clear and conspicuous sign....'Unless and until the Food and Drug Administration does its job, this food disclosure legislation is the first and only line of defense New Yorkers have against these potentially unsafe foods,' said Commissioner Mark Green....An estimated one to two percent of the population at large, and four to six percent of small children, have food allergies. Food that is normally safe for an allergy sufferer could become dangerous if it has been genetically altered with proteins from a food to which they are allergic. 'When it comes to a new, unproven technology that enters our bodies, the burden of proof should be on the technology, not on consumers as potential guinea pigs,' said Commissioner Green." (p9)

"Legislative Update: New York City Proposes First-of-Kind Law on Posting of Genetically Engineered Food." geneWATCH v9 n1-2, Aug 1993. p9,11.

FOOD POISONING--U.S. (v19)

"An estimated 9,000 Americans die each year and another 6.5 million become sick from bacterial foodborne illnesses. That is far, far too many for a nation that prides itself on having one of the world's safest food supplies. In addition, the Food and Drug Administration and the Food Safety and Inspection Service estimate that foodborne illnesses cost the United States between $6 and $23 billion annually in medical expenses and lost productivity." (pE75)

Torricelli, Robert G. (Rep.-N.J.). "H.R. 3751, Katie O'Connell Safe Food Act," Congressional Record (2 Feb 1994). Daily ed. pE75-76. (ISSN0363-7239).

"Approximately 9 million people get sick from food-borne illnesses every year; almost 10,000 die (MOTHER JONES, 7-8/92). An estimated one-third of all food poisoning comes from poultry and red meat. And the problem isn't going away: According to officials at the national Centers for Disease Control and the FDA, the number of diseases associated with meat has been steadily rising for the past two decades." (p10)

Devitt, Tiffany. "Jack in the Box: Reporting Avoided Meaty Issues." EXTRA! v6 n3, Apr-May 1993. p10-11. (ISSN0895-2310).

FOOD PRICES--U.S. (v19)

"The CPI [Consumer Price Index] for cereals and bakery products rose 3.4 percent last year--up 4.5 percent for cereals and up 4.1 percent for bread. Those increases were partially offset by a 0.2-percent decline in the CPI for flour and prepared flour mixes. Most of the price rise can be attributed to stronger demand as consumers switched to more basic foods to prepare at home. For example, cereal is relatively inexpensive on a per-serving basis, easy to fix, and is considered healthy. Also in order to economize, consumers working outside the home are more likely to carry a brown bag lunch rather than buying lunch at a local eatery, thus one source of stronger demand for bread." (p39)

Parlett, Ralph. "News of Food Prices: Food Prices Rose Moderately for the Third Consecutive Year." Food Review v17 n1, Jan-Apr 1994. p36-39.

"The CPI [Consumer Price Index] for eggs rose 8.1 percent--the highest increase of all the food categories in 1993. This followed a 10.6-percent decline the year before. Very small changes in egg supplies elicit large changes in prices. Egg production expanded in 1992--driving prices down and pressuring producer profits. In 1993, producers held production gains to a minimum. With stronger export demand reducing supplies available for the domestic market, prices increased." (p39)

Parlett, Ralph. "News of Food Prices: Food Prices Rose Moderately for the Third Consecutive Year." Food Review v17 n1, Jan-Apr 1994. p36-39.

"With consumers cutting back on spending and other effects of the slow pace of economic recovery, food prices, as measured by the Consumer Price Index (CPI), rose at a slower rate than the CPI for all other goods and services for the third consecutive year. Food prices in 1993 increased 2.2 percent above 1992 levels....Prices for food purchased in grocery stores rose 2.4 percent, while the cost of food purchased in restaurants and fast food establishments rose only 1.8 percent. These increases compare with a 3-percent rise in price levels of all other goods and services. Adjusted for inflation, however, food prices in 1993 declined--just as they did in the previous 2 years." (p36)

Parlett, Ralph. "News of Food Prices: Food Prices Rose Moderately for the Third Consecutive Year." Food Review v17 n1, Jan-Apr 1994. p36-39.

FOOD RELIEF (v19)

FOOD RELIEF--AFRICA

"About 22 million people in Africa need emergency food aid this year, says Francis Mwanza, a spokesman for the UN's World Food Programme (WFP) in Rome. That compares with 27 million last year, when Somalia was still recovering from famine, and Ethiopia was still dealing with large numbers of people displaced by a long civil war. Last year, civil conflict was the most common reason for food aid to Africa. This year, about a third of the need can be attributed to crop failures, mostly due to drought, Mr. Mwanza notes." (p4)

Press, Robert M. "International: Africa Experts Call for More Than Relief as Famine Recurs." The Christian Science Monitor v86 n48, 2 Feb 1994. p4. (ISSN0882-7729).

FOOD RELIEF--U.S.

"Catholic Charities USA's recent annual survey of its agencies revealed that in 1992 Catholic Charities served 14.4 million people, up from 12.3 million in 1991. Most of this increase came from those requesting emergency aid. The number of children coming to agencies for food increased from 1,493,252 to 2,704,788. In 1981, one in four clients received emergency aid; in 1992 it was three in four....At least 2.5 million, and as many as 4.9 million, older Americans suffer from hunger and 'food insecurity,' according to a national study conducted by the Urban Institute." (p7)

"Policy Briefs: Food Insecurity and Demand for Emergency Food on the Rise, Surveys Find." Foodlines v10 n5, Feb-Mar 1994. p7. (ISSN0736-0010).

FOOD STAMP PROGRAM--U.S. (v19)

"New technology, called Electronic Benefits Transfer (EBT), may be the answer to reducing costs and preventing abuse of the Food Stamp Program. Fraud and overpayments in the Food Stamp Program are currently estimated to cost the Federal Government $1 billion per year. Although the exact number and dollar value of counterfeit food stamp coupons may never be known, the food and nutrition service estimates that $1.2 million in counterfeit coupons were discovered between 1986 and 1992. The nationwide implementation and use of an EBT system would reduce fraud and discourage the diversion of benefits." (pS693)

Conrad, Kent (Sen.-N.Dak.). "Eliminating Waste and Fraud in Federal Nutrition Programs by Adopting a National Electronic Benefits Transfer System," Congressional Record (2 Feb 1994). Daily ed. pS693. (ISSN0363-7239).

"Use of government food stamps has reached an all-time high. Some 27 million Americans put bread and milk on the kitchen table with food stamps. But according to the government, under-the-table trafficking in food stamps reached $1 billion last year, also an all-time high....Fraud in the food stamp program has increased slowly since the program was launched in 1968, when 2.2 million Americans received $173 million worth of stamps. The program gained little in numbers during the 1980s. Rapid increases began in 1990 as unemployment benefits ran out for laid-off workers, more and more poor working families stayed below the poverty line because of inflation, and the number of single mothers with babies began to increase. Today, with the US still feeling effects from the last recession, the food stamp program costs a staggering $30 billion a year." (p1)

Holmstrom, David. "Food Stamp Use--and Abuse--Reaches All-Time High in US." The Christian Science Monitor v86 n76, 15 Mar 1994. p1,4. (ISSN0882-7729).

FOOD SUPPLY (v19)

see also AGRICULTURE

"Per capita grain yields are down from peak production years by 28% in Africa, 16% in Latin America and 4% in Asia. Today all are grain importers (Brown, 1991). In 1980 the world produced 710 lb of grain/person; today it is 699 lb, and projections are for 653 lb in the year 2000 (Ehrlich, 1991). This recent study, projecting a decrease of 0.9% in food production against a population increase of 1.8%, indicates that the result will be 800 million deaths in a 20-year period. Data from 1990 show that over one billion or 20% of the world population does not receive enough food 'for an active work life' and another 9% or 477 million people either receive an insufficient amount of food for the normal growth of a child or minimal activity as an adult (Millman, 1991)." (p52)

Paddock, William. "Our Last Chance to Win the War on Hunger." Carrying Capacity Network v4 n1, 1994. p52-65. (ISSN1066-5404).

"After decades of steady growth, the world's food supply is no longer keeping up with population increases. Production of meat, fish, and grains per person has slowed to the point where the earth may have reached its 'carrying capacity,' with the result that nearly one in five (or 1 billion people) is malnourished. This is the sobering conclusion of the Worldwatch Institute's annual 'State of the World' report....The growth in annual food production peaked in the 1980s, according to data gathered by the Worldwatch Institute, a Washington-based think tank. Between 1989 and 1993, the fish catch per person dropped 7 percent. After peaking in 1984, per capita grain output by last year had fallen 11 percent." (p10)

Knickerbocker, Brad. "Economy: The Balance between Food and People Has Become Threatened." The Christian Science Monitor v86 n37, 18 Jan 1994. p10. (ISSN0882-7729).

FOOD SUPPLY--AFRICA, SUB-SAHARAN (v19)

FOOD SUPPLY--AFRICA, WEST (v19)

FOOD SUPPLY--DEVELOPING COUNTRIES (v19)

FOOD SUPPLY--ERITREA

"Eritrea's new government did everything right. Seeds, oxen and ploughs were distributed; trees were planted, dams and terraces built; the area under cultivation was expanded by 25%. The rains arrived in 1993, but too late, too light or, occasionally, too heavy. Then came locusts, grasshoppers and rats. Crop failure was estimated at 80%, and it was back to food aid for some two-thirds of Eritrea's 2.5m population." (p49)

"International: The Horn of Africa: Famine at the Gate." Economist v331 n7861, 30 Apr 1994. p46,49. (ISSN0013-0613).

FOOD SUPPLY--ETHIOPIA

"Ethiopia is only one of six countries in the Horn of Africa where the rains have failed over the past year, requiring a massive infusion of emergency food rations. According to America's Agency for International Development (USAID), more than 17m people in Ethiopia, Eritrea, Sudan, Somalia, Djibouti and Kenya, two-thirds of them victims of drought, are 'at risk' of starvation....Yet even with a government that has opened up market systems and brought peace, and even when rains are bountiful, Eithiopia must import food, around 1m tonnes a year. In 1985, when the famine was at its height and thousands were dying each day, 1.3m tonnes were needed to feed 8m people at risk of starvation. Today comparable figures are used when aid workers talk merely of a 'crisis in the making'." (p46,49)

"International: The Horn of Africa: Famine at the Gate." Economist v331 n7861, 30 Apr 1994. p46,49. (ISSN0013-0613).

FOOD SUPPLY--LATIN AMERICA (v19)

FOOD SUPPLY--SOUTH ASIA (v19)

FOOD SUPPLY--ZAMBIA (v19)

FOODBORNE DISEASES (v19)

FOOT--U.S. (v19)

FOOTWEAR INDUSTRY--U.S. (v19)

FORCE AND ENERGY

see also NUCLEAR ENERGY

FORCE AND ENERGY--RESEARCH

"A new approach towards energy Research and Development (R&D) is needed. International Energy Agency governments' energy R&D budgets are currently heavily skewed in favor of fossil fuels and nuclear power. Only 12.5 percent of the total budget of $7,675 million is allocated to renewables and energy conservation: over 70 percent is allocated to fossil fuels and nuclear power....Given that fossil fuel combustion and nuclear power are so-called 'mature' technologies, no government R&D should be provided in the future except for the safe decommissioning of old plants, and ensuring appropriate waste management systems and techniques for existing stockpiles of waste. R&D should be substantially re-directed to energy efficiency and renewables, with a challenging target of 50 percent within five years." (p33)

"Energy Facts: Solar Water Heating Potential." Solar Industry Journal v4 n2, 1993. p33.

FORCED LABOR--BRAZIL

"A recent Americas Watch report 'Forced Labor in Brazil Revisited' (November 30, 1993) offers firsthand evidence that confirms the findings of earlier reports: in the inaccessible forests of the central and western states of Brazil large landowners use forced labor to cut and burn enormous tracts of land for the purpose of turning the forest into cattle pasture....the report also describes forced labor and conditions that approximate forced labor in other agricultural and industrial endeavors throughout Brazil....The 1992 report of the Commission of the Land Pastoral (CPT) notes a significant increase in the number of cases and persons exposed to non-traditional forced labor in recent years. Of the 18 cases of forced labor involving 16,442 workers, only four cases (128 workers) involved deforestation. The vast majority of the more than 16,000 laborers subjected to forced labor conditions were engaged in the following less traditional activities: sugar cane cutting (3,893 laborers); carbon production (8,800 laborers); coffee picking (60 laborers); lumber clearing and related activities (450 laborers); forcible eviction of land occupiers (60 laborers); other agricultural labor (3,051 laborers). In 1991 the CPT reported a total of 8 cases involving 4,883 laborers in traditional and non-traditional forced labor situations." (p1)

"Brazil: Forced Labor Revisited." NewsNotes v19 n1, Jan-Feb 1994. p1-2. (ISSN1064-1556).

FOREIGN ASSISTANCE

see ECONOMIC ASSISTANCE

FOREIGN BANKS AND BANKING

see BANKS AND BANKING, FOREIGN

FOREIGN BUSINESS ENTERPRISES

see BUSINESS ENTERPRISES, FOREIGN

FOREIGN DEBTS

see DEBTS, EXTERNAL

FOREIGN EXCHANGE RATES--KOREA (SOUTH) (v19)

FOREIGN INVESTMENTS

see INVESTMENTS, FOREIGN

FOREIGN LANGUAGE

see LANGUAGE AND LANGUAGES

FOREIGN STUDENTS

see STUDENTS, FOREIGN

FOREIGN STUDY--JAPAN--U.S. (v19)

FOREIGNERS

see IMMIGRANTS

FOREST DEPLETION

see DEFORESTATION

FOREST FIRES

see also DEFORESTATION

FOREST FIRES--OREGON

"In October 1991 someone deliberately set fire to Oregon's Willamette National Forest, burning 9,000 acres in an un-loggable, spotted owl habitat preserve. As Western timber jobs continue to decline and weather gets drier, more forest fires sparked by arson could flare up, AP reports. Arson is profitable because it creates jobs, first for those who fight the fire and then for those who do the salvage logging. For example, the Willamette fire in Warner Creek took two weeks and $10 million to stop. Environmentalists say the prospect of employment, especially through the salvage-logging program, encourages people to torch trees. 'Here's an agency that puts out Smokey the Bear posters saying 'Only You Can Prevent Forest Fires,' and then they run programs that reward arson,' says Mark Hubbard of the Oregon Natural Resources Council." (p4)

"Arson Feared this Summer." High Country News v25 n14, 9 Aug 1993. p4. (ISSN0191-5657).

FOREST PRODUCTS INDUSTRY--CANADA (v19)

FOREST PRODUCTS INDUSTRY--JAPAN--U.S.

"Japan's value-added wood product imports from the United States decreased between 1989 and 1992. In absolute terms, the value of value-added wood product imports from the United States fell by 13.56 percent. Moreover...such value-added imports fell as a percentage of total U.S. wood product imports into Japan during the same period. The decline in the ratio of U.S. value-added imports to wood product imports into Japan is in marked contrast to the U.S. industry's performance in the rest of the world where U.S. exports of value-added products as a share of total U.S. wood products exports increased 9.58 percent between 1989 and 1992. Moreover, the absolute value of U.S. wood product exports to the rest of the world increased by 38.50 percent during the 1989-1992 period. These data indicate that no relative progress has been made in actually opening the Japanese market to value-added wood product imports from the United States." (p75-76)

U.S. Senate. Committee on Finance. "United States-Japan Trade Negotiations." Hearing, 8 Nov 1993. Washington, D.C.: GPO, 1994. (ISBN0160435625). (Y4.F49:S.hrg.103-399).

FOREST PRODUCTS INDUSTRY--U.S.

"As a single national association, AFPA [the American Forest & Paper Association] represents a vital national industry which accounts for over 7 percent of the total U.S. manufacturing output. The industry employs some 1.4 million people, and ranks among the top 10 employers in 46 states, with an annual labor cost of about $46 billion. The forest and paper products industry generates sales of $200 billion annually. As a significant exporter of global markets, with exports of $17 billion in 1992, the industry makes an important contribution to the U.S. balance of payments." (p41)

Lovett, Stephen M. (International Vice President, American Forest & Paper Assoc.). U.S. Senate. Committee on Finance. "Renewing 'Super 301.'" Hearing, 14 Jun 1993. Washington, D.C.: GPO, 1993. (ISBN016043372X). (Y4.F49:S.hrg.103-332).

"With...shipments of approximately $200 billion annually, the forest products industry accounts for 7 percent of U.S. manufacturing output. With an annual payroll of $46 billion, the industry employs some 1.4 million people, and ranks among the top 10 employers in 46 states. With exports of $17 billion in 1992, the industry makes an important...contribution to the U.S. balance of payments. Exports are vital to the forest and paper industry. For the last five years, upwards of 50 percent of the growth in output for both wood and paper products has been attributable to exports. This, in turn, has enabled us to maintain domestic employment levels, despite the recession in the overall U.S. economy. In order to maintain strong export growth, our industry is committed to aggressively developing foreign markets, and supporting initiatives by our government to remove trade barriers to our exports. Japan is a priority export market for our industry. The total Japanese market for paper and allied products, at approximately $60 billion, ranks it second among world markets. By the same token, the Japanese wood products market, at $27 billion, ranks third in the world." (p66)

Smith, Maureen R. (International Vice President, American Forest and Paper Assoc.). U.S. Senate. Committee on Finance. "United States-Japan Trade Negotiations." Hearing, 8 Nov 1993. Washington, D.C.: GPO, 1994. (ISBN0160435625). (Y4.F49:S.hrg.103-399).

FORESTS AND FORESTRY

see also LUMBER TRADE; RAIN FORESTS

"On April 23, EARTH ISLAND JOURNAL hosted a press conference at the headquarters of the Rainforest Action Network (RAN) to herald what could be a partial solution to the destruction of the Earth's forests--paper made from plants other than trees....Nearly half of the estimated 16 billion acres of forests that once blanketed the Earth have already been destroyed. In many parts of the world today, forests are being felled, not to build homes, but to produce paper. It is estimated that 40 percent of the trees cut today are turned into pulp for paper boxes, tissues and printing. 'Imagine the impact if we could immediately halt 40 percent of the clearcutting now going on in the world's forests,' [RAN executive director Randall] Hayes noted. 'With kenaf [plants], we have that opportunity!'" (p19)

Smith, Gar. "JOURNAL Pioneers Tree-Free Paper." Earth Island Journal v8 n3, Sum 1993. p19. (ISSN1041-0406).

FORESTS AND FORESTRY--BRITISH COLUMBIA

"In each of the past three years, British Columbia has cut more than 73 million cubic meters of timber, enough to load a convoy of logging trucks parked end-to-end for 120 kilometers (75 miles) each day, year-round. The Ministry of Forestry calculates the harvest to be 25 percent above the 'sustained yield.' Even worse, about three-quarters of the timber cut is mature or ancient forest (150 to more than 2,000 years old). While clear-cuts are restricted to no more than 16 hectares in the United States, they typically range between 30 and 300 hectares in British Columbia. Combined with other industrial practices like short rotation cycles, herbicides, and replanting grids of monoculture trees, such clearcutting destroys the natural evolution of this complex ecosystem." (p34)

Denniston, Derek. "Wrong Turns: The Temperate Rainforest: Canada's Clear-Cut Secret." World Watch v6 n4, Jul-Aug 1993. p9,34. (ISSN0896-0615).

FORESTS AND FORESTRY--CALIFORNIA (v19)

FORESTS AND FORESTRY--CAMBODIA

"A 1960 survey found 13.2 million hectares of forest inside Cambodia, or 73% of the total land area, but war and logging have taken a heavy toll since then. In 1990, the UN Food and Agriculture Organization estimated that Cambodia still had 4.4 million hectares of 'closed forests' and another 1.8 million hectares of 'semi-closed forests'." (p13)

Salayakanond, Wirasak. "Asia: Plunder in the Jungle." Panoscope n34, Jan 1993. p12-13. (ISSN0951-8819).

FORESTS AND FORESTRY--CANADA (v19)

FORESTS AND FORESTRY--CHIAPAS (MEXICO)

"The extraction of wood from Chiapas' forests continues. Between 1981 and 1989, 2,444,777 cubic meters (86,897,195 cubic feet) of precious woods, conifers and tropical trees were taken out of Chiapas, destined for the Federal District, Puebla, Veracruz and Quintana Roo. In 1988 wood exports brought a revenue of 24 billion pesos ($7.7 million), 6000 percent more than in 1980." (p30)

Marcos, Subcommandante. "Defending the Commons: A Reality Tour of the Heart of Chiapas." Earth Island Journal v9 n2, Spr 1994. p30-31. (ISSN1041-0406).

FORESTS AND FORESTRY--COLORADO--SPORTS

"Ski resort expansion is booming in Colorado. Since 1990, the Forest Service has approved 90,000 acres of new ski terrain in Colorado, a whopping 57 percent increase. The agency has another 80,000 acres both inside and outside existing permit boundaries that it can consider for further ski development. Critics say the Forest Service is approving ski expansions without a plan. 'No one in the Forest Service sits down and says, "Where do we want to put new ski areas,"' says Tom Lustig, a staff attorney with the National Wildlife Federation in Boulder. 'It's driven by the developer, and the Forest Service almost never says no.'" (p4)

Larmer, Paul. "Does Aspen Need Thousands More Skiers?" High Country News v25 n18, 4 Oct 1993. p4-5. (ISSN0191-5657).

FORESTS AND FORESTRY--EMPLOYMENT--OREGON

"Only 6 percent of all employment in Oregon is timber related, and 39,000 new non-timber jobs are being added each year. From 1979 through 1986, 11,000 jobs in the forest products industry were lost while timber production increased. When you pass through towns out here, you realize that the most obscene aspect of this entire issue is the constant parade of fully loaded log trucks past idled and rusted mills to bustling export docks." (p8)

Welles, Caitlin E. "Writing Letters to the Editor Can Be Key to Your Cause." Audubon Activist v8 n3, Nov 1993. p8. (ISSN0898-915X).

FORESTS AND FORESTRY--GREAT BRITAIN

"Some Conservative ministers want to sell off Britain's state-owned forests....Arguments about selling the Forestry Commission's 1,128,000 hectares (4,355 sq miles) of land, four-fifths of which is forest, will come to a head this month....The business of growing, cutting and processing trees employs 41,000 people in Britain. Forestry people, mercantilists to a man, point out that the country does not produce nearly enough timber to be self-sufficient. In 1992 Britain imported 6.3 billion [pounds sterling] ($9.5 billion) of wood products and exported only 2.1 billion [pounds sterling] worth. Commercial tree-planting was once encouraged by tax rebates." (p57) "The government could decide to step up piecemeal land sales. Some 60% of Britain's forests are already privately owned. In 1992-93 the Forestry Commission sold 9,300 hectares for 14m [pounds sterling]....Long-term annual returns on investment in high-quality forests now average about 6%. Since income from timber sales is tax-free, that is a respectable 10% to anyone who pays income tax at the maximum marginal rate of 40%. However the commission has fallen behind its target of selling 100,000 hectares this decade. Privatisation enthusiasts argue that piecemeal sales will not attract big investors." (p60)

"Britain: Forestry: Private Woods." Economist v330 n7849, 5 Feb 1994. p57,60. (ISSN0013-0613).

FORESTS AND FORESTRY--IDAHO (v19)

FORESTS AND FORESTRY--INDIA

"By far the most evident degradation of Himalayan resources has occurred in the forests. While no reliable data on changes in forest cover exist for the region as a whole, state foresters in India estimate that since 1950, at least 40 percent of the forest cover in the Indian Himalaya has been lost to clearing for farmland, urban growth, and commercial logging. A comparable estimate for Nepal is about 20 percent loss. Commercial cutting began in earnest in 1865, when the British negotiated a 20-year lease for all state forests in the Garwhal Himalaya for 10,000 rupees per year. The contract paid off richly: between 1869 and 1885, the British hauled away 6.5 million railway ties from perhaps the largest, thickest deodar forest in the world. Following the success of the Chipko 'tree-hugging' movement in the mid-1970s to stop commercial felling in Uttar Pradesh, the Indian government halted the industry throughout the Indian Himalaya at least until 1996. Now, the primary regions of commercial clearing are in Sichuan and Yunnan provinces of China." (p15)

Denniston, Derek. "Saving the Himalaya." World Watch v6 n6, Nov-Dec 1993. p10-21. (ISSN0896-0615).

FORESTS AND FORESTRY--NEW ZEALAND

"Since 1990 the New Zealand government has sold the rights to the management and harvesting of 361,000 hectares of forests, in rolling 35-year leases, realising NZ$1.4 billion ($800m). It did not sell the land because of arguments over Maori rights and public access. New Zealand wood processors have had to pay more for their logs but...[director of Forestry Investment Management Robert] Rickman maintains that the industry is 'more efficient and completely revitalised'. Planting has increased from about 11,000 hectares a year to 60,000." (p60)

"Britain: Forestry: Private Woods." Economist v330 n7849, 5 Feb 1994. p57,60. (ISSN0013-0613).

FORESTS AND FORESTRY--RUSSIA

"Like ancient China, Russia once had a wall to protect itself against invaders--but this wall was green. From the 14th to the 18th century, Russia's czars kept a thick belt of forest uncut along their southern border to block attacks by Tatar nomads roaming the sparsely forested plains of Central Asia. Within the belt, the Russians dug trenches and felled trees to make the forest impassible to the nomads' cavalry and wagons. Most of the 'Green Wall of Russia' still stands today, ranging from one to 10 kilometers thick. Originally some 375 miles long, 84 percent still remains preserved, centuries after much of the surrounding land has been cleared for farmland." (p11)

Recknagel, Charles. "In Brief: The Green Wall of Russia." E Magazine v4 n6, Dec 1993. p11-12. (ISSN1046-8021).

"Despite the wealth of resources they contain, Siberian forests are extremely fragile. Many forest regions are quite arid, receiving as little as 25 to 30 centimeters of rain per year, equivalent to some areas in Arizona. Fires cause almost as much deforestation as does timber harvesting. Under these harsh conditions trees grow slowly. The forests also suffer from air pollution. Acid rain from Russia's nickel, aluminum and lead smelters has produced rings of dead trees--Russia's 'black forests'--sometimes more than 200 kilometers in diameter. Timber harvesting and the sinking of logs during transport have killed many of Siberia's rivers. Large dam projects have flooded thousands of hectares of forest land. But in a Russia free from the trade barriers imposed by the Soviet Forest Ministry, logging will be the greatest threat to Siberia's forests. Trees are a quick cash crop. Logs are easier to extract than oil or minerals and are readily exchanged for hard currency and technology. Russian forests are already disappearing at a rate of 12 million hectares a year." (p18)

Levin, Julia. "Siberia for Sale." Surviving Together v11 n2, Sum 1993. p17-19. (ISSN0859-6286).

FORESTS AND FORESTRY--THAILAND (v19)

FORESTS AND FORESTRY--U.S.

"'Twenty years ago [in the U.S.] there were deposits required on (wood) pallets,' Andy Mahler said. 'Now it's cheaper to cut down trees to build new pallets than to recycle them.' Former forest chief Dale Robertson has said that 51 percent of all hardwood lumber went into building between 500 and 600 million shipping pallets in 1991. Mahler adds that 57 percent of these pallets were 'either landfilled, incinerated or otherwise disposed of after only one use.' In Ohio alone, he says, 18,000 acres of forest a year goes 'directly to the landfills after a brief incarnation as a shipping pallet.'" (p32)

Letto, Jay. "Go East Young Timberman!" E Magazine v5 n1, Feb 1994. p26,30,32-33. (ISSN1046-8021).

"Saving what remains of the nation's old-growth forests, will require some sacrifice by US citizens. The 1992 PULP AND PAPER INTERNATIONAL YEARBOOK reports that the average American consumes 697.4 pounds of paper each year. The global average is 96.8 pounds. Most of this total consists of packaging consumers discard after a single use. US imports of wood products are contributing to the destruction of forests around the world. Each year the US consumes more than 16 billion cubic feet of wood; more than 25 percent of it is imported from other nations. The US imports 60 percent of its solid wood and 70 percent of its pulp from Canada." (p21)

Smith, Gar. "Clinton's Timber Plan Compromise." Earth Island Journal v8 n3, Sum 1993. p21. (ISSN1041-0406).

"Every year in the United States, nearly 900 million trees are cut down to provide raw material for American paper and pulp mills. More than 500,000 tons of wood pulp go into the manufacture of disposable diapers. It is these paper products which make up 40 percent of what goes into landfills. In effect, America is cutting down its forests and burying them in landfills as garbage. Before the advent of the industrial revolution in 1860, America's forests were considered limitless. Today, the lower 48 states have less than five percent of their original forests. What remains, according to the Wilderness Society, is 4.7 million acres, of which only 1.4 million acres are protected in national wilderness areas, forests and parks. The remaining unprotected trees are found in 3.3 million acres of pristine ancient forests. This wilderness is either privately owned or located on National Forest land and Bureau of Land Management land in Alaska, Washington, Oregon and Northern California." (p26)

Gertzweig, Dov. "Seeing the Forest for the Trees: The Global Challenge to Preserve the World's Forests." Earth News v4 n3, May-Jun 1993. p24-28. (ISSN1068-9400).

"Since 1950 more than 20 million acres of federal forest land have been clearcut and nearly a half-million miles of roads have been constructed to access the logging sites. The Forest Service, many are surprised to learn, is the world's largest roadbuilding institution. Most of these timber sales have been heavily subsidized by U.S. taxpayers. Last year alone the Forest Service lost more than $500 million on its timber-sale program. One study estimates that since 1970 losses from national forest timber sales may have exceeded $10 billion. Even worse, of course, is the damage this logging has wrought on the wildlife, rivers, and wildlands of the nation's public lands. With less than 5 percent of the native forest left in the West (and a fraction of 1 percent east of the Mississippi), many of the ecosystems across the continent are in a state of functional collapse." (p13)

St. Clair, Jeffrey. "Clinton and the Ancient Forests: Year One." Lies of Our Times v5 n3, Mar 1994. p11-14. (ISSN1046-7912).

"As forests around the world are torched or cut, environmentalists track the numbers of hectares deforested and of species lost. But there's another, less commonly known indicator of forest decline: the shrinking size of the trees that remain. The average diameter of timber felled in the Pacific Northwest of the United States, for instance, declined from 14 inches in the mid-1970s to 7 inches a decade later--and is continuing to fall, says Steve Loken of the Center for Resourceful Building Technology in Missoula, Montana." (p30)

Douglis, Carole. "Making Houses Out of Trash." World Watch v6 n6, Nov-Dec 1993. p30-32. (ISSN0896-0615).

FORESTS AND FORESTRY--U.S.--SPORTS

"Environmentalists have long charged that the [U.S.] Forest Service never saw a ski area it didn't like. Indeed, the agency rarely rejects proposals for new ones. But a growing number of defunct ski areas are straining the agency's longstanding love affair with the industry. In Colorado, reclamation work for the Pikes Peak and Berthoud ski areas alone is expected to cost at least $400,000. The cost of reclaiming an area called Geneva Basin, closed since 1986, is unknown....On Pikes Peak, near Colorado Springs, Colo., where a ski area went bankrupt in 1985, the Forest Service has already spent $250,000 on a reclamation job that is far from complete. It plans to leave a small landfill on site to bury such items as cinder blocks, a bathtub and pieces of the old ski lodge and out-buildings." (p4)

Noreen, Barry. "When Ski Areas Fail, Taxpayers Clean Up." High Country News v25 n9B, 17 May 1993. p4. (ISSN0191-5657).

FORMER SOVIET REPUBLICS

see also AIDS (DISEASE)--FORMER SOVIET REPUBLICS; ETHNOLOGY--FORMER SOVIET REPUBLICS; FOSSIL FUELS--CHINA--FORMER SOVIET REPUBLICS; ISRAEL--FORMER SOVIET REPUBLICS--EMIGRATION AND IMMIGRATION; JEWS--FORMER SOVIET REPUBLICS; NATURAL RESOURCES--FORMER SOVIET REPUBLICS; NUCLEAR DISARMAMENT--FORMER SOVIET REPUBLICS; NUCLEAR POWER PLANTS--FORMER SOVIET REPUBLICS--PUBLIC OPINION; RADIOACTIVE WASTES--FORMER SOVIET REPUBLICS; SOIL DEGRADATION--FORMER SOVIET REPUBLICS; U.S.--COMMERCE--FORMER SOVIET REPUBLICS

"Gathered under a single flag, they would nearly outnumber Canadians. Instead, 25 million ethnic Russians are scattered among 14 new countries from the Baltic Sea to China. Both the czars and the commissars dispatched Russian colonists to subdue other nationalities and to reap the bounties of their lands, but with the fall of the Soviet Union, the privileged status of these Russians in what Moscow calls the 'near abroad' evaporated....Tensions are greatest where the ethnic Russian populations are largest. In Latvia, Russians make up 34 percent of the population and Latvians 52 percent. In Kazakhstan, ethnic Russians and Kazakhs each account for nearly 40 percent of the population. Only 22 percent of Ukraine's people are Russians, but they are concentrated in the eastern part of the country and in Crimea, raising fears in Kiev that they may try to rejoin Russia. In last month's elections, more than 80 percent of Crimean voters ignored warnings from Kiev and voted in favor of a plebiscite on secession." (p40-41)

Stanglin, Douglas/Pope, Victoria. "World Report: Desperate Trips at the End of Empire." U.S. News & World Report v116 n14, 11 Apr 1994. p40-42. (ISSN0041-5537).

FORMER SOVIET REPUBLICS--ECONOMIC CONDITIONS (v19)

FORMER SOVIET REPUBLICS--HEALTH AND HYGIENE (v19)

"In 1988, delegates to the Nineteenth Communist Party Conference in Moscow learned that 53 percent of all Soviet school children were considered to be in poor health. Health researchers found in early 1992 that not only were two out of every five young men reporting for compulsory military duty unfit to serve, but that only 20 to 25 percent of high school graduates were classified as healthy, says [Murray] Feshbach. An estimated 75 percent of all women in the former USSR have a problem with their pregnancy." (p2)

Kalish, Susan. "Life Expectancy Falling, Morbidity Rising in Former USSR." Population Today v21 n1, Jan 1993. p1-2. (ISSN0749-2448).

FOSSIL FUELS

see also COAL

FOSSIL FUELS--CHINA--FORMER SOVIET REPUBLICS

"The use of fossil fuel accounts for 95 percent of China's primary energy consumption, comparable to an equivalent amount for the former Soviet Union and 87 percent for the U.S. Of China's 500,000 gigawatt (GW) hours of energy production, 65 percent are from coal, 14 percent from oil, and one percent from gas. In terms of global consumption of fossil fuel, 23 percent originates in the U.S., 18.5 percent in the former Soviet Union, and 8.4 percent in China. China's energy and industrial carbon emissions, obviously in large part coming from coal, amounted to 650 million metric tons (mmt) in 1990, with methane accounting for 4.8 mmt (the CO2 equivalent of 90 mmt)." (p4)

Wilson, Nancy C. "China Faces Hard Energy Choices: Booming Economy, Soaring Emissions." Climate Alert v6 n3, May-Jun 1993. p1,4-7.

FOSTER CHILDREN--U.S. (v19)

FOSTER HOME CARE--NEW YORK (NY) (v19)

FOSTER HOME CARE--U.S. (v19)

"While growing numbers of prospective parents wait or go elsewhere to adopt babies, the number of U.S. infants placed in foster care increased 37 percent between 1984 and 1990, according to researchers Ira M. Schwartz, former U-M faculty member who now is the dean of the University of Pennsylvania School of Social Work, and colleagues Robert M. Ortega and Shenyang Guo at the U-M Center for the Study of Youth Policy. The researchers studied the cases of more than 5,000 American infants, finding that more than half the babies placed in foster care were still there after four years. They also found that, in 1987, nearly three-fourths of the babies had been placed in several foster care settings." (p1-2)

News release. "Children's Issues." University of Michigan News and Information Services 26 Apr 1994. p1-3.

FOUNDATIONS (ENDOWMENTS)

see CHARITABLE USES, TRUSTS, AND FOUNDATIONS

FRANCE (vNCE)

FRANCE--ARMED FORCES--APPROPRIATIONS AND EXPENDITURES

"The [French] government is committed to keeping the overall growth of its budget below 5 per cent. Defense expenditures today represent 3.38 per cent of GDP [gross domestic product] down from 4 per cent a decade ago and 6 per cent in 1960." (p9)

Valls-Russell, Janice. "Triggering Controversy: A French Blueprint for Security." New Leader v77 n3, 14 Mar 1994. p8-9. (ISSN0028-6044).

FRANCE--ECONOMIC CONDITIONS

"Last July 'Anglo-Saxon speculators' concluded that French unemployment (at that time 11.5%) was too high to be politically sustainable, that high real interest rates could not be maintained and that it was time to attack the franc. Europe's exchange-rate mechanism fell apart. Six months later unemployment has risen further (to 12%), real interest rates have hardly budged--yet the franc is now back within the old 'narrow band' of the ERM....Despite predictions of minimal growth this year (estimates range from most forecasters' 0.5% to the government's own 1.4%), and despite an expected rise in unemployment to nearly 13% by the end of 1994, the government has not budged." (p49)

"Europe: Edouard Balladur and the Triumph of Politics." Economist v330 n7849, 5 Feb 1994. p49-50. (ISSN0013-0613).

FRANCE--EMIGRATION AND IMMIGRATION (v19)

FRANCE--EMPLOYMENT

"With [France's] more than 3 million unemployed (nearly 12 per cent of the economically active population), the unemployment fund deficit grew from 23.9 billion francs in 1992 ($4.1 billion) to 38 billion at the end of 1993 ($6.5 billion)." (p553)

"News Briefs: France: Emergency Cuts in Social Spending." International Labour Review v132 n5-6, 1993. p552-553. (ISSN0020-7780).

FRANCE--POPULATION

"Characteristic of post-demographic-transition countries of Europe, France's fertility level is well below replacement level. With a total fetility rate (TFR, or average lifetime births per woman) of 1.8 in 1992, France is experiencing societal aging. Lower death rates and longer life expectancies contribute to societal aging, which puts new demands on France's highly educated workforce....Aging is more evident in the rural areas of France, due to working-age people migrating towards urban jobs. In the countryside, 23 percent of the population is age 60 or older, compared to 19 percent in urban areas. Only 27 percent of rural residents are ages 20 to 39, compared with a national average of 30 percent. The proportion of 20- to 39-year-olds rises to 32 percent in cities of more than 100,000 people, and to 34 percent in the Paris area." (p4)

Hershey, Sharon. "France Faces Societal Aging." Population Today v21 n4, Apr 1993. p4. (ISSN0749-2448).

FRANCE--SOCIAL CONDITIONS

"Even among practising Catholics [in France], the church's teaching on moral issues goes largely unheeded. Contraception is almost universally practised. Abortion ends one pregnancy in five. One in three babies is born out of wedlock. One marriage in three ends in divorce." (p64)

"Europe: The Spirit, Yes--Priests, No." Economist v329 n7843, 25 Dec 1993. p64. (ISSN0013-0613).

FRANCHISES (RETAIL TRADE)--U.S.

"When most Americans think of franchises, they think of McDonald's. While the burger giant is the nation's largest franchise business, it is only a small part of an $800 billion sector that employs nearly 8 million people. A franchise is simply a business that sells an investor the right to distribute a product or service using the product's trade name and business system. Franchisees usually pay a regular royalty and an initial start-up fee. And franchises are booming. On the average, a new franchise opens every 6 1/2 minutes, according to

the International Franchise Association." (p23)
Miniter, Richard. "Women's Successes Smash Business Myths." Insight v10 n8, 21 Feb 1994. p20-23. (ISSN1051-4880).

FRAUD--U.S. (v19)

FREE ENTERPRISE--CHINA (v19)

FROGS

Frogs "do taste a little like chicken. The French call them 'grenouelle,' and eat some 3,000-4,000 metric tons of frog's legs each year. That adds up to a staggering 60 to 80 million frogs--a tenfold increase in the last 20 years. Local supplies of 'edible frogs' ('Rana esculenta') were outstripped in the 1950s. The majority of frogs eaten in France today are Asian bullfrogs from Indonesia and Bangladesh which are now declining as well. India outlawed Asian bullfrog exports in 1987 to counter insect outbreaks coincident with the frog's decline. It has since increased pesticide use and introduced exotic frog species. Asian bullfrogs, meanwhile, continue to be smuggled out of India to be sold in France as 'Bangladesh frogs.'" (p25)
Suckling, Kieran. "Global Mass Extinctions Baffle Scientists." Earth First! v14 n1, 1 Nov 1993. p25.

FRUIT TRADE--U.S. (v19)

FUELWOOD (v19)

FUJIAN (CHINA)--ECONOMIC CONDITIONS

"Fujian, the ancestral home of 8 million overseas Chinese, including most in Indonesia, was one of China's poorest provinces as economic reform began in the late 1970s. Now, in a pattern repeated along the eastern Chinese seaboard, the economy is growing at more than 25 percent annually, and Fujian has become second only to its larger neighbor, Guangdong, as a destination for foreign investment. According to the official Economic Daily newspaper, more than 11,000 foreign joint ventures totaling $17 billion have been approved in the province in the last 15 years, although less than one-quarter of that amount has been invested." (p14)
Tefft, Sheila. "Overseas Investors Elicit Praise and Protests in Fujian Province." The Christian Science Monitor v86 n87, 30 Mar 1994. p13-14. (ISSN0882-7729).

FUNGI--U.S. (v19)

FUNGICIDES

"According to the National Academy of Sciences, fungicides account for about 60% of the total dietary oncogenic (tumor-producing) risk from pesticides--a risk greater than that from herbicides and insecticides combined. About 42% of the dietary risk comes from fungicide use on 10 crops, and about 18% of the total risk comes from fungicide use on four fruit crops--oranges, apples, peaches, and grapes. Moreover, a number of the most commonly used fungicides such as benomyl...are incorporated into food (systemic), and cannot be washed off (NRC 1987). The safety of postharvest fungicides is a special problem, as most of them are carcinogenic in animal tests, and yet they are added directly to harvested food. Their use is permitted because fresh fruit and vegetables have been exempt from Food and Drug Administration Delaney Amendment regulation that forbids the presence of animal carcinogens in processed foods (UCAIC 1989)." (p1)
Quarles, William. "Update: Biological Control of Postharvest Fruit Disease." IPM Practitioner v15 n5-6, May-Jun 1993. p1-11. (ISSN0738-968X).

FUR GARMENTS--U.S.--PUBLIC OPINION

"Public opinion polls vary depending on the phrasing of the questions and who's doing the asking. A PARENTS Magazine poll found that 85 percent of respondents disapprove of wearing fur and 63 percent believe that the killing of animals for furs should be prohibited by law. A poll by USA TODAY shows 20 percent in favor of banning fur sales and 74 percent who say people should be able to buy and wear fur if they want. The FRIC [Fur Retailers Information Council] study found that 25 percent of their sample felt that the fur trade should speak out more strongly about the 'right to wear fur,' with the figure at 40 percent for fur owners." (p18)
Pardue, Leslie. "Currents: Fur Flies as Debate Rages." E Magazine v4 n6, Dec 1993. p18-19. (ISSN1046-8021).

FUR TRADE--U.S. (v19)

FURNITURE INDUSTRY AND TRADE--U.S.

"The [U.S.] furniture industry once could expect about $16,000-worth of home furnishings purchases for every new home that was built. Today, consumers spend less than one-half of that--about $7,000. The latest boom in ready-to-assemble (RTA) furniture sales is helping to recharge the market. RTA furniture--about a $2 billion business within the furniture industry--is growing from a 10 percent category into a 20 percent category, [Britt] Beemer says." (p11)
Coolidge, Shelley Donald. "Couches, Chairs, Tables, Lamps: Consumers Are Buying Once More." The Christian Science Monitor v86 n37, 18 Jan 1994. p11. (ISSN0882-7729).

GAMBIA

see CONTRACEPTION--GAMBIA

GAMBLERS--U.S. (v19)

GAMBLING--ATLANTIC CITY (NJ)

"In Atlantic City, the site of the first major gambling operation on the east coast, $3.22 billion came into the city's gambling establishments in 1992. Of that, about $240 million, or 8 percent, of the earnings of the casinos actually ended up in the hands of State and local governments to be used for services. Those who have followed the course of the gambling industry in Atlantic City, and its effects on the surrounding communities, believe that the communities have come up short--most of the benefits fall to the casinos and not to the communities." (pS16474)
Simon, Paul (Sen.-Ill.). "Statements on Introduced Bills and Joint Resolutions," Congressional Record (19 Nov 1993). Daily ed. pS16433-16501. (ISSN0363-7239).

GAMBLING--ATLANTIC CITY (NJ)--YOUTH (v19)

GAMBLING--LAS VEGAS (NEV)

"Only one American city changes its telephone directories twice a year. Las Vegas must, because its metropolitan area has the fastest-growing population in the country: from 465,000 people in 1980 to more than 970,000 today. The growth is driven by the gambling industry, which employs two-thirds of Las Vegas's workers and pays more than half its taxes. Over the past five years the casino operators have taken on 35% more employees and built five new gambling centres, making the dusty boulevard called the Strip home to nine of the world's ten largest hotels....Las Vegas drew 7.3% more visitors last year than in 1992. Its hotel occupancy rate is still rising--to stand now at 87%, compared with a national average of 67%, even though 20,000 new rooms have been built in the past five years. The 357-foot-high black pyramid of the new Luxor hotel and casino has an indoor river, virtual-reality rides, and slot machines winking at every turn." (p31)
"American Survey: Las Vegas: Fifty Ways to Lose Your Wallet." Economist v330 n7856, 26 Mar 1994. p31. (ISSN0013-0613).

GAMBLING--MISSISSIPPI

The Center for Policy Research and Planning in Jackson "estimates that Mississippi will take in $70 million in gambling taxes in fiscal 1993-94 and $75 million the next year. That's a lot in a state with a population of only 2.6 million and the nation's lowest per capita income--$9,648 in 1989, according to the 1990 census. One out of every four Mississippi residents lives below the poverty level....The state collected $41 million in license fees and taxes on gross casino revenue. An additional $13.6 million went to localities with casinos. During the fiscal year that ended last July, the state collected $33.6 million in gambling taxes and license fees out of total general fund collections of $2 billion...." (p8)

Lee, Anita. "Mississippi Stakes All on Riverboat Gambling." Planning v59 n12, Dec 1993. p8-13. (ISSN0001-2610).

GAMBLING--U.S. (v19)

"Gambling has become one of the largest growth industries in this country; in 1991, legal gambling generated over $300 billion in betting, up over $90 billion from 1987. State and local governments and native American tribes, strapped for financial resources, are turning to gambling as a source of revenue that involves neither cutting services nor increasing taxes. In 1991, State governments took in over $8 billion in monopoly profits from gambling. Thirty-three States have established State lotteries. Casino gambling is being developed in more and more cities and native American reservations across the country." (pS16474)

Simon, Paul (Sen.-Ill.). "Statements on Introduced Bills and Joint Resolutions," Congressional Record (19 Nov 1993). Daily ed. pS16433-16501. (ISSN0363-7239).

"Casino gambling was once confined to Nevada and New Jersey's Atlantic City. Now six other cash-starved states have approved it, and another 15 are expected to do so in 1994. In addition, a spate of court decisions, allowing Indians to run full-blooded casinos on their tribal lands, has given birth to 57 casinos on reservations in a dozen states. The number of visitors to Atlantic City fell by 10% when Foxwoods, a casino owned by the Mashantucket Pequot tribe in Ledyard, Connecticut, opened in February 1992. Some 22.4m people are expected to have visited Las Vegas in the course of 1993, an increase of only 2.3% over the previous year's 21.9m. Conventions have helped stave off disaster, with attendances up 24% over 1992. Last year, hotels in Las Vegas took in $4.2 billion from gamblers and $2.4 billion from conventioneers. But the city struggles to cope." (p64)

"Business: Gambling in America: King Kirk's Castle." Economist v329 n7842, 18 Dec 1993. p61,64. (ISSN0013-0613).

"A new gambling industry survey indicates that casino gambling has grown explosively in the United States. Four years ago, only two states--New Jersey and Nevada--offered casino-style gambling. Now, 23 states offer the roll of dice and spinnning roulette wheels. Another dozen states are considering legislation approving casinos. According to the survey by Harrah's Casinos and the polling firm Yankelovich Partners, the number of 'household' visits to casinos has almost doubled since 1990. In 1993, the number of visits was 92 million, up from 46 million visits in 1990. (A 'household' visit, as defined in the survey, averages out to 1 1/2 persons from the same family.)...Estimated casino revenue for 1993 is $12.9 billion, up from $8.3 billion in 1990." (p3)

Holmstrom, David. "Casino Gambling Surges in US, Tempting More Teenagers." The Christian Science Monitor v86 n59, 17 Feb 1994. p3. (ISSN0882-7729).

"All states but Hawaii and Utah allow some form of legalized gambling. The proceeds are usually targeted for a politically popular cause: downtown improvements, education, programs for the elderly and the disabled. Since New Hampshire established the first state lottery in 1964, 37 states have followed suit. Lotteries provided $11.45 billion in tax revenues in 1992. Since Iowa started the first riverboat gambling operation in 1991, six states have launched some 40 boats. Riverboat gambling is soon expected to be approved in at least eight other states. Connecticut, which granted a monopoly on slot-machines to the Mashantucket Pequot tribe, now receives $113 million a year in revenues, making the Foxwoods casino the state's single largest taxpayer." (p22)

"The Home Forum: Moral Issues of Our Times: Gambling's Illusiveness." The Christian Science Monitor v86 n38, 19 Jan 1994. p22. (ISSN0882-7729).

"Nationally, 37 states have lotteries and 10 have non-Indian-run casinos....S. Timothy Waputo, executive director of the National Indian Gaming Association...said Indian casinos bring jobs and revenues to tribes. In 21 states, 78 tribes have entered gaming compacts with governors, he said." (p3)

Ross, Elizabeth. "National: Critics Worry about Gambling Consequences in New England." The Christian Science Monitor v86 n88, 31 Mar 1994. p3. (ISSN0882-7729).

"The 37 state lotteries typically return about half of their ticket revenues (totalling $24 billion in 1992) in prize money. About 8 percent covers administrative costs. The remaining 42 percent goes into state revenues....It is also a regressive tax--low-income people paying a larger share of their income for lottery tickets than the well-to-do. In Florida, for example, those earning less than $10,000 a year have been spending an average 1.3 percent of their income on lottery tickets; those earning more than $70,000 a year use less than three-tenths of 1 percent of their income on tickets." (p11)

Francis, David R. "States May Not Find Jackpot in Gambling." The Christian Science Monitor v86 n74, 11 Mar 1994. p11. (ISSN0882-7729).

"Casinos...operate or are authorized in 23 states, and 95 percent of all Americans are expected to live within a three or four-hour drive of one by the year 2000....Low-stakes casinos attract visitors to old mining towns in Colorado and South Dakota, and Indian tribes operate 225 casinos and high-stakes bingo halls nationwide. Add church bingo, card rooms, sports wagering, dog and horse racing and jai alai to the mix and it becomes clear why Americans legally wagered $330 billion in 1992--a 1,800 percent increase over 1976." (p43) "Although most gambling experts believe that only 1 percent to 3 percent of Americans have a serious gambling problem at any given time, a July 1993 Gallup Poll funded by...[the Council on Compulsive Gambling of New Jersey] suggests that the figure may be closer to 5 percent." (p46)

Popkin, James/Hetter, Katia. "U.S. News: America's Gambling Craze." U.S. News & World Report v116 n10, 14 Mar 1994. p42-43,46. (ISSN0041-5537).

GAMBLING--U.S.--PUBLIC OPINION

"In 1938, 47 percent of those surveyed in a Gallup poll said that government lotteries 'would produce an unwholesome gambling spirit' in the country. By 1993, only about one-third thought that gambling is immoral. Fifty-four percent of American adults have purchased lottery tickets, according to a 1992 survey; nearly 25 percent say they have formed a weekly lottery habit." (p22)

"The Home Forum: Moral Issues of Our Times: Gambling's Illusiveness." The Christian Science Monitor v86 n38, 19 Jan 1994. p22. (ISSN0882-7729).

GAMBLING--U.S.--YOUTH

"Critics of gambling say its rapid growth in the US has a dark side, particularly among youngsters and teenagers. 'Kids today have grown up in an atmosphere where gambling is promoted by the state, churches, and synagogues, and the availability of it is everywhere,' says Tom Cummings, director of the Massachusetts Council on Compulsive Gambling. 'We are getting more and more calls from desperate high schools asking us to put on programs to help kids deal with gambling.' A council study of the effects of illegal gambling on 3,000 students found that 32 percent of students who do not gamble said they felt their refusal to partake in it was not normal. 'There was tremendous peer pressure on them to gamble,' Mr. Cummings says. In 1992, some 280,000 teenagers were denied entrance to Atlantic City casinos, and another 29,000 were led out of the casinos." (p3)

Holmstrom, David. "Casino Gambling Surges in US, Tempting More Teenagers." The Christian Science Monitor v86 n59, 17 Feb 1994. p3. (ISSN0882-7729).

GANGS

see also JUVENILE DELINQUENTS

GANGS--CALIFORNIA (v19)

GANGS--CHICAGO (ILL)

"Many youth in our cities today believe that becoming a gang member is their most worthwhile option. The loyalty among gang members provides a seemingly secure family, and the profits from gang-related illegal activities such as drug trafficking are a powerful draw. However, the life of a gang member is often a very violent one. Gang-related crime and violence continue to increase at an alarming rate. In Chicago alone, gang-related homicides per year rose from 38 in 1980 to 101 in 1990. Already, many neighborhoods, both in urban and rural areas, are virtually controlled by gangs. At a hearing held in Chicago by the Office of Justice Programs, one mother testified that one of the few sentences her 2-year-old child knows is: 'Get down, get down, they're shooting.' In Chicago, it has come to this." (pS2643)

Simon, Paul (Sen.-Ill.). "Statements on Introduced Bills and Joint Resolutions," Congressional Record (9 Mar 1994). Daily ed. pS2638-2643. (ISSN0363-7239).

GANGS--LOS ANGELES (CALIF)

"Although there has been a gang truce with several of the Crips and Bloods gangs in South Central and Watts districts in Los Angeles since the riots of 1992, on the other side of town in East Los Angeles the gang wars still continue. East L.A. has long been a neglected neighborhood, with a predominantly Mexican population. It has one of the nation's highest school drop-out rates and youth unemployment hovers at 75 percent. Teenage pregnancy is at an all-time high in this community. There is an aspect of suicide among many of these gang kids. They are between 10 and 21 years old and their options have been cut off: no education, no work, no opportunities for advancement. They stand on street corners and parks, flashing gang signs, inviting bullets....In 1992, Los Angeles police cited these statistics: 100,000 gang members, 1,000 gangs, nearly 600 people killed." (p22)

Rodriguez, Joseph. "Gang Life in Los Angeles: The East Side Story." APF Reporter v16 n2, 1994. p21-29. (ISSN0913-4562).

GANGS--NEVADA (v19)

GANGS--RUSSIA

"For all their tentacles abroad, Russian crime groups clearly pose the biggest problems for Russians at home. 'Organized crime,' said Boris Yeltsin...'is trying to take the country by the throat.' In a report delivered to Yeltsin...Russia's Analytical Center for Social and Economic Policies stated the problem in stark terms. 'The growth of organized crime,' the report said, 'threatens the continued political and economic development of Russia and creates conditions that could help bring national socialists to power.'...According to police statistics, interviews and other data examined in the Yeltsin report, approximately 150 criminal gangs control some 40,000 private and staterun companies within Russia. An estimated 80 percent of all Russian businessmen pay protection money to gangsters, the amounts ranging between 10 and 20 percent of gross revenues. That can amount to as much as half a company's profits, and it translates into consumer prices between 20 percent and 30 percent higher than they otherwise would be." (p45)

Duffy, Brian/Trimble, Jeff. "World Report: The Wise Guys of Russia." U.S. News & World Report v116 n9, 7 Mar 1994. p41-43,45-47. (ISSN0041-5537).

GANGS--U.S. (v19)

"Research designed to estimate the numbers and characteristics of youth gangs in the United States has not been conducted since [Walter] Miller's study [in the late 1970's]. However, Spergel and his colleagues (Spergel et al., 1990, 1991) completed a nationwide assessment of promising approaches to preventing and intervening in youth gangs. In the course of this research Spergel made the following observations: The scope and seriousness of the youth gang problem nationally is not clearly or reliably known. Police officials in 35 emerging and chronic gang-problem cities estimated the presence of 1,439 gangs and 120,636 gang members. Based on law enforcement and media reports, criminal youth gangs or gang members are to be found in nearly all 50 States....The age range of gang members has expanded in recent decades. Members remain in gangs longer. Extreme gang violence is concentrated in the older teen and young adult range. The average age of the arrested gang offender is 17-18. The average age of the gang homicide offender is 19-20." (p36)

Wilson, John J./Howell, James C. (Office of Juvenile Justice and Delinquency Prevention). U.S. House. Committee on Education and Labor. "Hearing Regarding the...Report Entitled 'A...Strategy for Serious...Juvenile Offenders.'" Hearing, 28 Oct 1993. Washington, D.C.: GPO, 1994. (ISBN0160433983). (Y4.Ed8/1:103-34).

"A 1993 study of youth violence by the University of Hawaii's Social Science Research Institute has found a high correlation between gang activity, weapons and drug use. Gang membership, they reported, is clearly associated with chronic delinquency. Gang members were 10 times more likely than non gang members to carry a weapon in the past year, 10 times more likely to have been frequently involved in gang fights, and four times more likely to use drugs or alcohol and at least five times more likely to steal or buy drugs than non gang members." (p39)

Stephens, Ronald D. (Executive Dir., National School Safety Center, Westlake Village, CA). U.S. Senate. Committee on Labor and Human Resources. "Recess from Violence: Making Our Schools Safe." Hearing, 23 Sep 1993. Washington, D.C.: GPO, 1993. (ISBN0160433096). (Y4.L11/4:S.hrg.103-313).

"On the federal level, Sen. Bob Dole decided that the best answer to the gang problem was not by investing in proven success stories like boys and girls clubs or community recreation programs, but rather by making it a federal crime to belong to a gang or encouraging someone to join a gang. The FBI estimates that there are over 200,000 organized gang members in the United States. Does he really expect us to believe that with the present 40,000 federal prison cells, a dent will be made in the number of youths involved in gangs? And, does he expect that with a construction cost of between $25,000 and $50,000 per cell, America and its trillion dollar debt can afford to build an additional 100,000 cells?" (p7 secB)

Strong, Jerome. "Prevention vs. Punishment." Ann Arbor News 30 Jan 1994. p7 secB.

A survey "Youth Violence: Gangs on Main Street, U.S.A." reports that gang activity and violence has increased in nearly one-third of 94 small cities with populations of 50,000 to 150,000. (p5)

"Partnerships." Education Week v13 n19, 2 Feb 1994. p5. (ISSN0277-4232).

"There are now over 30 identifiable Tongs in the United States. The largest are the Big Circle, originally from Hong Kong, which traffics heroin in New York City; United Bamboo, from Hong Kong and Taiwan, which specializes in extortion, gambling, gun smuggling, and heroin; and the Fuk Chien, originating in the Fukien Province of the People's Republic of China, which is involved in gun smuggling and heroin. The Fuk Chien also has the dubious distinction of being the most dangerous and violent of the Chinese Tongs. In addition to these three, the eastern U.S. has the Ghost Shadows, Flying Dragons, Tung On, and Ping On Tongs; the western U.S. has the Wah Ching (Youth of China). One of the more interesting phenomenon is the Viet Ching. These are Chinese-Vietnamese who are in Chinese Tongs. These individuals function in highly mobile groups, often with no name, and are in a state of constant flux in size and membership. They are profit-motivated and specialize in robberies and burglaries. There seems little question that the secret societies formed in China several centuries ago will become the feared crime groups of the future in the United States." (p34)

Tracy, Sharon. "The Evolution of the Hong Kong Triads/Tongs into the Current Drug Market." Journal of Third World Studies v10 n1, Spr 1993. p22-36. (ISSN8755-3449).

GANGS--UTAH

"Once thought to only be a problem of...[the U.S.'s] largest cities, gangs have invaded cities like Salt Lake City, UT. The problem of gang violence is of great concern to the citizens of...[Utah]. According to the Salt Lake Area Gang Project, a multijurisdictional task force created in 1989 to fight gang crime in the Salt Lake area, there are at least 215 identified gangs in...[the] region with over 1,700 members. Juvenile involvement in Utah's gangs is substantial, accounting for 34 percent of gang membership. Members are usually from 15 to 22 years of age." (pS457)

Hatch, Orrin G. (Sen.-Utah). "The Need to Retain the Anti-Gang Provision of the Crime Bill," Congressional Record (1 Feb 1994). Daily ed. p457-458. (ISSN0363-7239).

GAS, NATURAL

see NATURAL GAS

GASOLINE--TAXATION (v19)

GASOLINE--TAXATION--MISSISSIPPI (v19)

GASOLINE--TAXATION--U.S. (v19)

GAY PARENTS--U.S.

"Although the concept of 'lesbian mother' or 'gay father' may seem a contradiction in terms (Baptiste, 1987), 6 million to 14 million children are reared by gay men and lesbians (Editors of the Harvard Law Review, 1990; Wittlin, 1983). Estimates of the numbers of lesbian mothers in the United States range from 1.5 million (Hoeffer, 1981) to 5 million (Falk, 1989; Gottman, 1990)." (p27)

Hare, Jan. "Concerns and Issues Faced by Families Headed by a Lesbian Couple." Families in Society v75 n1, Jan 1994. p27-35. (ISSN1044-3894).

GAYS--U.S. (v19)

"Only 1 percent of American men are gay. That was the way many media outlets reported the findings of a survey released in April 1993 by the Alan Guttmacher Institute. Some conservatives jumped on this figure to argue, with dubious logic, that gays were therefore less deserving of civil rights protection. Both the journalists who reported the survey and the right-wing commentators who exploited it often failed to note some serious problems with the 1 percent (actually, 1.1 percent) figure. For one thing, the figure includes only men whose sexual activity has been exclusively homosexual for the past 10 years--a criterion that would disqualify countless men who identify themselves as gay. Some press reports did raise the question of whether everyone who denied having any homosexual experiences was being completely candid. In a follow-up story (4/25/93), for example, the NEW YORK TIMES noted that people are more likely to acknowledge socially disapproved behavior in a written questionnaire than in the face-to-face interviews used by the Guttmacher survey." (p14)

"The Disappearing Gay Male." EXTRA! v6 n4, Jun 1993. p14. (ISSN0895-2310).

A "campaign in Colorado to pass a constitutional amendment prohibiting legislation to protect homosexuals from discrimination was successful. It was adopted Nov. 3 by 53% of those voting. Since then, hate attacks including verbal abuse and physical assaults have escalated sharply against homosexuals in that state, with 45 reported in Nov. 1992 compared with five in Nov. 1991. In Kansas City, 37% of 900 lesbians and gays surveyed by a Mayor's Commission reported verbal assaults, threats, and name-calling. An additional 32% reported being beaten, attacked, bashed or otherwise physically hurt. Fourteen percent reported discrimination from police or the legal system. Overall, the report found that gays and lesbians in the Kansas City area live in a constant justifiable fear of being hurt physically or economically because of their homosexuality." (p11)

Swomley, John M. "Fundamentalists' Narrow-Mindedness: Not Based on the Bible." Human Quest v207 n2, Mar-Apr 1993. p11-12. (ISSN0897-8786).

GAYS--U.S.--ARMED FORCES--PUBLIC OPINION (v19)

GAYS--U.S.--CRIMES AGAINST

"For the past 9 years, NGLTF [National Gay and Lesbian Task Force Policy Institute] has issued an annual report examining anti-gay violence in America." Their most recent report, entitled "Anti-Gay/Lesbian Violence, Victimization, and Defamation in 1993" "indicates an overall decrease in the number of anti-gay incidents reported in Boston, Chicago, Denver, Minneapolis-St. Paul, New York City, and San Francisco. The reported incidents include harassment, threats, physical assault, vandalism, arson, police abuse, kidnaping, extortion, and murder. The six cities documented a total of 1,813 of these incidents in 1993. This represents a 14-percent decrease over the all-time high reported in 1992, and the first annual decline after 5 years of a steady and dramatic rise in the number of anti-gay incidents. Although promising, these figures still represent a 127 percent increase from the number of episodes reported 5 years ago. Only Denver experienced an increase in the number of reported incidents. The report attributes this increase to the passage of amendment 2, an anti-gay statewide ballot initiative in Colorado. Following passage of that initiative, 41 percent of the year's 204 anti-gay incidents occurred in a 2-month time span. Overall, Denver reported a 12-percent increase." (pS4007)

Simon, Paul (Sen.-Ill.). "Commending the National Gay and Lesbian Task Force Policy Institute for Their Efforts to Combat Antigay Violence," Congressional Record (25 Mar 1994). Daily ed. pS4007. (ISSN0363-7239).

"Antigay violence is a frequently occurring problem for gay adolescents [in the U.S.]. According to Martin and Hetrick (1988), 40% of a client population suffered some form of violence as a result of their homosexual orientation. Family members accounted for 49% of the violence, which included incest." (p165)

Dempsey, Cleta L. "Health and Social Issues of Gay, Lesbian, and Bisexual Adolescents." Families in Society v75 n3, Mar 1994. p160-167. (ISSN1044-3894).

GAYS--U.S.--PUBLIC OPINION (v19)

"Homophobia is an irrational fear of being gay, lesbian, or bisexual or of being in contact with someone who is same-sex oriented. Acts of prejudice and overt hostility toward gays may be witnessed by impressionable people who then recreate these same actions, thus perpetuating homophobia (Fricke, 1981). Many people in our society do not perceive it as wrong to physically or emotionally abuse gays (Whitlock, 1989). In subtle support of homophobia, 24 states and Washington, D.C., have laws stating that homosexual behavior is wrong and criminal (Cohn, 1992). In a 1992 NEWSWEEK poll, 53% of respondents considered homosexuality unacceptable, and 45% felt that gay civil rights were a threat to the American family and family values (Wilson, 1992). Despite these prejudices, 10% of our population is believed to be gay, lesbian, or bisexual." (p160)

Dempsey, Cleta L. "Health and Social Issues of Gay, Lesbian, and Bisexual Adolescents." Families in Society v75 n3, Mar 1994. p160-167. (ISSN1044-3894).

GAYS--U.S.--SUICIDAL BEHAVIOR

"Suicide is the third leading cause of death among teenagers (Fikar, 1992). However, researchers have failed to examine sexual orientation in their inquiries about adolescent suicide (Remafedi, Farrow, & Deisher, 1991), and the media often identify many suicides as accidents to avoid the issue of homosexuality (Sanford, 1989). The U.S. Public Health Service's 'Report of the Secretary's Task Force on Youth Suicide' stated that gay and lesbian youth account for 30% of all teen suicides (Fikar, 1992). Whereas 1 in 10 heterosexual teens attempts suicide, 2 to 3 of every 10 gay teens attempt suicide (Whitlock, 1989). A 1991 study of gay and bisexual males 14-21 years of age reported a 30% incidence rate for at least one suicide attempt by gay teens. Fifty percent of gay persons who attempted suicide reported more than one attempt." (p164)

Dempsey, Cleta L. "Health and Social Issues of Gay, Lesbian, and Bisexual Adolescents." Families in Society v75 n3, Mar 1994. p160-167. (ISSN1044-3894).

GAYS--U.S.--YOUTH

"Young homosexuals are two to three times more likely to attempt suicide than their heterosexual peers, according to a 1989 U.S. Health and Human Services Department report. Other surveys reveal more alarming figures: 45 percent of gay male teenagers and 20 percent of lesbian teenagers say they have experienced a verbal or physical assault in high school, and 28 percent of gay male youths drop out of school because of discomfort they experience there." (p37)

Portner, Jessica. "Creating a Safe Place." Education Week v13 n23, 2 Mar 1994. p36-37. (ISSN0277-4232).

GAZA STRIP

"The 363 square-kilometre Gaza Strip has a population of some 780,000, including 550,000 refugees from various parts of Israel who are registered with UNRWA, the United Nations Relief and Works Agency for Palestine Refugees in the Near East; 280,000 live in refugee camps, and 55 per cent are under 16 years of age. Per capita GDP [gross domestic product] is $800, as compared with $1,700 in the West Bank and $11,000 in Israel. The economically active population of the Gaza Strip is about 120,000." (p573)

"News Features: Occupied Territories: Gaza-Jericho: Jobs First." International Labour Review v132 n5-6, 1993. p571-579. (ISSN0020-7780).

GAZA STRIP--ECONOMIC CONDITIONS (v19)

GAZA STRIP--ISRAEL--WEST BANK--POPULATION

"Despite the dispersion of Palestinians and the immigration of Jews from other countries into Israel, the ratio of Palestinians to Jews in Israel, the West Bank, and Gaza combined has not changed over the past few decades. However, within Israel, the proportion of Palestinians in the population increased from 8 to 15 percent between 1950 and 1990, according to the ISRAEL STATISTICAL YEARBOOK. In 1990, Muslim women in Israel averaged 4.7 children, whereas Jewish women averaged 2.7 children. Within Israel, infant mortality for Muslims is around 16 infant deaths per 1,000 live births, almost twice as high as for Jewish newborns. The gap in infant mortality between Jews and Muslims widens when the populations of the West Bank and Gaza are taken into account." (p11)

Roudi, Nazy. "Spotlight: The Palestinians." Population Today v21 n1, Jan 1993. p11. (ISSN0749-2448).

GAZA STRIP--SOCIAL CONDITIONS

"Everything about Gaza seems extreme. In the summer it is an unbearably hot and steamy place. Rocky and barren, this strip of sand is 30 miles long and six miles wide at its broadest point. Three-quarters of a million people are crammed into its confines. Most Gazans--75 percent--are long-term refugees subsisting in camps that are among the world's most densely populated habitations. The Palestinians stranded in these miserable dwellings are forbidden by Israeli occupation authorities from planting a tree or adding a room. Other than their dreams of a homeland, the refugees have no escape from their cruel circumstances. No wonder the uprising against Israeli military rule began in Gaza, in Jabalia refugee camp. With 71,000 inhabitants, this is the largest and most squalid of the Palestinian camps, without trees or playgrounds. Narrow, unpaved alleys separate huts originally constructed as temporary shelters. Jabalia's poorest families have only two rooms for a dozen or more people. Guarded by Israeli soldiers, the entire settlement is sometimes sealed off for days at a time. Tension is always high." (p17)

Nimri Aziz, Barbara. "Mideast: Joy, Anger and Confusion in Gaza, A Land of Extremes." Toward Freedom v42 n8, Dec 1993-Jan 1994. p17,20. (ISSN0048-9898).

GAZA STRIP--WEST BANK--EMPLOYMENT

Skilled workers of the Gaza Strip and West Bank "have mostly sought work elsewhere, particularly in the Gulf States. By 1987, about 35 per cent of the employed population of the West Bank and 45 per cent of that in Gaza were working in Israel, with only 2 per cent employed in professional, technical and clerical occupations. In addition, about 40,000 Palestinians from the Occupied Territories went to work in the Gulf States in 1973-1982. By 1987 when the intifada began, about $675 million worth of external wage income was flowing into the Territories, mainly from Israel....In 1992 about 43 per cent of the combined workforce of the West Bank and Gaza Strip--then totalling some 320,000--was estimated to be unemployed or severely underemployed. Following the latest closure of the occupied territories in March 1993 the figure is thought to have risen to more than 60 per cent, as only 20,000-40,000 Palestinians out of a previous total of some 116,000 were allowed to continue to commute to work in Israel." (p575-576)

"News Features: Occupied Territories: Gaza-Jericho: Jobs First." International Labour Review v132 n5-6, 1993. p571-579. (ISSN0020-7780).

GAZA STRIP--WEST BANK--POPULATION

"The stock of [Palestinian] migrants who have left the West Bank and Gaza Strip since the beginning of 1969 is estimated at...337,000....by 1993 the stock of migrants was equivalent to roughly 17 per cent of the Palestinian population of the West Bank and Gaza Strip....Migration has been a major outlet for the increase in the size of the labour force resulting from high population growth. Indeed, the population's rate of natural increase, being the difference between crude birth and death rates, accelerated from roughly 2.2 per cent in the late 1960s to more than 4 per cent in the West Bank and more than 5 per cent in the Gaza Strip in the early 1990s....Improvements in living standards and in the provision of basic services led to a decline in the crude death rate from approximately 20 per thousand in the late 1960s to 5 per thousand in the late 1980s and early 1990s....Although crude birth rates declined slightly in the 1970s and early 1980s, they started increasing in the late 1980s and early 1990s. By 1991 they were among the highest in the world, estimated at 46 per thousand in the West Bank and 56 per thousand in the Gaza Strip." (p658)

Shaban, Radwan A. "Palestinian Labour Mobility."

International Labour Review v132 n5-6, 1993. p655-672. (ISSN0020-7780).

GENETIC ENGINEERING

see also ANIMAL GENETIC ENGINEERING; BIOTECHNOLOGY INDUSTRIES; FERTILIZATION IN VITRO

"One genetically engineered food product has already proven unsafe. In 1989 and 1990 a suspicious blood disease began showing up among people who had taken a nutritional supplement containing the amino acid L-tryptophan. Subsequently, the FDA recalled most preparations of L-tryptophan, and it is now believed to be responsible for twenty-seven deaths and over 1,500 serious illnesses. L-tryptophan never received FDA review, since the agency does not approve 'dietary supplements' prior to their marketing. But the product had been manufactured by Japan's Showa Denko company, using genetically altered bacteria; whether the supplement's toxicity was related to this phase of its creation remains very much an unresolved question." (p24)

Russell, Dick. "Miracle or Myth?" Amicus Journal v15 n1, Spr 1993. p20-24. (ISSN0276-7201).

"At a time when much effort is being put into the search for reliable alternatives to animal testing, animal welfare and rights activists are also deeply concerned that genetic engineering will lead to a further increase in animal experimentation. In the ten years since the production of the world's first genetically engineered animal, this area of research has increased rapidly. In the U.K. alone, the BUAV (British Union for the Abolition of Vivisection) reports some 62,455 transgenic animals produced in 1991, an increase of twenty-nine percent over the previous year. To make matters worse, the limitations of transgenic laboratory animals to produce reliable models of human disease are becoming more and more apparent. As a result, it is likely that scientists will increasingly seek to use animal species that are closer to us in evolutionary terms, such as transgenic dogs, pigs and primates." (p5)

Jennings, Vernon. "Transgenic Transgressions?" geneWATCH v9 n3-4, Jan 1994. p4-5.

GENETIC ENGINEERING--U.S.--PUBLIC OPINION

"Even as the first benefits of the genetic revolution begin to trickle in, people [in the U.S.] have started to wonder what those benefits will cost. A TIME/CNN poll found respondents profoundly ambivalent about genetic research and deeply divided over its applications. Asked whether they would take a genetic test that could tell them what diseases they were likely to suffer later in life, nearly as many people said they would prefer to remain ignorant (49%) as said they would like to know (50%). Most people strongly oppose human genetic engineering for any purpose except to cure disease or grow more food. A substantial majority (58%) think altering human genes is against the will of God....Of those polled, 90% said they thought it should be against the law for insurance companies to use genetic tests to decide whom to insure." (p48)

Elmer-DeWitt, Philip. "Science: The Genetic Revolution." Time v143 n3, 17 Jan 1994. p46-53. (ISSN0040-781X).

GENETICS

see also SPECIES

GENETICS--INDIGENOUS PEOPLES

"The Human Genome Diversity Project (HGDP), an informal consortium of universities and scientists in North America and Europe, has launched an effort to take blood, tissue and hair samples from hundreds of 'endangered' Indigenous human communities worldwide....HGDP's initial five-year effort hopes to collect human DNA samples from a minimum of 400 Indigenous communities, involving 10-15,000 individuals at a cost of $23-35 million. Some HGDP scientists already have begun collecting samples independently from Indigenous people in northern Chile, Southeast Asia and along the Nile. The project should be fully underway by late 1993 or early 1994. The cost of collecting DNA, at $2300 per sample, will be more than the gross national product of the world's 110 poorest countries. 'The millions of dollars to be spent on the HGDP could fund healing and community development for those Indigenous peoples,' counters the World Council of Indigenous Peoples." (p13)

"Patenting Indigenous Peoples." Earth Island Journal v8 n4, Fall 1993. p13. (ISSN1041-0406).

GENOCIDE

see also HOLOCAUST, JEWISH (1939-1945)

"Despite the overwhelming evidence, Turkey continues to deny the Armenian genocide. In an attempt to rewrite history by burying the truth, the Turkish Government is refusing to acknowledge its past guilt. This continued denial is an insult to the memory of the 1.5 million who perished at the hands of the Turks. Turkey must acknowledge its guilt in the Armenian genocide and come to terms with its past. I fear that we have...not learned anything from this experience. Hitler said 'Who will remember the Armenians?' No one did and 6 million Jews and 5 million others were exterminated. Then came Pol Pot, who killed 1 million Cambodians. Now, to date, the Bosnian Serbs have killed perhaps 200,000 people in Bosnia. When will the killing stop? George Santayana said that those who fail to...[heed] the lessons of history, are doomed to repeat them. Never has this been more true." (pS4388)

D'Amato, Alfonse (Sen.-N.Y.). "79th Anniversary of the Armenian Genocide," Congressional Record (19 Apr 1994). Daily ed. pS4385-4388. (ISSN0363-7239).

GENOCIDE--ARMENIA

"The systematic elimination of the Armenians began in 1894 evidenced by the deaths of close to 200,000 Armenians over a 2-year period. Over the next three decades, the Armenian people were methodically uprooted from their homeland, tortured, starved, and killed. April 24, 1915 marked the beginning of the infamous 1915 genocide when hundreds of Armenian religious, political, and intellectual leaders were rounded up, exiled, and eventually murdered. To further weaken the Armenian people, the 250,000 Armenians serving in the Ottoman Army during World War I were disarmed and placed in forced labor battalions where they were either starved or executed while the rest of the adult males were taken from their homes and killed. Left without any protection, the women, children, and elderly were raped, tortured and marched out of their homeland through the Southern Anatolian deserts where they suffered from extreme temperatures and lack of food and water. Over the course of the next few years, 1.5 million Armenians were killed, and more than 500,000 exiled from the Ottoman Empire." (pH2478)

Lewis, Jerry (Rep.-Calif.). "Commemorating the 79th Anniversary of the Armenian Genocide," Congressional Record (19 Apr 1994). Daily ed. pH2473-2489. (ISSN0363-7239).

GEORGIA

see LOANS--GEORGIA; OLYMPIC GAMES (1996: ATLANTA, GEORGIA); PRISONERS--GEORGIA; PUBLIC WELFARE--GEORGIA

GEORGIA--COMMERCE--MEXICO (v19)

GEORGIA (REPUBLIC)

see WAGES--GEORGIA (REPUBLIC)

GEORGIA (REPUBLIC)--ECONOMIC CONDITIONS (v19)

GEOTHERMAL POWER PLANTS

"A National Geothermal Association study found that for a typical geothermal project conducted by a U.S. developer, 40 percent of the total expenditures come back to the United States in the form of jobs or purchases. Roughly 50 percent of the expenditures remain in the host country, directly stimulating the economy. Estimates of the size of the geothermal market in developing countries range to more than $6 billion per year over the next 20 years, with Mexico ranking near the top of the list for potential development. Tapping Mexico and other export markets for geothermal could produce $20-$40 billion of direct economic benefits to the U.S. economy over the next 20 years. Mexico has the largest installed geothermal capacity in Latin America, with over 720 MW [megawatts], and an additional 120 MW under construction, and another 330 MW planned by 1999." (p65)

White, William (Deputy Secretary of Energy, U.S. Dept. of Energy). U.S. House. Committee on Energy and Commerce. "NAFTA: Energy Provisions and Environmental Implications." Hearing, 22 Sep 1993. Washington, D.C.: GPO, 1994. (ISBN0160440459). (Y4.En2/3:103:70).

GEOTHERMAL POWER PLANTS--U.S. (v19)

GERMANS

"Altogether there are reckoned to be 3.5m ethnic Germans in Eastern Europe and the former Soviet Union. These include some 300,000-500,000 in Poland, 53,000 in the Czech Republic and Slovakia and up to 220,000 in Hungary." (p20)

"Minorities: That Other Europe." Economist v329 n7843, 25 Dec 1993. p17-18,20. (ISSN0013-0613).

GERMANY

see also APPRENTICES--GERMANY; BEVERAGE CONTAINERS--GERMANY--GREAT BRITAIN--RECYCLING; COMPOST--GERMANY--U.S.; CONSUMPTION (ECONOMICS)--GERMANY--NETHERLANDS--U.S.; CRIME--GERMANY; EMPLOYEE FRINGE BENEFITS--GERMANY; FERTILITY, HUMAN--GERMANY; FIREARMS--GERMANY--CRIME; HATE CRIMES--GERMANY; INFLATION (FINANCE)--BRAZIL--GERMANY--JAPAN; LABOR COSTS--GERMANY; PESTICIDES--GERMANY; POPULATION FORECASTING--GERMANY; RACISM--GERMANY--YOUTH--PUBLIC OPINION; REFUGEES--GERMANY

GERMANY--COMMERCE--RUSSIA (v19)

GERMANY--ECONOMIC CONDITIONS (v19)

"The incumbent party, Helmut Kohl's Christian Democrats (CDU) [in Germany], has been in power for 12 years. Kohl has done well in foreign policy....He told the German people that reunification would be a piece of cake. It would cost West Germans 'petty cash.' The East would soon be a 'flourishing landscape.' Petty cash has turned out to be 150 billion Deutsche marks per year (about $88 billion). Unemployment in the East is running more than 15 percent--and the former communist party is the fastest-growing political force there, pulling better than 20 percent in recent local elections, an 'Ostalgia' that few would have predicted. Kohl is also blamed, as George Bush was, for the stagnant national economy, for unemployment rates (9 percent, nationally) that are the highest in 40 years. There is a growing fear that Germany...is becoming inefficient, that it is falling behind as an international competitor, that it can no longer afford its workers' paradise lifestyle (the highest gross wages in the world, an average eight weeks off per year, all manner of health and unemployment and pension benefits). Kohl is trailing by 8 points in recent polls and losing altitude." (p46)

Klein, Joe. "International: What's German for 'Ross Perot'?" Newsweek v123 n5, 31 Jan 1994. p46. (ISSN0028-9604).

GERMANY--EMPLOYMENT (v19)

"Of the 130,000 people working for employment companies [in Germany], 40 per cent were participating in ABM [or Arbeitsbeschaffungsmassnahmen] job creation measures, 35 per cent in vocational and retraining schemes, and 25 per cent were on short time. At the turn of the year, these companies accounted for 13 per cent of all ABM places, 14 per cent of all 'zero' short-time working and 5 per cent of people in vocational and retraining schemes. Whereas short-time work is currently no longer of importance, more recent surveys indicate that there has been a general shift towards ABM job creation measures, particularly among more recently founded employment companies." (p613)

Wiedemeyer, Michael/others. "Employment Promotion Companies in Eastern Germany: Emergency Measures or a Basis for Structural Reform?" International Labour Review v132 n5-6, 1993. p605-621. (ISSN0020-7780).

The steep rise in unemployment in Germany "was only curbed by the introduction of a broad range of labour market instruments on a scale previously unknown in Germany. Initially (summer 1991) over 2 million employees were placed on short-time working under special regulations, but when the latter expired at the beginning of 1992, it became increasingly difficult to conceal the growing disparity between labour demand and labour supply and, by mid-1993, 1.15 million people were officially registered as unemployed. A further 1.6 million were then participating in various labour market employment programmes, although this number is now in decline; some 400,000 were attending vocational and retraining courses; and 270,000 were engaged on state-run job creation schemes...compared to almost 400,000 in the previous year. In addition, some 210,000 were working short time and 900,000 were receiving supplementary early-retirement benefit (paid until they reach retirement age) or had taken early retirement under other schemes." (p606-607)

Wiedemeyer, Michael/others. "Employment Promotion Companies in Eastern Germany: Emergency Measures or a Basis for Structural Reform?" International Labour Review v132 n5-6, 1993. p605-621. (ISSN0020-7780).

GERMANY--ENVIRONMENTAL ASPECTS (v19)

GERMANY--HISTORY--UNIFICATION, 1990

"By 1989 ransom [in Germany] was big business, the price per head ranging from DM 96,000 ($60,000) for important cases to DM 4,500 for family reunification. Nearly 34,000 political prisoners and 2,000 separated children were 'bought free,' and more than a quarter of a million families were reunited, at a total cost of DM 3.5 billion." (p6-7)

Hottelet, Richard C. "What Ostpolitik Has Wrought." New Leader v76 n15, 27 Dec 1993. p6-8. (ISSN0028-6044).

GERMANY--JAPAN--U.S.--ECONOMIC CONDITIONS

"American unit-labour costs in manufacturing declined by an average of 6.4% a year...in 1985-93, compared with a rise of 6.6% in Japan and 4.2% in Germany. And American exports during the period shot ahead, rising, in volume, by an annual average of 8.6%; Japan managed only 2.3% and Germany 1.7%. Stephen Roach, chief economist at Morgan Stanley, says that productivity gains in the four previous cyclical upturns accounted for about half the growth in GDP [gross domestic product] through the first 2 1/2 years of recovery. In the ten quarters to September 1993, productivity grew at an annualised rate of 2.4%--the same rate as the economy." (p66)

"Business: Ready to Take On the World." Economist v330 n7846, 15 Jan 1994. p65-66. (ISSN0013-0613).

GERMANY--JAPAN--U.S.--MANUFACTURES (v19)

GERMANY--POLITICS AND GOVERNMENT (v19)

GERMANY (EAST)

see FERTILITY, HUMAN--GERMANY (EAST); MARRIAGE--GERMANY (EAST)

GHANA--ECONOMIC CONDITIONS

Ghana's "economy grew by an impressive 4% annually in 1988-92. But to achieve this, Ghana has been drip-fed by...[an International Monetary Fund and World Bank] determined to nurture a success in Africa. Little private foreign investment has followed, and it has gone into gold, not into manufacturing.

Ghanaians are still among Africa's poorest people: GDP [gross domestic product] per person is $450. Ghana's national savings rate averaged 7.5% of GDP over 1987-91, compared with 33% for the fast-growing East Asian 'tiger' economies; its gross domestic investment rate is only 16% of GDP." (p22)

"Africa: A Flicker of Light." Economist v330 n7853, 5 Mar 1994. p21-22,24. (ISSN0013-0613).

GIFTS--JAPAN

"The biggest issuers of gift certificates [in Japan] are department stores: they circulate over Y500 billion ($4.6 billion) worth each year--about 4% of their total annual sales of Y12 trillion ($110.6 billion). Supermarket certificates amount to Y70 billion ($646 million) annually, a relatively small component in the overall figure....Shopping centers and local market streets across the country also issue coupons. The value of certificates issued by credit companies and large travel agents is rising by 30% per year, accounting for about Y70 billion ($646 million) in certificates last year, because they can be redeemed at any department store in Japan. Coupons for specific products are increasing faster than ever. In this category, beer tickets, redeemable at any liquor store, are especially popular. Issued by retailer associations and the four major brewers, they are worth about Y215 billion ($2 billion) annually." (p46)

Moriya, Tsutomu. "Facts of Life: Gift Certificates: A Token of One's Affection." Look Japan v39 n454, Jan 1994. p46. (ISSN0456-5339).

GOLD INDUSTRY (v19)

GOLD INDUSTRY--BRAZIL

"Thousands of Brazilians are believed to be at risk from genetic defects and irreversible brain damage caused by mercury contamination in more than 2,000 gold-mining sites and 13 rivers around the country. Researchers at the University of Para, working with colleagues from universities in Denmark and Japan, found that 14% of people living near gold-mining sites in the Amazon have mercury in their bodies in excess of levels considered acceptable by the World Health Organization. If this finding is representative of the mercury levels at all sites, more than one million people in Brazil are at immediate risk. Garimpeiros use mercury in a chemical process to separate gold from other material. They inhale mercury vapour while they work, so they are at the highest risk of exposure. But the vapour also pollutes the air and falls back to earth when it rains, contaminating people and crops. Mercury spilled in rivers poisons fish and contaminates irrigated vegetables." (p19)

Trujillo, Decio, Jr. "Focus: Mining: Yanomami Suffer a Fresh Invasion." Panoscope n35, Apr 1993. p18-19. (ISSN0951-8819).

GOLD INDUSTRY--INDONESIA

"When Australian experts announced that with intensive exploitation, Indonesia could produce 50 tonnes of gold a year, this might have sounded like good news for Indonesians. But for those living near the gold deposits, it has meant dispossession, homelessness, loss of livelihood and, in one case at least, death. Since the corporate gold rush began in 1986, huge tracts of land, especially forested areas, have been granted to Indonesian and foreign mining companies. For example, one-third of Central Kalimantan, or almost 2 million hectares, has been allocated to companies under 99 different gold-mining contracts. By 1989, 25 million hectares of land in Indonesia had been granted to mining companies, though many of the contracts were later abandoned." (p16)

Sartika, Dewi. "Focus: Mining: Human Costs of a Corporate Gold Rush." Panoscope n35, Apr 1993. p16. (ISSN0951-8819).

GOLD MINES AND MINING

"Australia, with 234 tons production [of gold], this year became the world's third largest gold-producing area, after North America (477 tons) and South Africa (601 tons), pushing out the Commonwealth of Independent States." (p8)

Foster, Catherine. "Economy: New Gold Mining Activity Surges Ahead in Australia." The Christian Science Monitor v86 n34, 12 Jan 1994. p8. (ISSN0882-7729).

GOLF--U.S. (v19)

GOLF COURSES--EUROPE

"The golf course has been one of Western Europe's better job factories. The continent now has some 6m golfers, who spend an average of $1,700 a year each on their addiction. This $10 billion golf industry is already bigger than wine-making--and it accounts for roughly 150,000 jobs. A biggish course can employ 50 people directly--to say nothing of the architects, construction staff, equipment suppliers, clothing makers, golf writers and other hangers on....In 1992 alone, 255 new golf courses opened in Western Europe, nearly 6% of the total ever built there....The continent's relative beginners have been confronted with punishingly difficult courses, where woods and lakes swallow up their balls. Some 93% of French golfers have a handicap of 16 or more--ie, they hack....As America's home market matures--it had 14,375 courses at the end of 1992, 18 holes for every 22,000 golfers, compared with 18 for every 84,000 in Europe--big firms are turning their eyes to Europe." (p67)

"Business: In the Bunker." Economist v330 n7844, 8 Jan 1994. p67. (ISSN0013-0613).

GOLF COURSES--MYRTLE BEACH (SC)

"With 82 courses dotting the Grand Strand area [of Myrtle Beach, S.C.], visitors from around the world flock year-round to this golfing paradise. 'Nowhere else in the world can you drive 30 minutes and play 80 golf courses,' said John Faidley, head professional of Beachwood Golf Club, one of the first 15 courses opened in 1968....The first course--now called 'The Granddaddy,' Pine Lakes International--opened in 1927. By 1960, six courses were in place. The building progressed until a boom in the last 12 years, when more than 50 courses opened. Tourism officials say 2.77 million rounds of golf were played in the area in 1991. At the current rate, more than 100 courses and about 4 million rounds are being projected by the year 2000." (p8 secC)

Mattson, Mike. "Quality, Quantity Greet Golfers at 82 Area Courses." Ann Arbor News 30 Jan 1994. p8 secC.

GOLF COURSES--THAILAND--ENVIRONMENTAL ASPECTS

"A golf boom has been sweeping the country [of Thailand] for several years, with 140 courses now in operation, 160 more in the planning stage, and an eventual total of 1,000 predicted....In a country already ravaged by pollution, where unrestricted logging has reduced forest cover from 53 percent of the land to just 18 percent, golf courses are contributing to further the environmental damage. Drought conditions in recent years have exacerbated a serious water shortage in Thailand, and each golf course consumes enough water for a village of 1,200 people. The courses are covered mainly in Bermuda grass, which to survive in the tropics requires large amounts of fertilizers and pesticides, which contaminate underground water supplies and nearby rivers." (p45)

Sesser, Stan. "The Course of Corruption." Mother Jones v18 n3, May-Jun 1993. p44-47,67-70,72,74-76. (ISSN0362-8841).

GOLF COURSES--U.S.

The "Bush years brought about one of the greatest golf course construction booms in the history of what is now a $25-billion-a-year industry. In 1991 and 1992, new U.S. courses opened at the rate of almost one a day; today, another 2,000 are in various stages of planning or construction. But with 27 million golfers scrambling for tee times, the lords of golf insist the country's 14,000 courses are still overcrowded and that the construction of new courses must continue apace into the 21st century." (p73)

Selcraig, Bruce. "Greens Fees." Sierra v78 n4, Jul-Aug 1993. p70-77,86-87. (ISSN0161-7362).

GOLF COURSES--U.S.--ENVIRONMENTAL ASPECTS

"Environmental concerns about golf courses come at a time when the game is undergoing its biggest expansion in history. An estimated 23.5 million people in the U.S. play golf on more than 14,000 courses. An average of 300 new courses, each consuming about 140 acres, open every year, according to the National Golf Federation (NGF). South Carolina alone has 325 golf courses covering 48,000 acres. Golf is more than a sport; it's a big business, with a powerful lobby and millions of dollars to spend on public relations. The NGF says that, in 1989, Americans spent $20 billion on greens fees. Nationally, the annual price tag for golf course upkeep is $6 billion." (p56)

Chepesiuk, Ron. "The Greening of America." Wildlife Conservation v96 n4, Jul-Aug 1993. p54-59,81. (ISSN1048-4949).

"The golf industry is working hard to improve its image. In cooperation with the Audubon Society of New York State, the United States Golf Association (USGA) launched The Audubon Co-operative Sanctuary Program for Golf Courses (ACSP) in 1991. For a $100 annual fee, participating golf courses register with ACSP, which then sends them a resource inventory handbook, asking specific questions about their property (for example, course size and the nature of the surrounding habitat). The ACSP uses this data to identify existing site conditions and come up with wildlife management strategies. More than 500 golf courses in the U.S. and three foreign countries have signed up....Meanwhile, the USGA Turf Grass Research Committee has spent $3.5 million over the past nine years to develop new grasses that require less water, toxic chemicals, and care. A new and improved strain of buffalo grass that stays green with considerably less water than other turf species is expected to be available this year." (p56)

Chepesiuk, Ron. "The Greening of America." Wildlife Conservation v96 n4, Jul-Aug 1993. p54-59,81. (ISSN1048-4949).

GOVERNMENT AND BUSINESS

see INDUSTRY AND STATE

GOVERNMENT ASSISTANCE

see ECONOMIC ASSISTANCE, DOMESTIC

GOVERNMENT DEBTS

see DEBTS, PUBLIC

GOVERNMENT EMPLOYEES

see CIVIL SERVICE

GOVERNMENT SECURITIES--U.S. (v19)

GOVERNMENT SPENDING POLICY (v19)

GOVERNMENT SPENDING POLICY--AFRICA, NORTH--MIDDLE EAST (v19)

GOVERNMENT SPENDING POLICY--CHINA (v19)

GOVERNMENT SPENDING POLICY--CONGO (BRAZZAVILLE)

"Even during Congo's moderate first seven years of independence, the state's budget increased fourfold. After 1968 the budget continued to expand as the government tried to provide housing, relatively generous pensions and health care in keeping with its socialist orientation. Much of this budget was spent on the ever-expanding civil service, which grew from 3300 in 1960 to 73,000 in 1986, or more than one quarter of the work force. Moreover, the 'civil service' does not include parastatal workers, university staff, party officials or the 20,000 troops in the Congolese national army, which are another aspect of government 'over-employment.' In 1987 the civil service salaries alone absorbed 38 percent of the budget. Meanwhile, the national budget deficit ballooned to about 18 percent of GDP [gross domestic product] in 1990." (p56)

Clark, John F. "Socio-Political Change in the Republic of Congo: Political Dilemmas of Economic Reform." Journal of Third World Studies v10 n1, Spr 1993. p52-77. (ISSN8755-3449).

GOVERNMENT SPENDING POLICY--GREAT BRITAIN (v19)

GOVERNMENT SPENDING POLICY--GREAT BRITAIN--U.S. (v19)

GOVERNMENT SPENDING POLICY--KOREA (SOUTH)

"The Korean state clearly plays an integral and multifaceted role in national economic development....state policy controls the nation's transnational economic linkages. Two additional indicators of government activity are the state's tendency, since 1966, to generate more revenues (as a proportion of GDP [gross domestic product]) and to spend more money (as a proportion of GDP). For example, central government revenues (as a proportion of GDP) expanded from 15.9% in 1966 to 24.0% in 1988. This indicator reached as high as 24.9% between these two years. Total government expenditures expanded from 18.2% in 1966 to 21.3% in 1988, reaching as high as 25.3% during this time period. Both indicators could be interpreted as state strength, as the central government possesses the capacity to raise more income and to spend it on development projects. Interestingly, the Korea state often has engaged in deficit spending during the time period examined here. For 14 of the 23 years between 1966 and 1988, Korean government spending has been higher than government revenues. This spending has been largely in public corporations that invest in infrastructure related to electricity, highways, railroads, and other projects (Amsden 1989)." (p325-327)

Bradshaw, York W./others. "Transnational Economic Linkages...Dependent Development in South Korea, 1966-1988: A Time-Series Analysis." Social Forces v72 n2, Dec 1993. p315-345. (ISSN0037-7732).

GOVERNMENT SPENDING POLICY--NICARAGUA

"Among the main proposals in the [Nicaraguan] government's social policy are developing a community employment program, reviving the program to provide a glass of milk and biscuits to primary school children, prioritizing resources for basic health care, providing special attention to pregnant women, offering nutritional education, financing employment-generating projects, building houses, releasing credit for industrial and urban production and putting into effect a labor code, a family code and a new welfare law. This list contrasts sharply with the numerous social programs planned for 1992 and 1993 with outside funding, which the government failed to execute. In this period, it spent only 37% of its allocated budget. Although foreign aid for social programs has decreased by 85% in the past two years, the government's social policy offers no strategy for how to spend the scant resources expected this year." (p4)

"Politics: Government Presents Social Policy: An Incoherent Plan." Barricada Internacional v14 n369, Jan 1994. p4-5. (ISSN1013-9567).

GOVERNMENT SPENDING POLICY--RUSSIA (v19)

GOVERNMENT SPENDING POLICY--TAXATION--U.S. (v19)

GOVERNMENT SPENDING POLICY--U.S. (v19)

see also ENTITLEMENT SPENDING

"Taxes and debt [in the U.S.] have never been higher. Our unproductive, bloated Federal Government spends 24% of the GNP [gross national product]. With the states and localities, the cost reaches to almost 42%, an enormous burden on our people. For the first time in our history--in fact in the history of any Western industrial democracy--there are more people working in government at all levels than in manufacturing: 18.7 million in government and 18.1 million in manufacturing. Government employment has almost tripled in 30 years--four times faster than the population--while manufacturing especially in the last two decades, has been in steady decline." (p101)

Gross, Martin L. (Author of "The Government Racket: Washington Waste from A to Z."). U.S. Senate. Committee on Governmental Affairs. "Improving Government Organization and Performance." Hearing, 11 Mar 1993. Washington, D.C.: GPO, 1994. (ISBN0160435838). (Y4.G74/9:S.hrg.103-401).

"According to a 1993 Congressional Research Service study, every $3 billion spent on civilian economic stimulus nets 12,000 more jobs than the same spending on the military. The 'military Keynesian' strategy of relying on military spending to stimulate the economy was never the best economic strategy, but it is now one the [U.S.] literally cannot afford." (p11)

Strong, Susan C. "The Business of Peace." Boston Review v19 n2, Apr-May 1994. p11-13. (ISSN0734-2306).

Cobb County, Georgia, a suburb of Atlanta, "pulled down almost $3.4 billion from Washington in fiscal 1992. A good chunk came from the Pentagon, which owns a huge, Lockheed-operated aircraft manufacturing plant in Marietta, the county seat. Nobody would call Cobb an economic disaster area; the 1990 median family income was $41,297, 37 percent better than the national median. But even minus military contracts, Cobb was absorbing federal dollars at a $2,308-a-day clip. This was in a year when Washington spent $290.2 million more than it collected, when the national debt (the cumulation of annual deficits) had more than tripled in just 10 years and hit $4.064 trillion." (p21-22)

Overby, Peter. "White-Picket Welfare." Common Cause Magazine v19 n3, Fall 1993. p21-26. (ISSN0271-9592).

"As deficits grow, as the national debt mounts, so do the interest payments made to service that debt. Besides crowding out other fiscal priorities, these amount to a highly regressive transfer of wealth. At least 17 percent of these payments go overseas. In fact, interest payments to wealthy foreigners make up the largest foreign aid program in history. According to the President's budget, in 1993, the U.S. Government sent $41 billion overseas in interest payments. That's almost exactly twice as much as all spending on actual international programs, including foreign aid and operating our embassies abroad, which totalled $20.6 billion. Annual gross interest on the debt now runs about $300 billion, making it now the second largest item of Federal spending, and equal to almost 60 percent of all personal income taxes. In fact, if no Federal debt ever had been accumulated in the first place, the government would run a $286 billion surplus over the 1995-99 period." (pS2115)

Craig, Larry E. (Sen.-Idaho). "Balanced Budget Amendment," Congressional Record (1 Mar 1994). Daily ed. pS2081-2159. (ISSN0363-7239).

"In 1959, [U.S.] Social Security taxes and income taxes at the Federal level took 12.6 percent of the income of the average family in America. Today, those same taxes take 24.2 percent, almost twice as much. Why? Because we ran deficits, because we borrowed money, and because then Congress came back and raised taxes. If we want to reinvigorate the American dream, we have to stop the growth of Government and put Government on a budget like everybody else. The only way we are going to do that is with a balanced budget amendment to the Constitution." (pS2093)

Gramm, Phil (Sen.-Tex.). "Balanced Budget Amendment," Congressional Record (1 Mar 1994). Daily ed. pS2081-2159. (ISSN0363-7239).

"In the last 30 years, the [U.S.] Federal Government has balanced its budget only once. For the last 25 years, Congress has maintained a perfect record of spending more than it raised. The Congressional Budget Office has estimated as far out as the year 2004 when the annual deficit will be $365 billion and interest payments will be $334 billion. The interest on the national debt will increase by nearly $1.7 trillion by the year 2000. This vast sum could finance the entire 1994 budget. In fact, if we could somehow eliminate the interest payments, we could close the budget deficit. In 1992, we sent nearly $40 billion overseas in interest payments. Compare this to the $38 billion spent, annually on all nutrition programs, including food stamps, Women, Infants and Children and school lunch programs." (pS2097)

McConnell, Mitch (Sen.-Ky.). "Balanced Budget Amendment," Congressional Record (1 Mar 1994). Daily ed. pS2081-2159. (ISSN0363-7239).

"The [U.S.] debt is $4.4 trillion...our Federal budget spends $1.5 trillion each year....In 10 minutes' time, we will pay $5.5 million in interest payments in this Nation. If we did not have to pay this interest, that would equate to adding 100 police officers to State and local governments. In just 10 minutes' time, that $5.5 million that we are spending in interest would pay to immunize more than 45,000 children. It would provide a year of Head Start for almost 1,500 kids. In the 4 days that the Senate has debated the balanced budget amendment, we have paid $3.2 billion in interest. That $3.2 billion could have reduced taxes $40 for every taxpaying family, $10 a day." (pS2069)

Kempthorne, Dirk (Sen.-Idaho). "Balanced Budget Amendment," Congressional Record (1 Mar 1994). Daily ed. pS2045-2081. (ISSN0363-7239).

"The record of the last 43 years shows that the American economy has been willing to give up about 19.5 cents out of every dollar it produces--period. Congress can try to raise revenues by raising taxes, but higher taxes reduce incentives to work, save, and invest. That means economic activity ebbs and jobs are lost. Ultimately, the government still gets about 19.5 cents out of each dollar, but there are fewer and fewer dollars. In the short term, tax hikes may cause additional dollars to flow into the Treasury. But these dollars have not gone to lower the deficit. The record clearly shows that for every dollar of taxes raised, Congress spends that dollar and more." (pS2090)

Mack, Connie (Sen.-Fla.). "Balanced Budget Amendment," Congressional Record (1 Mar 1994). Daily ed. pS2081-2159. (ISSN0363-7239).

"This year, interest on the debt will gobble up nearly 14 percent of our total Federal outlays....Entitlements consume another 54 percent of the budget, and by 1998 entitlement spending will surpass the $1 trillion mark and consume nearly 60 percent of all Federal outlays. Discretionary spending--the money that we actually debate every year--makes up a little more than a third of our current budget. And that percentage shrinks every year as a larger and larger share must go to mandatory interest payments and entitlement benefits. Defense spending makes up less than 20 percent of outlays. International spending programs is slightly more than 1 percent and domestic spending is about 17 percent." (pS2099)

Kerrey, Robert J. (Sen.-Nebr.). "Balanced Budget Amendment," Congressional Record (1 Mar 1994). Daily ed. pS2081-2159. (ISSN0363-7239).

"Since 1969, [U.S.] Federal spending has increased on an annual basis more than 800 percent. Now, in 1969, it was a guns-and-butter year, and yet the entire Federal spending from 1969 through 1973, 5 years, is less than Bill Clinton's 1994 budget for 1 year. Sixty percent of next year's deficit will consist of the new spending that Congress has added to 1993 levels. Spending is running out of control. And yet the Clinton budget proposes additional spending of $1.475 trillion on top of the current levels for the years 1994 through 1998. Spending is out of control, and record tax increases are occasioned by this insatiable appetite for more and more spending." (pH1382)

Cox, Christopher (Rep.-Calif.). "Balanced Budget Constitutional Amendment," Congressional Record (16 Mar 1994). Daily ed. pH1373-1414. (ISSN0363-7239).

"If we [the U.S.] take all the dollars that we have spent to win the cold war since the time Harry Truman first decided it was necessary to contain the Soviet Union until it changed, and, if we divide that money by the number of taxpaying American families in the country today, the cost of winning that war was $82,000 per family." (pH10881)

Obey, David R. (Rep.-Wis.). "Government Reform and Savings Act of 1993." Congressional Record (22 Nov 1993). Daily ed. pH10729-10893. (ISSN0363-7239).

"Take four programs: Social Security, other Government civilian retirement, military retirement, and Medicare-Medicaid. Those four, plus interest, in 1963 were 24 percent of our budget. In 1973, they were 37 percent; those four, plus interest. In 1983, 47 percent; 1993, 56 percent. Absent any change in the law, in the year 2003, they will be 69 percent of all the money we spend. That means one of two things. Either all other programs get squeezed--Amtrak, education, the Environmental Protection Agency, the Forest Service, airport safety....or we raise taxes to pay for it, or we borrow." (pS1913)

Packwood, Bob (Sen.-Oreg.). "Balanced Budget Amendment," Congressional Record (25 Feb 1994). Daily ed. pS1895-1915. (ISSN0363-7239).

The February 9, 1994 "NEW YORK TIMES had an editorial which addressed the trade-offs we make inadvertently. It points out the fact that despite the $4 trillion Federal debt and the sacrifices that the President's budget calls on Americans to make, the Pentagon is actually scheduled to get more money next year than this. The Clinton administration is seeking $264 billion in defense spending authority for 1995, up $2.8 billion from 1994. As the TIMES points out, 'Unless Mr. Clinton finds the courage to trim defense, he will be forced to short-change domestic investment for years to come.' Those are the same investments we need to make if we are going to create jobs and raise U.S. living standards. They are the investments we need to make to increase funding for education and to fight crime." (pS1259)

Kerrey, J. Robert (Sen.-Nebr.). "Bosnia," Congressional Record (9 Feb 1994). Daily ed. pS1257-1269. (ISSN0363-7239).

"In the period 1980-88, taxes were reduced and military expenditures doubled. The result has been large federal deficits and diversion of funds from the domestic economy into military spending. As of July 13, 1989, our federal debt had increased to $2.8-trillion--a heavy economic and personal burden. The diversion of funds into military activities made us less competitive in world markets by sacrificing research, inventiveness, quality, and favorable pricing. The Japanese, not burdened by military requirements, picked up the gap, increased research and development for civilian goods, and sharply increased their share of sales in international markets. As a result, the U.S. trade balance slipped from a surplus of $15.5-billion in 1980 to a deficit of $119.1-billion in 1988." (p7)

Platt, Stanley K. "The Follies of the Eighties." Human Quest v208 n1, Jan-Feb 1994. p7. (ISSN0897-8786).

"While Clinton has promised to reduce military spending by $60 billion over the next five years, that amount is minuscule when one looks at the larger numbers. Military spending will only fall from $1.42 trillion to $1.36 trillion over this period....During the Cold War, 60% of our military expenses went to defend the United States and its allies against the 'Soviet Threat.' This so-called threat has evaporated, yet the Pentagon plans to spend only 17% less in 1997 than it did in 1992. Only 22.6% of the military budget goes for the defense of U.S. territory--56% goes to protect NATO countries, 12% goes to protect Japan and the Pacific Rim, and 8.6% to protect the Middle East. The U.S. is now spending 50% more on defending Europe than it spends on economic development, the environment, housing, education, and children combined." (p1)

Bound, Aida/Ickowitz, Amy. "Where Is the Common Sense in the Budget? Military Budget." Program & Legislative Action Apr-May 1993. p1-2.

"Federal spending now represents about 22 percent of gross domestic product [in the U.S.] and is expected to drift down to about 21 percent over the next five years. In the 1960s, federal spending averaged 19.1 percent of GDP [gross domestic product]; for the 1970s and 1980s, the figures were 20.6 percent and 23.1 percent, respectively. But although federal spending now represents a bigger share of the economy than in the 1960s and 1970s and only a slightly smaller share than in the 1980s, a pronounced change has taken place in its composition. In a nutshell, the government today spends more on entitlement (chiefly benefit) programs and on net interest, and less on other activities, than in the past...." (p34)

U.S. Congressional Budget Office. "The Budget Outlook." The Economic and Budget Outlook: Fiscal Years 1995-1999 Jan 1994. Washington, D.C.: GPO, 1994.

GRADUATES, COLLEGE

see COLLEGE GRADUATES

GRAIN TRADE (v19)

see also CORN INDUSTRY; SORGHUM INDUSTRY; WHEAT TRADE

"The production of grain, perhaps the most basic economic measure of human well-being, increased 2.6 fold from 1950 to 1984. Expanding at nearly 3 percent per year, it outstripped population growth, raising per capita grain consumption by 40 percent over the 34-year period, improving nutrition and boosting consumption of livestock products--meat, milk, eggs, and cheese--throughout the world. That period came to an end, ironically, around the time the United States withdrew its funding from the United Nations Population Fund. During the eight years since 1984, world grain output has expanded perhaps one percent per year. In per capita terms, this means grain production has shifted from its steady rise over the previous 34 years to a decline of one percent per year since then--a particularly troubling change both because grain is a basic source of human sustenance and because of the likely difficulty in reversing it...." (p20)

Brown, Lester R. "A Decade of Discontinuity." World Watch v6 n4, Jul-Aug 1993. p19-26. (ISSN0896-0615).

GRAIN TRADE--CHINA (v19)

GRAIN TRADE--EUROPE--RUSSIA

"Russia produces 700 kilograms of grain per capita while Western Europe produces about 500 kilograms per capita. Yet, Western Europe exports grain, whereas Russia imports it. The key element of this problem in Russia, the irrational use of and losses in harvested agricultural products, is caused by the lack of infrastructure (e.g. roads and storage) and the antiquated food processing industry." According to an estimate by Sergei Bobylev, "the present volume of losses amounts to 25-40 percent of agricultural products." (p31)

Bobylev, Sergei. "Sustainable Agriculture: An Ecological Approach to Russian Agriculture." Surviving Together v11 n3, Fall 1993. p31-32. (ISSN0859-6286).

GRAIN TRADE--EUROPEAN ECONOMIC COMMUNITY--U.S. (v19)

GRAIN TRADE--MEXICO--U.S. (v19)

GRAIN TRADE--RUSSIA--U.S. (v19)

GRAIN TRADE--U.S.

U.S. "Wheat exports rose to 35.6 million tons, valued at $4.7 billion. Although there were declines to China, the FSU [former Soviet Union], and Japan, expanded shipments to Latin America, Southeast Asia, and Africa more than offset the declines. Rice exports increased almost 600,000 tons, valued at nearly $800 million. The United States exported 30,000 tons to Japan in 1993, but gains to other markets pushed rice higher in 1993. The largest gain was to Iran which imported 200,000 tons of rice, up from 46,000 in 1992. Exports also grew to Latin America, Europe, and Africa." (p2)

U.S. Dept. of Agriculture/Greene, Joel. "Agricultural Exports Decline in 1993." Foreign Agricultural Trade of the United States Jan-Feb 1994. p2.

GRAIN TRADE--U.S.--TRANSPORTATION (v19)

GRANDPARENTS--U.S. (v19)

GRAPEFRUIT INDUSTRY--U.S. (v19)

GRAZING--U.S.--FEES (v19)

"The current [grazing fee] rate is $1.86 per animal unit month, enough forage to feed a cow and calf, five sheep or a horse. The fee will go up to $1.98 on March 1 because of normal fluctuations in the formula used to determine the rate. President Clinton's fiscal 1995 budget assumes that the fee will initially go up to $2.76 per animal unit month. [Interior Secretary Bruce] Babbitt's fee proposal, which is still on the table, would raise grazing fees over three years to $4.28." (p430)

Camia, Catalina. "Government & Commerce: Environment: Babbitt Offers Interest Groups More Input in Lands Policy." Congressional Quarterly Weekly Report v52 n7, 19 Feb 1994. p430. (ISSN0010-5910).

"While national and state livestock associations claim that [a grazing] fee increase and land-use reforms will drive ranch families off the land, Reid says the vast majority of ranchers will be unaffected. The compromise bill would raise grazing fees over the next three years from $1.86 to $3.45 per animal unit month (AUM). That is barely a third of the average fee on private land in the West and below state fees in all but Arizona. Small ranchers will be least affected. According to the Bureau of Land Management, 42 percent of all ranchers who use BLM land have permits for 100 AUMs or less. For them, the grazing fee increase will cost at most a total of $53 the first year, $106 the second and $159 thereafter." (p3)

Hinchman, Steve. "Western Roundup: Senate Dukes It Out with Babbitt." High Country News v25 n21, 15 Nov 1993. p3. (ISSN0191-5657).

GRAZING DISTRICTS--OREGON--PUBLIC OPINION

"Although the media sometimes have biased the problem associated with livestock grazing on federal lands, the majority of the public appears to be rather apathetic about this issue. In a survey of recreationists on federal rangelands in Oregon, most did not object to limited livestock grazing under extensive management schemes....However, they showed a strong aversion to areas intensively managed for livestock involving heavy fencing, brush control, seeding, etc. There was a tolerance for livestock in upland grassland areas but heavy intolerance for livestock around streams and mountain meadows. With the exception of anglers, there was a negative response to fences. Anglers reacted more favorably to fences than other groups, because they perceived exclusion of cattle vital to maintenance of the fishery. In this survey 84 percent of the recreationists were unfamiliar with the term multiple use, and more than 98 percent showed a complete lack of understanding of what range management practices involve." (p166-167)

Holcheck, Jerry L. "Policy Changes on Federal Rangelands: A Perspective." Journal of Soil and Water Conservation v48 n3, May-Jun 1993. p166-174. (ISSN0022-4561).

GRAZING DISTRICTS--U.S.

"Only 2 percent, or about 27,000, of the nation's ranchers use public lands. Additionally, the grazing program is dominated by large corporate ranchers, not by the small independent rancher revered in Western myth. A recent General Accounting Office report shows that only 10 percent of permit-holders on BLM [Bureau of Land Management] land account for almost two-thirds of the animals allowed to graze those lands. On Forest Service lands, only 6 percent of permit-holders control about 50 percent of the cattle." (p4-5)

Cusick, Steve. "After Years of Abuse, Federal Policy on Western Lands Is Ripe for Reform." Audubon Activist v8 n3, Nov 1993. p1,4-5. (ISSN0898-915X).

"Based on 1988 data, about 2.6 percent of the livestock feed needs in the U.S. are provided by federal lands....However, in the 11 western states federal lands provide for 12 percent of the total forage requirement. Livestock producers in Nevada are most dependent on federal lands (43 percent). Although total amount of forage provided by federal lands is small in comparison with the total forage base, some 20 to 22 percent of the yearling beef cattle in the USA have spent a portion of their lives on federal lands....Because of a lack of alternative forage resources, federal lands play a vital role in meeting seasonal livestock forage needs in many western states. Therefore, it is probable federal lands have a bigger role in meat production in the 11 western states than indicated by their percent of total feed needs." (p170)

Holecheck, Jerry L. "Policy Changes on Federal Rangelands: A Perspective." Journal of Soil and Water Conservation v48 n3, May-Jun 1993. p166-174. (ISSN0022-4561).

"U.S. Department of Interior (1990) data...show 40 to 45 percent of federal rangelands are conservatively grazed and would generally be considered in satisfactory condition by ranchers and environmentalists alike. Another 35 to 40 percent are grazed heavier than ideal for wildlife, long-term ecological sustainability, and maximum economic return, but the condition of these lands is either stable or in a very slow decline. About 15 to 25 percent are undergoing serious degradation from improperly controlled livestock grazing. Interestingly enough, the motive for heavy grazing (higher profits) is based on a falsehood. Various studies from different types of rangelands have shown that although heavy grazing may be more profitable than conservative grazing for a few years, in the long run (5 to 10 years) it generally gives a lower rate of return and increases financial risk...." (p168)

Holecheck, Jerry L. "Policy Changes on Federal Rangelands: A Perspective." Journal of Soil and Water Conservation v48 n3, May-Jun 1993. p166-174. (ISSN0022-4561).

GRAZING RIGHTS

see PASTURE, RIGHT OF

GREAT BRITAIN

see also ABORTION--GREAT BRITAIN; ADVERTISING--CIGARETTE INDUSTRY--GREAT BRITAIN; ALCOHOLIC BEVERAGES--TAXATION--FRANCE--GREAT BRITAIN; AUTOMOBILE INDUSTRY AND TRADE--GREAT BRITAIN; BEVERAGE CONTAINERS--GERMANY--GREAT BRITAIN--RECYCLING; BRAND NAME PRODUCTS--CANADA--GREAT BRITAIN--U.S.; CHILD SUPPORT--GREAT BRITAIN; COUNTERFEITS AND COUNTERFEITING--GREAT BRITAIN--U.S.; CRIME--GREAT BRITAIN--SAFETY MEASURES; DEFORESTATION--GREAT BRITAIN; DEPARTMENT STORES--GREAT BRITAIN; DOWN'S SYNDROME--GREAT BRITAIN; EDUCATION, HIGHER--GREAT BRITAIN; EXERCISE--GREAT BRITAIN--U.S.; FIREARMS--GREAT BRITAIN;

FORESTS AND FORESTRY--GREAT BRITAIN; IMMIGRANTS--AUSTRALIA--CANADA--GREAT BRITAIN--U.S.; INCOME--GREAT BRITAIN; MINORITIES--EMPLOYMENT--GREAT BRITAIN; NARCOTICS, CONTROL OF--GREAT BRITAIN; NUCLEAR ENERGY--GREAT BRITAIN; POSTAL SERVICE--GREAT BRITAIN; PRISON SENTENCES--GREAT BRITAIN; RETAIL TRADE--GREAT BRITAIN; SELF-EMPLOYED--CANADA--GREAT BRITAIN; SINGLE-PARENT FAMILY--GREAT BRITAIN; TAXATION--GREAT BRITAIN; TRADE-UNIONS--GREAT BRITAIN; TRAFFIC CONGESTION--GREAT BRITAIN; UNEMPLOYMENT--AUSTRALIA--GREAT BRITAIN; VIOLENCE--GREAT BRITAIN; WIND POWER--GREAT BRITAIN; WOMEN--EMPLOYMENT--GREAT BRITAIN

GREAT BRITAIN--ARMED FORCES (v19)

GREAT BRITAIN--ARMED FORCES--APPROPRIATIONS AND EXPENDITURES

"The Labour Party used to argue that Britain should cut its defence spending to the levels of continental Europe. A Conservative government is going some way towards implementing that policy. Having spent 5.3% of GDP [gross domestic product] on defence ten years ago, Britain spent 3.8% in 1992-93, and will, on current plans, spend 2.9% in 1996-97. That would be, proportionally, as much as Portugal now spends, and less than France--though substantially more than Italy, Germany or Spain. Still more cuts are on the way....Last December the Treasury announced that it wanted to trim 750m [pounds sterling] ($1.1 billion) from the 22.8 billion [pounds sterling] defence budget that had been planned for 1996-97." (p64)

"Britain: Defence Spending: Postponing Pain." Economist v331 n7861, 30 Apr 1994. p64-65. (ISSN0013-0613).

GREAT BRITAIN--ECONOMIC CONDITIONS (v19)

"Believe it or not, Britain's recovery has been under way for almost two years. The snag is that, yet again, Britons are consuming too much and investing too little. Since the recession ended in the first quarter of 1992, consumer spending has risen by nearly 5%. In contrast, business investment has continued to stagnate: in the fourth quarter of last year it was roughly 20% below its peak in early 1990....This time the economy seems even more unbalanced than in the comparable period of the previous recovery. Between the first quarter of 1981 (when the recession ended) and the end of 1982, investment expanded by 16%, while consumer spending rose by only 2.9%....Why has investment remained so subdued?...Corporate debt rose from 100% of GDP [gross domestic product] in 1980 to more than 170% in 1992. In contrast, American companies' debt stood at only 70% of America's GDP at its peak in 1990. The need of British firms to repay some of their debt is the best explanation for their limited investment plans." (p64)

"Britain: The Economy: Invest or Die." Economist v330 n7853, 5 Mar 1994. p64-65. (ISSN0013-0613).

"Look no further than the consumer for the cause of Britain's climb out of recession. Since the recovery began in the second quarter of 1992, consumer spending has risen by 4.8%, accounting for virtually all the increase in GDP [gross domestic product]. Investment, in contrast, is still lower than it was two years ago. This upturn has depended much more on the consumer than the previous one in the early 1980s: in the first seven quarters of that recovery, consumption increased by only 2.4%." (p67)

"Britain: Waiting for the Whammy." Economist v330 n7856, 26 Mar 1994. p67-68. (ISSN0013-0613).

GREAT BRITAIN--EMIGRATION AND IMMIGRATION (v19)

GREAT BRITAIN--MANUFACTURES

"Ever since British manufacturing began a long decline relative to other countries, there has been no shortage of those peddling a quick fix--or moaning and fretting. The results, to say the least, have proved disappointing. In no other large developed country has manufacturing output remained virtually static over the past two decades. In the same period manufacturing output in Germany grew by 25%, in France 27%, Italy 85% and Japan 119%." (p65)

"Britain: Competitiveness: Hooray for Intervention." Economist v331 n7861, 30 Apr 1994. p65. (ISSN0013-0613).

GREAT BRITAIN--RACE RELATIONS

"British Crime Survey figures record what they call [racial] 'incidents'. Incidents include attacks but cover a much wider range of behaviour. The Metropolitan Police state that 31% of incidents relate to criminal damage, 24% to abusive language, 17% to assaults causing injury, and 13% to common assaults which result in no visible injury. The 'victims' of racial incidents in the Metropolitan Police area are 49% Asian, 23% black, 22% white and 6% other." (p4)

"Race Quango's Climb-Down on Attack Figures." Freedom Today v18 n6, Dec 1993. p4.

GREAT BRITAIN--SOCIAL CONDITIONS (v19)

GREAT BRITAIN--U.S.--EMPLOYMENT

"During the 1980s service-sector jobs grew by more than enough to offset the decline in manufacturing employment (although in the recession of the early 1990s service-sector jobs fell in some countries). Nor does the increase merely reflect burgeoning government spending. Indeed, the private sector provided the bulk of new service jobs: in the 1980s the state's share of service-sector employment fell from 36% to 27% in Britain and from 23% to 20% in America....In fact, in both America and Britain there have been more jobs in services than in manufacturing for the whole of this century. And services' share of jobs is still growing....In 1970 27% of America's workers were in manufacturing; by 1993 the figure had fallen to 16%. Meanwhile, services' share had climbed from 66% to 78%. In Britain there has been a similar shift: since 1970 the proportion of jobs in manufacturing has dropped from 37% to 20%, while that in services has risen from just over half to 73%." (p91)

"Schools Brief: The Manufacturing Myth." Economist v330 n7855, 19 Mar 1994. p91-92. (ISSN0013-0613).

GREAT LAKES

"The Great Lakes watershed is home to some 100 species and 31 ecological communities that are rare or imperiled worldwide. Half of them are either unique or best represented in the 210,000-square-mile basin, according to a recent report by the Nature Conservancy, a private environmental group. At least 38 million Americans and Canadians rely on the lakes to some degree for their livelihood, drinking water, and recreation. Despite reports of 'Rust Belt' decline, the basin is still the industrial hub for North America, churning out more paper, steel, and automobiles than any other region." (p12)

Tyson, James L. "Cover Story: Delicate Ecosystem, Heavy Industry." The Christian Science Monitor v86 n75, 14 Mar 1994. p11-13. (ISSN0882-7729).

GREECE

see FIREARMS--GREECE--CRIME

GREECE--ECONOMIC CONDITIONS (v19)

GREEN MARKETING

"In...Oregon, the 400 envirotech companies currently employ nearly 14,000 people. Moreover, the average salary paid in the envirotech field is around $31,000--nearly $9,000 higher than the next closest industry. Both numbers will grow in the next 10 years. In fact, all signs point to a boom before the turn of the century for U.S. environmental technology companies. The global envirotech market is currently worth $200 billion a year, and is expected to reach $600 billion over the next 6 years. Hundreds of American companies currently have a substantial lead over their foreign competitors in the production of

environmental technologies, goods, and services." (pH2391)
Furse, Elizabeth (Rep.-Oreg.). "Environmental Export Promotion Act of 1994," Congressional Record (18 Apr 1994). Daily ed. pH2387-2392. (ISSN0363-7239).

"The international market for environmental goods and services is growing rapidly. It currently stands at $270 billion annually, and is likely to grow to $400-$600 billion by the end of the decade." (pH2389)
Gejdenson, Sam (Rep.-Conn.). "Environmental Export Promotion Act of 1994," Congressional Record (18 Apr 1994). Daily ed. pH2387-2392. (ISSN0363-7239).

GREEN MARKETING--EUROPE (v19)

GREEN MARKETING--PUBLIC OPINION

"Environmental concerns are growing in many countries, so adding environmental benefits to your products may also add appeal in the global marketplace. Arguments against the North American Free Trade Agreement often pointed out looser environmental regulatory and enforcement practices in Mexico, for example. But public concern about the environment is three times greater in Mexico than it is in the U.S. according to a 1992 study conducted by Roper for S.C. Johnson and Sons. It is twice as great in Canada. In both Mexico and Canada, two-thirds of adults agree that environmental protection laws have not gone far enough, compared with fewer than half of U.S. adults." (p29)
Stisser, Peter. "A Deeper Shade of Green." American Demographics v16 n3, Mar 1994. p24-29. (ISSN0163-4089).

GREEN MARKETING--U.S. (v19)

"In 1990, fewer than half of Americans fell into the three environmentally active camps. In 1993, 55 percent do. Other surveys confirm this trend. Two-thirds of Americans have noticed environmental claims on packaging in the past year, and half have purchased 'green' products since 1990." (p26)
Stisser, Peter. "A Deeper Shade of Green." American Demographics v16 n3, Mar 1994. p24-29. (ISSN0163-4089).

"If U.S. firms manage to capture 20 percent of the growth anticipated in the overseas environmental market, an estimated 300,000 new American jobs will be created over the next 7 years. In...Connecticut, for instance, increased envirotech exports will increase employment at over 500 environmental firms throughout the State." (pH2389)
Gejdenson, Sam (Rep.-Conn.). "Environmental Export Promotion Act of 1994," Congressional Record (18 Apr 1994). Daily ed. pH2387-2392. (ISSN0363-7239).

"Cleaning up the environment and preventing pollution creates jobs. Already in the US, 70,000 environmental companies with sales of $130 billion employ one million workers. Internationally, revenues are $270 billion and climbing. A lead trade publication, THE ENVIRONMENTAL BUSINESS JOURNAL, projects the global environmental industry will grow 51 percent from 1991-1996, reaching over $400 billion in revenue, making it one of the biggest industries in the world." (p12)
LeCain, Eleanor Mulloney. "Feature: Green Business Is Booming." Positive Alternatives v3 n4, Sum 1993. p12-13. (ISSN1065-0075).

GREENHOUSE EFFECT, ATMOSPHERIC--CHINA

"Currently, China's contribution to the world total of global emissions of greenhouse gases amounts to about seven percent. But if China continues its present course of explosive expansion, if world growth rates slow, and if China does not aggressively develop a noncarbon energy system, in a worst case scenario the nation could account for 40 percent of world emissions by the year 2050 (Lu Yingzhong, 1989.)" (p1)
Wilson, Nancy C. "China Faces Hard Energy Choices: Booming Economy, Soaring Emissions." Climate Alert v6 n3, May-Jun 1993. p1,4-7.

"While China's current greenhouse gas emission numbers are low, the nation is the fastest growing major contributor to the gases associated with global warming. With its potential fossil fuel consumption and growing population it is possible total Chinese CO2 emissions will reach 1.6 billion tons by 2020 and 2.25 by the year 2050. This 2050 estimate is uncomfortably close to the present CO2 emissions total from all industrial countries of 2.7 billion tons." (p4)
Wilson, Nancy C. "China Faces Hard Energy Choices: Booming Economy, Soaring Emissions." Climate Alert v6 n3, May-Jun 1993. p1,4-7.

GREENHOUSE GASES

"The United States still lags behind several countries that adopted ambitious climate plans prior to the Earth Summit. The Netherlands has a detailed, comprehensive program to cut its emissions 5 percent by 2000, and Denmark is aiming for a 20 percent cut by 2005. And to be fair, these countries start with per capita emissions that are already 30 percent below the U.S. level. Measured by its own goal of 'stabilizing' emissions, the U.S. plan still falls short, since it allows production of the most important greenhouse gas, carbon dioxide, to rise 3 percent by 2000, and even more in later years. (The European Community, which has also promised to stabilize emissions, now projects a similar overshoot--a 4 percent increase by 2000.) The U.S. plan is also a far cry from what scientists believe ultimately will be required to stabilize the earth's climate--a 60 to 80 percent cut in global emissions, replacing most of today's fossil fuels with renewable energy." (p2)
Flavin, Christopher. "Editorial: Climate Change in Washington." World Watch v7 n1, Jan 1994. p2. (ISSN0896-0615).

GREYHOUND RACING--U.S.

"Greyhound racing is the sixth most-attended spectator sport in the United States. According to statistics from the National Greyhound Association (NGA), over 45,000 dogs race at 61 tracks around the country annually. To maintain this business, an astonishing number of greyhounds, 48,263 in 1991, are bred and registered each year. Of these dogs, as many as 9,648, or 20%, of the greyhounds born are not registered as racers. Including these 9,648 dogs, 22,500 former racers at the tracks, and 16,115 registered racers for whom no positions are available on the tracks, a total of 48,263 greyhounds are disposed of each year. Only 7,000 of these are adopted." (p14)
"Shelter Shop: New Book Encourages Adoption of Racing Greyhounds." Shelter Sense v16 n4, Apr 1993. p14. (ISSN0734-3078).

GRIZZLY BEAR

"The [U.S. Federal] government on Dec. 9 released its 180-page plan for saving grizzlies in the 28,000-square-mile Yellowstone region and other parts of the Northern Rockies. The document took five years and three drafts to complete, and will serve as a 'cookbook' for bear recovery for the next five years. Grizzlies were listed as a threatened species in 1975, after populations in the lower 48 states dropped from 100,000 to less than 1,000. The new document is an update of a 1982 plan to restore bears to self-sustaining numbers. It covers 38,000 square miles and six recovery zones in the United States and Canada. An estimated 236 grizzlies currently populate the Yellowstone region, and females with cubs live in 16 management areas." (p10)
Welch, Craig. "Grizzly Recovery Plan Could Doom Bears, Critics Say." High Country News v25 n24, 27 Dec 1993. p10. (ISSN0191-5657).

GRIZZLY BEAR--ALASKA

"Today there is some kind of conservation officer 'behind every bush,' yet as wildlife bureaus grow, our most magnificent mammal retreats steadily toward the Canadian border. Of the 6000 grizzlies officially reported as remaining in areas owned by the United States, 5000 are in Alaska. Only five states have any at all. There seems to be a tacit assumption that if grizzlies survive in Canada and Alaska, that is good enough." (p20)

Leopold, Aldo. "The Land Ethic." Carrying Capacity Network v4 n1, 1994. p10-24. (ISSN1066-5404).

GRIZZLY BEAR--BRITISH COLUMBIA

"Estimates of grizzly [bear] numbers in B.C. [British Columbia] are so disparate as to be practically useless: they vary from 3,000 (independent researchers) to 12,000 (Wildlife Branch). About 6,000 is the figure The Grizzly Project is most comfortable with. B.C. is one of the last places in the world where grizzly bears are hunted legally, and legal hunting is the major cause of mortality. The 'magic number' the Wildlife Branch works with is a ceiling of 4 percent mortality from all causes, further broken down to 6 percent for males and 2 percent for females. We are far from that. For example, in 1989 at least 765 grizzlies were killed by humans in B.C., an amount equal to the entire U.S. grizzly population. Of these, 337 were hunted legally, 85 were estimated to have been wounded by hunters and not recovered, 68 were killed as 'nuisance bears' (mostly around logging and mining camps), an estimated 260 were poached, and 15 were killed in accidents with vehicles and machinery. Even using the government's inflated 12,000 population estimate, we lost 6.3 percent of our grizzlies in that one year. If you use the more realistic 6,000 figure, it's about 13 percent. This does not even count the many dozens of cubs orphaned when their mothers are killed, legally or illegally, intentionally or not." (p7)

Batycki, Candace. "Reports from the Field: Biting the Bullet for Grizzly Survival in B.C." Northwest Conservation Sum 1993. p7-8.

GRIZZLY BEAR--NORTH CASCADES NATIONAL PARK (WASH)

"Although exceedingly rare today, grizzlies once roamed throughout the North Cascades and most of what is now Washington state....A small population of grizzly bears inhabits the North Cascades, perhaps 10 to 20 on the U.S. side, and a dozen or so in British Columbia. Renowned grizzly bear biologists Frank and John Craighead have identified seven characteristics of ecosystem 'suitability' for maintaining viable grizzly populations. These are space, isolation from humans, sanitation, denning habitat, safety from human-induced mortality, an abundance of vegetation or habitat types, and food....The North Cascades Ecosystem consists of over 6.5 million acres in the United States, 68 percent of which has no open roads and 39 percent which is protected as parks or wilderness, and an adjacent 5 million acres of habitat in British Columbia....Jon Almack [member of an Interagency Grizzly Bear Working Group] has estimated that the North Cascades core--the land already protected in parks and wilderness--can sustain anywhere from 85 to 130 bears. Biologists believe, however, that at least 1,670 to 2,000 bears are needed to sustain a single viable population." (p14)

Snetsinger, Susan. "The North Cascades through the Eyes of the Grizzly." Northwest Conservation Win 1994. p14.

GRIZZLY BEAR--U.S.

"Texas lost its last grizzly about 1890, California in 1922, Oregon 1931, and Arizona 1935....Canada has 25,000 or so [grizzly bears], and Alaska another 40,000. In the lower 48 states, however, grizzly populations are less secure. The big bears are tough to count, but best guessers put the total at fewer than 1,000. Grizzly territory has been chopped by humans into unconnected islands of habitat. Today, the big bears exist on a mere 2 percent of their original range in the lower 48, in five separate and isolated populations (although some adjoin Canadian grizzly habitat): By far the largest population, at least 391 grizzlies, inhabits the Northern Continental Divide area of Montana, which encompasses about 9,600 square miles along the continent's backbone. Glacier National Park and the Bob Marshall Wilderness are part of this ecosystem. A minimum of 228 grizzlies roam 9,500 square miles in Yellowstone National Park and the surrounding territory in Wyoming, Montana, and Idaho. About 1,000 mountainous square miles in northern Idaho, known as the Selkirk ecosystem, contain perhaps 25 grizzlies. Named for the Cabinet Mountains and the Yaak River in northwest Montana, the Cabinet-Yaak ecosystem covers 2,600 square miles and has 15 to 20 grizzlies. A few grizzlies remain in the North Cascades, in the state of Washington." (p48)

Turbak, Gary. "Getting Along with Griz." Wildlife Conservation v96 n6, Nov-Dec 1993. p44-53,79. (ISSN1048-4949).

GROCERY TRADE--TAIWAN

"In 1987 a mere 3% of the Taiwanese population bought groceries in a 'modern' shop, such as a supermarket. By 1993 that figure had risen to 50%." (p64)

"Business: Asian Retailing: Teach Me Shopping." Economist v329 n7842, 18 Dec 1993. p64-65. (ISSN0013-0613).

GROSS DOMESTIC PRODUCT

"In the early 1990s Austrian per capita GDP [gross domestic product] was $16,592, Finland's $23,196, Norway's $21,334, and Sweden's $22,443, compared with the EC [European Community] average of $14,805. They are all small countries of between 4-8.5 million inhabitants, with open economies in which trade accounts for 35-40% of GDP, most of it (55-60%) with the Union." (p20)

Lintner, Valerio. "The Economics of EU Enlargement." Economics and Business Education v2 n5, Spr 1994. p17-22.

GROSS DOMESTIC PRODUCT--ISRAEL

"Services [in Israel] make up 51% of GDP [gross domestic product], manufacturing and construction 44%; agriculture's share is only 5%. A well-trained workforce (15% of all workers are described as engineers or technical specialists) has helped to create some successful export-oriented high-tech companies, more than 40 of them listed on American stockmarkets." (p16)

"Survey: Israel: Milk and Honey." Economist v330 n7847, 22 Jan 1994. p58(15-16,19). (ISSN0013-0613).

GROSS DOMESTIC PRODUCT--MEXICO

"Despite Mr [Carlos] Salinas's reforms and an inflow of about $25 billion in foreign capital, Mexico's GDP [gross domestic product] probably grew by only about 0.5% in 1993, down from 2.6% in 1992. In the third quarter of 1993, output shrank by 1.2%, the first drop since 1986. While bigger companies raise cheap funds on international capital markets and prepare to take on the world, smaller ones are struggling to cope with real interest rates of up to 15% and thousands have gone bust. Officials attribute the present slowdown mainly to a sluggish world economy and to the prolonged uncertainty over NAFTA's [North American Free Trade Agreement's] fate in Congress which held up investment decisions: after growing by 20.4% in 1992, private investment rose by only 2.8% in the first three quarters of 1993. The government expects a rebound to 6.4% in 1994: so long as political violence does not spread." (p20)

"Mexico: The Revolution Continues." Economist v330 n7847, 22 Jan 1994. p19-21. (ISSN0013-0613).

GROSS NATIONAL PRODUCT--U.S.

"David Morris of the Institute for Local-Self-Reliance calls free trade 'the first global religion,' which has only one commandment: 'Thou Shalt Put No Obstacles in the Way of Any Resource Flow.' The effect? Morris cites the Swiss economist Paul Bairoch who says that in 1750 per capita GNP [gross national product] was about the same in both developed and undeveloped countries. In 1930 the ratio was about four to one in favor of the developed nations. Today it is over eight to one." (p4)

"NAFTA & the Incorporation of America." Progressive Review n321, Jan 1994. p4-6.

GUANGDONG (CHINA)--ECONOMIC CONDITIONS

"The real engine of growth in China today is the foreign-invested industrial sector, most of which is concentrated in southern China, mainly in Guangdong. Considered on its own, Guangdong province is far and away the fastest growing economy in the world. Guangdong's industrial output climbed by nearly 20 per cent per year from 1980 to 1990, and 27 per cent in 1991. Guangdong is now China's leading industrial producer, and it also leads the nation in foreign investment, retail sales, and exports. With considerable natural resources and a population of 68 million--more than South Korea, Taiwan, Hong Kong and Singapore put together--a capitalist Guangdong has the potential not just to become Asia's 'Fifth Dragon' but perhaps even to outstrip them all. Guangdong's success has been powered by exports, which have grown by close to 30 per cent per year in recent years. Industrial growth has been led by Guangdong's private and foreign-invested enterprises, which together grew by 45 per cent in 1990 while exports from this sector grew by nearly 60 per cent." (p90-91)

Smith, Richard. "The Chinese Road to Capitalism." New Left Review n199, May-Jun 1993. p55-99. (ISSN0028-6060).

GUATEMALA

see also DEFORESTATION--GUATEMALA; LIFE EXPECTANCY--GUATEMALA; WETLANDS--GUATEMALA

GUATEMALA--MEXICO--SOCIAL CONDITIONS (v19)

GUATEMALA--POLITICS AND GOVERNMENT

"For a country more used to murder, torture and lesser infringements of the rights of man, the peaceful resolution of a political drama through an honest national referendum on January 30th came as something of a surprise [in Guatemala]....'A page has been turned,' declared Mr [Ramiro] de Leon [Carpio]. 'Now we can concentrate on the economy and the fight against corruption.' The economy is doing all right: output grew by about 4% last year and inflation was roughly 11%. Corruption will be another story. And why did only 16% of the electorate vote (319,000 for the reforms, 61,000 against)? It may be that many Guatemalans would happily turn the page on all their politicians, Mr de Leon included." (p48)

"International: Guatemala: Semi-Democratic." Economist v330 n7849, 5 Feb 1994. p48. (ISSN0013-0613).

GUATEMALA--POPULATION

"At current rates, Guatemala's population would double in 22 years. The population is 45 percent Indian, 45 percent Mestizo or Ladino (mixed Spanish and Indian), 5 percent white, 2 percent black, and 3 percent other. Although Spanish is the official language, over 40 percent of the population speak one of 23 indigenous tongues as a first language." (p7)

Lang, Anne. "Spotlight: Guatemala." Population Today v22 n4, Apr 1994. p7. (ISSN0749-2448).

GUINEA

see MINES AND MINERAL RESOURCES--GUINEA

GUINEA-BISSAU--ECONOMIC CONDITIONS

Guinea-Bissau "is staggering under servicing obligations (including arrears) averaging 210 per cent of exports in 1991-93--actual payments are far less--and total debt is an impossible 933 per cent of exports for 1993 alone. The irony for this small country is that in the late 1980s it had Africa's highest average ratio of development aid to GDP [gross domestic product] (over 61 per cent), and now has the third heaviest debt burden. Despite such difficulties, the [World] Bank predicts faster annual growth of 4 per cent over the next five years. The main impetus is to come from agriculture, although prospects for substantially higher export revenue are limited due to steadily falling prices for cashew nuts, the major export, in recent years. These contributed to a 24 per cent deterioration in terms of trade in 1986-91." (p22)

Bentsi-Enchill, Nii K. "Guinea-Bissau Struggles for Development." Africa Recovery v7 n1, Jun 1993. p22-25.

In Guinea-Bissau, "Agriculture now accounts for three-quarters of export earnings, and over half of GDP [gross domestic product]. One indicator of the sector's potential is that only 30 per cent of arable land is currently farmed, which is just two-thirds of 1950s levels. Subsistence farming predominates, with only 10 per cent of farmed land occupied by modern, market-oriented private farms and state farms....Fisheries are the second most important export item, and the major under-exploited resource. Revenue from licenses granted to foreign trawlers was around $6 mn in 1988, but by 1990 direct exports had fallen to $2.1 mn from a 1981 peak of $4.6 mn. In view of what the government described in 1990 as 'ludicrously poor profits' from the license fees, it hopes to create a national fleet to join the long-established or recent joint ventures with Russian, Algerian, French and Portuguese companies. Industry remains very small-scale, employing around 1 per cent of the workforce. The state sector represents 60 per cent of production, and provides half the jobs, but most firms are functioning at some 25 per cent of capacity. With only $1 mn in net direct foreign investment in 1990, the government is reviewing investment and labour laws and pointing to investment opportunities in agro-industry and in phosphate mining." (p25)

Bentsi-Enchill, Nii K. "Guinea-Bissau Struggles for Development." Africa Recovery v7 n1, Jun 1993. p22-25.

GUN CONTROL--LAW AND LEGISLATION

see FIREARMS--LAW AND LEGISLATION

GUNS

see FIREARMS

GUNSHOT WOUNDS--LOS ANGELES (CALIF) (v19)

GUNSHOT WOUNDS--U.S.--COSTS (v19)

GYPSY MOTH--U.S. (v19)

HAINAN ISLAND--ECONOMIC CONDITIONS (v19)

HAITI

see also BIRTH WEIGHT, LOW--HAITI; INFLATION (FINANCE)--HAITI; INSURGENCY--HAITI; POOR--HAITI; REFUGEES, HAITIAN--FLORIDA

HAITI--ECONOMIC CONDITIONS (v19)

"Currently, the Haitian economy is in free fall. The economy shrank by ten percent during fiscal year 1992, and another drop of five to eight percent is expected when final 1993 figures come in. Some 100,000 jobs have been lost since the coup, and real wages fell 40% in 1992 alone. The Aristide government ran a small budget surplus in 1991, but coup leaders finished fiscal year 1992 with a deficit of 450 million gourde ($36 million U.S.)--over one third of total government expenditures. Haitian government revenues were projected to plunge another 20% in fiscal 1993." (p37)

Tilly, Chris. "Letter from Abroad: Haiti's Agony." Dollars and Sense n192, Mar-Apr 1994. p16-19,36-37.

"The Haitian economy started declining in 1981, slid downhill rapidly after 1987 and sank still lower following the 1991 coup. The country's gross national product fell 6.2 percent in 1991 and 12.6 percent in 1992." (p16)

James, David. "Embargo Forces Haiti's Last Gasp." Insight v10 n12, 21 Mar 1994. p14-17. (ISSN1051-4880).

HAITI--POLITICS AND GOVERNMENT

"Monthly human rights reports compiled by the Washington Office on Haiti indicate that state terror remained a problem until Aristide's election, when it declined dramatically. In the 18-

month period immediately preceding Aristide's inauguration, 330 killings attributed to the military were documented, though the actual number is undoubtedly higher. In the eight months Aristide was in office, only 26 documented political killings were recorded; two-thirds of these were attributed to the army, which bitterly opposed Aristide. (See Washington Office on Haiti, 'Human Rights Violations in Haiti.') In the wake of Aristide's overthrow, political deaths have soared. Amnesty International released a report in January 1992, stating that 'reliable information indicates that over 1,500 civilians have been killed' since the coup, although 'these figures could substantially underestimate the extent of the human rights crisis in Haiti.'" (p22)

"Human Rights in Haiti." EXTRA! v6 n1, Jan-Feb 1993. p22. (ISSN0895-2310).

HAITI--POPULATION

"With the rate of natural population increase at 2.9% (a doubling time of 24 years), Haiti has sent a steady stream of people into the slums, into the mountains, and into surrounding countries--estimates are that up to one in five Haitians now live in the U.S., the Dominican Republic, or the Bahamas. Haiti's mountainous regions are now mostly deforested and their fragile soils eroded. Simple subsistence is becoming impossible for many because the land has simply been depleted. Long term political stability, and stemming the tide of refugees, would mean making Haiti livable again for its inhabitants--a gargantuan task, especially considering the nation's rapid population growth. Putting the numbers in perspective, 31,401 fleeing Haitians were intercepted by the Coast Guard last year, precipitating domestic crisis over where to put them, but Haiti's natural population increase is about 185,000 per year. In other words, the U.S. and other countries could accept 185,000 Haitian immigrants per year in perpetuity without beginning to reduce the island's human burden." (p4)

"Hot Topics: Caribbean Crisis in Perspective: Haiti as the Harbinger." Carrying Capacity Network Clearinghouse Bulletin v3 n2, Mar 1993. p3-4. (ISSN1066-5404).

"Haiti has the highest birth and death rates and the highest rate of natural increase in the Western Hemisphere. Forty percent of the population is under age 15. With a population of 6.5 million, in a land area slightly larger than the state of Maryland, population density measures over 600 inhabitants per square mile, a little less dense than Connecticut. There is an extreme economic disparity between the capital and the rural provinces, where about 72 percent of Haiti's people live. In 1990, the wealthiest 1 percent of the population accounted for 44 percent of national income. On average, per capita GNP [gross national product] is the lowest in the Caribbean, $370 in 1991, but in the countryside it is only about $100." (p7)

Barberis, Mary. "Spotlight: Haiti." Population Today v22 n1, Jan 1994. p7. (ISSN0749-2448).

HAITI--SOCIAL CONDITIONS (v19)

"Haiti is the poorest country in the Western Hemisphere. The depth of its poverty is truly stunning. One child in ten dies in infancy, a rate comparable to sub-Saharan Africa. According to the U.S. Agency for International Development (USAID), nearly half of all households consume less than three quarters of the recommended caloric intake, and nearly half lack safe drinking water. Estimates of illiteracy range from 65% to 90%. An early 1980s World Bank report described the plight of Haiti's poor--who make up 81% of the country's seven million people--as 'a condition of life so characterized by malnutrition, illiteracy, disease, squalid surroundings, high infant mortality, and low life expectancy as to be beneath any reasonable definition of human decency.'" (p16)

Tilly, Chris. "Letter from Abroad: Haiti's Agony." Dollars and Sense n192, Mar-Apr 1994. p16-19,36-37.

HANDICAPPED--CHINA (v19)

HANDICAPPED--EMPLOYMENT--U.S.

"School psychologists work with non-disabled children and their disabled peers. Children with disabilities must not be overlooked when policies are developed to ease the transition from school to work. The reality is that a very significant percentage of the disabled are presently unemployed (36 percent), underemployed (15-30 percent), and ill-prepared to be employed (SRI, 1992)." (p49)

Gorin, Susan (Executive Dir., National Assoc. of School Psychologists, Silver Spring, MD). U.S. House. Committee on Education and Labor. "Hearing on School-to-Work Transition." Hearing, 15 Jul 1993. Washington, D.C.: GPO, 1994. (ISBN0160440858). (Y4.Ed8/1:103-42).

"According to a Census Bureau report...only 52 percent of people [in the U.S.] with disabilities are working, and only 23 percent of those with a severe disability....other surveys have shown that over the past 15 years, the percentage of people wth disabilities not working has remained constant, or even increased....According to a 1992 GAO [General Accounting Office] study, 45 percent of families headed by a person with a disability, and 65 percent of single parents or single persons with a disability, live in poverty." (pS4336)

Dole, Bob (Sen.-Kans.). "Statements on Introduced Bills and Joint Resolutions," Congressional Record (14 Apr 1994). Daily ed. pS4334-4350. (ISSN0363-7239).

HANDICAPPED--NEW YORK (NY)--TRANSPORTATION (v19)

HANDICAPPED STUDENTS--U.S.

"In the past 11 years there has been little attention to students with disabilities, although they comprise 10 percent of all students and are among those most in need of education reforms [in the U.S.]. For example, Goals 2000 aims for a 90-percent high school graduation rate. Even without reform, the graduation rate among nondisabled students has been growing, to 83 percent today. But among students with disabilities... graduating with either a diploma or a certificate dropped from 60 percent to 52 percent between 1986 and 1989." (pS745)

Dole, Bob (Sen.-Kans.). "Goals 2000: Educate America Act," Congressional Record (3 Feb 1994). Daily ed. pS742-751. (ISSN0363-7239).

HARBORS--ASIA

"There are few better gauges of East Asia's economic boom than the region's crowded docks. In Singapore and Hong Kong, Asia already boasts the world's two busiest ports: last year each handled over 9m TEUs (or 20-feet equivalent units, the standard container measure), twice as much as in 1989. Both are pouring money into expansion: Hong Kong alone talks of handling a staggering 32m TEUs by 2011....Malaysia's three big ports--Penang, Port Klang and Johor--are building hard to double capacity from the current level of 1.2m TEUs." (p70-71)

"Business: Trade in Asia: The Rise of Ports Like Klang." Economist v331 n7858, 9 Apr 1994. p70-72. (ISSN0013-0613).

HARBORS--LOS ANGELES (CALIF) (v19)

HARBORS--U.S. (v19)

HATE CRIMES--EUROPE (v19)

HATE CRIMES--GERMANY (v19)

"Since November 1992 hate crimes [in Germany] have decreased by almost two-thirds; in October 1992, 17 percent of East and 12 percent of West Germans justified violent means against non-Germans, whereas only 8 percent in East and 5 percent in West Germany did so in January 1993; the number of adolescents willing to vote for parties of the extreme Right has been cut in half since September 1992." (p49)

Diedrich, Maria. "Born Guilty?" Transition v3 n2, 1993. p34-

51. (ISSN0041-1191).

HATE CRIMES--U.S. (v19)

"In 1991, there were 4,755 hate-related crimes reported under the [U.S.] Hate Crimes Statistics Act. Racial bias was the motivation behind 60 percent of these crimes, followed by religious bias crimes at 20 percent, and ethnic and sexually oriented crimes at 10 percent. This data was based on information submitted by only 32 States, and falls far short from predictions by several racial, ethnic and religious organizations, who claim that the numbers of hate crimes exceed the tens of thousands annually." (pH945)

Velazquez, Nydia M. (Rep.-N.Y.). "Improving America's Schools Act of 1994," Congressional Record (2 Mar 1994). Daily ed. pH920-959. (ISSN0363-7239).

HAWAII--ECONOMIC CONDITIONS (v19)

HAWAII--JAPAN--ECONOMIC CONDITIONS (v19)

HAY TRADE--U.S.

"The average hay price received by [U.S.] farmers in 1992/93 rose to $73.20 per ton, up $2.00 from the previous year. However, prices remained below the peak of $85.40 reached in 1989/90. The 1992/93 increase snapped 2 consecutive years of price declines....While prices for alfalfa hay rose, the average farm price for all other hay fell in 1992/93. Alfalfa hay prices received for the year increased 5 percent to $78.40 per ton. Record alfalfa prices were set in 1988/89 at $93.83 per ton. Because supplies of all other hays were supported by improved production, prices fell almost $3 to only $57.60 per ton in 1992/93, the lowest since 1987/88." (p12)

U.S. Dept. of Agriculture. "Hay Supplies Decline in 1993/94; Quality Questioned." Feed Situation and Outlook Report Nov 1993. p11-12.

HAZARDOUS SUBSTANCES--U.S.--TRANSPORTATION

"As the volume of hazardous materials shipped by rail has increased, so has the number of serious hazardous materials problems. Although rail accident rates are lower than in 1980, most of the decline had taken place by 1986. Since then, overall accident rates have leveled off or begun to rise. For trains carrying hazardous materials, accidents increased 28%. According to the Department of Transportation, 1,130 hazardous material incidents were reported in rail transportation in 1991, an increase of 36% since 1982. From the viewpoint of safety oversight, the trend of increasing safety problems is just as troubling. The Federal Railroad Administration (FRA) is responsible for issuing and enforcing safety rules along the nation's railroad system. In 1989, the FRA relied on only 28 hazardous materials inspectors nationwide to inspect an estimated 85 railroads, 15,000 shippers and over one million carloads of hazardous materials. This number has increased only recently to 42 inspectors. Over a five-year period from 1985 to 1989, FRA inspections had identified an increasing number of safety defects and violations." (p806)

Fleming, Mac A. (Chairman, Committee on Legislation, Railway Labor Executives' Assoc.). U.S. House. Committee on Appropriations. "Department of Transportation and Related Agencies Approp. for 1994 (Part 7A)." Hearing, Washington, D.C.: GPO, 1993. (ISBN0160411033). (Y4.Ap6/1:T68/4/994/pt.7A).

HAZARDOUS SUBSTANCES--U.S.--TRANSPORTATION--ACCIDENTS

"The U.S. Department of Transportation's database of hazardous materials spill reports has documented between eighty and a hundred spills a year for the past three years....These represent a small proportion of the total number of pesticide spills because only about 60 percent of spills that should be reported to the database actually are reported, and the many spills that occur from carriers (trucks, trains, and boats) without an interstate license have no reporting requirement. Spills of hazardous materials recorded in the database have been occurring with increasing frequency. A recent study by the LOS ANGELES TIMES showed that the number reported spills each year increased by 37 percent in the decade between 1982 and 1991. No such study has been done for pesticide spills specifically." (p8)

Cox, Caroline. "From Factories and Tank Cars to You: Hazards of Manufacturing and Transporting Pesticides." Journal of Pesticide Reform v13 n2, Sum 1993. p2-3,6-10. (ISSN0893-357X).

HAZARDOUS WASTE SITES

"According to a landmark study of 'Toxic Wastes and Race,' by the Commission for Racial Justice of the United Church of Christ, three out of five African Americans live in communities with one or more abandoned toxic waste sites. Three of the five largest commercial hazardous waste facilities, themselves accounting for 40% of all such landfill capacity in the U.S., are located in Black and Latino communities. The nation's largest hazardous landfill is located in a small town in Alabama that is 90% Black. A Greenpeace study, 'Playing with Fire,' in 1990, showed much the same to be true of incinerators. The population of people of color in communities with existing trash incinerators is 89% higher than the national average." (p1)

"Fight Toxic Racism!" Turning the Tide v6 n2, Mar-Apr 1993. p1.

HAZARDOUS WASTE SITES--ALABAMA

"The largest toxic waste dump...[in the U.S.] sprawls across 2,700 acres of Sumter County [in Alabama], its trenches as much as a half-mile long and 600 feet wide. Trucks hauling hazardous waste from 48 states and foreign countries pass through its gates 24 hours a day. According to the Census Bureau, approximately 16,000 people live in the rolling hills of west central Alabama that surround the waste dump. More than 11,000 residents are African American. Unemployment is 14 percent. Annual income averages barely $10,000....Spills, explosions, fires, and evacuations have plagued the dump. Truckers cited for drunk driving have spilled poisonous phenol and nitrobenzene that they were transporting to Emelle. In 1989, state troopers found 740 violations among 312 trucks shipping waste to Emelle and took 51 vehicles out of service." (p17)

Kiker, Kaye/Askew, Cleo. "The Emelle Megadump." Southern Exposure v21 n4, Win 1993. p17. (ISSN0146-809X).

HAZARDOUS WASTE SITES--HOUSTON (TEX)

"In Houston, TX...all the municipal landfills and 6 of eight garbage incinerators were placed in African American neighborhoods between the 1920's and 1970's. From 1970-78, three of four new privately owned landfills were placed in Black communities. With 28% of Houston's population, they had 82% of the garbage dumps. Similar patterns have been reported in L.A., Chicago, and numerous other cities." (p1)

"Fight Toxic Racism!" Turning the Tide v6 n2, Mar-Apr 1993. p1.

HAZARDOUS WASTE SITES--U.S. (v19)

"National Cement burns, in an aging cement kiln, 75 million gallons of toxic waste a year. The only such toxic incinerator in the western United States, it is perched above the apex of the two largest earthquake faults in the Western Hemisphere, the San Andreas and Garlock faults. National Cement stores 400,000 gallons of liquid hazardous waste, half a mile from the Los Angeles aqueduct and over the recharge area for one of California's largest aquifers. Trucks carrying the wastes must cross the aqueduct to deliver their poisonous cargo. The land surrounding National Cement, designated critical recovery habitat for the endangered California Condor, is now hopelessly compromised." (p6)

Patterson, Burr, Jr./Williams, Jane Melanie. "Desert Rats." Earth First! v13 n7, 1 Aug 1993. p6.

HAZARDOUS WASTE SITES--U.S.--AFRO-AMERICANS (v19)

HAZARDOUS WASTE SITES--U.S.--FINANCE (v19)

HAZARDOUS WASTE SITES--U.S.--MINORITIES

"Findings of the United Church of Christ report, 'Toxic Wastes and Race in the United States': Communities with one commercial hazardous waste dump had, on average, twice as many minority residents as communities without a waste site (24% versus 12%). Communities with two or more such waste dumps, or with one of the nation's five largest landfills, had three times as many minority residents as communities without a waste site....Three of the five largest commercial hazardous waste landfills in the US were in predominantly African American or Hispanic communities. Metropolitan areas with the greatest number of uncontrolled toxic waste sites had large African American populations. These include: Memphis (173 sites), St. Louis (160), Houston (152), Cleveland (106), Chicago (103) and Atlanta (94)." (p14)

"Focus: Environmental Justice." Panoscope n37, Oct 1993. p14. (ISSN0951-8819).

HAZARDOUS WASTE SITES--WASHINGTON (STATE)

In Hanford, Washington the federal government is struggling "to control the most expensive environmental cleanup project in American history. Until the summer of 1993, conventional scientific wisdom had set the price tag for the 30-year cleanup at...$50 billion. But that figure may be too low by a factor of six, according to a University of Tennessee estimate....Three hundred billion dollars...is three times the total cuts in federal defense spending planned through 1998. That much money over the next five years would emloy 200,000 people in the armed services and 1.9 million workers in the defense industry. Yet, even $300 billion does not count the demolition and removal of radiation-contaminated buildings from the Hanford site. Hanford is where the U.S. government chose to produce the bulk of its weapon-grade plutonium, for the atomic bombs that ended World War II and for the hydrogen bombs that sustained the Cold War. In their top-secret rush to produce fuel for weapons of mass destruction, technicians at the 560-square-mile federal site dumped at least 440 billion gallons of contaminated water into the sandy dirt. Another 61 million gallons of waste were pumped into 177 underground tanks, some of them as large as the Capitol dome and at least 68 of which leak." (p6)

Harden, Blaine. "Bad Comedy at America's Biggest Environmental Mess." APF Reporter v16 n2, 1994. p5-9. (ISSN0913-4562).

HAZARDOUS WASTE TREATMENT FACILITIES--U.S. (v19)

HAZARDOUS WASTES (v19)

see also POLLUTION

"Five years ago, a United Nations-sponsored meeting in Basel, Switzerland, set the groundwork for regulating the trade in hazardous materials. Since then, 103 countries have banned imports of such materials, and 13 of 24 industrially advanced nations in the Organization for Economic Cooperation and Development (OECD) have announced support for an export ban....Greenpeace, the most aggressive environmental group on trade and dumping of hazardous wastes, has cataloged more than 500 attempts to export more than 200 million tons of waste from OECD members to non-OECD nations since the 1989 meeting in Basel. Of that amount, 5.3 million tons have been dumped abroad, reports Jim Puckett of Greenpeace, who nonetheless calls this 'the tip of the iceberg.'" (p1,16)

Knickerbocker, Brad. "US Joins Global Effort by Curbing Some but Not All Exports of Waste." The Christian Science Monitor v86 n69, 4 Mar 1994. p1,16. (ISSN0882-7729).

"The paradox of the toxic-waste dilemma is this: The stricter an industrial nation's green laws, the more hazardous waste it tends to export. Germany, with perhaps the most stringent environmental regulations in Europe, tops the list by shipping more than half a million tons annually across its borders. It is followed by Belgium, the Netherlands, Switzerland and the United States. Exact statistics are elusive, but roughly 2 million tons of toxic detritus is exported each year from North America and Europe. Some hazardous waste moves as legitimate recyclable material--lead from car batteries, for example--and some is essentially worthless." (p64,66)

Satchell, Michael J. "Science & Society: Deadly Trade in Toxics." U.S. News & World Report v116 n9, 7 Mar 1994. p64,66,68. (ISSN0041-5537).

HAZARDOUS WASTES--OHIO

"With a rated burning capacity of sixty thousand tons a year and permission to nearly triple that intake with new construction, the hazardous-waste incinerator in East Liverpool, Ohio, is the largest such facility in the world, the largest in the country, or the second-largest in the country, depending on whom you ask. Despite its size, the incinerator is situated smack in the middle of East Liverpool, a small, depressed, industrial city of fewer than fourteen thousand people...." (p44) "The incinerator is situated approximately four hundred yards from an elementary school...the school is...just below the top of the smokestack, which is licensed to emit vaporized lead, mercury, and some three hundred other compounds. The incinerator is also... a stone's throw from the Ohio River, a major source of drinking water for millions of people....Moreover, the site is in one of the nation's premier atmospheric inversion areas, where the weather will cause it to blanket the region with emissions two days out of every three. When both kilns...are up and running, Ohio will have more than one-fifth of the nation's total hazardous-waste burning capacity. The builder of the facility, WTI [Waste Technologies Industries], estimates that the incinerator will annually consume at least five thousand truckloads of toxins." (p46)

Davis, L. J. "Clinton's Compromise: Where Are You Al?" Mother Jones v18 n6, Nov-Dec 1993. p44-49. (ISSN0362-8841).

HAZARDOUS WASTES--U.S. (v19)

"The military's thousands of toxic sites include some of the most dangerous in the country: More than 120 sit atop the Environmental Protection Agency's (EPA's) Superfund National Priority List of the nation's most polluted real estate. The military still generates nearly a ton of hazardous wastes every minute, more than even the largest multinational corporations. Any way you measure it, our military is a vast industrial enterprise. It oversees some 20,000 nuclear weapons and enormous fleets of planes, tanks and vehicles. Military installations are home to some 40,000 underground storage tanks for fuel and other chemicals, four times as many as Exxon has--even with its gas stations. But the military does not have a history of being sensitive to the environment." (p37)

Shulman, Seth. "Operation Restore Earth." E Magazine v4 n2, Mar-Apr 1993. p36-43. (ISSN1046-8021).

"There's the issue of how the [U.S.] military handles its environmental contracts. In one case in Tuscon, Arizona, a lucrative, state-of-the-art water treatment facility contract was granted by the Air Force to Hughes Aircraft--the same firm that ran the plant for decades and caused the solvent pollution in the first place. In 1981, after finding levels of trichloroethylene (TCE) as high as 400 parts per billion, 80 times higher than the maximum permitted by federal and Arizona law, the state closed municipal wells serving nearly 50,000 people. With TCE levels as high as 16,000 parts per billion in the groundwater below the plant itself, Hughes officials admitted to having dumped TCE into the desert soil for decades. Now, as Congressman Mike Synar (D-OK) noted, Hughes has 'been paid at a profit to pollute,' for all these years because of its relationship with the Air Force. In any other Superfund situation, a private firm like Hughes would be penalized for its pollution--by footing the bill itself for the cleanup." (p42)

Shulman, Seth. "Operation Restore Earth." E Magazine v4 n2, Mar-Apr 1993. p36-43. (ISSN1046-8021).

In May 1993, "the EPA finally released the 1991 Toxics Release Inventory, detailing how much of certain toxic chemicals were released into the environment by manufacturers that year....Texas and Louisiana have reduced their releases by 350 million pounds (46 percent) and 273 million pounds (37 percent) respectively [since base year of 1988], but they still have the highest amount of releases by far. At 458 million pounds for Louisiana and 410 million pounds for Texas, these two states released 25 percent of the total for the nation. Tennessee's 215 million pounds was third highest in the country. Among the 1991 top five releasing states, only Tennessee is not also one of the top five decreasers since 1988. Ohio and Indiana (fourth and fifth in 1991) have reduced their releases by 67 million pounds and 78 million pounds respectively, placing them fourth and fifth in decreases since 1988. Virginia has had the third largest reduction since 1988, with its 80 million fewer pounds taking it from 6th to 16th place." (p6)

Pendergrass, John. "Around the States." Environmental Forum v10 n4, Jul-Aug 1993. p6. (ISSN0731-5732).

HAZARDOUS WASTES--U.S.--MILITARY BASES

"As anyone who has studied the challenges of converting military bases or privately owned weapons plants knows, virtually all major defense facilities in the United States are plagued with severe hazardous waste contamination, including toxic substances such as solvents, heavy metals, and PCB's; munitions and explosive wastes; and radioactive wastes. Nationwide, major bases approved for closure in 1989 and 1991 contain a total of 1137 active cleanup sites. Fourteen of those installations are included on EPA's [Environmental Protection Agency's] 'Superfund' National Priorities List. This year's list of bases marked for closure or major realignment contained a total of 824 more contamination sites. Eleven of those bases are also on the Superfund list." (p4)

Siegel, Lenny. "Focus: Military Detox Time: How to Clean Up the Bases." Positive Alternatives v3 n4, Sum 1993. p4-5. (ISSN1065-0075).

HAZARDOUS WASTES--U.S.--POLITICS AND GOVERNMENT (v19)

HAZARDOUS WASTES--U.S.--TRANSPORTATION

"The Department of Transportation estimates that over 500,000 movements of hazardous materials occur each day in the United States, with over 4 billion tons moving each year." (pH10539)

Dingell, John D. (Rep.-Mich.). "Hazardous Materials Transportation Act Amendments of 1993," Congressional Record (21 Nov 1993). Daily ed. pH10536-10541. (ISSN0363-7239).

HAZARDOUS WASTES--U.S. DEPT. OF DEFENSE (v19)

HAZARDOUS WASTES--ZAMBIA

"Zambia is one of Africa's most industrialised countries with indiscriminate dumping of waste on the outskirts of towns. There is massive pollution from the copper mines--Zambia Consolidated Copper Mines is the country's biggest single air and water polluter. Petrochemical and fertiliser plants are a further problem. A report by the National Council for Scientific Research highlighted increasing trade in hazardous waste disposal. Between 1980 and 1986, 23,144 tonnes of dangerous chemicals were imported. The capital Lusaka, with a population of 1 million, has had virtually no controlled refuse collection and disposal. Most cities and towns are extremely dirty with uncollected refuse and poor sanitation, especially in townships and shanty compounds. In 1992 more than 500 people died from cholera caused by contaminated drinking water. Many more die from dysentery and related diseases." (p24)

Chisupa, Katongo. "Tackling the Polluters: Zambia Backs Words with Deeds." Panoscope n38, Jan 1994. p24-25. (ISSN0951-8819).

HEAD--WOUNDS AND INJURIES--U.S. (v19)

HEAD START PROGRAMS--U.S.

"Since 1965, nearly 14 million children from low-income families have participated in Head Start, most of them 3- and 4-year-olds. By law, virtually all of them are from families whose incomes are below the federal poverty line, $14,800 for a family of four. Still, the program serves fewer than half the eligible children. Despite a 50 percent increase in enrollment since 1989, to nearly 714,000 last year, Head Start today includes only 53 percent of eligible 4-year-olds and 21 percent of eligible 3-year-olds." (p541-542)

Katz, Jeffrey L. "Social Policy: Cover Story: Head Start Funding Nears Legislative Crossroads." Congressional Quarterly v52 n9, 5 Mar 1994. p541-543,546-547.

"Despite the significant expansion of the Head Start Program over the last four years, Head Start still only serves fewer than half of the eligible children in the Nation. In California and throughout the country, childhood poverty is growing faster than the program can expand. As a result, even though Head Start participation has increased to nearly 714,000 children--a 50-percent increase since 1989--only half of the four-year-olds and a fifth of the eligible three-year-olds are enrolled, and, according to the GAO [General Accounting Office], only 1 percent of poor families and toddlers are able to participate." (pS4709)

Feinstein, Dianne (Sen.-Calif.). "Head Start Amendments of 1994," Congressional Record (21 Apr 1994). Daily ed. pS4691-4727. (ISSN0363-7239).

"A University of Michigan study indicates that one key reason for long-term Head Start 'fade out' is the low quality of the subsequent education these children receive." (p1) Valerie E. Lee, U-M professor of education and graduate student Susanna Loeb "investigated the link between children's educational experience in preschool and the quality of schools they attended as eighth-graders, using a national sample of nearly 15,000 students in 975 public and private schools. About 14 percent of the students in the nationally representative sample attended Head Start preschools, 44 percent attended other types of preschools and 42 percent did not attend preschool. As expected, Lee and Loeb found wide background differences among the three groups, with the family income of Head Start graduates less than half that of students who attended other preschools. Over 41 percent of former Head Start students are Black, and 16 percent are Hispanic. Their parents have less education, on average, than those of the other two groups." (p2)

News release. "Lee." University of Michigan News and Information Services 1 Apr 1994. p1-2.

HEALTH BEHAVIOR--U.S. (v19)

HEALTH CARE COSTS

see MEDICAL CARE, COST OF

HEALTH FACILITIES

see also HOSPITALS

HEALTH FACILITIES--U.S.--FINANCE

"According to a recent article in the industry publication MODERN HEALTHCARE, profit margins at nursing homes continued to rise in 1990 even though Medicaid recipients continued to dominate the resident mix. Industry experts attributed much of the cash flow to increased Medicaid revenues as a result of successful Boren Amendment litigation. The average total pre-tax profit margin for all nursing facilities was 2.52% in 1990, up from 1.96% in 1989 and 1.63% in 1988. For-profit homes had the highest margin; government run homes, the lowest. MODERN HEALTHCARE also recently reported the results of an AHA [or American Health Association] survey showing that hospitals enjoyed nearly a 23% increase in total profits in 1991. The AHA's survey of acute-care hospitals reveals that total hospital profits rose to more than $10 billion in 1991, up from $8.2 billion in 1990. Total hospital revenues increased by 11%." (p7)

"Update: Medical Industry Profits Continue to Boom." Health Advocate n175, Win 1993. p7.

HEALTH INSURANCE

see INSURANCE, HEALTH

HEALTH MAINTENANCE ORGANIZATIONS--U.S. (v19)

"HMO [Health Maintenance Organization] membership has doubled since 1986, from 25 million people to an expected 50 million this year. Not only are HMOs less expensive than fee-for-service medicine, their premium hikes have fallen for five straight years, from 16 percent in 1990 to 5.6 percent in 1994. A 1993 study concluded that if all Americans went to HMOs the 19 percent chunk of GDP [gross domestic product] projected for health care in 2000 would shrink to 15 percent." (p37)

Barnes, Fred. "Health Care Costs Are Going Down." American Spectator v27 n2, Feb 1994. p36-39. (ISSN0148-8414).

"Since 1990, the growth in HMOs [Health Maintenance Organizations] has been accelerating again. Enrollment grew 4.3 percent in 1991, 6.4 percent in 1992, and 4.5 percent in the first part of 1993 alone, according to Interstudy Publications, a Minnesota firm that tracks HMOs. HMO enrollment is now at 41 million people." (p18)

Ingwerson, Marshall. "US Health Costs Are Dropping--Before 'the Plan.'" The Christian Science Monitor v86 n24, 29 Dec 1993. p1,18. (ISSN0882-7729).

HEALTH MAINTENANCE ORGANIZATIONS--U.S.--PUBLIC OPINION (v19)

HEALTH SERVICES ADMINISTRATION--U.S.--COSTS (v19)

HEALTH STATUS INDICATORS (v19)

HEALTH STATUS INDICATORS--ARKANSAS (v19)

HEALTH STATUS INDICATORS--DEVELOPING COUNTRIES (v19)

HEALTH STATUS INDICATORS--MAINE (v19)

HEALTH STATUS INDICATORS--SRI LANKA (v19)

HEALTH STATUS INDICATORS--WOMEN (v19)

HEARING IMPAIRED--EDUCATION--U.S.

"Data from the Rehabilitation Services Administration (RSA) reveals that 19,479 people with hearing loss were rehabilitated in 1990. Of those, 5,500 were prelingually deaf and 743 were prevocationally deaf. However, of the remaining 13,236 who experienced a postlingual and postvocational hearing loss, only 625 were successfully rehabilitated that year, using RSA's status 26 criteria." (p26)

Howe, Marylyn. "Meeting the Needs of Late-Deafened Adults." American Rehabilitation v19 n4, Win 1993-1994. p25-29. (ISSN0362-4048).

HEARING IMPAIRED--U.S.

"It is important to note that 79 percent of the people with impaired hearing in the United States experience their hearing loss after the age of 19, with another 15 percent having onset between 3 and 18 years of age (Ries, 1992)....Out of the overall population of people with hearing loss, about 43 percent are over the age of 65. Over 30 percent of the people past age 65 have some degree of hearing loss, compared to 8.8 percent of the total population." (p16)

Kosovich, George N. "VR and People Who Are Hard of Hearing: Where Do We Go from Here?" American Rehabilitation v19 n4, Win 1993-1994. p16-19. (ISSN0362-4048).

"The 1990-91 HEALTH INTERVIEW SURVEY (HIS) of the National Center for Health Statistics shows that 8.8 percent of the United States population over the age of 3 experiences some degree of hearing loss (Ries, 1992). This represents about 22 million people. A little over half of these--about 11.5 million people--have hearing loss in both ears, and about half of this group are 65 years of age or older." (p17)

Kosovich, George N. "VR and People Who Are Hard of Hearing: Where Do We Go from Here?" American Rehabilitation v19 n4, Win 1993-1994. p16-19. (ISSN0362-4048).

"The HIS [or HEALTH INTERVIEW SURVEY] reports for 1990-91 show that nearly 84 percent of the total population of those with hearing loss in both ears had adult onset hearing loss. Out of 9.4 million people with adult onset hearing loss in both ears, about 5 million were between the ages of 19 and 65 (Reis, 1992). In fiscal year 1990, 35.6 percent, or 6,929, of all people disabled by hearing loss that were rehabilitated were identified as being hard of hearing and had lost their hearing after age 19. Also, 625 people, or 3.2 percent of this total rehabilitated hearing impaired population, were coded as having adult onset deafness." (p17)

Kosovich, George N. "VR and People Who Are Hard of Hearing: Where Do We Go from Here?" American Rehabilitation v19 n4, Win 1993-1994. p16-19. (ISSN0362-4048).

HEART--DISEASES--TREATMENT (v19)

HEART--DISEASES--U.S. (v19)

"In 1991, there were 720,000 deaths attributed to coronary heart disease. The American Heart Association estimates that about 1.5 million heart attacks occur each year, and that coronary heart disease costs Americans an estimated $52 billion in direct health care expenditures and lost productivity." (p2)

Frazao, Betsy. "Health Linked to Nutrition: The High Costs of Poor Diets." Food Review v17 n1, Jan-Apr 1994. p2-3.

HEART--DISEASES--U.S.--MORTALITY (v19)

HEART--SURGERY--CANADA--GERMANY--U.S. (v19)

HEART ATTACK

see MYOCARDIAL INFARCTION

HELIUM INDUSTRY--U.S. (v19)

"Concerns that natural gas supplies were drying up prompted Congress to replace the 1925 act with the Helium Act Amendments of 1960. The 1960 act was intended to conserve helium for essential Government services and to supply current and foreseeable needs of the Federal Government. The law authorized the Secretary to buy helium from private suppliers and store it for use by the Federal Government. Also the law authorized storage of helium, maintaining helium production and purification plants, as well as related helium storage, transmission and shipping facilities. Beginning in 1960, the Federal Government contracted with private companies to supply helium to the BOM [Bureau of Mines] facility. To finance purchases the Bureau borrowed $252 million from the Treasury, intending that future sales would recover the loan. But Federal demand failed to meet projections, and in 1973 the BOM canceled the contracts. This left the Bureau controlling the estimated 32 billion cubic feet helium stockpile, and a debt, which--including interest--is estimated at $1.3 billion. Since the 1960 act, the situation has changed dramatically. Today, there is a thriving, efficient U.S. private helium industry which last year provided and supplied an estimated 3 billion cubic feet of the 3.5 billion cubic feet which is sold worldwide." (pE376)

Vucanovich, Barbara F. (Rep.-Nev.). "Introduction of Helium Amendments Act of 1994," Congressional Record (8 Mar 1994). Daily ed. pE376. (ISSN0363-7239).

HEMOPHILUS INFLUENZAE--U.S. (v19)

HEPATITIS--U.S.

"At the present time...[in the U.S.] the risk of hepatitis B from blood components from transfusion is approximately one in 200,000 per unit of administration. For hepatitis C which is the agent causing so-called non-A non-B hepatitis, the risk is less than one in 3,300 per unit exposure. At these risk rates and with the current utilization patterns, that translates into fewer than 5,400 cases of hepatitis C per year in the United States and less than 100 cases of hepatitis B per year in the United States." (p34-35)

Epstein, Jay (Acting Dir., Office of Blood Research and Review, U.S. FDA). U.S. House. Committee on Energy and Commerce. "Blood Supply Safety." Hearing, 28 Jul 1993. Washington, D.C.: GPO, 1993. (ISBN0160432081). (Y4.En2/3:103-42).

HEPATITIS VIRUSES--U.S. (v19)

HERBICIDES--U.S.

"Herbicides are now sprayed on about 95% of U.S. corn acreage. In 1982, (13.8 million ha [hectare]) 34 million acres of U.S. corn accounted for 54% of all herbicide active ingredient--110 million kg (242 million lbs) out of 204.7 million kg (450 million lbs) total. This was a dramatic increase from 1971, when 48.7% or 45.8 million kg (101 million lbs) of the 94.0 million kg (207 million lbs) of herbicide were sprayed on cornfields. U.S. herbicide use is expected to increase 33%, or another 68 million kg (150 million lbs), by the year 2000. Yet, only minimal resources are being directed towards weed control alternatives (Chandler 1985)....Besides spending over $2 billion annually on herbicides, U.S. farmers spend another $1 billion on labor and application equipment." (p3)

Grossman, Joel. "Update: Box B: Tillage vs. Herbicides." IPM Practitioner v15 n7, Jul 1993. p3. (ISSN0738-968X).

"Over $2 billion per year is spent on row crop tillage [in the U.S.]....About half of all tillage between crops is done for the purpose of weed control; 2 to 5 cultivations provide effective row crop weed control for a cropping season. Herbicides began replacing tillage for weed control extensively in the 1970s because loose soil (after tillage) is much more susceptible to erosion than soil with ground cover or crop residues. There is more water runoff (meaning less for crops) from bare soil than from ground with a plant or residue cover. Tillage also requires energy and labor inputs....But it took selective herbicides plus new machines that simultaneously tilled the soil, planted seeds and killed weeds to make no-till a reality. By the 1970s, over 100 selective herbicides, 20 for corn alone, received EPA registration. Herbicides gradually evolved from supplemental tillage to replacing cultivation altogether (Triplett and van Doren 1977). By the year 2000 only 20 million ha [hectare] (49.4 million acres) are expected to be farmed conventionally, versus 62 million ha in no-tillage and 62 million ha (153.1 million acres) in minimum-tillage (Chandler 1985)." (p3)

Grossman, Joel. "Update: Box B: Tillage vs. Herbicides." IPM Practitioner v15 n7, Jul 1993. p3. (ISSN0738-968X).

"Each year in the United States, about 15 million acres of corn, 1.5 million acres of wheat, and 3 million lawns are treated with the herbicide dicamba. While its name is often not commonly recognized, this wide use, together with concerns about its toxicology and its effects on our environment, make it important to scrutinize dicamba's hazards." (p30) "Dicamba's median lethal oral dose (LD50; the amount that kills 50 percent of a population of test animals) is 1707 milligrams per kilogram (mg/kg) in rats. Female rats are killed by a smaller dose than are male rats. If we assume humans are as susceptible to dicamba as are laboratory animals, an oral dose of about 3.5 ounces would be required to kill an average-sized (60 kg) human." (p31)

Cox, Caroline. "Herbicide Factsheet: Dicamba." Journal of Pesticide Reform v14 n1, Spr 1994. p30-35. (ISSN0893-357X).

"In general, herbicide concentrations in the streams and rivers decrease with time after planting. Until this year, it was assumed that the decrease was partly due to breakdown of the herbicide in the soil, and partly because all available herbicide has been washed away. It was assumed that if there was more rain, concentrations would decrease. The surprise in 1993 was that the herbicide concentrations remained high even after record amounts of rainfall. Levels of atrazine were as high as 3.4 ppb [parts per billion] in the Iowa River at Iowa City, with 2.8 ppb in the city's drinking water. Alachlor, which is usually not detected in Iowa City's water, was present in both river water and the city's drinking water....USGS [U.S. Geological Survey] estimated that for several days during peak flows, the Mississippi carried more than 12,000 pounds (6 tons!) of atrazine per day past Thebes, Illinois. During the worst 40 days of flooding, the Mississippi dumped about 340,000 pounds of atrazine and 40,000 pounds of alachlor into the Gulf of Mexico. This compares with an average yearly loading of 310,000 pounds for atrazine and 36,000 pounds for alachlor. In addition to pesticide runoff, nitrate runoff also significantly increased during the 1993 floods and was 20 to 25 percent higher than expected." (p29)

Shistar, Terry. "News from Around: Research: Too Much Poisoned Water: Pesticides and the 1993 Mississippi River Flood." Journal of Pesticide Reform v13 n4, Win 1993. p29. (ISSN0893-357X).

HEROIN--HONG KONG

"Hong Kong is a major transit point for drugs into the United States. Most trafficking involves heroin number 4 (injectable). The wholesale price for heroin number 4 fluctuated in the first half of 1990 from a low of about $13,500 per kilogram (2.2 pounds) in January to about $18,000 per kilogram in April. Heroin found in Hong Kong originates in Southeast Asia and is moved into Hong Kong by air, overland from China, or by sea intermixed in the considerable international cargo which transits the Crown Colony. Hong Kong authorities estimate that upwards of one-half of all heroin now enters by way of southern China with a sizeable portion probably re-exported to the United States....Through October 1990, Hong Kong authorities seized approximately 176 pounds (80 kilograms) of heroin number 4, 154 pounds (70 kilograms) of heroin number 3 (smokeable), and 132 pounds (60 kilograms) of raw or prepared opium." (p31-32)

Tracy, Sharon. "The Evolution of the Hong Kong Triads/Tongs into the Current Drug Market." Journal of Third World Studies v10 n1, Spr 1993. p22-36. (ISSN8755-3449).

HEROIN HABIT--U.S. (v19)

HIDES AND SKINS INDUSTRY--MEXICO--U.S. (v19)

HIGH SCHOOL DROPOUTS--CHICAGO (ILL)

"In Chicago, an examination of dropout rates produced the following findings: The high school with the highest dropout rate in the city, 69.5 percent, had a dropout rate among athletes of only 7 percent. The high school with the second highest dropout rate among the city's general enrollment, 67 percent, had a dropout rate for athletes of 5 percent. Further, a high school with a dropout rate of 55.9 percent had a dropout rate among athletes of .8 percent (Harden, 1987)." (p96-97)

Smith, J. W., Jr. "A Research Review: Interscholastic Athletic Programs: A Positive Factor In School Reform." NASSP Bulletin v78 n559, Feb 1994. p93-98. (ISSN0192-6365).

HIGH SCHOOL DROPOUTS--EMPLOYMENT--U.S.

A four-year evaluation of a program to provide education and job training to school dropouts shows that the youths did improve their educational level, but the program had little effect on their employment. "Forty-two percent of the JOBSTART youths attained a general-equivalency diploma within the follow-up period, compared with 29 percent of those in the control group. In general, however, the study found no real payoff in earnings for JOBSTART participants." (p18)

"News in Brief." Education Week v13 n17, 19 Jan 1994. p18. (ISSN0277-4232).

HIGH SCHOOL DROPOUTS--U.S. (v19)

"The increasingly high number of at-risk middle and high school students--those in danger of dropping out of school because of academic failure or other problems--is a major concern in education today. At-risk students show persistent patterns of under-achievement and of social maladjustment in school, leading to their failure to finish high school. Indeed, the national dropout rate averages about 25 percent (Sklarz 1989), and for minorities, that rate is higher, with an average of 30 percent leaving school before they graduate (Liontos 1991). In Texas, the dropout rate for Hispanic Americans is 45 percent. Additionally, students in urban schools have much higher dropout rates than those in other areas: in Boston, Chicago, Los Angeles, Detroit, and other major cities, dropout rates range from 40 percent to 60 percent of the total school population (Hahn 1987)." (p137)

McMillan, James H./Reed, Daisy F. "At-Risk Students and Resiliency: Factors Contributing to Academic Success." Clearing House v67 n3, Jan-Feb 1994. p137-140. (ISSN0009-8655).

"Young people who attend school are less likely to engage in several serious health-risk behaviors, the U.S. Centers for Disease Control and Prevention has found. The C.D.C....published a study comparing risk behaviors in a group of about 7,000 12- to 19-year olds. Youths who were not enrolled in school were less likely to always wear seat belts when riding in cars and trucks, and more likely to ride in a vehicle driven by someone who was drunk, the C.D.C. researchers found. Nearly one-third of the out-of-school adolescents reported smoking cigarettes on one or more days in the month preceding the study, compared with one-fifth of the enrolled students." (p7)

Sklaroff, Sara. "Health." Education Week v13 n25, 16 Mar 1994. p7. (ISSN0277-4232).

HIGH SCHOOL DROPOUTS--U.S.--ECONOMIC CONDITIONS (v19)

HIGH SCHOOL GRADUATES--U.S.

"The big change in high school graduation rates came between 1910 and 1960. Graduation was rare at the beginning of this period: 8.8 percent of 17-year-olds achieved it. By 1960, 69.5 percent of 17-year olds received [a] high school diploma, by 1969, 77.1 percent. In 1980 this slumped to 71.4 percent; the Department of Education estimates that it was 73.8 percent last year. But the graduation rate has never risen above 77.1 percent, where it was in 1969. Is there any possibility that we will reach 90 percent 6 years from now--unless we fudge the numbers by including persons who received a GED or some equivalent later in life." (pS926)

Moynihan, Daniel Patrick (Sen.-N.Y.). "GOALS 2000: Educate America Act," Congressional Record (4 Feb 1994). Daily ed. pS910-932. (ISSN0363-7239).

HIGH TECHNOLOGY--U.S. (v19)

HIGHER EDUCATION

see EDUCATION, HIGHER

HIMALAYA MOUNTAINS REGION

"There are at least 131 national parks and protected areas covering about 863,000 hectares in the Himalaya, according to Dr. Hemantra Mishra, a biodiversity specialist with the World Bank in Washington, D.C. Tourist and development pressures prompted the creation of many of these areas, notably the Sagarmatha National Park in Nepal (1973), Nanda Devi in India (1982), and Royal Manas in Bhutan (1987). But even with these 131 refuges, more than 99.7 percent of the Himalaya is left officially unprotected." (p17)

Denniston, Derek. "Saving the Himalaya." World Watch v6 n6, Nov-Dec 1993. p10-21. (ISSN0896-0615).

HISPANIC AMERICANS (v19)

see also ABORTION--HISPANIC AMERICANS; AIDS (DISEASE)--AFRO-AMERICANS--HISPANIC AMERICANS; AIDS (DISASE)--HISPANIC AMERICANS; DIPLOMATIC AND CONSULAR SERVICE--HISPANIC AMERICANS; EDUCATION--HISPANIC AMERICANS; POOR CHILDREN--HISPANIC AMERICANS; STERILIZATION (BIRTH CONTROL)--HISPANIC AMERICANS; VIOLENCE--AFRO-AMERICANS--HISPANIC AMERICANS--MORTALITY

"Mexican-Americans make up the largest sub-group (62%) of the overall Hispanic population, living primarily in the western and southwestern United States. The median age of the Hispanic population is 25.9 years, compared to 33.2 for the non-Hispanic population. Within Hispanics, the median age for Mexican-Americans is 23.6. Among Mexican-Americans, 42.9% are 19 years of age or younger, which is the largest percentage for all the Hispanic subgroups (Current Population Reports, Bureau of the Census, 1988; 1990)." (p225-226)

Castaneda, Donna M. "A Research Agenda for Mexican-American Adolescent Mental Health." Adolescence v29 n113, Spr 1994. p225-239. (ISSN0001-8449).

"Immigrants have always settled in America's largest cities, and today's immigrants are not much different. Six of the 12 Hispanic subgroups identified in the 1990 census have more than 80 percent of their populations in the nation's 20 largest cities, and 3 others have between 70 and 79 percent....An example of an unusually high concentration of a Hispanic group in one city is 77 percent concentration of people of Dominican origin in the New York urbanized area. Greater New York also has 60 percent of the nation's Ecuadorians and 44 percent of Puerto Ricans. Los Angeles has 49 percent of the nation's Guatemalans and 47 percent of its Salvadoreans. Miami is home to 53 percent of Cuban Americans." (p49,52)

Winsberg, Morton. "Specific Hispanics." American Demographics v16 n2, Feb 1994. p44-49,52-53. (ISSN0163-4089).

"Several U.S. places have Hispanic populations that rival or even surpass the largest cities in their countries of origin. New York's Puerto Rican population is now more than double that of San Juan. New York also has the second-largest urban population of Dominicans in the world, and the third-largest Ecuadorian population. The Mexican, Salvadorean, and Guatemalan populations of urban Los Angeles are surpassed only by those of their respective capitals: Mexico City, San Salvador, and Guatemala City. Eighteen percent of all Hispanic Americans live in Los Angeles, and 12 percent live in New York. These two urban areas rank among the top-5 for 11 of the 12 Hispanic groups. Miami is on the top-5 list for 9 Hispanic groups, Washington, D.C. for 6, San Francisco for 5, and Houston and Chicago for 4." (p52)

Winsberg, Morton. "Specific Hispanics." American Demographics v16 n2, Feb 1994. p44-49,52-53. (ISSN0163-4089).

"Since the U.S. census first counted Hispanics in 1970, those who identify Mexico, Puerto Rico, and Cuba as their country of origin have comprised about three-fourths of the total U.S. Hispanic population. Hispanics from other Latin-American nations and cultures are less well-understood, but they constitute one-quarter of an estimated $170 billion consumer market....Among all Hispanics, the share of Mexicans has fallen from 62 percent of all U.S. Hispanics in 1970 to 61 percent in 1990. The Puerto Rican and Cuban shares have remained at about 12 percent and 5 percent, respectively. Hispanic Americans who don't have origins in these three countries are a small share of the nation's total Hispanic population, but they have been growing. Their numbers grew by slightly more than 2 million between 1970 and 1990. Immigrants of the new wave have been fleeing civil wars in Nicaragua, El Salvador, Guatemala, and Colombia. Others come for jobs or to rejoin family members already here." (p44,48)

Winsberg, Morton. "Specific Hispanics." American Demographics v16 n2, Feb 1994. p44-49,52-53. (ISSN0163-4089).

"The geographic concentration of specific Hispanic populations is...striking. Over four-fifths (83 percent) of Mexican Americans are located in the Southwest (74 percent in Texas and California alone), 68 percent of Puerto Ricans are in the Northeast (primarily New York and New Jersey), and 70 percent of Cubans are in the South, with 65 percent in Florida alone. Geographic concentrations like these make it important to look beyond national averages to better understand Latino Americans." (p21)

O'Hare, William P. "America's Minorities--The Demographics of Diversity." Population Bulletin v47 n4, Dec 1992. p2-47. (ISSN0032-468X).

HISPANIC AMERICANS--ECONOMIC CONDITIONS (v19)

"In 1991 Puerto Ricans had the highest poverty rate for individuals in the nation at nearly 40% of the total Puerto Rican population, compared to 33% for African-Americans, and 14.2% for the population at large. Although Census figures for 1991 report that African-Americans had the highest percentage of families living below the poverty line, at 32%, Puerto Rican families had more of their families living in poverty at 36%. Puerto Ricans are a highly urbanized group with 95% of all mainland Puerto Ricans living in urban areas and 75% living in central cities (mostly in the East and Midwest), representing the most urbanized ethnic group in the United States. Most of these cities have watched a deterioration of their low-skilled employment base in manufacturing and an explosion of poverty. Puerto Rican children have the unfortunate distinction of being the poorest in the nation. A study of Latino child poverty conducted by the Children's Defense Fund, indicates that 48.4% of Puerto Rican children were poor in 1989, compared to 44% of African-American children. More recent Census data reveals further deterioration in the socio-economic status of Puerto Rican children with a poverty rate of 58% in 1991, compared to 46% in the African-American community." (p160)

Pagani, Ruth (Public Policy Coordinator, National Puerto Rican Coalition, Inc.). U.S. House. Committee on Ways and Means. "Historical Trends in Poverty and Family Income." Hearing, 26 Oct 1993. Washington, D.C.: GPO, 1994. (ISBN0160435765). (Y4.W36:103-42).

"To apply the term 'at risk' to Mexican-American adolescents is somewhat inaccurate because it implies 'potentiality.' For a large proportion of these young people, their vulnerability is real. Half of the 26.7% of Hispanics living below the poverty line are under the age of 18. Hispanic children represent 11% of all children in the U.S., but they represent 21% of all children living in poverty (Current Population Reports, Bureau of the Census, 1990). If children and youth in general are less of a priority, Mexican-American children fare even worse. Support for needy children has never been substantial (Conger, 1988; Edelman, 1987; Inouye, 1988) and the second-class status of Mexican Americans compounds the problem. Racism as much as their age adds to the problem (Torres-Gil, 1986)." (p227)

Castaneda, Donna M. "A Research Agenda for Mexican-American Adolescent Mental Health." Adolescence v29 n113, Spr 1994. p225-239. (ISSN0001-8449).

HISPANIC AMERICANS--EDUCATION

"Although the educational attainment of Puerto Ricans continues to be low in comparison to that of whites [in the U.S.], it has been rising steadily since the late 1970s, surpassing that of all Hispanics since 1988. Their labor force participation, however, has not kept pace with educational attainment. For example, after slight increases between 1985 and 1989, the labor force participation rate for Puerto Rican males decreased steadily between 1989 and 1991, from 70 to 66%. These statistics strongly suggest that the explanation for the high rate of poverty among Puerto Ricans does not rest solely on behavioral factors. Since the late 1970s Puerto Ricans have consistently shown increasing rates of high school completion, from 36% in 1978 to 61% in 1992. College graduation rates show a similar pattern going from 4.2% in 1977 to 8.4% in 1992." (p162)

Pagani, Ruth (Public Policy Coordinator, National Puerto Rican Coalition, Inc.). U.S. House. Committee on Ways and Means. "Historical Trends in Poverty and Family Income." Hearing, 26 Oct 1993. Washington, D.C.: GPO, 1994. (ISBN060435765). (Y4.W36:103-42).

"Hispanics are among the most undereducated racial/ethnic groups in the...[U.S.]. Hispanic educational attainment has increased in absolute terms since 1970, but the gap between Hispanics and non-Hispanics continues to be wide. Compared to Blacks and Whites, Hispanics enter school later, leave school earlier, and are less likely to complete high school and enter or complete college. To illustrate, as of 1992, a little more than half of all Hispanics 25 years old and over (52.6%) compared to four-fifths of non-Hispanics 25 years old and over (81.5%) had completed four years of high school or more. Moreover, almost one in ten Hispanics (9.3%), compared to almost one in four non-Hispanics (22.3%) had completed four years of college or more." (p189)

Perez, Sonia M. (National Council of La Raza). U.S. House. Committee on Ways and Means. "Historical Trends in Poverty and Family Income." Hearing, 26 Oct 1993. Washington, D.C.: GPO, 1994. (ISBN0160435765). (Y4.W36:103-42).

HISPANIC AMERICANS--EDUCATION (HIGHER) (v19)

HISPANIC AMERICANS--EMPLOYMENT (v19)

"Hispanics are active participants in the [U.S.] workforce; Hispanic men are more likely to be working or looking for work than either Black or White men. In 1992, 79.6% of Hispanic and 74.3% of non-Hispanic males were in the civilian labor force. The labor force participation rate of Hispanic women is slightly less than that of White or Black women, although it has been increasing in recent years....both Hispanic males and females are most often employed in low-paying jobs with limited opportunities for advancement and few benefits, such as health insurance. Census data show that in 1992, about one in nine Hispanic males (11.4%), compared to more than one in four non-Hispanic males (27.4%), were employed in managerial or professional jobs--which in 1992 had median weekly earnings of $655. By contrast, 27.5% of Hispanic men, compared to 19.2% of non-Hispanic men, were employed as operators, fabricators, and laborers--with median weekly earnings of $357....because Hispanic workers, on average, have earnings far below those of non-Hispanics, the median family income gap between Hispanics and Whites is growing wider; the gap was $11,895 in 1980 and $15,355 in 1991." (p187)

Perez, Sonia M. (National Council of La Raza). U.S. House. Committee on Ways and Means. "Historical Trends in Poverty and Family Income." Hearing, 26 Oct 1993. Washington, D.C.:

GPO, 1994. (ISBN0160435765). (Y4.W36:103-42).

HISPANIC AMERICANS--PUBLIC OPINION (v19)

HISPANIC AMERICANS--SANTA FE (N.MEX)--ECONOMIC CONDITIONS

"Often obscured by the allure of Santa Fe's world-class opera, seven museums and some 150 galleries, is the fact that the average annual wage in Santa Fe County is still below $16,000, and almost 13,000 residents live at or below poverty level. But the resentment of many Hispanics toward planned communities, designer boutiques and, now, exclusive golf developments is rooted in more than class differences. Santa Fe's Hispanics are being displaced by affluent whites at close to the rate of 1 percent per year. Since 1970, the Hispanic population in this town of 60,000 has decreased from 65 percent to 49 percent, while that of Anglos has increased from 33 percent to 48 percent, according to state labor statistics. During the 1980s alone, some 23,000 newcomers--a majority from Southern California and Texas--settled in Santa Fe County. At the same time 3,500 Santa Fe families, most of them Hispanic, left town." (p1)

Selcraig, Bruce. "Fore! in Santa Fe." High Country News v25 n9B, 17 May 1993. p1,10-11. (ISSN0191-5657).

HISPANIC AMERICANS--TEXAS

"Laredo, Texas, is not big as urban areas go, with 99,258 people in 1990. But 94 percent of Laredo residents are Hispanic, and the overwhelming majority are of Mexican origin. The census count of Hispanics, also mainly Mexican, is 90 percent in Brownsville and 83 percent in McAllen, two other Texas border towns." (p52)

Winsberg, Morton. "Specific Hispanics." American Demographics v16 n2, Feb 1994. p44-49,52,53. (ISSN0163-4089).

HIV (VIRUSES) (v19)

"WHO [World Health Organization] estimates that since the start of the pandemic 14 million adults and one million children have been infected with HIV. Nine million of the adult infections have occurred in sub-Saharan Africa and 1.5 million in Latin America. Of the more than two million infections estimated to have occurred in Asia, most have happened in the past three years. WHO estimates that by the end of the century 30 to 40 million people may have been infected with HIV." (p1)

News release. "'HIV Vaccine Development at Crossroads', Says WHO Director of AIDS Research." WHO Press 10 Apr 1994. p1-2.

HIV (VIRUSES)--U.S.--MEDICAL PERSONNEL

"It is critical that health and mental health workers be knowledgeable and rational about HIV. Irrational fears, prejudice, and stress can lead to burnout and reduce the quality of health care services provided....As of March 1992 only 91 of the 218,301 cumulative reported AIDS cases (0.04%) were health care workers reporting no other risk for HIV infection. Further, HIV-infected blood exposure in the workplace has only been confirmed as the mode of transmission for 3 cases (CDC, 1992)." (p81)

Knox, Michael D./others. "The HIV Mental Health Spectrum." Community Mental Health Journal v30 n1, Feb 1994. p75-89. (ISSN0010-3853).

HIV INFECTIONS

see also AIDS (DISEASE)

"WHO [World Health Organization] figures released today (Sunday 12 December 1993) show that the number of HIV infections since the start of the HIV/AIDS epidemic has topped 15 million worldwide. The largest number of new infections has been in Africa, where the cumulative total is now close to 10 million--an increase of 1.5 million over the last year." (p1)

News release. "1.5 Million New HIV Infections in Africa Pushes Global Total to Over 15 Million." WHO Press 10 Dec 1993. p1-2.

HIV INFECTIONS--ABIDJAN (COTE D'IVOIRE)

"Researchers, led by Kevin De Cock of Project RETRO-CI in Abidjan and the US Centers for Disease Control in Atlanta, followed a consecutive sample of 19,701 women of reproductive age attending a mother and child health clinic in Abidjan [Cote d'Ivoire]. Between 1988 and 1992, the prevalence of HIV-1 among these women rose from 5% to 9.2%, while the prevalence of HIV-2 decreased from 2.6% to 1.5%." (p5)

"Science: Declining HIV-2?" WorldAIDS n31, Jan 1993. p5. (ISSN0954-6510).

HIV INFECTIONS--AFRICA

"Daan Mulder, Jane Kengeya-Kayondo and their colleagues at the Uganda Virus Research Institute, and the UK Medical Research Council AIDS programme in Entebbe, have surveyed almost 10,000 people in 15 villages near Masaka...[in Africa's] southwest....Overall, more than half of all adult deaths, including teenagers, were linked with HIV. In adults aged between 25 and 44, more than 80% of deaths were linked with the virus....The prevalence of HIV in the population overall was almost 5%, and 8% for the adult and teenage population. There is one new case of infection in every 100 people each year." (p5)

"Science: Counting Uganda's Rising Toll." WorldAIDS n29, Sep 1993. p5. (ISSN0954-6510).

HIV INFECTIONS--AFRICA--PRISONERS

"The situation in African prisons is worrying. A study from Cote d'Ivoire found HIV prevalence rates of 25% among over 1,700 inmates, and 7% among prison staff....A study of Algerians in prison between 1987 and 1989 showed an HIV prevalence of 1.3%, about 10 times the rate among blood donors (0.16%) which is taken to be representative of the population at large since donations are voluntary and generally made by relatives at the time of hospital treatment." (p4)

"Marrakech Conference Report: Prison Fears Grow." WorldAIDS n32, Mar 1994. p4. (ISSN0954-6510).

HIV INFECTIONS--ASIA

"In parts of Asia today HIV is spreading as fast as it did in Africa a decade ago. With its enormous population, Asia is about to overtake Africa. Soon more Asians than Africans will be getting infected each year. WHO [World Health Organization] estimates that there have now been over 15 million HIV infections since the start of the epidemic--14 million in teenagers and adults, 1 million in children born to HIV-infected mothers. By the year 2000, WHO predicts that the current global figure will more than double, to between 30 and 40 million infections. But the epidemic expansion will be most dramatic in Asia. Today's cumulative infection total of over 2 million Asians is expected to quintuple to over 10 million infections by the year 2000." (p1)

News release. "'Asian Business Leaders Crucial in Fight Against AIDS', Says WHO AIDs Executive Director." WHO Press 14 Apr 1994. p1-3.

HIV INFECTIONS--BLOOD DONORS

"In the US, paid donors were seven times more likely to be infected with HIV than voluntary donors; one study in Mexico found the ratio even higher, at 70:1. Another study in Bombay, India found that 172 of 200 professional blood donors were HIV positive." (p9)

Brown, Phyllida. "Briefing: A Question of Life and Death." WorldAIDS n32, Mar 1994. p6-9. (ISSN0954-6510).

HIV INFECTIONS--BRAZIL--PRISONERS

"Between 1988 and 1990, 4,000 of Rio de Janeiro's 13,000 prisoners underwent compulsory HIV testing under the supervision of the State's Prison Department: 11% tested positive. In Sao Paulo, a 1992 WHO [World Health Organization] study based on

State Prison Department surveys revealed HIV prevalence levels of 20% among men and 28.7% among women, out of a total of 24,000 prisoners." (p2)

Longo, Paulo Henrique/de Oliveira, Sylvio. "Inside Story: A Hope in Hell?" WorldAIDS n30, Nov 1993. p2. (ISSN0954-6510).

HIV INFECTIONS--HONG KONG

"Heterosexual sex has become the most common means of transmission of HIV in Hong Kong, according to researchers at Hong Kong's Health Department. By April this year, a total of 359 cases of HIV, including 81 cases of AIDS, had been recorded in Hong Kong." (p4)

Kahane, Tony. "News: Hong Kong's Heterosexual AIDS." WorldAIDS n29, Sep 1993. p4. (ISSN0954-6510).

HIV INFECTIONS--INDIA

"Dr Gilada [of the Indian Health Organisation] has been monitoring the prevalence of HIV among Bombay's hijra prostitutes since 1986 when 24 hijras were tested for HIV. Only one tested positive. The following year, Dr Gilada tested 106 hijra prostitutes. This time three tested positive. By 1989, 11% of hijra prostitutes were testing positive for HIV. Last year, Dr Gilada found 40% of hijra prostitutes were infected with HIV." (p11)

"AidsWatch: India: A Fatal Profession." WorldAIDS n27, May 1993. p11. (ISSN0954-6510).

HIV INFECTIONS--INDIA--NEPAL--PROSTITUTES

"Up to 25% of prostitutes are HIV positive in some Indian cities--and the rate is even higher for Nepali prostitutes, reaching 35% in places, according to the Kathmandu-based Women's Rehabilitation Centre, who provide support for some returning girls....An estimated 25,000 girls, many of them infected with HIV, are engaged in prostitution in Kathmandu....AIDS is already a political issue in the Himalayan kingdom, where at least 5,000 people are estimated infected with HIV." (p11)

"AidsWatch: Nepal: Fighting against Fate." WorldAIDS n32, Mar 1994. p11. (ISSN0954-6510).

HIV INFECTIONS--MALAYSIA

"Widespread testing and the frequent sharing of needles among IDUs [injecting drug users] has lead to a soaring increase in identified HIV cases among drug users. In 1990, they accounted for 628 cases. Today, 80% of the 6,225 reported HIV cases in Malaysia (which has the second highest number of reported cases in Asia after Thailand) are drug users." (p3)

Segaram, Satay. "News: Streets of Shame." WorldAIDS n30, Nov 1993. p3. (ISSN0954-6510).

HIV INFECTIONS--MOTHERS

"In Europe the median rate of vertical transmission [of HIV] from mother to child was 16.6%, plus or minus 1.5%; while in Africa the rate was 28.1%, plus or minus 2.5%--a large and lamentable difference. This picture of transmission rates in Africa was backed up by a conference paper from a team at the Muhimbili University College of Health Sciences in Dar es Salaam, Tanzania. Studying new mothers in their clinic, they found that 12.5% were HIV positive, and that the vertical transmission rate was a minimum of 20% and a maximum of 34%, very much in accord with [a study by a team from Bordeaux University led by Dr. Francois Dabis]....The extra information from the Tanzanian study is the 12 month survival rate for the children. The survival rate for children born to HIV positive mothers was 84% against 96% for HIV negative mothers; the survival rate for HIV positive children was 47% against 95% for HIV negative children, when the mother was HIV positive." (p5)

Winsbury, Rex. "Science: Mother-to-Child HIV." WorldAIDS n32, Mar 1994. p5. (ISSN0954-6510).

HIV INFECTIONS--SOUTH AFRICA

"When the blood transfusion services [in South Africa] first started screening for HIV in 1985, approximately one in every 4,200 black people were found to be HIV positive. Today the figure is one in 79 black men and one in 60 black women, compared with one in 2,000 white men and one in 45,000 white women." (p1)

Armstrong, Sue. "Apartheid's AIDS Legacy." WorldAIDS n32, Mar 1994. p1. (ISSN0954-6510).

HIV INFECTIONS--SOUTH AFRICA--WOMEN

"Among black women [in South Africa] attending antenatal clinics the HIV infection rate increased by almost 400% between 1990 and 1992 (from 0.89% to 3.22%) according to surveys, while the comparable figures for white women were 0.06% to 0.09%. For coloured--or mixed race--women, the infection rate doubled from 0.16% to 0.33% in the same period." (p1)

Armstrong, Sue. "Apartheid's AIDS Legacy." WorldAIDS n32, Mar 1994. p1. (ISSN0954-6510).

HIV INFECTIONS--TANZANIA

"Research conducted last year by the African Medical Research Foundation (AMREF) along the Dar es Salaam to Makambako highway [in Tanzania] suggested disturbingly high levels of HIV among truck drivers and the prostitutes: the study showed that up to 31% of truckers were HIV positive, and that 55.7% of the prostitutes catering for the truckers were also infected with the virus. The study also showed that around 18% of truck drivers had untreated syphilis." (p4)

Ndejembi, Edna. "News: Tanzania's Truckers at High Risk of HIV." WorldAIDS n29, Sep 1993. p4. (ISSN0954-6510).

HIV INFECTIONS--THAILAND--PROSTITUTES

"Prostitutes [in Thailand], particularly the poorer ones in cheap brothels and hotels who cater for the domestic market and are less likely to use condoms, are hard hit by HIV. In Bangkok, 35% of these are thought to be infected, compared with 4% of women engaged in 'indirect' prostitution through massage parlours, bars and clubs, most of them geared to a better-off clientele, including foreigners. The worst affected region is the north: in Chiang Mai, 10% of blood donors, 61% of drug users, up to 35% of prostitutes and 1.5% of women visiting antenatal clinics are HIV positive. The implications on the regional spread of HIV are worrying: northern women form a large percentage of Thai sex workers abroad--in Japan, Singapore, Hong Kong and Macao." (p7)

Lintner, Bertil/others. "Briefing: Asia's AIDS Crossroads?" WorldAIDS n28, Jul 1993. p7. (ISSN0954-6510).

HIV INFECTIONS--U.S. (v19)

"Researchers tested the blood of 7,992 US volunteers over 18 from 1988 to 1991 and found 29 or 0.36% were HIV positive--a result which suggested an overall figure of 550,000 Americans infected. But the survey only dealt with people who agreed to cooperate and did not test prisoners or homeless people--groups which are known to have proprotionately higher rates of HIV." (p5)

"Science: U.S. Testing." WorldAIDS n32, Mar 1994. p5. (ISSN0954-6510).

HIV INFECTIONS--VIETNAM

"Vietnam's first case of HIV was reported in 1990. By the end of 1992, still only eight cases had been notified. But this year [1993] there are disturbing signs of a rapid acceleration in the spread of HIV--from just 15 cases in February to 332 by May." (p1)

Kahane, Tony. "Vietnam Under Fire." WorldAIDS n28, Jul 1993. p1. (ISSN0954-6510).

HMONG (ASIAN PEOPLE)--U.S. (v19)

"The Hmong population, a hill tribe people from Laos, has become heavily concentrated in three states: California, Minnesota, and Wisconsin. In 1980, 26 percent of the Hmong population of the United States resided in Minnesota due to active efforts by

Lutheran Churches there to resettle refugees. The remainder were scattered about the nation in response to the Task Force's mandate for dispersal. By 1990, 52 percent of the Hmong population lived in California, centered on 'Hmong capitals' in California's Central Valley communities of Fresno, Merced, Sacramento, and Stockton. Another 36 percent lived in Minnesota and Wisconsin, concentrated in the Minneapolis-St. Paul area and in a broad swath of central Wisconsin communities including La Crosse, Eau Claire, Manitowoc, and Sheboygan, as well as in Milwaukee." (p35)

Gober, Patricia. "Americans on the Move." Population Bulletin v48 n3, Nov 1993. p2-40. (ISSN0032-468X).

HOCKEY--CANADA

"While the number of Canadian men and boys playing hockey has fallen in recent years, the number of women playing has more than doubled in three years. More than 14,000 women played organized hockey in Canada in 1992, up sharply from a little more than 7,000 in 1990, according to the Canadian Amateur Hockey Association (CAHA). Meanwhile, male players fell from 481,000 two years ago to 424,000 last year, the CAHA says. The Ontario Women's Hockey Association (OWHA), which boasts the largest female hockey program in the world, says membership grew from about 4,500 to more than 6,300 players in the same period." (p16)

Clayton, Mark. "Sports: In Canada, Women's Hockey Rises Unchecked." The Christian Science Monitor v86 n50, 4 Feb 1994. p16. (ISSN0882-7729).

HOLIDAYS

Great Britain "has only eight public holidays. Many Japanese enjoy eight over Christmas alone, and 21 altogether. Americans and continental Europeans get fewer public holidays over Christmas, but more later: there are 16 public holidays a year in the United States, 14 in Gerrnany and 11 in France. Where England is unusual is in the distribution of its holidays. Three fall at Christmas, four more between Easter and the end of May, leaving just one for the rest of the year. (The government, in the face of opposition from industry, has just dropped plans to move one holiday from May to October.)" (p16)

"Leaders: Don't Bank on It." Economist v329 n7843, 25 Dec 1993. p16. (ISSN0013-0613).

HOLOCAUST, JEWISH (1939-1945)

"Adolf Eichmann called the failure to round up and deport Denmark's Jews his greatest operational defeat. Of the 7,800 Jews in Denmark in October 1943 (a number that includes the 1,300 children of mixed marriages), more than 7,200 escaped to Sweden, where they survived the war. When they returned home they received an unforgettably warm welcome. Their homes and belongings in Denmark had not been touched." (p7)

Goldberger, Leo. "The Rescue of the Danish Jews." Dimensions: A Journal of Holocaust Studies v7 n3, 1993. p3-8. (ISSN0882-1240).

"On October 2, 1940, Ludwig Fischer, the Nazi governor of the city, ordered the creation of the Warsaw ghetto. The Jews immediately began organizing a prodigious network of medical, social, and cultural self-help, in the hope of making life less harsh for the 500,000 men, women, and children pressed together in a part of the city originally intended for 80,000 inhabitants. Ghetto: a section of a city cut off from the world, a kind of leprosarium whose patients are isolated because they belong to the Jewish people. The idea was born one day in 1516, in the mind of a Venetian doge. In Warsaw in 1940, the ghetto became one of the largest 'cemeteries for the living,' reserved for a people condemned to disappear." (p36)

Halter, Marek. "Forcing Open the Gates of History." Dimensions: A Journal of Holocaust Studies v7 n2, 1993. p34-39. (ISSN0882-1240).

"The Nazis' Terezin--a model camp, a safe haven, a paradise ghetto--fooled an International Commission of the Red Cross and the rest of the world. However, the 'residents'--the prisoners--had a more accurate slang name for Terezin. They called it the schleuse, 'the sluice-gate.' For Terezin was a transit camp, a way station on the route to the death camps in Poland. Of the 140,000 people sent to Terezin, 87,000 prisoners left it in transports going east, mostly to Auschwitz and virtually certain death; over 33,430 prisoners died in Terezin itself from maltreatment, disease, starvation, and other afflictions. Of the 15,000 children sent to Terezin, fewer than one in 10 survived; about 17,000 inmates lived to see liberation on May 7, 1945." (p26)

Couture, Andrea M. "Nazism and Modern Culture: Terezin: Art, Propaganda and Memory." Dimensions: A Journal of Holocaust Studies v7 n1, 1993. p26-29. (ISSN0882-1240).

HOME-BASED BUSINESSES--U.S. (v19)

HOME CARE SERVICES--U.S.

"The need for outside help is like a growth hormone for the multi-billion-dollar home-health-care industry. Home-care spending was expected to reach $21 billion in 1993, according to a report issued early in the year by the National Association for Home Care. Registered nurses provide the bulk of medical care at home, while home-care aides help people remain independent. On a given day, aides may scramble eggs, change adult diapers, or brush a patient's teeth. The sparing use of physicians and hospitals keeps costs down. The average home-care visit cost an estimated $66 in 1993, compared with an estimated $1,500 in Medicare charges for an average day in the hospital." (p44)

Braus, Patricia. "When Mom Needs Help." American Demographics v16 n3, Mar 1994. p38-41,44-45. (ISSN0163-4089).

"'Data collection in home care is in its infancy,' says Karen Pace, director of research for the Washington, D.C.-based National Association for Home Care. 'There are bits and pieces, but nothing that tells the whole story.' The National Medical Expenditures Survey, last conducted by the Agency for Health Care Policy and Research in 1987, found that almost 6 million people received formal home-care services. But paid home care is only a fraction of home-care services. Most estimates suggest that at least two-thirds of all home-care assistance is provided free of charge by family or friends, says Pace." (p40)

Braus, Patricia. "When Mom Needs Help." American Demographics v16 n3, Mar 1994. p38-41,44-45. (ISSN0163-4089).

HOME OWNERSHIP--U.S. (v19)

HOME OWNERSHIP--U.S.--PUBLIC OPINION (v19)

HOME SCHOOLING--U.S. (v19)

HOMELESS CHILDREN

Peter Dalgish, founder and executive director of Street Kids International "defines street children as 'kids who live, work, and sleep in the streets, who have limited contact with their parents, and are under age 16.' Estimates of the numbers of street children worldwide run from UNICEF's guess of 30 million up to 100 million. Many are found in South American cities. Dalglish says there may be 150,000 street kids in Africa, spread out over some 50 cities. But no one is very sure about the numbers anywhere. Counting them is 'almost impossible; they move around so much,' says David Blumenkrantz of Undugu Society, a private group based in Nairobi that helps street children. A 1989 study by Kenyan researchers estimated there were 3,600 street children in Nairobi, but that 'sounds low' today, Mr. Blumenkrantz says." (p12)

Press, Robert M. "Cover Story: More African Kids Take to the Streets." The Christian Science Monitor v86 n51, 7 Feb 1994.

p11-13. (ISSN0882-7729).

HOMELESS PERSONS--BOGOTA (COLOMBIA)

There are approximately 20,000 homeless people in Bogota, Colombia, "according to the Andean Commission of Jurists, Colombian Section, in Bogota. Census figures released last year from the New Life Halfway House...say Bogota has 4,000 homeless children over 15 years of age and 3,500 under 14." (p14)

Dermota, Ken. "Justice: 'Social Cleansing' Targets Street Children." The Christian Science Monitor v86 n30, 6 Jan 1994. p14. (ISSN0882-7729).

HOMELESS PERSONS--FRANCE--GREAT BRITAIN (v19)

HOMELESS PERSONS--LOS ANGELES (CALIF) (v19)

HOMELESS PERSONS--SAN FRANCISCO (CALIF)

"'San Francisco is outlawing everything but walking for homeless people--then calling us criminals when we stop to rest, sleep, eat or drink,' said Paul Boden of the Coalition on Homelessness. 'Of course, some homeless people are guilty of these kinds of offenses, because they have nowhere else to go,' said Marcia Rosen, staff attorney with the Lawyers' Committee. 'San Francisco has one of the highest rates of homelessness in the nation. Yet the City funds, at most, 1,400 shelter beds to accommodate the approximately 11,000 to 16,000 homeless men and women in San Francisco.'" (p1)

"Homeless Plaintiffs File Federal Suit to Halt Mayor Jordan's Matrix Program." ACLU News v58 n1, Jan-Feb 1994. p1,6.

"During 1992, 81,366 individuals were turned away from shelter facilities located throughout San Francisco. The United States Conference of Mayors Task Force on Hunger and Homelessness issued a joint policy statement in July concluding, in part, that a lack of shelters and hotel rooms has forced people to sleep in parks and doorways." (p4)

Wood, Daniel B. "National: San Francisco's Homeless Plan Is under Fire." The Christian Science Monitor v86 n10, 9 Dec 1993. p4. (ISSN0882-7729).

HOMELESS PERSONS--U.S. (v19)

A 26-city survey shows that families with children now account for an equal share of the homeless [in the U.S.] as do single men: about 43 percent. Children account for about 30 percent of the homeless population. (p8)

"Children and Families." Education Week v13 n17, 19 Jan 1994. p8. (ISSN0277-4232).

"On the basis of more than 100 local, state and national studies of the homeless [in the U.S.], [Ms. Alice] Baum and [Mr. Don] Barnes estimate that between 65 and 85 percent of the homeless are mentally ill, alcoholic, drug dependent or some combination of the three. Merely providing temporary shelter to individuals with such problems is a disservice to them, as well as a waste of scarce funds. In fact, only one-third of the homeless take advantage of the public benefits that are available to them." (p11)

Neuman, Elena. "Cities Get Tough with the Homeless." Insight v10 n7, 14 Feb 1994. p6-13. (ISSN1051-4880).

HOMELESS PERSONS--U.S.--MENTALLY HANDICAPPED (v19)

HOMELESS PERSONS--U.S.--PUBLIC OPINION

"Polls show that the [U.S.] public has conflicting attitudes toward the homeless....A 1992 NEW YORK TIMES/CBS News poll found that the younger the respondent, the less sympathetic he or she tended to be. Fifty-five percent of those surveyed between the ages of 18 and 29 said that they had become so used to seeing the homeless they were no longer upset by the sight, whereas 45 percent of those between 30 and 44, and only 30 percent of those older than 45, responded similarly." (p9)

Neuman, Elena. "Cities Get Tough with the Homeless." Insight v10 n7, 14 Feb 1994. p6-13. (ISSN1051-4880).

"Some 81 percent of Americans would pay higher taxes for government programs to curtail homelessness, according to a Harris poll commissioned by BUSINESS WEEK magazine last year. Eighty-two percent of the 2,503 people surveyed last July in a PARADE magazine poll said governments should not bar the homeless from libraries, parks, mass transit, and other public places." (p4)

Tyson, James L. "National: Cities Crack Down on Homeless." The Christian Science Monitor v86 n40, 21 Jan 1994. p4. (ISSN0882-7729).

HOMEMAKERS--U.S.

"Women still are the primary homemakers in most households. But in one in five American households, men do most of the shopping. And if recent trends continue, one in three American households will have a male homemaker by the turn of the century....Between 1986 and 1993, the number of men designated as their household's primary shopper grew from fewer than 13 million to more than 20 million....Men who live alone and single fathers were 58 percent of male homemakers in 1993. But this share declined from 72 percent in 1986, mostly because married men are rapidly gaining shopping responsibilities. Husbands are now 24 percent of male homemakers, triple the share found in 1986. About 10 percent of all husbands are the designated homemaker, up from 2 percent in 1986. The third category of male homemakers, claiming 18 percent of the segment in 1993, are men in miscellaneous families and nonfamilies with no young children present. More than one-third (35 percent) of these households have male homemakers, a higher proportion than found in married couples but lower than found among singles and single fathers. If men keep up the recent pace, the number of male homemakers will rise to more than 35 million in 2000." (p59)

Crispell, Diane. "Demographic Forecasts: Mr. Mom Goes Mainstream." American Demographics v16 n3, Mar 1994. p59. (ISSN0163-4089).

HOMEOPATHY--U.S. (v19)

HOMEOWNERS--U.S.

"The Current Population Survey indicates that the total homeownership rate in the U.S. fell from 67 percent in 1982 to 64 percent in 1992. The only households that saw increases in homeownership rates were married couples without children under age 18, most of whom were older empty-nest families. The decline resulted from two trends: stagnant or declining incomes and a lack of affordable housing." (p55)

Crispell, Diane. "Demographic Forecasts: Getting Home." American Demographics v16 n1, Jan 1994. p55. (ISSN0163-4089).

HOMEOWNERSHIP--U.S.

"Homeowners [in the U.S.] have refinanced $1 trillion worth of mortgages in the past two years. Consumer debt service, which has fallen to less than 16% of aftertax income after peaking at over 18% in early 1991, will fall even further in 1994. Since the end of the 1990-91 recession, household net worth is up by some $1.3 trillion, three-quarters of the gain coming from rising stock and bond markets. The housing market has benefited the most from low interest rates. Sales of existing homes were running at their highest level in more than a decade in the fall of last year, and associated outlays for household furnishings and appliances were strong for much of 1993." (p61)

Farrell, Christopher/others. "Industry Outlook: Introduction: It Won't Take Your Breath Away, But...." Business Week n3353, 10 Jan 1994. p60-63,66. (ISSN0007-7135).

HOMEWORK--U.S.

"Recent data regarding sixth grade students [in the U.S.] show that the five most prominent disturbances of studying and doing homework at home are the phone (52 percent); television (51 percent); family members (walking in and out of the room, parents asking questions, siblings teasing, etc., 40 percent); general noises (vacuum cleaner, washing machine, doorbell, etc., 38 percent); and radio, stereo, or tape recorder (37 percent). Other problems include insufficient sleep, pets, background conversations, and siblings who are crying. In a related study, it has been found that the most positive influence on the amount of time spent on homework is the parent, and the most negative effect is television and a household with no quiet place for studying." (p60)

Ornstein, Allan C. "Toward Increased Learning: Homework, Studying, and Note Taking: Essential Skills for Students." NASSP Bulletin v78 n558, Jan 1994. p58-70. (ISSN0192-6365).

"The amount of homework performed by the individual student [in the U.S.] is related to academic performance. In the international educational achievement tests, conducted in 19 countries including the United States, and involving 133,000 elementary and secondary schools, the number of hours per week was significantly related to achievements. According to [Herbert J.] Walberg, graded homework or homework commented upon can raise, on the average, the typical student from the 50th to 70th percentile in cognitive performance. Graded homework has nearly three times more effect on student outcomes than nongraded homework." (p59)

Ornstein, Allan C. "Toward Increased Learning: Homework, Studying, and Note Taking: Essential Skills for Students." NASSP Bulletin v78 n558, Jan 1994. p58-70. (ISSN0192-6365).

HOMICIDE

see also EUTHANASIA; JUVENILE HOMICIDE; POISONING; SUICIDE

HOMICIDE--AFRO-AMERICANS (v19)

"At recent homicide rates, about 1 of every 133 Americans will become a murder victim. For males of African-American descent, the proportion is estimated to be at, current rates, 1 in every 30....In some areas it is the No. 1 killer of young African-American males....on the south side of Chicago, 23 percent of students reported seeing a murder in their neighborhood--1 out of 4 kids, that is--34 percent witnessed a stabbing. That is almost 3 out of 9; 39 percent had seen a shooting, or 4 out of every 10...." (pH2628)

Dornan, Robert K. (Rep.-Calif.). "The Validity of the White-water Investigation," Congressional Record (21 Apr 1994). Daily ed. pH2625-2632. (ISSN0363-7239).

HOMICIDE--BRAZIL--YOUTH (v19)

HOMICIDE--COLOMBIA (v19)

HOMICIDE--DETROIT (MICH)--YOUTH (v19)

HOMICIDE--U.S.

"Male homicide mortality [in the U.S.] increased an average of 6.3 percent per year from 1960 to 1967, 1.2 percent per year from 1968 to 1978, and 0.4 percent per year from 1979-91....For women, homicide mortality increased by 4.2 percent per year from 1960 to 1967, 1.8 percent per year from 1968 to 1978, and by 0.2 percent per year from 1979 until 1991." (p16-17)

Seltzer, Frederic. "Trend in Mortality from Violent Deaths: Suicide and Homicide, United States, 1960-1991." Statistical Bulletin v75 n2, Apr-Jun 1994. p10-18. (ISSN0790-8334).

"The dark world of homicide investigation [in the U.S.] has changed radically for the worse. In the bygone era of seemingly omniscient gumshoes, virtually all murders were solved--that is, 'cleared' from the books through arrest, death or at least identification of a perpetrator. But the clearance rate has been dropping for more than 30 years--from a national rate of 92 percent in 1960 to a rate of 65 percent in 1992. The actual number of uncleared murders rose from 701 in 1960 to 8,152 in 1991. In many of the nation's biggest cities, the numbers look even worse: Los Angeles detectives cleared just 58 percent of that city's murders in 1992. In Washington, D.C., the clearance rate in 1993 was a disheartening 45 percent. And even if the cops clear a case with an arrest, that doesn't necessarily mean the suspect is convicted or imprisoned." (p28,30)

Witkin, Gordon/others. "U.S. News: More Murder Mysteries." U.S. News & World Report v116 n14, 11 Apr 1994. p28,30-34. (ISSN0041-5537).

HOMICIDE--U.S.--EMPLOYEES (v19)

HOMICIDE--WASHINGTON (D.C.)

"In Washington, there were 148 murders in 1985; in 1993, there were 467. In Los Angeles, the murder totals have mushroomed from 750 a year in the mid-1980s to 1,058 last year, but the number of homicide detectives has risen only modestly, from 228 in 1986 to 254 today....In just the past few months, Washington has suffered a head-spinning pace of murders--17 in 9 days, 4 in 5 hours, 3 in 35 minutes--and detectives are bouncing from scene to scene." (p32)

Witkin, Gordon/others. "U.S. News: More Murder Mysteries." U.S. News & World Report v116 n14, 11 Apr 1994. p28,30-34. (ISSN0041-5537).

HOMOSEXUAL PARENTS

see GAY PARENTS

HOMOSEXUALITY

"On average, lesbians experience their first same-sex activity at the age of 20 years and identify themselves as lesbians within the next three years (Troiden, 1988). The majority of gay males have had homosexual experiences by age 15. Many gay adolescent males recall identifying themselves as gay at the approximate age of 14. Although it is true that from 17% to 37% of American males engage in some homosexual experimentation, adolescent homosexuality is not a passing phase on the road to adult heterosexuality." (p160)

Dempsey, Cleta L. "Health and Social Issues of Gay, Lesbian, and Bisexual Adolescents." Families in Society v75 n3, Mar 1994. p160-167. (ISSN1044-3894).

"A genetic factor [in sexual orientation] is...supported by family studies. In a comprehensive review of these studies, Richard C. Pillard found substantial evidence that sexual orientation is familial. Several of these studies have used samples of lesbians and or gay men and have found that relatives are more likely to be homosexual than would have occurred by chance. The most well known is a 1952 study done by Franz J. Kallman involving two sets of twins, one identical and one fraternal. In the forty sets of monozygotic twins (one egg) all were concordant for sexual orientation while only one-third of the dizygotic twins (two egg) were concordant. An on-going study by Milton Diamond, Frederick Whitam, and J.E. Dannemiller was first reported in 1987. At that time there were ten sets of monozygotic twin brothers among the sample, and they found an 80 percent concordance for homosexuality. There are now thirty pairs of twins in the sample, eighteen monozygotic and twelve dizygotic, and the findings remain similar. There is a 72 percent concordance for homosexuality among the one-egg twins and a 33 percent to 50 percent concordance for homosexuality among the two-egg pairs. This high percentage of concordance, particularly among the monozygotic twins, is a powerful argument for a genetic factor in the causal sequence for homosexuality." (p42)

Bullough, Bonnie/Bullough, Vern. "The Causes of Homosexuality: A Scientific Update." Free Inquiry v13 n4, Fall 1993. p40-42,44-47. (ISSN0272-0701).

HOMOSEXUALS

see GAYS

HONDURAS

see also AIDS (DISEASE)--HONDURAS

HONDURAS--ECONOMIC CONDITIONS

"The newly elected president of Honduras, Carlos Roberto Reina, a former lawyer and diplomat, served six years on the Inter-American Court of Human Rights and is considered by many to be both honest and capable. He has pledged that his government will bring a 'moral revolution' to Honduras, beginning with a 'code of ethics for public officials'. He has also promised to decrease military spending, reduce the $600 million budget deficit, and wage a war on crime, poverty, and human rights abuses. At the same time the new president plans to continue the structural adjustment program initiated by his predecessor which, according to the CHRISTIAN SCIENCE MONITOR (Dec. 1, 1993), has resulted in some financial stability for Honduras at the cost of higher food prices, but with a concurrent increase in absolute poverty from 68 to 73 percent of Honduras' five million people. Although Honduras received about $1.4 billion in U.S. aid in the 1980s the annual per capita income, according to the World Bank, fell from $720 in 1985 to $580 in 1991. Politicians and business leaders assert that much of the aid money was embezzled or used for programs that encouraged support for U.S. policies, especially during the contra war, but did not bring any long term benefits to Honduras." (p8)

"Honduras: A New President." NewsNotes v19 n1, Jan-Feb 1994. p8. (ISSN1064-1556).

HONESTY--U.S.--TESTING

"Superficially, the most persuasive support for the validity of honesty tests comes from studies examining their ability to predict counterproductive behaviors in the workplace. In general, honesty tests have been found to forecast theft and related misbehaviors in the workplace at better than chance levels (Goldberg et al. 1991). But the magnitude of these predictive correlations tends to be quite low; most are in the 0.1 to 0.3 range, indicating that honesty tests account for between roughly 1 to 9 percent of the differences among individuals in job-related dishonesty (one obtains these percentages by squaring the correlations). The remaining 90 percent or more of these differences typically remain unpredicted by honesty tests. Moreover, honesty tests yield a very high false positive rate. Using the cut-offs recommended by test publishers, between 73 and 97 percent of individuals who receive failing scores on such tests are not found to later commit theft on the job (Office of Technology Assessment 1990, cited in Guastello and Rieke 1991)." (p39)

Lilienfeld, Scott O. "Do 'Honesty' Tests Really Measure Honesty?" Skeptical Inquirer v18 n1, Fall 1993. p32-41. (ISSN0194-6730).

HONEY TRADE--U.S. (v19)

"The gap between production and consumption [of honey] in the United States is approximately 100 million pounds, with imports of honey from China helping to fill that gap at the low end for industrial use. Any restrictions on imports of honey from China would likely lead to increased imports from other countries rather than significantly increased market share for U.S. producers. Although rising somewhat since 1991, U.S. honey inventories are not large by historical experience, either in absolute amounts or relative to consumption. Honey stocks reported by the U.S. Department of Agriculture were much higher in the mid-1980's (about 75 percent of consumption in 1985 and 1986), before falling to their lowest level in a decade in 1991 (26.6 percent of consumption). The 1993 stocks were 37.8 percent of consumption, well below the 1980-1993 average level of 46.4 percent. The U.S. government has supported honey producers since 1950, in part, to ensure enough honeybees would be available for crop pollination." (pH2617)

Clinton, William J. (President-U.S.). "Imports of Honey from China--Message from the President of the United States," Congressional Record (21 Apr 1994). Daily ed. pH2617. (ISSN0363-7239).

HONG KONG

see also HEROIN--HONG KONG; HIV INFECTIONS--HONG KONG; INVESTMENTS, FOREIGN--CHINA--HONG KONG; RENTAL HOUSING--HONG KONG; TOURIST TRADE--CHINA--HONG KONG

HONG KONG--COMMERCE (v19)

HONG KONG--COMMERCE--CHINA (v19)

HONG KONG--ECONOMIC CONDITIONS

"Hong Kong is in the third year of an economic and stockmarket boom that has raised the Hang Seng stockmarket index 239% since the end of 1990, to a record of nearly 10,250 on December 13th. The American dollar value of Hong Kong's GDP [gross domestic product] per person in 1993 will prove to have been some $19,000: more than Britain's ($16,000). When GDP per person is calculated instead on a purchasing-power basis, Hong Kong in 1991 was the world's sixth-richest country--and has probably moved up from there, since it has spent the past two years growing at least twice as fast as the five others that were then ahead of it. The unemployment rate is 2%, which means that in reality it has more jobs than job-seekers." (p36)

"Asia: It's Already 1997 in Hong Kong." Economist v329 n7842, 18 Dec 1993. p36-38. (ISSN0013-0613).

HONG KONG--PUBLIC OPINION

"A...gauge of Hong Kong feeling may come from a survey by the Hong Kong Baptist College. Some 46% of those questioned would seek to leave the territory after 1997 if changes proved 'unsuitable'. About 42% had 'no trust at all' in China's willingness to administer the Basic Law [the mini-constitution written by the Chinese for Hong Kong after 1997]. Fully 95% opposed reunification with China, most of them presumably wanting independence. Only 15% wanted Hong Kong to remain British." (p35)

"Asia: Hong Kong: Things to Come." Economist v331 n7860, 23 Apr 1994. p34-35. (ISSN0013-0613).

HOSPITAL UTILIZATION--U.S. (v19)

"In 1991, [U.S.] children ages 5 to 17 years had 3.3 hospital discharges per 100 persons, compared to 19.4 among 25 to 44 year olds and 11.7 among 45 to 64 year olds. (National Center for Health Statistics, 1992)." (p60)

Hughes, Dana (Senior Policy Analyst, Inst. for Health Policy Studies). U.S. House. Committee on Energy and Commerce. "Medicaid Managed Care in California." Hearing, 20 Apr 1993. Washington, D.C.: GPO, 1994. (ISBN0160434122). (Y4.En2/3:103-52).

HOSPITALS

see also PRIVATIZATION--HOSPITALS--MASSACHUSETTS

HOSPITALS--CALIFORNIA

"The major difference between non-profit and for-profit hospitals is that non-profit hospitals receive billions of dollars in tax breaks from federal, state, and local governments. And yet studies show that these hospitals often do not provide a community benefit anywhere equal to the tax breaks they receive. A US General Accounting Office report of May 1990 titled 'Better Standards Needed for Tax Exemption' studied hospitals in five states, including California. That study documented the dichotomy between non-profit hospitals which really do try to fulfill a charitable mission, and those which do not. The GAO report found the following: Ten non-profit hospitals in the state of California with 11% of the state's non-profit inpatient beds provided 26% of the state's non-profit uncompensated care....Fifty non-profit hospitals in California had total uncompensated care costs of $55 million while the value of their tax exemption totalled $92 million....When only charity care is considered, fully 71% of California nonprofit hospitals provided less charity care than the value of their tax exempt status." (p15)

U.S. House. Committee on Energy and Commerce. "HMO Financial Practices." Hearing, 27 May 1993. Washington, D.C.: GPO, 1993. (ISBN0160432782). (Y4.En2/3:103-45).

HOSPITALS--JAPAN--DATA PROCESSING (v19)

HOSPITALS--OREGON

"In a recent study, HCIA Inc., a firm that analyzes the hospital industry, examined 5,600 hospitals around the [the U.S.]...and ranked the 100 best performers. Oregon led the Nation with 11 out of the 100 top performers--more than any other State. The efficiency rankings of independently-owned acute care hospitals were based on first, shortening lengths of stay, second, reducing mortality and morbidity rates, and third, improving facilities. In addition to the HCIA report, data collected in 1992 by the American Hospital association indicates that despite its high percentage of population over 65: Oregon has the shortest average length of hospital stay in the nation--5.05 days versus 7.12 days national average; Oregon ranks among the lowest in hospital inpatient days in the Nation--502.4/1000 versus 866.6/1000 national average; Oregon ranks 36th in adjusted expenses per hospital admission--$682 lower than the national average; and Oregon ranks 42d in hospital expenses per capita--21 percent below the national average. This phenomenal success can be attributed to the State of Oregon's local control over health care. Oregon has decided not to regulate the cost of health care and the hospitals have responded by working hard with business to cut costs." (pS522-523)

Hatfield, Mark O. (Sen.-Oreg.). "Oregon's Hospitals Are Among the Most Efficient in the Nation," Congressional Record (1 Feb 1994). Daily ed. pS522-523. (ISSN0363-7239).

HOSPITALS--U.S. (v19)

"A study by the Western Consortium for the Health Professions, Inc. from May of 1987 found that 'in 1984-85, California nonprofit community hospitals provided $82 million in uncompensated charity care. During that period, federal and state income tax and property tax revenues lost as a result of tax exemption were $300 million....This analysis of taxes forgone was very likely an underestimate because it failed to include net non-operating revenues in hospital profits. Complete inclusion of net non-operating revenues would imply their estimate of total taxes would rise by $181 million to $481 million. And a study released May 1993 of Boston hospitals by Nancy Kane of the Harvard School of Public Health found that 'those hospitals with the least financial resources are among the strongest in their local commitment to Boston, to uninsureds, or to minority populations.'" A May 1990 report by the General Accounting Office "and the Kane report both note that hospitals which exhibit a lack of care to the indigent are more profitable. Yet these profitable hospitals are exactly the ones which disproportionately benefit from exemption of federal and corporate income taxes." (p16)

U.S. House. Committee on Energy and Commerce. "HMO Financial Practices." Hearing, 27 May 1993. Washington, D.C.: GPO, 1993. (ISBN0160432782). (Y4.En2/3:103-45).

"Until 1989, hospitals could hold newly arrived patients for 24 hours for 'observation' without 'admitting' them. During this time the patient was an outpatient and was charged more....But in 1989, the Health Care Financing Administration (HCFA), which runs Medicare, eased the 24-hour rule....Although the great majority of hospital patients are 'admitted,' long outpatient stays are booming, says the Prospective Payment Assessment Commission (ProPAC), a government watchdog group. ProPAC checked hospital records and found that in 1991, the last year studied, there were 168,631 patients kept for two days or more but never formally admitted. This is up from 60,666 in 1989, the first year HCFA authorized exceptions to the 24-hour rule." (p6-7)

McLeod, Don. "Some Hospital Patients Left Hanging." AARP Bulletin v35 n2, Feb 1994. p6-7. (ISSN1044-1123).

"Very recently, the Health Care Information Association (HCIA) and Mercer Health Care Provider Consulting released a study naming the '100 Top U.S. Hospitals--Benchmarks for Success.' The study identified 100 of the best-performing general acute care hospitals in the United States, using 1992 Medicare cost report and discharge data. Specialty hospitals and merged facilities have been deliberately excluded from the study....If all hospitals were able to perform to the standards of the top 100 hospitals named in this study, the health care industry would see spectacular results; hospital charges would decline by $40 billion and expenses would decline by $28 billion; hospital average lengths of stay would drop by a day or more; mortality rates would drop 12 percent; and morbidity rates would drop 13 percent." (pS445)

Durenberger, Dave (Sen.-Minn.). "Congratulations to Minnesota Hospitals Honored in the Top 100 Performing Hospitals Nationwide," Congressional Record (31 Jan 1994). Daily ed. pS445. (ISSN0363-7239).

"For years hospitals [in the U.S.] have said they are in hard financial times--running a profitable hospital has become increasingly difficult. To be sure, a number of hospitals have closed their doors in recent years--50 of them in 1992 alone. But two separate reports show that hospital profit margins that year showed an increase. The larger of the two reports, the American Hospital Association's 'HOSPITAL STATISTICS' report, found that acute-care hospitals earned $11.9 billion in 1992--an 18 percent increase over 1991's $10 billion profit. Based on financial data from nearly 5,300 acute-care hospitals, the AHA reported that the average total profit margin in 1992 was 4.6 percent, up from 4.3 percent in 1991." (p1)

"Whatever Happened to Bad Times?" People's Medical Society Newsletter v13 n1, Feb 1994. p1,7. (ISSN0736-4873).

HOSPITALS--U.S.--ADMINISTRATION--COSTS (v19)

"The American Hospital Association has...made winning antitrust concessions a top lobbying priority. The AHA claims that antitrust enforcement is chilling beneficial hospital mergers and joint ventures. However, when you look at the facts, their claims don't hold up. Since 1987, there have been over 225 hospital mergers. Of that number, only 22 have required intensive investigation and only 7 have been challenged. Moreover, Federal authorities have not challenged a single joint venture or buying arrangement among hospitals. This is hardly a record of antitrust enforcement run amuck. The fact is that the antitrust laws have not been used to block hospital deals that would benefit local communities by consolidating unused hospital beds, reducing wasteful competition for high technology equipment, or saving a financially unstable hospital from closing its doors. Rather, the antitrust laws have been used to block mergers that were likely to increase prices and to keep HMOs out of the market." (p130)

Metzenbaum, Howard M. (Sen.-Ohio). U.S. Senate. Committee on Finance. "Antitrust Issues in the Health Care Industry." Hearing, 7 May 1993. Washington, D.C.: GPO, 1993. (ISBN0160434505). (Y4.F49:S.hrg.103-373).

"There are several sources of waste and inefficiency in the current U.S. health system that make us believe that we can rapidly slow the rate of growth in U.S. health costs. First, experts estimate that as much as 25 percent of U.S. health care costs are spent on administration. Estimated savings for simplifying claims forms and from other measures to automate and standardize administration are between $4.2 to $5 billion. In addition, estimates for reducing hospital and physician salary expenses from simplifying billing functions range between $50 to $60 billion a year....Second, as much as 25 percent to 33 percent of procedures in the United States are estimated to be marginally necessary or inappropriate. Although not all of these procedures can be eliminated, they represent almost $200 billion in marginal spending (assuming the lower estimate). If just one-fifth of these marginal procedures could be eliminated, we could save $40 billion a year. Third, GAO [General Accounting Office] has estimated that as much as 10 percent of medical spending represents fraud, waste and abuse. That is another $80 billion a year. Again, if just one-fifth of that could be eliminated, we would save another $16 billion a year." (p11)

U.S. House. Committee on Energy and Commerce. "Health Care Reform (Part 1)." Hearing, 28 Sep 1993. Washington, D.C.: GPO, 1994. (ISBN0160435692). (Y4.En2/3:103-59).

HOTELS, TAVERNS, ETC.--LAS VEGAS (NEV) (v19)

HOURS OF LABOR (v19)

see also HOLIDAYS

HOURS OF LABOR--EUROPE--JAPAN--U.S. (v19)

HOURS OF LABOR--JAPAN (v19)

HOURS OF LABOR--RUSSIA

"The preconception that domestic concerns are strictly and properly the responsibility of women survived decades of proclaimed socialist equality [in Russia]. In the family realm patriarchal stereotypes appeared the strongest. Collective responsibility for home and child care, declared to be a condition of women's liberation, never materialized. Food shortages, eternal lines, permanently sick children and indifferent doctors, and a dearth of the most basic household appliances and services have turned women's lives in Russia into a stressful and unrelenting ordeal. Women sleep less than men and engage in less entertainment. According to various studies, mothers and wives spend 2.5 times as much time on domestic chores than fathers and husbands spend. The total weekly working hours of a typical woman, including her professional and domestic obligations, are 76.3 compared to 59.5 for a man." (p45)

Mirovitskaya, Natalia. "Women: Women and the Post-Socialist Reversion to Patriarchy." Surviving Together v11 n2, Sum 1993. p44-46. (ISSN0859-6286).

HOURS OF LABOR--U.S. (v19)

HOURS OF LABOR, FLEXIBLE--U.S. (v19)

HOUSE CONSTRUCTION--U.S.

The Center for Resourceful Building Technology in Missoula, Montana "has recently completed a demonstration house incorporating the best resource-saving materials and techniques available....While the average house today uses 5.7 board-feet of dimensional lumber and 2.7 square feet of sheathing (mostly plywood) per square foot of floor area, this house used 4.0 board feet of lumber, and 2.5 square feet of sheathing (including only 3 panels of plywood) per square foot of floor area. In addition, it used one lineal foot of engineered lumber (such as I-joists) per square foot of floor area. No attempt was made to relate this to the number of trees cut, but the difference seems significant since about 2/3 of the dimensional lumber was 'finger-jointed', that is, made from short pieces of wood that might otherwise have gone to waste. The engineered lumber, too, is made from chips and strands and need not come from 'sawtimber' trees. Only 3491 board-feet of lumber (1.45 board-feet per square foot of floor area) was good old, garden-variety sawn lumber." (p9)

Foss, Tim. "Sustainable Culture: The Other Side of the Timber Supply Coin." Inner Voice v5 n5, Sep-Oct 1993. p9.

HOUSEHOLD APPLIANCES--U.S.--RECYCLING (v19)

HOUSEHOLDS

see also COST AND STANDARD OF LIVING

"In all industrial countries except the former Soviet Union, the average household size shrank over the past two decades. For instance, the average United States household continued to shrink, from 3.1 persons in 1970 to 2.6 in 1990. That trend also characterizes most countries in Latin America and eastern Asia. For example, China's average household declined from 4.4 persons in 1982 to 4 in 1990. On the other hand, in African and south and west Asian countries, the average household size seems to have increased. In Algeria, for example, it rose from 5.9 persons in 1966 to 7 in 1987." (p44)

Seufert-Barr, Nancy. "International Year of the Family, 1994: The Smallest Democracy: At the Heart of Society." UN Chronicle v31 n1, Mar 1994. p43-45. (ISSN0251-7329).

HOUSEHOLDS--AFRO-AMERICANS

"African Americans are marrying at much later ages than Hispanics and whites, which is reflected in their timing and paths for leaving home. Average ages at first marriage were lower for blacks than whites before World War II but have been about two years higher in recent years. In 1988, for example, the median marriage age was 26 years for black women versus 24 years for white women. In the past, blacks were more likely than whites to remain home until marriage; in the 1980s, black twentysomethings were only 65 percent as likely as non-Hispanic whites, and barely half as likely as Hispanics to remain home until marriage." (p27)

Goldscheider, Frances/Goldscheider, Calvin. "Leaving and Returning Home in 20th Century America." Population Bulletin v48 n4, Mar 1994. p2-35. (ISSN0032-468X).

HOUSEHOLDS--U.S. (v19)

"A displaced homemaker is a woman whose principal activity has been homemaking and who has lost her main source of income because of divorce, separation, widowhood, a spouse's disability or long-term unemployment, or lost eligibility for public assistance....Displaced homemakers [in the U.S.] often face huge obstacles when looking for a job. Four in ten work part-time or seasonally, but 60 percent do not work at all. Low educational attainment and labor force participation rates explain why 57 percent of displaced homemakers live in households at or below the official poverty threshold. Yet displaced homemakers are making progress in school and in the labor force. The proportion of displaced homemakers with high school diplomas increased from 44 percent in 1980 to 55 percent in 1989. About 20 percent of displaced homemakers had at least some college education in 1989, ccompared with 18 percent in 1980....Among displaced homemakers aged 35 to 64, the labor force participation rate for those with some college education was 58 percent in 1989, compared with 45 percent for high school graduates and 28 percent for high school dropouts. " (p6)

"Dear Dr. Demo: Stuck at Home." American Demographics v16 n2, Feb 1994. p6. (ISSN0163-4089).

"The number of displaced homemakers [in the U.S.] grew about 12 percent in the 1980s, from 14 million to nearly 16 million, according to the U.S. Census Bureau. A displaced homemaker is a woman whose principal activity has been homemaking and who has lost her main source of income because of divorce, separation, widowhood, a spouse's disability or long-term unemployment, or lost eligibility for public assistance....The proportion of displaced homemakers who are widows decreased slightly in the 1980s, from 67 percent to 65 percent. The share displaced by divorce or separation grew at the same pace, to about one-third of the total. Nearly 90 percent of displaced homemakers aged 65 and older are widowed, while nearly 90 percent of displaced homemakers under age 35 are divorced or separated. Homemakers aged 35 to 64 are slightly more likely to be displaced by divorce or separation than by widowhood (55 percent are divorced, and 43 percent are widowed.)" (p6)

"Dear Dr. Demo: Stuck at Home." American Demographics v16 n2, Feb 1994. p6. (ISSN0163-4089).

"In 1992, there were 3.3 million couples living together outside marriage in the United States, about double the number in 1980 and over six times the number in 1970. In about one-quarter of these households in 1992, at least one partner was under age 25; and in about one-half the households, neither partner had ever been married." (p21)

Goldscheider, Frances/Goldscheider, Calvin. "Leaving and Returning Home in 20th Century America." Population Bulletin v48 n4, Mar 1994. p2-35. (ISSN0032-468X).

"New data have become available that allow us to see patterns of leaving and returning home in the United States during most of the 20th century. In the National Survey of Families and Households (NSFH), a nationally representative sample of 13,000 men and women age 19 and older were interviewed in 1987-88 about the age when they 'first left home for four months or more' and why they left...." (p10) "Altogether the survey data span most of the 20th century. This allows us to connect the timing of leaving home to the major events of the 20th century, from the 1920s to the current twentysomething generation, who came of age in the 1980s." (p11)

Goldscheider, Frances/Goldscheider, Calvin. "Leaving and Returning Home in 20th Century America." Population Bulletin v48 n4, Mar 1994. p2-35. (ISSN0032-468X).

"The 1990 [U.S.] Census showed that 21 percent of all 25-year-olds living in households were living with their parents--up from 15 percent in 1970." (p3)

Goldscheider, Frances/Goldscheider, Calvin. "Leaving and Returning Home in 20th Century America." Population Bulletin v48 n4, Mar 1994. p2-35. (ISSN0032-468X).

"The more traditional their views about the importance of family versus employment responsibilities for women, the more the young people [in the U.S.] in this survey--and particularly the women--expected to remain at home until they married, and the more likely they actually did so. Traditional-minded young men were more than 20 percentage points more likely than like-minded young women to expect to leave home before marriage (69 percent for men versus 48 percent for women)." (p8)

Goldscheider, Frances/Goldscheider, Calvin. "Leaving and Returning Home in 20th Century America." Population Bulletin v48 n4, Mar 1994. p2-35. (ISSN0032-468X).

"With perhaps uncharacteristic wit, the Census Bureau has adapted the name of a popular movie to title its new report on single-person households: 'Home Alone in 1989.' Nearly one in four U.S. households is a one-person household, according to the report. The number of one-person households has doubled over the past 20 years from 11.2 million to 22.4 million in 1989....People age 65 and older accounted for 39 percent of those living alone in 1989. The median age of householders living alone was 57." (p10)

"Take a Number." Population Today v21 n2, Feb 1993. p10. (ISSN0749-2448).

HOUSEHOLDS--U.S.--AGED (v19)

HOUSEHOLDS--U.S.--WOMEN

"The proportion of young women [in the U.S.] who left home prior to marriage, but not to attend school, rose sharply with each succeeding cohort of young women, from about 16 percent for those reaching adulthood in 1945-58, to 33 percent among those turning 18 between 1973 and 1979. About 40 percent of the young women of the 1980-87 cohort who had left home, did so for reasons other than to marry or attend school." (p17)

Goldscheider, Frances/Goldscheider, Calvin. "Leaving and Returning Home in 20th Century America." Population Bulletin v48 n4, Mar 1994. p2-35. (ISSN0032-468X).

HOUSING

see also AIDS (DISEASE)--HOUSING--U.S.; DISCRIMINATION IN HOUSING--U.S.; HOUSEHOLDS; MINORITIES--U.S.--HOUSING; PUBLIC HOUSING--CHICAGO (ILL); RENTAL HOUSING--HONG KONG

HOUSING--ASPEN (COLO)

"Inside Aspen city limits, a single-family home sold for an average of $1.2 million last year....Towns like the former ranching and coal mining town of Carbondale, 32 miles away, have become bedfroom for commuters. And commute they do: 31,000 vehicle trips were counted into and out of Aspen from downvally on a weekday last August, up from a daily average of 15,000 in 1972. Growth pressures on Aspen have been unremitting. Pitkin County, which includes Aspen and the nearby ski resort of Snowmass Village, added a million square feet of commercial space between 1975 and 1989. Commercial passenger counts at the Pitkin County airport jumped from about 100,000 in 1977, to 218,000 in 1991. Second...homes are so prevalent that the 1990 census found 40 percent of the county's residences unoccupied." (p9)

Clifford, Harlan C. "Aspen: A Colonial Power with Angst." High Country News v25 n6, 5 Apr 1993. p8-11. (ISSN0191-5657).

HOUSING--CALIFORNIA (v19)

"CAR [California Association of Realtors] reports that home sales totaled 437,710 in 1993, up 2.2 percent from 1992, when a revised 428,170 houses were sold. The increase is the second consecutive year that sales of homes have risen. The median price for a home declined to $188,870 in 1993 from $197,360 in 1992, according to CAR. And the organization says the level of unsold, single family homes declined in 1993, largely because of a drop in listings, compared with 1992. Condominium sales fell 17.7 percent in 1993 from 1992, while the median price dropped 3.9 percent to $140,100 in 1993 from $145,790 in 1992." (p7)

Wood, Daniel B. "Economic Reports: California Home Sales Up despite Spate of Disasters." The Christian Science Monitor v86 n56, 14 Feb 1994. p7. (ISSN0882-7729).

HOUSING--CARACAS (VENEZUELA) (v19)

HOUSING--CHINA (v19)

HOUSING--JAPAN

"House builders have done well from the government's anti-recession measures. About a fifth of mortgage loans come from the government's Housing Loan Corporation, which has received a total of Y5.5 trillion from previous economic stimuli. Readily available mortgages, along with lower land prices, caused real spending on houses to rise 2.3% last year, after falls in 1991 and 1992 of 8.2% and 6.7% respectively." (p35-36)

"Asia: The Good News from Japan." Economist v330 n7848, 29 Jan 1994. p35-36. (ISSN0013-0613).

HOUSING--NEW YORK (NY)

"Over the past 12 years, some $1 billion in public and private funds has been injected into new and rehabilitated housing in the South Bronx--enough money to write each resident a $7,000 check. Twenty-two thousand new housing units have been created or are in various stages of development, including 13,000 in the last five years. Perhaps most important, people began coming back to the South Bronx. From 1980 to 1990, the population of the South Bronx grew from 280,790 to 293,780. A fresh wave of immigrants helped the South Bronx revive: 1990 census figures show 20 percent of the area's population is foreign born. A new South Bronx had evolved, with 58 percent of its people listed as Hispanic, another 37 percent black non-Hispanic, 1 percent Asian

and 1 percent white non-Hispanic." (p14)
Chittum, Samme. "Tales from the Bronx." Neighborhood Works v16 n6, Dec 1993-Jan 1994. p13-14,39.

HOUSING--U.S. (v19)

"Housing provided much of the good news for real estate last year, as low interest rates enticed many first-time buyers [in the U.S.]. Sales of existing single-family homes totaled 3.7 million, up 5%-plus. The National Association of Realtors (NAR) predicts that sales of existing homes will grow 10% this year, and that prices will rise to a median $110,900 from $106,000 in October, 1993. Single-family home starts, after rising 6% in 1993, to about 1.2 million, should jump 10% in 1994, to 1.37 million, predicts the National Association of Home Builders (NAHB)." (p108)
Woolley, Suzanne. "Finance: Real Estate: A Time to Rebuild." Business Week n3353, 10 Jan 1994. p108. (ISSN0007-7135).

"Single-family housing starts [in the U.S.] in 1993 reached about 1.1 million, compared with 1992's 1.04 million. Multifamily housing starts slid slightly, to 156,000, but are projected to rise to near 200,000 in 1994 as demand starts to outstrip supply." (p127)
Woolley, Suzanne. "Real Estate: The Investment Spectrum: A Firm Footing at Last." Business Week n3352, 27 Dec 1993. p126-127. (ISSN0007-7135).

"In 1992, the typical new home [in the U.S.] had 1,920 square feet, up from 1,385 in 1970. Three quarters had central air conditioning, compared with only one third in 1970. Over the years, there's been a constant shift from smaller to larger houses." (p51)
Samuelson, Robert J. "Judgment Calls: Here's Some Good News, America." Newsweek v123 n5, 31 Jan 1994. p51. (ISSN0028-9604).

"Pent-up demand for new housing and jobs [in the U.S.], caused by the recession and tight monetary conditions of the early-1980s, burst forth in mid-decade when housing and labor market conditions loosened. New employment surged (from -1.7 percent in 1982 to +4.8 percent in 1984), unemployment fell (from 9.7 percent in 1982 to 7.0 percent in 1985), and home mortgage rates declined (from 14.5 percent in 1982 to 11.1 percent in 1985). Between 1982 and 1985, the number of existing single-family homes sold climbed 62 percent (from 2.0 to 3.2 million), the number of housing starts rose 64 percent (from 1.1 to 1.7 million), and the number of new apartments completed grew by an impressive 212 percent (from 117,000 to 365,000). This peculiar coincidence of housing and labor market conditions brought a brief return to the high mobility levels of the 1950s and 1960s." (p7)
Gober, Patricia. "Americans on the Move." Population Bulletin v48 n3, Nov 1993. p2-40. (ISSN0032-468X).

HOUSING--U.S.--COSTS (v19)

HOUSING--U.S.--FINANCE (v19)

"According to a report by the National Commission on Children...the cost of housing nationally went from 28 percent of the average family's budget in 1970 to 44 percent in 1990." (p9-10)
Lemann, Nicholas. "Mysteries of the Middle Class." New York Review of Books v41 n3, 3 Feb 1994. p9-13. (ISSN0028-7504).

HOUSING--U.S.--SINGLE PEOPLE (v19)

HOUSING, DISCRIMINATION

see DISCRIMINATION IN HOUSING

HOUSING SUBSIDIES--U.S.

"The federal government is wasting tax dollars by operating inefficient buildings. California, Texas, Iowa, and several other States have successful programs that have profitably invested in buildings during the past several years. These programs have increased the efficiency of State structures and stimulated the local construction industries. In his effort to learn from the States and improve the use of tax dollars, the President will emphasize investments in energy retrofits that have short payback periods: for instance, the budget includes $2 billion over the next 5 years for energy retrofits in federal buildings that we expect will have an average payback time of about 5 years; and some of the $3-4 billion a year that HUD spends subsidizing the energy bills of 5 million low income households (about 7 percent, or $200-300 million) could be invested in energy retrofits that would pay back in less than 5 years and represent a lasting decrease in energy bills." (p321)
Gibbons, John H. (Director, Office of Science and Technology Policy). U.S. House. Committee on Appropriations. "Depts. of Veterans Affairs and Housing and Urban Development...Approp. for 1994 (Part 2)." Hearing, Washington, D.C.: GPO, 1993. (ISBN0160410754). (Y4.Ap6/1:V64/4/994/pt.2).

HOUSTON (TEX)

see HAZARDOUS WASTE SITES--HOUSTON (TEX)

HUMAN DEVELOPMENT INDEX

The United Nations Development Programme's 1993 'Human Development Report' "ranks nations using the Human Development Index (HDI), which combines life expectancy, education and basic purchasing power into a broader-based indicator of development than the traditional income or output measures. Since its first use four years ago, African countries' rankings have remained constant. Over two-thirds of the 61 countries ranked 'low' in human development in 1993 are African." (p4) "The 1993 report notes that disaggregating a national HDI ranking by group or region can reveal stark internal deviations in human development from the national average. In the United States, for example, whites rank first in the world in human development (ahead of Japan), whereas blacks rank 31st (alongside Trinidad and Tobago), and Hispanics rank 34th (alongside Estonia). When adjusted for gender disparities, all countries' HDI rankings, including African ones, fail to improve, meaning that no country treats its women as well as it does its men." (p5)
Collins, Carole. "Growth Not Benefiting People: UNDP." Africa Recovery v7 n1, Jun 1993. p4-5.

HUMAN FERTILITY

see FERTILITY, HUMAN

HUMAN RIGHTS

"'At least half of humanity on planet Earth suffers in one form or another a violation of basic human rights,' said [former President, Jimmy] Carter matter-of-factly. 'Contrary to what some believe, the human rights situation is not getting better--it's getting worse, and rapidly. In the four months of this year, there have been 123,000 human rights complaints filed to the United Nations. All last year, there were only 43,000 complaints filed. This means that for each month there are 10 times more complaints as there were last year.'" (p11)
Rogers, Adam. "Jimmy Carter Speaks Out against Human Rights Abuses." Earth News v4 n3, May-Jun 1993. p11-13. (ISSN1068-9400).

HUMAN RIGHTS--COLOMBIA--EL SALVADOR (v19)

HUMAN RIGHTS--YUGOSLAVIA

"The situation in former Yugoslavia continues to deteriorate and human rights abuses, particularly against women, continue unabated....In December [1992], US officials submitted a list naming 10 individuals they argue should be prosecuted for crimes against humanity. Some of the crimes identified by ASSOCIATED PRESS are the August 21 massacre of more than 200 Muslim men and boys by Bosnian Serb police in central Bosnia, the May-June murders of 2,000 to 3,000 Muslim men, women, and children by Serbian forces near Brcko, bombings and killings in Bajalunka, as well as the destruction of a Croatian town in fall 1991 that resulted in the forced expulsion of its inhabitants." (p3)

Tepper, Robert J. "Monitoring Human Rights ." Window on the World v24 n2, Mar 1993. p1-3,5.

HUMANE SOCIETIES

see ANIMAL WELFARE--SOCIETIES, ETC.

HUNGARIANS--ROMANIA--POLITICAL ACTIVITY (v19)

HUNGARIANS IN BUSINESS--ROMANIA (v19)

HUNGARY--ECONOMIC CONDITIONS (v19)

HUNGER (v19)

HUNGER--BRAZIL

"Not long after taking to the streets to call for the impeachment of President Ferdinand de Collor, Brazilians have taken up another cause: ending the hunger and poverty that haunt 32 million lives. Today, more than 500,000 Brazilians are participating in the numerous local committees of Citizenship Action against Hunger, Poverty and for Life....At Banco do Brasil, the leading state-run bank, employees are donating their lunch vouchers to the movement. In one office, about $4000 worth of vouchers was collected in a single day. Paulo Bezerra, a bank employee in Belo Horizonte, is amazed. 'I have never seen my workmates so much touched,' he says. 'After so long only thinking of ourselves, we all want to do something because the situation is dramatic.' Bezerra is right. In his city alone, over 400,000 people--20 percent of the population--have a 'food deficit,' according to Maria Regina Nabuco, Belo Horizonte's food supply officer. Hunger will kill 190,000 children in Brazil this year, adds Angela Guadagnin, mayor of Sao Jose dos Campos in Sao Paulo State." (p11)

Godinho, Marcio. "Brazil: A Movement to End the Misery." Toward Freedom v43 n1, Feb 1994. p11. (ISSN0048-9898).

HUNGER--DEVELOPING COUNTRIES

"According to the UN, about 790 million residents of the developing world suffer from chronic undernourishment. Another 2 billion have what FAO [Food and Agriculture Organization] calls 'hidden hunger'--unbalanced diets with deficiencies in specific nutrients that can lead to mental and physical problems." (p4)

Grier, Peter. "Foreign Aid: Outlook Is Poor in 1994 for Hungriest Nations." The Christian Science Monitor v86 n21, 24 Dec 1993. p4. (ISSN0882-7729).

HUNGER--MASSACHUSETTS--CHILDREN (v19)

HUNGER--U.S.

"Hunger is a problem that affects all segments of the [U.S.] population, and a recent study by the Urban Institute reports that elderly Americans--both above and below the poverty line--are also at risk of hunger. Between 2.5 and 4 million elderly Americans, 40% of whom have incomes above the poverty line, suffer from hunger or worry about getting enough food...." (p5)

"New Hunger Study Finds Many Elderly 'Food Insecure.'" Frontier Win 1994. p5.

"The good news is that a great many children and adults in the United States don't go to bed hungry every night. The bad news is that there are nearly 26 million of these Americans who have to get food from food pantries, soup kitchens, homeless shelters, and other food programs served by Second Harvest, a 185-member national food-bank network. Based in Chicago, Second Harvest is the largest hunger-relief organization in the US. Released this week by Second Harvest, an 18-month study of the thousands of emergency food programs in the US found that 10.4 percent of the population now has to be provided with food. And 45.5 percent of the food recipients did not expect to need food assistance as little as three months ago....The study revealed that 31.6 percent of the households receiving food help have someone in the family who is working, but that 73 percent of the households earn less than $10,000 in annual income. While the poverty rate between 1989 and 1992 rose 5 percent in central cities, it increased 21 percent in the suburbs." (p3)

Holmstrom, David. "National: 1 in 10 Americans Receive Food Aid, Many for First Time." The Christian Science Monitor v86 n74, 11 Mar 1994. p3. (ISSN0882-7729).

"The most visible hunger in America can be found on city streets, where crudely lettered cardboard signs spell out desperate appeals: 'Need food' or 'Hungry and homeless--please help.' But hidden away in other places around the country--in urban apartments, suburban homes, small towns, and rural areas--are millions of other hungry people whose needs are less well known. Nearly 26 million adults and children--1 in 10 Americans--do not have enough to eat, according to Second Harvest, a Chicago-based network of 185 food banks serving 42,000 charitable agencies across the nation. Almost half of those needing assistance are under the age of 17." (p22)

"Editorials: Counting the Hungry." The Christian Science Monitor v86 n77, 16 Mar 1994. p22. (ISSN0882-7729).

HUNGER--U.S.--AGED (v19)

HUNGER--U.S.--CHILDREN (v19)

HUNTING

see also POACHING

HUNTING--U.S.

"Three in four American hunters stalked big game in 1991, and virtually all big-game hunters go for deer. Much smaller shares go after turkey (16 percent), elk (6 percent), bear (3 percent), or other large animals such as moose (4 percent). More than half of American hunters hunt small game. The most popular small-game animals are rabbits and squirrels, followed by pheasant, quail, and grouse. About 3 million people hunt for migratory birds such as ducks. Fewer than 1.5 million hunt animals they are unlikely to eat, such as raccoons, foxes, and woodchucks." (p37)

Crispell, Diane. "Targeting Hunters." American Demographics v16 n1, Jan 1994. p34-38,40. (ISSN0163-4089).

HUNTING--ZIMBABWE (v19)

HURRICANES

"The post-war coastal boom coincided with a fluke of nature: a long lull in the hurricane cycle. Current weather-forecasting theory holds that hurricanes are linked to West African storm patterns and work in cycles of roughly 20 years. Indeed, in the 1950s, nine hurricanes squarely hit the Outer Banks. In the next 19 years, just one struck. Not one major hurricane hit the U.S. mainland between Camille in 1969 and Hugo in 1989. For the next couple of decades, meteorologists say, we should expect more and harsher hurricanes. If that proves true, National Hurricane Center director Robert Sheets told a Senate hearing last year, 'we will see multibillion-dollar losses of property almost every year and potential large loss of life because of the rapid coastal development.'" (p14)

Overby, Peter. "Beachfront Bailout." Common Cause Magazine v19 n2, Sum 1993. p12-17. (ISSN0271-9592).

HURRICANES--U.S.

"The Galveston hurricane of 1900, which killed 6,000, is the nation's worst natural disaster. Camille hit Mississippi with 175-mph winds and gusts of nearly 200 mph, causing the sea to surge 25 feet above high tide. Although Hugo came ashore in a forest, it still was big enough to cause $7 billion in property losses. Last year's Hurricane Andrew cost insurers $16.5 billion when it struck southern Florida; the total loss, including roads and other infrastructure and uninsured property, may reach $40 billion. If Andrew had veered through Miami, losses could have hit $50 billion. But by 1985, some 75 percent of coastal dwellers had never experienced a direct hit by a big hurricane. Those who remember earlier storms are growing old, moving away or being ignored." (p14-15)

Overby, Peter. "Beachfront Bailout." Common Cause Magazine

v19 n2, Sum 1993. p12-17. (ISSN0271-9592).

HYDROELECTRIC POWER
see WATER-POWER
HYPERTENSION--AFRO-AMERICANS (v19)
HYPERTENSION--U.S. (v19)
HYSTERECTOMY--U.S. (v19)
ICE CREAM INDUSTRY--U.S. (v19)
IDAHO
see AGRICULTURE--IDAHO; PESTICIDES--IDAHO; SALMON--IDAHO
IDAHO--ECONOMIC CONDITIONS (v19)
IDIOSYNCRATIC DRUG REACTIONS--U.S.--AGED (v19)
ILLEGAL ALIENS
see ALIENS, ILLEGAL
ILLEGITIMACY--U.S. (v19)
ILLEGITIMATE CHILDREN--U.S. (v19)
ILLINOIS
see ALIENS, ILLEGAL--CALIFORNIA--ILLINOIS; EDUCATION--ILLINOIS--FINANCE; FARM INCOME--ILLINOIS; POOR--ILLINOIS; PRISONERS--ILLINOIS; PUBLIC WELFARE--ILLINOIS; TEENAGE PREGNANCY--ILLINOIS
ILLINOIS--EMPLOYMENT (v19)
ILLINOIS--MANUFACTURES (v19)
ILLITERACY
see LITERACY
IMMIGRANTS (v19)
see also ALIENS
IMMIGRANTS--AUSTRALIA--CANADA--GREAT BRITAIN--U.S.

"In 1991 America accepted eight times as many permanent settlers per head of population as Britain. Canada took nine times as many, and Australia seven times as many. Between 1983 and 1991 the numbers accepted by America, Canada and Australia rose by 226%, 158% and 47% respectively. The number of permanent settlers in Britain rose by a mere 1%." (p66)

"Britain: Immigration: Unclaimed Benefits." Economist v331 n7861, 30 Apr 1994. p65-67. (ISSN0013-0613).

IMMIGRANTS--CALIFORNIA (v19)

"From 1985 to 1990, as immigration levels rose, California exported more than 38,000 poverty migrants to Washington, Oregon, Nevada and Arizona, and lost only 3,200 poverty migrants to the rest of the country....In addition, California lost more than 85,000 households with incomes below $35,000 and 145,000 people with less than college education to its four nearby states....210,000 poverty immigrants moved into Los Angeles County from 1985 to 1990 but the county had a net loss of 88,000 poverty residents due to out-migration." (p1-2)

News release. "Frey." University of Michigan News and Information Services 30 Mar 1994. p1-2.

IMMIGRANTS--CANADA (v19)
IMMIGRANTS--EMPLOYMENT--U.S. (v19)

"Businesses are hiring visitors from other nations with temporary work visas in order to fulfill minority quotas established by the 1964 Civil Rights Act and 1972 Equal Employment Opportunity Act. According to these laws, employers are required to submit federal reports which depicts the ethnic and racial composition of their workers....Last year, 163,000 temporary workers entered the U.S., most arriving from Asia, Latin America and Africa. This figure is a 260 percent increase from 1964 when the Civil Rights Act was enacted. Although the current number of imported workers is relatively low, they are becoming more prevalent in U.S. organizations. (SAN JOSE MERCURY NEWS, October 11, 1993)." (p4)

"Businesses Use Imported Labor to Cheat on Minority Quotas." FAIR Immigration Report v16 n1, Jan 1994. p4.

IMMIGRANTS--EUROPE (v19)
IMMIGRANTS--FRANCE (v19)
IMMIGRANTS--HONG KONG (v19)
IMMIGRANTS--ISRAEL (v19)
IMMIGRANTS--JAPAN

"Many Japanese-Brazilians and Japanese-Peruvians have entered the country [of Japan] since the revision of the Immigration-Control Law. According to Justice Ministry statistics, the number of Japanese-Peruvian entries increased rapidly after 1989 and peaked at 22,025 in 1991. The figure dropped by over 20% to 15,784 in 1992, but the number of Japanese-Peruvians overstaying their visas began to rise." (p5)

Sekiguchi, Chie. "Settling In?" Look Japan v39 n455, Feb 1994. p4-7. (ISSN0456-5339).

IMMIGRANTS--LOS ANGELES (CALIF)

"Do immigrants overuse welfare and other social programs and underpay taxes? Two recent, much-publicized reports claim that they do. A 1992 Los Angeles County study alleged that immigrants cost the country $947 million in social services in 1991, but paid county taxes of only $139 million. Another study by Donald Huddle extrapolated from the Los Angeles report to conclude that, nationally, immigrants drained the public treasury of $45 billion. Subsequent research by Jeffrey Passel and Rebecca Clark of the Urban Institute has shown that the Los Angeles figures overestimated immigrant social service costs by one-third and underestimated their taxes by nearly one-half. Moreover, the Los Angeles report itself estimated that the total taxes (local, state, and federal) paid by these immigrants exceed their total social service costs by $1.8 billion. The discrepancy emerged because most tax revenue flows to Washington, while many of the program costs are borne locally." (p33)

Defreitas, Gregory. "Fear of Foreigners: Immigrants as Scapegoats for Domestic Woes." Dollars and Sense n191, Jan-Feb 1994. p8-9,33-35.

IMMIGRANTS--PERU

"This year also marks the 94th anniversary of the first wave of Japanese immigration to Peru, one of the first non-Asian countries to receive Japanese immigrants. The current Japanese community in Peru (80,000 people, representing less than 0.4% of the total population) plays a significant role in Peruvian society. With the June 1990 change in the Immigration Law of Japan, the ranks of Peruvians in Japan have swelled. Now there are approximately 40,000 Peruvians working in Japan." (p13)

Aquino, Carlos. "Foreign Voices: Carlos Aquino: Peruvians-Japanese Ties." Look Japan v39 n451, Oct 1993. p13. (ISSN0456-5339).

IMMIGRANTS--U.S. (v19)
see also PUBLIC WELFARE--U.S.--IMMIGRANTS

"According to the 1900 census, 24,326 Japanese lived in the United States. Of these, only 410 were married women. In 1910, there were 5,581 married women in a U.S. Japanese population of 72,157; and in 1920, there were 22,193 in a U.S. Japanese population of 111,010. As a result of this, a practice that became known as 'picture bride' marriage developed. Most Japanese immigrant men couldn't afford to travel back to Japan for a bride, so requests were made to their parents, relatives, or friends in Japan to find prospective brides for them. Since these types of marriages often involved the exchange of photographs between Japanese men in the United States and Japanese women in Japan, the practice was referred to by Americans as picture bride marriages....The Immigration Station in San Francisco on Angel Island...estimates the number of picture brides admitted as between 1912-1919 as 5,273." (p7)

Mukai, Gary. "Japanese Immigration to the United States: With a Focus on Picture Brides." Access n119, Oct-Nov 1993.

p6-8.

"Immigrants coming from Arab nations still represent less than 3 percent of all immigrants coming to the United States, but their numbers are growing. In 1992, more than 27,000 people from Arab nations immigrated to the United States--68 percent more than those who came ten years earlier. These figures do not include Palestinians migrating from Israel or from the occupied territory. Among the 78,400 immigrants who arrived between 1990 and 1992, 17,500 are from Lebanon. That's more than one in every five recent Arab immigrants. People from Egypt (13,300) and Jordan (12,700) each account for about one in six Arab immigrants. Those coming from Syria (8,700) ranked fourth, accounting for one in nine recent arrivals. And Iraq (7,400) ranked fifth, making up less than one in ten immigrants." (p27,30)

El-Badry, Samia. "The Arab-American Market." American Demographics v16 n1, Jan 1994. p22-27,30. (ISSN0163-4089).

"Immigration from the Middle East picked up dramatically in the 1960s. In fact, more than 75 percent of foreign-born Arab Americans in 1990 had immigrated after 1964, compared with 52 percent of the total foreign-born U.S. population. The largest share (44 percent) came to the U.S. between 1975 and 1980, compared with just 24 percent of all foreign-born persons. This recent flood is due in large part to the Immigration Act of 1965, which ended a quota system that favored immigrants from Europe. Most post-1965 Arab immigrants have been Moslems with even more education than their predecessors. However, a 1991 survey suggests that about half of Arab Americans identify themselves as Christians." (p24-25)

El-Badry, Samia. "The Arab-American Market." American Demographics v16 n1, Jan 1994. p22-27,30. (ISSN0163-4089).

"Only about 15,000 adults a year come to the U.S. from Africa, but they're worth a look. Nearly 88 percent of adults who immigrate from Africa to the U.S. have a high school education or higher. The national average for native-born Americans is 77 percent. Only 76 percent of Asian immigrants and 46 percent of Central-American immigrants are high school graduates." (p9)

Speer, Tibbett. "Business Reports: Immigration: The Newest African Americans Aren't Black." American Demographics v16 n1, Jan 1994. p9-10. (ISSN0163-4089).

"According to the U.S. Immigration and Naturalization Service, the country added close to a million legal immigrants in 1992, along with an estimated 200,000 to 300,000 illegal immigrants. The number of immigrants has risen dramatically every decade since the 1930s, with more than 7 million recorded from 1981 through 1990--the second highest ever after the first decade of the twentieth century. Largely as a result of such statistics, the Census Bureau has recently revised upward its 1989 projection for overall U.S. population--for the second time. Whereas the earlier estimate had the population topping off at 300 million in the year 2040, the new figures have it growing past 400 million through 2050. The current population is 260 million." (p1)

Baumgarten, Fred. "Should Environmentalists Adopt an Immigration Policy?" Audubon Activist v8 n3, Nov 1993. p1,4. (ISSN0898-915X).

"Dade County, Florida, where one of every four students is a recent immigrant, pays $474 for every new immigrant student per year. This cost totaled over $24 million during the 1991-1992 school year....A study by George J. Borjas of the University of California at San Diego states that immigrants contributed about $36 billion to welfare in the 1980s but consumed $56 billion in welfare." (p2)

"Costs Prove 'Borderless World' Advocates Wrong." FAIR Immigration Report v16 n2, Feb 1994. p2.

"Triads are thought to be moving control over their criminal enterprises overseas, including the United States, in anticipation of Hong Kong's returning to the control of the People's Republic of China in 1997. Most Chinese in the United States are foreign born. There has been an increased growth in the Chinese population which is expected to continue and quicken as 1997 nears. It is estimated that 10 to 25% of the 5.6 million persons living in Hong Kong today will leave for the United States and Canada." (p33-34)

Tracy, Sharon. "The Evolution of the Hong Kong Triads/Tongs into the Current Drug Market." Journal of Third World Studies v10 n1, Spr 1993. p22-36. (ISSN8755-3449).

"Current projections from the [U.S.] Census Bureau anticipate a net addition of 880,000 immigrants a year until 2050, composed of about 324,000 Hispanics, 323,000 non-Hispanic Asians, 174,000 non-Hispanic whites, and 60,000 non-Hispanic blacks. The compounding effects of annual immigration at these levels are behind the projected rise in the share of minorities in the population from 25 percent in 1990 to 47 percent in 2050. If net immigration had halted in 1991, non-Hispanic whites would account for over 62 percent of the population in 2050 and blacks would be the largest minority, according to the Census Bureau." (p15)

O'Hare, William P. "America's Minorities--The Demographics of Diversity." Population Bulletin v47 n4, Dec 1992. p2-47. (ISSN0032-468X).

"While the immigrant component of the African-American population is quite small relative to Hispanics and Asians, many African immigrant groups swelled in size over the decade. The number of Ethiopians more than quadrupled, while the number of Ghanians grew by 175 percent, Kenyans by 167 percent, and Nigerians by 123 percent. Nigerians remained the largest African immigrant group during the 1980s, numbering 60,000 in 1990. The Caribbean, however, is the source of most U.S. immigrants of African descent. Severe political and economic problems in Haiti in recent years helped boost the number of Haitians in the United States from 92,000 in 1980 to 229,000 in 1990. In addition, the 1990 Census counted 343,000 American residents from Jamaica, and 119,000 from Trinidad and Tobago. And, many black Hispanics were undoubtedly among the 357,000 U.S. residents from the Dominican Republic counted in the 1990 Census. The influx of Caribbean immigrants helped raise the number of black Hispanics from 391,000 to 1.3 million between 1980 and 1992." (p11)

O'Hare, William P. "America's Minorities--The Demographics of Diversity." Population Bulletin v47 n4, Dec 1992. p2-47. (ISSN0032-468X).

IMMIGRANTS--U.S.--ECONOMIC CONDITIONS (v19)

IMMIGRANTS--U.S.--POLITICS AND GOVERNMENT--PUBLIC OPINION (v19)

IMMIGRANTS--U.S.--PUBLIC OPINION (v19)

IMMUNIZATION (v19)

IMMUNIZATION OF CHILDREN (v19)

According to a report entitled "The Children's Vaccine Initiative: Achieving the Vision" by the U.S. National Academy of Science, "Vaccines are among the most cost-effective health interventions known. Through vaccination programs smallpox was eradicated. Many believe that smallpox caused more disease and sickness than any other infectious illness. Public health officials in the Americas are about to declare victory over another infectious disease controlled by vaccination: poliomyelitis. 80% of world's infants are adequately immunized against measles, tetanus, pertussis, diphtheria, tuberculosis and polio, up from 5% just twenty years ago. A full 20% of the world's children, many in the poorest and most remote areas of the globe, are unvaccinated. More than 2 million deaths and 5 million cases of disability still occur annually as a result of diseases (such as measles and 'Haemophilus influenzae') that are preventable by vaccination. Underimmunization is also a problem in the United States, particularly among economically disadvantaged children living in rural and urban areas." (p111)

Orme, Thomas W. (American Council on Science and Health). U.S. House. Committee on Science, Space, and Technology. "Risk Assessment Research." Hearing, 16 Nov 1993. Washington, D.C.: GPO, 1994. (ISBN016043615X). (Y4.Sci2:103/85).

"Despite the importance of getting children off to a healthy start in life, our record in immunizing children against preventable diseases is abysmal--fewer than 60 percent of American preschool children are fully immunized, and rates are as low as 30 percent in some states. If El Salvador could suspend a civil war for three separate days every year for seven years so that children could be immunized and if China, still among the twenty poorest countries in the world, can reach an immunization rate of nearly 95%, there is no excuse for the American failure to reach all children." (p181)

Weill, James D. (General Counsel, Children's Defense Fund). U.S. Congress. Joint Economic Committee. "The 1993 Economic Report of the President." Hearing, 27 Jan 1993. Washington, D.C.: GPO, 1994. (ISBN0160440300). (Y4.Ec:Ec7/2/993/pt.1).

IMMUNIZATION OF CHILDREN--CHINA--EGYPT--KOREA (NORTH)--U.S. (v19)

IMMUNIZATION OF CHILDREN--COMPLICATIONS--U.S.

"The National Vaccine Information Center formed in 1989 by Dissatisfied Parents Together (DPT) receives thousands of calls about vaccine-caused problems. They helped to secure passage of the National Childhood Vaccine Injury Act of 1986 (PL99-666) creating a mechanism for vaccination reporting and compensation, the Vaccine Adverse Events Reporting System (VAERS). In a 20-month period from November '90 to July '92, VAERS received 17,221 injury reports (including 360 deaths) from mandated vaccinations of children from two months to seven years. As of 1993, 3,000 cases have not yet been heard and the budget has been exhausted. Recent bills do nothing to adequately fund the compensation system to pay the thousands of existing vaccine injury and death claims now pending." (p8)

Newfield, Marcia. "Vaccinations: A Shot in the Dark." New Directions for Women v22 n5, Sep-Oct 1993. p8. (ISSN0160-1075).

IMMUNIZATION OF CHILDREN--U.S. (v19)

IMPORTS--FALKLAND ISLANDS (v19)

IMPORTS--MEXICO

Though import growth has slowed along with the economy, Mexican companies have shifted, probaby permanently, to a greater dependence on imports. Officials point out that "Mexico's non-oil exports have been growing faster than those of South Korea and Singapore since 1985, but there are also fears that the export-growth rate of 15% recorded in the first eight months of 1993 will fall sharply once the domestic market revives. Rogelio Ramirez de la O, an economic consultant, says that each unit of investment in Mexico since 1988 has pulled in 1.8 units of imports, while the equivalent figure for Chile has been only 1.1. He argues that with NAFTA [North American Free Trade Agreement] in place and the budget balanced, Mexico can afford to tackle the current-account deficit by letting the peso slide further against the dollar, without reviving inflation; a fall to the bottom of the band fixed by the central bank would mean a devaluation against the dollar of about 13% over the next 18 months." (p21)

"Mexico: The Revolution Continues." Economist v330 n7847, 22 Jan 1994. p19-21. (ISSN0013-0613).

IMPORTS--U.S. (v19)

"Capital goods now account for some 40% of U.S. merchandise exports, of which more than half normally go to other industrial nations. At the same time, foreign-made equipment, which now accounts for 25% of U.S. imports, continues to make sharp inroads in U.S. capital-goods markets. Even as the dollar declined, the import share of domestic nonautomotive equipment spending has climbed from 30% in 1986 to some 50% today." (p26)

Koretz, Gene. "Economic Trends: The Capital-Goods Trade Surplus Is Shrinking Fast." Business Week n3355, 24 Jan 1994. p26. (ISSN0007-7135).

"Fiscal 1993 [U.S.] grain and feed imports totaled $1.6 billion, up 6 percent from fiscal 1992. Volume fell 9 percent to 4.9 million tons due to smaller corn and barley imports. Wheat imports slowed during the last quarter to 1.6 million tons on rising prices. Corn and barley shipments fell 63 and 62 percent, respectively, while rice increased 15 percent to 197,000 tons." (p21)

U.S. Dept. of Agriculture. "Import Commodities." Outlook for U.S. Agricultural Exports 30 Nov 1993. p20-21.

"Horticultural imports [in the U.S.] totaled $6.9 billion in fiscal 1993, increasing 2 percent from fiscal 1992. Fruit imports are down 10 percent, because of a 26-percent downturn in juice imports. Vegetable and tree nut import values increased 14 and 17 percent, respectively, from fiscal 1992 shipments. Orange juice shipments remained steady, but value fell dramatically due to a 40-percent decrease in import price. Apple juice imports fell 26 percent as quantity remained steady." (p21)

U.S. Dept. of Agriculture. "Import Commodities." Outlook for U.S. Agricultural Exports 30 Nov 1993. p20-21.

"U.S. agricultural imports for fiscal 1993 were $24.5 billion, slightly higher than the previous year. Competitive import value increased 2 percent to $18.9 billion, but noncompetitive imports fell 4 percent to $5.5 billion....In fiscal 1993, beef and veal import values fell 1 percent, while the value of pork and dairy products increased. Live cattle imports from Mexico and Canada continued to increase, 39 and 21 percent, respectively....Dairy product imports increased to $860 million in fiscal 1993." (p20-21)

U.S. Dept. of Agriculture. "Import Commodities." Outlook for U.S. Agricultural Exports 30 Nov 1993. p20-21.

INCINERATORS--GERMANY--SWEDEN--U.S. (v19)

INCOME--AFRO-AMERICAN WOMEN (v19)

INCOME--AFRO-AMERICANS

"In 1992, Black families [in the U.S.] lost purchasing power. The median income for Black families was $21,161, which was a drop from the 1991 median of $21,548 (in unadjusted dollars). For White families in 1992, the median income was $38,909, an increase from the 1991 level of $37,783 (in unadjusted dollars)." (p136)

Tollett, Erica E. (Senior Public Policy Analyst, National Black Child Devel. Inst.). U.S. House. Committee on Ways and Means. "Historical Trends in Poverty and Family Income." Hearing, 26 Oct 1993. Washington, D.C.: GPO, 1994. (ISBN0160435765). (Y4.W36:103-42).

INCOME--FLORIDA--AGED (v19)

INCOME--GREAT BRITAIN

"During Labour's period of office [in Great Britain] in 1974-79, the real take-home pay of a married man on average earnings fell by 0.2% a year. By contrast, in the past 15 years of Tory rule, it rose by an average of 2.3% a year...." (p59)

"Britain: That Sinking Feeling." Economist v330 n7848, 29 Jan 1994. p59-60. (ISSN0013-0613).

INCOME--KOSOVO--SERBIA--SLOVENIA

"According to World Bank figures for 1990--the last year for which reliable data are available--per capita income in Kosovo amounted to only $662, making it by far the poorest region in

Europe, even more depressed than neighboring Albania. On the other hand, per capita income in Serbia was $2,238, three-and-a-half times as great. (In Slovenia, the wealthiest republic of Yugoslavia, per capita income was $5,918, close to ten times that in Kosovo.)" (p26)

Neier, Aryeh. "Kosovo Survives!" New York Review of Books v41 n3, 3 Feb 1994. p26-28. (ISSN0028-7504).

INCOME--MEXICO (v19)

INCOME--U.S. (v19)

"Both the number and proportion of year-round, full-time workers with low annual earnings rose sharply between 1979 and 1990 [in the U.S.]. For purposes of the following discussion, low annual earnings are earnings less than the poverty level for a four-person family. The 1979 threshold for low annual earnings was $6,905, corresponding to $3.45 per hour for 50 40-hour weeks. The 1990 threshold was $12,195, or $6.10 per hour for the same amount of work....In 1979, there were 7.8 million workers who fell into the low annual earnings category, representing 12.1 percent of all year-round, full-time workers. By 1990, the absolute number was 14.4 million (an 85 percent increase over 1979) and the proportion had risen to 18.0 percent (up 49 percent over the period). As high as these figures are, they would be much worse if they included people who were strongly attached to the labor market, but had not been fully employed (i.e., who had spent part or all of the year looking for work or who had worked less than a 35-hour week for involuntary reasons). When these workers and the year-round, full-time workers are added together, the data reveal a national economy in which more than a quarter of all workers strongly attached to the labor force had low annual earnings in 1990 (25.7 percent)." (p179)

Jones, Linda R. Wolf (Director, Income Security Policy, Community Service Society of N.Y.). U.S. House. Committee on Ways and Means. "Historical Trends in Poverty and Family Income." Hearing, 26 Oct 1993. Washington, D.C.: GPO, 1994. (ISBN0160435765). (Y4.W36:103-42).

"Between 1967 and 1992, the inflation-adjusted median income of 65-plus households jumped 61 percent to $17,160 from $10,667--more than double the 27 percent increase for those 45 through 64. Incomes of those 15 through 24 actually declined 18 percent over the 25-year span." (p7)

Lewis, Robert. "'These Are Not the Best of Times.'" AARP Bulletin v35 n1, Jan 1994. p7. (ISSN1044-1123).

"For the first time, the Bureau of Labor Statistics' Consumer Expenditure Survey has published detailed spending data for both the merely comfortable and the truly affluent. The 1992 results of this annual survey include data for households with incomes of $50,000 to $69,999, and of $70,000 or more. Previously, the top income break was $50,000. By the new measure, the moderately affluent account for 11 percent of households, and the most affluent are 10 percent. Both groups of upper-income households are dominated by dual-earner married couples with children. They have an average of 3.1 persons, compared with 2.5 persons on average and fewer than two for households with incomes below $10,000. Despite their size, affluent families still have plenty of money to go around. The per capita after-tax income of households earning $50,000 to $69,999 averaged $17,000 in 1992. Among the most affluent, it averaged more than $30,500. The U.S. average that year was $12,000." (p11-12)

Crispell, Diane. "Business Reports: Households: The Very Rich Are Sort of Different." American Demographics v16 n3, Mar 1994. p11-13. (ISSN0163-4089).

"Although [U.S.] households reporting $100,000-plus incomes represent just 3% of the U.S. population, they provide a hefty 34% of government revenues." (p28)

Koretz, Gene. "Economic Trends: Affluent, Dual-Income Families Get Creamed by the Feds." Business Week i3352, 27 Dec 1993. p28. (ISSN0007-7135).

"Degree holders in the higher-salary ranks accounted for only 2.7 million or 38 percent of degree holders in service occupations in 1981; by 1991 there were 4.3 million degree holders earning wages in the top quartile--47 percent of all college graduates in service occupations....In 1981 the chance that a college degree holder would hold a lower-paying job in the service sector was 29 percent; by 1991 that likelihood had fallen to 25 percent. The probability of a degree holder having a high-paying job in service in 1981 was 18 percent; a decade later that probability has grown to 22 percent. The service sector was the only category in which the likelihood of attaining the top quartile of all salaries grew in the course of the 1980s. The good news for degree holders--and ultimately for colleges and universities--is that the ratio of degree holders drawing top earnings in the service sector increased dramatically between 1981 and 1991." (p35)

"The Landscape: Where the Jobs Are: College Graduates and Job Prospects." Change v26 n1, Jan-Feb 1994. p33-36. (ISSN0009-1383).

"It is not difficult to see why U.S. working men and women are concerned about NAFTA [North American Free Trade Agreement], and why the arguments against NAFTA have become so impassioned. When adjusted for inflation, the earnings of full-time male workers in the United States have actually declined over the past 20 years. For the bottom 60 percent of male U.S. workers average real wages fell 20 percent between 1973 and 1992. As Lester Thurow has pointed out, the earnings potential of the bottom two-thirds of the U.S. work force is collapsing. Is it any wonder that these workers feel vulnerable to any perceived threat to their jobs or wages? How can we fault them if they do not share the enthusiasm for NAFTA of those comfortably ensconsed in academic, Government, and corporate offices?" (pS16619)

Harkin, Tom (Sen.-Iowa). "North American Free-Trade Agreement Implementation Act," Congressional Record (20 Nov 1993). Daily ed. pS16602-16622. (ISSN0363-7239).

"The wealthiest 1 percent of Americans (with an average yearly income of $567,000) saved more than $71 billion last year--a big chunk of the budget deficit--from federal tax breaks enacted since 1978, according to Citizens for Tax Justice calculations....corporate income taxes supplied about 25 percent of federal revenues in the 1960s, but only 7 percent today (MULTINATIONAL MONITOR, 2-3/93)." (p8)

Cohen, Jeff/Solomon, Norman. "Clinton Update: When Clinton 'Soaks the Rich,' Pundits Drip." EXTRA! v6 n3, Apr-May 1993. p8. (ISSN0895-2310).

"Since 1973, American trade with other nations has doubled while the value of American weekly paychecks has fallen 18%. In the last decade alone, the number of young men working full time who earn only a poverty wage has increased 100%. Whole communities, like South Central Los Angeles; Camden, New Jersey; Flint, Michigan; and Toledo, Ohio; to name only a few, have suffered continuing economic and social decline. The economy got bigger--our national income per capita grew 28%--but the benefits were channeled to those with the highest incomes. Inequality grew, not so much because of the Reagan tax cuts as many assume, but because the structure of the American economy was significantly deregulated and internationalized and thereby tilted to favor corporate executives, investors and business lawyers to the detriment of almost everyone else. What was lacking here--and it still is--was not expanding foreign trade, but government policies that ranked community well-being as our most important national priority." (p20)

Brown, Edmund G., Jr. "Free Trade Is Not Free." Earth Island

Journal v8 n4, Fall 1993. p20-21. (ISSN1041-0406).
"Currently the richest 1 percent of the [U.S.] population makes more than the total income of the bottom 40 per cent. And thanks to unprogressive tax cuts during the Reagan years--when executive pay skyrocketed--the after-tax earnings of the richest 1 per cent of the population have jumped 136 per cent since 1977, while for the bottom 20 per cent they have inched forward a meager 1 per cent....this tax structure palpably affects our budget deficit, because every 1 per cent levy on the incomes of the wealthiest 10 per cent of Americans would add more than $17 billion to government resources." (p18)

Chase, Edward T. "The High Price of High Incomes." New Leader v76 n14, 13 Dec 1993. p17-18. (ISSN0028-6044).

"According to FORBES magazine's most recent compendium, America's four hundred richest individuals or families have amassed fortunes of at least $300 million. (This list changes every year; but people lose their place because of bad luck or ineptitude, not governmental incursions.) In 1991, the most recent year for figures, the Internal Revenue Service received 52,019 returns declaring annual incomes in excess of $1 million. In 1978, only 8,964 returns declared incomes of $1 million in today's dollars, so households at that level have increased sixfold in not much over a decade. At this bracket, salaries account for less than a quarter of all income, with the rest coming mainly from dividends, interest, and capital distribution and gains. Between 1978 and 1991, again using constant dollars, the median family income for the nation as a whole went from $35,594 to $36,841, an increment of barely 3.5 percent." (p22)

Hacker, Andrew. "Unjust Desserts?" New York Review of Books v41 n5, 3 Mar 1994. p20-24. (ISSN0028-7504).

"According to the most recent Census Bureau study, the 57.7 million men aged 25 to 64 who worked during 1992 had a median income of $22,467, while for the 49.3 million women, the median came to $16,277....In families with a single wage earner the median income came to $26,292, whereas those with two or more workers achieved $45,779." (p23)

Hacker, Andrew. "Unjust Desserts?" New York Review of Books v41 n5, 3 Mar 1994. p20-24. (ISSN0028-7504).

"In 1992, the 1,059 partners in ten of New York's largest law firms averaged $957,000 as their shares of their firms' profits. Some physicians affiliated with the country's leading medical schools received incomes exceeding $1 million. Executives did even better. Among fifty companies recently examined by FORTUNE magazine, each compensated its leading executive in excess of $5 million, rising to $11 million at Philip Morris and $15 million at General Electric. Corporate salaries are commonly augmented by stock awards. The current chairman of Coca-Cola, for example, has already amassed a portfolio of more than $300 million." (p20)

Hacker, Andrew. "Unjust Desserts?" New York Review of Books v41 n5, 3 Mar 1994. p20-24. (ISSN0028-7504).

"Isabel Sawhill and Mark Condon of the Urban Institute calculated last year that if economic productivity [in the U.S.] had grown as rapidly between 1973 and 1990 as it did from 1948 to 1973, the average family's income today would be 35 percent higher than it is now. Many members of the middle class became middle class only a generation or two ago, thanks precisely to the post-World War II boom--in polls, only 37 percent of Americans identified themselves as middle class in 1952, and only 44 percent in 1964. Today more than 80 percent do." (p9)

Lemann, Nicholas. "Mysteries of the Middle Class." New York Review of Books v41 n3, 3 Feb 1994. p9-13. (ISSN0028-7504).

"Household incomes reflects the number of earners in a household as well as the income of each earner. There is some evidence that an increase in the number of two-earner African-American households rather than a rise in personal earnings is primarily responsible for the growing affluence among blacks. African-American households tend to have fewer workers compared with other racial and ethnic groups, however. In 1992, 46 percent of white households (including white Hispanic households) had two or more workers, compared with 36 percent of black households and 49 percent of Hispanic households. In 1990, 18 percent of Asian families had three or more earners, compared with 14 percent of non-Hispanic white families." (p35)

O'Hare, William P. "America's Minorities--The Demographics of Diversity." Population Bulletin v47 n4, Dec 1992. p2-47. (ISSN0032-468X).

"A salary survey of members of the National Association of Business Economists [in the U.S.] showed that men earned $67,000 on average in 1992, while women earned $13,500 less, or $53,500." (p11)

Horn, Patricia. "Walls Are Falling for Women in Economics, but Slowly." The Christian Science Monitor v86 n28, 4 Jan 1994. p11. (ISSN0882-7729).

"A recent study by a group of economic historians at Harvard University concludes that the share of net worth--assets minus debts--held by the top 1 percent of households in the United States jumped from below 20 percent in 1979 to more than 36 percent in 1989. The fifty years prior to that decade had witnessed a growing redistribution of wealth, but that trend has been dramatically reversed since the new economics took over. How long can we accommodate such inequities with good conscience? The truth is that with the weakening of class solidarities, the social forces to correct them are not as strong as in the past. Should these inequities, moreover, become the target of grievance groups based on race, religion, or any other such primordial factor--which is not unlikely given their growing strength--conflicts could become really ugly, as the riots in places like Los Angeles, and Rostock remind us." (p80)

Hyden, Goran. "Back to the Future?" Transition v3 n2, 1993. p70-82. (ISSN0041-1191).

INCOME--U.S.--WOMEN

"In general, wives who work part-time (whether or not husbands work) add a median of 14 percent to the [U.S.] family income. They may not work just for money, but to keep current with their jobs or to maintain job benefits. Wives who work full-time bring home more than twice the share of family income that part-timers do, at 38 percent. Black wives who work full-time contribute slightly more than white and Hispanic wives do, mostly because the gender income gap is much smaller for blacks. Furthermore, black wives are more likely than white wives to work full-time, so overall, the median share of family income they bring to the table is higher than for whites, 38 percent versus 31 percent." (p16)

Krafft, Susan. "Business Reports: Income: Why Wives Earn Less Than Husbands." American Demographics v16 n1, Jan 1994. p16-17. (ISSN0163-4089).

INCOME DISTRIBUTION

"Disparity of income has doubled in the last thirty years: today the richest 20% of the people consume 150 times more of the world's goods than the poorest 20%. More and more people are being excluded from development, whether they live in 'less developed' countries or in 'industrialized' countries." (p2)

Griesgraber, Jo Marie. "Bretton Woods: After 50 Years, Time for a New World Vision." Center Focus n119, Jan 1994. p1-3.

"The United Nations Development Programme (UNDP) has just published its 'Human Development Report 1993.'" (p1) "The 1993 'Report' opens with a grim status report on development in the world: 'More than a billion of the world's people languish in absolute poverty, and the poorest fifth find the richest fifth enjoy more than 150 times their income. Women still earn only half as much as men--and despite constituting more than half the votes, have great difficulty securing even 10% representation in parliaments. Rural people in developing countries still receive less than half the income opportunities and social services available to their urban counterparts. Many ethnic minorities still live like a separate nation within their own countries.'" (p2)

Griesgraber, Jo Marie. "Development: From Exclusion to Inclusion: The 1993 Human Development Report." Center Focus n113, Sep 1993. p1-3.

INCOME DISTRIBUTION--ATLANTA (GA) (v19)

INCOME DISTRIBUTION--BRAZIL (v19)

INCOME DISTRIBUTION--COSTA RICA

"Per capita income in Costa Rica has been rising steadily since 1984, to its current $2,300 annually, enough to make the country receive a 'semideveloped' rating. But the wealth has been unevenly divided. Despite a decade of 4 percent real growth rates, the poverty index hovers at around 20 percent of the population." (p11)

Dye, David. "Economy: Costa Rica's Economy Bears Fruit of Ten Years of 'Structural Adjustment.'" The Christian Science Monitor v86 n62, 23 Feb 1994. p11. (ISSN0882-7729).

INCOME DISTRIBUTION--SOUTH AFRICA

"According to 1991 data, 51% of white households had an income greater than $1,200 per month. For Africans, only 1.2% reached this figure; secondly, according to the South African Catholic Bishops' Conference, less than 5% of the population own 88% of the personal wealth." (p1)

"South Africa: Major Obstacles to Liberation Remain." NewsNotes v19 n2, Mar-Apr 1994. p1-2. (ISSN1064-1556).

INCOME DISTRIBUTION--U.S. (v19)

"Family income inequality increased substantially in the United States over the last twenty years especially during the 1980s. The pre-tax cash incomes of the bottom forty percent of families were no higher at the end of a long economic expansion in 1989 than were the incomes of the bottom forty percent of families a decade earlier in real terms. In contrast, the incomes of the upper 20 percent of families were almost 20 percent higher in 1989 than those of analogous families in 1979. These differences did not narrow in the early 1990s." (p24)

Katz, Lawrence F. (Chief Economist, U.S. Dept. of Labor). U.S. House. Committee on Ways and Means. "Children and Families at Risk in Deteriorating Communities." Hearing, 7 Dec 1993. Washington, D.C.: GPO, 1994. (ISBN0160436567). (Y4.W36:103-43).

"From the 1970s to the early 1990s wage dispersion increased in the United States to levels greater than at any time since 1940. The hourly earnings of a full-time worker in the 90th percentile of the U.S. earnings distribution (someone whose earnings exceeded those of 90% of all workers) relative to a worker in the 10th percentile (someone whose earnings exceeded those of just 10% of all workers) grew by 20 percent for men and 25 percent for women from 1979 to 1989. The gap increased further in the early 1990s. Pay differentials by education and age increased. The college/high school wage premium doubled for young workers with weekly wages of young male college graduates increasing by some 30 percent relative to those of young males with twelve or fewer years of schooling. In addition, among workers without college degrees the wages of older workers rose relative to those of younger workers. The only earnings differential that fell was that between men and women, which dropped by 10 percent or so in all education and age groups in the 1980s." (p25)

Katz, Lawrence F. (Chief Economist, U.S. Dept. of Labor). U.S. House. Committee on Ways and Means. "Children and Families at Risk in Deteriorating Communities." Hearing, 7 Dec 1993. Washington, D.C.: GPO, 1994. (ISBN0160436567). (Y4.W36:103-43).

"Among whites as well as blacks, as the number of wage-earners and the level of probable earnings declines, poverty increases. Married couple-families have the lowest poverty rates; single-parent families with male heads have poverty rates considerably lower than single-parent families with childen that [are] headed by females of their own race. The relative poverty rates of these groups reflect the wage hierarchies in the U.S. labor market that have been distressingly consistent over the past decades: the median earnings of white males in 1992 was $31,012, of black males $22,369, Hispanic males, $20,049; white females, $21,659, black females $19,819, Hispanic females, $17,138. Thus, because female-headed black families have only one wage-earner and because they are likely to receive low wages when they do work, these families are more likely to be poor than other families." (p150)

McFate, Katherine (Joint Center for Political and Economic Studies). U.S. House. Committee on Ways and Means. "Historical Trends in Poverty and Family Income." Hearing, 26 Oct 1993. Washington, D.C.: GPO, 1994. (ISBN0160435765). (Y4.W36:103-42).

"In 1967, 2.9 percent of white families [in the U.S.] had real incomes less than $5,000 in 1990 dollars. Ten years later, 2.1 percent of white families had incomes below $5,000. And, by 1990, 2.5 percent of white families had incomes below $5,000, the same percent as in 1987. The percents for the intervening years all fall within the range of 1.9 percent to 3 percent. Thus, for the entire period of 1967 to 1990--a span of an entire generation--there was little change in the proportion of white families that were truly poor and disadvantaged. Of course there were substantial changes in the percentages of whites who were advantaged. The proportion of white families with incomes in excess of $100,000 in real dollars soared from less than 2 percent in 1967 to almost 6 percent in 1990. Just during the 1980s this well-off fraction of the white population expanded from around 3 percent in 1980 to 6.1 percent in 1989. The white rich got richer. The black rich, representing a correspondingly smaller percent of the black population, also got richer. Four-tenths of one percent of black families had incomes above $100,000 in 1967; five-tenths of black families had incomes above $100,000 in 1980. By 1990, however, 1.3 percent of black families had incomes in excess of $100,000." (p122-123)

Myers, Samuel L., Jr. (Hubert H. Humphrey Inst. of Public Affairs, Univ. of Minnesota). U.S. House. Committee on Ways and Means. "Historical Trends in Poverty and Family Income." Hearing, 26 Oct 1993. Washington, D.C.: GPO, 1993. (ISBN0160435765). (Y4.W36:103-42).

"The United States is, increasingly, an oligarchy. The richest 1 percent of our population now owns 37 percent of the wealth, more than the bottom 90 percent of the people. The CEO's of the FORBES 500 corporations earn 157 times more than their average worker, and the gap between the rich and the poor is wider than at any time since the 1920's. From 1983 to 1989, 55 percent of the increase in family wealth accrued to the richest half of 1 percent of families, while the lower-middle and bottom wealth classes lost over $250 billion dollars' worth of wealth." (pH478)

Sanders, Bernard (Rep.-Vt.). "What They're Not Talking about in Congress," Congressional Record (10 Feb 1994). Daily ed. pH478-479. (ISSN0363-7239).

INCOME TAX--JAPAN--U.S. (v19)

INCOME TAX--U.S. (v19)

INCOME TAX--U.S.--DEDUCTIONS (v19)

INDIA

see also AIDS (DISEASE)--INDIA; CHINA--INDIA--ECONOMIC CONDITIONS; DENTAL CARE--INDIA; ECONOMIC FORECASTING--INDIA; ELECTRIC POWER CONSUMPTION--INDIA; FORESTS AND FORESTRY--INDIA; HIV INFECTIONS--INDIA; INDUSTRIAL PRODUCTIVITY--INDIA; IRRIGATION--INDIA; MEDICAL CARE--INDIA; MINES AND MINERAL RESOURCES--INDIA; RICKSHAW MEN--CALCUTTA (INDIA); SEX OF CHILDREN, PARENTAL PREFERENCES FOR--INDIA; TIGERS--INDIA; UNTOUCHABLES--INDIA--SOCIAL CONDITIONS

INDIA--ECONOMIC CONDITIONS (v19)

INDIA--POPULATION

"India is caught in a demographic trap. Death rates have declined over the years but population growth has remained high, despite government family planning drives in the last decade. The country's population is 872 million, with an average growth rate of 2.35 percent a year in the last decade. Seventeen million are added every year....India is divided into 490 administrative districts, 90 of which have been identified as 'problem districts' accounting for 40 percent of the country's population. Along with Uttar Pradesh, 85 of the 90 problem districts belong to states like Bihar, Madhya Pradesh and Rajasthan. Leaders of these districts have been asked to formulate plans to check their populations....The eastern state of Bihar is perhaps the worst offender. Its Chief Minister, Laloo Prasad Yadav, has nine children. The Prime Minister of India, Narasimha Rao, has eight, and nearly 60 percent of his ministers have more than two." (p12)

Singh, Atiya. "India Tries to Bust the Baby Boom." Toward Freedom v42 n2, Mar 1993. p12,14. (ISSN0048-9898).

INDIA--SOCIAL CONDITIONS

"Although India was the first country in the world to articulate a policy to reduce its rate of population growth, it has often been criticized for what has been perceived as weak implementation of its program. It has also been criticized for its heavy focus on sterilization. We see India's program in a somewhat more favorable light. Contraceptive prevalence increased from 14 percent in 1970 to 34 percent in 1980 and to 43 percent in 1988, an average increase of 1.6 percentage points per year. The social and economic setting of which the program is a part is, however, daunting--low income per capita ($350), low annual rate of increase in GNP [gross national product] per capita from 1960 to 1990 (1.9 percent per year), relatively low life expectancy (58), high infant mortality (98 deaths per 1,000 live births), low literacy (48 percent), particularly among women (34 percent), and low female enrollment in primary and secondary schools (55 percent). Despite these unfavorable social and economic indicators, the TFR [total fertility rate] has gradually fallen from about 5.8 in 1960 to 4.2, a decrease of more than 25 percent." (p84)

Mauldin, W. Parker/Ross, John A. "Prospects and Programs for Fertility Reduction, 1990-2015." Studies in Family Planning v25 n2, Mar-Apr 1994. p77-95. (ISSN0039-3665).

INDIANA

see POLLUTION--INDIANA; TEENAGE PREGNANCY--INDIANA

INDIANS OF NORTH AMERICA

see also AIDS (DISEASE)--INDIANS OF NORTH AMERICA--CANADA; UNEMPLOYMENT--INDIANS OF NORTH AMERICA; URANIUM INDUSTRY--INDIANS OF NORTH AMERICA

"It is inarguable that Native Americans face some of the most dire economic and social circumstances of any people in the United States. The facts are disturbing: The average per capita income of the Navajo Nation is only $4,106, one-fourth less than the average American. Unemployment on reservations averages four-to-five times that of other regions of the United States, and the percentages of Navajos living in poverty is an astounding 56.1 percent, four times higher than the rest of the country. More than 15 percent of Indian homes lack basic sanitation facilities, a rate eight times worse than the rest of the United States." (pS16768)

McCain, John (Sen.-Ariz.). "Statements on Introduced Bills and Joint Resolutions," Congressional Record (20 Nov 1993). Daily ed. pS16719-16785. (ISSN0363-7239).

"The American Indian, Eskimo, and Aleut minority population... combines peoples with different pasts and disparate presents. They are linked because their civilizations were thriving here before Europeans and others began to settle the continent. The 1990 Census counted 1.9 million American Indians, including 148,000 Hispanic Indians, along with 57,000 Eskimos and 24,000 Aleuts. American Indians claim membership to over 500 tribes, but one-half of all Indians identify with one of the eight largest tribes. The Cherokee, Navajo, Chippewa, or Sioux tribes are the largest, claiming four out of ten American Indians....Higher birth rates among Indians, better census reporting, and perhaps a resurgence of ethnic pride helped increase the American-Indian population by 28 percent between the 1980 and 1990 Censuses. The Navajo, Choctaw, Chippewa, and Apache grew by 38 to 64 percent over the decade, for example, and the count of Aleuts increased by 68 percent, far more than could be accounted for by natural increase." (p12)

O'Hare, William P. "America's Minorities--The Demographics of Diversity." Population Bulletin v47 n4, Dec 1992. p2-47. (ISSN0032-468X).

INDIANS OF NORTH AMERICA--ALCOHOL USE (v19)

INDIANS OF NORTH AMERICA--EDUCATION

"Schools in the United States are failing a disproportionate number of minority students....The condition of Native American students, however, appears to be especially alarming. It is evident not only in high nonenrollment (10%), overageness (75% at least one grade behind), and low achievement test scores (Chadwick, Bahr, & Strauss, 1977; Sanders, 1987) but also in the disproportionate numbers of Native American school children diagnosed as having 'emotional disorders' (Yates, 1987) or placed in special education and learning disabled programs. A 1988 Bureau of Indian Affairs report noted that 11% of Native American sophomores in public and private schools were enrolled in special education programs, and 36% were classified as being handicapped. By comparison, only 7% of Hispanic students and 9% of Black students were in special education programs (O'Brien, 1990)....Studies also show that Native American teenagers have a lower self-image than any other minority group, the highest rate of suicide (Youngman & Sadongei, 1974), and the highest dropout rate (O'Brien, 1990). According to the National Center for Educational Statistics (1988), their dropout rate is 35.5%, compared with 27.9% for Hispanics and 22.2% for Black students." (p169)

Nel, Johanna. "Preventing School Failure: The Native American Child." Clearing House v67 n3, Jan-Feb 1994. p169-174. (ISSN0009-8655).

INDIANS OF NORTH AMERICA--HEALTH AND HYGIENE

"In response to President Nixon, the Congress passed the Indian Self-Determination and Education Assistance Act in 1974 and it was signed into law by President Ford on January 4, 1975. Major amendments were enacted in 1988 in an effort to improve the implementation of the Act. Today, approximately $531 million of the funds appropriated to the BIA [Bureau of Indian Affairs] are administered by tribal governments under self-determination contracts. There are over 400 contracts between Indian tribes and the IHS [Indian Health Service] involving about $497 million annually. Indian tribes contract with the IHS for the operation of 8 fully accredited hospitals, 347 health centers, and 70 service units." (pS4570)

McCain, John (Sen.-Ariz.). "Statements on Introduced Bills and Joint Resolutions," Congressional Record (20 Apr 1994). Daily ed. pS4554-4574. (ISSN0363-7239).

"American Indians suffer higher rates of fetal alcohol syndrome (FAS) and diabetes than any other population in the United States. Each year in New Mexico, more than 36 babies are born with FAS, compared to the national average of 2 FAS births per 1,000 births. Even more significant, New Mexico health officials estimate that the combined FAS rate for our State's 22 Indian tribes is 2 to 5 times that of the national average. Statistics on diabetes are also grim. In New Mexico, the rate of diabetes is nearly twice the national rate; and nationally, Native Americans are 10 times more likely to have diabetes than the non-Hispanic white population." (pS4014)

Bingaman, Jeff (Sen.-N.Mex.). "An Amendment to Senate Concurrent Resolution 63 Regarding the Indian Health Service," Congressional Record (25 Mar 1994). Daily ed. pS4013-4014. (ISSN0363-7239).

"Among Native Americans, a large proportion of the population dies before the age of 45. Cirrhosis and diabetes are two chronic diseases that afflict Native Americans more frequently than other groups. Diabetes is now so prevalent that in many tribes more than 20 percent of the members have this disease." (pS4045)

Hatch, Orrin G. (Sen.-Utah). "Preventive Health Services and Health Professions Amendments Act of 1993," Congressional Record (25 Mar 1994). Daily ed. pS4037-4047. (ISSN0363-7239).

INDIANS OF NORTH AMERICA--NUTRITION

"Four years ago, [nature writer Gary Paul] Nabhan began to investigate how the loss of traditional crops affected the health of Native peoples in his area. Since the 1940s, when Native Americans entered the cash economy and began consuming store-bought, Anglo foods, they have suffered from a host of diseases previously unknown to them. Today in the Southwest, Native Americans have the highest incidence of diabetes in the world; one in every two adults over age thirty-five is afflicted. After discovering that many traditional foods including mesquite, cholla cactus buds, prickly pear fruit and pads, and chia seeds actually help slow the rate of sugar released into the bloodstream, Nabhan conducted a study at the National Institute of Fitness where he and six O'odham and one Hopi health-worker ate four to six servings of Native, slow-release foods a day. 'By walking or running between five and nine miles a day, we tried to duplicate the physical activity levels that their grandparents would have had.' Over the two-week period, they observed a three-and-a-half pound drop in average weight; a percent and a half loss in fat weight per person; and about a weekly 30 to 35 point drop in blood sugar and cholesterol levels." (p19)

Goodstein, Carol. "People: Seeding the Desert." Amicus Journal v15 n3, Fall 1993. p16-19. (ISSN0276-7201).

INDIANS OF NORTH AMERICA--POPULATION (v19)

INDIANS OF NORTH AMERICA--SOCIAL CONDITIONS (v19)

"The percentage of Indian people in poverty in New Mexico is 46 percent. The national Indian poverty rate is 30.9 percent, while the Nation as a whole has a poverty rate of 13.1 percent. For Indian families headed by females, 50.4 percent of the families are living in poverty, which compares to a national figure of 31.1 percent. According to the 1990 census the percentage of unemployed Indian males and females in New Mexico who are considered in the work force is 21.2 percent and 16.4 percent respectively. This compares with national Indian unemployment rates of 13.1 percent for both Indian males and females. The national unemployment rate is 6.4 percent. For the entire United States, 20.3 percent of persons over the age of 25 have a bachelor degree or higher education, while only 9.3 percent of Indian people have attained this level of education." (pE579)

Richardson, Bill (Rep.-N.Mex.). "Introduction of a Bill to Provide Social Service Block Grants Directly to Indian Tribes," Congressional Record (24 Mar 1994). Daily ed. pE578-579. (ISSN0363-7239).

INDIANS OF NORTH AMERICA--U.S.--GAMBLING

"The Indian Gaming Regulatory Act of 1988 allowed Indians to operate, on their reservations, any sort of gambling that was not banned in their states....In Connecticut, the Mashantucket Pequots, whose casino complex is now the largest in the country, make $200m a year. In Florida, the Seminole tribe reduced the share of its budget contributed by the federal government from 60% in 1979 to 20% in 1984. On the western reservations, where gambling is newer, the Agua Caliente tribe in Palm Springs has gone into partnership with Caesars World to build a $20m casino and mall. And the Fort McDowell Yavapai tribe, 40 miles east of Phoenix, Arizona, already earns $4m-5m gross a month from poker machines. In all, revenue generated nationwide by Indian gambling runs at $5.8 billion a year." (p34)

"Cowboys and Indians: Once Upon a Time in the West." Economist v329 n7843, 25 Dec 1993. p31-34. (ISSN0013-0613).

INDIANS OF NORTH AMERICA--WOMEN--EDUCATION (v19)

INDIGENOUS PEOPLES--BRAZIL

"In this International Year of Indigenous Peoples, the 200,000 indigenous people of Brazil run the risk of losing the rights guaranteed them by the nation's 1988 Constitution. As the massacre of at least 73 Yanomami Indians in the northern state of Roraima in mid-August demonstrates, securing these rights is literally a matter of life and death....The massacre of Yanomami Indians is a direct consequence of the denial of indigenous peoples' right to land and life. 20,000 Yanomami, many still highly isolated from the outside world, inhabit the forests of the Brazil-Venezuela border. About 10,000 Yanomami live on the Brazilian side. A gold rush began there in the mid-1980s, and by 1987, 80,000 gold prospectors had invaded the land, bringing with them malaria and other epidemic diseases. Between 1987 and 1991, 2000 Yanomami died as a result of the invasion." (p12)

"Brazil: Massacre of the Most Vulnerable." NewsNotes v18 n5, Sep-Oct 1993. p12-13. (ISSN1064-1556).

INDIGENOUS PEOPLES--EL CHOCO (COLOMBIA)

"Along Colombia's Pacific coast lies one of the most biologically diverse tropical rainforest regions left on Earth. Known as El Choco, this verdant terrain has, until recently, managed to escape the nefarious claws of development with 83% of the forest still intact....Approximately 110,000 Indigenous people live in El Choco from eleven different tribal groups. The dominant nations are the Embera, Waunana and Awa. They have been driven from their traditional lands and live in isolated groups throughout the region. As a result of a long struggle, the Indigenous people have won legal title to 64 'resguardos' which cover approximately five percent of El Choco." (p27)

"Colombia: Plan Pacifico Threatens to Destroy Untouched Rainforest." Abya Yala News v7 n1-2, Win-Spr 1993. p27. (ISSN1056-5876).

INDIGENOUS PEOPLES--NICARAGUA

"During the '80s, northeastern Nicaragua along the Coco River was turned into a bone-chilling battlefield. The counterrevolution, with its headquarters in Honduras, set up military bases in the tropical rainforests without taking into account the various ethnic groups living in their ancestral lands. The end of the war opened the way for this traditionally isolated area to once again exist in peace. In November 1991, pressured by national and international environmental groups, President Violeta Chamorro declared the creation of a 2,900 square mile (7,500 sq km) natural reserve, equivalent to 8% of the national territory, in the department of Jinotega and the North Atlantic Autonomous Region....Currently, some 8,000 Sumus (95% of the total in Nicaragua) and almost 4,000 Miskitos live within the reserve limits along the banks of the Coco River, the Bocay River and other smaller rivers. The biggest concern, however, is the unknown number of mestizos who constantly enter in order to exploit the rich natural resources or to search for lands to settle." (p14)

Valenzuela, Matias. "Bosawas Reserve: Pressures on Nature." Barricada Internacional v13 n362, Jun 1993. p14-16. (ISSN1013-9567).

INDIGENOUS PEOPLES--ONTARIO

"It is estimated that roughly 180,000 of Ontario's estimated 9.7 million residents are aboriginal people. Almost two-thirds of this population is believed to live off reserves. There are approximately 127 distinct reserve communities in Ontario. About 25 percent of these are accessible only by air. Another four percent are classified as being 'remote' (more than 350 km from a 'major center,' which is defined as communities with populations of 2,500 or more). Forty-six percent of these reserve communities are classified as 'rural' (50-350 km from a 'major' center). The remaining 25 percent are described as being within 50 km of a 'major center.'" (p89)

Tetu, Ronald P. "Reviews of Professional Periodicals: Canadian Journal of Criminology." Federal Probation v58 n1, Mar 1994. p88-90. (ISSN0014-9128).

INDONESIA

see also EAST TIMOR (INDONESIA)--MORTALITY; ECONOMIC ASSISTANCE, AMERICAN--INDONESIA; FERTILITY, HUMAN--INDONESIA; GOLD INDUSTRY--INDONESIA; POOR--INDONESIA; WAGES--INDONESIA

INDONESIA--ARMED FORCES--APPROPRIATIONS AND EXPENDITURES (v19)

INDONESIA--ECONOMIC CONDITIONS (v19)

INDONESIA--SOCIAL CONDITIONS (v19)

"Commensurately with BKKBN's [National Family Planning Coordinating Board's] establishment and expansion, Indonesia experienced dramatic gains in economic welfare and women's status. Improvements in economic welfare resulted from a rapid expansion of the education system, combined with periods of strong economic growth. Enrollment rates of children age 7-12 increased from under 50% in 1961, to 60% in 1971 and to 94% in 1985 (Biro Pusat Statistik 1975, 1983, 1987). Poverty rates fell from about 40% in the late 1970s to about 22% in the late 1980s (World Bank 1990b). National household expenditure surveys show that price-adjusted nonfood expenditures increased by nearly 60% from 1978 to 1984 (Lembaga Demografi 1988). Real wages increased by 65% for women and by 40% for men between 1980 and 1987 (Ananta et al. 1990)." (p37)

Gertler, Paul J./Molyneaux, John W. "How Economic Development and Family Planning Programs Combined to Reduce Indonesian Fertility." Demography v31 n1, Feb 1994. p33-63. (ISSN0070-3370).

"Between 1960 and 1990, life expectancy [in Indonesia] rose by 20 years to 61. Its IMR [infant mortality rate] is still high at 70, but has been cut in half during the last three decades. Adult literacy increased from 39 to 77 percent from 1960 to 1990, and enrollment ratios of primary and secondary school increased slightly more. Women's literacy increased from 26 to 68 percent during the same period. Indonesia has a strong family planning program, and contraceptive prevalence increased from 9 percent in 1973 to 50 percent in 1991, a high average annual increase of 2.28 percentage points a year. The TFR [total fertility rate] decreased by almost two births per woman (1.94) from 1960 to 1990, more than halfway toward replacement from its level of 5.42 in 1960." (p84)

Mauldin, W. Parker/Ross, John A. "Prospects and Programs for Fertility Reduction, 1990-2015." Studies in Family Planning v25 n2, Mar-Apr 1994. p77-95. (ISSN0039-3665).

INDUSTRIAL HYGIENE--ONTARIO

"The management and labor representatives who head the Ontario Provincial Workplace Health and Safety Agency testified on the Senate OSHA [Occupational Safety and Health Administration] Reform Bill (S.575) before the Senate Labor and Human Resources Committee on the effectiveness of joint committees and the need for legislation to mandate this kind of approach. They reported that in Ontario the workplace fatality rate is one-half that in the United States, 4.3/100,000 workers versus 9/100,000 workers. For construction, the Ontario fatality rate is one-third the rate in the United States (11/100,000 workers versus 32/100,000 workers). The experience of Ontario's workplace safety program demonstrates that a systematic approach to safety and health at the workplace that includes programs, joint committees and training and education can be effective in addressing job hazards and reducing injuries and illnesses." (p90-91)

Donahue, Thomas B. (Secretary-Treasurer, AFL-CIO). U.S. House. Committee on Education and Labor "Hearings on H.R. 1280, Comprehensive Occupational Safety and Health Reform Act." Hearing, 28 Apr 1993. Washington, D.C.: GPO, 1994. (ISBN0160434033). (Y4.Ed8/1:103-35).

INDUSTRIAL HYGIENE--OREGON

"Since 1989, there has been a marked decrease in the number of Oregon's industrial fatalities. The incidence rate of workers injured or diseased, per hundred workers, has also decreased significantly in both the public and private sector. The national trend over this time period has been approximately an 11% increase in incidence rates, while Oregon has decreased approximately 10%. In 1990, Oregon had a 12.2% reduction in workers' compensation pure premiums; another 11% reduction in 1991, and an 11.4% reduction in 1992. Oregon is the only state accomplishing this magnitude of reduction and it is largely a consequence of occupational safety and health initiatives. From 1989 through 1992, the savings to Oregon employers has been over $1.5 billion in direct and indirect costs due in part to the incidence rate declines. But most important is the effect on Oregon workers. These incidence rate reductions mean our workers and their families have less human suffering and social-economic problems associated with occupational injuries, illnesses and fatalities." (p48-49)

Pompei, John A. (Administrator, Oregon Occupational Safety and Health Div., Dept. of Insurance and Finance). U.S. Senate. Committee on Labor and Human Resources. "The Occupational Safety and Health Act: Making the Case for Reform." Hearing, 14 Jul 1993. Washington, D.C.: GPO, 1993. (ISBN0160433738). (Y4.L11/4:S.hrg.103-334).

INDUSTRIAL HYGIENE--TEXAS

"In...Texas, over 500 deaths occurred on the job in 1991 in the private sector. The most hazardous job...is in construction. Seventeen percent of the fatalities in the same period were in the area of construction. The level of fatalities under current OSHA [Occupational Safety and Health Administration] are excessive not only in construction but in all areas. Fatalities, though, are not the only excessive cost. Injuries and illnesses contribute an economic cost in Texas alone of $3.7 billion for 1991. That figure does not include medical costs which are $2.3 billion in the same year. It may be said that reform of OSHA has too high a cost....However, there are other costs which need attention other than monetary cost. The cost to our future is also too high. In 1991, over 1,000 injuries and illnesses were reported in Texas for children under the age of 18. Twenty-three percent of the injuries were for teenagers between the ages of 11 and 13. No reform can make the workplace completely safe. However, protection of all workers, especially under-18 workers, need to be strengthened without overburdening business." (p124)

Green, Gene (Rep.-Tex.). U.S. House. Committee on Education and Labor. "Hearings on H.R. 1280, Comprehensive Occupational Safety and Health Reform Act." Hearing, 28 Apr 1993. Washington, D.C.: GPO, 1994. (ISBN0160434033). (Y4.Ed8/1:103-35).

INDUSTRIAL HYGIENE--U.S. (v19)

"According to government figures, each year an average of 2,100 deaths and 250,000 serious injuries occur in construction workplaces in...[the U.S.], and according to the National Institute of Occupational Safety and Health (NIOSH), construction fatalities and injuries are underreported by approximately 60%." (p177)

Georgine, Robert A. (President, Building and Construction Trades Dept., AFL-CIO). U.S. House. Committee on Education and Labor. "Hearings on H.R. 1280, Comprehensive Occupational Safety and Health Reform Act." Hearing, 28 Apr 1993. Washington, D.C.: GPO, 1994. (ISBN0160434033). (Y4.Ed8/1:103-35).

"Each year, more than 10,000 workers are killed by workplace hazards [in the U.S.]--that's one worker every hour of the day. Each year, more than 6 million workers are injured on the job, and 60,000 are permanently disabled. And as many as 100,000 workers die each year from the long-term effects of occupational diseases. Many of these are preventable tragedies. Yet the response of OSHA [Occupational Safety and Health Administration] has been completely inadequate. OSHA inspections are rare. OSHA has only 1,200 inspectors to inspect five million workplaces. At its current rate of inspection, OSHA will inspect each worksite once every 79 years....The costs to our Nation for work-related injuries are staggering--a full $83 billion is spent each year to pay for poor planning." (p15)

Woolsey, Lynn C. (Rep.-Calif.). U.S. House. Committee on Education and Labor. "Hearings on H.R. 1280, Comprehensive Occupational Safety and Health Reform Act." Hearing, 28 Apr 1993. Washington, D.C.: GPO, 1994. (ISBN0160434033). (Y4.Ed8/1:103-35).

"In addition to human suffering, accidents and illnesses on the job also exact a substantial economic toll on society. For example, in one study examining accidents of all types, the Rand Institute for Civil Justice reported that workplace accidents cost the nation $83 billion annually. This includes $51.7 billion in lost production--the equivalent of 2 million work-years annually--and $31.5 billion in medical costs associated with injuries. This $83 billion almost equals the total cost of all non-work-related accidents put together, even though work accidents make up only twenty percent of all accidents. And Rand did not even take into account costs due to workplace illnesses." (p41-42)

Reich, Robert B. (Secretary of Labor, U.S. Dept. of Labor). U.S. House. Committee on Education and Labor. "Hearings on H.R. 1280, Comprehensive Occupational Safety and Health Reform Act." Hearing, 28 Apr 1993. Washington, D.C.: GPO, 1994. (ISBN0160434033). (Y4.Ed8/1:103-35).

"More than 10,000 workers die from job injuries every year. Every year, 1,700,000 Americans are hit with disabling injuries on the job, and 390,000 are diagnosed with various occupational diseases. We must do a better job to protect these workers." (p2)

Ford, William D. (Rep.-Mich.). U.S. House. Committee on Education and Labor. "Hearings on H.R. 1280, Comprehensive Occupational Safety and Health Reform Act." Hearing, 28 Apr 1993. Washington, D.C.: GPO, 1994. (ISBN0160434033). (Y4.Ed8/1:103-35).

"Some...workplace injuries and illnesses are caused by newly recognized hazards like poor indoor air quality, infectious diseases and ergonomic hazards. In the last 10 years the number of reported cases of cumulative trauma disorders related to poor job design have increased by over 600 percent [in the U.S.], with over 225,000 cases reported in 1991....But many injuries and fatalities are caused by hazards that have been long recognized like unshored trenches, faulty scaffolding, failure to de-energize and 'lock-out' dangerous equipment during maintenance and repair. Many cases of occupational disease are still occurring from exposures to toxics like lead and silica which have been recognized as hazardous for decades. According to the National Institute for Occupational Safety and Health (NIOSH) and the Centers for Disease Control and Prevention (CDC) from 1985 to 1990, 536 cases of silicosis were reported from just four states--Michigan, New Jersey, Ohio and Wisconsin. And for 1992, NIOSH reported 21,241 cases of elevated blood lead levels among adults from an 18-state surveillance program, of which 95 percent are estimated to be work-related." (p84)

Donahue, Thomas B. (Secretary-Treasurer, AFL-CIO). U.S. House. Committee on Education and Labor. "Hearings on H.R. 1280, Comprehensive Occupational Safety and Health Reform Act." Hearing, 28 Apr 1993. Washington, D.C.: GPO, 1994. (ISBN0160434033). (Y4.Ed8/1:103-35).

"The picture of workplace injury and disease in America is...sobering when looked at in an historical context. Since the enactment of the Occupational Safety and Health Act in 1970, 250,000 workers have lost their lives due to traumatic injuries. According to the National Safety Council, since 1971, the number of occupational fatalities has decreased from 13,700 to 9,900 in 1991 and the rate of occupational fatalities has decreased from 17 fatalities per 100,000 workers to 9 fatalities per 100,000 workers....According to the Bureau of Labor Statistics (BLS), the rate of workplace injuries has also declined from 10.9/100 workers in 1972 to 8.4/100 workers in 1991....However, serious workplace injuries, those that result in time off the job or restricted activity have actually increased from 3.3/100 workers in 1972 to 3.9/100 workers in 1991. And according to the BLS, the time lost due to the serious injuries has also increased from 47.0 lost workdays/100 workers to 86.5 lost workdays/100 workers during the same time period." (p83)

Donahue, Thomas B. (Secretary-Treasurer, AFL-CIO). U.S. House. Committee on Education and Labor. "Hearings on H.R. 1280, Comprehensive Occupational Safety and Health Reform Act." Hearing, 28 Apr 1993. Washington, D.C.: GPO, 1994. (ISBN0160434033). (Y4.Ed8/1:103-35).

"About 7,000 workers per year are killed on the job in the United States; another 50,000 to 100,000 die from occupational illnesses, and as many as 10 million workers are wounded badly enough to have to seek medical care. In addition to the traditional occupational problems, within the past 10 years, we have witnessed the appearance of modern occupational epidemics of cumulative trauma disorders, occupational stress, and complaints about the quality of the indoor environment. The cost of these problems...is enormous." (p7)

Millar, Donald (Director, National Inst. for Occupational Safety and Health). U.S. Senate. Committee on Labor and Human Resources. "The Occupational Safety and Health Act: Making the Case for Reform." Hearing, 14 Jul 1993. Washington, D.C.: GPO, 1993. (ISBN0160433738).

(Y4.L11/4:S.hrg.103-334).

"Although we have made some progress since 1970, injury rates remain appallingly high. One hundred thousand Americans die each year from on-the-job safety accidents and occupational disease, and another 1.8 million suffer disabling injuries.... Thousands of American workers have been killed or injured unnecessarily because of standard-setting delays that, unbelievably, have lasted up to 17 years. Seven million public sector employees have no Federal or State OSHA [Occupational Safety and Health Act] protection at all." (p1)

Metzenbaum, Howard M. (Sen.-Ohio). U.S. Senate. Committee on Labor and Human Resources. "The Occupational Safety and Health Act: Making the Case for Reform." Hearing, 14 Jul 1993. Washington, D.C.: GPO, 1993. (ISBN0160433738). (Y4.L11/4:S.hrg.103-334).

"Since the Occupational Safety and Health Act was passed 23 years ago, we have made progress toward 'assuring safe and healthful working conditions' for the workers of...[the U.S.]. When the Act was passed, about 14,500 workers were fatally injured on the job each year. Over 2 million workers were disabled annually through job-related accidents. There were an estimated 390,000 cases of occupational illness each year. All of the official estimates have come down since the Act was passed, although the work force has grown by about 50 percent." (p9)

Millar, Donald (Director, National Inst. for Occupational Safety and Health). U.S. Senate. Committee on Labor and Human Resources. "The Occupational Safety and Health Act: Making the Case for Reform." Hearing, 14 Jul 1993. Washington, D.C.: GPO, 1993. (ISBN0160433738). (Y4.L11/4:S.hrg.103-334).

"Ten thousand Americans die every year from occupational injuries--almost 40 each working day. Up to 100,000 more die from occupational disease--almost 400 each working day. Every five seconds, a worker is injured on the job. Since August 1991, when we first introduced the OSHA [Occupational Safety and Health Act] Reform bill, more than 192,000 more workers have died from on-the-job injuries and work-related disease. These numbers are unacceptable." (p3)

Kennedy, Edward M. (Sen.-Mass.). U.S. Senate. Committee on Labor and Human Resources. "The Occupational Safety and Health Act: Making the Case for Reform." Hearing, 14 Jul 1993. Washington, D.C.: GPO, 1993. (ISBN0160433738). (Y4.L11/4:S.hrg.103-334).

"More than 1,700 public employees are killed on the job each year, while half a million public employees suffer disabling workplace injuries, AFSCME [or American Federation of State, County and Municipal Employees] said. The overall rate of occupational injuries and illnesses is at its highest level in 13 years, the Bureau of Labor Statistics reported, rising faster in 1992 than at any time since passage of OSHA [Occupational Safety and Health Administration] in 1970." (p1,3)

"Clinton Administration Gets Behind Drive for OSHA Reform." AFL-CIO News v39 n3, 31 Jan 1994. p1,3. (ISSN0001-1185).

"Ten years have elapsed since Public Citizen wrote to President Reagan requesting that the federal government individually notify 240,450 workers exposed to hazardous materials at 258 worksites surveyed in 69 epidemiological studies funded and conducted by the National Institute for Occupational Safety and Health (NIOSH), a part of the Health and Human Services Department's Centers for Disease Control and Prevention (CDC). Today--a decade later--fewer than 30 percent of these workers covered by only a handful of studies have been notified. Public Citizen has learned that, due to underfunding of its Screening and Notifications Section, NIOSH has individually notified a maximum of only 71,180 (29.6 percent) of the original 240,450 workers, leaving 169,270 still in the dark about health risks from on-the-job exposure. Those who were notified had been exposed at 55 (21.3 percent) of the 258 worksites." (p1)

"Unfinished Business." Health Letter v10 n3, Mar 1994. p1-2. (ISSN0882-598X).

"Nine out of every 100 full-time American workers can expect to be hit by job-related illnesses and injuries in 1994, according to statistics revealed by the Bureau of Labor Statistics. That comes out to more than 6.8 million people. This represents a substantial increase since 1984, when the figure stood at only 8.4 percent." (p1)

"Gov't Safety Statistics Show a Dramatic Rise in Work-Related Illnesses and Injuries." Maritime Newsletter v26 n1, Jan 1994. p1. (ISSN0161-9373).

"Burlington [Industries] is particularly proud of its medical surveillance program, instituted in December 1970, after Dr. Harold ('Bud') Imbus came to Burlington to head its medical department. No other textile company has come close to Burlington in studying byssinosis [or brown lung] among its workers. Burlington built its public image as a combatter of byssinosis largely on its 1971 study of 10,133 employees exposed to cotton dust. The Burlington study established that 18 percent of the 1,266 workers in the preparation departments, the dustiest mill areas, had 'classic byssinosis symptoms.' The study also showed that 4.5 percent of all the workers tested had byssinosis. A 1976 Burlington study, according to Dr. Imbus, showed that out of a sample of 12,519 employees, 1.09 percent had byssinosis." (p60)

Conway, Mimi. "Health and Wealth: Cotton Dust Kills, and It's Killing Me." Southern Exposure v21 n1-2, Spr-Sum 1993. p59-62. (ISSN0146-809X).

INDUSTRIAL PRODUCTIVITY (v19)

"Using the latest available international data, the report [compiled after a study by the McKinsey Global Institute] finds that American manufacturing companies lead Japan in productivity by 17 percent and Germany by 21 percent. The McKinsey analysis also shows that American workers are more efficient than Japanese workers in 4 of 9 industries and more productive than German workers in 7 of 9." (p58)

Collins, Sara. "Business: America Cranks It Up." U.S. News & World Report v116 n12, 28 Mar 1994. p57-58,60. (ISSN0041-5537).

INDUSTRIAL PRODUCTIVITY--ASIA (v19)

INDUSTRIAL PRODUCTIVITY--CHINA--INDIA (v19)

INDUSTRIAL PRODUCTIVITY--GREAT BRITAIN (v19)

INDUSTRIAL PRODUCTIVITY--INDIA

"India is benefiting from the emerging-market mania that has swept up investors around the world. Economic reforms since 1991 have restored macroeconomic balance in the country and slashed red tape. But IMF [International Monetary Fund]-induced austerity is not always a recipe for rapid growth, and India looks more a tortoise than a tiger. Industrial production grew by 1.5% in the year to March 1993 and in the six months that followed by just 1.6% over the same period a year earlier. Indian companies raised a record 210 billion rupees ($6.9 billion) through new share issues alone in 1993, so a boom in investment and output could be around the corner. Even so, paying 48 times historical earnings for shares looks crazy. Yet that is the average price at which shares in the Bombay Sensitive Index are selling." (p81)

"Finance: Indian Shares: Over Sensitive." Economist v330 n7849, 5 Feb 1994. p80-81. (ISSN0013-0613).

INDUSTRIAL PRODUCTIVITY--RUSSIA

"Russian industry has been crippled....The Yeltsin/Gaidar approach--never thought through clearly, repeatedly revised, and often misrepresented--has stripped away research and development funds, assuring that Russia will not be able to maintain the technological level it had in Soviet times." (p5) "Defense orders were slashed by more than 60 per cent in the first year of the reforms, and have not been restored. In addition, military industries are owed the equivalent of $1.5 billion. Thus the backbone of Russian productive power, built up during the Cold War years, has been broken. Overall, the headlong plunge into a free-price mode without setting up the mechanisms of a market economy has led to a 30 per cent decline in Russian industrial production over the past two years, and the real income of workers, taking inflation into account, has plummeted 43 per cent." (p6)

Hopkins, Mark. "The Challenge Facing Chernomyrdin." New Leader v77 n2, 14 Feb 1994. p5-7. (ISSN0028-6044).

INDUSTRIAL PRODUCTIVITY--U.S. (v19)

INDUSTRIAL SAFETY

see also HAZARDOUS SUBSTANCES

INDUSTRIAL SAFETY--U.S.

"The incidence rate [in the U.S.] of reported injuries and illnesses [in private industry workplaces] rose from 8.4 per 100 full-time workers in 1991 to 8.9 cases per 100 workers in 1992. Of the 6.8 million non-fatal injuries and illnesses, about 6.3 million were injuries that resulted in lost worktime, medical treatment other than first aid, loss of consciousness, restriction of work or motion or transfer to another job. The remainder were work-related illnesses, the majority of which involved cumulative trauma disorders." (p2)

O'Neill, Colleen M. "Job Injury Data Shows 'Law Failing.'" AFL-CIO News v39 n1, 3 Jan 1994. p2. (ISSN0001-1185).

"Ergonomics, the science of human movement in the workplace, used to focus mostly on the shop floor--where workers wrestled with difficult, often dangerous machinery. But now it is being applied to office environments and the kind of injuries they generate. The carpal tunnel syndrome and other repetitive motion conditions are the culprits, says Dan Kett, regional vice president with the insurance brokerage Johnson and Higgins in Detroit." (p51) "In offices in 1980, carpal tunnel syndrome represented 18 percent of all work-related physical ailments. 'Now there are a little more than 50 percent in offices,' he says....Despite the rise of the carpal tunnel syndrome, these conditions are not nearly the costliest to employers. That distinction belongs to the low back injuries, a category with 2.5 million new cases a year. 'They represent about 10 percent of the cases, and 80 percent of the costs,' Kett says. These low-back injuries are mostly suffered by relatively young persons, between 25 and 44, who, too often, think nothing of hefting boxes and tossing around heavy sacks. The victims can be anyone from a nurse turning over a 250-pound patient to a delivery person hoisting boxes himself--instead of using the right equipment to raise them." (p52-53)

Hoffman, Gary. "Troubleshooters." Corporate Detroit v10 n12, Dec 1993. p51-53.

"Forklifts are notoriously dangerous. TRANSPORTATION & DISTRIBUTION, an industry trade magazine, reported approximately 42,000 accidents involving forklifts in 1990. Government statistics and industry literature show that tipovers have been the primary cause of classifiable forklift deaths over the years, and published studies verifying forklift instability have been available since 1957. Commonly counterweighted to balance heavy loads, empty forklifts can be dangerously unsteady, with even moderate turns initiating tip-overs. Worse, a forklift tends to fall slowly at first, deceiving the operator into thinking there's time to jump to safety. But moments later the forklift slams to the ground like a mousetrap, catching the operator and all too often causing dismemberment, crushing injury, or death. A seat belt would keep the operator in the protective cab, increasing his or her chances of surviving unharmed....an industry analyst estimates that some sixty thousand Caterpillar forklifts potentially without seat belts could still be in use in the U.S. alone." (p13)

Petersen, Julie. "Outfront: Cat's Big Secret: Killer Forklifts." Mother Jones v18 n6, Nov-Dec 1993. p13. (ISSN0362-8841).

INDUSTRIALIZATION--KOREA (SOUTH)--TAIWAN

"Today, less than 20% of Taiwan's labour force are farmers; and of the country's 1.2 million farmers, only 11% work the land full-time. Most earn the major portion of their income from non-agricultural pursuits. As one analyst has remarked, 'farming has become the real 'sideline' for most farm families.'...High-speed growth has been socially destabilising in other ways. While absolute incomes have certainly risen in Taiwan, South Korea and Singapore, so, too, has income inequality. In South Korea, for instance, the share of the national income going to the bottom 40% of the population declined from 19.3% to 17.7% between 1965 and 1985, while the share going to the top 20% rose from 41.8% to 43.7%." (p4)

Bello, Walden. "World: Growing Pains of the Asian 'Tigers.'" Panoscope n35, Apr 1993. p2-5. (ISSN0951-8819).

INDUSTRY AND STATE--CHINA

"By 1989, the [Chinese] government conceded that half of state-owned industries were effectively bankrupt and 'have only been kept going by regular infusions of government bank loans.' Instead of productivity gains providing rising revenues, subsidies to loss-making state and collective firms soared....By the late 1980s such subsidies grew to consume well over a third of central government expenditures. In 1991 price subsidies cost some 33 billion yuan ($6.1 billion) while 56.6 billion yuan ($10.5 billion) was allocated to bailing out money-losing state firms. As more and more firms fell into insolvency and could not pay for their inputs, vast 'debt chains' emerged. Firm debt arrears rose from 110 billion yuan in 1989 to 150 billion in 1990 'and is growing'. In 1990-91 the government wrote off these debts with a huge infusion of cash, i.e. transferring the losses to the central government, and thereby adding to the record deficits of recent years." (p68)

Smith, Richard. "The Chinese Road to Capitalism." New Left Review n199, May-Jun 1993. p55-99. (ISSN0028-6060).

"In 1991, China's state-owned firms accounted for just 53 per cent of industrial output, down from over 80 per cent a decade ago, and the figure is steadily dropping. Some 37 per cent of industrial output was produced by the quasi-capitalist collectively owned rural industrial sector and 10 per cent by the private capitalist sector, including the increasingly important foreign capitalists. While the output of state industries grew by 8 per cent in 1991, that of industries owned by collectives grew by 18 per cent, and private sector output rose by 24 per cent. But the fastest growth was sustained by foreign-invested firms, who furnish 5 per cent of total output--joint ventures between foreign capitalists and both privately owned and local government-owned firms. Their turnover shot up by a phenomenal 56 per cent. If present trends continue, not only will the market share of the economy soon overtake the state sector, but the collective sector itself will gradually merge with, or be overwhelmed by, the private capitalist sector." (p86)

Smith, Richard. "The Chinese Road to Capitalism." New Left Review n199, May-Jun 1993. p55-99. (ISSN0028-6060).

INDUSTRY AND STATE--CONGO (BRAZZAVILLE)

"The biggest millstone around the neck of the Congolese economy...may be its numerous parastatals. [President Alponse] Massemba began the process of 'parastatal accumulation' by nationalizing the first foreign-owned enterprise and creating the first national marketing office. [President Marien] Ngoaubi continued the process, accelerating it with the rise of state revenues in the mid-1970s. By May 1978 there were some sixty-odd state enterprises in Congo; by the mid-1980s there were approximately 85. These enterprises employed some 30,000 persons, representing another 16 percent or so of persons employed in the modern sector. Desirable as the creation of parastatals was to create employment and promote industrialization, their cost to the Congolese economy has been high. As Radu and Sommerville have observed, 'By 1987 it was clear to everyone in Congo, excepting the most dogmatic radicals on the left, that the parastatal sector is one of the main reasons the country cannot pay its bills, remains dependent upon foreign aid, and has to import most of its food.' Virtually every Congolese parastatal continued to lose money at the end of the 1980s despite repeated government campaigns to improve their efficiency. Altogether, the debt of Congo's parastatals accounted for 28 percent of its total external debt in 1986." (p56-57)

Clark, John F. "Socio-Political Change in the Republic of Congo: Political Dilemmas of Economic Reform." Journal of Third World Studies v10 n1, Spr 1993. p52-77. (ISSN8755-3449).

INDUSTRY AND STATE--GREAT BRITAIN (v19)

INDUSTRY AND STATE--JAPAN--PUBLIC OPINION

"On commission from the Ministry of Foreign Affairs, Urban Connections, a Tokyo-based research firm which analyzes issues related to Japanese foreign policy, conducted a survey of the opinions of foreign-affiliated companies in Japan concerning deregulation and their specific suggestions for improvement. Responses were received from 349 companies (24.9% of the 1,403 firms to which questionnaires were sent), with 240 commenting in detail about their specific requests. More than half of foreign companies indicated that regulatory restrictions make doing business in Japan more difficult than in other countries (52%). Many of the remaining companies were either neutral (22%) or offered no opinion (16%). Only 10% expressed clear disagreement with this view." (p8)

Rossman, John. "Deregulation Survey: Foreign Companies: Loosen Up." Look Japan v39 n456, Mar 1994. p8-10. (ISSN0456-5339).

INDUSTRY AND STATE--U.S. (v19)

"At the end of 1991, 59 different [executive] agencies were working on approximately 4,900 regulations. Federal regulatory spending has grown to more than $13 billion annually. The cost to the private sector of complying with regulations is approximately $430 billion annually." (pE3113)

Chapman, Jim (Rep.-Tex.). "The Regulatory Sunset Act of 1993," Congressional Record (24 Nov 1993). Daily ed. pE3113. (ISSN0363-7239).

"The premier paper on the cost of Federal regulation [in the U.S.], entitled the 'Cost of Regulation,' was prepared for the GSA Regulatory Information Service Center by Thomas Hopkins in August 1992. This analysis estimated that the Federal regulation cost to the private sector and State and local governments was $581 billion, or $5,934 per household, in 1993. It should be noted that the $5,934 per household is in addition to $11,881 in taxes paid per household, for a total Federal burden of $17,816 per household. Other economists estimate the private sector and State and local compliance burden to be as high as $860 billion per year. It is time for Congress and the regulators to have better information on the cost of new legislation and regulation, and to be accountable to individuals, consumers, businesses, and State and local governments for those costs." (pS2612)

Nickles, Don (Sen.-Okla.). "The National Competitiveness Act: Jobs, Partnerships, and Defense Conversion for America," Congressional Record (9 Mar 1994). Daily ed. pS2602-2613. (ISSN0363-7239).

"Undergirding Clinton's drive for an industrial policy and the corporate state are a number of faulty assumptions. We have previously noted that contrary to what our president has said, productivity in this country has not lagged in recent times. Now economist Robert J. Samuelson notes in NEWSWEEK that business investment, as a percent of gross domestic product, was higher in the 1980s than in the 1970s and nearly 30% higher than in the 1950s. Samuelson also notes that research and development--which Clinton intends to subsidize heavily--jumped dramatically in the 1980s, up 52% compared [to] the 12% gain in the previous decade." (p8)

"Weather Report: Land of the Free." Progressive Review n316, Apr 1993. p7-9.

INFANTS--AFRICA, SUB-SAHARAN--MORTALITY (v19)

INFANTS--CARE--U.S. (v19)

INFANTS--CUBA--MORTALITY

"Cuba has just announced that its infant mortality rate dropped to 10.2 deaths per thousand live births in 1992, placing it among the world's 25 nations who have achieved the lowest infant mortality. This is especially significant when one considers that in 1959, the first year of the revolution, Cuba had a rate of 60 deaths per thousand live births. The United States had an overall infant mortality rate of 10.1 in 1987, but our rate among urban Afro-Americans was more than 22, while in Cuba the rate is the same for the entire population." (p25)

Rose, Irma Garcia/Rose, William. "Dateline Havana: Prevention Is the Watchword in Cuban Health Care." Cuba Update n3-4, Summer 1993. p25. (ISSN0196-0830).

"Infant mortality is the number of babies who die before the age of one year for every 1,000 live births. THE WALL STREET JOURNAL published (10/19/88) a table listing infant mortality rates in 20 industrialized countries, using the latest figures available for each country (1985-87). Japan had the lowest: 5.2 deaths. The United States was 20th with 10.4 deaths. In 1987, with an infant mortality rate of 13.3, Cuba ranked 23rd in the world. Cuba's achievement is by far the lowest rate of infant deaths in Latin America and comparable to that in industrialized nations." (p22)

Franklin, Jane. "Dateline Havana: Some Vital Statistics about Health Care in Cuba." Cuba Update n3-4, Summer 1993. p22. (ISSN0196-0830).

INFANTS--HEALTH AND HYGIENE--U.S.--COSTS (v19)

INFANTS--MORTALITY (v19)

INFANTS--U.S.--MORTALITY (v19)

see also SUDDEN INFANT DEATH SYNDROME--U.S.

A report from the National Commission to Prevent Infant Mortality "cited statistics indicating that the United States has a higher rate of infant deaths than Japan, Canada, and most European countries. It also noted that African-American infants had a mortality rate of 17.6 deaths per 1,000 births, while only 7.3 of 1,000 white children died before age 1." (p21)

"News in Brief: Infant Mortality." Education Week v13 n16, 12 Jan 1994. p21. (ISSN0277-4232).

"The U.S. infant mortality rate reached an all-time low of 9.8 deaths per 1,000 births in 1989 (National Center for Health Statistics (NCHS) 1992). Despite this noteworthy achievement and its indication of improvements in survival status among this nation's youngest population, concern over infant mortality differentials between African-Americans and Anglos (non-Hispanic Whites) persist (Baldwin 1986; Collins & David 1992; David & Collins 1991; Geronimus 1992; LaVeist 1992; Moss & Carver 1992; Partin 1992; Schoendorf et al. 1992; Wise & Pursley 1992; Paneth 1990; Yankauer 1990). For 1989, the last year in which complete figures are currently available, the infant mortality rate for African Americans was 18.6 (per 1,000 births) while the rate for Anglos was 8.1, more than a two-fold difference (NCHS 1992)." (p529) "This social problem is even more pressing when we look at the widening ratio of infant mortality rates between racial groups. The African-American to Anglo infant mortality ratios were 1.6 in 1950, 1.9 in 1960, 2.0 in 1980, and about 2.2 by 1989...(NCHS 1992; Yankauer 1990). Additionally, the infant mortality rate among African Americans is not even close to meeting the 1990 goal of 12 deaths per 1,000 births that the U.S. Public Health Service set for all minority groups in 1979." (p530)

Hummer, Robert A. "Racial Differentials in Infant Mortality in the U.S.: An Examination of Social and Health Determinants." Social Forces v72 n2, Dec 1993. p529-554. (ISSN0037-7732).

INFANTS--U.S.--SOCIAL CONDITIONS (v19)

INFERTILITY

see also FERTILITY, HUMAN; STERILIZATION (BIRTH CONTROL)

INFERTILITY--U.S.

"Roughly 5 million Americans of varying socioeconomic profiles suffer from infertility, meaning they have been unable to conceive a child after a year of unprotected, regular intercourse. Of that group, '50% to 70% of couples can get pregnant by standard approaches' that stop well short of exotic, invasive procedures, says Dr. David Adamson, a Palo Alto (Calif.) infertility specialist. Even when two completely healthy people have intercourse at exactly the right time, explains Dr. Cappy Rothman, a male-infertility specialist in Los Angeles, there's only a 20% to 30% chance of conceiving. That's why physicians like to give nature a year to work unassisted. Couples may increase the odds by using over-the-counter ovulation predictor tests and limiting or avoiding entirely their use of alcohol, cigarettes, medications, and drugs....Once considered a woman's problem, fertility trouble is now known to be caused 40% or more of the time by 'male factors,' primarily problems with sperm, such as count or motility (movement). The primary female factors include ovaluation problems (about 20%), tubal blockage (30%), and cervical chemistry that is hostile to sperm, even producing antibodies to them (5%). Age alone can be a negative: Women over 35 have increasing trouble conceiving and in carrying a baby to term." (p88)

Hamilton, Joan. "Personal Business: Health: Infertility: What You Should Know." Business Week n3362, 14 Mar 1994. p88-89. (ISSN0007-7135).

INFLATION (FINANCE) (v19)

"Inflation has slowed in most developed economies outside the United States over the last two years, which should further moderate U.S. inflation. Between 1991 and the end of last year, consumer price inflation slowed from 5.6 percent to about 2 percent in Canada, from 3.3 percent to about 1.3 percent in Japan, from 5.9 percent to about 1.5 percent in the United Kingdom, and from 3.1 percent to about 2.2 percent in France. In a notable exception to this pattern, inflation in Germany increased over the same period, but a restrictive monetary policy and recession are beginning to bring down the inflation rate." (p15)

U.S. Congressional Budget Office. "The Economic Outlook." The Economic and Budget Outlook: Fiscal Years 1995-1999 Jan 1994. Washington, D.C.: GPO, 1994.

INFLATION (FINANCE)--ARGENTINA--BRAZIL

"In both Brazil and Argentina,...prices were rising at about 3,000% a year as the 1980s ended. The figure in Argentina (and Chile and Mexico) today is around 10%; in Brazil it was 450% or so in 1991, 1,000% in 1992, 2,000% last year, and by now it is well on its way to 3,000%." (p15)

"Leaders: Nuts in Brazil." Economist v330 n7849, 5 Feb 1994. p15. (ISSN0013-0613).

INFLATION (FINANCE)--BRAZIL--GERMANY--JAPAN

"For 22 countries, rich and poor...[the ECONOMIST] examined over 30 indicators which sum up the economic, social, cultural and political aspects of life." (p39) "High rates of inflation can make everyday life very complicated. Unless you have a degree in advanced mathematics, avoid Brazil, where annual inflation has averaged 472% over the past decade--it is currently running at around 2,000%. Japan or Germany (where inflation has averaged 2%) are a safer bet." (p40)

"Where to Live: Nirvana by Numbers." Economist v329 n7843, 25 Dec 1993. p39-42. (ISSN0013-0613).

INFLATION (FINANCE)--CANADA

Canada's central banker John Crow "succeeded in chopping inflation from 5 percent to 2 percent between 1990 and 1992. Canadian inflation is still resting peacefully at about 2 percent, among the lowest in the industrialized world." (p7)

Clayton, Mark. "Economy: Canada Gets New Central Banker: Same Policy, but Less Baggage." The Christian Science Monitor v86 n21, 24 Dec 1993. p7. (ISSN0882-7729).

INFLATION (FINANCE)--CARIBBEAN AREA--LATIN AMERICA

"Inflation [in Latin America and the Caribbean], once endemic, is now under control, except in Brazil. For the first time, ECLAC [Economic Commission for Latin America and the Caribbean] could record it below 15% in more than half the 19 countries covered, and in seven of these below 10%." (p60)

"International: Latin America: Doing Well." Economist v329 n7843, 25 Dec 1993. p60. (ISSN0013-0613).

INFLATION (FINANCE)--EUROPE

"In France and Denmark, GDP [gross domestic product] is shrinking. In both countries, one worker in eight is on the dole. Inflation, at 2.2% in France and 1.6% in Denmark, is hardly rampant. True, Spain's inflation rate is higher, at 4.7%; but with unemployment at 22%, there is little danger of overheating." (p101-102)

"Finance: Exchange Rates: Nothing Like the Old Days." Economist v329 n7843, 25 Dec 1993. p101-102. (ISSN0013-0613).

INFLATION (FINANCE)--HAITI

Inflation in Haiti "ran 33 percent in 1992, the first year after the coup, then shot up to 45 percent in 1993 when the oil embargo was imposed. U.S. Embassy sources estimate that the inflation rate will top 50 percent in 1994; prices already have increased 25 percent this year. The Haitian government has worsened the problem with shortsighted fiscal policies. Haiti's central bank prints money to meet public payrolls, and the total government payroll, about $7 million a month, is increasing steadily to meet rising living costs. Since the embargo is choking most normal sources of government income, those costs can be met only by printing money." (p15)

James, David. "Embargo Forces Haiti's Last Gasp." Insight v10 n12, 21 Mar 1994. p14-17. (ISSN1051-4880).

INFLATION (FINANCE)--LATIN AMERICA (v19)

"In Mexico, inflation dropped from 15.5 percent in 1992 to 9.5 percent in 1993; in Argentina, from 23 percent to 11 percent; in Chile, from 15.3 percent to 12 percent. Some of the smaller countries made even more dramatic gains. Jamaica reduced inflation from 77.3 percent to 18 percent, Ecuador from 54.6 percent to 36 percent, Costa Rica from 21.7 percent to 12 percent, and Guyana from 26.3 percent to 10 percent. The exception to the anti-inflationary trend was Brazil, where political uncertainty, lack of progress on policy reforms, price adjustments by state enterprises and a system of generalized indexation were largely responsible for a sharp increase in inflation, from 1,000 percent in 1992 to 1,800 percent in 1993." (p4-5)

"The Region: Growth: Latin America's 'Found Decade.'" IDB v21 n3, Mar 1994. p4-5.

INFLATION (FINANCE)--SOUTH AFRICA (v19)

INFLATION (FINANCE)--U.S. (v19)

"Inflation averaged 12 percent in the late 1970's and in 1980, 4 percent during the mid-eighties, and 3 percent in 1992 and 1993. Inflation partly reflects the costs of production, and growth in these costs has moderated because of large gains in worker productivity in recent years. During 1992, nonfarm business productivity, the best measure of economy-wide worker productivity, rose 3.6 percent. That's the biggest 1-year increase since the early 1960's; productivity growth in 1993 was a slower 1.9 percent." (pS3411)

Domenici, Pete V. (Sen.-N.Mex.). "Congressional Budget Concurrent Resolution," Congressional Record (22 Mar 1994). Daily ed. pS3403-3415. (ISSN0363-7239).

"'The battle against inflation has been won: the industrial world has entered a golden age of stable prices.' Such claims have become louder as average inflation in OECD [Organization for Economic Cooperation and Development] economies has fallen to 2 1/2%, the lowest for 30 years....Pushing inflation down is relatively easy during a recession or early in a recovery. The hard part is judging when to tighten policy to prevent it rising as the economy picks up steam. This is the unenviable test now facing Alan Greenspan, chairman of America's Federal Reserve. The American economy grew at an annual rate of no less than 5.9% in the fourth quarter of 1993; yet, for the moment, inflation (2.7% in the year to December) seems under control. It is also widely accepted that measures such as America's consumer-price index (CPI) may overstate actual inflation by a full percentage point." (p18)

"Leaders: Is Inflation Dead?" Economist v330 n7849, 5 Feb 1994. p18. (ISSN0013-0613).

INFORMAL SECTOR (ECONOMICS)--DEVELOPING COUNTRIES (v19)

INFORMAL SECTOR (ECONOMICS)--HUNGARY (v19)

INFORMATION SERVICES--U.S.

"American business more than doubled its spending on computers and other information-processing equipment between 1960 and 1992. The share of 'information' equipment in total producer investment in durable equipment rose from about 17 percent in 1960 to 36 percent by 1992....Professor [Frank] Lichtenberg completed a study published recently by the National Bureau of Economic Research (NBER), a nonpartisan research group in Cambridge, Mass, that addresses the questions: What is the relative contribution of expenditures on information-services equipment and personnel to a company's output? Is it at least as high as those resources used in other ways by a firm to provide output? The study found that information-services (IS) spending boosts a company's output (or reduces costs) about six times as much as the same amount spent on production workers. Computer experts are paid 2.5 to 3 times as much as production workers. But the resulting increase in output means 'they are more than worth it,' Lichtenberg says." (p9)

Francis, David R. "Economy: US Companies Double Spending on Computers--and It Pays Off." The Christian Science Monitor v86 n71, 8 Mar 1994. p9. (ISSN0882-7729).

INFORMATION TECHNOLOGY--U.S.

"Merit Network Inc.--the University of Michigan-based computer networking pioneer--has been given an $11.1 million National Science Foundation grant to help keep the pieces of the global Internet glued together. Under the five-year grant, Merit and the University of Southern California's Information Sciences Institute will work together as 'routing arbiters' to insure that some 3,000 separate computer networks remain connected to the global data system. Merit President Eric M. Aupperle said the grant ensures that Merit will continue to play a central national role in running Internet, the global network that links more than 2 million computers and an estimated 20 to 40 million users of the network. Traffic on Internet has been increasing by 10 percent a month in an information explosion that shows no signs of moderating." (p2 secC)

Cain, Stephen. "Local: Merit Grant to Keep Internet on Line." Ann Arbor News 15 Feb 1994. p2 secC.

"In a new study...[economist Frank Lichtenberg] looks at how investment in information-systems (IS) technology and personnel affected the production of several hundred [U.S.] manufacturing and service companies in recent years. Lichtenberg's findings, based on the relationship of individual companies' use of IS equipment and labor to their output, suggest that such technology investments have been anything but ill-conceived. While they account for only about 10% of labor costs and 10% to 15% of total capital expenditures, computer equipment and employment jointly contribute some 21% of the output of the companies studied. Although IS personnel represent only 3% or so of the work forces of the companies studied and are paid two to three times as much as other workers, the average IS employee is six times more productive than are non-IS co-workers." (p20)

Koretz, Gene. "Economic Trends: Computers May Really Be Paying Off...." Business Week n3358, 14 Feb 1994. p20. (ISSN0007-7135).

"The electronic information industry's revenue was $11.6 billion in 1992, and is increasing at 14% annually, according to the Boston-based research firm the Yankee Group. This mostly consists of people using computers to retrieve information (not video) or interact with other computers; it's a crude version of what will one day exist. And home shopping, which has been the buzz-phrase of merger-mania because it stands to reap the benefits of interactive TV technology, is growing at an alarming rate. Six months after Fox Broadcasting's maverick boss Barry Diller took over QVC, the second largest home shopping channel, its market value jumped from $1.2 billion to more than $3.4 billion, according to BUSINESS WEEK." (p11)

Reed, Betsy. "Economy in Review: The Wealth of Information: How Media Empires Plan to Amass It." Dollars and Sense n192, Mar-Apr 1994. p8-11,35.

"It was always hoped that information technology (IT) would make workers more productive. But even as computers doubled their share of America's installed capital base--rising from 7% in 1980 to 14% in 1991--economists looked in vain for evidence that they really do enable fewer workers to produce more, higher-valued output....Stephen Roach, an economist at Morgan Stanley, was one of the first to notice the surprising lack of measurable benefits from investments in IT. He agrees that benefits are at last starting to emerge, but says that Mr Brynjolfsson is too optimistic about the pace of change. For evidence, he points to America's service industries, which spent nearly $900 billion on IT in the 1980s, more than 80% of the total invested. Although services' share of overall employment grew from 65% in 1980 to 77% in 1990, its productivity stagnated. That of manufacturing grew at 2% a year. With the 1990s, argues Mr Roach, this began to change. Recession cut the growth of white-collar jobs in service industries from an average 3-4% a year in the 1980s to virtually zero in 1991." (p74)

"Business: What Computers Are For." Economist v330 n7847, 22 Jan 1994. p74. (ISSN0013-0613).

INFORMATION TECHNOLOGY--U.S.--POLITICS AND GOVERNMENT (v19)

"Government can become more cost-effective, efficient, and 'user-friendly' through the use of information technology. Fast communication makes it possible for teams to work closely on a project even if team members are physically distant from one another, which presents an opportunity to flatten existing organizational structure, form effective cross-disciplinary problem-solving groups, and expand the definition of the workplace and workforce. Often, though, efficiency gains from the new technology can only be captured if changes are made in the structure of organizations and the way they are managed. The Federal Government spends over $26 billion annually on information technologies and services. Thus Federal use of these technologies can have a significant influence on the information technology market and can improve quality and timeliness of service and improve access to government information." (p320)

Gibbons, John H. (Director, Office of Science and Technology Policy). U.S. House. Committee on Appropriations. "Depts. of Veterans Affairs and Housing and Urban Development...Approp. for 1994 (Part 2)." Hearing, Washington, D.C.: GPO, 1993. (Y4.Ap6/1:V64/4/994/pt.2).

"The [U.S.] Federal government is the largest single user of information technology in the world spending more than $24 billion in fiscal year 1992 on information technology, with a 10 percent annual growth rate, and spending billions more to run its existing computer systems. Federal expenditures represent 6 percent of the total U.S. and 3 percent of the worldwide expenditures on information technology. Clearly, the effective use and management of this technology is critical to government, if government is going to deliver services citizens require within existing and future budget constraints. In the past 12 years, the Federal government has made increasingly larger investments in information technology and automation initiatives, while keeping government employment at the same level as 1960." (p350)

Wagner, G. Martin (Deputy Commissioner, Information Resources Management Service). U.S. House. Committee on Appropriations. "Treasury, Postal Service, and General Government Approp. for Fiscal Year 1994 (Part 5)." Hearing, Washington, D.C.: GPO, 1993. (ISBN0160410053). (Y4.Ap6/1:T71/994/pt.5).

INFORMATION TECHNOLOGY--UTAH

"With fewer than 2m people in its 82,000 square miles (212,000 square kilometres), Utah remains one of the least populous states in America. Yet the 40-mile strip between Salt Lake City and Provo contains the world's second-biggest swathe of software and computer-engineering firms after California's Silicon Valley. More than 1,120 information technology (IT) companies, ranging from industry leaders such as Novell to small multimedia start-ups with names such as Electronic Cottage International, generate $5 billion a year in sales--a figure growing at 7% a year. Starting more or less from scratch a decade ago, Utah's IT industry employed more than 63,000 people at the last count in 1992....The Utah Information Technologies Association expects local IT companies to employ another 14,500 by 1995. By then, one in ten people in the state's 770,000-strong workforce will be 'knowledge workers' earning 50% more than the national average." (p69)

"Business: Technology in Utah: Software Valley." Economist v331 n7860, 23 Apr 1994. p69-70. (ISSN0013-0613).

INFRASTRUCTURE (ECONOMICS)--CALIFORNIA

In California "Caltrans (which maintains highways) has increased its earthquake retrofit budget since the Bay Area quake of 1989. But the agency still spends more actual dollars on 'landscape maintenance' along freeways than on safeguarding citizens against earthquakes. In the last four fiscal years, Caltrans has spent $213 million on 'landscaping maintenance' vs. $174.9 million on retrofits either completed or under construction. Millions were spent spraying pesticides along freeways and watering ice plants when only $1.36 million could have rapidly retrofitted the section of the Santa Monica Freeway that collapsed." (p10 secA)

Hayden, Tom. "Blame Neglect, Not Nature for Los Angeles Catastrophe." Ann Arbor News 3 Feb 1994. p10 secA.

INFRASTRUCTURE (ECONOMICS)--EUROPE

"Comparisons between the quality and durability of roads constructed in European countries and those constructed in the United States are often made without pointing out the significant differences between the two systems. Recent U.S. tours to European countries to review highway construction practices have highlighted these differences: European countries invest heavily up front to build deep, strong pavements and roadway subgrades or foundations. While the average highway design life in the U.S. is 20 years, in Europe it is at least 30, and often 40, years. The average price of motor fuel in Europe is about $4.00 per gallon, with taxes representing about 63 percent, or $2.50, of the cost. Of this, an average $1.25 per gallon is spent on road construction and maintenance. Many European roads also operate toll facilities providing additional needed revenues for construction, operation, and maintenance which are not diverted...[to] other purposes." (p2626)

U.S. House. Committee on Appropriations. "Department of Transportation and Related Agencies Approp. for 1994 (Part 7B)." Hearing, Washington, D.C.: GPO, 1993. (ISBN0160411041). (Y4.Ap6/1:T68/4/994/pt.7B).

INFRASTRUCTURE (ECONOMICS)--U.S.

"There is an unquestioned need for increased transportation infrastructure investment. National estimates by the Federal Highway Administration show that we would have to invest $9.5 billion a year more than is currently being spent, just to maintain the nation's highways at 1989 conditions. To significantly improve conditions would require more than doubling current national investment, from about $36 billion per year to $75 billion each year. The U.S. Department of Transportation also projects a capital funding need for transit systems of $7.5 billion a year....In Nevada, the ten-year estimate of highway financing needs relative to projected income shows about $1.5 billion, coming from all sources, to deal with $3 billion in essential need." (p1150)

Miller, Bob (Governor of Nevada). U.S. House. Committee on Appropriations. "Department of Transportation and Related Agencies Approp. for 1994 (Part 7A)." Hearing, Washington, D.C.: GPO, 1993. (ISBN0160411033). (Y4.Ap6/1:T68/4/994/pt.7A).

"A TIME magazine article last summer simplified the process of building long-lasting roads. The base of a typical 40-year European [road] is five-to-six feet deep while its American counterpart is two-to-three feet deep. The upper layers are comparably heavier, and the European road has a tough, weather-resistant surface incorporating the latest materials. The difference between European and American road building is largely one of philosophy and of the willingness to commit financial resources to durability. Deeper, longer-lasting European roads simply are more expensive. Highway construction costs in Europe are about double those in the United States, and they spend about 50 percent more for materials than we do. For the past 37 years, we in the United States have been preoccupied with building the Interstate system. The emphasis was on getting the roads completed and into use as quickly as possible. That, in many ways, was a political decision to expedite construction of the Interstate system." (p138)

Ruane, T. Peter (President, CEO, American Road & Transportation Builders Assoc.). U.S. House. Committee on

Appropriations. "Department of Transportation and Related Agencies Approp. for 1994 (Part 8)." Hearing, Washington, D.C.: GPO, 1993. (ISBN0160410657). (Y4.Ap6/1:T68/4/994/pt.8).

"A recent study by the Federal Highway Administration (FHWA) estimates that $46.2 billion was needed in 1992 just to keep highway and bridge performance at its 1991 level, and that only $35.9 billion was actually spent. The same study estimates that the cost to maintain 1991 performance and condition will average $51.6 billion per year over the next twenty years, and that the cost to improve system capacity by 40 percent and eliminate the backlog of highway deficiencies will average $67.3 billion." (p23-24)

Hulten, Charles R. (Professor, Economics, University of Maryland). U.S. House. Committee on Appropriations. "Department of Transportation and Related Agencies Approp. for 1994 (Part 8)." Hearing, Washington, D.C.: GPO, 1993. (ISBN0160410657). (Y4.Ap6/1:T68/4/994/pt.8).

"According to Congressional Budget Office estimates, capital spending by state and local government, expressed in 1990 dollars, rose more or less steadily throughout the 1950s and 1960s and peaked in 1972. A steep decline in real capital expenditure set in after 1972 and it was not until 1986 that the 1972 level was once again attained. And, as a share of GDP [gross domestic product], infrastructure capital spending averaged 1.8 percent in the 1960s and then fell to an average of 1.5 percent during the 1970s and to 1.2 percent during the 1980s. This decline is seen as evidence of a massive under investment in public capital." (p22)

Hulten, Charles R. (Professor, Economics, University of Maryland). U.S. House. Committee on Appropriations. "Department of Transportation and Related Agencies Approp. for 1994 (Part 8)." Hearing, Washington, D.C.: GPO, 1993. (ISBN0160410657). (Y4.Ap6/1:T68/4/994/pt.8).

"The Department of Transportation's 1993 needs report indicated that we need to invest over $50 billion annually, at all levels of government just to maintain this Nation's Federal-aid system conditions--let alone improve them--which is far above the annual public sector investment of $33 billion. The report further stated that 45 percent of this Nation's bridges are obsolete or deficient and over 65 percent of its highways and roads need repair." (pS16461)

Baucus, Max (Sen.-Mont.). "Statements on Introduced Bills and Joint Resolutions," Congressional Record (19 Nov 1993). Daily ed. pS16433-16501. (ISSN0363-7239).

"Infrastructure is a big piece of our economy. The United States has about $1 trillion invested in public works capital. It spends $100 billion annually on operating, maintaining, and adding new public works. Transportation, also, is around 15 percent of our gross domestic product. Furthermore, we drive and move an incredible 3.5 trillion passenger miles." (p12)

Rivlin, Alice M. "Budgeting for Performance." Intergovernmental Perspective v20 n1, Fall 1993-Win 1994. p11-13,26. (ISSN0362-8507).

"According to the Civil Engineering Research Foundation, the current value of the nation's concrete-based structures exceeds $6 trillion. And a lot of that concrete needs fixing. A study by the Portland Cement Association shows that 10 percent of federal roads require immediate repair or replacement. And the American Association of State Highway & Transportation Officials rates 40 percent of U.S. highways below minimum engineering standards. According to the U.S. Department of Transportation, 230,000 of the 575,000 bridges it monitors are 'structurally deficient or functionally obsolete.' The numbers are equally depressing for the nation's airport runways, water conduits and sewers. The researchers have other gloomy figures, too, like within a decade bad roads will cost us $50 billion a year in traffic delays." (p25)

Wolkomir, Richard. "Inside the Lab and Out, Concrete Is More Than It's Cracked Up to Be." Smithsonian v24 n10, Jan 1994. p23-31. (ISSN0037-7333).

INFRINGEMENT OF COPYRIGHT

see COPYRIGHT INFRINGEMENT

INHERITANCE AND TRANSFER TAX--U.S. (v19)

INK (v19)

INSTITUTIONS, ASSOCIATIONS, ETC.

see ASSOCIATIONS, INSTITUTIONS, ETC.

INSURANCE

see also SAVING AND THRIFT

"The Japanese insurance market is the second largest in the world after the United States, with a premium volume of $308 billion. After almost 50 years, the foreign share of the Japanese market is only 2.9 percent. This contrasts with foreign penetration in the United States which is almost 10 percent....Worldwide insurance premium income today is approximately $1.4 trillion. The insurance sector is critical to the U.S. economy and its expansion into other markets is essential to the growth of jobs and expansion here at home." (pS3120)

Roth, William V., Jr. (Sen.-Del.). "Community Developing Banking and Financial Institutions Act of 1993," Congressional Record (17 Mar 1994). Daily ed. pS3117-3127. (ISSN0363-7239).

INSURANCE--JAPAN

"The Japanese insurance market is the second largest in the world after the U.S., with a premium volume of $308 billion in 1991. Of this, $82 billion came from property and casualty insurance and $226 billion from life insurance. U.S. insurers have operated in Japan since the late 1940s. Eleven companies do so at present. U.S. companies respect the Japanese market and value the business they have been able to do. Many U.S. insurers have longstanding friendships with Japanese insurers. However, for many years, U.S. insurers have been commercially frustrated by a system of traditional, excessively strict, but vague and largely unwritten insurance regulation that virtually eliminates true innovation. In addition, local market practices, including market arrangements between local insurers and their affiliated client companies, severely limit our horizons. These conditions effectively confine foreign insurance operations to a number of niches (often collectively called the 'third area') within the larger Japanese market. Thus, after almost 50 years, the foreign share of the Japanese property and casualty market (the 'second area') is only 2.9% and, of this, almost half comes from the third sector. This contrasts with foreign penetration in the U.S. in the range of 8% to 10%, depending on definitional variations." (p90)

U.S. Senate. Committee on Finance. "United States-Japan Trade Negotiations." Hearing, 8 Nov 1993. Washington, D.C.: GPO, 1994. (ISBN0160435625). (Y4.F49:S.hrg.103-399).

INSURANCE--MEXICO (v19)

INSURANCE, DEPOSIT

see DEPOSIT INSURANCE

INSURANCE, DISASTER

"Some feel that Lloyd's of London which carries about 30 percent of international catastrophe reinsurance, is overextended. Recently Lloyd's capacity has contracted, and the price of reinsurance has risen steeply. A string of losses--more than $1 billion in 1988, $3.3 billion in '89, an estimated $2.4 billion in '90 and close to $2 billion in '91--has raised fears that the 300-year-old company rests on a shaky foundation. According to Jeremy Leggett, Director of Research for Greenpeace, Lloyd's List has no more than $250 to $300 million in catastrophe reinsurance available on a global basis for a single company. With losses greater than $1 billion for individual companies, catastrophe insurance is insufficient for large insurers, forcing the industry to rethink its basic practice." (p5)

Wilson, Nancy C. "Surge of Hurricanes and Floods Perturb Insurance Industry." Climate Alert v6 n4, Jul-Aug 1993. p1,4-7.

INSURANCE, DISASTER--U.S.

"A recent spate of natural disasters--many of them topping $1 billion in insured losses--has shaken the insurance industry in the U.S. and around the world. The $3 billion of insured loss from Hurricane Hugo in 1989 broke all records for losses, but only 3 years later losses from Hurricane Andrew hit $17 billion. There is the sobering thought that the staggering scope of losses could have been much worse if the storms had followed a different route, if the path of Andrew had veered directly over Miami instead of 10 miles away in southern Dade County. The Great Flood of '93 on the Mississippi--although little of it was covered by private insurance--raises profound questions about future protection from disaster." (p1)

Wilson, Nancy C. "Surge of Hurricanes and Floods Perturb Insurance Industry." Climate Alert v6 n4, Jul-Aug 1993. p1,4-7.

INSURANCE, FLOOD--U.S. (v19)

INSURANCE, HEALTH

see also HEALTH MAINTENANCE ORGANIZATIONS

INSURANCE, HEALTH--EMPLOYMENT--U.S.

"Many small businesses are piggybacking off the health-care packages of companies employing the spouses of their employees. That makes small businesses unlikely candidates for voluntary employer health insurance programs, according to University of Michigan's School of Public Health. The school conducted a survey of 2,200 small businesses on their attitudes toward health-care reform. It was done in part to gauge the effectiveness of a voluntary universal health-care program for small businesses. Among those surveyed: 40 percent currently offer no health insurance. 61 percent have no interest in doing so. 26 percent are unequivocally interested. 13 percent might be interested....About 32 percent of small business employees in the survey obtained coverage from their spouses' health plans....Moreover, employees of the survey respondents prefer bigger paychecks rather than health-care benefits. About 58 percent of the employees preference for wages were characterized as a 'very' or 'somewhat' important factor in not receiving health insurance." (p3 secE)

Bridgeforth, Arthur, Jr. "Survey: Small Firms Count on Workers' Spouses for Insurance." Ann Arbor News 5 May 1994. p3 secE.

"Employers [in the U.S.] pay about 86 percent of health insurance premiums for workers. The average employer share varies by income from about 83 percent for families with incomes below $10,000 to 89 percent for families with incomes above $200,000." (pxiii)

U.S. Congressional Budget Office. "Summary." The Tax Treatment of Employment-Based Health Insurance Mar 1994. Washington, D.C.: GPO, 1994.

"Employment-based health insurance [in the U.S.] covers about 60 percent of the population. Excluding employers' contributions for that insurance from income and payroll taxes will cost the federal government about $74 billion in 1994." (p2)

U.S. Congressional Budget Office. "Introduction." The Tax Treatment of Employment-Based Health Insurance Mar 1994. Washington, D.C.: GPO, 1994.

INSURANCE, HEALTH--SOUTH DAKOTA (v19)

INSURANCE, HEALTH--U.S. (v19)

see also MEDICAID; MEDICALLY UNINSURED PERSONS

"Companies and other employers provided primary health insurance for 55.6% of Americans in 1992, the latest year available, down from 59.7% in 1988, according to EBRI's [Employee Benefit Research Institute] tabulations of Census Bureau statistics....That represents more than 10 million workers and dependents who either lost coverage or didn't get it when they started a new job....Some of the uninsured have sought refuge in Medicaid, where the number of recipients soared 40% between 1988 and 1992, to 20.5 million people, according to EBRI....The ranks of uninsured have risen by 15% since 1988, to 38.8 million, according to EBRI." (p171)

Bernstein, Aaron. "The Workplace: Commentary: Why Universal Health Coverage Is Smart Medicine." Business Week n3364, 28 Mar 1994. p171. (ISSN0007-7135).

"The Congressional Budget Office has maintained its credibility as an objective nonpartisan agency in its report assessing the Clinton health reform plan. The report concludes that the plan will increase the Federal deficit by over $74 billion from 1995-2000, contradicting the administration's contention that it will decrease the deficit by $58 billion over that period. The report therefore supports what we have been saying all along--that the President's plan is inadequately financed. It will harm our economy....the CBO report recognizes that truth-in-budgeting requires that the Clinton plan must be considered on-budget. If not, the American people would not have an accurate assessment of the economic effect of the plan. The report concludes that our Government will grow by about 20 percent as a result of the Clinton plan. It confirms what should be very clear--that, when the Government requires private entities to pay health insurance premiums, this is effectively a tax that must be considered as part of the Federal budget." (pS1308)

McCain, John (Sen.-Ariz.). "CBO Report on the Clinton Health Care Plan," Congressional Record (9 Feb 1994). Daily ed. pS1308-1309. (ISSN0363-7239).

"Adopted in 1974 to help guarantee union pension benefits, ERISA [Employee Retirement Income Security Act] is having an enormous impact on health care costs in America. In fact, many people argue that ERISA is the nation's health care crisis because it allows large corporations and their employees--about two-thirds of the nation's work force--to choose not to participate in state mandates and national insurance pools. In the process, it leaves small businesses, the self-employed and the unemployed to bear added costs." (p6) "Many people with prior medical conditions cannot afford health insurance. To provide coverage for these people, 27 states have set up special high-risk pools....In all but six states, the high-risk pool has been funded with an assessment on insurance companies, which pass the costs on to customers. Self-insured companies are challenging these pools, arguing that under ERISA, their health programs cannot be tapped for the benefit of other people....Among companies with more than 5,000 employees, about 80 percent are self-insured. Among companies with fewer than 500 employees only 41 percent are self-insured." (p8)

Tucker, William. "Loophole Hobbles Health Coverage." Insight v10 n9, 28 Feb 1994. p6-9. (ISSN1051-4880).

"Reports of health insurance fraud have been skyrocketing in recent years. According to the Health Insurance Association of America, the number of fraud cases investigated by health insurance companies has increased 75 percent in the past two years, and two-thirds of those claims were filed by health care providers. In economic terms, that represents anywhere from $28 billion to $94 billion in losses--losses that are passed on to consumers. In a 1993 survey, the association found that more than 90 percent of insurers have uncovered fraudulent claims." (p12)

Sileo, Chi Chi. "Rip-Offs Depress Mental Health Care."

Insight v10 n4, 24 Jan 1994. p11-15. (ISSN1051-4880).

"Many Americans have health insurance policies under which an insurer pays 80 per cent of the stated cost and the policyholder pays 20 percent. Unfortunately, some consumers may pay more than 20 percent of the actual cost, because their insurance companies have negotiated discounts with hospitals and other providers. When the insurer receives the bill, it pays 80 percent of the negotiated discount, yet the policyholder is required to pay 20 percent of the full charge." (p25)

Inlander, Charles. "Power Guide to Health: The Smart Patient." Mother Jones v18 n3, May-Jun 1993. p25. (ISSN0362-8841).

"In the short run, a universal coverage plan [in the U.S.] might require as much as $30 billion to $50 billion in additional Federal spending on the uninsured. Where will the nation find the funds? It might treat as taxable income the employer-paid health-insurance premiums for families whose income is in the upper 50 percent. Or one might also ask the well-to-do to chip in 1 percent of their income. Whatever the source for these funds, the question is: how can a nation with a G.N.P. [gross national product] of $6 trillion, with one of the lowest average tax burdens in the industrialized world and which is already spending $820 billion on health care for the well-insured, proclaim to the world that it cannot come up with the $30 billion to $50 billion to give every family the protection enjoyed in the rest of the industrialized world?" (p4)

Reinhardt, Uwe E. "Health Insurance for All--Now." New Patriot v6 n2, Mar-Apr 1993. p4.

"One insurance form. That's the crux of Clinton's plan to simplify the American health-care system. The form is expected to reduce mountains of paperwork, freeing health-care workers to do that for which they were trained. Simplifying paperwork will be beneficial to be sure, although providers will reap more from it than consumers. And the standardization of benefit packages will further simplify paperwork. But even a cursory glance at Clinton's 239-page draft shows that the plan is anything but simple. And it gets worse. The final legislation is 1,336 pages." (p6)

"The Magnificent Six." People's Medical Society Newsletter v12 n6, Dec 1993. p4-8. (ISSN0736-4873).

"The number of nonelderly Americans receiving public [insurance] coverage steadily increased between 1989 and 1992. That is, 33.4 million, or 15.1 percent of the total nonelderly population received public coverage in 1992 compared with 31.7 million (14.5 percent) in 1991, 29.2 million (13.5 percent) in 1990, and 26.2 million (12.3 percent) in 1989...." (p27)

Snider, Sarah C. "Who Are the Medically Uninsured in the United States?" Statistical Bulletin v75 n2, Apr-Jun 1994. p20-30. (ISSN0790-8334).

"Based on data from the Bureau of the Census's Current Population Survey, approximately 103 million nonelderly adults (ages 18 to 64), or 66 percent of that age group, were covered by employment-based insurance in 1992....In addition, 69 percent of children were covered. The next biggest source of coverage for nonelderly adults was privately purchased insurance, which covered 9 percent of that group. Medicaid covered 17 percent of children and 5 percent of adults. A significant fraction of the nonelderly population had no insurance: 17 percent of adults and 13 percent of children. In contrast, primarily because of Medicare, only 1 percent of the elderly were uninsured." (p8)

U.S. Congressional Budget Office. "Background." The Tax Treatment of Employment-Based Health Insurance Mar 1994. Washington, D.C.: GPO, 1994.

INSURANCE, HEALTH--U.S.--COSTS (v19)

INSURANCE, HOMEOWNERS--U.S. (v19)

INSURANCE, LIFE--U.S.

"Of the many nooks and crannies in the multibillion-dollar world of life insurance, the curiously-named 'viatical settlements' business occupies one of the least conspicuous. Prudence compels it to remain that way, for the industry, just four years old, is engaged in the sensitive task of arranging finances for the dying. It does so by offering terminally ill life-insurance policy-holders a chance to collect their own death benefits months before they die (hence 'viatical', derived from the Latin for travelling money). Typically, a viatical settlement company will pay 60-80% of a policy's face value for the right to assume the premium payments and become the beneficiary....AIDS patients, of whom there are some 350,000 in America, account for nearly 90% of viatical customers....Cancer patients make up much of the rest, says the National Viatical Association (NVA), a trade group that represents 40 of the 54 viatical companies operating in America." (p74)

"Finance: American Insurance: Deathly Pale." Economist v330 n7844, 8 Jan 1994. p74-75. (ISSN0013-0613).

INSURANCE, UNEMPLOYMENT

"Like every other western European country, France is suffering from an acute shortage of jobs. And as is also the case with neighboring nations, France's unemployed receive comparatively generous state benefits, which are becoming increasingly burdensome to taxpayers....Benefits received by an unemployed individual are currently calculated on the basis of the person's age, employment history and the wages he or she previously earned. For example, someone younger than 50 who has worked 14 months in the past two years will be entitled to two-and-a-half years of compensation payments. For the first four months, this same person receives the full amount of income he or she last earned. The state pay-out is then reduced by 15 percent every three months. Full benefits continue for a longer period in the case of a laid-off worker over 50 years of age." (p8)

Razali, Anne. "Welfare State: France's System Creaks Under Growing Burdens." Toward Freedom v42 n6, Oct 1993. p8. (ISSN0048-9898).

INSURGENCY

see also TERRORISM

INSURGENCY--HAITI

"In the time since the collapse of the Governors Island Accord, the human rights situation in Haiti has grown perilously worse, deteriorating to a point that many believe...surpasses even the height of the Duvalier era. A report that was released...by Human Rights/Watch Americas and the National Coalition for Haitian Refugees illustrates the case quite clearly. The report notes that political killings and suspicious murders in Haiti rose from a reported 9 last May and 5 last June to a total of 34 in July, 33 in August, more than 60 in September, and more than 80 in October. The number of killings has remained at or near the rate to the present day. In fact...some estimate that between 3,000 and 4,000 people have lost their lives in Haiti since the overthrow of President Aristide for the simple crime of supporting the return of President Aristide to their country." (pS4467)

Dodd, Christopher J. (Sen.-Conn.). "Statements on Introduced Bills and Joint Resolutions," Congressional Record (19 Apr 1994). Daily ed. pS4465-4478. (ISSN0363-7239).

INTELLIGENCE LEVELS--U.S.

"Because African-Americans average 15 points lower than whites do on standardized IQ tests, critics for a generation have condemned such measures as culturally biased. Indeed, the tests are so snakebit by litigation that many schools and most employers are afraid to use them. A 1988 survey found a consensus among 661 psychologists that IQ tests in fact measure intelligence reasonably well. Yet few of these scholars care to

express such views outside obscure technical journals." (p89)
Parshall, Gerald. "Face-Offs: Genes, Race and Intelligence." U.S. News & World Report v115 n25, 27 Dec 1993. p89. (ISSN0041-5537).

INTELLIGENCE SERVICE--RUSSIA--U.S.

"At the height of the cold war, some 65 percent of America's intelligence budget was focused on the Soviet threat; today, intelligence sources say, that figure is down to about 40 percent of a $29 billion budget. Yevgeni Mokeev, a public relations officer with the Russian Foreign Intelligence Service--the successor to the KGB--says Moscow has closed about 30 foreign listening posts once aimed mainly at monitoring U.S. activities." (p30,32)
Roberts, Steven V./others. "Cover Story: Why There Are Still Spies." U.S. News & World Report v116 n9, 7 Mar 1994. p30,32. (ISSN0041-5537).

INTEREST RATES (v19)

INTEREST RATES--GERMANY (v19)

INTEREST RATES--U.S. (v19)

"Low interest rates [in the U.S.] are a boon to companies....Net interest payments by nonfinancial corporations now consume 20% of corporate cash flow, down from a peak of 30% in late 1989. And a low cost of capital will boost business spending on productivity-enhancing equipment. Since the end of 1990, the cost of capital to U.S. companies--the blended cost of debt and equity financing--has dropped from 5.6% to 3.5%, calculates Mark Zandi, economist at Regional Financial Associates Inc. And capital equipment spending has risen at an 11% annual rate since mid-1991." (p61)
Farrell, Christopher/others. "Industry Outlook: Introduction: It Won't Take Your Breath Away, But...." Business Week n3353, 10 Jan 1994. p60-63,66. (ISSN0007-7135).

INTERNAL MIGRATION

see MIGRATION, INTERNAL

INTERNATIONAL BANK FOR RECONSTRUCTION AND DEVELOPMENT (v19)

INTERNATIONAL BUSINESS ENTERPRISES (v19)

INTERNATIONAL BUSINESS ENTERPRISES--U.S. (v19)

INTERNATIONAL RELATIONS (v19)

INTERNATIONAL TRADE (v19)

INTERNSHIP PROGRAMS--U.S.

"More and more, the internship is becoming the key to permanent employment. Last year, 26 percent of all graduates hired by companies had worked as interns, versus 9 percent the year before, according to an annual report on corporate hiring by Northwestern University in Chicago." (p9)
Coolidge, Shelley Donald. "Pay May Be Poor, but Some Internships Throw in a Car." The Christian Science Monitor v86 n109, 29 Apr 1994. p9. (ISSN0882-7729).

INTERRACIAL ADOPTION--U.S.

"In 1972...the National Association of Black Social Workers (NABSW) gained fame by vilifying the nascent practice of transracial adoption, branding it 'cultural genocide.'... Although the 1968 law permitting transracial adoptions was never changed, in one year the number was cut in half, to 1,569. By 1975, the last year official numbers were kept, it was down to 800." (p6) "Other studies counter the NABSW's claim that agencies make no efforts to recruit black families. To increase the list of prospective black parents, public agencies recruit from welfare rolls, and accept single parents and people in their 50s and 60s, categories that would automatically be excluded from white lists. A 1986 study found that 50 percent of minority adoptive families had incomes below $20,000, compared with 14 percent for nonminority families and 20 percent had incomes below $10,000, compared with 2 percent in nonminority families. All those at the bottom of the black list are considered before anyone on the white list....A study by the Packard Foundation in California found white families far more willing than black ones to adopt older and disabled children. Surveying midwestern states, the study found that 40 percent of transracially adopted children are disabled, 23 percent have psychological problems and 33 percent have been sexually abused." (p7)
"All in the Family." New Republic v210 n4, 24 Jan 1994. p6-7. (ISSN0028-6583).

"The overwhelming majority of couples [in the U.S.] waiting to adopt a child are white, and about half of the adoptable children in foster care, in every state, are black. Simple math would put some of those black children in white homes. But for twenty years taboos against race-mixing have kept thousands of black children in foster care, even while white couples on waiting lists are willing to adopt them. Sometimes the taboo against transracial adoption is taken to extraordinary extremes: a black child will be pulled out of a white foster home as soon as the couple expresses an interest in adoption, a practice courts have consistently upheld. The results have been grim. A 1993 study by U.C. Berkeley professor Rick Barth shows that a black child in California's foster care system is three times less likely to be adopted than a white child. Future prospects are even grimmer, as the number of children in the nation's foster care system has exploded from 275,000 in 1986 to 500,000 today, making it far more likely that conditions in foster homes will be less than ideal." (p6)
"All in the Family." New Republic v210 n4, 24 Jan 1994. p6-7. (ISSN0028-6583).

INTERRACIAL MARRIAGE--U.S.

"For much of U.S. history, most states had laws prohibiting marriage between individuals of different races. The last of these laws (in Virginia and South Carolina) were struck down by a U.S. Supreme Court ruling in 1967. Between 1970 and 1980, the number of recorded interracial married couples tripled, from 300,000 to over 900,000 and marriages between Hispanics and non-Hispanics grew from 600,000 to 900,000. In 1991, there were an estimated 1 million interracial married couples and 1.2 million Hispanics married to non-Hispanics. Mixed-race marriages made up about 2 percent of the 53 million married couples in 1991. About 7 percent of marriages involving an African American were interracial. However, one-quarter of those of other races (primarily Asian Americans) were married to someone outside their own race in 1991. And, just over one-fourth of married Hispanics had a non-Hispanic spouse in 1991." (p14)
O'Hare, William P. "America's Minorities--The Demographics of Diversity." Population Bulletin v47 n4, Dec 1992. p2-47. (ISSN0032-468X).

INTERSTITIAL CYSTITIS--U.S. (v19)

INTOXICATION

see ALCOHOLISM

INVESTMENT ADVISERS--U.S. (v19)

INVESTMENTS

see also CAPITAL INVESTMENTS; MUTUAL FUNDS; STOCK-EXCHANGE

INVESTMENTS--CHINA (v19)

INVESTMENTS--GERMANY (v19)

INVESTMENTS--JAPAN--U.S. (v19)

INVESTMENTS--NIGERIA (v19)

INVESTMENTS--U.S. (v19)

"Despite a reputation as one of the lousiest investments of the 1980s, limited partnerships are becoming a popular way for affluent families to transfer wealth and trim estate taxes. 'Anyone with $1 million or more in investments or a successful family business should consider it,' says Alexander A. Bove Jr., a Boston attorney and author of THE COMPLETE BOOKS OF WILLS & ESTATES. People at this level usually face the maximum estate-tax liability and can save as much as 60% or more. And they're valid in every state except Louisiana. Allowing parents to give away wealth without giving up control is only one of the advantages. Another is that stocks, real estate, and other assets put in a limited partnership can sometimes be valued at 10% to 60% below market value for gift-tax reasons. The discount reflects the restrictions on family-partnership interests that make them difficult to buy or sell. The partnerships also provide protection from creditors in lawsuits and bankruptcy proceedings." (p94) "Experienced estate-planning attorneys typically charge $1,000 to $2,500 to draft the partnership document, but the tab can swell to $5,000 or more. It may cost up to $2,000 just to have a professional appraiser determine the market value of assets to help figure the discount. Still, family limited partnerships can be worth the effort...." (p95)

Scherreik, Susan. "Personal Business: Estate Planning: How to Share the Wealth and Keep Control." Business Week n3354, 17 Jan 1994. p94-95. (ISSN0007-7135).

"Professionally managed futures funds and pools have enjoyed enormous growth of late--but with mixed success. Total assets in these funds have jumped from about $1 billion in 1985 to $23 billion today, according to Managed Account Reports (MAR) in New York, which tracks the performance of futures-fund managers....MAR's index of 511 public funds and private pools rose a handy 15.2% in 1993, but in 1986, the index fell 11.5%." (p112-113)

Stone, Amey. "Personal Business: Commodities: Futures: Dare You Defy the Odds?" Business Week n3360, 28 Feb 1994. p112-113. (ISSN0007-7135).

"Hedge funds have approximately $75 billion under management. The hedge funds apparently leverage that capital with bank loans ranging from $5 to $20 for every $1 under management. In other words, these funds could conceivably control anywhere between $375 billion and $1.5 trillion in financial clout. The funds can then further leverage that amount by buying options and other derivatives. To place hedge fund financial clout in perspective, the average daily volume of currency transactions is estimated in the $1 trillion range, while the world's largest stock exchange, the New York Stock Exchange, has a daily trading volume of roughly $10 billion." (pH2155)

Gonzalez, Henry B. (Rep.-Tex.). "Banks, Derivatives and Hedge Funds," Congressional Record (24 Mar 1994). Daily ed. pH2154-2157. (ISSN0363-7239).

"Americans' growing propensity to invest is reflected in a new national monthly poll, the American Capital Index, sponsored by American Capital Management and Research....The poll...showed that Americans are choosing a wide variety of investment options: 75 percent have savings accounts; 24 percent own real estate other than their primary residences; 31 percent report they own stocks, and 27 percent own bonds. A surprisingly large 29 percent have invested in mutual funds." (p18)

Weinstein, Bernard L. "Opinion/Essays: Americans Find Balance between Saving and Spending." The Christian Science Monitor v86 n65, 28 Feb 1994. p18. (ISSN0882-7729).

"American investors are flocking to buy stock in...foreign corporations....They are purchasing shares of individual companies in the form of American depositary receipts, or ADRs. ADRs of about 1,300 foreign firms trade on U.S. stock markets, with one ADR certificate equaling a given number of shares of stock. In 1993, total ADR trading volume on the New York and American exchanges and Nasdaq topped $200 billion, up from $94 billion in 1991 and $41 billion in 1988. With an average of 15 new ADRs a month, the trend shows no signs of topping out. It's easy to comprehend the enthusiasm. Last year, Merrill Lynch's ADR Composite Index, which tracks 184 ADRs and is the only index of its kind, chalked up a 29.9 percent gain. That was far ahead of the 10.1 percent gain in the Standard & Poor's 500-stock index and just slightly below the average 30.2 percent return for international stock funds. Some ADRs enjoyed triple-digit returns. From March 1, 1993, to Feb. 28, 1994, for example, the ADR price of the Signet Group, the U.K.'s largest retailer of fine jewelry, surged 400 percent to $9.38." (p65)

Hannon, Kerry. "Investing: Live Here, Invest Abroad." U.S. News & World Report v116 n13, 4 Apr 1994. p65. (ISSN0041-5537).

"The 'risk premium' that lenders demand for tying up their money in long-term investments has averaged a little more than 3 percentage points above the inflation rate in the past 19 years. With inflation running around 3 percent and the 30-year Treasury bond rate hovering just above 6 percent, interest rates don't seem poised to make any radical moves." (p46)

Hage, David. "Predictions: Have Mortgage Rates Hit Bottom?" U.S. News & World Report v115 n25, 27 Dec 1993. p46. (ISSN0041-5537).

INVESTMENTS, AMERICAN (v19)

"An agency of the federal government has taken on the role of subsidizing the movement of U.S. factories to other nations....This agency is the Overseas Private Investment Corporation, an extension of the Department of Commerce. In fiscal 1981, this agency made financial commitments of $101 million in direct loans and loan guarantees. These projects involved an aggregate total investment of $4.5 billion, of which U.S. investors provided $1.9 billion, host countries $2.1 billion, third nations $559 million and multilateral lending institutions $62 million." (p3)

"Unfiltered News." Acres, U.S.A. v24 n1, Jan 1994. p3.

INVESTMENTS, AMERICAN--EUROPE (v19)

"About 40% of all American profits earned abroad derive from Western Europe, where American firms have invested $240 billion, or nearly 50% of their total foreign investment. Three-fifths of all foreign investment in America is estimated to have come from Western Europe." (p22)

"America and Europe: A Ghost at the Feast." Economist v330 n7851, 19 Feb 1994. p21-22,24. (ISSN0013-0613).

INVESTMENTS, AMERICAN--HUNGARY--RUSSIA (v19)

INVESTMENTS, AMERICAN--INDONESIA (v19)

INVESTMENTS, AMERICAN--KOREA (SOUTH) (v19)

INVESTMENTS, AMERICAN--MEXICO (v19)

"Much of the argument against the NAFTA [North American Free Trade Agreement] is based on concerns that the agreement will spur large outflows of U.S. investment to Mexico. The fear is that this would reduce investment and employment in the U.S., and in the long run lead to the elimination or reversal of the U.S. trade surplus with Mexico. The logic of this argument breaks down when the facts are examined. U.S. investment in Mexico is a very small fraction of U.S. investment overseas, and an even smaller part of overall U.S. investment....cumulative U.S. investment in Mexico was only 2.7 percent of cumulative U.S. overseas investment in 1992....U.S. investment in Mexico on an annual basis is only a fraction of 1 percent of total U.S. non-residential investment, which was about $536 billion in 1992. Some have said that the NAFTA could lead to a doubling of foreign direct investment in Mexico. Even if this 'high-end' projection becomes reality, however, U.S. investment in Mexico will equal less than 1 percent of overall U.S. non-residential investment." (p13)

London, Paul A. (Acting Under Secretary of Commerce for Economic Affairs). U.S. Senate. Committee on Governmental Affairs. "NAFTA Job Claims: Truth in Statistics?" Hearing,

10 Nov 1993. Washington, D.C.: GPO, 1994. (ISBN0160435048). (Y4.G74/9:S.hrg.103-386).

INVESTMENTS, AMERICAN--SOUTH AFRICA

"As a result of the disinvestment campaign that reached its peak in the mid-1980s, U.S. investment in South Africa dropped from $3 billion to $1 billion and more than 200 companies sold or closed their South African operations. In July 1991, then-President Bush lifted most federal sanctions, and this year, after Nelson Mandela himself spoke in favor of it, Congress raced to lift the remaining sanctions. Seven of the 30 states that restricted investment in South Africa have repealed those laws, seven more will do so by the end of the year and 14 more will lift sanctions in 1994. Thirty-five of the 100 cities with similar investment restrictions have ended them." (p31-32)

Ruddy, Frank. "Fair Comment: South Africa Offers Hope, in Good Time." Insight v9 n52, 27 Dec 1993. p31-32. (ISSN1051-4880).

INVESTMENTS, EUROPEAN--ASIA--LATIN AMERICA (v19)

INVESTMENTS, FINNISH--ESTONIA (v19)

INVESTMENTS, FOREIGN (v19)

see also DEBTS, EXTERNAL; EXPORT PROCESSING ZONES

INVESTMENTS, FOREIGN--AFRICA

"Net foreign direct investment (FDI) in Africa rose in 1991 to $3 bn, according to the UN's 1993 'World Investment Report,' but overall its share of flows to developing countries--which totalled $36 bn in 1991--has been steadily falling since the early 1980s. For sub-Saharan Africa, FDI flows have averaged little more than $500 mn in recent years. Of portfolio investment--mainly bonds and other forms of commercial paper--the continent sees virtually nothing, although this is the fastest growing sector in financial flows to developing countries. From a mere $7.6 bn in 1989, these flows--in gross terms--had risen to some $20 bn by 1991 and to over $30 bn by 1992, according to the World Bank's 1993 'Global Economic Prospects and the Developing Countries.' While Africa was raising well over $100 mn a year through the bond market in the late 1970s, only Algeria raised finance this way in 1991, according to Bank figures. Overseas investment in African stocks and shares is also virtually non-existent." (p6)

"Tapping the Private Investment Pool." Africa Recovery v7 n1, Jun 1993. p6-8.

"Pointing to the volatility of Africa's FDI [foreign direct investment] receipts, the UN says they rose to $2.5 bn in 1991, some 21 per cent over 1990, but still below the $2.7 bn annual average for the 1985-1990 period. A sharp downturn is projected for 1992, with FDI falling by 33 per cent, attributable, in part, to recession and slow growth in industrialized countries. The 1991 surge in FDI mainly benefitted African oil-exporting countries, with Nigeria alone receiving over $700 mn, compared to the $586 mn total going to all non-oil African countries. In Angola, oil exploration and mining accounted for most of the over $660 mn received in FDI that year. Despite the focus on the extractive sectors, the share of non-oil producers in Africa's total FDI rose from 20 per cent in 1986-88 to 28 per cent in 1989-91, primarily due to a sharp rise of investment in Morocco (to $320 mn), attracted by strong growth, liberal investment laws and duty-free access to the European Community for manufactures with at least 40 per cent local content, says the UN report." (p12)

Bongang, Benn. "Africa's Route to Foreign Investment." Africa Recovery v7 n2, Oct 1993. p12.

INVESTMENTS, FOREIGN--AFRICA, SUB-SAHARAN

"For non-oil, sub-Saharan Africa, FDI [foreign direct investment] remains an elusive source of funds, despite continued liberalization of investment laws and the establishment of 'one-stop' centres intended to speed up the investment process. Accounting for over 35 per cent of global aid flows, the region gets less than 1 per cent of FDI, with the return on investments falling from some 30 per cent in the 1960s to 2.5 per cent 20 years later. For every country, such as Benin or Tanzania, which has set out to attract foreign investment, countries once favoured by investors, such as Cameroon, Congo and Cote d'Ivoire, have seen flows plummet along with once buoyant growth rates. The small size of domestic markets limits potential returns to manufacturing investors, the UN points out, and underlines the need to accelerate the efforts now under way to stimulate economic integration." (p6)

"Tapping the Private Investment Pool." Africa Recovery v7 n1, Jun 1993. p6-8.

INVESTMENTS, FOREIGN--ASIA (v19)

"Japan will soon displace the U.S. as the main market for Asia-Pacific manufactured goods and resources. It has already replaced the U.S. and Europe as the main investor and provider of economic aid to the region. In 1990, the Japanese invested a total of $6.6 billion in Malaysia, Indonesia, Thailand, Vietnam, China and the Philippines. In contrast, the U.S. invested only $3.5 billion, and the European community $2.7 billion. In addition, Japan provided more than $12 billion in aid to these countries between 1985 and 1989 for infrastructure projects designed to facilitate Japanese corporation expansion." (p21)

"Asia-Pacific Economic Growth: Threats and Opportunities." NewsNotes v19 n1, Jan-Feb 1994. p21-22. (ISSN1064-1556).

INVESTMENTS, FOREIGN--CANADA (v19)

INVESTMENTS, FOREIGN--CHILE (v19)

INVESTMENTS, FOREIGN--CHINA (v19)

INVESTMENTS, FOREIGN--CHINA--HONG KONG

"China is now Hong Kong's biggest trading partner, accounting for a third of the territory's total trade. As much as a third of Hong Kong's currency is circulating in China. Hong Kong firms have made perhaps two-thirds of the cumulative foreign direct investment (FDI) in the mainland. It shows: Hong Kong companies employ 3m factory workers in some 25,000 factories in China, about six times as many such workers as they employ in Hong Kong itself. China, for its part, has easily outstripped its American and Japanese rivals to become, with a stock of FDI as high as $20 billion, the biggest foreign investor in Hong Kong." (p36)

"Asia: It's Already 1997 in Hong Kong." Economist v329 n7842, 18 Dec 1993. p36-38. (ISSN0013-0613).

INVESTMENTS, FOREIGN--CUBA (v19)

"At latest count, there were over 80 joint venture firms in Cuba, with another 140 proposals under study. Cuba has bent over backward to make the island attractive to foreign capital and trade: decentralizing what was once a highly centralized commerce; generating a broader range of investment opportunities, from full joint ventures, to cooperative production arrangements, and management and marketing agreements, and giving Latin American and Caribbean firms the chance to own up to 100% of stock in joint concerns. In the last few months, there has been a rash of management contracts signed for wholly-owned Cuban hotels, and announcements from a number of investors that they are planning to plow profits from their current business with Cuba into new tourism development projects. Tourism is the most dynamic sector of the Cuban economy, growing at an annual rate of 30%, and guaranteeing one of the fastest returns on the dollar possible." (p11)

Reed, Gail. "Dateline Havana: Reshaping the Cuban Strategy: Thoughts from Cuban Economists." Cuba Update n6, Nov-Dec 1993. p11-12. (ISSN0196-0830).

INVESTMENTS, FOREIGN--DEVELOPING COUNTRIES (v19)

INVESTMENTS, FOREIGN--EUROPE, EASTERN (v19)

INVESTMENTS, FOREIGN--FRANCE

"After years of keeping foreign companies at arms' length, France is pulling them into its embrace. Figures not yet officially released by the Bank of France estimate that $10 billion of foreign direct investment (FDI) flowed into the country last year. This is marginally less than 1992's record $12 billion, which put France alongside Britain as the most popular place for investors among big industrial states....True, Japan heads the table as the country that increased its stock of FDI most in percentage terms between 1990 and 1992....However, the Japanese were starting from a low base and their stock of FDI at the end of 1992 was a mere $16 billion compared with France's $101 billion ($111 billion by the end of 1993). Measured in dollar terms, France's stock of FDI grew even faster than America's or Britain's (the two traditional leaders), though it is still smaller than theirs." (p55)

"Europe: France's Foreign Affair." Economist v330 n7850, 12 Feb 1994. p55. (ISSN0013-0613).

INVESTMENTS, FOREIGN--HAINAN ISLAND (v19)

INVESTMENTS, FOREIGN--INDONESIA

"Total foreign investments in Indonesia were $7.5 billion at the end of 1993, down 30 percent, or approximately $3 billion, from the $10.3 billion in 1992. One reason for the decline was a drop in investments from Japan. From 1957 through September 1993, Japan was involved in 555 investment projects in Indonesia, totaling $13.56 billion. In 1992, there were 48 Japanese investment projects in Indonesia totaling $1.5 billion. That dropped sharply in 1993, with 38 projects at a cost of $496 million." (p10)

Ho, Sie Pek. "Economic Reports: Jakarta Pushes Investment." The Christian Science Monitor v86 n35, 13 Jan 1994. p10. (ISSN0882-7729).

INVESTMENTS, FOREIGN--ISRAEL

"Direct foreign investment in Israel has increased from $439 million in 1991 to $633 million in 1992, notes a recent Bank of Israel report. Indirect investment through the purchase of shares of Israeli companies on US exchanges is more than $1.8 billion, the report states." (p9)

MacLachlan, Suzanne L. "Economy: Israel Draws US Investors Despite Faltering Peace Process." The Christian Science Monitor v86 n29, 5 Jan 1994. p9. (ISSN0882-7729).

INVESTMENTS, FOREIGN--JAPAN--U.S. (v19)

"In 1992, major foreign investments in Japan more than doubled over the previous year. There were 43 new foreign, corporate investment initiatives, compared to 18 in 1991, of which half were U.S. companies. By contrast, Japanese companies cut their investments in the U.S. in half in 1992, making $1.9 billion of acquisitions against $3.9 billion in 1991....Foreign direct investment in the United States in 1992 was at a level of $30.9 billion, down from $152.1 billion from the previous year...." (p32)

Hatch, Orrin G. (Sen.-Utah). U.S. Senate. Committee on Finance. "Renewing 'Super 301.'" Hearing, 14 Jun 1993. Washington, D.C.: GPO, 1993. (ISBN016043372X).

INVESTMENTS, FOREIGN--LATIN AMERICA (v19)

"Asian bankers and businessmen, scared off by Latin America's debt crisis during the 1980s, have on the whole been content to leave the region to the United States (which accounts for nearly two-thirds of its annual $8 1/2 billion of foreign direct investment and over half of its $270 billion of external trade)....The Japanese are especially wary. During the late 1960s and 1970s, they invested heavily--especially in Brazil, home to some 2m ethnic Japanese--in everything from shipbuilding to textiles and cars. The 1980s debt crisis and recession wiped out many of these investments. Latin America, which took a fifth of Japan's overseas direct investment during the early 1980s, by 1991 received only 8%." (p42,44)

"International: East Asians and Latin America: Tale of Two Dragons." Economist v329 n7842, 18 Dec 1993. p42,44. (ISSN0013-0613).

"Latin America continued to benefit from large inflows of capital in 1993, thanks in large part to slow growth and low interest rates in the industrial countries, and also to investor confidence in Latin America. An estimated $52.8 billion entered the region in 1993. As in previous years, most of the capital flows were concentrated in a few countries, with Mexico receiving 53 percent, Argentina, 23 percent, and Chile, Colombia and Peru a combined 13 percent. These resources financed the region's 1993 current account deficit and allowed an additional accumulation of $15.6 billion in international reserves." (p5)

"The Region: Growth: Latin America's 'Found Decade.'" IDB v21 n3, Mar 1994. p4-5.

INVESTMENTS, FOREIGN--MAURITIUS (v19)

INVESTMENTS, FOREIGN--MEXICO (v19)

INVESTMENTS, FOREIGN--MOROCCO (v19)

INVESTMENTS, FOREIGN--RUSSIA

"Countries that fail to repay loans are not cut off from foreign money...though those with spotless credit histories certainly find borrowing easier. Consider Russia. Despite its failure to service some $20 billion of bank debt, the country attracted around $700m of direct investment from foreign companies last year. Though less than the much smaller economies of Hungary and the Czech Republic pulled in, that sum is not negligible." (p93)

"Finance: Eastern Europe Comes In from the Cold." Economist v330 n7855, 19 Mar 1994. p93-94. (ISSN0013-0613).

INVESTMENTS, FOREIGN--SINGAPORE (v19)

INVESTMENTS, FOREIGN--U.S. (v19)

"U.S. executives...are increasingly seeking their companies' fortunes beyond America's borders--from Mexico to Malaysia. International sales by U.S. multinationals--from exports, direct investment, or joint ventures--were $1.2 trillion in 1991, 29% of corporate revenues. As economic globalization boosts demand in developing economies, and as trade barriers fall because of NAFTA [North American Free Trade Agreement] and the recently revised General Agreement on Tariffs & Trade, that trend is likely to accelerate....In the U.S. aerospace business, exports account for a record 34% of sales--up from less than 10% in the 1960s. Moreover, U.S. companies are raising production and adding people offshore: United Technologies Corp's Otis Co. Elevator unit logs 80% of its sales internationally, and five out of six employees work outside the U.S." (p62)

Ellis, James E. "Industry Outlook: Introduction: Why Overseas? 'Cause That's Where the Sales Are." Business Week n3353, 10 Jan 1994. p62-63. (ISSN0007-7135).

"In the first nine months of 1993, US investors bought nearly $8 billion worth of equities in emerging markets, compared with $5.6 billion in the whole of 1992 and very little at all in the 1980s. This buying accelerated still further in the last quarter of 1993." (p19)

Bell, Geoffrey/Kaess, Lisa. "Opinion/Essays: Grabbing Asia's Economic Tiger by the Tail." The Christian Science Monitor v86 n52, 8 Feb 1994. p19. (ISSN0882-7729).

INVESTMENTS, FOREIGN--VIETNAM

"Vietnam offers U.S. companies a cheap, hard-working, highly literate and well-trained work force with an entrepreneurial spirit. It offers a consumer market of 71 million people. U.S. companies now can compete with Asian and European firms that have been landing lucrative contracts for development projects in Vietnam. More than 850 foreign investment projects worth nearly $8 billion have been approved by Vietnam since 1988."

(p18)
"Vietnam: Normalization and Human Rights Concerns." NewsNotes v19 n2, Mar-Apr 1994. p17-18. (ISSN1064-1556).

INVESTMENTS, FRENCH--U.S.

"French business in the United States is a lot more than champagne and perfume. Companies from France are active in the United States in everything from heavy-duty trucks to yogurt to antacid to building materials. Overall, the US Commerce Department reports that French investment in the United States at the end of 1992 totaled $23.8 billion. Some 1,866 French affiliates in the United States employed some 363,000 people in 1991, the latest year for which figures are available." (p16)

Lever, Robert. "Business: More Than Champagne and Perfume." Europe n332, Dec-Jan 1993-94. p16. (ISSN0191-4545).

INVESTMENTS, JAPANESE--ASIA (v19)

INVESTMENTS, JAPANESE--ASIA--U.S. (v19)

INVESTMENTS, JAPANESE--EUROPE (v19)

INVESTMENTS, JAPANESE--GREAT BRITAIN (v19)

INVESTMENTS, JAPANESE--U.S. (v19)

IOWA (v19)

see also AGRICULTURAL LAWS AND LEGISLATION--IOWA--PUBLIC OPINION; FOOD INDUSTRY AND TRADE--IOWA; SPORTS--IOWA

IOWA--COMMERCE--MEXICO (v19)

"Mexico is Iowa's third largest export market, supporting 3,123 Iowa jobs in 1992. Since Mexico began to lower its tariff rates in 1987, Iowa's merchandise exports to Mexico have more than tripled, from $66 million to $200 million. NAFTA [North American Free-Trade Agreement] is expected to result in a net gain of 870 jobs in Iowa; good, export-related jobs which pay better than non-export related jobs." (pE2966)

Lightfoot, Jim (Rep.-Iowa). "North American Free-Trade Agreement Implementation Act," Congressional Record (20 Nov 1993). Daily ed. pE2966. (ISSN0363-7239).

IOWA--ECONOMIC CONDITIONS (v19)

IRAN--SOCIAL CONDITIONS

"Iran has the potential of reducing fertility sharply and rapidly. It has a GNP [gross national product] per capita of $2,490, three-fourths of its labor force is nonagricultural, life expectancy is 65 years, the infant mortality rate is relatively low at 52 deaths per 1,000 live births, and primary plus secondary school enrollment ratios are high at 90 percent for males and 75 percent for females. Adult literacy, however, is relatively low at about 43 percent for females and 65 for males. The United Nations estimates the TFR [total fertility rate] for 1985-90 as 6.5, a decrease of only three-quarters of a child from 1960-65, when it was 7.3." (p87)

Mauldin, W. Parker/Ross, John A. "Prospects and Programs for Fertility Reduction, 1990-2015." Studies in Family Planning v25 n2, Mar-Apr 1994. p77-95. (ISSN0039-3665).

IRAN. NAVY

"Iran already operates the most powerful navy in the Persian Gulf. According to the 1992-93 edition of the International Institute of Strategic Studies's publication THE MILITARY BALANCE, it operates 3 destroyers, 3 frigates, 33 patrol and coastal units--including 10 missile craft--and 14 support vessels." (p45)

Kraska, James. "Gatekeepers of the Gulf." Proceedings v120 n3, Mar 1994. p44-47. (ISSN0041-798X).

IRAQ

see also CHILDREN--IRAQ--MORTALITY; DEBTS, EXTERNAL--IRAQ; SANCTIONS (INTERNATIONAL LAW)--IRAQ--ECONOMIC CONDITIONS

IRAQ--ARMED FORCES (v19)

IRAQ-KUWAIT CRISIS, 1990-1991--ENVIRONMENTAL ASPECTS

"Climatologists were wrong in predicting that soot and smoke released by oil wells set on fire during the 43-day Gulf conflict in January and February 1991 would, in one month, shade more than a fifth of the Earth's surface and disrupt the Asian monsoon. Instead, the damage was much more acute and localised. About 600 Kuwaiti wells blazed for up to nine months and the 1,000 million barrels of burning oil emitted a 15,000 square kilometre cloud of smoke, soot and toxic carcinogenic chemicals. Tonnes of sulphur and nitrogen oxide were released, turning into nitric and sulphuric acid, falling as acid rain, largely on Kuwait, Iraq, Iran and Turkey....Tens of millions of barrels of crude oil from damaged wells swamped more than 60% of Kuwait. An estimated 6 million barrels flowed into the shallow and confined Gulf waters killing water fowl, dugongs (sea cows), turtles and fish, and causing severe marine pollution." (p12)

Jansen, Michael. "Gulf War: What Gulf-Clean-Up?" Panoscope n38, Jan 1994. p12-13. (ISSN0951-8819).

IRELAND

see also CONTRACEPTION--IRELAND--PUBLIC OPINION; ECONOMIC FORECASTING--IRELAND; NORTHERN IRELAND--RELIGION; TERRORISM--IRELAND

IRELAND--HISTORY--CIVIL WAR--COSTS

"The ending of political violence by the IRA would bring the most immediate benefits to Northern Ireland where the people and the economy have suffered so much over the past 25 years. But there would also be enormous benefits in the Republic where much needed funds are diverted to security measures. The restoration of normal conditions in the border areas would mean a welcome increase in tourism and the extension of a network of cross-border cooperation in economic and cultural sectors. A recent study estimates the annual cost of the Northern conflict to the Republic because of extra security and losses in tourism at almost $200 million. In Northern Ireland the figure is almost $500 million." (p13)

Carroll, Joe. "Member Country Report: Ireland: High Hopes." Europe n335, Apr 1994. p12-13,15. (ISSN0191-4545).

IRELAND--HISTORY--CIVIL WAR--MORTALITY

"In the last 25 years, more than 3,000 people have been killed in Northern Ireland, roughly two-thirds of them civilians. More than 35,000 have been injured or maimed. There have been nearly 10,000 explosions." (p8)

Dettmer, Jamie. "Fragile Hope Blossoms in Northern Ireland's Bloody War." Insight v10 n3, 17 Jan 1994. p6-11. (ISSN1051-4880).

IRELAND--POPULATION--RELIGION

"Northern Ireland, with its roughly 60 percent Protestant majority, has...been a part of the United Kingdom for nearly 75 years. The rest of Ireland, with its 95 percent Catholic majority, went on to achieve sovereignty. Relations between the partitioned portions of the island have remained tense, as the dominant religious group in each sector adopted measures intended to reinforce its status." (p6)

Kelley, Kevin J. "Ireland: A Short History of the Longest War." Toward Freedom v43 n1, Feb 1994. p5-6. (ISSN0048-9898).

IRRIGATION--BANGLADESH

"International Development Enterprise (IDE), a Swiss-funded group, has now developed...the Deep-set Treadle Pump that will make it possible to irrigate vast tracts of arid highlands. William Derrenger, director of IDE, calls the pump 'a miracle in the context of Bangladesh's needs. This is the kind of appropriate technology that development agencies have always dreamt of.' One recent study suggested that food production could be increased by up to 50 percent in Bangladesh if landless and marginal farmers are equipped with the pump. More than 100,000 were sold in the country last year, bringing the number in operation to some 700,000. And now interest in the pump is growing in countries like India, Vietnam and Brazil, where it may be introduced for farmers in the Amazon basin." (p10)

Zaman, Roushan. "What Works: A Simple Tool That Can Help Feed Millions." Toward Freedom v41 n8, Dec 1992-Jan 1993. p8,10. (ISSN0048-9898).

IRRIGATION--INDIA

"During the British raj [in India], canal charges provided a commercial rate of return on investment. Today revenues cover only 7.5% of the cost of operating and maintaining irrigation systems. The subsidy costs the taxpayer 23 billion rupees ($735m) a year, and there is not enough money for repairing or desilting canals, so the whole canal network is deteriorating....State electricity boards are losing around 50 billion rupees a year, largely because of subsidies to farmers operating pumps. The cost of power from new thermal stations is around 2.50 rupees per unit. Yet farmers pay 0.35 rupees per unit or less in many states, and three southern states give power free to small farmers....Apart from wasting money, the subsidy hurts farmers. Excessive pumping means the water table has fallen precipitously in many areas, drying up shallower tubewells. In coastal areas, the overuse of fresh water has sucked in sea-water, destroying freshwater aquifers permanently. Why do state governments persist in such profligacy? Because farmers count for a lot in a democracy where 70% of voters live in rural areas. Every party promises cheaper water and power. Giveaways may cost a lot in the long run, but at election time they look like a price worth paying." (p33)

"Asia: Where India's Reforms Get Stuck." Economist v330 n7847, 22 Jan 1994. p33-34. (ISSN0013-0613).

IRRIGATION--U.S.

"In the south central United States, water for irrigation is pumped from the huge Ogallala aquifer, at rates demonstrably above recharge capacity. Extraction has been encouraged by tax laws that contain a water depletion allowance. Rather than internalizing the negative external effects of irrigation, they have actually been encouraged. In seventeen western states, 40 to 50 million acres are under irrigation, accounting for 90 percent of water consumption. It is estimated that 90 percent of the capital costs of irrigation conducted under the federal Bureau of Reclamation is subsidized for irrigating farmers. Farmers in the West San Joaquin Valley of California, for example, pay less than 10 percent of the delivery cost of water." (p103)

Runge, C. Ford. "Trade Liberalization and Environmental Quality in Agriculture." International Environmental Affairs v5 n2, Spr 1993. p95-128. (ISSN1041-4665).

ISLANDS--INDONESIA (v19)

ISRAEL

see also BUSINESS ENTERPRISES--ISRAEL; EDUCATION--ISRAEL; GAZA STRIP--ISRAEL--WEST BANK--POPULATION; GROSS DOMESTIC PRODUCT--ISRAEL; INVESTMENTS, FOREIGN--ISRAEL; MEDICAL CARE--ISRAEL; UNEMPLOYMENT--ISRAEL; WATER-SUPPLY--ISRAEL--JORDAN

ISRAEL--ARMED FORCES (v19)

ISRAEL--ARMED FORCES--APPROPRIATIONS AND EXPENDITURES (v19)

ISRAEL--COMMERCE

Israel has "free-trade agreements with the United States, the European Union and the European Free-Trade Association. But over the past three years it has been dismantling import barriers unilaterally. The aim is to spur competition by increasing trade with third countries--and particularly with the fast-growing economies of Asia and Latin America. Although the government has succumbed to pleas from some domestic producers--in textiles, for example--to slow down their rate of exposure to new competition, tariffs continue to fall. In 1992 imports from third countries increased by 15%, and the new markets swallowed well over half of the increase in Israeli exports." (p16)

"Survey: Israel: Milk and Honey." Economist v330 n7847, 22 Jan 1994. p58(15-16,19). (ISSN0013-0613).

ISRAEL--ECONOMIC CONDITIONS (v19)

"Israel, with a population of 5.4 million and a GNP [gross national product] of $69.5 billion in 1993, has a per capita income of nearly $13,000. The Government of Israel (GOI) has been relatively successful in stabilizing the economy in the face of a massive inflow of immigrants which has increased the population by around 10 percent since the end of 1989. Real GDP [gross domestic product] growth has averaged around 6 percent per year over the past three years, employment has risen at an annual rate of 4 percent, the market based exchange system has improved export competitiveness, and inflation has been reduced to around 11 percent....However, unemployment increased from 8.9 percent in 1989 to 11.2 in 1992 before declining to 10.5 percent in 1993. While GDP growth has slowed to around 4 percent in 1993, expanding business investment and governmental infrastructure investment coupled with sustained export growth provide the basis for a resumption of 6 percent average annual GDP growth in 1994 and 1995." (pE471)

Hamilton, Lee H. (Rep.-Ind.). "Aid Reports on Egypt and Israel," Congressional Record (17 Mar 1994). Daily ed. pE470-472. (ISSN0363-7239).

"With a per capita GDP [gross domestic product] of around $13,000, Israelis are about as rich as Irishmen or Spaniards....In...[1985], Israel stood briefly on the verge of economic collapse: with 400% inflation, a soaring budget deficit and rapidly shrivelling foreign-exchange reserves. A Labour-Likud coalition government, acting in concert with frightened employers and unions, introduced an emergency economic-stabilisation programme. This included a temporary wage freeze, higher taxes, public-spending cuts and a currency devaluation followed by the pegging of the shekel to the dollar....In the short run, the plan was a marvellous success. It curbed inflation and tamed the budget deficit. Since it was implemented, Israel's GDP has grown by an average of nearly 5% a year....Foreign debt has fallen from 80% of GDP in 1985 to around 25% now." (p15)

"Survey: Israel: Milk and Honey." Economist v330 n7847, 22 Jan 1994. p58(15-16,19). (ISSN0013-0613).

ISRAEL--EMIGRATION AND IMMIGRATION (v19)

ISRAEL--FORMER SOVIET REPUBLICS--EMIGRATION AND IMMIGRATION

"Since 1989, when the Soviet Union decided to let its Jewish citizens emigrate, more than 500,000 of them have reached Israel, raising the country's population by more than 10%....Most of the newcomers reached Israel in 1990 (200,000) and 1991 (176,000). Desperate to escape the Soviet Union during a time of chaos, many flew into Ben Gurion airport in the pauses between the salvoes of Scud missiles that Iraq fired at Israel during the Gulf war. As news has trickled home about the hardships in Israel, the inflow has slowed. Fewer than 80,000 arrived in 1992, and only about 60,000 in 1993. But up to 1m Jews in Russia and other ex-Soviet republics have inquired at one time or another about Israeli visas. If the job market in Israel improves, or conditions deteriorate any more at home, the trickle could swiftly turn back into a flood." (p10)

"Survey: Israel: A Coat of Many Colours." Economist v330 n7847, 22 Jan 1994. p58(10,13-14). (ISSN0013-0613).

ISRAEL--MANUFACTURES (v19)

ISRAEL--RELATIONS--U.S. (v19)

ITALY

see also FERTILITY, HUMAN--ITALY; FIREARMS--ITALY

ITALY--CORRUPT PRACTICES

"How widespread is [corruption in Italy]...? Do bent administrators and businessmen still take and pay bribes? Is the Mafia strangling legitimate businesses?...Now comes a broad survey from those who are likely to encounter the tentacles of organised crime, the younger members of Confindustria, the industrialists' organisation. The survey was put together by Pino Arlacchi, a sociologist and one of Italy's top Mafia experts....Two years of police investigation and almost daily arrests have still not deterred the incorrigibly corrupt, according to the survey. Some 85% of the 800 members of the association who were polled say that bribes used to be paid to secure public contracts before Milan magistrates launched their 'clean hands' inquiry in 1992. Although about 80% say that matters have improved since, they admit that the notorious 'bustarelle' (envelopes) still change hands. And 13% say there has been no improvement at all. That proportion rises to 31.8% in the area the survey calls 'regions at risk--Mafia-plagued Sicily, Calabria and Campania...." (p53)

"Europe: Italy: Still Crooked." Economist v330 n7849, 5 Feb 1994. p53-54. (ISSN0013-0613).

ITALY--ECONOMIC CONDITIONS (v19)

ITALY--EMPLOYMENT (v19)

ITALY--OFFICIALS AND EMPLOYEES (v19)

JACKSONVILLE (FLA)

see RACISM--JACKSONVILLE (FLA)

JAPAN

see also AIRLINES--JAPAN; ALCOHOLISM--JAPAN; AUTOMOBILE INDUSTRY AND TRADE--JAPAN--U.S.; BALANCE OF TRADE--JAPAN--U.S.; BOTTLED WATER--JAPAN; BUDGET DEFICITS--JAPAN--U.S.; BUSINESS ENTERPRISES--JAPAN--U.S.; CANCER--JAPAN--MORTALITY; CIVIL SERVICE--JAPAN; COCAINE INDUSTRY--JAPAN; COMPUTER INDUSTRY--JAPAN; COMPUTER SOFTWARE INDUSTRY--JAPAN--U.S.; CYCLING--DENMARK--JAPAN--NETHERLANDS; DEBTS, EXTERNAL--JAPAN; DEPARMENT STORES--JAPAN; DISCRIMINATION IN EMPLOYMENT--JAPAN; EDUCATION--JAPAN; ELECTRONIC INDUSTRIES--JAPAN--U.S.; EUROPE--JAPAN--U.S.; FERTILITY, HUMAN--JAPAN; FIREARMS--EUROPE--JAPAN--U.S.; FOREST PRODUCTS INDUSTRY--JAPAN--U.S.; GERMANY--JAPAN--U.S.--ECONOMIC CONDITIONS; GIFTS--JAPAN; HOUSING--JAPAN; IMMIGRANTS--JAPAN; INDUSTRY AND STATE--JAPAN--PUBLIC OPINION; INFLATION (FINANCE)--BRAZIL--GERMANY--JAPAN; INSURANCE--JAPAN; INVESTMENTS, FOREIGN--JAPAN--U.S.; MEDICINE--JAPAN; MIGRANT LABOR--JAPAN; MUSIC TRADE--JAPAN; NARCOTICS, CONTROL OF--JAPAN; PAPER INDUSTRY--JAPAN--U.S.; PATENTS--EUROPE--JAPAN--U.S.; PATENTS--JAPAN; PETROLEUM CHEMICALS INDUSTRY--JAPAN; POPULATION FORECASTING--JAPAN; RETAIL TRADE--JAPAN; ROBOTS--JAPAN; SEMICONDUCTOR INDUSTRY--JAPAN; SEMICONDUCTOR INDUSTRY--STEEL INDUSTRY AND TRADE--JAPAN; SQUIDS--JAPAN; STEEL INDUSTRY AND TRADE--JAPAN; STOCK-EXCHANGE--JAPAN--U.S.; STUDENTS, FOREIGN--JAPAN; SUGAR TRADE--JAPAN; SUGARCANE--JAPAN; SWEETENERS--JAPAN--U.S.; TECHNOLOGY--JAPAN--TRAINING; UNEMPLOYMENT--EUROPE--JAPAN--U.S.; VEGETABLE TRADE--JAPAN; VISITORS, FOREIGN--JAPAN; YEN, JAPANESE--EVALUATION

JAPAN--ARMED FORCES--APPROPRIATIONS AND EXPENDITURES (v19)

JAPAN--COMMERCE--AFRICA

"South Africa is Japan's biggest partner in the continent, accounting for 25.4 per cent ($1.7 bn) of Japanese exports to Africa in 1992 and 52.5 per cent ($1.9 bn) of its imports. Other countries with substantial trade links with Japan were Nigeria and Kenya (7.8 and 2.6 per cent respectively of Japanese exports), and Zambia and Mauritania (6.8 and 4.2 per cent respectively of Japan's imports)." (p35)

Swinnerton, R. C. F. "Japan Raises Its Profile in Africa." Africa Recovery v7 n3-4, Dec 1993-Mar 1994. p34-35.

JAPAN--COMMERCE--EUROPEAN ECONOMIC COMMUNITY

"The huge surplus that Japan has been running with the EC [European Community] for years threatens to reach politically intolerable levels. Taking a non-confrontational approach, the EC and Japan have started to jointly analyze the root causes of the chronic trade imbalance to find remedies. An important part of this process is the Trade Assessment Mechanism, implemented to monitor and analyze market performance of EC exports to Japan. After declining in 1989, the surplus soared again in 1991 and reached a staggering $31.2 billion in 1992, propelled by a 5.6% increase in Japanese exports and a 1.6% drop in imports from the EC. Some 50% of the surplus was due to the concentration of Japanese exports in a few sectors: cars, electronic data processing equipment, telecommunications equipment, and electronic components. The drop in imports was largely due to the collapse of the bubble economy and reduced consumer spending in Japan." (p20)

Hallstrom, Conje. "Foreign Voices: Conje Hallstrom: EC Access." Look Japan v39 n452, Nov 1993. p20. (ISSN0456-5339).

JAPAN--COMMERCE--U.S. (v19)

"The case for numerical targets rests on the idea that Japan's economy is controlled to an unusual degree by government bureaucrats, who conspire with firms to keep out foreign products. In these circumstances, runs the argument, the mere absence of tariffs is not enough to make Japan a 'fair' trader. If foreign firms are to penetrate Japan, foreign governments need the help of Japan's bureaucrats. Hence numerical targets, under which Japanese officials become responsible for making Japanese firms buy more from abroad. This argument has been tested since 1986, when America talked Japan into promising American firms a 20% share of the Japanese market for semiconductors. In narrow terms that agreement has worked fairly well: America's share of Japan's market rose from around 9% to just over 20%. Now that it has slipped just below 20%, the Americans are waxing indignant (even though their own semiconductor industry is now booming, for reasons that appear to have little to do with the quotas America squeezed out of Japan.) The trouble is that agreements like these increase rather than diminish the power of government officials, whose excessive influence over companies was supposed to be the cause of the problem in the first place." (p17)

"Leaders: Mismanaged Trade." Economist v330 n7847, 22 Jan 1994. p17-18. (ISSN0013-0613).

JAPAN--ECONOMIC CONDITIONS (v19)

"It has long been recognized that the Japanese economy performs in a manner which sets it clearly apart from other major industrialized countries in general and the G-7. This is very evident when looking at the macroeconomic dimensions of the problem; at Japan's massive current account surplus, which now constitutes the major asymmetry in the world economy today; and at its low level of manufactured goods imports and inward flow of foreign direct investment. In 1991, for example, manufactured goods imported by the U.S. accounted for 6.9

percent of GDP [gross domestic product], an average of 7.4 percent for the rest of the G-7, excluding Japan, but only 3.1 percent for Japan. Among the OECD [Organization for Economic Cooperation and Development] countries, Japan has by far the lowest percentage of the global stock of inward direct investment; just 0.7 percent, as compared to 38.5 percent in Europe and 28.6 percent in the United States." (p42)

Barshefsky, Charlene (Deputy U.S. Trade Representative). U.S. Senate. Committee on Finance. "United States-Japan Trade Negotiations." Hearing, 8 Nov 1993. Washington, D.C.: GPO, 1994. (ISBN0160435625). (Y4.F49:S.hrg.103-399).

"In 1993 department-store sales [in Japan] were down 6.6% on the previous year; and vehicle output dropped 10.2%, the steepest decline since 1945....Meanwhile yet another round of trade talks with America ended in stalemate. This was no coincidence, since Japan's downturn widens its trade surplus by dampening demand for imports....The Americans want Japan's imports, which currently come to around 7% of GDP [gross domestic product], to approach the 14.6% that is the average for OECD [Organization for Economic Cooperation and Development] countries....Japan's recession worsens trade tension, but the opposite is also true: it is harder these days for Japan to export its way out of trouble. In 1980, its economy shocked by high oil prices, Japan's current-account deficit was worth 1.0% of GDP, leaving room for export-led recovery. This time the surplus stands at 3.3% of GDP. America demands that it should shrink to 2%, so Japan needs a domestic cure for its recession. Hence the enthusiasm for more public spending." (p35)

"Asia: The Good News from Japan." Economist v330 n7848, 29 Jan 1994. p35-36. (ISSN0013-0613).

In Japan, "Real GDP [gross domestic product] growth, which was a robust 3.3% in fiscal 1991, slowed to an anemic 0.5% in fiscal 1992. This year, it will probably be negative. Even the Economic Planning Agency has finally backed down from its declaration that the economy had bottomed out. On November 29, the Nikkei share price average dipped below 16,000, the lowest of the year. Why have business conditions failed to recover in spite of the stimulus packages of April and September, and record-low interest rates? On the surface, the government seems to be doing everything in its power. Expansionary fiscal policies produced 13.3% growth in public fixed asset formation during fiscal 1992 and an estimated 17.1% growth during fiscal 1993. But public asset formation accounts for only 6.7% of GNP [gross national product], and public asset growth of 17% means only a 1% boost for the GNP. Consumption, meanwhile, which represents about 60% of GNP, is forecast to contract this year. Likewise, private-sector capital investment, 20% of the GNP, will be down an estimated 7%." (p20)

Ueda, Kazuo. "Viewpoints: Economic Stimulus: Fiscal Stimulation." Look Japan v39 n455, Feb 1994. p20. (ISSN0456-5339).

"In Japan, the economy registered almost zero growth in 1993, and forecasters anticipate less than 1 percent growth this year. As of late 1993, industrial production was continuing the decline that began in early 1992, and it still shows no signs of recovery. Labor market indicators also continued to weaken. The ratio of job offers to applicants fell during 1993, and the unemployment rate, which rose from 2.2 percent in 1992 to approximately 2.5 percent in 1993, is forecast to increase further this year....Corporations have significant overcapacity, reducing the need for capital spending, and Japanese firms are also undergoing restructuring. Japan's financial system is saddled with many bad loans, and real estate prices continue to weaken. Income tax cuts amounting to about 1.5 percent of GNP [gross national product] are being considered, but political problems have delayed passage of the cuts, which now appear unlikely to be implemented until mid-1994." (p11)

U.S. Congressional Budget Office. "The Economic Outlook." The Economic and Budget Outlook: Fiscal Years 1995-1999 Jan 1994. Washington, D.C.: GPO, 1994.

"Economists note that the savings rate in Japan has stabilized over the past year at about 15 percent of take-home pay, after rising from 14.1 percent in 1990. This means that as the government injects more money into the economy, consumer spending may increase. That's important because consumer expenditures represent about 57 percent of Japan's GDP [gross domestic product]." (p71)

Butler, Steven. "Predictions: Will Japan Inc. Boom Again in '94?" U.S. News & World Report v115 n25, 27 Dec 1993. p71. (ISSN0041-5537).

JAPAN--EMIGRATION AND IMMIGRATION (v19)

JAPAN--EMPLOYMENT (v19)

"One reason for Japan's ability to bounce back quickly from previous recessions was its policy of lifetime employment. Instead of sacking workers, Japan's big companies can cut costs by reducing the overtime and bonus payments that account for more than a quarter of their pay bills....So far Japan is clinging to the old methods: the official unemployment rate is still only 2.7%. Firms have tried to avoid real sackings, preferring instead to freeze recruitment, transfer workers to subsidiaries, encourage early retirement and trim working hours. For all its past virtues, lifetime employment is now a hindrance....Hidden unemployment--in the form of gross overmanning--is now estimated at 2m-3m. The longer the recession goes on, the greater the risk that unneeded workers will have to be sacked." (p18)

"Leaders: Remade in Japan." Economist v329 n7842, 18 Dec 1993. p18. (ISSN0013-0613).

JAPAN--POLITICS AND GOVERNMENT--PUBLIC OPINION (v19)

In August 1993, Morihiro Hosokawa was selected "as Japan's 79th prime minister....In his first address as prime minister, Hosokawa proclaimed that his Cabinet represents 'not just one stop in the passage of history, but the starting point for a new history.' He proclaimed his administration the 'political reform government' and announced that the first task and highest priority of the Cabinet would be to carry out political reforms this year....Hosokawa also...expressed deep regret and apologies for Japan's aggressive actions during WWII, including its colonization of neighboring countries. Lower House Speaker Doi, speaking about Japan's responsibility for the war at an August 15 memorial ceremony for Japan's war dead, said, 'We have yet to come to an understanding with the people of Asia,' thereby confirming the Hosokawa coalition government's stance on Japan's war responsibilities. According to an early September survey in ASAHI SHIMBUN, 72% of Japanese approve of this position....When asked what their greatest expectation for the Hosokawa government was, 33% of the respondents to the poll said 'economic measures.' In mid-September, Hosokawa announced a Y6.15 trillion ($58 billion) package of emergency economy stimulus measures....In a subsequent ASAHI SHIMBUN survey, 69% were pessimistic about the effectiveness of the measures." (p11)

Mineshige, Miyuki. "Japanese Politics: Hosokawa Cabinet: First Steps." Look Japan v39 n452, Nov 1993. p10-11. (ISSN0456-5339).

JAPAN--POPULATION

"For several centuries before and during the Tokugawa Period (1603-1868), the population [of Japan] held steady at roughly 30 million, but under the militaristic Meiji government (1868-1912), with the spread of education and the improvement of sanitary standards, the population boomed. Moreover, after Japan's defeat in WWII came a revolution in health-care technology. These factors served to push the Japanese average life expectancy up from over 40 years to over 80. After the war, the birth rate went into a steady decline; at present, there is an average of only 1.5 births per woman in Japan. This process produced a sharp upswing in the proportion of the population considered elderly." (p26)

Utsunomiya, Toshio. "Sci-Tech Feature: Helping the Elderly: The Bright Gray Future." Look Japan v39 n451, Oct 1993. p26-27. (ISSN0456-5339).

JAPAN--RELATIONS--U.S.--PUBLIC OPINION (v19)

JAPAN--U.S.--INDUSTRIES (v19)

JAPAN--UNITED NATIONS

According to Ku Tashiro, a member of the International Civil Service Commission of the United Nations, "With a population of 120 million, Japan's ratio to the global population of 5.5 billion is 2.2%. Japan's personnel representation in the UN is 2.4%. Presently, the ratio of Japan's GNP [gross national product] to that of the total world GNP is over 15%. Japan's monetary contribution to the UN is 12.45%. Considering these figures, it may be safe to say that they roughly match." (p6)

Nishimura, Kunio. "Cover Story: International Contributions: UN-Representative Japan." Look Japan v39 n452, Nov 1993. p4-7. (ISSN0456-5339).

JEWS--FORMER SOVIET REPUBLICS

"The Mountain Jews are the largest part of the population of Oriental Jews in the former Soviet Union, numbering about 140,000 according to Lev Bardani, the Baku-based representative of the Jewish Agency for Israel responsible for this region. Aside from the Mountain Jews, some 20,000 Bukharan Jews (they speak a similar Jewish dialect of Persian) remain in the former Soviet Central Asian republics of Uzbekistan and Tajikistan. Tens of thousands have already emigrated to Israel. Most Mountain Jews, about 35,000, live in Azerbaijan, the majority of them in Baku. The next-largest concentration, about 20,000, is in the Russian autonomous republic of Dagestan. The largest concentration still in the mountains...[live in Krasnaya Sloboda, a] town of about 5,500 Jews across the Gudiyal-Chai River from the city of Kuba, founded some 350 years ago by Jews fleeing pogroms." (p36)

Sneider, Daniel. "Civil Society: The Mountain Jews of Azerbaijan and Russia." Surviving Together v11 n2, Sum 1993. p36-37. (ISSN0859-6286).

JEWS--SOVIET UNION--EMIGRATION AND IMMIGRATION (v19)

JEWS--U.S.--PUBLIC OPINION (v19)

JEWS--UKRAINE (v19)

JOB CREATION--EUROPEAN ECONOMIC COMMUNITY (v19)

JOB CREATION--U.S. (v19)

JOB HUNTING--U.S.--AGED (v19)

JOB SECURITY (v19)

JOB TRAINING

see OCCUPATIONAL TRAINING

JORDAN

see WATER-SUPPLY--ISRAEL--JORDAN

JORDAN--ECONOMIC CONDITIONS (v19)

JOURNALISTS--U.S.--POLITICAL AND SOCIAL VIEWS (v19)

JUAREZ (MEXICO)

see POLLUTION--EL PASO (TEX)--JUAREZ (MEXICO)

JUDGES

see also COURTS

JUDGES--U.S. (v19)

According to U.S. Chief Justice William H. Rehnquist, "In 1953, there were 218 federal district judges and 65 judges of the Court of Appeals....Today those numbers are 649 district judges and 175 judges of the Court of Appeals." (p94)

Reske, Henry J. "Your ABA: Troubling Review." ABA Journal v80, Jan 1994. p94. (ISSN0747-0088).

JUDGES--U.S.--ATTITUDES (v19)

JUDICIAL POWER--U.S. (v19)

JUDICIARY

see COURTS

JUNK BONDS--U.S.

"The number of Yankee bonds (dollar-denominated securities sold in America by foreign issuers) launched by companies rated below investment grade has now begun to grow. In 1992 there were $450-worth of such issues, estimates Donaldson Lufkin Jenrette (DLJ), a Wall Street firm. In 1993 there were $2.7 billion-worth--about 5% of all new junk issued. The growth should continue. Joseph Bencivenga, the head of high-yield research at Salomon, expects new issues of emerging-country junk in America at least to double in 1993." (p79)

"Finance: Junk Bonds: Emerging, Converging." Economist v330 n7848, 29 Jan 1994. p79. (ISSN0013-0613).

JUVENILE DELINQUENCY

see also GANGS; SCHOOL VIOLENCE

JUVENILE DELINQUENCY--CALIFORNIA--U.S. (v19)

JUVENILE DELINQUENCY--U.S. (v19)

"Recent F.B.I. statistics reveal disturbing trends in the commission of violent crimes by juveniles ages 10-17 [in the U.S.]. The violent crime arrest rate for these minors in 1990 exceeded the 1980 rate by 27 percent. In part, this trend resulted from a 79 percent increase in the number of juveniles ages 10-17 who committed murders with guns over the same period. In 1990, nearly 75% of these juvenile murder offenders used guns, primarily handguns, for their crimes. In addition, in 1990, juvenile violation of weapons laws surged to its highest level ever." (p93)

U.S. Senate. Committee on the Judiciary. "Children and Gun Violence." Hearing, 9 Jun 1993. Washington, D.C.: GPO, 1994. (ISBN0160439280). (Y4.J89/2:S.hrg.103-393).

"The overall rate of violent crime by juveniles is on the rise [in the U.S.]. The violent crime arrest rate for juveniles aged 10-17 rose by 27 percent between 1980 and 1990. Juvenile homicide, in particular, is on the rise. According to a Northeastern University report, arrest rates for criminal homicide among 13-14 year old males increased by 140 percent between 1985 and 1991. Among 15 year old males the increase was 217 percent; among 16 year old males, 158 percent; for 17 year old males 121 percent, and for 18-20 year old males 131 percent. More and more juvenile crime is being committed with guns. Between 1980 and 1990 there was a 79-percent increase in the number of juveniles committing murder with guns. In New York City, arrests on gun charges of children ages 7 to 15 rose by 75 percent between 1987 and 1990. Juveniles are the greatest victims of the rise in juvenile crime. People between the ages of 16 and 24 are more likey to be victims of handgun crime than any other group. Firearms are now the second leading cause of death for youths aged 15-19. The rate of firearm homicide for that age group rose 141 percent between 1985 and 1990." (p83)

Brady, Sarah (Chair, Handgun Control, Inc.). U.S. Senate. Committee on the Judiciary. "Children and Gun Violence." Hearing, 9 Jun 1993. Washington, D.C.: GPO, 1994. (ISBN0160439280). (Y4.J89/2:S.hrg.103-393).

"What sadder commentary can there be on the failure to instill moral values and respect for the sanctity of human life in our youth when, over the last decade, violent crime by juveniles has more than doubled in the United States. In 1982 there was a murder was committed by a juvenile approximately every 40 days. In 1992 a murder committed by a juvenile every 12 days. In 1982 a juvenile committed a rape every 26 days; by 1992 it was every 8 days. The statistics on violent behavior may partially include every race and income group, but those who ignore the fact that there is an overwhelmingly disproportionate impact on poor, black and hispanic inner city youths are not focusing on where the problem lies." (p73)

Lamson, Susan R. (Director, Federal Affairs Division, NRA-ILA). U.S. Senate. Committee on the Judiciary. "Children and Gun Violence." Hearing, 9 Jun 1993. Washington, D.C.: GPO, 1994. (ISBN0160439280). (Y4.J89/2:S.hrg.103-393).

"Analysis of self-reported measures of violent offending employed in the National Youth Survey (NYS) for the period 1976 to 1980 indicates that from ages 12 to 17, about 5 percent of juveniles at each age were classified as 'serious violent' (a combination of both serious and violent offense categories) offenders. 'Serious violent' offenders, on average, commit 132 delinquent offenses annually with 8 of them being 'serious violent' offenses. Most serious and violent juvenile careers last about 1 year, and nearly 10 percent of 'serious violent' offenders have a career length of 5 years or more (Elliot et al., 1986)." (p23)

Wilson, John J./Howell, James C. (Office of Juvenile Justice and Delinquency Prevention). U.S. House. Committee on Education and Labor. "Hearing Regarding the...Report Entitled 'A...Strategy for Serious...Juvenile Offenders.'" Hearing, 28 Oct 1993. Washington, D.C.: GPO, 1994. (ISBN0160433983). (Y4.Ed8/1:103-34).

"In 1971 Massachusetts closed its training schools and replaced them with a network of decentralized community-based services and a few, small secure-care units for violent juvenile offenders. This constituted the most sweeping reform in youth corrections in the United States since the establishment of juvenile training schools and juvenile courts in the 19th century. Massachusetts demonstrated that juvenile corrections need not be centered around large training schools....The National Council on Crime and Delinquency conducted a 10-year followup study in 1984-85. Designed to examine the effectiveness of current youth services for delinquent youth, it compared the Massachusetts juvenile corrections programs with those of California. It revealed that youth who spent 5 months in a Massachusetts program followed by supervision in the community had a rearrest rate of 51 percent, while youth who spent 14 months in a California institution had a rearrest rate of 70 percent. Of those released from Massachusetts correctional programs, only 23 percent were reincarcerated while 62 percent were reincarcerated in California." (p40)

Wilson, John J./Howell, James C. (Office of Juvenile Justice and Delinquency Prevention). U.S. House. Committee on Education and Labor. "Hearing Regarding the...Report Entitled 'A...Strategy for Serious...Juvenile Offenders.'" Hearing, 28 Oct 1993. Washington, D.C.: GPO, 1994. (ISBN0160433983). (Y4.Ed8/1:103-34).

"In 1991 there were an estimated 2.3 million arrests of juveniles [in the U.S.]. More than 100,000 of these arrests were for violent crimes, and more than 700,000 were for serious property crimes. These arrests represented 16 percent of all arrests, 33 percent of all burglary arrests, 26 percent of all robbery arrests, 16 percent of all rape arrests, 14 percent of all aggravated assault arrests, and 14 percent of all murder arrests (Snyder et al., 1993)." (p34)

Wilson, John J./Howell, James C. (Office of Juvenile Justice and Delinquency Prevention). U.S. House. Committee on Education and Labor. "Hearing Regarding the...Report Entitled 'A...Strategy for Serious...Juvenile Offenders.'" Hearing, 28 Oct 1993. Washington, D.C.: GPO, 1994. (ISBN0160433983). (Y4.Ed8/1:103-34).

"Juvenile arrests [in the U.S.] are increasing, particularly for violent offenses. Juvenile arrests for violent crimes increased 41 percent from 1982-1991. In 1991, the juvenile arrest rate for violent offenses reached its highest level in history. In the 10-year period between 1982 and 1991, the number of juvenile arrests for murder increased by 93 percent and aggravated assault arrests increased by 72 percent (Snyder, 1993)." (p19)

Wilson, John J./Howell, James C. (Office of Juvenile Justice and Delinquency Prevention). U.S. House. Committee on Education and Labor. "Hearing Regarding the...Report Entitled 'A...Strategy for Serious...Juvenile Offenders.'" Hearing, 28 Oct 1993. Washington, D.C.: GPO, 1994. (ISBN0160433983). (Y4.Ed8/1:103-34).

"Juvenile court caseloads are increasing [in the U.S.], largely as a result of increasing violent delinquency. From 1986 through 1990, the number of delinquency cases actually disposed by juvenile courts increased 10 percent. During the same period, juvenile courts disposed of 31 percent more violent cases, including 64 percent more homicide and 48 percent more aggravated assault cases (Snyder et al., 1993a)." (p20)

Wilson, John J./Howell, James C. (Office of Juvenile Justice and Delinquency Prevention). U.S. House. Committee on Education and Labor. "Hearing Regarding the...Report Entitled 'A...Strategy for Serious...Juvenile Offenders.'" Hearing, 28 Oct 1993. Washington, D.C.: GPO, 1994. (ISBN0160433983). (Y4.Ed8/1:103-34).

"The Philadelphia birth cohort study (Wolfgang, Figlio, and Sellin, 1972) found that 'chronic offenders' (five or more police contacts) constituted 6 percent of the cohort and 18 percent of the delinquents. They were responsible for: 62 percent of all offenses: 68 percent of the UCR Index offenses. About two-thirds of all violent offenses: 61 percent of homicides; 75 percent of rapes; 73 percent of robberies; 65 percent of aggravated assaults; 66 percent of the offenses that involved injuries. A 15-year followup of a 10-percent sample of the original Philadelphia birth cohort (Wolfgang, Thornberry, and Figlio, 1987) examined the cohort's police records through age 30. This study provided important information on the extent to which chronic juvenile offenders maintained their deviant careers through their early adult years. The study found that offenses increased in seriousness into adulthood, arrests declined steadily after age 18 (providing initial documentation of the 'maturation process'), and about one-quarter of the adults had no records as juveniles." (p37-38)

Wilson, John J./Howell, James C. (Office of Juvenile Justice and Delinquency Prevention). U.S. House. Committee on Education and Labor. "Hearing Regarding the...Report Entitled 'A...Strategy for Serious...Juvenile Offenders.'" Hearing, 28 Oct 1993. Washington, D.C.: GPO, 1994. (ISBN0160433983). (Y4.Ed8/1:103-34).

"According to statistics recently published by the U.S. Justice Department's office of juvenile justice and delinquency prevention, juvenile arrests for violent crimes increased by 50 percent--double the adult increase--between 1987 and 1991. Juvenile arrests for murder rose 85 percent, four times the increase for adults. By the end of that period, juvenile arrests for murder, forcible rape, robbery, and other violent crimes had reached an all-time high and accounted for 17 percent of all arrests for such crimes. The juvenile-justice also notes, however, that only 5 percent of juvenile arrests are for violent offenses, and a small proportion of juvenile offenders commit most of the violent and serious crime....As the National Center for Juvenile Justice points out, adults still commit more than 90 percent of homicides." (p26)

Schmidt, Peter. "Age of Reckoning." Education Week v13 n24, 9 Mar 1994. p24-27. (ISSN0277-4232).

JUVENILE DELINQUENTS

see also GANGS

JUVENILE DELINQUENTS--U.S.

"Between 1984 and 1990, the number of annual admissions of juveniles to adult prisons increased 30 percent [in the U.S.], from 9,078 to 11,782. Data from the 1987 National Correctional Reporting Program, which provided information on juvenile prison admissions for a sample of States, indicated that about 8 percent were convicted of murder or manslaughter, 40 percent were convicted of a personal offense (typically a robbery--18 percent); 48 percent were convicted for a property offense (more than half of those convicted for a property offense had burglary as their most serious commitment offense); and about 5 percent were sentenced to prison for a drug crime (OJJDP 1991, 1993)." (p35)

Wilson, John J./Howell, James C. (Office of Juvenile Justice and Delinquency Prevention). U.S. House. Committee on Education and Labor. "Hearing Regarding the...Report Entitled 'A...Strategy for Serious...Juvenile Offenders.'" Hearing, 28 Oct 1993. Washington, D.C.: GPO, 1994. (ISBN0160433983). (Y4.Ed8/1:103-34).

JUVENILE DETENTION HOMES--U.S.

"In a 1991 national study of conditions of confinement in juvenile detention and correctional facilities [in the U.S.] (Parent et al., 1993), institutional crowding was found to be a pervasive problem. Thousands of juvenile offenders, more than 75 percent of the confined population, were housed in facilities that violated one or more standards related to living space (facility design capacity, sleeping areas, and living unit size). Between 1987 and 1991, the percentage of confined juveniles living in facilities in which the daily population exceeded design capacity increased from 36 percent to 47 percent. Crowding was found to be associated with higher rates of institutional violence, suicidal behavior, and greater reliance on the use of short-term isolation. Sixty-five percent of all juvenile correctional administrators interviewed said their facilities had crowding problems." (p39)

Wilson, John J./Howell, James C. (Office of Juvenile Justice and Delinquency Prevention). U.S. House. Committee on Education and Labor. "Hearing Regarding the...Report Entitled 'A...Strategy for Serious...Juvenile Offenders.'" Hearing, 28 Oct 1993. Washington, D.C.: GPO, 1994. (ISBN0160433983). (Y4.Ed8/1:103-34).

"The number of admissions into public and private juvenile custody facilities [in the U.S.] has increased 19 percent over the past decade--from 638,309 to 760,644 facility admissions (Krisberg et al., 1992). In 1978 there were 2,220 juvenile facility admissions for every 100,000 juveniles in the population; by 1988 the admission rate had increased 34 percent to 2,974. The vast majority of admissions in 1988 were public facility admissions (81 percent), although private facilities experienced a greater increase from 1978 through 1988 in the number of admissions (104 percent compared with a 9-percent increase for public facilities). Detention center admissions accounted for 81 percent of public facility admissions in 1988 and, although the detention center proportion of admissions was relatively stable, there was an 11 percent increase from 1978 through 1988 in the number of admissions to detention centers. There was also a substantial increase in private detention center admissions (373 percent, from just under 2,000 to more than 9,000)." (p35)

Wilson, John J./Howell, James C. (Office of Juvenile Justice and Delinquency Prevention). U.S. House. Committee on Education and Labor. "Hearing Regarding the...Report Entitled 'A...Strategy for Serious...Juvenile Offenders.'" Hearing, 28 Oct 1993. Washington, D.C.: GPO, 1994. (ISBN0160433983). (Y4.Ed8/1:103-34).

JUVENILE HOMICIDE--U.S.

"In the United States, juvenile homicide has been increasing....between 1984 and 1989 the number of youths arrested for murder nationwide in the United States more than doubled from 1,004 to 2,208. One study showed that youths under eighteen years of age now make up about ten per cent of all homicide arrests in the United States." (p88) "A study of seventy-two teenagers who had been charged with murder between 1977 and 1985 showed that most had parents who had been divorced, about half had truanted from school and been expelled eventually and a number but by no means all, had multiple arrests for other offences committed. Most of the offenders were boys....Blacks constitute at least twenty per cent of Americans under eighteen...[but] accounted for more than fifty per cent of youths arrested for homicide crimes. Hispanic children make up eight per cent of the juvenile population but more than twenty-five per cent of the homicide arrests." (p89)

Lowenstein, L. F. "Why Children Kill." Contemporary Review v264 n1537, Feb 1994. p88-90. (ISSN0010-7565).

JUVENILE JUSTICE, ADMINISTRATION OF--GREAT BRITAIN--U.S. (v19)

JUVENILE JUSTICE, ADMINISTRATION OF--ILLINOIS (v19)

JUVENILE JUSTICE, ADMINISTRATION OF--U.S. (v19)

KANGAROOS

"Sales [of kangaroo] were slight for decades. But, of late, the 'roo trade has boomed, helped in part by an exception to the U.S. Endangered Species Act that ended a seven-year U.S. embargo on red and grey kangaroo products in 1981. Cullers aren't just killing 'roos to get them off farmers' fields. They're killing them because 'roo products make for big business. The 84,304 kangaroo skins the United States imported in 1990 is nearly triple the number imported in 1987. Domestic sales of meat are up, largely because laws in Australia have changed. The stringy, protein-rich flesh, once deemed too worm-infested for human consumption, is now served in all six of the country's states. International diners embrace kangaroo meat as a delicacy. In Denmark, for instance, one restaurant serves $36 plates of marinated kangaroo 'medallions.'" (p18)

Donahue, Bill. "Special Report: Kangaroos." Animals v127 n1, Jan-Feb 1994. p14-19. (ISSN0030-6835).

"Only rough estimates (based on aerial surveys) exist of the populations of the three most commercially exploited roos: the red, eastern grey and western grey. Conservation groups consider the U.S. Fish and Wildlife Service's (USFWS) figure of 18 million an overestimate. Meanwhile, 1992's legal kill quota for these three species totals 5.2 million, and the illegal kill is undetermined. The Humane Society of the United States (HSUS) estimates that, in the past, the illegal kill was greater than the legal kill. Australia sets its quota based on market demand for the leather say kangaroo advocates, rather than on biologically sound wildlife management principles. In 1992, Australia underwent the second most severe drought in its history, notes [Marian] Newman, and there was a huge, natural die-off of kangaroos. Yet the kill quota was the highest ever." (p14)

Couturier, Lisa. "Currents: The Low Down Under." E Magazine v4 n1, Feb 1993. p14-15. (ISSN1046-8021).

KANGAROOS--AUSTRALIA (v19)

"Extensive logging of Queensland's rainforests has threatened the long-term survival of both Lumholtz's and Bennett's tree kangaroos. In just 200 years, 75 percent of Australia's rainforests have been cleared, resulting in a patchwork of separate habitats that could fit into a circle barely 93 miles wide. Small, isolated populations are more susceptible to the long-term effects of inbreeding, including lowered disease resistance. Fragmented forest habitats, therefore, increase the vulnerability of many species to extinction. Fortunately, the rainforests of Australia are now listed and protected as World Heritage Land." (p10)

Hutchins, Michael/Sleeper, Barbara. "Out on a Limb." Animals v126 n6, Nov-Dec 1993. p8-10. (ISSN0030-6835).

KAZAKHSTAN

see ETHNOLOGY--KAZAKHSTAN

KENAF

"The fast-growing kenaf (rhymes with 'giraffe') plant originated in Africa. A member of the hibiscus family, kenaf is related to cotton and is similar in appearance to sugar cane or bamboo. Starting from seed, a kenaf plant can reach a height of 14 feet in five months. In US Department of Agriculture (USDA) field trials, kenaf was found to produce 6-10 tons of raw fiber per acre--three to five times more tons per acre per year than southern white pine. While chemically intensive wood-pulp paper processing only recovers 50 percent of the weight in fiber of the original timber, a mill processing kenaf can recover 90 percent of the original weight. According to the USDA, existing paper mills can be easily adapted to produce kenaf paper." (p19)

Smith, Gar. "JOURNAL Pioneers Tree-Free Paper." Earth Island Journal v8 n3, Sum 1993. p19. (ISSN1041-0406).

KENTUCKY--COMMERCE--MEXICO (v19)

KENYA

see also AIDS (DISEASE)--KENYA; EDUCATION--KENYA; FERTILITY, HUMAN--KENYA; SCHOOLS--KENYA; URBANIZATION--KENYA

KENYA--ECONOMIC CONDITIONS (v19)

KENYA--SOCIAL CONDITIONS

"Kenya has a relatively low life expectancy (58 years), high IMR [infant mortality rate] (69), low GNP [gross national product] per capita ($370), and high fertility (a TFR [total fertility rate] of 6.8), even after the relatively recent drop in the rate of more than one child per woman. Adult literacy increased from 20 percent in 1960 to 69 percent in 1990, and the gross enrollment ratio in primary plus secondary schools increased from 29 percent to 72 percent during the same period. Kenya has greatly strengthened its family planning program, and contraceptive prevalence increased by 20 percentage points from 1977-78 to 1988-89, a relatively high average of 1.8 points of increase a year." (p87)

Mauldin, W. Parker/Ross, John A. "Prospects and Programs for Fertility Reduction, 1990-2015." Studies in Family Planning v25 n2, Mar-Apr 1994. p77-95. (ISSN0039-3665).

KIDNAPPING

see ABDUCTION

KIDNAPPING--U.S. (v19)

KIDNAPPING, PARENTAL

"Each year hundreds of American children are kidnaped by a parent and held hostage overseas. As a result, the child's other parent is left to face the trauma of losing a son or daughter, with little recourse under the law to regain custody or even have contact with the child. Thousands of families have been torn apart in this manner. Since 1973 there have been nearly 4,000 reported cases of international child abduction, with more than 600 cases in 1992 alone." (pS16865)

Riegle, Donald W., Jr. (Sen.-Mich.). "International Parental Kidnaping," Congressional Record (20 Nov 1993). Daily ed. pS16865. (ISSN0363-7239).

KIDNAPPING, PARENTAL--U.S.

"More than 300 children are taken to live in foreign countries each year by a parent that does not have legal custody of the child. The State Department has recorded over 2,800 of these cases since 1975, but many experts believe that this figure is low. The actual number of cases may be closer to 10,000. The rate at which such kidnapings are increasing also provides cause for action. Since May 1983, the number of cases known to the State Department has jumped 84 percent." (pH10313)

Sensenbrenner, F. James, Jr. (Rep.-Wis.). "International Parental Kidnaping Crime Act of 1993," Congressional Record (20 Nov 1993). Daily ed. pH10312-10314. (ISSN0363-7239).

KIDNEYS--DISEASES--U.S.--TREATMENT

"About 170,000 Americans receive dialysis because of hereditary disorders or complications of diabetes, high blood pressure or other diseases. A study in the Sept. 30, 1993, NEW ENGLAND JOURNAL OF MEDICINE found that 55 percent of 13,473 patients studied were getting inadequate dialysis, increasing the risk of death by 28 percent. Studies show that the average dose of dialysis prescribed is less than the minimum standard and that the dose delivered is even less....Only about 2 percent of American dialysis patients spend more than 12 hours a week on dialysis, compared with 80 percent of Japanese patients and 77 percent of Western European patients. A unit in Lyon, France, dialyzes patients 22 to 24 hours a week--and has the best survival statistics in the world. Among industrialized nations, by contrast, America's dialysis patients fare the worst. A study in the May 1990 AMERICAN JOURNAL OF KIDNEY DISEASES found that after adjusting for age and medical problems the five-year mortality rate for dialysis patients in the United States was 15 percent higher than in Japan." (p58-59)

Brink, Susan. "Health: Dialysis by the Numbers." U.S. News & World Report v116 n6, 14 Feb 1994. p58-59. (ISSN0041-5537).

KIRGIZSTAN--ECONOMIC CONDITIONS

"After the collapse of the Soviet Union, each of the newly formed states made an effort to accomplish economic reforms on its own. Many trading ties that existed for decades disappeared. Of course, those ties were part of the Soviet government's central planning system, which aimed to eliminate all independence in the regions and bring any action under Moscow's authority. This strictly centralized system ruined the communist regime and had to be discarded. However, its abrupt dismantling has caused great difficulties for all the newly created countries. It's been especially hard for a small state like Kirgizstan, which was almost completely dependent on the other states. The machine-building complex in Kirgizstan was closely connected to Russia and Ukraine, for instance. The results of three years of reforms in the economy are not encouraging. Today, more than 100 large industrial enterprises either don't operate an entire day or have a shortened work week. One out of three industrial workers has lost his job. Close to 70 percent of the republic's population lives below the poverty line--and this includes many of those who used to be well-to-do. The average income of retirees is 20m soms per month, but the average cost of living is 68 soms per month." (p54)

Andreev, Nikolai. "Kirgizstan: Grappling with Democracy." Bulletin of the Atomic Scientists v50 n1, Jan-Feb 1994. p52-55. (ISSN0096-3402).

KIRGIZSTAN--SOCIAL CONDITIONS

An "issue of great concern is that people of non-Kirgiz nationality are leaving the republic. More than 100,000 have left Kirgizstan already; 70,000 of them went to Russia. Out of 109,000 Germans, only 70,000 are left, and every second person, it seems, plans to leave the republic. It is tragic that those who leave are the ones most needed in the local economy because of their scarcity: experts, professionals, and intellectuals....Yet another danger to peace in Central Asia, particularly Kirgizstan, is Islamic fundamentalism. The West fears that southern regions of the former Soviet Union will end up in the embrace of Islam....Local Muslim leaders have come up with the slogan, 'A mosque for every village.' They are building them, despite everything. Kirgizstan has suffered great destruction as a result of earthquakes in 1992; losses amount to 14 billion rubles. Schools are not being rebuilt, homes are not being rebuilt--but mosques are being constructed. Organizers manage to find everything necessary: money, building materials, and laborers." (p55)

Andreev, Nikolai. "Kirgizstan: Grappling with Democracy." Bulletin of the Atomic Scientists v50 n1, Jan-Feb 1994. p52-55. (ISSN0096-3402).

KOLA PENINSULA (RUSSIA)

see also EDUCATION--KOLA PENINSULA (RUSSIA)

KOLA PENINSULA (RUSSIA)--EMPLOYMENT

"About 730 000 people were employed in the Kola region [in northern Russia] in 1990, of which 75% (548 000) were engaged in the national economy....The number of workers increased as the economy developed. From 1960 to 1990 the level increased 1.9 times, reaching 468 400 by 1991. As the Kola Peninsula is industrially developed, the greatest number of workers and employees have been engaged in material production: 334 600 people, or 71.4%. Of this total, 32.5% (152 200 people), are engaged in industry, 12.2% (57 200) in construction, and 9.7% (45 600) in transport. About 133 800 people, or 28.6%, are engaged in the tertiary sector (OYSMO, 1992)...." (p8-9)

Luzin, Gennady P./others. "The Kola Peninsula: Geography, History and Resources." Arctic v47 n1, Mar 1994. p1-15. (ISSN0004-0843).

KOLA PENINSULA (RUSSIA)--POPULATION

"The Kola Peninsula is the most densely populated part of the Russian North and contains 66% of the population of the Russian Arctic. In 1992 the population density in the Kola Peninsula was 7.9 people-km, which exceeded the other polar areas of the country by 30-50 times (OYSMO, 1992). There are more than 200 settlements in the region, with 92% of the population living in 12 cities and 42% in the administrative centre of Murmansk, which has a population of almost a half million (472 900)....Three cities, Apatity, Severomorsk, and Monchegorsk, have a population between 60 000 and 90 000, and the others have fewer than 60 000 people...." (p8)

Luzin, Gennady P./others. "The Kola Peninsula: Geography, History and Resources." Arctic v47 n1, Mar 1994. p1-15. (ISSN0004-0843).

KOREA (NORTH)--ECONOMIC CONDITIONS

"Because North Korea is the world's most insular economy, the few connections it does have with the world outside assume disproportionate importance. Industry is already working at only 30-50% capacity and food is short. Between them, China, Japan and Russia account for over two-thirds of North Korea's trade. China supplies oil. Russia provides coal. Japan is the single biggest source of hard currency through the $600m-1 billion that is sent home each year by Koreans in Japan. If these three countries started to squeeze, North Korea would soon feel the pinch. Even South Korea, which officially frowns on business contacts, helps subsidise North Korea by allowing it to run a big deficit in direct and indirect trade." (p16)

"Leaders: One Raspberry Too Many." Economist v330 n7856, 26 Mar 1994. p16. (ISSN0013-0613).

"The CIA's 1978 assessment was that, as of early 1976, the North Korean economy was out-producing the South in per capita terms in almost every sector. Even the official Seoul figures concede that per capita GNP [gross national product] in the North was greater than that in the South up until 1975. The planned growth rates for the 1980s, if achieved, would have put North Korea's industrial output by 1990 on a par with that of the advanced countries of Western Europe and Japan at the end of the 1970s....There were no wholly reliable statistics, but the best estimates (from the JETRO [or Japan External Trade Organization] analysts) were that industrial output might have grown at an average of about 6.3 per cent between 1985 and 1990,... although crucial sectors like electric power were in 1988 still below what had been claimed for them in 1984, and wastage was thought to be at a high level. No increase had even been claimed in agricultural output since 1984. However the growth rate for the economy seems to have dropped from around two per cent in 1989 to minus 3.7 per cent in 1990 and minus 5.2 per cent in 1991, making those the worst years since 1953. Although the official target for the third Seven-Year Plan (1987-93) was for an average annual growth rate of ten per cent, there was serious trouble in most sectors of the economy." (p33-34)

McCormack, Gavan. "Kim Country: Hard Times in North Korea." New Left Review n198, Mar-Apr 1993. p21-48. (ISSN0028-6060).

KOREA (SOUTH)

see also CORPORATIONS--KOREA (SOUTH)--FINANCE;GOVERNMENT SPENDING POLICY--KOREA (SOUTH); INDUSTRIALIZATION--KOREA (SOUTH)--TAIWAN; SEX OF CHILDREN, PARENTAL PREFERENCES FOR--KOREA (SOUTH); STOCK-EXCHANGE--KOREA (SOUTH); TRADE-UNIONS--KOREA (SOUTH)

KOREA (SOUTH)--ECONOMIC CONDITIONS (v19)

"Many economists see the economy [in South Korea] growing by 6% to 7% this year, up from last year's 4.7%--a level that many Koreans consider disastrous. The steam is coming from capital investment and exports, which rose 7.6% last year and should grow 8% again this year. The strong yen and productivity improvement are making Korean ships, semiconductors, and autos attractive enough for the country to run its first current account surplus in several years." (p51)

Neff, Robert/Nakarmi, Laxmi. "International Outlook: South Korea: An Unexpected Ally for Business." Business Week n3358, 14 Feb 1994. p51. (ISSN0007-7135).

"Even during the recession raw growth rates in South Korea have not looked too terrible by rich-world standards: 5% in 1992 and 5.6% last year. But in a country that invests more than 35% of nominal GDP [gross domestic product] in upgrading and expanding capacity, anything less than 5-6% growth is likely to cause problems. The number of jobless jumped from 2.3% of the workforce in 1991 to 3.2% in early 1993, which hurts when there are no unemployment benefits....Interest rates are at a record low, inflation is a manageable 6.8%, and private capital spending jumped up so sharply in the first quarter of 1994 that some of Korea's ever-cautious bureaucrats are starting to talk about overheating. The country is back to more or less full employment and labourers from Pakistan and the Philippines are sneaking into the country to do the tough and dirty jobs that most Koreans refuse." (p36)

"Asia: South Korea: Not That Sort of Girl." Economist v331 n7860, 23 Apr 1994. p35-36. (ISSN0013-0613).

"Korean real GNP [gross national product] growth slowed to about 4.2 percent in 1993, a sharp drop from growth rates of 8.4-9.3 percent in 1990-1991. The recent slowdown in economic growth and related government policy dampened demand for some high-value agricultural products, but this is generally seen as a short-term reversal. The 5-year economic plan approved this summer is expected to gradually introduce interest rate cuts and business deregulation that will spur growth. The government is also boosting infrastructure spending and lowering income and corporate taxes to aid the recovery in 1994." (p13)

U.S. Dept. of Agriculture. "Regional Highlights: South Korea." Outlook for U.S. Agricultural Exports 30 Nov 1993. p13-14.

KOSOVO

see EDUCATION--KOSOVO; INCOME--KOSOVO--SERBIA--

SLOVENIA

KURDS

see also ECONOMIC ASSISTANCE, AMERICAN--KURDS

KURDS--TURKEY

"Since modern Turkey's establishment in 1923, Kurds, who presently comprise about 11 million of Turkey's 57 million population, have faced varying pressure to deny their cultural distinctiveness. While Moslem, they maintain distinct language and cultural forms. Through expressions of their Kurdish identity, civil disobedience, or at the extreme, open rebellion, Kurds have sought to promote and preserve their culture and rights. Since 1987, eight provinces where Kurds reside have withered under a state of emergency which authorizes a regional governor and the military to curb political, media and cultural activity....The violent prelude to upcoming local elections has highlighted threats to the democratic process and underlined the inability of Kurds to gain political representation or exercise other basic rights. In the past 2 years, shadowy death squads have killed 70 members of the pro-Kurdish Democratic Party (DEP), which holds 18 of 450 seats in the Turkish Parliament, including a Member of Parliament. Twenty party offices have been bombed. Over 300 DEP election candidates have been arrested and changes in electoral laws--reportedly made on security grounds--have made it extremely difficult for voters in Kurdish regions to cast their ballots." (pS2231)

DeConcini, Dennis (Sen.-Ariz.). "Turkish Democracy Imperiled," Congressional Record (2 Mar 1994). Daily ed. pS2231-2232. (ISSN0363-7239).

KUWAIT

see IRAQ-KUWAIT CRISIS, 1990-1991--ENVIRONMENTAL ASPECTS; MINES (MILITARY EXPLOSIVES)--CAMBODIA--KUWAIT--MOZAMBIQUE

KYRGYZSTAN

see AGRICULTURE--KYRGYZSTAN

LABOR, FORCED

see FORCED LABOR

LABOR COSTS (v19)

see also EMPLOYEE FRINGE BENEFITS; WAGES

LABOR COSTS--BELGIUM (v19)

LABOR COSTS--GERMANY (v19)

"German unions' past success has come at the cost of firms' competitiveness: average labour costs per unit of output are now around 25% higher than in other big rich economies, while in the early 1980s they were around 10% lower than the average. Not only are pay-packets fat; non-wage benefits such as sick pay and social-security taxes add another 80% on top of wages. The awkward truth now is that, in order to restore competitiveness to German industry--and to bring German unemployment back below its current, horrendous level of 4m--real labour costs must be cut sharply....Total unemployment in Germany now stands at nearly 12% of the labour force." (p15)

"Leaders: Metall Bashing." Economist v330 n7851, 19 Feb 1994. p15-16. (ISSN0013-0613).

LABOR COSTS--U.S. (v19)

LABOR PRODUCTIVITY--GERMANY--JAPAN--U.S. (v19)

LABOR PRODUCTIVITY--MEXICO (v19)

LABOR SUPPLY

see also UNEMPLOYMENT

"Greater economic integration throughout both the developed and developing regions can help the world grapple with the unbalanced distribution of the growing world labor force. In the mid-1990s, over 75 percent of the world's labor force resides in the developing world where the working-age population is younger, less experienced, and less educated than in the more developed regions. Because of their higher fertility--and therefore higher population growth rates--over 90 percent of the increase in the world's labor force in the next quarter century will occur in areas where both human and physical capital are relatively scarce. The developing-country share of the world labor force will increase to 83 percent by 2025." (p2)

Bloom, David E./Brender, Adi. "Labor and the Emerging World Economy." Population Bulletin v48 n2, Oct 1993. p2-39. (ISSN0032-468X).

LABOR SUPPLY--AFRICA--WOMEN

"Women are the linchpin of Africa's national economies. In Mali, for example, a UNICEF study found that women spend more than 15 hours a day doing physical labour. In Zimbabwe, according to a recent Ministry of Energy/Swedish Beijer Institute survey, women and children perform 73 per cent of farm labour, 62 per cent of livestock care, 81 per cent of fuel-gathering and chopping, and 96 per cent of routine domestic tasks. It is the combination of farm work and domestic tasks that tips the balance of African labour so heavily onto the backs of women. This arrangement is not only burdensome for women, but also involves a wasteful, inefficient use of one of Africa's most valuable resources--women's work. Such inefficiency hampers productivity and is a deterrent to development. Experts, such as economist Ingrid Palmer in a recent International Labour Organization (ILO) report, point out that Africa can no longer afford to squander the energies, time, talents and health of half its population on inefficient, time-consuming menial labour." (p17-18)

Morna, Colleen Lowe/others. "Women's Work: Africa's Precious Resource." African Farmer n7, Sep 1992. p16-27.

LABOR SUPPLY--AGED

"The world labor force is becoming older because of both accounting and behavioral changes. The average age of the world labor force remained at about age 34 between 1950 and 1990, reflecting the counter-balancing effects of a small increase in the average age of the labor force in the developed economies and a slight decrease in the developing countries. In 1990, the average age of the labor force for all developed countries was about four years older than that in developing countries. But the average labor force age will begin a slow ascent in developing countries as we enter the 21st century because of slower population growth and increased life expectancy. Between 1990 and 2025, the average age of the labor force is expected to increase from 37 to 38 years in developed countries and from 33 to 36 years in developing countries." (p6-7)

Bloom, David E./Brender, Adi. "Labor and the Emerging World Economy." Population Bulletin v48 n2, Oct 1993. p2-39. (ISSN0032-468X).

LABOR SUPPLY--ASIA--LATIN AMERICA (v19)

LABOR SUPPLY--DEVELOPING COUNTRIES (v19)

LABOR SUPPLY--EGYPT--FRANCE

"The labor forces of Egypt and France, two countries of similar population size, illustrate both the demographic 'accounting' effects of population structure as well as behavioral effects on the labor force. Two-thirds of France's 1986 population were between 15 and 65 years of age, compared with just over one-half of Egypt's 1986 population. Not surprisingly, France's labor force was larger--24 million compared with 13 million in Egypt. In addition to the large age-structure differences, the labor force behavior is very different in the two countries....The most obvious difference is the low propensity of Egyptian women to work outside the home. Only 6 percent of Egyptian women were counted in the formal labor force in 1986, compared with 36 percent of French women in that same year. Egypt's low female labor force participation compounds the effects of the young age structure, widening the gap in labor force size." (p10-11)

Bloom, David E./Brender, Adi. "Labor and the Emerging World Economy." Population Bulletin v48 n2, Oct 1993. p2-39.

(ISSN0032-468X).

LABOR SUPPLY--SOUTH AFRICA (v19)

LABOR SUPPLY--U.S. (v19)

"More American companies are turning to telecommuting to solve some very tough problems. Some are driven by the need to shrink real estate budgets. Others want to comply with new laws such as the Americans with Disabilities Act. And employers are using telecommuting as a way to meet worker demands for a better balance between work and family. Already, 7.5 million workers, or 6% of the U.S. labor force, spend at least a few days a month at home working for their companies during business hours, says researcher Link Resources Corp....About one-third of them are contract workers. But the biggest addition to the total has been among salaried employees. In this group, the stay-at-home population has grown 21.5% to 5.1 million, in the past year." (p46D)

Armstrong, Larry/Tilsner, Julie. "Top of the News: Corporate Strategies: 'The Office Is a Terrible Place to Work'." Business Week n3352, 27 Dec 1993. p46D. (ISSN0007-7135).

LABOR SUPPLY--U.S.--WOMEN (v19)

LABOR SUPPLY--VIETNAM

"Foreign investors are looking at Vietnam with ever increasing interest. The country's labor force is not only extremely inexpensive--per capita income in 1992 was about $200--it is well-educated (at 88%, the literacy rate is significantly higher than other developing countries'); and its population is growing--with a birth rate of about 2%, the population is expected to exceed 100 million in 2010." (p3)

Tsuboi, Yoshiharu. "Japanese Perspective: Vietnam: Plan for Vietnam." Look Japan v39 n456, Mar 1994. p3. (ISSN0456-5339).

LABOR SUPPLY--WOMEN

"The surge in female labor force participation in the industrial world has been a defining feature of the latter half of the 20th century. In the United States, the percentage of women over age 15 in the labor force grew from 34 to 57 percent between 1950 and 1991. On average, about 41 percent of women of all ages in industrial countries were engaged in economic activities in 1990, and the percentage was over 30 in all but a handful of industrial countries." (p8)

Bloom, David E./Brender, Adi. "Labor and the Emerging World Economy." Population Bulletin v48 n2, Oct 1993. p2-39. (ISSN0032-468X).

LABORERS

see BLUE COLLAR WORKERS; EMPLOYEES

LAKES--MAINE (v19)

LAMB MEAT INDUSTRY--U.S. (v19)

LAND TENURE--ALASKA (v19)

LAND TENURE--CHINA (v19)

LAND TENURE--SOUTH AFRICA

"During four decades of apartheid, some 3.5 million black South Africans were evicted from their homes or dispossessed of land under an experiment in social engineering that sought to relegate blacks to independent but impoverished tribal homelands. The evictions left whites in control of 87 percent of the land." (p6)

Battersby, John. "International: Mfengu Land Settlement Sets Precedent in South Africa." The Christian Science Monitor v86 n88, 31 Mar 1994. p6. (ISSN0882-7729).

LAND TENURE--U.S. (v19)

"More than 800,000 people belong to the 1,000 land trusts nationwide [in the U.S.], according to the Land Trust Alliance, a national organization that serves as a clearinghouse for land trust information." (p25) "More than 50 land trusts a year are created across America. 'It's just amazing,' Hocker said. 'We don't see any slowdown in the formation of land trusts. For example, they're growing now in other sections of the country--in the Southeast and increasingly in the Midwest.' Wisconsin, for example, held a meeting in September 1992 that attracted close to 25 land trusts." (p26)

Merriman, Kristin. "Land Trusts." Outdoor America v58 n1, Win 1993. p25-27.

"Of the 833 million acres of private farmland [in the U.S.], 40 percent is held by owners or organizations who do not themselves operate farms. Moreover, in 1992 farms with sales in excess of $100,000 controlled 54 percent of all U.S. land in farms, even though they constituted but 16.4 percent of the total number of farms. No matter how the numbers are cut, medium-size farms continue to fall to the economic power concentrated in the nation's corporatized food sector, bearing out the mid-'80s prediction by the Office of Technology Assessment that by the turn of the century, 75 percent of the nation's food will be produced by 50,000 'super farms.'" (p9)

Ostendorf, David. "Focal Point: Those Who Control the Land Control People." Prairie Journal v4 n2, Sum 1993. p8-9.

LAND USE (v19)

see also PUBLIC LANDS

LAND USE--ETHIOPIA (v19)

LAND USE--GREAT BRITAIN (v19)

LAND USE--KAZAKHSTAN (v19)

LAND USE--MICHIGAN

"Urban sprawl, as it is referred to by planners, is the increased use of rural areas near cities to build new industrial plants, shopping malls and new residential subdivisions.... According to a story in...[the] ANN ARBOR NEWS, the population in Southeast Michigan will increase by 6 percent over the next 16 years. Unless policies change, that population will consume about 40 percent of land that is now rural....And it is not just Southeast Michigan that is threatened. Cherry orchards near Traverse City and farmland from Kalamazoo to Grand Rapids is also endangered. In fact, the U.S. Department of Agriculture says Michigan has lost 5 million acres of farmland since 1960." (p8 secA)

"Land Use." Ann Arbor News 8 Feb 1994. p8 secA.

LAND USE--NAMIBIA

In Namibia "some 74 per cent of the best arable land is owned by some 4,000 white farmers, using an average 8,600 hectares each, mainly for lucrative livestock production exported to South Africa and the European Community. Over 120,000 black households share an average of 200 hectares each on the remaining farmland, for subsistence farming and livestock. Most of them live below the poverty line on overcrowded, communal lands scarred by overgrazing, desertification and drought." (p9)

Bellando, Eddi. "Namibia Confronts the Land Question." Africa Recovery v7 n2, Oct 1993. p9,26.

LAND USE--U.S. (v19)

LAND USE--ZAMBIA (v19)

LANDFILLS

see FILLS (EARTHWORK)

LANGUAGE AND LANGUAGES

see also BILINGUALISM

LANGUAGE AND LANGUAGES--LOUISIANA

"State language experts estimate that less than 5 percent of the more than 1.1 million Cajuns in Louisiana speak French as their first language, down from 90 percent-plus 60 years ago." (p7)

Boulard, Garry. "Windows on America: Louisiana Cajuns Celebrate Bid to Promote Their Culture." The Christian Science Monitor v86 n23, 28 Dec 1993. p7. (ISSN0882-7729).

LANGUAGE AND LANGUAGES--MALAYSIA

"Unemployment [in Malaysia] is 3.3%, the lowest on record, and industry is crying out for English-speaking graduates who can cope with foreign investors and international trade. Local universities do not seem to be producing the goods. Mohamed Ariff, dean of economics at University of Malaya, reckons that nine out of ten of local university students are unable to string an English sentence together correctly. Malaysia's university system discriminates in favour of the Malays by reserving a majority of places for them, at the expense of Chinese. But, if Mr Ariff is correct, they do not learn good English. Many Chinese do, by studying at private colleges; and a third of Malaysian students are educated at foreign universities, at a cost of $1 billion a year, 40% of which is paid by the government in scholarships, most of which go to Malays." (p37)

"Asia: Malaysia: The Language of Progress." Economist v330 n7846, 15 Jan 1994. p37-38. (ISSN0013-0613).

LANGUAGE AND LANGUAGES--PAPUA NEW GUINEA

"Language is...[a] problem in Papua New Guinea where 75% of the Pacific's first peoples live. There are 860 languages spoken by Papua New Guinea's 3 million tribal peoples. In 1976, a tribe was discovered which was unaware of the existence of other tribes." (p6)

McKenna, Neil. "Briefing: A Disaster Waiting to Happen: Papua New Guinea." WorldAIDS n27, May 1993. p5-9. (ISSN0954-6510).

LANGUAGE AND LANGUAGES--STUDY AND TEACHING--U.S. (v19)

LANGUAGE AND LANGUAGES--STUDY AND TEACHING--U.S.--PUBLIC OPINION

"A 1985 poll in Dade County, FL, revealed that 98 percent of Dade County Hispanic parents agreed that it was essential for their children to speak and write English perfectly--versus 94 percent of the Anglo parents....Thomas Sowell, in his book 'Inside American Education,' cited numerous surveys proving that the great majority of Hispanic parents--more than three-fourths of Mexican-American parents and more than 80 percent of Cuban-American parents--are opposed to the teaching of Spanish in the schools at the expense of English." (pH1714)

Taylor, Gene (Rep.-Miss.). "Improving America's Schools Act of 1994," Congressional Record (21 Mar 1994). Daily ed. pH1684-1725. (ISSN0363-7239).

LANGUAGE AND LANGUAGES--SUDAN

"Sudan, Africa's largest country, stretches from the Sahara desert in the north to rich agricultural areas in the south. The vast country is linked together by the White and Blue Nile rivers which meet at the capital Khartoum on their northward path to Egypt. Four times the size of Texas, Sudan encompasses dozens of ethnic groups and hundreds of distinct tribes speaking over a hundred different languages, making Sudan a microcosm of the African continent. The 18 million people who live in the northern part of Sudan are predominantly Arabic-speaking Muslims with ethnic roots traceable to North Africa and the Middle East. The six million people of the south, in general, share a distinctly African heritage, speak mostly tribal languages and English, and practice mainly tribal religions or Christianity. Yet, non-Arab ethnic groups such as the Nuba people and the Fur tribe live in the northern region as do animists and Christians, while many ethnically African Sudanese practice Islam in both the north and south." (p10)

Buchanan, Rob. "Hidden Wars: Sudan." Nonviolent Activist v10 n2, Mar-Apr 1993. p10-13. (ISSN8755-7428).

LAOS--ECONOMIC CONDITIONS (v19)

LAS VEGAS (NEV)--POPULATION (v19)

"The Las Vegas metropolitan area has experienced phenomenal growth for the last 12 years. Between 1980 and 1992, population has increased by over one-third. During 1989, it was estimated that over 6,000 persons moved to Las Vegas each month. By 1993, the rate had 'slowed' to 3,500 persons per month. Forecasts prepared for the region indicate that by the year 2000, well over 1.0 million persons will reside in the Las Vegas Valley. As the 'entertainment capital of the world,' Las Vegas welcomed over 20 million visitors in 1992. With over 86,000 rooms available, Las Vegas is a world class destination resort that affords a wide variety of recreational opportunities and unparalleled convention and meeting facilities. On any given day, the actual population of Las Vegas, defined as residents and tourists, exceeds 1.5 million persons." (p2081)

Gibson, Lee (Planning Coordinator, Regional Transportation Commission). U.S. House. Committee on Appropriations. "Department of Transportation and Related Agencies Approp. for 1994 (Part 7B)." Hearing, Washington, D.C.: GPO, 1993. (ISBN0160411041). (Y4.Ap6/1:T68/4/994/pt.7B).

LATCHKEY CHILDREN--U.S.

"No one knows how many American children become tiny guardians for younger brothers and sisters while parents are at work. Estimates of latchkey children range from 2 million to 15 million, or from 7 to 45 percent of all elementary school kids. A national survey in 1990 by the U.S. Department of Education found that 44 percent of 5-to-12-year-olds whose mothers were employed had no care arrangements at all. WEEKLY READER, a children's publication, asked sixth graders about their after-school situations. Of 30,000 12-year-olds, half were home alone and almost 7,000 more were home with a sibling." (p26)

Creighton, Linda L. "U.S. News: Kids Taking Care of Kids." U.S. News & World Report v115 n24, 20 Dec 1993. p26-27,30-33. (ISSN0041-5537).

LATIN AMERICA

see also CARIBBEAN AREA--LATIN AMERICA--ECONOMIC CONDITIONS; CHAGAS' DISEASE--LATIN AMERICA; CHOLERA--AFRICA--LATIN AMERICA; DEBT--AFRICA--LATIN AMERICA; DEBTS, EXTERNAL--AFRICA--LATIN AMERICA; FERTILITY, HUMAN--LATIN AMERICA; FOOD INDUSTRY AND TRADE--LATIN AMERICA--U.S.; INFLATION (FINANCE)--CARIBBEAN AREA--LATIN AMERICA; INFLATION (FINANCE)--LATIN AMERICA; INVESTMENTS, FOREIGN--LATIN AMERICA; LOANS--LATIN AMERICA

LATIN AMERICA--ECONOMIC CONDITIONS (v19)

"In Mexico and the other nations of Latin America,...high interest rates, capital flight, recession, and low commodity prices--combined to form a vicious cycle of debt, deficits, devaluations, and negative growth rates from which they have yet to escape. By 1982, an estimated $93 billion, much of it money controlled by multinational corporations operating in Latin America, had been moved from the region--$36 billion from Mexico alone. Since then, total capital flight has risen to more than $400 billion, $50 billion of it from Mexico. Between 1981 and 1988, total debt for the region increased by about 40 percent, and the net transfer of capital (via interest payments) reached a level of 4.1 percent of the gross domestic product per annum. By way of comparisons, the punitive net transfer of capital forced upon Germany after World War I by the 1919 Treaty of Versailles was only 2.5 percent of the GDP [gross domestic product]." (p4)

Burke, Melvin. "The Human Costs of NAFTA." Humanist v53 n5, Sep-Oct 1993. p3-9. (ISSN0018-7399).

"The 1990s continue to be Latin America's 'found decade' as the countries of the region in 1993 posted the third straight year of positive economic growth after the 'lost decade' of the 1980s. The region last year achieved a 3.3 percent increase in its gross domestic product, according to IDB's '1993 Annual Report.' This compares with 2.9 GDP [gross domestic product] in 1992....Brazil last year rebounded from a 1 percent decline in GDP in 1992 to a healthy 4 percent increase as a result of rapidly expanding exports and more consumer spending....In 1993, 12 countries grew at rates of 3-5 percent, and eight grew at rates of 0-3 percent....Among the region's seven largest countries, which account for more than 95 percent of regional output, only Mexico and Venezuela had rates of growth below 2 percent in 1993." (p4)

"The Region: Growth: Latin America's 'Found Decade.'" IDB v21 n3, Mar 1994. p4-5.

LAUNDRY--U.S.

"Commercials almost never show men doing the laundry, but nearly one-fifth of men do at lest seven loads a week. Men don't do as much laundry as women, but the washday gap may be closing. In the dual-career 1990s, laundry is going unisex. Forty-three percent of women wash at least seven loads of laundry a week, compared with 19 percent of men, according to a survey conducted for Lever Brothers Company, manufacturers of Wisk detergent. Men do 29 percent of the 419 million loads of laundry Americans wash each week." (p13-14)

Sandor, Gabrielle. "Business Reports: Markets: Attention Advertisers: Real Men Do Laundry." American Demographics v16 n3, Mar 1994. p13-14. (ISSN0163-4089).

LAUNDRY--U.S.--PUBLIC OPINION

A "Lever Brothers survey found that 79 percent of wives trust themselves most to do the laundry. Only 7 percent trust their spouses the most, followed by 6 percent who trust their mothers, and 3 percent who trust their adult children." (p14)

Sandor, Gabrielle. "Business Reports: Markets: Attention Advertisers: Real Men Do Laundry." American Demographics v16 n3, Mar 1994. p13-14. (ISSN0163-4089).

LAW--CHINA (v19)

LAW ENFORCEMENT--U.S. (v19)

"If this country continues to send people to jail at the present rate, half the population will be behind bars by the year 2053....Are we going to solve all of our social problems by locking up millions of people without ever addressing what causes these problems in the first place? That's what the U.S. Senate did Nov. 19, stuffing 22 billion taxpayer dollars into the pockets of the fastest growing industry in America--the prisons. What sense does it make to spend $22 billion on more prisons and cops and not spend one cent on the root causes of crime?" (p2)

"Editorial: The Crime Bill: Answering Poverty with Jails." People's Tribune v20 n49, 6 Dec 1993. p2.

LAW ENFORCEMENT--U.S.--COSTS (v19)

LAW FIRMS--U.S. (v19)

LAWNS--U.S.

"Lawns are so popular that they have become big business and are represented in Congress by their own lobbying groups and industry associations. The number of people involved in lawn and turfgrass care is mindboggling: an estimated 56 million Americans take some part in caring for their own lawns, according to National Gardening Association. For many of them, maintaining a lawn is the only intimate contact they have with the earth. Turfgrass is a $25 billion industry in the United States employing more than 500,000 people. And sale of lawncare items alone is a $4 billion dollar industry, according to Eliot and Beverly Roberts at the Lawn Institute in Pleasant Hill, Tennessee." (p16)

Lerner, Steve. "People: Suburban Wilderness." Amicus Journal v16 n1, Spr 1994. p14-17. (ISSN0276-7201).

LAWNS--U.S.--ENVIRONMENTAL ASPECTS

"In the United States, 25 to 30 million acres of lawns are cut about every 11 days during the growing season (Skow, 1991; HortIdeas, 1993). According to a recent EPA study, the amount of pollution emitted by a lawn mower in one hour is equivalent to that of a car driven 50 miles (HortIdeas, 1993). We can reclaim some of that free time and lessen our contribution to environmental problems by decreasing lawn size and trimming needs. A lawn that has a simple flowing shape and no internal obstacles is much easier to mow than one with square corners and awkward projections. One way to modify existing lawns is to replace sharp angles with perennial flower beds, ground covers, low-growing evergreens, mulches, or even structures, such as benches. A lawn broken into several separate parts will also be more time consuming and difficult to mow than one that is unified." (p5)

Hughes, Megan. "Your Lawn: More Fun, Less Work, Better for the Environment." Kerr Center for Sustainable Agriculture Newsletter v19 n7, Sep-Oct 1993. p5.

LAWSUITS

see ACTIONS AND DEFENSES

LAWYERS--CHINA (v19)

LAWYERS--EMPLOYMENT--U.S. (v19)

LAWYERS--SALARIES, ETC.--U.S. (v19)

LAWYERS--U.S. (v19)

see also ADVERTISING--LAWYERS--U.S.

"The number of female lawyers rose from 62,000 in 1980 to 140,000 in 1988, while the number of African-American, Latino, and Asian-American practitioners increased from 23,000 in 1980 to 51,000 in 1989." (p23)

Tobias, Carl. "Opinion/Essays: Keeping the Covenant on the Federal Courts." The Christian Science Monitor v86 n56, 14 Feb 1994. p23. (ISSN0882-7729).

LAWYERS--U.S.--FEES (v19)

LAWYERS--U.S.--PUBLIC OPINION (v19)

LEAD--TOXICOLOGY--CHINA

"Ten leading makers of china dishes have agreed to reduce the lead in their products by 50% and use vivid on-plate stickers to tell consumers which china patterns present lead hazards, under a settlement reached with EDF [Environmental Defense Fund] and the California Attorney General....Although the agreement, reached under California's landmark Proposition 65, covers sales of china in California only, industry representatives predicted a 'worldwide' impact on the entire industry, as china makers scramble to avoid the warning stickers by eliminating lead from their products. Lawyers for the 10 defendant companies predicted that at least another 200 major manufacturers would promptly bind themselves to the same requirements, to protect against Prop. 65 liability." (p1)

"China Makers Agree to Cut Lead 50%." EDF Letter v24 n2, Mar 1993. p1,8. (ISSN0163-2566).

LEAD--TOXICOLOGY--SOUTH CAROLINA

"Data from South Carolina, which may have the best records on lead hazards in child-care facilities in the nation, show that lead hazards in child-care facilities are...widespread. In South Carolina, out of 3,206 child-care facilities and foster homes inspected by the state over the last six years, 556 (18%) had lead hazards. In the case of one child-care center with lead hazards in Charleston, S.C., over 40% of the children in the center were found to have toxic levels of lead in their blood. The most widespread source of lead is paint manufactured before 1978, when a federal ban on lead in paint took effect. Nearly 90% of all schools were built before 1980 and so potentially contain lead paint. Over 50% of schools were built before 1960, when use of heavily leaded paint was most widespread. As this old paint deteriorates or is disturbed, it sheds toxic lead dust, which children contact and swallow." (p7)

U.S. House. Committee on Energy and Commerce. "Hazards of Lead in Schools and Day Care Facilities." Hearing, 15 Sep 1993. Washington, D.C.: GPO, 1993. (ISBN0160432839). (Y4.En2/3:103-46).

LEAD--TOXICOLOGY--U.S.

"The Department of Housing and Urban Development has reported that there are about 57 million homes with lead paint and 20 million homes with lead hazards. Since there are about 100 million homes in the United States, this means that 1 out of every 5 homes contains a lead hazard at this time." (p2)

Moorhead, Carlos J. (Rep.-Calif.). U.S. House. Committee on Energy and Commerce. "Hazards of Lead in Schools and Day Care Facilities." Hearing, 15 Sep 1993. Washington, D.C.: GPO, 1993. (ISBN0160432839). (Y4.En2/3:103-46).

LEAD-POISONING IN CHILDREN

see PEDIATRIC TOXICOLOGY

LEASE AND RENTAL SERVICES--U.S. (v19)

LEBANON--HISTORY--CIVIL WAR, 1975- (v19)

"Lebanon's export potential, including agriculture, was badly damaged during the war, with losses put at $600 million; 50 percent of the country's cold-storage capacity was knocked out, 15,000 hectares (37,000 acres) of forest gutted by shellfire, animal stocks were depleted, and irrigation systems were put out of action." (p24)

Meadows, Ian. "Lebanon: Up from the Ashes." Aramco World v45 n1, Jan-Feb 1994. p16-29. (ISSN1044-1891).

LEBANON--INDUSTRIES

"Pre-war industrial exports represented between 10 and 15 percent of Lebanon's gross domestic product, but the civil war damaged some 200 plants and led to wholesale emigration of workers, leaving this sector of the country's economy functioning at barely 25 percent of capacity." (p23)

Meadows, Ian. "Lebanon: Up from the Ashes." Aramco World v45 n1, Jan-Feb 1994. p16-29. (ISSN1044-1891).

LEBANON--POPULATION

"Lebanon's population of 3.5 million is fairly evenly spread over Beirut (581,000), Beirut's suburbs (681,000), Mount Lebanon (635,000), North Lebanon (690,000), South Lebanon (598,000) and the Bekaa Valley (410,000). The World Bank notes how events in South Lebanon have caused the perennial flight of mostly poorer people from that troubled area to Beirut and other urban centers, with all the socio-economic pressures that result. Lebanese birth rates showed a notable decline between 1982 and 1987. Yet the largest segment of Lebanon's population is in the 10-to-20 age group; a corresponding shrinkage in the 20-to-30 group is due largely to emigration, said to have been in excess of 300,000 people. Some 700,000 children were enrolled in state schools in 1992, over 90 percent of the 5-to-20 age group." (p20)

Meadows, Ian. "Lebanon: Up from the Ashes." Aramco World v45 n1, Jan-Feb 1994. p16-29. (ISSN1044-1891).

LEGAL ASSISTANCE TO THE POOR--U.S.--FINANCE (v19)

LEPROSY (v19)

LEPROSY--TREATMENT (v19)

LESBIANS--U.S. (v19)

LIBERIA--HISTORY--CIVIL WAR (v19)

LIFE EXPECTANCY (v19)

"The correlation between wealth and health...is borne out by the statistics on life expectancy, which is lower in the poorer nations and higher in the wealthier ones. An infant born in Niger has a life expectancy of 38. Its sister or brother in the human family that is born Japanese expects to live more than twice as long, to 79. Only two of thirty sub-Saharan African nations have life expectancies over 60; Sixteen range through the 40s and ten through the 50s. Eleven million children die unnecessarily each year, as well as 7 million adults. Maternal mortality rates are thirty times higher in poorer countries than in wealthy ones. In general, the burden of disease is five times higher per capita in the worst off nations than in the healthiest ones." (p1)

Hug, Jim, SJ. "Healthcare: Global-Local Links." Center Focus n118, Nov 1993. p1-5,7.

"National or regional differences in life expectancy have always been stark. The average citizen of a developing country lived to the same age--40 years old--in 1945 as the average Western European in 1830, and it wasn't until around the end of World War II that the average Third World person survived even that long. Western Europe's rate had long since shot upward, reaching 70 years old shortly after the Third World reached 40 years. Today, the average for the developing countries is 62 years, compared to 75 in the industrialized countries." (p33)

Kane, Hal. "Trends: Can Money Buy a Longer Life?" World Watch v6 n6, Nov-Dec 1993. p32-34. (ISSN0896-0615).

LIFE EXPECTANCY--DEVELOPING COUNTRIES (v19)

LIFE EXPECTANCY--ECONOMIC CONDITIONS

"Saudi Arabia's oil money has helped to boost its average income to $7,000 a person, but its people only live to an average age of 69--no longer than the average Sri Lankan, who earns less than $500 per year. The Sri Lankans, it turns out, have support services comparable to those of many Saudis. Likewise, in Gabon, where oil money has raised per capita incomes to more than six times those of Sri Lanka, the average life expectancy is only 54, probably because much of the Gabonese population does not have access to even minimal health services. Japan, on the other hand, exemplifies how both the quality and length of life can be improved when a country uses its wealth toward that end. Japan was devastated at the end of World War II, but by the mid-1950s, the malnutrition of the 1940s had virtually disappeared, literacy rates were high, and virtually all Japanese citizens had been given access to clean water, sanitation, and basic medical care. Although Japan was still a poor country in the 1950s, the life expectancy of Japanese men went up by 15 years during that decade. For the country's population as a whole, life expectancy rose by 20 years over a 20 year span--from 50 years old in 1950 to 70 in 1970." (p32)

Kane, Hal. "Trends: Can Money Buy a Longer Life?" World Watch v6 n6, Nov-Dec 1993. p32-34. (ISSN0896-0615).

LIFE EXPECTANCY--EDUCATION--U.S.

"In 1960, more than 70 percent of Americans age 85 to 89 had eight or fewer years of education; by 2015, this proportion will plummet to between 10 and 15 percent." Kenneth Manton of Duke University estimates "that men currently age 65 can expect 15.6 additional years of life: 13.7 years for the less-educated (eighth grade or less), compared with 16.3 years for those with more education (ninth grade plus). This difference is much greater for women, who can expect to live 24.3 years past age 65 if they have more education, compared to 18 years if they have less. While educated women in particular can expect more years of active life, the risk of spending some years in a nursing home will also increase." (p3)

"The Riche Report: Demographic Complexities Multiply for Social Security." Population Today v21 n12, Dec 1993. p3. (ISSN0749-2448).

"Particularly significant is the rise in Russia's crude death rate. In 1992 it reached 12.2 per 1,000, up from 11.2 per 1,000 in 1990. Life expectancy is dropping. In 1992, life expectancy at birth for men fell to 62.0 years (down from 63.9 in 1990). It fell from 74.4 to 73.8 years for Russian women during the same two-year period. Projections show a further drop in 1993, to 61 years for males and 73 years for females." (p2)

Haub, Carl. "Russia's New Revolution: A Demographic Baby Bust." Population Today v22 n4, Apr 1994. p1-2. (ISSN0749-2448).

LIFE EXPECTANCY--GUATEMALA

"Life expectancy in Guatemala remains among the lowest, and child mortality among the highest in the Western Hemisphere.

While average life expectancy is 63 years, it is only 44 years for Indians. Only three in ten births are attended by trained medical professionals. Adolescent pregnancy is high and survey data show that half of all women have given birth before age 20. One in nine children die before they reach age five; diarrhea is the leading cause of death. Contraceptive use is among the lowest in the hemisphere. Only 23 percent of married women use contraception, but there is evidence of substantial unmet demand. The Guatemalan total fertility rate is 5.2 births per woman, but most women consider four children ideal." (p7)

Lang, Anne. "Spotlight: Guatemala." Population Today v22 n4, Apr 1994. p7. (ISSN0749-2448).

LIFE EXPECTANCY--U.S. (v19)

"Life expectancy at birth for blacks overall was 69.1 years in 1990 compared to 76.1 years for whites. For black males, life expectancy was 64.5 years in 1990, a decline since its high of 65.3 years in 1984. For white males, the life expectancy is 72.7 years, 8.2 years longer than for African-Americans. Blacks also have higher age-adjusted death rates than whites for 15 leading causes of death. In the instance of homicide and HIV infection, the gap between black and white mortality rates is wider than for any chronic disease. Although infant mortality declined among both blacks and whites between 1980 and 1990, it was still more than twice as high among blacks than whites. In fact, black mothers with a college degree have a higher infant mortality rate than white mothers with less than a high school education." (pH10980)

Stokes, Louis (Rep.-Ohio). "The Minority Health Improvement Act of 1993." Congressional Record (22 Nov 1993). Daily ed. pH10980-10981. (ISSN0363-7239).

LIFE EXPECTANCY--U.S.--WOMEN

"Women today are living longer than ever before and their longevity rates are surpassing those of men. 'Women's life expectancy at birth is 78.3 years; men's is 71.5. Women over 40 now make up 20.5 percent of the U.S. population,' according to THE NEW OUR BODIES, OURSELVES published by The Boston Women's Health Book Collective. Midlife, often defined as approximately the years between 45 and 65, is imbued with a crescendo of changes for many women. These changes, which can occur in rapid succession, often include separation from a spouse, either through death or divorce, loss of an elderly parent, and departure of the children from the home. Of similar importance is the profound adjustment a woman goes through as she deals with the physiological changes and concomitant health, social and cultural issues related to menopause." (p1)

"Perspectives on Menopause." Perspectives in Health Promotion and Aging v8 n3, 1993. p1,3,7-9.

LIFE INSURANCE

see INSURANCE, LIFE

LIGHT BULBS--ENERGY CONSUMPTION

"Compact fluorescent bulbs use only one-fourth the electricity of conventional lights, provide equal or better lighting, and last 13 times longer than incandescent bulbs. During its extended life, a compact fluorescent bulb will save $40 to $60 in electricity alone. In addition, one such bulb will prevent the burning of 400 pounds of coal, the emission of about 1 ton of carbon dioxide, 21 pounds of sulfur dioxide, a broad array of toxic emissions, as well as the solid waste associated with coal ash and the 13 incandescent bulbs it replaces." (p32)

Grant, William. "Power to Spare." Outdoor America v58 n1, Win 1993. p31-33.

LIGHTNING--U.S. (v19)

LIMITED PARTNERSHIP--U.S. (v19)

LIQUOR INDUSTRY--LOS ANGELES (CALIF) (v19)

LITERACY

"To compare literacy rates around the world...[World Education Report 1993] defined an illiterate as a person over age 15 who could not read or write a simple text. By this measure, it said, there were 946 million illiterates in the world in 1980. By 1990, this figure had fallen to 905 million, and it is expected to drop to 869 million or lower by the year 2000." (p7)

"UNESCO Report: Illiteracy Down Worldwide, Problems Mount in Some Regions." Reading Today v11 n4, Feb-Mar 1994. p7. (ISSN0737-4208).

"In the past four decades, the number of adults who can read has increased by about 1.8 billion worldwide--a net growth of some 120,000 people a day. This continuing improvement in global literacy--from 56 percent of the population in 1950 to about 74 percent today--represents encouraging progress. But it also hides troubling disparities between industrial and developing nations and between men and women. In 1970, some 94 percent of adults over age 15 were considered literate in industrial countries, compared with only 45 percent in the Third World. Since then, literacy rates in the developing countries have gained ground impressively, climbing to 65 percent....In 1970, about 70 percent of the world's men were able to read, but only 54 percent of the women. By 1990, both sexes had increased in overall literacy but the gap between the two had narrowed only slightly--by 2 percentage points." (p36)

"Vital Signs." World Watch v7 n1, Jan 1994. p36-37. (ISSN0896-0615).

LITERACY--PORTUGAL (v19)

LITERACY--TANZANIA

"Tanzanians worry that they may be heading for ignorance. In 1989 the country's official literacy rate was put at 92 percent, totaling 15 million adults, but now there are not nearly enough books for all the country's readers. 'The shortage of books is seriously undermining intellectual development,' says novelist and newspaper editor Wilson Kaigarula. Tanzania produces about 50 titles a year (including small government booklets). By comparison, Britain produces 60,000 a year." (p19)

Tagama, Herald. "Arts & Letters: Book Famine Starves the Knowledge-Hungry." Toward Freedom v[42] n3, Apr-May 1993. p19. (ISSN0048-9898).

LITERACY--U.S. (v19)

"The NALS--a project of the National Center for Education Statistics and the Division of Adult Education and Literacy of the U.S. Department of Education--reported that while America today is a better educated and a more literate society than any time in its history, many adults still lack the literacy skills needed to function in today's technologically advanced society. 'This report is a wake-up-and-smell-the-coffee kind of call not only nationwide, but locally,' said [coordinator of the Ann Arbor Public Schools Adult Education Program, Sara] Aeshbach....The NALS surveyed 26,091 adults--estimated to represent an adult population of some 191,000. The study was conducted in 1992 and released in late 1993....The survey showed that between 21 and 23 percent of the respondents--representing some 40 to 44 million individuals nationwide in population terms--performed in the lowest level of the three literacy scales. Many adults in this level were able to total an entry on a deposit slip, locate the time and place of a meeting on a form, and identify a piece of specific information in a brief news article. Many individuals in the Level 1 range were born in other countries, attended school up to the eighth grade, were elderly or had a disability, illness or impairment, according to the report." (p3 secC)

Cobbs, Liz. "Local: Group Calls for Aid for Adult Learners." Ann Arbor News 27 Feb 1994. p3 secC.

"Last fall [U.S.] Education Secretary Richard Riley released a study indicating that only 59 percent of our fourth graders could meet basic reading standards for their age, and that 75 percent of our high school seniors could meet their basic standards. These figures are even more alarming in light of the fact that many of the kids in dire need of improvement have already dropped out of school by grade 12." (pS81)

Riegle, Donald W., Jr. (Sen.-Mich.). "Cosponsorship of S. 1150--Goals 2000 Educate America Act," Congressional Record (25 Jan 1994). Daily ed. pS81. (ISSN0363-7239).

LITERACY--WOMEN

"Although the literacy gap is shrinking, two thirds of the world's illiterates are female; 600 million women cannot read, and 90 million school-age girls are not in school. Uneducated women everywhere have high birthrates, low earnings and short lives. Yet even a few years of education for girls can be a magic bullet, leading to smaller, healthier families, less economic dependence and less vulnerability to abusive husbands." (p48)

MacFarquhar, Emily/others. "World Report: The War against Women." U.S. News & World Report v116 n12, 28 Mar 1994. p42-45,48. (ISSN0041-5537).

LITERACY, COMPUTER

see COMPUTER LITERACY

LITERARY PROPERTY

see COPYRIGHT

LIVER--TRANSPLANTATION--U.S.

"The actual number of individuals [in the U.S.] dying [awaiting a liver transplant] has increased due to the dramatic increase in the number of individuals waiting on the national patient waiting list. However, the overall death rate among these individuals has varied, with a decrease between 1991 and 1992. The national statistics on the death rate of liver transplant patients are as follows: 1988, 9.0 percent; 1989, 9.8 percent; 1990, 8.2 percent; 1991, 9.3 percent; and 1992, 8.5 percent." (p127)

Bond, Wanda W. (United Network for Organ Sharing). U.S. House. Committee on Energy and Commerce. "Organ Transplant and Bone Marrow Donor Reauthorization." Hearing, 22 Apr 1993. Washington, D.C.: GPO, 1994. (ISBN0160434653). (Y4.En2/3:103-54).

LIVESTOCK

see also CATTLE; POULTRY; SWINE

"Since 1980-82 the world's flock of chickens has grown by 132% to a feathery 17.2 billion, of which 11 billion live in Asia. Its herds of sheep and goats are up by 13%, to 1.8 billion, and its cattle by a modest 4% to 1.3 billion. Livestock is multiplying even faster than humanity. What it eats and what it excretes cause environmental damage in many parts of the world." (p102)

"Science and Technology: Home to Roost." Economist v330 n7856, 26 Mar 1994. p102. (ISSN0013-0613).

"An animal unit is 1,000 pounds of live weight. Thus, for example, a 1,300-pound dairy cow is 1.3 animal units; 333 chickens weighing 3 pounds each is 1.0 animal unit; and 5 hogs weighing 200 pounds each is 1.0 animal unit." (p85)

Beegle, Douglas B./Lanyon, Les E. "Nutrient Management Legislation in Pennsylvania." Journal of Soil and Water Conservation Supplement Mar-Apr 1994. p84-86.

LIVESTOCK--U.S.

"The number of beef cattle [in the U.S.] not on feed rose over 800,000 units [in 1993/94], while dairy cattle numbers, including both cows and heifers, declined 250,000. The gain in beef cattle not on feed is attributable to increased numbers of cows--the result of higher returns over the past several years. The gain in cattle numbers, coupled with a decline in hay supplies, has lowered the hay supply per RCAU [roughage consuming animal units] for 1993/94 to only 2.26 tons, a drop of 2 percent. This figure has now fallen for 2 years in a row, following 3 years of increases." (p12)

U.S. Dept. of Agriculture. "Hay Supplies Decline in 1993/94; Quality Questioned." Feed Situation and Outlook Report Nov 1993. p11-12.

"Small-scale livestock producers [in the U.S.] are under pressure both from corporate agribusiness and consumers. In the last 15 years, the pace of livestock industrialization has snowballed. The number of independent family hog producers, one of the last bastions of small-scale livestock production, has dropped to 250,000 from 750,000 in 1974. Estimates suggest only 100,000 hog producers will be left by the year 2000, if current trends continue." (p3)

"Is There a Future for Livestock on Sustainable Farms?" Land Stewardship Letter v11 n2, Spr 1993. p3.

LIVESTOCK--U.S.--GROWTH (v19)

LIVESTOCK INDUSTRY

see ANIMAL INDUSTRY

LIVING, COST OF

see COST AND STANDARD OF LIVING

LOAN FUNDS, STUDENT

see STUDENT LOAN FUNDS

LOANS

see also MORTGAGES; STUDENT LOAN FUNDS

LOANS--AFRICA

"'Lending for FY93 reaches record $23.7 billion,' screamed the headlines in a recent WORLD BANK NEWS, the World Bank's weekly newsletter. Sandwiched in the middle of the story was the revelation that despite rising lending to other regions, 'new lending commitments to Africa from (the Bank) in fiscal 1993 totaled $2.8 billion, a $1.2 billion decline from the amount committed in fiscal 1992 ($4 billion).'" (p4)

Tafirenyika, Masimba. "Center Focus: World Bank Overhauls Its Africa Strategy." Center Focus n113, Sep 1993. p4-5.

LOANS--AFRO-AMERICANS

"After studying lending practices at 9,300 United States financial institutions and more than 6.4 million loan applications, in 1991 the Federal Financial Institutions Examination Council (FFIEC) reported that the rejection rates for conventional home mortgages were 33.9% for African Americans, 21.4%...[for] Latinos, 22.4% for American Indians, 14.4% for Anglos, and 12.9% for Asians. Overall, African Americans were rejected for home loans more than twice as often as Anglos. Loan denial rates for African Americans varied widely among large urban centers. For example, one in three African American loan applicants was rejected in the Boston, Houston, St. Louis, Pittsburgh, and Phoenix metropolitan areas. The lowest loan rejection rate for African Americans occurred in the Washington, DC, Baltimore, Oakland, and San Diego metropolitan areas." (p35-36)

Bullard, Robert D. "Urban Habitat Program: Residential Apartheid in Urban America." Earth Island Journal v8 n4, Fall 1993. p35-36. (ISSN1041-0406).

LOANS--DEVELOPING COUNTRIES

"Already in the 1960s a rapid expansion of private bank lending to developing countries was well under way. This expansion accelerated after the oil shock of 1973-74. With the sudden increase of oil prices, the OPEC countries as a group witnessed enormous current account surpluses. These loanable funds were used as syndicated loans by commercial banks operating in Euromarkets. In 1973, private bank lending was only $5.7 billions per annum and it increased at an average rate of 49.3% per annum afterwards. It reached the peak of $76.8 billions per annum in 1981....During these years most of private capital flows were accounted for by medium and long-term private bank lending. However, the situation changed dramatically after 1982, when Mexico announced a 'de facto' default on its debts.

Thereafter the volume of private bank lending to non-oil developing countries declined sharply. By 1988, it dropped to a minimum of $0.7 billions per annum. The decline in private bank lending to developing countries in the 1980s has been more rapid than its expansion in the 1970s." (p332)

Amirahmadi, Hooshang/Wu, Weiping. "Private Capital Flows and Developing Countries." Journal of Third World Studies v10 n1, Spr 1993. p327-357. (ISSN8755-3449).

LOANS--DEVELOPING COUNTRIES--U.S.

U.S. "loans [to the Third World], granted to our favorite dictators and oligarchs so that they could purchase U.S. luxury goods and export capital to the West, are now the burden of the poor, who had nothing to do with them. Susan George estimates that debt service alone amounted to a capital flow of $418 billion from South to North from 1982 to 1990, six times the value of Marshall Plan aid in today's dollars. This includes the countries of sub-Saharan Africa, where starvation and misery are rampant in part thanks to the much-admired U.S. policy of 'constructive engagement,' which helped South Africa inflict 1.5 million deaths and more than $50 billion in damage in the neighboring countries in that period while maintaining its illegal hold on Namibia." (p7)

Chomsky, Noam. "Letter from Lexington: The United States on Human Rights." Lies of Our Times Sep 1993. p6-9. (ISSN1046-7912).

LOANS--EUROPE, EASTERN (v19)

LOANS--GEORGIA

"Even as the second-mortgage industry has come under siege in Georgia, small-loan companies in the state continue to operate under some of the worst lending laws in the nation. With the help of sympathetic legislator-businessmen...the small-loan industry has blocked attempts to improve fair-lending laws. The industry PAC [political action committee], Consumer Credit People for Responsible Government, tells members that campaign contributions are crucial to their profits, because the industry is 'a creature of the General Assembly.' Last year, the industry dished out more than $28,000 to state lawmakers. Such influence-buying has paid off. Georgia law allows small-loan companies to collect stunning interest rates: from 123 percent on a $50 loan to 45 percent on a $1,000 loan." (p36)

Hudson, Mike/Feuerstein, Adam. "SE Special Section: Reforming High Finance." Southern Exposure v21 n3, Fall 1993. p33-36. (ISSN0146-809X).

LOANS--LATIN AMERICA

"The end of 1993 brought to a close the latest of the Bank's four-year capital cycles, a period in which massive IDB [Inter-American Development Bank] lending helped Latin America embark on a new path of economic reform and growth. A large part of the Bank's $21.5 billion in financing in the 1990-93 seventh capital increase period was aimed at helping the region's countries open up their economies, shift economic initiative from the public to the private sector, and streamline government operations. A quarter of total lending for the period--$5.6 billion--went for 34 operations to help governments carry out such reform programs, noted IDB President Enrique V. Iglesias in his year-end message before the Bank's Board of Executive Directors....Recovering from their worst crisis since the Great Depression, the Latin American economies achieved aggregate growth of about 10 percent in 1993....The region's countries attracted more than $150 billion in external resources during the period." (p7)

"The Bank: Four-Year Surge in Lending." IDB v21 n1-2, Jan-Feb 1994. p7.

LOBBYING--CANADA

"Ottawa's government-business relationship is indeed changing, settling into a slower pace. The heady days and fast-growth of the 1980s, when lobbying grew into a $200 million (Canadian; US$ 148 million) industry, are now gone. Today there are about 700 so-called 'hired gun' lobbyists who consult for a fee. There are another 2,300 lobbyists working for trade associations and other groups." (p12)

Clayton, Mark. "Points of the Compass: Ottawa." The Christian Science Monitor v86 n62, 23 Feb 1994. p12-13. (ISSN0882-7729).

LOBBYING--U.S. (v19)

LOBBYISTS--U.S. (v19)

LOBSTER INDUSTRY--MAINE (v19)

LOCAL TRANSIT

see also BUS LINES

LOCAL TRANSIT--BRAZIL

"The city of Curitiba, Brazil, is using exclusive bus lanes to speed mass transit. This idea, which we unsuccessfully proposed for DC back in the 70s, allows Curitiba's busses to travel at an average speed of 20 mph, carrying 3.2 times as many passengers per hour as standard busses. The system took six months to install. Says Mayor Jaime Lerner, 'That means you don't have to waste a generation building a subway.' Curitiba's bus system carries 1.3 million passengers annually, reports the BRAZILIAN MONTHLY, four times the number as Rio's subway. The system uses boarding tubes and advance payment of fares and has resulted in 28% of the city's car drivers switching to mass transit." (p10)

"The Idea Mill: Urban Ecology." Progressive Review n316, Apr 1993. p10.

LOCAL TRANSIT--LOS ANGELES (CALIF)

"In January 1993, we opened the first 4.4 mile segment of the Metro Rail 'Red Line' which eventually will become a 22-mile subway, connecting downtown Los Angeles with the East-side, the West-side and the San Fernando Valley. This subway is the 'back bone' of the system, with most other rail lines feeding into it. The Federal share of this project is 50 percent, with the state and local governments paying the remaining 50 percent....The second phase of the 'Red Line' is scheduled to open in 1996 (with three stations opening), and the remainder will open in 1998. This will add 6.7 miles to our subway, extending it West into the Mid-Cities area, and Northwest into Hollywood....The third phase of the subway has been authorized by the Congress for a Federal commitment of $1.23 billion." (p1330)

Torres, Esteban E. (Rep.-Calif.). U.S. House. Committee on Appropriations. "Department of Transportation and Related Agencies Approp. for 1994 (Part 7B)." Hearing, Washington, D.C.: GPO, 1993. (ISBN0160411041). (Y4.Ap6/1:T68/4/994/pt.7B).

Los Angeles County Metropolitan Transportation Authority (MTA) "operates the most cost-efficient major bus system in the United States, carrying each passenger at an average cost of 21 cents per mile, according to 1991 national data. As MTA's rail network expands, the need for buses to act as an effective feeder system is expected to grow from the current peak fleet of 2,000 to nearly 4,000 within the next 30 years. Today, MTA buses carry more than 1.3 million passengers, every day and 416 million each year on 205 routes covering 326,337 miles. Our service area is one of the largest in the United States, covering 1,442 square miles that include four counties. MTA passengers can board a bus at any of approximately 19,650 bus stops throughout the region. MTA continues to operate some of the most crowded buses in the country, carrying an average of 18.4 riders at any given time on one of its buses. The average passenger load is 43% over the average of its peers, and 13% higher than the number two transit operator, Detroit's Department of Transportation." (p1371)

Alatorre, Richard (Chairman, Los Angeles County Metro Transportation Authority). U.S. House. Committee on

Appropriations. "Department of Transportation and Related Agencies Approp. for 1994 (Part 7B)." Hearing, Washington, D.C.: GPO, 1993. (ISBN0160411041). (Y4.Ap6/1:T68/4/994/pt.7B).

LOCAL TRANSIT--U.S. (v19)

LOCAL TRANSIT--U.S.--FINANCE (v19)

LOGGING--ALASKA

"In the 1950s...[Ketchikan Pulp and Alaska Pulp] mills were given 50-year contracts guaranteeing them a profit. When international pulp prices plunged in 1990, the Forest Service, in a thoughtful gesture, cut the price for timber that had already been purchased, and refunded the difference. This resulted last year in cash refunds from the Treasury totaling $9.8 million, in addition to $12.3 million in credits for future timber. Those credits will buy a lot more in the Tongass [National Forest] than they would anywhere else: the Forest Service charges only $2.26 per thousand board feet for timber with an export value of $500 to $2,500 per thousand board feet. It's only because of this bargain-basement price that Alaska's mills can afford to turn the old-growth forest into low-value cellulose stew. Over the years, Ketchikan Pulp and Alaska Pulp have bought out or driven out of business 102 smaller logging enterprises; they now hold exclusive sway over almost all of the Tongass. Together they have chewed through more than 8 billion board feet of Sitka spruce and western hemlock. Two-thirds of the cut, most of it in the form of 'dissolving pulp,' is shipped to Asia, where the old-growth habitat of the goshawk and marten is made into rayon, cellophane, and, more recently, disposable diapers." (p56-57)

Rauber, Paul. "Priorities: The $64 Million Question." Sierra v78 n4, Jul-Aug 1993. p55-57. (ISSN0161-7362).

LOGGING--BRAZIL

"For decades, loggers have invaded Indigenous lands in Brazil with impunity, creating violent confrontations with Indian people, and devastating the environment. Now, a Brazilian judge has ordered a halt to timber extraction from Indian lands in the eastern Amazon state of Para. According to estimates, between 1985 and 1990, over 640,000 cubic meters of valuable mahogany were extracted from Indian lands in Para, which required the construction of over 3000 km of illegal logging roads." (p18)

"Brazil: Stopping the Clearing of Timber from Indigenous Lands." Abya Yala News v7 n1-2, Win-Spr 1993. p18. (ISSN1056-5876).

LOGGING--CAMBODIA

"Thai timber merchants are not the only ones taking advantage of the power vacuum in Cambodia to plunder its jungles. Singaporean, Japanese and Taiwanese loggers are active, and buyers of the wood also include Vietnam and France. Statistics kept by the Phnom Penh administration show that timber exports from Cambodia have quadrupled in the past two years to 1.2 million cubic metres a year, mainly due to increased demand from Thailand, Singapore and Japan. Environmentalists blame deforestation for flash floods that hit Kompong Speu district near Phnom Penh in August 1991, causing massive damage. They warn that if the logging continues, the next disaster could be much worse, and that war-ravaged Cambodia simply cannot survive such blows." (p13)

Salayakanond, Wirasak. "Asia: Plunder in the Jungle." Panoscope n34, Jan 1993. p12-13. (ISSN0951-8819).

LOGGING--SARAWAK (MALAYSIA) (v19)

"With primary forests in peninsular Malaysia becoming rapidly depleted, the industry increasingly has turned to Sarawak. Between 1963 and 1985, 30 percent of the forested land of Sarawak was logged. In 1985, 670,000 acres were logged, providing 39 percent of Malaysian production and generating $1.7 billion in foreign exchange. Another 14.3 million acres--60 percent of Sarawak's forested land--are held in logging concessions. The banks of the Baram River in Sarawak's Fourth Division are lined for miles with stacked logs awaiting export. Although petroleum accounts for a far larger percentage of Sarawak's export earnings than timber, revenues from the oil fields flow almost entirely to the federal government. By contrast, the Sarawak government controls the forestry sector in the state. As of 1985, licensed logging concessions in Sarawak totaled 14.2 million acres; 23 percent had been exploited and the rest was scheduled for logging." (p16)

Davis, Wade. "State of the Peoples: Societies in Danger: Death of a People: Logging in the Penan Homeland." Cultural Survival Quarterly v17 n3, Fall 1993. p15-20. (ISSN0740-3291).

LONDON (ENGLAND)

see CONJUGAL VIOLENCE--LONDON (ENGLAND)

LOS ANGELES (CALIF)

see also COMMUTING--LOS ANGELES (CALIF); CRIME--LOS ANGELES (CALIF)--ALIENS, ILLEGAL; EARTHQUAKES--LOS ANGELES (CALIF); GANGS--LOS ANGELES (CALIF); IMMIGRANTS--LOS ANGELES (CALIF); LOCAL TRANSIT--LOS ANGELES (CALIF); MEDICAL CARE--LOS ANGELES (CALIF); POOR--LOS ANGELES (CALIF); PUBLIC WELFARE--LOS ANGELES (CALIF); REFUSE AND REFUSE DISPOSAL--LOS ANGELES (CALIF); RIOTS--LOS ANGELES (CALIF); TRANSPORTATION--LOS ANGELES (CALIF); VIOLENT CRIMES--LOS ANGELES (CALIF); VOTING--LOS ANGELES (CALIF)

LOS ANGELES (CALIF)--ECONOMIC CONDITIONS

Los Angeles County: "has a population of 9.1 million--almost half of whom are either on Medicaid (1.6 million)--which is called 'Medi-Cal' in California--or are uninsured (2.7 million per U.S. census data). The percentage of uninsured in the county exceeds that of any major urban area in the Nation. [It] is the most populated county in the United States and is larger than 42 States and 162 countries. [It] continues to struggle economically in the midst of the deepest recession since the Great Depression. Current unemployment exceeds 11 percent. Recent Rand studies indicate that: (1) Defense cuts will adversely impact Los Angeles six times greater than the average jurisdiction throughout the United States and (2) absent Los Angeles County, California has economically outperformed the rest of the Nation during the recent national recession." (p19)

Gates, Robert C. (Los Angeles County Director of Health Services). U.S. House. Committee on Energy and Commerce. "Medicaid Managed Care in California." Hearing, 20 Apr 1993. Washington, D.C.: GPO, 1994. (ISBN0160434122). (Y4.En2/3:103-52).

LOS ANGELES (CALIF)--EMPLOYMENT

"A gloomy study prepared by the Aerospace Taskforce of the Los Angeles Economic Roundtable predicts that as many as 350,000 jobs (40-50 per cent of the county's current high-tech workforce) may be eventually lost to defence cutbacks and plant relocations. This attrition, moreover, will impact non-whites disproportionately: Blacks and Latinos, less than 20 per cent of the aerospace workforce, constitute an extraordinary 53 per cent of the layoffs so far. The picture in non-durable, civilian manufacturing (two-thirds Latino in composition) is no less bleak. Labour-intensive industries have not bothered to wait for the formal signing of a free-trade treaty with Mexico but are already breaking for the border. The Southern California furniture industry, for example, is undergoing comprehensive 'maquiladorization' as thousands of $5-per-hour jobs held by Latino immigrants in Los Angeles' central manufacturing district are transformed into $5-per-day jobs in Tijuana's 'maquila' belt. In addition, thousands of other blue-collar jobs have been shifted, not south, but east of the California border, to 'union-free' industrial parks outside Las Vegas, Phoenix and Salt Lake City. Consequently, from South El Monte to Paramount, unemployment rates in Los Angeles' older, predominantly Latino, factory suburbs have risen punitively to 15-25 per cent." (p46)

Davis, Mike. "Who Killed Los Angeles? Part Two: The Verdict Is Given." New Left Review n199, May-Jun 1993. p29-54. (ISSN0028-6060).

LOS ANGELES (CALIF)--POLITICS AND GOVERNMENT (v19)

LOTTERIES--PENNSYLVANIA (v19)

LOUISIANA--COMMERCE--MEXICO (v19)

LOW BIRTH WEIGHT

see BIRTH WEIGHT, LOW

LUMBER TRADE--JAPAN--U.S. (v19)

LUMBER TRADE--NORTHWEST, PACIFIC (v19)

LUMBER TRADE--U.S. (v19)

"As the slow U.S. recovery and grim economies overseas depressed demand, paper prices fell for the fourth year in a row in 1993. Operating profits for the paper segments of the 19 largest companies plummeted 40%, [Dean Witter Reynolds Inc. analyst Evadna] Lynn says. At best, industry executives predict, prices and profits may recover this year to the depressed levels of 1992 as average capacity utilization surpasses the breakeven rate of 93%....Over the previous five years, 60% of the industry's 9.6% production hike went for export, says American Forest & Paper Assn. economist Richard Storat. But in 1993, key Scandinavian currencies weakened against the dollar and Europe's and Japan's economies dived. After years of growth, U.S. paper exports fell about 6% in 1993, says Lynn. She expects them to grow 5% in 1994 as economies abroad rebound in the second half." (p90)

Yang, Dori Jones. "Natural Resources: Forest Products: Splinters Everywhere." Business Week n3353, 10 Jan 1994. p90. (ISSN0007-7135).

"While companies [in the U.S.] that depend on federal logging suffer, larger competitors that control private timber are cashing in on a runup in prices caused by tighter supplies. In 1993, the average price of framing lumber rose 40%, to roughly $395 per thousand board feet, pushing wood operating profits up 57% at the 19 biggest producers, says Dean Witter Reynolds Inc. analyst Evadna Lynn....Lumber demand will be up substantially and production may rise only 3% because of capacity constraints and the timber ban. So Lynn expects prices to surge 15%, with wood profits jumping at least 50%." (p90)

Yang, Dori Jones. "Natural Resources: Forest Products: Splinters Everywhere." Business Week n3353, 10 Jan 1994. p90. (ISSN0007-7135).

"For three decades, the Columbia River Scaling and Grading Bureau (CRSB) has been one of the largest companies of its type in the West. CRSB employees 'scale' logs on trucks that roll off national forests in Alaska, California, Oregon and Washington--that is, they measure and inspect the logs, estimate the percentage of rot and defect in them, and come up with a figure of how much marketable timber they contain. From these figures, the Forest Service determines how much money it--and, in turn, we taxpayers--are paid for the logs. But for three decades, apparently, CRSB has been ripping us off. One former CRSB scaler, Paul Knapp, has already been sentenced to two years in prison for intentionally undervaluing some $1.5 million worth of logs. An Oregon timber company, Bugaboo, avoided trial in the case by paying a $1.6 million out-of-court settlement. And this October, CRSB and a second Oregon timber company, Thomas Creek, are scheduled to stand trial for allegedly defrauding the Forest Service of up to $15 million." (p1)

Stiak, Jim. "Logging Firms Rob a Lax Agency." High Country News v25 n15, 23 Aug 1993. p1,11. (ISSN0191-5657).

"According to a 1990 assessment by the Forest Service, the yearly demand for construction lumber in the United States alone is expected to rise by some 13 billion board-feet by the year 2040, while the demand for paper and fiberboard is projected to more than double. Indeed, according to a 1988 study by the Wood Products Promotion Council and the USFS Forest Products Lab, the average house had grown from about 1400 square feet in 1968 to almost 2000 square feet in 1988. Even more disturbing, the average 1988 house used more lumber per square foot of floor area than the 1968 house. In short, while we in the Forest Service forge ahead with our well-intentioned Ecosystem Management and either voluntarily or under duress keep reducing the 'cut,' Americans are building ever-more, ever-larger houses and using increasing reams of paper." (p9)

Foss, Tim. "Sustainable Culture: The Other Side of the Timber Supply Coin." Inner Voice v5 n5, Sep-Oct 1993. p9.

"'Engineered lumber' products...are winning market share as America's old-growth forests cease to provide a sure supply of structural beams for construction. Builders are turning to engineered lumber as a high-tech substitute offering higher quality at a competitive cost. The products, made from meshing wood fibers together to create large beams of up to 66 feet, also offer environmental benefits: Where traditional sawn lumber uses about 50 percent of each log, engineered lumber uses as much as 80 percent, and can use tree varieties that are small, fast-growing, and abundant....A typical new home in the United States or Canada uses more than $250 of engineered lumber, up from $165 in 1992. But the potential market is much bigger: more than $2,000 a home or a $3.5 billion potential market, says Robert Toomey, an analyst at Piper Jaffray. That does not include the market for commercial/industrial buildings or other applications." (p7)

Trumbull, Mark. "Economy: Engineered Lumber Rivals Standard Beams." The Christian Science Monitor v86 n41, 24 Jan 1994. p7. (ISSN0882-7729).

LUNGS--CANCER--CUBA (v19)

LUNGS--CANCER--EUROPE--WOMEN (v19)

LUNGS--CANCER--U.S.

"The scientific record in support of a correlation between ETS [environmental tobacco smoke] and lung cancer is very strong. Of the 30 epidemiologic studies from 8 countries analyzed in...[an] EPA report, 24 (80%) show a correlation between ETS and lung cancer. Nine of the studies show a statistically significant increase in cancer rates for persons exposed to ETS. In the case of an individual study, a 'statistically significant' increase in lung cancer means that the possibility that chance could explain the increase is low--5% or less. In the case of the 30 ETS studies, the possibility that chance could explain the occurrence of 9 studies with statistically [significant] results is even lower--less than 0.01%. The link between ETS exposure and lung cancer becomes a virtual certainty when one examines the results of the 17 most sophisticated studies, which differentiated among levels of ETS exposure. All 17 of these studies show increased cancer risks in the highest exposure group, with 9 being statistically significant. The probability of these results occurring by chance is less than 1 in 10 million. Fourteen of the studies provided enough data to examine whether there is a dose-response relationship between the level of ETS exposure and the incidence of lung cancer. All 14 studies show a positive dose-response relationship...." (p160-161)

U.S. House. Committee on Energy and Commerce. "Environmental Tobacco Smoke." Hearing, 21 Jul 1993. Washington, D.C.: GPO, 1993. (ISBN016043355X). (Y4.En2/3:103-51).

LUPUS ERYTHEMATOSUS--U.S. (v19)

"Doctors estimate that there are about 500,000 Americans known to be suffering from lupus. It is estimated that another 500,000 have not been diagnosed. Known cases of lupus outnumber those of leukemia, muscular dystrophy, or multiple sclerosis. While lupus affects both men and women, 9 out of 10 people struck with lupus are women. Although people of all ages contract lupus, the disease has its most significant impact on young women during the childbearing ages of 15 to 45. People of all ethnic backgrounds are stricken with lupus, but it attacks African-American, Hispanic, and some Asian and Native American women three times more frequently than white women. Within those ethnic groups hardest hit, rarely is there a person who has not been directly or indirectly affected by a friend, relative, or loved one who is suffering from lupus. One in every 250 African-American women can expect to be stricken." (pE649)

Meek, Carrie P. (Rep.-Fla.). "H.R. 2420, Lupus Legislation Cosponsors," Congressional Record (13 Apr 1994). Daily ed. pE649-650. (ISSN0363-7239).

LYME DISEASE--U.S. (v19)

MACAO--POPULATION (v19)

MACEDONIA--POPULATION

"According to Macedonian officials, in addition to the large Albanian minority there are 40,000 Serbs in...[Macedonia] (the Serbs claim there are 300,000). There are also about 100,000 Turks, perhaps 55,000 gypsies, 20,000 Greeks and 8,000 Vlachs, whose closest ethnic ties are with Romania." (p18)

"Minorities: That Other Europe." Economist v329 n7843, 25 Dec 1993. p17-18,20. (ISSN0013-0613).

MACEDONIA--SERBIA--ARMED FORCES (v19)

MACHINE-TOOL INDUSTRY--U.S.

"U.S. makers of factory machinery will have good times in 1994. Industrial production is rising, capacity utilization has climbed to 83%, interest rates remain low, and auto and other durable consumer-goods makers are buying more equipment....As a big market, and one of the healthiest, the U.S. is attracting more machine-tool imports again--up 14% for the first nine months of last year." (p73)

Schiller, Zachary. "Manufacturing: Machinery: No Rust on This Market." Business Week n3353, 10 Jan 1994. p73. (ISSN0007-7135).

MADAGASCAR

see also DEBTS, EXTERNAL--MADAGASCAR; DEFORESTATION--MADAGASCAR

"Madagascar, the Earth's fourth largest island, is believed to have broken off from the African continent about 100 million years ago. This abrupt separation from the mainland created a unique ecology. Homo sapiens arrived only 2,500 years ago in a wave of successive migrations from Africa and Indonesia. Today, of the 200,000 plant and animal species thus far identified, 150,000 are endemic to the island....Just over 11 million people live on this island of more than 226,658 square miles about 230 miles off the east coast of Africa. Even with an infant mortality rate of 12.2 percent, the population soared during the 1980s at an annual growth rate of 2.9 percent, well above the 2 percent growth in gross domestic product (GDP). This disparity in growth rates resulted in a 3.4 percent decline in per capita GDP in what the World Bank calls one [of] the world's ten poorest countries. With 65 percent of the population engaged in subsistence agriculture during that decade, there was considerable pressure on the remaining forested areas. Slash-and-burn or 'tavy' agriculture and the use of wood or charcoal for 81 percent of all fuel needs resulted in a decline in forested acreage from 21 percent of the island in the early 1980s to 10 percent by 1990." (p60)

Tucker, Michael. "A Proposed Debt-for-Nature Swap in Madagascar and the Larger Problem of LDC Debt." International Environmental Affairs v6 n1, Win 1994. p59-68. (ISSN1041-4665).

"Madagascar, the Earth's fourth largest island, is believed to have broken off from the African continent about 100 million years ago. This abrupt separation from the mainland created a unique ecology. Homo sapiens arrived only 2,500 years ago in a wave of successive migrations from Africa and Indonesia. Today, of the 200,000 plant and animal species thus far identified, 150,000 are endemic to the island. It is this biological diversity and uniqueness that make saving Madagascar's rainforest a pressing issue among the world's conservationists. Just over 11 million people live on this island of more than 226,658 square miles about 230 miles off the east coast of Africa. Even with an infant mortality rate of 12.2 percent, the population soared during the 1980s at an annual growth rate of 2.9 percent, well above the 2 percent growth in gross domestic product (GDP). This disparity in growth rates resulted in a 3.4 percent decline in per capital GDP in what the World Bank calls one [of] the world's ten poorest countries." (p60)

Tucker, Michael. "A Proposed Debt-for-Nature Swap in Madagascar and the Larger Problem of LDC Debt." International Environmental Affairs v6 n1, Win 1994. p59-68. (ISSN1041-4665).

MADISON (WIS)--EMPLOYMENT (v19)

MADRIZ (NICARAGUA)--SOCIAL CONDITIONS

Absalon "Gonzalez has no doubt whatsoever that the social and economic situation in Madriz has gone from bad to worse in the last few years. Like the rest of...[Nicaragua], the department [the region of Madriz] suffers from a high level of unemployment. An estimated 80% of the workers in the region are unemployed or underemployed. According to a survey carried out by the Community Movement, only 40% of the department's 102,000 inhabitants can meet their basic needs. Some 70% of children under five suffer from malnutrition. Another sign of the misery is the cholera epidemic, which continues to spread. Last November there were 520 cases of cholera in Madriz, and 11 people have died from the disease." (p12)

Andersson, Susanne. "Madriz Campesinos Survive: With a Little Help from Their Friends." Barricada Internacional n370, Feb 1994. p11-13. (ISSN1013-9567).

MAGAZINE ADVERTISING

see ADVERTISING, MAGAZINE

MAINE

see SEA URCHINS--MAINE

MALARIA

"According to World Health Organization estimates, there are some 300-500 million clinical cases of malaria per year, 90% of them in Africa, and 1.5-3 million deaths, one million of them African children under five years of age. Of the 10% of clinical cases outside Africa, India alone accounts for 38% of cases, and Brazil (mainly from Amazonia) accounts for 11%. Some 70% of cases outside Africa come from just seven countries: in decreasing order of incidence these are India, Brazil, Sri Lanka, Afghanistan, Thailand, Viet Nam, and Colombia." (p4)

News release. "Malaria Vaccine Could Be Developed Soon: Global Effort Needed." WHO Press 13 Feb 1994. p1-7.

"WHO [World Health Organization] estimates that there are some 300-500 million clinical cases of malaria per year, 90% of them in Africa, and 1.5-3.0 million deaths, at least one million of them African children under five years of age. About 10% of the estimated clinical cases are from outside Africa. In terms of reported incidence, India counts for 38% of cases, and Brazil accounts for 11% (mainly from Amazonia). Some 70% of cases outside Africa come from just seven countries: in decreasing order of incidence these are: India, Brazil, Sri Lanka, Afghanistan, Viet Nam, and Cambodia." (p5)

News release. "Chinese Herb Remedy Beats Multidrug-Resistant Malaria." WHO Press Apr 1994. p1-7.

MALARIA--AFRICA

"A person in Kilombero, Tanzania, suffers an average 300 bites a year from malaria-infected mosquitoes (which carry the disease from person to person)--and in the rainy seasons in February and May as many as 20-25 infected bites a night--some 100 times the rate in Columbia. As a result, at any moment more than two out of three people in Kilombero are infected with malaria parasites. Moreover, some 15-20% of the malaria parasites in the area already show resistance to the front-line drug to control malaria attacks, chloroquine." (p2)

News release. "Malaria Vaccine Could Be Developed Soon: Global Effort Needed." WHO Press 13 Feb 1994. p1-7.

MALARIA--AFRICA--COSTS (v19)

MALARIA--AFRICA--MORTALITY (v19)

MALARIA--TREATMENT

"A scientific study on the malaria treatment of multidrug-resistant malaria in Thailand has shown that the drug being tested was so effective it reduced the death rate three-fold when compared with quinine. And at the same time a related drug has helped Viet Nam reduce malaria mortality by a factor of five since 1991....When the results were analysed last month, they proved that intramuscular injections of 'artemether'--a derivative of extracts of the Chinese herb Artemisia annua L.--has saved the lives of 87% of patients with severe malaria, compared with intravenous quinine, the standard therapy for severe cases, which saved only 64%. With quinine, 18 of 50 patients died; with artemether, only 6 of 47 died." (p1)

News release. "Chinese Herb Remedy Beats Multidrug-Resistant Malaria." WHO Press Apr 1994. p1-7.

MALARIA--VIETNAM

"Viet Nam represents a classic case of malaria in Asia, where the disease typically hits non-immune workers and families entering new development areas, such as rubber plantations. In 1991, malaria mortality in Viet Nam reached historic levels, with over 4000 deaths. In response, the Vietnamese Government increased malaria control spending ten-fold to US$ 7 million a year in 1994, and with WHO advice and support, enacted a detailed malaria control plan, focused sharply on reducing malaria mortality and on the main problem areas--particularly in mountainous and highland areas. The result was a decrease in deaths from malaria in Viet Nam by 44% in 1992 compared with 1991, and a further 64% in 1993 compared with 1992. The programme's targets for 1994 continue to be ambitious--a reduction of the number of clinical cases of malaria by 20%, mortality by a further 30%, and of epidemics by 50% compared with 1993." (p3)

News release. "Chinese Herb Remedy Beats Multidrug-Resistant Malaria." WHO Press Apr 1994. p1-7.

MALAYSIA

see also AGED--CARE--MALAYSIA; CONTRACEPTION--MALAYSIA; DEFORESTATION--MALAYSIA; ETHNOLOGY--SARAWAK (MALAYSIA); HIV INFECTIONS--MALAYSIA; LANGUAGE AND LANGUAGES--MALAYSIA; LOGGING--SARAWAK (MALAYSIA)

MALAYSIA--ARMED FORCES--APPROPRIATIONS AND EXPENDITURES

"South-East Asia's defence imports are forecast to grow by 16% from 1991 to 1996. This disguises the fact that some countries are spending more heavily than others, with Malaysia in the vanguard. Its defence spending has risen from 0.5% of GDP [gross domestic product] in 1991 to 4.5% now. Over the next 15 years, it is planning to spend 6% of GDP on defence." (p33)

"Asia: Malaysia: Flying High, Shooting Higher." Economist v329 n7842, 18 Dec 1993. p33. (ISSN0013-0613).

MALAYSIA--ECONOMIC CONDITIONS (v19)

MALAYSIA--SOCIAL CONDITIONS

"Malaysia's economy has grown at an average annual rate of 4 percent for three decades and its GNP [gross national product] per capita is more than $2,300. Literacy is relatively high at 78 percent, and the enrollment ratio of primary plus secondary school is almost as high. Life expectancy is 70 years, and the IMR [infant mortality rate] is low--16 deaths per 1,000 live births. Contraceptive prevalence increased from 6 percent in 1966-67 to 51 percent in 1984, an average annual increase of 2.44 percentage points." (p84)

Mauldin, W. Parker/Ross, John A. "Prospects and Programs for Fertility Reduction, 1990-2015." Studies in Family Planning v25 n2, Mar-Apr 1994. p77-95. (ISSN0039-3665).

MALI

see DENTAL CARE--MALI; MEDICAL CARE--MALI

MALNUTRITION (v19)

MALNUTRITION--AFRICA, SUB-SAHARAN--ASIA (v19)

MANAGED CARE PLANS (MEDICAL CARE)

see also HEALTH MAINTENANCE ORGANIZATIONS

MANAGED CARE PLANS (MEDICAL CARE)--U.S.

"Currently, about 3.6 million Medicaid beneficiaries, roughly 12 percent of the total Medicaid population, are enrolled in managed care programs in 36 States. The overwhelming majority of these beneficiaries are low-income women and children. According to the General Accounting Office, another 13 States plan to implement managed care programs by January of next year. Moreover, many of the States that now have managed care programs plan to expand them." (p1)

Waxman, Henry A. (Sen.-Calif.). U.S. House. Committee on Energy and Commerce. "Medicaid Managed Care in California." Hearing, 20 Apr 1993. Washington, D.C.: GPO, 1994. (ISBN0160434122). (Y4.Ed2/3:103-52).

MANDATES--HAWAII--OHIO--TENNESSEE (v19)

MANDATES--TENNESSEE (v19)

MANDATES--U.S. (v19)

"According to an October, 1993 survey by the U.S. Conference of Mayors, the top ten most expensive mandates, eight of which are environmental, will cost cities with 30,000 or more in population over $50 billion in the next few years. This is just the tip of the iceberg because there are 14,950 smaller cities not included in this study. The National Association of Counties reports that counties spend about $4.8 billion annually to comply with just 12 unfunded Federal mandates." (pE179)

Clinger, William F., Jr. (Rep.-Pa.). "Stop Us before We Mandate Again," Congressional Record (10 Feb 1994). Daily ed. pE179. (ISSN0363-7239).

"The U.S. Conference of Mayors declared last October 27 'National Unfunded Mandates Day,' and mayors across the country held press conferences in their city halls to raise awareness of the issue. In Washington, D.C., October 27 became the day of the dueling press conferences when NRDC [Natural Resources Defense Council] and other environmental groups decided to head the mayors off at the pass by holding their own press conference an hour earlier in the same hotel. The mayors, in conjunction with a variety of other groups representing local governments, produced a flurry of figures. Enforcing the Clean Water Act alone will cost 314 cities surveyed $29.5 billion over the next five years. Cities spend approximately 11 percent of their budgets enforcing mandates. Pointing to the root of the problem, the National League of Cities says that while in 1965 the federal government devoted 48 percent of its spending to capital grants to state and local governments; by 1998, the White House Office of Management and Budget (OMB) projects only

15 percent will go to local and state coffers." (p11)
Ruben, Barbara. "Mandating Controversy." Environmental Action v26 n1, Spr 1994. p10-12. (ISSN0013-922X).

"According to a study of 314 cities by the accounting firm of Price Waterhouse and commissioned by the US Conference of Mayors, unfunded federal mandates cost the cities $6.5 billion in 1993 and will cost $54 billion during 1994-98. The study found that the cities were spending 11.7 percent of their budgets to meet required federal programs. The cost is rising because of the increase in such federal mandates. In 1961, there were only two programs--today, there are 66, ranging from Clean Air and Water Acts to Voting Rights." (p2)
Scherer, Ron. "National: Mayors Balk at Washington Telling Them How to Spend Their Money." The Christian Science Monitor v86 n31, 7 Jan 1994. p2. (ISSN0882-7729).

MANUFACTURES

see also FURNITURE INDUSTRY AND TRADE; GREAT BRITAIN--MANUFACTURES; MEXICO--MANUFACTURES; MICHIGAN--MANUFACTURES; U.S.--MANUFACTURES

"It is still common to refer to OECD [Organization for Economic Cooperation and Development] members as the 'industrialised economies'. Common, yet quite wrong. Manufacturing firms now employ just one worker in six in America, one in five in Britain and one in three in Germany and Japan....the decline of manufacturing in the past two decades has been steepest in Britain, where manufacturing employment has tumbled by almost half since 1970. In most other countries the fall has been slower. In the same period, America has shed 8% of its manufacturing jobs; France has lost 18%; and Germany has lost 17%. Japan, however, is a notable exception--it has added about 20% to manufacturing payrolls over the same period." (p91)
"Schools Brief: The Manufacturing Myth." Economist v330 n7855, 19 Mar 1994. p91-92. (ISSN0013-0613).

MAORI (NEW ZEALAND PEOPLE)

"The Maori birthrate has declined a little over the last three decades, but generally Maori population growth has been considerably more rapid than that of European New Zealanders. The 1991 census reported that 37.5 percent of Maori are under the age of fifteen, compared with 23 percent of non-Maori. Not only is the Maori population growing at a faster rate than the 'Pakeha,' but also a massive migration of Maori from the countryside to the cities has occurred since World War II. Although 75 percent of Maori lived in rural areas before 1945, 80 percent live in cities today." (p13)
Barr, Hugh. "Toward a Bicultural Education System: The Experience of New Zealand." National Forum v74 n1, Win 1994. p12-15. (ISSN0162-1831).

MAQUILADORA INDUSTRY

see OFFSHORE ASSEMBLY INDUSTRY

MARIHUANA--COMMONWEALTH OF INDEPENDENT STATES (v19)

MARIHUANA--U.S. (v19)

MARIHUANA--U.S.--YOUTH

"Drug use among American young people has been making a clear comeback in the past two years. That is the conclusion of University of Michigan research scientists Lloyd Johnston, Patrick O'Malley, and Jerald Bachman, all at the University's Institute for Social Research." (p1) "In 1993 the proportion of students reporting any use of marijuana in the prior 12 months was 9 percent for eighth-graders, 19 percent for 10th-graders, and 26 percent for 12th-graders....Put another way, the proportion of eighth-graders using marijuana has increased by half in the last two years, while the proportion of 10th-grade users increased by about a quarter and the proportion of 12th-grade users by about a fifth." (p2)
News release. "Drug Survey." University of Michigan News and Information Services 27 Jan 1994. p1-6.

MARKETING

see also GREEN MARKETING; RETAIL TRADE

MARKETING--U.S.

"Call it the odor of money....In one experiment [in the U.S.], customers inspecting Nike sneakers in a floral-scented room were likely to pay about $10 extra for them. In a Las Vegas test, gamblers pumped 45 percent more coins into slot machines in odorized rooms, says [Chicago's Smell and Taste Treatment Foundation director Alan] Hirsch. Brawny garbage bags now emit a fresh-linen scent, says Stanley Manne of Chicago Transparent Products, partly to get customers in grocery aisles to notice them. And JMB Retail Properties is considering using scents at its 60 regional malls nationwide to compete for customers....Environmental Protection Agency (EPA) scientists recently tested about 30 everyday scented items such as perfumes, soaps and shampoos. The most toxic chemical found was methylene chloride, a main ingredient in paint strippers, says EPA scientist Lance Wallace. Other common chemicals are the pine scent 'alpha pinene' (which causes mutations in bacteria), the lemon scent 'limonene' (a possible carcinogen), ethanol, linolool (both alcohols), and the petrochemical toluene (which can cause headaches and is found in some gasolines)." (p10)
Deneen, Sally. "In Brief: Scents and Cents." E Magazine v4 n4, Jul-Aug 1993. p10. (ISSN1046-8021).

MARKETING RESEARCH--U.S. (v19)

MARRIAGE

see also DIVORCE; INTERRACIAL MARRIAGE--U.S.; U.S.--ARMED FORCES--MARRIAGE

MARRIAGE--AFRO-AMERICANS (v19)

MARRIAGE--ANNULMENT--CATHOLIC CHURCH (v19)

MARRIAGE--GERMANY (EAST)

"If the collapse of East German Communism and the subsequent rapid transition to the market system have had an especially profound effect upon natality within marriage, they have had a similarly dramatic impact on the formation of such unions themselves. Like birth trends, aggregate figures on new marriages in the GDR [German Democratic Republic] evidenced a certain stability between 1980 and 1988....Just as with births, registered marriages in Eastern Germany commenced a precipitous slide after 1989. By 1992 the number of marriages celebrated was a mere 37 percent of the 1989 total. Marriage rates per thousand persons in Eastern Germany fell nearly equally sharply. Whereas Eastern Germany's marriage rate had been consistently higher than Western Germany's during the 1980s, by 1992 it was less than half as high....Between November 1989 and June 1990, the tally of marriages appears to have been largely unaffected by the radical political events that were unfolding. For the period January-June 1990, for example, Eastern Germany recorded 97 percent as many marriages as it had during the same six months in the previous year. Wedding totals collapsed in July 1990. For that month registered marriages were down 41 percent from July 1989; despite seasonal fluctuations, the trend has continued downward since." (p143-145)
Eberstadt, Nicholas. "Demographic Shocks after Communism: Eastern Germany, 1989-93." Population and Development Review v20 n1, Mar 1994. p137-152. (ISSN0098-7921).

MARRIAGE--TANZANIA

"According to...[a Tanzanian] survey, 20% of married men and 15% of married women are unfaithful to their partners--and four out of five men believe it is a sign of manhood for a man to have extra-marital sex. Three-quarters of the women were unfaithful for money or presents, to further their careers, or because their husbands failed to satisfy them sexually. Only one in five urban respondents and 4% of rural respondents said they used condoms in these cases." (p4)
Ndejembi, Edna. "Ignorance and AIDS Myths 'Rife'." WorldAIDS

n30, Nov 1993. p4. (ISSN0954-6510).

MARRIAGE--U.S. (v19)

"Between 1960 and 1992, the median age at first marriage [in the U.S.] rose from 22.8 to 26.5 years for men and from 20.3 to 24.4 years for women....The marriage delay afforded young adults of the 1980s time to spend in a variety of living arrangements. They lived longer with parents than did young adults of the 1960s and 1970s, who had married at somewhat younger ages; and they lived away from parents longer than unmarried young people had done in the past." (p4)

Goldscheider, Frances/Goldscheider, Calvin. "Leaving and Returning Home in 20th Century America." Population Bulletin v48 n4, Mar 1994. p2-35. (ISSN0032-468X).

"In 1991, almost 2,371,000 couples married [in the U.S.], a drop of 3 percent from 1990. The marriage rate per 1,000 population was 9.4 percent, lower than it has been since 1965. This represents a drop of 11 percent since 1981. During the 1980s, the marriage rate dropped even faster for people between ages 15 and 44 (when 90 percent of people marry). For people in this age group, the marriage rate dropped 11 percent for men (from 90.0 to 79.8 per 1,000) and 14 percent for women (from 103.1 to 89.0 per 1,000). About half as many couples divorced as married in 1991--1,187,000 couples, an increase of 1 percent over 1990. The divorce rate was 4.7 per 1,000 population, unchanged since 1988." (p4)

"Vital Signs Show Societal Aging." Population Today v21 n1, Jan 1993. p4. (ISSN0749-2448).

MARRIAGE, INTERRACIAL

INTERRACIAL MARRIAGE

MARYLAND

see CHILD CARE WORKERS--MARYLAND; CRIMINAL JUSTICE, ADMINISTRATION OF--MARYLAND; MEDICAL CARE, COST OF--MARYLAND

MASS MEDIA--AFRICA

"A number of contributors to...[a] collection of essays, entitled 'Africa's Media Image', argue that much Western coverage of the continent is biased and ill-informed....Most of the essayists do agree that Africa receives proportionately less attention from the Western press than almost any other part of the world. Only 8 percent of U.S. foreign correspondents were based in Africa in 1986, notes Bosah Ebo, as compared to 31 percent in Europe, 23 percent in Latin America and 18 percent in Asia. One commonly voiced excuse for the lack of coverage, observes Africa News editor Tami Hultman, is that only a tiny portion of the U.S. population has an interest in Africa. But what about African-Americans, who comprise 12 percent of the country's population? asks Hultman. Sadly, as Charles Bodie notes..., the African-American press has generally done only slightly better than the white-owned media in reporting on Africa. But the scant attention given Africa in the black-controlled U.S. press is due more to insufficient resources, Bodie suggests, than to blacks' indifference toward the continent." (p18)

Kelley, Kevin J. "Media: Africa's Bad Press: Warranted or Unfair?" Toward Freedom v[42] n3, Apr-May 1993. p18. (ISSN0048-9898).

MASS MEDIA--U.S.--PUBLIC OPINION

"A majority of children who watch television news or read newspapers say that media stories depicting children typically involve violence or drugs, according to a survey. The nationwide survey of 850 children, done for the California-based advocacy group Children Now, found that 65 percent of children ages 11 to 16 watch television news regularly, and 44 percent read a newspaper. Sixty-one percent of the children who follow the news said the image of children they see portrayed usually involves crime or drugs....However, 80 percent said news coverage is basically fair, and 65 percent said that without coverage by the news media, people would do less to help children in trouble." (p6)

"Media." Education Week v13 n24, 9 Mar 1994. p6. (ISSN0277-4232).

MASS TRANSIT

see LOCAL TRANSIT

MASSACHUSETTS

see CIGARETTE TAX--MASSACHUSETTS; PETS--MASSACHUSETTS; PRIVATIZATION--HOSPITALS--MASSACHUSETTS; PRIVATIZATION--MASSACHUSETTS; PRIVATIZATION--MEDICAL CARE--MASSACHUSETTS; PRIVATIZATION--MENTAL HEALTH--MASSACHUSETTS

MATERIALISM--U.S.

"In 1946, FORTUNE magazine heralded the arrival of a 'dream era...The Great American Boom is on.' By 1950, young families were moving into 4,000 new houses each day, and filling those houses with baby carriages, clothes dryers, dishwashers, refrigerators, washing machines and--especially--televisions. The head of President Eisenhower's Council of Economic Advisers canonized the new economic gospel: The American economy's 'ultimate purpose,' he proclaimed, was 'to produce more consumer goods.' Subsequent generations have faithfully agreed. On average, people in the U.S. today own twice as many automobiles, drive 2.5 times as far, use 21 times as much plastic and travel 25 times as far by air as their parents did in 1950." (p29)

Durning, Alan Thein. "American Excess--Are We Shopping Our Planet to Death?" E Magazine v4 n1, Feb 1993. p26-31. (ISSN1046-8021).

MATHEMATICAL ABILITY--U.S.--TESTING

"In the First International Study of Achievement in Mathematics, conducted over a period of several years in the mid-1960's, American 13-year-olds tied for 10th place in mathematics out of 12 countries participating. In the same study, our 12th-graders were dead last. In the follow-up study conducted between 1983 and 1986, our 13-year-olds seemed to fare slightly better. Their mathematics scores were about in the middle, with five nations scoring higher and seven lower--seven others scored the same as the United States. But American students in the last year of secondary school scored almost last; out of 15 countries studied, only Thailand and Hungary had lower scores. In 1991, we were 13th out of 14 countries in mathematics achievement of 13-year-olds on the International Assessment of Educational Progress. Only Jordan scored worse. In science achievement, the United States was 12th out of 14 nations. Our rankings have not improved over the last three decades." (pS926)

Moynihan, Daniel Patrick (Sen.-N.Y.). "GOALS 2000: Educate America Act," Congressional Record (4 Feb 1994). Daily ed. pS910-932. (ISSN0363-7239).

MATHEMATICS--STUDY AND TEACHING--U.S. (v19)

MAYORS--U.S. (v19)

MEASLES--U.S. (v19)

MEAT INDUSTRY AND TRADE

see also BEEF INDUSTRY; CATTLE TRADE; PORK INDUSTRY AND TRADE; POULTRY INDUSTRY; SWINE

"The Meat Import Law's trigger level for 1994 has been set at 1,218.9 million pounds, product weight, down 3.2 percent from last year. Voluntary restraint agreements have been reached with Australia and New Zealand for 664.9 million and 406.6 million pounds, respectively, down 4.3 percent from 1993." (p2)

U.S. Dept. of Agriculture. "VRA's Agreed to for 1994." Livestock, Dairy and Poultry Situation and Outlook 25 Jan 1994. p2.

"The growth in meat production, like that of grain, is slowing. Between 1950 and 1987, world meat production increased from 46 million tons to 161 million tons--boosting the amount per person from 18 kilograms in 1980 to 32 kilograms (about 70 pounds) in 1987. Since then, however, it has not increased at all. The one percent decline in per capita production in 1992 may be the beginning of a gradual world decline in per capita meat production, another major discontinuity." (p22)

Brown, Lester R. "A Decade of Discontinuity." World Watch v6 n4, Jul-Aug 1993. p19-26. (ISSN0896-0615).

MEAT INDUSTRY AND TRADE--CHINA (v19)

MEAT INDUSTRY AND TRADE--U.S. (v19)

"While 40 percent of all American meat and poultry processors are State inspected, State-inspected operations slaughter and process only about 5 percent of the total American meat supply. What does this tell us about these businesses? Simply that they are small mom and pop operations who, like all small businesses, are in a day-to-day struggle to find new markets and keep their doors open. From this perspective, the current prohibition against State-inspected meat traveling in interstate commerce works a particular hardship on those family meat and poultry operations close to a State border since they cannot market their product across that boundary line. That's why we are losing about 5 percent of these businesses every year. In fact, we barely have more than 3,000 State-inspected meat and poultry processors left in our country--only 20 percent of what we had 25 years ago." (pE3028)

Gunderson, Steve (Rep.-Wis.). "Opening Our Borders to State-Inspected Meat: An Exercise in Equity," Congressional Record (22 Nov 1993). Daily ed. pE3028. (ISSN0363-7239).

"For all of 1993, beef prices averaged 3.6 percent above 1992 and pork prices were 3.1 percent higher. Because of higher red meat prices, consumers chose more poultry, pulling poultry prices up 4.2 percent." (p38)

Parlett, Ralph. "News of Food Prices: Food Prices Rose Moderately for the Third Consecutive Year." Food Review v17 n1, Jan-Apr 1994. p36-39.

U.S. "Beef exports declined 2 percent to just under $2 billion because of a $95-million and $61-million drop in exports to Mexico and Korea, respectively, negating a $120-million gain to Japan. But expanded pork exports kept total meat exports at last year's $3.3 billion. Pork exports received a substantial boost in the last quarter of 1993 with sales to the former Soviet Union (FSU). The United States shipped the FSU nearly $26 million worth of pork in 1993, compared with $340,000 in 1992. Poultry meat exports jumped 19 percent to $1.1 billion on continued gains to Mexico, the Middle East, and Hong Kong." (p2)

U.S. Dept. of Agriculture/Greene, Joel. "Agricultural Exports Decline in 1993." Foreign Agricultural Trade of the United States Jan-Feb 1994. p2.

MEDICAID (v19)

"Because of economic and political pressures to contain soaring Medicaid costs, managed care is commonly viewed as a mechanism to reduce costs primarily and to achieve other benefits, such as improve access to care, secondarily. Given this pressure, it is ironic that Medicaid managed care programs tend to focus on AFDC [or Aid to Families with Dependent Children] beneficiaries, since the potential savings that can be expected from the population are relatively small. Indeed, expenditures associated with the AFDC population are too insignificant compared to all Medicaid costs to achieve major savings. While low income families comprise 72% of all Medicaid beneficiaries, they account for only 29% of the expenditures. (Kaiser Commission on the Future of Medicaid, 1992)." (p61-62)

Hughes, Dana (Senior Policy Analyst, Inst. for Health Policy Studies). U.S. House. Committee on Energy and Commerce. "Medicaid Managed Care in California." Hearing, 20 Apr 1993. Washington, D.C.: GPO, 1994. (ISBN0160434122). (Y4.En2/3:103-52).

"State spending [in the U.S.] on Medicaid nearly tripled in the past decade, consuming a greater and greater portion of limited State budgets. In 1992, Medicaid absorbed 17 percent of State spending, up from 10 percent just 5 years earlier. In fact, with the exception of education, States spend more on health care than any other item in their budget. Like other employers, States have seen the cost of health insurance continue to escalate. Nationally, States spent almost $11 billion to insure their workers and retirees last year, up 45 percent over the past 7 years, from $200 million in 1986 to $465 million in 1993." (pS2671)

Kennedy, Edward M. (Sen.-Mass.). "State Savings under Health Reform," Congressional Record (10 Mar 1994). Daily ed. pS2671. (ISSN0363-7239).

MEDICAID--COSTS--SUBSTANCE USE (v19)

MEDICAID--MEDICARE

"While the private sector has begun to get a grip, the federal government allows its health-care programs to roar out of control. 'Medicare and Medicaid have tripled since 1982,' Clinton correctly told an entitlements summit in Bryn Mawr, Pennsylvania, in December. Medicare spending jumped 12 percent in 1992. Medicaid is expected to grow 16.6 percent in 1993. That's just at the federal level. State outlays for Medicaid rose 30 percent from 1991 to 1992. By 1996, states will spend more on Medicaid than on education." (p37)

Barnes, Fred. "Health Care Costs Are Going Down." American Spectator v72 n2, Feb 1994. p36-39. (ISSN0148-8414).

"When most people [in the U.S.] think of federally financed health care, they usually think of Medicare and Medicaid, the two largest programs of government expenditures. Gross federal outlays for Medicare totaled $143 billion in 1993; for Medicaid, $76 billion." (p2)

U.S. Congressional Budget Office. "Introduction." The Tax Treatment of Employment-Based Health Insurance Mar 1994. Washington, D.C.: GPO, 1994.

MEDICAID--MEDICARE--COSTS (v19)

MEDICAL CARE

see also CHRISTIAN SCIENTISTS--MEDICAL CARE; DENTAL CARE; HEALTH FACILITIES; MANAGED CARE PLANS (MEDICAL CARE); MANAGED CARE PLANS (MEDICAL CARE)--U.S.; PRIVATIZATION--MEDICAL CARE--MASSACHUSETTS

"If we review the available information we will find that even in those countries that supposedly provide universal [health] coverage, a significant portion of the population is actually not covered. For instance, in France universal coverage is defined as 95 percent coverage. The best they have ever achieved is 5 percent uninsured. If you look closer to home at Hawaii, which has had an employer mandate for 20 years, you will find the uninsured rate is 8.1 percent. A recent analysis by Andrew Dick found that high rates of coverage has more to do with the characteristics of the population than the effectiveness of an employer mandate." (pH2844)

Hefley, Joel (Rep.-Colo.). "An Employer Mandate Won't Work," Congressional Record (28 Apr 1994). Daily ed. pH2843-2844. (ISSN0363-7239).

MEDICAL CARE--AUSTRALIA--U.S.

"As the United States Congress wades deeper into the difficult debate over reforming the nation's health care, it might want to take a look down under. Australia went through a similar experience in the 1970s. It had a system similar to the present American system, and faced the same difficult issues of reform....Australia's 12-year-old universal health insurance system is funded by a flat 1.5 percent levy on gross income over A$10,000 (US$7,100) for singles, as well as through general revenue....Costs have been consistently held to 8 percent of GDP [gross domestic product], says Lesley Russell, manager of public affairs for the drug company Merck, Sharpe & Dohme. Health care costs in the US account for 14 percent of GDP, and are expected to rise to 19 percent within five years, she notes....Administrative costs in Australia in 1987 were US$19 per capita; in the US they were $95." (p8)

Foster, Catherine. "International: Australians Offer US Tips on Health Care." The Christian Science Monitor v86 n109, 29 Apr 1994. p8. (ISSN0882-7729).

MEDICAL CARE--CALIFORNIA

"California's Medicaid program--Medi-Cal --provides health care coverage to more than 5 million women, children, and aged or disabled people in this State. Between 1980 and 1992, enrollment in Medi-Cal climbed to 79 percent, while the cost of the program tripled. We now spend almost $14 billion dollars a year for Medi-Cal services, amidst a growing recognition that these services are not provided in a system that makes sense. During the 1980's, California was the fastest growing state in the nation, swelling to more than 30 million residents. During this same period, the number of Californians without health insurance climbed to nearly one-fourth of the population. These two factors contributed to a tremendous jump in the number of those who depend on state and federally funded programs for health care. Between 1980 and 1992, enrollment in Medi-Cal, the State's publicly financed health care system for the poor, climbed 79 percent--from 2.96 million to 5.2 million beneficiaries. At the same time, the cost to taxpayers for providing this care has more than tripled to $14 billion." (p9)

Coye, Molly Joel (Director, California State Dept. of Health Services). U.S. House. Committee on Energy and Commerce. "Medicaid Managed Care in California." Hearing, 20 Apr 1993. Washington, D.C.: GPO, 1994. (ISBN0160434122). (Y4.En2/3:103-52).

"Health insurance is evolving from a mechanism for simply paying doctors' and hospitals' bills into a means of managing health risks and costs. The results are dramatic: In California, where half the population is now enrolled in HMOs and other 'managed care' plans, costly hospital days for every 1,000 people fell by more than a third from 1980 to 1992. To maximize savings, virtually all Americans must be enrolled in similar systems 'where their incentives to stay well are matched by providers' incentives to keep them well,' contends C. Duane Dauner, president of the California Association of Hospitals and Health Systems." (p43)

Dentzer, Susan. "On the Economy: Precious Principles of Health Reform." U.S. News & World Report v116 n6, 14 Feb 1994. p43. (ISSN0041-5537).

MEDICAL CARE--CANADA (v19)

A survey by Statistics Canada "estimated the number of people waiting for some kind of medical service and also collected information on the people's incomes, making it possible to determine whether those with high and low incomes have an equal probability of waiting for medical services. Those with annual incomes of $60,000 to $79,000 (Canadian) have a 4.7 percent probability of waiting, and those with annual incomes over $80,000 have a 4 percent probability. By contrast, every other income group has a probability of 7 percent or more, and most exceed 8 percent." (p27)

Matthews, Merrill, Jr. "Symposium: Global Budgets Force Rationing." Insight v10 n12, 21 Mar 1994. p25-27. (ISSN1051-4880).

MEDICAL CARE--CANADA--U.S. (v19)

"One important element of health care rationed by the Canadian system is technology. For example, Seattle (population 490,000) has more CAT scanners (used to detect brain tumors) than the entire province of British Columbia (population 3 million). There are more MRI scanners in Washington state (population 4.6 million) than in all of Canada (population 26 million). While critics of the U.S. health care system claim that the United States has too much technology, all the evidence suggests that Canada has too little--as a result of the conscious decision made by government officials. Canada also rations by making people wait. A recent 12,000-person survey conducted by Canada's official statistical agency led to an estimate that almost 1.4 million people (out of a total population of 26 million) are waiting for some medical service ranging from a visit to their general practioner to nursing home admission. Of those, more than 177,000 are waiting for surgical procedures." (p26-27)

Matthews, Merrill, Jr. "Symposium: Global Budgets Force Rationing." Insight v10 n12, 21 Mar 1994. p25-27. (ISSN1051-4880).

"If you are seriously ill, the best place to be is in the United States. Among all industrialized nations, the United States has the highest cure rates for stomach, cervical and uterine cancers, the second highest cure rate for breast cancer and is second to none in treating heart disease....In Canada medical technology is rationed to dangerously low levels. The United States has 3.26 open-heart surgery units per million people; Canada has only 1.23 units per million. Cardiovascular disease is Canada's number one health problem, yet open-heart surgery units and catheterization equipment are kept in such short supply that the average wait for urgent (not elective) surgery is eight weeks. The shocking result is that in Canada, a cardiac patient is ten times as likely to die waiting in line for surgery as on the operating table. In the United States, there is no wait." (p25)

McCaughey, Elizabeth. "No Exit." New Republic v210 n6, 7 Feb 1994. p21-25. (ISSN0028-6583).

MEDICAL CARE--EMPLOYMENT--U.S. (v19)

MEDICAL CARE--EUROPE (v19)

MEDICAL CARE--FRANCE (v19)

MEDICAL CARE--GEORGIA--PUBLIC OPINION (v19)

MEDICAL CARE--GREAT BRITAIN (v19)

MEDICAL CARE--INDIA

"Far from ensuring efficiency, as the World Bank claims, competition in health care provision leads to false expectations and unnecessary high-tech care, and can leave consumers at the mercy of unscrupulous practitioners....The high-tech, profit-orientation of many Indian doctors has led to a boom in medical technology. India's medical electronics industry grew more than tenfold between 1972 and 1986, when it was worth US$10 million....Private hospitals and diagnostic centres must recoup the costs of their expensive machinery, so they try to persuade doctors to order unnecessary tests. Centres often offer doctors 20-40% of the test fee when they refer a patient....Despite the problems with the private sector, 70% of Indians use it, while only 30%--the poorest--use the public health service. Although more than 80% of urban residents have a government health facility within one kilometre, a study in five cities showed that even two-thirds of slum dwellers used private clinics. The poor spent up to one-quarter of their income on private health care, according to a survey by the National Council for Applied Economic Research. This is because treatment in the government-run sector is often poor." (p22-23)

Sharma, Kalpana. "World: Unhealthy Competition: India's Private Sector Cashes in on Health." Panoscope n37, Oct 1993. p22-23. (ISSN0951-8819).

MEDICAL CARE--ISRAEL

"Dr. Farouq Abdul Rahim, Chair of the Jordanian Medical Association, told us that on average U.S. $22-25 is spent for health care per person each year in the Occupied Territories compared with $450 per year for Israelis in Israel. Suhaila Tarazi, Senior Administrator for the Al-Ahli Arab Hospital in Gaza told us only about 20 percent of Palestinians in the Occupied Territories have health insurance. Dr. Arafat Hidmi, Medical Director for the United Nations Relief and Works Agency (UNRWA) told us that the infant mortality rate in the UNRWA camps is about 17 per 1,000 live births, but outside the camps in the Occupied Territories the rate is nearly 70 infant deaths per 1,000 live births." (p4)

Hall, David. "PSR/Washington Conducts Fact-Finding Mission to Israel and Occupied Territories." Vital Signs v6 n1, Apr 1993. p4.

MEDICAL CARE--LOS ANGELES (CALIF)

Los Angeles County's "Department of Health Services is the anchor of the county's health care safety net, operating six public hospitals, including the Nation's largest--LAC+USC Medical Center--six comprehensive ambulatory care centers and over 40 community health centers. The hospitals rank first, fourth, seventh, ninth, tenth and seventeenth among the State's 500 hospitals in terms of Medi-Cal/indigent care disproportionality. Fifty percent of the county's trauma runs are served by three of our hospitals. With an annual operating budget of $2.3 billion and 26,000 employees, the department provides: 170,000 admissions, 500,000 ER visits; 4.6 million ambulatory/public health visits; 50,000 births annually, 30 percent of all Medi-Cal inpatient services and 80 percent of all uncompensated care within the county." (p20)

Gates, Robert C. (Los Angeles County Director of Health Services). U.S. House. Committee on Energy and Commerce. "Medicaid Managed Care in California." Hearing, 20 Apr 1993. Washington, D.C.: GPO, 1994. (ISBN0160434122). (Y4.En2/3:103-52).

MEDICAL CARE--MALI

"Since 1989, Mali has seen a new type of health institution emerge in the form of Community Health Centres, founded on three fundamental principles so that each Centre is: created by the community; run by the community; managed by the community." (p18) "The 15 urban centres in Bamako now cover a total population of some 250 000, or around 30% of the city's population. They handle a total of more than 80 000 consultations a year, all undertaken by medical practitioners; this amounts to 20% of all general medical consultations officially carried out in Bamako. The 9300 deliveries at the centres, following regular prenatal consultations and under the care of state-registered midwives, represent nearly 30% of all births recorded in the city, and there are now more than 2000 new family planning consultations each year." (p19)

Balique, Hubert/others. "Mali's New Private Sector." World Health n6, Nov-Dec 1993. p18-20. (ISSN0043-8502).

MEDICAL CARE--MARYLAND (v19)

MEDICAL CARE--MEXICO

"In Mexico's rugged Sierra Madre mountains, over one hundred remote, poor communities provide for their own basic healthcare. Their village health workers, and the training clinic at the base of the mountain, form a unique cooperative network known as Project Piaxtla. Villages formerly plagued by preventable diseases now treat at least 90% of their health problems with a basic set of medicines." (p14) "Another clinic/community organizational effort focused on decreasing the debt of local farmers. Before 1977, if farmers in the Sierra Madre mountain region ran out of corn to eat or plant, they were forced to borrow corn from rich landowners at outrageous prices (sometimes 300% interest). This often led farmers into a desperate cycle of debt, poverty and disease. To break the cycle, Ajoya health workers and poor farmers organized cooperative corn banks that loan corn at 50% interest (in corn). This more manageable fee keeps the farmers free from heavy debt, while making the corn bank available to more people each year. Many surrounding villages saw the benefits of community seed banks, and organized them with Ajoya's help." (p15)

Janes, Danielle. "Piaxtla: Village-Organized Healthcare." Rain v14 n3, Spr 1993. p14-19.

MEDICAL CARE--MONTANA (v19)

MEDICAL CARE--OREGON

"The Oregon Health Plan is a homegrown project. Although Oregon is a reasonably prosperous state, 16% of its 2.8m residents lacked any health coverage before the plan took effect. By devising a list of accepted treatments, Oregon hopes that limited Medicaid dollars can be stretched to cover 395,000 people--120,000 more than were covered last year. The plan is expected to cost $169m from now until the end of 1995, with the state picking up 37% of that and the federal government the balance. To pay for its share, Oregon tapped into its general fund and charged smokers (those convenient cash cows) an additional 10 cents a pack in tax." (p27)

"American Survey: Oregon Health Care: Trying to Be Tough." Economist v331 n7860, 23 Apr 1994. p27. (ISSN0013-0613).

MEDICAL CARE--U.S. (v19)

"There can be no dispute that America is going through a severe healthcare crisis. Fully 35 million Americans are uninsured and an additional 15 million Americans are underinsured. Tens of millions more have endured lower wage increases over the years in order to maintain their existing health coverage, and many live in a state of fear that they will lose their coverage anyway. Nationally, healthcare cost increases continue to far outpace the rate of general inflation, and healthcare spending continues to rise as a percent of GNP [gross national product]. This crisis has lead to greater scrutiny of how the healthcare industry is financed and supported in the U.S. And this, rightly, is leading to an overdue reinvestigation of the role of non-profit healthcare institutions, particularly hospitals, in the provision of healthcare. Non-profit institutions remain the core of the hospital industry--fully 59% of community hospitals in the US are non-profit. And by virtue of their non-profit status, these hospitals receive billions of dollars in tax breaks from federal, state, county, and municipal governments." (p14)

U.S. House. Committee on Energy and Commerce. "HMO Financial Practices." Hearing, 27 May 1993. Washington, D.C.: GPO, 1993. (ISBN0160432782). (Y4.En2/3:103-45).

"Any projection of the number of [medically] uninsured will be subject to some error. Still, in 1991, the number was 35.4 million in the Current Population Survey. In 1992, the number had grown to 37.4 in spite of the improvements in the economy which caused the number of employed to grow by half a million and the number of persons employed full time for the entire year to grow by over a million. If the number of uninsured increases by the same amount as in 1992, the number of uninsured in 1993 will be over 39 million....Perhaps improvements in the economy will cause the number of employed persons with insurance (as part of their wages) to increase rapidly enough to keep the number of uninsured from growing to 39-40 million. Firm estimates will be available in late 1994." (p20)

U.S. House. Committee on Energy and Commerce. "Health Care Reform (Part 1)." Hearing, 28 Sep 1993. Washington, D.C.: GPO, 1994. (ISBN0160435692). (Y4.En2/3:103-59).

"Health care is one of the largest sectors of...[the U.S.] economy, accounting for 14 percent of our Gross National Product--$900 billion each year. There is no doubt that reforms are needed. There are many problems with our current way of providing and financing health care: runaway medical inflation, overwhelming malpractice liability, administrative inefficiencies, and the difficulties of ensuring health insurance to under- and un-insured populations." (p2)

Schaefer, Dan (Rep.-Colo.). U.S. House. Committee on Energy and Commerce. "Health Care Reform (Part 1)." Hearing, 28 Sep 1993. Washington, D.C.: GPO, 1994. (ISBN0160435692). (Y4.En2/3:103-59).

"A new study [in the U.S.] suggests that people who belong to health maintenance organizations (HMOs) are more satisfied with their care than are members of traditional health-insurance plans. About 85 percent of HMO members say they are satisfied with their insurance policies, compared with 72 percent of those with conventional indemnity plans, according to the Sachs Group of Evanston, Illinois....The study compared responses from 5,000 households who were enrolled in either an HMO, an indemnity plan, or a preferred provider organization (PPO). Indemnity insurance plans are most common: 58 percent of all insured Americans are enrolled in such a plan, according to Richard Coorsh of the Health Insurance Association of America. Indemnity plans...feature deductibles and allow subscribers to switch physicians or seek care from a specialist....The second most common type of plan is the PPO, which covers 20 percent of all Americans. These plans are...organized by large employers who negotiate special rates from doctors and hospitals....Nearly as many are enrolled in HMOs (19 percent), which generally do not have deductibles and instead feature a small co-payment for care." (p17-18)

Braus, Patricia. "Business Reports: Health Care: HMOs Get High Marks from Their Members." American Demographics v16 n2, Feb 1994. p17-18. (ISSN0163-4089).

"Hospitals [in the U.S.] have lent their own employees to schools to help guidance departments evaluate psychiatric and substance abuse problems. While these actions are not illegal, they could create an atmosphere that pushes students into institutional care they did not need. Estimates put the level of fraud perpetrated by certain actors in the health care industry at $70 billion dollars. The GAO [General Accounting Office] estimates the fraud could reach $100 billion by 1995. This figure dwarfs the estimated $5 billion lost through criminal fraud in the entire savings and loan debacle. Most authorities estimate that health care fraud and abuse encompasses 5 to 15 percent of this nation's overall medical costs--this at a time when health insurance premiums have skyrocketed out of reach for a significant portion of our citizens." (pE529)

Bryant, John (Rep.-Tex.). "Mental Health Care Providers Bounty Prevention Act," Congressional Record (23 Mar 1994). Daily ed. pE529-530. (ISSN0363-7239).

Eighty-five "percent of Americans do have insurance, and more than 81 percent of these individuals are satisfied with their coverage. Even among the 15 percent of the population who lack insurance, fewer than half are uninsured for extensive periods of time. Moreover, the care that is received by all Americans--including the uninsured--is the envy of the world. Consequently, the approach to health care reform that we should take is to build upon what is good in the system, and correct what is flawed." (pS290)

McCain, John (Sen.-Ariz.). "Statements on Introduced Bills and Joint Resolutions," Congressional Record (27 Jan 1994). Daily ed. pS286-291. (ISSN0363-7239).

"Two million Americans lose their health insurance each month. This is according to a report released September 15th by Families USA, a consumer group fighting for health and long term care reform. 'Some lose insurance for a month or two. Some for a year or more. But, however brief, it's a terribly dangerous time for a family. If a child gets seriously ill, it can destroy a family's security forever,' said Ron Pollack, executive director. States with the highest number of people who lose health insurance each month: CA (306,000); TX (173,000); NY (130,000); FL (113,000); IL (90,000); OH and PA (89,000); MI (76,000); NC (64,000); GA (62,000); VA (55,000); LA (51,000); MA (50,000)." (p1)

"Health Care Reform." Family Day Care Bulletin Oct 1993. p1.

"The Clinton's health-care program adds an additional $389 billion in new spending over the first five years. It includes: $65 billion for the new Medicare long-term care benefits; $66 billion for the new Medicare drug benefit; $29 billion for public health and administration; $116 billion in subsidies for low-income firms and workers, $10 billion to subsidize the tax deduction for self-employed workers; $45 billion for a contingency cushion and $58 billion for deficit reduction. The income to pay for these programs will come from: $124 billion in Medicare savings; $89 billion in tobacco taxes and assessments on corporations that form their own alliances; $65 billion in Medicaid savings; $47 billion in savings from federal programs; and $71 billion in revenue gains. Whether the predictions are accurate and the funding adequate remains to be seen. Critics and supporters alike have said such costs are difficult to predict. As one Blue Cross official reminded an audience at a recent conference, Medicare costs were five times greater than what was projected in its first year. Further, there is no surfire way to predict the cost of the new services the uninsured and underinsured will seek. The cost of subsidizing early retirement benefits, too, is hard to predict, since subsidies may increase early retirements." (p5)

"The Magnificent Six." People's Medical Society Newsletter v12 n6, Dec 1993. p4-8. (ISSN0736-4873).

"In a new study, the Employee Benefit Research Institute offers some 'facts' on health insurance, gleaned from the government's 'Current Population Survey' of March 1993. Eighty-three percent of nonelderly Americans and 99 percent of elderly Americans (aged 65 and over) were covered by either public or private health insurance in 1992. Although some of the nonelderly had public health insurance (15 percent), private insurance was the most common source of coverage--usually obtained through an employment-based plan. In contrast, nearly all of the elderly (96 percent) were covered by Medicare. In 1992, 38.5 million nonelderly Americans did not have health insurance, up from 36.3 million in 1991. Among those 38.5 million Americans, most were working adults (56.7 percent), while the remainder were children (25.4 percent) and nonworking adults (17.8 percent). Nearly one-half of all uninsured workers were either self-employed or working in firms with fewer than 25 employees in 1992." (p10)

Coolidge, Shelley Donald. "Economic Reports: Who Doesn't Have Health Insurance?" The Christian Science Monitor v86 n45, 28 Jan 1994. p10. (ISSN0882-7729).

"The Clinton administration and Congress are taking aim at health-care fraud, a sleeping giant that experts say costs taxpayers $90 billion a year....The General Accounting Office (GAO) estimates that fraud consumes 10 percent of the health-care budget. A recent review of 21 hospitals by the Office of Inspector General (OIG) turned up $50 million in unallowable costs, including alcohol, entertainment, marketing, and donations." (p4)

Appel, Adrianne. "National: US Government Targets Health-Care Fraud." The Christian Science Monitor v86 n50, 4 Feb 1994. p4. (ISSN0882-7729).

"'Home health care and home-infusion therapy were supposed to reduce costs by having patients discharged from hospitals earlier than normal and cared for at home,' said Michael Mangano, HHS [U.S. Dept. of Health and Human Services] principal deputy inspector general at a September hearing of an Energy and Commerce Committee subcommittee. Instead, the amount Medicare contractors paid per beneficiary for home infusion rose 63 percent from 1990 to 1991, from an average of $4,243 to $6,923, the OIG [Office of Inspector General] found....The OIG uncovered three types of kickback schemes between home-infusion-therapy firms and doctors: direct payment for referrals, stock ownership based on amount of referrals, and payment for falsifying papers declaring a patient needed infusion therapy." (p4)

Appel, Adrianne. "National: US Government Targets Health-Care Fraud." The Christian Science Monitor v86 n50, 4 Feb 1994. p4. (ISSN0882-7729).

"Employment-based health coverage [in the U.S.] is shrinking fast: In 1987, 72 percent of the work force was covered by private group health insurance, but by 1992 that number had fallen to 68 percent. What's more, roughly 75 million people are now enrolled in publicly funded health insurance, ranging from Medicare to programs for state and local workers. That's three times the number enrolled in Canada's taxpayer-funded health insurance system. American's public insurance pool could well grow to 110 million, or about 40 percent of the population, by the time most baby boomers have turned 65 and qualified for Medicare. If employer-based coverage erodes further, more galloping health outlays will be heaped onto tomorrow's taxpayers." (p43)

Dentzer, Susan. "On the Economy: Precious Principles of Health Reform." U.S. News & World Report v116 n6, 14 Feb 1994. p43. (ISSN0041-5537).

"The...principle that should be preserved [in President Clinton's health care reform plan] is universal coverage, or the guarantee that all Americans will have health insurance. Some pundits argue that the nation can't afford insurance for the roughly 15 percent of the population that is without it at any given time. But every other large industrialized nation except South Africa has universal coverage--and the World Bank reports that in 1990 the United States, with 1 out of 20 of the world's people, spent nearly $4 of every $10 that the entire globe spent on health care. Meanwhile, U.S. health outlays will undoubtedly rise from 14 percent of gross domestic product now to almost 19 percent by the year 2000. Achieving universal coverage, done carefully, merely means having the political will to spread this gigantic pot of health dollars among more Americans." (p43)

Dentzer, Susan. "On the Economy: Precious Principles of Health Reform." U.S. News & World Report v116 n6, 14 Feb 1994. p43. (ISSN0041-5537).

MEDICAL CARE--U.S.--DATA PROCESSING

"An orthopedic surgeon in Billings, Montana, examines a skin graft on a car-crash victim more than 230 miles away. Using a live video hookup, the surgeon advises the primary physician in rural Glendive on how to remove the staples and care for the wound....The videoconference saves the patient a nine-hour round trip to Billings....Just three years ago, only two states had telemedicine experiments. More than 20 states now have them, says Dr. Jane Preston, president of the American Telemedicine Association in Austin, Texas. Medical videoconferencing could save Americans $39 billion a year on everything from kidney dialysis to remote consultations, according to a study by Arthur D. Little of Cambridge, Massachusetts....U.S. citizens logged over 1 trillion miles of travel for medical purposes in 1992, according to Preston. 'Even if only one-quarter of this travel could be accomplished by videoconferencing, the savings to the country would be astronomical,' she says. Preston also directs a system that connects specialists in Austin with four rural facilities in nearby Giddings. In early results, the 2,800 patients included in the systems saved up to 22 percent over traditional delivery systems." (p6)

Heather, Rebecca Piirto. "Multimedia: Electronic House Calls." American Demographics v16 n3, Mar 1994. p6. (ISSN0163-4089).

MEDICAL CARE--U.S.--MORTALITY

"According to a May 11, 1993 (pages A-12) article in the SAN FRANCISCO EXAMINER, a recent study conducted by doctors, lawyers, and analysts at Harvard University provided disturbing figures about the leading cause of accidental death in the US: medical treatment. The article said the 'investigation... concluded that 150,000 Americans are killed annually by medical treatment, with more than half of those deaths attributable to doctors' negligence.' The Harvard research team concluded that 'Medical injury...accounts for more deaths than all other types of accidents combined, and dwarfs the mortality rates associated with motor vehicle accidents (50,000 a year) and occupational-related mishaps (6,000 a year).' The group went on to say that 'Not too many, but rather too few suits were brought for the negligent medical injuries inflicted on patients.'" (p43)

Channon, Gloria/Lyford, Joe, Jr. "Health Watch." Propaganda Review n10, Sum 1993. p43.

MEDICAL CARE--U.S.--PUBLIC OPINION

"Asked whether 'under President Clinton's health care plan, if it is passed,' you would have more or fewer choices as to doctors and other aspects of medical care than at present, 42 percent of respondents said fewer, just 16 percent more, while 39 percent said they would expect to have about the same degree of choice. And 56 percent thought the 'total amount of money (they) pay for medical care' would increase, just 14 percent that it would decrease, and 28 percent that it would remain about the same. Fifty-three percent responded that under the Clinton approach they thought 'there would be too much government involvement in (their) health care,' just 8 percent too little, and 36 percent about the right amount. As to whether they would be better or worse off under the Clinton plan, only 28 percent thought better off, 37 percent worse, and 31 percent that the plan would basically have no effect on them." (p22)

Ladd, Everett Carll. "The Home Forum: How Americans View Plans for Health-Care Reform." The Christian Science Monitor v86 n40, 21 Jan 1994. p22. (ISSN0882-7729).

MEDICAL CARE, COST OF (v19)

MEDICAL CARE, COST OF--EUROPE--JAPAN (v19)

MEDICAL CARE, COST OF--EUROPE--U.S.

"President [William Clinton] contends that 'there's a lot we can learn from the Germans,' whose national health program provides comprehensive coverage at a mere 9% of gross domestic product, compared with 14% in the U.S. But what the President isn't factoring in is the cost employers pay, on top of wages, to support the system. In fact, across the European Community, benefits costs--mostly for health insurance--are twice those in the U.S. The EC now admits that such costs are a big reason why the U.S. created 20 million jobs in the 1980s while Europe produced barely any." (p78)

Javetski, Bill. "Cover Story: These Days, Europe's Safety Net Looks More Like a Noose." Business Week n3355, 24 Jan 1994. p78. (ISSN0007-7135).

MEDICAL CARE, COST OF--MARYLAND

"According to the Maryland Health Services Cost Review Commission, the state agency that sets hospital rates in Maryland, in 1992, for the seventeenth consecutive year, the cost of a hospital admission in Maryland rose 3.77%, a rate below the national average of 8.44%. In 1976, the cost of an admission in Maryland was more than 25% above the national average; in 1992, the cost per admission was 14% below the national average. The Commission believes that its success in slowing the annual increase in hospital costs is a result of hospitals responding to the incentives of the Maryland rate setting system to become more efficient. The rate setting system used in Maryland takes a quasi-public utility approach in which rates are set for each hospital department based upon reasonable costs, and are later adjusted for such items as levels of uncompensated care, inflation, volume changes and productivity. Institutions that increase productivity or otherwise lower costs are rewarded under this system." (p62-63)

Cooper, Ellen S. (Chief, Antitrust Division, State of Maryland). U.S. Senate. Committee on Finance. "Antitrust Issues in the Health Care Industry." Hearing, 7 May 1993. Washington, D.C.: GPO, 1993. (ISBN0160434505). (Y4.F49:S.hrg.103-373).

MEDICAL CARE, COST OF--MASSACHUSETTS (v19)

MEDICAL CARE, COST OF--MEXICO--U.S. (v19)

MEDICAL CARE, COST OF--MICHIGAN

"In the last 10 years, the average Michigan family's health payments rose 257 percent faster than wages. If health care inflation continues unabated, in the year 2000--just 7 years from now--Michigan families can expect to spend, on average, over $11,000 per year on health care, compared to average annual expenditures of $4,569 per family in 1991." (pE3048)

Levin, Sander M. (Rep.-Mich.). "Health Care Reform," Congressional Record (24 Nov 1993). Daily ed. pE3047-3049. (ISSN0363-7239).

MEDICAL CARE, COST OF--U.S. (v19)

"Medicare, the federal health-insurance program for elderly people, covered just one-third of all paid home health care in 1992. Medicaid, the federal program for the poor, paid 25 percent, and private health insurance paid just 6 percent of all paid home care in 1992. Out-of-pocket expenses accounted for 31 percent of total home-care costs in 1992. A caregiver's personal contribution can be even higher. Among individuals who received any paid home-care services in 1992, the average cost was $3,100. One-third of these costs came out-of-pocket, according to a 1993 report of home-care expenses by Families USA Foundation. Caregivers with low-to-middle family incomes between $13,500 and $23,500 paid the highest share out-of-pocket, an average of half of their home-care costs." (p44-45)

Braus, Patricia. "When Mom Needs Help." American Demographics v16 n3, Mar 1994. p38-41,44-45. (ISSN0163-4089).

"The rate of growth in medical spending is dropping precipitously. Every month brings a fresh decrease in what the U.S. Labor Department calls 'price inflation for consumer medical goods and services.' It was 5.8 percent for the year ending last August, 5.7 percent for October, 5.5 percent for November. That's still nearly twice the rate of general inflation, but a lot better than 1989 (8.5 percent) or 1990 (9.6 percent). In fact, the 5.5 percent increase is the lowest since January 1974. Better yet, the 4.9 percent rise in the third quarter of 1993 was the lowest quarterly hike since 1973. And it's a good bet medical inflation will fall further....For the first time in years, the percentage of payroll costs devoted to health and dental insurance dropped from 8.4 percent in 1991 to 8.1 percent in 1992, according to a U.S. Chamber of Commerce study of 1,100 firms." (p36)

Barnes, Fred. "Health Care Costs Are Going Down." American Spectator v27 n2, Feb 1994. p36-39. (ISSN0148-8414).

"Steelcase and the University of Michigan have studied 4,000 Steelcase employees for nine years. The ongoing study is putting numbers behind what has largely been a common-sense hunch--that getting workers to reduce health risks will lower a company's health-care costs....For a business, the Steelcase study shows if workers get out of shape, the company loses money. A worker who is a consistently high health risk cost Steelcase an average $1,677 in annual medical claims, while a consistently low-risk worker cost $638....The savings will depend on the workforce. At Steelcase the average worker is 44 years old, turnover is low and 75 percent are men. The specific health-care costs would be different at a largely white-collar, female-dominated workplace." (p8 secB)

Murphy, Chris. "Business: Wellness Programs Boost Bottom Line, U-M Study Says." Ann Arbor News 13 Jan 1994. p8 secB.

"Medical prices grew at the slowest rate in 20 years in 1993, but increasing volume--especially in the 40% of health care financed by the government--pushed overall spending up 10.2% last year, to an estimated $903.3 billion. Another double-digit rise is expected in 1994. Curtailing spending has its risks: Health services have been an economic bulwark since 1990, adding 1.4 million jobs. But business and government can no longer stomach the kind of increases that are projected to lift health care's share of the nation's economy from one-seventh to one-fifth by the year 2000." (p97)

McNamee, Mike/Schiller, Zachary. "Services: Health Care: Prepping for Radical Surgery." Business Week n3353, 10 Jan 1994. p97. (ISSN0007-7135).

"More than 7.1 million people [in the U.S.] are expected to receive some [medical] care in their homes in 1994. That's up from 5.9 million in 1987, the industry's trade group says. Home care, which provides the services of nurses and aides, and home infusion therapies, which include delivery of drugs intravenously, are expected to grow 35% in 1994, according to the Commerce Dept.--three times faster than the rest of the health-care industry. The other industry segment, durable medical equipment, such as oxygen tanks and wheelchairs, is also growing fast. The federal government is picking up a sizable percentage of the tab. Medicare and Medicaid expenditures for home care ballooned to $18 billion last year, from just $8 billion in 1990, according to HOME HEALTH LINE, an industry newsletter. The Health Care Financing Administration, which manages Medicare expenses, predicts a 166% increase in its home-care spending by 1996." (p70-71)

Himelstein, Linda/others. "Social Issues: Is Fraud Poisoning Home Health Care?" Business Week n3362, 14 Mar 1994. p70-73. (ISSN0007-7135).

"At 12.7% of its Gross Domestic Product (GDP), the U.S. spent about 5% more of its 1990 GDP on healthcare than is average for our level of income and education and achieved about 5 years less of life expectancy. Spending nearly $2,800 per capita, the U.S. ranked 11th in the world with a life expectancy of 76. Greece achieved the same life expectancy with an outlay of $358 per capita, and Chinese life expectancy was 69, with a health services outlay of $11 per capita." (p2)

Hug, Jim, SJ. "Healthcare: Global-Local Links." Center Focus n118, Nov 1993. p1-5,7.

"In 1940...[the U.S.] spent $4 billion on health care. In 1960, total national health expenditures were $27.1 billion. In 1965, the year Government became a health service payor for millions of Americans through Medicare and Medicaid, national health spending had increased to $41.6 billion. Over the next 15 years, national health spending quintupled, reaching more than $250 billion in 1980. Over the next decade, health spending more than doubled again, and by 1991, this Nation was spending $751.8 billion on health care. Put another way, in 1960 we spent 7.8 percent of our gross domestic product on health care. By 1991, that number was 14.1 percent. Not only has Government's entry into a major portion of our health care market not had a positive effect on the cost of care, but, rather, many of us believe Government's intrusion into the marketplace has been a major factor in the enormous increase in health spending." (pH2399)

Goss, Porter J. (Rep.-Fla.). "At What Cost Reform?"

Congressional Record (19 Apr 1994). Daily ed. pH2399. (ISSN0363-7239).

"Rising health care costs are threatening our standard of living. The average American worker would be making $1,000 a year more today if health care accounted for the same proportion of wages and benefits as in 1975. Unless we act, health care costs will lower real wages by almost $600 per year by the end of the decade and nearly $1 in every $5 Americans spent will go to health care. Small businesses create most of the new jobs in America and while most want to cover their employees, more and more cannot. Under the current health care system, cost pressures are forcing a growing number of small business owners to scale back or drop health insurance for their employees. Small businesses spend 40 cents of every health insurance dollar for administration--eight times as much as large companies. And only 1 in every 3 companies with fewer than 500 workers today offers its employees a choice of health plan." (pS16715-16716)

Clinton, William (President, U.S.). "Report of Proposed Legislation Entitled 'The Health Security Act of 1993'-- Message from the President--PM 74," Congressional Record (20 Nov 1993). Daily ed. pS16715-16717. (ISSN0363-7239).

The U.S. spent "$1 trillion on health care today--more than on defense, education, and Social Security pensions combined--and it will be $2 trillion by 2000. Yet, we have over 2,000,000 Americans losing their health insurance each month. And of those, one million will go without insurance for half-a-year and 100,000 will never get their insurance back. And let me tell you the truly shocking part of all this--the vast majority of the people who lose their health care coverage are middle-class Americans who pay premiums, work hard, play by the rules." (pS16810)

Rockefeller, John D., IV (Sen.-W.Va.). "The Health Security Act," Congressional Record (20 Nov 1993). Daily ed. pS16787-16829. (ISSN0363-7239).

"In 1980, health care for the average American family cost $2,500 a year. This year it's about $6,500. If we don't do anything to reform the system, by the end of the decade, an average family will be spending $14,000 a year just for health care. If we do nothing to stop this, American workers will continue to lose $655 in income each year by the end of the decade. Small businesses will continue to face skyrocketing premiums, and a full third say they will be forced to drop insurance. Large employers will have to pay as much as $20,000 a year for each employee." (pH860)

Bonior, David E. (Rep.-Mich.). "Health Care in America," Congressional Record (24 Feb 1994). Daily ed. pH859-862. (ISSN0363-7239).

"In 1980, total Federal spending for health--which is mostly for Medicare and Medicaid--accounted for about 12 percent of all Federal spending; this amount rose to 15.4 percent in 1990. If our system remains unchanged, Federal spending on health is estimated to nearly double to 29 percent by the year 2000. Much the same is happening in the States. State spending on health care accounted for about 8 percent of total State expenditures in 1980, increasing to 12.5 percent in 1990. This percentage is expected to grow to 19 percent by the year 2000, with all the increase attributable to rising Medicaid costs." (pE3048)

Levin, Sander M. (Rep.-Mich.). "Health Care Reform," Congressional Record (24 Nov 1993). Daily ed. pE3047-3049. (ISSN0363-7239).

In the U.S., "the average cost to employers to provide health insurance to their workers increased by over 140 percent, from $1,645 per worker per year in 1984 to $3,968 in 1992. Ultimately, it is employees who bear much of the burden of these increases in the form of lower wages, or the reduction or even elimination of health insurance benefits. Escalating prices affect not only our pocketbooks, but our global competitiveness. American employers spent 107 percent of corporate after-tax profits in health care in 1991, compared to only 48 percent in 1980. These exploding health care expenditures drive up the cost of labor, raise the retail prices of American goods and services, and severely restrict our ability to compete in the global marketplace." (pE3048)

Levin, Sander M. (Rep.-Mich.). "Health Care Reform," Congressional Record (24 Nov 1993). Daily ed. pE3047-3049. (ISSN0363-7239).

"There are upwards of 40 million Americans uninsured, many millions more that are underinsured. Every month, 2 million people lose their heatlh coverage. Health care costs are approaching $900 billion a year. And this year...health care costs will go up over $100 billion. So the total health care costs of this country after this year will be near $1 trillion. Even though health care costs will go up over $100 billion this year, our health care will not be any better. If health care costs are not brought under control, Americans will be spending $1 out of every $5 they earn on health care in less than 7 years. That is by the year 2000." (pS759)

Reid, Harry (Sen.-Nev.). "America's Health Care in Crisis," Congressional Record (3 Feb 1994). Daily ed. pS759-760. (ISSN0363-7239).

In the U.S. "Drug, alcohol and tobacco abuse costs society between $140 billion and $238 billion a year....The costs of just three STDs [sexually transmitted diseases]--gonorrhea, herpes and chlamydia--reached $5.4 billion in 1990....there are around 350,000 reported cases [of AIDS], and the number is expected to grow significantly. Given that the average lifetime cost of treating an HIV-positive patient is more than $100,000, the costs of treating current AIDS patients will total more than $300 billion....Around one-third of the 150,000 deaths per year from injuries are suicide- or crime-related; more than 2 million Americans suffer from nonfatal violence each year. According to the Centers for Disease Control, the cost of firearm-related homicides alone exceeds $14 billion annually." (p33)

Harder, Cherie. "Fair Comment: Clinton's Health Reforms Fail to Cap Irresponsible Behavior." Insight v10 n5, 31 Jan 1994. p33-34. (ISSN1051-4880).

MEDICAL CARE, COST OF--U.S.--PUBLIC OPINION (v19)

MEDICAL PERSONNEL

see also HIV (VIRUSES)--U.S.--MEDICAL PERSONNEL

MEDICAL PERSONNEL--MALPRACTICE--U.S.

"A very small percentage of physicians cause the majority of malpractice injuries [in the U.S.]. In 1991 state medical boards took only 3.4 serious disciplinary actions for every 1,000 physicians. Malpractice insurance costs doctors and hospitals about $9 billion a year, or 1 percent of the nation's total health care costs. Estimates of the cost of 'defensive medicine'--tests and procedures ordered to protect health care providers from lawsuits--range from $15 billion to $27 billion a year. Most personal injury lawyers charge a contingent fee of one-third the settlement of jury award, a rate-of-return of $3,000 to $4,000 an hour in successful cases. Other legal costs often eat up another 20 or 30 percent of the award. Total contingent fee income per year for personal-injury cases is about $14 billion." (p18)

Kemper, Vicki. "The Numbers Game." Common Cause Magazine v19 n3, Fall 1993. p18. (ISSN0271-9592).

MEDICAL PERSONNEL--MALPRACTICE--U.S.--COSTS (v19)

MEDICAL PERSONNEL--NORTH DAKOTA--VERMONT (v19)

MEDICAL PERSONNEL--U.S.--MINORITIES

"Despite some laudable efforts over the past 20 years, minorities remain seriously underrepresented in the health professions. In 1992 the number of African Americans,

Hispanics, and Native Americans enrolled in medical schools reached 10.3 percent, yet these groups represent 22 percent of the U.S. population. Minorities comprise only 3.5 percent of health faculty and researchers." (p1-2)

News release. "Need for More Minority Health Professionals Goes Beyond Past Calls for Social Equality, Justice." Institute of Medicine News 14 Apr 1994. p1-3.

MEDICAL RESEARCH

see MEDICINE--RESEARCH

MEDICAL TECHNOLOGY--U.S.

"About 10% of the nation's 6,600 hospitals have figured out the advantages of information technology and are in the midst of massive reengineering efforts....The remaining 90% have no choice but to follow, due to Medicare's edict that all providers must submit claims electronically by 1996. Most are still sent on paper. On top of that, health-care reform will almost certainly include mandates for measuring the efficacy of treatment, which means information must be easily available." (p105)

Arnst, Catherine/Zellner, Wendy. "Information Processing: Information Management: Hospitals Attack a Crippler: Paper." Business Week n3359, 21 Feb 1994. p104-106. (ISSN0007-7135).

"Health care is 5 to 10 years behind the rest of American industry when it comes to computers. The industry that gobbles up some 13% of the gross domestic product is spending only 1% to 2% of its operating budget on information technology. That compares with 10% for banking, 6% to 7% for insurance, and 4% for manufacturing. In fact, health care is the only major industry still keeping paper records. The records aren't even very useful: About 30% of patient information needed during a typical clinicai visit is missing--stuck in a different file, according to an Institute of Health study." (p104)

Arnst, Catherine/Zellner, Wendy. "Information Processing: Information Management: Hospitals Attack a Crippler: Paper." Business Week n3359, 21 Feb 1994. p104-106. (ISSN0007-7135).

"As the health care debate rages, medical technology, despite facing a bruising regulatory regime, effectively controls health care costs by bringing lifesaving technologies to market. In addition, exporting medical products has generated a trade surplus that has risen from $1.1 billion in 1987 to $4 billion in 1992. Unfortunately, the small companies which comprise the bulk of the industry are highly vulnerable. The FDA [Food and Drug Administration], which regulates the industry, has nearly destroyed the sector with an approval process that takes so long that businesses are forced to move production offshore....In fiscal year 1991, the average clearance time was 102 days. By fiscal year 1993, it had risen to 195 days. Equally disturbing, there is a current backlog of over 5,100 device applications at the FDA--a 50-percent jump in outstanding applications since 1991." (pH1175)

Ramstad, Jim (Rep.-Minn.). "Concurrent Resolution on the Budget--Fiscal Year 1995," Congressional Record (10 Mar 1994). Daily ed. pH1170-1242. (ISSN0363-7239).

MEDICALLY UNINSURED PERSONS--U.S. (v19)

"Nationally, more...[than] one-half of the uninsured in 1990 were full-time workers and their families. More than 1 million of those who lost their health insurance in 1991 were earning between $25,000 and $40,000 annually, and almost one-half of the uninsured go without health insurance for 2 years or more....People without health insurance end up paying, on average, about 20 percent of the cost of any health care they might receive. But those of us with insurance are charged, on average, 130 percent of the cost of the care we receive. The excess amounts we pay help defray the costs of caring for those without insurance." (pE3048)

Levin, Sander M. (Rep.-Mich.). "Health Care Reform," Congressional Record (24 Nov 1993). Daily ed. pE3047-3049. (ISSN0363-7239).

"In 1992 the U.S. civilian, noninstitutionalized population approached 252 million persons, up some 3.5 percent since 1989....Over this same period, however, the proportion of the total population (i.e., the elderly plus the nonelderly) that was medically uninsured increased by 12.1 percent. Since 1989, the number of these uninsureds rose by 4.2 million, reaching 38.9 million Americans in 1992. This 1992 total was 2.3 million persons higher than in 1991 and was a larger increase than that experienced from 1989 to 1991. In 1992, 17.4 percent of all nonelderly Americans were medically uninsured, up from 16.6 percent of this population in 1991." (p21-22)

Snider, Sarah C. "Who Are the Medically Uninsured in the United States?" Statistical Bulletin v75 n2, Apr-Jun 1994. p20-30. (ISSN0790-8334).

"In 1980, 11 percent of the [U.S.] population was uninsured; by 1993, that proportion had increased to 15 percent. The number of uninsured people increased by 55 percent during that interval....In 1992, about 72 percent of the 35 million uninsured people in the United States were part of a family with a working adult. Another 13 percent were members of families in which the head of the household was temporarily laid off or looking for work. Only 15 percent of uninsured people lived in a household whose head was out of the labor force." (p8)

U.S. Congressional Budget Office. "Background." The Tax Treatment of Employment-Based Health Insurance Mar 1994. Washington, D.C.: GPO, 1994.

MEDICALLY UNINSURED PERSONS--U.S.--CHILDREN (v19)

MEDICARE (v19)

MEDICINAL PLANTS

"While less than one percent of the world's 265,000 known plant species have been analyzed for their medicinal properties, 25 percent of our medicines come from that tiny fraction. And often, the realization of their value is garnered first from indigenous people. In an effort to encourage tribal people to record their knowledge, pass it on to the next generation and protect useful species, Mark Plotkin, director of plant programs for the Washington DC-based Conservation International, is setting up 'Sorcerer's Apprentice' programs, throughout Latin America. 'We're trying to use this type of 'ethnopharmacopeia' to generate a cultural re-awakening and convince these people not to throw away their entire culture because some missionary or government official says everything you know is primitive and stupid,' explains Plotkin." (p14)

Goodstein, Carol. "Currents: Sorcerers' Apprentices." E Magazine v4 n2, Mar-Apr 1993. p14-16. (ISSN1046-8021).

MEDICINE--JAPAN

"The term 'kampo' refers to Japanese herbal medicine in the Chinese tradition. Its storehouse of knowledge is based on Chinese medical texts that date as far back as 4,000 years. The Chinese classic 'Shen Nong's Materia Medica,' for example, was written 2,000 years ago and presents detailed descriptions of herbs, classifying their purpose, uses, efficacy and effects. Some 5,700 herbs were selected and tested in developing medicine in ancient China; about 100-200 are commonly used today as the basis for Japanese kampo drugs, known collectively as 'kampoyaku.' In addition to herbs, kampoyaku incorporate minerals and animal organs, as well as extracts from berries, roots and trees. More unusual ingredients include snakes, sea horses, and powdered pearls." (p34)

Ross, Catrien. "Body and Soul: Chinese Medicine: Kampo Makes a Comeback." Look Japan v39 n451, Oct 1993. p34-35. (ISSN0456-5339).

MEDICINE--RESEARCH--CALIFORNIA

"Kaiser Permanente's Division of Research in Oakland is among the most highly regarded epidemiological research centers in the...[U.S.]. Significant findings have resulted from research into cancer, cardiovascular epidemiology, gerontology, nutrition and alcohol and tobacco use. Division of Research scientists recently identified a 60-75 percent reduction in fatal cancer of the rectum and distal colon in persons who received screening sigmoidoscopies compared with individuals who did not. These findings were published in THE NEW ENGLAND JOURNAL OF MEDICINE in March 1992. The Southern California Region also conducted a five-year study at 10 hospitals that concluded that normal birth after prior Caesareans is possible and safe for many women. Of 6,000 women studied, 75 percent were able to deliver normally after Caesarean births. A study tracking 7,000 women after three years is being completed that is expected to be the definitive study on vaginal births after Caesareans." (p58)

U.S. House. Committee on Energy and Commerce. "HMO Financial Practices." Hearing, 27 May 1993. Washington, D.C.: GPO, 1993. (ISBN016042782). (Y4.En2/3:103-45).

MEDICINE--RESEARCH--U.S.

"The National Institutes of Health (NIH), the leading research group in the world, has played a critical role in promoting new technologies that reduce health care costs. In a recent report, NIH estimated that at least $9 billion could be saved in medical costs for just $4.3 billion invested in research. Some projects that help realize these savings include: Discovery of a bacteria that causes ulcers which can be treated with an antibiotic which could save as much as $816 million a year in treatment costs; the National Institute of Allergy and Infections Diseases developed a treatment for neonatal herpes which will reduce premature mortality and severe neurological handicaps, potentially saving as much as $183 million a year in therapy costs; the National Institute on Aging and the National Heart, Lung and Blood Institute has found that screening and medication could reduce strokes and heart attacks for elderly patients with hypertension which will save as much as $48.5 million in treatment costs each year. Also, since a University of Pittsburgh study found that tonsillectomies are not needed in the majority of cases, utilization of this procedure decreased 50 percent, saving as much as $401 million a year in treatment costs." (pE731)

Coyne, William J. (Rep.-Pa.). "The Health Research Act," Congressional Record (20 Apr 1994). Daily ed. pE731-732. (ISSN0363-7239).

MEDICINE--U.S.

"More than 25%, perhaps closer to 50% of our medicines are still natural, or at least purified or modified natural substances. The figure could be much higher. In spite of the fact that modern Americans are tending to prefer natural medicines, dyes, foods, etc., the pharmaceutical industry is trending towards the synthetics. A major reason is it costs nearly $100 million to prove a drug safe and efficacious here in the U.S. An herb can't legally be sold as a medicine until it has been proven safe and efficacious. If the drug company proves that, e.g., sweet annie (Artemisia annua) cures malaria, how does it recoup its $100 million investment if the world grows its own sweet annie and self-medicates?" (p13)

Duke, James A. "Annuals and Biennials in the Permaculture Scenario." International Permaculture Solutions Journal v1 n2. p13-17. (ISSN1046-8366).

MEDICINE--U.S.--AGED (v19)

MEDICINE--U.S.--VETERANS

"Hundreds of medications are dispensed and administered every day in [U.S.] Veterans Affairs Medical Centers (VAMCs). The national rate of medication errors is reported at 12 medications errors per 10,000 dosages of medications administered. Most medication errors result from a failure to follow the proper procedures. Each VAMC Nursing Service has policies and procedures for administration of medications. Medication administration procedures are clear, specific and consistent across nursing services. These procedures define the steps to be followed to ensure that the right medication is given in the right dosage, to the right patient via the right route at the right time. Medications are documented in the patient's chart on the Medication Administration Record." (p70)

U.S. House. Committee on Appropriations. "Depts. of Veterans Affairs and Housing and Urban Development...Approp. for 1994 (Part 1)." Hearing, Washington, D.C.: GPO, 1993. (ISBN0160408709). (Y4.Ap6/1:V64/994/pt.1).

MEDICINE, ALTERNATIVE

see ALTERNATIVE MEDICINE

MEDICINE, PREVENTIVE--U.S.

"Early intervention programs, such as thinking that education begins at birth and preparation begins before birth...are going to save us money. We know all the figures: A dollar invested in comprehensive preschool education like Head Start saves $3 later on. A dollar invested in immunizations saves $10 in later medical costs. A dollar invested in comprehensive prenatal care saves about $4 in later health costs. One dollar invested in the WIC [Women, Infants, and Children] programs for pregnant women saves an additional $3 in Medicaid costs. These are investments that up front save us money and make our lives better." (pS623)

Harkin, Tom (Sen.-Iowa). "Goals 2000: Educate America Act," Congressional Record (2 Feb 1994). Daily ed. pS605-634. (ISSN0363-7239).

MEDITATION--U.S. (v19)

MEDITERRANEAN--POPULATION (v19)

MELANOMA--U.S.

"Melanoma now strikes thirty-two thousand Americans each year and kills sixty-eight hundred. But before 1950 it was quite rare. Two other skin cancers, basal and squamous cell skin tumors, were dermatologists' major concern. These slow-spreading cancers usually occur in white men over forty-five who work outdoors or live near the equator. They are by far the nation's most prevalent cancers, with 600,000 new diagnoses each year, but they rarely prove fatal, with successful treatment in 99 percent of cases." (p34)

Castleman, Michael. "Power Guide to Health: Beach Bummer." Mother Jones v18 n3, May-Jun 1993. p32-37. (ISSN0362-8841).

MENINGITIS--U.S. (v19)

MENOPAUSE--U.S.--HORMONE THERAPY

"The number of U.S. women ages 45 to 64 taking estrogen jumped nearly 30 percent between 1990 and 1993, from 5.8 million to 7.4 million. Prescriptions written for estrogen supplements nearly tripled between 1985 and 1993, and the market has barely been tapped--three fourths of women 45 to 64 aren't on hormones. Long the domain of gynecologists who prescribe it for menopause symptoms such as hot flashes, estrogen is now attracting attention for its potential to prevent disease." (p60,63)

Rubin, Rita. "News You Can Use: Estrogen Anxiety." U.S. News & World Report v116 n13, 4 Apr 1994. p60,63-64. (ISSN0041-5537).

MENTAL ILLNESS (v19)

MENTAL ILLNESS--TREATMENT--U.S. (v19)

MENTAL ILLNESS--U.S. (v19)

"At the time Governor Harriman met with Dr. Hoch in 1955, there were 93,314 adult residents of mental institutions maintained by New York State. As of August 1992, there were 11,363." (p12)

Moynihan, Daniel Patrick. "Defining Deviancy Down." American

Educator v17 n4, Win 1993-94. p10,12-18. (ISSN0148-432X).
"Nearly half of all American men and women have experienced at least one episode of psychiatric disorder during their lifetimes--a significantly higher number than had been found in previous surveys, according to a national study conducted by the University of Michigan. The problems ranged from periods of major depression, recalled by 21.3 percent of the women interviewed, to simple phobias, such as fear of flying, which was reported by 6.7 percent of the men. The first-of-its-kind study of the incidence and severity of mental illness--based on detailed face-to-face interviews with more than 8,000 people between the ages of 15 and 54--also found that nearly a third of those questioned had experienced a diagnosable psychiatric episode within the previous year." (p1 secA)

Cain, Stephen. "Mental Ailments Widespread--Study." Ann Arbor News 14 Jan 1994. p1,10 secA.

"Mental illness affects all social, ethnic, and national groups. Approximately 40 million Americans, one out of five adults, suffer from diagnosable mental disorders. Available statistics reveal that out of this 40 million, between 7 and 12 million children suffer from serious mental disorders. One-third of our elderly population suffers from significant symptoms of mental illness. Approximately one-third of homeless individuals have psychiatric disorders. Often, these individuals have been discharged from hospitals and receive inadequate follow-up services. Individuals who are HIV positive are vulnerable to mental illness as well. Approximately 20 to 25 percent of those with the HIV virus will develop psychiatric problems along with the first signs of this disease; more than 60 percent of AIDS patients will ultimately suffer neuropsychiatric consequences. Statistics also reveal that the vast majority of the 30,000 who commit suicide annually have a mental or addictive disorder." (pS3793)

Simon, Paul (Sen.-Ill.). "Mental Health Awareness Week," Congressional Record (24 Mar 1994). Daily ed. pS3793. (ISSN0363-7239).

"Nearly half of all Americans between the ages of 15 and 54 have experienced an episode of psychiatric disorder at some time in their lives, and nearly 30 percent have had such an episode at some time in the last year, according to the first national survey to administer psychiatric interviews to a sample of the general population....The most common disorders identified in the study, conducted through the U-M Institute for Social Research (ISR): major depression, with 17 percent of the population experiencing an episode at some time in their lives and over 10 percent in the last year; and alcohol dependence, with 14 percent experiencing a problem at some time in their lives and more than 7 percent in the last year....The next most common disorders are social phobias, such as extreme fear of speaking in public or meeting new people, and simple phobias, such as fear of flying, with 13 percent and 11 percent, respectively, of the population experiencing the disorders in their lives, and 8 percent and 9 percent, respectively, in the last year." (p1)

News release. "Kessler." University of Michigan News and Information Services 13 Jan 1994. p1-4.

In a study of 8,000 Americans by the University of Michigan's Institute for Social Research, "Approximately one in every four respondents reported a lifetime history of at least one substance use disorder and a similar number reported a history of at least one anxiety disorder, such as phobias, panic or generalized anxiety disorder....The highest overall rates of mental illness occur between the ages of 25 and 34, then decline with age. The rates of almost all disorders decline with income and education, with the exception of lifetime substance use disorders, which are significantly higher in the middle education group than among those with either the lowest or highest educations." (p2)

News release. "Kessler." University of Michigan News and Information Services 13 Jan 1994. p1-4.

MENTAL ILLNESS--U.S.--COSTS (v19)

"In 1989, McDonnell Douglas introduced a managed mental health employee assistance plan. Their plan focused on each individual patient, on a case-by-case basis, and managed long-term care. During the first year, they reduced their per capita cost by 34 percent. Psychiatric inpatient costs decreased by 50 percent and chemical dependency costs dropped 29 percent. And overall, employee absenteeism is lower and turnover rates were reduced. These results have been repeated time and time again at companies like Federal Express, Digital, Honeywell, and First National Bank of Chicago--all of them have success stories. All of them have taken the time to treat mental illness and substance abuse just like any other physical illness to make prevention and treatment a priority and in doing so, they've not only saved money, they've saved lives." (pH1143)

Bonior, David E. (Rep.-Mich.). "Health Reform Should Cover Mental Illness, Substance Abuse," Congressional Record (9 Mar 1994). Daily ed. pH1142-1143. (ISSN0363-7239).

MENTALLY HANDICAPPED--U.S.

"The deinstitutionalization policies [in the U.S.] of the 1960s and 1970s effectively moved a substantial proportion of persons with mental retardation from institutions to community-based residential settings. Census data estimates (reported in Bruininks, Rotegard, Lakin, & Hill, 1987) indicate a steady growth in the number of residential patients in public institutions from 1900 until 1967. Starting in 1968, the institutionalized population dropped from 194,000 to 120,000 in 1980. Most of these individuals moved into their family's homes, privately managed community residential facilities, or specially licensed foster homes." (p29-30)

Reischl, Thomas M./Wordes, Madeline. "Collaborative Evaluation of a Volunteer Monitoring Program to Improve Group Homes for Adults with Mental Retardation." Community Mental Health Journal v30 n1, Feb 1994. p29-43. (ISSN0010-3853).

"A U.S. Conference of Mayors survey found that one-third of the nations' homeless suffer from severe mental illness; a University of Washington study concluded that 10 to 15 percent of inmates in state prisons are seriously mentally ill." (p62)

Sabar, Ariel. "Privatizing the Poor." Mother Jones v19 n2, Mar-Apr 1994. p62. (ISSN0362-8841).

MENTALLY ILL--U.S.--SUBSTANCE USE (v19)

MERCHANT MARINE--CHINA (v19)

MERCHANT MARINE--SALARIES, ETC.--U.S. (v19)

MERCHANT MARINE--U.S. (v19)

"In 1988, when the Commission on Merchant Marine and Defense was asked to explore the condition of America's Maritime Industry, it was revealed that the U.S. merchant marine force is unable to meet our Nation's minimum defense requirements. The Commission concluded that the state of U.S. maritime affairs poses...a 'clear and growing danger to the national security in the deteriorating conditions of America's maritime industries.' In response to these findings, the Commission warned that, 'unless decisive action is taken to reverse this downward trend, by the year 2000, the number of ships will be reduced by one-half to 220 vessels; the proportion of the U.S. ocean trade carried in U.S. vessels will drop from approximately 4 to 1 percent; the number of merchant fleet shipboard billets and merchant seamen will be about one-half their current size, and the shipyard industrial base will continue to shrink at an alarming rate.'" (pS16481)

Cohen, William S. (Sen.-Maine). "Statements on Introduced

Bills and Joint Resolutions," Congressional Record (19 Nov 1993). Daily ed. pS16433-16501. (ISSN0363-7239).

MERCY KILLING
see EUTHANASIA

MEREBANK (SOUTH AFRICA)
see POLLUTION--MEREBANK (SOUTH AFRICA)

METAL CASTINGS INDUSTRY--U.S. (v19)

METHANE (v19)

METHOXYNAPHTHYL CARBAMATE
see CARBARYL

METHYL TERTIARY BUTYL ETHER

"A recent paper published by the University of Oklahoma concludes that the health and environmental risks associated with MTBE [methyl tertiary butyl ether] have not been fully evaluated. The report stated that MTBE appears not to biodegrade once released into the environment, creating a potentially dangerous environmental/public health concern. In sharp contrast to MTBE, other oxygenates, including ethanol, biodegrade rather quickly. A University of Oklahoma study found that after 249 days, there was no evidence of the anaerobic destruction of MTBE, indicating that it may never biodegrade. Another study has found that fish absorb MTBE from the water into their body. The fish concentrates the MTBE about 1.5 times, for example, if the water is 10 ppm MTBE, the fish would contain 15 ppm. The RFG program is expected to create a market for between 400,000 and 700,000 barrels per day of oxygenate. If MTBE is the only oxygenate used, and ethanol is precluded, the potential for groundwater contamination is increased accordingly." (pS16641)

Grassley, Charles E. (Sen.-Iowa). "Reformulated Gasoline Program," Congressional Record (20 Nov 1993). Daily ed. pS16633-16644. (ISSN0363-7239).

METRIC SYSTEM--U.S. (v19)

MEXICO
see also AGRICULTURE--MEXICO; BALANCE OF TRADE--MEXICO--U.S.; BANKS AND BANKING--MEXICO; BEEF INDUSTRY--MEXICO--U.S.; CHEMICALS--MEXICO--ACCIDENTS; CHIAPAS (MEXICO); COLOMBIA--MEXICO--SOCIAL CONDITIONS; CONSUMER BEHAVIOR--MEXICO; CORN INDUSTRY--MEXICO; DAIRY PRODUCTS INDUSTRY--MEXICO--U.S.; ELECTRIC POWER CONSUMPTION--MEXICO; EXPORTS--MEXICO--U.S.; GROSS DOMESTIC PRODUCT--MEXICO; IMPORTS--MEXICO; INVESTMENTS, AMERICAN--MEXICO; IOWA--COMMERCE--MEXICO; MEDICAL CARE--MEXICO; NATURAL GAS--MEXICO--U.S.; NATURAL RESOURCES--CANADA--MEXICO--U.S.; NORTH AMERICAN FREE TRADE AGREEMENT--MEXICO; OFFSHORE ASSEMBLY INDUSTRY--ENVIRONMENTAL ASPECTS--MEXICO; OFFSHORE ASSEMBLY INDUSTRY--MEXICO--U.S.; PETROLEUM INDUSTRY AND TRADE--MEXICO; POLLUTION--EL PASO (TEX)--JUAREZ (MEXICO); POOR--MEXICO; RURAL-URBAN MIGRATION--MEXICO; TELECOMMUNICATION--MEXICO; U.S.--COMMERCE--MEXICO; WAGES--MEXICO

MEXICO--COMMERCE (v19)

MEXICO--COMMERCE--U.S. (v19)

"USITC [United States International Trade Commission] data...shows that U.S. exports to Mexico have risen by about $25.6 billion since 1987, while imports of U.S. components from Mexico have risen only about $4.2 billion....the real-world alternative to many assembly operations in Mexico is the movement of such operations--in part or lock, stock and barrel to Southeast Asia or elsewhere. In these cases, the losses to the U.S. in terms of jobs would be much greater because the job-creating connections to the U.S. of these third countries are usually significantly weaker than the Mexican connection. For example, the U.S. content of products made by U.S. companies in Asia is 20 percent, while the U.S. content of products made by U.S. companies in Mexico is 70 percent....USTR [United States Trade Representative], using data from the ITC that extends a recent GAO [General Accounting Office] analysis through 1992, estimates that about 78 percent (about $30.9 billion) of U.S. exports to Mexico were for consumption in Mexico. Reimports of U.S. components from Mexico totalled 21.9 percent ($8.7 billion) of U.S. exports in 1992, a share that has fallen by one third since 1987." (p10-11)

London, Paul A. (Acting Under Secretary of Commerce for Economic Affairs). U.S. Senate. Committee on Governmental Affairs. "NAFTA Job Claims: Truth in Statistics?" Hearing, 10 Nov 1993. Washington, D.C.: GPO, 1994. (ISBN0160435048). (Y4.G74/9:S.hrg.103-386).

MEXICO--ECONOMIC CONDITIONS (v19)

"To hear the debate, you might...conclude that Mexicans are too poor to buy anything of real value from Americans. Yet, the fact is that the average Mexican spends 34 percent more on American goods than the average European and 14 percent more than the average Japanese consumer. It is true that millions of Mexicans live in poverty. Yet, 30 percent of the country lives on a wage that one might consider middle or upper-middle class. People who buy computers and other such items. That amounts to 25 million people, the size of the population of Canada!" (pS16689-16690)

Baliles, Gerald L. (Former Governor-Va.). "North American Free-Trade Agreement," Congressional Record (20 Nov 1993). Daily ed. pS16678-16700. (ISSN0363-7239).

Economic growth has "been slowed because Mexico's more open and competitive environment has obliged many firms to scrap plant and machinery installed in the protectionist era sooner than would normally have been the case; and to adjust to sharp changes in the relative prices of capital, labour, energy and imported goods. Energy prices, for example, are now 50% higher in real terms than they were in 1982. Capital was also cheaper then, and many imported goods were inaccessible. According to Jesus Reyes Heroles of GEA, an economic consultancy, companies in industries such as textiles, leather goods and petrochemicals were stuck with the wrong technology when relative prices changed. Despite growth in investment from 17% of GNP [gross national product] in 1988 to 22% in 1992, the economy's capital stock is barely bigger than it was a decade ago....the biggest cloud over Mexico's growth prospects is a current-account deficit that reached $22.8 billion, or 6.8% of GDP [gross domestic product], in 1992." (p21)

"Mexico: The Revolution Continues." Economist v330 n7847, 22 Jan 1994. p19-21. (ISSN0013-0613).

Mexico's President Carlos "Salinas's economic policies have widened already-huge disparities of wealth. Mexico now has seven dollar-billionaires, according to FORBES magazine--as many as Britain. Some have grown rich from a privatisation programme which brought large capital sums to the state but which also converted public monopolies into private ones. At the other extreme, despite sharply increased social spending by the government, 16% of Mexico's population--13.5m people--is officially classified as living in 'extreme poverty' and another 23.6m as 'poor'. The government claims, improbably, that unemployment is only 3.7%; private-sector economists say that 25-30% of the labour force is out of work or scraping a living in the informal economy." (p19)

"Mexico: The Revolution Continues." Economist v330 n7847, 22 Jan 1994. p19-21. (ISSN0013-0613).

The Mexican economy has "changed in some areas beyond recognition under...[President Carlos] Salinas. The budget has been in surplus; foreign debts have been renegotiated; private investment has become the driving force of what was previously a state-led economy; import tariffs have been cut--the highest is now 20%, compared with more than 100% ten years ago; inflation, running at 159% annually in 1987, fell to 8% in 1993; more than 390 state-owned companies have been privatised, raising $23 billion; the consititution has been amended to allow communal farmers to own their land and do deals with private investors; regulations hindering private business have been systematically scrapped." (p20)

"Mexico: The Revolution Continues." Economist v330 n7847, 22 Jan 1994. p19-21. (ISSN0013-0613).

"A National Autonomous University study reported in 1991 that the number of...[Mexicans] living in 'extreme poverty' increased from 18 million to 20 million in the two years after [President Carlos] Salinas took office. The number living in 'poverty' climbed from 51 million to 55 million. Likewise, real wages dropped almost 40 percent in the last decade, and the ranks of the un- or underemployed swelled. Workers' share of aggregate personal income declined from 36 percent in the mid-1970s to 25 percent in 1988, and 23 percent in 1992." (p21)

Sims, Beth. "Poverty and Patronage in Mexico." Lies of Our Times May 1993. p20-21. (ISSN1046-7912).

"The restructuring of the economy seriously damaged Mexico's productive base, causing hundreds of thousands of small businesses to fold, and raising under- and unemployment to nearly 40% of the economically active population. The legally established minimum daily wage is just slightly over US$4 while the 'canasta basica' (cost of food and bare minimums) costs at least four times that amount. Even government statistics recognize that there are now more than 40 million Mexicans (out of a total 90 million) living in poverty and, of those, 17 million live in absolute poverty. Second and third degree child malnutrition had been unknown in Mexico since the 40s but is now back in alarming incidence, particularly in rural areas." (p9)

"Mexico: Chiapas Uprising." NewsNotes v19 n2, Mar-Apr 1994. p9-10. (ISSN1064-1556).

MEXICO--ENVIRONMENTAL ASPECTS (v19)

MEXICO--MANUFACTURES

"Big companies [in Mexico] have worked hard in the past three or four years to become more competitive. They have shed peripheral businesses, cut workers and found foreign partners with new technologies and markets. Some have expanded into the United States or elsewhere through acquisition. Many are now highly efficient. Their efforts have contributed to a steady productivity rise in manufacturing industry, up 19% between 1990 and 1992. But many smaller companies have barely begun to work out what they need to do to compete, and are holding the economy back." (p20-21)

"Mexico: The Revolution Continues." Economist v330 n7847, 22 Jan 1994. p19-21. (ISSN0013-0613).

MEXICO--POLITICS AND GOVERNMENT

Mexico's President Carlos Salinas "has tried to improve tax collection; social spending has risen by 85% since he took office in 1988; military spending has never been high....Unlike most of Latin America, Mexico is not a recognisable democracy with alternating governments. A strong, centralised bureaucracy has ruled the country since the revolution, with the Institutional Revolutionary Party (PRI) as its electoral vehicle. Elections have been marked by fraud and other biases in the PRI's favour. For decades, this system guaranteed stability and--because presidents, despite their enormous power, cannot be re-elected--periodic renewal. More recently, it has had the strength to force through economic reform. Now it has become a liability. At the top, it stifles independence of thought and impedes accountability. At the bottom, state and municipal governments cannot hope to respond to the inequalities (which NAFTA [North American Free Trade Agreement] will exacerbate) between a prosperous north and a poor south with the 15% of the budget that they now get." (p13)

"The Clash in Mexico." Economist v330 n7847, 22 Jan 1994. p13-14. (ISSN0013-0613).

MEXICO--POPULATION

"In the 40 years before 1940, the population of Mexico grew 52% (from 13 to 19.8 million). A serious population growth? Yes, but manageable. However, in the next 40 years it grew by 251% (from 19.8 to 69.4 million). A serious growth? No. A frightening and unmanageable explosion. What happened in Mexico happened in varying degrees throughout the developing world." (p55)

Paddock, William. "Our Last Chance to Win the War on Hunger." Carrying Capacity Network v4 n1, 1994. p52-65. (ISSN1066-5404).

"The 1990 Census of Mexico returned a much lower count for the country as a whole than expected, 81 million rather than the expected 87 or 88 million. Mexico City, expected to come in at 19 or 20 million people, was found to have a much lower count of 15 million. Debate continues on whether or not the enumeration suffered from an unusual undercount or if people moved out following the 1985 earthquake, but it does not seem likely that the numbers will be adjusted." (p2)

Haub, Carl. "Tokyo Now Recognized as World's Largest City." Population Today v21 n3, Mar 1993. p1-2. (ISSN0749-2448).

MEXICO--RELIGION (v19)

MEXICO--SOCIAL CONDITIONS (v19)

MEXICO--U.S.--RURAL CONDITIONS

"The preamble to the NAFTA [North American Free Trade Agreement] speaks to a goal of sustainable development. For rural North America we can't think of a more pressing need. In 1990, 50 percent of all rural children in Mexico were malnourished and 43 percent of all rural families lived below the poverty line. And while rural conditions in the United States are absolutely better, they are surprisingly close to Mexico's and more important, they are deteriorating fast. In 1991, the rural poverty rate (16.1%) was higher than the metropolitan poverty rate (13.7%). In 1990, 3.6 million rural children--about 23 percent--lived below the poverty line. And unemployment is 26 percent higher in rural areas than in urban areas of the U.S." (pSR4)

"Special Report: Sustainable Rural Development in North America and the North American Free Trade Agreement." Center for Rural Affairs Newsletter Apr 1993. pSR1-4.

MEXICO, GULF OF

see PETROLEUM INDUSTRY AND TRADE

MEXICO, GULF OF--ENVIRONMENTAL ASPECTS (v19)

MIAMI (FLA)--POPULATION

"Before World War II, Miami's largest minority was black, including both African Americans and peoples of the Bahamas and other Caribbean islands. But during the late 1950s, the Hispanic population began to grow....In 1970, there were 300,000 Hispanics in Dade County. By 1990 that number had more than tripled to 954,000--nearly half of the population of the Miami metro area....During the 1980s, large numbers of black immigrants from the Caribbean began to arrive....Also during the 1980s, the number of non-Hispanic whites living in the city declined by a total of 170,000 people, while the non-Hispanic white population of the two counties to Miami's North grew by 310,000." (p4)

Winsberg, Morton. "1994 PAA Conference Site: Hispanics Dominate Miami's Demography." Population Today v22 n4, Apr 1994. p4. (ISSN0749-2448).

MICHIGAN

see also AUTOMOBILE INDUSTRY AND TRADE--

MICHIGAN; CHILD WELFARE--MICHIGAN; CHILDREN--MICHIGAN--SOCIAL CONDITIONS; CRIME--MICHIGAN; EDUCATION, HIGHER--MICHIGAN; EDUCATION--MICHIGAN; FERTILIZATION IN VITRO--MICHIGAN; FIREARMS INDUSTRY AND TRADE--MICHIGAN; LAND USE--MICHIGAN; MEDICAL CARE, COST OF--MICHIGAN; POLLUTION--CALUMET REGION (LAKE MICHIGAN); POOR CHILDREN--MICHIGAN; PRISONERS--MICHIGAN--COSTS; PRISONS--MICHIGAN; SCHOOLS--MICHIGAN--PUBLIC OPINION; TOBACCO INDUSTRY--MICHIGAN; TRAFFIC ACCIDENTS--MICHIGAN; TRAFFIC SAFETY--MICHIGAN; TRANSPLANTATION OF ORGANS, TISSUES, ETC.--MICHIGAN; WAGES--MICHIGAN; YOUTH--MICHIGAN--SEXUAL BEHAVIOR

MICHIGAN--ECONOMIC CONDITIONS (v19)

"During a press conference and subsequent speech to a crowd of 1,000 at the Economic Club of Detroit...[Governor John] Engler gushed a stream of positive economic statistics that have been compiled on his watch. Some 4.3 million people are working in Michigan today--'more men and women on payrolls than ever before in our history,' Engler said. The state's 7 percent unemployment rate last year was the lowest in 15 years. And after announcing that state government ended 1993 with a surplus of $312 million, Engler boasted that Michigan is on 'the superhighway to recovery.'...Engler said his role was to cut taxes six times while eliminating a budget deficit of $1.8 billion that he inherited from Gov. James Blanchard. The tax cuts, he said, are why U.S. NEWS & WOLRD REPORT recently rated Michigan's economic recovery as the best among the nation's largest industrial states." (p1 secE)

Haglund, Rick. "Engler Surfs on Wave of Good Economic News." Ann Arbor News 30 Jan 1994. p1 secE.

"The Michigan economy has enjoyed significant advantages over the nation in the past year, both in terms of economic growth and in consistency. The state's economy, as proxied by Comerica Bank's Michigan Business Activity Index, has expanded by nearly a 6 percent real rate over the past year, or more than double the rate of growth recorded at the national level. What's more, this robust rate of growth has translated into a 3 percent gain in the level of employment in the state compared with just a 1.7 percent gain for the nation. The strong growth in Michigan employment has pushed the unemployment rate down 1.2 percentage points versus only a six-tenths of one percent decline in the national unemployment rate." (unpaginated)

Bills, James M. "Michigan to Maintain Growth Advantage over the Nation." Economic Newsletter 1993. unpaginated.

"Governor John Engler in his 1994 'State of the State' address described conditions as he sees them in Michigan....He spoke of the new jobs created in the state over the last year and how this has significantly improved the state's image as a place for people to find work. The truth is that 128,000 new jobs were created in this state in 1992, most of them part-time and temporary positions that paid close to minimum wage. January's unemployment records show that 351,000 people are looking for work. These facts are from the Michigan Employment Security Commission that Engler heads. So, by their own figures, there are many more people looking for work than there are jobs available. Add to these unemployment numbers the 285,000 families receiving ADC [or Aid to Families with Dependent Children] benefits, the 114,000 who receive SSI [or Supplemental Security Income] benefits, the 14,000 who receive State Disability Benefits, and the 150,000 plus who used to be on General Assistance. That's almost one million people unemployed. But the governor, with smoke and mirrors, speaks of better economic times?!?" (p5)

Taylor, Maureen D. "Michigan: What's the Real 'State of the State?'" People's Tribune v21 n6, 7 Feb 1994. p5.

"How much credit can [Governor John] Engler rightly claim for Michigan's recovery? Probably a lot less than he thinks he's entitled to, say David Littmann, Comerica Bank's senior economist and Donald Grimes, a University of Michigan economist. Littmann...[says] Engler deserves credit for 20 percent of the good economic news. He balanced the state budget without an income tax hike, eliminated General Assistance and signed a bill that wiped out the state inheritance tax. But 80 percent of Michigan's impressive recovery is due to favorable national economic factors, Littmann said. Chief among them: low interest rates, which have fattened pocketbooks and allowed consumers to buy more cars, many of them made in Michigan, and other big-ticket items....Comerica's Michigan Business Activity Index rose an average 8.9 percent during [Governor James] Blanchard's first three years in office, three times the 2.9 percent rise during Engler's first three years. Littmann attributes Michigan's economic jump in the 1980s to the hefty tax cuts during Ronald Reagan's presidency. Engler has been suffering, relatively speaking, because of tax hikes during the Bush and Clinton administrations." (p1 secE)

Haglund, Rick. "Engler Surfs on Wave of Good Economic News." Ann Arbor News 30 Jan 1994. p1 secE.

MICHIGAN--MANUFACTURES

"According to the most recent data published by the U.S. Small Business Administration, Michigan had the second-lowest number of new company formations in the nation. Further, the same report on national economic indicators shows Michigan leading the nation with the highest rate of business dissolutions. Given this data, it should come as no surprise that Michigan, once the manufacturing powerhouse of the Great Lakes states, now lags far behind its Midwest rivals in manufacturing growth. An analysis compiled by State Policy Reports found that Michigan ranks only 33rd in the nation for the number of new manufacturing facilities announced between 1990 and 1992. At 8.8 new facilities per million residents, Michigan ranks below Illinois, Indiana, Ohio, Wisconsin and Missouri; Michigan also lags far behind the national average of 15.9 new manufacturing facilities per million residents." (p8 secA)

Corbin, Gary. "Opinion: Editorials: Engler's Economic Development Policy Too Little, Too Late." Ann Arbor News 19 Jan 1994. p8 secA.

MICROCOMPUTERS--PRICES--U.S. (v19)

MICROCOMPUTERS--U.S. (v19)

MICROWAVE DEVICES

A "microwave clothes dryer, which could prove to be as revolutionary in the laundry room as the microwave oven has been in the kitchen, may be commercially available as early as 1996, according to the Electric Power Research Institute (EPRI) in Palo Alto, Calif. The dryer offers significant advantages in speed and efficiency over standard dryers, says John Kesselring, manager of residential systems for EPRI, which is developing the dryer. The new machines are about 25 percent more energy-efficient than conventional dryers; prototype microwave dryers for the home can dry normal loads 20 percent faster than conventional dryers and commercial microwave dryers 60 percent faster; and drying temperatures are significantly lower--about 95 degrees F compared with 110-160 degrees F for conventional dryers." (p9)

Coolidge, Shelley Donald. "Economic Reports: Microwave Clothes Dryers May Recast Laundry Room." The Christian Science Monitor v86 n59, 17 Feb 1994. p9. (ISSN0882-7729).

MIDDLE CLASSES--DEVELOPING COUNTRIES (v19)

MIDDLE EAST

see also FERTILITY, HUMAN--MIDDLE EAST; WEAPONS INDUSTRY--MIDDLE EAST--U.S.

MIDDLE EAST--ARMED FORCES

"A brief comparison of regional air forces indicates...that Iran trails its neighbors significantly. With 206 aircraft of which only 40 MIG 29s can be considered advanced, Iran must survive alongside the Gulf Cooperation Council countries with 624 aircraft that include such advanced planes as F-15s, Mirage 2000s, and Strike and Interceptor Tornados. Saudi Arabia alone has on order or in operation over 150 F-15s. More alarming in Iran's view is the fact that even after Desert Storm Iraq still has 261 tactical aircraft....In terms of military budgets, Iran has spent less than $3 billion per annum over the past four years. Saudi Arabia, on the other hand, with a population only 16 percent of that of Iran, expended $13 billion and $31.5 billion on arms in 1990 and 1991 respectively. Between 1985 and 1992, Saudi Arabia and Iraq together received arms deliveries totaling $79.6 billion, while Iran's deliveries amounted to $13.5 billion during the same period." (p103)

Bill, James A. "The United States and Iran: Mutual Mythologies." Middle East Policy v2 n3, 1993. p98-106. (ISSN1061-1924).

MIDDLE EAST--ECONOMIC CONDITIONS

"The Gulf war has intensified the economic crisis [for the Middle East]. There have been some losers and some winners, but the area as a whole has been a net loser. According to the IMF [International Monetary Fund], the Gulf crisis led to a 4% drop in GDP [gross domestic product] for the Middle East as a whole, a 2.5% rise in the rate of inflation, and a decline in the region's current account from a $10 billion surplus to a $43 billion deficit." (p90)

Bahgat, Gawdat. "Democracy in the Middle East: The American Connection." Studies in Conflict and Terrorism v17 n1, Jan-Mar 1994. p87-96. (ISSN1057-610X).

MIDDLE EAST--POLITICS AND GOVERNMENT (v19)

MIGRANT LABOR--JAPAN

"According to the Japanese government, there were 279,000 illegal migrant workers in Japan in 1992....Migrant workers want Japan to legalize the presence of undocumented workers, something already done in Europe, North America and Australia, and to guarantee them fundamental human rights prescribed in Japan's constitution and in international worker rights conventions. In 1990, Japan limited the admission of foreign unskilled workers to those with Japanese ancestry, known as 'Nikkeis'. More than 200,000 Latin Americans of Japanese descent have gone to Japan in search of jobs and better pay. As a result, thousands of Asian migrant workers were expelled and replaced with Nikkeis. Although they have legal status, Nikkeis face the same exploitation as other migrant workers. Many foreign workers are brought into Japan illegally by organizations linked to or controlled by Yakuza gangsters. Others enter as tourists but soon end up under Yakuza control in order to secure jobs." (p17)

"Asian Migrant Workers Face Exploitation." NewsNotes v19 n1, Jan-Feb 1994. p17-18. (ISSN1064-1556).

MIGRATION, INTERNAL

see also RURAL-URBAN MIGRATION

MIGRATION, INTERNAL--AFRO-AMERICANS

African Americans with a college education "are most strongly drawn to high-amenity areas with large and growing professional job bases. They favor Maryland, Georgia, Florida, Virginia, and California....Maryland and Georgia each received a net migration of over 12,800 college educated blacks in the late 1980s. California, Florida, and Virginia receive over 5,000 each. African-American college graduates are likely to head toward large cosmopolitan areas, both inside the South (Atlanta, Washington, Baltimore, Dallas/Fort Worth, Miami, and Orlando) and outside the South (Los Angeles, San Francisco/Oakland, Philadelphia)." (p2)

Frey, William H. "Black College Grads, Those in Poverty Take Different Migration Paths." Population Today v22 n2, Feb 1994. p1-2. (ISSN0749-2448).

MIGRATION, INTERNAL--CALIFORNIA (v19)

"Since 1990, foreign migrants have continued to flow to the Golden State, but the state's allure for native-born migrants has faded. Allied Van Lines, one of the world's largest moving companies, has charted the extraordinary turnabout in California's attractiveness to Allied's customers, who tend to be upper middle class. Over half (57 percent) of Allied's customers are college graduates and one-half have annual incomes in excess of $40,000. For the first time in 1989, there were more outbound than inbound Allied movers for California....By 1992, inbound customers represented only 37 percent of Allied's relocation activity in the Golden State. The net out-migration of domestic migrants, many of whom are non-Hispanic whites, and the net in-migration of foreign migrants, most of whom are Asian and Latino, accelerates the dramatic change in California's ethnic composition that has already occurred in recent years." (p26)

Gober, Patricia. "Americans on the Move." Population Bulletin v48 n3, Nov 1993. p2-40. (ISSN0032-468X).

MIGRATION, INTERNAL--CHINA

"China's dramatic economic transformation is resulting in an internal migration of historic proportions....Chinese officials estimate that this 'floating population' numbers more than 105 million. Roughly 50 million rural migrants are already believed to be living in 23 of China's larger cities, according to the nation's State Statistical Bureau. With the number of rural unemployed currently surpassing 100 million--and growing perhaps 13 million a year--the trend of growing rural-to-urban migration is expected to worsen." (p23)

Smith, Paul J. "Opinion/Essays: China's Reforms Go Awry as Peasants Surge to Cities." The Christian Science Monitor v86 n72, 9 Mar 1994. p23. (ISSN0882-7729).

MIGRATION, INTERNAL--ETHIOPIA

"When drought struck in 1984-85, the Ethiopian government sped up a 12-year-old programme to move farmers from overcrowded hillsides in the north to less densely populated regions farther south. The target during the famine was to relocate 1.5 million hungry people to more fertile areas. About 500,000 actually moved, in a programme that was poorly planned and crudely executed. Of those, 100,000 may have died as a result of being moved, according to Nestanet Asfaw, international coordinator of the Ethiopian Rehabilitation Campaign. With the overthrow of Mengistu Haile Mariam in 1991, so many people started trekking the hundreds of kilometres back to their old villages that this mass 'de-resettlement' has become a national crisis....By July 1992, 300,000 people had made the long and often arduous trek either back to their original homes or to transit stations. In the past year, the number deciding to move has steadily increased." (p23)

Amado, Addise. "Focus: Resettlement: Africa: Resettled Thousands Head for Home." Panoscope n36, Jul 1993. p23. (ISSN0951-8819).

MIGRATION, INTERNAL--MOZAMBIQUE

"A good 1992/93 harvest and sustained progress towards ending hostilities have reduced Mozambique's food aid requirements. However, they have also accelerated the return of refugees and increased demand for such resettlement needs as farm tools and seeds....In late February, UN Secretary-General Boutros Boutros-Ghali said that about half of the 4-4.5 million people internally displaced by the civil war had returned to their villages. A further 621,000 people--about 40 per cent of those who fled to neighbouring countries--had also gone back home."

(p4)
"Emergencies Pose Continuing Challenges: Mozambique." Africa Recovery v7 n3-4, Dec 1993-Mar 1994. p4.

MIGRATION, INTERNAL--OREGON (v19)

MIGRATION, INTERNAL--U.S.

"Between 1985 and 1991, nearly 2m people moved from other states to the 'intermountain west'--Washington, Oregon, Arizona, Idaho, Nevada, Utah and Montana--in search of space and the simple life. Wherever ranching land coincides with spectacular mountain scenery, old ranches are being sold and broken up into 'ranchettes' of anything from 20-100 acres, and sometimes as few as two....For the past three years, the Rocky Mountain West has led the country in growth of population and employment, and in housebuilding, while the amount of land devoted to ranching and farming has fallen by 5%." (p32)
"Cowboys and Indians: Once Upon a Time in the West." Economist v329 n7843, 25 Dec 1993. p31-34. (ISSN0013-0613).

"After 1920, millions of blacks left the rural South for northern industrial cities, propelled by poor job prospects and oppressive social conditions. This migration stream dramatically altered the distribution of African Americans in the United States, as well as the ethnic makeup of major U.S. cities. In 1900, 90 percent of the country's black population lived in the South, largely in rural areas. By 1970, almost half of all African Americans lived outside the South." (p11)
Gober, Patricia. "Americans on the Move." Population Bulletin v48 n3, Nov 1993. p2-40. (ISSN0032-468X).

"The largest net interregional flow [in the U.S.] in 1990-1991 was between the weakest and the strongest regional economies, the Northeast and the South....The sheer magnitude of this flow was surprising--it was larger than all other net flows combined. In 1990-1991, 565,000 persons moved from the Northeast to the South while only 195,000 flowed in the opposite direction. This net imbalance created a highly efficient migration stream, redistributing some 370,000 persons from the Northeast to the South in that year alone." (p18)
Gober, Patricia. "Americans on the Move." Population Bulletin v48 n3, Nov 1993. p2-40. (ISSN0032-468X).

"Between 1990 and 1991 the Northeast continued to send large numbers of out-migrants to the South: 565,000 persons went South (about two-thirds of these moving from New York State to Florida), according to the Census Bureau. Only 195,000 headed in the opposite direction, yielding a net of 370,000 people flowing South....The South retained its reputation as a magnet, with net in-flows of 26,000 from the Midwest and 38,000 from the West. Net flows were roughly equal from the Northeast to the Midwest (99,000) and to the West (116,000)." (p4)
Gober, Patricia/Haub, Carl. "U.S. Migration: South Retains Its Magnetism; Midwest Rallies." Population Today v22 n1, Jan 1994. p4-5. (ISSN0749-2448).

MILITARY ASSISTANCE, AMERICAN--BOSNIA AND HERCEGOVINA--COSTS (v19)

MILITARY ASSISTANCE, AMERICAN--EGYPT

"Despite the hope that Egypt would scale down its military forces, it has vastly increased its military capabilities since [the] Camp David [accords]. Here the United States has helped with $20 billion of arms and economic aid, over $7 billion of which was forgiven as a result of Egypt's participation in the Gulf war. In the fifteen months following the war, Egypt purchased $2.4-billion worth of arms, a huge increase over 1990. Egypt is now building the largest air force in the Middle East. In addition, thanks to the strategic relationship it has developed with the United States as a result of Camp David, Egypt is producing the main American battle tank, the A-1 Abrams; has a license to produce the most up-to-date two-dimensional U.S. radar system; and is cooperating with the U.S. in developing a third-generation shoulder-carried anti-tank missile." (p37)
Isaac, Jean. "The Real Lessons of Camp David." Commentary v96 n6, Dec 1993. p34-38. (ISSN0010-2601).

MILITARY ASSISTANCE, AMERICAN--JORDAN (v19)

MILITARY ASSISTANCE, AMERICAN--PUBLIC OPINION

"According to a recent (March 1993) poll of 1,020 adult Americans sponsored by Americans Talk Issues and conducted by Greenberg Research, pollster to President Clinton and the Democratic National Committee: 68% of Americans want to let the rest of the world bear more of the burden of resolving disputes and providing humanitarian assistance, while only 25% say the US is the only superpower and has to take the lead because nobody else will. A bare 7% want to focus exclusively on US problems and reject providing any military force for UN interventions. While 84% approve of using US military force for humanitarian reasons as we did in Somalia, five options are preferred to using 'overwhelming force.' They are: 'use diplomatic initiatives to negotiate peace agreements,' 'use enough military intervention to deliver food and other supplies to the people,' 'use trade embargoes,' 'prohibit all arms sales to warring parties,' and 'not allow the currency and bonds of the country to be traded on world markets.'" (p19)
"Two New Polls Find Americans Support Sending US Military...." Veterans for Peace Journal n23, Sum 1993. p19. (ISSN1063-9381).

MILITARY ASSISTANCE, AMERICAN--SOMALIA (v19)

MILITARY BASES--U.S. (v19)

"The Pentagon has announced plans to close or reduce our presence at 854 military sites overseas, a large majority of which are in Europe. America has already closed 427 military sites in Europe. The facilities we leave behind represent a significant investment of American taxpayer dollars--about $6.5 billion, according to the Defense Department--in the collective security of the West. An estimated $3.89 billion of that investment is in Germany, where we have already left over 60 percent of the military sites slated for closure. Through a series of residual value agreements, some allies have agreed to repay us for the value of what we leave behind. We ought to turn those commitments into cash. But so far we haven't. Over the past few years, we have collected less than $50 million out of the $6.5 billion the facilities are worth." (pS505)
Lautenberg, Frank R. (Sen.-N.J.). "Foreign Relations Authorization Act," Congressional Record (1 Feb 1994). Daily ed. pS492-520. (ISSN0363-7239).

MILITARY BASES, AMERICAN--PANAMA (v19)

MILITARY CONTRACTS

see DEFENSE CONTRACTS

MILITARY SUPPLIES INDUSTRY

see DEFENSE INDUSTRIES

MILITARY WEAPONS (v19)

"In general, missiles that travel farther must travel faster to achieve the distance; missiles that travel shorter distances travel slower to limit the distance traveled. Overcoming this fact of physics requires an increase in missile complexity and in missile cost that no country has been willing to pay. All modern strategic missiles travel much faster than 5 km/sec., while all current and foreseeable theater missiles travel 5 km/sec or less." (pS3903)
Warner, John W. (Sen.-Va.). "Some of the Subjects Receiving Attention," Congressional Record (25 Mar 1994). Daily ed. pS3900-3903. (ISSN0363-7239).

"In 1992, Ukraine sold Iran eight SS-N-22 supersonic 'Sunburn' antiship missiles for $600,000 apiece. Presently, the U.S. Navy has no electronic countermeasures that can defeat the Sunburn--

which travels 15 feet above the waves at about 1,900 miles per hour and executes evasive S-turns as it approaches its target." (p45-46)

Kraska, James. "Gatekeepers of the Gulf." Proceedings v120 n3, Mar 1994. p44-47. (ISSN0041-798X).

MILITARY WEAPONS--BOSNIA--SERBIA

"Arms are so plentiful in Serbia that it was exporting weapons to, among others, Somali warlords. Bosnians, by contrast, were lightly armed. The military gap between Bosnia and Serbia is one to ten in light weapons, one to 300 in heavy armaments including tanks and artillery. Landlocked and encircled, Bosnians cannot get arms unless the embargo is lifted. Their easy slaughter has been made possible by the arms embargo of the great powers, and in effect ratified by the UN." (p12)

Ahmad, Eqbal. "Roundtable Discussion: At Cold War's End: A World of Pain." Boston Review v18 n3-4, Jun-Aug 1993. p10,12-14. (ISSN0734-2306).

MILITARY WEAPONS--CZECHOSLOVAKIA (v19)

MILITARY WEAPONS--ENVIRONMENTAL ASPECTS

"Global military spending is about US$ 950,000 million a year and nuclear weapons powers allocate up to 60% of science research funds to defence and space programmes (most space programmes have military uses). In the post-cold war climate, there is a clear case for diverting these funds to environment protection and research into sustainable development. Many industrialised countries have adopted eco-friendly rhetoric, yet they continue environmentally-hostile high-tech military activities, mostly in secret. The United States claims to be reducing its use of aerosols and refrigerants containing chlorofluorocarbons (CFCs) which damage the ozone layer, yet it launches 1,200 rockets and missiles annually for research and testing. Each rocket releases 75-150 tonnes of ozone-depleting exhausts. Military supersonic jets and B-52 bombers, which fly above 15,800 metres, also harm the ionosphere and ozone layer." (p30)

Sharma, Dhirendra. "In My View: Confront Military Spending." Panoscope n38, Jan 1994. p30. (ISSN0951-8819).

MILITARY WEAPONS--IRAN (v19)

MILITARY WEAPONS--IRAQ (v19)

MILITARY WEAPONS--RUSSIA

"Today, with or without the complicity of current and former military officers, Russian crime groups have declared open season on the Russian Army and Navy. Last year, the Russian Defense Ministry reported 6,430 cases of theft of weapons from military depots, compared with 3,923 cases in 1992. Among the stolen items: tanks, rocket launchers and Kalashnikov assault rifles." (p46)

Duffy, Brian/Trimble, Jeff. "World Report: The Wise Guys of Russia." U.S. News & World Report v116 n9, 7 Mar 1994. p41-43,45-47. (ISSN0041-5537).

MILITARY WEAPONS--U.S. (v19)

An analysis by the General Accounting Office "shows that it costs a maximum of $23 billion to get 500 alert Minuteman III missiles good for 30 years. By contrast, spending $58 billion would extend the life of 432 Trident missiles, but not for 30 years. That's because the Trident submarines have to be retired after their hull life reaches 30 years. The first submarine would thus have to be retired in 2011 and one more each year after that. Then, many of these submarines will require a missile backfit costing $12 billion, when the expected service life of the submarine will be no more than 8 years." (p11)

Dorgan, Byron L. (Sen.-N.Dak.). U.S. Senate. Committee on Governmental Affairs. "Evaluation of the U.S. Strategic Nuclear Triad," Hearing. 10 Jun 1993. Washington, D.C.: GPO, 1994. (ISBN016043971X). (Y4.G74/9:S.Hrg.103-457).

"Our total ammunition stockpile [in the U.S.] is about 2 million tons, but very little of that is the high-quality kind of ammunition we are going to need in the event of war....Going from the least valuable to the most valuable, first of all, about 5 percent of the stockpile is excess ammunition....Nobody even knows whether any of them would work, they are completely useless. About 30 percent of the stockpile has been given to the allies over a period of time....The experts say that is not usable either. Then about 25 percent of the stockpile is usable for training. This is poor quality, less modern ammunition. It is also less reliable....Then there is about 25 percent of the stockpile which is called discretionary, which means that in theory the commanders in the field would have the discretion to use that in the event of an actual major regional contingency." (pH395) "That leaves the ready-for-war ammunition, which is 15 percent of the stockpile, less than 350,000 tons, or not enough to fight even one Desert Storm as envisioned by the Department of Defense when it was preparing for Desert Storm." (pH396)

Talent, James M. (Rep.-Mo.). "The Hollowing of U.S. Forces," Congressional Record (9 Feb 1994). Daily ed. pH394-396. (ISSN0363-7239).

"We are supposed to have stockpiled enough ammunition to fight two major regional contingencies at the same time, and actually in 11 of 18 critical categories, we are so short that it would take more than 12 months of production, given the existing industrial base, to bring us up to the level necessary to fight one. Here are some examples. We currently do not have sufficient quantities in go-to-war stocks, high-quality stocks, of 25 millimeter ammunition. That is the ammunition that goes in the Bradley fighting vehicle, which is the basic armored vehicle of the Army. It would take more than a year for the industrial base to meet the requirements for 25 millimeter ammunition. We currently do not have sufficient go-to-war ammunition of .50 caliber ammunition either. That is the basic ammunition that is used in the machine guns on our tanks, and the machine guns used by our infantry, a very basic requirement, obviously, for the Army, and we are 12 months away from having an adequate stockpile. We currently do not have stocks of 30 millimeter ammunition that is used by the Apache helicopter, which is our most up-to-date, modern, and effective attack helicopter. It does not do any good to have helicopters and tanks and armored cars if you do not have ammunition." (pH396)

Talent, James M. (Rep.-Mo.). "The Hollowing of U.S. Forces," Congressional Record (9 Feb 1994). Daily ed. pH394-396. (ISSN0363-7239).

"According to Eric Hoskins, M.D., a public health specialist and medical coordinator of the Harvard Study Team that surveyed health and welfare in post-war Iraq, U.S. and allied coalition tanks, artillery and attack planes fired at least 10,000... [armor-piercing shells made of depleted uranium (DU)] during the six-week long Persian Gulf War dispersing 40 tons of DU throughout the theatre of combat in Iraq and Kuwait. When fired, the DU shell core bursts into a searing flame that helps to pierce tank armor and ignites diesel vapors inside the tank burning the crew alive. On detonation, Hoskins explained, DU shells also release airborne uranium particles that are deposited in the bones, organs and body cells of those exposed. DU, like lead, is also chemically toxic and can damage the kidneys or lungs. It was DU's radioactivity, detected on destroyed coalition military vehicles, that forced the Pentagon to concede some friendly-fire casualties it had earlier denied because, as Hoskins notes, Iraqi weapons were not equipped with DU projectiles." (p9)

Genesio, Jerry. "Atomic Radiation, Agent Orange, and Now, Depleted Uranium." Veterans for Peace Journal n23, Spr 1993. p9. (ISSN1063-9381).

MILK PRODUCTION--U.S.

"In 1965, the Northeast, Lake States, Corn Belt, and Northern Plains together accounted for over 71 percent of U.S. milk production. By 1992, these four regions made up under 60 percent. In contrast, the Mountain and Pacific regions together accounted for 26 percent of U.S. milk production in 1992, double their combined share in 1965." (p16)

U.S. Dept. of Agriculture/Fallert, Richard. "Commodity Spotlight: Dairy Shifts to West & Southwest." Agricultural Outlook Dec 1993. p16-17,19.

"The Pacific region has exhibited the strongest sustained growth of any region, more than doubling its share of U.S. milk production from 1965 to 1992. The region is now second largest in milk production in the U.S., accounting for 19 percent in 1992, up from just 9 percent in 1965. In August 1993, California was the largest milk producing state--calculating monthly--just passing Wisconsin. Likewise, the Mountain states have nearly doubled their share of U.S. milk production since 1965, from 3.7 percent to over 7 percent in 1992." (p17)

U.S. Dept. of Agriculture/Fallert, Richard. "Commodity Spotlight: Dairy Shifts to West & Southwest." Agricultural Outlook Dec 1993. p16-17,19.

"The South currently accounts for about 10 percent of U.S. milk production, down from 13 percent in 1975. However, within the region the decline has varied. While Appalachia's share dropped from nearly 7 percent in 1965 and 1975 to 5.4 percent in 1992, the Southeast's share actually rose from 3 percent in 1965 to 3.8 in 1975, before dropping to 3.3 in 1992. Strong growth in cow numbers in Florida accounts for most of the Southeast's growth." (p17)

U.S. Dept. of Agriculture/Fallert, Richard. "Commodity Spotlight: Dairy Shifts to West & Southwest." Agricultural Outlook Dec 1993. p16-17,19.

"The Southern Plains states have increased their share of U.S. milk production to 4.5 percent in 1992, up from 3.5 percent in 1965. Large herd operations in Texas have accounted for most of this regional growth." (p19)

U.S. Dept. of Agriculture/Fallert, Richard. "Commodity Spotlight: Dairy Shifts to West & Southwest." Agricultural Outlook Dec 1993. p16-19.

"While the Midwest (Lake States, Corn Belt, and Northern Plains) accounted for over half of U.S. milk production in 1965, the region's share was barely 40 percent in 1992. The biggest decline occurred in the Corn Belt, whose share dropped from 17.1 to 11.2 percent. The Corn Belt experienced its largest drop in national share from 1965 to 1975." (p17)

U.S. Dept. of Agriculture/Fallert, Richard. "Commodity Spotlight: Dairy Shifts to West & Southwest." Agricultural Outlook Dec 1993. p16-17,19.

"Recently, the FDA has allowed some dairy farmers [in the U.S.] to use the genetically engineered milk production booster BGH (Bovine Growth Hormone) on a trial basis. The GAO [General Accounting Office] has recommended that the FDA halt its plans to approve the commercial sale of BGH. Not only are the hormonal and allergenic effects of BGH-laced milk unknown, but cows given the hormone have 33 percent more udder infections and consequently require even more antibiotics. 'BGH is a solution looking for a problem,' says Columbia University nutrition professor Dr. Joan Dye Gussow. Taxpayers spend millions in annual subsidies to buy surplus milk. BGH use would flood the market with further surpluses, making the smaller dairy farms unprofitable; only the largest, most mechanized 'dairy factories' would survive." (p52)

Bria, Rosemarie. "Food & Health: Milk a Natural? Think Again." E Magazine v4 n2, Mar-Apr 1993. p52-54. (ISSN1046-8021).

"Nationwide, milk production [in the U.S.] rose between 1980 and 1992 by almost 20 percent, to more than 150 billion pounds annually. At the same time, production per cow increased 30 percent. That efficiency gain allowed the US dairy herd to shrink to just under 10 million cows--a million fewer than in 1980, USDA statistics show." (p10)

Pendleton, Scott. "Economy: Dairy Industry Moves Southwest Seeking Warmer, Drier Climate." The Christian Science Monitor v86 n40, 21 Jan 1994. p10. (ISSN0882-7729).

MILWAUKEE (WIS)

see COMMUTING--MILWAUKEE (WIS)

MINES (MILITARY EXPLOSIVES) (v19)

"Today, despite the dramatic rise in public and media interest in dealing with this problem, far more mines are being strewn than are being cleared. In the former Yugoslavia, 3 million mines have been scattered in the past 2 years. Millions of mines contaminate Georgia, Azerbaijan, and Tajikistan....In Angola, over one-third of the country is infested with mines. In Afghanistan, where tens of thousands of people have been maimed, 8 out of 10 mine victims die before they reach a hospital. In northern Somalia, there are 23,000 amputees. Over two-thirds are under the age of 15. Over a third of all mine casualties are women and children." (pS2017)

Leahy, Patrick J. (Sen.-Vt.). "Landmines," Congressional Record (28 Feb 1994). Daily ed. pS2016-2017. (ISSN0363-7239).

"The State Department recently released a report entitled 'Hidden Killers: The Global Problem with Uncleared Landmines' which depicts the destructive effects of some 85 million landmines that remain uncleared in some 62 nations around the world. The International Red Cross estimates that landmines kill roughly 800 people a month. Mines also prevent countries from recovering from war by impeding farming and blocking refugees from returning to their homelands. In East Asia alone, there reportedly are 15-23 million landmines deployed in eight countries, many of them left over from the Vietnam War. The existence of landmines in such mass quantities poses a daily danger to non-combatant civilians--especially to children. Asia Watch reports that, in Cambodia alone, up to 700 amputations are performed every month on victims of landmines." (p22)

"Arms Proliferation: Proposed Extension of Landmine Moratorium." NewsNotes v18 n6, Nov-Dec 1993. p22-23. (ISSN1064-1556).

"The US estimates there are 85 million to 110 million land mines scattered around some 62 countries. According to the International Committee of the Red Cross, nearly 10,000 people are killed or maimed by those land mines each year....Land mines are indiscriminate. In northern Somalia, about 75 percent of the victims of mine injuries are children under the age of 15..." (p4)

Press, Robert M. "Global Effort Grows to Ban Export and Sale of Land Mines." The Christian Science Monitor v86 n17, 20 Dec 1993. p4. (ISSN0882-7729).

"Finding and removing each antipersonnel mine, which sells for about $3, costs from $300 to $1,000. In more than 60 countries--a third of the world's nations--85 to over 100 million mines of various designs, including those buried during the Second World War, wait ready to explode. They do not discriminate between soldier and civilian or adult and child. Each week, 150 or more people--a fifth to over a half of them children--are killed by mines. Many others are maimed." (p77)

Fruchtbaum, Harold. "Feature: UN De-Mining: A Campaign against 'Blind Terrorism.'" UN Chronicle v31 n1, Mar 1994. p77. (ISSN0251-7329).

"The difficulties and dangers of...[land mine removal] cannot be overstated. In 10 months of non-UN de-mining operations in

Kuwait, where millions of mines were sown during the Gulf War, 84 foreign and local experts were killed in the process. At least 16 United Nations staff members have died and 62 have been injured in similar operations in Afghanistan, where approximately 30 United Nations teams operate. At the United Nations Cambodian Mine Action Centre, it takes a team of 20 trained workers a week to clear a piece of jungle the size of two football fields. It has been estimated that with current technology, at a rate of 30 square kilometres a year, it could take more than 4,300 years to clear 20 per cent of the land in Afghanistan...." (p4-5)

Ruel, Susan. "The Scourge of Land Mines: UN Tackles Hidden Peacetime Killers." United Nations Department of Public Information n1415, Nov 1993. p1-6.

MINES (MILITARY EXPLOSIVES)--ANGOLA

"As if the threat of renewed civil war is not enough to stop agricultural production and keep the majority of the population in urban centers there is the added danger of an estimated 10 million landmines buried in Angola. Although these land mines on an average cost $20, the UN estimates the direct and indirect cost of removal at $300 to $1,000 per mine. According to UN Under-Secretary for Humanitarian Affairs Jan Eliasson, the UN has not been able to raise any contributions from member nations to even begin the task of landmine removal in Angola." (p7)

"Angola: Civil War Continues to Rage." NewsNotes v19 n2, Mar-Apr 1994. p7. (ISSN1064-1556).

MINES (MILITARY EXPLOSIVES)--CAMBODIA

"The land mining of Cambodia began in 1970, during the Vietnam War. American, Cambodian and Vietnamese soldiers, and Cambodian rebel groups, booby-trapped and land-mined bridges, fields, rice paddies, access roads, footpaths and water sources. Needless to say, none kept systematic records. Unfortunately, mine-clearing techniques--people crawling on their stomachs and prodding the earth in front of them, or teams of trained dogs sniffing out the mines--have improved little since the trench warfare of World War I. And the sheer number of mines can be overwhelming. In April 1991, a U.S. Agency for International Development team de-mined just one kilometer of land near an old Vietnamese military post and unearthed 6,000 'anti-personnel' mines." (p12-13)

Rosenberger, Jack. "In Brief: Cambodian Land Mines: Vietnam's Shattering Legacy." E Magazine v4 n2, Mar-Apr 1993. p12-13. (ISSN1046-8021).

"Cambodia's 12-year civil war may have been the first in history in which more people were killed by mines than by any other armament. Today, with one mine for every two inhabitants, Cambodia is thought to have the world's highest percentage of disabled people: one out of 236 Cambodians is an amputee, compared with 1 per 22,000 in the United States. And the toll keeps mounting: in the words of a U.S. prosthetist, 'Cambodia is being de-mined an arm and a leg at a time.'" (p2-3)

Ruel, Susan. "The Scourge of Land Mines: UN Tackles Hidden Peacetime Killers." United Nations Department of Public Information n1415, Nov 1993. p1-6.

MINES (MILITARY EXPLOSIVES)--CAMBODIA--KUWAIT--MOZAMBIQUE

"The United Nations, which has become the world's biggest mine-clearing agency, estimates that it will cost $30m-40m to remove some 2m mines in Mozambique; demining activities in Cambodia will cost $10m-12m a year for the next 5-10 years. Kuwait, littered with mines by a ruthless Iraq, is paying private-sector contractors $700m to clean the place up. Kuwait can afford that, more than the rest of the world spends on demining. Mine-free rich countries--and a handful of them, with China, are the ones that profitably supplied most of the mines--could afford as much, if they chose. Most infested countries, poor and war-shattered, can pay only with limbs and lives." (p45)

"International: Landmines: A Man with a Stick, and Luck." Economist v330 n7852, 26 Feb 1994. p45. (ISSN0013-0613).

MINES (MILITARY EXPLOSIVES)--CAMBODIA--YUGOSLAVIA

"Peace has returned to Cambodia after 12 years of war, but Cambodians are still dying or getting their arms and legs blown off at the rate of 200 to 300 a month by some 4 million land mines left behind on the killing fields. United Nations experts say this macabre scenario is being repeated from Angola to Afghanistan, as tens of thousands of civilians are killed or mutilated by the estimated 85 to 100 million mines scattered like seeds of death across the globe. Even as the United Nations takes up a major new effort to deal with this menace, thousands more mines are being planted--in the former Yugoslavia alone, at a rate of several thousands a week." (p1)

Ruel, Susan. "The Scourge of Land Mines: UN Tackles Hidden Peacetime Killers." United Nations Department of Public Information n1415, Nov 1993. p1-6.

MINES (MILITARY EXPLOSIVES)--COSTS

"U.N. [United Nations] de-mining experts estimate that, while the cheapest landmine can be purchased for about three dollars, it costs an average of $1000 to subsequently extract one mine from the earth. When the socio-economic impact in terms of lost development, strains on medical and rehabilitative services and the impact on the environment are added to the cost, the impact of this supposedly 'cost-effective' weapon becomes truly staggering." (p22)

"Arms Proliferation: Proposed Extension of Landmine Moratorium." NewsNotes v18 n6, Nov-Dec 1993. p22-23. (ISSN1064-1556).

MINES (MILITARY EXPLOSIVES)--DEVELOPING COUNTRIES (v19)

MINES AND MINERAL RESOURCES

see also COPPER MINES AND MINING; GOLD MINES AND MINING; URANIUM MINES AND MINING

"Power in the mining industry is concentrated in few hands. The Swedish Raw Materials Group estimates that, in 1990, more than a third of the value of all Western mineral products was owned by fewer than 20 companies. Just two companies, Anglo American of South Africa and Rio Tinto Zinc (RTZ) of Britain, controlled 13% of this wealth. Next came the state mining corporations of Chile and Brazil, with around 6%." (p11)

Moody, Roger. "Focus: Mining: South Counts the Cost of North's Bonanza." Panoscope n35, Apr 1993. p11-13. (ISSN0951-8819).

MINES AND MINERAL RESOURCES--ARIZONA (v19)

MINES AND MINERAL RESOURCES--BOLIVIA (v19)

MINES AND MINERAL RESOURCES--CANADA (v19)

MINES AND MINERAL RESOURCES--CHINA (v19)

MINES AND MINERAL RESOURCES--CHINA--MORTALITY (v19)

MINES AND MINERAL RESOURCES--EMPLOYMENT--U.S.

"The [U.S.] mining industry insists it cannot afford any more job losses. According to the Bureau of Labor Statistics, the industry lost 51 percent of its jobs between 1979 and 1992. Mining accounts for less than 1 percent of the non-agricultural jobs in the United States....There are roughly 140,000 people who dig for hard-rock minerals in the West, including an estimated 15,000 to 20,000 who mine on federal lands." (p18)

Camia, Catalina. "Government & Commerce: Environment: Severity of Job Loss at Issue in Mining Law Overhaul." Congressional Quarterly v52 n1, 8 Jan 1994. p18-20.

MINES AND MINERAL RESOURCES--ENVIRONMENTAL ASPECTS

"About 60% of the world's uranium and half the North's alluvial gold has been extracted from the territory of indigenous peoples. The single largest source of diamonds is just one sacred Aboriginal site in Australia. It is estimated that about 10% of the industrialised world's iron ore, 10-20% of its bauxite, probably 20% of its copper and large proportions of its manganese, tin, nickel, phosphates, lead and zinc are also taken from the lands and waters of native peoples. The industry's most vulnerable victims are usually its least heeded. The devastation caused by mining has been regarded as an acceptable price to pay for industrialisation and military might; not surprisingly, the US and Russia are the most mined nations of all. The US pays the price for this with waste heaps that stretch for many thousands of hectares, and acid mine drainage and heavy metal releases that have contaminated an estimated 15,000 kilometres of US waterways. In Russia, mining has blighted entire regions, such as the Kola Peninsula and the city it serves, Norilsk, which in 1988 spewed out 2.3 million tonnes of pollutants, more than 6% of the republic's total." (p11)

Moody, Roger. "Focus: Mining: South Counts the Cost of North's Bonanza." Panoscope n35, Apr 1993. p11-13. (ISSN0951-8819).

MINES AND MINERAL RESOURCES--GUINEA

"Worldwide opposition is growing to a plan for a massive, environmentally and socially destructive iron mine on the peaks of the Nimba Mountains, in Guinea....The giant opencut mine would threaten up to 500 animal species, including leopards, forest buffalo, pygmy hippopotami, the chimpanzees of Boussou--whose use of rudimentary tools has been documented--and the viviparous toad, the only tailless amphibian that gives birth to live young....Financed by an international consortium known as the Nimba International Mining Company (NIMCO), the mine would pollute the region's water and air, devastating the local subsistence farming economy." (p5)

"Opposition Builds to Destructive West African Mine." EDF Letter v24 n3, May 1993. p5. (ISSN0163-2566).

MINES AND MINERAL RESOURCES--INDIA

"The North Karanpura Valley [in India] is nearly 70 kilometers (43 miles) long where it channels the Damodar River. More than one-third of the valley is forested, and five major rivers and 37 streams flow to the once-mighty Damodar. The forests of the ecologically rich upper valley are home to Indigenous peoples, tigers, elephants, spotted deer, langur monkeys and gaur bison....The Piperwar mine and a second mine at Ashoka will destroy 29 villages occupied by tribal groups including the Munda, Ganju, Oraon and Santal. One-third of the total land area--more than three million hectares (7.41 million acres) containing forests, fields and streams--will be destroyed and 12,500 people will be driven from land that their ancestors have occupied for 1000 years." (p26)

Imam, Bulu. "Defending the Commons: Mines Threaten the Damodar Valley." Earth Island Journal v9 n2, Spr 1994. p26. (ISSN1041-0406).

MINES AND MINERAL RESOURCES--NEVADA (v19)

"The Goldstrike Mine in Nevada is the highest-producing gold mine in the United States. Operated by American Barrick Resources, a Canadian company, the mine is on public land, owned and managed by the BLM [Bureau of Land Management]. Total ore reserves at Goldstrike are estimated by the company to be 20.1 million ounces. Barrick marketed its output for $422 per ounce in 1992, according to the company. Reform of the Mining Law would mean that Barrick would pay the American people a fraction of the gold wealth it is taking from American soil--a royalty. Yet if it can complete the 'patenting' process in time, it will escape the royalty because its mine will become private land, for $5 per acre. In fact, Barrick filed a series of patent applications last year. If these patents are issued, Barrick will pay $5,190 to the Treasury for a resource with a gross value of $8.482 billion at 1992 prices." (p31)

Hocker, Phil. "Mining Reform Is an Urgent National Priority." Environmental Forum v10 n4, Jul-Aug 1993. p31-32. (ISSN0731-5732).

"The Goldstrike mine is an accounting feat as well as an engineering marvel. Barrick has $100 million invested in rolling stock, with each tire for its 190-ton trucks costing $15,000. [Mr. John] McDonough [manager of the mine] says the trucks burn $150 an hour in diesel fuel on the six-mile haul spiraling up from the bottom of the pit. Although the drivers are among the highest paid workers in Nevada, their labor at $15-to-$20 an hour represents just a fraction of the cost of running equipment. Every piece of machinery and every ton of ore at the Goldstrike is tracked by a remote control computer system. 'The objective is to keep everything moving,' says McDonough. The firm mines as fast as it can because, whether it mines fast or slow, it must pump out the same amount of groundwater. The mine has 30 wells around the pit, each of which cost roughly $500,000 to dig, and they pump 65,000 gallons of water a minute to keep the pit from flooding. Pumping has lowered the aquifer around the pit by almost 1,200 feet." (p8)

Christensen, Jon. "Two Nevadans in Search of Mining Reform." High Country News v25 n18, 4 Oct 1993. p8-15. (ISSN0191-5657).

MINES AND MINERAL RESOURCES--U.S.

"In 1990 alone, mining companies took an estimated $3.6 billion in minerals from public lands. Much of that money went abroad. According to a National Wildlife Federation report, 16 of the top 25 gold mines in the United States are owned wholly or in part by foreign companies. One such mine, the Summitville operation in Colorado, was abandoned by its Canadian owners in 1992, saddling taxpayers with $60 million worth of cleanup to be done." (p4)

Cusick, Steve. "After Years of Abuse, Federal Policy on Western Lands Is Ripe for Reform." Audubon Activist v8 n3, Sep 1993. p1,4-5. (ISSN0898-915X).

"There are currently about 3,800 active mines or plans for mines on Forest Service and BLM [Bureau of Land Management] lands. Many of the active operations are highly toxic 'heap-leach' gold mines, where cyanide is used to extract particles of gold from tons of rock. On Forest Service lands alone, there are 25,000 abandoned mine sites, affecting an estimated 400,000 acres of federal land. The Mineral Policy Center, an environmental group based in Washington, D.C., estimates that 10,000 miles of streams have been permanently degraded by mine drainage, heavy metals, and other pollution. The EPA says it will cost at least $2.4 billion to clean up the worst sites." (p4)

Cusick, Steve. "After Years of Abuse, Federal Policy on Western Lands Is Ripe for Reform." Audubon Activist v8 n3, Sep 1993. p1,4-5. (ISSN0898-915X).

"A reform designed by Congress to remove inactive or illegitimate claims from public land is doing just that. Miners abandoned more than 50 percent of their claims Aug. 31 when the Bureau of Land Management began charging a $100 annual fee. Before Congress acted, the agency required no rent, although claim holders had to show $100 worth of improvement or exploration on each claim each year. Nationally, holdings dropped from over 1 million to 520,000 as the Aug. 31 renewal deadline passed. In Nevada, the U.S.'s largest hard-rock producer, the reform trimmed 270,000 claims to 130,000. In Oregon and Washington, holdings plummeted 62 percent, from 37,000 to 14,000, and in Idaho, miners dropped over 26,000 of their 57,000 claims. The reform raised $52 million, well short of the $97 million anticipated." (p7)

Hinnen, Todd. "Miners Drop 480,000 Claims to Avoid Fees." High Country News v25 n21, 15 Nov 1993. p7.

(ISSN0191-5657).

MINES AND MINERAL RESOURCES--U.S.--SAFETY MEASURES (v19)

MINNEAPOLIS (MINN)--ECONOMIC CONDITIONS (v19)

MINNESOTA

see MOTORCYCLES--MINNESOTA--SAFETY MEASURES; POLLUTION--MINNESOTA

MINORITIES

see also CHILDREN OF MINORITIES--U.S.--SOCIAL CONDITIONS; EDUCATION, HIGHER--U.S.--MINORITIES; EDUCATION--U.S.--MINORITIES; HAZARDOUS WASTE SITES--U.S.--MINORITIES; MEDICAL PERSONNEL--U.S.--MINORITIES; NARCOTICS, CONTROL OF--U.S.--MINORITIES; POOR--U.S.--MINORITIES; PRISONERS--NEW ZEALAND--U.S.--MINORITIES; SEXUAL HARASSMENT OF WOMEN--U.S.--MINORITIES; UNEMPLOYMENT--U.S.--MINORITIES

MINORITIES--BOSTON (MASS) (v19)

MINORITIES--EMPLOYMENT--GREAT BRITAIN

"Of the 2.6m Britons who belong to ethnic minorities, almost all arrived after 1950, or are the children of those who did. Most such immigrants arrived with fewer qualifications, on average, than Britain's whites. Yet today: Members of ethnic minorities are more likely to create jobs than whites. According to the government's 1991 census, 12.8% of working whites were self-employed that year, compared with 15.1% for ethnic minorities. Self-employment does not only mean running a one-man corner shop. Of ethnic-minority businesses, 42% employ others. Only 34% of white-owned businesses do. Members of ethnic minorities are fast overtaking the skill levels of whites. Between 1988 and 1990 37% of white 16-19-year-olds were in full-time education, according to the government's Labour Force Survey. The figure for members of ethnic minorities was 56%." (p66)

"Britain: Immigration: Unclaimed Benefits." Economist v331 n7861, 30 Apr 1994. p65-67. (ISSN0013-0613).

MINORITIES--U.S.

"Minorities now account for more than half the population in many of the nation's largest cities. Of the eight U.S. cities with over a million residents, only two (San Diego and Philadelphia) have populations in which non-Hispanic whites are the majority; and non-Hispanic whites are likely to lose their majority status in these cities within a few years. The combined populations of the four major minority groups made up 41 percent of San Diego's population, and 48 percent of Philadelphia's population in 1990. Among the 20 largest U.S. cities, 9 are a majority non-Hispanic white, 4 are a majority African American, and 1 city has a majority Hispanic population...." (p23,25)

O'Hare, William P. "America's Minorities--The Demographics of Diversity." Population Bulletin v47 n4, Dec 1992. p2-47. (ISSN0032-468X).

MINORITIES--U.S.--ATTITUDES (v19)

MINORITIES--U.S.--HOUSING

"Since minorities are disproportionately poor, many cannot afford to move to more expensive suburbs. In 1987, for example, minorities comprised 49 percent of residents of public or subsidized housing. About one in ten white renters lived in public or subsidized housing in 1987, compared with 29 percent of black, 27 percent of American-Indian, 16 percent of Latino, and 12 percent of Asian renters." (p27)

O'Hare, William P. "America's Minorities--The Demographics of Diversity." Population Bulletin v47 n4, Dec 1992. p2-47. (ISSN0032-468X).

MINORITIES--U.S.--PUBLIC OPINION

"Minority groups not only share animosity toward white Americans, they have widespread prejudices toward each other, according to a poll released...by a major ecumenical group. The poll found 'a yawning gulf between white and minority group perceptions about America,' said the group founded in 1927 as the Naitonal Conference of Christians and Jews. Eight in 10 black respondents in the poll believe members of their race lack the opportunities enjoyed by whites. Six in 10 Hispanics and nearly as many Asian Americans express the same sentiment....Louis Harris' LH Research conducted the survey, which also asked respondents if they agreed with generalizations about minorities. Some findings: The idea that blacks 'want to live on welfare' was agreed with by 31 percent of Asian Americans, 26 percent of Hispanics and 21 percent of whites surveyed. Sixty-eight percent of Asian Americans polled agreed with the claim that Hispanics 'tend to have bigger families than they are able to support.' About half of white and black respondents agreed. More than four in 10 blacks and Hispanics and 27 percent of whites concur with the stereotype that Asian Americans are 'unscrupulous, crafty and devious in business.'" (p5 secA)

Goldberg, Howard. "Nation & World: Prejudice Cuts Across the Board, Poll Finds." Detroit Free Press 3 Mar 1994. p5 secA.

MINORITIES IN TELEVISION BROADCASTING--U.S. (v19)

MINORITY AGED--U.S.

"To date, older Americans are the age group least affected by the nation's growing racial and ethnic diversity. But...the older population will also become more diverse as more minorities join the ranks of 'senior citizens.' Between 1992 and 2010, for example, the number of minority elderly (ages 65 and older) will increase from 4.5 million to 7.9 million--a 76 percent increase, compared with a 15 percent increase among non-Hispanic white elderly. Minority elderly represented 14 percent of the population age 65 and older in 1992, but by 2010 their share will grow to 20 percent, and by 2040, to 31 percent--more than double the current share. Asians and Hispanics will be the fastest growing segments of the older population. As a result of these changes, policies, programs, and even commercial products targeted at today's older population may need to be reassessed to see if they will meet the needs of tomorrow's elderly." (p18-19)

O'Hare, William P. "America's Minorities--The Demographics of Diversity." Population Bulletin v47 n4, Dec 1992. p2-47. (ISSN0032-468X).

MINORITY CHILDREN

see CHILDREN OF MINORITIES

MISSISSIPPI

see GAMBLING--MISSISSIPPI

MISSISSIPPI RIVER

see FLOOD CONTROL--MISSISSIPPI RIVER

MISSOURI

see TRAFFIC ACCIDENTS--MISSOURI--YOUTH

MISSOURI RIVER--NAVIGATION (v19)

MOBILE TELEPHONE

see CELLULAR RADIO

MOLDOVA

"In August 1990, Moldova's parliament declared the republic's independence. For the first time in history, Moldova acquired statehood. In 1991, Mircha Snegur--the Communist Party head of Moldova--was elected the first president." (p41) "The National Front [a popular political movement] launched a campaign that called for the unification of Moldova with Romania. (United by a common language and culture, the two were a single country until 1940.) This call for consolidation with Romania quickly led to armed conflict. The Pridnestrovie region--a narrow strip on the eastern shore of the Dneistr River that runs through Moldova from north to south--announced that it would secede from the republic and form a separate state. Most Moldovan industry is located in this region, and a quarter of the country's population of 4 million live there. This area produces 40 percent of the gross national product. About 60 percent of Pridnestrovie's population are Russians and Ukrainians, and only 30 percent of the population is Moldovan." (p42)

Gamova, Svetlana. "Moldova: A Three-Way Split." Bulletin of the Atomic Scientists v50 n1, Jan-Feb 1994. p41-43. (ISSN0096-3402).

MOLESTING OF CHILDREN

see CHILD MOLESTING

MONEY

see also COINS; COUNTERFEITS AND COUNTERFEITING; DOLLAR, AMERICAN

MONEY--AUSTRALIA

"The Reserve Bank of Australia is making money out of plastic, to hinder counterfeiters....The medium is harder for forgers to perfect. Opaque except for a small transparent window, plastic money can incorporate complex optical tricks that cannot be photocopied, as well as other security devices....Plastic money has other advantages over its paper rival. It lasts up to eight times as long--no small consideration when 90% of the notes printed each year simply replace paper ones. And it can be recycled." (p101)

"Finance: Counterfeiting: Plastic Is Beautiful." Economist v329 n7843, 25 Dec 1993. p101. (ISSN0013-0613).

MONEY--CANADA--CIRCULATION (v19)

MONEY--U.S. (v19)

MONEY--VALUATION--RUSSIA

"Russia was one of the few countries in the world where foreign currencies were accepted as freely as the national one. But the ruble has taken a beating since the 1991 Soviet collapse, and many people prefer the stable dollar. At the beginning of 1993, one United States dollar was worth 570 rubles. Today, one dollar is worth about 1,270 rubles." (p4)

Sloane, Wendy. "Russians Mutter as Moscow Bans Sales in Hard Currencies." The Christian Science Monitor v86 n28, 4 Jan 1994. p4. (ISSN0882-7729).

MONEY LAUNDERING--U.S.

"The Treasury Department has estimated that $110 billion is laundered through our financial system each year. Some think the number may be as high as $300 billion. Whatever the figure, it is an extraordinary problem, representing the lifeblood of the drug trade. However, since enactment of the Bank Secrecy Act in 1970, which requires that a currency transaction report (CTR) be filed for each monetary transaction over $10,000, nearly 54 million reports have been filed with the Federal Government. Well intended as the 1970 law may be, such a large data base has not proven conducive to effectively using many reports." (pH1563)

Leach, James A. (Rep.-Iowa). "General Leave," Congressional Record (21 Mar 1994). Daily ed. pH1562-1564. (ISSN0363-7239).

MONEY SUPPLY--U.S. (v19)

MONGOLIA

see WAGES--MINIMUM WAGE--MONGOLIA

MONTANA

see also PASTURE, RIGHT OF--MONTANA

MONTANA--ECONOMIC CONDITIONS

"Bozeman's growth is among the fastest in the state [of Montana]. In 1988, the total value of buildings permitted by the city was $8 million. In 1993 it jumped to $40 million. The boom has many of the earmarks of a gold boom, a regular phenomenon in this state. But instead of precious metals, it's a boom in the quality of life, as people scour the Rockies for a crime-free small or mid-sized town that has what many newcomers call a 'sense of community.'...While the demand on real estate has shot home prices up, salaries in these small towns stay low. The average price of a home in Bozeman is $101,000, while four years ago that same house went for about $65,000. Salaries of many people who work at Montana State University, for example, are among the lowest in the nation. Montana's per capita income in 1990 was $11,200. The result: Buying real estate is no longer an option for many average Bozemanities." (p4)

Robbins, Jim. "Montana Town Puts Out Unwelcome Mat." High Country News v26 n1, 24 Jan 1994. p4. (ISSN0191-5657).

MONTANA--POPULATION (v19)

MONTENEGRO--SERBIA--ECONOMIC CONDITIONS

"Even...tighter sanctions have not devastated the economy [in Montenegro and Serbia] by themselves. But they have accelerated its collapse. The cost of the war, on top of all the usual travails of an economy emerging from communism, have also done their work. Today 60% of workers in industry, services and administration are unemployed. Industry is working at 20-30% of its pre-war capacity; GNP [gross national product] has fallen by half since 1989; hyperinflation has taken hold; 40% of all economic activity is believed to take place on the black market. Though small companies duck and weave through the embargo, big ones cannot survive. The huge Elektronska Industrija from Nis was on the point of beginning production of 1m television sets for the domestic and export markets just before the war. Now it cannot get imported parts nor export a single set." (p44)

"Europe: The Sanctions Alternative." Economist v330 n7850, 12 Feb 1994. p44. (ISSN0013-0613).

MOOD (PSYCHOLOGY) (v19)

MORMON CHURCH

"In addition to being one of the fastest-growing churches in the world, the Mormons operate a world-wide conglomerate that ranges from insurance to broadcasting. It is estimated that the church collects at least $5 billion a year from its businesses and its tithes; faithful members donate 10% of their gross earnings....Beginning with a handful of believers in 1830, they now have 8.7m members, double the number 12 years ago. And that could be only the beginning. Rodney Stark, a sociologist at the University of Washington, predicts that by 2080 Mormonism will be the world's great faith, with as many as 280m members." (p30)

"American Survey: Mormons: At Day's End." Economist v331 n7858, 9 Apr 1994. p30. (ISSN0013-0613).

MOROCCO--ECONOMIC CONDITIONS (v19)

MOROCCO--SOCIAL CONDITIONS

"Morocco's GNP [gross national product] per capita increased at an average annual rate of 2.3 percent from 1960 to 1990, and was $950 in 1990. Its life expectancy increased from 48 to about 61 years from 1960-65 to 1985-90, and its IMR [infant mortality rate] decreased by 29 points to 58. Adult literacy increased rapidly, but from a low level of only 14 percent in 1960; its level in 1990 was still relatively low at 49 percent. Female literacy followed the same pattern, but at a much lower level; it increased from 6 to 38 percent. The pattern of primary plus secondary school enrollment was the same, but the female enrollment ratio was only 41 percent in 1990. Morocco's family planning program was very weak in 1972, with a score of only 13, but it has increased steadily, to a score of 57 in 1989. Similarly, contraceptive prevalence rose from 20 percent in 1980 to 41.5 percent in 1992. Its TFR [total fertility rate] was 7.15 in 1960-65, but it has fallen by more than 40 percent, to 4.2 in 1992." (p86)

Mauldin, W. Parker/Ross, John A. "Prospects and Programs for Fertility Reduction, 1990-2015." Studies in Family Planning v25 n2, Mar-Apr 1994. p77-95. (ISSN0039-3665).

MOROCCO--TUNISIA--SOCIAL CONDITIONS

"Morocco and Tunisia are part of the Maghreb region of North Africa, and they share two fundamental cultural traits: Arab culture and the religion of Islam. They also have similar demographic features: high population growth rates (around 2.3 percent annually), high fertility rates (total fertility rates are 4.8 in Morocco and 4.1 in Tunisia), as well as rapidly decreasing illiteracy and infant mortality rates (United Nations, 1991)." (p355)

Obermeyer, Carla Makhlouf. "Reports: Culture, Maternal Health Care, and Women's Status: A Comparison of Morocco and Tunisia." Studies in Family Planning v24 n6, Nov-Dec 1993. p354-365. (ISSN0039-3665).

MORTALITY

see also ACCIDENTS--U.S.--MORTALITY; AGED--MORTALITY; AIDS (DISEASE)--U.S.--MORTALITY; AIDS (DISEASE)--ZIMBABWE--MORTALITY; ANIMALS--U.S.--MORTALITY; CANCER--JAPAN--MORTALITY; CANCER--U.S.--MORTALITY; CARDIOVASCULAR SYSTEM--DISEASES--U.S.--MORTALITY; CHILD ABUSE--U.S.--MORTALITY; CHILDREN--CUBA--MORTALITY; CHILDREN--IRAQ--MORTALITY; CONSTRUCTION WORKERS--U.S.--MORTALITY; DIARRHEA IN CHILDREN--DEVELOPING COUNTRIES--MORTALITY; DIET--MORTALITY; EAST TIMOR (INDONESIA)--MORTALITY; FIREARMS--U.S.--CHILDREN--MORTALITY; FIREARMS--U.S.--MORTALITY; FIREARMS--U.S.--YOUTH--MORTALITY; FIRES--U.S.--MORTALITY; INFANTS--CUBA--MORTALITY; INFANTS--U.S.--MORTALITY; IRELAND--HISTORY--CIVIL WAR--MORTALITY; MEDICAL CARE--U.S.--MORTALITY; MOTORCYCLES--U.S.--MORTALITY; OCCUPATIONAL MORTALITY; POOR--U.S.--MORTALITY; PREGNANCY--COMPLICATIONS--MORTALITY; PREGNANCY--MORTALITY; RADON--U.S.--MORTALITY; RUSSIA--MORTALITY; TOBACCO HABIT--U.S.--MORTALITY; TOYS--U.S.--ACCIDENTS--MORTALITY; TRAFFIC ACCIDENTS--U.S.--MORTALITY; TRANSPORTATION--U.S.--MORTALITY; U.S.--MORTALITY; VIOLENCE--AFRO-AMERICANS--HISPANIC AMERICANS--MORTALITY; VIOLENCE--SOMALIA--MORTALITY; VIOLENCE--U.S.--YOUTH--MORTALITY

MORTALITY--AFRICA

"WHO [World Health Organization] estimates that since 1983, maternal mortality has increased by 3% to 9% in some regions of Africa. African women aged 15-44 years have a life-time risk of maternal death of 1 in 23, in contrast to 1 in 35 in South Asia, 1 in 131 in Latin America and 1 in 1825 in the industrialized countries. Despite the fact that infant mortality declined from 76 per 1000 live births in 1985, to 68 per 1000 live births in 1991 worldwide, there are still 4.2 million newborn infant deaths each year, of which 3 million die in the first week of life." (p1) "The study showed that: failure in diagnosis or correct case management by the doctors or midwives was noted in over 40% of the maternal deaths; shortcomings in the facilities were noted in over 10% and neglect by the woman seeking care was noted in over 50% of deaths. Only 7% of the deaths were considered unavoidable, and over 50% of the problems could have been detected during antenatal care." (p2)

News release. "Women and Children Continue to Suffer Ill-Health." WHO Press 20 Jan 1994. p1-2.

MORTALITY--SOUTH AFRICA (v19)

MORTALITY--TEXAS (v19)

MORTALITY--U.S. (v19)

"In 1989 motor vehicle injuries were the fourth leading cause of death [in the U.S.]. However, in 1990, the latest year for which data are available, an increase in deaths from diabetes mellitus and a decrease in deaths from motor vehicle injuries moved motor vehicle injuries to fifth place. The largest number of deaths in 1990 was from heart diseases, followed by cancer, and pulmonary diseases. It is interesting to note that homicides and AIDS deaths were each less than half of the motor vehicle deaths but have received much greater public interest, and in the case of AIDS, research support of a different order of magnitude than motor vehicle deaths....In 1990, motor vehicle injuries were the fourth leading cause of premature death prior to age 65. Cancer, suicide/homicide and heart diseases had greater numbers of premature deaths. The common measure of premature death is Years of Potential Life Lost referenced to age 65. This measure significantly undercounts the importance of diseases of the aged, however, it is the only time series data available." (p28)

Smolkin, Howard (Acting Administrator, National Highway Traffic Safety Admin.). U.S. House. Committee on Appropriations. "Department of Transportation and Related Agencies Approp. for 1994 (Part 4)." Hearing, Washington, D.C.: GPO, 1993. (ISBN0160410738). (Y4.Ap6/1:T68/4/994/pt.4).

"Since 1970, the death rate in auto accidents [in the U.S.] is down one third; cars are safer, more people use seat belts. On-the-job deaths have dropped by more than one quarter (from 14,000 to 10,000) since 1960, although the labor force has doubled." (p51)

Samuelson, Robert J. "Judgment Calls: Here's Some Good News, America." Newsweek v123 n5, 31 Jan 1994. p51. (ISSN0028-9604).

MORTALITY--UGANDA

"Long years of civil war and insurgency made Uganda's crude death rate (over 20 per 1,000) one of the worst in sub-Saharan Africa. Now AIDS is expected to raise the rate by about 6 per 1,000 between 1995 and 2000. Some 6-10 per cent of Ugandans are HIV-positive, a quarter of them women of child-bearing age. Already 30 per cent of children are orphans in some districts. Slow progress in infant and child mortality rates is being reversed, with malaria, pneumonia, and diarrhoea the main killers of children under five--who account for over half of hospital deaths. Infant deaths are running at some 70 per cent above the average for low-income countries. Widespread malnutrition means that some 45 per cent of surviving children suffer from stunted growth, one of the highest levels in Africa." (p18)

"Expanding Social Services with Limited Funds." Africa Recovery v7 n2, Oct 1993. p18-19.

MORTGAGE LOANS--U.S. (v19)

MORTGAGES--U.S. (v19)

see also DISCRIMINATION IN MORTGAGE LOANS

"The Borrower's Right of Prepayment, included in federal banking laws since 1968, allows most homeowners to pay off all or part of their mortgage early without incurring a penalty. Most homeowners who prepay either add a small amount to each month's payment or make an additional payment equal to their monthly bill once a year. The savings can be substantial, especially if the additional payments are made in the early years of a loan. For example, a person who makes an extra payment of $815.35 during the 24th month of a $100,000, 30-year mortgage eliminates $8,838.09 of future interest charges. Many people prefer 30-year loans because the monthly payments are lower and more manageable than those on a 15-year mortgage. They intend to reduce interest costs by periodically making additional payments as their budget allows." (p3 secD)

Turner, Mike. "It May Pay to Prepay Part of Principal." Ann Arbor News 18 Apr 1994. p3 secD.

"Since the beginning of 1992, average rates on 30-year, fixed mortgages have fallen, from 8.24% to as low as 6.74% in October, according to the Federal Home Loan Mortgage Corp. That slide prompted a massive wave of refinancings that now is subsiding,

even as 30-year rates have crept back up to around 7.2%." (p138)
Holland, Kelley. "Personal Business: Mortgages: Missed Out on Refi Madness? Don't Despair." Business Week n3353, 10 Jan 1994. p138. (ISSN0007-7135).

MOTHERS
see HIV INFECTIONS--MOTHERS; SINGLE MOTHERS; WORKING MOTHERS

MOTHERS--MORTALITY (v19)

MOTHERS--U.S. (v19)

MOTHERS, WORKING
see WORKING MOTHERS

MOTION PICTURE INDUSTRY--EUROPE--U.S.
"A look at European cinema-ticket receipts and audiences for 1993 shows that American films dominate the hit list in almost every European country. In Britain the top 19 films were all American, with Kenneth Branagh's 'Much Ado About Nothing' taking 20th place. Spanish films had less than 20% of their home market and German films just 9% of theirs. Hollywood films had 90% of the Italian market. Only France still has a worthwhile national film industry, and domestically-produced films there commanded 37% of the market. A low-brow French comedy, 'Les Visiteurs', was the most popular film in France last year. It had box-office receipts of $82m compared with $38m for 'Jurassic Park', which was the biggest money-spinner in Britain, Italy and Germany." (p89)
"Arts, Books and Sport: Movies Eclipse Films." Economist v330 n7849, 5 Feb 1994. p89-90. (ISSN0013-0613).
"Out in the marketplace, the Europeans who make films and television programmes have been overwhelmed by their American rivals. Hollywood productions account for about 80% of the European Union market for feature films, compared with 60% ten years ago." (p52)
"Europe: Battling for the Box." Economist v331 n7858, 9 Apr 1994. p52. (ISSN0013-0613).

MOTION PICTURE INDUSTRY--EUROPEAN ECONOMIC COMMUNITY--FRANCE (v19)

MOTION PICTURE INDUSTRY--EUROPEAN ECONOMIC COMMUNITY--U.S. (v19)

MOTION PICTURE INDUSTRY--FRANCE--U.S. (v19)

MOTION PICTURE INDUSTRY--HUNGARY (v19)

MOTION PICTURE INDUSTRY--POLAND (v19)

MOTION PICTURE INDUSTRY--U.S. (v19)
"Hollywood produces what the public wants. Since the end of World War II Hollywood has made almost 450 war films, most (280) about World War II but a significant number about Korea (60) and Vietnam (50). The psychological significance of these numbers is important, for what we see influences what we do and what we expect others, especially our politicians, to do for us." (p3-4)
"The Media and Images of War: Perception versus Reality." Defense Monitor v23 n4, 1994. p1-8. (ISSN0195-6450).
"In a season highlighted, or low-lighted, depending on your aesthetic sense, by tales of marauding dinosaurs, sleuthing fugitives, and Yuppie lawyers, motion pictures took in over $5 billion in ticket sales in 1993--up 8 percent from last year....Exact box-office figures vary, depending on whose calculus is being used. Analyst Art Murphy of the HOLLYWOOD REPORTER, a trade publication, puts the total receipts for the year at $5.2 billion. His counterpart at DAILY VARIETY, Leonard Klady, estimates it at closer to $5.04 billion. All agree, however, that 1993 was a record year. Mr. Murphy says it surpassed the previous mark set in 1989 ($5.03 billion); Mr. Klady, the one set last year ($4.65 billion)." (p4)
Armstrong, Scott. "National: Tinseltown Marks Best Year Ever in Tickets Sold." The Christian Science Monitor v86 n30, 6 Jan 1994. p4. (ISSN0882-7729).
"In 1992, 72 percent of all first-time directors were veterans of film school, compared with 35 percent in 1980. 'The projection is that by the year 2000, almost 90 percent of new directors will have gone to film school,' says Gilbert Cates, dean of the School of Theater, Film and Television at UCLA." (p94)
Hardigg, Viva. "Graduate Schools: Arts & Architecture: Full House at Film School." U.S. News & World Report v116 n11, 21 Mar 1994. p94-95. (ISSN0041-5537).

MOTION PICTURE INDUSTRY--U.S.--ENVIRONMENTAL ASPECTS
"Paramount...faxed Greenpeace and Rainforest Action network to inform them that they were going to stop purchasing all rainforest wood by October 4. Hollywood uses at least 250,000 4'x10' sheets of lauan plywood annually. Lauan is extracted from Southeast Asia, Indonesia and Malaysia. The demand for lauan is a principle cause of deforestation in Indonesia, estimated at 2.5 million acres per year." (p12)
Johnson, Michelle. "Hollywood Out of the Rainforest!" Earth First! v14 n1, 1 Nov 1993. p12.
"Every year, the Los Angeles film industry consumes more than 250,000 sheets of 4x10-foot lauan plywood....Fortunately, the entertainment industry's lauan dependence does not need to continue. Viable substitutes are now available....These include Medite II (a medium-density, urea-formaldehyde-free fiberboard made from wood scraps) and Homosote (a fiberboard made from recycled paper)....Warner's Vice President of Studio and Production Affairs, Lisa Rawlins, says the decision to use Medite will actually save the company money. Warner had been paying $10.40 a sheet for lauan plywood, while Medite sells for $6.90 a sheet." (p40)
Kupfer, David. "The Greening of Hollywood." Earth Island Journal v8 n3, Sum 1993. p40-41. (ISSN1041-0406).

MOTION PICTURES--FRANCE--U.S. (v19)

MOTION PICTURES--U.S.
"Aging boomers make up an increasing part of the first-run [U.S.] movie audience. In 1981, 24 percent of total yearly admissions to movies were to those aged 16 to 20, according to the Motion Picture Association of America (MPAA). By 1992, only 15 percent of admissions were aged 16 to 20. Attendance of 40-to-49-year-olds rose from 6 percent to 16 percent during the same period. Attendance of middle-aged adults has jumped in each of the last three years. Although figures are not available, attendance of young children has probably risen along with that of their parents." (p52)
Pampel, Fred/others. "Marketing the Movies." American Demographics v16 n3, Mar 1994. p48-49,52-54. (ISSN0163-4089).
"Nearly half of [U.S.] teenagers go to the movies at least once a month, compared with just one in four adults. Young people are not always discriminating viewers: rather than wait for recommendations and reviews, they often go to movies as soon as they open. They are more likely to go on impulse, are more attracted by big-name stars, and are heavily influenced by television advertising." (p48)
Pampel, Fred/others. "Marketing the Movies." American Demographics v16 n3, Mar 1994. p48-49,52-54. (ISSN0163-4089).

MOTOR VEHICLES
see also ALL TERRAIN VEHICLES; AUTOMOBILES; ELECTRIC VEHICLES; MOTOR CYCLES; TRUCKS

MOTOR VEHICLES--CHINA--THAILAND
"It's fair to say that consumers in parts of the Third World are moving up the pollution curve. Things that use power and things that emit fumes are currently the things most in demand. Ek Chor China Motorcycle recently issued shares on the New York Stock Exchange. The company's prospectus reports that in 1987,

when China's per capita GDP [gross domestic product] surpassed the $1000 mark, the country was manufacturing 730,000 motorcycles per year. Per capita income has since increased by about 12 percent annually, but motorcycle production has climbed at a rate of 21 percent a year....China is not the only country experiencing this phenomenon. In Thailand, vehicle sales soared by 35 percent in both 1992 and 1993. Some 1.3 million cars and 700,000 motorcycles are now causing traffic nightmares in Bangkok." (p17)

Hanson, Eric. "Asia: With Wealth Comes Filth." Toward Freedom v43 n1, Feb 1994. p17,20. (ISSN0048-9898).

MOTOR VEHICLES--U.S.

In the U.S. "the number of vehicle miles traveled by the nation's cars has doubled. Today, some 250 million motor vehicles transport Americans two trillion miles a year, up 50 percent from 1970 (compared with population growth during the same period of 15 percent). Every year, we add four million cars and trucks to our roads." (p7)

Kay, Jane Holtz. "Transportation: Hell on Wheels." Planning v60 n1, Jan 1994. p7-10. (ISSN0001-2610).

MOTORCYCLES--LAW AND LEGISLATION--U.S. (v19)

MOTORCYCLES--MINNESOTA--SAFETY MEASURES

"Minnesota motorcyclists lobbied the State legislature to enact the toughest licensing standards in the Nation. They also implemented self-funded comprehensive rider education programs and public awareness programs which have won over 20 national awards and can now serve as a model for other States. In Minnesota, bikers do it because good behavior is rewarded by good health--not because someone in Washington is trying to force them to. That is why the Motorcycle Industry Council rated Minnesota the second safest State in the Nation in which to ride a motorcycle. Since the repeal of its mandatory helmet law, the number of licensed motorcyclists in Minnesota has doubled. Today, Minnesota has experienced a 77-percent reduction in cyclist fatalities from the record high numbers which were recorded in 1980--all that in only 25 years. All this happened because Minnesota motorcyclists and lawmakers realized that there is no substitute for ongoing traffic safety education and tough licensing provisions." (pS1289)

Durenberger, Dave (Sen.-Minn.). "Statements on Introduced Bills and Joint Resolutions," Congressional Record (9 Feb 1994). Daily ed. pS1284-1290. (ISSN0363-7239).

MOTORCYCLES--U.S.

"Illinois' economy is suffering because we don't have a helmet law. The average acute health care cost for an injured Illinois motorcyclist in 1988 was $6530. The long term care for a brain injured person can range up to $5 million. Over half of the injured motorcyclists had no health insurance. The acute care costs of the 5,484 injured motorcyclists in 1988 was $35.3 million--almost half of which was paid with public funds." (p7)

Cullerton, John J. (State Sen.-Ill.). U.S. House. Committee on Appropriations. "Department of Transportation and Related Agencies Approp. for 1994 (Part 7A)." Hearing, Washington, D.C.: GPO, 1993. (ISBN0160411033). (Y4.Ap6/1:T68/4/994/pt.7A).

MOTORCYCLES--U.S.--ACCIDENTS (v19)

MOTORCYCLES--U.S.--ACCIDENTS--MORTALITY (v19)

MOTORCYCLES--U.S.--MORTALITY

"The [U.S.] national average of motorcycle fatalities per 100 accidents is 2.95. States with rider education programs and no helmet laws, however, have the lowest average death rate, 2.56 fatalities per 100 accidents. States with mandatory helmet laws and no rider education programs have a significantly higher rate of 3.09 fatalities per 100 accidents. Police accident reports indicate that well over 45 percent of motorcyclists involved in accidents did not have a motorcycle license, 92 percent did not have any rider training and more than half had less than 6 months riding experience. 62 percent of the accidents and 50 percent of the fatalities involved riders between the ages of 17-26. Clearly, mandating helmet use will not address the real problem of rider inexperience and lack of training." (pS1288)

Campbell, Ben Nighthorse (Sen.-Colo.). "Statements on Introduced Bills and Joint Resolutions," Congressional Record (9 Feb 1994). Daily ed. pS1284-1290. (ISSN0363-7239).

MOTORCYCLES--U.S.--SAFETY MEASURES

"Of the top 12 [U.S.] States with the best motorcycle safety records, only one has a helmet law. On the other hand, half of the 12 States with the worst safety records have helmet laws. Comparing States with and without mandatory helmet laws as a whole, figures show that for the 14-year-period between 1977 and 1990, States with mandatory helmet laws had 12.5 percent more accidents and 2.3 percent more fatalities than States that did not mandate helmet usage." (pS1288)

Campbell, Ben Nighthorse (Sen.-Colo.). "Statements on Introduced Bills and Joint Resolutions," Congressional Record (9 Feb 1994). Daily ed. pS1284-1290. (ISSN0363-7239).

MOUNTAINS

"Mountains and highland areas cover one-fifth of the earth's surface and are home to more than 10% of the world's population. Many millions more depend on them for food, timber, minerals and, most importantly, water. The rivers of the Himalaya are a source of life and livelihood for half a billion people on the plains of Asia. But development projects often ignore the unique hazards of mountain areas: big dams straddle fault lines, roads are built on unstable slopes. The people most familiar with the dangers are disregarded while the projects are being planned and then frequently displaced to make way for them. Despite their ecologically prudent relationship with their environment, mountain dwellers have traditionally been marginalised by the policies of the plains and today are further disadvantaged in the name of economic development." (p27)

Bexley, Jo. "Books: Assault on the Mountains." Panoscope n34, Jan 1993. p27. (ISSN0951-8819).

MOUTH--CARE AND HYGIENE

"According to data presented at a recent meeting in Geneva, more than 800 million people throughout the world now benefit from fluorides, the most common naturally occurring fluorine chemical compounds, as a means of controlling caries and maintaining oral health. This is mostly achieved through the fluoridation of water...(210 million people), salt (50 million) or toothpaste (450 million). Ground water in its natural condition almost always contains fluorides, but in concentrations that vary widely from one place to another." (p1)

News release. "WHO Advocates Affordable Fluoride Toothpastes for the Developing Countries." WHO Press 15 Feb 1994. p1-2.

MOVING, HOUSEHOLD (v19)

"A certain measure of mobility is required for members of a modern society to obtain an education, raise families, find jobs, and realize personal goals. Between 1990 and 1991, 17 of every 100 Americans moved to a different home. Nearly 7 percent moved there from a different county, state, or country....The elevated levels of mobility in American society, however, are not universal across the developed world. Nor are they unique. In addition to the United States, mobility rates of more than 17 percent are found in Canada, Australia, and New Zealand. Greater stability distinguishes the populations of France, Sweden, Great Britain, Switzerland, Israel, and Japan, where annual mobility rates range from 9 to 15 percent. More rooted still are residents of the Netherlands, Austria, Belgium, and Ireland where fewer than 9 percent of the population moves to another home each year." (p2-4)

Gober, Patricia. "Americans on the Move." Population Bulletin v48 n3, Nov 1993. p2-40. (ISSN0032-468X).

MOVING, HOUSEHOLD--EDUCATION--U.S.

"One in six, or half a million, of the nation's 3rd graders have attended at least three different schools since the 1st grade, and those children are much more likely to be low achievers than those who have not changed schools, according to a new General Accounting Office report. The report is based on an Education Department study of 15,000 3rd graders in 235 schools in the 1990-91 school year. Of those who changed schools frequently, 41 percent were below grade level in reading and 33 percent were below grade level in math, compared with 26 percent and 17 percent of those who did not change schools." (p21)

"News in Brief: G.A.O. Finds Mobility Hurts Student Progress." Education Week v13 n23, 2 Mar 1994. p21. (ISSN0277-4232).

MOVING, HOUSEHOLD--U.S. (v19)

"There are far more housing transactions in high-mobility than in low-mobility settings. In 1992, for example, there were almost twice as many sales of existing single-family homes, condominiums, and cooperatives in Texas than in New York (242,000 versus 130,000) even though the states are roughly equivalent in population. Colorado, with less than one-half of Massachusetts' population, had 25 percent more real estate transactions (71,900 verus 57,600). Nevada and Maine have almost identical populations, but there were 131 percent more sales in Nevada than in Maine (25,000 versus 10,800)." (p8)

Gober, Patricia. "Americans on the Move." Population Bulletin v48 n3, Nov 1993. p2-40. (ISSN0032-468X).

MOZAMBIQUE

see also DEBTS, EXTERNAL--MOZAMBIQUE; EDUCATION--MOZAMBIQUE; MIGRATION, INTERNAL--MOZAMBIQUE; MINES (MILITARY EXPLOSIVES)--CAMBODIA--KUWAIT--MOZAMBIQUE

MOZAMBIQUE--ECONOMIC CONDITIONS

"Mozambique...has the advantage of significant economic potential: fertile land, extensive forests, known mineral deposits, plentiful off-shore fishing areas, considerable hydro-electric capacity and a large labour force. Though the long era of Portuguese colonial rule had left most of this potential untapped, the early years of independence brought some hopeful prospects for the country's development. There was a broad range of export crops--cashew nuts, sugar cane, cotton, tea and sisal--and agricultural production increased by nearly 9 per cent between 1977 and 1981. In 1975 the Moatize coal mine was producing nearly 600,000 tonnes, out of Mozambique's confirmed coal reserves of some 6 bn tonnes. Iron ore and gold were also produced, and there were deposits of bauxite, manganese, platinum, diamonds, natural gas and uranium. The Cabora Bassa hydro-electric dam, begun in colonial times, had an enormous generating capacity, enough to cover Mozambique's own needs and to sell large amounts to South Africa and other neighbouring countries....Now the poorest country in the world in terms of per capita GDP [gross domestic product], and emerging from a decade-and-a-half of war, Mozambique itself has few of the financial resources needed to take on the challenge of reconstruction." (p15-16)

Harsch, Ernest/Laishley, Roy. "UN Mobilizes for Peace: Mozambique: Out of the Ruins of War." Africa Recovery Briefing Paper n8, May 1993. p1-20.

"The scale of Mozambique's tragedy is difficult to grasp. Out of a total population of some 16 million people, an estimated 4-5 million--more than a quarter--were driven from their homes by the decade and a half of fighting, and more recently by drought. Some 200,000 children have been orphaned and another quarter million separated from their families or otherwise severely traumatized. Nutritional levels remain among the lowest anywhere, especially among children, and disease is rife and spreading. Mozambique today is the poorest country in the world, with a gross national product of just $70 per person. Two-thirds of all Mozambicans are estimated to be living in extreme poverty. This largely reflects the destruction wrought through civil war and persistent external destabilization." (p3)

Harsch, Ernest/Laishley, Roy. "UN Mobilizes for Peace: Mozambique: Out of the Ruins of War." Africa Recovery Briefing Paper n8, May 1993. p1-20.

"More than a decade of war, much of it South African-backed destabilisation, has made Mozambique one of the world's poorest countries. The average annual per capita income of US$ 80 is the same as the price of a meal for two at some of Maputo's posh restaurants. World Bank and IMF-backed structural adjustment measures which forced the removal of food subsidies exacerbated the problem, leading to a sharp rise in malnutrition. Tens of thousands of rural Mozambicans fled the war and settled in the relative safety of already overpopulated towns and cities. With only 300,000 formal sector jobs in a country of 15 million people, nearly all urban adults and many children must find work on the fringes of the economy." (p21)

Waterhouse, Rachel. "Focus: The Informal Sector: 'Ow! My Stomach Hurts.'" Panoscope n38, Jan 1994. p21. (ISSN0951-8819).

MULTIPLE PERSONALITY--U.S. (v19)

MULTIPLE SCLEROSIS--TREATMENT--U.S. (v19)

MULTIPLE SCLEROSIS--U.S.

"A quarter-million Americans have MS [multiple sclerosis], a disease of the central nervous system that includes a gamut of symptoms, from paralysis and vision loss to slurred speech, fatigue and poor coordination. It affects women more than men and mostly strikes people in their 20s and 30s who lived the first 15 years of their life in cold climates. Its cause is unknown." (p24)

Ansett, Patricia. "M.S. News: Steroids Can Delay MS Onset, Study Finds." Rollin' Times Jan 1994. p24.

MUNICIPAL BONDS--U.S. (v19)

"Yields on high-grade tax-exempt bonds are now within only 0.2% of Treasury bonds of the same maturity, so the aftertax yield of the munis is much higher. With top tax rates increasing to 39.6%, munis would have to yield close to 0.4% less than comparable Treasuries for the aftertax return to be the same. If the spread between muni and Treasury yields were to widen to that extent, it would produce a substantial rise in bond prices." (p118)

Holland, Kelley. "Municipal Bonds: The Investment Spectrum: Another Munificent Year for Munis." Business Week n3352, 27 Dec 1993. p118. (ISSN0007-7135).

MUNITIONS

see MILITARY WEAPONS

MUNITIONS INDUSTRY

see WEAPONS INDUSTRY

MURDER--CANADA--U.S. (v19)

MURDER--CANADA--U.S.--MINORITIES (v19)

MURDER--COLOMBIA--U.S.

"The United States today has 11 murders per 100,000 members of the population. Colombia, despite brave efforts by public officials, registers 70 per 100,000--about the same as Washington, D.C." (p34)

Barone, Michael. "On Politics: Slouching toward Dystopia." U.S. News & World Report v115 n24, 20 Dec 1993. p34. (ISSN0041-5537).

MURDER--EMPLOYMENT--U.S. (v19)

MURDER--ISRAEL (v19)
MURDER--RIO DE JANEIRO (BRAZIL) (v19)
MURDER--SAO PAULO (BRAZIL) (v19)
MURDER--U.S. (v19)
MURDER--U.S.--YOUTH (v19)

"The rate of murders [in the U.S.] by white youths has doubled since 1986, and the rate by black youths has tripled, says James Fox, dean of the College of Criminal Justice at Northeastern University in Boston. In Washington State, juveniles accounted for 1.5 percent of all murder convictions in 1984 and 5.4 percent in 1992....Moreover, Mr. Fox says: 'This is nothing compared to what we'll see for the next 10 years.' He says the number of teens in America will climb by 23 percent by 2005, including a 28 percent rise among blacks and 46 percent among Hispanics. Kids in those fast-growing minority groups are more likely to grow up in poverty and with disrupted neighborhoods or families." (p8)

Trumbull, Mark. "National: As Youth Crime Rises, So Do Reform Ideas." The Christian Science Monitor v86 n62, 23 Feb 1994. p8. (ISSN0882-7729).

MURDERERS--U.S. (v19)
MUSHROOMS--U.S. (v19)
MUSIC TRADE--JAPAN

"According to the Recording Industry Association of Japan, the country produced 415,450,000 CDs, tapes, and records last year for sales of Y641.7 billion ($6 billion). This represents 6% growth by volume and 2% growth by sales over 1991, and is a new high for the industry. Yet while the record industry is booming, manufacturers of audio/visual equipment are in a slump. At the September 1992 mid-term, Sony Music Entertainment Japan, which owns the contracts for Dreams Come True and many other popular entertainers, posted 49% annualized current profit growth. Its parent company, Sony, the world's largest manufacturer of audio/visual equipment, saw its profits decline by 0.8%. The software market is helping to keep the hardware market afloat." (p40)

Yamamoto, Akihiko. "Culture: Popular Music: Singing Along." Look Japan v39 n451, Oct 1993. p40-42. (ISSN0456-5339).

MUSLIMS--U.S.

"The number of Moslems in the U.S. is larger than the total Arab-American population: estimates range from 3 to 4 million. American Moslems are divided by their use of language, the different forms of Islam, and the cultural gap between more assimilated immigrants and recent arrivals....About one in four Moslem Americans is black. In fact, blacks account for most of the country's native-born Moslems, according to Dr. Ihsam Bagby of the Islamic Resource Institute in California." (p10)

El-Badry, Samia. "Business Reports: Religion: Understanding Islam in America." American Demographics v16 n1, Jan 1994. p10-11. (ISSN0163-4089).

MUTUAL FUNDS

A "byproduct of the growth in investment companies over the past decade has been a significant increase in the internationalization of the fund industry. Since 1981, assets of funds that invest primarily in foreign markets have skyrocketed from under $2.5 billion to almost $95 billion. Over 480 investment companies invest a majority of their assets in securities of non-U.S. issuers. Investment companies also have been an important source of capital for emerging markets. Sixty-two open-end and closed-end international funds with $10 billion in assets concentrate their investments in emerging markets in Latin America, Asia and Eastern Europe." (p148)

Levitt, Arthur (Chair, U.S. Securities and Exchange Commission). U.S. House. Committee on Energy and Commerce. "Mutual Fund Industry." Hearing, 22 Jul 1993. Washington, D.C.: GPO, 1994. (ISBN0160436060). (Y4.En2/3:103-62).

"The hottest mutual fund action in 1993 was not in the U.S. but overseas. The average equity mutual fund was up 16.5%, besting the 9.25% total return in the Standard & Poor's 500-stock index. But a good share of that boost came from the stellar performance of international equity funds....While U.S. diversified equity funds were up only 10.8%, they still beat the S&P. That wasn't bad considering that in most years they lag the S&P, on average, by about two percentage points. Out of 19 stock-fund categories, all but one beat the S&P index and 16 made double-digit gains." (p110)

Spiro, Leah Nathans. "Mutual Funds: The Investment Spectrum: A Very Good Year--Especially on the Fringes." Business Week n3352, 27 Dec 1993. p110-112. (ISSN0007-7135).

MUTUAL FUNDS--CANADA

"Canadian baby boomers, worried about the lowest interest rates in 30 years, have fled from the safety of guaranteed deposits to mutual funds. And many Canadians are choosing to move their money into mutual funds that invest in the stock market....Sales of equity-based mutual funds in Canada were up by 163 percent last year. Canadians showed even more confidence in foreign markets: Sales of foreign equity funds rose by 178 percent in 1993, according to the Investment Funds Institute of Canada. Even the number of funds increased last year, rising to 633 from 549. While five-year term deposits (the traditional favorite of retirement plans) have been returning just 5 percent, the returns from Canadian-based equity funds have been impressive. Canadian markets were up 29 percent last year, and most equity-based mutual funds reflected that rise." (p8)

Langan, Fred. "Economy: More Canadians Move Their Money into Mutual Funds." The Christian Science Monitor v86 n48, 2 Feb 1994. p8. (ISSN0882-7729).

MUTUAL FUNDS--EUROPEAN ECONOMIC COMMUNITY (v19)
MUTUAL FUNDS--ITALY (v19)
MUTUAL FUNDS--U.S. (v19)

see also BOND FUNDS--U.S.

"Because mutual funds have proved to be a way by which middle-income individuals and families can receive the same benefits of professional money management and diversification of investments as wealthy individuals, funds have played a significant role in opening the securities markets to millions of Americans. By 1992, 27% of U.S. households owned mutual funds. According to [Investment Company] Institute data, the number of individual mutual fund shareholders as of the end of 1992 was approximately 38.2 million; the median age of fund shareholders is 46; mutual fund shareholders have a median household income of $50,000, average financial assets of $114,000 (excluding real estate and assets in employer-sponsored retirement plans), and an average of $43,500 invested in mutual funds." (p87)

Fink, Matthew P. (President, Investment Company Institute). U.S. House. Committee on Energy and Commerce. "Mutual Fund Industry." Hearing, 22 Jul 1993. Washington, D.C.: GPO, 1994. (ISBN0160436060). (Y4.En2/3:103-62).

"From 1982 to 1992, the number of investment companies increased by 133 percent and industry assets increased by 344 percent. Yet the SEC [Securities and Exchange Commission] staff, which is devoted to mutual fund regulation, increased by only 74 percent. And as the SEC recently testified, quote, 'the situation is ironic given that last year, the SEC collected over $80 million in fees from mutual funds but was only allowed to use $18 million of those fees with a $62 million balance diverted to pay for other Federal spending.' Thus, mutual funds are paying far more in SEC fees than they are receiving back in terms of SEC regulation." (p79)

Fink, Matthew P. (President, Investment Company Institute). U.S. House. Committee on Energy and Commerce. "Mutual Fund Industry." Hearing, 22 Jul 1993. Washington, D.C.: GPO,

1994. (ISBN0160436060). (Y4.En2/3:103-62).

"Fueling the growth of the investment company industry [in the U.S.] has been the rechanneling of money from other financial services intermediaries. Between 1980 and 1992, for example, assets of life insurance companies grew only 20% as fast as mutual fund assets. During this same period, bank deposits grew only 12% as fast....One analyst estimated that as much as 40% of mutual fund net cash inflow has come from bank deposits." (p143) "Three factors have prompted banks to enter the mutual fund business: low interest rates for traditional bank products, a desire to maintain a relationship with bank customers seeking higher rates of return, and a search for fee income. The sustained period of low interest rates has probably been the most influential factor contributing to the rapid growth of bank mutual funds. During the past five years, bank mutual funds have grown from 213 portfolios with $35.4 billion in assets to 1,017 portfolios with $181.1 billion in assets, making bank-managed funds one of the fastest growing segments of the mutual fund industry...." (p144)

Levitt, Arthur (Chair, U.S. Securities and Exchange Commission). U.S. House. Committee on Energy and Commerce. "Mutual Fund Industry." Hearing, 22 Jul 1993. Washington, D.C.: GPO, 1994. (ISBN0160436060). (Y4.En2/3:103-62).

"In 1982, the total amount of investors' money managed by mutual funds [in the U.S.] was $297 billion. Today, it is more than seven times as much: $2.1 trillion. For most of 1992 and so far in 1993, the net amount of money given to mutual fund managers to invest has been increasing by $1 billion every business day. Ten years ago, there were 857 mutual funds. Today there are nearly five times as many and a new one opens up for business almost every day....Now, people who are not familiar with mutual funds might dismiss these figures. Some might observe rather cynically that it is just another example of the rich getting richer....First, 40 million Americans, more than 1 out of 4 households, own shares in a mutual fund. And second, 18 percent of Americans who own mutual funds, nearly 8 million people, have annual household incomes below $30,000. Fifty percent of fund owners make less than $50,000." (p1-2)

Markey, Edward J. (Rep.-Mass.). U.S. House. Committee on Energy and Commerce. "Mutual Fund Industry." Hearing, 22 Jul 1993. Washington, D.C.: GPO, 1994. (ISBN0160436060). (Y4.En2/3:103-62).

"In April 1993, there were 4,081 separate mutual fund portfolios, an increase of 624% from the 564 that existed at the beginning of the 1980s. During that same time period, total mutual fund assets soared from $135 billion to $1.7 trillion, an increase of more than 1,100%....The percentage of U.S. households that own mutual funds quadrupled from 6%, or 12.1 million accounts, to 27%, or 77 million accounts....On average, since January 1992, roughly $20 billion of new money has flowed into mutual funds each month....As these numbers illustrate, mutual funds have become a major component of the U.S. and world capital markets." (p140)

Levitt, Arthur (Chair, U.S. Securities and Exchange Commission). U.S. House. Committee on Energy and Commerce. "Mutual Fund Industry." Hearing, 22 Jul 1993. Washington, D.C.: GPO, 1994. (ISBN0160436060). (Y4.En2/3:103-62).

"In the 50 years since the enactment of the Investment Company Act of 1940 and particularly in the last decade, the growth of the mutual fund industry has been nothing short of explosive. Today mutual funds serve as one of the...largest financial intermediaries [in the U.S.] with more than 4,000 funds holding over $1.6 trillion in investor assets. A large part of the industry's recent growth is attributable to the individual investors. In 1992, $1.02 trillion or 64 percent of all mutual fund assets were held by individuals. Currently, one out of every four American families has invested in at least one mutual fund." (p3)

Fields, Jack (Rep.-Tex.). U.S. House. Committee on Energy and Commerce. "Mutual Fund Industry." Hearing, 22 Jul 1993. Washington, D.C.: GPO, 1994. (ISBN0160436060). (Y4.En2/3:103-62).

"Investors have increasingly chosen investment companies and the most popular form, mutual funds, as their primary savings and investment vehicle. Over one-quarter of American households have put savings into mutual funds. And total mutual fund assets now stand at $1.9 trillion, an increase of more than 1,100 percent since 1980. Roughly $20 billion of new money flows into mutual funds each month....The funds themselves have become major players in the financial markets. Stock mutual funds in 1992 accounted for 96 percent of the new money flowing into exchange-listed stocks. Funds also account for significant U.S. investment in foreign markets. Mutual funds and other investment companies have become major purchasers of municipal, mortgage-backed, and asset-backed securities. Fund investments in these instruments have reduced borrowing costs for municipalities, and that is significant; they also have improved the access to and the cost of credit for millions of homeowners and consumers. Product innovation, the ever-expanding array of new types of funds, and enhanced investor services have been equally important characteristics of the industry during the last 2 decades." (p135)

Levitt, Arthur (Chair, U.S. Securities and Exchange Commission). U.S. House. Committee on Energy and Commerce. "Mutual Fund Industry." Hearing, 22 Jul 1993. Washington, D.C.: GPO, 1994. (ISBN0160436060). (Y4.En2/3:103-62).

"Most mutual funds [in the U.S.] now are organized in investment company 'complexes,' which are large groups of mutual fund portfolios covering a wide range of investment objectives that have a common investment adviser, underwriter, or sponsor. There are about 600 such complexes ranging in size from the largest complex of 203 portfolios and over $200 billion in assets to the smallest with 2 portfolios and $5 million in assets. The 100 largest complexes manage about 83% of the industry's assets. In most cases, investors can, with a telephone call, switch between funds in the same complex and change their investment strategy. During both the 1987 market break and the sharp interest rate spike earlier that year, for example, most redeeming shareholders did not 'cash out' but rather moved their holding to a money market fund or other fund portfolio within their complex." (p145)

Levitt, Arthur (Chair, U.S. Securities and Exchange Commission). U.S. House. Committee on Energy and Commerce. "Mutual Fund Industry." Hearing, 22 Jul 1993. Washington, D.C.: GPO, 1994. (ISBN0160436060). (Y4.En2/3:103-62).

"Most of the new money currently going into mutual funds is currently coming from people who...already own fund shares rather than first-time investors. For example, over the last 2 years, as a result of sales fund assets increased by about 30 percent but the percentage of householding owning mutual funds only increased by 4 percent, indicating that most of the new money is coming from existing shareholders....increased market activity by mutual funds, pension plans, and other institutional investors actually helps to decrease stock market volatility. Moreover, an analysis of the 1987 stock market rate indicates that mutual funds were able to meet most shareholders' redemptions from their cash reserves rather than through forced sales of portfolio securities. Thus, in 1987 and future years, mutual funds are able to act as shock absorbers helping to cushion against sharp rise changes." (p79-80)

Fink, Matthew P. (President, Investment Company Institute). U.S. House. Committee on Energy and Commerce. "Mutual Fund

Industry." Hearing, 22 Jul 1993. Washington, D.C.: GPO, 1994. (ISBN0160436060). (Y4.En2/3:103-62).

"Mutual funds and other investment companies have had a profound impact on the daily operation of the financial markets. Stock mutual funds have become a dominant force in the markets as individuals increasingly choose mutual funds as their stock market investment vehicles. Stock mutual funds are by far the largest net purchasers of U.S. equities. In 1992, stock funds accounted for 96% of the new money flowing into exchange-listed stocks. On some days, the country's largest mutual fund manager and its brokerage subsidiaries generate as much as 10% of the total trading volume on the New York Stock Exchange." (p146-147)

Levitt, Arthur (Chair, U.S. Securities and Exchange Commission). U.S. House. Committee on Energy and Commerce. "Mutual Fund Industry." Hearing, 22 Jul 1993. Washington, D.C.: GPO, 1994. (ISBN0160436060). (Y4.En2/3:103-62).

"Mutual funds are the most popular and well known type of investment company, representing approximately 86 percent of all investment company assets. Mutual funds pool the money of many investors and invest it in a wide range of stocks, bonds, or money market instruments, consistent with the investment objectives of the fund. Mutual funds are professionally managed, thereby allowing investors to delegate investment decisions--such as which securities to hold, when to buy, and when to sell." (p81) "For many years, mutual funds concentrated in common stocks of American companies. As recently as 1971, 94 percent of industry assets were in equity funds. However, in response to changing investor needs and changes in the marketplace, the industry broadened its product lines in the 1970s and 1980s, and introduced new types of funds, such as money market funds, municipal bond funds and international equity funds. Today, mutual fund assets are distributed in approximately equal amounts among the three broad categories of fund types: equity funds, bond and income funds, and money market funds." (p82)

Fink, Matthew P. (President, Investment Company Institute). U.S. House. Committee on Energy and Commerce. "Mutual Fund Industry." Hearing, 22 Jul 1993. Washington, D.C.: GPO, 1994. (ISBN0160436060). (Y4.En2/3:103-62).

"Mutual funds indeed have been a great American success story. The modern industry started in 1940 with 68 funds with less than $500 million in assets. Today we have over 4,000 funds with over $1.7 trillion in assets....institutional investors...own over 36 percent of fund assets today. The growth in mutual funds can be attributed both to appreciation of portfolio securities and to new sales....we have had very strong stock and bond markets, so over the last 9 years, 43 percent of the growth was due to appreciation of portfolios and 57 percent to new sales." (p78)

Fink, Matthew P. (President, Investment Company Institute). U.S. House. Committee on Energy and Commerce. "Mutual Fund Industry." Hearing, 22 Jul 1993. Washington, D.C.: GPO, 1994. (ISBN0160436060). (Y4.En2/3:103-62).

"The availability of mutual funds through banks has increased dramatically since 1990. Banks can sell both funds advised by entities unaffiliated with the bank ('nonproprietary funds') or funds in which the bank or its affiliate acts as the fund adviser ('proprietary' funds). Bank distribution is accomplished through both direct marketing and sales force distribution. The [Investment Company] Institute recently completed the first comprehensive survey of mutual fund sales through banks. The findings indicate that during 1991 banks accounted for over $28 billion, or 13 percent, of total sales of equity and bond and income funds. Of these sales, 55 percent were of nonproprietary funds, while 45 percent were of proprietary funds. The results for the first half of 1992 were quite similar. During the first six months of 1992, banks accounted for over $23 billion, or 14 percent, of sales of equity and bond and income funds. Similarly, 60 percent of these sales were of nonproprietary funds, while 40 percent were of proprietary funds. It is important to note that a significant portion of the sales of proprietary funds are the result of banks investing trust and custody assets under their management in their proprietary funds, rather than retail sales." (p92-93)

Fink, Matthew P. (President, Investment Company Institute). U.S. House. Committee on Energy and Commerce. "Mutual Fund Industry." Hearing, 22 Jul 1993. Washington, D.C.: GPO, 1994. (ISBN0160436060). (Y4.En2/3:103-62).

"The growth in mutual fund assets is attributable in significant part to the capital appreciation of portfolio securities owned by mutual funds due to increases in stock and bond prices. For example, during the period from January 1984 to present, mutual fund assets [in the U.S.] increased by $1.3 trillion. The increase in assets of equity and bond and income funds over this period was $938 million, of which 43% was due to capital appreciation of portfolio securities and the remaining 57% was due to net sales of fund shares." (p88-89)

Fink, Matthew P. (President, Investment Company Institute). U.S. House. Committee on Energy and Commerce. "Mutual Fund Industry." Hearing, 22 Jul 1993. Washington, D.C.: GPO, 1994. (ISBN0160436060). (Y4.En2/3:103-62).

"The investment company industry [in the U.S.] has grown dramatically since 1980. Investors are increasingly choosing investment companies as their primary savings and investment vehicle. Since 1980, investment company assets have grown at a compound annual rate of 21.7%, doubling every four years. By far the most popular form of investment company is the open-end management investment company, commonly known as a mutual fund. Mutual funds now hold almost 16% of all household discretionary assets, more than twice the figure of 10 years ago, and account for 84% of the $2.1 trillion dollars in investment company assets...." (p139)

Levitt, Arthur (Chair, U.S. Securities and Exchange Commission). U.S. House. Committee on Energy and Commerce. "Mutual Fund Industry." Hearing, 22 Jul 1993. Washington, D.C.: GPO, 1994. (ISBN0160436060). (Y4.En2/3:103-62).

"The retirement plan market has played an important role in mutual fund growth [in the U.S.]. Recent data indicate the popularity of mutual funds as a vehicle through which to invest retirement dollars. By the end of 1992, retirement assets accounted for 21 percent of total mutual fund assets....As many companies switch from defined benefit plans (where the employer makes investment decisions) to defined contribution plans, such as 401(k) plans, more individual employees are selecting their own investments. The growth of these defined contribution corporate retirement plans has been dramatic. In 1975, only 11.2 million participants were covered by corporate defined contribution plans as compared to the 27.2 million participants covered by corporate defined benefit plans. By 1990, however, approximately 38.5 million employees were covered by corporate defined contribution plans as compared to only 28.8 million employees in corporate defined benefit plans. It is anticipated that by the year 2000 corporate defined contribution plans will have 52.3 million participants with assets of $2,258 trillion, while corporate defined benefit plans will have 29.7 million participants and assets of $1,847 trillion." (p90-91)

Fink, Matthew P. (President, Investment Company Institute). U.S. House. Committee on Energy and Commerce. "Mutual Fund Industry." Hearing, 22 Jul 1993. Washington, D.C.: GPO, 1994. (ISBN0160436060). (Y4.En2/3:103-62).

"What else can you call it but mutual-fund mania? Investors

pumped $128.2 billion into equity mutual funds last year. That's about 10% more than they invested in 1991 and 1992 combined, each of which were record years, too....So far, fund buyers have been rewarded handsomely. In 1993, diversified U.S. funds racked up an average 13.8% total return (appreciation plus reinvestment of dividends and capital gains)--soundly beating the Standard & Poor's 500-stock index by nearly four percentage points. And with the Dow Jones industrial average pushing 4000, 1994 is off to a rousing start as well. With the huge drop in long-term interest rates, the conservative funds that hold some fixed-income securities also beat the S&P 500. Even precious-metals funds, perennial laggards, went on a tear in 1993, up 97%. The average one-year return for all 760 equity funds in the 1994 BUSINESS WEEK Mutual Fund Scoreboard was a juicy 20%--boosted by fat profits from funds investing overseas." (p72)

Laderman, Jeffrey A. "Cover Story: The Best Mutual Funds." Business Week n3358, 14 Feb 1994. p72-75,77. (ISSN0007-7135).

"The U.S. mutual fund industry is clearly a tremendous growth industry, and a prime example of the preeminent role our country's financial services industry play in the global financial marketplace. Since 1980, industry assets have increased from about $135 billion to more than $1.8 trillion, with hundreds of millions more flowing into funds every day. Increasingly, foreign investors have participated in the U.S. securities markets, providing vital investment capital that fuels the growth of American enterprise." (pS16491)

McCain, John (Sen.-Ariz.). "Statements on Introduced Bills and Joint Resolutions," Congressional Record (19 Nov 1993). Daily ed. pS16433-16501. (ISSN0363-7239).

"Mutual-fund investors couldn't help making money in 1993, no matter where they turned. Stock funds gained an average of 12.5 percent, according to Lipper Analytical Services, handily beating the 10.1 percent total return of the Standard & Poor's 500-stock index. Small-company growth funds were up 17 percent, and even Grampa's equity-income and utility funds rose more than 13 percent. And those gains look like 'frijoles' next to foreign-stock funds' 39.4 percent showing. As long-term interest rates continued their slide, corporate bond funds gained an average 8.2 percent; tax-free municipal-bond funds returned 8.8 percent." (p62)

Kaye, Steven D. "News You Can Use: 1994 Investment Guide: The Best Mutual Funds." U.S. News & World Report v116 n5, 7 Feb 1994. p62-63. (ISSN0041-5537).

"Of the mutual funds that invest in 'emerging markets' like China, Malaysia and Turkey, even the laggards registered gains of more than 30 percent in 1993, compared with the U.S. market's 10 percent increase. Shares of the very best performers more than doubled in price. The Turkish Investment Fund gained 151.64 percent, for example; the Asia Pacific Fund, 109.04 percent. Save for the recuperating gold funds, results like that haven't been seen since the last stages of the biotech frenzy." (p78)

Egan, Jack. "On Money: Investing Where Less Is More." U.S. News & World Report v116 n5, 7 Feb 1994. p78. (ISSN0041-5537).

"The average fund investor now has $43,500 in mutual funds, nearly 40 percent of his or her financial assets. Yet even as the states rise, choosing funds grows more daunting. Some 3,400 stock and bond funds are now in business--1,500 of which are new in the last two years." (p81)

Morse, Robert J. "Exclusive Rankings: The Best Funds for '94." U.S. News & World Report v116 n5, 7 Feb 1994. p81-82. (ISSN0041-5537).

MYOCARDIAL INFARCTION--U.S.--WOMEN

"Heart disease isn't just a man's problem: 247,000 women die of heart attacks each year. It is the number one killer of women in the...[U.S.], and too often, women ignore the warning signs." (p26)

Grant, John. "Health: Strong Medicine." Corporate Detroit v11 n1, Jan 1994. p23-24,26,28.

MYRTLE BEACH (SC)

see GOLF COURSES--MYRTLE BEACH (SC)

NAIROBI

see BLOOD--NAIROBI

NAMES--U.S.

"Just 10 percent of married women in the U.S. use something other than their husband's last name, according to a poll conducted for AMERICAN DEMOGRAPHICS by NFO Research of Greenwich, Connecticut. Unwieldy as they can be, hyphenated names are used by 5 percent of couples, while just 2 percent of married women use their maiden name exclusively. About 3 percent of women use other alternatives. This category includes Hillary Rodham Clinton, who uses her maiden name as a middle name. Some women even switch names, using their maiden name professionally and their husband's name for social or legal purposes." (p9)

Brightman, Joan. "Business Reports: Trends: Why Hillary Chooses Rodham Clinton." American Demographics v16 n3, Mar 1994. p9. (ISSN0163-4089).

"MODERN BRIDE magazine asked recently engaged women about their name plans after marriage. Among women under age 25 who had made a decision one way or the other, 16 percent planned to use something other than their finance's name. But among engaged women aged 30 or older, the share was 47 percent. Older brides are reluctant to part with a name that forms an integral part of their identities, says Robert Tomasson, deputy society editor for THE NEW YORK TIMES. Based on an informal audit of wedding announcements in the newspaper, the share of new brides choosing to keep their maiden name or to use a hyphenated name rose from 22 percent to 26 percent between 1988 and 1993." (p9)

Brightman, Joan. "Business Reports: Trends: Why Hillary Chooses Rodham Clinton." American Demographics v16 n3, Mar 1994. p9. (ISSN0163-4089).

NAMIBIA

see EDUCATION, HIGHER--NAMIBIA; LAND USE--NAMIBIA

NANNIES--U.S. (v19)

NARCOTIC TRAFFIC

see DRUG TRAFFIC

NARCOTICS--CENTRAL ASIA (v19)

NARCOTICS, CONTROL OF (v19)

NARCOTICS, CONTROL OF--COLOMBIA (v19)

NARCOTICS, CONTROL OF--GREAT BRITAIN

"On February 11th Michael Howard, the home secretary [of Great Britain], tabled an amendment to his Criminal Justice bill. He wants to raise the maximum fine for possession of marijuana and other soft drugs from 500 [pounds sterling] ($750) to 2,500 [pounds sterling]....Increased fines will indeed have little or no effect. Policemen often turn a blind eye to marijuana. When they do not, they usually issue a mere caution. The percentage of people caught with marijuana who are fined fell from about 65% to 25% between 1982 and 1992. Magistrates are already reluctant to levy fines. The average fine for carrying marijuana is 86 [pounds sterling]. Only 365 people were fined more than 200 [pounds sterling] in 1992." (p67)

"Britain: Marijuana: Pot Panned." Economist v330 n7851, 19 Feb 1994. p67. (ISSN0013-0613).

NARCOTICS, CONTROL OF--JAPAN

"According to National Police Agency statistics, in 1992 about 31 kg of cocaine were seized and 133 people, most of them in their twenties, were arrested for cocaine-related crimes. This was four times the number of arrests and 20 times the amount of the drug than in 1988. (For comparison, 637kg of the drug were seized in the US in 1990.) Most of the cocaine comes from Colombia or the US. It is expected that drug smuggling from the US to Japan will increase as drug control in the US becomes stricter." (p46)

Matsumoto, Mina. "Facts of Life: Cocaine: White Lines." Look Japan v39 n455, Feb 1994. p46. (ISSN0456-5339).

NARCOTICS, CONTROL OF--U.S. (v19)

"Drug interdiction has been a significant part of [U.S.] Customs mission. During the 1980's, cocaine became the primary illegal drug of choice. In the decade from 1981-1991, Customs seized 855,334 pounds of cocaine. Last fiscal year alone, 244,597 pounds were seized. Customs was able to achieve these successes through the integration of investigative, inspectional, and intelligence programs with an aggressive interdiction strategy that includes interdiction of...smuggling aircraft, interdiction of marine vessels, improved selective targeting at ports of entry, expanded use of canine teams, and the development of high technology methods of conducting drug detection examinations. The source areas for narcotics, especially cocaine, shifted in the 1980's to Mexico, the Caribbean, and South and Central America. Customs responded by deploying significant, additional resources to the Southwest border, enhancing the Southwest border facilities through a comprehensive capital improvements initiative, and providing the very latest in detection technology to that border area." (p43)

Weise, George J. (Commissioner, U.S. Customs Service). U.S. Senate. Committee on Finance. "U.S. Customs Service, USTR, and ITC Budget Authorization for Fiscal Years 1994 and 1995." Hearing, 28 Jun 1993. Washington, D.C.: GPO, 1993. (ISBN0160433754). (Y4.F49:S.hrg.103-337).

"'Sentences for drug dealers clearly have gotten crazy, but it doesn't do any good because there is an infinite supply of suppliers,' [Lloyd] Johnston [of the University of Michigan's Institute for Social Research] said. 'We are stretching the limits of prison capacity, which means we don't have space for, say, the people who commit three violent felonies.' Indeed, U-M [University of Michigan] Population Studies Center researcher W. Scott Boggess noted that 6,859 people were sent to state prison [in Michigan] on drug charges in 1979--8 percent of the total serious crimes--but that the number jumped to 51,507 in 1988--25 percent of the total for serious crimes. Nationwide, 21.3 percent of all people in state prisons were there for drug crimes, according to the latest figures available." (p10 secA)

Cain, Stephen. "Drug Study Finds National Relapse." Ann Arbor News 31 Jan 1994. p1,10 secA.

"From 1981 to 1988...the Drug Enforcement Administration reported a 400-percent increase in the number of seizures of clandestine labs. In late August 1989, the Chemical Diversion and Trafficking Act (CDTA) went into effect and this trend was immediately reversed. The Chemical Diversion and Trafficking Act of 1988 was the first comprehensive legislative effort by a major nation to control the diversion of chemicals as an element of its effort to deal with the illicit drug problem. The CDTA demonstrated that this is an effective approach to drug control which can be implemented with modest administrative burdens to Government and industry. Laboratory seizures declined to 521 in 1990 and to 375 in 1991. This decline has validated the effectiveness of 'chemical control' as a law enforcement tool." (pS16899)

Gorton, Slade (Sen.-Wash.). "Comprehensive Drug Abuse Program," Congressional Record (20 Nov 1993). Daily ed. pS16897-16899. (ISSN0363-7239).

"One aspect of Clinton's antidrug policy seems clear.... Interdiction no longer will have the same priority status it enjoyed in the Reagan and Bush years. Bush's administration, for example, concentrated 70 percent of its annual $12 billion antidrug outlay on interdiction, spending more on this strategy than did all the presidents from Nixon to Reagan." U.S. Attorney General Janet "Reno has questioned publicly the wisdom of spending billions on interdiction, noting that only about 25 percent of the drugs entering the southeastern United States are confiscated. Three times as much would have to be seized, she has said, before a real dent could be made in consumption--a goal which, she admitted, would be 'economically prohibitive.'...An estimated 400 metric tons of cocaine continues to flow across U.S. borders annually, of which about 100 tons are seized." (p14)

Horvitz, Leslie Alan. "Federal Drug Policy: Hard Habits to Break?" Insight v10 n9, 28 Feb 1994. p12-16. (ISSN1051-4880).

"Marc Mauer, the asistant director of Washington, DC's Sentencing Project, calculates that drug arrests increased during the 1980s by 88 percent, and that one out of every four prison inmates is now serving time or awaiting trial for a drug offense. (In 1983 it was one in eleven.) Nearly 60 percent of federal prison inmates have been convicted of drug offenses, receiving on average eight-year sentences, twice the length of the sentences given in 1980. In state prisons, drug offenders make up 22 percent of inmates, up from 6 percent. One third are in prison for possession and two thirds for sale or manufacture, but the distinctions have less to do with street behavior than with plea bargaining." (p36-37)

Rothman, David J. "The Crime of Punishment." New York Review of Books v41 n4, 17 Feb 1994. p34-38. (ISSN0028-7504).

"Speaking before the 1991 National Guard Association Conference, Lt. General John B. Conway, Chief of the National Guard Bureau, said: 'Our commander in chief has declared war on drugs. Our mission as America's National Guard in this war is clear: make America drug-free in as short a time as possible using any means necessary no matter what the cost.'...So between January and August of last year [1992], the National Guard made nearly 20,000 arrests, searched 120,000 cars and searched over 1200 buildings. There are now 7000 NG troops on drug duty, with an annual budget of about $300 million." (p7)

"Weather Report: Land of the Free." Progressive Review n316, Apr 1993. p7-9.

NARCOTICS, CONTROL OF--U.S.--MINORITIES

"Drug law enforcement and punishment [in the U.S.] are aimed mostly at minorities, and the 'war on drugs' is in large part a war on blacks. The proportion of blacks among all those arrested for drug possession increased from 22 percent in 1981 to 37 percent in 1990. In Baltimore, among adult offenders, blacks are five times more likely than whites to be arrested for drug offenses; among juveniles, blacks are ten times more likely. Of all drug possession offenders who received a prison sentence in New York, 91 percent were black or Hispanic; in California, 71 percent of those sentenced to prison for drug possession were black or Hispanic." (p37)

Rothman, David J. "The Crime of Punishment." New York Review of Books v41 n4, 17 Feb 1994. p34-38. (ISSN0028-7504).

NATIONAL DEBT

see DEBTS, PUBLIC

NATIONAL MONUMENTS--NEW MEXICO

"With or without a road through it, Petroglyph National Monument is hardly pristine. Its 7,000 acres of grassland, as barren as anywhere in arid New Mexico, allow visitors to retreat into isolation even as rush-hour traffic cruises nearby. But signs of humanity are everywhere. There are the old mattresses and concrete rubble that people have dumped. Volunteers recently hauled 160 tons of trash out of one of the monument's canyons, although the dumping has dropped off in recent years....Some attacks on the monument were sanctioned by the military. In 1919, the National Guard used part of the area for target practice for close to a year. It left behind a seven-foot-tall bunker, made of stone, concrete and dirt, that landowners tore down a year ago so a subdivision could rise in its place." (p13)

Davis, Tony. "Petroglyphs Have Drawn Fire for Decades." High Country News v25 n20, 1 Nov 1993. p13. (ISSN0191-5657).

NATIONAL PARKS AND RESERVES

see also WILDERNESS AREAS

"The Park Service recently approved a pilot project requiring those engaging in 'dangerous activities' to pay for their rescue. In remote places this can be expensive. The Park Service spent $3 million to retrieve stranded climbers in 1992, including $430,000 for 23 rescue missions on Alaska's Mount McKinley, $150,000 for a four-day search in Yosemite National Park, and $50,000 for a two-week search in Olympic National Park. Rescue fees have never before been charged in the United States. But mountaineers must make a down payment covering emergency response before each climb in Nepal and Pakistan. In Europe, a program much like the Park Service's has resulted in affordable rescue insurance, reports the LOS ANGELES TIMES." (p5)

"Hotline: The Cost of Being Lost." High Country News v25 n19, 18 Oct 1993. p5. (ISSN0191-5657).

NATIONAL PARKS AND RESERVES--CALIFORNIA

"There are 20 national park units within the State of California with 22,192 acres of authorized but unacquired lands--22,000 acres of private citizens' lands that has been authorized by Congress to be national parks but which this Congress and the preceding ones will not pay those Americans for. We execute takings in this Congress with the blithe supposition that, somehow or another, nobody will notice. And, after all, if it is for a national park we ought to be able to take it out of the hides of Americans. They ought to be grateful to have it stolen from them--because that is what we have done. So you have 22,000 acres now in the State of California--let alone the hundreds of thousands of acres that exist around the rest of America--that belong to private American citizens which this Congress will not pay for. And the preceding Congresses have not paid for." (pS4055)

Wallop, Malcolm (Sen.-Wyo.). "California Desert Protection Act of 1993," Congressional Record (11 Apr 1994). Daily ed. pS4054-4056. (ISSN0363-7239).

NATIONAL PARKS AND RESERVES--U.S. (v19)

"Although national parks, monuments, recreation areas, and other sites administered by the National Park Service are the most heavily visited federal lands, they are by no means the only ones open to the public. The Bureau of Land Management--the largest public-lands agency, with more than 270 million acres under its jurisdiction--has 76 scenic and recreational areas for public use; the Forest Service (a branch of the U.S. Department of Agriculture) allows camping, hiking, and other outdoor activities on 143 national forests, 19 national grasslands, and two scenic trails; and the U.S. Fish and Wildlife Service grants public access to hundreds of national wildlife refuges." (p3)

Naar, Jon. "Wonders of the West Offer Alternative to Wasteful Past." Audubon Activist v8 n3, Sep 1993. p3. (ISSN0898-915X).

"Although the [U.S.] National Park Service is already unable to take care of the lands and facilities entrusted to its care, the agency faces continual pressure for expansion of its responsibilities. Golden Gate National Recreation Area has nearly tripled in size from its original authorization of 23,000 acres less than 25 years ago. Golden Gate is currently seeking nearly $70 million for a variety of life safety projects, asbestos removal, historic building preservation, restroom improvements, and so forth. The same funding shortfall exists at other national parks in the State of California. For example, Sequoia National Park has identified a shortfall of $140 million to fix up its existing facilities, and Yosemite National Park needs $342 million. This funding shortfall exists throughout the National Park System. A report recently submitted to Congress documents a 37-year backlog in funding for major park facilities and a 26-year backlog in funding for previously authorized land acquisition, assuming no inflation and no expansion of the park system." (pE483-484)

Duncan, John J., Jr. (Rep.-Tenn.). "Introduction of Presidio Preservation Act," Congressional Record (17 Mar 1994). Daily ed. pE483-484. (ISSN0363-7239).

"Vast as it is, Grand Canyon National Park has reached the limits of its carrying capacity. More than 5 million tourists now clog the South Rim each year, and the National Park Service estimates that the number will reach 7 million by the year 2010. The Grand Canyon shares a package tour with Disneyland. At any given hour of the day, 6,000 cars vie for fewer than 1,500 parking spaces, and the average wait for a spot is now two hours. Canyon hotels recommend that reservations be made a full year in advance....Many of the trails leading from the South Rim to the Colorado River--at least those trails that aren't glued down with mule excrement--are being eroded away by foot traffic faster than they can be repaired. By some estimates, more than 250,000 people raft through the canyon each year. They camp on narrow beaches that have already been badly eroded by variable releases of water from Glen Canyon Dam. The combined action of dam and frolickers threatens to destroy those riparian beaches entirely, and with them dozens of native plant and animal species." (p16)

McNamee, Gregory. "How the Auto and Airplane Teamed Up to Destroy the Grand Canyon." High Country News v25 n22, 29 Nov 1993. p16. (ISSN0191-5657).

"Hunters and anglers visit national wildlife refugees more than 6 million times a year; other wildlife-related recreation, such as birding and wildlife photography, results in 30 million refuge visits. At the Great Smoky Mountains National Park, the nation's most popular, visitation is up 3 percent from 1991; people came to the park 8.9 million times in 1992. On Bureau of Land Management (BLM) lands, visitors spent 539,779,000 hours in 1992--a 9 percent increase from 1991--and 96,537 recreational use permits were issued. National forests withstood 691 million visits in 1992." (p11)

Marshall, Laury. "Take a Number Please! Outdoor Recreationists Flock to Public Lands." Outdoor America v59 n1, Win 1994. p11-14.

"The 14,000-acre Indiana Dunes National Lakeshore contains more than 1,400 species of plants, ranking third in plant diversity in the entire National Park System. The Indiana Dunes State Park was created in 1926 as a result of recognition about the importance of the dunes. However, to pass the first related bill establishing the Indiana Dunes National Lakeshore took until 1966. More than 10 million people live within a two-hour drive of the dunes, and close to 2 million people visit each year." (p23)

Anderson, Thomas. "IWLA News: Indiana Dunes." Outdoor America v58 n2, Spr 1993. p23.

NATIONAL PARKS AND RESERVES--U.S.--FEES (v19)

NATIONAL PARKS AND RESERVES--UTAH

"Consider a few statistics gleaned from Utah's national parks. In 1982 the number of visitors recorded at Arches was 339,415; in 1992 it was 799,831--more than a 100-percent increase in 10 years. The number of tourists who passed through Canyonlands in 1982 was 98,310; by 1992 it had quadrupled to 396,911. During the same period Bryce's annual visitations increased from 704,796 to a whopping 1,477,324; Zion's from 1,361,750 to 2,687,848; Capitol Reef's from 323,458 to 729,324. And the same pattern is true for Natural Bridges, Cedar Breaks, and Rainbow Bridge national monuments and the Glen Canyon National Recreation Area." (p98)

Stegner, Page. "Red Ledge Province." Sierra v79 n2, Mar-Apr 1994. p92-98,100,144-146. (ISSN0161-7362).

NATIONAL RIFLE ASSOCIATION (v19)

"Sleeping or not, the NRA is a giant. With more than 3.3 million dues-paying members--900,000 of them added in the last 12 months--the NRA dwarfs other political organizations. The U.S. Chamber of Commerce has 215,000 members; the National Federation of Independent Businesses has 600,000 members; the Republican National Committee roughly 300,000. Handgun Control Inc., has 300,000 members." (p79)

Norquist, Grover G. "Politics: Democrats Misfire on Guns." American Spectator v72 n2, Feb 1994. p78-80. (ISSN0148-8414).

NATIONAL SCHOOL LUNCH PROGRAM--CRIMES AGAINST (v19)

NATURAL DISASTERS--U.S. (v19)

NATURAL FOODS INDUSTRY--JAPAN--U.S. (v19)

NATURAL FOODS INDUSTRY--U.S. (v19)

NATURAL GAS--MEXICO (v19)

NATURAL GAS--MEXICO--U.S.

The North American Free Trade Agreement "will...enhance opportunities for cross-border trade in natural gas. Under NAFTA, U.S. natural gas suppliers can negotiate directly with Mexican end-users for the sale and export of natural gas. Projections have placed U.S. increases in exports of this environmentally-friendly form of energy at 800 million cubic feet per day in the next 5 years. Last year, natural gas demand in Mexico was approximately 1.1 trillion cubic feet. It is believed that if Mexico's natural gas industry is developed, natural gas consumption can grow to 1.4 trillion cubic feet by the year 2000 and generate $450 million annually to U.S. gas producers." (p5)

Klug, Scott L. (Rep.-Wis.). U.S. House. Committee on Energy and Commerce. "NAFTA: Energy Provisions and Environmental Implications." Hearing, 22 Sep 1993. Washington, D.C.: GPO, 1994. (ISBN0160440459). (Y4.En2/3:103/70).

NATURAL GAS--SIBERIA--U.S.

"In Arizona many of the natural gas wells have hydrogen contents of less than 0.1% but it is not uncommon to find wells with 0.1 to 1% hydrogen. In some cases the hydrogen content is as high as 4.2% (Steve Rauzi, 1993)....Within the lower 48 states of the U.S., hydrogen contents of up to 15% have been reported. About 30 to 40% of all natural gas wells in the U.S. are believed to have hydrogen values of greater than 1% (Howard Meyer, 1993). In Siberia a gas field was even reported to contain up to 43% hydrogen (Nechayeva, 1968). Hydrogen in natural gas is a concern to gas extraction companies because hydrogen gas lowers the volumetric heat production of a fuel. As a result the higher the hydrogen content is, the lower the burn value will be." (p5)

Melchiorre, Erik B. "Hydrogen Potential from Existing Natural Gas Wells." Hydrogen Today v4 n1, 1993. p1,5.

NATURAL GAS--U.S.

"U.S. gas exports to Mexico have generally been on the rise and are projected to grow dramatically in the future. Between 1991 and 1992, natural gas exports more than doubled, going from 78 billion cubic feet to 190 BCF. The Energy Information Administration projects that, with NAFTA [North American Free Trade Agreement], gas exports will rise to over 300 BCF by the year 2000, with another 100 BCF heading north to Canada. This is more than eight times the amount of gas we exported to these two nations in 1990." (p13)

White, William (Deputy Secretary of Energy, U.S. Dept. of Energy). U.S. House. Committee on Energy and Commerce. "NAFTA: Energy Provisions and Environmental Implications." Hearing, 22 Sep 1993. Washington, D.C.: GPO, 1994. (ISBN0160440459). (Y4.En2/3:103/70).

NATURAL RESOURCES

see also CONSERVATION OF NATURAL RESOURCES; FISHERIES; FORESTS AND FORESTRY; MINES AND MINERAL RESOURCES; WATER-POWER; WATER-SUPPLY

NATURAL RESOURCES--CANADA--MEXICO--U.S.

"Proven U.S. reserves of oil and gas will be depleted in less than a decade if current rates of production and consumption continue, or if significant new reserves are not discovered and/or existing field recovery not enhanced. Yet, the United States, with these dwindling reserves, is currently producing 24 percent of world gas production and 12 percent of world oil production. In contrast, Mexico has a reserves-to-production ratio of greater than 50 years for both oil and gas, producing only two percent of world gas production and 4 percent of world oil production. The United States has twice the proven gas reserves of Mexico, but one-half the oil reserves. Canada has a reserves/production ratio of 17 years for oil and 25 for gas and is producing six percent of world gas production and 2.5 of oil production." (p93)

U.S. House. Committee on Energy and Commerce. "NAFTA: Energy Provisions and Environmental Implications." Hearing, 22 Sep 1993. Washington, D.C.: GPO, 1994. (ISBN0160440459). (Y4.En2/3:103/70).

NATURAL RESOURCES--FORMER SOVIET REPUBLICS

"The estimated resource reserve for Russia and the other New Independent States is enormously impressive. In oil, the estimated reserves are 57 billion barrels, almost $1.3 trillion; in manganese some 500 million short tons, $192 1/2 billion; in gold 8,710 metric tons, a value in excess of $105 billion; in nickel 8.1 million short tons, some $57 1/2 billion in value; in vanadium, some 4 million metric tons, more than $30 billion in value; platinum, 6 million kilograms, almost $23 1/2 billion in value; in silver, 50,000 metric tons, in excess of $7 billion in value; and in chromite, 129 million metric tons, almost $6 1/2 billion in value, totaling some $1.7 trillion...." (pS313)

Specter, Arlen (Sen.-Pa.). "Privilege of the Floor," Congressional Record (28 Jan 1994). Daily ed. pS312-317. (ISSN0363-7239).

NATURAL RESOURCES--U.S.

"Were consumption per capita [in the U.S.] to continue at even 2 percent (only two-thirds the rate we have grown in the last 25 years), it would double in 35 years and quadruple in 70 years. If one multiplies the projected increase in consumption with the 2.6-fold increase in population, the globe would consume 20 times the physical resources we consume today. Of course, we can and will reduce the environmental damage and resource consumption of economic growth, but however successful we are, there will be huge increments of growth demand on our land, water, climate, and resources. Can the ecosystem possibly absorb the wastes which flow out of these numbers?" (p15)

Lamm, Richard D. "The Environment: Growth in a Finite World." Humanist v53 n5, Sep-Oct 1993. p13-15. (ISSN0018-7399).

NATURE CONSERVANCY

Nature Conservancy, a "non-profit organization, which employs more than 1,500 people, specializes in debt-for-nature swaps. The organization buys part of the country's debt from commercial banks at a reduced rate--sometimes only 10 cents on the dollar--and then works with the debtor country's central bank to convert the debt into local currency, which is used to fund local environmental projects. Nature Conservancy usually implements these projects through local non-governmental organizations, and they have used this method to convert some US $100 million of Latin America's debt. Eighteen Latin American countries are currently involved with the organization's projects, which protect over 20 million acres (eight million hectares) of tropical forests." (p33)

"Latin American Focus: Region: Environmental Group Focuses on Latin America." Barricada Internacional v14 n369, Jan 1994. p33. (ISSN1013-9567).

NEPAL

see HIV INFECTIONS--INDIA--NEPAL--PROSTITUTES

NEPAL--ECONOMIC CONDITIONS (v19)

NETHERLANDS

see CONSUMPTION (ECONOMICS)--GERMANY--NETHERLANDS--U.S.; CYCLING--DENMARK--JAPAN--NETHERLANDS; ENERGY CONSERVATION--DENMARK--NETHERLANDS

NETWORKS, COMPUTER

see COMPUTER NETWORKS

NEUROPATHY--CUBA

"The neuropathy epidemic that struck 50,000 Cubans was brought under control in early September, but researchers are still sifting through clues to identify its causes....Fearing that dietary imbalances may have conspired with unknown toxins to cause the outbreak, the Cuban government ordered the production and free distribution of vitamin supplements to the entire population, beginning in May. By September, the pharmaceutical industry had turned out 1.8 billion of the tablets, which combine B-complex with vitamin A, folic acid and nicotinamide....international experts have been unanimous in their praise for the resources Cuba has devoted to the epidemic, and the quality of care and research--especially given the dramatic economic crisis the country is facing....by June Cuba had already invested $70 million in prevention, treatment and study of the disease. The total cost now hovers closer to $100 million." (p15)

Reed, Gail. "Update: Health Watch Neuropathy Epidemic Over: The Causes Still a Mystery." Cuba Update n6, Nov-Dec 1993. p15. (ISSN0196-0830).

NEVADA

see MINES AND MINERAL RESOURCES--NEVADA; WATER-SUPPLY--NEVADA

NEVADA--ECONOMIC CONDITIONS (v19)

NEW ENGLAND

see also FISHERIES--NEW ENGLAND

NEW ENGLAND--ECONOMIC CONDITIONS (v19)

"After a prolonged and deep recession, New England's economy is showing signs of improvement, economists say. And due to lower interest rates, the residential construction industry is one sector making slow but steady gains. In Massachusetts, a bellwether state for the region, more people are buying and building houses. The region's home sales increased 19 percent over sales a year ago, says Yolanda Kodrzycki, an economist at the Federal Reserve Bank of Boston....Over the past four years, New England has seen the worst of the national recession. The economic slump began here in 1989, and since then the region has lost 800,000 jobs. It has endured sharp cutbacks in its defense, computer, and financial industries while state governments faced serious revenue shortfalls and budget crises." (p8)

Ross, Elizabeth. "New England: Northeast States Creep Slowly Out of Recession." The Christian Science Monitor v86 n27, 3 Jan 1994. p8. (ISSN0882-7729).

NEW HAMPSHIRE

see BIRTH CONTROL--NEW HAMPSHIRE

NEW JERSEY

see BIOLOGICAL DIVERSITY--NEW JERSEY; PUBLIC LANDS--NEW JERSEY--OREGON

NEW MEXICO

see ALCOHOLISM--NEW MEXICO; NATIONAL MONUMENTS--NEW MEXICO; PASTURE, RIGHT OF--NEW MEXICO; WILDLIFE REFUGES--NEW MEXICO

NEW ORLEANS (LA)--ECONOMIC CONDITIONS

"According to Vincent Maruggi, assistant director of the University of New Orleans's division of business and economic research...the black upper class in New Orleans has barely grown at all in recent years, while the poverty rate among African-Americans remains one of the highest in the United States. 'Both the white upper-economic class and the black upper-economic class in New Orleans are shrinking,' Mr. Maruggi says....According to the 1990 US Census, there are only slightly more than 1,600 black households in the city with combined incomes of more than $50,000. More than 75,000 black households fall below the $25,000 mark, and, of that number, some 26,000 households earned less than $5,000 annually. Such dire statistics have made New Orleans the third-poorest city in the country, with a poverty rate that has increased from 26 percent to 31 percent in the last decade alone....According to city figures, as much as 80 percent of last year's murders took place in the poorest sections of this aging city." (p3)

Boulard, Garry. "National: Leaders in New Orleans Aim to Stem Crime Wave Among Young Black Males." The Christian Science Monitor v86 n44, 27 Jan 1994. p3. (ISSN0882-7729).

NEW PRODUCTS--U.S. (v19)

NEW YORK--MANUFACTURING--EMPLOYMENT (v19)

NEW YORK (NY)

see also ALIENS, ILLEGAL--NEW YORK (NY); CRIME--NEW YORK (NY); FIREARMS--NEW YORK (NY); HOUSING--NEW YORK (NY); PEDIATRIC TOXICOLOGY--NEW YORK (NY); SCHOOLS--NEW YORK (NY); TOBACCO INDUSTRY--NEW YORK (NY)

NEW YORK (NY)--ECONOMIC CONDITIONS (v19)

NEW YORK (NY)--EMPLOYMENT

"Look at New York City. The U.S. economy began to pick up in mid-1991, but the city's upturn didn't emerge for another year. Since 1987, total private-sector employment declined by nearly 360,000 jobs, even as the total municipal work force rose by 15,000, according to the city's Office of Management & Budget." (p42)

Farrell, Christopher/others. "Top of the News: City Government: Rudy Revs Up the Chainsaw." Business Week n3359, 21 Feb 1994. p42. (ISSN0007-7135).

NEW YORK (NY)--INTERNATIONAL STATUS (v19)

NEW YORK (STATE)

see AIDS (DISEASE)--NEW YORK (STATE)--PRISONERS

NEW YORK (STATE)--COMMERCE--MEXICO (v19)

NEW ZEALAND

see ECONOMIC FORECASTING--NEW ZEALAND; FORESTS AND FORESTRY--NEW ZEALAND; MAORI (NEW ZEALAND PEOPLE); PRISONERS--NEW ZEALAND--U.S.--MINORITIES; RAILROADS--NEW ZEALAND--SWEDEN

NEW ZEALAND--ECONOMIC CONDITIONS (v19)

NEWFOUNDLAND

see PUBLIC WELFARE--NEWFOUNDLAND

NICARAGUA

see also AGED--NICARAGUA; COCAINE INDUSTRY--NICARAGUA; CONTRACEPTION--NICARAGUA; CRIME--NICARAGUA; DRUG TRAFFIC--NICARAGUA; EDUCATION, HIGHER--NICARAGUA; EDUCATION--NICARAGUA; ETHNOLOGY; GOVERNMENT SPENDING POLICY--NICARAGUA; INDIGENOUS PEOPLE--NICARAGUA; MADRIZ

(NICARAGUA)--SOCIAL CONDITIONS; PESTICIDES--NICARAGUA; POLITICAL PARTIES--NICARAGUA--PUBLIC OPINION

NICARAGUA--ECONOMIC CONDITIONS

"The recession [in Nicaragua] will affect not only the economic indicators for 1993 but also the possibility of a future recovery. As the hole gets deeper, it becomes increasingly hard to climb out. If by the year 2000 the country wants to match the per capita gross domestic product it had in 1990, it would need to grow 4.4% a year. If the recovery is delayed, we will need at least 5% or 6% annual growth to reach this level. The government's current path allows little or no room for changes. This is proven by its plans for 1993 and the coming years, which are simply to continue the same institutional and economic reforms and to block any attempt to draw up an agenda which prioritizes social issues and economic recovery." (p24)

"The Structural Adjustment Plan: Digging Its Own Grave." Barricada Internacional v14 n369, Jan 1994. p22-24. (ISSN1013-9567).

"The Chamorro government has carried out a draconian structural adjustment program [in Nicaragua] that has brought the 5-digit inflation they inherited down to 3.8% for 1992. Its privatization program has been nearly completed, transferring state enterprises and farms to landless peasants, factory workers, and former combatants from both sides as well as to former owners and new national and international investors. The government recently renegotiated its debts and is considered in 'good standing' with multilateral and bilateral creditors, but the impact has been soaring unemployment and underemployment, and drastically cut social services. The United Nations Development Program's index of human development indicators shows Nicaragua slipping from 85th of 173 countries in 1990 to 11th in 1993. A lack of domestic and foreign investment and falling international prices for coffee and other main products have also been devastating." (p11)

"Nicaragua: Progress and Problems." NewsNotes v18 n5, Sep-Oct 1993. p10-11. (ISSN1064-1556).

NICARAGUA--HEALTH AND HYGIENE

"A recent report issued by the Minister of Health and UNICEF indicates the seriousness of the daily situation faced by most ordinary Nicaraguans. In 1993, 500,000 cases of influenza have been reported, with 22 deaths in the first two weeks of June--as well as 2000 cases of dengue fever, 5000 cases of diarrhea each week, and 941 cases of cholera, with 87 deaths. In the latest health crisis, 800 persons have been bitten by rabid animals and one has died. In addition, the per capita income in Nicaragua is $431; over 39% of the population live in critical to extreme poverty; infant mortality is 71.8 deaths per 1000 live births and maternal mortality is 159 deaths per 1000 live births--both are rising; 42% of the deaths in Nicaragua are of children under 5 years old; 24% of the children between the ages of 7 and 12 are not in school; and illiteracy is now over 25%." (p9)

"Nicaragua: National Dialogue." NewsNotes v18 n4, Jul-Aug 1993. p8-9. (ISSN1064-1556).

NICARAGUA--POPULATION

"According to a study by the United Nations Fund for Population Activities (UNFPA), Nicaragua is experiencing a population explosion that, if it continues at its present rate, will increase the country's population to 8 million in the next 20 years. Currently, Nicaragua has 4.2 million inhabitants. According to Jairo Palacio, director of UNFPA in Nicaragua, the country's population grows at a yearly rate of 3.7%, 'the highest in the Americas and one of the highest in the world.' The UNFPA representative said that, on top of being the country with the highest growth rate in the Western Hemisphere and the second highest in the world, Nicaragua is characterized by other worrisome demographic statistics. For example, it has a remarkably high number of young mothers, since 22% of all births are given by mothers between the ages of 15 and 19. Many have traditionally said that Nicaragua is 'a country of young people,' but Palacio stressed that this is not exactly the case. Instead, said Palacio, 47.9% of Nicaraguans are younger than 15 years old, thus making it a country of 'children.'" (p22)

"Briefly: A Country of Children." Barricada Internacional v13 n364, Aug 1993. p22. (ISSN1013-9567).

"Nicaragua has one of the highest birth rates in the world: 4.6 children per woman. Given this, and the fact that 45.6% of the population is under 15 and 50.5% of women are sexually active before they turn 18, the only possible outcome is population growth. According to a report by the Ministry of Social Action, Nicaragua's population has quadrupled since 1950. However, while the population continues to grow, social and economic conditions are deteriorating. Unemployment has now surpassed the 60% level, illiteracy has increased to 30%, the maternal mortality rate has become one of the highest in Latin America and over 70% of the population lives in poverty. Given these statistics, even government reports recognize that Nicaragua is the poorest country in the continent." (p25)

"Periscope: Women Use Contraceptives without Permission." Barricada Internacional v14 n369, Jan 1994. p25. (ISSN1013-9567).

NIGER--EDUCATION

"In Niger, where conditions are especially bad, a child goes to school for an average of 2.1 years. If the figure is adjusted for grade repetition, it falls to 1.8 years. If the length of the school year is factored in, the figure is 306 days....If this Nigerian child is a girl, the figure falls to 204 days, and the lack of textbooks means this girl will really receive only 60 to 80 days of effective schooling in her lifetime." (p7)

"UNESCO Report: Illiteracy Down Worldwide, Problems Mount in Some Regions." Reading Today v11 n4, Feb-Mar 1994. p7. (ISSN0737-4208).

NIGERIA

see BUDGET DEFICITS--NIGERIA

NIGERIA--ECONOMIC CONDITIONS (v19)

NONNUTRITIVE SWEETENERS--U.S.--CHILDREN

A study of 48 children aged three to ten who were given diets containing sucrose, aspartame (Nutrasweet) and saccharin showed that neither their behavior nor their cognitive function was significantly affected by the sweeteners. "Even the 23 children whose parents had described them as 'sugar sensitive' showed no ill effects from the sweeteners." (p8)

Sklaroff, Sara. "Special Education." Education Week v13 n22, 23 Feb 1994. p8. (ISSN0277-4232).

NONPROFIT ORGANIZATIONS--U.S. (v19)

"Since 1982 more and more foundation dollars are for program support, increasing from 28% of all foundation grant dollars in 1982 to 41% in 1992. General support, meanwhile, the type of money all nonprofits love, was 13% in 1992, essentially unchanged from the early 1980s. Capital grants (22%), research (10%), student aid (5%) and emergency and technical assistance (1%) round out the parade of types of support." (p4)

"Trends in Foundation Giving: Social Welfare Programs Receive Lion's Share." Responsive Philanthropy Win 1994. p16,4.

"The Foundation Center in New York...reports that 'more than two-thirds of 1992 (foundation) grants were made for programs that serve the general public.' Targeting children and youth was the biggest shift, going from 7.3% of total foundation giving in 1980 to 13.3% in 1992, the latest data available from the Foundation Center. Minorities giving doubled, going from 4.8% to 9.6% during the same period. Women and girls grantmaking tripled, expanding from 1.7% in 1980 to 5.3% in 1992. And the disabled as a focus for grants also expanded, but not as much, increasing from 1.6% to 3.8%. Not faring so well were the elderly/aging population. 'Funding...peaked in the mid-1980s; since 1987, it has stayed around the 2.5% level,' according to the Foundation Center." (p16)

"Trends in Foundation Giving: Special Populations Get More and More Dollars." Responsive Philanthropy Win 1994. p16,4.

"Throughout the 1980s, social welfare programs received the largest share of foundation dollars, even more than education received, and the trend is continuing. According to data recently released by the Foundation Center, social welfare programs received 32% of foundation funds in 1992, compared to education's 25% share. This represents a megabuck rise of over $800 million in 1992 dollars from 1979, when social welfare programs received 23% of all foundation giving, according to NCRP [National Committee Responsible Philanthropy] calculations. (Total foundation giving in 1992 was $9.3 billion, according to the Foundation Center report, FOUNDATION GRANTS INDEX, 1994, Introduction.)" (p16)

"Trends in Foundation Giving: Social Welfare Programs Receive Lion's Share." Responsive Philanthropy Win 1994. p16,4.

"United Way of America reports that total designations (as opposed to undesignated gifts which United Way citizens committees allocate among recipient agencies) increased 42.5% from 1989 to 1991. This represents a much more rapid increase than the 6% increase in all United Way revenues during that time....Non-member recipients of funds through United Way campaigns now account for 19% of all designations, an average of around $150,000 per United Way. Nationally, these designated dollars directed 'outside the United Way system' represent about 2.4% of total United Way campaign dollars." (p5)

"Donor Choice Bigger Than Ever for United Ways but Only 2.4% of Total Pledges Reach Non-Members." Responsive Philanthropy Sum 1993. p5-6.

The National Committee for Responsive Philanthropy issued a Special Report, "Charity in the Workplace, 1992," saying that "United Ways, while appearing to be growing great guns during the 1970s and 1980s, actually grew only 2% in inflation-adjusted dollars. Gross National Product grew 48% and total private giving grew 54% in inflation-adjusted dollars during this same 20-year period, 1970 to 1990." (p2)

"United Ways' Growth Curve Bodes Ill for Those Needing $." Responsive Philanthropy Win 1994. p2-3.

NONVIOLENCE

"Walter Wink, professor of biblical interpretation at Auburn Theological Seminary...opened...[a United States Institute of Peace workshop on alternatives to war] with his paper, 'Beyond Just War and Pacifism,' advocating nonviolence as the only Christian choice, based on the teachings of Jesus. Wink noted a growing dissatisfaction with just war theory within religious circles. (This theory appraises the use of force on the basis of a set of standards: the authority to order the use of force, the reasons for using force, and acceptable conduct under conditions of armed conflict.) Wink suggested that just war criteria should be renamed 'violence reduction criteria' and that governments should be encouraged to wage war with less brutality and ferocity. The criteria would be aimed at avoiding warfare before it starts and decreasing its atrocities once it begins. Recently, there has been an increase in the use of nonviolence, according to Wink. In 1989 alone, 13 nations experienced nonviolent revolutions, and all except the one in China were successful. More than 3.3 billion people--64 percent of the world's population--have been involved in nonviolent revolutions in this century, he added." (p8)

"Religious Perspectives on Pacifism and Nonviolence in International Conflicts." United States Institute of Peace Journal v6 n5, Oct 1993. p8-9. (ISSN1046-7513).

NORTH AMERICA--ECONOMIC CONDITIONS (v19)

NORTH AMERICAN FREE TRADE AGREEMENT (v19)

"Since NAFTA [North American Free Trade Agreement] negotiations were announced, U.S. exports to Mexico have grown very rapidly--an average of roughly 20 percent a year from 1990 to 1992. To reach 900,000 jobs by 1995, U.S. exports to Mexico would need to grow by about 12 percent a year over the next 3 years (reaching an estimated $57 billion in 1995 with jobs per billion dollars declining at a 3.7 percent annual rate to 15,755 in that year)....the U.S. has a large trade surplus with Mexico that clearly indicates net job creation, and is likely to persist. In 1992, the U.S. had exports of over $40 billion to Mexico and an overall surplus of $5.4 billion with that country. Only eight years ago in 1985, when Mexico was in a severe depression and its economy tied up in knots, the U.S. had exports of only about $12 billion to Mexico and a trade deficit of $5.5 billion with that country. U.S. workers have gained enormously from Mexican economic growth and the NAFTA positions them to continue to do so. In fact, the U.S. has a much bigger surplus in manufacturing with Mexico than we have overall with that country. This is because we import about $4.3 billion worth of oil from Mexico. In 1992, the U.S. surplus with Mexico on manufactured goods was $7.5 billion." (p12)

London, Paul A. (Acting Under Secretary of Commerce for Economic Affairs). U.S. Senate. Committee on Governmental Affairs. "NAFTA Job Claims: Truth in Statistics?" Hearing, 10 Nov 1993. Washington, D.C.: GPO, 1994. (ISBN0160435048). (Y4.G74/9:S.hrg.103-386).

"The [Clinton] Administration has claimed that 200,000 U.S. jobs will be created as a result of NAFTA [North American Free Trade Agreement]. Studies by other groups claim that this figure could exceed 2 million....On the negative side of the ledger, several studies have estimated that NAFTA will cause a loss of anywhere from 34,000 to 900,000 U.S. jobs. Most economists will tell you that the science, or rather the art of economics is an imperfect study of an imperfect world....we would be well served to view the predictions of any of these NAFTA studies with a jaundiced eye and a grain of salt. Unfortunately, the Administration has tossed a figurative grain of salt over its shoulder and to the wind and has embraced the 200,000 jobs figure as the gospel truth without taking into account a number of important factors." (p1)

Glenn, John (Sen.-Ohio). U.S. Senate. Committee on Governmental Affairs. "NAFTA Job Claims: Truth in Statistics?" Hearing, 10 Nov 1993. Washington, D.C.: GPO, 1994. (ISBN0160435048). (Y4.G74/9:S.hrg.103-386).

"Thanks to the improved trade climate that NAFTA [North American Free Trade Agreement] negotiations have helped to foster, our energy trade with Canada and Mexico is already generating jobs for Americans....In 1992 we sold these two nations more than 185 thousand barrels per day of oil and petroleum products, over 160 billion cubic feet of natural gas, about 16 million tons of coal and coke and almost 9 billion kilowatt-hours of electric power, with a combined value of over $2 billion. Using the average labor intensity for production in each of these sectors, these exports generated more than 100,000 jobs across the American economy....Canada and Mexico are important suppliers of energy to our nation. In 1992 these two countries together supplied 24 percent of our net oil imports and Canada supplied 98 percent of natural gas imports." (p12)

White, William (Deputy Secretary of Energy, U.S. Dept. of Energy). U.S. House. Committee on Energy and Commerce. "NAFTA: Energy Provisions and Environmental Implications."

Hearing, 22 Sep 1993. Washington, D.C.: GPO, 1994. (ISBN0160440459). (Y4.En2/3:103/70).

"NAFTA [North American Free Trade Agreement] will create the world's largest open market. It will have a population of 370 million; it will have a GDP [gross domestic product] of $7 trillion. It is an unparalleled opportunity for Americans, for the United States as a whole, and for Minnesota in particular. Since Mexico started to remove its trade barriers, Minnesota exports to Mexico have grown by 191 percent. In 1992 alone, last year, we had $261,420,000 worth of exports to Mexico. Sales of Minnesota products to Mexico will dwarf this figure once we pass NAFTA, remove the remaining trade barriers, and begin to expand trade around the world. We have already experienced great growth in exports as a result of the United States-Canada Free-Trade Agreement. Minnesota exports to Canada have increased 65 percent over the last 4 years as a result of the free trade agreement. In 1992 alone, Minnesota's exports to Canada totaled $1.8 billion." (pS16605)

Durenberger, Dave (Sen.-Minn.). "North American Free-Trade Agreement Implementation Act," Congressional Record (20 Nov 1993). Daily ed. pS16602-16622. (ISSN0363-7239).

"Statistics compiled by Harry Browne and Beth Sims of the Resource Center in Albuquerque, New Mexico reveal that the industrial Midwest has been victimized repeatedly by corporate flight to Mexico....Ohio has lost over 15,000 jobs while Indiana and Illinois have each lost over 6500. From the Missouri River to eastern Ohio over 45,000 jobs have been exported to Mexico. Because of the difficulty in accessing information from companies which directly link plant closings in the U.S. to plant openings in Mexico, these figures are conservative. An example of under-reporting job loss is evidenced by two studies on Iowa. While the Browne/Sims study reports that Iowa has lost 1700 jobs to Mexico, the DES MOINES REGISTER reported in 1986 that Iowa had lost over 2400 jobs. Of all jobs included in the Browne/Sims study 52 percent moved to Mexico after 1988. In another recently released study, Pat Choate of the Manufacturing Policy Project reported that 5.9 million manufacturing jobs in the U.S. are at risk of moving to Mexico. The Midwest--including Illinois, Indiana, Iowa, Kansas, Michigan, Minnesota, Missouri, Nebraska, North Dakota, Ohio, Oklahoma, South Dakota and Wisconsin--has over 1,520,000 jobs at risk under NAFTA, according to Choate." (p8)

O'Meara, Ben. "Focal Point: NAFTA: Who Wins, Who Loses?" Prairie Journal v4 n1, Spr 1993. p8-9.

NORTH AMERICAN FREE TRADE AGREEMENT--CANADA

"The NAFTA [North American Free Trade Agreement] will decimate the Canadian horticultural industry because fruits and vegetables will not be protected from lower-priced imports from the southern United States and Mexico. NAFTA guarantees the eventual removal of all import protection against predatory pricing policies. Canadian fruit and vegetable production is expected to compete directly with imports. Just how tough that will prove is illustrated in the example of iceberg lettuce. In 1992, it cost British Columbia growers $8.70 to produce a 24-head case of lettuce; while importers were bringing in U.S. lettuce at $3 per case." (p7)

Pugh, Terry. "The Nation: 'Free Trade' Undermines Canadian Agriculture." Prairie Journal v4 n1, Spr 1993. p6-7.

NORTH AMERICAN FREE TRADE AGREEMENT--CANADA--PUBLIC OPINION (v19)

NORTH AMERICAN FREE TRADE AGREEMENT--MEXICO

"Currently, 30 percent of Mexico's population lives in the countryside. Peasant farmers control more than half the surface area in Mexico, farming on plots averaging 15 acres. Their primary crops are basic grains, especially corn, dry edible beans, wheat and sorghum. For five decades, the government supported the production of these crops as part of a national food security policy. Under President Salinas, Mexico is converting from a food security policy to one based on the export of tropical products, winter vegetables, and beef to earn foreign exchange. The export crops are predominantly produced by agribusinesses, who are the real beneficiaries of free trade. Family farmers, who primarily produce basic grains, will be forced to compete with corn imports from the U.S. at half the price they currently receive. Studies predict that anywhere from 800,000 to 5 million people will be displaced from the countryside as a result of NAFTA [North American Free Trade Agreement] and national agricultural reforms." (p10)

Lehman, Karen. "Worldview: NAFTA: Not Good News for Mexico." Prairie Journal v4 n1, Spr 1993. p10-11.

NORTH AMERICAN FREE TRADE AGREEMENT--MEXICO--PUBLIC OPINION (v19)

NORTH AMERICAN FREE TRADE AGREEMENT--PUBLIC OPINION (v19)

NORTH AMERICAN FREE TRADE AGREEMENT--WOMEN

"The North American Free Trade Agreement (NAFTA) will disproportionately affect women, yet the voices of women workers have barely been heard in the mainstream media's discussion of the pact. NAFTA's most likely impact, according to the World Bank, will be on multinational corporations operating south of the U.S.-Mexico border and on those who work for them--predominantly women and girls. Multinationals already employ almost half a million people in Mexico, 70 percent to 80 percent of whom are women between the ages of 16 and 25. NAFTA may open up new job opportunities for these women, albeit in industries that pay as little as 40 cents an hour for 14- to 16-hour days, but the freer rein their employers will enjoy is widely expected to decrease what slim protection the women have had against violence and abuse in the workplace." (p12)

Flanders, Laura. "With Jobs at Stake, Women Are Ignored." EXTRA! v6 n1, Jan-Feb 1993. p12. (ISSN0895-2310).

NORTH CAROLINA

see PORK INDUSTRY AND TRADE--NORTH CAROLINA; POULTRY INDUSTRY--NORTH CAROLINA; PRISONERS--NORTH CAROLINA

NORTH CAROLINA--COMMERCE--MEXICO (v19)

NORTHERN IRELAND--HISTORY--CIVIL WAR (v19)

NORTHERN IRELAND--POLITICS AND GOVERNMENT (v19)

NORTHERN IRELAND--RELIGION

"Several weeks ago, Amnesty International released a troubling report entitled, 'Political Killings in Northern Ireland,' which noted that more than 350 people have been killed by security forces in Northern Ireland during the last 20 years. About half of those killed were unarmed individuals. Most were Catholic. Disturbingly, Amnesty International expressed the view that there was convincing evidence that British security forces in Northern Ireland practice a policy of deliberately killing suspects, rather than arresting them....To date, the British have still not responded to Amnesty's charges. Unfortunately, these kind of charges against British occupying forces in Northern Ireland are not new. While international media attention is often rightly given to the tragedy of IRA terrorism in Ireland, in the United States we do not often hear of the equally gruesome violence perpetrated by loyalist paramilitary groups against Catholics there." The "point...is not that one type of murder is worse than another, but rather that after more than 20 years and the deaths of more than 3,400 people over all, the time has come to stop simply laying blame at one side or another and bring peace to the whole of Ireland." (pH980)

Manton, Thomas J. (Rep.-N.Y.). "Peace in Northern Ireland," Congressional Record (2 Mar 1994). Daily ed. pH980-994. (ISSN0363-7239).

"Out of a population of 1.6 million [in Northern Ireland], only 110,000 live in truly mixed areas. Twenty years ago, only 43 voting districts were exclusively Catholic and 56 entirely Protestant; now the figures are 120 and 115 respectively." (p9)

Dettmer, Jamie. "Fragile Hope Blossoms in Northern Ireland's Bloody War." Insight v10 n3, 17 Jan 1994. p6-11. (ISSN1051-4880).

NORTHWEST, PACIFIC

see BIRDS--NORTHWET, PACIFIC; ECONOMIC FORECASTING--NORTHWEST, PACIFIC

NORWAY

see also PUBLIC WELFARE--NORWAY

NORWAY--ECONOMIC CONDITIONS (v19)

"As in the rest of western Europe, unemployment has increased inexorably in Norway in recent years. The number of jobless Norwegians has grown from 60,000 in 1985 to some 200,000 today, or 6.2 percent of the workforce....Despite the growing expense of joblessness benefits, the country derives ready income from its petroleum industry. In fact, Norway's current 'Oil Age' is sometimes compared to the Spanish Golden Age of the 16th century....The government does have a budget deficit, and the country's foreign debt amounts to $1720 per capita. Yet Norway's ledgers are expected to be fully balanced by 1996, due partly to the revenues resulting from oil exploitations...." (p6)

Brown, Ross. "Welfare State: A Colder Climate in Scandinavia." Toward Freedom v42 n6, Oct 1993. p6. (ISSN0048-9898).

NOSOCOMIAL INFECTIONS

"While the number of hospital-acquired infections nationwide has remained at an estimated 2 million annually, and infection rates in intensive care units (ICU) are decreasing, more and more of the bacteria that cause these infections are failing to respond to antibiotics, according to the chief of surveillance activity of the hospital infections program at the Centers for Disease Control and Prevention (CDC)....A CDC report in the Aug. 6, 1993 MORBIDITY AND MORTALITY WEEKLY REPORT found a 20-fold increase in the percentage of infection-causing enterococci bacteria resistant to the antibiotic vancomycin between Jan. 1, 1989 and March 31, 1993. Breaking down the figures by years, the researchers found that the percentage increased from .3 percent in 1989 to 7.9 percent in 1993. Patients in intensive care units (ICU) saw an increase from .4 percent to 13.6 percent." (p6)

"Nosocomial Infections Fight Back." People's Medical Society Newsletter v13 n1, Feb 1994. p6. (ISSN0736-4873).

NUCLEAR DISARMAMENT--FORMER SOVIET REPUBLICS

"One of the most important potential benefits of converting disarmament's nuclear legacy to power generation is that it would provide an opportunity to help the former Soviet Union resolve its own power generation crisis. The Soviet Union built 41 nuclear reactors to generate electricity. Eighteen of the units, which accounted for almost 29 percent of the Soviets' nuclear capacity, were known as Chernobyl-style reactors. Even though officials of the former Soviet Union recognize the dangers of these power plants, most of them have no option but to permit their continued operation....With the end of the Cold War and accompanying drastic reductions in nuclear weapons requirements, a substantial proportion of the region's nuclear scientists and engineers have suddenly found themselves unemployed....Providing these scientists with an opportunity to use their sophisticated training and skills in a civilian nuclear program could give them an incentive to stay in their country." (p23-24)

Copulos, Milton R. "Symposium: A Peace Dividend for Nuclear Power." Insight v10 n4, 24 Jan 1994. p22-24. (ISSN1051-4880).

NUCLEAR ENERGY

"Worldwide, there were 423 operable nuclear reactors at the start of 1993. While the United States maintains the largest number--roughly a quarter of the world total--17 other countries (including Germany and Japan) are more reliant on nuclear power for their electricity needs. Stopped cold in the United States, nuclear-power growth has also slowed to a trickle in most of the rest of the world. At the end of 1992, construction was actively under way at fewer than 50 plants worldwide, with almost a third of those in Japan (nine) and France (five). Most new reactors should be completed within the next few years. Given the expected rate of plant retirements, however, the Worldwatch Institute projects that by the turn of the century global nuclear capacity will be at most only slightly higher than it is today." (p80)

Greenberg, Phillip A. "Dreams Die Hard." Sierra v78 n6, Nov-Dec 1993. p78-85,102-103. (ISSN0161-7362).

NUCLEAR ENERGY--EASTERN EUROPE (v19)

NUCLEAR ENERGY--FRANCE

"Fifty-six French [nuclear] reactors account for 73 percent of the nation's electricity--a larger share than anywhere else in the world. But the heavily subsidized state-owned agency that operates France's $145-billion nuclear program has run at a loss for much of the past 20 years, accumulating a debt of $35 billion, and its financial future is unclear. Some observers--including the International Energy Agency, an arm of the industrialized nations' Organization for Economic Cooperation and Development--have questioned the wisdom of relying so heavily on nuclear power. The discovery of a serious generic flaw in France's vaunted standardized plant designs, for instance, could lead to disastrous nationwide electricity shortages." (p80)

Greenberg, Phillip A. "Dreams Die Hard." Sierra v78 n6, Nov-Dec 1993. p78-85,102-103. (ISSN0161-7362).

NUCLEAR ENERGY--GREAT BRITAIN

"Nuclear power's share of Britain's electricity generation has grown from 17% to 26%. Britain's advanced gas-cooled reactors (AGRs) performed better than any other sort of atomic reactors in the world last year. While output is up, controllable costs (ie, all except such things as interest payments and payments made under fixed contracts) are down by 30%. Productivity has more than doubled." (p58)

"Britain: No, Thanks." Economist v331 n7858, 9 Apr 1994. p57-59. (ISSN0013-0613).

NUCLEAR ENERGY--JAPAN (v19)

NUCLEAR ENERGY--U.S.

"Building on successes over the past several years--nuclear energy production costs have decreased on average by 4.4 percent from 1989 to 1991--the industry seeks to enhance safe and reliable operations through increased communications and shared operating experiences among utilities....increasing numbers of U.S. nuclear energy facilities are joining the ranks of the world's top energy facilities. Through cooperation, operating experience at these world-class facilities can be shared and applied at all U.S. nuclear power plants. To be clear, the average cost per kilowatt-hour of electricity from nuclear energy is 2.16 cents. This compares competitively with coal-fire electricity at 1.98 cents per kilowatt-hour. However, considering that the 10 most economical nuclear energy plants generate electricity for less than 1.5 cents per kilowatt-hour, it is clear that a system to pool the best operating knowledge could significantly lower the cost of electricity to millions of American ratepayers." (pS16528)

Wallop, Malcolm (Sen.-Wyo.). "Nuclear Power, A Necessary Option for our Energy Future," Congressional Record (19 Nov

1993). Daily ed. pS16528-16529. (ISSN0363-7239).

The U.S. Department of Energy's fiscal year 1994 budget request for $19.6 billion asks for "less money for nuclear weapons production and more for cleanup....Hard numbers tell the story. The [Clinton] administration's budget proposal backs research on commercial-fission nuclear reactors to the tune of $230 million, down only $30 million from this year's budget. Research into fusion power will receive $348 million next year. At the same time, research on solar, wind and other renewable energy resources will get $327 million, a 30 percent increase. And programs to promote energy efficiency and conservation will rise 35 percent to $789 million. These figures will still be dwarfed by defense spending in the energy budget. It will drop 18 percent but will nonetheless add up to $5.9 billion. And cleanup of the weapons complex will cost $6.5 billion next year, a billion dollars more than this year. Together, they absorb more than half the nation's energy budget." (p13)

Christensen, Jon. "Can Hazel O'Leary Reinvent the Energy Department?" High Country News v25 n11, 14 Jun 1993. p13. (ISSN0191-5657).

NUCLEAR ENERGY--U.S.--COSTS

"In a study for Greenpeace of nuclear power's costs since the industry's inception, Komanoff Energy Associates concluded that from 1950 to 1990, total U.S. expenditures on nuclear energy approached half a trillion dollars. The utility industry anted up $395 billion (in constant 1990 dollars), with another $97 billion coming from various federal government subsidies. Looking more closely at the latter, the Congressional Research Service calculated that nuclear energy soaked up 65 percent of all federal energy research-and-development funds from 1948 to 1992." (p102)

Greenberg, Phillip A. "Dreams Die Hard." Sierra v78 n6, Nov-Dec 1993. p78-85,102-103. (ISSN0161-7362).

NUCLEAR INDUSTRY--U.S.

"Despite the billions of dollars in taxpayer subsidies of the last four decades, the nuclear industry [in the U.S.] is in trouble. 'Nukes face a new crisis: competitive markets,' concludes a headline to a recent article in PUBLIC UTILITIES FORTNIGHTLY, a trade publication. According to Greenpeace's report, ratepayers and shareholders spent $396 billion between 1950 and 1990 (outside of taxpayer expenditures) to develop and maintain nuclear power, a number that far exceeds the value of the energy supplied." (p16)

Lapp, David. "Bankrolling Nuclear Power." Environmental Action v25 n1, Spr 1993. p12-16. (ISSN0013-922X).

NUCLEAR MEDICINE--U.S. (v19)

NUCLEAR POWER PLANTS--CALIFORNIA

"One California utility has found that life after nuclear power can be sweet. The Sacramento Municipal Utility District (SMUD), which had its Rancho Seco nuclear power plant shut by voters in 1989, has watched its bottom line turn from red to black. The last year that Rancho Seco ran, SMUD lost $575 million. Today, the utility is making money....Forced to quickly replace the nuke's power, SMUD now spends about $52 million a year--8 percent of its total revenue--on energy efficiency....In addition, SMUD is building four natural gas cogeneration plants, which produce steam for factories as well as electricity. The juice from these plants is expected to be cheap--about half the national average of 8 cents per kilowatt hour. SMUD is also pursuing the development of renewable fuels such as wind, solar and geothermal." (p12)

Stiak, Jim. "Nuclear-Free Utility." High Country News v25 n11, 14 Jun 1993. p12. (ISSN0191-5657).

NUCLEAR POWER PLANTS--EUROPE

"'There are now fifty-eight Soviet-designed civilian nuclear power stations operating from Central and Eastern Europe,' points out Carl Bildt, Sweden's prime minister. 'Of those, forty are of older design....If they were in the United States or Sweden, we would have closed them down yesterday.'... Estimates of how much it will cost to make these plants safe run into the billions. Eberhard von Koeber, executive vice president of the Swedish engineering firm Asea Brown Boveri (ABB), claims it could cost up to $50 billion to rehabilitate, decommission, and replace the most dangerous plants." (p36)

Hinrichsen, Don. "Russian Roulette." Amicus Journal v14 n4, Win 1993. p35-37. (ISSN0276-7201).

"For the troubled nations of...[Eastern Europe], the need for electricity is taking precedence over public demands that unsafe [nuclear power] plants be closed down permanently. Lithuania's Ignalina plant, though condemned by Western experts, is likely to remain on stream because it produces about 60 percent of the country's electricity. Similarly, Sosnovyi Bor generates 60 percent of the electricity for St. Petersburg; Kozloduy produces 40 percent of Bulgaria's electricity; Paks 40 percent of Hungary's; and fifteen reactors in Ukraine crank out 25 percent of the country's electricity needs (though only around six reactors are currently operating)." (p37)

Hinrichsen, Don. "Russian Roulette." Amicus Journal v14 n4, Win 1993. p35-37. (ISSN0276-7201).

NUCLEAR POWER PLANTS--FORMER SOVIET REPUBLICS--PUBLIC OPINION

"The public does not believe that nuclear power is safe. In an opinion poll of people who live near the South Ukrainian nuclear power plant and the Zaporozhskaya power plant, almost 70 percent of the general population--and 60 percent of those employed at the plants--said that nuclear power plants present a hazard to public health. Almost half of the general population wanted to move away, and half of the employees wanted to change jobs. The same safety concerns are expressed by people who live near other nuclear fuel cycle facilities, especially those that generate a large amount of liquid radioactive waste. By now the whole world knows about the 1957 accident at Kyshtym in the Chelyabinsk region. The explosion of a tank filled with high-level radioactive waste resulted in unprecedented radioactive contamination. Now, the Yenesei River in Siberia is contaminated by radionuclides from a reprocessing plant in Krasnoyarsk-26, and animals spread radioactive contamination from an area around the plutonium production plant at Tomsk-7." (p23-24)

Popova, Lydia. "Energy: Russia's Nuclear Elite on the Rampage." Surviving Together v11 n2, Sum 1993. p23-25. (ISSN0859-6286).

NUCLEAR POWER PLANTS--OREGON

On November 9, 1992, "A cracked steam tube released radioactive gas into...[the Trojan nuclear power plant in Oregon], and Trojan was temporarily closed for repairs. Two months later the temporary shutdown was made permanent." (p10) "At the heart of the matter is what could be the Achilles' heel of nuclear power: the steam generator tubes that carry cooling water through the hot reactors. The walls of these tubes are only 1/20 of an inch thick; to make them strong, Westinghouse and other reactor manufacturers used a metal alloy called Inconel 600, a chrome-nickel-iron alloy that has corroded faster than expected. Tubes that were supposed to last 35 years in Trojan failed after 16 years. This prompted the NRC [Nuclear Regulatory Commission] to loosen its safety regulations....NRC is now considering relaxing the rules for a number of other reactors. And according to the NRC, 71 of the nation's 108 commercial reactors use the Inconel 600 tubes." (p11)

Stiak, Jim. "Fatally Flawed Nuclear Power Plant Is Shut." High Country News v25 n11, 14 Jun 1993. p10-12.

(ISSN0191-5657).

NUCLEAR POWER PLANTS--SOVIET UNION--ACCIDENTS (v19)

NUCLEAR POWER PLANTS--U.S.

see also THREE MILES ISLAND NUCLEAR POWER PLANT (PA)

"Three U.S. nuclear plants have shut down in the last year, and the amount of U.S. electricity generated by nuclear power--about 20 percent--has begun to slip. New York investment brokers Shearson Lehman Brothers last year predicted that 25 nuclear plants in the nation may shut down within the decade because of soaring maintenance costs. While the industry tries to rescue itself, drawing up plans for a second generation of simpler and safer nuclear power plants, the nails in the coffin of the first generation are being hammered home." (p12)

Stiak, Jim. "Fatally Flawed Nuclear Power Plant Is Shut." High Country News v25 n11, 14 Jun 1993. p10-12. (ISSN0191-5657).

"Initial cost estimates for dismantling nuclear plants have proven to be as unrealistic as were those for building them 20 years ago. In 1988, the NRC [Nuclear Regulatory Commission] put the costs of decommissioning at $105 million to $135 million for large plants, depending on their type. The GAO [General Accounting Office] and others criticized those numbers as far too low, a conclusion eventually accepted by the industry itself. The utility that owns the comparatively small 175-megawatt (MW) Yankee Rowe plant has projected that decommissioning will cost $247 million, and recent estimates for dismantling the 330-MW Fort St. Vrain reactor stand at $333 million. A 1990 study by Public Citizen found that utilities' median estimates for decommissioning large reactors (700 to 1,299 MW) ranged between $191 million and $268 million (depending on the size class), with one plant coming in at a high of $466 million. Even those astronomical numbers were eclipsed by the recent $541-million estimate to dismantle the 1,100-MW Trojan plant, while Indiana Michigan Power looks to spend as much as $550 million each to decommission its two 1,000-MW Cook reactors." (p85)

Greenberg, Phillip A. "Dreams Die Hard." Sierra v78 n6, Nov-Dec 1993. p78-85,102-103. (ISSN0161-7362).

NUCLEAR POWER PLANTS--U.S.--COSTS

"Some analysts are predicting that a quarter of the 109 nuclear plants in the United States will shut down over the next decade due to increasing operation and maintenance costs....Utilities are finding that decommissioning the plants may cost as much or more than the original construction. Portland General Electric officials expect the shutdown at Trojan [a nuclear power plant in Oregon] to cost $420 million. The plant cost $460 million and opened in 1976. SMUD [the Sacramento Municipal Utility District] officials expect to spend $300 million to decommission Rancho Seco, which cost $350 million to build. The 330-megawatt Fort St. Vrain plant [in Colorado] cost $224 million to build and will cost $333 million to dismantle." (p7)

Bryce, Robert. "National: More Nuclear Plants Close as Costs Mount." The Christian Science Monitor v86 n28, 4 Jan 1994. p7. (ISSN0882-7729).

NUCLEAR POWER PLANTS--WASHINGTON (STATE)

"The Washington Public Power Supply System (WPPSS, pronounced 'Whoops') was born in the heady nuclear boom of the 1960s. Backed by Northwest utilities, its goal was to build five nukes in Washington state for $4 billion. Only one of the five--Unit #2 in Richland--was completed, and it cost $3.2 billion, about eight times the original estimate. When power demand didn't rise as quickly as predicted, construction of two of the other plants was halted in the early 1980s. That triggered the largest municipal bond default in U.S. history, as WPPSS reneged on $2.25 billion in revenue bonds. The default dried up financing for the other two plants." (p11)

Stiak, Jim. "WPPSS's Endless Saga." High Country News v25 n11, 14 Jun 1993. p11. (ISSN0191-5657).

NUCLEAR REACTORS--U.S.--ACCIDENTS

"Estimates of the costs of a major nuclear accident vary from the General Accounting Office's (GAO) estimate in 1987 that under average weather conditions losses from a major nuclear accident could be as high as $15 billion to a 1982 analysis by Sandia National Laboratory for the Nuclear Regulatory Commission (NRC), which found that under a worst-case scenario financial losses (not including on-site damages) could range from $56 billion to $314 billion, with 100,000 early deaths. The NRC estimates the chance of a major 'core melt' nuclear accident within the next 20 years is 45 percent." (p13)

Lapp, David. "Bankrolling Nuclear Power." Environmental Action v25 n1, Spr 1993. p12-16. (ISSN0013-922X).

NUCLEAR WASTES

see RADIOACTIVE WASTES

NUCLEAR WEAPONS

"World War II brought unprecedented physical destruction during the half-decade it raged on three continents. Yet in the half century since then, the United States, Soviet Union, China, Britain, and France have together produced some 128,000 nuclear warheads, 250 tons of weapons-grade plutonium, and 1,300 to 1,800 tons of highly-enriched uranium--and what remains of it today still has a destructive power roughly 1,600 times that of all of World War II put together." (p10)

Renner, Michael. "Updates: 'Finishing the Job.'" World Watch v7 n2, Mar-Apr 1994. p10-11. (ISSN0896-0615).

NUCLEAR WEAPONS--CHINA--U.S.--TESTING (v19)

NUCLEAR WEAPONS--COMMONWEALTH OF INDEPENDENT STATES (v19)

NUCLEAR WEAPONS--SOUTH ASIA

"South Asia is a nuclear hot spot. Two regional powers, India and Pakistan, are adversaries that have warred twice since the partitioning of Pakistan from India in 1947. Although neither country admits to possession of nuclear weapons, Leonard Spector of the Carnegie Endowment for Peace believes India has as many as 100 nuclear bombs that could be quickly deployed, and Pakistan between 15 and 20--enough to cause millions of deaths. Neither country has signed the Nuclear Nonproliferation Treaty (NPT). For these reasons, Spector writes, 'It is not far-fetched to suggest that the subcontinent has replaced Europe as the most likely area of conflict between nuclear-armed foes.' Mistrust between these two countries has led to a massive arms buildup, consuming more than 30 percent of both countries' annual budgets. Millions of Indians and Pakistanis live in abject poverty. A recent study by the Pakistan government said that over 55 percent of the population has no access to clean water and 45 percent lacks access to health care. Meanwhile, each country blames the other for the buildup and neither has been bold enough to call for unilateral disarmament. IPPNW [International Physicians for the Prevention of Nuclear War] hopes to change this." (p1)

Osewe, Patrick. "Confronting the Nuclear Threat in South Asia." Vital Signs v6 n1, Apr 1993. p1,3.

NUCLEAR WEAPONS--TESTING (v19)

"The testing history of...nuclear weapons states indicates that the United States has conducted some 1,050 nuclear tests and the former Soviet Union about 700. While Britain has tested significantly less than the United States or the former Soviet Union, it has tested more than has China. France, following its own independent nuclear policy, has conducted more than 200 tests." (p51)

Shen, Dingli. "Toward a Nuclear-Weapon-Free World: a Chinese Perspective." Bulletin of the Atomic Scientists v50 n2,

Mar/Apr 1994. p51-54. (ISSN0096-3402).

NUCLEAR WEAPONS--TESTING--HEALTH ASPECTS (v19)

NUCLEAR WEAPONS--U.S.

March 1, 1994 "is the fortieth anniversary of the Bravo shot, the detonation of the largest nuclear device ever tested by the United States. The 15-megaton Bravo blast was 1,000 times more powerful than the atomic bomb which devastated Hiroshima. It blanketed thousands of square miles with radioactive fallout, including inhabited atolls in the Marshall Islands, the Pacific island nation then administered by the United States under a trusteeship agreement with the United Nations....The aftermath of the Bravo debacle continues in the Marshall Islands....on one island of the Nation's most populous atoll, the rate of thyroid disease, including cancer, is 100 times higher than any place else in the world." (pH898)

Miller, George (Rep.-Calif.). "America's Responsibility to Disclose the Truth about Radioactive Fallout in the Marshall Islands," Congressional Record (1 Mar 1994). Daily ed. pH898-900. (ISSN0363-7239).

"The U.S. nuclear weapons complex is a vast industrial enterprise that sprang from the secret Manhattan Project effort to develop the atomic bombs dropped on Japan in 1945. Its 15 major facilities collectively occupy some 3,350 square miles--an area larger than Delaware, Rhode Island, and the District of Columbia combined--in 13 states and employ more than 100,000 people....In the half-century that it has existed, the nuclear weapons industry has manufactured nearly 70,000 nuclear warheads. It has produced about 89 metric tons of plutonium and more than 500 metric tons of highly enriched uranium, the primary radioactive materials in nuclear weapons. And it has carried out 1,076 nuclear explosions." (p2)

"Nuclear Threat at Home: The Cold War's Lethal Leftovers." Defense Monitor v23 n2, 1994. p1-3,7. (ISSN0195-6450).

"The number of resistance actions and arrests occurring outside of the mass campaign for a nuclear test ban has remained about the same for the last three years. Almost 1000 anti-nuclear arrests were reported in the United States and Canada in 1993. (In 1991 and 1992, more than twice that number were counted at the Nevada Test Site alone.) While the faith-based Nevada Desert Experience continued to bring resisters to the desert, for the first year since 1984, no mass secular resistance actions occurred at the test site. Secular and religious resisters both returned en masse to the Lawrence Livermore National Laboratory in California. For years, it has seemed that Livermore gave as much expertise to lobbying against a moratorium, as was given to designing the weapons for testing themselves. Thus, for the first time in eight years, more arrests were made at a location other than the Nevada Test Site. Livermore logged 285 arrests, compared to 230 at the test site." (p1)

Cohen-Joppa, Felice/Cohen-Joppa, Jack. "Nuclear Resistance 1993." Nuclear Resister n92, 20 Jan 1994. p1-2.

"The pace of anti-nuclear civil disobedience stayed steady through 1992, despite changes in the global and national political scene. Total arrests were up slightly from the previous year to almost 2,500, as were the number of sites where arrests occurred (40), and distinct actions reported (90). Political changes that have challenged the existence of many peace and anti-nuclear groups have also influenced the focus of resistance organizing. More and more often, nuclear disarmament actions were explicitly part of a broader based opposition to much of U.S. foreign and domestic policy. Also, the groups and individuals most involved in the anti-nuclear nonviolent direct action movement are as likely to be found risking arrest on other peace, social justice and environmental issues. The primacy of a nuclear test ban as an achievable goal for the anti-nuclear movement, plus the essential absence of risk involved in most civil disobedience at the Nevada Test Site, contributed again to the great majority of 1992 anti-nuclear arrests being recorded there. At least 2,017 arrests were recorded during more than 30 actions at the test site in 1992." (p1)

"Nuclear Resistance--1992." Nuclear Resister n88, 2 Apr 1993. p1,6.

NUCLEAR WEAPONS--U.S.--INVENTORY CONTROL

"The nuclear weapons freeze campaign put much of its efforts into nuclear freeze votes by city, town and county councils and local referenda. The freeze called for a bilateral (US-Soviet) freeze on the production of nuclear weapons. Based on figures from the Nuclear Weapons Freeze Campaign National Clearinghouse in St. Louis, Newcombe (1983) reported that 240 city councils, 466 New England town meetings and 63 county councils passed freeze resolutions, a total of 769. In addition, referenda were passed in over 50 cities and counties. This effort was followed by a comprehensive test ban campaign which had received support from 154 cities by 1987." (p4)

Alger, Chadwick F. "We Can Learn from People Who Think Globally and Act Locally." Access n118, May 1993. p1-7.

NUCLEAR WEAPONS--U.S.--TESTING

"When the atomic energy commission began exploding nuclear bombs in the Nevada desert in the early 1950s, it described the area's residents--the farmers and ranchers, schoolchildren and homemakers, Mormons and American Indians who would live under massive fallout clouds, bury their dead livestock and drink radioactive milk--as 'a low-use segment of the population.' Such was the official rationale for detonating 126 atmospheric nuclear bombs, some more powerful than those dropped on Hiroshima and Nagasaki, and some 800 underground nuclear 'tests' over a 40-year period." (p28)

Kemper, Vicki. "Report from Ground Zero." Common Cause Magazine v19 n2, Sum 1993. p28-31. (ISSN0271-9592).

NUCLEAR WEAPONS PLANTS--U.S.

"Between Oct. 1, 1990 and May 31, 1993, DOE [U.S. Dept. of Energy] paid contractors' attorneys $47 million to fight class-action lawsuits from people living near nuclear weapons plants. The lawsuits, filed at seven nuclear weapons plants, charge that radioactive and chemical contamination from discharges into the air and water have lead to ongoing health and emotional problems for nearby residents." (p6)

"Econotes: DOE's Growing Fallout." Environmental Action v26 n1, Spr 1994. p6. (ISSN0013-922X).

"The...17 major and 100 secondary nuclear bomb plants [in the U.S.] employ 150,000 workers, and subcontractors employ an additional 50,000. The plants themselves contain vast buildings where chemicals were mixed and leached, where radioactive metals were cut and ground and where potentially explosive mixtures of radioactive liquid wastes and toxic chemicals are stored in holding tanks for eventual disposal." (p51)

Pasternak, Douglas/others. "Special Report: Department of Horrors." U.S. News & World Report v116 n3, 24 Jan 1994. p47-48,51-52. (ISSN0041-5537).

NUNS--PUERTO RICO--U.S.

The number of Roman Catholic women in religious orders is dwindling as nuns grow older. "A recent LOS ANGELES TIMES poll of 1,049 nuns throughout the United States and Puerto Rico found the median age for the Catholic nuns to be 65. Just 3 percent of the nuns were 40 or younger, 37 percent were older than 70, and 12 percent were older than 80....In 1993, there were 94,022 nuns in the United States, compared with 106,912 in 1988 and 181,421--the peak figure--in 1966." (p8)

Lawton, Millicent. "Private Schools." Education Week v13 n24, 9 Mar 1994. p8. (ISSN0277-4232).

NURSE PRACTITIONERS--U.S. (v19)
NURSING--EDUCATION (HIGHER)--U.S. (v19)
NURSING--U.S.--PUBLIC OPINION (v19)
NURSING HOME CARE--U.S. (v19)
NURSING HOMES--U.S.

"In 1990, 1.8 million Americans lived in nursing homes. How fast that number grows will depend on changes in death rates and in the rates that older people live in nursing homes. The Brookings Institution forecasts 4 million residents by 2018. Researchers from Duke University project a lower total of between 2 and 3 million by 2020. The Urban Institute of Washington, D.C., projects up to 5 million people in nursing homes by 2030. But all forecasters agree that the nursing-home population will see explosive growth after 2021, when the oldest baby boomers reach age 75. The average boomer will be 85 years old in 2040." (p47)

Braus, Patricia. "Nursing Homes: The Hard Facts." American Demographics v16 n3, Mar 1994. p47. (ISSN0163-4089).

NUT INDUSTRY--U.S. (v19)
NUTMEG INDUSTRY--GRENADA (v19)
NUTRITION (v19)
NUTRITION--U.S. (v19)
NUTRITION--U.S.--PUBLIC OPINION (v19)
NUTRITION OF CHILDREN

see CHILDREN--NUTRITION

OATRIM

Not only did the volunteers who tried the new ARS-developed fat replacer, Oatrim "have a substantial drop in the artery-clogging LDL cholesterol without a decrease in beneficial HDL cholesterol; their glucose tolerance--ability to process sugar from a meal--improved significantly also....Oatrim reduced the volunteers' insulin levels 11 to 24 percent, depending on the level of beta glucan in the fat replacer. And glucagon, a hormone that has the opposite effect of insulin and moves glucose from body cells into the blood, dropped a significant 16 to 36 percent. As a result of these hormone changes, the volunteers' blood glucose levels were 7 to 12 percent lower after eating Oatrim than they were before. But the biggest surprise of the study may be Oatrim's main payoff: Most of the volunteers lost weight during the study, despite increases in their calories. As a group, they lost an average 4.5 pounds, says biologist Daniel Scholfield who worked with Hallfrisch and Behall." (p4)

McBride, Judy. "Two Thumbs Up for Oatrim." Agricultural Research v41 n12, Dec 1993. p4-7. (ISSN0002-161X).

OATS INDUSTRY--U.S. (v19)
OCCUPATIONAL HEALTH AND SAFETY

see INDUSTRIAL HYGIENE

OCCUPATIONAL MOBILITY--U.S. (v19)
OCCUPATIONAL MORTALITY--U.S. (v19)

"A recent NIOSH [National Institute of Occupational Safety and Health] study reports that work-related fatalities in the United States declined by 23 percent from 1980 to 1989, and work-related motor vehicle deaths (an area not yet addressed by OSHA [Occupational Safety and Health Administration]) along with workplace homicides accounted for approximately 35 percent of the total." (p234)

Jones, William T. (American Iron and Steel Inst.). U.S. House. Committee on Education and Labor. "Hearings on H.R. 1280, Comprehensive Occupational Safety and Health Reform Act." Hearing, 28 Apr 1993. Washington, D.C.: GPO, 1994. (ISBN0160434033). (Y4.Ed8/1:103-35).

"In 1974, the rate of Lost Workday Injuries and Illnesses [in the U.S.]--those incidents in which an employee loses, or must be placed on light duty, at least a full day--was 3.5 per 100 workers. The rate has fluctuated over the years, and in 1991, this rate was 3.9 per 100 workers. Although the fatality rate has declined, the Bureau of Labor Statistics estimated that in establishments of eleven or more employees 2,800 workers were killed on the job in 1991. Regrettably, these statistics do not describe the full extent of the danger at our workplaces. Workplace fatalities, as measured in the past, have been underestimated. In comparison to the BLS figures, the National Safety Council reported 9,900 workplace fatalities in 1991. In addition, reputable studies suggest that thousands of deaths resulting from occupational illnesses go unreported each year because we cannot link later disease to earlier workplace exposures." (p40)

Reich, Robert B. (Secretary of Labor, U.S. Dept. of Labor). U.S. House. Committee on Education and Labor. "Hearings on H.R. 1280, Comprehensive Occupational Safety and Health Reform Act." Hearing, 28 Apr 1993. Washington, D.C.: GPO, 1994. (ISBN0160434033). (Y4.Ed8/1:103-35).

The National Safety Council, "a clearinghouse on occupational safety issues based in Itasca, Ill., reported 14,200 work-related deaths in 1970, the year the [workplace safety] law was enacted. That figure had dropped to 13,000 in 1980 and 8,500 in 1992." (p610)

Masci, David. "Social Policy: Labor: Overhaul of Job Safety Law Gains Committee Approval." Congressional Quarterly v52 n10, 12 Mar 1994. p610.

"According to the Centers for Disease Control, just over 38,000 Americans died from firearms in 1991. Excluding suicides, the figure drops to 19,600--a death rate of eight per 100,000 people. By contrast, occupational diseases kill 75,000 Americans each year, many from breathing cotton or coal dust. Another 6,000 die from traumatic worksite incidents caused by faulty machines, electrocution, falls, homicides, vehicle accidents, fires, and suffocation. That's a combined rate of 32 work-related deaths per 100,000 people--four times the death rate from firearms." (p6)

Hall, Bob. "Watch Out--He's Got a Job!" Southern Exposure v22 n1, Spr 1994. p6. (ISSN0146-809X).

"Murderous episodes at [U.S.] job sites are growing, and a cottage industry of high-priced consultants is arising to exploit it. But like mass killings, they are relatively rare.
A Labor Department count for 1992 found 45 revenge-type murders by workers or former employees. A preliminary compilation for 1993 by the Chicago-based National Safe Workplace Institute that included killings in personal or family feuds tallied 70 cases. Although that toll is up from fewer than 20 per year during the 1980s, institute Director Joseph Kinney says it 'is hardly at epidemic proportions.'" (p27)

Gest, Ted/others. "U.S. News: Violence in America." U.S. News & World Report v116 n2, 17 Jan 1994. p22-24,26-27,30,32-33. (ISSN0041-5537).

OCCUPATIONAL TRAINING--GERMANY (v19)
OCCUPATIONAL TRAINING--U.S. (v19)

"Young dropouts benefit little from federally funded job-training programs, according to a long-term national study." A study of the Job Training Partnership Act indicates that adult women, who make up 30 percent of the participants, boosted their salaries by an average of 15 percent or $1,837, while adult males, 25 percent of the participants, increased their incomes by 8 percent, or $1,599, in the 30-month period after receiving training. But out-of-school teenagers, who comprised 23 percent of the participants, showed little or no increase in earnings in the 30-month period after training. (p23)

Olson, Lynn. "Young Dropouts Benefit Little from J.T.P.A., Study Finds." Education Week v13 n23, 2 Mar 1994. p23. (ISSN0277-4232).

OCCUPATIONS--GERMANY (v19)
OCEAN TRAVEL (v19)
OFF-ROAD VEHICLES
see ALL TERRAIN VEHICLES
OFFSHORE ASSEMBLY INDUSTRY--ENVIRONMENTAL ASPECTS--MEXICO (v19)

"The development of the Maquila zones along the U.S.-Mexican border has led to environmental degradation of the border area, even the WALL STREET JOURNAL has noted that '(the Maquiladoras') very success is helping turn much of the border region into a sinkhole of abysmal living conditions and environmental degradation.'...There have been many reports, scientific and journalistic, of how the pollution (air, ground and water) has affected the communities on both sides of the border. For example, industrial solvents dumped into the Rio Grande and released into the air from companies operating in Matamoros, Mexico have resulted in the birth of at least 80 babies with neural tube defects (many without brains 'anencephaly'). Most of the mothers have been impoverished Mexican-Americans living near the Rio Grande." (p121)

Hancock, Nolan W. (Citizenship-Legislative Dir., Oil, Chemical and Atomic Workers International Union). U.S. House. Committee on Energy and Commerce. "NAFTA: Energy Provisions and Environmental Implications." Hearing, 22 Sep 1993. Washington, D.C.: GPO, 1994. (ISBN0160440459). (Y4.En2/3:103/70).

The North American Free Trade Agreement "is likely to accelerate unsustainable development in Mexico, particularly along the border where 1,700 manufacturing plants employing about 500,000 workers now operate under the existing 'maquiladora' program. Although the program has been a financial boon, providing 37% of Mexico's foreign exchange, it has also led to environmental degradation and squalid living conditions for Mexican workers and their families. Groundwater has been poisoned by chemical dumping. Large numbers of poorly paid workers live in houses made of cardboard, packing crates, or cast-off plywood. Human waste in Ciudad Juarez, population 1.5 million, runs untreated into the Rio Grande. Birth defects exceed national averages. Shantytowns on the American side are growing so rapidly that their sprawl is best traced by aerial photographs." (p1,3)

"Free Trade Sets Sail: Dolphins, Wages, and NAFTA." Rocky Mountain Institute Newsletter v9 n1, Spr 1993. p1,3.

OFFSHORE ASSEMBLY INDUSTRY--MEXICO (v19)
OFFSHORE ASSEMBLY INDUSTRY--MEXICO--U.S. (v19)

"While the maquiladora sector in Mexico exports almost exclusively to the United States, only 46 percent of the 2,522 maquilas in existence in 1992 were completely or majority U.S.-owned. Some 48 percent were either completely or majority Mexican-owned; 2 percent (52 plants) were Japanese-owned. A growing portion of U.S. companies using assembly facilities in Mexico contract out the work to Mexican firms that provide assembly services." (p94)

Newquist, Don (Chair, U.S. International Trade Commission). U.S. House. Committee on Energy and Commerce. "Telecommunications Trade." Hearing, 3 Aug 1993. Washington, D.C.: GPO, 1994. (ISBN0160435919). (Y4.En2/3:103-60).

OFFSHORE ASSEMBLY INDUSTRY--U.S. (v19)
OHIO
see HAZARDOUS WASTES--OHIO; SCHOOL CHILDREN--FOOD--OHIO; WATER-SUPPLY--OHIO
OIL-SHALES--U.S. (v19)
OIL RESERVES
see PETROLEUM RESERVES
OIL SPILLS

"Four years since the Exxon Valdez spill, among the things that should be most remembered is that, although it was not the largest tanker spill in history, it was the most damaging--even including the 60-million-gallon Amoco Cadiz spill in 1978 and the recent 24-million-gallon Braer spill off the Shetland Islands. The Valdez spill occurred within a sound and inundated 1,200 miles of sensitive shoreline with heavy crude. It is the largest oil spill to occur in North America and remains the most destructive single event of oil pollution in North American history....Although human casualty in the sense of physical injury or death was low, mortality in nature was very high--3,500 to 5,500 sea otters, thousands of other sea and land mammals, 260,000 to 600,000 birds, unfathomable numbers of fish and shellfish, and incalculable tons of the plant and microscopic biota which make up the food web." (p37)

Keeble, John. "A Parable of Oil and Water." Amicus Journal v15 n1, Spr 1993. p35-42. (ISSN0276-7201).

"There are...a variety of environmental costs associated with petroleum production; oil spills are probably the most notorious. Almost 2 billion tons of crude oil are transported by sea every year. Of this, about 400,000 tons is released into the ocean through accidental spills and an even larger amount spills into the seas through routine activities like cleaning tankers. The cost of cleaning up spills is astronomical, in both economic and ecological terms. An average oil spill costs (based on claims made) about $28,000 per ton of oil spilled. In the case of the infamous Exxon Valdez spill in Alaska's Prince William Sound, costs of claims totalled $90,000 per ton of oil spilled. Ecological damage, of course, is much more difficult to calculate and nearly impossible to repair. For example, 20 years after the tanker S.T. Arrow spilled 16,000 tons of oil off Nova Scotia, much of the oil still remains on shore rocks and sand. Its biological activity is unknown....Large oil spills appear to be becoming more frequent. Five of the world's fifteen largest oil spills have occurred in the 1990s and spills totalled over 700,000 tons per year (enough to fuel every car in California for a day)." (p3,6)

Cox, Caroline. "From Factories and Tank Cars to You: Hazards of Manufacturing and Transporting Pesticides." Journal of Pesticide Reform v13 n2, Sum 1993. p2-3,6-10. (ISSN0893-357X).

OIL SPILLS--CASPIAN SEA

"Situated in southeastern Europe, the Caspian Sea is the largest closed reservoir in the world. It is bordered by five countries: Azerbaijan, Iran, Kazakhstan, Russia and Turkmenistan. The fate of the Sea was decided in the mid-20th century when Azerbaijan had to choose whether to base its economy on developing the oilfields on the sea floor or the valuable fish found in its waters. The country chose oil and thus brought upon itself the ills it now faces. The Sea is polluted by oil drilling and frequent leaks and accidents during transportation. Every year 288,000 tons of oil products are dumped into the sea, covering the entire surface with an oily film. The film blocks the passage of oxygen and light into the water, damaging seaweed and phytoplankton that depend for their existence on photosynthesis, and killing fish and zooplankton. The oil film also washes up on the beaches, affecting all those who live along the shore and disturbing migratory birds." (p14)

Hussein-Zadeh, Nigar. "Help Us Heal the Caspian Sea." Surviving Together v11 n2, Sum 1993. p14. (ISSN0859-6286).

OIL SPILLS--U.S.

"Four years after the grounding of the Exxon Valdez on Bligh Reef in 1989, oil spills continue to occur with alarming frequency: In 1992, the Shoko Maru spilled more than 96,000 gallons of crude oil into the Texas City Channel and a leak at an offshore well in Louisiana spilled at least 30,000 gallons; in 1991 alone, there were 677 spills in the Port of New Orleans, 398 spills in Port of Hampton Roads, 236 spills in Port of

Philadelphia, 130 spills in Seattle, and 116 spills in Boston Harbor. The amount of oil spilled in these ports alone in one year exceeded 300,000 gallons. The recent huge spills off foreign coasts--the Shetland Islands, the coasts of Spain and Indonesia--reinforce the importance of regulation." (p42)

Sankovitch, Nina. "Craft Warnings." Amicus Journal v15 n1, Spr 1993. p42-43. (ISSN0276-7201).

"Research by government scientists suggests that many sea bird and fish populations in the [Prince William] sound have just begun the process of recovery and are still in somewhat of a precarious state [since the Exxon VALDEZ oil spill in 1989]. Meanwhile, Exxon's findings show the same populations to have recovered to normal, healthy levels. Survey data from the U.S. Fish and Wildlife Service (FWS) reveal dramatic declines in the population size of many species and subsequent slow recovery rates. In the case of the common murre, the hardest hit of all sea birds with between 175,000 and 300,000 killed outright, FWS scientists believe that the breeding cycle has been so disturbed that it could take between 20 and 70 years to recover. Exxon claims that the murre is currently existing at pre-spill levels." (p10)

Brown, Wendy. "Has Prince William Sound Recovered from Oil Spill?" Blue Goose Flyer v19 n3, Jul 1993. p10.

"As a result of oil leaks and inefficiencies, each year America's oil system loses the energy equivalent of Australia's annual petroleum consumption. There is one spill a day in the US caused by leaking pipelines alone. America's oil pipeline network is more than four times the size of its interstate highway system. According to the Environmental Protection Agency, oil and gas wastes exceed the combined total of all municipal agricultural, mining and industrial wastes. Each year, nearly 170 million tons of oily wastes are generated by oil refineries and buried at refinery sites; another 18,000 tons make their way into community landfills. As much as 57 million tons of oil-field wastes are disposed of in landfills annually." (p11)

"America's 'Crude Awakening.'" Earth Island Journal v8 n4, Fall 1993. p11. (ISSN1041-0406).

OIL WELLS--SAUDI ARABIA--U.S.

"The United States has about 600,000 operating [oil] wells. Saudi Arabia has about 1,400. In 1992, U.S. oil productivity averaged 13.3 barrels per day per well. Saudi Arabia's wells averaged 5,800. Iran's averaged 4,880. Even in intensively drilled Venezuela, the average was 195 barrels per day per well. Compared with the United States, much of OPEC has barely moved into high gear in its potential drilling programs. In the Middle East, $15 a barrel prices provide ample returns on exploration and production costs in the neighborhood of $1 a barrel." (p54)

Nadler, Arnold. "Oil Prices: What to Expect and Why It Matters." Public Power v52 n1, Jan-Feb 1994. p46-48,50,52-54,56. (ISSN0033-3654).

OILS AND FATS--U.S. (v19)

OILSEED INDUSTRY (v19)

"Despite recent upward revisions for 1993/94 rapeseed and soybean production, current prospects for world oilseed production continue to decline to an estimated 223.1 million metric tons, down nearly 2 percent from last year. While foreign supplies of oilseeds are reaching record levels, the 16 percent drop in U.S. oilseed production more than offsets the gain. Global soybean production is projected at 112.1 tons, a 3.8 percent decline from last year's record of 116.5 million tons. Higher world rapeseed and sunflowerseed production are not enough to offset the drop in soybean, peanut, and cottonseed production." (p6)

U.S. Dept. of Agriculture. "World Oilseed Situation and Outlook for 1993/94." Oil Crops Situation and Outlook Report Jan 1994. p6-7.

"Total foreign oilseed production, up 4.4 percent, is record high. Stimulated by high oilseed prices, planted area and production is expanding in all the major producing areas, with the notable exception of the EU [European Union] and Eastern Europe. Favorable weather conditions in China, combined with economic incentives that stimulated oilseed planting, resulted in a record crop in 1993, up 5 percent over the previous year. Peanut production expanded 26 percent to a record 7.5 million tons as higher prices prompted farmers to increase area as opposed to cotton. Soybean production is estimated up 17 percent to 12 million tons as high domestic demand for protein meals and favorable autumn weather in north east China stimulated planting and boosted yields. Record planting in South America, up 9 percent, will push total oilseed production to 43.2 million tons." (p6)

U.S. Dept. of Agriculture. "World Oilseed Situation and Outlook for 1993/94." Oil Crops Situation and Outlook Report Jan 1994. p6-7.

OILSEEDS--EUROPEAN ECONOMIC COMMUNITY (v19)

OILSEEDS--INDIA (v19)

OILSEEDS--U.S. (v19)

OLIVE OIL INDUSTRY--U.S.

"In the US, consumption of olive oil increased 50 percent from 1987 to 1992, according to the US Department of Agriculture. Forecasted consumption for 1993 is 278 million pounds, putting per capita consumption at about one pound per person." (p12)

Conover, Kirsten A. "Food: Olive Oil Branches Out." The Christian Science Monitor v86 n68, 3 Mar 1994. p12. (ISSN0882-7729).

OLYMPIC GAMES (1996: ATLANTA, GEORGIA)

"The 1996 Centennial Olympic Games will focus the attention of the world on the United States and Atlanta, Georgia. In excess of two million visitors will demand transportation services while attending the 1996 Centennial Olympic Games. It is estimated that an average of 361,000 people daily will be involved in the Olympics experience. The Metropolitan Atlanta Rapid Transit Authority (MARTA) must be there to meet that demand by providing coordinated, efficient, and reliable public transportation." (p1343)

U.S. House. Committee on Appropriations. "Department of Transportation and Related Agencies Approp. for 1994 (Part 7B)." Hearing, Washington, D.C.: GPO, 1993. (ISBN0160411041). (Y4.Ap6/1:T68/4/994/pt.7B).

OLYMPICS, SPECIAL

see SPECIAL OLYMPICS

ONCHOCERCIASIS

"New data has convinced experts at the World Health Organization (WHO) that forty times as many Ugandans--some 1.2 million people in all--are infected with the parasite that causes river blindness (onchocerciasis) as was thought seven years ago, the last time estimates were reviewed. And similar figures are emerging from other countries in Africa (which accounts for more than 99% of cases). In Equatorial Guinea, for example, 60 000 are now judged to be infected, five times as many as previous estimates....River blindness is endemic in large areas of sub-Saharan Africa and in isolated areas of Latin America and Yemen. The Committee estimated that some 270 000 people are blind today as a result of the disease--and an equal number severely visually impaired, reducing their life expectancy by 65%. Hundreds of thousands also suffer from severe skin lesions--another manifestation of the disease." (p1-2)

News release. "Success in River Blindness Control Reveals Many New Cases: Massive Increase in Drug Delivery Planned." WHO Press 9 Dec 1993. p1-3.

ONION INDUSTRY--U.S. (v19)
OPERA COMPANIES--U.S. (v19)
OPTIC NEURITIS--CUBA (v19)
ORANGE INDUSTRY--U.S. (v19)
ORANGUTAN

"Found only in the Indonesian rainforests, orangutans number between 20,000 and 30,000 in the wild. Tottering on the verge of extinction makes them all the more profitable on the black market....The money made from...trade [in orangutans] is enormous. While a hunter gets $200 for a baby, the middleman can sell it for $1,000. Prices can soar to $30,000 for a circus or zoo--unless the final destination is the U.S., where an orangutan can fetch $50,000." (p14)

Speart, Jessica. "Currents: Poached Primates." E Magazine v4 n4, Jul-Aug 1993. p14-15. (ISSN1046-8021).

ORCHESTRA--U.S. (v19)
ORCHESTRA--U.S.--FINANCE (v19)
OREGON

see CONSERVATION OF NATURAL RESOURCES--OREGON; FOREST FIRES--OREGON; FORESTS AND FORESTRY--EMPLOYMENT--OREGON; GRAZING DISTRICTS--OREGON--PUBLIC OPINION; HOSPITALS--OREGON; INDUSTRIAL HYGIENE--OREGON; MEDICAL CARE--OREGON; NUCLEAR POWER PLANTS--OREGON; PUBLIC LANDS--NEW JERSEY--OREGON; TIMBER--OREGON; WATER--POLLUTION--OREGON

OREGON--ECONOMIC CONDITIONS (v19)
ORGAN DONATION

see DONATION OF ORGANS, TISSUES, ETC.

ORGANIZATIONS, NONPROFIT

see NONPROFIT ORGANIZATIONS

ORLANDO (FLA)

see AIRPORTS--ORLANDO (FLA)

OSTEOPOROSIS--U.S. (v19)

"The National Osteoporosis Foundation estimates that some 25 million Americans suffer from osteoporosis, which causes 1.5 million bone fractures a year, at an annual cost of $10 billion in medical charges. These costs are expected to rise to $200 billion per year by the year 2040. Osteoporosis affects mostly women--over half of all women over age 50. However, about 5 million men are also at risk for osteoporosis-related fractures--one third of all men by age 75." (p3)

Frazao, Betsy. "Health Linked to Nutrition: The High Costs of Poor Diets." Food Review v17 n1, Jan-Apr 1994. p3.

"Osteoporosis...is a condition characterized by exaggerated bone loss, which can lead to fractures. Usually, by age 35 a woman's bone mass has reached its maximum development. After age 35 she normally loses about one percent of bone density a year, on average about 10 percent a decade. In two-thirds of cases, insufficient nutrients are a significant antecedent. However, osteoporosis may also result from menopause induced by surgical removal of the ovaries, or chemotherapy or radiation therapy that causes the ovaries to become dysfunctional. The change in estrogen levels that accompanies natural menopause also may result in osteoporosis. After menopause, when there is a reduction in estrogen, nearly 25 percent of white, Asian, and brown-skinned women develop this condition. For reasons still unclear to scientists, black women are less likely to develop osteoporosis, or develop it at a later age than white women." (p3)

"Perspectives on Menopause." Perspectives in Health Promotion and Aging v8 n3, 1993. p1,3,7-9.

OSTRICHES--U.S.

"Although ostrich leather sells for premium prices, much of the excitement these long-legged livestock are generating is based on the meat they produce. Technically, an ostrich is a bird. But its meat looks and tastes like beef, not poultry.... According to a USDA bulletin, ostrich meat has about the same amount of cholesterol as lean turkey, 20 percent less than chicken or beef, and nearly 30 percent less than pork. An 85-gram serving of ostrich meat contains only 2 grams of fat. The same size serving of broiled chicken or turkey has about 3 grams of fat, beef 15 to 16 grams, and pork 19 grams....An ostrich steak weighing 5 to 6 ounces, served with a vegetable and a starch, is priced at $28--$6 to $8 more than most beef steaks on the restaurant's menu....Confidence in the future of ostriches as a livestock enterprise has driven prices steadily upward. Five to six years ago, young chicks sold for around $800 apiece. Today, a pair of 3-month-old chicks typically costs $8,000 to $9,000. A pair of yearlings may bring twice that much, even though they won't be capable of reproducing until they're 3 to 4 years old. A few top-producing birds reportedly have sold for more than $100,000 a pair." (p29)

Kessler, Karl. "Ostrich Burgers, Anyone?" Furrow v99 n2, Jan-Feb 1994. p29-30. (ISSN0016-3112).

OUTPLACEMENT SERVICES--U.S. (v19)

"Many of today's jobless are reporting to 'outplacement' operations for career counseling, leads on new jobs, tips on resume writing, a supportive office environment, and more....Between 1990 and 1993, the number of unemployed served by outplacement firms in the United States more than doubled, according to a September survey conducted by the Association of Outplacement Consulting Firms International (AOCFI) in Washington. Outplacement industry revenues increased from $392 million in 1990 to $625 million in 1992 and are expected to reach $700 million this year." (p1)

Ross, Elizabeth. "Outplacement Firms Grow in Number and Popularity as Companies Trim Down." The Christian Science Monitor v86 n23, 28 Dec 1993. p1,4. (ISSN0882-7729).

OVERUSE INJURIES--U.S. (v19)

"Workplace illnesses associated with stresses from repeated motions of wrists and limbs, such as carpal tunnel syndrome, which were barely recognized when OSHA [Occupational Safety and Health Administration] was created, now make up more than three-fifths of all occupational illnesses recorded by employers [in the U.S.]. In 1983 there were about 27,000 recorded cases of repetitive motion disorder. In 1991, nearly 224,000 repetitive motion disorder cases were reported by BLS [Bureau of Labor Statistics]. For instance, an ever-growing number of Americans spend their days in front of computer terminals--entering, manipulating, or retrieving data--and, therefore, musculoskeletal and nerve ailments to hands, arms, necks, and shoulders are becoming the occupational diseases of the information age." (p41)

Reich, Robert B. (Secretary of Labor, U.S. Dept. of Labor). U.S. House. Committee on Education and Labor. "Hearings on H.R. 1280, Comprehensive Occupational Safety and Health Reform Act." Hearing, 28 Apr 1993. Washington, D.C.: GPO, 1994. (ISBN0160434033). (Y4.Ed8/1:103-35).

"The Bureau of Labor Statistics documented that in 1989, the 147,000 cumulative trauma disorders represented more than half of all reported cases of occupational illness [in the U.S.]. These included carpal tunnel syndrome, a prominent type of cumulative trauma disorder in which the nerves in the wrist become chronically 'pinched,' resulting in a range of affliction ranging from mild pain to severe form, for example, one would not be able to write or type, handle a bag of groceries, or hold an infant. California has an occupational disease surveillance system which requires that physicians report all cases of occupational illness and injury to the state. Through this system, 72 cases of work-related carpal tunnel syndrome were reported in one county in 1986. A surveillance program funded by NIOSH [National Institute for Occupational Safety and Health] found one year later, in the same county, there were actually 3,400 cases of work-related carpal tunnel syndrome. That is 48 times the number of cases previously reported." (p10)

Millar, Donald (Director, National Inst. for Occupational Safety and Health). U.S. Senate. Committee on Labor and Human Resources. "The Occupational Safety and Health Act: Making the Case for Reform." Hearing, 14 Jul 1993. Washington, D.C.: GPO, 1993. (ISBN0160433738). (Y4.L11/4:S.hrg.103-334).

OZONE, ATMOSPHERIC

see ATMOSPHERIC OZONE

PAGERS--U.S. (v19)

PAINT--U.S. (v19)

PALESTINIAN ARABS (v19)

"Over 1.5 million Palestinians reside in nearby Jordan, where they now make up almost half of the population and most have full citizenship. The other two neighboring countries of Syria and Lebanon contain over 300,000 each. More than one-half million Palestinians were living elsewhere in the Middle East in 1990, including over 300,000 in Kuwait, although that number is thought to have fallen to around 30,000 after the 1991 Persian Gulf War. Outside the Arab world, the United States has the largest number of Palestinians. About 48,000 identified themselves as Palestinians by writing it on the 1990 Census. However, it is estimated that the number is probably around 100,000." (p11)

Roudi, Nazy. "Spotlight: The Palestinians." Population Today v21 n1, Jan 1993. p11. (ISSN0749-2448).

PALESTINIAN ARABS--CIVIL RIGHTS--ISRAEL (v19)

PALESTINIAN ARABS--ECONOMIC CONDITIONS (v19)

PAN AMERICAN HIGHWAY SYSTEM

"The 1.36 million acres (550,000 hectares) of tropical forest in Panama not crossed by the Pan-American Highway are once again threatened by people who want to fulfill the old dream of building a road that spans all of the Americas. Currently, drivers can go from Alaska to Panama and from Patagonia to Colombia, but there is an abrupt obstacle where the Central American isthmus meets South America, an area known as Darien....The idea of building that last stretch of highway, crossing the border between Panama and Colombia over forest-covered mountains, has been a dream for business groups but a nightmare for environmental activists. The Darien tropical forests are home to 2,325 different kinds of plants and 704 animal species, many of which are exclusive to this area." (p33)

"Latin American Focus: Panama: Pan-American Highway Endangers Jungle." Barricada Internacional v13 n363, Jul 1993. p33. (ISSN1013-9567).

PANAMA

see DRUG TRAFFIC--PANAMA--U.S.; PANAMA CANAL (PANAMA)

PANAMA CANAL (PANAMA)

Panama "Canal traffic levels in 1992 declined slightly as world trade returned to more normal patterns following the end of the Persian Gulf War. Additionally, the prolonged recession in the U.S. and Japan had a negative impact on our traffic levels. As a result, a number of canal cargoes experienced declines including manufactures of iron and steel, phosphates, ores and metals, refrigerated products, automobiles, chemicals and petrochemicals, minerals, and grains. These losses were only partially offset by gains in petroleum products, lumber, coal, and containerized cargo. The downturn in cargo shipments drove a reduction in oceangoing transits from 12,763 in fiscal year 1991 to 12,636 for 1992, and ship tonnage measured in Panama Canal net tons declined from 193 million tons to 190 million tons. This drop in traffic levels resulted in tolls revenue of $369 million, some $6 million below the $375 million produced in 1991. Total operating revenues (before deductions for capital contributions) were $507 million versus $512 million in 1991." (p208-209)

Guardia, Gilberto (Administrator, Panama Canal Commission). U.S. House. Committee on Appropriations. "Department of Transportation and Related Agencies Approp. for 1994 (Part 3)." Hearing, Washington, D.C.: GPO, 1993. (ISBN0160410649). (Y4.Ap6/1:T68/4/994/pt.3).

PANDAS (v19)

PAPER INDUSTRY (v19)

PAPER INDUSTRY--JAPAN--U.S.

"Access to the Japanese market is of crucial importance to the U.S. paper industry. After the U.S., Japan is the world's second largest producer and consumer of paper and paperboard. Japanese paper consumption is expected to grow at twice the U.S. rate into the next decade. Yet, import penetration in Japan is the smallest in the world. In 1992, paper and paper products imports from all sources accounted for 3.7 percent of Japanese paper and paperboard consumption and imports from the U.S. represented 1.8 percent of consumption. Comparable figures for import penetration of Europe and the U.S. are 30 percent and 14 percent, respectively. This situation is especially troublesome considering that Japan clearly does not have the resource base which would justify reliance on domestic products. Japan's government and its paper industry have argued that imports are low because of Japan's distance from major paper and paperboard exporting countries. However, Australia, which is just as remote, imports some 30 percent of the paper and paperboard it uses." (p69)

Smith, Maureen R. (International Vice President, American Forest and Paper Assoc.). U.S. Senate. Committee on Finance. "United States-Japan Trade Negotiations." Hearing, 8 Nov 1993. Washington, D.C.: GPO, 1994. (ISBN0160435625). (Y4.F49:S.hrg.103-399).

PAPER INDUSTRY--U.S. (v19)

"The U.S. is the world's largest producer of pulp, paper and paperboard. With annual sales of $128 billion, it is among the nation's top ten manufacturing industries. As a result of massive capital expenditures devoted to modernization and environmental improvements, the U.S. paper industry today ranks among the most competitive in the world. Exports have served as the major engine of demand growth in recent years--exports accounted for 60 percent of the growth in paper, paperboard and market pulp production from 1987 through 1992. Measured another way, exports of these products worldwide increased by a total of 56 percent over the same period." (p69)

Smith, Maureen R. (International Vice President, American Forest and Paper Assoc.). U.S. Senate. Committee on Finance. "United States-Japan Trade Negotiations." Hearing, 8 Nov 1993. Washington, D.C.: GPO, 1994. (ISBN0160435625). (Y4.F49:S.hrg.103-399).

International Paper "has the worst record in the paper and forest products industry for compliance with worker health and safety laws. From 1986 through 1992, IP paid $1.3 million in penalties. The U.S. Department of Labor cited IP for 1,329 violations, of which 86 were classified as 'willful.' In July 1991, IP pleaded guilty to five felony counts and paid a $2.2 million fine relating to hazardous waste violations and falsification of environmental reports to the government. This was the second largest federal fine ever for hazardous waste violations." (p3)

Scott, Ken/Moulton, Sean. "America's Least Wanted: The 1993 Campaign for Cleaner Corporations (C3)." CEP Research Report Nov-Dec 1993. p1-5. (ISSN0898-4328).

PAPER INDUSTRY--U.S.--RECYCLING (v19)
PAPUA NEW GUINEA
see LANGUAGE AND LANGUAGES--PAPUA NEW GUINEA
PARENTAL LEAVE--U.S. (v19)
PARKING LOTS--U.S.--COSTS

"The capital costs of a parking space range from $2000 to $5000 for a surface lot, and on up to $10,000 to $12,000 a space in a two- or three-story structure. (Debt interest can add an additional 7 to 10 percent.) Operations and maintenance, including sweeping, painting and resurfacing, is generally figured at 1.5 percent on the initial construction cost annually. Land costs vary widely by location, but can be calculated from the local cost for an acre of land: A parking space takes up 340 square feet for both the space and the aisle. There are about 128 spaces per acre. Other costs include utilities, security, insurance, parking enforcement and administration. If you divert five parking spaces from a project (freeing $10,000 to $25,000 of capital) and use two spaces to build a 680 square foot shower/changing room, and one space for lockers for a dozen bicycles, you still have 680 square feet to plant trees." (p2)

"Turning Asphalt into Biomass." IBF News n2, 1993. p2.

PAROLE--TEXAS (v19)
PART-TIME EMPLOYMENT (v19)
PART-TIME EMPLOYMENT--CANADA (v19)
PART-TIME EMPLOYMENT--NETHERLANDS--U.S. (v19)
PART-TIME EMPLOYMENT--U.S.

"Part-time workers are a growing segment of the U.S. labor force (Feldman, 1990). According to U.S. government statistics there are now about 19 million part-time workers, which is just over 20 percent of the labor force (Nardone, 1986). Since 1955 the proportion of part-time workers in the labor force has doubled. More recently there appears to be a notable shift towards a permanent part-time labor demand, particularly in retail trade (Kahne, 1985). From a total of 38 hours per week for nonsupervisory retail workers in 1960, the average figure has steadily declined to 28.9 hours per week in 1989. Seventy-five percent of the part-time labor force is employed in the retail and service industry (Feldman, 1990)." (p365)

Nkomo, Stella M./Fields, D. Michael. "A Field Study of Demographic Characteristics and Job Attribute Preferences of New Part-Time Employees." Journal of Business and Psychology v8 n3, Spr 1994. p365-375. (ISSN0889-3268).

PASSIVE SMOKING--LAW AND LEGISLATION--U.S. (v19)
PASSIVE SMOKING--U.S. (v19)

"Environmental tobacco smoke, also called secondhand smoke, is a mixture of the smoke given off by the burning end of a cigarette, pipe, or cigar and the smoke exhaled from the lungs of smokers. This mixture contains more than 4,000 substances, more than 40 of which are known to cause cancer in humans and animals and many of which are strong irritants. Exposure to secondhand smoke is called involuntary smoking or passive smoking. In January 1993, the Environmental Protection Agency (EPA) published an assessment of the respiratory health risks of passive smoking, entitled 'Respiratory Health Effects of Passive Smoking: Lung Cancer and Other Disorders.' The report concludes that exposure to environmental tobacco smoke is responsible for approximately 3,000 lung cancer deaths each year in nonsmoking adults in the United States and that it seriously affects the respiratory health of hundreds of thousands of children." (p128)

Browner, Carol (U.S. Environmental Protection Agency). U.S. House. Committee on Energy and Commerce. "Environmental Tobacco Smoke." Hearing, 21 Jul 1993. Washington, D.C.: GPO, 1994. (ISBN016043355X). (Y4.En2/3:103-51).

"Not surprisingly, given tobacco's deadly record, studies show the impact of environmental tobacco smoke [in the U.S.]...[is] pervasive and severe, especially where children are concerned. Experts agree that cancer is one deadly effect, and EPA estimates that environmental tobacco smoke causes 3,000 cancer deaths each year among nonsmokers....The U.S. Surgeon General has determined that more than 30,000 lives each year are lost as a result of heart disease from environmental tobacco smoke exposure. Environmental tobacco smoke also causes respiratory ailments, especially when children are concerned. Asthma is the most pervasive ETS health impact. EPA estimates that between 200,000 and 1 million American children suffer asthmatic attacks as a result of environmental tobacco smoke. ETS may even cause the onset of asthma in previously healthy children. Passive smoke causes lower respiratory infections such as pneumonia and bronchitis. More than 50,000 small children are afflicted by such serious infections each year because of ETS exposure, and many thousands are hospitalized. Children also suffer reduced lung function, respiratory irritation, and severe inner ear infections as a result of exposure to environmental smoke." (p1)

Waxman, Henry A. (Sen.-Calif.). U.S. House. Committee on Energy and Commerce. "Environmental Tobacco Smoke." Hearing, 21 Jul 1993. Washington, D.C.: GPO, 1993. (ISBN016043355X). (Y4.En2/3:103-51).

"According to a study of Environmental Tobacoo Smoke (ETS) recently published in the prestigious JOURNAL OF THE AMERICAN MEDICAL ASSOCIATION: ETS levels in restaurants were 1.6 to 2.0 times higher than in office workplaces. ETS levels in restaurants were 1.5 times higher than in a home with one or more smokers. ETS levels in bars were 3.9 to 6.1 times higher than in offices and about 4.5 times higher than in residences....As a result of this ETS exposure, waiters, waitresses, and bartenders have a 50% higher risk of getting lung cancer than other people; a conclusion borne out by at least six different epidemiological studies in a number of different states." (p5)

"Restaurant Smoking Bans Proliferating as Risks of Restaurant Smoking Become Known." ASH Smoking and Health Review v23 n4, Jul-Aug 1993. p5. (ISSN1046-907X).

"In January [1993], the Environmental Protection Agency (EPA) issued a major report which concluded that second-hand smoke is a toxic substance, like asbestos, which is responsible for approximately 3000 lung cancer deaths each year in the United States." (p1) Some of the EPA report's most significant findings are: "150,000 to 300,000 cases of pneumonia and bronchitis annually in infants and young children up to 18 months of age are attributable to exposure to ETS [environmental tobacco smoke]. 7,500 to 15,000 cases of respiratory illness in children due to ETS will result in hospitalization. ETS exposure increases the prevalence of fluid in the middle ear, a sign of chronic middle ear disease. ETS exposure in children irritates the upper respiratory tract and is associated with a small but significant reduction in lung function. ETS exposure increases the frequency of episodes and severity of symptoms in many of the nation's 2 to 5 million asthmatic children. The report estimates that 200,000 to 1,000,000 asthmatic children annually have their condition worsened by exposure to ETS. ETS exposure is a risk factor for new cases of asthma in children who have not previously displayed symptoms." (p4)

"EPA Issues Landmark Report on Passive Smoke." Tobacco-Free Youth Reporter v5 n1, Spr 1993. p1,4.

PASSIVE SMOKING IN CHILDREN--U.S. (v19)

"Infants and young children whose parents smoke are among the most seriously affected by exposure to secondhand smoke, with increased risk of lower respiratory tract infections such as pneumonia and bronchitis. EPA estimates that passive smoking is responsible for between 150,000 and 300,000 lower respiratory tract infections in infants and children under 18 months of age annually, resulting in between 7,500 and 15,000 hospitalizations each year. Children who have been exposed to secondhand smoke are also...more likely to have reduced lung function and symptoms of respiratory irritation such as cough, excess phlegm, and wheezing." (p130)

Browner, Carol (U.S. Environmental Protection Agency). U.S. House. Committee on Energy and Commerce. "Environmental Tobacco Smoke." Hearing, 21 Jul 1993. Washington, D.C.: GPO, 1994. (ISBN016043355X). (Y4.En2/3:103-51).

The Environmental Protection Agency "found that exposure to secondhand smoke is the source of a variety of illnesses in children. Exposure to secondhand smoke causes 150,000 to 300,000 lower respiratory tract infections such as bronchitis and pneumonia in young children each year; causes additional episodes of asthma and increased severity of asthma symptoms in children who already have asthma; and may be a risk factor for 8,000 to 26,000 new cases of asthma annually in children who would not otherwise become asthmatic. While much of the unnecessary exposure to secondhand smoke encountered by children takes place in the home, children are also vulnerable in other settings. For example, in a study released in February, the Centers for Disease Control found that more than 18% of the 3.9 million U.S. children in licensed or accredited day care centers may be exposed to secondhand smoke. These centers do not have a nonsmoking policy to protect the 752,000 children they serve. While we can't stop people from smoking in their own homes, there are places where the federal government has the authority, and the obligation, to protect children from exposure to secondhand smoke." (p122)

Durbin, Richard J. (Rep.-Ill.). U.S. House. Committee on Energy and Commerce. "Environmental Tobacco Smoke." Hearing, 21 Jul 1993. Washington, D.C.: GPO, 1993. (ISBN016043355X). (Y4.En2/3:103-51).

"Despite state laws and company rules against smoking, more than 752,000 children are at risk for potentially harmful smoke exposure while they are at the day care center, says the authors of a study published in the journal, PEDIATRICS. Secondhand smoke has been shown to cause lung cancer and a greater incidence of respiratory illness. (taken from WORKING MOTHER MAGAZINE, July 1993). In the '1993 Family Day Care Licensing Study' (The Children's Foundation, May 1993), twenty states still allow smoking in family day care homes with no restrictions. Eighteen more states allow smoking with varying restrictions, such as not in areas where food is prepared and served, or where children are present, or when [an] adult is in direct contact with a child. Indoor tobacco smoke contains 4,000 chemicals. Many of these cause cancer, either by themselves or in combination with other pollutants. Children are more at risk than adults because they breathe 2-3 times more pollutants for every pound they weigh than adults do." (p2)

"Protecting Children from Secondhand Smoke." Family Day Care Bulletin Oct 1993. p2.

"A study by the Centers for Disease Control published in PEDIATRICS on February 15, 1993, reports that 18% of the 3.9 million children in licensed or accredited day care centers [in the U.S.] may be exposed to secondhand smoke. Of the 2003 licensed day care centers surveyed in the study, only 55% were completely smoke-free. Many of the others restrict smoking only in certain areas and at certain times. Based on the findings in the EPA report on ETS [environmental tobacco smoke], this new CDC study strongly suggests that about 700,000 children may be exposed to toxic second-hand smoke in the very centers where their parents have sent them for living, nurturing care." (p4)

"Study Says Children in Day Care Centers Often Exposed to Smoke." Tobacco-Free Youth Reporter v5 n1, Spr 1993. p4.

PASTURE, RIGHT OF--MONTANA

"A report from the U.S. General Accounting Office found that 6 percent of ranchers control 32 percent of national forest grazing lands. Of the 90 million acres of Forest Service lands where grazing is now permitted, the 500 largest cattle and sheep operations control 29 million acres, the GAO found. Environmentalists pointed to the report as evidence that many ranchers could afford a higher grazing fee for their federal permits....Currently, the Bureau of Land Management and the U.S. Forest Service charge $1.86 per animal unit month compared to market rates on private lands ranging from $6.39 in Idaho to $10.13 in North Dakota. At the hearing, University of Montana economist John Duffield testified that he believes $8 per AUM is an equitable fee." (p9)

Wilkinson, Todd. "Bruce Babbitt on Western Land Use: 1993 Is the 'Year of Decision': Bozeman, Mont." High Country News v25 n9B, 17 May 1993. p9. (ISSN0191-5657).

PASTURE, RIGHT OF--NEW MEXICO

"The 145,000-acre Diamond Bar grazing allotment in New Mexico is a case study in arrogance. It is New Mexico's largest allotment and almost all the land--121,000 acres--is either in the Gila or Aldo Leopold wilderness areas. Grazed for more than a century, the Diamond Bar had not made money for a long time, and in 1981, the third owner in eight years went bankrupt....The ranch was sold in late 1985 to a family partnership for about $850,000, or roughly $715 per head. With only 100 acres of private land included, nearly all the value of the ranch was based on the public-land grazing permit." (p15)

Johnson, Steve. "Is the Gila Pasture or Wilderness?" High Country News v25 n21, 15 Nov 1993. p15. (ISSN0191-5657).

PASTURE, RIGHT OF--U.S.

"Barry Reiswig of the U.S. Fish and Wildlife Service...[is a] civil servant who went out on a limb, successfully, in order to convince his agency to do its job. Reiswig manages about 800,000 acres of wildlife preserves in southern Oregon and northern Nevada. He said he has transformed grazing on the Sheldon-Hart Mountain Refuge Complex despite opposition from some grazing permittees and the local Oregon congressman, Bob Smith. Reiswig did it...by convincing his agency (run by Bush appointee John Turner) and the public that the number of grazing AUMS [animal unit months] had to be reduced from 30,000 to a few thousand. His evidence consisted of scientific studies coupled with refutations of the science the ranchers put forward to prove that grazing was good for wildlife. According to Reiswig, no such studies exist. Grazing has been ratcheted down for the past several years, Reiswig said, and the increased beauty and productivity of the refuges are attracting attention and building a constituency for the change. According to Reiswig, the refuges are one of the very few large chunks of Western land whose landscape is not heavily shaped by livestock grazing." (p14)

Marston, Ed. "Reporter's Notebook: A Room Full of Heroes." High Country News v25 n22, 29 Nov 1993. p14-15. (ISSN0191-5657).

"Two-thirds of the Bureau of Land Management's public-grazing lands--well over 100 million acres--are in less than good condition; as many as 80 percent of the miles of riparian areas managed by the BLM are rated unsatisfactory; and ubiquitous erosion relentlessly carves living landscapes into dying badlands. The economics are appalling. In 1992, the BLM spent $89 million on range management and collected only $22 million in grazing fees, $11 million of which were returned to grazing districts for range improvement. Moreover, for every $4 the BLM spent in 1992 managing rangelands, ranchers earned only $3 in profits." (p16)

Hess, Karl, Jr./Holechek, Jerry L. "Babbitt Inherited a

Mess; His Plan Will Make It Worse." High Country News v25 n20, 1 Nov 1993. p16. (ISSN0191-5657).

PATENTS--EUROPE--JAPAN--U.S.

In a survey conducted by the General Accounting Office, "U.S. companies generally reported more widespread patent problems in Japan than in the United States or Europe....more than three times as many of the companies were dissatisfied with their overall patent experience in Japan as compared with that in the United States and Europe. Thirty-nine percent of the companies that had filed for patents in Japan were dissatisfied with their overall patent experience, while 13 percent were dissatisfied with their patent experience in the United States, and 3 percent with that in Europe....65 percent of the companies reported at least one major problem in obtaining patents in Japan. In contrast, 25 percent reported at least one major problem in Europe, and 17 percent reported at least one in the United States....Forty-two percent of the companies said that 'patent pendency' in Japan, or the length of time needed to obtain a patent, was a great problem. In contrast, only 6 percent said they had similar problems in Europe and 5 percent in the United States." (p72)

Mendelowitz, Allan I. (Director, International Trade, Finance, and Competitiveness, U.S. GAO). U.S. Senate. Committee on Finance. "United States-Japan Trade Policy." Hearing, 22 Jul 1993. Washington, D.C.: GPO, 1994. (ISBN0160434092). (Y4.F49:S.hrg.103-354).

PATENTS--JAPAN

"To develop an understanding of U.S. firms' patent experiences in Japan...[the General Accounting Office] surveyed 346 U.S. firms that were top U.S. patent holders (in terms of the number of patents held) in three sectors--chemicals, semiconductors, and biotechnology. Over 90 percent of the 300 firms that responded to our survey had filed patent applications in Japan in the past 10 years, and two-thirds held 10 or more Japanese patents....the majority of the responding companies were large, with almost 60 percent reporting annual sales of over $1 billion. Ninety percent were U.S. companies or subsidiaries of U.S. companies; 10 percent were U.S. subsidiaries of foreign firms (1 percent of these were subsidiaries of Japanese firms)....50 percent of the firms had filed for chemical patents, while 41 percent had filed for biotechnology patents, and 35 percent had filed for semiconductor patents." (p71)

Mendelowitz, Allan I. (Director, International Trade, Finance, and Competitiveness, U.S. GAO). U.S. Senate. Committee on Finance. "United States-Japan Trade Policy." Hearing, 22 Jul 1993. Washington, D.C.: GPO, 1994. (ISBN0160434092). (Y4.F49:S.hrg.103-354).

PATENTS--U.S. (v19)

PEACH INDUSTRY--U.S. (v19)

PEANUT INDUSTRY--MEXICO--U.S. (v19)

PEANUT INDUSTRY--U.S. (v19)

U.S. "Peanut production in 1993/94 is placed at 3.33 billion pounds, 957 million below last season. As a result of the lower supplies, domestic food use of peanuts is projected to decline to 2.04 billion pounds in 1993/94. Crush and exports in 1993/94 are expected to total 768 and 720 million pounds, respectively. Peanut prices in 1993/94 are expected to rise and average 30-30-31 cents per pound, above the previous season's 30-cents-per-pound average." (p3)

U.S. Dept. of Agriculture. "Summary." Oil Crops Situation and Outlook Report Jan 1994. p3.

PEDESTRIANS--U.S. (v19)

PEDESTRIANS--U.S.--MORTALITY (v19)

PEDIATRIC AIDS

see AIDS (DISEASE) IN CHILDREN

PEDIATRIC TOXICOLOGY--CALIFORNIA

"California accounts for a large proportion of the nation's children at risk for lead poisoning, as 1 out of every 8 children under the age of 6 in the United States lives in California (U.S. Census Bureau, 1990). Nearly 2.2 million housing units built before 1950 exist in California, and nearly all are likely to have lead-containing paint. Recent California studies of household interior paint lead levels showed 37% of the housing in the Oakland neighborhood, 25% in Sacramento, and 13% in the Los Angeles study area to exceed HUD [U.S. Dept. of Housing and Urban Development] levels for triggering abatement. In addition, millions of pounds of lead have been emitted into California's air this century and remain in the soil, accessible to the state's 2.87 million children under the age of six." (p9)

"Update: Health & the Environment: California Lead Industry Assessed as Part of Clean-up Effort." Health Advocate n175, Win 1993. p9.

PEDIATRIC TOXICOLOGY--NEW YORK (NY)

"About 14 million children less than 7 years of age are at great risk because they live in pre-1959 housing that contains the highest concentrations of lead-based paint....Young children live in at least 54 million residential housing units, where there is an extant inventory of 3 million or more tons of leaded paint....As their second home, about 80 percent of New York City Public Schools contain leaded paint; and in 1987, the Board of Education indicated that there were over 50,000 classrooms that required lead paint repairs....Today, as in previous decades, lead based paint remains the major source of childhood lead exposure and poisoning....The 90 percent phaseout of lead in gasoline in the early 1980's...has led to an estimated three-fold decrease in average blood lead values in children....Lead has marked effects on neurobehavioral development that are now widely pervasive in America's young children....These studies have directly and casually linked 'low level' lead exposure to impairments in I.Q. of 4-6 points and deficits in reading, spelling, mathematics, attention, abstract thinking and maturational development--skills that are necessary for academic success and future productivity in the workplace." (p69)

Rosen, John F. (Prof. of Pediatrics, Head, Div. of Environmental Science, Montefiore Medical Center). U.S. House. Committee on Energy and Commerce. "Hazards of Lead in Schools and Day Care Facilities." Hearing, 15 Sep 1993. Washington, D.C.: GPO, 1993. (ISBN0160432839). (Y4.En2/3:103-46).

Lead and asbestos "pose health risks when they are present in a damaged or deteriorated condition. The New York City public schools have a maintenance backlog of $600 million which does not include the normal annual upkeep of our buildings, preventive or routine maintenance, nor does it include our capital backlog of over $13 billion. Over 400 of our buildings need modernizations....With this kind of underfunding, schools get repainted only once every 60 years, if they get repainted at all. And if we don't alleviate the sources of the damage, such as leaking roofs or roofs that need complete replacement, we will have the problem over and over...again. The nationwide average of the number of schools constructed more than 50 years ago was 20 percent but in New York City, over 50 percent of our buildings were constructed more than 50 years ago. Using the Scorecard system and using an estimate of the surface area in all our schools, walls and ceilings and hallways, rooms and commonplace spaces, to remove all lead paint from all our buildings, that is over 330 million square feet of surface area, would...take $3.53 billion for all of our buildings....just the elementary schools alone would take over $750 million." (p54)

Linden, Amy (Chief Executive, Division of School Facilities, N.Y.C. Board of Education). U.S. House. Committee on Energy and Commerce. "Hazards of Lead in Schools and Day Care Facilities." Hearing, 15 Sep 1993. Washington, D.C.: GPO, 1993. (ISBN0160432839). (Y4.En2/3:103-46).

PEDIATRIC TOXICOLOGY--U.S.

"Lead poisoning is widely regarded as the most serious environmental threat facing young children in America. Even low levels of exposure can cause subtle brain damage and reduce a young child's IQ. But despite the magnitude of the health impact, schools and day care centers have largely ignored the hazard. A new report by the General Accounting Office...finds that only 9 out of 57 school districts surveyed inspect for lead paint hazards and only 3 inspect for lead-contaminated soils. Even worse, only 2 out of the 16 States surveyed by the GAO routinely inspect for lead paint hazards in child care facilities where the children are younger and especially vulnerable....the...[Subcommittee on Health and the Environment's] investigation into lead hazards in schools in New York City finds that 16 percent of New York City classrooms, nearly 1 out of every 6, appear to contain lead hazards. Likewise, information from South Carolina which has the Nation's best data on day care hazards, indicates that 18 percent of the day care centers in the State--nearly 1 out of every 5--were found to have lead hazards upon inspection." (p1)

Waxman, Henry A. (Sen.-Calif.). U.S. House. Committee on Energy and Commerce. "Hazards of Lead in Schools and Day Care Facilities." Hearing, 15 Sep 1993. Washington, D.C.: GPO, 1993. (ISBN0160432839). (Y4.En2/3:103-46).

"The Health and the Environment Subcommittee asked the Comptroller General of the General Accounting Office (GAO) to assess the extent of lead hazards in child-care facilities and schools [in the U.S.] and the steps being taken to eliminate these hazards....Major findings from the GAO report include the following: 7 of 16 states surveyed by GAO conduct no inspections of child-care facilities for lead hazards. Only 2 of the 16 states routinely inspect some childcare facilities for lead paint, the leading source of lead exposure. Only 1 of the 16 states inspects any child-care facilities for lead-contaminated soil, the second leading source of lead exposure. Out of 57 school districts in 10 states examined by GAO, only 9 districts inspect any schools for lead paint. Even fewer school districts (3 of 57) inspect any schools for lead-contaminated soil." (p6)

U.S. House. Committee on Energy and Commerce. "Hazards of Lead in Schools and Day Care Facilities." Hearing, 15 Sep 1993. Washington, D.C.: GPO, 1993. (ISBN0160432839). (Y4.En2/3:103-46).

The General Accounting Office "investigated the efforts of 57 school districts in 10 states (California, Florida, Illinois, Michigan, New Jersey, New York, North Carolina, Ohio, Pennsylvania, and Texas). These 57 school districts manage over 4,000 schools attended by 3.4 million children. As with child-care facilities, a pattern of neglect of lead hazards is revealed by the GAO report: None of the 10 states have an inspection program or inspection requirement to insure that schools are free of lead hazards....GAO found that most schools, if they inspect for lead hazards at all, investigate only one type of lead hazard: contaminated drinking water, which is often a less important source of lead exposure after paint and soil. The 1988 Lead Contamination and Control Act promoted testing for lead hazards in school drinking water. As a result of this law, numerous schools have tested for drinking water contamination. In fact, in 33 of the school districts surveyed by GAO, all schools have been tested for contaminated drinking water. A large number of the schools tested (15%) had lead levels in drinking water above federal guidelines." (p8-9)

U.S. House. Committee on Energy and Commerce. "Hazards of Lead in Schools and Day Care Facilities." Hearing, 15 Sep 1993. Washington, D.C.: GPO, 1993. (ISBN0160432839). (Y4.En2/3:103-46).

PEDIATRIC TOXICOLOGY--ZIMBABWE

"Children are at particular risk of poisoning as a result of swallowing chemicals that are commonly used around the home, and inhaling carbon monoxide in smoke. For example, a retrospective study of hospital admissions in Zimbabwe found that 90 (4%) of the 2236 children below 15 years of age admitted during 1980-89 were victims of carbon monoxide poisoning. They were mostly very young children who had been ill; as a form of curing the illness and 'sending bad spirits away' they were exposed to smoke, using traditional herbs, which were added to the fire or hot stone according to a local cultural belief." (p24)

Kasilo, Ossy M. J./Nhachi, Charles F. B. "Danger: Poison!" World Health n5, Sep-Oct 1993. p24-25. (ISSN0043-8502).

PENNSYLVANIA

see REFUSE AND REFUSE DISPOSAL--PENNSYLVANIA

PENSIONS--CHILE (v19)

"Government reforms, including privatization, have reached many levels of the economy. One of the most innovative changes was Chile's decision in 1981 to create a private (but mandatory) system to administer employee pension funds. Chilean workers are widely supportive of their program, which supplements a government-mandated minimum pension. They are required to contribute 10 percent of earnings to individual, privately managed retirement accounts. 'The combination of a steady flow of contributions, together with very high real rates of return (an average of 14.5 percent from July 1981 to July 1992), has meant a large accumulation of funds invested in the Chilean economy,' writes Peter Diamond in a paper published by the National Bureau of Economic Research....Three-quarters of Chilean workers own a piece of these funds, which now have assets of around $14 billion--about 40 percent of GDP [gross domestic product]." (p6)

Walters, David C. "Economy: Good News in Chile: Economy Is Growing, Unemployment Down." The Christian Science Monitor v86 n48, 2 Feb 1994. p6. (ISSN0882-7729).

PENSIONS--EUROPE, EASTERN

"Of all the threats to the economies of Eastern Europe and the former Soviet Union, one of the biggest is posed by their own old folk. The impact of old-age pensions on their budgets threatens to plunge some of them into crisis in the next couple of years....The cost of pensions, relative both to GDP [gross domestic product] and to government spending, has risen sharply since the end of communism. In Poland, for instance, pensions have risen as a proportion of GDP from 7% in 1988 to nearly 12% in 1992. Yet elderly people in some countries are in dire poverty. What has gone wrong? Part of the problem is that GDP itself has been shrinking. But the sheer number of people drawing pensions in many ex-communist countries is extraordinary: 13.5m out of a population of 52m in Ukraine, for instance, and 2.4m out of the 9m in Bulgaria." (p55)

"Europe: Old and Unaffordable." Economist v331 n7861, 30 Apr 1994. p55-56. (ISSN0013-0613).

PENSIONS--GREAT BRITAIN--U.S. (v19)

PENSIONS--U.S. (v19)

"For decades the so-called 'defined benefit' plan, in which retirees got regular payments from an employer-funded, professionally managed pension plan, was a hallmark of the American corporation. Today companies are rapidly switching to less costly 'defined contribution' retirement plans, such as 401(k)s, in which the employer makes regular contributions to an employee's retirement fund. Investing the money wisely so there's enough at retirement often is the employee's responsibility. As of 1990, the U.S. Labor Department said 45 percent of the work force had some kind of private pension coverage. Seventeen percent--nearly triple the percentage in 1975--were covered by a defined contribution plan. Thirteen percent were covered by a defined benefit plan and 15 percent by some combination of the two." (p3 secB)

Haglund, Rick. "Business: Employers Less Willing to Play Parent." Ann Arbor News 6 Feb 1994. p1,3 secB.

"Looking at studies done on the [National Retirement Income Policy prepared by the American Society of Pension Actuaries]...in the United States, one finds that the Carter administration reported in its 1981 President's Commission on Pension Policy study that retirees need from 85 percent at lower pay levels down to 50 percent at higher pay levels of preretirement income in order to maintain a reasonable standard of living. Colin B. England, FSA, published a study (1987) that took the approach of updating the President's Commission on Pension Policy report to reflect the many tax law changes that occurred in the 1980s. More recently, Georgia State University, in conjunction with the consulting firm Alexander and Alexander, produced a comprehensive study on the subject. Their approach was to utilize Department of Labor statistics on geographical preretirement expense patterns to project postretirement income needs patterns. This study produced tables showing retirement income replacement needs as high as 90 percent at a $15,000 per year preretirement income level to a low of 66 percent at a $90,000 annual preretirement level." (pE345)

Johnson, Nancy L. (Rep.-Conn.). "National Retirement Income Policy," Congressional Record (3 Mar 1994). Daily ed. pE345-347. (ISSN0363-7239).

PERU

see also AIDS (DISSEASE)--PERU; COCAINE INDUSTRY--BOLIVIA--COLOMBIA--PERU; IMMIGRANTS--PERU

PERU--ECONOMIC CONDITIONS (v19)

"The 1980s are known throughout Latin America as 'the lost decade,' a period when living standards dropped dramatically due to simultaneous recession and inflation. In Peru, where poverty was already acute and inequality extreme, the lost decade has brought catastrophe to many of the country's 21 million inhabitants. Salaries have fallen to 1960 levels; over half the workforce is now employed in off-the-books enterprises that afford them no job security or benefits; incidents of chronic malnutrition have increased alarmingly among young children. Much of this is the result of economic mismanagement. Successive governments with varying political programs have proven incapable of pulling Peru out of the economic ditch into which it stumbled in the late '70s." (p7)

Burt, Jo-Marie. "Peru: Keeping Hope Alive in the Shantytowns." Toward Freedom v[42] n3, Apr-May 1993. p7-8. (ISSN0048-9898).

PESO, MEXICAN--VALUATION (v19)

PESTICIDE RESIDUES IN FOOD--PHILIPPINES

"An FAO [Food and Agriculture Organization] regional director made the observation that Philippine farmers use ten times more pesticides than are necessary. From 1987 to 1989, the major pesticide companies in the Philippines put on the market 20 100 tonnes of pesticides. Pesticides sales grew by 70% between 1988 and 1992, and will amount to about US$ 120 million this year. It is not surprising that a study by the Bureau of Plant Industry in 1990 showed that pesticide residues in samples from locally sold vegetables and fruits such as string beans, eggplants, tomatoes and mangoes exceeded the maximum allowable levels set by WHO [World Health Organization]." (p26-27)

Quijano, Romeo/others. "Time to Blow the Whistle." World Health n5, Sep-Oct 1993. p26-27. (ISSN0043-8502).

PESTICIDE RESIDUES IN FOOD--U.S. (v19)

"According to the FDA [Food and Drug Administration], at least 38 percent of the food supply [in the U.S.] contains pesticide residues. This understates the actual amount because routine lab tests detect fewer than half of the pesticides applied to food. Many foods sampled by FDA had more than one pesticide residue; some had as many as twelve." (p172)

Meyerhoff, Albert H. (Senior Attorney, Natural Resources Defense Council). U.S. House. Committee on Energy and Commerce/U.S. Senate. Committee on Labor and Human Resources. "Safety of Pesticides in Food." Hearing, 21 Sep 1993. Washington, D.C.: GPO, 1994. (ISBN0160434912). (Y4.En2/3:103-55).

"Pesticide policy reforms are needed to reduce or eliminate risks posed by pesticides in food, in particular those foods of special importance in the infant and child diet, according to a new report ['Pesticides in Children's Food'] by the Environmental Working Group. Infants and children are routinely exposed to combinations of two or three pesticides per food, according to the report, which differs from the National Research Council report...in its method of determining risk. 'When cancer risks from just 8 pesticides in 20 fruits and vegetables are added, the average child exceeds the EPA lifetime one-in-one-million risk standard by his or her first birthday,' the report says. It also says millions of children in the United States receive up to 35 percent of their entire lifetime dose of some carcinogenic pesticides by age 5. It recommends a 'targeted pesticide risk reduction strategy that will gradually but completely phase out pesticides that present the greatest hazards to children.'" (p2)

"Pesticide Reforms Needed to Protect Children, Says Report." Alternative Agriculture News v11 n7, Jul 1993. p2. (ISSN8755-4941).

PESTICIDE RESISTANCE

"The bugs are winning. At the time the Delaney Clause was enacted [in 1958], 137 species of insects and mites had become resistant to chemical pesticides. Today, the number of resistant pests is almost 500 (as well as 100 species of plant pathogens and 48 species of weeds)." (p172-173)

Meyerhoff, Albert H. (Senior Attorney, Natural Resources Defense Council). U.S. House. Committee on Energy and Commerce/U.S. Senate. Committee on Labor and Human Resources. "Safety of Pesticides in Food." Hearing, 21 Sep 1993. Washington, D.C.: GPO, 1994. (ISBN0160434912). (Y4.En2/3:103-55).

PESTICIDES

see also FUNGICIDES; HERBICIDES

"Since World War II, pesticide toxicity has increased 10-fold (Pimentel, 1991); Third World annual use is now at 500 000 tons (D. Pimentel, personal communication) (adding about $US4 billion to their debt load)." (p57)

Paddock, William. "Our Last Chance to Win the War on Hunger." Carrying Capacity Network v4 n1, 1994. p52-65. (ISSN1066-5404).

PESTICIDES--COSTS

"Pesticides have both a direct and indirect cost. The direct cost of pesticide use is the purchase price plus the price of application. Worldwide, 2.5 million tons of pesticides costing $20 billion are applied each year. In the U.S. '500,000 tons of 600 different types of pesticides are used annually at a cost of $4.1 billion, including application costs.'" (p8) "The total short-term indirect costs of pesticide use are about $8 billion a year in the U.S. When this cost is added to the $4 billion of direct cost, total short-term costs are about $12 billion. The benefits from pesticide use due to larger yields and other reasons are estimated at $16 billion annually. Though there is an apparent profit of $4 billion from pesticide use, many short-term costs have not been estimated, and long-term costs such as water pollution are hard to quantify. In any event, pesticide use is not the bargain it seemed when applications began to proliferate in the 1950s. Only generations of the future will finally be able to calculate the true cost." (p9)

Quarles, Bill. "Journal Highlights: Indirect Costs of Pesticides." IPM Practitioner v15 n8, Aug 1993. p8-9. (ISSN0738-968X).

PESTICIDES--DEVELOPING COUNTRIES

"By 1986, the U.S. pesticide industry exported 34 percent of its total sales value ($1.4 billion) compared with 26 percent in 1965. Pesticide imports by developing countries grew from $328 million in 1967 to $1,489 million in 1986, or by roughly 350 percent. In developing countries, pesticides and fertilizer are aggressively marketed and subsidized, yet farm-level education (including the basic literacy necessary to read package instructions) is often lacking. Human poisoning in developing countries due to overapplication is common, but poorly documented. One estimate in seven countries of Central America was that pesticide poisonings occurred at a rate 1,800 times higher than in the United States. Robert Repetto has found that pesticide subsidies as a percentage of full retail costs were 56 percent in Colombia, 71 percent in Honduras, and 59 percent in Ecuador. In Africa, the same study found pesticide subsidies of 11 percent in Senegal, 33 percent in Ghana, and 17 percent in Egypt. In Indonesia and China, the subsidies were 18 and 81 percent respectively, for an overall average of roughly 50 percent." (p109)

Runge, C. Ford. "Trade Liberalization and Environmental Quality in Agriculture." International Environmental Affairs v5 n2, Spr 1993. p95-128. (ISSN1041-4665).

PESTICIDES--ENVIRONMENTAL ASPECTS--U.S.

The Environmental Protection Agency "estimates that one out of every ten public drinking water wells in the US contains at least one pesticide; their data indicate that nearly 10,000 community drinking water wells and over 440,000 domestic water wells contain pesticides. Seventy-four different pesticides have been found in groundwater which supplies drinking water for 32 states. Agriculture is also now the number one source of pollution of surface water; pesticides have found their way into countless lakes, rivers and waterways throughout the nation." (p172)

Meyerhoff, Albert H. (Senior Attorney, Natural Resources Defense Council). U.S. House. Committee on Energy and Commerce/U.S. Senate. Committee on Labor and Human Resources. "Safety of Pesticides in Food." Hearing, 21 Sep 1993. Washington, D.C.: GPO, 1994. (ISBN0160434912). (Y4.En2/3:103-55).

PESTICIDES--GERMANY

"The use of many pesticides has been restricted or eliminated in Germany. For example, in 1988 application of atrazine was eliminated in protection zone areas due to its potential to contaminate groundwater....The German government went one step further and canceled all atrazine agricultural use starting with the 1991 season. In total, the number of active ingredients permitted for agricultural use has declined from 308 in 1987 to 216 in 1990, a 30 percent reduction...." (p180)

Gassman, Philip W. "Pesticide Fate Research Trends within a Strict Regulatory Environment." Journal of Soil and Water Conservation v48 n3, May-Jun 1993. p178-187. (ISSN0022-4561).

PESTICIDES--IDAHO

"A survey of 261 [Idaho] potato growers' pest management practices in 1992 found that 97 percent check their crop at least weekly to catch pest problems early and 33 percent actively conserve and protect beneficial insects by restricting chemical use." (p9)

Flocchini, Jim. "Organic Agriculture: A Growth Industry in Idaho." Journal of Pesticide Reform v13 n1, Spr 1993. p8-9. (ISSN0893-357X).

PESTICIDES--NICARAGUA

In Nicaragua, "Over 60 agricultural workers have died due to the improper use of pesticides, especially DDT, while 1,200 others have been seriously intoxicated, according to preliminary findings of a study carried out by the Ministry of Health (Minsa) in Chinandega, 100 miles (160 km) north of Managua. According to the study, in cases in which the worker was poisoned, the pesticide either penetrated the skin or was ingested through the nose or mouth. Most of those affected were young people between the ages of 15 and 24 who sprayed the fields by hand." (p9)

"News: Economy and Labor: Pesticides Poison Workers." Barricada Internacional v13 n362, Jun 1993. p9. (ISSN1013-9567).

PESTICIDES--TOXICOLOGY--PHILIPPINES

"A United Nations report suggests that there are about two million poisonings and 10 000 deaths a year from pesticides; about three-quarters of the deaths occur in developing countries. In the Philippines, a recent report showed 1302 poisoning cases between January 1992 and March 1993 in the National Capital region alone; and a study in Central Luzon showed a 27% increase in mortality, which translated to about 900 farmers dying every year in one province alone due to exposure to pesticides." (p26)

Quijano, Romeo/others. "Time to Blow the Whistle." World Health n5, Sep-Oct 1993. p26-27. (ISSN0043-8502).

PESTICIDES--TOXICOLOGY--U.S.

The Environmental Protection Agency's "Incident Data System (IDS) received about 2,000 [pesticide] incident reports during 1992. By comparison, the American Association of Poison Control Centers surveillance system received 54,577 reports of pesticide exposure, 26,725 of which involved children under six years of age." (p75)

Browner, Carol M. (Administrator, U.S. Environmental Protection Agency)/others. U.S. House. Committee on Energy and Commerce/U.S. Senate. Committee on Labor and Human Resources. "Safety of Pesticides in Food." Hearing, 21 Sep 1993. Washington, D.C.: GPO, 1994. (ISBN0160434912). (Y4.En2/3:103-55).

PESTICIDES--U.S. (v19)

"A study by Texas A&M University...indicates [that] without pesticides and their availability...the domestically produced fruit and vegetables would drop by 70 percent." (p20)

Roberts, Pat (Rep.-Kans.). U.S. House. Committee on Energy and Commerce/U.S. Senate. Committee on Labor and Human Resources. "Safety of Pesticides in Food." Hearing, 21 Sep 1993. Washington, D.C.: GPO, 1994. (ISBN0160434912). (Y4.En2/3:103-55).

"Conventional pesticide use in the United States has increased dramatically, from 511 million to more than one billion pounds. Total pesticide use, including wood preservatives, disinfectants and sulfur now exceeds two billion pounds annually, eight pounds for every man, woman and child in the United States." (p172)

Meyerhoff, Albert H. (Senior Attorney, Natural Resources Defense Council). U.S. House. Committee on Energy and Commerce/U.S. Senate. Committee on Labor and Human Resources. "Safety of Pesticides in Food." Hearing, 21 Sep 1993. Washington, D.C.: GPO, 1994. (ISBN0160434912). (Y4.En2/3:103-55).

"For over 20 years, EPA [Environmental Protection Agency] has been required to complete the review of older pesticides. We have tried to amend the laws to get the job done in 1972, 1978, and 1988. Despite these attempts, GAO [General Accounting

Office] reports that of the almost 20,000 pesticide products under review since 1972, only 31 have been reregistered. At this rate, the process would take until the year 15,520 A.D. to complete." (p6)

Synar, Mike (Rep.-Okla.). U.S. House. Committee on Energy and Commerce/U.S. Senate. Committee on Labor and Human Resources. "Safety of Pesticides in Food." Hearing, 21 Sep 1993. Washington, D.C.: GPO, 1994. (ISBN0160434912). (Y4.En2/3:103-55).

"Pesticide production and use in the United States was 638,666,000 pounds a year in 1960 and has risen to over two billion pounds per year. A 1985 Chlorinated Pesticide Screening Test developed by Environ-Health Systems revealed that 99 percent of people worldwide had from 4 to 19 pesticides in their blood. The bodies of those born after 1946 will carry DDT, banned in 1974, as long as they live. New studies published by the JOURNAL OF THE NATIONAL CANCER INSTITUTE link the high incidence of breast cancer to DDT, PCBs, and other chlorinated hydrocarbons (broad-spectrum synthetic insecticides) in breast tissue. Cancer rates have soared to one in three persons, and cancer claims the lives of one in four. A growing body of evidence indicates that these chemicals also disrupt the human reproductive and immune systems." (p186-187)

Flynn, Charlotte (National Chair, Gray Panthers)/Smigel, Marjorie (Chair of Task Force on Environment, Gray Panthers). U.S. House. Committee on Energy and Commerce/U.S. Senate. Committee on Labor and Human Resources. "Safety of Pesticides in Food." Hearing, 21 Sep 1993. Washington, D.C.: GPO, 1994. (ISBN0160434912). (Y4.En2/3:103-55).

The Environmental Protection Agency "intends to capitalize on and expand a number of projects that have been started in the past few years. One of the most visible and successful is its biologicals program. Biological pesticides comprise the single fastest growing segment of registration activity. Since the first biological pesticide, 'Bacillus popilliae,' was registered in 1948, EPA has registered approximately 30 microbials and 50 biochemicals. Prior to 1985, registration of biologicals was rare, comprising at most 10% of all pesticides. In the past 2 years, 50% to 70% of all new pesticidal active ingredients registered have been biologicals." (p80)

Browner, Carol M. (Administrator, U.S. Environmental Protection Agency)/others. U.S. House. Committee on Energy and Commerce/U.S. Senate. Committee on Labor and Human Resources. "Safety of Pesticides in Food." Hearing, 21 Sep 1993. Washington, D.C.: GPO, 1994. (ISBN0160434912). (Y4.En2/3:103-55).

"'The damage resulting from nuclear radiation is the same as the damage resulting from the use of toxic genetic chemicals [pesticides],' [Italian scientist Americo] Mosca wrote. 'The use of fungicides of organic synthesis (Zineb, Captan, Phaltan, etc.) annually causes the same damage to present and future generations as atomic fallout from 29 H-bombs of 14 megatons--or damage equal to fallout of 14,500 atomic bombs, type Hiroshima.' Mosca computed that in the U.S., in the 1970s, yearly use of toxic genetic chemicals was about 453,000 tons, which caused damage equal to atomic fallout from 145 H-bombs of 14 megatons, or 72,000 atomic bombs, type Hiroshima." (p7)

"Organiculture: Backgrounding the Wave of the Future." Acres, U.S.A. v24 n1, Jan 1994. p6-8,10.

"'Weak federal laws and regulations, bureaucratic delay, and a suspect system of environmental and health effects assessment' are responsible for inadequate pesticide oversight, resulting in a dramatic increase in pesticide use since the publication of SILENT SPRING 30 years ago, according to a new report by the Natural Resources Defense Council. Pesticide use has increased from 540 million pounds annually in 1964 to 1 billion pounds in 1991, including 71 carcinogenic pesticides used on food crops, says the report. NRDC's pesticide reform goals, released with the report, are to improve the safety of the food supply; encourage the use of non-toxic agricultural alternatives to pesticides; and strengthen the nation's pesticide program by modernizing pesticide laws to better protect the public and environment." (p3)

"Inadequate Oversight Has Resulted in Increasing Pesticide Use, Says NRDC." Alternative Agriculture News v11 n7, Jul 1993. p3. (ISSN8755-4941).

"Among the estimated 126 pesticides currently in use on golf courses, three popular ones--chlorothalonil, 2,4-D, and trifluralin--have caused cancer in laboratory animals, according to Eugene, Oregon-based Northwest Coalition for Alternatives to Pesticides (NCAP). Golfers usually don't know what chemicals have been applied to their favorite courses because only about 20 states require clubs to post notices, and few elsewhere voluntarily inform the public. It's not uncommon for golfers and golf course workers to have adverse reactions to the array of chemicals used to maintain their turf grass. And in one well-publicized case, that reaction was fatal. Before Labor Day weekend in 1983, Navy Lieutenant George Prior...was playing golf at the Army-Navy Country Club in Arlington, Virginia. After his round he experienced headaches, fever, and nausea. Within three days a sunburn-like rash covered his body, and large blisters hung from his arms and back. He developed pneumonia and kidney failure, fell into a coma, and died some 20 days after the game. An autopsy found that Prior had been killed by a violent allergic reaction to one of golf's most common pesticides, chlorothalonil." (p75-76)

Selcraig, Bruce. "Greens Fees." Sierra v78 n4, Jul-Aug 1993. p70-77,86-87. (ISSN0161-7362).

PESTICIDES--U.S.--COSTS

"According to USDA [U.S. Dept. of Agriculture] and Environmental Protection Agency data, pesticide costs are a small fraction of farm production costs [in the U.S.], and farm production costs are only a fraction of the retail cost of food. In 1992, farmer production expenses amounted to about $145 billion, of which about $6 billion (4.13 percent) was for pesticides. Expenditures for food for off-premise use amounted to about $319 billion. So, farm pesticide costs amounted to 1.8 percent of food expenditures." (p123-124)

Womach, Jasper (Specialist in Agricultural Policy, Environment and Natural Resources Policy Div.). U.S. House. Committee on Energy and Commerce/U.S. Senate. Committee on Labor and Human Resources. "Safety of Pesticides in Food." Hearing, 21 Sep 1993. Washington, D.C.: GPO, 1994. (ISBN0160434912). (Y4.En2/3:103-55).

"Peanut pesticide costs in 1990 averaged $80.14 per acre, or $0.04 per pound. At a conversion rate of .528 pounds of peanut butter per pound of peanuts, pesticide costs amount to $0.076 per pound of peanut butter. The average annual 1992 retail price of peanut butter is $1.88 per one-pound jar....Florida orange pesticide costs in 1989/90 averaged $139.28 per acre, or $0.80 per 90-pound box. Using a conversion rate of 1.3 gallons of frozen concentrate per box of oranges, pesticide costs amount to $0.058 per 12-ounce can of frozen concentrate. The average annual 1992 retail price of frozen orange concentrate is $1.42 per 12-ounce can....Southern California broccoli pesticide costs in 1992/93 averaged $159.80 per acre, or $0.32 per carton. At 26 pounds per carton, pesticide costs amount to $0.012 per pound of fresh broccoli. The average annual 1992 retail price of fresh broccoli is $1.18 per pound." (p124)

Womach, Jasper (Specialist in Agricultural Policy, Environment and Natural Resources Policy Div.). U.S. House. Committee on Energy and Commerce/U.S. Senate. Committee on

Labor and Human Resources. "Safety of Pesticides in Food." Hearing, 21 Sep 1993. Washington, D.C.: GPO, 1994. (ISBN0160434912). (Y4.En2/3:103-55).

PESTICIDES--U.S.--PUBLIC OPINION

"Consumers [in the U.S.] perceive pesticides in the food supply as a matter of concern. A survey in 1984 found 76% of those surveyed were 'very concerned' or 'extremely concerned' and 96% were at least 'somewhat concerned' (UCAIC 1989). Yearly surveys by the Food Marketing Institute for 1984 through 1987 found about 75% of consumers considered pesticide residues in food as a 'serious hazard' (UCAIC 1988). In 1990, the percentage had increased to 80%. Food additives and gamma radiation treatments were also perceived as problems (Shewfelt and Prussia 1993)." (p10)

Quarles, William. "Update: Biological Control of Postharvest Fruit Disease." IPM Practitioner v15 n5-6, May-Jun 1993. p1-11. (ISSN0738-968X).

PESTICIDES--ZIMBABWE

"A study of health hazards resulting from the use of pesticides based on organophosphates among farm workers in Zimbabwe showed that most poisoning incidents occur during the spraying season, December to March. Another study, involving 942 people, found that 75% of urban poisoning cases were suicides and attempted suicides. The single most vulnerable group comprised those aged between 21 and 30 years. A sizeable amount of the health budget could be saved if stricter legislation were introduced in order to prevent access to pesticides by unauthorized persons." (p25)

Kasilo, Ossy M. J./Nhachi, Charles F. B. "Danger: Poison!" World Health n5, Sep-Oct 1993. p24-25. (ISSN0043-8502).

PESTICIDES INDUSTRY--U.S.

"According to U.S. Customs records (the only public source of pesticide export records) obtained and analyzed by FASE [Foundation of Advancement in Science and Education] almost 500 million pounds of pesticides were exported from the U.S. in 1991. This works out to be 27 pounds per hour and is an 11 million pound increase over 1990 figures also analyzed by FASE. (JPR 11(1):35)....FASE calculated that over 115 million pounds of exported pesticides, 95 percent of those that could be identified) are known or suspected to cause cancer, genetic damage, or adversely affect reproduction and development. More than half of U.S. pesticide exports go to developing countries that often have even less success at regulating pesticide use than does the U.S. In an excellent example of the outrageous amounts of hazardous chemicals leaving U.S. ports, FASE calculated that over 9 million pounds of paraquat were exported in 1991, enough to potentially provide a lethal dose to over a billion people. The amount of paraquat exported to Guatemala was enough to fatally poison each rural resident nearly 35 times." (p25)

Lind, Pollyanna. "News from Around: Research: Just What Pesticides Are Being Shipped from the U.S.? And Where Are They Going? Journal of Pesticide Reform v13 n2, Sum 1993. p25. (ISSN0893-357X).

PET OWNERS--U.S.

"Based on data from a recently commissioned telephone survey, The HSUS [Humane Society of the United States] has discovered some interesting characteristics about pet ownership and pet-owner attitudes across the nation. Among other findings, the survey revealed that cat owners are more likely (77%) to have their pet spayed or neutered than are dog owners (53%). And the study indicates that 14% of pet owners obtain their pet from an animal shelter, which corroborates a 1991 study by the American Animal Hospital Association." (p6)

"HSUS Releases National Statistics on Pet Ownership, Attitudes." Shelter Sense v16 n5, May 1993. p6-7,12. (ISSN0734-3078).

PETROLEUM--UNDERGROUND STORAGE--U.S.

"As of first quarter fiscal year 1993, 202,000 [petroleum] releases [from underground tanks], have been confirmed and reported to EPA. In fiscal year 1993, 148,000 cleanups have been initiated and 70,000 cleanups have been completed. The number of confirmed releases is expected to grow at a rate of about 50,000 releases per year until the rate begins to slow down at about 320,000 releases during fiscal year 1995. The rate of confirmed release continues to grow as each of the deadlines for leak detection are phased-in and owners and operators are closing facilities. In 1998, after the upgrading requirements are implemented, we are expecting another increase in the number of confirmed releases." (p457)

Browner, Carol M. (Administrator, Environmental Protection Agency). U.S. House. Committee on Appropriations. "Depts. of Veterans Affairs and Housing and Urban Development...Approp. for 1994 (Part 5)." Hearing, Washington, D.C.: GPO, 1993. (ISBN016041072X). (Y4.Ap6/1:V64/4/994/pt.5).

"To give a full picture of the underground storage tank problem in the U.S. requires more than an estimate of how many 'tanks' are now 'leaking.' First, many, if not most, releases from tank systems come from leaking piping or from spills and overfills, not leaking tanks. To estimate potential leaks, it may be helpful to consider a fixed universe. There were approximately 2 million regulated UST [underground storage tank] systems in operation when the [Environmental Protection] Agency's regulations took effect in 1988; the vast majority were unprotected bare steel. Leaks are more likely to occur in these older, unprotected tanks. While precise projections are not possible, EPA estimates that about 20 percent of these (up to 400,000) have had a release in the past, could now be leaking, or could have a release in the next several years." (p456)

Browner, Carol M. (Administrator, Environmental Protection Agency). U.S. House. Committee on Appropriations. "Depts. of Veterans Affairs and Housing and Urban Development...Approp. for 1994 (Part 5)." Hearing, Washington, D.C.: GPO, 1993. (ISBN016041072X). (Y4.Ap6/1:V64/4/994/pt.5).

PETROLEUM CHEMICALS INDUSTRY--JAPAN

"The average Japanese [petrochemical] company turns a mere 500,000 tonnes of ethylene gas into plastics every year--half the level deemed the minimum for a firm to survive in America. Meanwhile, protection blunted the incentive to update factories in Japan. Nicholas Smith, an analyst at Jardine Fleming, says that more than 70% of Japan's ethylene plants are more than 20 years old. With Japan's small, backward and over-manned petrochemicals businesses expected to lose as much as Y80 billion ($730m) in the year to March, the restructuring put off a decade ago is now unavoidable." (p65)

"Business: MITI's Identity Crisis." Economist v330 n7847, 22 Jan 1994. p65-66. (ISSN0013-0613).

PETROLEUM INDUSTRY AND TRADE (v19)

"After a half-decade of painful cost-cutting, oil companies were hoping that 1994 would be the second year of a gradual recovery. But crashing prices have caused them to change their view. Now, they're simply aiming to hold their ground. Most analysts look for flat earnings for the broad industry, reflecting sluggish demand, high environmental costs, and the lowest crude prices in five years--down some 15%, to about $14 a barrel, since OPEC failed to curb production at a late November meeting....Average crude price for 1994 will be around $17.75 a barrel, down from $18.52 last year but high enough to keep the industry in the black, says Oppenheimer Securities analyst Paul Ting....'What (OPEC) is doing now is illogical,' says Mobil Chief Executive Allen E. Murray. 'These countries are giving away $100 million a day in revenue rather than give up 2% to 3% in production.'...Small independent producers...account for 40% of

U.S. crude production....At under $15 a barrel, the 450,000 domestic stripper wells--which by definition yield under 10 barrels a day--become uneconomical, says longtime wildcatter Michel T. Halbouty. The Independent Petroleum Association of America figures at least 75,000 production jobs are at risk." (p87)

Burrows, Peter. "Natural Resources: Energy: A Trickle, Not a Gusher." Business Week i3353, 10 Jan 1994. p87. (ISSN0007-7135).

PETROLEUM INDUSTRY AND TRADE--ALASKA (v19)

PETROLEUM INDUSTRY AND TRADE--ASIA (v19)

PETROLEUM INDUSTRY AND TRADE--CHILE

"In Chile, a return to civilian rule and market-based economics has sparked economic growth and soaring petroleum consumption. From 1986 to 1991, oil consumption increased 43 percent, an annual rate of 7.4 percent." (p54)

Nadler, Arnold. "Oil Prices: What to Expect and Why It Matters." Public Power v52 n1, Jan-Feb 1994. p46-48,50,52-54,56. (ISSN0033-3654).

PETROLEUM INDUSTRY AND TRADE--CHINA

"With a population of over one billion and a surging economy,...[China] already is the world's third largest user of energy. Currently, petroleum consumption and production are in approximate balance at about 2.9 mbd [million barrels daily] (compared with U.S. consumption of about 17 mbd)....consumption is bound to increase at a rapid clip. Last year Chinese automobile factories turned out 180,000 cars. Imports more than doubled to 210,000. In the first half of 1993, total vehicle output jumped to 620,000, up 44 percent from a year earlier. Within a decade, the government hopes that Chinese factories will be producing three million vehicles a year, two thirds of them cars. Continuation of an estimated five percent a year increase in oil use, with domestic output remaining unchanged, will lead to nearly two mbd in imports in 10 years--an addition to world oil demand roughly equal to the total production from Kuwait or Nigeria today." (p56)

Nadler, Arnold. "Oil Prices: What to Expect and Why It Matters." Public Power v52 n1, Jan-Feb 1994. p46-48,50,52-54,56. (ISSN0033-3654).

PETROLEUM INDUSTRY AND TRADE--CONGO (BRAZZAVILLE)

"When Congolese production and oil prices increased in the early 1980s, the state's share of the oil receipts peaked at around $800 million. Ironically, though, Congo's petroleum sector has been a bane as well as a boon to its financial solvency and development planning. Instead of paying off its old debts with the 1979-1981 windfalls, the Congolese government again increased its expenditures; moreover, it continued to borrow heavily from abroad on the assumption that these revenues would be permanent. Then, as oil prices and revenues fell in the mid-1980s, the government had to borrow more. During the era of large petroleum profits, other export sectors declined, so that by the late 1980s, 90 percent of foreign exchange was earned by petroleum revenues. Meanwhile the government now gets about 70 percent of its income from oil revenues. In 1991 Congo's oil revenues were about $334 million, or 40 percent of their peak in the early 1980s, while its production probably topped out. Hence, oil has left Congo more rather than less dependent." (p57-58)

Clark, John F. "Socio-Political Change in the Republic of Congo: Political Dilemmas of Economic Reform." Journal of Third World Studies v10 n1, Spr 1993. p52-77. (ISSN8755-3449).

PETROLEUM INDUSTRY AND TRADE--CUBA

"Alternative energy sources aside, it's no secret that economic recovery in Cuba depends on oil. The sugar-for-crude barter deal struck with the Soviets once supplied Cuba with 13 million tons a year--but by 1989, the agreement was already falling through cracks. That year, total oil consumption in Cuba stood at 11.6 million tons; and by 1992, Cuban homes and offices were in the dark several hours a day, as the dipstick plunged to 6.9 million. This year, the island is shooting to purchase 6.2 million tons abroad (of this, up to three million in an oil-for-sugar deal with the Russians at world market prices), and to pump 1.3 million tons domestically (compared to 881,000 tons drilled in 1992)." (p45)

Reed, Gail. "Economic News: Where Will the Oil Come From?" Cuba Update n3-4, Summer 1993. p45. (ISSN0196-0830).

PETROLEUM INDUSTRY AND TRADE--MEXICO (v19)

"Mexican market for oil and natural gas field equipment purchases in 1991 was about USD 520 million. U.S. suppliers accounted for about USD 158 million of that demand. Pemex [the national oil company of Mexico] plans for 1993 call for 46 development wells, 38 in their offshore areas. Refinery construction expenditures in 1991...[were] USD 851 million, of which USD 272 million were for equipment. Projects included drilling platforms, oil pipelines, natural gas fuels pipelines, and processing plants. Plans call for a refinery in Salina Cruz to replace one shut down for environmental reasons near Mexico City. There is expected to be built a refinery of similar capacity at another site starting this or next year. Environmental technology upgrades include six existing plants, and eight new plants for production of gasoline additives for efficient and cleaner combustion." (p128)

Coleman, Lester (Exec. Vice President, Halliburton Co.). U.S. House. Committee on Energy and Commerce. "NAFTA: Energy Provisions and Environmental Implications." Hearing, 22 Sep 1993. Washington, D.C.: GPO, 1994. (ISBN0160440459). (Y4.En2/3:103:70).

PETROLEUM INDUSTRY AND TRADE--MEXICO--U.S.

"Foreign markets account for 80 percent of U.S. oil and gas field machinery, and the United States currently has a 70 percent share of Mexico's import market, which is expected to grow by 15 percent in 1993 and again in 1994." (p26)

Yerxa, Rufus (Deputy U.S. Trade Rep.). U.S. House. Committee on Energy and Commerce. "NAFTA: Energy Provisions and Environmental Implications." Hearing, 22 Sep 1993. Washington, D.C.: GPO, 1994. (ISBN0160440459). (Y4.En2/3:103/70).

PETROLEUM INDUSTRY AND TRADE--MEXICO, GULF OF

"A couple of years ago the Gulf of Mexico was known as 'the dead sea' within the energy industry. The gulf is back in fashion. It produces about 25% of America's gas (and 12% of its oil). The number of exploration rigs has increased to around 85. That is still less than half the total in the early 1980s, but there is talk of many more to come. The rise in the price of gas, from $1 per 1,000 cubic feet in the spring of 1992 to more than $2.50 now, is one reason for this optimism. Another is better technology." (p70)

"Business: Dead Sea Bubble." Economist v330 n7853, 5 Mar 1994. p70. (ISSN0013-0613).

PETROLEUM INDUSTRY AND TRADE--PERSIAN GULF REGION

"The media's acceptance of disinterested U.S. intervention in the Horn of Africa free of strategic calculation is in sharp contrast to a statement presented during U.S. Senate hearings on 1991 Defense Appropriations by Gen. H. Norman Schwarzkopf, then chief of the U.S. Central Command (USCENCOM) covering Southwest Asia, the Arab Peninsula, and the Horn of Africa: 'With Free-World economies increasingly dependent on the uninterrupted flow of Southwest Asian oil, the U.S. has a vital interest in maintaining the unrestricted access to governments, people, and resources of this region....This volatile region contains 77 percent of the Free World's proven oil reserves. While some estimates indicate that our own economically exploitable reserves could be depleted in 20 to 40 years, the Persian Gulf region will still have over 100 years of proven reserves, with many promising areas yet to be explored.'" (p14)

Petras, James/Vieux, Steve. "The Somali Invasion." Lies of Our Times Feb 1993. p14-16. (ISSN1046-7912).

PETROLEUM INDUSTRY AND TRADE--PRUDHOE BAY (ALASKA) (v19)

PETROLEUM INDUSTRY AND TRADE--RUSSIA (v19)

PETROLEUM INDUSTRY AND TRADE--U.S. (v19)

"During the 1980's, the number of U.S. refineries dropped from 314 to 184, a 42% decrease; refining capacity fell by 20%. The United States now imports more than one-half of its petroleum needs, and nearly 30% of this oil arrives in the form of refined products. Over 50,000 jobs have been lost in the refinery industry since 1982." (p119)

Hancock, Nolan W. (Citizenship-Legislative Dir., Oil, Chemical and Atomic Workers International Union). U.S. House. Committee on Energy and Commerce. "NAFTA: Energy Provisions and Environmental Implications." Hearing, 22 Sep 1993. Washington, D.C.: GPO, 1994. (ISBN0160440459). (Y4.En2/3:103/70).

"At the height of the oil boom in the early 1980s, companies drilled more than 1,000 wells and built more than 1,000 miles of roads in the Little Missouri Grasslands. Federal royalties brought $50 million a year to the U.S. Treasury. The boom leveled out at 500 producing wells. But the Forest Service is planning for 500 more wells and 300 miles of new roads in the northern two-thirds of the grasslands alone. Development has taken a heavy toll. Of the 500,000 acres of wilderness found in the 1970s, only about 100,000 acres scattered in small pockets remain undeveloped." (p9-10)

Hinchman, Steve. "Oil Firms Commandeer Badlands." High Country News v25 n7, 19 Apr 1993. p9-10. (ISSN0191-5657).

"Once consigned to the fossil-fuel scrap heap, oil shale might rise again thanks to a new process that produces crude oil for about $30 a barrel. The Lawrence Livermore National Laboratory, which developed the technology, says it wants to field test a 100-ton-per-day pilot project, probably in Colorado's Piceance Basin. Unocal Corp., which built and operated a 10,000-barrel-per-day shale plant north of Parachute, Colo., in the 1980s, is participating in the research. Shale beds in the area hold an estimated 600 billion barrels of recoverable oil, rivaling the Persian Gulf's reserves. Livermore researcher Robert Cena says the new technology is economical because it cooks rock more efficiently than the natural gas Unocal used in its failed process." (p3)

"Hotline: What Rough Beast...." High Country News v25 n7, 19 Apr 1993. p3. (ISSN0191-5657).

"One of the few certainties in the world of oil is that United States production will continue to decline. The only question is how fast. Notwithstanding the fact that our production is already about 20 percent lower than back in 1973, in 1992 the United States was still almost in a dead heat for first place among the world's oil producers. Former Soviet Union production averaged 9.0 mbd [million barrels daily]. Including natural gas liquids, U.S. production was 8.8 mbd. Saudi Arabia was at 8.4 mbd. Since 1985, when oil prices plunged, U.S. production has fallen by an average of 270,000 b/d per year. This accounts for about one quarter of the world's increase in demand for OPEC oil." (p54)

Nadler, Arnold. "Oil Prices: What to Expect and Why It Matters." Public Power v52 n1, Jan-Feb 1994. p46-48,52-54,56. (ISSN0033-3654).

PETROLEUM INDUSTRY AND TRADE--U.S.--TRANSPORTATION (v19)

"According to the East-West Center, a secondary impact [in Hawaii] of a severe oil supply disruption would be significant price hikes, with a doubling or even tripling of prices as a likely outcome, and a corresponding increase in inflation. Tourism could fall by as much as 50 percent, causing a 5-percent job loss in the U.S. Pacific islands, or roughly 28,000 jobs in Hawaii. A recession would likely follow, producing a much more severe downturn that could easily double the effects of the crisis. In other words, a severe oil supply disruption would create adverse downstream effects that would not be felt for several months, yet would continue for several years. The study paints a bleak portrait of the economic consequences of an oil emergency in Hawaii." (pS4555)

Akaka, Daniel K. (Sen.-Hawaii). "Statements on Introduced Bills and Joint Resolutions," Congressional Record (20 Apr 1994). Daily ed. pS4554-4574. (ISSN0363-7239).

PETROLEUM INDUSTRY AND TRADE--VIETNAM

"Oil is luring foreign investors to Vietnam. At present 110,000 barrels a day are being produced, up from 20,000 a day in 1989....Vietnam should be pumping at least 300,000 barrels a day by the turn of the century. Even allowing for rapid growth in domestic demand, this would provide net export earnings of $1.5 billion-2 billion a year." (p39)

"Asia: Vietnam's Gas-Fired, Oil-Charged Future." Economist v330 n7844, 8 Jan 1994. p39. (ISSN0013-0613).

PETROLEUM PRODUCTS--PRICES

"A poll by the International Energy Workshop in Vienna, Austria, produced [oil] price forecasts for 1990 no lower than $42 a barrel. The average forecast was $62, with predictions ranging up to $77. The actual price in 1990 turned out to be $20 a barrel. In 1978, the U.S. Department of Energy forecast that domestic production of oil in 1985 would be 10.6 mbd [million barrels daily]. A year later, DOE lowered its 1985 supply forecast by 1.1 mbd, while increasing the expected price by 125 percent....In 1982, the U.S. Department of Energy predicted that gas prices would reach $7 per thousand cubic feet (mcf) by 1990. Two years later, the Gas Research Institute forecast a price of about $5 per mcf by 1990. The actual U.S. wellhead average for 1990 was $1.71 per mcf." (p52)

Nadler, Arnold. "Oil Prices: What to Expect and Why It Matters." Public Power v52 n1, Jan-Feb 1994. p46-48,50,52-54,56. (ISSN0033-3654).

PETROLEUM PRODUCTS--PRICES--U.S. (v19)

PETROLEUM PRODUCTS--U.S.--STORAGE

"Petroleum is leaking from more than 200,000 of the nation's 800,000 to 900,000 aboveground petroleum storage tanks and piping, according to a recent EDF [Environmental Defense Fund] report, 'LAST But Not Least: Leaking Aboveground Storage Tank Threats, Costs, and Answers.' More than half the major storage facilities have large underground pools of petroleum that can migrate offsite if left unaddressed. Unlike underground storage tanks, which were regulated in the 1980's, aboveground tanks are essentially unregulated. They have leaked millions of gallons over decades, severely contaminating groundwater, damaging ecosystems, depreciating property values, and forcing families to relocate." (p3)

"Leaks Found at One in Four U.S. Petroleum Tank Farms." EDF Letter v24 n3, May 1993. p3. (ISSN0163-2566).

PETROLEUM REFINERIES--ENVIRONMENTAL ASPECTS

"At a typical [oil] refinery, 99.7% of the crude oil received is turned into a product such as gasoline or diesel fuel, and only 0.3% ends up as pollution. But for a community near an average-sized refinery, that 0.3% can mean over 10,000 gallons of oil released to the air, land, or water every day." (p2)

"EDF News Briefs: Preventing Pollution from the Oil Refinery Near You." EDF Letter v25 n1, Jan 1994. p2. (ISSN0163-2566).

PETROLEUM RESERVES (v19)

PETROLEUM RESERVES--ALASKA

According to U.S. Secretary of the Interior Manuel Lujan, "geologists now believe there is a 46 percent chance of finding anywhere up to 14 billion barrels of oil beneath the 1.5 million-acre coastal plain of the Arctic Refuge. (Governmental reports and environmental impact statements refer to the coastal plain as the '1002 area'; Gwich'in Indians refer to it as the 'Birthing Place'--the place where each spring the 186,000 Porcupine Caribou Herd migrates to, and where the cows give birth to their calves.) Four or five years ago, proponents of drilling in the refuge were saying there was a 19 percent chance of finding up to 3.2 billion barrels of oil. Later that figure was upped to 9.6 billion barrels. Now the figure has jumped to 14 billion barrels, and the odds of finding oil close to even money. At this rate, in a few years it wouldn't even be necessary to drill--the stuff would be bubbling to the surface of it own volition, spouting up like geysers of black gold!" (p20)

Ellison, Burns. "Traditional Roots: What Comes of Counting Caribou instead of Sheep." Land Report n46, Spr 1993. p19-22.

PETROLEUM RESERVES--SAUDI ARABIA (v19)

PETROLEUM RESERVES--U.S. (v19)

"We have a resource in place to insulate U.S. consumers from energy price shocks. When an oil crisis hits, we turn to the strategic petroleum reserve. This emergency reserve, located in Louisiana and Texas, currently holds 580 million barrels of crude." However, "Hawaii's only means of access to the strategic petroleum reserve is by tanker delivery from the Gulf of Mexico through the Panama Canal. Unlike the mainland, which has access to oil transported by pipeline, rail, and highway, all of Hawaii's crude oil and refined products arrive by ocean tanker. A total reliance on ocean deliveries makes Hawaii exceptionally vulnerable to a cutoff of oil supplies....The distance between the strategic petroleum reserve loading docks and Honolulu, by way of the canal, is 7,000 miles--more than one-quarter of the distance around the globe. The problems of the other Pacific territories are even more acute. American Samoa is 8,000 miles by ship from the SPR facilities, and Guam is over 10,000 miles distant from these reserves. Puerto Rico and the Virgin Islands face a similar predicament." (pS4554)

Akaka, Daniel K. (Sen.-Hawaii). "Statements on Introduced Bills and Joint Resolutions," Congressional Record (20 Apr 1994). Daily ed. pS4554-4574. (ISSN0363-7239).

PETS--MASSACHUSETTS

A survey by the Massachusetts Society for the Prevention of Cruelty to Animals "revealed that 36% of Massachusetts households have cats and/or dogs--22% cats and 21% dogs. According to the survey, 7% have both cat(s) and dog(s). The vast majority (more than 4 in 5) have owned the same kind of pet before. Among cat owners, 39% own more than one cat. The average number of cats per cat-owning household is 1.6. Most of the cat-owning housholds (86%) have a mixed-breed cat. Among dog owners, 19% own more than one dog. The average number of dogs per dog-owning household is 1.2. Purebreds occupy the majority (59%) of dog-owning households." (p8)

"MSPCA Survey Shows Interesting Results." Shelter Sense v16 n5, May 1993. p8-9. (ISSN0734-3078).

PETS--U.S. (v19)

"In 1992, the AKC [or American Kennel Club] registered a record 1.5 million new dogs, and the Cat Fanciers Association (CFA) registered 73,839 new cats. These figures don't include the countless unregisterable purebreds and purebred mixes produced by backyard breeders or the registerable purebreds whose owners never send in their registration paperwork. 'Many people have never bothered to send in their registration forms,' reports the AKC. 'The AKC for many years registered about half of the dogs actually eligible for registration.'" (p7)

Miller, Julie E. "Purebreds and Pet Overpopulation: The Case for a Breeding Moratorium." Shelter Sense v16 n8, Sep 1993. p3-12. (ISSN0734-3078).

"Pet owners obtained their pets from a variety of sources. According to the HSUS [Humane Society of the United States] survey, 52% got their pet from a friend, relative, or neighbor, 18% from a breeder, 14% from an animal shelter, 9% from a pet store, and 5% from a newspaper ad. Fourteen percent said their pets just showed up. (Respondents with more than one pet could indicate more than one source for their animals)....When respondents were asked where they would be most likely to get their next pet were they to get another one, 25% of them said the animal shelter. Of the remainder, 16% said a breeder; 15% said a friend, relative, or neighbor; 9% said a pet store; and 8% said a newspaper ad." (p7)

"HSUS Releases National Statistics on Pet Ownership, Attitudes." Shelter Sense v16 n5, May 1993. p6-7,12. (ISSN0734-3078).

"The HSUS [Humane Society of the United States] has gathered limited data indicating that intact dogs are two to three times more likely to bite than their sterilized counterparts. Unfortunately, when owners of at least one unsterilized dog were told that spayed or neutered dogs are less likely to bite, only 15% said they were more likely to have the animal sterilized. Four percent said they were less likely, and 76% said that the information had no effect on their decision." (p6) "Of the dog and cat owners with at least one unsterilized animal, 33% said they would be more likely to have their pet spayed or neutered if it saved them some money on insurance." (p7)

"HSUS Releases National Statistics on Pet Ownership, Attitudes." Shelter Sense v16 n5, May 1993. p6-7,12. (ISSN0734-3078).

PHARMACEUTICAL INDUSTRY--CANADA (v19)

PHARMACEUTICAL INDUSTRY--EUROPE--U.S. (v19)

PHARMACEUTICAL INDUSTRY--U.S.

"Largely because of growth in managed-care health plans, analysts say, the 10 largest U.S. drug companies will be lucky to earn $12.7 billion, up 4%. Sales may rise just 3.5%, to $64.7 billion....Sales and marketing expenses now consume 30% of drug revenues....With managed-care plans on the bandwagon, analyst Mariola B. Haggar of Salomon Brothers Inc. says more than 40% of U.S. prescriptions will be written for cheaper generic substitutes in 1994, up from 36% last year." (p85)

Weber, Joseph. "High Technology: Pharmaceuticals: A Big Dose of Uncertainty." Business Week n3353, 10 Jan 1994. p85. (ISSN0007-7135).

PHILADELPHIA (PA)

see also COMMUTING--PHILADELPHIA (PA); CRIMINAL JUSTICE, ADMINISTRATION OF--PHILADELPHIA (PA)

PHILADELPHIA (PA)--EMPLOYMENT

"For the past four years, employment in Philadelphia has declined at an average annual rate of 1.6 percent, and the city's current 9.2 percent unemployment rate is the seventh worst among the top 25 urban centers in America. Although Philadelphia's tourism-related employment increased by 22 percent in the 1980s, the gain paled compared with the 58 percent increase in tourism jobs across the nation." (p60)

Cohen, Warren. "Business: Cities Try to Bring Home the Bacon." U.S. News & World Report v116 n4, 31 Jan 1994. p59-60. (ISSN0041-5537).

PHILIPPINES
see also PESTICIDE RESIDUES IN FOOD--PHILIPPINES; PESTICIDES--TOXICOLOGY--PHILIPPINES

PHILIPPINES--ARMED FORCES (v19)

PHILIPPINES--SOCIAL CONDITIONS

"The Philippines have had a slow rate of increase in income per capita, averaging 1.3 percent a year from 1960 to 1990, to a figure of $720 in 1990. Life expectancy at birth is about 63 years, and the infant mortality rate is 45. Adult literacy is 90 percent, and primary plus secondary school enrollment is 97 percent, with females ranking at least as high as males. The rate of natural increase has fallen from about 3 percent in 1960-65 to 2.5 percent....A series of national surveys shows a drop in contraceptive prevalence from 38.5 percent in 1978 to 32.0 percent in 1983, and again from 45.8 percent in 1986 to 36.1 percent in 1988. Use of modern methods of contraception, excluding condoms, has increased in each successive survey, although the increase from 1986 to 1988 was only 20.7 percent to 20.9 percent....Total fertility rates declined from 6.29 in 1963-67 to 5.28 in 1978-82 (Casterline et al., 1988), and to 4.26 in 1983-87 (World Bank, 1991)." (p84-85)

Mauldin, W. Parker/Ross, John A. "Prospects and Programs for Fertility Reduction, 1990-2015." Studies in Family Planning v25 n2, Mar-Apr 1994. p77-95. (ISSN0039-3665).

PHOSPHATES--U.S.

"Today, industry publications indicate that the overall amounts of phosphates in household laundry detergent will decline to some 25,000 short tons in 1994. In 1976, the amount of phosphates in household detergents was estimated to be some 423,000 short tons. In addition, this decline will continue as a result of the recent decision by Procter & Gamble to convert its flagship product--Tide with Bleach--to a nonphosphate formulation. Procter & Gamble products are thought to account for about half of all household laundry products." (pS1522-1523)

Mitchell, George G. (Sen.-Maine). "Clean Lakes Legislation," Congressional Record (11 Feb 1994). Daily ed. pS1522-1523. (ISSN0363-7239).

PHOTOVOLTAIC POWER GENERATION--U.S. (v19)

PHYSICAL FITNESS--U.S. (v19)

PHYSICIAN SERVICES UTILIZATION--U.S. (v19)

PHYSICIANS' ASSISTANTS--U.S. (v19)

PHYSICIANS--EDUCATION--U.S. (v19)

PHYSICIANS--MALPRACTICE--GREAT BRITAIN (v19)

PHYSICIANS--MALPRACTICE--U.S. (v19)

PHYSICIANS--SALARIES, ETC.--U.S. (v19)

PHYSICIANS--SUPPLY AND DEMAND--U.S. (v19)

PHYSICIANS--U.S. (v19)

PINBALL MACHINES--U.S. (v19)

PIPELINES--U.S.--ACCIDENTS

"For the years 1988 to 1992, hazardous liquid pipelines [in the U.S.] averaged fewer accidents annually than the natural gas pipeline systems (transmission, distribution, and gathering combined). During that period, 1204 incidents were reported by natural gas pipeline operators as opposed to the 980 reported by hazardous liquid pipeline operators. Hazardous liquid pipeline incidents also resulted in fewer deaths and injuries than natural gas pipeline incidents. For the years 1988 to 1992, 114 deaths and 485 injuries resulted from natural gas pipeline systems as opposed to the 13 deaths and 110 injuries resulting from hazardous liquid pipeline systems." (p928)

U.S. House. Committee on Appropriations. "Department of Transportation and Related Agencies Approp. for 1994 (Part 5)." Hearing, Washington, D.C.: GPO, 1993. (ISBN0160410509). (Y4.Ap6/1:T68/4/994/pt.5).

PLAGUE

"Although human plague is often regarded as a terrible disease of the past--the 'Black Death' killed countless millions in Europe alone during the Middle Ages--it continues to claim lives in Africa, Asia, North America and South America, according to latest figures from the World Health Organization....A total of 267 cases, including 70 deaths, in Zaire in 1993 have been reported officially to WHO [World Health Organization]....For 1992, the last full year for which figures are available, nine countries reported a total of 1,768 cases, including 198 deaths, to WHO. During the 15 years from 1978 to 1992, 14,856 cases were reported, including 1,451 deaths, in 21 countries....The nine countries in which plague was known to have occurred in 1992 were Madagascar (198 cases, 26 deaths) and Zaire (390 cases, 140 deaths) in Africa; Brazil (25 cases, no deaths) and Peru (120 cases, four deaths) in South America; the United States of America (13 cases, 2 deaths); and among Asian countries, China (35 cases, six deaths), Mongolia (12 cases, four deaths), Myanmar (528 cases, three deaths) and Viet Nam (437 cases, 13 deaths)." (p1)

News release. "Plague Still a Killer Disease in Many Countries, Warns WHO." WHO Press 2 Mar 1994. p1-2.

PLANNED PARENTHOOD
see BIRTH CONTROL

PLANTS--U.S. (v19)

PLANTS, MEDICINAL
see MEDICINAL PLANTS

PLASTICS--U.S.--RECYCLING (v19)

"Plastics recycling rates are low and growing only lethargically. From 1991 to 1992, recycling of all plastics rose from 2.3% to 2.9%, while recycling of plastic packaging rose from 4.8% to 6.5%....Growth in production of virgin plastic outpaced growth in recycling by almost 10 to 1 for all plastics, and by almost 4 to 1 for plastic packaging....There have been few success stories in plastics recycling. One is that about 40% of plastic soft drink bottles are recycled, largely as a result of collection in states with bottle deposit programs. (But even here, increases in production have outstripped the growth in recycling.) And almost 25% of plastic milk and water jugs are recycled. Less than 2% of all other major types of plastic packaging is recycled, however. For example, polystyrene packaging (foam coffee cups, for example) was recycled at a rate of only 1.5% in 1992, barely up from the 1991 rate of 1.2%. These rates pale in comparison to the polystyrene industry's much-touted goal of recycling 25% of all polystyrene packaging by 1995." (p4)

Denison, Richard A. "EDF Column: It's Time to Take Another Look at Plastics Recycling." EDF Letter v24 n6, Nov 1993. p4. (ISSN0163-2566).

PLUTONIUM

"Plutonium is readily absorbed by the body and can remain there for decades. As little as .000001 ounce of plutonium-239, the radioisotope of plutonium used to fuel nuclear weapons, may be sufficient to cause lung cancer if inhaled in fine particles. With an estimated half-life of 24,000 years, half of the plutonium-239 that exists in 1994 will still be around in the year 25994. It will continue to emit radiation and remain a potential threat to life for about 10 half-lives--in other words, 240,000 years, or about 10,000 human generations!" (p2)

"Nuclear Threat at Home: The Cold War's Lethal Leftovers." Defense Monitor v23 n2, 1994. p1-3,7. (ISSN0195-6450).

"With the end of the Cold War, some 50 tons of excess plutonium resulting from the dismantlement of many thousands of nuclear weapons present 'a clear and present danger' to international security that must be dealt with promptly, concludes a new report from a committee of the National Academy of Sciences."

(p1) "In addition to plutonium used for weapons, there are hundreds of tons of civilian plutonium in spent fuel around the world, a by-product of the nuclear power industry. Another 60-70 tons are produced every year. Some of this material is being separated from the spent fuel for use as reactor fuel, although such an approach is currently more costly than using uranium. As of late 1992, some 86 tons of plutonium separated from spent fuel from nuclear reactors were in storage worldwide." (p4)

News release. "Specific Steps Must Be Taken to Reduce Plutonium Security Risks." National Academy of Sciences News 24 Jan 1994. p1-5.

PLUTONIUM--U.S.

"Currently, about 37 metric tons of weapons-grade plutonium is contained in nuclear warheads or stored at the government's weapons disassembly plant in the Texas Panhandle. The estimated cost of manufacturing the plutonium has exceeded $100 billion, which was arguably, in the aftermath of the Cold War, money well spent. Now, that same plutonium is a peace dividend or a giant headache, depending on your perspective, and the government is faced with the question of what to do with it." (p25)

Simonson, Scott. "Symposium: Don't Be Fuelish with Warheads." Insight v10 n4, 24 Jan 1994. p25-27. (ISSN1051-4880).

"It may...be argued that disposal of vitrified plutonium is less hazardous than disposal of the residue from reactor burning of the same plutonium, since the spent fuel still contains up to 70 percent of the original plutonium, and it contains...highly undesirable radioactive waste products....The cost of vitrification has to be considered in the context of the overall cost of nuclear waste cleanup as well as disarmament, which will exceed $200 billion, reports the [U.S.] Energy Department. Vitrifying and disposing of the entire 37 tons of existing plutonium will cost between $1 billion and $2 billion, according to the department's Savannah River Laboratories. Alternatively, burning plutonium will likely be even more costly. The Energy Department estimates that, even with the gain of electrical power from plutonium-fueled power plants factored in, the cost of producing and burning plutonium in the gas-cooled reactor would be approximately $2.7 billion." (p27)

Simonson, Scott. "Symposium: Don't Be Fuelish with Warheads." Insight v10 n4, 24 Jan 1994. p25-27. (ISSN1051-4880).

POACHING--YELLOWSTONE NATIONAL PARK

"Joel Scrafford, the U.S. Fish and Wildlife agent who assists in Yellowstone poaching investigations, says he has noticed a marked increase in poaching since 1989. Not only are rangers apprehending poachers at the park's borders, but they are also getting them two and three miles inside park boundaries, he says. But rangers must give priority to visitors and emergencies: 'Wildlife falls between the cracks,' he says. 'For every one poacher caught, nearly 90 percent aren't.' The estimated fewer than 10 percent of all poachers caught face penalties under the Lacey Act, including fines up to $250,000, confiscation of their equipment, and five years in prison." (p14)

McKeever, Lauren. "Poachers Zero in on Yellowstone's Prized Wildlife." High Country News v25 n24, 27 Dec 1993. p14. (ISSN0191-5657).

Donald E. Lewis, "A professional hunter who pleaded guilty in July to killing three elk in Yellowstone National Park in August had actually hunted in the premier national park for the last nine years, according to federal records....'This hunt in the park is the most blatant example of trophy poaching that I have encountered in my 30 years of investigating wildlife crime,' lead agent Joel Scrafford wrote in April to Assistant U.S. Attorney Christopher Crofts, the prosecutor handling the case. In Yellowstone Park alone, where wildlife is protected, Lewis and his companions killed approximately 14 elk since 1983, records show. Some years they set up hunting camps inside the park....A July plea bargain let Lewis and his hunting partner Arthur Sims, of Huntsville, Ala., each plead guilty by mail to three misdemeanor charges of poaching elk in the national park in 1991. U.S. Magistrate John Brooks of Casper, Wyo., fined each the maximum $5,000 for each of the three elk they pleaded guilty to killing and banned them from hunting and national parks for five years. Neither received any jail time, except for 60 days Lewis was already serving in Utah for poaching eight mule deer there." (p13)

Milstein, Michael. "Poacher Gets Light Sentence." High Country News v25 n24, 27 Dec 1993. p13-14. (ISSN0191-5657).

POISONING

see also FOOD POISONING

POISONING--ZIMBABWE

"Petroleum distillates such as kerosene or paraffin, if taken by mouth, may cause oedema (fluid) in the lung. A high prevalence of accidental paraffin poisoning of children has been reported among poor communities in countries as far apart as India, Turkey, Uganda and Zimbabwe. A study in Zimbabwe focusing on poisoning admissions in six major hospitals found that household chemicals represented the second biggest cause (1192 cases) of admissions, after traditional medicines (1378 cases). Some 12% were suicides or attempted suicides and 285 of the 1192 cases died. Paraffin alone accounted for about 20% of cases of poisoning in children involving household chemicals; most of the victims were under five years of age. In country areas without electricity, paraffin is the main source of fuel, and it is a commonly used cooking fuel in city slums." (p24)

Kasilo, Ossy M. J./Nhachi, Charles F. B. "Danger: Poison!" World Health n5, Sep-Oct 1993. p24-25. (ISSN0043-8502).

POLAND

see also DRUG TRAFFIC--POLAND; PRIVATIZATION--POLAND; SINGLE MOTHERS--EMPLOYMENT--POLAND

POLAND--ECONOMIC CONDITIOINS

"Despite the explosion in new firms [in Poland], unemployment was on the rise--from less than 3 per cent in 1989 to 10 per cent by 1991 (and to 16 per cent by 1993)....Meanwhile, far from tight budgets or monetary policy, the government ran deficits equivalent to 6-8 per cent of GDP [gross domestic product], and uncollectible bank loans approached 25-30 per cent of all outstanding loans. Far from maintaining a stable zloty, the currency fell more than 70 per cent in two years against the dollar. By late 1991, the Poles had wandered so far from therapists' [economists advocating 'shock therapy' economic reforms] demands that the International Monetary Fund (IMF)--assigned as the watchdog of the Polish transformation--suspended a $2.5 billion aid package in an attempt to pressure wayward Warsaw back on course." (p56)

Parker, Richard. "Clintonomics for the East." Foreign Policy n94, Spr 1994. p53-68. (ISSN0015-7228).

POLAND--ECONOMIC CONDITIONS (v19)

POLAND--POLITICS AND GOVERNMENT (v19)

POLAND--SOCIAL CONDITIONS

"Almost the entire population [of Poland] (97.6 percent) is ethnically Polish, with Germans and people from the former Soviet Union forming small minorities. Most of the country (95 percent) is Roman Catholic....Economic hardship and housing shortages have historically constrained childbearing, and Polish women average about 2.0 children in their lifetimes. This is a bit higher, however, than the Eastern European average of 1.8 children. About four-fifths of Polish women of reproductive age use contraception, according to the United Nations Population

Fund. However, fully half of these women use 'traditional' methods of birth control (withdrawal or the calendar rhythm method), which are less reliable than modern methods. Contraceptives produced within the country are not widely available, nor are they of good quality. As a result, many Polish women rely on induced abortion." (p11)

Sherk, Kirsten. "Spotlight: Poland." Population Today v21 n12, Dec 1993. p11. (ISSN0749-2448).

POLICE--ARIZONA (v19)

POLICE--GREAT BRITAIN (v19)

POLICE--LOS ANGELES (CALIF) (v19)

POLICE--POLAND (v19)

POLICE--SOUTH AFRICA (v19)

POLICE--SOUTH AFRICA--MORTALITY (v19)

POLICE--U.S. (v19)

"Today, 3.3 violent crimes are committed [in the U.S.] for every police officer. Twenty-five years ago, the ratio was exactly the opposite. Private businesses find it necessary to employ 1.5 million security guards, but there are only 535,000 police to protect the entire nation." (p67)

Zuckerman, Mortimer B. "Editorial: War on Crime, by the Numbers." U.S. News & World Report v116 n2, 17 Jan 1994. p67-68. (ISSN0041-5537).

POLICE--U.S.--COMPLAINTS AGAINST (v19)

POLICE--U.S.--JOB STRESS (v19)

POLICE--WASHINGTON (D.C.)

"Washington, DC, with a population of 589,000 has 5,213 police officers...Utah, with a population more than three times that of Washington DC--1.8 million versus 500,000--actually has fewer police officers--we only have 2,979--than the District of Columbia. Utah has only 16 officers per 10,000 population. In contrast, the District of Columbia has 89 officers per 10,000--nearly 3 times as many as almost every other jurisdiction. We need to get more officers to rural areas where the violent crime problem is increasing at a greater rate." (pS1315)

Hatch, Orrin G. (Sen.-Utah). "Drug Control and Rural Crime in America," Congressional Record (10 Feb 1994). Daily ed. pS1314-1315. (ISSN0363-7239).

"Qualification requirements for [Washington,] D.C. cops are lax. In May 1985, a recruit to the police academy could be expelled for failing two exams; 7 months later the same recruit had to fail six exams to be sent packing. Finally, in 1988, after 40 percent of graduating recruits failed the final comprehensive exam, the police academy abolished the test....Former Washington cop Montague Holmes states that because of the lax hiring procedures 'a lot of people who were in the drug rackets joined the police department. Some of them went straight when they joined the department, some of them didn't.' The [WALL STREET] JOURNAL reports that last year, 36 officers were indicted on charges such as dope dealing, sexual assault, murder, sodomy, and kidnaping. In another incident, thousands of confiscated weapons [were] being stolen from a police warehouse by employees. At least one of these weapons was later used in a murder." (pH10560)

DeLay, Tom (Rep.-Tex.). "New Columbia Admission Act," Congressional Record (21 Nov 1993). Daily ed. pH10559-10575. (ISSN0363-7239).

POLIOMYELITIS (v19)

"The number of countries reporting zero incidence of poliomyelitis rose to 141 in 1993, the highest ever recorded. A total of 7898 cases was registered in 46 countries during the year, or less than half of the 15 911 cases which occurred in 58 countries in 1992. These figures are contained in a report released...in Geneva by the World Health Organization (WHO)....In both 1989 and 1990, epidemics of approximately 5000 cases of paralytic poliomyelitis were recorded in China. Since those days, supplementary doses of oral polio vaccine to children less than four years of age were administered in 25 out of 30 provinces in China. As a result, the number of reported cases dropped to 344 in 1993. However, the biggest event was the first National Immunization Day when an estimated 100 million children under four years of age were vaccinated in December 1993, followed by a supplementary dose in January 1994. That was the biggest number of children ever immunized against a disease anywhere in the world." (p1-2)

News release. "Poliomyelitis Eradication: 141 Polio-Free Countries Reported in 1993." WHO Press 8 Apr 1994. p1-2.

POLIOMYELITIS--EUROPE

"Europe reported 187 cases of poliomyelitis in 1993; 161 cases--or 86% of the total--were reported from nine of the Newly Independent States of the former Soviet Union; Azerbaijan and Uzbekistan reported outbreaks of 64 and 68 cases respectively. Both of these outbreaks resulted from vaccine shortages which developed following independence. Inadequate vaccine supply for the Newly Independent States represents a continuing threat to the region....Against the backdrop of almost universal decline in the number of reported polio cases there is one Region--the Eastern Mediterranean--which reported a 24% increase in polio incidence last year. There were 2360 cases in 1993, while in 1992 there were 1901 registered cases. For the most part, the increase is due to large outbreaks of the disease in Pakistan and Sudan. Pakistan reported 1803 cases in 1993, a 72% increase over the 1046 cases reported in 1992." (p1)

News release. "Poliomyelitis Eradication: 141 Polio-Free Countries Reported in 1993." WHO Press 8 Apr 1994. p1-2.

POLITICAL ACTION COMMITTEES--U.S. (v19)

POLITICAL CORRECTNESS--U.S.

"Some dismiss political correctness (PC) as an irrelevance hyped up by the right; others see it as a leftist danger to the very fabric of American life; stil others argue that it is plain passe. Is America in the throes of neo-PC, anti-PC or post-PC? It is hard to tell. So much the better for the PC industry. For that is what political correctness has become. It is no longer a matter of who wins or loses the arguments. The arguments themselves are what sustain the industry. Competition in the PC business is not only healthy, it is essential. Few industries can boast such rapid growth as this one. A computer search by the NEW YORK TIMES found 103 newspaper references to 'political correctness' in 1988. In 1993 the number was roughly 10,000." (p27)

"American Survey: An All-American Industry." Economist v329 n7843, 25 Dec 1993. p27-28. (ISSN0013-0613).

POLITICAL CORRUPTION--RUSSIA (v19)

POLITICAL PARTICIPATION--U.S. (v19)

POLITICAL PARTIES

see also COMMUNIST PARTIES

POLITICAL PARTIES--NEPAL (v19)

POLITICAL PARTIES--NICARAGUA--PUBLIC OPINION

"A study sponsored by the United Nations Development Program has shown that most Nicaraguans surveyed have little or no faith in political parties or politicians as the legitimate mediators in the country's efforts to overcome the economic and political crisis. According to the study, those interviewed (43.5% of whom voted for the present government and 35% for the FSLN [Sandinista National Liberation Front]) think that the political parties are hampering the peace process. Some 66.3% believe that the parties have no interest in the most pressing concerns of the people and 49.1% said that, at the moment, they do not back any specific political party." (p7)

"News: Society: No Faith in Parties or Politicians." Barricada Internacional v13 n361, May 1993. p7. (ISSN1013-9567).

POLITICAL SCIENCE

"Faced with conditions that constitute nothing less than a planetary emergency, governments are stuck in a kind of global gridlock, unable or unwilling to break free of domestic politics or narrow self-interests to act for the common good. The world's governments spend some 2,000 times more on national arms than on U.N. peacekeeping. Meanwhile, 40,000 children die every day from lack of food and basic health care." (p8)

Yost, Jack. "Editorial: A Democratic United Nations." World Federalist News i24, Jun 1993. p8.

POLITICIANS, WOMEN

see WOMEN IN POLITICS

POLLUTION

see also AIR--POLLUTION; AUTOMOBILES--U.S.--POLLUTION CONTROL DEVICES; SOIL POLLUTION--U.S.; WATER--POLLUTION

see also AIR--POLLUTION; ELECTRIC POWER-PLANTS--ENVIRONMENTAL ASPECTS; SOIL POLLUTION; WATER--POLLUTION

POLLUTION--BLACK SEA

"'If no emergency measures are taken to save the [Black] sea, in 10 to 15 years it will die', says Simeon Nicolaev, director of the Rumanian Marine Research Institute in Constanta. Fish catches have dropped from 900,000 tonnes in 1986 to 100,000 tonnes in 1992 because of 'eutrophication', or over-fertilisation by organic matter from land-based sources. The Black Sea receives discharges from 17 countries through major rivers like the Danube, Don, Dnepr and Dnestr, plus domestic and industrial waste from the coastal states. This organic waste consumes oxygen in the water as it decomposes and then produces poisonous hydrogen sulphide as a byproduct. There is no dissolved oxygen below about 150 metres in the Black Sea and scientists have proclaimed these lower depths biologically dead." (p27)

Dvoretsky, Vladimir. "Tackling the Polluters: Time Running Out for Black Sea." Panoscope n38, Jan 1994. p27. (ISSN0951-8819).

POLLUTION--CALUMET REGION (LAKE MICHIGAN)

The Calumet Region of Lake Michigan "encompasses 140 square miles stretching from Chicago's Southeast Side to Northwest Indiana, including Gary, Hammond, Whiting and East Chicago, Ind., as well as the Illinois towns of Calumet City, Dolton and Burnham. Its population is diverse: 419,000 people--178,000 in Illinois, 241,000 in Indiana, 53 percent white; 42 percent black; 15 percent Hispanic. It is also the site for more than 25 percent of the nation's steel manufacturing....As a result, pollution is astounding. The Indiana portion of the region contains four Superfund sites on the National Priorities List, and as many as 52 sites designated as potential uncontrolled hazardous waste sites. The Grand Calumet River and Indiana Ship Canal, which contain between 4 million and 5 million cubic yards of contaminated sediments, receive point discharges totalling a billion gallons per day, 90 percent of their total flow. In addition, some 180 million pounds of contaminated sediment enter Lake Michigan each year from the harbor, creating a three-mile plume of pollutants which is approaching municipal water intakes." (p10-11)

"Industry's Polluted Legacy: The Calumet Region." Neighborhood Works v16 n5, Oct-Nov 1993. p10-11.

POLLUTION--CHICAGO (ILL)--HEALTH AND HYGIENE

People for Community Recovery (PCR) conducted "a health survey in 1992 of more than 800 project residents [on the south side of Chicago] with the help of the University of Illinois School of Health and Dr. Robert Ginsburg, a toxicologist formerly with Citizens for a Better Environment. This...assessment showed 27 percent of residents surveyed suffered from asthma, bronchitis or emphysema, and that 68 percent of those suffering from such ailments found their symptoms improving when they left the area for extended periods. Even more disturbing was the fact that more than half of the 270 pregnancies reported in the survey resulted in miscarriage, stillbirths, premature births or babies who required special medical care for birth defects or other serious health problems, according to Dr. Herbert White, Jr., regional medical director of occupational and environmental medicine at St. James Hospital in Chicago." (p10)

Sennett, Frank. "An Urban Refusal." Neighborhood Works v16 n5, Oct-Nov 1993. p9-13.

POLLUTION--DEVELOPING COUNTRIES (v19)

POLLUTION--EL PASO (TEX)--JUAREZ (MEXICO)

"El Paso, Texas, with only about 500,000 people and little heavy industry, has the seventh worst air pollution in the country. The city could lose Federal funds unless it can comply with the Clean Air Act, but it has already done just about all it can on its own to improve air quality....El Paso's dilemma is that a large part of its air pollution comes from across the border in Juarez, Mexico, beyond its control....In Juarez, rapid urbanization and widespread poverty have led to a variety of social problems, with limited revenues to address them. Population nearly doubled in the last 10 years, to 1.2 million, as people were drawn by the 'maquiladoras,' foreign-owned plants built after Mexico liberalized restrictions on foreign investment. There are some 300 to 350 maquiladoras in or near Juarez, mostly assembly plants that import parts and export finished products. Carbon monoxide, ground-level ozone, and particulate matter are serious air pollution problems in the Juarez area. Incomplete combustion of fuel--from automobiles, backyard brick ovens, trash fires, and spontaneous combustion in landfills--is a major source of these pollutants. Unpaved streets are a significant source of particulate matter, as are blowing soil, open-bed trucks, and quarries." (p7)

"El Paso Air Pollution: A Dilemma and a Novel Solution." EDF Letter v24 n4, Jul 1993. p7. (ISSN0163-2566).

POLLUTION--HEALTH AND HYGIENE (v19)

POLLUTION--INDIANA

"Nowhere is pollution in the [Great Lakes] basin more glaring than amid the factories and dunes along northwest Indiana's lakeshore....Steel mills on the lakeshore produce 25 percent of the nation's steel, alongside fossil fuel plants, four oil refineries, and many other factories. In the past century, industry has left behind five federally mandated Superfund toxic-waste cleanup sites and more than 400 other places requiring government-managed clean-ups. Moreover, one-third of the 452 underground storage tanks registered in the area leak harmful chemicals, according to the Indiana Department of Environmental Management. Much of the waste from the dunes flows into the Grand Calumet River in Gary and East Chicago, Ind., and the Indiana Harbor Ship Canal, an area widely considered the dirtiest of 42 polluted sites identified by the International Joint Commission....Each day, industries dump more than 1 billion gallons of waste into the river and canal, adding to the 5 million cubic yards of contaminated sediment already there. Each year some 150,000 cubic yards of the poisonous outflow drains into Lake Michigan." (p12)

Tyson, James L. "Cover Story: Delicate Ecosystem, Heavy Industry." The Christian Science Monitor v86 n75, 14 Mar 1994. p11-13. (ISSN0882-7729).

POLLUTION--MEREBANK (SOUTH AFRICA)

"Sunlight may be shimmering on the sandy beaches of Durban, but a thick cloud seems to hang perpetually over nearby Merebank, blocking much of the South African sunshine. The 40,000 mainly Asian and mixed-race residents of Merebank are surrounded by chemical plants spewing the noxious gases responsible for the hazy atmosphere. Two major oil refineries are situated within a mile-and-a-half radius of the community's center, while the giant Mondi Paper Co. and a chromium processing facility operate practically in the residents' backyards. An aerial view shows that the pollution is not confined to Merebank but also affects the approximately 200,000 people living in segregated townships to the south of Durban. The same perspective also reveals that the factories' waste streams merge into a single river of filth before emptying into the Indian Ocean at a favorite fishing spot. A 1990 health survey found that primary school children in Merebank have almost twice as much chance of acquiring coughs, colds, and flus than does a socially and economically similar group of children 10 miles away. In another survey, 70 percent of those interviewed in Merebank complained of respiratory disorders." (p6)

Kalan, Heeten. "Apartheid and the Environment: Polluting the Poor." Toward Freedom v42 n8, Dec 1993-Jan 1994. p6,8. (ISSN0048-9898).

POLLUTION--MINNESOTA

"The Minnesota Pollution Control Agency (MPCA) has identified coal combustion as the largest source of man-made mercury emissions in Minnesota. Once emitted from smokestacks, this highly toxic and persistent pollutant is transported through the atmosphere and deposited in watersheds. The MPCA has found that mercury concentrations in fish have been increasing at a rate of 3 percent to 5 percent a year. As a result, fish consumption advisories have been issued; presently, 97 percent of Minnesota lakes exceed the health restrictions of one meal of fish per week due to mercury contamination. Mercury pollution also threatens fish-eating birds and mammals, such as loons, otter and mink. A recent MPCA study revealed that Minnesota loon populations show elevated levels of mercury residues, causing disease, death and possibly reproductive impairments." (p32)

Grant, William. "Power to Spare." Outdoor America v58 n1, Win 1993. p31-33.

POLLUTION--POLAND (v19)

POLLUTION--TAIWAN

"Taiwan's reputation as being the dirtiest place in Asia is well deserved. The lower reaches of almost all the island's 44 rivers are nearing biological death due to unregulated industrial and human waste dumping. The government itself admits that 20% of farmland is now polluted by industrial waste water, so that about a third of the island's rice crop is contaminated beyond officially tolerated levels with heavy metals, including mercury, arsenic and cadmium. Not surprisingly, cancer is now the island's leading cause of death. Taiwan's air is no better. Suffused with high levels of sulphur dioxide, air quality in the capital is officially designated harmful 17% of the year by already lenient Taiwan standards. Asthma cases among children quadrupled between 1980 and 1990." (p2-3)

Bello, Walden. "World: Growing Pains of the Asian 'Tigers.'" Panoscope n35, Apr 1993. p2-5. (ISSN0951-8819).

POLLUTION--U.S. (v19)

POOR (v19)

"The areas of poverty in the...100 largest central cities [in the U.S.] are spreading. The incidence of neighborhoods in which at least 20 percent of families are poor has increased from 34 percent of cities' census tracts in 1980 to 39 percent in 1990. Neighborhoods which are extremely poor, those with a poverty rate of at least 40 percent, increased from 9.7 percent of city tracts in 1980 to 13.7 percent in 1990....The likelihood that a city resident would live in a distressed neighborhood, one with disproportionately high levels of poverty, joblessness, female headed families and welfare receipt has increased dramatically, from less than 1 in 50 in 1970 to more than 1 in 10 in 1990. The likelihood that a city dweller would live in an extremely poor neighborhood, 40 percent poverty rate or higher, more than doubled from 5.2 percent in 1970 to 10.7 in 1990." (p11)

Bane, Mary Jo (Asst. Secretary, Children and Families, U.S. Dept. of Health and Human Services). U.S. House. Committee on Ways and Means. "Children and Families at Risk in Deteriorating Communities." Hearing, 7 Dec 1993. Washington, D.C.: GPO, 1993. (ISBN0160436567). (Y4.W36:103-43).

POOR--AFRICA

The "recently published report on 'Implementing the World Bank's Strategy to Reduce Poverty' says that for poverty to fall, consumption in Africa must grow by at least 4.7 per cent a year. But the projected rate will at best be only 3.3 per cent, which is lower than in all other world regions. This grim news follows years of decline in which the number of poor in sub-Saharan Africa rose from 184 million in 1985 to 216 million in 1990. While this ratio of 47.8 per cent of the population is lower than in South Asia (49 per cent), poverty in that region is declining, and in sub-Saharan Africa the depth of poverty--how poor people actually are--is far worse than anywhere else in the world." (p30)

"Poverty Will Deepen in Africa: World Bank Poverty Report." Africa Recovery v7 n1, Jun 1993. p30.

POOR--AFRO-AMERICANS

"Black Americans have the highest poverty rate of any racial or ethnic group in the United States....This is not news. The black poverty rate has been about three times the white poverty for many years. About a third of the black population in the United States lives in poverty today. However, the number of African-Americans living in poverty today is greater than at any time in recent history: today, over 10.6 million black citizens live in poverty, 4.9 million are children, 887,000 are elderly. This has been a fairly steady increase, mirroring population increases overall....However, not only is poverty among black Americans more pervasive, it is more severe....today almost 12 percent of black households have incomes of less than $5,000 compared to just 3.6 percent of whites and 6.6 percent of Hispanics. This means that over 1.3 million black households have annual incomes of under $5000. And fully 42 percent of black households can be called low-income--i.e., have annual incomes of under $15,000. About 22 percent of white households had low incomes. In 1992, almost one of every four households in the United States had an income of less than $15,000--of these 22.7 million low income households, 4.7 million were headed by an African-American." (p148)

McFate, Katherine (Joint Center for Political and Economic Studies). U.S. House. Committee on Ways and Means. "Historical Trends in Poverty and Family Income." Hearing, 26 Oct 1993. Washington, D.C.: GPO, 1994. (ISBN0160435765). (Y4.W36:103-42).

"Poverty has been the condition for most Black Americans in this country until well into the twentieth century. In 1939, 'The odds that a black person would be in poverty (the ratio of the poverty to the nonpoverty populations) were 7 times higher than those for a white.' Beginning in the 1950s and for the next couple of decades, poverty began to decline for African Americans. But even in its decline, the poverty rate for Blacks was 30 percent in 1974 compared to 9 percent for Whites. Present trends in poverty for Black Americans demonstrate that African Americans are not escaping poverty at rates that we should be proud of as a rich and prosperous nation. In 1992, the Census report on poverty notes that the poverty rate for Blacks was 33.3 percent compared to 11.6 percent for Whites. In addition, 'Blacks constituted only 12.6 percent of all persons but 28.8 percent of the poor, a proportion that has fluctuated little since the mid-1960's.' Today, families in poverty are primarily made up of children and their single mothers. American society has tolerated disproportionately high poverty rates for African Americans for too long." (p136)

Tollett, Erica E. (Senior Public Policy Analyst, National Black Child Devel. Inst.). U.S. House. Committee on Ways and Means. "Historical Trends in Poverty and Family Income." Hearing, 26 Oct 1993. Washington, D.C.: GPO, 1994. (ISBN0160435765). (Y4.W36:103-42).

POOR--AFRO-AMERICANS--HISPANIC AMERICANS (v19)

POOR--EDUCATION--U.S.

"More than half the students in [U.S.] schools with the highest concentrations of poverty are low achievers--scoring below the 35th percentile on standardized tests--compared with only 8 percent of students in schools with the lowest poverty concentrations." (p71)

Zuckman, Jill. "Social Policy: Education: Clinton's Chapter 1 Formula Runs Aground in House." Congressional Quarterly v52 n2, 15 Jan 1994. p70-73.

POOR--HAITI

"President Aristide has described Haiti as 'a country that is poor because of the rich.'...Three-quarters of Haitians are peasants who survive on an income equivalent to $1.35 a day. Most struggle as sharecroppers or landless laborers or farm their own tiny plots of exhausted land, hemmed in by expenses that keep them poor. To start their crops, they borrow money at astronomical interest rates--20% per month is not uncommon--and they often have to rent land or tools. (A peasant group in the Central Plateau attests that since most peasants cannot afford the $10 to purchase a hoe, they rent a hoe at 80 cents per week!) The peasants sell their harvest to middle-people, who skim off another layer of profit. Finally, the government uses taxes on necessities and crops to extract 80% of the country's tax revenues from the peasantry, although nearly 90% of the national budget is spent in the city of Port-au-Prince." (p17)

Tilly, Chris. "Letter from Abroad: Haiti's Agony." Dollars and Sense n192, Mar-Apr 1994. p16-19,36-37.

POOR--HISPANIC AMERICANS (v19)

POOR--ILLINOIS

"In Illinois, poor families may be Caucasian, African American, or Hispanic. Although many live in urban settings, many other poor families live in rural communities. In 1960, 12% of Chicago's population lived in poverty; in 1990, it was 22% (U.S. Bureau of the Census, 1990). Although single women and children make up the majority of the poor, recent statistics indicate that in more than 40% of families who are now falling into poverty, both parents are working (Baracik & Shapiro, 1992)." (p47)

Williams, Betty L. "Essay: Reflections on Family Poverty." Families in Society v75 n1, Jan 1994. p47-50. (ISSN1044-3894).

POOR--INDONESIA

"The week before the TIMES published its paean to the virtues of President Suharto's economic record, the statisticians were at it again, insisting that 20,633 urban and rural villages out of a total of 65,554 throughout...[Indonesia] have been classified as 'poor.' This means that nationwide, impoverished villages account for 31.5 percent of the total. The regional breakdown, however, reveals that poverty is far more widespread in the outer islands, mostly in the eastern parts of the archipelago, than in Java and parts of Sumatra. The percentages range from 39.16 percent in Southeast Sulawesi and 40.32 percent in Aceh (North Sumatra) up to 53.96 percent in the Moluccas, 70.59 percent in East Timor, and 77.65 percent in West Papua. Such figures make a mockery of the World Bank's assertion, quoted by the TIMES, that 'conditions of abject poverty (have) dropped from 60 percent two decades ago to 15 percent today.'" (p8-9)

Budiardjo, Carmel. "Indonesian Tyranny: A Price Worth Paying." Lies of Our Times Nov 1993. p8-10. (ISSN1046-7912).

POOR--IOWA (v19)

POOR--LOS ANGELES (CALIF)

"Currently, the poorest of Los Angeles' poor receive $293 per month or $9.76 per day for General Assistance. Out of the 168,000 who are in this program statewide, 103,000 live in Los Angeles County. A proposal, now being reviewed by the county's Board of Supervisors, would cut this aid by 27 percent, down to $212 per month or $7 per day. The government is pushing the poor into a corner where the only alternative is to commit a crime to survive. This proposal, if approved, would save the county $103 million. These millions of dollars are going to be used to beef up the Sheriff's Department to the tune of 1,092 positions. Yet, unable to survive on $7 per day, many of L.A. County's poor will steal for food or rob someone to get the money to buy food. If they get caught they will end up in jail, where it will cost the county $34 per day to keep them behind bars." (p3)

De Rienzo, Guido. "L.A. Budget Hearings Squeeze the Poor." People's Tribune v20 n31, 2 Aug 1993. p3.

POOR--MEXICO (v19)

"According to government statistics, 37 million of 84 million Mexicans live in poverty, despite [President Carlos] Salinas's huge social works program. About 25 percent of Mexicans are farmers, but they receive only 8 percent of the national income." (p29)

Robinson, Linda/Conger, Lucy. "World Report: Mexico's Plague Year." U.S. News & World Report v116 n13, 4 Apr 1994. p28-30. (ISSN0041-5537).

POOR--SOUTH AFRICA

In South Africa, "Fifty-three per cent of Africans live below the poverty line compared to 2 per cent of all whites. The next government will have to do something about the millions unemployed; establish supplemental feeding programs for the 2.3 million people, including 1 million children, who are malnourished; begin programs to help the estimated 12 million people without adequate water supplies; and help electrify the homes of the 80 per cent of all Africans, who are without power." (p131)

Herbst, Jeffrey. "Creating a New South Africa." Foreign Policy n94, Spr 1994. p120-135. (ISSN0015-7228).

"The Development Bank of South Africa recently declared that more than 18 million of the country's 38 million population live below the accepted 'minimum living level' of 750 Rand (US$ 190) a month per household. Black people constitute 95% of people who live below the poverty line, and 8-9 million of these are 'completely destitute', according to the bank." (p10)

Parker, Heather. "Africa: Greening South Africa's Townships." Panoscope n38, Jan 1994. p10-11. (ISSN0951-8819).

POOR--U.S. (v19)

"Adults [in the U.S.] in poor neighborhoods differ in important ways from those in more affluent areas. The social composition of an increasing number of neighborhoods has deteriorated during the 1970s, resulting in an increase in neighborhoods of working-age males not attached to the labor force, households headed by a woman with children, households receiving welfare, and dropouts among the school-age population. Although the poverty rate remained fairly constant from 1970 to 1980, there was a 75 percent increase in the number of census tracts with concentrated poverty, and significantly, a 331 percent increase in the number of underclass neighborhoods." (p67)

Street, Lloyd (Dept. of Human Service Studies, Cornell

University). U.S. House. Committee on Ways and Means. "Children and Families at Risk in Deteriorating Communities." Hearing, 7 Dec 1993. Washington, D.C.: GPO, 1994. (ISBN0160436567). (Y4.W36:103-43).

"There is a clustering of poor people in the 10 largest [U.S.] metropolitan areas. Almost half of all poor persons live in the poorest neighborhoods--those in which at least 40 percent of all residents have poverty-level incomes. The number of persons living in such neighborhoods--referred to as concentrated poverty neighborhoods--is increasing. The 1970s saw a 29.5 increase in the number of poor people living in these neighborhoods, to an estimated 2.45 million. Comparable data is not yet available from the 1990 census. This growth was not evenly distributed. A little over half of all SMSAs [Standard Metropolitan Statistical Areas] showed no change or a decrease in concentrated poverty; the others, especially large cities in the Northeast and Midwest, showed increases in this concentrated poverty (Jargowsky and Bane, 1990; Farley, 1990)." (p66)

Street, Lloyd (Dept. of Human Service Studies, Cornell University). U.S. House. Committee on Ways and Means. "Children and Families at Risk in Deteriorating Communities." Hearing, 7 Dec 1993. Washington, D.C.: GPO, 1994. (ISBN0160436567). (Y4.W36:103-43).

"Today, there is an entire generation of people left isolated, economically depressed, and physically cut off from the social, economic, and cultural opportunities that most of us take for granted. Today, more than 2 million of America's families are poor despite having an adult member of the household work more than 30 hours a week. Today, one in five children under the age of 15 lives in poverty, and 50 percent of all black children under the age of six live in poverty. Today, crime, drugs, random violence, homelessness, AIDS, and inadequate services, diminish the quality of life to a level which can no longer be tolerated." (p9)

Cisneros, Henry G. (Secretary, U.S. Dept. of Housing and Urban Development). U.S. House. Committee on Appropriations. "Depts. of Veterans Affairs and Housing and Urban Development...Approp. for 1994 (Part 6)." Hearing, Washington, D.C.: GPO, 1993. (ISBN0160410754). (Y4.Ap6/1:V64/4/994/pt.6).

"With respect to racial composition of the poor, in 1990, whites constituted about two-thirds of the poor, blacks 29% and Hispanics about 18%. However, about 32% and 28% of black and Hispanic subsets of the populace, respectively, are poor, whereas only about 11% of whites are poor. The percentage of blacks in the population of the poor remained relatively constant (about 30%) between 1960 and 1990 whereas the percentage of Hispanics increased from 9% (1970) to 18% in 1990. However, earnings of black family-heads relative to whites has deteriorated. According to Darity and Myers, in 1976, the earnings ratio of black to white family-heads was .63, whereas in 1985, it was .59, which means that for every $100 earned by white family-heads in 1976, their black counterparts earned $63 which fell to $59 in 1985. Hence, over this period, relative earnings of black-family heads declined. Furthermore, the proportion of the poor residing in metropolitan areas increased from 44% in 1960 to 73% in 1990, and in the central cities, the resident poor increased from 27% to 42%. The poor are therefore concentrated in metropolitan areas and in the central cities, where blacks constitute a relatively large proportion." (p97)

Henry, C. Michael (Institution for Social and Policy Studies, Yale Univ.). U.S. House. Committee on Ways and Means. "Historical Trends in Poverty and Family Income." Hearing, 26 Oct 1993. Washington, D.C.: GPO, 1994. (ISBN0160435765). (Y4.W36:103-42).

"In 1991, an estimated 20 million people [in the U.S.], 56 percent of the poor, lived in households where someone worked during the year. An even larger share of poor families with children include a worker. Indeed, 5.5 million people live in poor families with children, which includes a member who worked full time, year-round." (p145)

Shapiro, Isaac (Exec. Director, Center for Budget and Policy Priorities). U.S. Congress. Joint Economic Committee. "The 1993 Economic Report of the President." Hearing, 27 Jan 1993. Washington, D.C.: GPO, 1994. (ISBN0160440300). (Y4.Ec:Ec7/2/993/pt.1).

"In 1991, some 6.9 percent of all [U.S.] workers were poor. In 1980, 6.7 percent were poor. Similarly, in 1991, some 2.6 percent of full-time workers were poor, essentially the same as the 2.5 percent rate in 1980. The trend among families with children is more adverse. Some 9.1 percent of families with children in which the head-of-household worked were poor in 1980. By 1991, the poverty rate among these families had risen to 11.2 percent." (p184)

Shapiro, Isaac (Exec. Director, Center for Budget and Policy Priorities). U.S. Congress. Joint Economic Committee. "The 1993 Economic Report of the President." Hearing, 27 Jan 1993. Washington, D.C.: GPO, 1994. (ISBN0160440300). (Y4.Ec:Ec7/2/993/pt.1).

"The U.S. Census Bureau reports that 200,000 persons age 65 and over slipped below the poverty line...[in 1992], boosting the number of those deemed poor to nearly 4 million. As a result, the 65-plus poverty rate rose to 12.9 percent from 12.4 percent in 1991. This was the third straight yearly increase, and marked the highest rate since 1983. (The 1992 rate for all persons was 14.5 percent.)...the Census Bureau reports 1992 poverty rates of 21.9 percent for young people under 18, 18 percent for those 18 through 24 and 16.2 percent for those 75 and older. Census says one out of five women 75 and over was poor in 1992, but only one in 10 men was. Elderly poverty was highest among black women 75 and over--43 percent of them were poor, compared to 32 percent of Hispanic women and 18 percent of white women." (p7)

Lewis, Robert. "'These Are Not the Best of Times.'" AARP Bulletin v35 n1, Jan 1994. p7. (ISSN1044-1123).

"Rural Americans are more likely to be poor than their urban relatives and the gap is growing. Fifty-one percent of rural residents fall into the two poorest quintiles, compared with 37 percent of those in metropolitan areas. In 1987, per capita rural income was only 73 percent of urban per capita income, down from 77 percent in 1979. Thirty-six percent of all rural children live near or below the poverty level, compared with 29 percent in urban areas." (p23)

U.S. Dept. of Agriculture/Stauber, Karl N. "Rural Development: The Diversity of Rural America." Agricultural Outlook Jan-Feb 1994. p23-24.

"National poverty statistics reported by the Congressional Research Service: 20.7 percent of families in which the head of the household had less than a high school education were poor; and 31.7 percent of families in which the head of the household was unemployed were poor. Only 5.7 percent of those families in which the head of the household was employed were poor, compared to the overall family poverty rate of 10.3 percent." (pS16667-16668)

Gorton, Slade (Sen.-Wash.). "The Need for Welfare Reform," Congressional Record (20 Nov 1993). Daily ed. pS16667-16668. (ISSN0363-7239).

"Despite the beginnings of an economic recovery, the U.S. child poverty rate rose for the fourth straight year in 1992. New data released by the U.S. Census Bureau indicates that the numbers of poor white, black and Latino children are at their highest levels since 1965. More than one in five American children (14.6 million) lived in poverty in 1992, up by 276,000 in 1991. An analysis of the Census data by the Children's Defense Fund (CDF) found: Despite a 2.6% growth in the nation's Gross Domestic Product in 1992, and a similar increase in consumer spending, the nation's childhood poverty edged up from 21.8% in 1991 to 21.9% in 1992." (p4)

"Issues in Brief: Number of Poor Children Hits Highest Level in 28 Years." Frontier Win 1994. p4.

"The current poverty figures [in the U.S.] also reflect trends in cash assistance programs, and here we find some very interesting trends over the last 30 years. We have greatly expanded cash assistance to the elderly in this country...and there has been a dramatic reduction in elderly poverty: 35% of the elderly were poor in 1960, 25% of the elderly were poor in 1970, and today 12 or 13% are poor. That's a great success story....As serious as hunger problems are today, they are significantly less severe than they were in the 1960's before the Food Stamp program or most other food assistance programs were widespread. A study in the late 1970's found the nutrition gap between the middle class and the poor narrowed substantially as food assistance programs were created and expanded." (p8)

Greenstein, Robert. "Did We Lose the War on Poverty." Frontier Win 1994. p8-9.

POOR--U.S.--AGED

"Despite a decades-long decline in elderly poverty, the number of older Americans in poverty has increased for the third consecutive year. Totaling nearly 4 million in 1992, they represent an estimated 12.9% of the population. The latest Census Bureau report shows that nearly half (47%) of the women, and a third of the men over age 65 are below two times the poverty level. While the poverty rate for persons of all races aged 65 and over is 12.9%, this statistic more than doubles to over 30% for the black population. According to the American Association of Retired Persons (AARP), in two basic age groups of older Americans, 60-64 and 65+, poverty increased between 1991 and 1992 for both men and women, with the largest increase in men over 65. Although men in this age group saw the single largest rise in poverty, rates among women increased in both age groups. Men between the ages of 60-64 saw a slight decrease from previous years." (p9)

Greenstein, Robert. "Did We Lose the War on Poverty." Frontier Win 1994. p8-9.

POOR--U.S.--ENERGY ASSISTANCE

"In 1990-1991, the United States had an estimated 1,125 million low-income households whose heat source was interrupted due to an inability to pay, according to a report to Congress by the Low Income Home Energy Assistance Program (LIHEAP). The program, which is funded by the US Health and Human Services Department, began in 1981 after the oil-price shocks of the 1970s that drove up the cost of home-heating fuel....By NCAF [National Community Action Foundation] calculations, 28 million Americans meet the federal income guidelines for energy assistance, but of those only 23 percent receive the benefits. The other 77 percent may have been denied benefits because they did not meet narrower state eligibility guidelines or the state programs had run out of funds, or because they never applied. Federal fuel assistance funds peaked at $2.1 billion in 1985. Since then those funds have fallen, along with state funding. State funding dropped from $17 million to $10 million between 1986 and 1992, according to NCAF." (p6)

Horn, Patricia. "National: Poor Pinched to Pay Energy Bill This Winter as States, US Cut Aid." The Christian Science Monitor v86 n62, 23 Feb 1994. p6. (ISSN0882-7729).

POOR--U.S.--MINORITIES

"The changes of the last two decades have had a very profound impact on minority young families, especially those that are black. The median earnings of the heads of young black families with children fell 71 percent from 1973 to 1990 (from $13,860 to $4,030 in 1990 dollars). Their total family incomes from all sources fell 48 percent. The median income of these young black families is now below the federal poverty line for a family of three. In 1973 it was nearly double that poverty line. Two out of three children in young black families now are poor." (p179)

Weill, James D. (General Counsel, Children's Defense Fund). U.S. Congress. Joint Economic Committee. "The 1993 Economic Report of the President." Hearing, 27 Jan 1993. Washington, D.C.: GPO, 1994. (ISBN0160440300). (Y4.Ec:Ec7/2/993/pt.1).

POOR--U.S.--MORTALITY

"A report published in the NEW ENGLAND JOURNAL OF MEDICINE on July 8 reveals that families with incomes of $9,000 or less have a death rate three times higher than families with incomes of more than $25,000. More important, the report found that the early deaths caused by poverty do not discriminate based upon color. For example, the death rate among poor African American men, according to the report, is 5.4 times the rate for African American males who are in higher income brackets. Similarly, the death rate for white men who make $9,000 a year or less is 6.7 times higher than that of white males whose incomes exceed $25,000 per year." (p2)

De Rienzo, Guido. "Guest Editorial: Fighting for Life." People's Tribune v20 n31, 2 Aug 1993. p2.

POOR CHILDREN--HISPANIC AMERICANS

"Although persons under 18 years of age represent more than one-third (34.7%) of the Hispanic population [in the U.S.], almost one-half (48.8%) of the Hispanic poor are children. In 1992, two of every five (39.9%) Latino children were poor, compared to almost half of Black (46.6%) and about one in six (16.6%) White children. Moreover, more than half of all Puerto Rican children (57.9%) lived below the poverty line." (p188)

Perez, Sonia M. (National Council of La Raza). U.S. House. Committee on Ways and Means. "Historical Trends in Poverty and Family Income." Hearing, 26 Oct 1993. Washington, D.C.: GPO, 1994. (ISBN0160435765). (Y4.W36:103-42).

POOR CHILDREN--MICHIGAN

"Washington has failed to acknowledge the desperation in our streets. Poverty is deeper today. Unemployment in our cities is greater. And, hopelessness has a meaner grip on our children than ever in the history of this nation. We now have 36 percent of Michigan children 18 and under who are living in poverty. Nationally one in five children lives in poverty. More than half of all children who live in families without a father are poor. Such high poverty rates among our children will create social and economic costs for our society for years to come. For example, the Michigan Department of Corrections budget in 1983 was $283 million dollars. Now, just 11 years later that same budget is over $1.2 billion dollars! And, still no one feels any safer than they did in 1983." (p7 secB)

Strong, Jerome. "Prevention vs. Punishment." Ann Arbor News 30 Jan 1994. p7 secB.

POOR CHILDREN--U.S. (v19)

"A generation ago white or married-couple young families or those headed by high school graduates were fairly well insulated from poverty [in the U.S.]." However, "In 1990 a child in a family headed by a parent under age 30 was: twice as likely to be poor as a comparable child in 1973; if living with both parents, two and a half times as likely to be poor as in 1973; and nearly three times more likely to have been born out-of-wed lock than his counterpart two decades ago." (p180)

Weill, James D. (General Counsel, Children's Defense Fund). U.S. Congress. Joint Economic Committee. "The 1993 Economic Report of the President." Hearing, 27 Jan 1993. Washington, D.C.: GPO, 1994. (ISBN0160440300). (Y4.Ec:Ec7/2/993/pt.1).

"The economic and social disaster facing young families with children has now reached virtually all of...young families [in the U.S.]. One in four white children in young families is now poor. One in five children in young married-couple families is now poor. And one in three children in families headed by a young high school graduate is now poor. Nearly three-fourths of the increase in poverty among young families since 1973 has occurred outside the nation's central cities. And poverty has grown most rapidly among young families with only one child." (p178)

Weill, James D. (General Counsel, Children's Defense Fund). U.S. Congress. Joint Economic Committee. "The 1993 Economic Report of the President." Hearing, 27 Jan 1993. Washington, D.C.: GPO, 1994. (ISBN0160440300). (Y4.Ec:Ec7/2/993/pt.1).

"In this day and age, no group is more vulnerable than children to the pressures of the city. Before they are old enough to know that life can be better, children in our inner cities awake to the presence of drugs, crime, guns, and violence. We know we are losing the game when in 1990, 20 percent of infants and toddlers lived in poverty. Three New Jersey cities had poverty rates for young children above 25 percent while in other cities and rural areas over 45 percent of all infants and toddlers live in poverty. We know that poor and near poor infants and toddlers are more likely to live in single parent families, are more likely to be immigrants or linguistically isolated, or live in families where the most educated parent has not completed high school. These characteristics place children at high risk for not having the essential support they need to learn effectively or grow to meet their full potential." (pS4712)

Bradley, Bill (Sen.-N.J.). "Head Start Amendments of 1994," Congressional Record (21 Apr 1994). Daily ed. pS4691-4727. (ISSN0363-7239).

"Since...[the U.S.] last reauthorized Head Start in 1990, the number of children growing up in poverty has increased dramatically--and so has the pressure on Head Start programs to help turn the tide. This is most true of the youngest and most vulnerable children--those under the age of 3. The General Accounting Office recently reported a 26-percent increase in the number of infants and toddlers growing up in poverty. Today one out of every five children is born into poverty--twice the rate for the elderly. In Springfield, MA, the figure is one out of every three. In Detroit, it is one out of every two. These figures are an indictment of our society and all that we stand for." (pS4702)

Kennedy, Edward M. (Sen.-Mass.). "Head Start Amendments of 1994," Congressional Record (21 Apr 1994). Daily ed. pS4691-4727. (ISSN0363-7239).

"The number of poor children under the age of 6 in America increased by more than 25 percent during the 1980's. These numbers are worse in urban areas: 47 percent of young children living in the capital of...Connecticut are poor, making Hartford the American city with the second highest child poverty rate. The youngest Americans are also the poorest Americans. Those with political power in this country--adults of working age and senior citizens--have markedly lower poverty rates. And the problem is growing worse: All but three States saw an increase in the number of poor infants and toddlers from 1980 and 1990. The opportunities for overcoming their disadvantages are few: In 1990, only about one in three children aged 3 or 4 participated in a preschool program." (pS4705)

Dodd, Christopher J. (Sen.-Conn.). "Head Start Amendments of 1994," Congressional Record (21 Apr 1994). Daily ed. pS4691-4727. (ISSN0363-7239).

"The US Department of Labor fixes $11,182 a year as the income a family of three needs to exist in minimal comfort. A dollar short of that level is officially defined as the condition of poverty. By 1990 there were four million more of our children whose families were thus identifiably poor than there had been in 1980, and their class has grown to represent one of every five Americans under eighteen." (p33)

Kempton, Murray. "A New Year's Wish." New York Review of Books v41 n3, 3 Feb 1994. p33. (ISSN0028-7504).

"A recent study by Tufts University in Medford, Mass., indicates that poverty among white, black, and Hispanic children under 18 in the US increased by a staggering 47 percent between 1973 and 1992. The result, says the Urban Institute in Washington, is that 1 out of 5 American children--more than 14 million--are in poverty today. That is twice the poverty rate of any other industrialized nation. 'Today, children are the poorest Americans,' reports the National Commission on Children. The majority of children in poverty are white, but about 44 percent of all black children are poor, and 36 percent of Hispanic children are poor. Poverty rates among Hispanic children are growing the fastest." (p2)

Holmstrom, David. "National: As Child Poverty Grows, Report Warns of Crisis." The Christian Science Monitor v86 n44, 27 Jan 1994. p2. (ISSN0882-7729).

POPULATION (v19)

see also AFRICA--POPULATION; AGED--POPULATION; ALBANIA--POPULATION; ALGERIA--POPULATION; ASIAN AMERICANS--POPULATION; ATLANTA (GA)--POPULATION; AUSTRALIA--POPULATION; CALIFORNIA--POPULATION; CHIAPAS (MEXICO)--POPULATION; CHINA--POPULATION; CITIES AND TOWNS--POPULATION; CRIMEA--POPULATION; DEVELOPING COUNTRIES--POPULATION; FAIRFAX COUNTY (VA)--POPULATION; FRANCE--POPULATION; GAZA STRIP--ISRAEL--WEST BANK--POPULATION; GAZA STRIP--WEST BANK--POPULATION; GUATEMALA--POPULATION; HAITI--POPULATION; INDIA--POPULATION; IRELAND--POPULATION--RELIGION; JAPAN--POPULATION; LAS VEGAS (NEV)--POPULATION; LEBANON--POPULATION; MACEDONIA--POPULATION; MEXICO--POPULATION; MIAMI (FLA)--POPULATION; NICARAGUA--POPULATION; RURAL POPULATION--RUSSIA; SLOVAKIA--POPULATION; SOUTH AFRICA--POPULATION; SOUTH ASIA--POPULATION; SOUTH CAROLINA--POPULATION; TAHITI--POPULATION; TEXAS--POPULATION; TURKMENISTAN--POPULATION; U.S.--POPULATION; UZBEKISTAN--POPULATION; WASHINGTON, D.C.--POPULATION

"The last forty years saw the fastest rise in human numbers in all previous history, from only 2.5 billion people in 1950 to 5.6 billion today. This same period saw natural habitats shrinking and species dying at an accelerating rate. The ozone hole appeared, and the threat of global warming emerged. Worse is in store. Each year in the 1980s saw an extra 85 million people on earth. The second half of the 1990s will add an additional 94 million people per year. That is equivalent to a new United States every thirty-three months, another Britain every seven months, a Washington every six days. A whole earth of 1800 was added in just one decade, according to United Nations Population Division statistics. After 2000, annual additions will slow, but by 2050 the United Nations expects the human race to total just over 10 billion--an extra earth of 1980 on top of today's, according to U.N. projections." (p16)

Harrison, Paul. "Sex and the Single Planet." Amicus Journal v15 n4, Win 1994. p16-18,21-23,26. (ISSN0276-7201).

"While sustainable technologies offer some hope of creating new ways of managing natural resources, the task will be prodigious. If consumption and population both double, technology will have to reduce environmental impact per unit of consumption by 75 percent just to maintain current levels of environmental damage.

Population, Paul Harrison writes, 'is the most promising field of action.' For example, Thailand has reduced its fertility rate (number of children per woman) from 6.1 to only 2.3 in twenty years. Sri Lanka, Indonesia, and other countries have had similar experiences. We already know what to do. Unfortunately, family planning services are by no means universally available." (p44)

Meyerson, Fred. "Reviews: The Third Revolution." Amicus Journal v14 n4, Win 1993. p43-44. (ISSN0276-7201).

"For 99.9% of the more than 1 million years that humans have inhabited the earth, the maximum world population was less than 6 million--fewer than the present population of New York City. Population growth during this long period was only about 0.001% per year....At the dawn of the industrial revolution in 1700, the world population stood at less than 1 billion. By 1900 the number had increased to about 1.6 billion. Over that entire 200-year period the average annual rate of population growth never exceeded 0.5% per year. The major increase in the population growth rate that occurred during the last 200 years coincided with the discovery and use of stored fossil energy resources such as coal, oil, and gas. Since then, the increased rate of population growth has closely paralleled the increased use of fossil fuel....The current world population stands at greater than 5 billion (PRB, 1987). Never in history have humans, by their sheer numbers, so dominated the earth and its resources. Demographers project that the world population will reach 6.1 billion by the year 2000, approach 8.2 billion by 2025 (UN, 1982), and probably reach 12 billion by the year 2100. Presently there seems to be no generally accepted way to limit this growth (NAS, 1971, 1975)." (p37)

Pimentel, David/Pimentel, Marcia. "The Demographic and Environmental Consequences of the Green Revolution." Carrying Capacity Network v4 n1, 1994. p37-44. (ISSN1066-5404).

"More alarming than sheer numbers is the status of the annual population growth rate. Around the beginning of the 20th century the rate of population growth increased sharply, first to 1%, and then to 1.5%, and eventually to 2% per year. The rate of increase peaked in the 1970s and at present has begun to decline very slowly. However, in 1988 the growth rate is still about 1.7% or about 1,700 times greater than it was during the first million years of human existence. In addition to the actual rate of growth, there is the age-structure that presently exists in the world population. A large proportion of the world population (e.g., 45% of Africa, 40% of Latin America, and 37% of Asia) is now within child-bearing age (PRB, 1987). In the long term this young age-structure will sustain the rapid population growth rate. For example, with more than half of the Chinese below the age of 20 years, even limiting births to one child per couple will not stop China's population growth (Coale, 1984). If 70% of the couples have only one child, the current population of slightly more than 1 billion (Coale, 1984) will still reach 1.2 billion by the year 2000 (Wren, 1982; Zhao, 1982)." (p38)

Pimentel, David/Pimentel, Marcia. "The Demographic and Environmental Consequences of the Green Revolution." Carrying Capacity Network v4 n1, 1994. p37-44. (ISSN1066-5404).

"The annual addition to the world's population is 95,000,000. With such numbers, we are changing this earth! We are crowding many other animals out of existence. More than 1.5 billion people were added since Earth Day I, 22 years ago. Two to 2.5 billion people could be fed an American diet. Six billion, if vegetarian. But, we have 5.3 billion now. So, some time in 1997 we use up the vegetarian solution." (p4)

Stetzel, Warren. "Gentle on the Land." Community Service Newsletter v41 n1, Jan-Feb 1993. p1-6.

"Scientists agree that the precise relationship between population and environmental destruction is not fully understood. We do know, however, that: Every year farmers around the world are trying to feed 90 million more people with 24 billion fewer tons of topsoil. Desertification from over-grazing and inefficient farming methods is taking 15 million acres out of use each year. Increasing demand for fresh water has diminished our water supplies by trillions of gallons above and below ground. In several regions of northern China, water tables are falling by 12 to 15 feet a year. Parts of Mexico City are sinking as underground aquifers are pumped dry. Approximately one billion people do not get enough food to function. Our species alone co-opts, consumes or eliminates 40 percent of the Earth's basic photosynthetic energy and appropriates two-thirds of the planet's land surface." (p22)

Fonda, Jane. "Forum: High Time for Some Population Intelligence." E Magazine v5 n1, Feb 1994. p22-24. (ISSN1046-8021).

"Slow and uncertain population growth characterized most of human history, with the level of one billion people attained only about 1850. But during the twentieth century population growth has exploded: two billion in 1930, three billion in 1960, four billion in 1975, and five billion in 1987, with more than six billion projected by the year 2000." (p7)

Ravenholt, R. T. "Taking Contraceptives to the World's Poor." Free Inquiry v14 n2, Spr 1994. p7-9,12-13. (ISSN0272-0701).

"As populations age, the child dependency ratio (persons under age 15 to those ages 15 to 64) usually falls and the old-age ratio increases. In developed countries, the child dependency ratio will slip from 32 to 29 between 1990 and 2025. At the same time, the old-age dependency ratio (those age 65 and older to those ages 15 to 64) will rise from 18 to 29. The net result is a projected rise of the overall dependency ratio--from 50 to 58 between 1990 and 2025." (p5)

Bloom, David E./Brender, Adi. "Labor and the Emerging World Economy." Population Bulletin v48 n2, Oct 1993. p2-39. (ISSN0032-468X).

"Instances of disparities in consumption patterns abound among different regions of the world. For example, private automobiles create environmental impacts through the heavy industry it takes to manufacture them, the oil it takes to power them, the roads they need to run on, and the scattered residential patterns they make possible. Four-fifths of the world's 445 million cars are in more developed regions. There are about 12 times as many people as cars in the world. But this proportion varies sharply: 75 people for every car in Africa, 52 people per car in Asia, and between two and five people per car in North America, Central America, Oceania, and Europe." (p2)

De Sherbinin, Alex/Kalish, Susan. "Population-Environment Links: Crucial, but Unwieldy." Population Today v22 n1, Jan 1994. p1-2. (ISSN0749-2448).

"World population has reached 5.6 billion this year and unless a significant number of people opt for smaller families, population will hit 7.9 billion by the year 2020, according to a report issued today by the United States Bureau of the Census. Nine of the 10 people added to the world's population by 2020 will come from developing countries, the report adds. One billion of them will come from Asia alone. Half of the world's population now lives in just six countries: China, India, the US, Indonesia, Brazil, and Russia." (p9)

Baldauf, Scott. "Economic Reports: Developing World Will Claim Huge Share of Population Growth." The Christian Science Monitor v86 n109, 29 Apr 1994. p9.

(ISSN0882-7729).

"World population, which is increasing by about 90 million a year, now stands at 5.5 billion. According to the UN's medium projection, that figure will rise to 8.9 billion by the year 2030 and level off at 11.5 billion by 2150. Most of that increase will come in developing countries, where many people in a relatively young populace are now reaching child-bearing years, and where food supplies already are a problem. For example, United States government demographers estimate that Nigeria will grow from its 1990 level of 87 million people to 278 million by 2030; Bangladesh from 114 million to 243 million; and India from 853 million to nearly 1.5 billion (more than China today)." (p10)

Knickerbocker, Brad. "Economy: The Balance between Food and People Has Become Threatened." The Christian Science Monitor v86 n37, 18 Jan 1994. p10. (ISSN0882-7729).

POPULATION--ENVIRONMENTAL ASPECTS

"Between 1961 and 1985 farmland in developing countries expanded by 0.6 percent a year. Technology change bore no blame for this spread: improved seeds and fertilizers reduced the land needed to produce each ton of food by 2.6 percent a year. The push to increase farm area came from population growth, running at 2.3 percent a year, and consumption of agricultural products per person, growing at 0.9 percent a year. These two factors accounted for 100 percent of the spread. Thus population growth was to blame for 72 percent of the increase in farmed land in developing countries. Using the same method, for the same period, we find that population growth accounted for 69 percent of the growth in livestock numbers in developing countries. By contrast, population growth accounted for only a quarter of the increase in air pollutants in the West between 1970 and 1988--increased consumption levels explained the rest. Population growth accounted for about 40 percent of the increase since 1960 in carbon dioxide emissions, which stoke global warming." (p22)

Harrison, Paul. "Counting Heads, Taking Stock." Amicus Journal v15 n45, Win 1994. p22. (ISSN0276-7201).

POPULATION FORECASTING (v19)

"The world's population is currently 5.6 billion and is expected to reach 6 billion by 2000. The coming generation will see 3 billion people entering their reproductive years, more than the entire world population in 1960. The population could reach 9 billion by 2025. Some parts of the world grow faster than others. If the current pace continues, the population of Africa will double in 20 years." (p22-23)

Waldrop, Judith. "Business Reports: International: This Is Not a Doomsday Scenario." American Demographics v16 n3, Mar 1994. p22-23. (ISSN0163-4089).

"The earth is now inhabited by more than 5.3 billion people. That number is expected to grow to 6.1 billion in the next seven years, and to more than 8.0 billion by the year 2025." (p14)

Darst, B. C./Murphy, L. S. "Keeping Agriculture Viable: Industry's Viewpoint." Journal of Soil and Water Conservation Supplement Mar-Apr 1994. p8-14.

"Mexico currently has a population of about 90 million. If it keeps up its current human growth rate of 2.3 percent, that number will rise to 180 million by 2023. The number of people in Guatemala, a country only slightly smaller than Ohio, could reach 20 million people in about 22 years. And Costa Rica's population, only 3.3 million people at present, may be nearing 6 million by 2025." (p19)

Hren, Ben/Bartolomeo, Nick. "Special Report: Carrying Capacity Project: Bordering on Explosive Growth." Outdoor America v59 n1, Win 1994. p15-22.

"With urban population growth worldwide estimated to increase by 46 per cent in the period 1985-2000 (and with African, Asian and Latin American levels set to grow by, respectively 108 per cent, 70 per cent and 49 per cent), the problem of building infrastructure to accommodate the urban poor and to make the urban environment habitable is becoming more and more challenging." (p8)

Miller, Steve. "Dossier: Improving the Urban Working Environment." World of Work n7, Mar 1994. p8-9. (ISSN1020-0029).

POPULATION FORECASTING--CHINA (v19)

POPULATION FORECASTING--GERMANY

"By 2015, the number of Germans over 65 will rise from 12m to nearly 18m. By 2030, on one estimate, 38% of Germans will be over 60, 16% under 20. According to the OECD [Organization for Economic Cooperation and Development], the present value of future pensions in Germany is 1.6 times current GDP [gross domestic product]." (p59)

"Europe: Welfare in Germany: Even Germans Can't Afford It." Economist v330 n7851, 19 Feb 1994. p59-60. (ISSN0013-0613).

POPULATION FORECASTING--GREAT BRITAIN (v19)

POPULATION FORECASTING--JAPAN

"The Ministry of Health and Welfare projects that in 2021 the number of persons living in Japan aged 65 and over will peak at 32.75 million, more than doubling the proportion of elderly in the total population to 25.6%. The convergence of four demographic factors are contributing to this shift: the 1947-1949 baby boom, declining infant mortality, longer life expectancy, and declining fertility rate...." (p16)

Mann, Elisa Akiko/Chiba, Hitoshi. "Economy Feature: MOF Seminar." Look Japan v39 n455, Feb 1994. p16-17. (ISSN0456-5339).

POPULATION FORECASTING--JAPAN--U.S.--AGED (v19)

POPULATION FORECASTING--LOS ANGELES (CALIF) (v19)

POPULATION FORECASTING--PALESTINE (v19)

POPULATION FORECASTING--U.S. (v19)

"When the oldest baby boomers hit age 50 in 1996, the mature market will explode. Between 1990 and 2000, the number of 18-to-34-year-olds will shrink by 9 million and lose $40 billion a year in spending power, while 12 million more Americans older than age 50 will be spending an additional $300 billion a year." (p18)

Sandor, Gabrielle. "Business Reports: Generations: Attitudes (Not Age) Defines the Mature Market." American Demographics v16 n1, Jan 1994. p18. (ISSN0163-4089).

"To an extent, the world's demographic future has been written. Already there are some 5.5 billion people living on earth. 'That there will be a lot more people on earth (in the next few decades) is a fact,' notes John Casterline, a sociologist and demographer at Brown University. Analyses of current rates of population growth and fertility decline suggest that global population will stabilize between 10 billion and 15 billion near the end of the next century. Even an impossibly sharp decline in fertilty to about two children worldwide by the end of this decade would translate into a stable population of over 8 billion people. By taking the right steps today, we can reasonably expect to achieve stabilization at around 11 billion. The real question, then, is not if, but how, to accommodate a global population at least twice the size of today's." (p9)

Jacobson, Jodi L. "Perspective: Population Mythology." Amicus Journal v16 n1, Spr 1994. p9-10. (ISSN0276-7201).

"The Census Bureau has increased its previous estimate of population growth [in the U.S.] in the 1990s by 42%, largely because of powerful immigration flows. This year alone, 1 million new immigrants are expected to arrive--many well-educated and all eager to work. If the Census Bureau's new population growth projections are right, the number of new household formations in the 1990s could hit 1.3 million a year, about the same as in the 1980s--and far better than the previous estimate of only 1.1 million." (p66)

Farrell, Christopher/others. "Industry Outlook: Introduction: The Baby Boomlet May Kick In a Little Growth." Business Week n3353, 10 Jan 1994. p66. (ISSN0007-7135).

"Where one American now stands, there could be two by 2050, according to the U.S. Census Bureau's recently released report, 'Population Projections of the United States, by Age, Sex, Race, and Hispanic Origin: 1992 to 2050.' Such a doubling of the current U.S. population from 255 to 500 million by 2050 is considered by the Census Bureau to be a 'high' projection. But even the Census Bureau's 'middle projection,' which is considered by the Bureau as the most likely to occur, indicates that we can expect a dramatic 50% increase in fellow Americans, from today's population of 255 to 383 million in the year 2050, should current demographic trends continue. Just four years ago, the Census Bureau projected that the U.S. population would peak at 304 million in 2038 and then decline. But that was before the Census Bureau recognized that fertility rates are likely to rise, before the Immigration Law of 1990 was passed, and before life expectancy projections were increased. Even if the Census Bureau's middle projection is correct, America's population will probably grow by at least another 150 million people within the next sixty years." (p1)

"500 Million Americans by 2050?" Carrying Capacity Network Clearinghouse Bulletin v3 n2, Mar 1993. p1-2,7. (ISSN1066-5404).

"Immigration is driving rapid population growth in the United States. The United States now has the fastest growing population of any nation in the industrialized world. Over half of our Nation's population growth is attributable to legal and illegal immigration. Largely because of our present immigration policies, the U.S. Census Bureau now estimates that our Nation's population will increase from its current size of approximately 250 to 392 million by the year 2050." (pS2800)

Reid, Harry (Sen.-Nev.). "Statements on Introduced Bills and Joint Resolutions," Congressional Record (10 Mar 1994). Daily ed. pS2779-2812. (ISSN0363-7239).

"The U.S. Customs Service, along with the American workforce at large, is rapidly changing in its demographics, and the cultural differences among us are greater than ever. Note these projections from the U.S. Department of Labor: Within just a few years, 75 percent of those entering the American workforce will be minorities and women; By the year 2000, women will make up about 47 percent of all American workers; minorities and immigrants will hold about 32 percent of all U.S. jobs; During the 1990's there will be approximately 5 million fewer employees entering the American workforce annually than there were in 1980; and Immigration patterns have changed, with Europe no longer being the major source of immigration into the United States as it was in our earlier history." (p14)

Brown, Karl. "Spotlight on Diversity." Customs Today v29 n1, Spr 1994. p14-15. (ISSN0897-1609).

The U.S. "population is growing due to immigration. From 1980 to 1989, 520,000 more people entered the U.S.--legally and illegally--than left each year. If these trends do not change in the near future, it is possible our population could increase by 256 million or more by the middle of the next century. By 2050, there could be a half-billion American citizens." (p19)

Hren, Ben/Bartolomeo, Nick. "Special Report: Carrying Capacity Project: Population: The Clear and Present Crisis." Outdoor America v59 n1, Win 1994. p15-22.

"New long-term projections released in December by the Census Bureau indicate that the nation is expected to become more diverse, older, and substantially more populous than previously thought....U.S. population, enumerated at 248.7 million in the 1990 census, would increase an additional 26 million over the 1990s, reaching 274.8 million in 2000 and ultimately 382.7 million by 2050. The projected population for 2050 is more than 80 million higher than the one projected in 1989 for the same date--the equivalent of adding two and one-half more Californias. Furthermore, the 1989 projections showed the U.S. population leveling off by about 2035. In the new projections, there is no end in sight to population growth." (p3)

Pollard, Kelvin. "Faster Growth More Diversity in U.S. Projections." Population Today v21 n2, Feb 1993. p3,10. (ISSN0749-2448).

"The US Census Bureau projects that by 2030 the number of people 65 and over will double to about 65.6 million. The 'baby boomers' will have reached retirement age and make up over 22 percent of the population." (p18)

Holmstrom, David. "As More Seniors Thrive over 85, Their Needs Take a Spotlight." The Christian Science Monitor v86 n79, 18 Mar 1994. p1,18. (ISSN0882-7729).

PORCUPINES--U.S.

"The 1980s boom in second home development led to a decrease in once healthy porcupine populations in rural areas now being carved up into small house lots. A porcupine needs 70 acres of continuous woods. Since its reproductive rate is low--females give birth to only one offspring a year--lost territory can lead to the slow demise of regional populations. This happened in lower Michigan, Pennsylvania's Poconos, Westchester County, New York and parts of Connecticut. And its' now happening in areas of Vermont, New Hampshire and Massachusetts." (p12)

Wapner, Kenneth. "In Brief: The Porcupine Man." E Magazine v4 n1, Feb 1993. p12-13. (ISSN1046-8021).

PORK INDUSTRY AND TRADE--CHINA (v19)

PORK INDUSTRY AND TRADE--EUROPEAN ECONOMIC COMMUNITY (v19)

PORK INDUSTRY AND TRADE--NORTH CAROLINA

"As corporate hog production grew in North Carolina, the total number of hogs produced there grew substantially, increasing by 83 percent between 1985 to 1992. That drew Smithfield's new plant to the state. Hog slaughter increased during the period, too, by one-third. But the number of pork producers fell by well over 50 percent during the same period, because the corporate producers soaked up available packing capacity." (p4)

"New Players, New Plays, New Playing Fields." Center for Rural Affairs Newsletter Sep 1993. p3-4.

PORK INDUSTRY AND TRADE--U.S. (v19)

"A new study by Kansas State University economists comparing the efficiency of 91 farrow-to-finish hog operations concludes that half the farms with fewer than 200 litters had costs below average for the whole group, and that over half the farms larger than that had costs above average. In fact, the most efficient farm had only about 150 litters per year. Even about one-third of the smallest farms (those with under 100 litters) had below average cost of production--further evidence that most efficiencies, even in today's very capital intensive pork industry, can still be captured by very small producers. Interestingly, the one-third of the producers who were most profitable got $.95 per hundredweight more for their hogs than the one-third who were least profitable. Profit may not have as much to do with efficiency as people like to think." (p1)

"Pork Restructuring Continues." Center for Rura Affairs Newsletter Dec 1993. p1.

"Iowa and the western Corn Belt remain the center of the pork industry, with about 80 percent of the hogs produced within 500 miles of Des Moines. The packing industry is even more concentrated in this region, and hogs are still imported here for slaughter, with market prices higher than other regions. But most of the new pork plants are in the Southeast, in the eastern Corn Belt, and on the southwest perimeter of the Great Plains. In these areas, corporate farming supplies most of the hogs, directly or under contract. In North Carolina, Smithfield [a pork packing company] contracts with corporate giants like Carroll's Farms, and with large integrators like Murphy Farms, which has 300 contract growers in that state alone. Indiana Packers, Inc, says it will eventually rely on contracts with a few growers." (p4)

"New Players, New Plays, New Playing Fields." Center for Rural Affairs Newsletter Sep 1993. p3-4.

"Commercial pork production in 1993 totaled slightly over 17 billion pounds, less than 1 percent below the 1992 record. Commercial slaughter totaled 93.1 million head, down 2 percent. The decline in slaughter was partially offset by heavier dressed weights, which averaged 183 pounds, up 2 pounds from 1992. The trend toward heavier hogs has continued since 1980 when dressed weights averaged 171 pounds." (p1)

U.S. Dept. of Agriculture. "Review of 1993." Hog Outlook 13 Jan 1994. p1-2.

PORNOGRAPHY--NEW YORK (NY) (v19)

PORTS

see HARBORS

PORTUGAL

see UNEMPLOYMENT--PORTUGAL

PORTUGAL--SPAIN--ECONOMIC CONDITIONS (v19)

POST-TRAUMATIC STRESS DISORDER--U.S.--VETERANS (v19)

POSTAL SERVICE--EMPLOYMENT--U.S.

"Restructuring the Postal Service began at the top with the number of officers dropping from 42 to 23. Headquarters staffing was reduced about 38 percent and the postal field structure was streamlined. The Postal Service's field management structure was also simplified and streamlined to make mail service more efficient, responsive, and competitive. In order to minimize the impact of the restructuring on employees, a retirement incentive of six months' pay and an early-out option was offered to all eligible postal employees. The six months' pay incentive was offered to certain groups of employees eligible for optional retirement or eligible for voluntary early retirement. More than 47,000 employees took advantage of a special retirement six-month lump sum salary incentive, reducing the number of career employees to approximately 688,000 by the end of 1992." (p62)

Runyon, Marvin (Postmaster General, CEO, U.S. Postal Service). U.S. House. Committee on Appropriations. "Treasury, Postal Service, and General Government Approp. for Fiscal Year 1994 (Part 2)." Hearing, Washington, D.C.: GPO, 1993. (ISBN0160406595). (Y4.Ap6/1:T71/994/pt.2).

POSTAL SERVICE--GREAT BRITAIN

"The [Great Britain] Post Office's monopoly on letter deliveries priced below 1 [pound sterling] ($1.50) justifies regulation, but not state ownership. Private-sector disciplines would drive down costs and, with tough regulation, prices. Unlike British Rail and British Coal (both due to be privatised soon) and most of its foreign counterparts, the Post Office has been in profit since the mid-1970s. In the fiscal year to the end of March 1993 the Post Office's pre-tax profits rose to 283m [pounds sterling] on sales of 5.3 billion [pounds sterling]. Its letter-delivery business, the Royal Mail, which provides around 80% of sales and 90% of profits, has cut its unit costs by 1.5% a year in real terms in the past decade and now employs a staff 5% smaller than four years ago." (p59)

"Britain: The Post Office: Post-Haste, Please." Economist v330 n7844, 8 Jan 1994. p59. (ISSN0013-0613).

POSTAL SERVICE--U.S. (v19)

"Competition to mail is growing, and it is coming from many different directions. For some time, post offices' parcels and express-mail businesses have been under attack by private couriers. America's post office now delivers only around 10% of American overnight mail; Federal Express, the market leader, carries over half. According to Triangle, a consultancy, public post offices account for less than 15% of the international express-mail market." (p69)

"Business: Hitting the Mail on the Head." Economist v331 n7861, 30 Apr 1994. p69-70. (ISSN0013-0613).

POTATO INDUSTRY--U.S. (v19)

"In the United States, about 60 percent of commercial potato production is of a single variety. This genetic uniformity may leave crops seriously vulnerable to disease, pest infestations, and changes in weather and soil conditions or even agricultural disaster, like a blight that destroyed 15 percent of the corn crop in the United States in 1970." (p27)

King, Jonathan W. "Breeding Uniformity." Amicus Journal v15 n1, Spr 1993. p25-28,30. (ISSN0276-7201).

POULTRY INDUSTRY

see also EGG TRADE

POULTRY INDUSTRY--EUROPEAN ECONOMIC COMMUNITY (v19)

POULTRY INDUSTRY--HONG KONG--U.S. (v19)

POULTRY INDUSTRY--NORTH CAROLINA

"In North Carolina, 4,200 farmers--more than a fifth of all poultry growers in the South--raise chickens and turkeys. But these are not the independent farmers one associates with tobacco and other agricultural products. Rather, 99 percent of all broilers and 90 percent of all turkeys are grown by farmers under contracts with large poultry corporations." (p120)

Yeoman, Barry. "Food Empires: Don't Count Your Chickens." Southern Exposure v21 n1-2, Spr-Sum 1993. p119-120. (ISSN0146-809X).

POULTRY INDUSTRY--U.S. (v19)

"The U.S. chicken industry is the largest and most competitive in the world. Production in 1991 was 20 billion pounds on a ready-to-cook weight basis with a wholesale value of $15 billion. U.S. output represents 35 percent of total worldwide broiler production. Total U.S. chicken exports in 1992 were over 1.5 billion pounds, valued at $676.5 million. But exports to Canada were only $90 million of the over $1 billion Canadian chicken market. With an open market, U.S. exports to Canada could increase annually to between $350 to $700 million, resulting in 7,000-14,000 new U.S. jobs." (p71)

U.S. Senate. Committee on Finance. "Renewal of Fast-Track Authority and the Generalized System of Preferences Program." Hearing, 20 May 1993. Washington, D.C.: GPO, 1993. (ISBN0160432154). (Y4.F49:S.hrg.103-285).

POWER, NUCLEAR

see NUCLEAR ENERGY

POWER PLANTS, GEOTHERMAL

see GEOTHERMAL POWER PLANTS

POWER PLANTS, NUCLEAR

see NUCLEAR POWER PLANTS

POWER RESOURCES--U.S. (v19)

PRAIRIES--ILLINOIS (v19)

PREFABRICATED HOUSES--U.S.

"'Manufactured homes' are the fastest growing form of housing in the...[U.S.]--with sales jumping 60 percent during the 1980s and 23 percent last year alone. The $6 billion-a-year industry also holds another distinction: it's been riddled with more fraud in recent years than just about any other business in America. In the mid-1980s, manufacturers representing more than half the mobile-home market were indicted for padding factory invoices in order to inflate profits they earned through loan programs run by federal housing and veterans agencies. Investigators said the scheme gouged more than $100 million from low- and moderate-income borrowers. Veterans officials estimated manufacturers padded invoices on at least 80 percent of the 295,000 mobile homes shipped in 1984." (p26)

"The Great Mobile Home Rip-Off." Southern Exposure v21 n3, Fall 1993. p26. (ISSN0146-809X).

PREGNANCY (v19)

see also DRUG ABUSE IN PREGNANCY; TEENAGE PREGNANCY

PREGNANCY--COMPLICATIONS (v19)

"A birth is a delicate event for the human species and entails certain risks. Yet more than 56 million deliveries take place each year without any skilled help--in many cases the mother is completely alone with her baby. Up to one in three pregnancies (not counting abortions) develop complications, such as haemorrhage, sepsis, hypertensive disorders and obstructed labour, and half of these--around 23 million--need skilled treatment. Around 12.5 million pregnancies are complicated by a disease such as malaria, hepatitis, tuberculosis or diabetes. For half a million women every year such complications prove fatal, and when the mother dies the risk of death for surviving children--especially for girls--increases by up to 50%. Some 15 million women develop long-term disabilities such as obstetric fistulae (constant leaking of urine or faeces due to severe damage to the birth canal), severe anaemia, pelvic inflammatory diseases, reproductive tract infections and infertility." (p30)

"WHO on....Making Motherhood Safer." World Health n5, Sep-Oct 1993. p30-31. (ISSN0043-8502).

"Complications that affect women during pregnancy and delivery also affect the fetus. Of the 12.9 million deaths a year of children under five, around one-third occur before the baby is one month old and three million occur during the first week of life, largely as a consequence of poorly managed pregnancies or inadequate care of the baby during the first critical hours of life. Many millions of babies who survive the birth process are badly damaged. For example, some 3% of newborn babies (3.6 million) suffer moderate or severe birth asphyxia following obstructed labour. Of these, about 800 000 die and an equal number suffer brain damage leading to cerebral palsy, seizures and serious learning disorders." (p30-31)

"WHO on....Making Motherhood Safer." World Health n5, Sep-Oct 1993. p30-31. (ISSN0043-8502).

PREGNANCY--COMPLICATIONS--MORTALITY

"Every year pregnancy means death for 500,000 women; 99 percent of these deaths occur in developing countries, and 250,000 of these women die from clandestine abortions. Although abortion is illegal in two-thirds of developing countries, fifty to sixty million abortions are performed yearly worldwide and almost half are illegal. For every death fifteen other women are left handicapped in some way." (p13-14)

Johnson, Bonnie. "Overpopulation and Reproductive Rights." Free Inquiry v14 n2, Spr 1994. p13-16. (ISSN0272-0701).

PREGNANCY--DEVELOPING COUNTRIES--MORTALITY (v19)

PREGNANCY--MORTALITY

"Even at the end of the 20th century, maternal mortality rates remain high in the developing world. In Afghanistan and Sierra Leone, for instance, according to the World Health Organization (WHO), one mother dies for every 100 live births--a rate 250 times higher than that of some European countries. And many maternal deaths in developing countries are attributed by WHO to excessive childbearing." (p15)

Sachs, Aaron. "Men, Sex, and Parenthood in an Overpopulating World." World Watch v7 n2, Mar-Apr 1994. p12-19. (ISSN0896-0615).

PREGNANCY, TEENAGE

see TEENAGE PREGNANCY

PREGNANCY TERMINATION

see ABORTION

PREGNANT WOMEN--U.S.--TOBACCO USE

"One of the first documented problems caused by maternal smoking is low birth weight and prematurity. Adequate birth weight is of major importance to the health and survival of the infant. Infants who are considered low birth weight (under 2,500 grams) have a mortality rate that is 30 times higher than those weighing more than 2,500 grams. A 1957 medical journal article reviewed earlier studies and its own retrospective epidemiological study to conclude that maternal smoking during pregnancy was significantly related with premature birth. It reported that smoking mothers were twice as likely as nonsmokers to have premature babies, and that the probability increased with the number of cigarettes smoked (dose-response relationship). This study was followed in 1959 by another retrospective study which corroborated and reinforced its findings. A 1961 prospective study also found a dose-response relationship between maternal smoking and low birth weight." (p6)

Tye, Joe. "Protecting Babies from Philip Morris & RJR Nabisco." Tobacco-Free Youth Reporter v5 n1, Spr 1993. p6.

PRENATAL CARE--U.S.

African American women are less likely than white women to receive warnings from their doctors about prenatal smoking and alcohol use, according to the National Center for Health Statistics. "Nearly 36 percent of black mothers reported never being told to quit smoking, compared with 29 percent of white mothers. More than 70 percent of white women said they received advice about the dangers of drinking alcohol during pregnancy; 60 percent of black women said they were given similar warnings. Also, wealthier women tended to receive more information on breast-feeding then did poorer women." (p4)

"News Roundup: Black Women Get Less Advice on Prenatal Care, Study Says." Education Week v13 n19, 2 Feb 1994. p4. (ISSN0277-4232).

"A study reported in MEDICAL CARE found that prenatal and infant nurse home visits improved a wide range of maternal and child health outcomes among poor, unmarried, teenage mothers. 'Effect of Prenatal and Infancy Nurse Home Visitation on Government Spending,' 31 MEDICAL CARE 155 (1993)....This study involved nurse home visits to poor first-time teenage mothers in rural New York, during the pregnancy and the first two years of the child's life, and then compared outcomes with other poor first-time teenage mothers who did not have the home visits....During the prenatal stage, the women who received home visits improved their health-related behaviors, such as reducing cigarette use and improving their diets, experienced greater informal social support, and made better use of the WIC [Women, Infants, and Children] program. The birth outcomes were similarly improved: there were 75% fewer premature births among smokers, and girls under 17 had children with higher mean birthweights. During the first two years of life, there was a 75% reduction in state-verified cases of child abuse, and a 56% difference in emergency room-visits for the children due to injuries and ingestions. During the first four years of life, the mothers who received home visits were participating by 80% more in the work-force, and bore 43% fewer subsequent children." (p11)

"Medicaid Developments: Prenatal Home Visits Cut Costs." Health Advocate n175, Win 1993. p11.

PRENATAL CARE--U.S.--COSTS

"The General Accounting Office recently studied an array of children's programs and concluded that the WIC [Women, Infants, and Children program] had the best documented return on investment of any federal early intervention program. The GAO concluded that each dollar invested in prenatal WIC benefits saves $2.89 in Medicaid, SSI [Supplemental Security Income], special education, and other health care costs within the first year after birth--and saves $3.50 over 18 years. Similarly, a study conducted for USDA by Mathematica Policy Research and issued in 1991 estimated that each dollar invested in prenatal WIC benefits saves between $1.92 and $4.21 in Medicaid costs during the first months after birth." (p190)

Shapiro, Isaac (Exec. Director, Center for Budget and Policy Priorities). U.S. Congress. Joint Economic Committee. "The 1993 Economic Report of the President." Hearing, 27 Jan 1993. Washington, D.C.: GPO, 1994. (ISBN0160440300). (Y4.Ec:Ec7/2/993/pt.1).

PRESCRIPTION PRICING--U.S.

"According to the Boston Consulting Group, sales of prescription drugs at full price [in the U.S.] have dropped to 25% of the total from 60% in 1987; and the average discount has risen to 16% of the list price, four times bigger than in 1987. Overall, the annual growth in the drug industry's revenues, which used to bound along at 14% or more in the 1980s, is likely to drop below 10% by 1996." (p91)

"Business: American Drug Firms: Kicking the Habit." Economist v329 n7843, 25 Dec 1993. p90-92. (ISSN0013-0613).

PREVENTIVE MEDICINE

see MEDICINE, PREVENTIVE

PRICES--U.S. (v19)

PRIME MINISTERS--PAKISTAN (v19)

PRIME RATE--CANADA (v19)

PRINCE EDWARD ISLAND--HEALTH AND HYGIENE (v19)

PRINTED CIRCUITS INDUSTRY--U.S. (v19)

PRINTING INK INDUSTRY--U.S. (v19)

PRISON SENTENCES--GREAT BRITAIN

"The British government...exercises plenty of discretion in how it deals with its 1,200 terrorist prisoners. The average life sentence served in Northern Ireland is 12-14 years, compared with the mandatory 20 for terrorist lifers in England. Since 1985, 250 have been released 'on licence'--meaning an immediate return to prison for any offence." (p77)

"Britain: Northern Ireland: Balancing Act." Economist v329 n7843, 25 Dec 1993. p77. (ISSN0013-0613).

PRISON SENTENCES--U.S. (v19)

PRISONERS

see also AFRO-AMERICAN PRISONERS; AIDS (DISEASE)--NEW YORK (STATE)--PRISONERS; AIDS (DISEASE)--U.S.--PRISONERS; HIV INFECTIONS--AFRICA--PRISONERS; HIV INFECTIONS--BRAZIL--PRISONERS; WOMEN PRISONERS--U.S.

"The United States leads the world with a rate of 455 incarcerated per 100,000 of the population. South Africa is a distant second with 311 per 100,000. To be sure,...a low rate of incarceration may reflect pervasive police brutality; in India, for example, police prefer to beat up petty criminals rather than imprison them. But such conduct is irrelevant to comparisons one might make with the Netherlands (40 per 100,000), or Japan (45), or France (81), or England (97). Moreover, the prison population is growing at the fastest rate in the world. Between 1980 and 1990, the number of inmates in state and federal prisons rose by 168 percent, from 330,000 to 883,000, and predictions are that the number will reach one million by 1994." (p34)

Rothman, David J. "The Crime of Punishment." New York Review of Books v41 n4, 17 Feb 1994. p34-38. (ISSN0028-7504).

PRISONERS--CIVIL RIGHTS--U.S. (v19)

PRISONERS--EMPLOYMENT--U.S.

"Convicts taking jobs from free citizens is a serious problem. There are now 1.3 million persons in prisons or jails. The United States has [the] highest incarceration rate in the world. I have heard it said--by those who would like to see private sector business using 'factories with fences,'--that 45 percent of the convicts could be working. That translates to nearly 600,000 jobs. But, the United States now has 8.7 million officially unemployed, and 16.4 million with a job-related income loss--one of every eight workers....Policies that artificially stimulate the employment of convicts is unwise and it is unjust." (p33)

Zalusky, John L. (Head, Office of Wages and Industrial Relations, AFL-CIO). U.S. Senate. Committee on Labor and Human Resources. "Implications of the Fair Labor Standards Act for Inmates...Private Industry, and Labor." Hearing, 28 Oct 1993. Washington, D.C.: GPO, 1994. (ISBN0160435064). (Y4.L11/4:S.hrg.103-385).

"Most prison labor involves making items for the State, such as license plates, to help cut the cost of the prisoners' confinement. The argument that prisoners are taking jobs away from people because we do not pay them minimum wage or the prevailing wage is...a red herring....The Bureau of Prisons told GAO [General Accounting Office] that their industries paid 15,300 prisoners average rates of 87 cents an hour, for 27.2 million regular work hours, and $1.75 an hour for 1.8 million overtime hours worked during fiscal year 1992. This amounts to $27 million for inmate compensation, or about $100 million less than what paying minimum wage would have cost. If we decide to pay inmates minimum wage, we can say goodbye...to prison work programs. The States will not be able to afford them, and neither will the Federal Government." (p5-6)

Reid, Harry (Sen.-Nev.). U.S. Senate. Committee on Labor and Human Resources. "Implications of the Fair Labor Standards Act for Inmates...Private Industry, and Labor." Hearing, 28 Oct 1993. Washington, D.C.: GPO, 1994. (ISBN0160435064). (Y4.L11/4:S.hrg.103-385).

PRISONERS--FRANCE--U.S.

"California...will enshrine in state law the idea that criminals convicted of three or more violent crimes should automatically be locked up for good. Washington state already has such a law, christened 'Three strikes, you're out.' Thirty other states are likely to follow suit. And Bill Clinton has just endorsed the idea for federal offences too....Over the past two decades, the prison population of America has soared. More than 450 people per 100,000 are in jail, the highest proportion in the world; in France, the figure is 81 per 100,000. Meanwhile, the rate of violent crime in America remains steady--rising by some measures, falling slightly by others, but still by far the worst in the rich world. The prisons are chronically overcrowded, a condition that often leads to early release. Now, with 'three strikes', the cells will be filled with whiskery old lags, enduring their forced retirement at state expense." (p16)

"Leaders: Three Strikes, You're Hoodwinked." Economist v330 n7849, 5 Feb 1994. p16,18. (ISSN0013-0613).

PRISONERS--GEORGIA

"The number of black offenders admitted to Georgia's prisons has more than tripled from 1981 to 1990, increasing from 4,470 to 13,690. For whites, prison admissions have decreased from 45 percent of the total prison admissions in 1981 to 33 percent of all admissions in 1990. Although they comprise approximately 27 percent of the population of Georgia, blacks represent about 65 percent of all arrests by the police and almost 67 percent of the state's prison population. Admissions to Georgia's prisons have changed from one black inmate for every white inmate in 1981 to two black inmates for every white inmate in 1990 (Rojek & Bachtel, 1990)." (p57)

Arthur, John A. "Correctional Ideology of Black Correctional Officers." Federal Probation v58 n1, Mar 1994. p57-66.

(ISSN0014-9128).

PRISONERS--GREAT BRITAIN (v19)

PRISONERS--ILLINOIS

"'In the last six years the population in Illinois prisons has grown by over 12,000,' says Howard Peters III, Illinois state director of corrections. 'We have 35,000 inmates now. This is the most in state history. We have built 15 new prisons in the last 15 years and are still overcrowded.'" (p7)

Holmstrom, David. "National: More Prisons Not a Cure to Crime, Experts Say." The Christian Science Monitor v86 n62, 23 Feb 1994. p7. (ISSN0882-7729).

PRISONERS--MARYLAND (v19)

PRISONERS--MICHIGAN (v19)

PRISONERS--MICHIGAN--COSTS

"It costs $22,000 per year to incarcerate someone in a Michigan prison. For the 80-90 percent who have serious substance abuse problems, the cost of a 180-day intensive treatment program would be $8,600. The cost of intensive group therapy for one year for those guilty of assaultive behavior and/or sexual offenses would be $10,000. Seventy percent of those who enter Michigan prisons have not earned a high school diploma or GED. Most do not have vocational skills. Education and job training are likely to produce better long-term results than incarceration....Other sanctions are known to be just as effective and cost far less. Intensive probation supervision saves $10,000 to $13,000 per offender in the states where it is used. Victim-offender mediation is often done by volunteers at very little cost to taxpayers." (p7 secC)

Ryder, Penny. "Other Voices: A Better Way on Crime." Ann Arbor News 27 Feb 1994. p7 secC.

PRISONERS--NEW ZEALAND--U.S.--MINORITIES

"The bicultural and bilingual situation of the Maoris in New Zealand is very similar to the African-American situation in the United States. Hugh Barr, in 'Toward a Bicultural Education System,' reports that Maoris, who make up 10 percent of the population, account for 45 percent of the prison population. Compare those figures with the equivalent figures--11 percent and 43 percent, respectively--for African-Americans (U.S. Bureau of the Census, 1992)." (p5)

Robinson, Helja Antola. "Weaving the Tapestry of Diversity." National Forum v74 n1, Win 1994. p3-5. (ISSN0162-1831).

PRISONERS--NORTH CAROLINA

"If you are interested in unusual exports, North Carolina will appeal to you. More than 200 people convicted in the state's courts are now incarcerated in Rhode Island or Oklahoma. The governor of North Carolina, James Hunt, has asked the legislature to authorise the housing of a total of 1,000 convicts in other states' prisons....Since December, North Carolina has signed two contracts in Rhode Island, one for housing 75 convicts at the Adult Correctional Institution in Cranston, the other for 230 at the Detention Facility Corporation in Central Falls. It has another contract for 240 convicts with the town of Hinton, Oklahoma, and the Hinton Economic Development Authority, and it is negotiating a deal with a private prison near Memphis, Tennessee....North Carolina's prisons were so crowded as to be unconstitutionally inhumane. The state, which had been stacking prisoners into three-tier bunks, agreed to provide dormitories with 50 square feet per inmate. But this meant keeping the prison population below a total of 21,400, by releasing on parole any number in excess of that....Over the past seven years the average time served by North Carolina's prisoners has dropped from 40% of the original sentences to 18.5%. Since June, 42 people on parole have been charged with murder." (p26)

"American Survey: Exporting Prisoners: Send Me Your Crooks." Economist v330 n7852, 26 Feb 1994. p26-27.

(ISSN0013-0613).

PRISONERS--SEXUAL BEHAVIOR

"A recent study in the Dominican Republic established an average HIV prevalence of 8.5% among young male prisoners. In the US, up to 8% of male prisoners and 15% of female prisoners in some areas are known to be HIV positive. Two years ago, AIDS became the leading cause of death in New York prisons. Sex between men in prison is a major route of HIV transmission....Australia found that 12% of inmates reported sexual activity in prison; another study in England produced a figure of 10%. These may be underestimates. Male rape is also a reality in most prisons. In some places, such as the US and South Africa, it is widespread." (p1)

Kahane, Tony. "Jail Condoms Call." WorldAIDS n30, Nov 1993. p1. (ISSN0954-6510).

PRISONERS--TEXAS (v19)

PRISONERS--U.S. (v19)

see also WOMEN PRISONERS--U.S.

"In a 1991 study reported by Patrick Langan in the journal SCIENCE, several explanations were offered for the increased use of imprisonment [in the U.S.] between 1974 and 1986. Increasing levels of reported crime and overall arrests accounted for 9 percent of the increase. More specific increases in arrests and imprisonment for drug crimes accounted for another 8 percent, and there is reason to believe that this figure has continued to grow. Changes in the proportion of young people in the U.S. population accounted for 20 percent of the increase." (p61)

Hagan, John (Member, Panel on High Risk Youth). U.S. House. Committee on Ways and Means. "Children and Families at Risk in Deteriorating Communities." Hearing, 7 Dec 1993. Washington, D.C.: GPO, 1994. (ISBN0160436567). (Y4.W36:103-43).

"Studies indicate that 80 per cent of the nation's prison population has a history of drug and alcohol abuse. Illinois has 300 beds only for substance abuse treatment for its 34,000 prisoners." (p40)

Bogira, Steve. "Pushing Treatment Instead of Prisons." APF Reporter v16 n2, 1994. p39-44. (ISSN0913-4562).

"According to figures provided by the U.S. Sentencing Commission, of the total 16,684 drug cases sentenced in Federal court in 1992, only 98--06 percent--of those sentenced to mandatory minimum sentences--were truly first-time offenders who had minimal involvement in the drug enterprise, did not carry a firearm, and did not cause death or serious injury to another. The notion that our Federal prisons are filled with people who should not be there is wrong. And, with respect to State prisons, bear in mind that in 1991, the Department of Justice found that 94 percent of all State inmates were either violent or repeat offenders, and over one-third of all inmates have been incarcerated before. Moreover, two-thirds of the violent inmates in State prisons had killed, raped, or injured their victims. Over half of the remaining 6 percent of State inmates had been convicted of drug trafficking or burglary. That is according to the Bureau of Justice Statistics survey of State prison inmates in 1991." (pS2432)

Hatch, Orrin G. (Sen.-Utah). "The Department of Justice Mandatory Minimum Study," Congressional Record (8 Mar 1994). Daily ed. pS2431-2432. (ISSN0363-7239).

"The Administrative Office of the United States Courts (1993) reports that the average annual per capita cost of housing an inmate in a Federal penal facility was $20,803 during fiscal year 1992....By the end of 1991, there were 823,414 individuals under penal jurisdiction. The growth rate represents an increase in prison populations of 150 percent since 1980 and translates into a need for approximately 1,000 new prison bed spaces weekly. It was reported that in mid-year 1991, local jails held 422,609 persons, 101 percent over the rated capacity of the Nation's jails." (p51)

Rackmill, Stephen J. "An Analysis of Home Confinement as a Sanction." Federal Probation v58 n1, Mar 1994. p45-52. (ISSN0014-9128).

"Last year federal and state costs for constructing and operating prisons and jails amounted to $25 billion. And building more and more US prisons over the last decade, along with tougher laws, has not significantly reduced crime or increased public safety. Between 1990 and 1992, the number of people behind bars increased by 160 percent. According to the Edna McConnell Clark Foundation in New York, US prisons and jails now hold 1 million inmates." (p7)

Holmstrom, David. "National: More Prisons Not a Cure to Crime, Experts Say." The Christian Science Monitor v86 n62, 23 Feb 1994. p7. (ISSN0882-7729).

A U.S. "federal report [states] that about 70 percent of inmates released on parole are rearrested for a serious offense within six years....The NRA [National Rifle Association]...wants to abolish parole and force prisoners to serve at least 85 percent of their sentences. Now, many are released after one-third of their terms." (p82)

Gest, Ted. "Face-Offs: A Battle for the Souls of Crime Fighters." U.S. News & World Report v115 n25, 27 Dec 1993. p82. (ISSN0041-5537).

PRISONERS--U.S.--ALIENS, ILLEGAL (v19)

PRISONERS--U.S.--COSTS (v19)

PRISONERS, WOMEN

see WOMEN PRISONERS

PRISONS

"Most...[Western Europeans and Americans] are ill-informed about various aspects of our system of justice. Thus it is not well-known that the United States has the highest per capita prison population of the world. To be precise, the U.S. incarceration rate is 455 per 100,000, second is South Africa with 311 prisoners, third is Sweden with 44. (During the last year of the Soviet Union, 1991, its rate was 268 per 100,000, which placed it third that year.)" (p3)

Neumaier, John J. "Quest for a More Human World." Veterans for Peace Journal n23, Spr 1993. p3-4. (ISSN1063-9381).

PRISONS--CALIFORNIA

"Use of probation is way down and parole violators are jailed more quickly. At least 35% of the more than 100,000 prisoners in California are technical parole violators. A parolee may, for example, be returned to prisons for having failed to report a job change to a parole officer. California has spent over 14 billion dollars for new prisons in the last decade! Can this be justified in a state whose public schools are closing for lack of state funds?" (p14)

Elvin, Jan. "Reflections on Lucasville: Have We Learned Anything Yet?" National Prison Project Journal v8 n3, Jul 1993. p14.

"The California prison system...currently has packed 120,000 felons into 50,000 cells. Don Novey, president of the California Correctional Peace Officers Association, says the crowding is so serious that 79 percent of convicted felons never spend time behind bars." (p4)

Dillin, John. "Cries against Crime Lead to Proposal for Regional Prisons." The Christian Science Monitor v86 n57, 15 Feb 1994. p1,4. (ISSN0882-7729).

PRISONS--GREAT BRITAIN (v19)

PRISONS--MICHIGAN (v19)

"We have gone the route of tougher prison sentences in the 1980s, which led to building more correction facilities to hold the inmates. By the end of 1992, Michigan was putting more people in prison and spending more on corrections than any state in the Midwest and yet Michigan had the highest crime rate in the Midwest. Last year, one-third of all new revenue in Michigan went to the Corrections budget, which reached $1.1 billion. That, according to the Corrections Department, amounts to $120...for every man, woman and child in the state." (p8 secA)

"Opinion: Editorials: Crime Reform." Ann Arbor News 19 Jan 1994. p8 secA.

PRISONS--TEXAS (v19)

PRISONS--U.S. (v19)

"Since the 1960s, America has quadrupled its prison population to the point at which it has the highest per capita rate of incarceration in the world. Yet, during the same period, violent crime increased 560 percent. So much for deterrence." (p30)

Colson, Charles W. "Fair Comment: Solution to Megacrime: Build Conscience." Insight v10 n10, 7 Mar 1994. p30,32. (ISSN1051-4880).

"In 1981 the question of the constitutionality of prison overcrowding came before the U.S. Supreme Court in 'Rhodes v. Chapman.'...The case began when a prisoner named Kelly Chapman filed a lawsuit to halt double-celling at Lucasville [Ohio]. He cited state veterinarian regulations requiring 43 square feet of space for a calf once it became five weeks old. 'I went around measuring the cell,' said Chapman, 'or my half of it. I have 32 square feet. I couldn't accept that a calf is entitled to more living space than a man.'" Today, "Forty-one states and the District of Columbia are under court order to reduce prison overcrowding and/or remedy unconstitutional conditions." (p14)

Elvin, Jan. "Reflections on Lucasville: Have We Learned Anything Yet?" National Prison Project Journal v8 n3, Jul 1993. p14.

"There are more people in prisons and jails in the US--1.4 million--than in any other country in the world, a number that has doubled since 1986. With an incarceration rate of 455 per 100,000, the US has the dubious distinction of being number one, while South Africa is a distant second with 311 per 100,000. England has 97, France 81, Japan 45. And the prison population in the US is also growing at the world's fastest rate." (p45)

Leiper, Stephen. "Propaganda Watch: Crime and Propaganda: Fear Is Up though Crime Is Down." Propaganda Review n11, Spr 1994. p44-46.

"For many Southern states, prison construction is now the biggest growth industry in the budget. According to the Bureau of Justice Statistics, more than 68,000 new prison beds were being built in the region last year at a cost of over $2 billion. Texas accounts for more than half the total. The Lone Star State is currently in the midst of the largest prison expansion in U.S. history, making room for another 37,800 prisoners. Over the past eight years, prison spending in Texas has leapt by 127 percent--while funds for higher education have risen by only two percent." (p4)

Bryce, Robert. "Roundup: The South behind Bars." Southern Exposure v21 n3, Fall 1993. p4. (ISSN0146-809X).

PRISONS--U.S.--COSTS

"Keeping people in prison places a large burden on state budgets. The Edna McConnell Clark Foundation, the leading private sponsor of programs for prison reform, estimates that in 1992 the US spent 25 billion dollars on its prison system, making it the second fastest growing item, after Medicaid, among state government expenditures. New York, for example, between 1983 and 1990 built twenty-seven new prisons at the short-term cost of 1.6 billion dollars, and eventual cost of 5.4 billion over thirty years if one includes the interest payable on state bonds floated for the construction." (p34)

Rothman, David J. "The Crime of Punishment." New York Review of Books v41 n4, 17 Feb 1994. p34-38. (ISSN0028-7504).

PRISONS--U.S.--FINANCE (v19)

PRISONS--U.S.--OFFICIALS AND EMPLOYEES (v19)

PRISONS--VENEZUELA

"More than 100 inmates died at the Sabaneta jail in Maracaibo,...[Venezuela's] second-largest city, on January 3rd in what was probably the most gory prison riot in Venezuela's history....The riot is the latest outrage in a black drama of jail violence that has plagued Venezuela. Its 32 main prisons house nearly 30,000 inmates, almost double the number for which they were designed....Things are made worse by the inefficient judicial system: the time from criminal charge to sentence averages 3 1/2 years." (p42-43)

"International: Venezuela: No Place to Be a Prisoner." Economist v330 n7844, 8 Jan 1994. p41-42. (ISSN0013-0613).

PRIVACY--U.S.--PUBLIC OPINION (v19)

PRIVACY, RIGHT OF--U.S.--PUBLIC OPINION

"According to a Harris-Equifax poll completed this fall, 80 percent of those polled were concerned about threats to their personal privacy. In fact, an example of the high level of concern is reflected in the volume of calls received by California's Privacy Rights Clearing House. Within the first three months of operation. The California Clearinghouse received more than 5,400 calls. The Harris-Equifax poll also reported that only 9 percent of Americans felt that current law and organizational practices adequately protected their privacy. This perception is accurate. The Privacy Act of 1974 was created to afford citizens broad protection. Yet, studies and reviews of the Act clearly indicate that there is inadequate specific protection, too much ambiguity, and lack of strong enforcement." (pS16493)

Simon, Paul (Sen.-Ill.). "Statements on Introduced Bills and Joint Resolutions," Congressional Record (19 Nov 1993). Daily ed. pS16433-16501. (ISSN0363-7239).

PRIVATE SCHOOL STUDENTS--U.S. (v19)

PRIVATE SCHOOLS--U.S. (v19)

PRIVATIZATION (v19)

PRIVATIZATION--ALBANIA

"The opening of Albania's borders in the spring of 1991, which provoked dramatic scenes of mass exodus, led to the adoption of a democratic regime in April 1992....In the countryside, where more than 60 per cent of Albanians live, cooperatives and State farms have been completely discarded and nearly three-fourths of the land has been privatized. But the new owners are hindered by the shortage of modern agricultural tools, the lack of spare parts and the cost of fertilizer and pesticides. Hard work earns little and it is not unusual to see entire families working in the fields with hand tools, sowing, hoeing or harvesting." (p22)

Fromont, Michel. "Regions: Reconstructing Albania from the Ruins." World of Work n7, Mar 1994. p22-23. (ISSN1020-0029).

PRIVATIZATION--CUBA (v19)

PRIVATIZATION--EUROPE, EASTERN

"In the past four years, Hungary has sold off barely 200 of its 2,000 state-owned firms to private investors; Poland has sold no more than 1,000 of 8,000. Romania planned to privatize 1,100 large companies in 1993; in fact, it sold 10. Only the Czechs--with their 'coupon' program for mass privatization--have seriously dented state ownership of production, but the program will not offer critical new capital to the now-private firms." (p61)

Parker, Richard. "Clintonomics for the East." Foreign Policy n94, Spr 1994. p53-68. (ISSN0015-7228).

PRIVATIZATION--GREAT BRITAIN (v19)

PRIVATIZATION--HOSPITALS--MASSACHUSETTS

"In January 1991, when Governor William Weld took office, the Massachusetts Health and Human Services (HHS) budget was growing at a rapid rate. The Governor's Special Commission on Hospital Consolidation was charged with evaluating the consolidation and restructuring of HHS facilities....Before Privatization: In both the public and private sectors, there were simply too many individual health care institutions and too many empty beds. The Commonwealth's public hospital system, built to accommodate more than 35,000 individuals, in 1991 cared for fewer than 6,200 clients." (p13) "After Consolidation and Privatization: Net operating savings for the Commonwealth as a result of facility closings total approximately $60 million to date, and capital expenditures avoided exceed $140 million....Nursing homes were able to absorb two-thirds of the patients from the closed public health hospitals....An estimated 5,000 new private sector jobs have been created in community-based settings." (p14)

Robinson, Mark/Wilson, Steve. "Privatization in Massachusetts: Getting Results." Government Union Review v15 n1, Win 1994. p1-55. (ISSN0270-2487).

PRIVATIZATION--LATIN AMERICA (v19)

PRIVATIZATION--MASSACHUSETTS

"In 1991, Massachusetts had the highest costs in the nation for prison health care--$43 million for 10,000 inmates. There were no cost controls, no means for central accountability, no controls on malpractice claims, and no standards of care for assessing how well services were being delivered. Since privatization, expenses are down and quality of care is up. Health care costs have been reduced from $4,300 to $2,600 per inmate per year, and in recognition of attainment of national standards for care, half of the facilities were accredited for the first time. Total savings to the Commonwealth: $8 million annually." (p12)

Robinson, Mark/Wilson, Steve. "Privatization in Massachusetts: Getting Results." Government Union Review v15 n1, Win 1994. p1-55. (ISSN0270-2487).

"In September 1992, the Massachusetts Highway Department (MHD) contracted with a Massachusetts-based company to provide comprehensive highway maintenance and drawbridge operation in Essex County....Before Privatization:...One foreman was employed for every 2.15 laborers. Overtime costs were very high--a foreman made as much as $40,000 in overtime. Sixty-five percent of MHD vehicles were beyond their useful life, and 12 percent were inoperable." (p15) "After Privatization: Savings from the first year of the contract: $2 million in direct operating costs, $1 million in reallocated equipment, and $1.5 million in reallocated personnel....Maintenance overtime costs were down by $252,000 from last year." (p16)

Robinson, Mark/Wilson, Steve. "Privatization in Massachusetts: Getting Results." Government Union Review v15 n1, Win 1994. p1-55. (ISSN0270-2487).

PRIVATIZATION--MASSACHUSETTS--PUBLIC OPINION

"A poll of Massachusetts residents conducted in 1993 by the Becker Institute found that 53 percent approved of 'proposals to turn over or privatize more state agencies to for-profit contractors,' while 39 percent disapproved. The favorable results are most notable in that the question suggested that entire functions of state agencies would be privatized, and that the contractors would be for-profit operators....In September 1993, these findings were confirmed by a second poll commissioned by the Boston Globe, which found that 45 percent of Massachusetts voters surveyed supported privatization, while 33 percent opposed it." (p22)

Robinson, Mark/Wilson, Steve. "Privatization in Massachusetts: Getting Results." Government Union Review v15 n1, Win 1994. p1-55. (ISSN0270-2487).

PRIVATIZATION--MASSACHUSETTS--SOCIAL SERVICES

"By fiscal year 1993 [in Massachusetts], revenue collections for the Department of Social Services (DSS) from federal and non-state sources had leveled off at $120 million to $130 million annually, yet a special commission appointed by the Governor found that as much as $200 million was available to the agency from outside sources. DSS's annual cost to generate these revenues was approximately $5 million, using a combination of in-house staff and consulting services. Through privatization, DSS expects to increase its annual level of revenue generation by at least 40 percent (from $125 million to $180 million per year) and reduce its per-dollar cost of revenue generation by 30 percent (from an average of 4.0 cents to 2.8 cents per dollar)." (p18)

Robinson, Mark/Wilson, Steve. "Privatization in Massachusetts: Getting Results." Government Union Review v15 n1, Win 1994. p1-55. (ISSN0270-2487).

PRIVATIZATION--MEDICAL CARE--MASSACHUSETTS

"In 1992, the Department of Mental Retardation (DMR) [in Massachusetts] began an extensive evaluation of institutional dietary and housekeeping services. The study focused on 5 facilities serving over 1,600 consumers with mental retardation. The Commonwealth was spending $9.7 million per year at the facilities for housekeeping and cleaning and $13.5 million for dietary and food services. More than 725 state employees were involved in the provision of these services. In FY94, contracts for both dietary and housekeeping services were awarded to three companies. The cost of these contracts for FY94 is $5.3 million for housekeeping and $7.75 million for dietary services. A conservative estimate of savings to the Commonwealth for FY94 is $10 million." (p20)

Robinson, Mark/Wilson, Steve. "Privatization in Massachusetts: Getting Results." Government Union Review v15 n1, Win 1994. p1-55. (ISSN0270-2487).

PRIVATIZATION--MENTAL HEALTH--MASSACHUSETTS

"The consolidation of state hospitals and the relocation of many patients to more clinically appropriate community-based settings are among the [Massachusetts Governor William Weld] administration's largest privatization endeavors. These facilities were operating in aggregate at only 18 percent of capacity when Governor Weld took office....Consider the documented savings from closing just one facility, the state school in Belchertown....The average cost per patient at Belchertown exceeded $100,000. The average placement cost in community settings is $79,000. Annual savings from just this one facility: $6,216,000. Costs at the Dever State School have run still higher. At an annual cost of as much as $125,000 per patient, Dever is the most expensive state-run facility in the United States. At $438 a day, Massachusetts had the highest per diem rates in the country for the care of people with mental retardation. The result was that 90 percent of individuals with mental retardation in the state were not being served." (p30,32)

Robinson, Mark/Wilson, Steve. "Privatization in Massachusetts: Getting Results." Government Union Review v15 n1, Win 1994. p1-55. (ISSN0270-2487).

PRIVATIZATION--MEXICO (v19)

PRIVATIZATION--POLAND

"Although Poland has made great strides in creating new small businesses, the private sector, which employs 47 per cent of the work force, still accounts for only 25 per cent of GDP [gross domestic product]. Similarly, the big public firms--so despised by the therapists [economists advocating 'shock therapy' economic reforms] as socialist dinosaurs--provide at least 60 per cent of Poland's exports. One disturbing result of the market reforms is huge disparities between individual and regional incomes....Nationwide, for every two new jobs--often at pitifully low wages and slight benefits--added by the private sector, one worker ends up unemployed." (p57)

Parker, Richard. "Clintonomics for the East." Foreign Policy n94, Spr 1994. p53-68. (ISSN0015-7228).

"In Poland...employees control (though they don't own) state companies. They direct a large portion of any profits toward their own wages, leaving little for investment. And with 16 percent of the labor force unemployed, workers will not accept layoffs for the sake of greater company efficiency. Neither are elected politicians keen to add to unemployment by forcing privatization. High unemployment also hinders job creation in private companies as taxes go up to pay for unemployment benefits. Poland, unlike Russia, has firmly constrained government subsidies to state firms....The subsidies amounted to 4.5 percent of GDP [gross domestic product] in 1989; 1.1 percent in 1993. Their gross profits have shrunk from 28 percent of sales in 1989 to 4 percent in the first 11 months of 1993. Some firms have shed workers to avoid losses but not to maximize profits as often occurs in private companies. Employment in Poland's non-farm private sector has swelled from 13 percent of total employment prior to reform to 36 percent at the end of 1992." (p10)

Francis, David R. "Economy: Economists Benefit from Cold War's End." The Christian Science Monitor v86 n79, 18 Mar 1994. p10. (ISSN0882-7729).

PRIVATIZATION--UKRAINE (v19)

PRIVATIZATION--UZBEKISTAN

The Uzbekistan "government statistics indicate that 7,000 industrial enterprises have been privatized. Government officials say that there are 1,000 joint ventures employing foreign capital and that 200 tons of Uzbek gold, deposited in Swiss banks, has attracted Western investments. Despite all of these pronouncements, Uzbekistan has no free-market economy. The ownership of 96 percent of government enterprises, collective farms, and ministries remains the same--only the names have been changed. Furthermore, private initiatives are overwhelmed by contradictory laws and decrees, exorbitant taxes, government interference, and mafia harassment." (p50-51)

"Uzbekistan: Tamerlane v. Marx." Bulletin of the Atomic Scientists v50 n1, Jan-Feb 1994. p48-51. (ISSN0096-3402).

PROBATION--U.S. (v19)

PRODUCE TRADE--MEXICO--U.S. (v19)

PRODUCE TRADE--U.S. (v19)

PRODUCTIVITY, AGRICULTURAL

see AGRICULTURAL PRODUCTIVITY

PRODUCTIVITY, INDUSTRIAL

see INDUSTRIAL PRODUCTIVITY

PRODUCTS LIABILITY--U.S. (v19)

PROFESSORS

see COLLEGE TEACHERS

PROPANE INDUSTRY--U.S. (v19)

PROPERTY--MADRID (SPAIN)--PARIS (FRANCE) (v19)

PROPERTY, AMERICAN

see AMERICAN PROPERTY

PROPERTY, LITERARY

see COPYRIGHT

PROPERTY TAX--U.S. (v19)

PROSTATE--CANCER (v19)

PROSTATE--CANCER--U.S. (v19)

PROSTITUTES

see HIV INFECTIONS--INDIA--NEPAL--PROSTITUTES; HIV INFECTIONS--THAILAND--PROSTITUTES

PROSTITUTES--JAPAN (v19)

PROSTITUTION--THAILAND

"Asia Watch, an American-based human-rights group, said the government [of Thailand] was turning a blind eye to the traffic in women and girls brought from Myanmar (Burma) to Thailand for forced prostitution....It is reckoned that some 20,000 women from Myanmar are at present in Thai brothels, with 10,000 new recruits each year. The total number of prostitutes in Thailand is put at between 800,000 and 2m. In 1992 the prime minister, Chuan Leekpai, said the government was cracking down on forced and child prostitution, but not on prostitution in general. 'I won't talk about what is impossible,' he said. Many Thai men, as well as foreigners, patronise the brothels. According to one survey, 75% of Thai men have had sex with a prostitute." (p32)

"Asia: The Slaves from Myanmar." Economist v330 n7849, 5 Feb 1994. p32. (ISSN0013-0613).

PROSTITUTION, JUVENILE (v19)

PUBERTY--NUTRITION

"Over the past 150 years, World Health Organization statistics reveal, the average age at which women begin to menstruate has fallen from 17 to 12.5 years. In his new book FOOD FOR LIFE, Dr. Neal Barnard claims that this drop parallels the rise of the meat industry and the subsequent increase in the world's consumption of meat....Barnard notes that in China, where people eat mostly rice and vegetables and rarely consume meat or dairy products, the average girl reaches puberty at 17. By contrast, the gradual introduction of meat into the Japanese diet has coincided with a drop in the age of puberty in Japan from 15 to 12.5 years in just 40 years." (p9)

Sterling, John. "Hamburgers and Premature Puberty." Earth Island Journal v8 n4, Fall 1993. p9. (ISSN1041-0406).

PUBLIC EMPLOYEES

see CIVIL SERVICE

PUBLIC HOUSING--CHICAGO (ILL)

"Last year...there were 50 homicides in the CHA [Chicago Housing Authority] complexes in Chicago. At the same time, those communities were living with the following statistics: An 89 percent poverty rate; a median family income of $5,400; only 32 percent of the adults had more than a high school education; unemployment averages of 60 percent; only 8.5 percent of the residents were employed in private sector employment, so the private sector has abandoned these areas altogether; and 45 percent of the residents being children under the age of 14. Now, when you aggravate that mix with drugs and guns--and they have confiscated almost 1,200 in the last year--and overcrowding--Robert Taylor has about 13,000 people, which is more than the population of most Illinois towns. So when you aggravate the situation, what you wind up with is the crisis of violence that we have." (pS4661)

Moseley-Braun, Carol (Sen.-Ill.). "Bankruptcy Amendments Act of 1993," Congressional Record (21 Apr 1994). Daily ed. pS4640-4665. (ISSN0363-7239).

PUBLIC HOUSING--U.S. (v19)

PUBLIC LANDS

see also GRAZING DISTRICTS; PASTURE, RIGHT OF

"Clinton sacrificed [U.S. Dept. of the] Interior's agenda to corral Western votes on the budget and free trade--raising questions about his environmental commitment. Against these realities [Interior Secretary, Bruce] Babbitt pits logic and economics. Interior, which controls 66% of public lands, has long sold rights to them at a bargain: On average, ranchers pay only one-fifth as much to run cattle on public range as on private land. And the government takes a bath: Last year, it cost $16.6 billion to manage resources the General Accounting Office says had yielded just $6.9 billion in revenues the previous year. Worse, Interior says it will cost $11 billion to clean up abandoned metal mines that threaten groundwater, mainly in the West. And it says 51% of federal range is in poor or fair condition." (p70)

Regan, Mary Beth. "Environment: Environmental Policy: Rough Ride for an Ex-Cowboy." Business Week n3360, 28 Feb 1994. p70-71. (ISSN0007-7135).

PUBLIC LANDS--ALASKA (v19)

PUBLIC LANDS--NEW JERSEY--OREGON

"Compare the State of New Jersey to one county in Oregon, Harney County....Harney County has 6 million acres of land, or 9,375 square miles--in one county. The State of New Jersey has 7,468 square miles....Harney has 74 percent, or 5 million acres, of Federal ownership. That equates to 7,812 square miles within the county. So the Federal ownership within one county of Oregon is larger than the whole State of New Jersey." (pS4222)

Hatfield, Mark O. (Sen.-Oreg.). "Payments in Lieu of Taxes Act," Congressional Record (13 Apr 1994). Daily ed. pS4210-4229. (ISSN0363-7239).

PUBLIC LANDS--U.S. (v19)

PUBLIC LANDS--UTAH (v19)

PUBLIC LANDS--WYOMING (v19)

PUBLIC OPINION (v19)

PUBLIC RADIO--U.S. (v19)

PUBLIC SCHOOLS--CALIFORNIA--PUBLIC OPINION (v19)

PUBLIC SCHOOLS--CHICAGO (ILL) (v19)

PUBLIC TELEVISION--U.S. (v19)

Based on a survey during the first half of 1992, "More than half (59 percent) of [U.S.] public television's evening programming was given to national, non-public affairs programming....National public affairs programs constituted 33 percent of the public television evening schedule, with news making up more than a third of this category (12 percent of the total). Current public affairs documentaries were 8 percent of programming, business and financial programs 5 percent, historical documentaries 4 percent and interview and talk shows 2 percent....Although the system is intended to reflect the local needs of communities, local programming took up only 7 percent of evening airtime in the period we examined." (p8)

Croteau, David/others. "Public Television & the Missing Public: A Study of Sources & Programming." EXTRA! v6 n6, Sep-Oct 1993. 6-14. (ISSN0895-2310).

"PBS [Public Broadcasting Service]--a national 'service' supplying programming to 346 public television stations that reaches 99 percent of America's television households--was established in 1969 to counteract the diet of programming--shoot-'em-up Westerns, short news programs and game, variety and comedy shows--supplied by the big three networks. PBS, however, is not a network. It owns no stations, and outside of about 10 hours of programming per week, it cannot force member stations to air programs at a specific time--or even at all. Instead, PBS funnels money for programming and provides technical support to those member stations." (p10)

Miniter, Richard. "As the Vast Wasteland Blooms, Can PBS Survive?" Insight v10 n10, 7 Mar 1994. p10-11. (ISSN1051-4880).

PUBLIC TELEVISION--U.S.--FINANCE

"The Reagan administration...called for and obtained reductions in the funding of public television. One result was an increased reliance on corporate 'underwriters' to fund public television. The percentage of public television's total budget that came from the federal government fell from 26 percent in 1980 to 16 percent in 1990, while corporate funding increased from 11 percent of the budget to 17 percent. Corporations are now the largest source of funds for programming produced by PBS's National Program Service, donating $90 million, or 30 percent of the whole--more than federal agencies and foundations combined." (p7)

Croteau, David/others. "Public Television & the Missing Public: A Study of Sources & Programming." EXTRA! v6 n6, Sep-Oct 1993. p6-14. (ISSN0895-2310).

PUBLIC UTILITIES
see also ELECTRIC UTILITIES; RAILROADS; WATER-SUPPLY

PUBLIC UTILITIES--U.S.
"A new study performed by Oak Ridge National Laboratory analyzed conservation investments for 1,200 utilities. Only 363 reported significant demand-side management programs and of these, thirteen utilities account for three-fourths of national conservation savings. Almost two-thirds of these 363 utilities reported savings of only .1 percent of 1990 power generation." (p42)
Asmus, Peter. "Saving Energy Becomes Company Policy." Amicus Journal v14 n4, Win 1993. p38-42. (ISSN0276-7201).
"Utilities [in the U.S.] will spend at least $2 billion on conservation programs this year, a figure that should rise to $10 billion a year by the end of the decade, according to the...Association of Demand-Side Management Professionals of Berkeley, California. All told, the group projects a $50 billion investment in utility energy efficiency--or demand-side management--programs in the 1990s, a figure that dwarfs utility commitments in previous decades." (p38)
Asmus, Peter. "Saving Energy Becomes Company Policy." Amicus Journal v14 n4, Win 1993. p38-42. (ISSN0276-7201).
"On a national basis, the average retail rate for all state and local government utilities [in the U.S.] was 5.88 cents per kWh in 1990. The estimated increase in revenue requirements to replace lost preference purchases would increase the 1990 average retail rate by slightly less than 1.1 mills (1.8 percent) to 5.99 cents per kWh. The impact on rates is similar for the average of all state and local government utilities in the states served by the five power marketing administrations. The average retail rate for these systems was 5.86 cents per kWh in 1990. The average retail rate would increase by about 1.2 mills (2.1 percent) to 5.98 cents per kWh....Nationally, the average retail rate for all cooperatives was 6.82 cents per kWh in 1990. The estimated increase in revenue requirements to replace lost preference purchases would increase the 1990 average retail rate by about 1.5 mills (2.2 percent) to 6.97 cents per kWh." (p64) "Nationally, the average retail rate of all investor-owned utilities was 6.77 cents per kWh in 1990. The decrease in revenue requirements resulting from increased preference purchases would decrease the 1990 average retail rate by about 0.4 mill (0.5 percent) to 6.73 cents per kWh." (p65)
Ulm, David H. "Rate Impacts of Federal Hydro Power." Public Power v52 n1, Jan-Feb 1994. p62-65. (ISSN0033-3654).

PUBLIC WELFARE
see also CHILD WELFARE; FOOD RELIEF; SOCIAL WORKERS; SUPPLEMENTAL SECURITY INCOME PROGRAM

PUBLIC WELFARE--CALIFORNIA (v19)
"The number of people on welfare in L.A. County has increased every month for the past four years! In June of 1993 alone, 32,000 new claims for AFDC [or Aid to Families with Dependent Children], general relief, food stamps, in-home supportive services or Medi-Cal were filed. This means that 1,600 new claims for public assistance were filed each day the office's doors were open during the month of June. Right now, 1,740,000 people are on some form of public assistance in L.A. County: or 20% of the population of the largest county in the 'golden state.'" (p4)
De Rienzo, Guido. "L.A. County: Robbin' The Hood on Behalf of the Sheriff." People's Tribune v20 n37, 13 Sep 1993. p4.
"California, which currently is spending $6 billion a year to support poor families with chidlren, is trying to nudge more of its 947,000 welfare parents into the work force. Only 7 percent now hold jobs." (p1) "The federal government currently spends a record $23 billion on Aid to Families with Dependent Children (AFDC)....Long term, California's plan is designed to fundamentally change the state's welfare culture. Michael Genest, deputy director of California's welfare programs, notes that while few welfare mothers currently work, 88 percent of poor, nonwelfare mothers do hold down jobs....Another key target of reform is teenage parents on welfare. In California, if they maintain a 'C' average in school, teen parents receive a $100 bonus per report card. Teen parents who receive failing grades are penalized $100. Graduating brings a $500 bonus." (p18)
Dillin, John. "Washington Eyes California's Model for Welfare Moms." The Christian Science Monitor v86 n77, 16 Mar 1994. p1,18. (ISSN0882-7729).

PUBLIC WELFARE--CANADA (v19)

PUBLIC WELFARE--CANADA--U.S. (v19)

PUBLIC WELFARE--EUROPEAN COMMUNITY--U.S. (v19)

PUBLIC WELFARE--FLORIDA--WISCONSIN--REFUGEES (v19)

PUBLIC WELFARE--GEORGIA
"In Georgia, a mother with one child receives $235 per month in welfare payments, less than one-half the official poverty rate. Yet welfare 'reformists' led by Governor Zell Miller want to scapegoat and punish these victims of the economic crisis even more. As more workers lost jobs to 'downsizing,' the number of welfare recipients increased dramatically (from 86,663 in 1988 to 139,355 in 1993). Rather than seek the answer in providing more well-paying jobs, the Georgia legislature passed legislation this year to withhold payments to mothers who conceive a child after being on welfare more than 24 months. In addition, a teen mother under 18 must live with a parent or guardian." (p9)
Slaughter, John. "Georgia Welfare Reform: 'We Have Got to Stand Up!'" People's Tribune v21 n1, 27 Dec 1993. p9.

PUBLIC WELFARE--HISPANIC AMERICANS (v19)

PUBLIC WELFARE--ILLINOIS
"Contrary to popular belief, most poor people work. In 1990, nearly two of three poor families with children had one or more workers in the family, many of whom worked more than 40 hours per week. Despite their efforts, however, the average income of these families was $615 per month. The Illinois Department of Public Aid, which dispenses public assistance grants to eligible families, regularly publishes its standard of need--the income needed for families to maintain a 'reasonable standard of health and decency.' For a family of four, the standard is $876. The department provides cash grants at approximately 40% of the standard, and this standard is approximately 70% of the national poverty level (Illinois Department of Public Aid, 1993)." (p47)
Williams, Betty L. "Essay: Reflections on Family Poverty." Families in Society v75 n1, Jan 1994. p47-50. (ISSN1044-3894).

PUBLIC WELFARE--LOS ANGELES (CALIF)
"Two years ago, a three-person family on the Aid to Families with Dependent Children (AFDC) program in Los Angeles County received $694 per month. Today, the same family has to make ends meet on $607 per month. This amounts to a 13 percent cut, or $87 per month less. Despite the fact that the number of people on some type of aid has increased by over 80 percent since 1986, the amount 'doled out' has continued to shrink." (p8)
De Rienzo, Guido. "Los Angeles County: As Numbers of Poor Grow, Aid Shrinks." People's Tribune v20 n49, 6 Dec 1993. p8.

PUBLIC WELFARE--NEWFOUNDLAND
"Every Canadian province has a problem of welfare finance, but Newfoundland's is the worst. Nearly half of all people employed there receive unemployment insurance in any given year; in rural areas, 70%. Spending on social services for a population of just under 600,000 costs C$22m a year--and over C$1 billion in

federally financed unemployment insurance." (p60)

"International: Canada: New-found Plans." Economist v329 n7843, 25 Dec 1993. p60. (ISSN0013-0613).

PUBLIC WELFARE--NORWAY

"Social security programs [in Norway] now account for one-quarter of all state expenditures, while one of every four Norwegians receives some kind of government benefit. Entire districts enjoy public largesse as well. Residents of Finmark County and of the northern part of Troms County, both deep inside the Arctic Circle, are eligible for a special tax deduction of up to $4300 a year per person. Children in these districts meanwhile each qualify for $520 extra in annual benefits, on top of the $1460 provided nationwide for the first child in a family. These pay-outs climb incrementally with each additional child, reaching an annual total of $1820 for the fourth child born into a Norwegian family. Many benefits seem amazingly magnanimous to foreign observers. Employees are automatically entitled, for example, to as many as 12 'sick days' per year. Similarly, parents get full pay for up to 10 days annually if they must stay at home to care for a sick child. A single parent with two children is eligible for 30 days a year of paid sick leave." (p6)

Brown, Ross. "Welfare State: A Colder Climate in Scandinavia." Toward Freedom v42 n6, Oct 1993. p6. (ISSN0048-9898).

PUBLIC WELFARE--U.S. (v19)

"Some of those who live in poverty cannot be expected to become self-supporting, others should not be. Among the former are some of the roughly two-thirds of low-income adults with very low levels of literacy; those affected by the 'widespread existence of learning disabilities' that the U.S. Department of Health and Human Services has noted among AFDC [or Aid to Families with Dependent Children] recipients (the U.S. Department of Labor estimates that 25-40% of those on welfare may have learning disabilities). Among the latter are those in the welfare system who 'are caring for seriously ill or mentally or physically impaired family members." (p199)

U.S. House. Committee on Ways and Means. "Historical Trends in Poverty and Family Income." Hearing, 26 Oct 1993. Washington, D.C.: GPO, 1994. (ISBN0160435765). (Y4.W36:103-42).

"Although Washington spends about $14 billion a year on welfare, that's only 1% of the federal budget. And that's down from 1.4% in 1970, largely because benefits have lagged behind inflation....About 30% of the 5 million adults on welfare leave the rolls before two years, studies show." (p92)

Bernstein, Aaron. "The Workplace: Commentary: Why Clinton's Workfare Won't Work." Business Week n3361, 7 Mar 1994. p92. (ISSN0007-7135).

"Federal and state AFDC [or Aid to Families with Dependent Children] expenses--states administer the programs and pay about half the costs--amount to about $23 billion in benefits annually plus $2.7 billion in administrative costs. The average monthly benefit is $377 per family. In addition, families on AFDC normally qualify for food stamps, free school meals and Medicaid, the federal-state health insurance program for the poor. They also may receive housing subsidies and assistance in paying their utility bills." (p118)

Katz, Jeffrey L. "Social Policy: Human Services: Clinton Plans Major Shift in Lives of Poor People." Congressional Quarterly Weekly Report v52 n3, 22 Jan 1994. p117-118,121-122. (ISSN0010-5910).

"The number of recipients on Aid to Families With Dependent Children (AFDC), the...[U.S.] main welfare program, had been fairly steady from 1971 to 1989, when the total was 10.9 million. (A recession had pushed the figure to 11.3 million recipients in 1976, but then the total eased). But the total has ballooned since 1989, increasing 30 percent to 14 million people in nearly 5 million families. Nearly one of seven children receives welfare. The weakened economy bears the brunt of the blame for swelling the welfare rolls; a rise in out-of-wedlock births also contributed." (p118)

Katz, Jeffrey L. "Social Policy: Human Services: Clinton Plans Major Shift in Lives of Poor People." Congressional Quarterly Weekly Report v52 n3, 22 Jan 1994. p117-118,121-122. (ISSN0010-5910).

"Welfare [in the U.S.] has changed from being a temporary safety net to a way of life. Studies show that 50 percent to 70 percent of welfare recipients leave AFDC [or Aid to Families with Dependent Children] within two years, but many of them later return to the welfare rolls for total stays that last eight or more years." (p118)

Katz, Jeffrey L. "Social Policy: Human Services: Clinton Plans Major Shift in Lives of Poor People." Congressional Quarterly Weekly Report v52 n3, 22 Jan 1994. p117-118,121-122. (ISSN0010-5910).

"In 1992, Federal spending for the broad category of social welfare programs accounted for half of all Federal spending--a total of $777 billion. Of that $777 billion, $285 billion was budgeted specifically for public assistance programs. This is more than the $273 billion we spent on defense, more than the $199 billion interest on the national debt, more than the $208 billion for all other Federal programs combined. Yet, for all of the money spent on social welfare programs, poverty has continued to rise. In Washington State there was a 19-percent increase in welfare caseloads between July 1990 and February 1992. Nationally, the numbers are just as dramatic. In the first 5 months of fiscal year 1992, Aid to Families with Dependent Children (AFDC) climbed to a record 4.685 million families, including 9.2 million children. This is 21 percent above the comparable 1990 level. These numbers suggest that our current efforts are doing little to transform dependence into independence, or that more money is not necessarily the answer." (pS16668)

Gorton, Slade (Sen.-Wash.). "The Need for Welfare Reform," Congressional Record (20 Nov 1993). Daily ed. pS16667-16668. (ISSN0363-7239).

"Scapegoating of low-income people [in the U.S.] has increased over the past 12 years. In the last year or so, this scapegoating has begun to focus specifically on welfare recipients. Since the beginning of 1992, dozens of states have either considered or have passed legislation that sharply reduces or cuts off benefits to welfare recipients based on their behavior in specific areas. These 'behavior modification' techniques, as they are known, have as their subtext the pernicious idea that people on welfare--and particularly mothers with small children receiving Aid to Families with Dependent Children (AFDC) are lazy, irresponsible, and not motivated to get off welfare unless they are prodded to do so through a system of monetary rewards and punishments. Thus, for example, the Family Development Initiative Act in New Jersey, the first such set of proposals to pass a state legislature, reduces or cuts off benefits for 'able-bodied' AFDC recipients with children over the age of two who 'refuse' to work or participate in state-mandated education or job training programs. The New Jersey law...encourages women to marry someone who is NOT their child's biological father by allowing such 'stepparent' couples to retain more of their combined income without losing AFDC benefits (up to 150% of poverty level)." (p3)

Astor, Kathy K. "Punishing Women Who Break the Rules of Patriarchy." New Directions for Women v22 n1, Jan-Feb 1993. p3-5. (ISSN0160-1075).

"The average welfare benefit [in the U.S.] is $367 a month or $4400 a year. This is almost $9000 less than the federal poverty line for a family of three. Of the 13 million AFDC [or Aid to Families with Dependent Children] recipients, only 4 million are adults, 90 percent of whom are women--many mothers of young children. In more than half of welfare homes, the youngest child is under 5 years of age. 10 percent of all single mothers are unemployed. The $4.25 an hour minimum wage is $2.75 an hour less than the $7.00 an hour needed to keep a family of four out of poverty. Of all AFDC mothers, 40 percent are African American, 38 percent are white, 16 percent are Latina, 2.7 percent are Asian, 1.3 percent are Native American, and 1.5 percent are of unknown race....Forty-seven percent of the population receives some kind of direct government benefit, with 5.1 percent of the population receiving AFDC." (p5)

"Did You Know...?" New Directions for Women v22 n1, Jan-Feb 1993. p3-5. (ISSN0160-1075).

In the U.S., "the welfare rolls stabilized in the early 1970's at about 3.6 million families and began to grow only with the 1989 recession. Even now, Aid to Families With Dependent Children...accounts for only 1 percent of the Federal budget, or about $22 billion a year. And rather than supporting families so generously as to encourage 'dependency,' the grants are painfully low, averaging $370 a month in 1992. No state brings families up to the poverty line, even when food stamps are included." (p7)

Abramovitz, Mimi/Piven, Francis Fox. "Scapegoating Women on Welfare." New Patriot v6 n5, Sep-Oct 1993. p7.

"At last, we seem to be moving toward a consensus on welfare reform [in the U.S.]. Many in Congress, on both sides, strongly support the proposition that the nation's main welfare program, Aid to Families with Dependent Children (AFDC), should be converted into a program emphasizing work. The catch, of course, is that it's expensive. Including day care and the other needed services, it costs at least $5,000 per year to educate or train a welfare mother, not counting the cash payments she receives. Just putting her to work costs $4,000 a year for day care, transportation and supervision. And there are 5 million AFDC families." (p9-10)

Offner, Paul. "Target the Kids." New Republic v210 n4, 24 Jan 1994. p9-10. (ISSN0028-6583).

PUBLIC WELFARE--U.S.--IMMIGRANTS

"A country with extensive welfare programs, such as the United States, cannot afford the large-scale immigration of less-skilled persons that we have today, explained economist George Borjas in a recent NATIONAL REVIEW article....Immigrant households make up only 21 percent of California's population, but receive one-third of all cash benefits distributed in the state. In 1970, immigrants were slightly less likely than natives to receive cash benefits such as AFDC [or Aid to Families with Dependent Children] or SSI [Supplemental Security Income]. By 1990, the situation had changed drastically: more than 9 percent of immigrant households received public assistance, as opposed to about 7 percent of native households. (NATIONAL REVIEW, December 13, 1993)." (p2)

"Economist Says Large-Scale Immigration Harmful." FAIR Immigration Report v16 n1, Jan 1994. p2.

PUBLIC WELFARE--U.S.--SINGLE-PARENT FAMILY

"In 1965, when [Sen. Daniel Patrick] Moynihan--then an assistant secretary of Labor--attributed social problems among blacks to unstable family structure, their rate of out-of-wedlock births was 26 percent. It is now 68 percent. In an October 1993 op-ed column in THE WALL STREET JOURNAL, Charles Murray, a fellow at the American Enterprise Institute, noted that in 1991, the babies born to single white women represented 22 percent of white births--just four percentage points less than the black rate that so alarmed Moynihan three decades ago. 'My proposition,' Murray wrote, 'is that illegitimacy is the single most important social problem of our time--more important than crime, drugs, poverty, illiteracy, welfare or homelessness because it drives everything else.'" (p121)

Katz, Jeffrey L. "Social Policy: Human Services: Clinton Plans Major Shift in Lives of Poor People." Congressional Quarterly Weekly Report v52 n3, 22 Jan 1994. p117-118,121-122. (ISSN0010-5910).

PUBLIC WELFARE--WISCONSIN

Wisconsin's Learnfare program, which cuts the welfare benefits of families whose thirteen- to nineteen-year-old children are truant from school, has few students using its case-management services which are intended to help students improve their attendance. In ten sample counties only 14 percent of 4,700 eligible teenagers responded to offers for these services. The evaluation showed that case-management can be effective when it is used, and that the challenge is to persuade more teens and their families to participate. (p14)

Cohen, Deborah L. "Learnfare's Services for Truants Not Often Tapped." Education Week v13 n23, 2 Mar 1994. p14. (ISSN0277-4232).

PUBLISHERS AND PUBLISHING--TAXATION--CANADA--GREAT BRITAIN--IRELAND (v19)

PUBLISHERS AND PUBLISHING--U.S. (v19)

PUERTO RICO

see AGRICULTURE--PUERTO RICO; NUNS--PUERTO RICO--U.S.

PUERTO RICO--POLITICS AND GOVERNMENT (v19)

PUMAS

"Humans are the greatest threat to [the survival of cougars]....In the 1500s Jesuit priests initiated extermination programs; between 1937 and 1970 the modern Animal Damage Control Agency killed 7,255 cougars. While domestic dogs kill some 20 people a year and bee stings kill 40, neither generates as much concern or fear as cougars. But, [Kevin] Hansen tells us, they have fatally attacked only 10 people since 1890." (p12)

Trewartha, Arden. "Bulletin Board: The American Lion." High Country News v25 n15, 23 Aug 1993. p12. (ISSN0191-5657).

QUALITY CONTROL--U.S. (v19)

QUALITY OF LIFE

see also COST AND STANDARD OF LIVING

"Despite new agricultural technologies, including the Green Revolution, and the fact that most arable land in the world is already in agriculture, a scarcity of food and essential nutrients exists for some people in all nations. The situation is especially acute in the developing countries. Estimates are that of the more than 5 billion humans that now exist in the world, from 1 to 1.5 billion are malnourished (Latham, 1984; Sivard, 1987; Pimentel, 1989). In addition to food shortages, the quality of life for this 10 to 30% of the world population is diminished or threatened by insufficient clean water, shelter, health care, and satisfying employment." (p37)

Pimentel, David/Pimentel, Marcia. "The Demographic and Environmental Consequences of the Green Revolution." Carrying Capacity Network v4 n1, 1994. p37-44. (ISSN1066-5404).

RABIES

"Worldwide, more than 33 000 people die of rabies each year, most of them in China and India. Human cases of rabies in Europe are relatively rare. Only eight such cases were reported in 1993--five in the Russian Federation, and one each in Latvia, Lithuania and Belarus. All were fatal, as were the 12 cases reported in Europe in 1992. But about 100 000 people a year in Europe seek vaccination after exposure to suspected rabid animals, imposing high costs on health services." (p2)

News release. "Spring Offensive against Rabies in Europe." WHO Press 20 Apr 1994. p1-3.

RABIES--EUROPE

"Since the first field trial of oral immunization of foxes against rabies in Switzerland in 1978--with vaccine contained in chicken heads--more than 59 million vaccine baits have been distributed in more than 15 countries in Europe and North America. This has resulted in a substantial drop in the number of rabies cases in animals in central Europe and a reduction in the number of contacts between humans and rabies-suspected animals. In France, only 261 cases of animal rabies were reported in 1993 against 2984 for 1990. In Germany, the number of rabies cases decreased from 5572 in 1990, to 853 in 1993. The figure for other countries also show this very promising trend." (p1)

News release. "Spring Offensive against Rabies in Europe." WHO Press 20 Apr 1994. p1-3.

RABIES--INDIA--U.S. (v19)

RABIES--U.S. (v19)

RACISM

see also ANTISEMITISM

RACISM--GERMANY--YOUTH--PUBLIC OPINION

In Germany, "a frighteningly large number of...young people willing to employ violent means against foreigners come from or still live in respectable middle-class homes; they attend high school or are working in regular jobs. And we do need to ask why it took our high school and university students--the daughters and sons of the rebels of 1968--months before organizing rallies against racism. We can no longer use the easy formula of the outcast when almost 40 percent of the young people (age 15-24) in West Germany and more than 50 percent in East Germany confess that they find the presence of foreigners in our country annoying; when almost 30 percent in West and more than 40 percent in East Germany think all foreigners should leave Germany. True, more than 90 percent of these young people profess their aversion to violence, skinheads, hooligans, but one percent or fifty thousand adolescents in Germany stated in a survey conducted by IBM in 1992 that they were willing and ready to use violent means against foreigners." (p45)

Diedrich, Maria. "Born Guilty?" Transition v3 n2, 1993. p34-51. (ISSN0041-1191).

RACISM--JACKSONVILLE (FLA)

"The Jacksonville Community Council, Inc., which monitors quality of life indicators for the Jacksonville Chamber of Commerce in Florida, now has information dating back to 1983 for most of its 74 indicators. Among other trends, JCCI's index marks increasing racial tensions in the community: in 1984, 28 percent of Jacksonville residents believed that racism is a problem; in 1987, 46 percent; in 1991, 67 percent." (p14)

Bardoe, Cheryl. "Reproducible Feature: Taking Stock: Indexes Serve as Tool for Sustainability." Neighborhood Works v16 n5, Oct-Nov 1993. p14-15.

RACISM--U.S.

"I am always amazed and puzzled by those Americans who argue persuasively and passionately on behalf of equal treatment for blacks while simultaneously supporting measures to deny the same people the opportunity for achieving equality. The issue at hand, namely, the drawing of race-based congressional districts, is a perfect example. In a 5 to 4 decision, the Supreme Court ruled that drawing congressional districts for the purpose of giving blacks an opportunity to be elected, dilutes the votes of white citizens. In the case of Shaw versus Reno, the high court discounted the fact that until the drawing of two congressional districts with a majority of black voters, North Carolina had not elected a black Member to Congress since 1901. The high court ignored the fact that for over 90 years a State with 35 percent black population had deliberately created white race-based districts which diluted the voting strength of black citizens." (pH1877)

Clay, William (Rep.-Mo.). "1965 Voting Rights Act under Attack," Congressional Record (22 Mar 1994). Daily ed. pH1870-1879. (ISSN0363-7239).

"A University of Michigan study...paints the first national portrait of social integration on college campuses....The study was presented...at the annual meeting of the American Educational Research Association by Sylvia Hurtado, assistant professor of education at the U-M School of Education's Center for the Study of Higher and Postsecondary Education. The study is based on a nationally representative sample of 6,000 college students at 390 schools, who were surveyed in 1987 and followed up 1991." (p1) "Hurtado and her colleagues...analyzed the incidence of exclusion or harassment based on racial or ethnic identity. About 53 percent of the African American students felt excluded from school activities because of their race/ethnicity, compared with about 24 percent of Asian Americans, 16 percent of Mexican Americans and 6 percent of whites. At the same time, 19 percent of whites said they had heard faculty make inappropriate remarks about minorities, compared with 51 percent of African Americans and 31 percent of Asian American students. Moreover, about 32 percent of African American and 30 percent of Asian American students said they were insulted or threatened by other students, compared with 10 percent of Mexican Americans and 9 percent of whites." (p2-3)

News release. "Hurtado." University of Michigan News and Information Services 31 Mar 1994. p1-3.

RACISM--U.S.--PUBLIC OPINION

"Just fifteen years ago, 23 percent of whites thought that blacks were born with less ability; now only 6 percent say they think so. Virtually no respondent, liberal or conservative, would give less government help to an unemployed black worker than to an unemployed white one. At the same time [social scientists and authors of THE SCAR OF RACE Paul M. Sniderman and Thomas Piazza]...found that large numbers of whites still hold negative stereotypes of blacks, and most make no effort at all to disguise their opinions. Large numbers of respondents (61 percent) told the pollsters that most blacks on welfare could get a job, that blacks could do better if they tried harder (43 percent), that black neighborhoods are run down (42 percent), that blacks have a chip on their shoulder (36 percent)." (p37)

Jacoby, Tamar. "After Bigotry." New Republic v210 n4, 24 Jan 1994. p36-39. (ISSN0028-6583).

RACISM IN THE PRESS--U.S.

"A report by Katherine McFate of the Joint Center for Political and Economic Studies (detailed by Michelle McQueen in the WALL STREET JOURNAL, 8/12/92) shows that the NEW YORK POST is engaging in racial fear-mongering. Although the media presents crime as being at a new height, the number of victims of violent crime has actually decreased by 9 percent from 1981 to 1990. The most common victims are black men, who are 50 percent more likely than white men and two and a half times more likely than white women to be the victim of a violent crime. And crime seldom has what the POST calls 'racial implications.' Only 18 percent of white victims of violent crime reported that their assailant was black. The real racial bias in the system is against African Americans: Blacks account for 29 percent of arrests, but 47 percent of prison inmates. But if all you see is the NEW YORK POST, you probably won't read about that." (p17)

"NEW YORK POST: Militant White Daily." EXTRA! v6 n1, Jan-Feb 1993. p17. (ISSN0895-2310).

RADIO BROADCASTING--U.S.

A study of National Public Radio "reviewed transcripts of all weekday broadcasts of 'All Things Considered' and 'Morning

Edition' from September through December 1991. The sample included 2,296 stories, which featured 5507 quoted sources. Government officials were 1414 (26 percent) of all sources. Journalists, writers and academics made up 22 percent.... Ordinary citizens...constituted 10 percent of sources.... Only 21 percent of NPR's sources were women--just 3 percentage points more than FAIR found in a 1990 study of 'Nightline's' guests (EXTRA!, Winter '90)." (p18) "One-third of NPR's segments addressed international events and two-thirds addressed U.S. domestic affairs. Of the domestic stories, 29 percent were about political issues, 24 percent dealt with social issues (e.g., sexual harassment or affirmative action) and 13 percent covered economics. Another 29 percent was cultural and arts reporting....Like commercial broadcasters, NPR's international coverage concentrated on Europe (55 percent of international stories) and downplayed events in the Third World. Only 12 percent of NPR's international coverage dealt with Asia (excluding the Mideast), 8 percent with Latin America and the Caribbean and 6 percent with Africa. These three regions together account for more than three-fourths of the world's population." (p19)

Ryan, Charlotte. "A Study of National Public Radio." EXTRA! v6 n3, Apr-May 1993. p18-21,26. (ISSN0895-2310).

RADIO IN POLITICS--U.S. (v19)

RADIO STATIONS--BOLIVIA

"Radionovelas broadcast by small native-language radio stations operated in Bolivia by peasant groups and the Roman Catholic church are as popular as any soap opera anywhere, with listener numbers soaring when they go on the air. The stories, which reach up to 2.5 million of Bolivia's 6 million people, relate directly and realistically to peasant life, and are aimed at stimulating thought and debate about the problems peasants face....Indigenous-language broadcasting was started in the 1950s to 'civilise' the Bolivian Indian population. But in the past 20 years, many stations have been run by the people themselves to recover traditional culture and reinforce community links. In all, 22 radio stations in the country are aimed at peasant listeners; 12 are church-run, while 10 are operated by peasant groups. Radio is an excellent tool for rural communication because a radio set is inexpensive and does not require a formal electricity supply, which in any case is not available in the countryside." (p19)

Dorna, Ivan Arias. "Focus: Communication: Two-Way Radio Nurtures a Culture." Panoscope n34, Jan 1993. p19. (ISSN0951-8819).

RADIO STATIONS--U.S. (v19)

RADIOACTIVE WASTES--FORMER SOVIET REPUBLICS

"The Yablokov Report, which was commissioned by President Boris Yeltsin...detail[s] the extent of Soviet nuclear disposal at sea. According to the report, the Soviet Union had dumped over 2.5 million curies of radioactive waste into the Arctic Ocean and other marine environments. By comparison, the accident at Three Mile Island in...Pennsylvania released 15 curies of radiation....since 1959, the former Soviet Union dumped 18 nuclear reactors, a reactor screen, 11,000 to 17,000 cannisters of nuclear waste, and hundreds of thousands of gallons of liquid radioactive waste....solid nuclear fuel waste totaling 10 million curies is currently stored aboard vessels in Murmansk Harbor....In October 1993, Russia dumped 900 tons of low-level radioactive waste in the Sea of Japan in violation of a previously agreed upon international moratorium." (pH1243)

Weldon, Curt (Rep.-Pa.). "H.R. 3982, the Ocean Radioactive Dumping Ban Act of 1994," Congressional Record (10 Mar 1994). Daily ed. pH1243-1244. (ISSN0363-7239).

"As many as 120 civilian underground explosions have been carried out in the USSR over the past four decades and about 1,000 more under military operation. There are 54 civilian nuclear power plants in the former USSR, operated in ways that would be considered less-than-safe by international standards. There are many radioactive waste sites, even in densely populated areas: 636 in Moscow; 200 in Omsk; 1,400 in St. Petersburg. These commonplace sources of radioactivity take a toll in morbidity, as do the dramatic events, such as the nuclear accident at Chernobyl in 1986. Over 650,000 people were exposed to radiation at Chernobyl, and a 1992 commission found 1,700 cases of thyroid cancer (200 of them children) believed to have resulted from that accident." (p2)

Kalish, Susan. "Life Expectancy Falling, Morbidity Rising in Former USSR." Population Today v21 n1, Jan 1993. p1-2. (ISSN0749-2448).

RADIOACTIVE WASTES--RUSSIA

"For 40 years, Russia has apparently dumped nuclear wastes into Arctic seas, buried them on the shores of the Arctic Ocean, and discharged them directly into inland lakes and rivers that flow into the Arctic, contaminating the watershed for hundreds of miles downstream. Nuclear weapons testing has been the biggest single source of radioactive contamination of the Arctic. The U.S.S.R. held nearly all of its high yield tests at Novaya Zemlya, an island in the Arctic Ocean, releasing a total of 300 megatons of radioactive fallout into the atmosphere, some of which drifted to Alaska and northern Canada." (p4)

Hajost, Scott A./Pfirman, Stephanie L. "EDF Column: Protecting the Arctic, Now and in the Future." EDF Letter v24 n1, Jan 1993. p4. (ISSN0163-2566).

"In Russia, 60,000 hectares have been polluted as the result of uranium and thorium mining and hydrometallurgical processing. Every ton of spent fuel that is processed will generate 5,000 cubic meters of high-level and 17 million cubic meters of low-level radioactive waste. Unlike Europe's coastal facilities, Russia's reprocessing plants, including a partially constructed new plant, are all inland, where their wastes contaminate the soil and poison the water. The poor state of Russia's railways will lead to accidents and spills of radioactive substances during transport. Russia is already the most radioactively polluted country in the world. An expansion of the nuclear industry will cause even more damage to public health." (p24)

Popova, Lydia. "Energy: Russia's Nuclear Elite on the Rampage." Surviving Together v11 n2, Sum 1993. p23-25. (ISSN0859-6286).

RADIOACTIVE WASTES--SOVIET UNION (v19)

RADIOACTIVE WASTES--U.S. (v19)

"In addition to subsidizing the price of nuclear fuel, taxpayers [in the U.S.] are given responsibility for fission's end product--radioactive waste. Under the Nuclear Waste Policy Act of 1982 nuclear utilities are required to pay only 0.1 cents per kilowatt-hour (kwh) of nuclear-generated electricity into a federal fund that will be used to find a permanent resting place for the highly radioactive waste. DOE [U.S. Department of Energy] proposes to store the waste for tens of thousands of years at Yucca Mountain in Nevada, despite numerous environmental problems and deep public opposition. The U.S. General Accounting Office (GAO) repeatedly has urged DOE to raise its waste disposal assessment fee. The agency estimates that unless the fee is raised, DOE will spend $4.1 billion (1988 dollars) more than it collects to dispose of high-level waste. GAO also warns that the financial condition of 11 of the 17 utilities that owe one-time fees of $2 billion to the fund for waste generated prior to 1983 'cast serious doubt on their ability to pay.'" (p14)

Lapp, David. "Bankrolling Nuclear Power." Environmental Action v25 n1, Spr 1993. p12-16. (ISSN0013-922X).

RADON--U.S.--MORTALITY

"The National Council on Radiation Protection (NCRP), a quasi-government agency aligned with the nuclear industry, recently estimated that indoor radon comprises about 55 percent of all radiation exposure. By contrast, they say radiation exposure from the entire nuclear fuel cycle (wastes, uranium tailings and reactor emissions) comprises only 0.1 percent, or 555 times less than radon. Says Alfred Craig, head of EPA's Radon Reduction Research and Development Program, 'Radon is clearly among the most serious causes of death in the country, and I predict that as we study the problem further, death rates will only increase.'" (p19-20)

Mead, Nathaniel. "Currents: Radon Revisited." E Magazine v5 n1, Feb 1994. p18-21. (ISSN1046-8021).

RAILROADS--CHINA (v19)

RAILROADS--NEW ZEALAND--SWEDEN

"Introducing commercial disciplines into railways makes them much more efficient. But the benefits seem to be obtained even where commercialised railways have not actually been privatised. Take New Zealand. The railways there have indeed been transformed since commercialisation in the 1980s, with jobs cut from 20,000 in 1981 to 5,000 now; and profits replacing losses. But the bulk of the transformation took place under public ownership. The railway was sold to Wisconsin Central Railway, an American firm, only in July. Or take Sweden, where competition was introduced from 1988. The railway employed 29,000 people in 1987, but now employs 18,000. Costs have fallen by 25-30%. And yet in Sweden only rural services have been opened to competition. Mainline services remain a monopoly of the state rail company, which has also won most of the contracts for rural services." (p75)

"Britain: The World of Railways." Economist v329 n7843, 25 Dec 1993. p75. (ISSN0013-0613).

RAILROADS--NORTHEASTERN STATES (v19)

RAILROADS--TEXAS

"The Texas TGV [high speed rail projects] will provide nonstop 200 MPH service between Houston and Dallas, between San Antonio, Austin and Dallas, and between Dallas DFW Airport and Fort Worth. This is a service area, commonly referred to as the 'Texas Triangle,' which contains 60% of the state's population and which generates over 75% of the state's gross domestic product....The rolling stock will be specially adapted for the Texas TGV and will be based on the design of the next generation of the operationally proven TGV Atlantique which currently operates at 186 MPH. This was the same design which established the world ground speed record for fixed guideway vehicles of 320 miles per hour in May of 1990. The system planned for Texas will go beyond the Atlantique; it will initially operate at 200 MPH and the system infrastructure is designed to accommodate speeds up to 250 MPH." (p226-227)

Salci, Larry E. (Texas TGV Corp.). U.S. House. Committee on Appropriations. "Department of Transportation and Related Agencies Approp. for 1994 (Part 7A)." Hearing, Washington, D.C.: GPO, 1993. (ISBN0160411033). (Y4.Ap6/1:T68/4/994/pt.7A).

RAILROADS--U.S. (v19)

"During FY92, the number of miles traveled by Amtrak passengers decreased 2.9 percent to 6.09 billion miles, down 182 million miles from FY91. However, total ridership increased from 40.1 million to 41.6 million passengers, including 21.3 million intercity passengers and 20.3 million commuter passengers transported by Amtrak. For the first time in over a decade, Amtrak revenues declined 2.5 percent to $1.32 billion. This forced Amtrak to continue to expand a series of corporate-wide actions to reduce its operating budget. In fact, costs company-wide were reduced sufficiently to maintain the railroad's revenue-to-cost ratio at .79. This is the highest ratio in Amtrak history and one of the best among passenger railroads in the world." (p639)

Claytor, W. Graham, Jr. (President, Chairman, National Railroad Passenger Corp. (AMTRAK)). U.S. House. Committee on Appropriations. "Department of Transportation and Related Agencies Approp. for 1994 (Part 5)." Hearing, Washington, D.C.: GPO, 1993. (ISBN0160410509). (Y4.Ap6/1:T68/4/994/pt.5).

"For the first time since 1975, revenues in FY 1992 actually declined ($34.2 million or 3.3 percent) compared to our record performance in FY 1991. While this should not obscure the fact that Amtrak generated well over $1.3 billion in passenger and other revenues during the year, our performance failed to meet even our modest expectations for the year. This is the result of weak passenger demand. The recession took a serious toll on demand for travel services. Passenger ticket revenues fell 3.5 percent, intercity ridership fell some 3 percent, and passenger miles declined from 6.3 billion to 6.1 billion. Three isolated events also significantly undermined ticket revenues: Hurricane Andrew virtually wiped out travel to the south for several weeks; a threatened rail passenger strike and actual freight railroad shutdown forced our passengers to use other travel modes; and a fratricidal airline fare war devastated long-distance rail demand during the peak summer months." (p520-521)

Claytor, W. Graham, Jr. (President, Chairman, National Railroad Passenger Corp. (AMTRAK)). U.S. House. Committee on Appropriations. "Department of Transportation and Related Agencies Approp. for 1994 (Part 5)." Hearing, Washington, D.C.: GPO, 1993. (ISBN0160410509). (Y4.Ap6/1:T68/4/994/pt.5).

"There is very little statistical operating and financial data available for shortlines. These non-Class I railroads have been exempt from filing such data since 1981. Based on available information, largely from industry trade groups, this segment of the railroad industry has grown since deregulation in 1980 by over 250 carriers to 522 in 1991. The vast majority of shortlines have operating revenues under $10 million. The number of miles-of-road-owned in 1991 was about 31,000. The impact of deregulation through the Staggers Rail Act of 1980 contributed significantly to the strong growth in shortlines by eliminating much of the regulatory burden on the rail industry." (p351-352)

Cothen, Grady (Assoc. Administrator for Safety, Federal Railroad Admin.). U.S. House. Committee on Appropriations. "Department of Transportation and Related Agencies Approp. for 1994 (Part 5)." Hearing, Washington, D.C.: GPO, 1993. (ISBN0160410509). (Y4.Ap6/1:T68/4/994/pt.5).

"On January 18, 1992, a DOT [U.S. Department of Transportation] specification 112 tank car containing 30,700 gallons of liquefied propane, a flammable gas, fractured along a circumferential weld when the train began to move at Dragon, Mississippi and lost its entire load of propane. Metallurgical examination revealed a 21 inch long preexisting crack at the origin of the fracture that had extended almost completely through the tank shell before the catastrophic failure. By March 11, 1992, 8 similar tank cars had been inspected and 4 of those tank cars were found to have cracks ranging from 2 to 30 inches long in the same location as the one that failed. Therefore, on March 13, 1992, the Safety Board issued an urgent Safety Recommendation to the FRA [Federal Railroad Administration] to require the appropriate inspection of a representative sampling of other dual diameter tank cars for similar defects. The inspection of 108 tank cars of the same design identified that 40 tank cars had cracks in the same location. And, 25 of the 40 tank cars had been tested and inspected during or after 1988: 13 of the 40 tank cars had been tested and inspected during 1991 and 1992." (p164)

Vogt, Carl W. (Chairman, National Transportation Safety Board). U.S. House. Committee on Appropriations. "Department of Transportation and Related Agencies Approp. for 1994 (Part 6)." Hearing, Washington, D.C.: GPO, 1993. (ISBN0160410746). (Y4.Ap6/1:T68/4/994/pt.6).

"MAGLEV is high-speed guided ground transportation which depends on magnetic forces for vehicle suspension, guidance and propulsion. It operates on electricity, making it clean and quiet. It is also safe, as the MAGLEV cars wrap around an elevated guideway and cannot derail. The capital costs, approximately $30 million per mile, are similar to those of new highways, but the system is far less damaging to the environment. HSR [high speed rail] systems have a lower capital cost, but higher operating and maintenance (O&M) cost. Since a MAGLEV system has no friction between vehicle and track with its attendant wear and tear, long term maintenance costs will be low compared to other rail systems. At speeds of 185 mph or more, MAGLEV consumes 32% less electricity per seat-mile than other types of HSR. MAGLEV can reach its top speed of 300 mph in a distance of 3 miles, compared to HSR which requires 15 miles to reach a speed of 190 miles. This ability to attain higher speeds with much faster acceleration than HSR will increase ridership by reducing travel times and allowing more stops. It can climb much steeper grades and take sharper curves than HSR....The speed of such a system (150 to 300 mph) complements the air and auto modes by providing a desirable alternative for trips in the 100 to 600 mile range." (p1273)

Brown, William S., III (Chairman, MAGLEV, Inc.)/Williams, Lynn R. (President, United Steelworkers of America). U.S. House. Committee on Appropriations. "Department of Transportation and Related Agencies Approp. for 1994 (Part 7A)." Hearing, Washington, D.C.: GPO, 1993. (Y4.Ap6/1:T68/4/994/pt.7A).

"Until fiscal year 1989, the FRA [Federal Railroad Administration] partially funded State safety inspection programs. The number of rail accidents had declined steadily in the preceding years and, according to a NARUC [National Association of Regulatory Utility Commissioners] survey, this welcome decline was in direct correlation to the increase in the number of States participating in the FRA's Railroad Safety Grants-in-Aid Program. Due to the elimination of Federal funding, rail operations are less safe than they should be. This cannot be Congress' desire. There were 568 motorists who were killed at public grade crossings in 1990 and in 1991, there were 608 deaths as a result of 5,386 crashes nationwide. The States' authority in railroad safety enforcement was preempted by the Railroad Safety Act of 1970, when power was delegated to the FRA and the DOT." (p193)

Ligon, Claude M. (Maryland Public Service Commission). U.S. House. Committee on Appropriations. "Department of Transportation and Related Agencies Approp. for 1994 (Part 7A)." Hearing, Washington, D.C.: GPO, 1993. (ISBN0160411033). (Y4.Ap6/1:T68/4/994/pt.7A).

"A safe, well-maintained and user-friendly rail network offers efficient movement of people and goods with reduced congestion, conservation of energy and protection of the environment, lower investment in infrastructure maintenance, and improved access for many who have limited access without a well-developed rail network. According to an unofficial estimate by the U.S. Office of Technology Assessment, the current costs of congestion are at least equal to the amount that all levels of government collectively spend on highways each year. Flight delays cost airlines and businesses at least $5 billion annually in the U.S. An expanded role for rail would mitigate this problem and reduce the need for new airports. Rail requires far less physical space than highways or airports, thus reducing land acquisition costs, and displacing fewer homes, jobs and natural resources. Despite the public attention given to prominent rail accidents, passenger rail is nearly 18 times more safe than automobile travel. The U.S. Highway Administration estimates that the cost of U.S. road accidents in 1988 was $358 billion." (p2711)

Collens, Lewis M. (Illinois Institute of Technology). U.S. House. Committee on Appropriations. "Department of Transportation and Related Agencies Approp. for 1994 (Part 7B)." Hearing, Washington, D.C.: GPO, 1993. (ISBN0160411041). (Y4.Ap6/1:T68/4/994/pt.7B).

"A maglev system could allow even faster speeds [than high-speed rail systems], but also would require an entirely new guideway infrastructure, making maglev more costly than all high-speed rail alternatives. Although successfully tested at 320 mph in Japan and 270 mph in Germany, no high-speed maglev system has ever been placed in revenue service. In fact, the Germans have not chosen to introduce maglev on major routes, but have proceeded, instead, to introduce a new high-speed train that uses conventional railway track--the Intercity Express or ICE trains. A maglev system could cost between $20 million and $60 million per mile. The National Research Council estimated a cost of $6.4 billion for a 200-mile maglev system, or about $32 million per mile." (p298)

Mead, Kenneth M. (Director, Trans. Issues Resources, Community, and Economic Dev. Division). U.S. House. Committee on Appropriations. "Department of Transportation and Related Agencies Approp. for 1994 (Part 8)." Hearing, Washington, D.C.: GPO, 1993. (ISBN0160410657). (Y4.Ap6/1:T68/4/994/pt.8).

"According to the National Research Council, the cost to upgrade an existing rail line to allow speeds of about 110 mph would be about $2.7 million per mile. Although not quite 'high-speed' as we have defined it, this would represent a significant improvement over current conditions. Speeds on most Amtrak routes are restricted to below 79 mph, and on some sections of track, considerably below 79 mph. To achieve speeds of up to 150 mph while continuing to use existing rail infrastructure would require electrification of the rights-of-way and construction of additional track to permit high-speed passenger trains to pass slower freight and commuter trains. The capital cost to achieve speeds approaching 150 mph could range up to $10 million per mile." (p295-296)

Mead, Kenneth M. (Director, Trans. Issues Resources, Community, and Economic Dev. Division). U.S. House. Committee on Appropriations. "Department of Transportation and Related Agencies Approp. for 1994 (Part 8)." Hearing, Washington, D.C.: GPO, 1993. (ISBN0160410657). (Y4.Ap6/1:T68/4/994/pt.8).

"Implementation of high-speed rail in the United States requires two fundamental improvements over conventional rail passenger operations: a railroad infrastructure capable of significantly faster operating speeds; and locomotives capable of high-speed operations. This country has considerable experience in building the infrastructure necessary for high-speed operations and Amtrak is presently utilizing that experience to upgrade the New York-Boston segment of the Northeast Corridor to permit up to 150 mph passenger operations. Unfortunately, while Amtrak's current Northeast Corridor electric locomotives operate at speeds up to 125 mph, this country has no similar experience in developing non-electric motive power capable of sustained passenger train operations at such speeds. Presently, the maximum operating speed for non-electric locomotives in the United States is about 105-110 mph, and acceleration capability diminishes as these speeds are approached." (p266)

U.S. House. Committee on Appropriations. "Department of Transportation and Related Agencies Approp. for 1994 (Part 8)." Hearing, Washington, D.C.: GPO, 1993. (ISBN0160410657). (Y4.Ap6/1:T68/4/994/pt.8).

"In 1988, the average number of passenger miles carried per gallon of fuel for automobiles was 34, and the best case automobile passenger miles per gallon of fuel was 80. A five car, single-level Amtrak train traveling at 80 miles per hour can carry 292 passenger miles per gallon of fuel, and an eight car, single-level Amtrak train traveling at 80 miles per hour can carry 335 passenger miles per gallon of fuel. Therefore, due to the greater fuel efficiency of the passenger train over the private automobile, energy savings will occur if there is displacement of automobile use." (p367)

Claytor, W. Graham, Jr. (President, Chairman, National Railroad Passenger Corp. (AMTRAK)). U.S. House. Committee on Appropriations. "Department of Transportation and Related Agencies Approp. for 1994 (Part 8)." Hearing, Washington, D.C.: GPO, 1993. (ISBN0160410657). (Y4.Ap6/1:T68/4/994/pt.8).

"In 1992, Amtrak compared the operating and maintenance costs of a conventional diesel electric locomotive with a hypothetical turbine-hydraulic locomotive and concluded the difference to be $3.62 per mile vs. a potential $6.56 per mile for a two locomotive, 8-car trainset. Based upon the British and Korean experiences, it is likely that a medium speed diesel engine could produce horsepower to weight ratios more comparable with the turbine at lower cost. Amtrak is committed, however, to exploring the potential that turbine power can offer and plans to support the New York State ISTEA Demonstration that will provide a fresh look at operating and maintenance costs of a modern modular turbine. We also believe that using a turbine electric drive, thus far only developed in one recent prototype by the French National Railroads in the mid-70's, can offer a means to improve the overall speed and load profile of the turbine in railway service." (p361)

Claytor, W. Graham, Jr. (President, Chairman, National Railroad Passenger Corp. (AMTRAK)). U.S. House. Committee on Appropriations. "Department of Transportation and Related Agencies Approp. for 1994 (Part 8)." Hearing, Washington, D.C.: GPO, 1993. (ISBN0160410657). (Y4.Ap6/1:T68/4/994/pt.8).

"Light weight is perhaps the most critical issue in high speed rail. The major benefit is lower maintenance costs associated with track wear. By way of comparison, recently designed turbine locomotives weigh about 81.5 tons for 3083 horsepower compared to 131 tons for a comparable diesel. This difference in weight is the equivalent of hauling an extra non-revenue producing passenger car for the life of the diesel locomotive with all the fuel consumption and wear that would be associated with this dead weight." (p401)

Nichols, Dennis B. (President, CEO, Turbomeca Engine Corp.). U.S. House. Committee on Appropriations. "Department of Transportation and Related Agencies Approp. for 1994 (Part 8)." Hearing, Washington, D.C.: GPO, 1993. (ISBN0160410657). (Y4.Ap6/1:T68/4/994/pt.8).

"Operating and maintenance (O&M) costs of HSGT [high speed ground transportation] systems are...likely to be high, relative to those for conventional rail for several reasons. Track and guideways must be maintained to very high standards, and safe operation of HSGT requires expensive signal and control systems. One analysis reported that track maintenance costs are 5 times higher for 125 mph trains than for trains traveling 60 mph. The O&M cost per train mile for a maglev system has been estimated to be about 20 percent higher than that for a high-speed rail system. However, as there is no U.S. experience with operating HSGT systems, O&M costs in the U.S. operating environment can only be roughly estimated until a system is actually put in operation." (p299-300)

Mead, Kenneth M. (Director, Trans. Issues Resources, Community, and Economic Dev. Division). U.S. House. Committee on Appropriations. "Department of Transportation and Related Agencies Approp. for 1994 (Part 8)." Hearing, Washington, D.C.: GPO, 1993. (ISBN0160410657). (Y4.Ap6/1:T68/4/994/pt.8).

"On November 1, 1993, the number of jumbo covered hopper cars (4,000 cubic feet capacity or more) in active service [in the U.S.] increased to 255,975, 3 percent above a year earlier. Privately owned rail cars accounted for the largest share of the growth, 7,884 cars. Railroad-owned cars increased 3,167 cars in the period. Jumbo covered hopper cars are used for a variety of dry bulk commodities in addition to grain." (p17)

U.S. Dept. of Agriculture. "Reduced Demand for Grain to Lower Rail and Barge Shipments." Feed Situation and Outlook Report Nov 1993. p17-19.

"This is Inman Yard: 425 acres of steel rail, gravel railbed, freight cars, grain hoppers, pin pullers, piggyback flatcars, switch engines and diesel locomotives. It is the main switching yard of the nation's fourth-largest railroad, the nerve center for a system that stretches across 20 states from Florida to Michigan and Virginia to Missouri....Inman Yard reveals an industry that has all but disappeared from the American imagination, but which still carries almost 40 percent of the nation's intercity freight. It also showcases a remarkable American renaissance, for railroads that were stagnating just 15 years ago are thriving again today. Rail productivity shot up 157 percent between 1983 and 1992, and freight shipments have reached record levels for seven straight years....Now that the nation's economy is gaining momentum, railroads are picking up steam. Coal shipments are up 15.3 percent from last year, while the volume of autos and auto parts has climbed 12.1 percent." (p46-47)

Hage, David. "Business: On the Right Track." U.S. News & World Report v116 n11, 21 Mar 1994. p46-47,49,52-53. (ISSN0041-5537).

RAILROADS--U.S.--ACCIDENTS

"Using calendar 1991, the last complete year of the Federal Railroad Administration's (FRA) accident statistics, there were 1,194 fatal injuries for 1991 in the industry. Of that total, 608 (50 percent) were in highway/rail accident/incidents. It is interesting to note that of the remaining 586 fatalities, 509 were trespassers. Preliminary FRA accident statistics for 1992 show 522 fatal injuries received in rail-highway crossing accident/incidents as compared to 556 for the same period in 1991." (p207)

U.S. House. Committee on Appropriations. "Department of Transportation and Related Agencies Approp. for 1994 (Part 6)." Hearing, Washington, D.C.: GPO, 1993. (ISBN0160410746). (Y4.Ap6/1:T68/4/994/pt.6).

RAIN FORESTS

"In 1989, Charles Peters, of the New York Botanical Garden's Institute of Economic Botany, completed a study that finally provided rainforest conservationists with the data they needed to prove that a rainforest is worth more intact than logged or burned for cash crops or cattle pasture, the usual fate of the 50 million acres of tropical forest lost worldwide each year. Peters and two colleagues found that the fruits and rubber that could be gathered from one hectare (2.5 acres) of Peruvian rainforest could net a harvester $422 a year, every year, which adds up to a far more secure future than the $1,000 that hectare would yield, just once, if it were cut for timber." (p34)

Jukofsky, Diane. "Can Marketing Save the Rainforest?" E

Magazine v4 n4, Jul-Aug 1993. p32-39. (ISSN1046-8021).

"British Columbia has been rapidly liquidating North America's largest and most productive temperate rain forest. With less than 40 percent still standing, foresters project that at current rates of logging, no ecologically viable stands of ancient rain forest will grow on British Columbian coasts 15 years from now. Cathedral groves of ancient Sitka spruce, Douglas fir, western hemlock, and red cedar are being razed at rates faster than the tropical deforestation in Indonesia and Brazil. With about 44 percent of the world's temperate rain forest already gone, the 23 million hectares (58 million acres) that remain are of incalculable biological value. (By comparison, the total area of tropical rain forest is about 610 million hectares.) The largest contiguous zone--the 'Amazon Basin' of temperate rain forest--is found along a narrow coastal strip between Oregon's Siuslaw River and the Alaskan Peninsula. But in Oregon and Washington, no intact watersheds of more than 500 hectares remain unlogged." (p9)

Denniston, Derek. "Wrong Turns: The Temperate Rainforest: Canada's Clear-Cut Secret." World Watch v6 n4, Jul-Aug 1993. p9,34. (ISSN0896-0615).

RAIN FORESTS--CANADA

"Clayoquot Sound is the 650,000-acre heart of western Vancouver Island. Ten mountainous river networks and numerous islands are covered with a blanket of ancient temperate rainforest. Like a green arch around the clearcut landscape of the central sound, five neighboring watersheds are home to the largest remaining expanse of coastal rainforest in Canada--a prime candidate for ecosystem protection. Only one of the watersheds, the 45,000-acre Moyeha River, is currently protected as part of Strathcona Provincial Park. For almost 15 years, local and regional environmental groups have been fighting to save the ecological integrity of Clayoquot Sound." (p14)

Sandmann, Holger. "Clearcut by Compromise in B.C.'s Clayoquot Sound." Northwest Conservation Spr 1993. p14.

RANCHERS--U.S.

"Ranchers still dominate the rural west [in the U.S.] both economically and politically. There are at least 30,000 of them, with properties that average 15,000-20,000 acres (6,000-8,000 hectares). Most run a standard cow-calf operation, under which calves are sent with their mothers to mountain pastures in the summer and fattened for autumn sales. For a few weeks each year, when the calves need branding or the herd needs bringing down from pasture, such ranches will employ real working cowboys, using horses, to reach places inaccessible by four-wheel drive." (p31)

"Cowboys and Indians: Once Upon a Time in the West." Economist v329 n7843, 25 Dec 1993. p31-34. (ISSN0013-0613).

RANCHES--ARIZONA--ECONOMIC CONDITIONS (v19)

RANCHES--COLORADO

"San Luis, Colorado--On a Monday afternoon in June at the height of the farming season, more than 100 people gathered in the parish hall here. They had come to discuss, in English and in Spanish, the fate of 77,000 acres known these days as the Taylor Ranch. The ranch is one of the largest, privately owned, undeveloped chunks of mountain range left in Colorado. For communities in the southern end of Costilla County, where farmers use the oldest irrigation ditches and water rights in the state, it's the top of the watershed....In 1960, Jack Taylor, a lumberman from North Carolina, bought the tract and fenced it....Taylor had gotten the ranch for a song: $500,000, or about $7 an acre. Some say that's because there was what a 1976 NEW YORKER article called 'a little cloud on the title.'" Today the asking price is between $22 and $32 million. (p1)

Rumsey, Becky. "A Lost Land Grant: Can It Be Reclaimed?" High Country News v25 n19, 18 Oct 1993. p1,10-12. (ISSN0191-5657).

RANCHES--U.S. (v19)

"America now boasts hundreds of ranches licensed to take in guests. On some, visitors must work for their supper; in 1989 more than 1,500 guests stayed on such ranches in Wyoming, adding an estimated $750,000 to the state economy. Then come the dude ranches proper, more than 200 of them nationwide at the last count. These are places where the stock are kept out of sight, where a leisurely horseback ride is the hardest work required, and where Evian slakes the rider's thirst. Dude-ranch chic, from figured boots ($99) to the Ralph Lauren Double RL jacket ($495) is pricey; the lodging, in properly murky cabins with temperamental plumbing, can run to more than $100 a day, including use of horse. Many northern dude ranches plainly make enough in a short season to keep a sketchy ranching operation, and dozens of horses, going all year." (p32)

"Cowboys and Indians: Once Upon a Time in the West." Economist v329 n7843, 25 Dec 1993. p31-34. (ISSN0013-0613).

"Federal subsidies lie at the heart of the West's marriage to nonsustainable ranching and its dogged resistance to change. This is most evident in the USDA Agricultural Stabilization and Conservation Service emergency feed program, which pays ranchers for half of the cost of feed they buy during drought. It encourages ranchers to stock their ranges at maximum levels, rather than to keep herds small enough to get through dry years. After all, why stock the range sustainably when the government will pay half the cost of the feed you need in poor years? And thanks to the program, poor years come regularly. On average, Western ranchers qualify for this subsidy four out of every 10 years. In both 1989 and 1990, neither of which were drought years, medium-sized ranches in southwestern New Mexico received about $3,600 annually from this subsidy." (p16)

Hess, Karl, Jr./Holechek, Jerry L. "Babbitt Inherited a Mess; His Plan Will Make It Worse." High Country News v25 n20, 1 Nov 1993. p16. (ISSN0191-5657).

RANCHES--UTAH--ECONOMIC CONDITIONS (v19)

RANGELANDS

see also GRAZING DISTRICTS

RANGELANDS--U.S.

"The United States has about 770 million acres of rangelands, from the wet grasslands of Florida to the desert shrub ecosystems of Wyoming and from the high mountain meadows of Utah to the desert floor of California. More than half of these rangelands are privately owned, 43 percent are owned by the federal government, and the remainder are owned by state and local governments." (p2)

"Minimum Ecological Standard Needed to Protect U.S. Rangelands." National Research Council News 6 Jan 1994. p1-4.

RAPE

"Anthropology confirms that if there is anything universal about the female condition it is vulnerability to assault. In the United States in 1991, the FBI recorded 106,593 rapes. And a survey of Third World women's groups in the late 1980s found violence the top common concern. A woman is raped in South Africa every 83 seconds. In Latin America, where macho culture breeds high levels of abuse, more than 100 women's projects are dedicated to fighting it." (p45)

MacFarquhar, Emily/others. "World Report: The War against Women." U.S. News & World Report v116 n12, 28 Mar 1994. p42-45,48. (ISSN0041-5537).

"'Violence against women is perhaps the most pervasive yet least recognised human rights abuse in the world', says Lori Heise of the Violence, Health and Development Project at Rutgers

University in the USA. The US Department of Justice reports that every six minutes in America a woman is raped, and other studies suggest that one in five American women is likely to be raped. In South Africa--thought to have the highest incidence of rape in the world--nearly 370,000 women are raped every year. In other words, a woman is raped every one and a half minutes....In South Korea, 17% of women report being victims of attempted or successful rape. In the Central African Republic, 22% of women questioned said their first experience of sexual intercourse had been rape...." (p6) "Studies across the USA show that 78% of prostitutes were raped before the age of 14, usually by a relative or friend of the family. In India, 80% of a group of prostitutes interviewed by the Housewives Federation had been cast out of their communities because of rape." (p9)

Armstrong, Sue. "Briefing: The Last Taboo." WorldAIDS n29, Sep 1993. p6-9. (ISSN0954-6510).

RAPE--PRESS COVERAGE--U.S.

"As Helen Benedict, professor at Columbia's Graduate School of Journalism, concluded, 'Given that a woman in...[the U.S.] is being raped every five minutes, according to the FBI, or every 3.5 minutes, according to another national survey, covering rape is an essential duty for the press.' 'Women are too often reported as victims, not because there's too much coverage of sex crime, but because it's covered in the wrong way,' said Benedict. 'Instead of looking at victims, the press should be looking at perpetrators; it should be looking at rape--and sexism. And that's what the press is utterly failing to do.'" (p7)

Flanders, Laura. "A FAIR Forum on Coverage of Women's Stories." EXTRA! v7 n1, Jan 1994. p7. (ISSN0895-2310).

RAPE--SOUTH AFRICA

"A recent study by South Africa's National Institute for Crime Prevention and Rehabilitation of Offenders (NICRO) reached some stark conclusions: one in four South African women will experience rape; there are 380,000 rape cases in South Africa each year; and 95% of rape victims are black." (p1)

Armstrong, Sue. "South Africa's Rape Epidemic Fuels HIV." WorldAIDS n27, May 1993. p1. (ISSN0954-6510).

RAPE--U.S. (v19)

"After quoting a Columbia creative-writing professor on the great number of students who write about their fear of reporting date rape, [Peter] Hellman asks, 'Is the problem really that pervasive? Or is a genuine case of date rape...the exception rather than the rule?' Hellman touts statistics from Barnard College showing not one rape reported by its 2,200 students during the previous year and Columbia with only two reported rapes out of 19,300 students. And after citing a survey by MS. magazine on the subject showing that 42 percent of women raped had told no one, he then states, 'It's a grim picture that the survey presents--perhaps grimmer than need be.' Hellman goes on: 'Columbia isn't alone in its dearth of reported rapes, and crime reports from 2,400 campuses across the country show fewer than 1,000 rapes for the year reported--less than half a rape per campus.'" (p3)

Weinzel, Lynn. "Crying Rape!" New Directions for Women v22 n3, May-Jun 1993. p3. (ISSN0160-1075).

"An analysis by researchers at the University of California at Los Angeles of L.A. rape victims, reported in the January 1989 AMERICAN JOURNAL OF PUBLIC HEALTH, reinforced the assumption that victims who fought back were more likely to be injured. The reseachers found that 67 percent of victims who responded aggressively were physically injured, compared with 35 percent of victims who didn't struggle. But they also found that for 23 of 29 women who fought back and yet were both raped and physically assaulted, the blows from the assailant came before the rape....A subsequent study of 274 rapes or attempted rapes in the March 1992 JOURNAL OF INTERPERSONAL VIOLENCE bore out the speculation; it showed that 85 percent of the women who scratched, kicked, bit, ran or screamed did so because the rapist had been violent first....A study in the November AMERICAN JOURNAL OF PUBLIC HEALTH of 150 Omaha women who were targets of rape showed conclusively that fighting back can stave off rape....the researchers, Janice Zoucha-Jensen and Ann Coyne of the University of Nebraska at Omaha School of Social Work, found that 96 percent of women who cried or pleaded with the assailant were raped anyway." (p74)

Brink, Susan. "Crime: The Case for Fighting Off a Rapist." U.S. News & World Report v115 n24, 20 Dec 1993. p74. (ISSN0041-5537).

RAPE--U.S.--CHILDREN (v19)

RAPE--U.S.--COLLEGE STUDENTS (v19)

RAPESEED INDUSTRY--EUROPEAN ECONOMIC COMMUNITY (v19)

RATE OF INTEREST

see INTEREST RATES

RATS (v19)

REAL ESTATE AGENTS (v19)

REBELLIONS

see INSURGENCY

RECYCLING

see also BEVERAGE CONTAINERS--GERMANY--GREAT BRITAIN--RECYCLING; BEVERAGE CONTAINERS--U.S.--RECYCLING; COMPUTERS--RECYCLING; PLASTICS--U.S.--RECYCLING; TIRES, RUBBER--U.S.--RECYCLING

RECYCLING (WASTE, ETC.)

"According to the Organization for Economic Co-operation and Development (OECD)--the club of 24 industrialized nations--in 1990 some 40 million tonnes of waste, worth $19 000 million, were exported for recycling worldwide. The industry employs 350 000 people and generates revenues of $38 000 million a year. Most of these profits go to OECD countries." (p7)

MacKenzie, Debora. "Europe's Toxic Waste." World Health n5, Sep-Oct 1993. p6-8. (ISSN0043-8502).

RECYCLING (WASTE, ETC.)--CANADA

"The Environmentally Sound Packaging (ESP) Coalition reports that Canada met its 1992 target of reducing packaging sent for disposal by 20 percent. Results from the Protocol's 1990 survey of 11,000 businesses showed that, of 13.5 million tonnes of packaging used, 54 percent was reused and 13 percent was recycled. The majority of the reduction is from institutional, commercial and industrial ('ICI') sources, which accounts for 70 percent of all packaging used in Canada. In addition, the 1992 goal required reductions mainly through waste reduction and reuse options. The province's high volume of returnable beer bottles and shipping pallets accounted for much of the reduction. ESP predicts the 1996 goal will be harder to meet since those reductions will need to come more from the residential programs." (p6)

"The State Scene: British Columbia." Wastelines v4 n3, Mar 1993. p6.

RECYCLING (WASTE, ETC.)--CHICAGO (ILL)

"As much as 80% of Chicago's residential solid waste stream is composed of materials that could be recycled. Each ton of recycled paper saves 3.3 cubic yards of landfill space. Compared to the manufacturing of paper from virgin materials, the manufacture of paper from recycled materials uses up to 64% less energy and 58% less water, and reduces water pollution by 35% and air pollution by 74%. For every 15,000 tons of solid waste landfilled each year, one job is created. The same amount recycled creates 9 jobs in sorting and preparing materials for market." (p19)

Bardoe, Cheryl. "Chicago's Sustainability Indicators."

Neighborhood Works v16 n5, Oct-Nov 1993. p16-20.

RECYCLING (WASTE, ETC.)--U.S. (v19)

"The Michigan Department of Transportation has always strived to be a leader in the use of recycled materials in highway engineering applications. Our interests are driven by a desire to increase the use of cost-effective products that improve our highway systems and to reduce the waste stream in our society, avoiding landfilling or useless disposal of renewable resources. One of our biggest successes to date is in the recycling of bituminous paving mixtures, which we began in 1977. This resource recovery effort has developed to the point where in a typical year the department's recycled asphalt pavement (RAP) program saves an estimated 525,000 tons of aggregate and 10,500 tons of asphalt cement, resulting in a savings of between 3.5 to 4.5 million dollars. In addition to the dollar savings, we avoid the necessity of disposing of some 1 million tons of old asphalt pavement per year." (p832)

Welke, Robert A. (Chief Engineer, Deputy Director, Bureau of Highways). U.S. House. Committee on Appropriations. "Department of Transportation and Related Agencies Approp. for 1994 (Part 8)." Hearing, Washington, D.C.: GPO, 1993. (ISBN0160410657). (Y4.Ap6/1:T68/4/994/pt.8).

Partners for Environmental Progress "rationalizes that plastic peanut butter jars are the environmental choice because they take up less room in the landfill. They estimate that because glass has a national recycling rate of 30 percent, about two-thirds of each jar (7.1 oz.) will end up in the landfill. On the other hand, assuming no recycling at all, plastic jars add only 1.7 oz. PEP fails to consider, however, the greater environmental costs of manufacturing plastic jars with petrochemicals. Also, as EAF's [Environmental Action Foundation's] solid waste policy analyst Resa Dimino points out, no one buys a third of a jar of peanut butter. To base a purchasing decision on the wasteful habits of the two-thirds of Americans that don't recycle is ludicrous, she says." (p7)

"Econotes: Plastic Logic." Environmental Action v25 n4, Win 1994. p7. (ISSN0013-922X).

RECYCLING (WASTE, ETC.)--U.S.--POLITICS AND GOVERNMENT (v19)

REDUCING--U.S. (v19)

REDUCTION OF ATMOSPHERIC OZONE

see ATMOSPHERIC OZONE--REDUCTION

REDWOOD NATIONAL PARK (CALIF) (v19)

REFUGEES (v19)

REFUGEES--AFRICA, SUB-SAHARAN (v19)

REFUGEES--GERMANY

"At a time when recently reunited Germany makes the front pages for nationalistic skinhead and neo-Nazi violence, this is an equally important story about its people. And it echoes in government camps across the country's 16 Lander, or states, where 350,000 refugees, the vast majority of them Croats and Bosnian Muslims, including thousands of traumatized youngsters, have found temporary shelter from the ongoing slaughter--or murderous 'ethnic cleansing'--conducted in the name of Serbian nationalism." (p8)

Oppenheimer, Paul. "Compassion vs. Nationalism in Germany." New Leader v77 n2, 14 Feb 1994. p8-11. (ISSN0028-6044).

"Germany has become a nation of intermingling cultures. There are now 6.5 million 'de facto' immigrants among its 80 million people." (p9) "Attacks on refugee homes and the homes of 'Gastarbeiter' [foreign workers] are frequent in both western and eastern sections of the country. The extensively reported murderous raids at Molln and Solingen in 1992 and '93, resulting in seven deaths, were simply the most perverse expressions of widespread brutality. As of mid-January, the Federal and local police had recorded a total of over 19,000 neo-Nazi criminal acts of all kinds dating from reunification, including at least 30 murders, assaults, arson, desecrations of Jewish cemeteries, and other types of vandalism." (p10)

Oppenheimer, Paul. "Compassion vs. Nationalism in Germany." New Leader v77 n2, 14 Feb 1994. p8-11. (ISSN0028-6044).

"Germany is the only Western nation that responded generously to the plight of Yugoslavian refugees. While Britain, Spain, Italy, Switzerland, and the United States host only token numbers, Germany has accepted more than 240,000 of these victims. Asylum seekers from the Third World, ethnic Germans, Yugoslavian refugees--a population of approximately 80 million Germans has taken in almost one million refugees from all over the world during the last two years--people who receive free housing, meals, medical care, and language training, plus a monthly allowance while waiting for the five years it usually takes German bureaucracy to investigate and decide each individual case. Germany pays an average of $10,000 annually for each asylum seeker. Small wonder that the communities, suffering from extreme budget problems and housing shortages, groan and rebel, and the voices of protest grow louder under the impact of the recession on the one hand and the skyrocketing costs for rebuilding a rundown East Germany on the other." (p38-39)

Diedrich, Maria. "Born Guilty?" Transition v3 n2, 1993. p34-51. (ISSN0041-1191).

REFUGEES--SERVICES FOR--U.S. (v19)

REFUGEES, AFGHAN

"About 1.6m Afghans remain in Pakistan and are unwilling to return home while the civil war continues. Iran has 2.3m refugees and some thousands have recently fled to Tajikistan and Uzbekistan. About 10,000 people have been killed in factional battles since the Najibullah government fell. Afghans are the largest group assisted by the United Nations High Commissioner for Refugees." (p37)

"Asia: Afghanistan: The Turncoat." Economist v330 n7844, 8 Jan 1994. p37. (ISSN0013-0613).

REFUGEES, AFGHAN--GOVERNMENT POLICY--IRAN (v19)

REFUGEES, BOSNIAN--CROATIA

"The United States can take simple measures to ensure that Croatia is positioned to counter Serbian expansionism. Providing for 260,000 Bosnian Muslim refugees has cost the Croatian government nearly $850 million in the past 2 years. The burden of accommodating 800,000 refugees and displaced persons within its borders has taken a staggering toll on the Croatian economy; the Croatian Government has spent $1.52 billion and in 1992 Croatia's citizens paid 60 percent of their own income, two-thirds going for social programs, to support refugee care. Yet Croatia has managed its wartime economy well: inflation is close to zero, internal reserves are strong and Croatia has not taken on any new foreign debt. As such, Croatia is an excellent candidate to receive loans, grants and aid from international monetary institutions to rebuild damaged infrastructure and other aspects of the economy; in combination with U.S. refugee assistance, financial aid to Croatia will alleviate common suffering, eliminate the need for a massive future economic bailout and as such will prove a wise investment." (pE623)

Lipinski, William O. (Rep.-Ill.). "Croatian-Bosnian Agreement," Congressional Record (12 Apr 1994). Daily ed. pE623-624. (ISSN0363-7239).

REFUGEES, CUBAN--U.S. (v19)

REFUGEES, EAST ASIAN (v19)

REFUGEES, HAITIAN--FLORIDA

"Refugee advocates protest that Haitian applications for asylum and for visas for relations are not being fairly processed by American officials. Of 55,000 asylum petitions since February 1992, only 5.5% were approved. Overworked and under-experienced immigration officials are alleged to have ignored valid reports of torture and killings. Most simply consider the Haitians to be economic migrants." (p31)

"American Survey: All Right, Just This Once." Economist v331 n7861, 30 Apr 1994. p31. (ISSN0013-0613).

REFUGEES, HAITIAN--U.S. (v19)

REFUGEES, INDOCHINESE

"Solutions are less newsworthy than problems; and sometimes they are hardly less ugly. A final solution of sorts has been agreed to in Geneva for the problem of the Indochinese boat people who have, for nearly 19 years now, been filling up camps around Asia. The Geneva meeting, convened by the United Nations High Commissioner for Refugees, brought together Vietnam and Laos, which produced the exodus; the countries of 'first asylum', such as Hong Kong and Indonesia, which have provided shelter and food; and the countries of resettlement, which have taken in those judged to be refugees. A 'comprehensive plan of action', adopted by these countries in 1989, has achieved one of its aims: the flood of boat-people departures has become a trickle. Just 55 left in 1992, and 777 in 1993....The 60,000 Vietnamese boat people scattered around Asia, and the 26,000 Laotians in camps in Thailand should be resettled or back home by the end of 1995. Hong Kong, which over the years has received 195,000 Vietnamese boat people, still has more than 26,000. Of these, more than 90% have been classified as economic migrants." (p36)

"Asia: Boat People: Final Solution." Economist v330 n7852, 26 Feb 1994. p36. (ISSN0013-0613).

REFUGEES, IRAQI--U.S. (v19)

REFUGEES, LIBERIAN

"On 8 March, UNHCR [UN High Commissioner for Refugees] asked major donors to disburse funds already pledged to support its efforts to help returning Liberian refugees....While some 75,000 refugees have returned during the past year, around 700,000 remain in neighbouring countries. Guinea hosts 415,000, Cote d'Ivoire 250,000, Ghana 20,000, Sierra Leone 600,000 and Nigeria 3,000. The urgency of UNHCR's task has increased with the approach of the rainy season, which will make parts of Liberia inaccessible after May." (p5)

"Emergencies Pose Continuing Challenges: Liberia." Africa Recovery v7 n3-4, Dec 1993-Mar 1994. p5.

REFUGEES, SOMALIAN

"Today, hundreds of thousands of Somalis are refugees, with 375,000 in Ethiopia, over 300,000 in Kenya, 150,000 in Saudi Arabia, and 20,000 in Yemen, according to the U.S. State Department. More than 300,000 people died in 1992 as a result of famine and civil strife, according to the United Nations, as reported by the State Department....Somali women have many children, as is characteristic of much of the Horn of Africa. The TFR (total fertility rate, or average births per woman) is 6.6. Even with a growth rate of 2.9 percent per year, the country is still quite sparsely populated with a population density of 34 people per square mile." (p11)

Musembi, Benedicta. "Spotlight: Somalia." Population Today v21 n2, Feb 1993. p11. (ISSN0749-2448).

REFUGEES, SOMALIAN--ETHIOPIA (v19)

REFUGEES, YUGOSLAVIAN--EUROPE (v19)

"Displacement of people generated by armed conflict in the former Yugoslavia has created the most notable population movement in Europe today. The UN High Commissioner for Refugees estimates the number of displaced persons at more than 2.5 million, with numbers steadily increasing as the war in Bosnia and Herzegovina continues. More than 2 million of these refugees are in regions of former Yugoslavia: an estimated 810,000 in Bosnia and Herzegovina, 630,000 in Croatia, 430,000 in Serbia, and 70,000 in Slovenia. Another almost half million refugees from former Yugoslavia are in five European countries: 220,000 in Germany, over 70,000 in Switzerland, 60,000 in Sweden, 57,500 in Austria, and 50,000 in Hungary." (p5)

Hershey, Sharon. "New U.N. Report Tracks Migration." Population Today v21 n4, Apr 1993. p5. (ISSN0749-2448).

REFUSE AND REFUSE DISPOSAL

see also HAZARDOUS WASTES; RECYCLING (WASTE, ETC.)

"The quantity of waste materials associated with raw material extraction often far exceeds the amount of useful product. For instance, about 160 tons of ore must be processed to yield a ton of virgin copper....The specific case of phosphate rock is worth illustrating....One thousand units of the ore, plus 793 units of sulfuric acid and 1,762 units of makeup water yields 555 units of salable phosphoric acid (for fertilizer) and 39 units of salable fluosilicic acid, which is used by the aluminum industry. But the process also yields 3,000 units of 'phosphogypsum,' which is unsalable because it is contaminated with radioactive thorium. Yet gypsum is concurrently being mined for use in building materials." (p38) In the U.S. in 1988, "purchased inputs (feedstocks) amounting to 60.3 million metric tons, plus another 33.8 million metric tons of oxygen from the atmosphere, yielded 39 million metric tons of 'finished' chemical products (such as plastics, synthetic rubber, synthetic fibers, solvents, anti-freeze, etc.) and generated 54.3 million metric tons of wastes, including 29.3 million metric tons of carbon dioxide and 2.3 million metric tons of unburned hydrocarbons (according to our estimate). If all these hydrocarbons were oxidized, both oxygen inputs and CO2 outputs would be correspondingly increased." (p39)

Ayres, Robert U. "Technological Trends." National Forum v74 n2, Spr 1994. p37-42,48. (ISSN0162-1831).

According to facts excerpted from THE GREEN CONSUMER by John Elkington, Julia Hailes, and Joel Makower, "Per-person daily household trash produced in Calcutta, India: 1.12 pounds; in New York City: 3.96 pounds....Plastic beverage bottles Americans go through every hour: 2.5 million. Styrofoam cups thrown away each year in the U.S.: 25 billion. Plastic containers dumped overboard daily by commercial fishing fleets: 640,000. Northern fur seals drowned each year by lost plastic fishing net: 500,000. Estimated number of sea birds, marine mammals, and fur seals killed each year as a result of eating or being strangled by plastics: 1 million, 100,000, and 50,000, respectively.... Trees wasted each week by Sunday newspapers not being recycled: 500,000. Homes that could be heated by the wood and paper thrown away each year: 5 million homes for 200 years....Gallons of water that can be contaminated by a single quart of motor oil: up to 2 million....U.S. drivers waste 100,000 barrels of oil each day simply because car tires are not inflated properly." (p11)

"Act Now!! For Eco-Justice." New Directions for Women v22 n2, Mar-Apr 1993. p11. (ISSN0160-1075).

REFUSE AND REFUSE DISPOSAL--CHICAGO (ILL)

"Chicago residents, on average, generate between 986 pounds and 1,205 pounds of solid waste per person each year. The 40% of Chicago households living in low-density housing (structures with 1 to 4 housing units) generate an average of 3.3 pounds of solid waste per person per day; the 60% of Chicago households living in high-density housing (more than 4 units) generate an average of 2.7 pounds of solid waste per person per day." (p19)

Bardoe, Cheryl. "Chicago's Sustainability Indicators." Neighborhood Works v16 n5, Oct-Nov 1993. p16-20.

REFUSE AND REFUSE DISPOSAL--EUROPE--U.S. (v19)

REFUSE AND REFUSE DISPOSAL--LAW AND LEGISLATION--U.S.

"New local and state regulations are improving the attractiveness of composting: in many states, towns must choose between sending less to the landfill and paying hefty fines. New Jersey's regulations, the most stringent in the nation, require that municipalities reach a 'materials recovery' goal--which can be achieved through both recycling and composting--of 60 percent by 1995. California's and Missouri's laws are only slightly less rigorous, requiring, respectively, garbage to be halved by 1998, and reduced by 40 percent by 1998. Yard waste--grass, leaves, and brush--is banned altogether from landfills in at least twenty-one states, and sewage sludge, an eminently compostable material, can no longer be dumped into the waters off our coastlines." (p39-40)

Hanson, Beth. "Pass the Humus." Amicus Journal v15 n3, Fall 1993. p38-42. (ISSN0276-7201).

REFUSE AND REFUSE DISPOSAL--LOS ANGELES (CALIF)

"According to a City of Los Angeles study done in cooperation with the Alliance of Motion Picture and Television Producers' Solid Waste Management Task Force, Hollywood's studios produced 46,000 tons of trash in 1991, but only 15 percent of this material was recycled or reused. Seventy percent of Hollywood's waste--more than 34 million pounds annually--is wood. Over the past year, Hollywood studios have begun working to reclaim this resource by transferring reusable wood to needy groups in LA. According to Bert Ball, director of the LA Cultural Affairs Department's 'Material for the Arts' program, 'We get not only lumber, but paper, paint, furniture; literally warehouses full of stuff from the industry.' The program has become the largest single donor to LA's independent theater community and also transfers needed resources to the LA school district. In its first year, Materials for the Arts kept more than 600 tons of resources out of landfills." (p40)

Kupfer, David. "The Greening of Hollywood." Earth Island Journal v8 n3, Sum 1993. p40-41. (ISSN1041-0406).

REFUSE AND REFUSE DISPOSAL--PENNSYLVANIA

"Pennsylvania has the dubious distinction of being the No. 1 importer of other peoples' garbage. It is garbage from New York, New Jersey, and now even Canada--not our garbage--that is filling up many of our landfills....In 1991, the amount of garbage imported was about 3 million tons; in 1992 we experienced a 26 percent increase which put us up to 3.6 million tons; and in 1993, although the final numbers are not yet in, it will be close to 4 million tons. If you include other types of waste imported, such as sludge and ash, it is closer to 5 million tons. Some of our largest Pennsylvania landfills are taking in almost 90 percent of their waste from out-of-State. The landfill space planned for handling our own trash is being eaten up, and the health and safety of our citizens is endangered with a proliferation of trash trucks on our highways." (pE463)

Clinger, William F., Jr. (Rep.-Pa.). "Introduction of Interstate Municipal Solid Waste Control Act," Congressional Record (17 Mar 1994). Daily ed. pE463-464. (ISSN0363-7239).

REFUSE AND REFUSE DISPOSAL--TOKYO (JAPAN) (v19)

REFUSE AND REFUSE DISPOSAL--U.S. (v19)

"The independent Port Import Export Research Service found that the ports of Los Angeles and Long Beach shipped more than 67 million pounds of waste plastic from recycling centers throughout Southern California and the Southwest in the six months ending in February [1993]. Almost all of the waste was sent to China via Hong Kong." (p15)

"Plastic Recycling Scam Exposed." Earth Island Journal v8 n3, Sum 1993. p15. (ISSN1041-0406).

"The economics of solid waste [will change the way AT&T does business]. If you look at the disposal cost in the 1970s, it was around $.75 a ton. In the 1980s it cost about $4 a ton, and in 1992 we're talking about approximately $150 a ton. For the year 2000...it will be well over $500. So disposing of plain manufacturing waste is going to be very expensive. At $.75 a ton, nobody's going to look at what they throw away. As the price goes up, we're starting to examine our waste stream, inventory it, and find that indeed there are valuable commodities that, if we keep separate, we can sell, or at least reduce their impact on the environment, and that's where the economy is." (p27)

"Forum Profile: AT&T's David Chittick." Environmental Forum v10 n3, May-Jun 1993. p24-29. (ISSN0731-5732).

"In 1990...American households consumed $110 billion worth of energy. That doesn't count the costs to the landscapes of Kentucky and Wyoming, to wild creatures and wilderness, to clean air and the earth's climate. As houses consume resources, they excrete wastes. The average household now produces each year about 3,500 pounds of garbage, 630,000 pounds of wastewater, and 25,000 pounds od carbon dioxide, along with smaller amounts of sulfur dioxide, nitrous oxide, and heavy metals." (p9)

"Sitting Lightly on the Land." Rocky Mountain Institute Newsletter v10 n1, Spr 1994. p9.

RELIGION

see IRELAND--POPULATION--RELIGION; NORTHERN IRELAND--RELIGION; TELEVISION AND RELIGION--U.S.; U.S.--RELIGION

RELIGION AND POLITICS--U.S. (v19)

RELIGIOUS EDUCATION--FRANCE

"There is little difference between private Catholic schools (catering for nearly a fifth of pupils) and the state schools [in France], save that religious education has been banned in state schools since 1882. There, teachers are forbidden to mention Jesus's birth even in the runup to Christmas. Small wonder, then, that ignorance of the most basic religious matters is widespread, even though 40% of parents still send their children to catechism classes after school hours. Polls suggest that half of those aged between 16 and 35 cannot say the Lord's prayer or a Hail Mary without a crib; three-quarters do not know what happened at Easter." (p64)

"Europe: The Spirit, Yes--Priests, No." Economist v329 n7843, 25 Dec 1993. p64. (ISSN0013-0613).

RELIGIOUS EDUCATION--U.S. (v19)

RENEWABLE ENERGY SOURCES

see also SOLAR ENERGY; WATER-POWER; WIND POWER

"Mexico...is currently using its own resources to electrify nearly 60,000 villages beyond the existing utility grid. Photovoltaics, wind and microhydro are the best least-cost options to provide electricity to these people, who would otherwise be unserved for generations....similar efforts are soon to begin in Indonesia (48,000 villages), India (39,000 villages), Sri Lanka (20,000 villages), Zimbabwe (4,500 villages) and Brazil (2,500 villages)....The World Bank has estimated that nearly three-fourths of the people in Indonesia live in the country's 62,000 rural villages, yet only 26 percent of village households are currently electrified. The government of Indonesia has set the goal of electrifying up to 75 percent of all villages by 1999." (p15)

Sheinkopf, Kenneth G. "Exporting Renewable Energy: A Guide for U.S. Industry." Solar Today v7 n6, Nov-Dec 1993. p14-19. (ISSN1042-0630).

RENEWABLE ENERGY SOURCES--AUSTRALIA (v19)

RENEWABLE ENERGY SOURCES--EUROPEAN ECONOMIC COMMUNITY--U.S. (v19)

RENEWABLE ENERGY SOURCES--U.S. (v19)

"More than 400 hundred million cattle, pigs, and chickens consume vegetable matter to produce over two billion tons of manure each year. If concentrated in one place this would cover an area of 1,000 square miles to a depth of two feet....One pound of dry cow dung produces about one cubic foot of biogas. One cubic foot of biogas per day is enough to cook meals for four people. About 225 ft...[cubed] of biogas is equal to a gallon of gasoline. Most engines can run on this much biogas to produce a horsepower constantly for 10 hours." (p17)

McAlister, Roy/McAlister, Sara. "Making Fuel from Wastes." Hydrogen Today v4 n2, 1993. p17.

"California generated over half of its new electricity capacity during the last decade from renewable sources. California has enough wind power for a city the size of San Francisco. Clean energy like wind power tends to be more labor intensive, using more workers to produce, install, and maintain the sources. A 1990 study by the Worldwatch Institute, 'Beyond the Petroleum Age: Designing a Solar Economy,' and other reports show that a dollar invested in efficiency and renewable energy can create from two to ten times as many jobs as a dollar spent on traditional fossil or nuclear energy. Additionally, clean energy jobs are often safer than fossil fuel or nuclear jobs. They involve few toxics, no radioactive materials, and no uranium or coal mining which have proven especially hazardous." (p12)

LeCain, Eleanor Mulloney. "Feature: Green Business Is Booming." Positive Alternatives v3 n4, Sum 1993. p12-13. (ISSN1065-0075).

"Biomass power plants use technology that is very similar to that used in coal-fired power plants. For example, biomass plants use similar steam-turbine generators and fuel delivery systems. However, coal is a more mature technology, which is reflected in higher power plant efficiencies. Today's biomass power plant efficiencies are typically 16 percent to 17 percent and the best units have efficiencies of about 25 percent. Modern coal-fired power plants, in contrast, are larger and have efficiencies of 30 percent to 35 percent. Coal achieves higher efficiencies because it has more energy per pound than biomass used as a bulk fuel and because biomass has a higher moisture content." (p22)

Bain, Richard L./Jones, Jim. "Renewable Electricity from Biomass." Solar Today v7 n3, May-June 1993. p21-23. (ISSN1042-0630).

"There are good to excellent resources for renewable hydrogen production globally and in most areas of the United States. Land and water requirements would be modest. With PV [photovoltaics] electrolysis alone, it would be possible to supply enough hydrogen for all light duty vehicles in the U.S.--using hydrogen fuel cells and assuming 2010 driving levels--with only 0.1 percent of the U.S. land area. Using wind power alone would require 2 percent of the U.S. land area (15 percent of the environmentally developable wind resource), and biomass alone would take 3 percent of the U.S. land area or 70 percent of the currently idled cropland...." (p18)

Ogden, Joan M. "Renewable Hydrogen Energy Systems." Solar Today v7 n5, Sept-Oct 1993. p17-18. (ISSN1042-0630).

RENEWABLE ENERGY SOURCES--U.S.--PUBLIC OPINION

"'Trends in Public Perceptions and Preferences on Energy and Environmental Policy,' a report published by the National Renewable Energy Laboratory (NREL), documents trends in public opinion on U.S. energy and environmental policy. To conduct the study, trends in items from a public opinion data base relating to energy, the environment, transportation, buildings, utilities, alternative fuels, and policy alternatives such as energy-efficient mortgages were compiled and analyzed. Data was taken from nearly 600 surveys taken between 1979 and 1992. Some of the findings are: An increasing majority of the public favors environmental protection even if that means having an inadequate supply of energy and most people polled favor a balance between economic growth and environmental protection. The public is willing to pay somewhat more for electricity, gasoline and other goods and services to protect the environment and most people support such measures as mandatory recycling and wildlife preserves....A large majority favors the development of renewable energy sources. In one poll on future energy supplies, 83% favored the development of renewables and energy efficiency and only 12% preferred more fossil fuel production." (p36)

"Energy Facts: Trends in Preferences for Environmental Protection versus Adequate Energy." Solar Industry Journal v4 n4, 1993. p36.

RENEWABLE ENERGY SOURCES--UKRAINE

"The 1986 Chernobyl disaster, along with sootbelching power plants and an ever increasing demand for energy has made Ukraine fertile ground for alternative energy. The windy Crimean Peninsula sits as a perfect home for 5,000 soon-to-be-built windmills. The windplant, which will be developed in four stages over a four-year period, will be the second largest in the world. The first phase of the project, to be completed in August [1993], is already underway. When finished, the windfarm will generate 500 megawatts of power, enough to supply more than 400,000 Ukrainian homes. The energy provided will help replace power from the remaining two Chernobyl reactors, scheduled to be shut down by the end of this year." (p27)

Ottoboni, Gina. "Energy: Capturing the Wind in Crimea." Surviving Together v11 n2, Sum 1993. p27. (ISSN0859-6286).

RENT CONTROL--U.S.--POLITICS AND GOVERNMENT

"Uncle Sam has his own landlord: the Public Buildings Service. Housed at the General Services Administration (GSA), the service has the mammoth job of maintaining more than 7,800 federal buildings with space for more than one million civil servants....The Public Buildings Service is financed through the Federal Buildings Fund, which Congress created in 1972 with the idea that agencies should pay market rent for their offices." (p7) "But Congress saw a way to 'save' money at the GSA's expense. In 1977 it ordered federal rents slashed by 10 percent. In 1983 it froze rents at the 1982 level. In 1984 it mandated rents at the '82 level plus 14 percent. Then President Reagan's Office of Management and Budget (OMB) stepped in. Needing quick-fix deficit reductions, OMB ordered no rent increases in 1985 or '86, years when commercial real estate rents were soaring. In 1987 GSA submitted newly appraised rates--and OMB slashed them 15 percent....These aren't just accounting tricks. By scamming the rent money, congressional budgeteers can effectively shift some overhead costs to the GSA, fattening the bottom line at their pet agencies....GSA figures that rent shenanigans have cost it $2.9 billion over the years--$5.1 billion in 1993 dollars, the equivalent of more than a year's rent for the entire government." (p8)

Overby, Peter. "No Sacred Cows: Low-Rent Neighborhood." Common Cause Magazine v19 n2, Sum 1993. p7-8. (ISSN0271-9592).

RENTAL AUTOMOBILES

see AUTOMOBILES, RENTAL

RENTAL HOUSING--HONG KONG

"With rents for prime residential housing [in Hong Kong] surging 84% since 1990, monthly rent for a modern 1,500-square-foot apartment now averages $6,590. Residential rates are likely to go up an additional 30% this year. The commercial sector is only slightly better, with office rents up 55%. Rents are expected to surge 45% in 1994." (p77)

Engardio, Pete. "Finance: Real Estate: The Year of the Landlord in Hong Kong." Business Week n3362, 14 Mar 1994. p77. (ISSN0007-7135).

RENTAL HOUSING--U.S. (v19)
REPETITIVE MOTION INJURIES
see OVERUSE INJURIES
RESEARCH
see also AGRICULTURE--RESEARCH--U.S.; EDUCATION--RESEARCH--U.S.--FINANCE; FEDERAL AID TO MEDICAL RESEARCH; FORCE AND ENERGY--RESEARCH; MEDICINE--RESEARCH; U.S.--RESEARCH

"Up to now, the U.S. Government's research and development budget has reflected the priorities of the cold war. According to official NSF [National Science Foundation] statistics, as recently as 1992 the Federal Government spent 59 percent of its research and development on defense and only 0.3 percent for the direct support of industrial development. Our major economic competitors, however, have chosen to emphasize the support of the new basic industrial technology. Their percentages of government research and development money used to support industry are impressive: in Germany, 13.3 percent; in France, 12.6 percent; in Italy, 14.3 percent. Other nations also provide major assistance to help their small manufacturers--Japan funds 170 assistance centers, for example. Today, with the cold war over and economic growth a higher priority than ever, it is appropriate--indeed imperative--that we use some of the Federal Government's $70 billion annual research budget to support the development of the new basic technologies and manufacturing practices that are absolutely central to national prosperity." (pS2396)

Hollings, Ernest F. (Sen.-S.C.). "Conclusion of Morning Business," Congressional Record (7 Mar 1994). Daily ed. pS2366-2410. (ISSN0363-7239).

RESEARCH--EUROPE--JAPAN--U.S. (v19)
RESEARCH--EUROPEAN ECONOMIC COMMUNITY--JAPAN--U.S. (v19)
RESEARCH--GERMANY--JAPAN--SWEDEN--U.S. (v19)
RESEARCH--GERMANY--JAPAN--U.S. (v19)
RESEARCH--JAPAN--U.S. (v19)
RESEARCH--U.S. (v19)
RESEARCH, INDUSTRIAL--U.S. (v19)
RESOLUTION TRUST CORPORATION (v19)

"The RTC [Resolution Trust Corporation] routinely considers whether targeted directors or officers have liability insurance coverage and the value of their recoverable assets during its investigation and litigation analysis of claims. The ultimate decision to pursue claims through litigation is based on both the strength of the claims and the likelihood of a cost-effective outcome. Of the $362 million recovered as of March 31, 1993, sixty-five (65%) percent has been paid by insurance companies and thirty-five (35%) percent from individuals." (p817)

U.S. House. Committee on Appropriations. "Depts. of Veterans Affairs and Housing and Urban Development...Approp. for 1994 (Part 6)." Hearing, Washington, D.C.: GPO, 1993. (ISBN0160410754). (Y4.Ap6/1:V64/4/994/pt.6).

RESPIRATORY INFECTIONS--TREATMENT--U.S. (v19)
RESPIRATORY INFECTIONS IN CHILDREN--AFRICA--MORTALITY (v19)
RESPIRATORY ORGANS
see also LUNGS
RESPIRATORY ORGANS--CANCER--U.S.

"In 1990 the age-adjusted death rate from respiratory cancer among women [in the U.S.] was 26.2 per 100,000 compared with 4.6 per 100,000 in 1950. Among men the corresponding death rates were 61.0 and 21.3 per 100,000, respectively." (p5)

Kranczer, Stanley. "International Cancer Mortality Comparisons." Statistical Bulletin v75 n1, Jan-Mar 1994. p2-10. (ISSN0790-8334).

RESTAURANTS--U.S. (v19)
RETAIL TRADE
see also ADVERTISING; FRANCHISES (RETAIL TRADE); SHOPPING; SHOPPING MALLS

"More and more, retailing is going global. By the year 2000, 90 percent of the world's 100 largest retailers will be operating globally, according to a recent report by Management Horizons, a retail consulting firm in Columbus, Ohio. That compares with the current 30 percent of the world's 100 largest retailers that operate globally, says Daniel Sweeney, an author of the report." (p7)

Coolidge, Shelley Donald. "Economy: Facing Saturated Home Markets, Retailers Look to Rest of World." The Christian Science Monitor v86 n56, 14 Feb 1994. p7. (ISSN0882-7729).

RETAIL TRADE--GREAT BRITAIN (v19)

"The rate of growth of retail sales [in Great Britain] has fallen from 4% last year to a little less than 3% now. A recent survey by the Confederation of British Industry said that the number of retailers reporting increased sales in the year to February out-weighed those whose sales dropped by just 10%--down from 15% in January. And according to a poll by Gallup, published on March 21st, 42% of Britons expect their households' finances to deteriorate during the coming year, while just 17% expect them to get better." (p67)

"Britain: Waiting for the Whammy." Economist v330 n7856, 26 Mar 1994. p67-68. (ISSN0013-0613).

RETAIL TRADE--JAPAN

"The Japan Department Stores Association has 118 members who together operate 273 stores. In 1992, Association members posted a total of Y9,520 billion ($85.7 billion) in sales, a decline of 3.3% from 1991. The results for 1993 are expected to be even worse, dropping by an estimated 6%-7%. Department stores currently account for about 7% of total retail sales, but two years of decline and the emergence of new competition have worked to erode this share." (p14)

Azukizawa, Yukiteru. "Strategic Restructuring: Department Stores: Shop Lifting." Look Japan v39 n456, Mar 1994. p14-15. (ISSN0456-5339).

RETAIL TRADE--U.S. (v19)

"Customer and employee theft are 'increasing fairly dramatically' across the industry, insists J. Stephen Yaeger, a senior manager with KPMG Peat Marwick's retail consulting practice....A University of Florida survey found average shrinkage [losses to paperwork errors, theft, and the like] to be 1.88% of sales, based on 1992 data--down from 1.91% the year before, but still higher than the 1.79% of 1990." (p36)

Zellner, Wendy. "Top of the News: Retailing: Sticky Fingers Are Rifling through Retail." Business Week n3364, 28 Mar 1994. p36. (ISSN0007-7135).

RETIREES--GREAT BRITAIN (v19)
RETIREMENT--U.S.

"The majority of Americans do not plan comprehensively for their retirement; they do not consider the potential outcomes of typical decisions made at or before retirement, such as: relocating, utilizing Medicare and supplemental insurance, living solely on Social Security and/or a pension, and experiencing extended periods of leisure time. Research shows that Americans only become aware of these issues as a reaction to their changed circumstances, when it is too late to alter major lifestyle decisions. Many people spend more time and effort planning a 2-week vacation than planning the 20-plus years they could spend in retirement. As the U.S. population ages, persons will live an increasingly greater percentage of their lives as retirees. According to the National Center for Health Statistics, the average life expectancy for a 65-year-old in 1950 was 13.9 additional years, while, in 1990, the average

65-year-old could expect to live 17 more years. In this 40-year period, the life expectancy has increased 3.1 years." (pS2209)

Graham, Bob (Sen.-Fla.). "Social Security Administration Independent Agency Act," Congressional Record (2 Mar 1994). Daily ed. pS2193-2218. (ISSN0363-7239).

"Social Security data, taken from the 1990 ANNUAL STATISTICAL SUPPLEMENT OF THE SOCIAL SECURITY BULLETIN, show that there has been a large drop in the average age of retirement (mean age) at which men and women receive their first Social Security regirement benefit. Between 1950 and 1989 the average retirement age fell five years for men and 4.6 years for women, with over 85 percent of the drop occurring by 1970. During the 1980s, as the average retirement age approached its floor of 62, the trend nearly leveled off. There is, however, still some room for further declines. This will happen if there is a continuation of the long-run trend of increasing proportions of recipients who start taking their benefits at age 62. By 1989, nearly half of men and three-fifths of women did so." (p6)

Gendell, Murray/Siegel, Jacob S. "Retirement Quandary: More Retirees at Younger Ages, Living Longer." Population Today v21 n3, Mar 1993. p6-7,9. (ISSN0749-2448).

"The fall in the average retirement age and the rise in longevity [in the U.S.] have resulted in a longer retirement period....Men who retired in the late 1980s can expect to spend on average about 16 years in retirement compared with about 12 years for men retiring in the early 1950s, an increase of over one-third. The increase for women is even greater, both in terms of absolute numbers (nearly 7 years) and relative change (an increase of about half). The fall in the average age at retirement also means that the percentage of the population of retirement age increased more--from 6 percent in 1950 to 14 percent in 1990--than did the population of 'normal' retirement age (65), and may do so in the future." (p7)

Gendell, Murray/Siegel, Jacob S. "Retirement Quandary: More Retirees at Younger Ages, Living Longer." Population Today v21 n3, Mar 1993. p6-7,9. (ISSN0749-2448).

RETIREMENT INCOME--U.S. (v19)

REVENUE--U.S. (v19)

"Federal revenues [in the U.S.] are expected to be $1.25 trillion in 1994, or 18.8 percent of GDP [gross domestic product]. They are projected to grow only a little faster than the economy in the next five years, reaching 19 percent of GDP in 1999. As a share of GDP, revenues will be slightly higher than typical levels of the past three decades. In 1960 through 1993, revenues averaged 18.6 percent of GDP. In only a few years did they reach or top 19 percent; in 1969 and 1970 (when taxes were hiked to help finance the Vietnam War); in 1979 through 1982 (years of high inflation, which preceded the Reagan Administration's tax cut and the accompanying indexing of income tax brackets to inflation); in 1987 (when taxpayers rushed to realize capital gains before tax reform, which repealed preferential rates on such income, took effect); and in 1989 (when final payments from the first full year of tax reform flowed in and the economy was still chugging along strongly)." (p48)

U.S. Congressional Budget Office. "The Budget Outlook." The Economic and Budget Outlook: Fiscal Years 1995-1999 Jan 1994. Washington, D.C.: GPO, 1994.

RHINOCEROSES

"Despite the best efforts of the Convention on International Trade in Endangered Species (CITES) and the international conservation community, rhino populations continue to plummet to an alarming level. In fact, of the five species of rhinos, fewer than 10,000 are left in the wild. In 1970, there were over 65,000 African black rhinos; today, there are less than 2,000 alive. Unless immediate steps are taken, this magnificent animal will cease to exist as a viable species throughout most, if not all, of its habitat." (pE390)

Fields, Jack (Rep.-Tex.). "Introduction of the Rhinoceros Conservation Act of 1994," Congressional Record (9 Mar 1994). Daily ed. pE390-391. (ISSN0363-7239).

"A 1992 study by Traffic International concluded that over 10 tons of rhino horn--representing some 3,000 rhinos--could be found on the shelves of Taiwan's pharmacies. Sources inside Taiwan estimate that an equal amount of horn may be held by dealers, speculators, private citizens and practitioners of Chinese medicine....Smugglers send most of their rhino horns to Taiwan via South Africa, one of the few countries in the world that maintains diplomatic relations with Taiwan. Dr. Martin [UN Special Envoy and world's leading expert on rhinos] has stated categorically that 'Confiscated packages of illegal wildlife goods are always addressed to Taipei (Taiwan's capital city).' South Africa's Endangered Species Protection Unit found that every one of the 189 rhino horns confiscated since 1989 were destined for Taiwan." (p5)

"Endangered Species Project Alert: Taiwan Is the End of the Line for Endangered Species." Earth Island Journal v8 n3, Sum 1993. p44(1-8). (ISSN1041-0406).

"None of the five species [of rhino] has declined more precipitously than the African black rhinoceros, whose numbers have plunged from 65,000 to 2,500 in less than 20 years. Once found throughout the African savanna, the black rhino now survives only in isolated pockets mainly in Zimbabwe, South Africa, Kenya, Namibia, and Tanzania. Protective laws within these countries and the virtual ban on international trade in horn have failed to stem the poaching. One technique to foil poachers that seems to be working in Kenya is based on a plan devised by South Africa in the 1920s to protect its rhinos. Like South Africa, Kenya has been concentrating its remaining animals in small, easily guarded sanctuaries such as Nairobi National Park outside the capital. After rhinos were reintroduced there in the early 1970s, the population grew to more than 60 by 1992. The park fits the profile of a successful rhino preserve: It is compact and well patrolled, and, with the help of funds provided by NYZS/The Wildlife Conservation Society, key areas have been fenced, allowing wildlife officials to keep close tabs on all its charges. Kenya now has more than 400 black rhinos and the Kenya Wildlife Service is translocating animals to additional sanctuaries. Still, this is a far cry from the 20,000 that roamed the country a mere 20 years ago." (p24)

Ricciuti, Edward R. "Rhinos at Risk." Wildlife Conservation v96 n5, Sep-Oct 1993. p22-31. (ISSN1048-4949).

"Since 1970,...about 85 percent of the world's rhinos have been killed for their horns. Today, only about 10,000 to 11,000 rhinos survive worldwide....Possibly the most endangered of all rhinos is the diminutive Sumatran, or hairy, rhinoceros. Living in thick forests like the Javan rhino, the Sumatran has been reduced to mostly scattered, nonviable populations on the Malay Peninsula and on the islands of Sumatra and Borneo. Its remote habitat is being logged, few animals are in protected areas, and none has ever bred in captivity. Their low densities and remote habitat make censusing extremely difficult. Perhaps 500 or more exist, but there are no reliable estimates." (p29)

Bolze, Dorene. "Where Have All the Rhinos Gone?" Wildlife Conservation v96 n5, Sep-Oct 1993. p29. (ISSN1048-4949).

RHINOCEROSES--AFRICA (v19)

RHINOCEROSES--AFRICA--ASIA (v19)

RHINOCEROSES--TIGERS (v19)

"In 20 years, the rhino count in Asia and Africa has plummeted from 100,000 to fewer than 10,000. In this century, Asia's tigers have dwindled from 100,000 to barely 5,000. At the current rate of poaching, both species will disappear from the wild in this decade. Driving the frantic pace of killing is profit. Rhino horn, used in China and Taiwan in traditional medicines, fetches up to $30,000 a pound. Powdered tiger bone, also used in medicine, can sell for $500 a gram. A tiger penis, regarded as food to enhance sexual vigor, goes for $1,700." (p22)

Satchell, Michael. "Outlook: Science & Society: An Issue for the White House: Tigers and Rhinos." U.S. News & World Report v116 n12, 28 Mar 1994. p22. (ISSN0041-5537).

RHINOCEROSES--ZIMBABWE

"Zimbabwe was the last stronghold of the black rhino. In the early 1980s it still had a thriving population of some 3,000 wild rhinos. Today it has fewer than 100. The Zambezi River valley, which once held nearly 2,000 of the beasts, was especially vulnerable to poachers coming in from Zambia. There may be a handful left there, but trackers cannot find them." (p50)

"International: Fumbi, Under Guard." Economist v330 n7853, 5 Mar 1994. p50. (ISSN0013-0613).

"Beset by fierce drought and economic woes typical of developing African nations, Zimbabwe has practically empty pockets. Its wildlife department, once one of the finest in Africa, is falling into disarray. Game scouts have been spread thin ever since the department had to lay off 264 of them. Only 100 full-time scouts now patrol the Zambezi Valley, an area of 4,800 square miles. The country's last-ditch effort to save its rhinos by de-horning them is an expensive proposition requiring helicopters and ground crews. The expense varies according to how far wildlife biologists must travel to find the animals. It cost Namibia $1,400 per animal to de-horn 20 rhinos scattered far and wide across its desert; Zimbabwe spent an average of $704 each to de-horn 59 rhinos that were grouped more densely. As the number of rhinos in Zimbabwe decreases, more money will be needed to pay for the time spent searching for them." (p25)

Ricciuti, Edward R. "Rhinos at Risk." Wildlife Conservation v96 n5, Sep-Oct 1993. p22-31. (ISSN1048-4949).

RHODE ISLAND (v19)
RICE TRADE (v19)
RICE TRADE--ASIA (v19)
RICE TRADE--AUSTRALIA (v19)
RICE TRADE--CHINA (v19)
RICE TRADE--JAPAN (v19)
RICE TRADE--MARKETING--JAPAN (v19)
RICE TRADE--MEXICO (v19)
RICE TRADE--THAILAND (v19)
RICE TRADE--THAILAND--VIETNAM (v19)
RICE TRADE--U.S. (v19)
RICE TRADE--U.S.--MINORITIES (v19)
RICKSHAW MEN--BANGLADESH

"Bangladesh's capital, Dhaka, is aptly called the 'city of rickshaws', with 200,000 plying its streets. A recent survey suggests the country has nearly a million such vehicles. Cycle rickshaws contribute 35% of the transport sector's gross domestic product (GDP)--10 billion Taka (US$ 250 million) a year, according to the government's Bureau of Statistics. This is more than double GDP input from Bangladesh's motorised vehicles. The rickshaw industry also provides work for 'mistries' (mechanics), painters, owners and spare parts dealers." (p17)

Zaman, Roushan/Biswas, Ranjita. "Pedal-Driven Power Is Non-Polluting but Painful." Panoscope n38, Jan 1994. p17. (ISSN0951-8819).

RICKSHAW MEN--CALCUTTA (INDIA)

"Rickshaws are...multiplying in Calcutta. Despite a freeze in new licences, between 35,000 and 50,000 criss-cross the city; the official figure is 6,000. Powerful people own hundreds of unlicensed vehicles and rent them out for lucrative fees. There are an estimated 75,000 to 100,000 rickshaw pullers earning little more than US$ 1 per day--out of which they pay rent and heavy bribes to the police. Unsuccessful attempts have been made to ban rickshaws in Calcutta since 1919. Recent plans to stop the trade provoked strong opposition from the rickshaw-puller community. 'In the village, we are treated as bonded labourers, so we escape to Calcutta to earn a living through sweat and blood. If we are banned, where do we go? Back to starving?' asks Ramdhunia, of Muzzafarpur district, in Bihar. The voluntary organisation Unnayan argues that rickshaw pulling is less 'barbaric' than mining and unloading freight. Given the poverty levels in rural India, just banning rickshaws would not solve the problem, they say. An alternative livelihood has to be found, as most pullers are landless. In Calcutta, 92% of pullers come from neighbouring Bihar state. Of these, 96% are married but only 7% can affort to bring their families to the city, according to Unnayan." (p17)

Zaman, Roushan/Biswas, Ranjita. "Pedal-Driven Power Is Non-Polluting but Painful." Panoscope n38, Jan 1994. p17. (ISSN0951-8819).

RIGHT OF PROPERTY--GERMANY (v19)
RIOTS--LOS ANGELES (CALIF)

"Few politicians or television pundits...have bothered to examine the official [Los Angeles] riot statistics collected in the appendices of the Webster report. It is revealing to learn, for example, that only 38 per cent of those arrested by the LAPD were Black, or that Latinos, in addition to being 51 per cent of the total arrestees, also constituted a majority of arson defendants. Moreover, the greatest density of riot-related 'incidents' occurred north of the Santa Monica Freeway within the Wilshire and Rampart LAPD areas, not in Southcentral LA. Indeed, nearly as many suspects were booked by the Rampart station alone--west of Downtown--as by all four of the stations included within the Department's South Bureau. Even the Hollywood station made twice as many arrests as the 77th Street station, which patrolled the supposed riot epicentre at Florence and Normandie. The arrest and incident data, in other words, imply that there were actually two, parallel Los Angeles uprisings last year. The first, which riveted the attention of the world, occured in South Los Angeles and adjacent parts of LA County, and was driven by Black anger, although it included significant participation of poor Mexican immigrants in the looting of stores and mini-malls. The second, largely invisible, riot occured in the preponderantly Latino Mid-city area...." (p37-38)

Davis, Mike. "Who Killed Los Angeles? Part Two: The Verdict Is Given." New Left Review n199, May-Jun 1993. p29-54. (ISSN0028-6060).

RIVER BLINDNESS

see ONCHOCERCIASIS

RIVERS--MISSOURI (v19)
ROADS

see also PAN AMERICAN HIGHWAY SYSTEM

ROADS--U.S.

"Overall, the highway system proposed by transportation Secretary Federico F. Pena...would include only 4 percent of the nation's roads. Those roads carry 40 percent of the country's drivers, though, and 75 percent of its commercial traffic." (p110) "The 1991 [surface transportation] law dictates that the National Highway System include all the interstates (45,000 miles of roadway), the Defense Department's Strategic Highway Network and major connectors (about 17,000 more), and the 21 'high-priority corridors' chosen by Congress as part of the same 1991 law (4,506 miles). The states were left to propose about

88,000 more miles of highways for the new system. To guide the states' choices, federal officials gave each a target based on the mileage of their heavily traveled roads. The states ultimately recommended about 94,500 miles for the new system, and the Transportation Department pushed that amount down to about 92,000." (p113)

Healey, Jon. "Government & Commerce: Transportation: Congress Focuses on Fewer, More Significant Roads." Congressional Quarterly Weekly Report v52 n3, 22 Jan 1994. p110-111,113-114. (ISSN0010-5910).

ROADS--U.S.--MAINTENANCE AND REPAIR

"More than 60 percent of the miles of paved highways in the U.S. need some form of surface rehabilitation. In 1988, the U.S. Department of Transportation classified 43 percent of the interstate system pavement as either fair or poor. Truck operating costs increase by 6.3 cents per mile when road conditions drop from 'good' to 'fair.'" (p828-829)

Mellott, Paul C., Jr. (Executive V.P., H.B. Mellott Estate Inc.). U.S. House. Committee on Appropriations. "Department of Transportation and Related Agencies Approp. for 1994 (Part 7A)." Hearing, Washington, D.C.: GPO, 1993. (ISBN0160411033). (Y4.Ap6/1:T68/4/994/pt.7A).

ROADS, CONCRETE--U.S.

"Standard concrete can withstand compressive pressures of about 3,000-5,000 pounds per square inch (psi). New high-performance concrete can take up to 20,000 psi, and its vigor is rising as scientists tinker. The Civil Engineering Research Foundation calculates that this new concrete should double pavement life from 30 to 60 years, for a savings of $423 million a year." (p30)

Wolkomir, Richard. "Inside the Lab and Out, Concrete Is More Than It's Cracked Up to Be." Smithsonian v24 n10, Jan 1994. p23-31. (ISSN0037-7333).

ROBBERY--GREAT BRITAIN (v19)

ROBOTS

"According to the International Federation of Robotics (IFR), the total number of industrial robots in operation worldwide at the end of 1992 was 570,000 units, of which around 61% were in use in Japan, 16% in Western Europe, 13% in Russia and Eastern Europe, and 8% in the US. As all of the industrial robots used in Japan are domestically produced, an estimated 70% of the world's robots are Japanese-made (estimated, because not all countries make public their production figures)." (p24)

Yonemoto, Kanji. "Sci-Tech Feature: Robots in Japan: Lending a Hand." Look Japan v40 n457, Apr 1994. p24-25. (ISSN0456-5339).

ROBOTS--JAPAN

"In 1992, 62% of industrial robots distributed in Japan were bound for the electric/electronics-machinery-manufacturing industry and the automobile industry. The most common use of the robots was assembly (34.2%), followed by welding (21.6%), machining (10.6%), and plastic molding (7.1%). Industrial robots for non-manufacturing industries accounted for a mere 2% of the total." (p25)

Yonemoto, Kanji. "Sci-Tech Feature: Robots in Japan: Lending a Hand." Look Japan v40 n457, Apr 1994. p24-25. (ISSN0456-5339).

ROLLER-SKATE HOCKEY--U.S. (v19)

ROMAN CATHOLIC CHURCH

see CATHOLIC CHURCH

RUBBER, ASPHALT

see ASPHALT-RUBBER

RUNNING--U.S.--WOMEN (v19)

RURAL-URBAN MIGRATION (v19)

RURAL-URBAN MIGRATION--AUSTRALIA (v19)

RURAL-URBAN MIGRATION--CHINA (v19)

RURAL-URBAN MIGRATION--MEXICO

"In 1959, 40 percent of Mexico's population was urban. Today, 72 percent of Mexicans are crowded into cities, contributing to serious social and environmental problems. This emptying of the Mexican countryside has many causes including a rapid shift toward a free market economy and government policies which have favored specialized agro export production. NAFTA [North American Free Trade Agreement] will extend and institutionalize the private and market forces that have contributed to so much dislocation. At least one study (Levy, Wijnbergen, 1991) suggests that if current policies continue, even without a NAFTA, about 1.2 million people would leave rural Mexico over the next decade. With NAFTA, the study predicts an additional 700,000 would be displaced. Most of these would be landless laborers, very small farmers, and farmers in the rain-fed or non-irrigated agricultural areas." (pSR1-2)

"Special Report: Sustainable Rural Development in North America and the North American Free Trade Agreement." Center for Rural Affairs Newsletter Apr 1993. pSR1-4.

RURAL CONDITIONS

see MEXICO--U.S.--RURAL CONDITIONS; RURAL CRIMES--U.S.; U.S.--RURAL CONDITIONS

RURAL CRIMES--U.S.

"According to sketchy data that has reached the National Crime Information Center (NCIC), and from state, county and municipal authorities throughout the...[U.S.], the rural peace of farming has become a thing of the past. Increasingly, farms are becoming targets for random shooting by heavily armed young people whose only goal is destruction. Houses, barns, and even livestock in the fields are their targets....Unless automatic weapons, grenades, or foreign military weapons are used, these shootings are matters for local jurisdiction, almost always the county sheriff. In more than 50 percent of the rural midlands, it takes 30 minutes or more for local officers to reach the site of the shootings. By that time, the young offenders have raced away in the car or cars they occupied. Overall through the midlands belt, according to best data available, more than 15,000 of these incidents have occurred during the past three years." (p22)

"Positioning Yourself for the Difficult Time Ahead." Acres, U.S.A. Aug 1993. p22.

RURAL POPULATION

see also FARMERS

RURAL POPULATION--RUSSIA

"Although women play a significant role in Russian agriculture and agriculture is central to the major socio-economic shifts in Russia, no scholarly analysis of the gender dimension of this sector has ever been undertaken. With the rural share of the population exceeding 30 percent, it is clear that agriculture in Russia is considerably more labor-intensive than in any other industrialized country. Women comprise a little less than half of the rural population and 44.3 percent of kolkhoz members. The age differential in the rural population is shown by the fact that the proportion of women is lowest among youth and highest in the elderly population." (p27)

Mirovitskaya, Natalia. "Women: The Double Burden Weighs Heavier on Rural Russian Women." Surviving Together v11 n3, Fall 1993. p27-30. (ISSN0859-6286).

RUSSIA

see also ADVERTISING--RUSSIA; ALCOHOLIC BEVERAGES--RUSSIA; BAIKAL, LAKE (RUSSIA)--ENVIRONMENTAL ASPECTS; BALANCE OF TRADE--RUSSIA; BIOLOGICAL DIVERSITY--BAIKAL, LAKE (RUSSIA); CHILD CARE--RUSSIA; COPPER MINES AND MINING--BAIKAL, LAKE (RUSSIA); CRIME--RUSSIA;

DIPHTHERIA--RUSSIA; DRUG ABUSE--RUSSIA; ECONOMIC ASSISTANCE, AMERICAN--RUSSIA; ECONOMIC ASSISTANCE--RUSSIA; FAMILY SIZE--RUSSIA; FARMS--RUSSIA; FERTILITY, HUMAN--RUSSIA; FOOD INDUSTRY AND TRADE--RUSSIA; FORESTS AND FORESTRY--RUSSIA; GANGS--RUSSIA; GRAIN TRADE--EUROPE--RUSSIA; HOURS OF LABOR--RUSSIA; INDUSTRIAL PRODUCTIVITY--RUSSIA; INTELLIGENCE SERVICE--RUSSIA--U.S.; INVESTMENTS, FOREIGN--RUSSIA; KOLA PENINSULA (RUSSIA); MILITARY WEAPONS--RUSSIA; MONEY--VALUATION--RUSSIA; RADIOACTIVE WASTES--RUSSIA; RURAL POPULATION--RUSSIA; TIGERS--RUSSIA; UNEMPLOYMENT--RUSSIA--SPAIN; WATER--POLLUTION--RUSSIA; WATER-POWER--RUSSIA; WOMEN--EMPLOYMENT--RUSSIA

RUSSIA--ARMED FORCES (v19)

"In 1988...the USSR's land forces comprised 1.6 million men equipped with some 60,000 tanks, produced at a rate of 3,500 a year. The 1992 military reform plans of the Russian Ministry of Defense projected a decline in the entire Russian armed forces to 1.5 million men, including no more than 600,000-700,000 in the ground forces. When and if a professional army is formed by the year 2000, there will no longer be a need for the enormous stockpiles of arms and equipment in cadre divisions which, in the past, were to be complemented by a massive mobilization of reservists in case of war....Consider the matter from another angle. Since 1988, the production of tanks has dropped fivefold, to 500-700 tanks a year." (p7)

Arbatov, Alexei. "Cooperative Security: The Military Problem: Russian Security or NATO Expansion?" Boston Review v19 n2, Apr-May 1994. p7-10. (ISSN0734-2306).

RUSSIA--ARMED FORCES--APPROPRIATIONS AND EXPENDITURES (v19)

RUSSIA--ECONOMIC CONDITIONS (v19)

"As evidence of progress [in Russia], the [Clinton] Administration cites [Boris] Yeltsin's privatization program, the elimination of some import and consumer subsidies, and a reduction in inflation from 29% a month last summer to the current 18% a month. The agency, however, contends that it has shown unprecedented largess toward the Russians, who already have received $2.5 billion since 1992 merely for promising to get on the path of reform. The IMF [International Monetary Fund] contends that Yeltsin hasn't followed through on his commitments. 'What shock therapy?' argues Ernesto Hernandez-Cata, who directs IMF negotiations with Russia. 'They have an unemployment rate of 6% or so. That's lower than anywhere in Western Europe.'" (p39)

Garland, Susan B. "Top of the News: Foreign Policy: A Sticky Summit." Business Week n3353, 10 Jan 1994. p38-40. (ISSN0007-7135).

"Over the past three years, Russia's output has declined by 38%. America's fell by a mere 30% in the Great Depression between 1930 and 1933. However,...a breakdown of the output figures tells a different--and less gloomy--story. Anyone who has tried to use a Russian-made video recorder or worn a pair of Russian shoes will rejoice that production of the former fell by 40% in 1993, and of the latter by 33%. Foreign consumer goods are now widely available across Russia. Yet in those consumer industries where Russian producers turn out competitive goods--televisions and fridges, for example--output increased in 1993 by 9% and 10% respectively." (p67)

"Business: Russian Industry: Carry On Comrade." Economist v330 n7846, 15 Jan 1994. p67-68. (ISSN0013-0613).

"Real incomes last year [in Russia] were 10% higher than in 1992, an improvement confirmed by a more down-to-earth measure: it now takes 40% of the average weekly income to buy a standard basket of food, down from 90% in January 1992....the average monthly wage in dollar terms had risen from $8 in January 1992 to $100 at the end of 1993--useful if you want to buy imports. Russia registered a $20 billion trade surplus last year." (p52)

"Europe: What Is About to Be Lost." Economist v330 n7847, 22 Jan 1994. p52. (ISSN0013-0613).

"Although most international comment on the Russian economy has focused on the disasters, with inflation approaching 1,000 percent a year and industrial output slumping by one third in the last 30 months, there is considerable good news. The CIA's latest published economic survey reckons that the private sector, which employed 15 percent of the work force in 1991, now employs 42 percent of Russian workers and accounts for about 40 percent of GDP [gross domestic product]. And although overall trade has declined, the shift from endemic trade deficits to what looks to be a trade surplus of $20 billion for the whole of 1993, has started to give the Russian government some room for maneuver. From less than $1 billion in late 1992, official foreign reserves are now $7 billion, which suggests that Western donors offering stabilization funds for the Russian currency should be able to count on some local help." (p9)

Walker, Martin. "Trade: The Key to Russia's Future." Europe n333, Feb 1994. p9. (ISSN0191-4545).

"The Russians need a rest now. For two tumultuous years President Boris N. Yeltsin took them through an ill-advised experiment that was supposed to destroy the old Soviet order and bring about a capitalist market system. Instead, it has produced a society of growing lawlessness and deepening poverty, an economy dominated by inefficient industrial monopolies, and a financial community increasingly controlled by a brutal mafia. The experiment, launched in January 1992 at the urging of economic adviser Yegor T. Gaidar, with strong encouragement from an International Monetary Fund that had faint knowledge of Russia's political and economic situation, has impoverished a third of the population. An estimated 40 to 50 million Russians currently live below the poverty line--that is, on an income of less than 66,000 rubles (about $40) a month. The top 10 per cent, the new rich, at present earns 10 times more than the poorest 10 per cent, and the income gap continues to widen, making this a country of conspicuous haves and virtually ignored have-nots." (p5)

Hopkins, Mark. "The Challenge Facing Chernomyrdin." New Leader v77 n2, 14 Feb 1994. p5-7. (ISSN0028-6044).

"Russia's rebound is impressive. The average monthly wage is now $87 per month--not much, but still eleven times what it was in January of 1992. Some 42 percent of all employed Russians now work for the private sector; 15 percent did so in 1991. Russia has a trade surplus and $7 billion in foreign reserves." (p9)

"Don't Panic." New Republic v210 n2-3, 10-17 Jan 1994. p9. (ISSN0028-6583).

RUSSIA--MORTALITY

"Murray Feshbach, a student of East European and Russian demography at Georgetown University in Washington, points out that the death rate in Russia rose by over 30% between 1989 and 1993, to 14.2 per thousand. For men aged between 16 and 59, it rose by 30% between 1992 and 1993 alone. On today's trends, a 16-year old boy in Russia has only a 60% chance of surviving to the age of 60. Indeed, Mr Feshbach estimates that life expectancy at birth for men fell by three full years, from 62 to 59, between 1992 and 1993." (p54)

"Europe: Eastern Germany: Living and Dying, in a Barren Land." Economist v331 n7860, 23 Apr 1994. p54. (ISSN0013-0613).

RUSSIA--SOCIAL CONDITIONS

"It should not be surprising that the mainstream media avoid open discussion of the raw economic leverage exerted on the Russians in defense of capitalist reforms in Russia. For one thing, these reforms have been a colossal failure. Gross national product fell 20 percent last year and continues to shrink (CHALLENGE, September-October 1993). Inflation is expected to be 'at least 2,000 percent this year' (THE BANKER, September 1993, p.12). The health standards of the Russian people have deteriorated dramatically. Last year 2,000 cases of diptheria were reported in Moscow alone compared to 4 in the United States. Twenty-five percent of children in Russia developed rickets or anemia in their first five years. Between 1990 and 1992, suicides in Russia tripled. (CURRENT, September 1993, p.21). Yet the West threw its weight behind more of the same, increasingly unpopular 'reforms' at every crucial juncture. As religious- and ethnic-based civil wars flare on the southern periphery of Russia--in Georgia, Armenia, Azerbaijan, and Tajikistan--the danger grows of a diversionary war in defense of Russians now living in the new republics and fueled by domestic misery in Russia itself. Celebrating the Yeltsin coup is one thing: taking responsibility for his disastrous policies, and their possibly tragic consequences, is another." (p9)

Petras, James/Vieux, Steve. "Behind the 'Democrat's Coup.'" Lies of Our Times Dec 1993. p8-9. (ISSN1046-7912).

RUSSIANS--KAZAKHSTAN--TAJIKISTAN--UZBEKISTAN (v19)

SAFETY BELTS, AUTOMOBILE

see AUTOMOBILES--SEAT BELTS

SAINT LAWRENCE SEAWAY (v19)

"During October of 1992...[the U.S.] released a contracted study effort to assess the economic impacts of the Great Lakes/St. Lawrence Seaway System. Major findings of the survey were that the Seaway System generates over 44,000 direct and induced jobs; $1.9 billion in annual personal income; $1.7 billion in corporate revenue; and $90.7 million in state and local taxes. The project was based on direct interviews with the maritime communities of sixteen U.S. lake port cities representing eighty percent of the tonnage moving through the System. The study is conservative by design in order to include only those impacts that are defensible." (p158)

Parris, Stanford E. (Administrator, Saint Lawrence Seaway Development Corp.). U.S. House. Committee on Appropriations. "Department of Transportation and Related Agencies Approp. for 1994 (Part 3)." Hearing, Washington, D.C.: GPO, 1993. (ISBN0160410649). (Y4.Ap6/1:T68/4/994/pt.3).

SALES PERSONNEL--U.S.--DATA PROCESSING (v19)

SALMON--IDAHO

"Although the Idaho Fish and Game Department blames eight hydroelectric dams for killing 77 to 95 percent of the migrating juvenile salmon, NMFS [the National Marine Fisheries Service] officials ruled the dams cause 'no jeopardy' to Snake River salmon....Charles Ray, salmon policy coordinator for Idaho Rivers United, said the dams killed an estimated 2.7 million juvenile chinook salmon during the spring migration, or about three-fourths of the wild run. 'If the feds all of a sudden decided that they'd make three-fourths of this year's bald eagle eggs into omelettes, the public would howl--it'd be an outrage, a national crime. But that's exactly what they're doing to the salmon,' Ray said." (p7)

Stuebner, Steve. "Idaho Gov. Andrus Takes on Eight Dams." High Country News v25 n19, 18 Oct 1993. p7. (ISSN0191-5657).

SALMON--U.S.

see also COHO SALMON--U.S.

"An estimated 10 to 15 million adult salmon spawned in the Columbia River and its tributaries 150 years ago. Today that number has been reduced to less than 500,000. Despite listings under the Endangered Species Act (ESA), wild salmon have continued to decline with the continuing degradation of their spawning, migratory, and ocean habitats." (p1)

"Western Salmon Get Help in Fighting an Upstream Battle." EDF Letter v24 n6, Nov 1993. p1,3. (ISSN0163-2566).

SALMON INDUSTRY--ALASKA (v19)

SALMONELLOSIS--U.S. (v19)

SALVATION ARMY--U.S.

The Salvation Army "is far larger than most people realize, claiming more than 5 million members in ninety-nine countries. Last year, it raised $726 million from private donations in the United States, more than any other nonprofit organization. (The Christmas kettles alone brought in $61 million.) All money raised locally is used locally. One of the principles of charity outlined in Army literature is that any social plan 'must be on a scale commensurate with the situation with which it proposes to deal.' In the United States last year the Army served at least 69 million free meals and provided shelter for 9.5 million homeless people." (p22)

Tisdale, Sallie. "Good Soldiers." New Republic v210 n1, 3 Jan 1994. p22-24,26-27. (ISSN0028-6583).

SAN FRANCISCO (CALIF)

see FISHES--SAN FRANCISCO (CALIF); HOMELESS PERSONS--SAN FRANCISCO (CALIF)

SANCTIONS (INTERNATIONAL LAW) (v19)

SANCTIONS (INTERNATIONAL LAW)--IRAQ--ECONOMIC CONDITIONS

"At national level, the United Nations embargo, imposed after Iraq's invasion of Kuwait in mid-1990, has cut off oil exports that were worth $15 billion a year. Down in the street the resultant shortages make themselves felt in prices. Sugar before the Gulf war cost 0.60 of a dinar per kilo; today's figure on the open market is 200 dinars. That is equivalent to about $1 at the black-market rate (though $625 at the long-fixed official one). Wheat flour costs around 30 dinars a kilo. An average wage is around 400 dinars a month. Government ration shops, 50,000 of them throughout the country, keep people alive; a family of six pays only about 30 dinars a month for its rations. But the rations meet only 50-70% of energy and protein needs and few vitamin needs. Urban Iraqis, harder hit than country people, must buy the rest on the open market or go without." (p46)

"International: Iraqis Count the Cost of Sanctions." Economist v330 n7851, 19 Feb 1994. p46. (ISSN0013-0613).

SANTA FE (N.MEX)

see HISPANIC AMERICANS--SANTA FE (N.MEX)--ECONOMIC CONDITIONS

SARAWAK (MALAYSIA)

see ETHNOLOGY--SARAWAK (MALAYSIA); LOGGING--SARAWAK (MALAYSIA)

SAUDI ARABIA

see BUDGET DEFICITS--SAUDI ARABIA; OIL WELLS--SAUDI ARABIA--U.S.

SAUDIA ARABIA--ARMED FORCES (v19)

SAVING AND INVESTMENT--ASIA, EASTERN (v19)

SAVING AND INVESTMENT--JAPAN (v19)

SAVING AND INVESTMENT--JAPAN--U.S. (v19)

SAVING AND INVESTMENT--U.S. (v19)

SAVING AND INVESTMENT--U.S.--RETIREMENT (v19)

SAVING AND THRIFT--U.S.

"The Wall Street Journal reported last December that not only are consumers charging more purchases to their credit cards, they have let their savings rate slide lower and lower. From a 5.2-percent rate in 1992, the savings rate for 1993 was just over 4 percent as of November....the U.S. savings rate has been far below that of our major competitors since the 1970's, when it was in the 9-to10-percent range. In fact, our savings rate is currently the lowest of all of the G-7 countries. In 1991, Germany's savings rate was 4.3 times ours and Japan's was nearly 9 times as high. Why is too low a savings rate bad for the economy? Basically, it is because it raises the cost of capital, forcing the Government and businesses to pay more for the use of money and putting the United States at a disadvantage internationally. The cost of capital has a direct bearing on the formation of businesses and on the creation of new jobs." (pS953)

Hatch, Orrin G. (Sen.-Utah). "Statements on Introduced Bills and Joint Resolutions," Congressional Record (4 Feb 1994). Daily ed. pS951-960. (ISSN0363-7239).

"In the early 1960s, federal borrowing absorbed 1 percent of net private savings in America; by 1992, it soaked up a whopping 71 percent. As a result, the United States now has the lowest savings rate in the industrialized world and must depend on foreign savers for its net investment." (p31)

Hewitt, Paul. "Fair Comment: Entitlements for the Elderly Drive Deficits." Insight v10 n6, 7 Feb 1994. p31. (ISSN1051-4880).

SAVINGS AND LOAN ASSOCIATION FAILURES--U.S. (v19)

SAVINGS AND LOAN ASSOCIATIONS--U.S. (v19)

SAVINGS BONDS--U.S.

"From 1987 until the current surge in Savings Bond sales started at the end of 1991, about 40 percent of dollar sales of Savings Bonds were sold through payroll savings. Payroll sales grew steadily in 1991 and 1992 but were only 27 percent of sales in 1992 because of the steep increase in over-the-counter sales, driven by the above-market 6 percent guaranteed rate. With the reduction in the guaranteed rate, we expect payroll sales once more to make up about 40 percent of total dollars in future." (p146)

Schneebeli, Richard J. (Acting Executive Dir., U.S. Savings Bonds Division). U.S. House. Committee on Appropriations. "Treasury, Postal Service...Approp. for Fiscal Year 1994 (Part 1)." Hearing, Washington, D.C.: GPO, 1993. (Y4.Ap6/1:T71/994/pt.1).

The United States Savings Bonds Division "promotes sales in both the payroll savings areas and in the over-the-counter markets. Dollar sales of $13.6 billion in fiscal year 1992 were the highest in the Program's 52 year history. The value of Savings Bonds held by Americans rose 11 percent in fiscal year 1992 to $150.3 billion, the highest in the history of the Bond program. The 1993 sales year has started off at an even brisker pace. January Sales were 2.55 billion dollars, the highest January ever in the history of the Program. To date the four month 1993 totals are $8 billion, 992 million. We feel that the Savings Bonds Program has continually demonstrated its value to the government and to the public. From 1941 to 1992, the public purchased over $300 billion, at issue price, of Savings Bonds. For many of our citizens, Savings Bonds have been the primary method of saving, and for the government they have provided a stable source of financing the public debt." (p110)

Schneebeli, Richard J. (Acting Executive Dir., U.S. Savings Bonds Division). U.S. House. Committee on Appropriations. "Treasury, Postal Service...Approp. for Fiscal Year 1994 (Part 1)." Hearing, Washington, D.C.: GPO, 1993. (Y4.Ap6/1:T71/994/pt.1).

SAXOPHONE--U.S. (v19)

SCANDINAVIA

see CANCER--SCANDINAVIA

SCHISTOSOMA--DEVELOPING COUNTRIES

"More than 200 million people living in 76 tropical developing countries are infected with bilharzia, according to World Health Organization (WHO) estimates. In some parts of Uganda, such as West Nile, the entire population has been infected at one time or another with the diesease, which is also known as schistosomiasis. In children, the sometimes fatal disease is associated with mental and physical retardation, and weakness. In adults, it causes anaemia, fatigue, tissue damage and cirrhosis of the liver. Globally, it kills at least 200,000 people every year. Almost 30 years ago, two Ethiopian doctors, Aklilu Lemma and Legesse Wolde Yohannes, discovered that the soapberry plant ('Phytolacca Dodecandra') could kill the freshwater snails that help transmit the disease. The plant, called 'endod' in Ethiopia and 'luwoko' in Uganda, has small berries which, when dried, powdered and mixed with water, create a foaming detergent traditionally used in Africa for washing clothes." (p5)

Aliro, Ogen Kevin. "Africa: Natural Soap Washes Away a Deadly Bug." Panoscope n35, Apr 1993. p5-6. (ISSN0951-8819).

SCHOLASTIC APTITUDE TEST--U.S. (v19)

Researchers Myra and David Sadker have criticized the S.A.T. tests for being biased against girls. "On the S.A.T., required for admission to many colleges, boys typically score 50 to 60 points higher than girls. A high school girl with an A+ grade-point average typically scores 83 points lower than a boy with the same G.P.A., the Sadkers say. On the Achievement Tests, which evaluate knowledge in a single subject area, boys in 1992 outscored girls on 11 of the 14 different versions of the test--from physics to American history to Latin. Girls outdid boys only in German, English composition, and literature." (p25)

Lawton, Millicent. "Girls Will--and Should--Be Girls." Education Week v13 n27, 30 Mar 1994. p24-27. (ISSN0277-4232).

SCHOOL ADMINISTRATORS--SALARIES, ETC.--U.S.

"Average increases in principals' salaries are on the rise again, although they remain well below what they were in the late 1980's, a new report shows. Salaries for the 1993-94 school year are about 3 percent higher than those of 1992-93 for principals of public elementary, middle, and high schools, according to the report released...by the National Association of Secondary School Principals. Average salary increases in the late 1980's were between 6 percent and 8 percent....High school principals this year are paid an average of $64,993, a 2.98 percent increase from last year. Middle school principals earn an average of $60,651, an increase of 3.35 percent, while elementary school principals earn an average of $56,906, a 3.52 percent increase. The highest salary reported in the survey was $108,674. The salary report is based on data collected by the Educational Research Service from more than 1,000 school districts." (p4)

"News Roundup: National: Principals' Salary Increases On the Upswing, Report Says." Education Week v13 n25, 16 Mar 1994. p4. (ISSN0277-4232).

SCHOOL ATTENDANCE--U.S.

"Truancy continues to be a major problem in many communities. In Los Angeles County, for instance, about 300,000 (out of 1.6 million) students are truant every day. According to the district attorney, youngsters who are truant are responsible for 85 percent of daytime crime. Truancy is a common denominator for most criminal activity. Similar percentages of truancy occur in many of our large urban areas. Truancy is one manifestation of the entire safe schools and communities matrix. When students are not in school they tend to disrupt local neighborhoods. But school safety is not simply a large city phenomenon; it cuts across suburban and rural districts as well." (p39)

Stephens, Ronald D. (Executive Dir., National School Safety Center, Westlake Village, CA). U.S. Senate. Committee on

Labor and Human Resources. "Recess from Violence: Making Our Schools Safe." Hearing, 23 Sep 1993. Washington, D.C.: GPO, 1993. (ISBN0160433096). (Y4.L11/4:S.hrg.103-313).

SCHOOL CHILDREN--FOOD--OHIO

"One experiment with universal breakfast has yielded dramatic results in Ohio. Hamilton City School District's Food Service Director, Linda Vaupel, initiated a universal school breakfast program at Van Buren Elementary School for a one-month trial period in October 1992. Sixty-eight percent of the students were eligible for free and reduced-price meals.... Teachers...noted a dramatic difference in the children who were eating breakfast. 'Those participating in the pilot project were more alert and ready to start the day,' principal Michael Farmer said. With such important progress noted by teachers, Van Buren continued the program beyond the one month period, and Hamilton County expanded universal breakfast into another eight elementary schools. Notably, Elementary Standardized Achievement Test scores in the schools serving universal breakfasts have increased markedly. 'The percentage of fourth and sixth grade students scoring in the top 50 percent nationwide increased significantly,' [Lisa] Hamler-Podolski noted. 'Fifty-seven percent of the students ranked in the top 50 percent nationwide in reading compared to only 29 percent in the previous school year.'" (p6)

"From the Field: Ohio City Experiments with Universal Breakfast." Foodlines v10 n3, Sep-Oct 1993. p6. (ISSN0736-0010).

SCHOOL CHILDREN--FOOD--U.S.

"In 1992, $675 million in subsidized commodities was donated to school lunch and breakfast programs. Those commodities--in the form of processed cheese, frozen or canned meats, canned fruits and vegetables, oils, butter, flour, and other staples--represent one fifth of each school meal. Many of those commodities are high in fat. Among the vegetable commodities, a bite-sized fatty potato product tops donations. That product gets 42 percent of its calories from fat, compared with a baked potato, with less than 1 percent calories from fat." (p18)

U.S. Dept. of Agriculture/Jacobson, Michael. "Food & Nutrition: USDA's Responsibility to Consumers." Agricultural Outlook Jan-Feb 1994. p17-18.

"The National School Lunch Program, which feeds some 25 million children daily, could be teaching good eating habits that will last a lifetime. USDA surveys, however, indicate that school lunches are far too high in fat and sodium. The average meal gets 38 percent of its calories from fat--compared with the recommended 30 percent--and half again more than the recommended level of saturated fat. Meals have twice the recommended amount of sodium. In other words, schools actually provide diets that are bad for children's health." (p17)

U.S. Dept. of Agriculture/Jacobson, Michael. "Food & Nutrition: USDA's Responsibility to Consumers." Agricultural Outlook Jan-Feb 1994. p17-18.

"A 1987 study conducted by physicians and university researchers in Massachusetts found that low-income elementary school children participating in the School Breakfast Program showed an improvement in standardized achievement test scores and improved attendance rates compared to similar students who did not eat breakfast at school....However, the program is not available to millions of low-income children who need it. This past school year, only 58.4 percent of the schools which offer the National School Lunch Program nationwide also offered breakfast, and only 34.9 percent of low-income students who receive free or reduced-price lunches participated in the breakfast program." (p4)

"Back to School Means More Than 'Three R's for Many Children." Foodlines v10 n3, Sep-Oct 1993. p1,4-5. (ISSN0736-0010).

SCHOOL DISTRICTS--U.S.

"Through [W. L.] Elder's work...based on the Merged File of Common Core Data Public Schools Universe and Public Agency Universe maintained by the National Center for Educational Statistics, a procedure has been established that permits development of a topology of school district locales (e.g., city, urban fringe, town, rural). In his landmark work, Elder presented the following data: Rural districts represented nearly half (47.2%, of the nation's 15,123 operating districts in 1989-1990. These 7,145 rural districts operated over one-fourth (22,412) of the 79,307 public schools in the country. Slightly more than 6-1/2 million students (16.6%) of the nearly 40 million public elementary-secondary school-age population attended these rural schools. More than one out of eight (13.4%) of the nation's 2.2 million teachers were employed by these rural districts (Elder, 1991)." (p17)

Stephens, Robert/Hunter, Bruce. "The Nation's Rural School Districts: Orphans in the School Reform Debate." Holistic Education Review v6 n1, Spr 1993. p16-24. (ISSN0898-0926).

SCHOOL EMPLOYEES--U.S. (v19)

SCHOOL FACILITIES--U.S. (v19)

SCHOOL VIOLENCE--CALIFORNIA (v19)

SCHOOL VIOLENCE--ILLINOIS (v19)

SCHOOL VIOLENCE--U.S. (v19)

"An August 1993 USA WEEKEND survey of 65,000 10th through 12th grade students from across the United States reported that: 37 percent do not feel safe at school; 43 percent avoid school restrooms; 55 percent said they knew someone who had brought a weapon to school, and 63 percent said they would learn more if they felt safer. The Lou Harris Poll, released in July 1993, underscored the fact that America's young people are immersed in a gun culture. Among the 2,500 students, aged 10 to 19, who were surveyed in 96 elementary, middle and senior high schools, 15 percent say they have carried a handgun on their person in the last 30 days and 4 percent (one in 25) say they have taken a handgun to school this past year. More startling perhaps is that 59 percent said they could get a handgun if they wanted one." (p39)

Stephens, Ronald D. (Executive Dir., National School Safety Center, Westlake Village, CA). U.S. Senate. Committee on Labor and Human Resources. "Recess from Violence: Making Our Schools Safe." Hearing, 23 Sep 1993. Washington, D.C.: GPO, 1993. (ISBN0160433096). (Y4.L11/4:S.hrg.103-313).

"Nearly 3 million thefts and violent crimes occur on or near school campuses every year. This equates to almost 16,000 incidents per school day, or one every six seconds. 1.9 million of these incidents are considered violent crimes, and they include rape, robbery, assault, and murder (Department of Justice, Bureau of Justice Statistics)....Although national records are not kept, data from the National School Safety Center indicate that approximately 30 persons were killed in schools, on their way to schools, or on school property during the last school year." (p14-15)

Kunin, Madeleine M. (Deputy Secretary, U.S. Dept. of Education). U.S. Senate. Committee on Labor and Human Resources. "Recess from Violence: Making Our Schools Safe." Hearing, 23 Sep 1993. Washington, D.C.: GPO, 1993. (ISBN0160433096). (Y4.L11/4:S.hrg.103-313).

"In Ann Arbor schools, there has been a steady increase of violence in recent years. District records show the number of suspensions for serious offenses (fighting, possession of weapons, etc.) has grown from a total of 55 incidents in 1987-88 to 115 in 1992-93....The increase is not reason for alarm, but is good reason to address violence in schools now, before Ann Arbor has a chance to be included in grim statistics reported elsewhere. According to a study by the Pew Partnership for

Civic Change, youth violence has reached epidemic proportions in larger cities and most U.S. cities of 50,000 to 150,000...also have begun to experience increases in crimes committed by teenagers. In Rochester, Minn., as an example, the Pew report said, there were rumors of gangs in 1990. In 1991, there was substantial evidence of gangs. In 1992, there were clear indicators that gangs had gained a stronghold. In 1993, there were regular reports of violence, fighting and other gang-related activities." (p6 secB)

"Opinion: Editorials: Schools: Community as a Whole Must Stand against Youth Violence." Ann Arbor News 20 Feb 1994. p6 secB.

"Much of the violent activity among teenagers takes place on school grounds. U.S. secretary of education Richard W. Riley has noted that each year about three million thefts and violent crimes occur on or near school campuses. That is about 16,000 incidents per school day. Violence at school is becoming almost as much a rural and suburban as an urban problem. A 1993 study by the National School Boards Association found that, of 720 school districts, 82 percent reported an increase in violence in their schools in the past five years. These increases are occurring across all geographic areas." (p3)

"Saving Youth from Violence." Carnegie Quarterly v39 n1, Win 1994. p1-5.

"A National School Boards Association survey shows that 82 percent of 729 school districts [in the U.S.] responding said that violence in their schools had increased over the past 5 years. In 1992, 2 percent of eighth graders, 4 percent of 10th graders and 3 percent of 12th graders nationwide reported that they regularly carried a weapon to school. In addition, 14 to 19 percent of eighth, 10th and 12th graders reported being threatened with a weapon; 25 to 29 percent reported being threatened without a weapon; and 5 to 9 percent reported being injured with a weapon in school. According to newspaper accounts between 1986 and 1990 at least 71 persons--65 students and 6 school employees--were killed by guns at school, 201 were severely wounded, and 242 were held at gunpoint." (pE235)

Mfume, Kweisi. "Congressman Mfume Supports Safe Schools Act," Congressional Record (23 Feb 1994). Daily ed. pE235-236. (ISSN0363-7239).

"There are no comprehensive statistics on school violence but according to a survey by the National School Boards Association: 82 percent of 729 school districts said violence had increased; 61 percent reported weapons incidents; 39 percent reported shootings or knifings; 23 percent reported drive-by shootings; 15 percent reported at least one rape; 78 percent reported student assaults on students; and 60 percent reported student assaults on students and teachers. Why does violence occur? According to an article in America's Agenda: 18 percent gang or drug disputes; 15 percent long standing arguments; 12 percent romantic disagreements; 10 percent fights over material possessions; and 13 percent accidents." (pS837)

Murkowski, Frank H. (Sen.-Alaska). "GOALS 2000: Educate America Act," Congressional Record (4 Feb 1994). Daily ed. pS835-846. (ISSN0363-7239).

"Nationally, violence in and around schools is occurring at alarming rates, as these statistics from a 1993 U.S. Justice Department report confirm: Nearly three million thefts and violent crimes occur on or near school campuses every year--one every six seconds. Fifteen percent of students questioned say their school has gangs, and 16 percent claim a student has attacked or threatened a teacher at the school. Nearly one out of five public school teachers reports being verbally abused by students. Eight percent report being physically threatened, while 2 percent say they have actually been physically attacked. Nearly 20 percent of all students in grades 9-12 report they have carried a weapon at least once." (p45)

Huml, Frank J. "Is Social-Skills Training One 'Missing Link'?" Education Week v13 n25, 16 Mar 1994. p45. (ISSN0277-4232).

"Nearly a quarter of teenagers [in the U.S.] fear for their physical safety while at school, according to preliminary findings released by the Gallup International Institute....at an American Medical Association conference on family violence, George H. Gallup Jr. said that 30 percent of 518 teenagers surveyed in 1992 and 1993 reported that their schools had serious problems with violent behavior in the classroom. Two-thirds said they had best friends who had been physically harmed within the past year. Of those assaulted, 10 percent were hurt by teachers or principals, and more than 25 percent were assaulted by other adults, the survey found. One in five of the teenagers surveyed reported that a friend had been assaulted with a knife or gun. One-fifth of the 13- to 17-year-olds participating in the study said their best friends had been victims of sexual assault, and 9 percent said they had a friend who had been raped. Mr. Gallup said the rape figure likely was underreported because boys are less likely than girls to be aware of sexual assaults on their friends." (p4)

"News Roundup: National: Many Teenagers Feel Fear at School, Survey Shows." Education Week v13 n26, 23 Mar 1994. p4. (ISSN0277-4232).

Eighty-two percent of 720 school districts surveyed by the National School Boards Association have said that violence has increased in their schools over the past five years. Board members in 78 percent of the districts said student assaults on other students were the most frequent form of violence, and 28 percent reported student attacks on teachers. To combat violence "seventy-eight percent of the districts surveyed use student suspensions, 70 percent work with social agencies, and 60 percent train their staffs in conflict resolution. Twenty-four percent of the districts send trained dogs into the schools to find drugs, 15 percent use metal detectors to search for weapons, and 11 percent use closed-circuit-television cameras on school buses." A study from the U.S. Justice Department says that "thirty-five percent of male high school students in crime-ridden urban neighborhoods said they carry a gun, and 22 percent of those students reported owning a gun....Forty-five percent of the students reported that they had been threatened with a gun or had been shot 'on the way to or from school' within the past few years." In a survey of teachers by the Metropolitan Life Insurance Company, 77 percent said they felt "very safe" at school. But among those who rated their schools' quality of education as fair or poor, only 44 percent feel safe. (p9)

Portner, Jessica. "School Violence Up over Past 5 Years, 82% in Survey Say." Education Week v13 n16, 12 Jan 1994. p9. (ISSN0277-4232).

"Violence in the [U.S.] public schools was the subject of the latest annual MetLife-sponsored teacher survey conducted by Louis Harris and Associates, Inc....As in previous surveys, the interview data were collected from a nationally representative random sample of subjects. The 1993 study differed from earlier surveys, however, by including three sample groups--teachers, students and law enforcement officials." (p2) According to the study "Schools in suburban/rural settings were reported as being 'very safe' by more than 80 percent of the teachers, but by only 53 percent of the students in these settings. Conversely, 6 percent of these students reported feeling 'not very' or 'not at all' safe compared to only 1 percent of the teachers....Ten percent of students versus 1 percent of teachers felt 'not very' or 'not at all safe' in their elementary schools." (p4)

Mushinski, Margaret. "Violence in America's Public Schools." Statistical Bulletin v75 n2, Apr-Jun 1994. p2-9.

(ISSN0790-8334).

"Violence in the [U.S.] public schools was the subject of the latest annual MetLife-sponsored teacher survey conducted by Louis Harris and Associates, Inc....As in previous surveys, the interview data were collected from a nationally representative random sample of subjects. The 1993 study differed from earlier surveys, however, by including three sample groups--teachers, students and law enforcement officials." (p2) According to the study "Eleven percent of teachers and 23 percent of students reported having been a victim of violence in or around their schools....The proportion of teachers who had been violence victims was almost three times higher among those in schools perceived as providing poor to fair quality education than among all the teachers as a whole (31 versus 11 percent, respectively) and 4.5 times higher among these teachers than those in schools perceived as providing an excellent quality education. Virtually all (95 percent) of the teachers who had been victims indicated that students had been involved in the violence." (p6)

Mushinski, Margaret. "Violence in America's Public Schools." Statistical Bulletin v75 n2, Apr-Jun 1994. p2-9. (ISSN0790-8334).

"Violence in the [U.S.] public schools was the subject of the latest annual MetLife-sponsored teacher survey conducted by Louis Harris and Associates, Inc....As in previous surveys, the interview data were collected from a nationally representative random sample of subjects. The 1993 study differed from earlier surveys, however, by including three sample groups--teachers, students and law enforcement officials." (p2) According to the study "While only 4 percent of the teachers did not report the violence to school officials or the police, half of the student victims either did not report the incident (45 percent) or were unsure as to whether or not it had been reported by a witness (5 percent). Boys were almost twice as likely as girls to be a victim of violence (30 versus 16 percent, respectively) and 39 percent of all students with poor grades versus 22 percent with good or fair grades had been a victim of violence." (p6-7)

Mushinski, Margaret. "Violence in America's Public Schools." Statistical Bulletin v75 n2, Apr-Jun 1994. p2-9. (ISSN0790-8334).

"Violence in the [U.S.] public schools was the subject of the latest annual MetLife-sponsored teacher survey conducted by Louis Harris and Associates, Inc....As in previous surveys, the interview data were collected from a nationally representative random sample of subjects. The 1993 study differed from earlier surveys, however, by including three sample groups--teachers, students and law enforcement officials." (p2) According to the study "Half the teachers versus 21 percent of the students and only 8 percent of law enforcement officials reported that no handguns or knives were regularly brought to school....Between 1 and 10 percent was the predominant response among each survey group when asked to estimate the proportion of students who regularly carried weapons to school. Even more alarming, 9 percent of students and 7 percent of law officials thought that this percentage exceeded 25 percent." (p7)

Mushinski, Margaret. "Violence in America's Public Schools." Statistical Bulletin v75 n2, Apr-Jun 1994. p2-9. (ISSN0790-8334).

"In a new study of 729 school districts by the National School Boards Association (NSBA), 82 percent of the districts reported significant increases in violence during the last five years. The report called violence in schools an 'epidemic' with 39 percent of the schools reporting a shooting or knifing last year and 23 percent reporting a drive-by shooting." (p4)

Holmstrom, David. "From the States: Violent Crime Is Down--But Not in Public Schools." The Christian Science Monitor v86 n35, 13 Jan 1994. p4. (ISSN0882-7729).

SCHOOL VIOLENCE--U.S.--PUBLIC OPINION

"A recent survey found that overall 37 percent of [U.S.] students don't feel safe in school. This is double the number found in a similar survey conducted in 1989. The survey also found that 50 percent of students know someone who switched schools to feel safer; 43 percent of public school students avoid school restrooms; 20 percent avoid hallways; and 45 percent avoid the school grounds. (USA TODAY WEEKEND August 13-15, 1993)." (p13)

Kunin, Madeleine M. (Deputy Secretary, U.S. Dept. of Education). U.S. Senate. Committee on Labor and Human Resources. "Recess from Violence: Making Our Schools Safe." Hearing, 23 Sep 1993. Washington, D.C.: GPO, 1993. (ISBN0160433096). (Y4.L11/4:S.hrg.103-313).

SCHOOL YEAR--GERMANY--JAPAN--U.S. (v19)

SCHOOL YEAR--U.S.

"The number of students in schools using year-round calendars is up for the 15th straight year, a report by the National Association for Year-Round Education says. More than 1.4 million students now do without the traditional summer vacation, the annual survey found. In the current school year, 366 districts in 32 states offer classes on a year-round basis." Eighty-five percent of the buildings having year-round schedules are elementary schools. The most popular calendar schedules students for 60 days in school followed by a 20-day break. Nearly 60 percent of year-round schools use an overlapping calendar. "By alternating student breaks, such schedules enable schools to increase their building capacity, since a portion of the enrollment is always on hiatus." (p6)

Harp, Lonnie. "Enrollment in Year-Round Schools Is Up Again." Education Week v13 n17, 19 Jan 1994. p6. (ISSN0277-4232).

SCHOOLS--BOSTON (MASS) (v19)

SCHOOLS--CUBA--FURNITURE, EQUIPMENT, ETC.

"Three million students begin classes September first in Cuba, and while no school has been shut down as a result of the economic crisis, there are severe shortages of school supplies. In a conversation with the Pastors for Peace 'Friendshipment' drivers in Havana, the Minister of Education's chief adviser, Eduardo Lara, pointed to several key items:...Cuban students and teachers use 50 million pencils in each academic year. They only have 2.5 million guaranteed for this term--500,000 of those from donations. Cuban pencil factories could guarantee at least half of the island's demand, but like most production plants, they lack raw materials and oil....Some 5.5 million shirts, blouses, pants and skirts would normally be distributed to students, at subsidized prices. However, only 603,300 of these uniforms are now in stock. The country needs cloth." (p16)

"Severe Shortages Hurt Schools." Cuba Update Supplement Sep 1993. p16.

SCHOOLS--KENYA

"The Kenyan 'state' has never been primarily responsible for maintaining secondary education. Shortly after Kenya gained political independence in 1963, President Jomo Kenyatta encouraged the country to form community-based 'self-help' development efforts in the spirit of 'harambee' (Barkan & Chege 1989). These projects asked local communities to pool their financial and labor resources for various developmental projects that required relatively little government involvement....Out of a total of 2,485 secondary schools in 1987, 1,497 were 'harambee' and another 353 were completely private schools (Republic of Kenya 1989)." (p352) "However, despite the construction of additional nongovernment schools, it is clear that 'harambee' institutions are neither cheaper than nor superior to government-maintained institutions (Mwiria 1990). In fact, the opposite is true in both cases. A comprehensive survey for 1980 showed that government-maintained day school fees ranged from 300 shillings ($40.4 U.S.) to 600 shillings ($81.8 U.S.) per year; by contrast, 'harambee' day school fees ranged from 450 shillings ($60.6 U.S.) to 1,200 shillings ($161.7 U.S.) a year (Hazlewood et al. 1989:23)." (p353)

Bradshaw, York W. "State Limitations, Self-Help Secondary Schooling, and Development in Kenya." Social Forces v72 n2, Dec 1993. p347-378. (ISSN0037-7732).

SCHOOLS--LOS ANGELES (CALIF) (v19)

SCHOOLS--MICHIGAN--PUBLIC OPINION

"In the Detroit metropolitan area, residents' opinions about the quality of the public schools in their districts varied widely. In...[a] survey, the respondents were asked the following questions: 'How would you rate the quality of the public schools in your school district? Would you say they are excellent, good, fair, or poor?'....Residents of Detroit gave the lowest ratings to their public schools of any area; more than 75% rated them either fair or poor. The ratings were substantially higher in other Wayne County communities. In Macomb and Oakland counties, fewer than 30% rated the public schools either fair or poor." (p129) "For the parents, the quality of the public schools in their own district was the most important factor affecting whether or not they would consider sending their children to school in another school district. Among those giving a poor rating to their public schools, 77% would consider it; among those giving an excellent rating, however, only 33% would consider it." (p130)

Strate, John M./Wilson, Carter A. "Public Opinion on School Choice." Urban Review v25 n2, Jun 1993. p123-137. (ISSN0042-0972).

SCHOOLS--NEW YORK (NY)

"In New York City, over half the city's schools are title I schools and benefit from its program, 666 schools out of a total of 1,105. An estimated 237,200 students receive title I services. The sad fact, however, is that 428,948 students are actually eligible because of educational deprivation, but there isn't enough funding to go around. To put it into perspective...in some parts of the country, if a school has 25 percent of its students at poverty level, it becomes a title I school. By contrast, in New York City a school must have 62.2 percent of its students at poverty level to satisfy the targeting requirements for the limited resources. Thus, a New York City school can have almost two-thirds of its students at poverty level and still not be included in the title I programs, a fact which provides a strong argument for the merits of the Clinton administration's original proposals to target more of the available resources at the Nation's poorest schools." (pH823)

Maloney, Carolyn B. (Rep.-N.Y.). "Improving America's Schools Act of 1994," Congressional Record (24 Feb 1994). Daily ed. pH798-857. (ISSN0363-7239).

SCHOOLS--U.S. (v19)

see also CATHOLIC SCHOOLS--U.S.

"The public school parent [in the U.S.] is about three times as likely as the private school parent to have an income below $15,000. The private school parent is more than twice as likely to have an income above $50,000. We hear about Catholic schools doing good work in cities, and that is true. However, only 2 percent of Catholic Schools overall fall in the lowest income quartile for students, and in the urban areas where nearly a fifth do, the public schools are twice as poor. The amazing thing is that these stark differences do not result in significantly different education outcomes. On our National Assessment for Educational Progress, high school seniors in private schools were only 7 points higher on a 500-point scale in math. And a larger percentage of the public school seniors actually scored at the top achievement level. This slight overall private school edge disappears completely when you control for the education levels of the parents." (pS853)

Hollings, Ernest F. (Sen.-S.C.). "Unanimous Consent Agreement," Congressional Record (4 Feb 1994). Daily ed. pS846-879. (ISSN0363-7239).

"Historically, 10,000 students is a large number for a school district. Our schools, we must remember, are an outgrowth of the one-room schoolhouses and school districts in rural America. With the exception of a few urban areas, even as late as the turn of the 20th century, most school districts consisted of three, four, or five schools and a few hundred students. As late as 1930, nearly 50% of American school districts had fewer than 300 students. By 1988, as many as 26% of the school districts (enrolling only 1.3% of the nation's students) had fewer than 300 students. Inversely, 4.1% of public schools were in school districts containing 10,000 or more students. There were only 171, or 1.1%, of the school districts with 25,000 or more students, but they accounted for 11.2 million students, or 28% of the nation's public school enrollment." (p167)

Ornstein, Allan C. "School Consolidation vs. Decentralization: Trends, Issues, and Questions." Urban Review v25 n2, Jun 1993. p167-174. (ISSN0042-0972).

SCIENCE--STUDY AND TEACHING--AFRO-AMERICANS (v19)

SCIENCE--STUDY AND TEACHING--ASIA--U.S. (v19)

SCIENCE--STUDY AND TEACHING--NEW YORK (STATE) (v19)

SCIENCE--STUDY AND TEACHING--U.S. (v19)

SCIENCE--STUDY AND TEACHING--U.S.--MINORITIES (v19)

SCIENCE--STUDY AND TEACHING--U.S.--WOMEN (v19)

SCIENCE AND STATE--U.S. (v19)

SCIENTISTS--CUBA--EMIGRATION AND IMMIGRATION (v19)

SEA URCHINS--MAINE

"On the watery first floor at Great Atlantic Seafood, Inc., rubber-booted workers methodically crack open, extract, and clean piles of fresh Marine sea urchin. These round, prickly shelled animals, no bigger than tennis balls, have become an important export commodity here....This relatively new seafood industry in Maine has grown rapidly over the past six years. In 1987, fishermen landed 1.4 million pounds of sea urchins; by the end of 1993, the figure surged to almost 27 million pounds. Most urchins were shipped live to Japan until a processing industry got under way two years ago. Now, at least six major urchin processors are based in Portland, while others have sprung up along the Maine coast. Processed Maine sea urchin can sell for between $10 to $40 a pound, says Lloyd Covens, co-owner of the Urchin Merchant, a processing plant in Portland." (p10)

Ross, Elizabeth. "New England: Maine Sea-Urchin Boom Faces a Prickly Future." The Christian Science Monitor v86 n46, 31 Jan 1994. p10. (ISSN0882-7729).

SEAFOOD INDUSTRY

"The current U.S. trade deficit for seafood stands at $3.3 billion. If we could reduce our seafood trade deficit by one-third through expanded aquaculture production, we would create 25,000 new jobs....Nearly one-quarter of global seafood consumption will come from fish farming by the year 2000. Based on population projections and assuming stable wild fishery harvests, world aquaculture production must double by the end of this decade and increase sevenfold in the next 35 years to keep pace with rising demand for seafood." (pS16528)

Wallop, Malcolm (Sen.-Wyo.). "Nuclear Power, A Necessary Option for our Energy Future," Congressional Record (19 Nov 1993). Daily ed. pS16528. (ISSN0363-7239).

SEARCHES AND SEIZURES--U.S. (v19)

SECONDHAND SMOKE

see PASSIVE SMOKING

SECRET SERVICE--U.S.

"In the first year, FY 1991, losses to financial institutions associated with financial institution fraud investigations by the Secret Service exceeded $450 million. The Service's investigative effort was accomplished at a cost of approximately $8.5 million. In fiscal year 1992, losses sustained by financial institutions in 471 financial institution fraud investigations conducted by the Secret Service exceeded $500 million; in addition the Service seized approximately $4.4 million in assets and arrested 341 individuals. Costs associated with these investigations were estimated to be $9.1 million. As of the end of February, 1993, the Secret Service is conducting 506 FIF investigations in 100 offices throughout the United States. In these investigations we have arrested 119 individuals and seized approximately $14.4 million, which represents an increase of approximately 227% over last fiscal year. Since the inception of the Service's FIF program, approximately 51% of all investigations involve losses in excess of $100,000 or failed financial institutions. In addition, only 12 of the 556 persons arrested resulted in a trial. The remaining cases were adjudicated prior to trial." (p1257)

U.S. House. Committee on Appropriations. "Treasury, Postal Service...Approp. for Fiscal Year 1994 (Part 1)." Hearing, Washington, D.C.: GPO, 1993. (Y4.Ap6/1:T71/994/pt.1).

"The [U.S. Secret] Service's major challenge in FY 1992 was to meet the protective requirements associated with the presidential campaign....protection begins before the national conventions when the Service begins to protect major candidates. Prior to the conventions, these candidates made a total of 452 domestic stops. After the Democratic National Convention, the Service assumed protection for Presidential nominee William Clinton and Vice Presidential nominee Albert Gore, Jr., and their spouses. These protectees made 550 domestic stops in FY 1992. In addition, President Bush and Vice President Quayle and their spouses made a total of 1,754 stops, including 57 foreign stops, during FY 1992. During this same period, that is, FY 1992, the Service's other permanent protectees made 1,562 domestic stops and 119 foreign stops. The Service also provided protection for 304 foreign heads of state and 69 accompanying spouses visiting the United States." (p1195)

Simpson, John P. (Deputy Asst. Sec., Regulatory, Tariff and Trade Enforcement). U.S. House. Committee on Appropriations. "Treasury, Postal Service...Approp. for Fiscal Year 1994 (Part 1)." Hearing, Washington, D.C.: GPO, 1993. (Y4.Ap6/1:T71/994/pt.1).

SECRETARIES--U.S.

"What once commonplace expression has all but vanished from the American workplace? 'Take a letter, Miss Smith.' That's because in the age of personal computers, fax machines and electronic mail, traditional secretarial jobs are going the way of the manual typewriter. From 1983 to 1993, the nation's corps of secretaries shrank by nearly 8 percent to about 3.6 million, notes Harvard economist James Medoff. At the same time, the proportion of these positions fell from about 3.9 percent to just 3 percent of the total number of civilian jobs....Paradoxically, as skill demands have risen, wages for the vast pool of clerical workers have still fallen in real terms To be sure, not everyone is hit: Professional Secretaries International, a 40,000-member association based in Kansas City, Mo., says its members' incomes now average about $27,000 and are gaining ground, with an elite 6 percent earning $41,000 or more. But overall, median weekly earnings for the nation's clerical workers were just $341 in 1992--roughly $18,000 annually--and in recent years they haven't kept pace with inflation." (p65)

Dentzer, Susan. "On the Economy: Secretaries Down the Chute." U.S. News & World Report v116 n12, 28 Mar 1994. p65. (ISSN0041-5537).

SECURITIES--RUSSIA (v19)

SECURITIES INDUSTRY--JAPAN (v19)

SECURITIES INDUSTRY--U.S. (v19)

SECURITY, INTERNATIONAL (v19)

SECURITY CLASSIFICATION (GOVERNMENT DOCUMENTS)--U.S.

"Despite sweeping changes in the international arena, the classification bureaucracy [in the U.S.] is stuck on autopilot, stamping top secret on nearly 7 million new documents each year. Ninety-five percent of these papers will be marked for indefinite restriction. Over the years, this has led to the buildup of tens of millions of secret documents, some truly sensitive, some not. Remaining under wraps, for instance, is the radar equation, a standard law of physics that has been in textbooks since the 1940's as well as some 6,000 U.S. inventions, some dating from the 1940's, whose authors are forbidden to publish, patent, or even discuss their work. The tremendous cost--borne by the U.S. taxpayer--for the personnel, processing and storage needed to handle all these classified documents is daunting enough. But we also need to consider that private American companies spend at least $14 billion a year to meet increasingly complex, overlapping, and sometimes contradictory controls on classified information." (pH10375)

Skaggs, David E. (Rep.-Colo.). "Conference Report on H.R. 2330 Intelligence Authorization Act for Fiscal Year 1994," Congressional Record (20 Nov 1993). Daily ed. pH10374-10381. (ISSN0363-7239).

SECURITY SYSTEMS--U.S. (v19)

SEDIMENTARY BASINS--GREAT LAKES (v19)

SEDIMENTARY BASINS--MICHIGAN (v19)

SEED INDUSTRY AND TRADE--U.S. (v19)

SEED INDUSTRY AND TRADE--U.S.--APPROPRIATIONS AND EXPENDITURES (v19)

SEGREGATION IN EDUCATION--U.S.

Segregation of the nation's black students now exceeds 1970 levels, according to a report from the National School Boards Association's Council of Urban Boards of Education. "'Given recent changes in the law and a widespread debate among Southern school boards about ending desegregation plans, the increase in segregation shown here could foreshadow much larger moves toward racial isolation in the future,' the study says." In the Northeast, segregation of blacks and Hispanics is worse, with about half of these minorities attending intensely segregated schools that are at least 90 percent minority." (p5)

Schmidt, Peter. "Desegregation Study Spurs Debate over Equity Remedies." Education Week v13 n16, 12 Jan 1994. p5. (ISSN0277-4232).

University of Michigan "researchers, Reynolds Farley and William H. Frey at the U-M Population Studies Center, compared 1980 and 1990 U.S. census data to determine segregation trends in 232 metropolises. Their findings are reported in the February issue of the AMERICAN SOCIOLOGICAL REVIEW...The average segregation index dropped from 69 in 1980 to 65 in 1990, and the number of moderately segregated metropolises (indexes of 54 or less) more than doubled from 29 in 1980 to 68 in 1990. The U-M researchers also noted that segregation decreased in 194 metropolitan areas during the 1980s and, in 85 of them, the indexes declined at least five points." (p1)

News release. "Segregation." University of Michigan News and Information Services 14 Feb 1994. p1-4.

SELF-EMPLOYED--CANADA--GREAT BRITAIN

"Canada...has put people to work by encouraging self-employment, which now represents 7 percent of all jobs in that country. The Canadian government offers welfare recipients training in entrepreneurship and some funding to help them operate new small businesses. About 73 percent of out-of-work Canadians who became self-employed have held their jobs for at least two years. In Britain, government programs have boosted the number of self-employed workers from 7.5 percent of the work force in 1979 to 11 percent today. About 650,000 British citizens have joined the government self-employment program." (p8)

Tyson, James L. "Economy: Countries Repeat Vows to Keep Focus on Jobs." The Christian Science Monitor v86 n78, 17 Mar 1994. p8. (ISSN0882-7729).

SELF-ESTEEM--U.S.

"Harvard professor Carol Gilligan, studying the psychological development of teenage girls in 1988, found that they experience a major drop in self-esteem as they reach adolescence. Only 29 percent of teenage girls said that they 'felt happy the way I am,' as opposed to 60 percent of nine-year-old girls. Gilligan suggests that this adolescent crisis in confidence is due to the conflict between the image that a girl has of herself with what society tells her a woman should be like." (p14)

Phillips, Kimberly. "How Seventeen Undermines Young Women." EXTRA! v6 n1, Jan-Feb 1993. p14. (ISSN0895-2310).

SELF-ESTEEM IN ADOLESCENCE--U.S. (v19)

SEMICONDUCTOR INDUSTRY

"In 1993, the world chip market reached just under $80 billion. In 1996 it is predicted to go to $100 billion, and in 2000 to reach almost $150 billion." (p14)

Shimura, Yukio. "Strategic Restructuring: Semiconductors: Forging the Happy Alliance." Look Japan v39 n454, Jan 1994. p14-15. (ISSN0456-5339).

SEMICONDUCTOR INDUSTRY--EMPLOYMENT--U.S. (v19)

SEMICONDUCTOR INDUSTRY--EUROPE (v19)

SEMICONDUCTOR INDUSTRY--JAPAN

"In the late 1970s...MITI [Ministry of International Trade and Industry] poured subsidies into the semiconductor industry, determined that Japan should catch up with American chip makers. At the same time, domestic firms were encouraged to buy their chips at home. By 1986 Japanese chip makers had overtaken their American rivals, and America's share of the Japanese market was down to 8.8%. At the time, many Americans praised Japan's 'invincible' industrial policy. In 1993, however, America captured 42% of the world's chip industry, measured by value, nudging Japan's firms (with 41%) from the top spot....And America is ahead in the smarter, more profitable chips, such as the microprocessors that form computers' brains." (p65)

"Business: MITI's Identity Crisis." Economist v330 n7847, 22 Jan 1994. p65-66. (ISSN0013-0613).

"The Japanese semiconductor industry is dominated by 10 large manufacturers of electrical and electronic equipment, each of which ranks among the world's top 20 electronics firms." (p14)

Shimura, Yukio. "Strategic Restructuring: Semiconductors: Forging the Happy Alliance." Look Japan v39 n454, Jan 1994. p14-15. (ISSN0456-5339).

SEMICONDUCTOR INDUSTRY--JAPAN--U.S.

"Since a given U.S. industry has a certain share of other foreign markets, it should have at least as large a slice of Japan's. U.S. computer manufacturers make that case, citing their success in Europe to argue that their Japanese share would be as high if the market weren't closed. But turn the argument around and it yields wacky conclusions. American chip makers have 43 percent of the world's semiconductor market but only a 20 percent share in Japan. By contrast, Japan's chip makers have 42 percent of the world market--but only 20 percent of the market in the United States. Does that mean that the U.S. market is closed to Japanese producers? 'That's obviously nonsense,' notes Stanton Anderson, a Washington attorney who counsels Japanese chip makers, but it's precisely the sort of snap judgment that could be drawn from a quick look at the numbers." (p76)

Dentzer, Susan. "On the Economy: Japan Trade and the Numbers Tease." U.S. News & World Report v116 n16, 25 Apr 1994. p76. (ISSN0041-5537).

SEMICONDUCTOR INDUSTRY--STEEL INDUSTRY AND TRADE--JAPAN

"In Japan, both steel and semiconductors are considered 'industrial staples,' but they differ in their growth potential. Japan currently produces about Y9 trillion ($83 billion) a year in steel compared to only Y3 trillion ($28 billion) in integrated circuits. But steelmakers can only look forward to growth of 1%-2% per annum, whereas semiconductor firms expect more than 10%--and early in the 21st century, chips are expected to overtake steel altogether." (p14)

Shimura, Yukio. "Strategic Restructuring: Semiconductors: Forging the Happy Alliance." Look Japan v39 n454, Jan 1994. p14-15. (ISSN0456-5339).

SEMICONDUCTOR INDUSTRY--U.S. (v19)

"When Government and industry work in partnership, we succeed. One clear example is the case of semiconductors. In the early 1980's, collusion and dumping by Japanese semiconductor companies threatened to drive the United States out of the semiconductor market entirely. We recognized the problem, and took action by working with American industry to create Sematech in 1987. Sematech is a phenomenal success...the chip industry reported that the American share of the world semiconductor market rose to 43 percent. For the first time since 1985, we have taken the largest share of the world market. This turnaround in the market equates to $3.4 billion more in yearly sales and the preservation of 16,500 American jobs. Because of this recovery, the American chip industry is now building three new semiconductor plants costing about $1 billion each. They will create 12,000 to 15,000...new jobs." (pS2937)

Riegle, Donald W., Jr. (Sen.-Mich.). "Trying Times at the White House," Congressional Record (15 Mar 1994). Daily ed. pS2934-2956. (ISSN0363-7239).

SENIOR CITIZENS

see AGED

SERBIA

see CROATIA--WARS--SERBIA; INCOME--KOSOVO--SERBIA--SLOVENIA; MILITARY WEAPONS--BOSNIA--SERBIA; MONTENEGRO--SERBIA--ECONOMIC CONDITIONS

SERBIA--ECONOMIC CONDITIONS (v19)

SERVICE INDUSTRIES (v19)

SERVICE INDUSTRIES--JAPAN--U.S. (v19)

SERVICE INDUSTRIES--MEXICO--U.S. (v19)

SERVICE INDUSTRIES--U.S. (v19)

"The need for a strong multilateral trade agreement for services is supported by the economic data on the U.S. service sector. In the United States, the service sector is the fastest growing component of the economy, employing over 77 percent of the workforce, accounting for nine out of ten new jobs, producing almost 70 percent of the GDP [gross domestic product], and even one-third of total United States exports. Every state has more people employed in service jobs than in manufacturing, agriculture or mining....From a global perspective, we are the leader in services trade. Services exports from the U.S. have grown steadily over the past several years, from $77 billion in 1986 to $167 billion in 1992--an increase of 116 percent. What we in the Coalition [of Service Industries] call the 'private services balance,' has been in surplus for over 20 years, and reached a record high of $59 billion in 1992, significantly offsetting the merchandise trade deficit of $96 billion." (p52)

Parker, Henry G., III (Coalition of Service Industries, Warren, NJ). U.S. Senate. Committee on Finance. "Renewal of

Fast-Track Authority and the Generalized System of Preferences Program." Hearing, 20 May 1993. Washington, D.C.: GPO, 1993. (ISBN0160432154). (Y4.F49.:S.hrg.103-285).

"The restaurant, apparel, food store, and hotel industries are sectors that are complaining bitterly about the impact of a health insurance mandate. They are also industries associated with a lot of minimum wage and lower paid workers....The Department of Commerce census data shows that between 1990 and 1991 there was a 1.26 percent decline in total private employment, but a 0.4 percent increase in the number of establishments open for business. In the total retail sector, there was a 1.09 percent decline in employment, which was less than the national total decline, while in the services sector there was a 2.69 percent increase in employment. In the eating and drinking establishment--restaurant--area, there was a job decline of 0.7 percent but an increase in the number of restaurants. In the apparel and accessory stores sector, employment increased 0.09 percent, while the number of stores declined. In food stores, there was a 0.3 percent decline in employment, but the number of stores increased. In the hotel and lodging sector, employment declined 1.34 percent but again the number of establishments increased by about 3.86 percent." (pE636)

Stark, Fortney Peter (Rep.-Calif.). "Health Care Reform and Employment," Congressional Record (13 Apr 1994). Daily ed. pE635-636. (ISSN0363-7239).

SEX CRIMES (v19)

see also CHILD MOLESTING; RAPE; SEXUAL HARASSMENT OF WOMEN

SEX CRIMES--U.S.

"Every hour, 10 women are raped, 240 women are beaten by their husbands or boyfriends. During the last 10 years, the rape rate has risen far more than 4 times as fast as the total crime rate. The Surgeon General reports that domestic battery has become the single largest cause of bodily injury to American women. Yet violence against women is grossly underreported, whether on the campus or in the home. Some studies conclude that only 34 percent of stranger rapes and 13 percent of acquaintance rapes are reported to authorities. No more than half of the domestic battery victims go to the police. More than half of the women homicide victims are killed by their husbands, ex-husbands, or boyfriends. More than half of the rape victims experience physical injuries other than the rape itself. The injury is contagious: Rape survivors are also 9 times more likely than other women to attempt suicide." (pH10359)

Sensenbrenner, F. James, Jr. (Rep.-Wis.). "Violence Against Women Act of 1993," Congressional Record (20 Nov 1993). Daily ed. pH10349-10370. (ISSN0363-7239).

"In...[the U.S.], every 5 minutes a woman is raped, every 15 seconds a woman is beaten by her husband or companion, and every year 4,000 women are killed by their abusers. Street and domestic violence costs our Nation 5.3 billion health care dollars annually. More than 30 percent of women in emergency rooms are there because of domestic violence, and more than 60 percent of the women in mental health wards are there because of ongoing abuse." (pH10359)

Morella, Constance A. (Rep.-Md.). "Violence Against Women Act of 1993," Congressional Record (20 Nov 1993). Daily ed. pH10349-10370. (ISSN0363-7239).

"Women are increasingly becoming the victims of violent crime like assault and rape [in the U.S.]. They are losing their freedom to live their lives fully because of fear of being attacked. A recent study found that due to the fear of rape, women are eight times less likely than men to walk alone in their neighborhood. Most women won't use public transporation after dark out of fear of being assaulted. Their fears are well-substantiated. In 1990, there were more than 680,000 rapes. The number of sexual assaults increased four times as fast as the total crime rate. All too often, women are restricted from leading normal lives because of fear of violence." (pH10359)

Moakley, John Joseph (Rep.-Mass.). "Violence against Women Act of 1993," Congressional Record (20 Nov 1993). Daily ed. pH10349-10370. (ISSN0363-7239).

SEX OF CHILDREN, PARENTAL PREFERENCES FOR--CHINA--KOREA (SOUTH) (v19)

SEX OF CHILDREN, PARENTAL PREFERENCES FOR--INDIA

"With India's ultrasound market expanding at 20 percent a year, sex selection may be increasing at least as fast. Studies of hospital births show between 6 percent and 15 percent more boys being born than nature's norm. The missing girls presumably were aborted or left to die." (p55)

MacFarquhar, Emily. "World Report: Echoes of Sita." U.S. News & World Report v116 n12, 28 Mar 1994. p54-55. (ISSN0041-5537).

SEX OF CHILDREN, PARENTAL PREFERENCES FOR--KOREA (SOUTH)

"Data from the recently released National Fertility and Family Health Survey of South Korea show that more Korean women are choosing to have sons rather than daughters. The sex ratio at birth in Korea has jumped from the normal 105 male births per 100 female births to an unusual 114 males per 100 females. Ultrasonic tests have helped make possible the rise in the sex ratio at birth. Less than 2 percent of women taking the test who found that their fetus was a boy decided to terminate the pregnancy. However, almost half of those whose fetus was a girl opted for abortion." (p8)

"News Clips: South Korea's Skewed Sex Ratio." Population Today v21 n3, Mar 1993. p8. (ISSN0749-2448).

SEX RATIO--CHINA

"China's reported sex ratio at birth increased steadily during the 1980s: from 108.5 boys per 100 girls in 1981, to 110.9 in 1986, 111.1 in 1987, and 113.8 in 1989. Significantly higher than the normal sex ratio of 106 male births per 100 female, the disparities increase even further by birth order. The reported sex ratio in 1989 was 104.9 for first-born children, but reached 120.9 for the second, 124.6 for the third, and 131.7 for the fourth child. Sex ratios based just on hospital births (births outside of hospitals are more likely to go unreported) have also risen, though less sharply." (p8)

"News Clips: China's Sex Ratio." Population Today v21 n12, Dec 1993. p8. (ISSN0749-2448).

SEX ROLE--U.S. (v19)

SEXUAL ABUSE OF CHILDREN

see CHILD MOLESTING

SEXUAL BEHAVIOR

see PRISONERS--SEXUAL BEHAVIOR; YOUTH--MICHIGAN--SEXUAL BEHAVIOR; YOUTH--U.S.--SEXUAL BEHAVIOR

SEXUAL HARASSMENT--CANADA--U.S.

"In a 1993 study, 73 percent of female residents [in the U.S.] reported being sexually harassed, mostly by male physicians. But when it came to patients, harassment was supposed to mean authoritative doctor abusing vulnerable patient." Dr. Susan Phillips and psychologist Margaret Schneider "discovered otherwise. Last May they mailed a survey to 599 of the 1,064 licensed female family physicians in Ontario. More than three quarters of those responding said they had been sexually harassed by a patient....Physicians contacted by NEWSWEEK agree that 'it happens all the time,' as urologist Eila Skinner of the University of Southern California puts it. But most downplay its significance, fearing that complaining casts them as victims, as women first and doctors second. The Canadian survey uncovered similar attitudes: 35 percent of the doctors said the incidents made them angry, 26 percent said they were afraid, 10 percent were indifferent and 9 percent were amused." (p54)

Begley, Sharon/others. "Society: Hey Doc, You Got Great Legs." Newsweek v123 n5, 31 Jan 1994. p54. (ISSN0028-9604).

SEXUAL HARASSMENT--U.S.--YOUTH (v19)

SEXUAL HARASSMENT IN EDUCATION--U.S. (v19)

SEXUAL HARASSMENT OF WOMEN--U.S. (v19)

"Nearly a fifth of all women teaching in public universities say they have been sexually harassed at their present institution, according to a new national survey. The findings also suggest that the harassment has a profoundly negative impact on how the victims view their colleagues, the university administration and their own marketability in the academic world, according to study co-author Eric L. Dey of the University of Michigan's Center for the Study of Higher and Postsecondary Education. However, the number of faculty women who have filed formal sexual harassment complaints is vanishingly small both at Michigan and at most other universities. At the U-M, for example, none of the approximately 50 sexual harassment complaints forwarded to the central administration between Nov. 1, 1991, and Dec 31, 1993, was filed by a female faculty member, said E. Kay Dawson, a lawyer and assistant to the provost." (p1 secA)

Cain, Stephen. "Women College Faculty Cite Frequent Harassment." Ann Arbor News 7 Apr 1994. p1 secA.

"Some 70 percent of working women [in the U.S.] have been the victims of sexual harassment, according to several recent surveys. According to the National Institute of Business Management, 1 out of 2 women reports having been sexually harassed in the workplace within the past 2 years. The Equal Employment Opportunity Commission reports that sexual harassment complaints have increased 125 percent nationwide since 1990....In a 1992 Working Women survey, more than 60 percent of those surveyed responded that they had been harassed; however, only 1 out of 4 reported the harassment to their employers. Many women do not feel that they can safely report the problem, and many fear retaliation. Only 1 of 5 women surveyed by Working Women believes companies and the government treat complaints of harassment justly. Over 90 percent think that companies and government must do more to prevent and stop the abuse. Harassment in any workplace, whether in the public or private sector, must not be tolerated." (pS1863)

Moseley-Braun, Carol (Sen.-Ill.). "Statements on Introduced Bills and Joint Resolutions," Congressional Record (24 Feb 1994). Daily ed. pS1860-1875. (ISSN0363-7239).

J. T. Cholewinski and J. M. Burge "studied twenty-one female nursing students [in the U.S.] who reported experiencing some form of sexual harassment while in nursing school. Of those reported experiences, 71% involved a male faculty member. Most of the subjects (90%) did not formally report the harassment. Out of 10% that did report the incidents to an official, no official action was taken regarding the faculty member. In addition, the researchers found that 20% of the student nurses told of sexual harassment incidents also occurring in the clinical environment. These interactions involved physicians and other personnel who either physically or verbally harassed the student nurses." (p54)

Goodner, Ellen/Kolenich, Diane. "Sexual Harassment in Nursing School." Imprint v41 n2, Feb-Mar 1994. p54-55,58. (ISSN0019-3038).

"Nearly one out of every seven women faculty members at American colleges and universities report that they have been sexually harassed on the job, according to a study presented...at the annual meeting of the American Educational Research Association. The first large-scale, national look at the extent and effects of sexual harassment of women faculty, the study is based on a survey of a representative sample of nearly 30,000 male and female faculty at nearly 270 public and private institutions of higher education." (p1) "About 7 percent of all faculty in the study said they had been harassed at their current institution, but the incidence was much higher among women faculty than among men. About 15 percent of the women faculty reported being harassed, compared with about 3 percent of the men....About 24 percent of full professors, compared with 9 percent of instructors and 13 percent of assistant professors reported having experienced harassment." (p2)

News release. "Dey." University of Michigan News and Information Services 1 Apr 1994. p1-3.

"Nearly one out of every seven women faculty members at American colleges and universities report that they have been sexually harassed on the job, according to a study presented...at the annual meeting of the American Educational Research Association. The first large-scale, national look at the extent and effects of sexual harassment of women faculty, the study is based on a survey of a representative sample of nearly 30,000 male and female faculty at nearly 270 public and private institutions of higher education." (p1) "The researchers...examined the incidence of harassment in different types of institutions and in academic departments, finding that the highest harassment rate is reported by women faculty in public universities (18 percent) while those at Catholic four-year colleges reported the lowest (10 percent). Across all types of institutions, the highest harassment rates were reported in departments of fine arts (22 percent) and English (20 percent) with the lowest reported rates in departments of mathematics and statistics (8 percent), the health related professions (9 percent) and the physical sciences (11 percent)." (p3)

News release. "Dey." University of Michigan News and Information Services 1 Apr 1994. p1-3.

SEXUAL HARASSMENT OF WOMEN--U.S.--MINORITIES

"Nearly one out of every seven women faculty members at American colleges and universities report that they have been sexually harassed on the job, according to a study presented...at the annual meeting of the American Educational Research Association. The first large-scale, national look at the extent and effects of sexual harassment of women faculty, the study is based on a survey of a representative sample of nearly 30,000 male and female faculty at nearly 270 public and private institutions of higher education." (p1) "The findings...show that Native American and Hispanic American faculty women are more likely to report harassment (20 percent and 19 percent, respectively) than white women faculty (15 percent), African Americans (13 percent) and Asian Americans (6 percent). After adjusting for length of service, the researchers found that African American faculty report more harassment than the other groups." (p3)

News release. "Dey." University of Michigan News and Information Services 1 Apr 1994. p1-3.

SEXUALLY TRANSMITTED DISEASES (v19)

SEXUALLY TRANSMITTED DISEASES--U.S. (v19)

SHANGHAI (CHINA)--ECONOMIC CONDITIONS

"According to the State Statistical Bureau, Shanghai now has China's most powerful urban industrial economy. Accounting for more than one-tenth of China's industrial output, the city saw its gross domestic product grow 14.5 percent in 1992. With more than 5,300 foreign-funded enterprises and more than 30 newly privatized state enterprises, Shanghai is in the forefront of the market changes that are edging out China's old command economy." (p6)

Tefft, Sheila. "International: Shanghi: Boom Town of the East." The Christian Science Monitor v86 n26, 31 Dec 1993.

p6. (ISSN0882-7729).

SHEEP INDUSTRY--EUROPEAN ECONOMIC COMMUNITY (v19)

SHEEP INDUSTRY--U.S. (v19)

SHEEP INDUSTRY--UTAH (v19)

SHIPBUILDING INDUSTRY--U.S. (v19)

SHIPBUILDING SUBSIDIES--FRANCE--GERMANY--ITALY--JAPAN (v19)

SHIPPING--TAXATION--U.S. (v19)

SHIPPING--U.S.

"There are now 377 oceangoing vessels and 77 Great Lakes boats under the US flat--less than half the number just two decades ago. The number of jobs aboard US oceangoing ships has plummeted from more than 50,000 in 1965 to less than 10,000 today--a decline that corresponds with a concomitant fall in related occupations, such as longshoremen and port pilots. US shipyards have been similarly hard-hit. The number of vessels under construction in the US fell from 97 in 1974 to one in 1992, according to the National Shipbuilding Initiatives. If that trend continues, the number of shipyard workers will drop from roughly 100,000 today to 28,000 in 1997, according to the Shipbuilders Council of America." (p2)

Boot, Max. "National: Shipping Industry Sails toward Subsidies." The Christian Science Monitor v86 n42, 25 Jan 1994. p2. (ISSN0882-7729).

SHIPYARDS--U.S. (v19)

SHOPPING--U.S. (v19)

"Shopping ranks third among Americans' leisure-time activities, just behind television and eating. But it is a costly pleasure. At least 15 million Americans are compulsive shoppers, with an estimated 40 million more struggling with overspending. The result of this consumer feast? Credit card debt has increased 30 percent in the last six years, and in homes of compulsive shoppers, more than 40% of the household income goes to pay for past purchases." (p23)

"Treatment News: Help for Compulsive Shoppers." Women & Recovery Fall 1993. p23.

SHOPPING MALLS--MINNEAPOLIS (MINN)

"In August 1993, the [4.2 million-square-foot] Mall of America reported that it had met its projections of over 35 million visits and more than $600 million in sales for the first 12 months. Visitors spend an average of three hours in the center, three times the national average for shopping malls." (p13)

"Mall of America officials have said they want to increase market penetration in the Twin Cities, which the Census Bureau says has the sixth-highest median household income of the largest 25 metropolitan areas ($36,600). Mall marketers are repositioning it as a user-friendly place, despite the 360 stores, amusement park, nightclubs, 14-screen cinema, and occasional traffic jams." (p14)

Wieffering, Eric. "Business Reports: Regions: What Has the Mall of America Done to Minneapolis?" American Demographics v16 n2, Feb 1994. p13-14,16. (ISSN0163-4089).

SHOPPING MALLS--U.S.

"The shift in U.S. retailing from neighborhood and downtown shops to huge suburban shopping malls has encouraged the consumer lifestyle. Our almost 35,000 shopping centers surpassed high schools in number in 1987. Over the past three decades, shopping center space has grown twelvefold: 2,000 new centers opened each year from 1986 to 1989. With so many competing malls, new ones may go to extremes to draw shoppers. The Mall of America, which opened in Bloomington, Minnesota last August, expects to attract more visitors each year than Mecca or the Vatican. Along with four department stores and more than 300 specialty shops, it offers a seven-acre Camp Snoopy theme park, a giant walk-through aquarium, a two-story miniature golf course, countless cinemas and restaurants, plus some 13,000 parking spaces." (p31)

Durning, Alan Thein. "American Excess--Are We Shopping Our Planet to Death?" E Magazine v4 n1, Feb 1993. p26-31. (ISSN1046-8021).

SHRIMP INDUSTRY--THAILAND (v19)

SICKLE CELL ANEMIA--LOUISIANA

"Red blood cells that contain normal hemoglobin remain round when they release oxygen. Cells with abnormal or sickle hemoglobin, upon releasing oxygen, become distorted into the shape of a sickle causing a chronic and painful anemia. Distorted, or sickled cells cannot traverse capillaries, further limiting oxygen supply to the body's tissues....the minority population in the State of Louisiana is about 1.29 million people. Of this number roughly 3,250 people are suspected of having the disease, and of this number, 25 percent will have the most acute and serious form, which is often fatal. Alarmingly, about 130,000 Louisianians carry the genetic trait for this illness." (pS16477)

Johnston, J. Bennett (Sen.-La.). "Statements on Introduced Bills and Joint Resolutions," Congressional Record (19 Nov 1993). Daily ed. pS16433-16501. (ISSN0363-7239).

SINGAPORE

see TOURIST TRADE--SINGAPORE; URBANIZATION--SINGAPORE

SINGLE-PARENT FAMILY--AFRO-AMERICANS (v19)

SINGLE-PARENT FAMILY--GREAT BRITAIN (v19)

"If Britain's divorce rate approaches 40 per cent, it has moved from the lowest in Europe to the highest, with the steepest rate of increase. As the rate of remarriage has also halved, this reinforces the fragmenting impact of rising divorce. But lone parenthood increasingly stems from the huge growth in 'never-married' mothers; with the one birth in ten outside marriage in 1979 becoming three in ten by the 1990s. A rising proportion of unmarried mothers are under 25 and, if one in ten lone parents now has three children or more, each birth may mark a liason with a different boyfriend. Moreover, by the 1990s around 7 out of 10 lone parents obtained all or much of their income from public assistance--payable without a 'seeking work' test until children are 16. Only 15 per cent have never been in receipt of Income Support, and dependence on public assistance has become a long-term rather than a short term phenomenon. In contrast, earnings are the main source of income for over 80 per cent of two parent families." (p18)

Morgan, Patricia. "A Critical Examination of the New Child Support Agency." Freedom Today v18 n6, Dec 1993. p18-19.

SINGLE-PARENT FAMILY--U.S. (v19)

see also PUBLIC WELFARE--U.S.--SINGLE-PARENT FAMILY

"Between 1973 and 1990, the median income of families [in the U.S.] with children headed by a parent under age 30 dropped 32 percent when adjusted for inflation. Economic hardship--whether from low wages, sustained poverty, or unemployment--significantly diminishes the emotional well-being of parents, with direct and indirect effects on children's health and well-being (McCord, 1990; Elder, 1992). Economic hardships are linked to family disintegration and to the increase in single-parent households....In all social classes, there has been significant growth in single parent households. Almost half of all marriages now end in divorce, about a quarter of all births are to unmarried women. The net result has been that about 25 percent of all children live with only one parent, usually the mother--a rate double that of 1970. Overall, about 50 percent of all children will reside in a single parent home before age 18, spending an average of 6 years with a single parent (Bumpass, 1984; Norton and Glick, 1986)." (p52)

Cook, Thomas D. (Professor, Center for Urban Affairs and

Policy Research, Northwestern Univ.). U.S. House. Committee on Ways and Means. "Children and Families at Risk in Deteriorating Communities." Hearing, 7 Dec 1993. Washington, D.C.: GPO, 1994. (ISBN0160436567). (Y4.W36:103-43).

"In addition to economic and programmatic influences, critical trends in the...demographic make-up [of the U.S.] have both enlarged and transformed the AFDC [or Aid to Families with Dependent Children] caseload. The number of female-headed families with children in the general population increased by 27 percent from 1979 to 1989; this construct now accounts for almost one quarter of all families with children. Within this group, the number of female-headed families that are poor grew by almost 40 percent overall from 1979 to 1989. While the number of female-headed families in poverty maintained by white and black women showed marked increases of 38 percent and 31 percent respectively, those maintained by Hispanic women soared by 79 percent over the same decade. This caused a surge in the proportion of AFDC adults who are Hispanic: Hispanics as a proportion of the adult caseload increased by 17 percent from 1979 to 1989....The number of families headed by women who have never been married--i.e., those women family heads who are the most likely both to be poor and to have the longest lengths of stay on AFDC--has also increased, in this case by over 160 percent from 1980 to 1990." (p178)

Jones, Linda R. Wolf (Director, Income Security Policy, Community Service Society of N.Y.). U.S. House. Committee on Ways and Means. "Historical Trends in Poverty and Family Income." Hearing, 26 Oct 1993. Washington, D.C.: GPO, 1994. (ISBN0160435765). (Y4.W36:103-42).

SINGLE-PARENT FAMILY--U.S.--ECONOMIC CONDITIONS (v19)

SINGLE MOTHERS--EMPLOYMENT--POLAND

"In Poland, lone mothers head about 18 per cent of families with dependent children. A recent study of over 900 unemployed lone mothers in Poland showed that 91 per cent lived below the poverty line, while 52 per cent had an income which reached only about half of the poverty line level. Most lone mothers said they had no savings. One-third had managed to get some kind of casual work, though a further 29 per cent said they had no chance of any work of this kind, since unemployment had meant them taking their children out of nurseries and nursery schools, whose services had increased dramatically in cost. Only six per cent of partners provided any help in caring or providing for their joint offspring. The overwhelming majority of these women (80 per cent) said that unemployment had been an extremely painful experience, describing themselves as being 'shattered', 'appalled', 'engulfed by a feeling of hopelessness', and full of 'fear for their own future and that of their children.'" (p79-80)

Watson, Peggy. "The Rise of Masculinism in Eastern Europe." New Left Review n198, Mar-Apr 1993. p71-82. (ISSN0028-6060).

SINGLE MOTHERS--U.S. (v19)

"It is not just poor, young, uneducated families that are increasingly headed by females. Even African American families with well-educated heads are increasingly headed by females....there is a steep growth in female-headed families among families with college educated heads since 1970. In 1991, nearly 30 percent of black families with college educated heads were headed by females up from 8 percent in 1970. This compares to a rise in the percent of white families headed by females among college graduates, which rose from 4 percent to 8 percent from 1970 to 1991. There is also little support for the view that the cause of the rise in black female-headed families is the attractiveness of welfare. The percent of black families headed by females continues to rise long after the growth in real AFDC [or Aid to Families with Dependent Children] benefits has come to a halt." (p123)

Myers, Samuel L., Jr. (Hubert H. Humphrey Inst. of Public Affairs, Univ. of Minnesota). U.S. House. Committee on Ways and Means. "Historical Trends in Poverty and Family Income." Hearing, 26 Oct 1993. Washington, D.C.: GPO, 1994. (ISBN0160435765). (Y4.W36:103-42).

A study released by the Carnegie Foundation "demonstrates the terribly high poverty rate for children under 3 being raised by single mothers. For children under 3 raised by single Hispanic mothers, the poverty rate approaches 75 percent. Between 1960 and 1988 the percentage of births in America to unmarried mothers rose from 5 percent to 26 percent. Between 1971 and 1991 the number of children under the age of 6 increased by less than 10 percent but the number of poor children under the age of 6 increased by 60 percent. The Carnegie Foundation report contained more than sobering statistics like these: it contains recommendations on how we might reverse them." (pS4705)

Dodd, Christopher J. (Sen.-Conn.). "Head Start Amendments of 1994," Congressional Record (21 Apr 1994). Daily ed. pS4691-4727. (ISSN0363-7239).

"There were nearly 4 million never-married mothers in the United States in 1992, almost double the number ten years earlier. With more than 35 million mothers between ages 15 and 44, about 12 percent of the country's mothers were never-married women. Nationally, one in four never-married women are mothers--the proportion rising to over 40% in Mississippi, according to the U.S. Census Bureau. The Bureau's unpublished estimate, taken from the June 1992 Current Population Survey, shows a national increase of 91 percent since 1982 in the number of never-married mothers between the ages of 18 and 44. The Census Bureau calculated this statistic for 39 states, plus the District of Columbia, which had more than 75,000 never-married women." (p4)

Rooks, Ronica N. "Motherhood Growing More Common among Never Married Women." Population Today v21 n11, Nov 1993. p4. (ISSN0749-2448).

"More than a million babies a year are born to unmarried women, nearly a third of all births in the United States. Although 70 percent of these births are to women age 20 and over, the birthrate among teenagers has been rising for five consecutive years. Projections show that if current trends continue, by the end of the decade 40 percent of all births in the US and an astonishing 80 percent of minority births will be to single mothers." (p22)

"Moral Issues of Our Times: Reaffirming the Family." The Christian Science Monitor v86 n48, 2 Feb 1994. p22. (ISSN0882-7729).

"The number of births to unmarried mothers in the US rose to 1.2 million in 1992, an 82 percent increase since 1980. The majority of these mothers are on welfare, costing some $50 billion annually in wefare payments, Medicaid, and food stamps." (p2)

Holmstrom, David. "National: As Child Poverty Grows, Report Warns of Crisis." The Christian Science Monitor v86 n44, 27 Jan 1994. p2. (ISSN0882-7729).

"When New York Sen. Daniel Patrick Moynihan wrote his 1965 warning about the disintegration of the black family, 26 percent of black births were to unwed mothers. Today, the figure among whites is 22 percent--only 4 percentage points lower. Meanwhile, the share of African-American births out of wedlock has soared to 68 percent, and we now have a criminal underclass that is terrorizing certain neighborhoods and producing horrors visible to all on local nightly newscasts." (p34)

Barone, Michael. "On Politics: Slouching toward Dystopia." U.S. News & World Report v115 n24, 20 Dec 1993. p34. (ISSN0041-5537).

SOIL CONSERVATION--U.S.

"One of the major goals of the Conservation Reserve Program (CRP) is to reduce water and wind erosion through the establishment of perennial grasses on more than 45 million acres of highly erodible and environmentally sensitive croplands [in the U.S.]....Averaged across all locations, soil organic carbon levels for CRP lands were 34 percent greater than those for cropland. Elimination of tillage, reduced soil erosion, accumulation of surface litter, and large amounts of root production on CRP grass plantings are probably responsible for these increases. Conservation Reserve Program lands gained an average of 1,000 pounds of carbon per acre per year. These results suggest that the 45 million acres enrolled in CRP have recovered about 45 percent of the 84 billion pounds of carbon released annually into the atmosphere from United States agricultural activities. These findings also illustrate that agriculturally-related carbon dioxide emissions may be effectively controlled through changes in land use and management systems." (p1)

Gebhart, Dick. "Some Agricultural Activities Are Related to Carbon Dioxide Emissions." Kerr Center for Sustainable Agriculture Newsletter v19 n8, Nov-Dec 1993. p1.

SOIL DEGRADATION--FORMER SOVIET REPUBLICS

"The rate of environmental degradation in Russian agriculture is much higher than in many of the other republics of the former Soviet Union. For example, over the past 25 years, the reduction of humus (the essential organic element of healthy soil) in Russia totaled 13 percent. In contrast, the average rate of humus reduction in the former Soviet Union was only 10 percent, while in Belarus, Lithuania, Latvia and Estonia, humus content grew from five percent to 14 percent. The qualitative degradation of arable land has reached a threatening rate and scale in Russia. Since 1971, salinity and acidic content have doubled. Areas that are damp or rocky have increased three-fold. Losses of organic matter in the soil have increased by half." (p31)

Bobylev, Sergei. "Sustainable Agriculture: An Ecological Approach to Russian Agriculture." Surviving Together v11 n3, Fall 1993. p31-32. (ISSN0859-6286).

SOIL EROSION--U.S.

"About 36.5 million acres of highly erodible or environmentally-sensitive cropland have been enrolled in the CRP [Conservation Reserve Program] under 10-year contracts." (p272) "Soil erosion reductions on CRP lands are nearly 700 million tons per year, or an average of 19 tons per acre. This is a 22 percent reduction in U.S. cropland erosion compared with conditions that existed prior to CRP and conservation compliance. Most CRP acres are planted in grass, but CRP also includes 2.4 million acres of trees, 2 million acres of special wildlife practices, 410,000 acres of wetlands, and 5,200 miles of filter strips along waterways. Annual rental payments average $50 per acre, with an annual $1.8 billion Federal government outlay." (p273)

Osborn, Tim. "The Conservation Reserve Program: Status, Future, and Policy Options." Journal of Soil and Water Conservation v48 n4, Jul-Aug 1993. p271-278. (ISSN0022-4561).

"Agricultural statistics...indicate that there is an average of 8.51 Mg/ha [milligrams/hectare] (3.8 tons per ac) of sheet and rill water erosion on U.S. cropland each year. Currently, there are about 134 million ha (330 million ac) of arable cropland tilled in the U.S. This means there are approximately 1.14 Mg (1.254 billion tons) of soil lost annually. Conservation practices carried out by SCS [or Soil Conservation Service] have established that the rate of soil erosion can be significantly decreased by allowing crop residue to remain on the soil surface. As little as 30 percent coverage of residue material across the soil surface can reduce soil erosion to 10 percent of its non-covered state. SCS has classified 49.8 million ha (123 million ac) as highly erodible lands (HEL) throughout the U.S. More than one third of the tilled U.S. cropland is included in this category. The Conservation Compliance Provision in the 1985 Food Security Act and the 1990 Food, Agriculture, Conservation, and Trade Act, requires farmers to implement management techniques on HEL to decrease soil erosion." (p207)

McMurtrey, J. E., III/others. "Research: Fluorescence and Reflectance of Crop Residue and Soil." Journal of Soil and Water Conservation v48 n3, May-Jun 1993. p207-213. (ISSN0022-4561).

SOIL FERTILITY--SOUTH AMERICA (v19)

SOIL POLLUTION--U.S.

"According to the Centers for Disease Control, 5 to 10 percent of all children eat dirt directly, a condition known as 'pica.' Dirt-eating is a major cause of lead poisoning in children; hence the worry in predominantly Latino and African-American West Dallas, Texas, which has been poisoned by a lead smelter for decades. While state and federal officials have known about the problem for at least ten years, not until this May did the EPA finally declare the smelter and neighborhoods within a mile and a half of it a Superfund site. Dirt is also the issue at another Superfund site in Fort Valley, Georgia, where this August several hundred mostly African-American residents were told not to let their children play in it anymore, as the soil in several neighborhoods around a pesticide factory was contaminated with 43 times the national average of arsenic." (p56)

Rauber, Paul. "Priorities: Corporate Crybabies." Sierra v78 n6, Nov-Dec 1993. p54,56,58-60. (ISSN0161-7362).

SOILS

"The constituents of a typical, fertile 1,000-square-foot garden are outlined below: if your garden area is only 500 square feet, divide by 2; if it is 3,000 square feet, multiply by 3. When organic matter is at the desirable level of 5%, this component of a 1,000 foot garden weighs about 2,500 pounds. It is composed of vegetable matter, decaying roots, compost, manure, leaves, kitchen wastes, humus and, most precious of all, live organisms....the bio-population includes trillions of voracious, incestuous, cannibalistic plant-creatures, some of which act as laboratories to produce nitrogen, humus, vitamins, hormones, and other 'special formula' foods. In 1,000 cubic feet of soil, this live part will weigh 40 to 60 pounds. Without it, the soil is dead,...and so are we....at least 20,000,000,000,000,000 of these small individuals are working, resting and eating in your 1,000-foot garden." (p18)

Fryer, Lee. "Home Grown." Acres, U.S.A. Feb 1994. p18-19.

"Soils are generally composed of 40-50 percent mineral particles (rock dust), 20-25 percent water (less in the upper layers, more in the lower), 20-25 percent gases (more in the upper layers, less in the lower as replaced by water) and 2-15 percent humus....Many soil organisms are extremely small, but they compensate in number for their tiny size. More than 70 different species have been collected from a square foot of rich forest soil. The total animal population of forest soils approaches 10,000 organisms per square foot." (p36)

Lewandowski, Stephen. "Defending the Commons: Wild Soils." Earth Island Journal v9 n2, Spr 1994. p36-37. (ISSN1041-0406).

"In most parts of the world there is more life beneath the surface of the soil than above it. In a few shovelfuls of forest soil there may be more than 1,000 different types of organisms and as many as 100 different types of mites. In a square meter there can be more than 10 million nematodes and protozoa, 1 million mites and springtails, and thousands of other invertebrates, including several hundred earthworms. Even in a teaspoon of soil there can be as many as 10 million bacteria and two kilometers of fungal filaments. The soil is indeed a living, breathing firmament in which the primary action taking place is the breakdown of organic matter and the release of plant nutrients." (p11)

Hill, Stuart B. "Common as Dirt: Our Sub-Terrestrial Allies Are Nature's Most Efficient Recyclers." Land Stewardship Letter v11 n4, Fall 1993. p11,15.

SOILS--U.S.

"Farmers in the state of Iowa, with the greatest concentration of prime farmland in the United States, have already destroyed half the topsoil. In parts of Ohio, farmers lose two bushels of topsoil for every bushel of corn harvested. Back in 1950, J. Russell Smith wrote that 'the soil washed out and blown out of the fields of the United States each year would load a modern freight train long enough to reach around the world 18 times.' All farmers and ranchers--as if working together--lose an inch of topsoil from the United States every 16 years. Nature takes 100 to 500 years to replace it. The history of American soil clearly demonstrates that we stand on the edge of an abyss. Our soil bank is nearly bankrupt." (p4)

Nollman, Jim. "The Soil Garden." Raise the Stakes n22, Win 1993-94. p4. (ISSN0278-7016).

SOLAR CARS

"Ironically, it is the limitations of a solar car that have become the key to its impact. The roughly six square meters of photovoltaic cells that can be put on a car roof only generate about 500 watts of power--less than one horsepower, or enough to light five 100-watt lightbulbs. Even when using batteries, such cars generally run on 2,000 watts (2.5 horsepower) or less....efficiency is the key....To maximize the speed and range of such a car, its energy needs must be reduced to a tiny fraction of those of a conventional car--forcing an entirely new approach to auto design." (p28-29)

Flavin, Christopher. "JumpStart: The New Automotive Revolution." World Watch v6 n4, Jul-Aug 1993. p27-33. (ISSN0896-0615).

SOLAR ENERGY--FLORIDA

"Florida Power and Light Company (FPL) has aggresssively promoted energy conservation programs for over a decade. Their early recognition of the potential role for solar energy prompted development of a solar domestic hot water incentive program, now in its eleventh year. As of 1992, the program was directly responsible for the installation of more than 43,000 systems....In 1985, the program was responsible for the installation of approximately 14,000 systems. As federal tax credits expired, installations dramatically dropped to 5,000 in 1986, then fell to a low of 931 in 1987. While the solar hot water industry suffered seemingly insurmountable losses, FPL remained committed to the technology and its incentive program. Installations have risen to 2,000 in 1992, and the trend is expected to continue for 1993." (p15)

Siciliani, John. "Prize Projects: Utility Solar Hot Water Programs: A Viable DSM Option." Solar Industry Journal v4 n3, 1993. p15.

SOLAR ENERGY--U.S.

"Last Earth Day, Public Citizen launched a new Sun Day campaign that treats Washington, DC as a clearinghouse to help local groups add solar to their agenda. The new campaign promotes concrete targets: reducing total energy consumption by 10 percent by 2010; tripling the output of renewable energy to become 25 percent of the total mix; and cutting our carbon dioxide emissions by one fifth--as Australia, Germany and other European countries plan to do. The Sun Day principles have an eclectic band of supporters: from Senators Paul Wellstone (D-MN) and Tom Harkin (D-IA); to the cities of Olympia, Washington, Tacoma Park, Maryland, and Ocala, Florida; to eco-leaders Denis Hayes and Hazel Henderson. And their network has grown to 600 local groups." (p17-18)

Downey, John. "Currents: Charge of the Solar Light Brigade." E Magazine v4 n1, Feb 1993. p15-18. (ISSN1046-8021).

"As long as solar energy is used to generate only a small fraction of our total electricity supply, there is little advantage to converting solar electricity into hydrogen for non-transportation applications. But as the PV [photovoltaics] and wind contributions grow to more than 10 to 15 percent of our electricity, energy must be stored for use on cloudy and windless days. The Department of Energy national laboratories estimated in 1990 that renewable energy, without energy storage, could account for at most 24 to 34 quads of energy by the year 2030, compared to 80 quads consumed now from all sources of energy....If a storage mechanism such as hydrogen was available, then renewables could contribute another 16 to 21 quads of energy by 2030. Total renewable energy contributions would be in the range of 45 to 50 quads, or more than half of our current energy consumption." (p11)

Thomas, C. E. 'Sandy'. "Solar Hydrogen: A Sustainable Energy Option." Solar Today v7 n5, Sep-Oct 1993. p11-13. (ISSN1042-0630).

"Solar domestic hot water (SDHW) systems vary widely in cost and savings. Batch heaters can be home-built for as little as $300....The cost of active systems adequate for families of two to five people range from $2,000 to $5,000....Savings from SDHW systems depend on water usage, system size, system design and local climate conditions....The cost of operating an electric water heater will range from about $200 to $800 per year depending on local electric rates. Natural gas prices are typically 50 to 60 percent less than electricity for heating water. Since a SDHW system can provide 50 to 100 percent of a family's annual hot water needs, the savings can amount to hundreds of dollars a year. For example, if a SDHW system costs $4,000 and saves $400 a year, then it takes about 10 years for the savings to 'pay back' the investment....Other costs to consider when purchasing a SDHW system are maintenance and system life....A recent study conducted by the Harrisburg campus of Pennsylvania State University of 255 closed-loop systems installed in the late 1970s in Pennsylvania showed that over a 10 year period, they required little maintenance. Eighty-six percent of the systems' owners were pleased with the performance of their system and average annual maintenance cost was $13." (p12-13)

Sheffer, Marcus B./Lau, Andrew S. "Solar Water Heating in Pennsylvania." Solar Today v8 n1, Jan-Feb 1994. p12-15. (ISSN1042-0630).

SOLAR ENERGY--U.S.--POLITICS AND GOVERNMENT

"Eight states and one territory have loan programs available for solar technologies and other energy conserving technologies. Arizona's...program makes loans to both the manufacturers of renewable energy or energy saving products and the customers who use those products. California...provides inexpensive (5 percent) loans to small businesses to demonstrate alternative energy technologies as well as loans to farms, local governments, schools, hospitals and businesses to use and/or advance alternative energy technologies. Idaho's...loan program provides a maximum of $50,000 over six years at 5 percent interest, and Iowa's makes loans over 3-12 years for solar technologies used in the public sector that have six-year paybacks or less. Mississippi...has a program that makes loans up to a maximum of $200,000 over seven years, and Oregon offers loans to a maximum of $20 million over 10-15 years at 7-10 percent interest. Puerto Rico has established a revolving renewable energy loan fund, while South Dakota...makes loans at 3 percent interest for solar measures with a payback of less than 10 years. Finally, Tennessee's...program offers loans to a maximum of $100,000 over seven years. Local governments are included in Tennessee's program." (p13)

Shirley, Larry E./Sholar, Jodie D. "State and Utility Financial Incentives for Solar Applications." Solar Today v7 n4, Jul-Aug 1993. p11-14. (ISSN1042-0630).

"Seven states have income tax credits for solar applications. California offers a tax credit of 10 percent of the cost of a solar electric system and Massachusetts has a 15 percent credit for renewable energy property up to a maximum credit of $1000. In Hawaii, a state tax credit is available for 35 percent of the cost of solar systems for single-family, multi-family and commercial buildings, with a maximum credit of $1750 per single-family house and $350 per multi-family unit. North Dakota offers a 15 percent credit spread evenly over three years for all solar technologies, and North Carolina has a tax credit of 25 percent of the cost of residential and commercial applications of active or passive solar systems up to a maximum of $1000. North Carolina also offers a 20 percent credit for solar industrial process heat applications up to $8000. In Oregon, residential property owners can....either take a credit of up to $1500 or multiply their first year's energy yield in kilowatt-hours by $.60 per dwelling to figure their credit. Business owners can take a commercial credit of 35 percent spread over five years. And Utah offers a credit of 25 percent of the cost of most residential solar applications, including photovoltaics, up to a maximum credit of $1500." (p12)

Shirley, Larry E./Sholar, Jodie D. "State and Utility Financial Incentives for Solar Applications." Solar Today v7 n4, Jul-Aug 1993. p11-14. (ISSN1042-0630).

SOLAR ENERGY INDUSTRIES--U.S. (v19)

SOLDIERS

see also AFRO-AMERICAN SOLDIERS

SOLDIERS--RUSSIA (v19)

SOLDIERS--U.S.--RETIREMENT

"In the last 5 years, there have been 206 individuals in the third or fourth star grades of admirals and generals to retire; 200 of the 206--all but 6--retired on their highest grade....Three were eligible to retire at the three star, but were not nominated by the President for that rank. In other words, of the six that did not receive the higher rank, three, for reasons best known to the President, were not so indicated. Three others were nominated by the President to retire, but were not confirmed to retire at the four-star or three-star grade by the Senate. It seems to me that these figures show that it is normal and customary for three and four grade generals and admirals to retire at the higher grade. But it is not automatic, which shows that we do take a look at these things. Both the President and the Senate review these retirements in great detail." (pS4431)

Exon, J. James (Sen.-Nebr.). "Executive Session," Congressional Record (19 Apr 1994). Daily ed. pS4420-4459. (ISSN0363-7239).

SOLDIERS, AFRO-AMERICAN

see AFRO-AMERICAN SOLDIERS

SOLVENTS INDUSTRY--U.S.

"Up to 58% of the nation's use of common industrial solvents (major sources of groundwater contamination) could be readily eliminated within 10 years using currently available methods, according to a path-breaking study released recently by EDF [the Environmental Defense Fund] and the Metropolitan Water District of Southern California (MWD). The collaboration of EDF and MWD, a major water utility that supplies most of the water used by 15 million southern Californians, was considered highly unusual when it began. The study looked at five main industrial solvents, for which current U.S. consumption is about 800,000 metric tons per year, and focused in detail on industry practices responsible for 92% of total U.S. use." (p1)

"Use of Industrial Solvents Can Be Greatly Reduced." EDF Letter v24 n1, Jan 1993. p1,3. (ISSN0163-2566).

SOMALIA

see also VIOLENCE--SOMALIA--MORTALITY

SOMALIA--HEALTH AND HYGIENE

"Somalia had a good main harvest in 1993, and cereal production in 1994 may reach 435,000 tonnes, well up on the past two years. UN agencies and non-governmental organization (NGOs) have dug and repaired hundreds of wells and restored water supplies throughout the country. But an outbreak of cholera in several parts of Somalia in late February indicated the fragility of the health situation. Still, malnutrition among children is now under 20 per cent, down from 60-80 per cent a year ago. About 75 per cent of children under 5 years of age have been immunized against various diseases, twice as many as before the civil war. Some 70,000 children attend rebuilt primary schools, again, more than before the crisis." (p6)

Malinowski, Tom. "UN Brokers Political Accord in Somalia." Africa Recovery v7 n3-4, Dec 1993-Mar 1994. p6.

SOMALIA--SOCIAL CONDITIONS (v19)

SORGHUM INDUSTRY--U.S. (v19)

"Sorghum use [in the U.S.] in June-August 1993 reached 90 million bushels, substantially above the previous 2 years. Strong demand from the livestock sector and lower prices boosted feed and residual use to 55.8 million bushels, accounting for nearly all the larger quarterly disappearance. Sorghum exports were 31.9 million bushels, little changed from the June-August 1992 period. FSI [food, seed and industrial] uses, estimated at 2.1 million, were up 0.3 million from a year earlier." (p8)

U.S. Dept. of Agriculture. "Sorghum Supplies to Fall 15 Percent in 1993/94." Feed Situation and Outlook Report Nov 1993. p7-8.

SOUTH AFRICA

see also AIDS (DISEASE)--SOUTH AFRICA; BUSINESS ENTERPRISES--SOUTH AFRICA; HIV INFECTIONS--SOUTH AFRICA; INCOME DISTRIBUTION--SOUTH AFRICA; INVESTMENTS, AMERICAN--SOUTH AFRICA; LAND TENURE--SOUTH AFRICA; POLLUTION--MEREBANK (SOUTH AFRICA); POOR--SOUTH AFRICA; RAPE--SOUTH AFRICA; VIOLENCE--SOUTH AFRICA; VOTING--SOUTH AFRICA; WOMEN--EMPLOYMENT--SOUTH AFRICA

SOUTH AFRICA--COMMERCE (v19)

SOUTH AFRICA--ECONOMIC CONDITIONS (v19)

"The economy of South Africa is in the worst recession in a century, and the prospect of improvement in the short term is not good. Apartheid, to borrow from Voltaire, was not only a crime; it was a mistake. Creating and maintaining an economic underclass has pulled the economy under. Unemployment is at 45 percent, and black South African youths are less educated and more poorly prepared to enter the work force today than their predecessors were when apartheid became legal in 1948." (p32)

Ruddy, Frank. "Fair Comment: South Africa Offers Hope, in Good Time." Insight v9 n52, 27 Dec 1993. p31-32. (ISSN1051-4880).

"The entire region [of Southern Africa] remains deeply scarred by the impact of apartheid destabilization. According to UN figures, over a million lives were lost and some $60.5 bn of damage [was] inflicted on neighbouring economies during the 1980s. South Africa's gross domestic product (GDP) is also much greater than the combined total of all 10 members of the Southern African Development Community (SADC)." (p24)

Davies, Robert. "Looking towards a New Southern Africa."

Africa Recovery v7 n3-4, Dec 1993-Mar 1994. p24-25.
"The future of the entire continent depends, in large measure, on what happens in South Africa. We are talking about a continent of 650 million of the world's most marginalized people, 235 million of whom are poor, 100 million of whom are malnourished, and 15 to 25 million of whom face hunger....At the very least, the transformation of South Africa could bring with it a considerable peace dividend for all the countries of southern Africa. The U.N. has estimated that South Africa's destabilization operations during the 1980s cost the neighboring countries $60 billion. And if Angola, Mozambique, Zimbabwe and South Africa were able to reduce their defense budgets to the per-capita spending level of, say, Canada or Japan, the collective savings of these four countries alone would be about $3.5 billion a year." (p21)

Sparks, Allister. "Writing Racism's Last Chapter." Toward Freedom v42 n1, Feb 1993. p1,20-21. (ISSN0048-9898).

SOUTH AFRICA--POLITICS AND GOVERNMENT

"With only five weeks to go until South Africa's first all-race elections, the white right-wing is in a state of unprecedented turmoil. Fearful of black majority rule, ardent Afrikaners are deeply divided over whether to take part in the voting and how to reach their goal of a separate homeland....The collapse of apartheid and the painstaking four-year transition to democracy have taken a heavy toll on Afrikaners who believed domination and privilege were their permanent heritage....Afrikaners account for nearly 60 percent of the country's white population of some 5 million, which in turn represents about 15 percent of all voters. Right-wing whites account for about 3 to 5 percent of the voting population. Of the 3 million white voters who took part in the 1992 referendum on racial reforms, 30 percent voted against the changes." (p6)

Battersby, John. "International: S. African Right Bitterly Divided." The Christian Science Monitor v86 n83, 24 Mar 1994. p6. (ISSN0882-7729).

SOUTH AFRICA--POPULATION

"According to the 1991 census of South Africa (as adjusted for under-enumeration), the population is about 75 percent black, 13 percent white, 8 percent 'coloured,' and 3 percent Asian (mostly Indian descent). Black South Africans are ethnically diverse and divided by language and traditions....One indicator of racial contrasts in South Africa is life expectancy, which is 72 years for whites, 68 years for Asians, 64 years for blacks, and 63 years for 'coloureds.' Total fertility rates (TFR, or average births per woman) also vary, with the TFR of white women below replacement level at 1.8, and that of blacks at 5.2 children. About half of South Africans are illiterate." (p7)

"Spotlight: South Africa." Population Today v22 n2, Feb 1994. p7. (ISSN0749-2448).

SOUTH AFRICA--PUBLIC OPINION

"A recent survey showed that only 14 percent of...[South Africa's] 5 million whites are prepared to move to a volkstaat [a white homeland] and that only 60 percent of [Gen. Constand] Viljoen's supporters consider it a viable option. Though terrorist attacks are expected from ultra-right-wing whites, who are reportedly stockpiling arms and ammunition, analysts believe the vast majority of Afrikaners will not leave their jobs, homes and families to take up the fight." (p70)

Ransdell, Eric. "Predictions: Will South Africa Find Peace?" U.S. News & World Report v115 n25, 27 Dec 1993. p70. (ISSN0041-5537).

SOUTH AFRICA--RACE RELATIONS

"According to the Survey of Eligible South African Voters commissioned by the International Republican Institute and conducted jointly by Public Opinion Strategies and Decision Surveys International (South Africa-based)....When asked their nationality, 16 percent of blacks replied South African or black South African, and 63 percent gave their African tribe; 83 percent of whites identified themselves as South Africans....A majority of blacks report household incomes of less than $250 per month, and 45 percent of whites earned between $1,150 and $2,900 a month." (p11)

Battersby, John. "Profile of Black Voters." The Christian Science Monitor v86 n65, 28 Feb 1994. p11. (ISSN0882-7729).

SOUTH AFRICA--SOCIAL CONDITIONS

"Four decades of apartheid [in South Africa] have left the first democratic government a fearsome economic imbalance. Black incomes per head are barely one-tenth those of whites; 95% of black families earn less than 750 rand ($220) a month, according to the Urban Foundation. Nearly half the labour force has no formal job. Some 7m (out of 28m) blacks live in shacks; 12m have no clean water; 14m cannot read. While white schools had 82,000 unfilled places in 1992, 1.5m black children got no schooling at all. The black pass-rate in the school-leaving exam dropped to just 35% last year." (p37)

"International: The Cost of Undoing Apartheid." Economist v330 n7849, 5 Feb 1994. p37-38. (ISSN0013-0613).

"With a population of 38 million, South Africa is the third largest country in sub-Saharan Africa (Nigeria and Ethiopia rank first and second). Its GNP [gross national product] per capita is moderately high at $2,500, although its rate of increase in income was a modest 1.3 percent from 1965 to 1990. Life expectancy is 60 years, and infant mortality is 55. The crude birth rate decreased from the low 40s in 1960-65 to about 32 in 1985-90. During the same period, the total fertility rate [or TFR] declined from 6.51 to 4.48 according to the United Nations and a national survey in 1987-89 reported a TFR of 4.58 among blacks, a decrease of more than 25 percent from 6.25 in 1970-75 (Freedman, 1992). This is the lowest TFR among blacks of any country in sub-Saharan Africa." (p86)

Mauldin, W. Parker/Ross, John A. "Prospects and Programs for Fertility Reduction, 1990-2015." Studies in Family Planning v25 n2, Mar-Apr 1994. p77-95. (ISSN0039-3665).

SOUTH AMERICA

see DEFORESTATION--CENTRAL AMERICA--SOUTH AMERICA--U.S.

SOUTH ASIA

see also NUCLEAR WEAPONS--SOUTH ASIA

SOUTH ASIA--POPULATION

"The Indian subcontinent contains more than one billion people, separated into four nations: India (897 million), Pakistan (128), Bangladesh (122), and Nepal (21). Each of these countries has a record of poverty, low literacy, high mortality, low life expectancy, and low income per capita." (p84)

Mauldin, W. Parker/Ross, John A. "Prospects and Programs for Fertility Reduction, 1990-2015." Studies in Family Planning v25 n2, Mar-Apr 1994. p77-95. (ISSN0039-3665).

SOUTH CAROLINA

see also LEAD--TOXICOLOGY--SOUTH CAROLINA

SOUTH CAROLINA--POPULATION

"The influx of new settlers has placed the eight coastal counties of South Carolina among the fastest growing areas in the Southeast. Berkeley County ranked sixth in the region for population growth during the 1980s, and Dorchester ranked eleventh. The rapid growth has also made tourism the second largest industry in the state, earning an estimated $3.3 billion a year. By the year 2010, experts predict, an additional 500,000 people will live on the South Carolina coast." (p53)

Nixon, Ron. "Cultures in Conflict." Southern Exposure v21 n3, Fall 1993. p53-56. (ISSN0146-809X).

SOUTH DAKOTA
see AGRICULTURE--SOUTH DAKOTA; TIMBER--SOUTH DAKOTA
SOUTHERN STATES
see DEFENSE INDUSTRIES--SOUTHERN STATES; DRUG ABUSE AND CRIME--SOUTHERN STATES
SOVIET UNION
see ENERGY CONSUMPTION--SOVIET UNION--U.S.
SOVIET UNION--ARMED FORCES (v19)
SOVIET UNION--ARMED FORCES--APPROPRIATIONS AND EXPENDITURES (v19)
SOYBEAN INDUSTRY--EUROPEAN ECONOMIC COMMUNITY (v19)
SOYBEAN INDUSTRY--U.S. (v19)

U.S. "Soybean export volume fell 400,000 tons to 19.4 million tons, but higher export unit values bolstered soybean value to $4.6 billion, a gain of 5 percent. Exports to Canada increased because of the reduced Canadian soybean and rapeseed crop in 1992. Exports also expanded to Southeast Asia. Shipments were down to Mexico, Europe, and Korea." (p2)

U.S. Dept. of Agriculture/Greene, Joel. "Agricultural Exports Decline in 1993." Foreign Agricultural Trade of the United States Jan-Feb 1994. p2.

U.S. "Soybean exports rose 5 percent to 20.4 million tons on increased shipments to the EC [European Community], Taiwan, and Southeast Asia. Shipments to the EC totaled 8.3 million tons, the largest since 1988, as rapeseed was scarce and South American exportable supplies were low last fall. Taiwan imported a record 2.4 million tons, and shipments to Southeast Asia were almost 900,000 tons." (p2)

U.S. Dept. of Agriculture/Greene, Joel. "Exports Rose Slightly in FY 1993." Foreign Agricultural Trade of the United States Nov-Dec 1993. p2-3.

"U.S. soybean yields plunged to 32.0 bushels per acre in 1993/94 because of weather of historic dimensions. A damp spring in the western Corn Belt began a spell of rainfall that persisted throughout the summer, leading to severe flooding along the Mississippi River basin. The Southeast had its driest and second hottest summer of this century. U.S. soybean acreage harvested fell to 56.4 million acres, the smallest since 1976/77. The 1993/94 U.S. soybean production of 1,809 million bushels is the smallest since 1988/89." (p3)

U.S. Dept. of Agriculture. "Summary." Oil Crops Situation and Outlook Report Jan 1994. p3.

SPACE SCIENCES--U.S.--PUBLIC OPINION (v19)
SPACE STATIONS--COSTS (v19)

"This year the space station has been through a major redesign and we have entered into a joint venture with the Russians which serves also as a critical initiative to bring post cold war Russia into the mainstream of global society. Through the redesign and Russian cooperation, we have cut $4 billion in costs from the space station...[and] will be operable 2 years earlier than originally planned in 1997 and completed in 2001, it will have 25 percent more volume, 57 percent more power, a larger area for microgravity experiments and room for six astronauts--two more than before." (pH10889)

DeLay, Tom (Rep.-Tex.). "Government Reform and Savings Act of 1993." Congressional Record (22 Nov 1993). Daily ed. pH10729-10893. (ISSN0363-7239).

SPAIN--ECONOMIC CONDITIONS (v19)

Spain's "economy is deep in recession. The economy shrank by around 1% last year. Unemployment, which briefly dropped below 16% at the start of the 1990s, has soared: the official rate is now 23%." (p56)

"Europe: Spain: The Iron Is Cold." Economist v330 n7848, 29 Jan 1994. p56. (ISSN0013-0613).

SPAIN--SOCIAL CONDITIONS (v19)
SPECIAL EDUCATION--U.S. (v19)
SPECIAL OLYMPICS

"The Special Olympics movement is worldwide in scope. There are nearly 1 million Special Olympics athletes worldwide and nearly 450,000 in the United States alone. There are more than 1 million family members in the United States who are actively involved with Special Olympics; that number increases to 2 million active families worldwide. There are more than 500,000 Special Olympics volunteers and 250,000 coaches worldwide." (pS1741)

Dodd, Christopher J. (Sen.-Conn.). "Statements on Introduced Bills and Joint Resolutions," Congressional Record (23 Feb 1994). Daily ed. pS1739-1744. (ISSN0363-7239).

SPECIES (v19)
see also ENDANGERED SPECIES

"In 1675 the Jesuit priest Anthanasius Kircher set out to calculate how many creatures were on the ark with Noah. Father Kircher determined that God's original complement of land animals consisted of 310 species. Today some 50,000 mollusks, 750,000 insects, 6,300 reptiles, 9,000 birds, and 4,000 mammals are known--a fraction of the 30 million species estimated to exist. Most of the thousands of new species found each year are insects and other little animals, but now and again larger species are discovered. In just one year, 1988, accounts were published about a newly described lemur from Madagascar, a monkey from Gabon, and a deer from western China. In 1990 a new type of lion tamarin was discovered on a small island only 40 miles from Sao Paulo, Brazil. An average of two bird species are discovered every year. During the past century, an average of one new whale has been described each decade--11 since 1908." (p6)

Walters, Mark Jerome. "Animals in Peril: Not Quite an Oryx." Animals v126 n5, Sep-Oct 1993. p6. (ISSN0030-6835).

"The overall impact of the human population, as measured by total energy use, is increasing at about 1.8 percent annually. That measure also approximates the rate of habitat destruction; coincidentally, conservation biologist Norman Myers's recent estimate of the rate of tropical forest destruction is also 1.8 percent annually. Overall, this implies a rate of extinction on the order of a half-percent of remaining species annually. If Earth contains, at a conservative estimate, 20 million species, that will mean a loss of about 100,000 species each year; by the end of the century, roughly one million species. On the other hand, if (as some scientists are convinced) there are 80 million species, one million is a vast understatement of the extinction problem. Besides reduction of habitat, there are other factors that can cause extinctions: human-transported pests, acid rain, toxic pollutants, possible rapid climate change. A predicted loss of one million species, then, rather than being a grossly inflated number, may instead appear to be a wildly optimistic fantasy in 20 years time." (p67)

Ehrlich, Paul R. "Bioessay: Is the Extinction Crisis Real?" Wildlife Conservation v96 n5, Sep-Oct 1993. p66-67. (ISSN1048-4949).

SPENDING, ENTITLEMENT
see ENTITLEMENT SPENDING
SPENDINGS TAX (v19)
SPORTS
see also BASEBALL; DISCRIMINATION IN SPORTS; OLYMPIC GAMES (1996: ATLANTA, GEORGIA); SOCCER; VOLLEYBALL; WATER SKIING
SPORTS--IOWA

"The State of Iowa fields over 2,500 girls' high school teams competing in...10 different sports. And every Iowa high school participates in at least three girls' sports--softball, basketball, and volleyball. In all, these 2,500 teams provide the opportunity for 71,600 girls to participate in interscholastic athletics. Iowa is the only State in America which sponsors high school co-ed tournaments in golf and in tennis. Also very noteworthy is the fact that this spring will mark the 75th anniversary of the Iowa Girls' High School State Basketball Tournament. Iowa girls' softball, golf, and tennis celebrates their 39th anniversary; track and field its 33d; cross country its 20th; swimming its 27th; and volleyball its 25th. And all of these programs were implemented well before title IX mandated girls' activities in 1972." (pS766)

Grassley, Charles E. (Sen.-Iowa). "National Girls and Women in Sports Day," Congressional Record (3 Feb 1994). Daily ed. pS765-766. (ISSN0363-7239).

SPORTS--U.S. (v19)

SQUIDS--JAPAN

"This was a bumper year for squid; the catch was so plentiful that squid could be had in Japanese stores for about Y100 ($1) a piece. The Japanese now consume more fresh squid than they do fresh sardines or salmon, averaging about 1.6kg per person per year. That means that roughly a third of the squid swimming in the Sea of Japan are eaten fresh each year. When processed foods are added in, the average Japanese consumes several kilograms of squid each year--roughly half the world catch. If that sounds like a lot, we should note that sea birds and sperm whales eat roughly ten times as much squid as humans do." (p30)

Umezu, Takeshi. "New Technology: Ocean Pollution: Squid Watch." Look Japan v39 n453, Dec 1993. p30-31. (ISSN0456-5339).

SRI LANKA

see AIDS (DISEASE)--SRI LANKA

STALKING--LAW AND LEGISLATION--U.S. (v19)

STANDARD OF LIVING

see COST AND STANDARD OF LIVING

STARCH INDUSTRY--U.S. (v19)

STATE GOVERNMENTS--U.S. (v19)

STEEL INDUSTRY AND TRADE

see also SEMICONDUCTOR INDUSTRY--STEEL INDUSTRY AND TRADE

STEEL INDUSTRY AND TRADE--EUROPE--JAPAN--U.S. (v19)

STEEL INDUSTRY AND TRADE--EUROPE--U.S. (v19)

STEEL INDUSTRY AND TRADE--JAPAN

"Japan is the world's second largest producer of steel. The industry grew at an astonishingly rapid clip during the 1950s and 1960s, as Japan rebuilt after the war. By FY 1973, gross crude steel production had reached 120 million tons. Then came the two oil crises, which not only slowed economic growth but forced steelmakers to shift their focus from quantitative expansion to qualitative improvement. The general trend since has been a decline in production volumes: in the late 1970s gross steel output averaged around 105 million tons. When the economy contracted in FY 1982, production dipped to around 96 million tons, but the next year it was back over the 100 million-tons line. During the high-yen slump, production again dropped back to 96 million tons in 1986, but expanded once more in the heyday of the 'bubble.' In FY 1990, production topped 110 million tons for the first time in 11 years. When the bubble ruptured, demand for steel shrank and producers were forced to cut their output. Gross steel production fell to 99 million tons in FY 1992, a drop of almost 7 million tons over 1991 and a return to the levels of the early 1970s." (p18)

Yoshida, Kazuhiko. "Strategic Restructuring: Steel: Reinforcing Itself." Look Japan v39 n455, Feb 1994. p18-19. (ISSN0456-5339).

STEEL INDUSTRY AND TRADE--LUXEMBOURG (v19)

STEEL INDUSTRY AND TRADE--U.S. (v19)

"The $42 billion [U.S.] basic steel industry is entering 1994 with high expectations. The leading companies broke into the black in the middle of last year, then produced flat out--filling domestic orders of 88 million tons, a 6% jump from depressed 1992. Order books are full through the first quarter, what with the economy growing and the auto and appliance industries raising production. Overall, steelmakers are banking on shipments to rise 3% this year, to 91 million tons, says Andrew Sharkey III, president of the American Iron & Steel Institute. Signaling this confidence, producers have announced price hikes of 4% in January and 2% in June on flat-rolled steel used in cars and appliances....The main problems facing steelmakers this year are recessions in Europe and Japan, which have led to oversupply and lower prices there. At the end of last year, for instance, the U.S. spot price for hot-rolled steel was $375 a metric ton vs. $260 for export from Europe. It costs $65 a ton to ship steel across the Atlantic. That gives an incentive to foreign steelmakers--who won a majority of the 84 trade cases U.S. companies filed against them last year alleging illegal dumping--to boost shipments from the 18 million tons they sent in 1993." (p74)

Baker, Stephen. "Manufacturing: Steel: Big Steel's Big Opportunity." Business Week n3353, 10 Jan 1994. p74. (ISSN0007-7135).

STERILIZATION (BIRTH CONTROL)--HISPANIC AMERICANS

"Sterilization rates as high as sixty-five percent for Latinas have been reported in some areas of the United States. New York Latinas have a sterilization rate seven times higher than white women and almost twice that of black women. At the time of the procedure, many Latinas did not realize that it was irreversible. We are not given adequate information so that we can give truly 'informed consent' for medical procedures that affect our reproductive choices." (p6)

Alvarez, Luz. "The Latina Reproductive Rights Movement." Guild Practitioner v50 n1, Win 1993. p4-8. (ISSN0017-5390).

STEROIDS

see ANABOLIC STEROIDS

STOCK-EXCHANGE

"It is telling that, in dollar terms, the worst performing big stockmarket in 1993 was America's. It rose by 14%--which would be respectable enough by the standards of a normal year. But compared with Britain's equity market (up 17%), Germany's (up 37%), or star performers such as Hong Kong and Malaysia, up a startling 124% and 101% respectively, its performance looks positively drab. Many of the world's stockmarkets (including, it would be said, America's) are at or near record levels." (p72)

"Finance: Stockmarkets: Flying High." Economist v330 n7844, 8 Jan 1994. p72. (ISSN0013-0613).

STOCK-EXCHANGE--ASIA (v19)

STOCK-EXCHANGE--INDONESIA--TURKEY (v19)

STOCK-EXCHANGE--JAPAN--U.S.

"Global money managers have been watching the gyrations on the Tokyo exchange with increasing caution. From a high of almost 39,000 points in late 1989, the Nikkei has dipped down to the 16,800-point level. Yet during that same period, US and many other global markets have continued to post market gains. The Dow Jones industrial average, for example, has climbed more than 50 percent since October 1990." (p9)

Halverson, Guy. "Economy: US, Global Markets Stay Strong Despite Japanese Tumble." The Christian Science Monitor v86 n10, 9 Dec 1993. p9. (ISSN0882-7729).

STOCK-EXCHANGE--KOREA (SOUTH)

"The government sets strict limits on South Korean companies' capital-raising abroad. In 1993, says Jardine Fleming, equity and equity-linked issues in foreign markets have come to $925m, up from $513m in 1992 but still small. Foreigners' unsatisfied demand for Korean shares can be judged from secondary-market prices. The government limits foreign investment in Seoul's stockmarket to 10% of any single stock; attractive, liquid shares have already hit this ceiling, and foreign investors trade Korean stocks among themselves at premiums ranging from 3% to 70% in the offshore over-the-counter market. A talked-of raising of the foreign cap to 15% will still leave foreigners wanting more. Meanwhile, the government also restricts the issue of new equity to South Korean investors. New equity and equity-related issues have come to 3.9 trillion won in 1993, up from 2 trillion won in 1992." (p102)

"Finance: South Korean Finance: Hastening Slowly." Economist v329 n7843, 25 Dec 1993. p102. (ISSN0013-0613).

STOCK-EXCHANGE--TAIWAN (v19)

STOCK-EXCHANGE--U.S. (v19)

STOCK OPTIONS--U.S. (v19)

"Fueled by a fresh onslaught of investors, small and large alike, options trading is indeed on the rise. In 1993, options volume rose 15% over 1992, reaching levels not seen since the 1980s....And although volume is still far below 1987 levels, the momentum continues to build." (p104)

Burns, Greg. "Finance: Markets: Options Don't Look So Scary Anymore." Business Week n3347, 7 Feb 1994. p104. (ISSN0007-7135).

STOCK OWNERSHIP--GREAT BRITAIN--U.S. (v19)

STOCK OWNERSHIP--TAIWAN (v19)

STOCK OWNERSHIP--U.S. (v19)

"It is sometimes argued that increased stock ownership by executives will result in better management and thus enhance corporate performance. A recent study reported in the [23 March 1993] WALL STREET JOURNAL, however, suggests strongly that significant stock ownership by executives has little effect on the economic well-being of the company. On the contrary, companies where employees own more than 10% of the stock overall outperform those companies without employee ownership. What may not be true of executive ownership may indeed be true if ownership is more broadly distributed." (p173)

Naughton, Michael/Kennedy, Robert G. "Executive Compensation: An Evaluation from the Catholic Social Tradition." Social Justice Review v84 n11, Nov 1993. p169-174.

STOCK PRICE INDEXES--EUROPE

"In 1993, Warsaw's 22-share stock market index...rose nearly 800%--in dollars--outdistancing such highfliers as Brazil, Thailand, and Turkey. But Warsaw is hardly the only Eastern European bourse to come alive. Budapest's jumped 24% last year, and shares on the Prague exchange have rocketed an average 138% since August, when the market set prices for 980 new issues." (p44)

Schares, Gail E. "International Business: Eastern Europe: Go East, Young Man--and Buy Stocks." Business Week n3354, 17 Jan 1994. p44-45. (ISSN0007-7135).

STOCK PRICE INDEXES--TAIWAN (v19)

STOCK PRICE INDEXES--U.S. (v19)

According to Larry Wachtel, a vice president with investment house Prudential Securities Inc., "Over the course of the past 44 years...market indexes have fallen in 24 years during February, compared with 20 years in which market indexes moved upward. By contrast, the market, as measured by the Standard & Poor's 500, moved up 29 times in March, and down 15 times." (p10)

Halverson, Guy. "Economy: Interest Rate Upturn Makes Markets Edgy." The Christian Science Monitor v86 n62, 23 Feb 1994. p10. (ISSN0882-7729).

STOCKS--U.S. (v19)

Nineteen ninety-three "was the year in which U.S. investors discovered the world. Through September, a stunning $98 billion flowed into foreign stocks and bonds, much of it from mom-and-pop investors crowding into mutual funds that herald the promise of 'emerging markets.' Warning that the big gains in U.S. stocks are past, fund managers and financial columnists are hyping the trend. The returns have been rich: foreign stocks chalked up gains averaging 32 percent last year--three times the average payback on U.S. equities--while foreign bonds overwhelmingly outperformed U.S. issues." (p37)

Levinson, Marc. "Business: Strong Dollar, Sad Faces." Newsweek v123 n3, 17 Jan 1994. p37. (ISSN0028-9604).

STORES, DEPARTMENT

see DEPARTMENT STORES

STOVES

"Improved cookstoves--designed both for more efficient use of fuel and reduced health risks to users--are creating a quiet revolution in the developing world. In China, where the changeover from traditional stoves has been most rapid, more than 140 million of the new stoves are in use. In Kenya, the figure is over half a million and rising. Similar stoves are gaining widespread popularity from Guatemala to India. Around the world, women are spreading the word about these new stoves that bring both reduced fuel costs and less smoky kitchens. Biomass fuels, which include wood, other plant matter, and animal wastes, are the principal sources of energy for at least 40 percent of the world's population. Most of the biomass energy (approximately 75 percent) is used for cooking. In rural areas, the most widely used means of burning this fuel is the traditional 'three-stone stove'--actually nothing more than three stones arranged in a triangle to support the base of a cooking pot. In the urban and peri-urban areas, unlike in the rural areas where both stones and wood are freely gathered, the three-stone stove is often replaced by charcoal stoves such as the traditional cylindrical metal stove of Kenya." (p34-35)

Chege, Nancy. "Trends: Cooking Up a More Efficient Stove." World Watch v6 n6, Nov-Dec 1993. p34-36. (ISSN0896-0615).

STRATEGIC DEFENSE INITIATIVE (v19)

STRESS (PSYCHOLOGY)--U.S. (v19)

STRIKES AND LOCKOUTS--U.S. (v19)

"Even a company's threat to use permanent replacements made unions [in the U.S.] think twice about going out on strike. The result was a dramatic decline in labor's use of its strike weapon. Through October [1993], there were only 31 walkouts involving 1,000 workers or more. That was down slightly from 35 for the same period last year and far lower than the 81 large strikes recorded in 1983." (p6)

Belsie, Laurent. "Economy: 1994 Holds Some Promise for Labor Unions." The Christian Science Monitor v86 n17, 20 Dec 1993. p6. (ISSN0882-7729).

STUDENT LOAN FUNDS--U.S. (v19)

"As early as 1985, the U.S. Government Accounting Office charged that two thirds of trade schools were lying to students--overstating job placement rates for graduates, for example, or offering 'free scholarships' that did not reduce tuition. It took Congress until 1990 to do anything about it. That year, more than 40 percent of all trade school students defaulted on their loans....All told, unpaid loans cost taxpayers $2.9 billion last year--or 44 cents out of every dollar spent on federal student loans." (p31)

Yeoman, Barry. "SE Special Section: 'The Perfect Job for You.'" Southern Exposure v21 n3, Fall 1993. p29-32.

(ISSN0146-809X).

"Major shifts in higher education finance [in the U.S.] have left more and more of the students footing the bill...in 1980 Pell Grants covered 41 percent of the average college bill, by 1990 they paid only 25 percent; additionally, eligibility rules have been tightened so that the percentage of those eligible has been reduced from 31.5 percent of entering freshmen in 1980 to 15.6 percent in 1988. Student borrowing through the federally guaranteed student loan program has increased from $4.8 billion ten years ago to $12.3 billion annually. Poor and middle-class students, however, are proving hard-pressed to pay this new bill. According to the American Council on Education (ACE), 43 percent of those graduating in 1984 were in debt for school expenses, and their average indebtedness was $5,470; by 1988 this indebtedness increased to $7,480. Government Accounting Office statistics indicate that of the $52 billion in student loans outstanding in 1991, some $12.3 was in default and that the annual default rate had increased tenfold over the past decade (from $239 million in 1980 to $3.6 billion in 1991)." (p82-83)

Spear, Bruce. "Multiculturalism Inc." Transition v3 n3, 1993. p72-86. (ISSN0041-1191).

STUDENTS

see also HANDICAPPED STUDENTS

STUDENTS--U.S.

"The College Board reports that three-quarters of young, full-time, dependent [U.S.] students held down jobs in 1989-90. Thirty percent of such traditional students had full-time jobs....The College Board reports that non-traditional students (defined as part-time, independent, or over age 24) are much more likely than traditional students (younger, full-time, and dependent) to work full-time during periods of enrollment: 46 percent worked full-time in 1989-90, compared with the 30 percent of traditional students cited earlier." (p6)

Kramer, Martin. "Forum: Earning and Learning." Change v26 n1, Jan-Feb 1994. p6-7. (ISSN0009-1383).

STUDENTS, COLLEGE

see COLLEGE STUDENTS

STUDENTS, FOREIGN--JAPAN (v19)

"In 1982, Japan had only 8,116 foreign students in its various educational institutions, compared with the US's 311,882 and France's 119,336. Yasuhiro Nakasone, the prime minister at the time, was appalled that Japan was lagging so far behind. He believed that increasing the number of foreign students would not only internationalize Japanese society, but would also contribute to the international community by providing educational opportunities to students from developing countries. His proposal, now known as the '100,000 by 2000 plan,' soon became the centerpiece of the ministry's campaign for internationalization. By 1992, the ministry was almost halfway to its goal; there were 48,561 foreign undergraduates, graduate students, research students, and students of vocational schools in Japan, an eight-fold increase in less than a decade. Over 90% of these students were from other Asian countries." (p10)

Saphir, Ann. "Foreign Students: 50,000 and Counting: Open and Shut?" Look Japan v39 n451, Oct 1993. p10-12. (ISSN0456-5339).

STUDENTS, FOREIGN--U.S.--APPROPRIATIONS AND EXPENDITURES (v19)

STURGEONS

"As an anadromous species, sturgeon spawn in rivers, then swim out into the ocean for twelve to fifteen years before returning to reproduce. Sturgeon fishing has traditionally taken place on rivers, not in ocean waters; sturgeon caught at sea were incidental to other targeted catches. But a recent increase in ocean, or intercept fishing, is believed to be rapidly accelerating the decline in sturgeon. The value of sturgeon eggs remains high; at $50 per pound of eggs, a single female with fifty to sixty pounds of roe can sell for close to $3,000. However, the tremendous upsurge in ocean fishing for sturgeon since the mid-1980s, has been aimed at the sturgeon's meat. Smaller male and female fish are caught and smoked, bringing a retail price of about $40 a pound, or as much as $2,500 for an average-size fish. In the last few years, all coastal states except New York and New Jersey have banned the harvest of sturgeon in their waters in an effort to let the stocks recover. Recent regulations adopted by New York State limit season and size, and leave New Jersey as the only state not complying with the Atlantic States Marine Fisheries Commission Sturgeon Plan. Intercept fishing in New Jersey waters can continue at 1990 levels, when 200,000 pounds of sturgeon were taken." (p25)

Lee, Cara. "Siege of the Hudson River: High-Tech Fishing Mars a Sturgeon Sanctuary." Amicus Journal v16 n1, Spr 1994. p22-28. (ISSN0276-7201).

SUBSIDES

see also HOUSING SUBSIDIES

SUBSIDIES--GERMANY (v19)

SUBSIDIES--U.S.--TRANSPORTATION

"All modes of transportation [in the U.S.] receive public subsidies for infrastructure or operations. All freight and passenger modes competing with rail receive an enormous subsidy. The freight rail carriers receive almost nothing by way of subsidy. The freight truck mode receives a subsidy of about $4 billion a year by virtue of the underpayment for damage to the highway system. Freight barges get something under $1 billion a year as the Corps of Engineers builds and operates their rights of way. Passenger subsidies are as skewed. In 1990, Amtrak received a $340 million subsidy in a $2 billion operating budget. However, during that same year the government collected about $3.9 billion in aviation user taxes, but spent about $7.1 billion on aviation programs. The difference is a $3 billion annual subsidy for private sector airline operations." (p406)

Nichols, Dennis B. (President, CEO, Turbomeca Engine Corp.). U.S. House. Committee on Appropriations. "Department of Transportation and Related Agencies Approp. for 1994 (Part 8)." Hearing, Washington, D.C.: GPO, 1993. (ISBN0160410657). (Y4.Ap6/1:T68/4/994/pt.8).

SUBSIDIES, AGRICULTURAL

see AGRICULTURAL SUBSIDIES

SUBSTANCE ABUSE

see also ALCOHOLISM; DRUG ABUSE; TOBACCO HABIT

SUBSTANCE ABUSE--U.S. (v19)

"In establishing substance abuse as a disability which qualifies for benefits under the SSI [Supplemental Security Income] programs, Congress placed two conditions on the payment of benefits to substance abusers: first, the substance abuser must receive treatment; and second, a third party, such as a friend or relative, must collect the benefits on behalf of the substance abuser. Unfortunately, both of these protections have failed. For example, up until last month, the SSA [Social Security Administration] had set up programs to monitor and enforce the treatment requirement in only 18 states. In fact, 26 States have never had an agency approved by SSA to monitor treatment. Fewer than one-third of the approximately 250,000 drug addicts and alcoholics are required to get treatment or have someone else collect their benefits for them. Of the $1.4 billion in benefits flowing to drug addicts and alcoholics on the SSI and disability programs, less than $320 million of these payments are even covered by these protections. So, over $1.1 billion in payments are exposed to widespread abuse--with no controls in place." (pS1420)

Cohen, William S. (Sen.-Maine). "Disability Drug Abuse

Prevention and Rehabilitation Act of 1994," Congressional Record (10 Feb 1994). Daily ed. pS1420-1421. (ISSN0363-7239).

"In 1990,...a study [was done] of rural drug abuse by the GAO [General Accounting Office]. The results were startling, and demonstrated that drug and alcohol abuse are a major problem in rural States. Life-time prevalence of substance abuse by rural 18 year olds in 1988 occurred at a similar rate to urban youths, for alcohol, cigarettes, stimulants, inhalants, tranquilizers, and heroin. The arrest rates for alcohol and drug abuse per thousand residents is similar between rural States and nonrural States." (pS16423)

Harkin, Tom (Sen.-Iowa). "Violent Crime Control and Law Enforcement Act," Congressional Record (19 Nov 1993). Daily ed. pS16422-16423. (ISSN0363-7239).

SUBSTANCE ABUSE--U.S.--COSTS

Dr. Herbert Kleber, a drug official for the Bush administration "estimates that with an additional $2.9 billion--beyond the $2.5 billion in the 1994 budget--some 480,000 new slots could be created in drug treatment facilities, enough to treat an additional 1.3 million addicts a year. For a total of $15 billion, he says, alcoholics could be treated, too. This sounds like a good investment considering that the costs of alcohol and drug abuse--including productivity losses and costs related to crime--added up to $166 billion in 1990." (p5)

Baker, Beth. "No Sacred Cows: Drug Treatment on Demand." Common Cause Magazine v19 n4, Win 1993. p5-6. (ISSN0271-9592).

SUBSTANCE ABUSE--U.S.--PHYSIOLOGICAL EFFECT (v19)

SUBSTANCE USE

see WELFARE RECIPIENTS--U.S.--SUBSTANCE USE

SUDAN

see also FERTILITY, HUMAN--SUDAN; LANGUAGE AND LANGUAGES--SUDAN; WATER-SUPPLY--EGYPT--SUDAN

SUDAN--HISTORY--CIVIL WAR

The "exhaustive report, 'Quantifying Genocide in the Southern Sudan: 1983-1993' by Millard Burr of the U.S. committee on Refugees, is based on systematic compilation of year-by-year field reports and internal Sudanese documents. It concludes that the death toll in Sudan is, sadly, not diminishing. The report estimates that some 300,000 persons died in southern Sudan during 1992 and the first 5 months of 1993--nearly 4,000 deaths per week for 17 months--making it one of the deadliest periods ever in Sudan. One of every five southern Sudanese has died from the war or from war-related causes, according to the report, and 4 of every 5 southern Sudanese have been uprooted from their homes at some time since 1983. More than 300,000 southern Sudanese are refugees, and some 5 million Sudanese from the south and north are internally displaced." (pE185)

Wolf, Frank R. (Rep.-Va.). "Final Offensive by Sudanese Government Demands United States Attention," Congressional Record (11 Feb 1994). Daily ed. pE185. (ISSN0363-7239).

"Civil war, ranging the mainly Muslim and Arab north against the 3 1/2m-4m people of the mainly Christian and black-African south, has ravaged southern Sudan for 28 of the country's 38 years of independence. More than 500,000 people have been killed in the latest, 11-year, cycle of violence. Though successive governments have always maintained they are merely trying to regain control of their country, the religious--and ethnic and linguistic--divide has been made worse by the attempts of the government, led by Colonel Omar Bashir, to impose Islamic rule." (p45)

"International: The Blessings of Religion." Economist v331 n7858, 9 Apr 1994. p45. (ISSN0013-0613).

"The statistics for the civil war [in Sudan] to date are horrific--the U.S. Office of Foreign Disaster Assistance estimates that 2.5 million people need emergency assistance and are at risk; 1.8 million southern Sudanese have fled to the north; and according to the U.S. Committee for Refugees 1.3 million people have already died from the war, famine, and disease between 1983-1993--and yet new numbers will be added due to the latest government offensive against the south." (p2)

"Sudan: 100,000 Displaced as Government Begins Offensive." NewsNotes v19 n2, Mar-Apr 1994. p2-3. (ISSN1064-1556).

"Since 1983, war and famine in Sudan have killed an estimated half a million children, women and men, with perhaps 250,000 dying in 1987-88 alone. An additional 50,000 have been disabled due to the conflict. It has been impossible to compile precise figures, and the real toll may, in fact, be higher. Approximately 4 million southern Sudanese have been displaced as a result of the civil war. Many have sought refuge in squatter camps around Khartoum and other northern Sudanese towns while millions more fled to camps within the south. In addition, hundreds of thousands have gone to Ethiopia, Kenya, Uganda and the Central African Republic. The war is estimated to cost the Khartoum government more than $1 million a day." (p12)

"Fast Facts." Nonviolent Activist v10 n2, Mar-Apr 1993. p12. (ISSN8755-7428).

SUDAN--POLITICS AND GOVERNMENT--RELIGION (v19)

SUDDEN INFANT DEATH SYNDROME--U.S.

"Sudden Infant Death Syndrome (SIDS) is a fatal disorder which kills thousands of infants in the United States each year. SIDS is one of the leading causes of death in the United States for infants 1-week to 1-year old, claiming the lives of over 7,000 babies in America each year. That is one of every 500 live births, or nearly one baby every hour of every day. More children die of SIDS in one year...[than] all infants who die of cancer, heart disease, pneumonia, child abuse, AIDS, cystic fibrosis, and muscular dystrophy combined. SIDS takes the lives of infants from all areas of America, all cultures and all socio-economic backgrounds. It is a major contributor to the high rate of infant mortality in the United States." (pS16953)

Riegle, Donald W., Jr. (Sen.-Mich.). "Statements on Introduced Bills and Joint Resolutions," Congressional Record (22 Nov 1993). Daily ed. pS16936-16955. (ISSN0363-7239).

SUGAR SUBSTITUTES--U.S. (v19)

SUGAR TRADE (v19)

SUGAR TRADE--CHINA (v19)

SUGAR TRADE--CUBA (v19)

"Sugar is...[Cuba's] number one industry and top hard currency earner. However, lack of fuel and spare parts teamed up with serious flooding to sabotage the 1992-93 harvest, which came in at 4.28 million tons, down from 7.3 million the year before. The disaster cost the island $450 million in lost sales. According to Political Bureau member Carlos Lage, there are expectations for modest improvement for the 1993-94 season, but full recovery won't be in the offing until the following year. A $350-million credit line from Russia includes an undisclosed amount for what Council of Ministers' Vice-president Lionel Soto calls 'a permanent financing mechanism' for the sugar industry. According to the agreement signed in July, the Russian side will guarantee the lion's share of the fuel for cane-harvesters and transportation; as well as fertilizers, herbicides, tires and spare parts for the mills. (The dearth of fertilizers for the last harvest is indicative of the dimension of the problems: in 1990, Cuba applied 750,000 tons of fertilizers to the fields, but by 1992, there were only 95,000 tons available.)" (p13)

Reed, Gail. "Dateline Havana: Cuba's Economic Recovery Rests on Sugar." Cuba Update n6, Nov-Dec 1993. p13. (ISSN0196-0830).

SUGAR TRADE--EUROPEAN ECONOMIC COMMUNITY (v19)

SUGAR TRADE--JAPAN

"Over the past decade, leading raw sugar suppliers to the Japanese market were Australia (averaging 599,000 tons or 32 percent annually), Thailand (508,230 tons or 27 percent), Cuba (308,000 tons or 16 percent), and South Africa (300,000 tons or 16 percent). Australia's share of the market has been steady-to-rising, and Thailand's share is trending up, reflecting the expansion of its industry with the help of Japanese investment....South Africa's share of the market also has been fairly steady, but shipments fell substantially in 1992 and 1993 due to a devastating drought that wiped out South Africa's short-turn ability to export. Cuba's share of the market has shown the most year-to-year variation, reflecting competing commitments with the former Soviet Union and more recently the contraction of Cuba's exportable surplus." (p31)

U.S. Dept. of Agriculture/Buzzanell, Peter J. "Japan's Sweetener Industry--Emerging Trends and Policy Issues." Sugar and Sweetener Situation and Outlook Report Dec 1993. p20-39.

SUGAR TRADE--LOUISIANA (v19)

SUGAR TRADE--U.S. (v19)

"For fiscal 1993, the destination of U.S. refined sugar exports were dominated by shipments to Canada of 110,641 metric tons and to Mexico of 65,579 tons, accounting for 42 and 25 percent of the total, respectively. During fiscal 1992, refined sugar exports totaled 68,922 tons to Canada and 69,146 tons to Mexico. U.S. refined sugar exports traditionally also flow into the Caribbean: Haiti imported 32,633 tons in fiscal 1993, versus 59,110 in fiscal 1992, and Jamaica imported 36,961 in 1993 and 46,517 in 1992. Smaller amounts flow into the Bahamas and Lesser Antilles, where U.S. packaged sugar products have an established market." (p15)

U.S. Dept. of Agriculture. "U.S. Sugar." Sugar and Sweetener Situation and Outlook Report Dec 1993. p11,13,15-17.

"Sugar use in bakery and cereal products [in the U.S.] registered a record quarter in July-September of 484,000 tons, refined, and total use for fiscal 1993 was 1.70 million tons. This was up 5.1 percent from the year before and accounted for 21 percent of total deliveries for human consumption for fiscal 1993. This solid performance reflects strong demand for bakery and cereal products, heightened by the new trend toward 'jumbo products,' i.e. larger-sized biscuits and sweet rolls many food manufacturers now offer....Of total fiscal 1993 U.S. sugar deliveries, 4.24 million tons (46.7 percent) were beet sugar and the remainder was cane sugar. This compares with beet sugar deliveries of 3.90 million tons in fiscal 1992 that accounted for 44.2 percent of the total." (p13)

U.S. Dept. of Agriculture. "U.S. Sugar." Sugar and Sweetener Situation and Outlook Report Dec 1993. p11,13,15-17.

SUGARCANE--JAPAN

"For climatic and agronomic reasons, sugarcane [in Japan] is grown exclusively on smaller islands in Kagoshima and Okinawa Prefectures....The current decline in sugarcane area is attributed largely to the advancing age of growers and labor shortages. However, sugarcane remains among the most suitable crops for the southern-most islands, where growing conditions are generally difficult due to shallow soils and frequent typhoons. With few alternative crops, the region depends heavily on cane production. For example, 48 percent of the cultivated land in the Okinawa Prefecture is devoted to about 22,000 hectares of sugarcane. In 1992, MAFF [or Japan's Ministry of Agriculture, Forestry and Fishery] estimated that there were an estimated 42,527 sugarcane farms in Japan, 31 percent in Kagoshima and 59 percent in Okinawa Prefecture. The average size of a sugarcane farm in Japan is about 1.7 hectares, with about 0.5 hectares devoted to cane in a given season...." (p22)

U.S. Dept. of Agriculture/Buzzanell, Peter J. "Japan's Sweetener Industry--Emerging Trends and Policy Issues." Sugar and Sweetener Situation and Outlook Report Dec 1993. p20-39.

SUICIDAL BEHAVIOR

see GAYS--U.S.--SUICIDAL BEHAVIOR

SUICIDE--GREAT BRITAIN--JAPAN--U.S. (v19)

SUICIDE--U.S. (v19)

"In 1991 firearms and explosives accounted for 65 percent of the suicides committed [in the U.S.] by men and just under 40 percent of those by women. Poisonings were the second most common means of suicide among women (close to 37 percent of these deaths) but third among men (just over 13 percent). Hangings were the second leading method used by men (15.1 percent) and third by women (13.4 percent). Jumping to one's death ranked fourth for both men and women, accounting for 2.0 and 3.5 percent of the suicides, respectively." (p14)

Seltzer, Frederic. "Trend in Mortality from Violent Deaths: Suicide and Homicide, United States, 1960-1991." Statistical Bulletin v75 n2, Apr-Jun 1994. p10-18. (ISSN0790-8334).

SULPHUR DIOXIDE--U.S.

"The Clean Air Act will reduce the U.S.'s total SO2 [sulfur dioxide] emissions by 10 million tons from 1980 levels by the year 2000. It also grants each power plant permission to release a certain amount of those emissions, usually less than it released before. The Environmental Protection Agency (EPA) gives each plant one emissions 'allowance' permit for each ton of SO2 that the plant may now release. These permits may be bought and sold, so long as the plants have one permit at the end of the year for each ton of SO2 they've released. If a plant holds its emissions below its allotted level, it may sell its extra permits to another plant that can't make the cut. (The Act also reduces nitrous oxide emissions, the other major component of acid rain, but not with a trading system.)" (p54)

Goffman, Joseph. "Forum: Learning to Love Emissions Trading." E Magazine v4 n1, Feb 1993. p54-55. (ISSN1046-8021).

SUNFLOWER SEED INDUSTRY--EUROPEAN ECONOMIC COMMUNITY (v19)

SUNFLOWER SEED OIL INDUSTRY--U.S.

"Despite the increase in sunflower acreage [in the U.S.], low yields and adverse weather shrank 1993/94 production, which is estimated at 1.18 million metric tons. Crushers are expected to use 816,000 metric tons, down from 923,000 a year ago, as expected exports of sunflower oil drop to 248,000 metric tons, down 6.7 percent from the previous season. Despite the lower crush, stocks are expected to shrink even lower, pushing prices of all sunflowers to a record high excluding 1983/84. The season-average price received by farmers is expected to range between $11.75 and $12.75 per hundred-weight." (p3)

U.S. Dept. of Agriculture. "Summary." Oil Crops Situation and Outlook Report Jan 1994. p3.

SUPERCONDUCTING SUPER COLLIDER (v19)

SUPERFUND PROGRAM (v19)

"The one thing everyone can agree on is that Superfund is a catastrophe. In 13 years, the Environmental Protection Agency has put 1, 270 toxic-waste sites on its Superfund list. Only 49 have been completely cleaned. Much of the $12 billion spent has paid for lawsuits to force companies to pay for the cleanups....The role of the insurance industry in the cleanup is even more contentious. Most policies written before 1986 didn't exclude toxic-waste coverage. So companies facing Superfund charges have tried to stick carriers with the bill. A 1992 study of four insurers found that 88% of their Superfund costs went to pay for suits over claims." (p41)

Regan, Mary Beth. "Washington Outlook: Can Clinton Clean Up the Superfund Morass?" Business Week n3358, 14 Feb 1994. p41. (ISSN0007-7135).

"The federal 'superfund' provides money for the cleanup of hazardous and toxic wastes that have been released into the ground or water. It was created in 1980 under the Comprehensive Environmental Response, Compensation and Liability Act (PL 96-510). The law established the principle that polluters, not taxpayers, should pay to clean up toxic waste sites. But the law has been criticized for sparking too many court cases and not enough cleanup actions. Congress also has been concerned that local governments are unfairly burdened because the law's strict liability provisions allow cities to be sued. As of May 1993, only 54 of the nation's 1,202 priority sites have been cleaned up." (p3384)

Hook, Janet/others. "Special Report: Cover Story: Democrats Hail 'Productivity,' but Image Problems Remain." Congressional Quarterly v51 n49, 11 Dec 1993. p3355-3406.

"Hazardous waste sites are not being cleaned up in a timely manner. Litigation and delay have become the standard operating procedure for the Superfund program. After 13 years and approximately $18 billion spent on the Superfund program, only 12 percent or about 150 sites on the Superfund priority list have been cleaned up. Only 4 percent have actually been delisted. The average time it takes to clean up a site is a staggering 10 to 15 years, costing $25 to $30 million per site." (pS3965)

Smith, Bob C. (Sen.-N.H.). "Statements on Introduced Bills and Joint Resolutions," Congressional Record (25 Mar 1994). Daily ed. pS3954-3985. (ISSN0363-7239).

"The Environmental Protection Agency has so far discovered over 1,300 Superfund sites around the Nation. Some 73 million Americans live within 4 miles of those sites, and numerous studies have shown that people living near these sites suffer significantly higher risks of cancer, birth defects, and other serious health problems. Their problems are only compounded by the economic devastation that these communities face, as property values are devalued and they are unable to leave the very sites that are poisoning them." (pS1085)

Lautenberg, Frank R. (Sen.-N.J.). "Statements on Introduced Bills and Joint Resolutions," Congressional Record (7 Feb 1994). Daily ed. pS1047-1086. (ISSN0363-7239).

"After spending more than $12 billion dollars since Superfund began in 1980, the [U.S. federal] government has managed to clean up fewer than 100 chemical dump sites. Furthermore, the extent of the problem is enormous. There may be as many as 439,000 contaminated sites, plus six million underground storage tanks, 15 to 25 percent of which are already leaking. Since cleanup efforts have largely failed, the government has two choices: to either excavate contaminated sites and store the toxic soil in immense steel-reinforced concrete buildings (thus creating an embarrassing monument to technical failure), or convince the public to accept low levels of toxins in their soil, air, water, homes and bodies." (p55)

Montague, Peter. "Forum: Sign of the Times?" E Magazine v4 n4, Jul-Aug 1993. p54-55. (ISSN1046-8021).

"The Congressional Office of Technology Assessment (OTA) has estimated that Superfund cleanups may eventually be needed for 9,000 sites at a cost of up to $500 billion. And Superfund is only one government program. Cleanups will also be required at sites covered by the Resource Conservation and Recovery Act ($234 billion), or administered by the Department of Defense ($30 billion), and the Department of Energy ($240 billion). Under present estimates, the U.S. will be spending $185 billion per year on cleaning up toxic and radioactive waste by the year 2000. By comparison, the current annual defense budget is $240 billion." (p39)

Burke, William K. "The Booming Business in Waste." E Magazine v4 n3, May-Jun 1993. p38-43. (ISSN1046-8021).

"Under the EPA's system for ranking Superfund sites, Triumph [Idaho] scored higher than any other toxic-waste site in the nation. A score of at least 28.5 is required for listing; Triumph scored 90.33. EPA officials base the scores on levels of arsenic and lead in residents' yards, toxic dust in the air, and heavy metals in the tailings piles. EPA contractors in two tests also recorded high lead readings in a 48-foot-deep drinking water well--tests which are still disputed today--and shut it down....Triumph residents and Idaho National Engineering Laboratory hydrologists Greg Norrell argue that the EPA and its contractor, Seattle-based Ecology And Environment Inc., botched soil and groundwater tests, which led to erroneous conclusions about environmental and health dangers. Norrell and a Denver-based law firm that specializes in Superfund law have recalculated Triumph's hazardous-ranking score based on their own analysis of the relative health dangers. The result: 28.3, or two-tenths below the threshold of Superfund listing." (p10)

Stuebner, Steve. "Triumph, Idaho, to EPA: Get Out." High Country News v25 n17, 20 Sep 1993. p1,10-11. (ISSN0191-5657).

"When Butte and Anaconda [in Montana] were designated as the nation's largest Superfund site in the early 1980s, it was a stigma from which the depressed towns thought they'd never recover. Not only did they have to cope with high arsenic and lead levels in the blood of their children, but they thought they'd never attract new businesses and people. The mine had recently laid off 5,000 high-paid, blue-collar workers, leaving only contaminated dust and a handful of jobs....First the town prospered by making a mess, and now the town prospers by cleaning it up. Butte's pollution is so vast and complicated that the world's best engineers flock to it. In the last five years, tens of millions of federal dollars have poured into Butte, EPA has opened an office, ARCO has established cleanup offices in Butte and Anaconda, and a half dozen high-tech firms moved here to field-test ideas and vie for contracts. Conventional copper mining currently employs about 330 people, but the clean-up industry employs almost three times as many." (p12)

Williams, Florence. "Seeking Treasure in Butte's Trash." High Country News v25 n22, 29 Nov 1993. p12. (ISSN0191-5657).

"In Superfund's first 12 years, the federal government spent $7.7 billion, while the private sector spent roughly $6.3 billion on the program. In contrast, the gross domestic product of the US is more than $6 trillion....No one is satisfied with a program that has boosted income for some lawyers but completed cleanup of relatively few sites. By September 1993, 217 of the 1,289 sites on the national priorities list had seen completion of construction work related to cleanup. Through January, 56 sites had been completely cleaned up." (p8)

Feldmann, Linda. "Clinton Proposals Will Rejig Superfund." The Christian Science Monitor v86 n47, 1 Feb 1994. p8-9. (ISSN0882-7729).

SUPERMARKETS--U.S. (v19)

SUPPLEMENTAL SECURITY INCOME PROGRAM--U.S. (v19)

"From 1973 to 1993...the average annual growth rate in the real wages of workers covered by Social Security has been virtually stagnant at only 0.45 percent. The surge in productivity of the past two years...has led some economists to speculate that we may now be experiencing a turn-about that goes beyond the cyclical improvement in productivity that typically occurs during this phase of an economic expansion. Yet even if we imagined that this sudden jump in US worker productivity points toward a permanent doubling in the future growth rate of real wages (to 0.90 percent per year), this still remains below the official long-term assumption employed in the intermediate Social Security Administration forecast (1.10 percent per year)." (p40)

Peterson, Peter G. "Entitlement Reform: The Way to Eliminate the Deficit." New York Review of Books v41 n7, 7 Apr 1994. p39-47. (ISSN0028-7504).

SUPPLEMENTAL UNEMPLOYMENT BENEFITS--CANADA (v19)

SUPPORT OF CHILDREN

see CHILD SUPPORT

SURGERY--COMPLICATIONS--U.S. (v19)

SURGERY, UNNECESSARY--U.S. (v19)

SWEDEN

see also RAILROADS--NEW ZEALAND--SWEDEN

SWEDEN--ARMED FORCES--GAYS (v19)

SWEDEN--ECONOMIC CONDITIONS (v19)

SWEDEN--EMPLOYMENT

"Four years ago white-collar unemployment in the Swedish public sector totaled just 2.2 percent. Now it is 8 percent and rising. Women, especially, are suffering since they dominate the state work force in endangered sectors like health care and education. In 1990, 89 percent of Swedish women worked--the highest proportion in the industrialized world. Today the rate is down to 83 percent." (p62)

Knight, Robin/others. "Business: Europe Tries to Cope with Half a Loaf." U.S. News & World Report v116 n7, 21 Feb 1994. p59,61-62. (ISSN0041-5537).

SWEDEN--MANUFACTURES (v19)

SWEET POTATO INDUSTRY--U.S. (v19)

SWEETENER INDUSTRY--U.S.

"HFCS [high fructose corn syrup] exports, including crystalline fructose, totaled 103,700 tons, slightly more than the 102,500 in fiscal 1992. Canada is the largest importer, though increasing quantities go to Mexico. In fiscal 1993, 42,300 tons were shipped to Canada, and 33,100 to Mexico, together accounting for about three-fourths of total U.S. HFCS exports. While U.S. HFCS exports to Canada dropped by nearly 29 percent from fiscal 1992, U.S. exports to Mexico jumped by nearly two-thirds. U.S. exports of crystalline fructose in fiscal 1993, included in total HFCS exports, totaled 20,200 tons, up sharply from fiscal 1992's 12,600 tons." (p18)

U.S. Dept. of Agriculture. "U.S. Corn Sweeteners." Sugar and Sweetener Situation and Outlook Report Dec 1993. p17-19.

"The United States continued to be a net importer of HFCS [high fructose corn syrup] in fiscal 1993. HFCS imports, mostly from Canada, rose to 207,500 tons, up from 179,000 in fiscal 1992. Crystalline fructose imports, used in dry beverage mixes and other uses, are included in the HFCS total, but were relatively small (less than 1,000 tons in fiscal 1992, and less than 500 tons in fiscal 1993). Higher HFCS imports in 1993 were partly in response to tight supply conditions resulting from the Midwestern floods." (p18)

U.S. Dept. of Agriculture. "U.S. Corn Sweeteners." Sugar and Sweetener Situation and Outlook Report Dec 1993. p17-19.

"U.S. imports of sweeteners from Japan are largely in the form of the high-intensity sweeteners aspartame...and saccharin....U.S. imports from Japan, the primary source of foreign supply of aspartame, averaged 1,419 tons (1990-92), valued at $45.2 million. For the first 9 months of 1993, imports of aspartame were 1,614 tons, valued at $56.2 million. U.S. saccharin imports from Japan averaged 378 tons (1990-92) and were valued at $2.5 million. Japan accounted for 39 percent of total saccharin imports, second only to South Korea. These imports are used to supplement U.S.-produced aspartame and saccharin in the growing diet food and beverage product market." (p35)

U.S. Dept. of Agriculture/Buzzanell, Peter J. "Japan's Sweetener Industry--Emerging Trends and Policy Issues." Sugar and Sweetener Situation and Outlook Report Dec 1993. p20-39.

SWEETENERS--JAPAN--U.S.

"While Japan and the United States do not trade sugar, they do have trade in other sweeteners and sweetener byproducts. U.S. exports of crystalline fructose...to Japan have been increasing in recent years averaging 3,948 tons valued at $4.1 million (1990-1992) and 3,421 tons valued at $2.1 million in the January-through-September period of 1993. Japan is currently the largest market for U.S. manufactured crystalline fructose where it is used in products such as dry beverage bases. U.S. exports of beet pulp...a primary byproduct of processing sugarbeets, have averaged 316,080 tons (1990-92) accounting for 52 percent of total exports. The average value of these exports to Japan was $38.2 million. Beet pulp is largely used as a feed for Japan's dairy industry that is concentrated on the island of Hokkaido. Beet pulp exports totaled 244,396 tons and were valued at $29.6 million in the January-September 1993 period, up in terms of volume and value from the same period in 1992." (p35)

U.S. Dept. of Agriculture/Buzzanell, Peter J. "Japan's Sweetener Industry--Emerging Trends and Policy Issues." Sugar and Sweetener Situation and Outlook Report Dec 1993. p20-39.

SWEETENERS--U.S. (v19)

see also NONNUTRITIVE SWEETENERS--U.S.--CHILDREN

"Corn sweetener use in the United States totaled 10.13 million tons in fiscal 1993, up 3.1 percent from the previous year. The composition of estimated corn sweetener use by the food and beverage industry was HFCS-55 [high fructose corn syrup with 55-percent fructose, dry basis], 3.97 million tons; HFCS-42 [42-percent fructose, dry basis], 2.85 million; glucose syrup, 2.71 million tons; and dextrose, 605,000 tons." (p17) "Glucose syrup deliveries for domestic foods and beverages in fiscal 1993 totaled 2.70 million tons, up 1.5 percent from the previous year. Glucose syrup is used in a wide variety of food products and does not display the strong, season pattern that HFCS does. Dextrose deliveries for use in domestic foods and beverages in fiscal 1993 totaled 605,000 tons, up 5 percent from fiscal 1992. While dextrose is the smallest of the three main corn sweeteners, it still accounts for around 6 percent of total U.S. corn sweetener use in domestic foods and beverages." (p18)

U.S. Dept. of Agriculture. "U.S. Corn Sweeteners." Sugar and Sweetener Situation and Outlook Report Dec 1993. p17-19.

"Fiscal 1993 combined production of corn sweeteners [in the U.S.] (HFCS [high fructose corn syrup], glucose syrup, and dextrose) totaled 10.82 million tons, up 3.2 percent from the previous year. The U.S. corn wet-milling industry used 629 million bushels of corn. This represented only 6.6 percent of the total corn crop, but 41 percent of the food, seed, and industrial use category. HFCS production in fiscal 1993 totaled 6.9 million tons, up nearly 4.1 percent from the preceding year. HFCS-55 (55-percent fructose, dry basis) continues to be the dominant corn sweetener in the United States, with output at 4.02 million tons, up 5 percent from 1991/92." (p17)

U.S. Dept. of Agriculture. "U.S. Corn Sweeteners." Sugar and Sweetener Situation and Outlook Report Dec 1993. p17-19.

SWIMMING--U.S. (v19)

SWINE--DISEASES--U.S. (v19)

SWINE--PRICES--U.S.

"Despite abundant supplies of pork and poultry, hog prices

averaged $46 per cwt [hundredweight] in 1993, up $3 from 1992. Hog prices received some support from reduced supplies of Choice beef and pork in first-half 1993 and a recovering general economy. Also, another year of narrow farm-retail spreads supported prices. Spreads declined about 2 percent in 1993, about the same decline as in 1992." (p1)

U.S. Dept. of Agriculture. "Review of 1993." Hog Outlook 13 Jan 1994. p1-2.

SWINE--U.S.

"The rise of corporate hog farming means bigger farms--and fewer farmers. The size of the average hog farm in the South has almost quadrupled since 1974, from 29 pigs to 111 last year. Over that same period, three-fourths of all hog farmers in the region--more than 235,000 farmers--have been driven out of business....corporate farms crowd thousands of hogs into confinement sheds on a single site, generating more manure than they are often able to absorb. More hogs mean more environmental hazards. 'The potential for catastrophic problems is greater for 1,000 sows than for 100 sows,' notes Jim Barker, a swine specialist at North Carolina State." (p126)

Cecelski, David/Kerr, Mary Lee. "Food Empires: Hog Wild." Southern Exposure v21 n1-2, Spr-Sum 1993. p125-126. (ISSN0146-809X).

SYRIA--ARMED FORCES (v19)

SYRIA--RELATIONS--FORMER SOVIET REPUBLICS (v19)

TAHITI--POPULATION

"Tahiti, a 402-square-mile volcanic island in the Windward Society Islands, is the largest island in French Polynesia. The French nuclear testing program encouraged migration from the outlying islands to Tahiti. The results have been an extremely high cost of living, a lack of sewage and waste disposal facilities, inadequate health care and crowded, inadequate housing, problems that are particularly acute for those from outer islands. Between 1956 and 1989, the population of the Windward Society Islands rose 235 percent." (p38)

Kelly, Marion. "Tahitians." Cultural Survival Quarterly v17 n3, Fall 1993. p38. (ISSN0740-3291).

TAIWAN

see ANIMAL INDUSTRY--TAIPEI (TAIWAN); ANIMAL INDUSTRY--TAIWAN; GROCERY TRADE--TAIWAN; INDUSTRIALIZATION--KOREA (SOUTH)--TAIWAN; POLLUTION--TAIWAN

TAIWAN--COMMERCE--U.S. (v19)

TAIWAN--ECONOMIC CONDITIONS (v19)

TAJIKISTAN--HISTORY--CIVIL WAR

"For almost four years, Tajikistan has been going through an economic and political struggle that has turned into civil war. Varying estimates put the loss of life in this war at 20,000-50,000. Hundreds of thousands of people have left the country. From 1989 to 1992, more than 200,000 Russians left and 100,000 Tajiks fled to neighboring Afghanistan. More than 500,000 Tajiks and Uzbeks--so called 'internal refugees'--moved to safer regions of the country." (p56)

"Tajikistan: Another Afghan War?" Bulletin of the Atomic Scientists v50 n1, Jan-Feb 1994. p56-59. (ISSN0096-3402).

"The continuing civil war in Tajikistan has devastated the republic, destroyed its economy and plunged it back into the Middle Ages. Out of a population of 5.4 million, an estimated 30,000 people have been killed since 1991, tens of thousands have been wounded and more than half a million are refugees in their own homeland, while another estimated 250,000 people have fled to Russia, Uzbekistan, Afghanistan and Pakistan. Tajikistan has become the major destablizing element in Central Asia and neighboring states." (p31)

Rashid, Ahmed. "Challenges of Sovereignty: The Dramatic Repercussions of Tajikistan's Civil War." Surviving Together v12 n1, Spr 1994. p31-33. (ISSN0859-6286).

TANZANIA

see AIDS (DISEASE)--EDUCATION--TANZANIA; HIV INFECTIONS--TANZANIA; LITERACY--TANZANIA; MARRIAGE--TANZANIA

TARIFF

"On July 7, 1993, four of the seven countries attending the economic summit in Tokyo announced that they had reached a major agreement on tariff reductions. The United States, the EC [European Community], Japan, and Canada (the quadrilateral, or quad) agreed to cut tariffs on industrial goods. Under the agreement, tariffs would be reduced to zero on 8 products: pharmaceuticals, medical equipment, construction equipment, steel, beer, furniture, farm equipment, and distilled spirits. (The steel tariff cuts were contingent upon completion of a separate multilateral steel agreement currently being negotiated, and some of the other tariff cuts included exceptions.) Tariffs would be harmonized on certain chemical products. Peaks in tariffs would be reduced for three groups of products: ceramics, glass, and textiles and apparel. Finally, tariffs would be cut by an average of at least 33% on 5 products: scientific equipment, wood, paper, nonferrous metals, and electronics." (p10)

U.S. House. Committee on Energy and Commerce. "Telecommunications Trade." Hearing, 3 Aug 1993. Washington, D.C.: GPO, 1994. (ISBN0160435919). (Y4.En2/3:103-60).

TARIFF--MEXICO--U.S. (v19)

TARIFF--U.S.

"U.S. Trade Representative Mickey Kantor told the House Ways and Means Committee earlier this year that he expects the GATT [General Agreement on Tariffs and Trade] to generate tax revenue sufficient to cover the expected reduction in revenues due to lower tariff revenues. It is expected that GATT will result in $7 to $21 billion in additional economic activity in the first year after enactment and increase to $100 to $200 billion per year once fully implemented. This increased economic activity will result in billions of dollars of tax revenue to the Federal Government each year. However, the paygo rules do not allow these increased revenues to be used to offset the tariff losses." (pH2202)

Ewing, Thomas W. (Rep.-Ill.). "Introduction of Legislation to Amend Budget Rules as They Apply to Trade Agreements," Congressional Record (12 Apr 1994). Daily ed. pH2201-2202. (ISSN0363-7239).

TAXATION

see also AIRLINES--TAXATION--U.S.; ALCOHOLIC BEVERAGES--TAXATION--FRANCE--GREAT BRITAIN; AUTOMOBILES--TAXATION--U.S.

"For 22 countries, rich and poor...[the ECONOMIST] examined over 30 indicators which sum up the economic, social, cultural and political aspects of life." (p39) "Nobody likes the taxman, but in some countries he is greedier than others. Taxes accounted for no less than 75% of GDP [gross domestic product] in Brazil in 1991, in part because of the impact of hyperinflation on the tax system. Sweden has the second highest taxes, at 50% of GDP, almost double America's 27%. The Bahamas (5%) or Hong Kong (11%) are for those who wish to minimise their tax bill." (p40)

"Where to Live: Nirvana by Numbers." Economist v329 n7843, 25 Dec 1993. p39-42. (ISSN0013-0613).

"Governments raise most of their revenues from taxes that drive a 'wedge' between the labour costs that firms pay and the cash that workers take home. These taxes make workers less eager to work and firms less keen to hire them." (p70) "The size of the tax wedge varies among countries....In Japan income taxes and employees' and employers' social security taxes amount to 16% of the cost of employing an average production worker. America also has a slim wedge, 24%. But in Europe, the distortion is generally much bigger, often because of high employers' taxes: in Italy, the tax wedge is a whopping 51%." (p71)

"Schools Brief: A Bad Case of Arthritis." Economist v330 n7852, 26 Feb 1994. p70-71. (ISSN0013-0613).

TAXATION--GERMANY--U.S. (v19)

TAXATION--GREAT BRITAIN

In Great Britain, "the rate of VAT [value-added tax] has been raised sharply, from 8% to 17.5%. Although the total income-tax burden has fallen from 11.2% of GDP [gross domestic product] in 1978-79 to an expected 9.6% of GDP in 1994-95, VAT has jumped from 3.1% to 6.7% of GDP." (p59)

"Britain: That Sinking Feeling." Economist v330 n7848, 29 Jan 1994. p59-60. (ISSN0013-0613).

TAXATION--GREAT BRITAIN--PUBLIC OPINION (v19)

TAXATION--U.S. (v19)

"In 1992, about 11 million taxpayers filed their returns electronically. For them, filing electronically generally meant faster refunds than if they had filed paper returns and greater assurance that their returns were received and accepted by IRS and that their computations were correct. For IRS, electronic filing meant that returns could be processed and stored more efficiently and with less rework. IRS data showed, for example, that the error rate for electronic returns during the 1992 filing season was 2.8 percent compared to 18 percent for paper returns. IRS expects to receive about 14 million electronic returns in 1993." (p912)

Stathis, Jennie S. (Director, Tax Policy & Admin. Issues, General Gov. Div., U.S. GAO). U.S. House. Committee on Appropriations. "Treasury, Postal Service...Approp. for Fiscal Year 1994 (Part 1)." Hearing, Washington, D.C.: GPO, 1993. (Y4.Ap6/1:T71/994/pt.1).

"In the last year, we more accurately defined accounts receivable to exclude all accounts determined not collectible as well as duplicate assessments against corporate officers for delinquent payroll taxes already included as assessed against the business. Using this new definition, as of September 30, 1992, ARDI [the Accounts Receivable Dollar Inventory] was $71 billion. This represents a 27% increase over the FY 1989 base year figure of $56 billion. It includes an Allowance for Doublful Accounts (ADA) estimated at $43 billion. ADA is an accounting procedure that estimates the portion of accounts receivable which IRS believes will not be collected for various reasons including hardship, bankruptcy, errors, etc. After removing the ADA, an estimated net accounts receivable of $28 billion is left. This $28 billion figure represents a more realistic estimate of the value of accounts receivable." (p820)

U.S. House. Committee on Appropriations. "Treasury, Postal Service...Approp. for Fiscal Year 1994 (Part 1)." Hearing, Washington, D.C.: GPO, 1993. (Y4.Ap6/1:T71/994/pt.1).

"Individuals' compliance levels, according to IRS estimates, have remained fairly steady at about 85 percent over the last 20 years. Among individuals, however, self-employed taxpayers tend to have lower compliance. TCMP [the Taxpayer Compliance Measurement Program] data has regularly shown that compliance among sole proprietors--or self-employed taxpayers who keep formal business records--is 15 to 20 percentage points lower than for other individual taxpayers (e.g., wage earners). Among those who do not keep formal business records--such as roadside vendors and moonlighting craftsmen--compliance is much lower. Although IRS lacks similar trend data for this group, IRS has estimated that this type of self-employed individual only voluntarily reports about 13 percent of his or her business income. As with the other taxpayer groups, IRS' audit coverage of tax returns from individuals has declined. Between 1980 and 1992, covrage for all individuals dropped from 2 percent to 0.9 percent. For sole proprietors, IRS' rate fell from 2.8 percent to 2.3 percent." (p989)

U.S. House. Committee on Appropriations. "Treasury, Postal Service...Approp. for Fiscal Year 1994 (Part 1)." Hearing, Washington, D.C.: GPO, 1993. (Y4.Ap6/1:T71/994/pt.1).

"It seems prudent to maintain a certain level of audit coverage for all taxpayer groups. Beyond that, IRS' enforcement efforts should be targeted to more noncompliant populations. Between 1980 and 1987, for example, small corporate compliance, as measured by IRS' Taxpayer Compliance Measurement Program (TCMP), dropped from 81 percent to 61 percent. At the same time, IRS' audit coverage of small corporations dropped from 6 percent to about 1 percent. This rate increased to 2.5 percent in 1992. Until IRS has evidence of improved compliance by small corporations, audit coverage should be maintained at least at this level. The compliance of large corporations is not measured through TCMP and no one really knows their compliance levels. IRS' audit coverage for these corporations also has been dropping. Between 1980 and 1992, audit coverage dropped from 37.2 percent to 29.1 percent for all large corporations and from 76.8 percent to 43.7 percent for the largest corporations (those $100 million or more in assets)." (p989)

U.S. House. Committee on Appropriations. "Treasury, Postal Service...Approp. for Fiscal Year 1994 (Part 1)." Hearing, Washington, D.C.: GPO, 1993. (Y4.Ap6/1:T71/994/pt.1).

"Not surprisingly, the smaller part of the [tax] gap [in the U.S.] is the tax taxpayers report on their returns, but do not pay voluntarily and timely. This so-called 'remittance' gap [for 1992] accounts for $13.3 billion or 10.5 percent of the total. Because it is self-assessed, all of that $13.3 billion flows into our accounts receivable inventory. The largest part of the gap, and the most troublesome part in terms of our ability to collect it, is the reporting gap--the amount of tax liability not voluntarily reported on returns. The reporting gap accounts for $113.7 billion or 89.5 percent of the $127 billion estimate." (p779)

Dolan, Michael P. (Acting Commissioner, Internal Revenue Service). U.S. House. Committee on Appropriations. "Treasury, Postal Service...Approp. for Fiscal Year 1994 (Part 1)." Hearing, Washington, D.C.: GPO, 1993. (Y4.Ap6/1:T71/994/pt.1).

"The following represents the latest IRS information on the major components of the income tax reporting gap: Sole Proprietors (includes 'informal suppliers,' primarily cash businesses like sidewalk vendors who generally work alone)--28.7 percent; Corporations--25.2 percent; Capital Gains (combination of unreported capital gains and miscalculation of basis)--7.8 percent. As one might expect the actual dollars are on a steep increase--a 300 percent jump in the last 20 years. But after accounting for inflation, tax law changes, and population and income growth over the years, we find that the annual gap has been more or less constant." (p781)

Dolan, Michael P. (Acting Commissioner, Internal Revenue Service). U.S. House. Committee on Appropriations. "Treasury, Postal Service...Approp. for Fiscal Year 1994 (Part 1)." Hearing, Washington, D.C.: GPO, 1993. (Y4.Ap6/1:T71/994/pt.1).

An "innovative approach to filing was offered during the 1992 filing season; approximately 125,000 taxpayers filed their returns using touch-tone telephones. TeleFile, which was tested on a limited basis in Ohio, was available to certain taxpayers who were eligible to file a 1040EZ return. We continued the TeleFile test in Ohio this year with a major enhancement. Taxpayers...used a 'voice signature' at the end of the telephone call instead of sending in a signature on paper. This is an important step in developing a completely paperless return process and reducing the time and expense for both the taxpayer and the IRS. During this year's filing season, we received 147,000 returns with 68,400 utilizing the voice signature option. There are plans to expand TeleFile to seven states in 1994, based upon the positive evaluation of the 1992 and 1993 tests." (p1316)

Dolan, Michael P. (Acting Commissioner, Internal Revenue Service). U.S. House. Committee on Appropriations. "Treasury, Postal Service...Approp. for Fiscal Year 1994 (Part 1)." Hearing, Washington, D.C.: GPO, 1993. (Y4.Ap6/1:T71/994/pt.1).

"When state and local taxes are included, Government now takes over one-third of the income of the average [U.S.] family. During the past four decades, the tax protection for families has shrunk to one-quarter of what it was in the 1950s. If the dependent deduction had kept pace with inflation and per capita income, it would stand at over $8,000 a person this year, according to the Urban Institute, rather than the 1992 level of $2,300. Furthermore, two-thirds of the average working mother's earnings go to paying for increases in Federal taxes over the past several decades rather than providing additional income for her family. Uncle Sam gets more out of Mom's paycheck than do her own children." (pH1194)

Wolf, Frank R. (Rep.-Va.). "Concurrent Resolution on the Budget--Fiscal Year 1995," Congressional Record (10 Mar 1994). Daily ed. pH1170-1242. (ISSN0363-7239).

"In 1950, a family of four [in the U.S] with an average income paid only 2 percent of its annual income to the Federal Government while today that family pays 24 percent in income and payroll taxes. When State and local taxes are included, the tax burden exceeds one-third of the family's income. In 1950, close to 80 percent of family income was protected from Federal income tax through the personal exemption. Today the personal exemption only shields 20 percent of that income. Since 1960, a family with 2 children has seen their tax burden increase 43 percent--and a family with 4 children has seen a rise of 223 percent." (pS3490)

Lott, Trent (Sen.-Miss.). "Congressional Budget Concurrent Resolution," Congressional Record (23 Mar 1994). Daily ed. pS3477-3502. (ISSN0363-7239).

"Let's look at Jeff and Becky Smith. This is an average Utah family where Jeff is produce manager for a grocery store and earns $31,000 a year. Becky, his wife, works part time as a nurse and makes $13,000 a year. The Smiths have three children. The Smiths may not know it, but they would be better off financially if they were to divorce and Becky take two of the kids. Under current law, the Smiths pay $3,810 as a married couple filing jointly. If Jeff and Becky were to divorce, however, their combined single taxes would only be $910. This represents a marriage penalty of $2,900 a year. If the 1993 tax changes had not been enacted last year, the marriage penalty would have been $2,522, so the tax on Jeff and Becky's marriage license has gone up by $378 a year." (pS3654)

Hatch, Orrin G. (Sen.-Utah). "Congressional Budget Concurrent Resolution," Congressional Record (24 Mar 1994). Daily ed. pS3631-3659. (ISSN0363-7239).

"Single people and married couples with no children face just about the same tax rates as they did in 1960. But for a couple with two children, average taxes have risen about 43 percent. A family with four children has found their tax bill more than tripled. The reason is simple. The personal exemption--the way the Tax Code adjusts for family size--has been eroded by inflation and neglect....According to the Urban Institute, if the value of the personal exemption for taxpayers with children had been adjusted for inflation and real growth in income since 1948, it would have been $8,652 in 1993. Today, it stands at $2,350." (pS3610)

Coats, Dan (Sen.-Ind.). "Congressional Budget Concurrent Resolution," Congressional Record (24 Mar 1994). Daily ed. pS3599-3615. (ISSN0363-7239).

"Studies by the Congressional Budget Office show that it is the wealthier taxpayers who are holding on to their capital assets to avoid paying the tax. One CBO study found that when the capital gains tax was over 40 percent in the mid-1970's, taxpayers in the top 1 percent of income accounted for just 33 percent of all taxable capital gains. But when the capital gains tax rate was cut to 20 percent in 1981, the top 1 percent accounted for 55 percent of all realized capital gains....The evidence gathered since the passage of the 1986 Tax Reform Act shows that capital gains paid by the wealthy have declined. In 1985, Americans with incomes over $500,000 per year paid $12 billion in capital gains taxes. This amount had dropped to $10 billion in 1991, adjusted for inflation, confirming that wealthier taxpayers are holding on to their assets." (pS954)

Hatch, Orrin G. (Sen.-Utah). "Statements on Introduced Bills and Joint Resolutions," Congressional Record (4 Feb 1994). Daily ed. pS951-960. (ISSN0363-7239).

"Studies show that, since the late 1960's, every time that the tax rate on capital gains has risen, the amount of capital gains realized by taxpayers has fallen. Conversely, every time that rates have fallen, realizations of capital gains have gone up. To illustrate this, consider that revenues from capital gains dropped from $41 billion in 1987 to $26 billion in 1991, despite the fact that the top tax rate on capital gains went from 20 percent to 28 percent....When the capital gains tax rate jumped from 20 percent to 28 percent in 1987, a terrible thing happened. Seed capital for new businesses began to dry up. Between 1986 and 1991, venture capital financing of small businesses fell from $4.2 billion to $1.4 billion. In 1986, 1,512 firms received venture capital financing. By 1991, that number was down to 792." (pS955)

Hatch, Orrin G. (Sen.-Utah). "Statements on Introduced Bills and Joint Resolutions," Congressional Record (4 Feb 1994). Daily ed. pS951-960. (ISSN0363-7239).

"The history of the economic effects of capital gains tax rate changes suggests that lowering the tax on capital gains increases revenue to the Treasury....evidence indicates that raising the tax rate results in lower revenue. In 1990, the Treasury took in 10 percent less revenue at the 28 percent capital gains rate than it did in 1985 at the 20 percent rate. In 1991, the Government collected 22 percent less from the capital gains tax than it did in 1985....there is an estimated $8 trillion of unrealized capital gains in the United States. For the most part, taxpayers can choose when they want to unleash this tremendous amount of capital. Our tax policies are obviously holding them back, to the detriment of our economy. Let us find a way to harness these resources and reap the benefits." (pS956)

Hatch, Orrin G. (Sen.-Utah). "Statements on Introduced Bills and Joint Resolutions," Congressional Record (4 Feb 1994). Daily ed. pS951-960. (ISSN0363-7239).

"Last fall, the World Resources Institute issued a study, 'Green Fees: How a Tax Shift Can Work for the Environment and the Economy,' which estimated that a variety of these taxes could generate $100 to $150 billion in revenues while unleashing the economy to grow by another $45 to $80 billion. Our current income taxes, on the other hand, retard economic growth by 40 to 60 cents for every dollar collected. As the report noted, 'At present, the only way most people can reduce their tax bill is to work less and earn less income.' In his State of the Union address, Clinton mostly proposed to hike taxes the old fashioned way: Raising the top rate for personal income taxes from 31 to

36 percent, and for corporate income taxes from 34 to 36 percent. But he also made history by proposing an energy tax." (p35)

Nixon, Will. "Bill & Al's Green Adventure." E Magazine v4 n3, May-Jun 1993. p30-36. (ISSN1046-8021).

"The IRS estimates that there are 3.4 million Americans working as independent contractors who should be reclassified as employees. The Small Business Administration estimates that there are roughly 5 million independent contractors nationwide." (p10)

Bovard, James. "The IRS Wages War on the Self-Employed." Insight v10 n4, 24 Jan 1994. p6-10. (ISSN1051-4880).

TAXATION--U.S.--PUBLIC OPINION (v19)

TEA TRADE--U.S.

"From its accidental discovery by China's Emperor Shen Nung in 2737 B.C., when tea leaves blew into a pot of water he was boiling, tea has evolved into the world's most popular drink. Although the U.S. ranks 7th in tea consumption, well behind countries like India, Russia and England, tea manufacturers are striving to overcome Americans' coffee habit by targeting the 90s trend toward healthier lifestyles. It's working: U.S. tea profits are now $250 million annually, double that of a decade ago. Indeed, the surge in tea sales, particularly decaffeinated and herbal blends, is attributed to people 'cutting back on coffee'--often associated with heart attacks and stress--'and switching to tea,' says Bob Crawford, CEO for R.C. Bigelow which, with Thomas J. Lipton, comprises the lion's share of America's tea market. Although regular tea also contains caffeine, it has only 36 milligrams per cup compared to 100 for coffee." (p48)

Lane, Hilary. "Food & Health: Sip-by-Sipping in the 90s." E Magazine v4 n5, Sep-Oct 1993. p48,50-51. (ISSN1046-8021).

TEACHERS (v19)

TEACHERS--U.S.

"Forty-one states and the District of Columbia have developed alternatives to the traditional education school route to licensing teachers during the past decade, according to a new report. Most of the licensing programs...have been designed specifically to bring talented people with bachelor's degrees into teaching, the study says, rather than to alleviate teacher shortages." (p8)

Bradley, Ann. "41 States, D.C. Have Alternative Teacher Licensing." Education Week v13 n17, 19 Jan 1994. p8. (ISSN0277-4232).

TEACHERS--U.S.--INFLUENCE--PUBLIC OPINION (v19)

TEACHING--U.S.

"In classrooms, question-asking on the part of teachers and students takes up a significant portion of the day....We know that questions serve many important educational functions, enabling individuals to seek information (Hunkins, 1972), obtain clarification, and receive confirmation, among other uses (Good, Slavings, Harel, & Emerson, 1987)....What comes as something of a surprise, however, is the disproportionate emphasis on teacher, rather than student, questions in the educational literature (see Wilen, 1987; 1991). We know, for instance, that questions take up nearly 67 percent of teachers' turns at talk (Dillon, 1981; Dillon, 1988a), with teachers averaging about two questions per minute directed at their classes." (p27) "One consistency in much of the classroom interaction research is the relative paucity of question asking by students. While Edwards and Westgate (1987) found that pre-school children initiated more than half of the questions asked when interacting with their parents, in nursery school, children ask less than five percent of the questions (Tizard & Hughes, 1984). High school seniors, it has been observed, ask less than fifteen percent of all questions in their classrooms (Bridges, 1988)." (p28)

Daly, John A./others. "Question-Asking Comfort: Explorations of the Demography of Communication in the Eighth Grade Classroom." Communication Education v43 n1, Jan 1994. p27-41. (ISSN0363-4523).

TECHNOLOGY

see also INFORMATION TECHNOLOGY--U.S.; MEDICAL TECHNOLOGY--U.S.

"For 22 countries, rich and poor...[the ECONOMIST] examined over 30 indicators which sum up the economic, social, cultural and political aspects of life." (p39) "The richer the country the more props of modern life there will be--from fax machines to microwaves. But even among rich countries there are huge differences. Sweden tops the telephone league, with 68 lines for every 100 people. By comparison, Spain has only 32--fewer than any other industrial economy. America has the most cars: 589 for every 1,000 people, more than twice as many as in Japan. If you loathe cars, head for China or India (only 2 per 1,000)." (p40)

"Where to Live: Nirvana by Numbers." Economist v329 n7843, 25 Dec 1993. p39-42. (ISSN0013-0613).

TECHNOLOGY--DEVELOPING COUNTRIES

"There are over 450 million TV sets in the developing world--one for every 10 people (compared with one for every two in the developed world), according to 1992 BBC surveys. Radios outnumber television sets by 2 to 1. The number of VCRs in developing countries has increased by more than 80 percent in the past five years and is now estimated at about 55 million." (p5)

Piotrow, Phyllis Tilson. "'Entertainment Education:' An Idea Whose Time Has Come." Population Today v22 n3, Mar 1994. p4-5. (ISSN0749-2448).

TECHNOLOGY--JAPAN--TRAINING

"One of the most serious concerns of people engaged in technical cooperation is how to make a technology transfer more effective and widely disseminated. The Japan International Cooperation Agency (JICA) has been tackling this concern. The Third Country Training Program (TCTP), in operation since 1975, and the In-Country Training Course...initiated this year, are good examples of the agency's endeavors....TCTPs have been carried out mainly under the auspices of organizations or institutes to which JICA has previously extended project-type technical cooperation or grant aid. In fiscal 1992 the agency carried out a total of 62 TCTP courses in 22 countries, accepting some 1,000 trainees from 126 nations; in fiscal 1993, 80 courses in 22 countries will be carried out." (p6)

Nishimura, Kunio. "Cover Story, Part II: Third Country Training: Effective Cooperation." Look Japan v39 n451, Oct 1993. p6-8. (ISSN0456-5339).

TECHNOLOGY--U.S. (v19)

"A 1991 report by the Office of Technology Assessment noted that the U.S. share of world exports had fallen from 14 percent in 1970 to 10 percent 16 years later. Even more disturbing, the report noted that average weekly wages in manufacturing in the United States have fallen from more than $380 in 1978 to roughly $340 in 1990, in inflation-adjusted figures. Moreover, numerous reports from the Commerce Department and the Department of Defense over the past several years indicate that in several critical technologies, the United States is losing ground to either Europe or Japan." (pS2629)

Dodd, Christopher J. (Sen.-Conn.). "National Competitiveness Act," Congressional Record (9 Mar 1994). Daily ed. pS2625-2633. (ISSN0363-7239).

TECHNOLOGY--U.S.--PUBLIC OPINION (v19)

"One in five American adults is a 'techthusiast' who is most likely to purchase or subscribe to emerging technological products and services, according to a study by Backer Spielvogel

Bates (BSB) of New York City. These 37 million adults are younger, more affluent, and better-educated than the average American. Despite their technical bent, they watch less television than average and read more magazines and newspapers. With a median household income of $56,500, techthusiasts can afford to take a chance on new gadgets. They can also make sense of new technologies because they have completed a median of slightly more than 14 years of school, compared with less than 13 for the general population....Techthusiasts are younger than the average American adult, with a median age of 38. 'Younger people are a bit more receptive to the changes these technologies may bring,' says Craig Gugel, senior vice president and executive director of media research and technology for BSB." (p38)

Mitchell, Susan. "Technophiles and Technophobes." American Demographics v16 n2, Feb 1994. p36-40,42. (ISSN0163-4089).

"Some people [in the U.S.] wouldn't touch a computer if you paid them. Technology is to them as snakes, spiders, and heights are to other fear-filled people. Fear of technology may be the phobia of the 1990s, according to a survey by Dell Computer Corporation of Austin, Texas....One-fourth of American adults have never used a computer or programmed a VCR. A similar share are not comfortable using a computer on their own. More striking is the nearly one-third of adults who are so intimidated by computers that they are afraid they will break them. In this group are found the most serious technophobes: nearly one-fourth of the phobes, or about 8 percent of all adults, are uncomfortable setting a digital alarm clock....Nine in ten teenagers are comfortable using a range of technical devices, from answering machines and VCRs to compact-disc players and computers. Only 74 percent of older adults can claim this level of ease, according to the Dell survey." (p38-39)

Mitchell, Susan. "Technophiles and Technophobes." American Demographics v16 n2, Feb 1994. p36-40,42. (ISSN0163-4089).

TEENAGE PREGNANCY--ILLINOIS

"In a small, but sharp triumph for welfare reform, an innovative program in Illinois has helped hold the line on the rise in the number of teenagers bearing children. Teenage mothers accounted for 12.9 percent of total births in the state in 1992, according to the Illinois Department of Public Health. Although the number is only a slim improvement over the 13 percent figure for 1991, it is the lowest tally since 1988....The program, dubbed Parents Too Soon, chiefly aims to decrease the incidence of teenage pregnancy by counseling abstinence and, in local areas that approve it, contraceptive use." (p9)

Tyson, James L. "National: State Program Offers Welfare Improvements for Illinois, Nation." The Christian Science Monitor v86 n46, 31 Jan 1994. p9. (ISSN0882-7729).

TEENAGE PREGNANCY--INDIANA

"A program currently operating in Indiana has successfully addressed the needs of pregnant teens and, as a result, has increased the birthweight of their babies and improves the potential that they will return to high school after they give birth. This program, the 'Have a Healthy Baby' program, focuses on prenatal nutrition and wise lifestyle choices for pregnant teens and adults. It is taught in 138 high schools in Indiana and is designed to address the issues of daily nutritional choices and the relationship of life-style choices, such as drugs, alcohol and smoking, which affect the health of the baby. Only 2.6 percent of the 1,716 females enrolled in the program gave birth to low birthweight infants, compared to Indiana's average of 6.7 percent of births being low birthweight. The savings to the Medicaid system from this program are estimated at over $4 million. In addition, these teens are more likely to stay in school while pregnant and return to school after they give birth, giving them a better chance of obtaining a job that would make them self-sufficient." (pH1809)

Long, Jill L. (Rep.-Ind.). "Improving America's Schools Act of 1994," Congressional Record (22 Mar 1994). Daily ed. pH1794-1809. (ISSN0363-7239).

TEENAGE PREGNANCY--LATIN AMERICA (v19)

TEENAGE PREGNANCY--U.S. (v19)

"Concern about the high rate of teen pregnancy in the United States has been growing. This concern has increased because of the severe risk of developing human immunodeficiency virus infection. In 1989, more than 50 percent of teenagers were sexually active, although only 10 percent of those actually got pregnant. Of this 10 percent, many also have multiple pregnancies, contributing to the highest teen pregnancy rate in the developed world. Though the overall teen pregnancy rate has not increased during the past decade, the rate for groups below age seventeen is rising (Kleinfeld and Young 1989)." (p143)

Ripple, Rochelle P. "Intergenerational Education: Breaking the Downward Achievement Spiral of Teen Mothers." Clearing House v67 n3, Jan-Feb 1994. p143-145. (ISSN0009-8655).

"Every day in the United States over three thousand teenagers become pregnant. The rate of teen pregnancy in the United States is higher than in most other industrialized nations. It is twice as high as in Canada, Great Britain, and France, three times as high as in Sweden, and seven times as high as in the Netherlands (Office of Educational Research and Improvement 1991). The pregnancy rate in America among the fifteen- to nineteen-year-old group rose a little over 14 percent between 1973 and 1985 (National Commission on Children 1991). About 20 percent of teenage pregnancies result in miscarriage and 30 percent in abortion (Simons et al. 1991). The percentage of live births among unmarried mothers rose from nearly 5 percent in 1960 to more than 25 percent by 1988 (National Commission on Children 1991)." (p224)

Dorrell, Larry D. "A Future at Risk: Children Having Children." Clearing House v67 n4, Mar-Apr 1994. p224-227. (ISSN0009-8655).

"The statistics on teenage pregnancy in modern America are alarming. Every sixty-four seconds, a teenage mother gives birth (Simon, Finley, and Young 1991)....As many of 25 percent of teenage mothers will become pregnant with their second child within one year of giving birth to their first child (Committee for Economic Development 1987). Seven-tenths of 1 percent of all first pregnancies occur before the age of thirteen. Over 17 percent of all first pregnancies occur before the age of eighteen (Simons et al. 1991)." (p224)

Dorrell, Larry D. "A Future at Risk: Children Having Children." Clearing House v67 n4, Mar-Apr 1994. p224-227. (ISSN0009-8655).

"According to U.S. Public Health Service reports, 71 percent of all teenage parents have adult partners over age 20. California and U.S. vital statistics reports show that men over age 20 cause five times more births among junior high-age girls than do boys their own age, and 2.5 times more births among high school girls than high school boys do. Even though many more pregnancies among teenage females are caused by men older than 25 than by boys under 18, media reports and pictures depict only high schoolers. By their choice of terms and images, the media blame the young and female while giving the adult and male a break." (p9)

Males, Mike. "Bashing Youth: Media Myths about Teenagers." EXTRA! v7 n2, Mar-Apr 1994. p8-11. (ISSN0895-2310).

TELECOMMUNICATION (v19)

see also ARTIFICIAL SATELLITES IN TELECOMMUNICATION; COMPUTER NETWORKS; RADIO BROADCASTING; TELEPHONE; TELEVISION

"Japan purchases just 5 percent of its telecommunications goods and services from foreign companies while the United States and the European Community (EC) countries buy about 25 percent from foreign firms. Last year the Untied States had a $75 billion overall merchandise trade deficit with Asia and a $50 billion deficit with Japan. Many of the Western European countries also lag behind the United States in open markets. The American trade surplus with the European Community shrunk to $9 billion last year, a drop of nearly 50 percent from the 1991 level." (pE2981)

Markey, Edward J. (Rep.-Mass.). "The Telecommunications and Financial Services Fair Trade Act of 1993," Congressional Record (20 Nov 1993). Daily ed. pE2981. (ISSN0363-7239).

"A lot of public information, available for free on paper from local libraries or government agencies, commands a stiffish price when bought from a computerised service. An annual subscription to the Federal Code of Regulations, $400 in printed form, costs $21,750 in the electronic version. Data gathered by the National Oceanographic and Atmospheric Administration's latest earth-resources satellite (which set American taxpayers back $36m) are available only through a private company that charges $2,500 to $5,900 a year. The Federal Reserve Board's quarterly reports on the financial health of banks used to be given away but now cost $500 apiece in digital form....converting text and images (eg. photographs, charts and paintings) into digital form can be costly. That is one reason why less than 1% of mankind's documented knowledge has been captured in digital form. Computer archives go back only 12 years (ie, to when newspapers began using computerised type-setting). This leaves more than 99% of the world's knowledge in books, reports and other publications gathering dust on library shelves." (p35-36)

"America's Information Highway: A Hitch-Hiker's Guide." Economist v329 n7843, 25 Dec 1993. p35-36,38. (ISSN0013-0613).

TELECOMMUNICATION--DEVELOPING COUNTRIES (v19)

TELECOMMUNICATION--MEXICO

"Mexico has just 8 phone lines for every 100 residents, compared with 55 per 100 in the U.S. But it's adding new ones at a rate 12% per year--823,000 in 1993 alone. Revenues generated by that expansion should keep money rolling in for the rest of the decade. In fact, Lehman Brothers Inc. Senior Vice-President Marianne G. Bye thinks Telmex is already so flush with cash that it will boost its dividend 60% in 1994, after raising it 88%, to 98 [cents] a share, in 1993. 'You cannot go wrong with a company that sells for 10 times earnings and has profit growth of 15% a year,' agrees Oscar A. Castro, portfolio manager of the Montgomery Global Communications Fund. 'It's one of the cheapest telecom stocks in the world.'" (p97)

Glasgall, William/others. "Global Markets: Strategies for Stocks: Bells Are Ringing--All Over the World." Business Week n3352, 27 Dec 1993. p96-97. (ISSN0007-7135).

"For Mexico, NAFTA [North American Free Trade Agreement] is an opportunity to attract to its economy the private capital which fled the country during the 1980s; to compensate for the reduced public loans which have been diverted to Eastern European countries by the IMF [International Monetary Fund]; and to join an exclusive, powerful trade bloc in the hemisphere. The NAFTA-like 'pro-market' reforms of the Salinas administration already have lured billions of dollars back to Mexico. Since 1989, the Mexican stock exchange has increased sevenfold; this expansion was fueled by the 'privatization' (sale) of public enterprises such as TELMEX, the national telecommunications system. Mexico will pay at least part of its massive foreign debt by selling such public assets to private businesses. For example, the Mexican government sold TELMEX for $3.7 billion and exchanged that money for $7.2 billion of discounted Mexican debt. Privatized TELMEX now has a stock value of $28 billion--but the phones in the country do not operate any more efficiently, and neither real investment nor employment has been increased by this speculative activity." (p8)

Burke, Melvin. "The Human Costs of NAFTA." Humanist v53 n5, Sep-Oct 1993. p3-9. (ISSN0018-7399).

TELECOMMUNICATION--U.S. (v19)

TELECOMMUNICATION--U.S.--SWITCHING SYSTEMS (v19)

TELECOMMUNICATION SATELLITES

see ARTIFICIAL SATELLITES IN TELECOMMUNICATION

TELECOMMUTING--U.S. (v19)

TELEMARKETING--U.S. (v19)

TELEPHONE

see also CELLULAR RADIO

"Invented by Alexander Graham Bell, a Scottish-born American, in 1876, the telephone conquered the United States long before it found favour elsewhere. Even in the 1950s America had more telephones than the rest of the world. Access to the telephone came to be seen as a right of American citizenship: the idea was even enshrined in the country's 1934 Communications Act. With time, other countries followed. Some have even surpassed America in the universality of their telephone service. America has 45 telephones lines per 100 inhabitants; Monaco has more than 80 and Sweden close to 70. Telephones remain a tool of the rich. North America, with just 5% of the world's population, has 31% of its telephones. Western Europe, with 8% of the population, has another 30% of the telephones. Africa, in contrast, accounts for 12% of the world's population and less than 2% of its telephones. The whole of Asia, accounting for over half the world's population, owns just 7% of its telephones." (p48-49)

"Modern Wonders: The Messenger." Economist v329 n7843, 25 Dec 1993. p48-49. (ISSN0013-0613).

TELEPHONE, MOBILE

see CELLULAR RADIO

TELEPHONE COMPANIES--U.S.

"The $60 billion industry that provides long-distance telephone service is dominated by three communications giants--AT&T, MCI and Sprint, which together account for $51 billion in annual revenues." (p426) "Long-distance calls that begin and end within a state's boundaries account for $13 billion, or about 21 percent, of the long-distance industry's $60 billion in revenues, according to industry figures. The 398 smaller long-distance carriers rely on such calls the most, for roughly half of all their traffic; the rest comes from the small portion of interstate business they have managed to keep away from the big three long-distance carriers." (p427)

Mills, Mike. "Government & Commerce: Telecommunications: Telephone Wars: Forcing Hill to Broker Information Age." Congressional Quarterly Weekly Report v52 n7, 19 Feb 1994. p426-427,429. (ISSN0010-5910).

TELEPHONE COMPANIES--U.S.--TECHNOLOGY (v19)

TELEVISION

see also VIOLENCE IN TELEVISION

TELEVISION--HONG KONG (v19)

TELEVISION--POLAND (v19)

TELEVISION, CABLE

see CABLE TELEVISION

TELEVISION, PUBLIC

see PUBLIC TELEVISION

TELEVISION ADVERTISING--U.S. (v19)

TELEVISION ADVERTISING--U.S.--PUBLIC OPINION (v19)

TELEVISION AND CHILDREN--U.S. (v19)

TELEVISION AND RELIGION--U.S.

"More than 100 million people in the United States attend

worship services every week, 40 million read the Bible every day, and nearly 9 of every 10 Americans profess an affinity for a particular religion. Yet the major TV networks rarely deal with religious topics--and when they do, they are usually critical. So says, the conservative Media Research Center (MRC). After a year-long study of network morning and evening news shows, it found that religion was the focus of only 1 percent of news programming....After monitoring 18,000 news reports last year on the evening broadcasts of CBS, ABC, NBC, CNN, and PBS, the MRC tallied only 212 that dealt with religious matters. Out of about 23,000 news reports on morning talks shows, only 197 dealt with religion. A survey of more than 1,000 hours of prime-time broadcasts on NBC, CBS, ABC, and Fox counted only 116 mentions of religion." (p1)

Dillin, John. "Media: TV Networks Blind to Role Religion Plays in the US, Major Study Says." The Christian Science Monitor v86 n71, 8 Mar 1994. p1,4. (ISSN0882-7729).

TELEVISION BROADCASTING

see also CABLE TELEVISION; PUBLIC TELEVISION

TELEVISION BROADCASTING--EUROPE

"For 40 years most European countries had two or three channels, provided by a state-owned broadcaster and paid for mainly through taxes or license fees. A few places, such as Britain and Italy, dabbled with commercial TV. In Germany the two state channels could take advertising--in five minute blocks, for 20 minutes a day, except Sundays and holidays. In the 1980s a wave of deregulation broke over the old order of broadcasting in virtually every European country....In 1980 there were 40-odd TV channels in what is now the European Union. Today there are 150, over a third delivered by satellite." (p12)

"Survey: Television: Wired Planet." Economist v330 n7850, 12 Feb 1994. p56(12-13). (ISSN0013-0613).

TELEVISION PROGRAMS--LAW AND LEGISLATION--EUROPE

"French law requires that 60 percent of all television programming be produced by companies within the European economic community and half of this total--or 30 percent--must be by French companies. In Britain, the independent networks are advised by government regulators that, outside of sports and cultural programming, no more than 14 percent of broadcasts should be non-European owned. Portugal, Greece and Italy all have screen quotas. In Italy, this means that theaters are required by law to show Italian films 25 days per quarter. Last year the European economic community decided that, starting in 1993, at least 51 percent of all television programming in member nations must be of European origin." (p6)

Munro, J. Richard. "Exported Images: Boon or Invasion?" Media & Values n61, Win 1993. p6-7. (ISSN0149-6980).

TEMPORARY EMPLOYMENT--U.S. (v19)

"Over the past few years, increasing demand for temporary professionals has created a whole new industry. The editor of EXECUTIVE RECRUITER NEWS told FORTUNE magazine recently that he estimates the number of temporary firms working strictly with executives and professionals has nearly tripled, from 40 in 1990 to 100 today. Overall, the United States is home to 7,000 temporary-employment agencies. The number of people working for these companies soared more than 200 percent in the past decade, from 472,000 to 1.6 million today. Some estimates show as many as one in four Americans is now part of this work force, hired to cope with unexpected or temporary challenges." (p1 secE)

Moilanen, Kathy Ann. "Temporarily Yours: As-Needed Workers Provide Flexibility." Ann Arbor News 23 Jan 1994. p1,3 secE.

"Almost two years into an economic recovery, it has become clear that the American labor market has changed significantly. 'The size of the American contingent work force...has ballooned over the past decade,' John Sweeney, president of the Service Employees International Union told a Senate Labor and Human Resources subcommittee at a special conference Feb. 8. 'Today, temporary, contract, and part-time employees represent 25 to 30 percent of the entire work force.'...one segment of the labor market is booming: temporary employees--people who work for agencies that coordinate jobs for them. From 1980 to 1993, the number of 'temps' quadrupled, from 400,000 to 1.6 million. Temporary employees compose 1.5 percent of the work force. In fact, positions filled by temps represent one out of every six new jobs created since December 1991." (p10-11)

Tucker, William. "The Changing Face of America's Work Force." Insight v10 n11, 14 Mar 1994. p10-13. (ISSN1051-4880).

TENNESSEE

see WATER--POLLUTION--TENNESSEE

TERRORISM

see also BOMBINGS

TERRORISM--IRELAND

"According to RUC [Royal Ulster Constabulary] sources, Protestant loyalists account for a majority of the 80 murders committed last year in West Belfast. Official figures show that 210 Protestants were arrested for terrorist offenses in 1993, versus 122 for the IRA [Irish Republican Army]." (p45)

Arostegui, Martin. "Christmas in Belfast." National Review v46 n1, 24 Jan 1994. p45. (ISSN0028-0038).

TERRORISM--ISRAEL (v19)

TERRORIST BOMBINGS

see BOMBINGS

TERRORISTS--U.S.

A recent study by Brent L. Smith and Kathryn D. Morgan investigated the age, gender, education, ethnicity, and occupation of officially designated American terrorists. Their study found that the "average age of right-wing terrorists in America was 39, significantly higher than the average age of domestic left-wing group members. Over one third of the right-wing terrorists were over age 40. In contrast, fewer than 20% of the leftist terrorists were over 40. Much of this difference is found in the leadership of the Christian Identity Movement. Four of those acquitted at the national trial of white supremacists in 1988 were over 60 years of age....Even examination of the members of Puerto Rican separatist groups, the FALN and the Macheteros, as well as members of El Rukns, the New African Freedom Fighters, and other leftists indicted for terrorist activities, reveals a membership averaging in their thirties. Fifty percent of the leftist extremists indicted for terrorist related activities during the 1980s were between 31 and 40 years of age." (p51-52)

Smith, Brent L./Morgan, Kathryn D. "Terrorists Right and Left: Empirical Issues in Profiling American Terrorists." Studies in Conflict and Terrorism v17 n1, Jan-Mar 1994. p39-57. (ISSN1057-610X).

TESTING

see HONESTY--U.S.--TESTING; MATHEMATICAL ABILITY--U.S.--TESTING; NUCLEAR WEAPONS--TESTING

TESTING FOR DRUG ABUSE

see DRUG TESTING

TETANUS

"The number of infants dying each year from tetanus in the first three weeks of life has been cut in half since 1980 and is now estimated at 500 000 worldwide. In addition, over 30 000 deaths of women from the same cause are being prevented each year....In 1989, the World Health Assembly committed WHO [World Health Organization] to achieving the elimination of the disease by 1995, which in many countries accounted for up to 25% of all infant deaths in the early 1980s. Elimination is defined as less than one case of tetanus for every 1000 births occurring in each administrative district throughout the world....Priority support should be given to countries accounting for 80% of the estimated global neonatal tetanus cases: Bangladesh, China, Ethiopia, India, Indonesia, Kenya, Nepal, Nigeria, Pakistan, Somalia, Sudan, Uganda, Viet Nam, Zaire....In 1980, fewer than 5% of women in developing countries had received the recommended course of at least two vaccinations against tetanus, a figure that by 1993 had risen to 43% in spite of the steady increase in the total population." (p1)

News release. "Elimination of Neonatal Tetanus Will Save 1 Million Newborns Annually." WHO Press 25 Jan 1994. p1-2.

TETANUS IN NEWBORN INFANTS--EGYPT (v19)

TETANUS IN NEWBORN INFANTS--MORTALITY (v19)

TEXAS

see also ACTIONS AND DEFENSES--TEXAS; AGRICULTURE--TEXAS; AIRPORTS--TEXAS; CARBON DIOXIDE--TEXAS; CHILDREN--TEXAS--SOCIAL CONDITIONS; ECONOMIC FORECASTING--TEXAS; HAZARDOUS WASTE SITES--HOUSTON (TEX); HISPANIC AMERICANS--TEXAS; INDUSTRIAL HYGIENE--TEXAS; POLLUTION--EL PASO (TEX)--JUAREZ (MEXICO); RAILROADS--TEXAS; TRANSPORTATION--FRANCE--TEXAS; WATER-SUPPLY--TEXAS

TEXAS--ECONOMIC CONDITIONS (v19)

"If Texas were a nation, its gross product would be the 10th largest in the world....Texas has led the nation in job growth for five years. It is the only state among the largest 15 that did not lose manufacturing jobs last year. It gained 15,000 jobs in 1993, and 165,000 total new jobs in all industries. The North American Free Trade Agreement will be more of a benefit to Texas than any other state, [economist Ray] Perryman says. The value of Texas goods exported to Mexico rose by $12 billion between 1987 and 1992 to stand at $19 billion--three times as much as from second-place California." (p11)

Pendleton, Scott. "Economy: As Texas Economy Expands, State Pins Future on Educating Youth." The Christian Science Monitor v86 n50, 4 Feb 1994. p11. (ISSN0882-7729).

TEXAS--POPULATION

"Among the 15 most populous states, Texas has the highest percentage of people 17 years old and under. It leads the United States in immigration of young families. Six of the 10 fastest-growing regions in the country are in Texas." (p11)

Pendleton, Scott. "Economy: As Texas Economy Expands, State Pins Future on Educating Youth." The Christian Science Monitor v86 n50, 4 Feb 1994. p11. (ISSN0882-7729).

TEXTILE INDUSTRY

see also COTTON TRADE

TEXTILE INDUSTRY--EMPLOYMENT--U.S. (v19)

TEXTILE INDUSTRY--ENVIRONMENTAL ASPECTS--U.S. (v19)

TEXTILE INDUSTRY--EUROPE--U.S. (v19)

TEXTILE INDUSTRY--U.S. (v19)

"For 1993, U.S. Customs charged $10,845,000 worth of illegally transshipped textile merchandise to China's quota restraint levels, and $4,058,141 to Pakistan's quota restraint levels, based upon the entered value of the merchandise. These figures are based on actual entries. Customs estimates another $150,000,000 worth of illegally transshipped textile merchandise has either been seized, denied entry, or is pending further information before charges are recommended. For 1994, the Agency estimates charging $30,000,000 worth of illegally transshipped textile merchandise to the foreign government's quota restraint levels and another $200,000,000 that will be seized, denied entry, or detained awaiting further information." (p18)

Weise, George J. (Commissioner, U.S. Customs Service). U.S. Senate. Committee on Finance. "U.S. Customs Service, USTR, and ITC Budget Authorization for Fiscal Years 1994 and 1995." Hearing, 28 Jun 1993. Washington, D.C.: GPO, 1993. (ISBN0160433754). (Y4.F49:S.hrg.103-337).

"In 1974, the total value of textile and apparel imports was $4.2 billion [in the U.S.]. By 1993, the value of imports grew by 1000 percent to $42 billion. Despite this exponential growth, textile enforcement resources and manpower has not even begun to keep pace. Customs agents...inspected 10 percent of the containers crossing our borders [in the 1970s]. Now they are lucky if they inspect 1 percent. What has been the result? Today, foreign countries and foreign companies smuggle as much as $4 billion every year in illegal textiles and apparel. These illegal imports violate international trade agreements and take thousands of jobs away from American workers." (pH2320)

Spratt, John M., Jr. (Rep.-S.C.). "The Gap between Fact and Fiction in the Clinton Administration," Congressional Record (14 Apr 1994). Daily ed. pH2260-2322. (ISSN0363-7239).

"During calendar year 1993, U.S. textile exports rose to a record 2.5 billion pounds, nearly 4 percent above 1992. Similarly, textile imports reached 6.8 billion pounds, also a record. The textile trade deficit continues to increase, reaching nearly 4.3 billion pounds, up 500 million from a year ago. Total domestic consumption (U.S. mill consumption plus net textile product trade balance) reached 19.6 billion pounds. U.S. per capita fiber consumption reached a record 76 pounds compared with 72.6 in 1992. The trade deficit represented nearly 22 percent of domestic consumption last year." (p2)

U.S. Dept. of Agriculture. "Record Textile Trade in 1993." Cotton and Wool Update 11 Mar 1994. p2.

THAILAND

see AIDS (DISEASE)--THAILAND; DENTAL CARIES--THAILAND; DEVELOPING COUNTRIES--BRAZIL--THAILAND; FERTILITY, HUMAN--THAILAND; FISHERIES--THAILAND; GOLF COURSES--THAILAND--ENVIRONMENTAL ASPECTS; HIV INFECTIONS--THAILAND--PROSTITUTES; MOTOR VEHICLES--CHINA--THAILAND; PROSTITUTION--THAILAND; WATER-SUPPLY--THAILAND

THALASSEMIA

"Thalassaemia major is a common inherited disorder characterized by severe anaemia. A limited number of patients may be cured by bone marrow transplantation from identical siblings, but for the large majority there is no cure....The disease occurs with a high frequency in a belt extending through the Mediterranean coasts and islands, the Middle East and Indian subcontinent to the Far East. Worldwide there are at least 70 million carriers, and at least 42 000 patients with thalassaemia major are born each year....In Sardinia, the Italian island in the Mediterranean with 1.5 million inhabitants, the disorder has a carrier frequency of 12.6%. This means that one couple out of every 60 is at risk of having a child with thalassaemia major, and the incidence of this disease among newborn babies is 1:250 live births." (p26)

Cao, Antonio. "Preventing a Genetic Disease." World Health n6, Nov-Dec 1993. p26-27. (ISSN0043-8502).

THEATER--U.S. (v19)

THREE MILE ISLAND NUCLEAR POWER PLANT (PA)--HEALTH ASPECTS

"'Three Mile Island Revisited,' a 30-minute documentary hosted by award-winning environmental journalist Karl Grossman, makes a chilling case that people did die as a result of TMI [or Three Mile Island nuclear power plant]....When TMI-neighbor Jane Lee conducted a door-to-door survey using forms provided by a sympathetic epidemiologist, she discovered that only 'a very small percentage' of the area's residents had been contacted by state health department officials....Lee's 'cancer map' provides one of the documentary's most horrifying images. Small, colored circles pasted onto a map of Harrisburg show a massive clot of cancer cases representing 500 homes. Lee's survey showed that cancers in this region were 600 percent above expected occurrences. Lee's map reveals 23 cancer deaths, 45 'living cancers,' 53 benign tumors, 39 thyroid disorders and 209 respiratory problems." (p24)

Smith, Gar. "The Deadly Legacy of 'America's Chernobyl.'" Earth Island Journal v8 n3, Sum 1993. p24. (ISSN1041-0406).

THROMBOSIS--U.S. (v19)

THYROID GLAND--CANCER--BELARUS--UKRAINE (v19)

TIGERS

see also RHINOCEROSES--TIGERS

"Tigers stalked the earth long before the evolution of 'Homosapiens'; the early relatives of the world's largest cat began to evolve over 50 million years ago. Since 1900, when there were over 100,000 tigers, the world's tiger population has plummeted by over 95 percent. Fewer than 5,000 tigers survive in the wild. The Caspian, Bali and Javan species of tigers have become extinct since 1950, and China tigers have become so rare that they are now considered biologically extinct. Only 200 Siberian tigers--the world's largest cat--survive in isolated habitats; they too could be hunted to extinction within two years. The remaining populations of Bengal, Sumatran, and Indochinese tigers all suffer from relentless poaching; the high market demand for tiger bone may lead to their extinction in the wild within the next five years." (p4)

"Endangered Species Project Alert: Taiwan Is the End of the Line for Endangered Species." Earth Island Journal v8 n3, Sum 1993. p44(1-8). (ISSN1041-0406).

TIGERS--INDIA

"Many biologists now reject the figures presented in the last all-India tiger census in 1989, which estimated that 4,334 tigers roamed within Indian borders. Most experts, says [Peter] Jackson, think the actual figure was more like 3,000. Still, even that figure is a dramatic improvement over the 2,500 tigers estimated in India in the mid-1960s." (p12)

Montgomery, Sy. "Ranthambhor's Missing Tigers." Animals v126 n4, Jul-Aug 1993. p8-10,12. (ISSN0030-6835).

TIGERS--RUSSIA

"The Amur tiger, also known as the Ussuri or Siberian tiger, inhabits the southern corner of the Russian Far East....The Amur tiger has already survived one population crisis--fifty years ago its numbers dropped to 40 due to excessive hunting; only World War II brought the killing to a halt. Now the tiger is on the verge of another crisis. Current population estimates range from 200-300. Approximately 50 live in Khabarovskiikrai and approximately 200 in Primorskiikrai....The occasional tiger is shot by local villagers for preying on domestic livestock, but in the current harsh economic climate hunting has become the main source of income for many residents of tiger country. Currently, a tiger pelt can fetch upwards of $10,000 on the international market while the fine for poaching is only 4 million rubles, or roughly $2,500." (p36)

Chisholm, B. J. "Environment: Cooperation in the Taiga: The Key to Saving the Amur Tiger." Surviving Together v12 n1, Spr 1994. p36-39. (ISSN0859-6286).

TIMBER (v19)

TIMBER--OREGON

"The volume of timber cut in Oregon peaked in 1952, when nearly 10 billion board-feet of wood fell on public and private lands. By 1962, the rate of cutting had declined by half. (Today, the debate focuses on whether the forests can cough up 1 billion board-feet in the three coastal states without threatening the existence of the owl and hundreds of other species.) In Washington, the pace of cutting peaked decades earlier, mainly at the hands of loggers working for Weyerhaeuser Co., the Tacoma timber giant that had purchased millions of acres from the Northern Pacific Railroad. The clearing of forest lands is a pattern dating back before the American revolution. Clearcutters had earlier leveled lands in the Midwest, South and East. The debate today is whether the last stands, and the fragile resources they support, should be left alone." (p14)

Koberstein, Paul. "Reporter's Notebook: Is the Northwest Ready to Live Within Its Forests?" High Country News v25 n7, 19 Apr 1993. p14. (ISSN0191-5657).

TIMBER--SOUTH DAKOTA

"In 1983, the Black Hills National Forest was the first in the lower 48 states to adopt a 10-year plan for managing its resources. By the end of this year, it will be the first to issue a 10-15 year revision. At the center of the debate is timber harvesting. Critics say the current plan supports timber harvest levels so high they destroy the forest's unique ecology. During the 1980s, timber harvests in the Black Hills increased nearly 50 percent, to 118 million board-feet in 1992. The 1983 plan for the 1.2 million-acre forest expected ever-increasing timber yields well into the 21st century....According to the Sierra Club, the Black Hills are sliced by 7,000 miles of forest roads, compared to only 1,500 miles of roads in the similarly sized Bighorn National Forest, 200 miles to the east in Wyoming. While the Bighorns have 195,500 acres of designated wilderness, the Black Hills have a scant 10,700 acres, less than 1 percent of the entire forest." (p3)

Nachison, Andrew. "Western Roundup: On this Forest, Multiple Use Is Logging, and Logging." High Country News v25 n17, 20 Sep 1993. p3. (ISSN0191-5657).

TIMBER--U.S.

"'The [timber] industry [in the U.S.] is still in the Northwest,' explains Jeff Olson, forest economist for The Wilderness Society, but between 1978 and 1987 'the nation's seven largest manufacturers of lumber and wood products reduced their capacity in the Northwest by 35 percent and simultaneously increased their capacity in the South by 121 percent.' Big timber started vacating the Northwest long before the owl injunction tied up federal forests in 1991. Richard Haynes, program manager for social and economic research at the U.S. Forest Service, reports that in the Northwest in 1988, the total timber volume was 13 billion board feet (bbf), but by 1992 it had dropped to 7.2 bbf. In the South the total volume grew from 12.7 bbf in 1988 to 14.4 bbf in 1992. And the trend continues: From July 1992 through July 1993, production in the South increased 1.7 percent, while on the West Coast it decreased 12 percent." (p27)

Letto, Jay. "Go East Young Timberman!" E Magazine v5 n1, Feb 1994. p26-30,32-33. (ISSN1046-8021).

"The White House has ordered the Forest Service to reduce federal timber sales that lose money. The agency's proposal, released earlier this year, would end logging in 62 of the country's 156 national forests, many of them in the East. According to [Mathew] Jacobson, the Allegheny National Forest in Pennsylvania--because it has 'some of the best cherry in the world'--is the 'only one in the East that makes any money.' But he fears that closing other forests will put pressure to cut more in the Allegheny. A recent study of the Allegheny's economy revealed that, while the forest's wood-products industry brings in $48.4 million a year and provides jobs for 970 people, recreation brings in $91 million and employs 2,700 people." (p30)

Letto, Jay. "Go East Young Timberman!" E Magazine v5 n1, Feb 1994. p26-30,32-33. (ISSN1046-8021).

"Although timber is stolen by a variety of methods...scaling may be the most popular. According to a House of Representatives Appropriations Committee report released this March, 'Report on the U.S. Forest Service Administration of Timber Contracts,' 80 percent of the dollar value of stolen timber can be traced to fraudulent scaling. CRSB alone, some Forest Service officials told the House investigators, may have defrauded the government out of $50,000 a month for 25 years." (p1)

Stiak, Jim. "Logging Firms Rob a Lax Agency." High Country News v25 n15, 23 Aug 1993. p1,11. (ISSN0191-5657).

TIME--U.S.--SYSTEMS AND STANDARDS--ACCIDENTS AND INJURIES (v19)

TIRE INDUSTRY--U.S. (v19)

TIRES, RUBBER--U.S. (v19)

TIRES, RUBBER--U.S.--RECYCLING

"An average passenger car tire weighs about 20 pounds. Approximately 50 to 60 percent of the tire is usable as CRM [crumb rubber modified asphalt]. At 20 pounds per ton, that's two tires per ton of HMA [hot mix asphalt]. Rubber modified asphalt costs between 50 and 100 percent more than conventional HMA. HMA costs about $30 per ton. Using the more conservative 50 percent increase, rubber modified asphalt costs $45--or $15 more per ton. That's $7.50 per tire to dispose of them in HMA. That still leaves somewhere around 40 to 50 percent of the tire that can't be used in HMA to be otherwise disposed of." (p818)

Thompson, Robert M. (Past Chairman, National Asphalt Pavement Association). U.S. House. Committee on Appropriations. "Department of Transportation and Related Agencies Approp. for 1994 (Part 8)." Hearing, Washington, D.C.: GPO, 1993. (ISBN0160410657). (Y4.Ap6/1:T68/4/994/pt.8).

"The United States is faced with the seemingly daunting task of finding ways to dispose of the 285 million tires that are discarded each year and the estimated 2 to 3 billion tires currently stored in stockpiles....Scrap tires can be an efficient, economical and environmentally-benign energy resource (tire-derived-fuel or TDF). They are being successfully used as supplemental or primary fuel in cement kilns, pulp/paper mills, electric utilities, pyrolysis units and dedicated tires-to-energy facilities. Last year, 57 million scrap tires were used by these industries. The potential TDF usage within five years is predicted to be 230 million scrap tires." (p824)

U.S. House. Committee on Appropriations. "Department of Transportation and Related Agencies Approp. for 1994 (Part 8)." Hearing, Washington, D.C.: GPO, 1993. (ISBN0160410657). (Y4.Ap6/1:T68/4/994/pt.8).

TISSUE DONATION

see DONATION OF ORGANS, TISSUES, ETC.

TOBACCO--TAXATION

see CIGARETTE TAX

TOBACCO FARMS--U.S. (v19)

TOBACCO HABIT

see also CIGARETTE HABIT

TOBACCO HABIT--CUBA--URUGUAY--HEALTH ASPECTS (v19)

TOBACCO HABIT--EUROPE (v19)

TOBACCO HABIT--EUROPE--MORTALITY (v19)

TOBACCO HABIT--POLAND (v19)

TOBACCO HABIT--U.S. (v19)

"Spit tobacco use is increasing at an astonishing rate, particularly among America's young people. This phenomenon is causing alarm among the country's leading health experts who are predicting an oral cancer epidemic of disastrous proportions if current trends aren't stopped now. Here are a few facts that have come out of recent studies: In 1970, most users of snuff were men, aged 50 and over. But by 1985, boys aged 16 to 19 were using snuff twice as much as men! In 1990-91, nearly 1 in 5 high school males surveyed used spit tobacco. Spit tobacco use increased by 40% among college athletes between 1985 and 1989. In states like Tennessee and Montana, up to one-third of high school boys use spit tobacco. Use of spit tobacco is a special problem for Native American youth. In several areas of the country, Native American use exceeds 50%. Ninety-one percent of Sioux County's male seventh graders in North Dakota now use spit tobacco. The average age of first use among users recently surveyed was nine years old. Spit tobacco has high levels of nitrosamines, a cancer causing agent legally regulated by the federal government in foods--but not in tobacco products. The average snuff user is exposed to nearly 300 times more nitrosamine than a non-smoker." (p7)

"Spit Tobacco and Roll-Your-Own Tobacco: Tobacco's Cheap Attack on Youth: Spit Tobacco a National Epidemic." Tobacco-Free Youth Reporter v5 n1, Spr 1993. p7,20-21.

"The most ingenious and effective means of building widespread acceptance for the use of spit tobacco was by associating it with our national passion, professional sports. Recent government figures show that 45% of major and minor league baseball players use spit tobacco, providing a not-too-subtle example to loyal young fans, who want to emulate their heroes in every way. Pitcher Nolan Ryan remembers that when he joined the majors 20 years ago, nearly one-third of the players smoked, but no one dipped snuff. During the 1980s, things began to change, with players now rejecting cigarettes for snuff. Says Ryan, 'The switch came with free samples of dip coming into the clubhouse.'" (p20)

"Inspector General Warns of Dangers of Spit Tobacco." Tobacco-Free Youth Reporter v5 n1, Spr 1993. p7,20.

TOBACCO HABIT--U.S.--COSTS (v19)

TOBACCO HABIT--U.S.--MORTALITY

"More than 430,000 Americans die each year of tobacco-related causes. The annual cost: $68 billion in health-care expenses and lost productivity, estimates the Congressional Office of Technology Assessment. That's more than the $46.7 billion Americans spend on tobacco. And while there is no evidence that cigarette makers are deliberately boosting nicotine levels to hook new smokers, as some critics charge, companies clearly manipulate levels...and are aware of the substance's druglike power." (p34)

Carey, John. "Top of the News: It's Time for Regulators to Stop Blowing Smoke." Business Week n3362, 14 Mar 1994. p34. (ISSN0007-7135).

TOBACCO INDUSTRY

see also CIGARETTE INDUSTRY

TOBACCO INDUSTRY--ANN ARBOR (MICH)

"Teens and children as young as 12 swept through 79 stores in Ann Arbor, Michigan one July day, and left 63 of the shops after buying a pack of cigarettes. The youth volunteered their time to this fourth sting conducted by 'Smokebusters 2000,' an Ann Arbor, Michigan group composed of area doctors, the County Health Department and the local heart association, lung association and cancer society, with funding from state and county boards of health. The 80% success rate was consistent across all four surveys." (p16)

"Local News: Cities & Towns: Ann Arbor Youth Buy Smokes with 80% Success." Tobacco-Free Youth Reporter v5 n2, Sum 1993. p16.

TOBACCO INDUSTRY--ARGENTINA (v19)

TOBACCO INDUSTRY--BRAZIL (v19)

TOBACCO INDUSTRY--CHILE (v19)

TOBACCO INDUSTRY--CHINA (v19)

TOBACCO INDUSTRY--COLOMBIA (v19)

TOBACCO INDUSTRY--EUROPE, EASTERN (v19)

TOBACCO INDUSTRY--GUATEMALA (v19)

TOBACCO INDUSTRY--KENTUCKY (v19)
TOBACCO INDUSTRY--LATIN AMERICA (v19)
TOBACCO INDUSTRY--MICHIGAN

A University of Michigan study "found that in 1992, the total number of tobacco-related jobs in...[Michigan] was 19,127. Of those, 7,843 jobs were directly related to the sale and distribution of tobacco products. Another 11,284 spin-off jobs were generated by increased purchases from Michigan suppliers due to tobacco product sales; spending by people whose incomes came from tobacco sales; and government jobs supported by cigarette excise tax revenues." (p2)

News release. "Tobacco." University of Michigan News and Information Services 4 Mar 1994. p1-4.

TOBACCO INDUSTRY--NEW YORK (NY)

"A New York City Department of Consumer Affairs undercover investigation in April [1993] found 85% of stores surveyed in Manhattan were illegally selling cigarettes to teens. In a one-day sweep on April 26th, six teen volunteers went undercover to buy cigarettes at twenty-one Manhattan groceries, delis, newsstands, drugstores, and smoke shops. All but three stores sold cigarettes to the kids....New York's Tobacco Product Regulation Act bans tobacco sales to anyone under the age of 18 and requires sellers to ask for photo identification if the customer looks younger than 25. Stores are also banned from selling loose cigarettes and must post signs indicating that it is illegal to sell cigarettes to minors....Retailers face fines of up to $300 for failing to post the sign and $300 for selling to a minor. A second violation within a two-year period carries a maximum penalty of $500, and for a third violation, a $1000 fine and mandatory suspension of the cigarette dealer's license." (p16)

"Local News: Cities & Towns: 85% of NYC Stores Sell to Minors." Tobacco-Free Youth Reporter v5 n2, Sum 1993. p16.

TOBACCO INDUSTRY--TAXATION--U.S. (v19)
TOBACCO INDUSTRY--U.S. (v19)

see also ADVERTISING--TOBACCO INDUSTRY--U.S.

"Pension systems, retirement funds, and universities across the...[U.S.] have been profiting from tobacco stock for years. A 1990 study by divestment activist Dr. Gregory Connolly details some $21 billion worth of tobacco stock held by state pension funds, insurance companies, investment funds, banks, college endowments, and academic retirement funds as of December 1987. The state of Texas alone holds nearly $400 million in tobacco stock, including $250 million in its Teacher Retirement System. Connolly, head of the Massachusetts Office for Non-Smoking and Health, has also uncovered $7 billion worth of tobacco stock held by 37 state retirement funds. The California system contains some $500 million in tobacco investments--even though the state is considered a leader in anti-smoking initiatives." (p11-12)

Root, Jay. "The Fight to Switch." Southern Exposure v21 n3, Fall 1993. p11-14. (ISSN0146-809X).

"Compared with the 1992 [U.S. tobacco] season, changes in prices by grade and production areas varied. The season-average price, $1.688 for gross sales (including resales), is 3.8 cents below last year. Average prices were down 6.7 cents in the old and middle belt of North Carolina and Virginia, 2.9 cents in the eastern North Carolina belt, 2.8 cents in the Georgia-Florida belt, and 2.5 cents in the North Carolina-South Carolina border belt. Among the 64 markets having sales, season averages ranged from $1.59 to $1.73 a pound." (p9)

U.S. Dept. of Agriculture. "Flue-Cured." Tobacco Situation and Outlook Yearbook Dec 1993. p8-10.

"Flue-cured tobacco marketings fell 53 percent from 1975 to 1986, before increasing 35 percent by 1992. Marketings fell 1 percent in 1993. Still, the 1993 outturn was 38 percent below 1975's marketings; the 1993 effective quota was 43 percent lower than in 1975. The declines stemmed from reduced use due to decreased cigarette production, less tobacco per cigarette, and substitution of imported flue-cured and air-cured for domestic flue-cured. Between 1975 and 1986, domestic use of flue-cured fell one-third before increasing in 1987 to about 80 percent of 1975's use. Domestic disappearance fell in 1988, rose in both 1989 and 1990, fell in 1991, but rose again in 1992." (p10)

U.S. Dept. of Agriculture. "Flue-Cured." Tobacco Situation and Outlook Yearbook Dec 1993. p8-10.

"The 259,616 American jobs now involved in growing, warehousing, manufacturing, supplying, and selling tobacco products have already dropped and will continue to drop even if no tax increase is enacted. Cigarette production has increased over the past decade, but tobacco related jobs have fallen--due to cost-cutting actions taken by tobacco manufacturers. While U.S. tobacco consumption slowly drops, tobacco exports worldwide are rising dramatically. In 1983, 667 billion cigarettes were manufactured in the United States, compared with 695 billion in 1991. The primary causes of recent tobacco-related job losses is increased mechanization of the production process, while declines in U.S. tobacco farming are caused by the tobacco companies' new policy of importing cheaper foreign tobacco. Over the past ten years, tobacco industry profits have risen, but tobacco farmers have not shared in the wealth. The IRS reports that between 1981 and 1987 tobacco's net income nearly doubled from $2.3 billion to $4.4 billion. At the same time, the tobacco crop value to farmers actually fell. Between 1980 and 1991, farmers' share of the retail tobacco dollar fell from 7% to 3%, while the manufacturers' share rose from 37% to 50%." (p20)

"National News: The Truth about Tobacco, Health, Jobs." Tobacco-Free Youth Reporter v5 n3, Fall 1993. p5,20.

A December, 1992 report, "International Trade: Advertising and Promoting U.S. Cigarettes in Selected Asian Countries," emphasizes that "the dichotomy between U.S. trade goals and U.S. health policy objectives...[which] the GAO [General Accounting Office] reported in 1990 continues to exist, and as a result, American tobacco advertising and promotions are on the rise in these countries. According to USA TODAY (June 9, 1993), between 1991 and 1992, American cigarette exports increased from 179 billion to 206 billion cigarettes. Citing international sources, the May 1993 ASH BULLETIN reported, 'in the developed world, cigarette consumption fell by 6.2% between 1986 and 1991, while in poorer countries it grew by 17.4%. Worldwide, international brands such as Marlboro and Camel are likely to take a bigger share of the market as consumers shift to American-blend cigarettes.'" (p15)

"International News: Report Confirms Flawed Policy." Tobacco-Free Youth Reporter v5 n2, Sum 1993. p15.

TOBACCO USE

see BASEBALL PLAYERS--U.S.--TOBACCO USE; PREGNANT WOMEN--U.S.--TOBACCO USE; YOUTH--U.S.--TOBACCO USE

TOMATO INDUSTRY--U.S. (v19)
TOOTH DECAY

see DENTAL CARIES

TORTURE--TURKEY (v19)
TOURIST TRADE (v19)

see also CUSTOMS ADMINISTRATION AND TOURISTS

TOURIST TRADE--AFRICA

"The World Tourism Organization reports that, in 1990, Africa earned about $4.8 billion from tourism--only three percent of the world's annual tourism dollars, but substantial for this part of the world. There are no statistics on how much came specifically from nature tourism, but Jerry Mallett of the

Adventure Travel Society says Africa 'has tremendous nature tourism potential.' And Wylie Whisonant, Jr., of the U.S. Travel and Tourism Administration, believes ecotourism signifies a change in attitude: 'People are looking for adventure and mystery in a natural setting.'" (p12)

Geffen, Alice. "In Brief: Ecotouring Out of Africa." E Magazine v4 n3, May-Jun 1993. p12. (ISSN1046-8021).

TOURIST TRADE--ALASKA--VANCOUVER (CANADA) (v19)

TOURIST TRADE--AUSTRALIA

"According to the Australian Tourism Commission (ATC), Down Under attracted nearly 3 million international visitors in 1993, a record. Despite the recession, tourism is up 6.5 percent over last year from both the United States and Japan. But that's nothing compared to the massive influx from Asia: it's up a remarkable 85 percent from Korea, and 75 percent from Hong Kong." (p20)

Foster, Catherine. "A Letter from Sydney: Trying the Exotic Down Under." The Christian Science Monitor v86 n83, 24 Mar 1994. p20. (ISSN0882-7729).

TOURIST TRADE--CHINA

"Tourism in China has been playing an important role in the country's economic development. Despite the setback by the Tiananmen Square incident in 1989, China's annual receipts have kept increasing by more than 10% since the 1980s. In 1992, 37 million tourists visited China, earning hard currency of U.S. $3.6 billion (National Tourism Administration of China 1992). Tourism in the Heilongjiang Province of Northeast China is growing at an even faster pace. Since 1989, annual receipts have increased by more than 30%, making the province's tourism sector one of the nation's fastest growing sectors (Tourism Administration of Heilongjiang Province 1993)." (p65)

Xinluo, Zhao. "Research Notes & Communications: Barter Tourism: A New Phenomenon Along the China-Russia Border." Journal of Travel Research v32 n3, Win 1994. p65-67. (ISSN0047-2875).

TOURIST TRADE--CHINA--HONG KONG

"Last year Chinese nationals paid more than 950,000 visits to Hong Kong...Hong Kong residents, meanwhile, visited the mainland almost 21.5m times in 1992--an average of more than three visits for each of the territory's 6m people." (p36)

"Asia: It's Already 1997 in Hong Kong." Economist v329 n7842, 18 Dec 1993. p36-38. (ISSN0013-0613).

TOURIST TRADE--CHINA--U.S.

"The CHINA DAILY reported that almost 700,000 Chinese went abroad on personal business last year. Only 4% of first-time applicants were refused exit permits, compared with 20% in 1992. Many Chinese who want to go abroad on holiday or to study are refused permission not by China but by the countries they want to visit. The United States is particularly strict, fearing that Chinese allowed in for a holiday may stay on in the land of the free." (p32)

"Asia: China and America: The Rights Row." Economist v330 n7849, 5 Feb 1994. p32. (ISSN0013-0613).

TOURIST TRADE--CUBA (v19)

TOURIST TRADE--CUBA--U.S. (v19)

TOURIST TRADE--EMPLOYMENT (v19)

TOURIST TRADE--EUROPE--JAPAN--U.S. (v19)

TOURIST TRADE--FLORIDA (v19)

"With at least 10 tourists killed in the past year, Florida's sun and fun reputation and its $31 billion-a-year tourism industry are on the line....According to the Florida Department of Commerce and Interpol, Canadians are 120 times more likely to be victims of crime in their country than in Florida. The British are 79 times more likely to be victimized at home and Germans are 75 times more apt to be crime victims in their homeland. Florida Department of Law Enforcement statistics show that crimes against non-residents (tourists, migrants, the homeless, airline personnel, etc.) account for only 3.2 percent of crimes committed in the state. But that must be balanced against the stark statistics released in October by the FBI, which ranked Dade County--the Miami area--as having the worst crime rate of the country's large metropolitan areas." (p5 secD)

Smith, Karen Feldman. "Tourism Industry Tries to Reduce Visitors' Fears." Ann Arbor News 16 Jan 1994. p5 secD.

TOURIST TRADE--GREECE--MIDDLE EAST--TURKEY (v19)

TOURIST TRADE--LAS VEGAS (NEV) (v19)

TOURIST TRADE--MEXICO--U.S. (v19)

TOURIST TRADE--NEPAL (v19)

TOURIST TRADE--NEW JERSEY (v19)

TOURIST TRADE--SINGAPORE

"Singapore received a total of 5.32 million visitors in 1990, a figure about double the number of its citizens and permanent residents of 2.69 million. Considering that Singapore is a city state without much scenic endowment bestowed by nature, it is remarkable that it has been able to rank third among Asia Pacific destinations, after that of Malaysia (7.08 million) and Hong Kong (5.93 million) and ahead of Thailand (5.30 million) and Japan (3.24 million). In 1990, the major group of arrivals was that from the ASEAN [or Assn South East Asian Nations] region (27%), followed closely by those from Europe and North America (24%). Japan generated about 18% of the arrivals. In a survey of visitors carried out by the Singapore Tourist Promotion Board, about 74% of those who visited Singapore in 1990 indicated the likelihood of returning within two years. While 62% of these visitors came here solely for the purpose of holiday, the rest were for business (13%), in transit (9%), a combination of business and holiday (4%), and other purposes. The average length of stay of these tourists amounted to 3.3 days, down from the peak of 3.8 days in 1982." (p44)

Ah-Keng, Kau. "Assessing the Market Receptivity of a New Theme Park in Singapore: An Exploratory Study." Journal of Travel Research v32 n3, Win 1994. p44-50. (ISSN0047-2875).

TOURIST TRADE--TURKEY

"In 1984, Turkey received barely 400,000 visitors; in 1992, the number of visitors soared to 7.5 million and the 10 million mark is surely not far away. Tourism in Turkey has developed with lightning speed. It accounted for 16.9 per cent of export earnings in 1989, passed the 25 per cent mark by 1990 and is heading higher still." (p24)

Fromont, Michel. "Regions: Turkey Manages a Boom in Tourism." World of Work i6, Dec 1993. p24-25. (ISSN1020-0029).

TOURIST TRADE--U.S. (v19)

"Tourism is one of our largest industries, ranking as the No. 1 employer in 13 States...and last year domestic and foreign travelers spent $380 billion on tourism activities in the United States. It is a clean industry creating good jobs. At this moment, tourism is a major export success story for the U.S. economy. Last year, international visitors to the United States spent a total of $74 billion, and foreigners spent $20 billion more here than Americans spent traveling abroad. As the market for world tourism grows by leaps and bounds, it is imperative that the United States have a comprehensive strategy for maintaining our favorable balance of trade in this industry. The United States still enjoys the largest share of the world tourism market at 19.3 percent, and any decline in that share represents million of dollars lost to U.S. hotels, motels, theme parks, camps, attractions, restaurants, and retailers." (pS2162)

Hollings, Ernest F. (Sen.-S.C.). "Nomination of C. Gregory Farmer as Under Secretary of Commerce for Travel and Tourism," Congressional Record (1 Mar 1994). Daily ed. pS2162. (ISSN0363-7239).

"The largest single category of U.S. services exports is travel--especially tourism--which totaled $56.5 billion in 1993, or about 30 percent of all services exported that year. But that doesn't mean that Americans spent this much money traveling abroad; rather, it means that foreign travelers spent that sum staying in hotels or sightseeing throughout the United States. Nothing was really 'exported,' but because foreigners paid Americans for a 'product' made in the United States, their purchases were analogous to importing American goods and thus were recorded as U.S. exports. Conversely, when Americans went abroad last year, they 'imported' $42.3 billion of travel services." (p47)

Dentzer, Susan. "On the Economy: Exporting the Truth on Trade." U.S. News & World Report v116 n13, 4 Apr 1994. p47. (ISSN0041-5537).

TOURISTS AND CUSTOMS ADMINISTRATION

see CUSTOMS ADMINISTRATION AND TOURISTS

TOXIC WASTES

see HAZARDOUS WASTES

TOXICOLOGY

see CARBARYL--TOXICOLOGY; LEAD--TOXICOLOGY; PEDIATRIC TOXICOLOGY; PESTICIDES--TOXICOLOGY; VETERINARY TOXICOLOGY--U.S.

TOXICOLOGY, VETERINARY

see VETERINARY TOXICOLOGY

TOYS--U.S.

"Toy revenues [in the U.S.] grew 5.3 percent in 1993, reaching $17.5 billion, up from $17 billion in 1992, according to John Amerman, chairman of Mattel Inc., and the new chairman of the TMA [or Toy Manufacturers of America]. But video-game sales rose 18 percent in 1993, which helped push overall toy sales up. Without the electronic games, toy revenues rose slightly less than 2 percent. Industry officials anticipate sales posting a revenue gain of around 6 percent in 1994." (p9)

Halverson, Guy. "Economy: Thousands of New Playthings, and Not a Child in Sight." The Christian Science Monitor v86 n60, 18 Feb 1994. p9. (ISSN0882-7729).

TOYS--U.S.--ACCIDENTS--MORTALITY

"According to the Consumer Product Safety Commission, between January 1980 and July 1991, 284 children under the age of 10 years choked to death. Of these deaths, 186 involved children's products, including balloons, marbles, small balls, and other toys. Between January 1, 1992 and September 30, 1993, 30 children died from toy-related causes, with almost half of that number (14) caused from choking. In addition, the Commission estimates that in 1992 alone, there were 177,200 toy-related injuries serious enough to be treated in hospital emergency rooms, with almost one-half of the injuries to children under 5 years old." (pS16889)

Gorton, Slade (Sen.-Wash.). "Child Safety Protection Act," Congressional Record (20 Nov 1993). Daily ed. pS16885-16892. (ISSN0363-7239).

"Each year, approximately 30 children die from toy-related causes, and thousands more are injured. In 1992 alone, 177,200 children were treated in hospital emergency rooms for toy-related injuries....According to the CPSC [Consumer Product Safety Commission], between January 1984 and June 1, 1993, 212 toddlers were reported to have drowned in 5 gallon-type buckets when they fell head first into a bucket containing water or other liquid. In addition, each year approximately 130 more toddlers are taken to hospital emergency rooms for treatment." (pS16889)

Bryan, Richard H. (Sen.-Nev.). "Child Safety Protection Act," Congressional Record (20 Nov 1993). Daily ed. pS16885-16892. (ISSN0363-7239).

TOYS--U.S.--CHILDREN--MORTALITY (v19)

TRACTORS--U.S.

"In spite of disastrous crops for many Midwestern farmers last season, 1993 corn prices declined 8 percent from 1991, while the cost of a 40- to 100-horsepower tractor rose 8 percent, according to USDA's Economic Research Service. One tractor can cost an entire year's worth of a family's production and income. In 1975, a new 110-129 horsepower tractor cost about 7,000 bushels of corn. In 1980 it cost 10,000 bushels, and in 1990 the price nearly doubled to 19,000 bushels." (p10)

"How Many Bushels of Corn Will Buy a Tractor?" Land Stewardship Letter v12 n1, Win 1994. p10.

TRADE

see COMMERCE

TRADE-UNIONS--CANADA--U.S.--WOMEN

"According to a study by Susan Eaton, published by the International Labor Organization, the female membership of unions in Canada and the United States has more than doubled in the past 30 years, but women have made little headway into top-level union posts. One example: the report, 'Women Workers, Unions, and Industrial Sectors in North America,' points out that 240,000 women are members of the International Brotherhood of Electrical Workers, or 31% of its total membership; but none of the top international officers are women. The 78-page report also notes: Two-thirds of new union members are women." (p8)

"Books on Women at Work." Union Democracy Review n94, Jun 1993. p8.

TRADE-UNIONS--GREAT BRITAIN (v19)

"Trade-union membership [in Great Britain] is down from 12m in 1979 to 7.5m now. New laws have made union organising much more difficult. The latest requires unions to obtain written permission from each employee for union dues to be deducted directly from their pay packets. The unions are working hard to collect these signatures, but a further fall in membership could result. Yet there are signs that the unions' fortunes may have stopped declining. With less power, they have become more popular. An opinion poll in September 1993 showed that 79% of respondents agreed that trade unions are necessary to protect people's interests at work." (p65)

"Britain: Trade Unions: The Monks' Tale." Economist v330 n7853, 5 Mar 1994. p65. (ISSN0013-0613).

TRADE-UNIONS--KOREA (SOUTH)

"Since 1987 [in Korea] significant legal reforms and far-reaching industrial relations developments have taken place. For example, total union membership increased from 1,050,000 in July 1987 to 1,932,000 in December 1989 in a labour force of some 19 million. Union members then decreased to 1,735,000 in December 1992, a density of approximately 18.5 per cent of permanent employees and the trend appears to be stable. Collective bargaining is now an important means of improving employee working conditions." (p581)

Park, Young-bum. "Industrial Relations and Labour Law Developments in the Republic of Korea." International Labour Review v132 n5-6, 1993. p581-582. (ISSN0020-7780).

TRADE-UNIONS--MINERS--U.S. (v19)

TRADE-UNIONS--U.S. (v19)

"Major collective bargaining settlements reached in 1993 provided smaller wage increases than the contracts they replaced, reflecting a puttering economy for most of the year and a focus by union negotiators on job security and maintaining benefit levels. The 395 new major agreements last year covering 2.1 million workers in private industry called for wage gains averaging 2.3 percent in the first year and 2.1 percent annually over the contract term. The Bureau of Labor Statistics said the replacement contracts averaged 2.9 percent, less than the 3.7 percent average wage gains in the prior settlements. The BLS standard for a major contract is a bargaining unit of 1,000 or more workers. For bargaining units of 5,000 or more workers, 73 settlements were reached in 1993 covering 1.4 million workers....Of the 395 major settlements, 252 were for 36 months or longer. Of the 2.1 million workers, 90 percent will get pay increases, 9 percent will have no rate change and wages will be reduced for 1 percent." (p6)

Oravec, John R. "Economy: Pacts Reflect Economic Ripples." AFL-CIO News v39 n4, 7 Feb 1994. p6. (ISSN0001-1185).

"Union membership [in the U.S.] as reported by the Department of Labor, rose in 1993 for the first time in 14 years. Unions had 16.6 million members in 1993, compared with 16.4 million members in 1992, enough to keep the overall unionized percentage of the work force the same, with continued private-sector decline more than offset by a growth in public employee unionism." (p7)

Lucore, Robert E. "Bargaining: Tough Year of Negotiation Ends on High Note." AFL-CIO News v39 n7, 21 Mar 1994. p7-10. (ISSN0001-1185).

"Union membership [in the U.S.] declined by 157,000 in the import-battered manufacturing sector last year [1993] with the loss of 370,000 factory jobs; it rose in construction by 23,000; declined in wholesale and retail trade by 35,000; and increased in mining by 9,000. Overall, the proportion of union members remained at 15.8 percent as the labor force of wage earners increased by 1.4 million to 105.1 million. Some 9.6 million union members were in the private sector, where they constituted 11.2 percent of the work force, while 7 million were government employees, representing 37.7 percent of the public sector work force. Union members made up 32.9 percent of the work force in communications and public utilities; 28.7 percent in transportation; 20 percent in construction; and 19.2 percent in manufacturing." (p1)

Oravec, John R. "Membership and Union Advantage Moving Ahead." AFL-CIO News v39 n5, 21 Feb 1994. p1,10. (ISSN0001-1185).

"Union membership has shrunk from a high of 35 percent of the work force in 1945 to 22 percent in 1980 to 16 percent today--the lowest since the turn of the century. Only 16 million of 103 million American workers belong to unions--the same as in 1955, when 50 million people were in the work force. The collapse of union representation in the private sector is even more dramatic. Only 11 percent of private workers are now unionized, and the figure probably will sink below 10 percent before the end of the century. Overall union membership has been sustained only by the explosion of unionization in the public sector, which has risen from nearly zero in 1950 to 39 percent today." (p8)

Tucker, William. "Unions Work Toward a Comeback." Insight v10 n2, 10 Jan 1994. p6-11. (ISSN1051-4880).

"The United Auto Workers...has shrunk from 1.4 million members in 1980 to fewer than 900,000 today, while steelworkers union membership has fallen from 1.2 million to fewer than 600,000.... unions' share of the American work force has dropped from 22 percent to a humble 16 percent." (p58)

Hage, David/others. "Business: Unions Feel the Heat." U.S. News & World Report v116 n3, 24 Jan 1994. p57-58,60-61. (ISSN0041-5537).

TRADE-UNIONS--U.S.--WOMEN (v19)

TRADE BALANCE

see BALANCE OF TRADE

TRAFFIC ACCIDENTS--GREAT BRITAIN (v19)

TRAFFIC ACCIDENTS--MICHIGAN

"Drivers in Michigan afflicted with early Alzheimer's disease (AD) are no more likely to pose a health hazard on roads than other elderly motorists, according to a University of Michigan study. 'The results show very few differences between AD drivers, either immediately prior to or following official diagnosis, and a comparable group of drivers not known to have AD,' saysPatricia F. Waller, director of the U-M Transportation Research Institute (UMTRI)....Through the use of driving records available from the state of Michigan, each early AD driver was compared before and after diagnosis with five similar non-AD motorists based on year of birth, gender and county of residence. The study found that the vehicle crash rate of early Alzheimer's patients was 'virtually identical' to that of non-AD drivers. In the five-year pre-diagnosis period, 'AD patients experienced 6.8 collisions per 100 years of driver licensure compared with 6.2 for non-AD drivers,' Waller says....In addition, Waller says no difference exists between the two groups in terms of crash severity. More than 80 percent of collisions for both early AD- and non-AD drivers involve property damage only (i.e., no injuries), with little difference in the amount of damage incurred." (p1-2)

News release. "Driving/Alzheimers." University of Michigan News and Information Services 17 Jan 1994. p1-3.

TRAFFIC ACCIDENTS--MISSOURI--YOUTH

"In Missouri drivers under the age of 21 account for 7.7 percent of licensed drivers, yet in 1991, they were involved in 29.5 percent of all traffic accidents and 26.4 percent of fatal accidents. In 1991, a total of 277 Missourians were killed and 21,171 injured in accidents involving young drivers. That translates to a young driver death or injury accident every 24.5 minutes." (pS16878)

Danforth, John C. (Sen.-Mo.). "High Risk Drivers Act of 1993," Congressional Record (20 Nov 1993). Daily ed. pS16875-16879. (ISSN0363-7239).

TRAFFIC ACCIDENTS--U.S. (v19)

see also DRINKING AND TRAFFIC ACCIDENTS--U.S.

"The National Highway Traffic Safety Administration estimated that the costs...[to] society from all U.S. motor vehicle crashes and injuries that occurred in 1990 were $137.5 billion. The estimate reflects the economic loss of crashes, including lost productivity, property damage, and health care costs. We must recognize, however, that the cost estimate fails to reflect the more devastating costs associated with crashes, the emotional costs of injuries and lost lives. If the current trends continue, over the next 10 years, an estimated 400,000 people will be killed and over 5 million will be hospitalized as a result of highway crashes. We can prevent a substantial portion of the loss by reducing the number of crashes experienced by high risk drivers. In 1991, drivers under the age of 21 experienced the highest crash involvement rate per licensed driver. Nationally, although only 7.4 percent of licensed drivers are between the ages of 16 and 20, they account for 15.4 percent of all driver fatalities." (pS16878)

Danforth, John C. (Sen.-Mo.). "High Risk Drivers Act of 1993," Congressional Record (20 Nov 1993). Daily ed. pS16875-16879. (ISSN0363-7239).

TRAFFIC ACCIDENTS--U.S.--AGED

"According to a 1993 study, drivers 75 years and older were involved in 11.5 fatal crashes per 100 million miles driven, as compared to 2 fatal crashes per 100 million miles for drivers aged 35 to 59. It is estimated that by 2030, those 65 and older will represent 22 percent of the population. In light of the aging American population and the higher propensity of accidents, the concerns of older drivers need to be addressed." (pS16878)

Danforth, John C. (Sen.-Mo.). "High Risk Drivers Act of 1993," Congressional Record (20 Nov 1993). Daily ed. pS16875-16879. (ISSN0363-7239).

TRAFFIC ACCIDENTS--U.S.--AGED--MORTALITY (v19)

TRAFFIC ACCIDENTS--U.S.--COSTS

"A recent analysis has shown that from 1966 to 1990 a fatality reduction of 243,000 lives can be attributed to highway safety programs [in the U.S.]. This life saving saved society $171 billion, based on an estimated $702,000 per fatality. These same programs also reduced the number of injuries, saving society an estimated additional $381 billion. The total cost to society of these programs was estimated to be $162 billion, including government costs as well as cost to the consumer to pay for additional safety features on vehicles. That is, society paid $162 billion to save $552 billion, a ratio of 3.4. Looked at another way, society 'profited' from these programs by $390 billion, an annual average of nearly $16 billion. NHTSA [National Highway Traffic Safety Administration] budgets, which provided much of the leverage for these savings were typically in the $200 to $300 million range, providing a societal return ratio well in the double digit range. True benefit/cost analysis requires an estimate of what society would be willing to pay to avert a fatality. Agency research has shown that value to be $2.6 million for motor vehicle related fatalities. The overall benefit/cost ratio is thus 3.7 times the cost saving ratio, or 12.6." (p189)

Smolkin, Howard (Acting Administrator, National Highway Traffic Safety Admin.). U.S. House. Committee on Appropriations. "Department of Transportation and Related Agencies Approp. for 1994 (Part 4)." Hearing, Washington, D.C.: GPO, 1993. (ISBN0160410738). (Y4.Ap6/1:T68/4/994/pt.4).

"According to a recent report of the National Highway Traffic Safety Administration (NHTSA), traffic fatalities cost the country $137.5 billion a year in lost productivity, medical costs, property damage, insurance administration, and legal and court costs. One third of the first year costs of motor vehicle injuries are paid for by the taxpayer in the form of Medicaid and Medicare payments. Another substantial portion of costs is in the form of lost tax revenues to federal, state and local treasuries. Based on the NHTSA report, fatal crashes alone cost $31.2 billion in 1990--$702,281 for each traffic death. If the societal cost of $702,281 per fatality is applied to the 1,962 reduction in the number of fatalities which occurred between 1991 and 1992, then the U.S. avoided $1.38 billion in medical and other costs during that time period. NHTSA also calculated that in 1992, severe injuries declined 3,256 from 1991 levels. At an average cost of $373,393 for each severe injury, an additional cost of $1.21 billion was avoided as a result of highway safety improvements." (p611)

Arena, James (Director, Highway Traffic Safety). U.S. House. Committee on Appropriations. "Department of Transportation and Related Agencies Approp. for 1994 (Part 7A)." Hearing, Washington, D.C.: GPO, 1993. (ISBN0160411033). (Y4.Ap6/1:T68/4/994/pt.7A).

TRAFFIC ACCIDENTS--U.S.--MORTALITY (v19)

"Between 1990 and 1991 (the most recently available international information) the United States reduction in fatalities was 7 percent (44,599 to 41,462). A review of available information for other countries shows that France experienced a 7 percent reduction and the Netherlands had a 6 percent reduction. Japan experienced a 1 percent reduction in fatalities during this time period. A review of available information on fatality rates per 100 million vehicle kilometers traveled for 1991 shows the U.S. at 1.2, followed by the Netherlands at 1.3. The fatality rate in France was 2.2, while the rate in Japan was 1.8." (p190)

Smolkin, Howard (Acting Administrator, National Highway Traffic Safety Admin.). U.S. House. Committee on Appropriations. "Department of Transportation and Related Agencies Approp. for 1994 (Part 4)." Hearing, Washington, D.C.: GPO, 1993. (ISBN0160410738). (Y4.Ap6/1:T68/4/994/pt.4).

"Last year's motor vehicle death toll [in the U.S.] declined to the lowest level since 1962. The estimated 39,200 fatalities reported for 1992 were 5 percent below the 41,462 deaths in 1991, and sharply lower than the 1990 figure of 44,599. The resulting fatality rate was at an historic low in 1992, falling to 1.8 deaths per 100 million vehicle miles traveled (VMT). Nevertheless, vehicle crashes still constitute more than 90 percent of transportation-related fatalities in this country. Vehicle crashes remain the number one cause of death for persons aged 5-32 and the biggest cause of serious injuries....The medical cost of motor vehicle crash injuries is conservatively estimated to be $14.4 billion annually. Nearly thirty percent of these costs, over $4 billion dollars, are paid by medicare and medicaid." (p5)

Smolkin, Howard (Acting Administrator, National Highway Traffic Safety Admin.). U.S. House. Committee on Appropriations. "Department of Transportation and Related Agencies Approp. for 1994 (Part 4)." Hearing, Washington, D.C.: GPO, 1993. (ISBN0160410738). (Y4.Ap6/1:T68/4/994/pt.4).

"NHTSA [National Highway Traffic Safety Administration] has estimates of traffic fatalities [in the U.S.] beginning in 1899, based on data from the National Center for Health Statistics and state accident summaries....in 1975, NHTSA's Fatal Accident Reporting System began operations. Data on vehicle miles traveled is reported as far back as 1921. Based on available information, the historical high fatality rate was 24.1 deaths per 100 million VMT, which occurred in 1921, the first year of VMT data availability. Therefore, this probably was not the actual highest fatality rate. For more recent times, the fatality rate was 5.5 in 1966. The fatality rate has continued to decline since 1966 to the currently preliminary estimate of 1.8 for 1992." (p24)

Carr, Bob (Rep.-Mich). U.S. House. Committee on Appropriations. "Department of Transportation and Related Agencies Approp. for 1994 (Part 4)." Hearing, Washington, D.C.: GPO, 1993. (ISBN0160410738). (Y4.Ap6/1:T68/4/994/pt.4).

"In 1991, more than 9,100 people died in traffic crashes [in the U.S.] involving more than 8,200 15- to 20-year old drivers. That is more than 22 percent of all fatalities that occurred on our nation's highways in 1991. Moreover, young drivers comprise only 7.1 percent of licensed drivers, but account for 14.9 percent of all driver fatalities according to the latest figures from the National Highway Traffic Safety Administration (NHTSA). Further, while young drivers do only 20 percent of their driving at night, over half of the crash fatalities of adolescent drivers occur during nighttime hours." (p31)

Vogt, Carl W. (Chairman, National Transportation Safety Board). U.S. House. Committee on Appropriations. "Department of Transportation and Related Agencies Approp. for 1994 (Part 6)." Hearing, Washington, D.C.: GPO, 1993. (ISBN0160410746). (Y4.Ap6/1:T68/4/994/pt.6).

In 1992 the U.S. "saw significant continued progress in reducing highway fatalities. For the first time in 30 years--since 1962--the total number of fatalities was below 40,000 (preliminarily set at 39,500). This is 15,000 fewer fatalities than the record high of 54,589 in 1972. By any measure this progress is a major achievement, especially when you consider the increases in the number of vehicles on the road (up 63%), the number of drivers (up 43%) and the number of vehicle miles traveled (up 71%) that have occurred since 1972. The preliminary 1992 data appear to follow the progress made in 1991, according to the just released

Fatal Accident Reporting System (FARS) report. The overall fatality rate per 100 million vehicle miles traveled was 1.8 in 1992, in 1991 it was 1.9 (down from 2.1 in 1990). Moreover, in 1991 (the last year data available) fatalities of passenger car and light truck occupants each experienced declines....Compare this record around the globe and you'll quickly find that this nation--despite our greater number of drivers, vehicles and miles traveled--is a leader in traffic safety. For example, in 1989, the latest year with comparable data, the U.S. was tied with Great Britain for the lowest rate at 2.3 fatalities per 100 million vehicle miles." (p2314)

Hanna, Tom (President, American Automobile Manufacturers Association). U.S. House. Committee on Appropriations. "Department of Transportation and Related Agencies Approp. for 1994 (Part 7B)." Hearing, Washington, D.C.: GPO, 1993. (ISBN0160411041). (Y4.Ap6/1:T68/4/994/pt.7B).

TRAFFIC ACCIDENTS--U.S.--YOUTH

"According to the National Highway Traffic Safety Administration, the age 21 laws throughout the...[U.S.] have saved an estimated 12,300 lives through 1991. Due primarily to the enactment and enforcement of age 21 laws, the proportion of alcohol related fatal crashes among drivers under the age of 21 was reduced from 53 percent in 1980 to a low of 29 percent in 1987. This proportion has begun to rise in the last 3 years going back up to 33 percent." (p152)

Vogt, Carl W. (Chairman, National Transportation Safety Board). U.S. House. Committee on Appropriations. "Department of Transportation and Related Agencies Approp. for 1994 (Part 6)." Hearing, Washington, D.C.: GPO, 1993. (ISBN0160410746). (Y4.Ap6/1:T68/4/994/pt.6).

"The statistical evidence is strong for prohibiting any level of alcohol in the blood of a young driver. As stated in the [National Transportation Safety] Board's March 11, 1993, letter to the States discussing this problem, '...young drivers are over-represented in traffic safety crashes and deaths [in the U.S.]. Thus, they continue to be a major traffic safety concern. In 1990, according to the NHTSA [National Highway Traffic Safety Administration], drivers aged 15-20 years comprised only 7.1 percent of licensed drivers (11.9 million of 168.99 million), but accounted for 14.9 percent of all driver fatalities (3,568 of 23,904 driver fatalities). Further, while young drivers do only 20 percent of their driving at night, over half the crash fatalities of adolescent drivers occur during nighttime hours....first-year drivers (primarily ages 16 and 17) have twice the average number of crashes and, on a miles-driven basis, four times the number of crashes involving more experienced drivers.'" (p152)

Vogt, Carl W. (Chairman, National Transportation Safety Board). U.S. House. Committee on Appropriations. "Department of Transportation and Related Agencies Approp. for 1994 (Part 6)." Hearing, Washington, D.C.: GPO, 1993. (ISBN0160410746). (Y4.Ap6/1:T68/4/994/pt.6).

TRAFFIC ACCIDENTS--U.S.--YOUTH--MORTALITY (v19)

TRAFFIC ACCIDENTS AND DRINKING

see DRINKING AND TRAFFIC ACCIDENTS

TRAFFIC CONGESTION--BANGKOK (THAILAND) (v19)

TRAFFIC CONGESTION--BOGOTA (COLOMBIA)

"Projections for the future, north and south, are...alarming: Bogota, Colombia, a city of 3.8 million in 1980, is expected to grow to 8 million in the year 2000. While it had a very low motorization rate of 4% in 1980, by 2000, every tenth inhabitant is expected to own a car. The car population will grow from 150,00 to 800,000. At the same time, the population density is expected to decrease slightly (with suburbanization), causing the average trip length to grow and mobility to increase slightly (from 1.5 to 1.92 trips per day.) Combining all these factors, the required road space will have to increase by 500% (Urs Heierli, 'Environmental Limits to Motorization.')" (p1)

"Transport & Development: Sustainable Access." IBF News n2, 1993. p1-2.

TRAFFIC CONGESTION--GREAT BRITAIN

"Britain is planning to make its highways a key testing ground in a bid to curb pollution and boost the quality of life of its citizens....The Major government is already committed to introducing a system of electronic tolls on national roads within the next decade. The prime minister says a rising scale of gasoline taxes will be introduced in the next few years. The aim is to reduce what he calls the 'social cost' of road use, mainly air and noise pollution, traffic congestion, and accidents. This social cost can be quantified, says David Pearce, professor of environmental economics at London University, who estimates it at between 23 billion and 26 billion [pounds sterling] ($34 billion-$39 billion) a year.... Government figures indicate that if no effort is made to curb cars on Britain's roads, by 2025 the volume of traffic will be double that in 1989. Britain, a relatively small country with a population of about 57 million, has a concentrated and complex road network." (p4)

MacLeod, Alexander. "International: Remember Rio? Britain to Tax Polluters." The Christian Science Monitor v86 n48, 2 Feb 1994. p4. (ISSN0882-7729).

TRAFFIC CONGESTION--U.S. (v19)

"Americans lose 1.25 billion hours a year in traffic congestion. The Union of Concerned Scientists estimate that two billion gallons of gasoline are wasted each year in traffic tie-ups. Currently, congestion costs the American economy between $10 billion and $30 billion per year. This figure could reach $50 billion a year in 2005 when highway congestion will triple as forecasted by the General Accounting Office. Traffic congestion imposes direct costs upon individuals by increasing personal travel time and vehicle operating costs in terms of fuel and motor oil consumption. For example, the California Chamber of Commerce estimated that traffic delays and rough roads costs motorists $135 per year in lost time and another $97 in fuel and maintenance costs. The Texas Transportation Institute estimated the 1986 per capita cost of congestion (user cost and additional fuel cost) at $330 without the added cost of higher insurance premiums associated with more congestion-related accidents, and $440 per capita including the insurance adjustments." (p829-830)

Mellott, Paul C., Jr. (Executive V.P., H.B. Mellott Estate Inc.). U.S. House. Committee on Appropriations. "Department of Transportation and Related Agencies Approp. for 1994 (Part 7A)." Hearing, Washington, D.C.: GPO, 1993. (ISBN0160411033). (Y4.Ap6/1:T68/4/994/pt.7A).

"Driving a car [in the U.S.] is getting less convenient all the time. Seventy percent of metropolitan rush-hour traffic is now stop-and-go, a 30-percent increase since 1983. Billions of hours--100 million hours a year in the San Francisco Bay Area alone--are lost as commuters sit fuming in traffic jams. And not only the drivers are fuming, as their idling cars pump pollutants into the air. In a 1989 study, University of California at Irvine economics professor Kenneth Small put the health costs of this 'excess pollution' conservatively at $8.4 billion a year--and that doesn't include noise pollution, water pollution from highway runoff, and the contribution of all that carbon dioxide to global warming." (p45-46)

Rauber, Paul. "Priorities: Key to Gridlock?" Sierra v79 n2, Mar-Apr 1994. p45-47. (ISSN0161-7362).

TRAFFIC REGULATIONS--U.S. (v19)

TRAFFIC SAFETY--MICHIGAN

"Researchers stationed at 168 intersections and freeway exits throughout...[Michigan] last fall observed 64.4 percent of drivers and front-seat passengers wearing safety belts, a 13 percent increase from summer 1992. In addition, 99 percent of motorcyclists sighted were wearing helmets." (p1) "Conducted in the state's 28 most populous counties, the study involved 17,719 front-seat occupants in 13,669 passenger cars. It also included 177 motorcyclists, all but one of whom were wearing helmets." (p2)

News release. "Seatbelts." University of Michigan News and Information Services 15 Mar 1994. p1-2.

TRANS-ALASKA PIPELINE (ALASKA) (v19)

TRANS-RACIAL ADOPTION

see INTERRACIAL ADOPTION

TRANSPLANTATION OF ORGANS, TISSUES, ETC. (v19)

TRANSPLANTATION OF ORGANS, TISSUES, ETC.--GREAT BRITAIN--U.S. (v19)

TRANSPLANTATION OF ORGANS, TISSUES, ETC.--MICHIGAN

"Last year, Organ Procurement Agency of Michigan received 423 referrals from hospitals flagging potential donors, up slightly from 1992. However, in 23 percent of those cases, objections from next-of-kin prevented transplants. Ninety-seven potential organ donors were lost last year because doctors could not get proper consent. That figure has steadily increased since 1990, when only 20 percent--72 families--raised an objection....Overall, organ donations in Michigan held steady last year after peaking in 1991, and demand continues to outstrip the supply. In 1993, 163 Michigan residents donated organs upon death, up one from 1992 but still down from an eight-year high of 175 in 1991. The Ann Arbor-based procurement agency, which also goes by the name Gift of Life, has a waiting list of 1,707 state residents who need an organ transplant. The wait has proved too long for some. Since the beginning of the year, 28 transplant candidates have died because their doctors could not acquire organs in time." (p7 secA)

Nord, Thomas. "Fewer Opting for Organ Donations." Ann Arbor News 12 Apr 1994. p7 secA.

TRANSPLANTATION OF ORGANS, TISSUES, ETC.--U.S. (v19)

"As of February 28, 1993, there were 22,799 patients waiting for kidney transplants [in the U.S.] and that number is expected to increase at the annual rate of 20%. Despite the expanding need for organs, the number of cadaveric organ donors has improved only slightly. There were only 4,548 cadaveric organ donors in 1992, an increase of only 0.4% over the number of cadaveric donors (4,530) in 1991. This can be compared to 4,085 cadaveric organ donors in 1988." (p147)

Bowden, A. Bruce (National Kidney Foundation, Inc.). U.S. House. Committee on Energy and Commerce. "Organ Transplant and Bone Marrow Donor Reauthorization." Hearing, 22 Apr 1993. Washington, D.C.: GPO, 1994. (ISBN0160434653). (Y4.En2/3:103-54).

"Because of the tremendous success of transplantation [in the U.S.], more and more people are being placed on the national transplant waiting list. Every 20 minutes, a new patient is added to the national list for an organ transplant. The list has more than doubled since 1987 and has reached a record high of approximately 31,000 individual names. The disparity between the number of people waiting for a transplant and the number of donor organs available is not expected to abate because of the increased success rate of transplantation and the broadening of criteria for patients being considered for transplants. Tragically, the number of patients who die while waiting for an organ transplant has increased dramatically during the last three years. In 1992, more than 2,500 adults and children died while on the national list. Transplantation is a medical miracle that is being sidetracked by the unavailability of a sufficient number of organs. While patients are dying due to the limited number of organs, the waste of perfectly healthy organs occurs daily." (p86)

Bollinger, R. Randal (President, United Network for Organ Sharing). U.S. House. Committee on Energy and Commerce. "Organ Transplant and Bone Marrow Donor Reauthorization." Hearing, 22 Apr 1993. Washington, D.C.: GPO, 1993. (ISBN0160434653). (Y4.En2/3:103-54).

"Despite efforts throughout the...[U.S.] to increase the number and rate of organ donation, donation rates have remained relatively flat. While there was an 11 percent increase in the number of donors in 1990 over the annual rate in the late 1980s, we have reached another plateau in the last few years. It is not possible to link flat donation rates with any one specific cause. Variables such as seat belt and helmet laws, the possibility of transmitting fatal infections and lack of public awareness have been cited as possible factors. Now we are learning that a general mistrust in the medical system and the race and ethnicity of the requestor may influence the decision to donate. Also, studies have shown that not all potential donor families have been approached about donation. This is a delicate and personal issue and we cannot expect universal acceptance overnight." (p32-33)

Harmon, Robert G. (Administrator, Health Resources and Services Admin.). U.S. House. Committee on Energy and Commerce. "Organ Transplant and Bone Marrow Donor Reauthorization." Hearing, 22 Apr 1993. Washington, D.C.: GPO, 1993. (ISBN0160434653). (Y4.En2/3:103-54).

"In 1991, HCFA [Health Care Financing Administration] paid for the transplantation of over 7,000 kidneys, 117 livers and 282 hearts [in the U.S.]. Over 70 percent of kidney transplants and procurement costs nationwide in 1991 were paid by Medicare for a total of $368 million. HCFA's role in monitoring the performance of OPO's [organ procurement organizations] is to ensure that they operate efficiently, and effectively account for Medicare and Medicaid's share of the OPO's costs of making organs available for these transplants." (p35)

Buto, Kathleen A. (Dir., Bureau of Policy Dev., Health Care Financing Admin.). U.S. House. Committee on Energy and Commerce. "Organ Transplant and Bone Marrow Donor Reauthorization." Hearing, 22 Apr 1993. Washington, D.C.: GPO, 1994. (ISBN0160434653). (Y4.En2/3:103-54).

"In 1992, 16,475 individuals received organ transplants [in the U.S.]. Twenty years ago such progress in the science of transplantation and the quality of life of transplant patients would have been unthinkable. However, it is clear that the pace of science has exceeded the awareness of the American people about the importance of organ donation. To date, there are more than 30,000 potential transplant patients on the national waiting list....The increasing disparity between the number of organs available and the list of waiting patients makes it vitally important to ensure that organs are distributed equitably." (p10)

Bliley, Thomas J., Jr. (Rep.-Va.). U.S. House. Committee on Energy and Commerce. "Organ Transplant and Bone Marrow Donor Reauthorization." Hearing, 22 Apr 1993. Washington, D.C.: GPO, 1994. (ISBN0160434653). (Y4.En2/3:103-54).

"In the last 3 years, thanks to vastly improved technology and outcomes, the number of patients [in the U.S.] in a position to receive and who want a transplant has skyrocketed, from 13,115 on the UNOS [United Network for Organ Sharing] Registration list in 1987 to over 30,000 as of February of this year. Yet the numbers of donations has only increased from approximately 6,000 in 1988 to 7,000 in 1991....There is a critical need for increased awareness, and not only among the general public. The fact is that of the more than 6000 critical care hospitals in the United States only about 1 in 6 actually produce donors. Even if only half of the remaining hospitals produced two donors a year, we would vastly reduce the organ shortage in this country. Unfortunately, many of the physicians in these hospitals know little, if anything, about donation. There is a critical need to educate. Yet last year the Department of Transportation had only $400,000 to spend on donor awareness programs....We need at least $2 million in well utilized funds to do a good job on donor awareness. Hopefully, we can coordinate these efforts with the fine work of the Coalition on Donation which is now working on a major Ad Council campaign." (p66)

Penington, Jeff (President, Transplant Recipients International). U.S. House. Committee on Energy and Commerce. "Organ Transplant and Bone Marrow Donor Reauthorization." Hearing, 22 Apr 1993. Washington, D.C.: GPO, 1994. (ISBN0160434653). (Y4.En2/3:103-54).

"The number of transplants and patients requesting transplants have consistently increased each year [in the U.S.] and more patients are either dying at some transplant centers or their condition is deteriorating due to the inequitable allocation of organs as they wait for a suitable match. According to UNOS [United Network for Organ Sharing], in 1989 2,191 transplants were performed nationwide and 830 patients remained on a waiting list. Of the 830 waiting list patients, 300 were on life-support. In 1990, the number of liver transplants increased to 2,555. Approximately 1,880 patients remained on a waiting list. Of those patients on the waiting list, 300 were life-support patients; 200 were non-life-support/intensive care patients; 480 were hospitalized patients; and 900 were home-bound patients." (p117-118)

Tazakis, Andreas (Assoc. Professor of Surgery, University of Pittsburgh School of Medicine). U.S. House. Committee on Energy and Commerce. "Organ Transplant and Bone Marrow Donor Reauthorization." Hearing, 22 Apr 1993. Washington, D.C.: GPO, 1994. (ISBN0160434653). (Y4.En2/3:103-54).

"The primary purpose of the OPTN [Organ Procurement and Transplantation Network] has been to provide a national system [in the U.S.] for listing potential transplant recipients and matching recipients with suitable organs in an equitable manner. The priorities in managing the OPTN have been to provide equal access to transplantation for an ever-growing number of patients in need. Today, more than 30,000 patients are on the OPTN waiting list. Since the last reauthorization we have witnessed a 35 percent increase in the number of patients on the waiting list, while the rate of organ donation has remained relatively flat. The increase in the number of transplants is due to the increased recovery of multiple organs from one donor, and not to a substantial increase in the number of donors. Thus, the task of the OPTN to match organs and recipients has become increasingly more difficult to accomplish each year." (p23-24)

Harmon, Robert G. (Administrator, Health Resources and Services Admin.). U.S. House. Committee on Energy and Commerce. "Organ Transplant and Bone Marrow Donor Reauthorization." Hearing, 22 Apr 1993. Washington, D.C.: GPO, 1994. (ISBN0160434653). (Y4.En2/3:103-54).

"From 1988 to 1992, the annual number of people waiting for transplants rose by 66 percent to nearly 50,000 in 1992. In the same time period, the number of organ donors grew by only 31 percent, with 4,497 donors providing 15,715 organs in 1992. But, even more compelling is the fact that, during this 5-year time period, over 10,000 people died waiting for an organ transplant. At present, over 30,000 Americans are waiting for an organ transplant; tragically, between five and seven people die each day because an organ is not available for transplant." (pS3661)

Hatch, Orrin G. (Sen.-Utah). "Program," Congressional Record (24 Mar 1994). Daily ed. pS3661-3667. (ISSN0363-7239).

TRANSPORTATION

see also BICYCLE COMMUTING; HAZARDOUS SUBSTANCES--U.S.--TRANSPORTATION; HAZARDOUS WASTES--U.S.--TRANSPORTATION; LOCAL TRANSIT; PETROLEUM INDUSTRY AND TRADE--U.S.--TRANSPORTATION; RAILROADS; ROADS; SHIPPING; SUBSIDIES--U.S.--TRANSPORTATION

TRANSPORTATION--CALIFORNIA

"Los Angeles, and the entire State of California, recognizes that there are transportation shortfalls and we are actively working to improve the quality of life for every resident of the state. In addition to a one cent sales tax that is dedicated to transportation improvements, Los Angeles has adopted a 30 year plan that envisions expenditures totaling $186 billion for various transportation projects and improvements. With a population of nearly 9 million people, I am pleased that a light rail system is currently under construction and operating, and should be completed soon." (p1311)

Feinstein, Dianne (Sen.-Calif.). U.S. House. Committee on Appropriations. "Department of Transportation and Related Agencies Approp. for 1994 (Part 7B)." Hearing, Washington, D.C.: GPO, 1993. (ISBN0160411041). (Y4.Ap6/1:T68/4/994/pt.7B).

TRANSPORTATION--COSTS

"Federal funding for transit declined precipitously during the eighties, a total of 52% in real terms in the last twelve years. In 1981, transit received 20% of all U.S. Department of Transportation (DOT) budget authority. By 1991, transit's share of DOT budget authority had dropped to less than 11%, about half of what it was a decade earlier....In 1981, federal assistance represented 78% of transit capital spending in urbanized areas; by 1989 the federal share had dropped to 61%. In 1981, federal assistance was 15% of all transit operating revenue; by 1990 the federal share had dropped to under 5%. Federal operating assistance appropriated for urbanized areas declined by 56% in constant dollars between 1980 and 1992. In contrast, between 1980 and 1990, fares increased by 32% in constant dollars and state and local operating aid increased by 69% in real terms. In 1981, highways received two dollars in federal funds for every federal transit dollar. In 1991, highways received four and one-half dollars in federal funds for every transit dollar. Over the past decade, federal budget authority for highways increased 60% while budget authority for transit declined by 30%." (p740)

U.S. House. Committee on Appropriations. "Department of Transportation and Related Agencies Approp. for 1994 (Part 7A)." Hearing, Washington, D.C.: GPO, 1993. (ISBN0160411033). (Y4.Ap6/1:T68/4/994/pt.7A).

TRANSPORTATION--EUROPE--U.S.

"Population densities in Europe are much higher than in the U.S. While the United States has 70 persons per square mile, Germany has more than 500 persons per square mile. In addition, within European urban areas the population is more concentrated and is more often connected to intercity rail passenger stations by intraurban rail networks. Rates of automobile ownership are also lower in Europe. While there are roughly .6 automobiles per person in the United States, there are only .32 cars per person in the United Kingdom and .41 cars per person in France. The competitive situation is also very different in Europe. The cost of driving, for example, is much lower in the United States. Gasoline prices in the United States average around $1.15 per gallon, but are over $3.25 per gallon in Germany and nearly $4.70 in Italy. The United States also has a well developed system of airports and airline fares, especially since deregulations, are relatively low. Airline yields (fares per passenger mile) are nearly three times higher for scheduled airline service within Europe than in the United States. Europeans are much more likely to fly on air charters for leisure trips and these fares are closer to U.S. fares." (p340)

U.S. House. Committee on Appropriations. "Department of Transportation and Related Agencies Approp. for 1994 (Part 8)." Hearing, Washington, D.C.: GPO, 1993. (ISBN0160410657). (Y4.Ap6/1:T68/4/994/pt.8).

TRANSPORTATION--FRANCE--TEXAS

"The distance from Paris to Lyon is 265 miles. The Dallas to Houston distance is approximately 245 miles (231 miles, according to a federal source). The point-to-point city population to be linked in France by the Paris to Lyon line in 1982 was 2.59 million. The 1990 point-to-point city population for the Dallas-Fort Worth to Houston route is 3.53 million. A comparison of metropolitan areas shows Paris to Lyon, in 1982, connected 9.68 million; Dallas-Fort Worth to Houston, in 1998, will connect 8.98 to 9.23 million people, according to population projections. In 1982, gasoline cost about $1.50 a gallon in France. In Texas, gasoline currently oscillates around $1.15, but will increase to more than $1.25 by 1995, if the proposed BTU tax is enacted (how much more depends upon the price of oil in 1995 and the increases in federal and state taxes). In 1982, the approximate cost of a Paris to Lyon auto trip, (inclusive of gas, depreciation, maintenance, etc.) was $71. In Texas, the approximate cost of an auto trip from Dallas to Houston (inclusive) is about $62 (1990). Airline travel between Paris and Lyon was available in 1982 and cost approximately $88. In Texas, air travel, Dallas to Houston, costs approximately $79 in 1993." (p260-261)

Salci, Larry E. (Texas TGV Corp.). U.S. House. Committee on Appropriations. "Department of Transportation and Related Agencies Approp. for 1994 (Part 7A)." Hearing, Washington, D.C.: GPO, 1993. (ISBN0160411033). (Y4.Ap6/1:T68/4/994/pt.7A).

TRANSPORTATION--LOS ANGELES (CALIF)

"The initial $1.665-billion grant from the Federal Highway Administration to repair LA's roads [after the Northridge quake] 'will not result in earthquake-safe driving,' [Ms. Jan] Lundberg contends. APM [the Alliance for a Paving Moratorium] is backing an alternative that is safer, cheaper, quicker and guaranteed to create more jobs. 'Light rail costs only $10-16 million per mile, compared to as much as $1 billion per mile for new freeways. One train car replaces as many as 100 passenger cars. Rail speeds worldwide average more than 40 kilometers per hour (25 mph) compared to cars, which average about 21 km/hr. (13 mph). Death rates for motor vehicle drivers are about ten times higher than for rail travelers.' Noting that US cars burn 7.3 billion gallons of fuel per year at a cost of $41 billion, while adding 73 million tons of CO2 to the atmosphere, Lundberg believes that it is time to go beyond APM's call for a moratorium on new road construction." (p18)

"After the Quake: A Call for a Car-Free LA." Earth Island Journal v9 n2, Spr 1994. p18. (ISSN1041-0406).

TRANSPORTATION--U.S.

"The FTA [Federal Transit Administration] (then UMTA) program started in 1964, and the first outlays of $47 million were realized in 1965. At that time, 8.3 billion passengers boarded transit vehicles...[in the U.S.], in all modes. Transit patronage fell to 7 billion in 1975, which was its low point. By that year, the FTA program had grown to $2.443 billion. Today, transit patronage is back up to 8 billion passenger trips. A decline that had begun in the mid-1940's was halted in just 15 years, from 1965 to 1980. Transit has undergone significant growth in the extension of transit service to larger geographic areas between 1980 and 1990. Transit bus route miles grew by 24 percent, while commuter rail route miles grew by 15.6 percent and rapid rail grew by 27.5 percent. On a passenger miles basis, mass transit patronage increased by 8 percent from 35.2 billion passenger miles in 1980 to 38 billion passenger miles in 1990. This includes rapid and light rail transit patronage which increased over 30 percent in that period. By comparison, carpooling suffered in both share of trips and in absolute numbers, declining by 12.3 percent between 1983 and 1990 in person miles per vehicle mile." (p867)

McManus, Robert H. (Acting Administrator, Federal Transit Administration). U.S. House. Committee on Appropriations. "Department of Transportation and Related Agencies Approp. for 1994 (Part 4)." Hearing, Washington, D.C.: GPO, 1993. (ISBN0160410738). (Y4.Ap6/1:T68/4/994/pt.4).

"Travel delays in the Nation's largest urbanized areas (UZAs) now cause two billion hours of time to be lost annually. Over the next 20 years, congestion will increase more than 400 percent on the Nation's freeway systems and over 200 percent on other roads, according to the Federal Highway Administration (FHWA). During this period, annual delay in travel time will increase by 5.6 billion hours. The cost of congestion on urban freeways alone, according to a Transportation Research Board report, will increase to $50 billion per year by 2005. Transit provides a low-cost alternative to congestion. The investment costs of transit compare favorably with those of highway construction. Major urban highways can cost $100-120 million per mile, while busways can be built for $4-12 million per mile, light rail for $10-20 million per mile, and heavy rail for costs comparable to or lower than major highways. Transit can substantially reduce congestion. Every bus full of passengers at rush hour removes at least 40 cars from traffic, every full rail car removes 75-125 cars from traffic, and every van full of passengers removes 13 cars from traffic. One high-occupancy vehicle (HOV) lane carries the same number of people as three regular highway lanes." (p747)

U.S. House. Committee on Appropriations. "Department of Transportation and Related Agencies Approp. for 1994 (Part 7A)." Hearing, Washington, D.C.: GPO, 1993. (ISBN0160411033). (Y4.Ap6/1:T68/4/994/pt.7A).

"The 1990 census provides the most recent update on travel patterns. Between 1980 and 1990, significant changes occurred in travel behavior. During this decade, while the population grew by slightly under 10% (to 248.7 million), the number of new workers grew by 19.1% (to 115 million) and vehicles by 17%. In spite of this large rise in workers and vehicles--and perhaps the greatest surprise of the survey--most alternative forms of commuting (e.g. carpooling, vanpooling) fell off precipitously, with carpooling decreasing by over 30% (to just over 13-percent). Interestingly, while telecommuting remains a rather small percentage (3-percent), it nonetheless represented the only--and in fact rather dramatic--growth (up 50-percent) of the alternative commute options....The reasons surrounding this paradoxical growth in both commuting and single auto use have been captured by both quantitative and qualitative accounts. According to the 1990 NTPS survey, over 75% of the population now live in urban areas, and more significantly, over 50% now commute from a suburban residence to a suburban office setting (DOT, 1991)." (p624)

Horan, Thomas A. (Ph.D., Institute of Public Policy, George Mason University). U.S. House. Committee on Appropriations. "Department of Transportation and Related Agencies Approp. for 1994 (Part 8)." Hearing, Washington, D.C.: GPO, 1993. (ISBN0160410657). (Y4.Ap6/1:T68/4/994/pt.8).

"U.S. productivity in the logistics and transportation sector has increased dramatically in the 80's. For instance, logistics costs as a percent of GNP [gross national product] have dropped from 14.7% of GNP in 1981, to 11.0% in 1990. Inventory, as a percent of total sales, has declined dramatically, from 26% in 1981, to 20% in 1990. This is largely due to a more efficient and reliable transportation system that allows us to centralize and reduce inventories, while delivering them reliably and in less time than ever before. Freight transportation expenditures as a percent of GNP have dropped from 8.1% of GNP on average in the 1970's to 6.3% in 1989. Measured another way, the rail freight system increased its productivity by 9.7% in 1992 according to the Labor Department, and the trucking industry's productivity increased by 4.5% in 1992." (p171)

Taylor, John C. (Dept. of Marketing, School of Business Admin., Wayne State University). U.S. House. Committee on Appropriations. "Department of Transportation and Related Agencies Approp. for 1994 (Part 8)." Hearing, Washington, D.C.: GPO, 1993. (ISBN0160410657). (Y4.Ap6/1:T68/4/994/pt.8).

"The enhanced use of transit--increased ridership--must be part of any viable strategy to move our nation toward energy independence. Transportation is responsible for 63% of U.S. oil consumption, and oil imports are nearly 70% of our annual trade deficit. Transit is an inexpensive way to conserve energy. We estimate that every commuter who switches from driving alone to using transit saves 200 gallons of gasoline per year. If 10% of urban commuter trips were replaced by transit, more than 300,000 barrels of oil would be saved each day." (p745)

U.S. House. Committee on Appropriations. "Department of Transportation...Approp. for 1994 (Part 7A)." Hearing, Washington, D.C.: GPO, 1993. (ISBN0160411033).

"Consider...[the U.S.] taxicab industry. The federal Department of Transportation in 1983 found that 87% of the 103 cities studied had restricted entry into the business in some way. Chip Mellor of the Institute for Justice points out that 'In Denver, for instance, only three companies are allowed to operate, and the city has denied every application from new taxicab companies since 1947.' Other cities like Chicago and LA are closed, Boston requires a $60,000 permit fee and New York a $140,000 medallion. Mellor notes that another transportation department study found that taxi industry restrictions cost the consumer $800 million a year and that removing them would create 38,000 new jobs." (p4)

Smith, Sam. "The 'Free Market' Entrance Fee." Progressive Review n317, May 1993. p4-5.

TRANSPORTATION--U.S.--MORTALITY

"America's transportation system again showed safety improvements in 1992 as fewer accidents and deaths were reported compared to previous years. Although only preliminary data is available at this time, it would appear that in 1992 fewer than 40,000 people died on our transportation systems. Transportation-related fatalities in 1991 totalled 43,554, compared with 47,014 in 1990. In aviation, preliminary statistics show the number of fatalities aboard commuter airplanes dropped to 21 in 1992--from 77 a year earlier. Large commercial carriers registered four fatal accidents and 33 fatalities in 1992, compared to the same number of fatal accidents and 50 deaths the year before. The 33 fatalities represent the lowest number of deaths since 1986, when five persons died in that category. In general aviation, although there were fewer fatal accidents (408), more people (812) were killed in 1992 than the previous year. The comparable numbers for 1991 were 414 fatal accidents and 746 deaths." (p9)

Vogt, Carl W. (Chairman, National Transportation Safety Board). U.S. House. Committee on Appropriations. "Department of Transportation and Related Agencies Approp. for 1994 (Part 6)." Hearing, Washington, D.C.: GPO, 1993. (ISBN0160410746). (Y4.Ap6/1:T68/4/994/pt.6).

TRANSPORTATION AND STATE--U.S. (v19)

TRAVEL

see also AIR TRAVEL; AUTOMOBILE TRAVEL; CUSTOMS ADMINISTRATION AND TOURISTS

TREATMENT

see DRUG ABUSE--TREATMENT--U.S.; KIDNEYS--DISEASES--U.S.--TREATMENT; MALARIA--TREATMENT

TROUT--WASHINGTON (STATE)

"In Washington, the bull trout is extinct from much of the mainstem Columbia and its tributaries, including the Okanogan, Lower Yakima, Stehekin/Lake Chelan and Walla Walla rivers. It has been extirpated from about 58 percent of its former range in Montana, at least 12 major Oregon rivers, and the Coeur d'Alene river of Idaho. Studies show that 90 percent of Montana's bull trout stream populations are at moderate to high risks of extinction, and 83 percent have that status in northern Idaho. Throughout its range east of the Cascades, and especially in the Greater Columbia Mountains and Northern Rockies ecosystems, significant declines in bull trout populations have been reported in all but pristine, often roadless, upper headwater streams." (p10)

Murphy, Chris. "Retrieve the Bull Trout from the Brink of Extinction." Northwest Conservation Win 1994. p10.

TRUCK DRIVERS--U.S.--DRUG USE (v19)

TRUCKING--EMPLOYMENT--U.S.

"The Nation's trucking industry generates close to $300 billion in revenues, with the ICC [Interstate Commerce Commission]-regulated sector representing just over a quarter of that total. Intrastate (including local) movements, private carriage, and other exempt movements comprise the rest. Estimates of employment in the trucking industry vary widely. Some sources claim figures as high as 8 million persons. But this figure presumably includes numerous part-time workers. We believe that a reasonable estimate of total full-time industry employment today (including all non ICC-regulated private carriers) would be closer to 4 million. We have no comparable estimate for ten years ago, however, the U.S. Bureau of Labor Statistics (BLS) provides an indication of the trend in trucking employment excluding an undefined proportion of private carriers. BLS indicates that 1.38 million individuals were employed in trucking services in 1981 compared to 1.90 million in 1991." (p159)

McDonald, Gail C. (Chair, Interstate Commerce Commission). U.S. House. Committee on Appropriations. "Department of Transportation and Related Agencies Approp. for 1994 (Part 5)." Hearing, Washington, D.C.: GPO, 1993. (ISBN0160410509). (Y4.Ap6/1:T68/4/994/pt.5).

TRUCKING--U.S.

"Unlike rail, where the past decade has seen significant declines in employment, the trucking industry has had employment growth over this period. And, according to Department of Labor estimates, long-term employment growth in trucking will continue to be strong through 2005. For one sector of the motor carrier industry, the for-hire trucking and warehousing sector (Standard Industrial Code (SIC) 42), the Bureau of Labor Statistics projected 410,000 new trucking industry jobs would be created from 1990 to 2005, with employment rising from 1.638 million to 2.048 million over this period." (p159)

McDonald, Gail C. (Chair, Interstate Commerce Commission). U.S. House. Committee on Appropriations. "Department of Transportation and Related Agencies Approp. for 1994 (Part 5)." Hearing, Washington, D.C.: GPO, 1993. (ISBN0160410509). (Y4.Ap6/1:T68/4/994/pt.5).

"Trucking is the nation's largest freight transportation mode. The trucking industry employs 7.6 million people--more than the populations of 42 of the 50 United States. We have gross freight revenues equal to 5% of the gross domestic product--a total of $278 billion per year. Trucks haul 77% of all manufactured goods and transport 42% of the total tonnage shipped by all modes--2.7 billion tons of freight annually....for the ten year period ending in 1991, the fatal accident rate for commercial trucks was down 40%, even though travel actually increased by 38.7%. In 1991, more people died from falling in their own home than died in accidents involving commercial trucks." (p2647)

Donohue, Thomas J. (President, CEO, American Trucking Associations, Inc.). U.S. House. Committee on Appropriations. "Department of Transportation and Related Agencies Approp. for 1994 (Part 7B)." Hearing, Washington, D.C.: GPO, 1993. (ISBN0160411041). (Y4.Ap6/1:T68/4/994/pt.7B).

TRUCKS--CRASHWORTHINESS--U.S.

"While a vehicle may be relatively safe in the overall driving environment, an assessment of the safety risk in a particular crash mode, e.g., side crashes, may indicate an unreasonable safety risk. The agency's [National Highway Traffic Safety Administration's] analysis showed that in fatal side crashes, GM model year 1973-1987 full size pickup trucks had a fatality rate per million registered vehicle-years of 32.08, compared to the Ford full-size pickup truck rate of 28.04, and the Dodge pickup truck rate of 25.02. Further, in these side impact fatal crashes, GM pickups had a rate of fire-related fatalities that is 2.4 times greater than that of similar Ford pickups (2.83 to 1.16). Finally, in those crashes in which fire caused the fatality (i.e., in which fire was found to be the 'most harmful event'), the rate for GM pickups is 3.5 times greater than the Ford rate (1.47 for GM and .42 for Ford). It is important to recognize that the issue here is not the 'general performance' of these GM pickup trucks. Rather, it is whether the trucks contain a specific defect that creates an unreasonable risk to motor vehicle safety." (p242)

Boehly, William A. (Associate Administrator for Enforcement, National Highway Traffic Safety Admin.). U.S. House. Committee on Appropriations. "Department of Transportation and Related Agencies Approp. for 1994 (Part 4)." Hearing, Washington, D.C.: GPO, 1993. (ISBN0160410738). (Y4.Ap6/1:T68/4/994/pt.4).

TRUCKS--U.S.--ACCIDENTS (v19)

"In 1991 [in the U.S.], there were 2,519 total occupant fatalities in small pickup trucks, of which 121 (about 5 percent) involved occupants in the pickup truck bed. The fatality rate for these vehicles was 226.6 per 100 million registered vehicles, or a relative fatality rate of 1.2 compared with all passenger vehicles (182.0 per 100 million registered vehicles). If none of these 121 fatalities had occurred, the fatality rate per 1,000 registered vehicles would have been 5 percent lower, or 214.9 per 100 million registered vehicle years, which equates to a relative fatality rate of 1.2; the difference is lost in the rounding. Therefore, fatalities in the pickup truck bed is a relatively small problem." (p373)

Boehly, William A. (Associate Administrator for Enforcement, National Highway Traffic Safety Admin.). U.S. House. Committee on Appropriations. "Department of Transportation and Related Agencies Approp. for 1994 (Part 4)." Hearing, Washington, D.C.: GPO, 1993. (ISBN0160410738). (Y4.Ap6/1:T68/4/994/pt.4).

"Federal accident data indicate that although combination trucks account for only 1.8 percent of all U.S. highway accidents, they are involved in 6.7 percent of all fatal accidents. The number of fatal accidents per 100 million miles for combination trucks is nearly double that of passenger cars. More than 5,000 people are killed every year in the United States in heavy truck accidents." (p29)

Vogt, Carl W. (Chariman, National Transportation Safety Board). U.S. House. Committee on Appropriations. "Department of Transportation and Related Agencies Approp. for 1994 (Part 6)." Hearing, Washington, D.C.: GPO, 1993. (ISBN0160410746). (Y4.Ap6/1:T68/4/994/pt.6).

TRUCKS--U.S.--WEIGHT

"The FHWA [Federal Highway Administration] has had more than 10 years of experience using data provided by the States to evaluate the effectiveness of State vehicle size and weight enforcement programs. While year-to-year comparisons of such information as trucks weighed and citations issued provide some indication as to the effectiveness of the State's program, the basic questions 'What are the magnitude and location of the overweight truck problem?' remain unanswered. The 1990 State certifications showed that more than 149 million trucks were weighed of which nearly 623,000 were found to be overweight. This information demonstrates very good compliance with about 0.4 percent of all trucks weighed found in violation. However, data from WIM [Weight-In-Motion] surveys and weigh scale bypass studies show much higher percentages of trucks to be overweight. In these surveys and studies, it is not uncommon to find 10 to 20 percent of trucks weighed to be overweight. Data from the weigh stations as reported in the State certifications, therefore, appear to underrepresent the number of overweight trucks in actual operation." (p371)

U.S. House. Committee on Appropriations. "Department of Transportation and Related Agencies Approp. for 1994 (Part 3)." Hearing, Washington, D.C.: GPO, 1993. (ISBN0160410649). (Y4.Ap6/1:T68/4/994/pt.3).

TRUCKS--WEIGHT--GOVERNMENT POLICY--U.S.

"States [in the U.S.] determine the fees to be charged for overweight [vehicle] permits as well as penalties to be assessed for violating vehicle size and weight laws. Current permit fee and overweight fine schedules are reported annually to the Congress in FHWA's [Federal Highway Administration] publication 'Overweight Vehicles--Penalties & Permits.' In 1989, the average permit fee for a 4000-pound gross weight overload was $16.78, and the average overweight fine was $182.25. Permit fees ranged from no charge to $60 for 4000 pounds overweight. The fine for 4000 pounds overweight ranged from $10 to $700. If the cost of pavement damage ranges between 4 and 16 cents per ESAL-mile, the cost of an 84,000-pound truck traveling 100 miles would be between $16 and $64. ESAL stands for 18,000-pound equivalent single axle load and is the primary measure of pavement wear used in the United States." (p372-373)

U.S. House. Committee on Appropriations. "Department of Transportation and Related Agencies Approp. for 1994 (Part 3)." Hearing, Washington, D.C.: GPO, 1993. (ISBN0160410649). (Y4.Ap6/1:T68/4/994/pt.3).

TUBERCULOSIS (v19)

"While intensive public health initiatives and advanced treatments helped stem the spread of tuberculosis in the 20th century, the disease has increased worldwide since 1985 and kills 3 million people each year. The TB bacterium, which can develop into full-blown tuberculosis, is now carried by one third of the world's population. More than 15 million people in the United States are infected with the bacterium and have a 10% chance of suffering from active tuberculosis during their lives." (p10)

Nightingale, Marisa. "Tuberculosis: A Killer Comes Back." Frontier Spr 1994. p10-11.

"An individual can have TB [tuberculosis] that is resistant to one or more of the front-line antituberculosis drugs. The term multidrug-resistant TB (MDR-TB) refers to TB that is resistant to two or more antituberculosis drugs....MDR-TB is very difficult and costly to treat (Centers for Disease Control 1992a; National MDR-TB Task Force 1992). If a patient has MDR-TB, the duration of treatment increases from six months to between eighteen to twenty-four months, and cure rates decrease from nearly 100 percent to under 60 percent (National MDR-TB Task Force 1992). Total MDR-TB treatment costs can reach approximately $150,000, which is about ten times the costs of drug-susceptible TB treatment; and the costs of drugs for MDR-TB can reach $6,000, or approximately twenty-one times the costs of drugs for drug-susceptible TB (Institute of Medicine 1992)." (p111)

Gittler, Josephine. "Controlling Resurgent Tuberculosis: Public Health Agencies, Public Policy, and Law." Journal of Health Politics, Policy and Law v19 n1, Spr 1994. p107-147.

TUBERCULOSIS--AUSTRALIA (v19)
TUBERCULOSIS--CANADA (v19)
TUBERCULOSIS--CHINA (v19)
TUBERCULOSIS--EUROPE (v19)
TUBERCULOSIS--ITALY--SWITZERLAND--U.S. (v19)
TUBERCULOSIS--JAPAN (v19)
TUBERCULOSIS--MEXICO (v19)
TUBERCULOSIS--MORTALITY (v19)
TUBERCULOSIS--NEW ZEALAND (v19)
TUBERCULOSIS--TANZANIA (v19)
TUBERCULOSIS--U.S. (v19)

"The rise of tuberculosis in recent years is placing a heavy and unexpected additional burden on the health care system. Thirty thousand new active cases are reported each year in the United States, with over 1,700 deaths, up from 22,000 in 1985. The most ominous development is the alarming increase in drug-resistant highly infectious strains of the disease that have caught the country unprepared." (pS16983)

Kennedy, Edward M. (Sen.-Mass.). "Preventive Health Amendments of 1993," Congressional Record (22 Nov 1993). Daily ed. pS16982-16983. (ISSN0363-7239).

"In the early 1970s, federal budget officials [in the U.S.] all but declared victory in the war on tuberculosis. Mandatory childhood screenings, mobile X-ray vans and powerful new drugs had helped reduce the killer lung disease from more than 80,000 reported cases in 1953 to fewer than 40,000 a year. So, between the late 1960s and the early 1980s, federal spending on TB control was slashed from more than $15 million annually to less than $5 million. And for 10 years up to 1982, federal TB grants were eliminated....But then, in clinics from San Francisco to Harlem, public health officials noted an alarming resurgence in TB among whole new categories of patients: Asian refugees, middle-class men diagnosed with AIDS and the homeless. Between 1985 and 1992, the number of new TB cases reported shot up by 20 percent. By the time Washington caught up with the crisis, solutions had become far more expensive. TB appropriations for the Centers for Disease Control and Prevention jumped to $46 million in fiscal 1992, then to $104 million in 1993." (p52-53)

Hage, David. "Business: Weeding Out Waste." U.S. News & World Report v116 n1, 10 Jan 1994. p51-53. (ISSN0041-5537).

TUBERCULOSIS--U.S.--COSTS (v19)
TUBERCULOSIS--U.S.--FARMERS

"Farmworkers have different and more complex health problems than the general population. They suffer more frequently from infectious diseases than the general population. These include diseases related to poor sanitation like dysentary, hepatitis, typhoid fever, and other respiratory and intestinal ailments. Recently, the growing incidence of tuberculosis among farmworkers was widely reported in the press. Parasitic infections afflict farmworker adults and children an average of 20 times more than the general population, and estimates of prevalence of these infections range from 27-59% in this group." (p87-88)

Schneider, Cynthia G. (Staff Attorney, Migrant Legal Action Program). U.S. House. Committee on Energy and Commerce. "Medicaid Managed Care in California." Hearing, 20 Apr 1993. Washington, D.C.: GPO, 1994. (ISBN0160434122). (Y4.En2/3:103-52).

TUITION
see COLLEGE COSTS

TUNISIA
see also MOROCCO--TUNISIA--SOCIAL CONDITIONS

TUNISIA--ECONOMIC CONDITIONS

"Fiscal reforms, including the introduction of a value-added tax in 1988, have boosted revenues [of Tunisia], enabling the government to reduce the budget deficit to some 2 per cent of gross domestic product (GDP) in 1993 from nearly 6 per cent in 1989." (p26) "Above all, since 1987, Tunisia has enjoyed average growth of 5 per cent a year. This is despite two successive years of drought--1988-89--and a sharp drop in earnings from tourism in 1990-91. With a successful family planning programme reducing the population growth rate to under 2 per cent, Tunisia's overall per capita income has continued to register steady improvement." (p27)

Marks, Jon. "Tunisia Moves beyond Adjustment." Africa Recovery v7 n3-4, Dec 1993-Mar 1994. p26-31.

TURKEY
see also KURDS--TURKEY; TOURIST TRADE--TURKEY

TURKEY--EMPLOYMENT

"Low union density means that a large proportion of workers do not get the benefits of unionization and collective bargaining. In 1990, for example, about 21 per cent of wage/salary earners [in Turkey] were unionized or covered by collective agreements. Among employees covered by the Social Insurance Scheme the figure was about 45 per cent (Koray, 1992). The highest density occurred in industries heavily concentrated in the public sector: 95 per cent in general services and in communications, 94 per cent in national defence, 86 per cent in the sugar industry, 82 per cent in the energy sector, and 73 per cent in railways. In the SEEs [state economic enterprises], however, union membership declined between 1985 and 1990, because of a major change in employment practices introduced in 1984 under the legislation that launched the privatization programme (Legislative Decree No. 233, of 8 June 1984)." (p692)

Dereli, Toker/Zeytinoglu, Isik Urla. "Public Sector Industrial Relations on the Eve of Mass Privatization in Turkey." International Labour Review v132 n5-6, 1993. p689-702. (ISSN0020-7780).

TURKEY--SOCIAL CONDITIONS

"Turkey is the only country in the Middle East that is likely to reach replacement fertility by 2015. Its GNP [gross national product] per capita grew by an average of 2.6 percent per year during the period 1965-90, to $1,630 (World Bank, 1992). Life expectancy was 65 years in 1985-90, and infant mortality fell by 60 percent from 1960-65 to 1985-90, to a level of 68 deaths per 1,000. Female literacy was 71 percent in 1990, with total adult literacy at 81 percent. Female primary plus secondary school enrollment doubled from 35 percent to 72 percent from 1960 to 1990....Contraceptive prevalence outran program improvements, rising steadily from 22 percent in 1963 to 37 percent in 1973, 51 percent in 1983, and 63 percent in 1988. The country's TFR [total fertility rate] fell from 6.11 in the early 1960s to 3.79 in the late 1980s, a decrease of 2.3 births per woman." (p86)

Mauldin, W. Parker/Ross, John A. "Prospects and Programs for Fertility Reduction, 1990-2015." Studies in Family Planning v25 n2, Mar-Apr 1994. p77-95. (ISSN0039-3665).

TURKEY INDUSTRY--EUROPEAN ECONOMIC COMMUNITY (v19)
TURKEY INDUSTRY--MEXICO--U.S. (v19)
TURKEY INDUSTRY--MINNESOTA (v19)
TURKEY INDUSTRY--U.S. (v19)
TURKMENISTAN (v19)
TURKMENISTAN--POPULATION

"Turkmenistan's population of 4.2m is scattered over a vast area, 90% of it covered by the Obe Kara Kum, or Black Sands. Among the Turkmen are some 400,000 ethnic Russians and other Russian-speakers." (p42)

"Asia: Turkmenistan: Beloved Still." Economist v330 n7847, 22 Jan 1994. p42. (ISSN0013-0613).

UGANDA

see COFFEE INDUSTRY--UGANDA; DEBTS, PUBLIC--UGANDA; MORTALITY--UGANDA

UGANDA--ECONOMIC CONDITIONS (v19)
UKRAINE--ECONOMIC CONDITIONS (v19)
ULCERS (v19)
ULTRASONICS IN OBSTETRICS--INDIA (v19)
ULTRAVIOLET RADIATION

"For the first time, scientists at the Unviersity of Chicago have been able to establish an absolute increase in ultraviolet radiation in a populated area. Episodic increases as large as 45% above historical values have been estimated for some recent periods based on readings in southern Argentina. This means that the average ultraviolet increases projected for the year 2000 are already periodically exceeded at some locations. Moreover, these increases occurred at summer solstice, when damaging consequences are most likely to occur." (p4)

Oppenheimer, Michael. "EDF Column: Clearing Up the Confusion about Ozone Depletion." EDF News v24 n5, Sep 1993. p4.

"Recent scientific findings show the 1992 and 1993 global ozone levels to be the lowest since records of satellite observations started in 1978. A 10% reduction in ozone could lead to as much as a 15-20 per cent increase in UV exposure....Increased exposure to ultraviolet radiation stunts plant growth, adversely affects photosynthesis and diminishes disease resistance.... Excessive ultraviolet radiation exposure is known to be associated with increase in skin cancers, diseases of the eye and a reduced ability of the body to combat infectious diseases." (p1)

News release. "Ultraviolet Radiation Can Seriously Damage Your Health." WHO Press 17 Dec 1993. p1-2.

UNEMPLOYMENT (v19)

"According to most estimates, the NAIRU [non-accelerating-inflation rate of unemployment] has been rising in OECD [Organization for Economic Cooperation and Development] countries since the 1960s. And most studies reckon it to be higher in Western Europe than in America or Japan. One [study entitled 'Unemployment: Macroeconomic Performance and the Labour Market', by R. Layard, S. Nickell and R. Jackman] puts Japan's NAIRU in the 1980s at 2%, compared with 6% in America and 8% in Britain and France." (p70) "Payments to unemployed people, and their duration, vary widely between countries....In America, a production worker's 'replacement rate'--the ratio of unemployment benefit to wages--averaged 36% in 1990, and benefit was paid for 26 weeks at most. In Holland, by contrast, unemployment pay averaged 75% of wages and lasted for up to three years." (p71)

"Schools Brief: A Bad Case of Arthritis." Economist v330 n7852, 26 Feb 1994. p70-71. (ISSN0013-0613).

"Few people remember when unemployment in OECD [Organization for Economic Cooperation and Development] countries averaged a modest 2-3% of the labour force during the 1950s and 1960s. Today, a record 35m people, or 8.5%, are on the dole, up from 25m as recently as 1990. Some countries have been hit harder than others: Japan's official jobless rate is only 2.9%, Spain's is a horrendous 23.1%. Indeed, Europe as a whole is an unemployment black spot: the average jobless rate in the European Union (EU) is expected to hit 12% this year, almost double America's 6.5%. It was not always so. In the 1960s and 1970s America's unemployment rate was twice Western Europe's....It is only since the early 1980s that Europe has had a higher rate than America. While America's current jobless rate is slightly lower than in 1980, Europe's dole queues have lengthened unremittingly over the past two decades, from 2.4% in 1970, to 6% in 1980, to almost 12% now." (p74)

"Schools Brief: Labour Pains." Economist v330 n7850, 12 Feb 1994. p74-75. (ISSN0013-0613).

"In the OECD [Organization for Economic Cooperation and Development] as a whole, the total labour force--all those working or seeking work--rose from 42.8% of the population in 1966...to 47.3% of the population in 1989 (the most recent year easily available). The percentage of the OECD population which was working increased also, from 41.6% to 44.2%--but not as much. The balance was made up by unemployment: the average OEC unemployment rate rose from 2.7% to 6.4% of the labour force." (p58)

Munford, Michael. "Unemployment and the Problem of Work." Quadrant v38 n1-2, Jan-Feb 1994. p56-60. (ISSN0033-5010).

"The unemployment rate has hit some record highs and lows: During the Great Depression of the 1930s, the unemployment rate was about 25 percent; in the early 1950s, the unemployment rate was in the 2.5 percent range, which oddly enough might have been below full employment. When economists say 'full employment,' they are referring to the unemployment rate below which inflation worsens. Economists now consider the full employment rate at 5.5 to 6 percent unemployment. Once the jobless rate reaches this level, the Federal Reserve often begins to hike interest rates." (p11)

Scherer, Ron. "Briefing: Unemployment in the US: Jobless Figures Will Change." The Christian Science Monitor v86 n31, 7 Jan 1994. p11. (ISSN0882-7729).

UNEMPLOYMENT--ALBANIA

"Unemployment, led by factory closings, layoffs in businesses which are being restructured, and the flood of mostly unqualified young people onto the labor market, is rapidly increasing. It reached 23 per cent according to the Ministry of Labor, though according to trade unions the figure is twice as high....Another major problem is the increase in various forms of economic and social exclusion. The unemployment compensation system is overburdened. Some 250,000 unemployed receive a modest benefit, but an ever higher percentage of those out-of-work--who are either not entitled to or have exhausted their benefits--find themselves with no resources whatsoever. Furthermore, Albania must face up to the problem of former political prisoners who, along with their families, number nearly 500,000 people in urgent need of social protection, vocational training and reinsertion." (p22)

Fromont, Michel. "Regions: Reconstructing Albania from the Ruins." World of Work n7, Mar 1994. p22-23. (ISSN1020-0029).

UNEMPLOYMENT--AUSTRALIA--GREAT BRITAIN

"If more people seek work, unemployment will rise, and it will be more difficult to get a job, even if there are just as many jobs available....In Britain, for example, the total number of people working in 1989 was 26.5 million, or 46.2% of the population: both these figures were higher than at any time since 1969, and possibly higher than at any time ever. Yet in the same year, 1.7 million people were unemployed: 6.1% of the labour force: more unemployment than at any time in the fifties, sixties or seventies. More jobs had not got rid of unemployment, because the number of people seeking work had grown even more....In 1989, 46.3% of the Australian population was working. This was the highest percentage ever recorded. In the same year, 2.8% of the Australian population, or 5.7% of the Australian labour force, was unemployed." (p57-58)

Munford, Michael. "Unemployment and the Problem of Work." Quadrant v38 n1-2, Jan-Feb 1994. p56-60. (ISSN0033-5010).

UNEMPLOYMENT--CALIFORNIA

"The unemployment rate [in California], 8.7 percent, is 2.3 points above the national average. Employment, which peaked at 13 million at the end of 1990, is a million jobs short of that total today." (p35)

Levinson, Marc/Murr, Andrew. "Special Report: Getting Back to Business." Newsweek v123 n5, 31 Jan 1994. p35-36. (ISSN0028-9604).

"Over the past three years, 526,000 Californians have lost their jobs, 90 percent of them in the south. In Los Angeles County alone, nearly 400,000 have been tossed out of work." (p31)

Roberts, Steven V./others. "Special Report: Breaking Point." U.S. News & World Report v116 n4, 31 Jan 1994. p26-32,36. (ISSN0041-5537).

UNEMPLOYMENT--CANADA (v19)

UNEMPLOYMENT--CHINA

"The total of urban unemployed [in China] in 1990 amounted to 3.8 million or about 2.6 per cent of the urban workforce. Over the 1991 to 1995 period it is estimated that employment will need to be found for about 36 million city residents and 100 million rural people. Estimated unemployment rates do not include surplus of underemployed labor; some estimates suggest that state-owned enterprises usually employ 15 to 20 per cent more labor than they actually require." (p24-25)

von Rohland, Hans. "Regions: Social Security in China: The Shattered Rice Bowl." World of Work n7, Mar 1994. p24-25. (ISSN1020-0029).

UNEMPLOYMENT--EUROPE

"Most voters [in Europe], while plainly worried about persistently high unemployment and the growing threat to social services, are uncertain about how to respond. Young people in particular, who are usually the main source of social innovation, are now generally apathetic and quiescent. Rather than becoming actively involved in politics, they devote their time to worrying about a bleak economic future. Unemployment rates for individuals aged 16-24 offer ample causes for fear and despair. In France, the jobless figure for this group stands at 23 percent; in Italy, it is 28 percent; and in Spain, more than one in every three young people is without work." (p5)

Baldwin, Geoffrey. "Farewell to Europe's Welfare State." Toward Freedom v42 n6, Oct 1993. p4-5. (ISSN0048-9898).

UNEMPLOYMENT--EUROPE--JAPAN--U.S.

"How does America's unemployment match up against that in other countries? Official figures say that Japan's jobless figure is far lower than America's, at only 2.9%, whereas most European economies have 10% or more....Using...results, [from the Bureau of Labor Statistics,] Tapan Datta, an economist at American Express Bank, estimates that at the end of 1993 America's 'effective' unemployment rate (including discouraged and involuntary part-time workers) was as high as 9.3%. But Japan has even more discouraged workers, particularly women. Adding in these, Japan's jobless rate is 9.6%. Europe, by contrast, tends to have fewer discouraged workers. In France, adding them in lifts unemployment only from 12.0% to 13.7%." (p25)

"American Survey: The Overlooked Housekeeper." Economist v330 n7849, 5 Feb 1994. p25. (ISSN0013-0613).

UNEMPLOYMENT--EUROPE, EASTERN--WOMEN

"With economic reform and the introduction of a competitive labour market, women have become particularly vulnerable to unemployment in all of Eastern Europe. The exception is possibly Hungary, where women's willingness to work for very low wages has created a preference for female workers in some sectors. In Poland, the proportion of the unemployed who are women is growing steadily. By April 1992, they constituted nearly 53 per cent of the unemployed, as opposed to 45 per cent of the workforce. In the former GDR [German Democratic Republic], women's unemployment rates have risen much faster than men's. Between mid-1989 and mid-1991 they rose by 500 per cent, compared with 300 per cent for men. Of those registered unemployed in Romania in September 1990, 85-90 per cent were women. In Czechoslovakia, Bulgaria, and Albania, women represent about 60 per cent of the unemployed." (p78)

Watson, Peggy. "The Rise of Masculinism in Eastern Europe." New Left Review n198, Mar-Apr 1993. p71-82. (ISSN0028-6060).

UNEMPLOYMENT--EUROPEAN ECONOMIC COMMUNITY (v19)

UNEMPLOYMENT--EUROPEAN ECONOMIC COMMUNITY--U.S. (v19)

UNEMPLOYMENT--FRANCE

"Currently 1 of every 4 French youths aged 18 to 26 is out of work. And with many economists citing France's minimum wage of 5,900 francs (about $1,000) a month as a heavy impediment to hiring, most observers believe that the minimum wage will have to be addressed if high youth unemployment is to be reduced." (p3)

LaFranchi, Howard. "International: Students Pound the Streets and Paris Beats a Retreat." The Christian Science Monitor v86 n87, 30 Mar 1994. p3. (ISSN0882-7729).

UNEMPLOYMENT--GERMANY (v19)

UNEMPLOYMENT--GREAT BRITAIN--U.S. (v19)

UNEMPLOYMENT--INDIANS OF NORTH AMERICA

"The average unemployment rate on Indian reservations stands at 56 percent as compared to 7 percent for the rest of the country. Per capita income ranks the lowest for American Indians as compared to the rest of the U.S. population. In addition, the lack of financial infrastructure and even basic banking services make it virtually impossible for tribes to create new jobs, revitalize their communities, and enhance local business development." (pH10524)

Furse, Elizabeth (Rep.-Oreg.). "Regulatory Reform Act of 1993," Congressional Record (21 Nov 1993). Daily ed. pH10500-10524. (ISSN0363-7239).

UNEMPLOYMENT--ISRAEL

According to Yair Tsaban, Israel's minister for absorption, "unemployment among the Russian immigrants has fallen to 17% from 36% two years ago. He concedes that about two-thirds of those who have found jobs are not yet employed in their original professions, and that some never will be. With 9,000 doctors, for example, Israel had more physicians than it needed even before the new immigration brought in 4,000 more. For Russian women, and older men, any kind of work can be hard to find. But the statistics show that after a couple of years in the labour market immigrants begin to climb up to better jobs. One encouraging sign is that about 70,000 Russian families, a third of the total, have felt confident enough about their future in Israel to take out home loans." (p13)

"Survey: Israel: A Coat of Many Colours." Economist v330 n7847, 22 Jan 1994. p58(10,13-14). (ISSN0013-0613).

UNEMPLOYMENT--LOS ANGELES (CALIF) (v19)

UNEMPLOYMENT--NORTHERN IRELAND (v19)

UNEMPLOYMENT--PHILADELPHIA (PA) (v19)

UNEMPLOYMENT--PORTUGAL

"Latest official unemployment figures [in Portugal] are close to 6 percent--a 35 percent increase in the number of jobless, with the hardest hit sectors being textiles, footwear, retail, and construction. Unemployment appears ready to climb to between 7 and 8 percent of the work force in 1994, still low compared to the EU average of about 11 percent. But some believe the true rate is disguised when part-time work and unpaid wages are taken into account. The population still has to contend with the lowest wages in the EU and an insufficient social security system." (p29)

Provan, Sarah. "Member Country Report: Portugal." Europe n333, Feb 1994. p28-29. (ISSN0191-4545).

UNEMPLOYMENT--RUSSIA--SPAIN

"For 22 countries, rich and poor...[the ECONOMIST] examined over 30 indicators which sum up the economic, social, cultural and political aspects of life." (p39) "Unemployment is something which some governments try to lie about. For example, Russia boasted an official jobless rate of only 0.8% of the workforce in 1992....But independent estimates suggest that it is really 7-10%. Spain is more honest, admitting to the highest unemployment rate (18.4%) of the 22 countries." (p40)

"Where to Live: Nirvana by Numbers." Economist v329 n7843, 25 Dec 1993. p39-42. (ISSN0013-0613).

UNEMPLOYMENT--SPAIN (v19)

"Official figures put the number of people [in Spain] without work at the end of 1993 at 3.55 million--or 22.99 percent of the working population. Last year alone, 345,000 jobs were lost, pushing memories of the Barcelona Olympics and Spain's 1492-1992 celebrations firmly into the background." (p6)

Tremlett, Giles. "International: Layoff Law Spurs Strike in Spain." The Christian Science Monitor v86 n45, 28 Jan 1994. p6. (ISSN0882-7729).

UNEMPLOYMENT--U.S. (v19)

"Unemployment rates, while they cannot and should not be ignored for policymaking purposes, are more likely to be indicative of short-term shifts in the economy than they are representative of long-term trends and changes in society itself. Between 1970 and 1990, unemployment rates [in the U.S.] moved in a range that went from a low of 4.9 percent in 1970 and 1973 to a high of 9.7 percent in 1982. The unemployment rate for 1990 was 5.5 percent, rising to 6.7 percent in 1991 to reflect the weaker economy at that time. There has been no consistency over the past decade in the relationship between the adult male unemployment rate and the adult female unemployment rate, with the male rates being higher in some years and the female rates in others. On the other hand, the unemployment rates of blacks (specifically) and minorities (generally) were at least 5 percentage points higher than the rates for whites throughout the 1980s. In the early 1980s, the spread between black and white unemployment rates was roughly 9 or 10 percentage points, closing to a 6 or 7 percentage point difference in the latter half of the decade." (p183)

Jones, Linda R. Wolf (Director, Income Security Policy, Community Service Society of N.Y.). U.S. House. Committee on Ways and Means. "Historical Trends in Poverty and Family Income." Hearing, 26 Oct 1993. Washington, D.C.: GPO, 1994. (ISBN0160435765). (Y4.W36:103-42).

"Last year was not a good year for American workers and their families. It started with unemployment at 7.1 percent, it ended with unemployment at 7.3 percent, and unemployment stayed above the 7 percent figure all year. The average number of people unemployed each month was 9.4 million, which means that some 23 million people or more were jobless at least once sometime during the year. In addition, there were more than a million people who were so discouraged by the lack of jobs that they simply gave up looking, plus over six million who worked at part-time jobs because they could not find full-time jobs....The unemployment rate for December, in fact, was five-tenths of 1 percentage point higher, higher than the unemployment rate at the recession trough in March of 1991." (p4)

Sarbanes, Paul S. (Sen.-Md.). U.S. Congress. Joint Economic Committee. "The 1993 Economic Report of the President." Hearing, 27 Jan 1993. Washington, D.C.: GPO, 1994. (ISBN0160440300). (Y4.Ec:Ec7/2/993/pt.1).

"While the nation's jobless rate took a welcome drop from 6.8 percent in October to 6.4 percent in November--the lowest mark since the depths of the Bush recession in 1991--problems remain for the U.S. work force as major corporations initiated another flurry of layoffs. The Bureau of Labor Statistics reported that the number of jobless workers declined by 534,000, but that still left 8.3 million on the unemployment rolls and only 3.6 million were drawing jobless benefits. Although payrolls expanded by 208,000, the average duration of unemployment worsened from 18.6 weeks to 19.3 weeks. More than 3 million workers were jobless 15 weeks or longer. Jobs creation is still lagging far behind the pace of recovery from two previous recessions, AFL-CIO economist Markley Roberts said....Roberts noted that more than 15 million workers remain unemployed or under-employed. They include the 8.3 million officially jobless, 1.1 million discouraged workers and 6 million confined to part-time jobs because they can't find full-time work." (p10)

Oravec, John R. "Economy: Jobless Rate Fall Masks Underlying Weaknesses." AFL-CIO News v38 n26, 13 Dec 1993. p10. (ISSN0001-1185).

"The [U.S.] Department of Labor's January 1994 unemployment report, released February 4, is the first one based on the Census Bureau's redesigned survey, which covers 60,000 households. In tests conducted between September 1992 and August 1993, the old survey generated a 7.1 percent unemployment rate, while the new survey resulted in a 7.6 percent rate. That's a difference of about 600,000 people. For women workers, the new survey's unemployment rate was 6.8 percent, or 0.8 percent higher. The survey redesign is the first CPS [Current Population Survey] overhaul in 40 years. It was prompted by many changes in society and the economy, including large increases in women's labor force participation and the growth of alternative work schedules. 'People don't necessarily just work full-time any more,' says Labor Statistics Commissioner Katherine G. Abraham. 'People don't necessarily have just one job. The original design of the questionnaire was not well suited to capturing this assorted activity.'" (p10-11)

Dunn, William. "Business Reports: Labor Force: The CPS Gets a 40-Year Makeover." American Demographics v16 n2, Feb 1994. p10-12. (ISSN0163-4089).

"An increasing number of people [in the U.S.] are joining the ranks of displaced workers, those employees who have lost their jobs and probably won't find a similar one in their area or any other. The statistics are alarming: in 1992 75 percent of laid-off workers were permanently laid off--this represents the highest annual figure since 1967 when this category of workers was first tracked. Since the 1970's, the percentage of unemployed workers out of work for 6 months or longer has increased steadily from 11 to 16 percent in the 1990's. In fact, in 1993 21 percent of the unemployed hadn't worked in at least 6 months, the second highest annual rate since World War II." (pE147)

Gejdenson, Sam (Rep.-Conn.). "The Expanded Training Opportunities Act," Congressional Record (9 Feb 1994). Daily ed. pE147. (ISSN0363-7239).

"Unemployment [in the U.S.] is falling overall to 6 percent, but black unemployment is rising to 13 percent--50 percent for our youth. The gap between rich and poor is wider now. Our schools are becoming more segregated, not less. A savage inequality in funding for education helps track some children for Yale and some for jail. The ghettos and barrios of our cities are poorer, more isolated and more desperate. Our youth are killing each other in the streets with no regard for human life." (p10)

Jackson, Jesse L. "My Turn: What Would Dr. King Say?" Newsweek v123 n4, 24 Jan 1994. p10. (ISSN0028-9604).

"Last year, 645 [U.S.] companies announced layoffs of at least 601,537 employees. By the end of the year, the layoffs were averaging 3,000 victims per day. Six hundred thousand human beings. That's more than 10 times the number of U.S. soldiers killed in Vietnam. And those are just 1993's economic casualties! The largest companies in the United States have been throwing at least 400,000 people overboard every year since 1980. The sad truth about this is that many of these people will never find work again." (p2)

"Editorial: Whose Recovery?" People's Tribune v21 n3, 17 Jan 1994. p2.

"When the heads of the so-called G-7 countries--the world's leading capitalist economies--meet in Detroit in March to discuss worldwide unemployment, they most likely will point to high technology as the savior of their troubled economies. But while Clinton and the others push the high tech solution, 200,000 scientists and four percent of engineers in the United States are out of work. Computer giant IBM, which employed 406,000 workers in 1986, will employ only 215,000 by 1995. Other companies like Digital Equipment, Data General and Apple in the United States have been through rounds of layoffs. The same thing is happening in Europe at companies like Groupe Bull in France and Olivetti in Italy....The G-7 conference won't discuss the real problems or their solutions." (p8)

"High Tech and the Jobs Summit: Put Unemployed Engineers and Scientists to Work!" People's Tribune v21 n11, 14 Mar 1994. p8.

"It is becoming routine to lay off employees--particularly middle managers--in the American workplace. A 1993 WALL STREET JOURNAL article noted that according to the Bureau of Labor Statistics, a record 1.4 million executives, managers, and administrative professionals have lost their jobs since 1989." (p18)

Price, Adrienne E. "Opinion/Essays: When Uncle Sam's Budgeteers Go after Middle Managers." The Christian Science Monitor v86 n66, 1 Mar 1994. p18. (ISSN0882-7729).

UNEMPLOYMENT--U.S.--MINORITIES

"The real wages and employment rates of young, less-educated [U.S.] males have fallen dramatically over the past quarter-century. This deterioration has been true for white and Hispanic males, but it has been even worse among black males. It has shown up in terms of both increased unemployment and decreased labor force participation. The nonemployment rate for 20-to-24 year old nonwhite males increased from 22 percent in 1964 to 42 percent in 1992. Much of this decline involves persistent joblessness--individuals are essentially jobless 52 weeks out of the year." (p30)

Katz, Lawrence F. (Chief Economist, U.S. Dept. of Labor). U.S. House. Committee on Ways and Means. "Children and Families at Risk in Deteriorating Communities." Hearing, 7 Dec 1993. Washington, D.C.: GPO, 1994. (ISBN0160436567). (Y4.W36:103-43).

UNEMPLOYMENT--U.S.--YOUTH (v19)

UNITED NATIONS (v19)

"Among the disturbing aspects of the recent explosion in the UN's peace-keeping responsibilities is the fact that military operations are seemingly better funded than their humanitarian component, and also drain resources away from the UN's work on longer-term development goals. The UN is now spending $3 on peace-keeping for every $1 it spends on development assistance, India's Ambassador to the UN Hamid Ansari told an April session of the Special Committee on Peace-keeping. 'It is astounding,' UNICEF Executive Director James Grant told the agency's Executive Board on 29 April, that governments had committed billions to peace-keeping operations to protect relief, but the mobilization of relief only scraped by. He pointed out that over $1 bn had been spent on the military intervention in Somalia while only 10 per cent of the $166.5 mn appeal by the UN Department of Humanitarian Affairs for relief and reconstruction work in 1993 had so far been contributed." (p17)

Laishley, Roy. "UN Peace-Keeping Challenges Mounting on Continent." Africa Recovery v7 n1, Jun 1993. p1,16-17.

"In 1987, there were five peacekeeping operations, with some 10,000 soldiers, with an annual budget of $233 million. At the present time, there are some 17 operations, with 70,000 soldiers costing around $3.5 billion a year. There is an additional peacekeeping request made for Georgia, one of the new independent states of the former Soviet Union, where there is a request for some 2,500 to 3,000 peacekeepers. However Russia is the only country willing to send troops there. There are now some 28,000 peacekeeping forces in the Balkans, which is some 6,000 below strength. The peace talks which are now underway with respect to Angola may well lead to a request for peacekeeping forces there." (pS3644)

Specter, Arlen (Sen.-Pa.). "Congressional Budget Concurrent Resolution," Congressional Record (24 Mar 1994). Daily ed. pS3631-3659. (ISSN0363-7239).

"The numbers are stunning. Around 70,000 peacekeepers from 70 countries are serving in 17 UN missions across the world....The pace has been fast; more operations have been launched in the past few years than in all the 40 years of the cold war; there are seven times more peacekeepers in the field than six years ago. But the UN's members are no better at paying for what they get: the current cost is estimated at $3.2 billion a year, of which one-third is unpaid." (p52)

"International: United Nations: Sea of Blue." Economist v331 n7861, 30 Apr 1994. p52. (ISSN0013-0613).

"During the UN's first 43 years, 13 peace-keeping missions were sent into the field. 13 peace-keeping missions were undertaken in the next 43 months--from 1988 until the end of 1992. In the first nine months of 1993 six more peace-keeping missions were established. Although peace-keeping as we now know it is not specifically mentioned in the UN Charter, its essence is implicit in the preamble's reference to 'unite our strength to maintain international peace and security,' and provision of Chapters VI and VII for 'pacific settlement of disputes' and 'action with respect to threats to the peace...and acts of aggression.'" (p1)

Nichols, Sue. "New Dimensions of UN Peace-Keeping." Window on the World v24 n6, Win 1993-94. p1,15.

UNITED NATIONS--AFRICA (v19)

UNITED NATIONS--APPROPRIATIONS AND EXPENDITURES (v19)

UNITED NATIONS--ARMED FORCES (v19)

UNITED NATIONS--ARMED FORCES--CANADA

"Canada, a country that has participated in virtually every United Nations peacekeeping operation, appears on the verge of revamping and downsizing its historic peacekeeping role. Canada has been at the forefront of UN peacekeeping since former Prime Minister Lester Pearson won the Nobel Peace Prize for his plan to separate combatants with UN troops during the 1956 Suez crisis. But while peacekeeping remains a popular idea, the reality of the two-year Bosnian war combined with a new government intent on cutting deficits and defense spending, is forcing a redefinition of Canada's peacekeeping mission and its priorities....Bosnia is by far Canada's largest peacekeeping commitment, accounting for four-fifths of the 2,322 troops Canada has deployed in 15 UN peacekeeping missions worldwide.

That is almost 2,000 fewer than were deployed in 1992. Canada pulled peacekeepers out of Cyprus last year and shut its NATO Air Force bases in Europe. Peacekeeping doesn't come cheap. It cost the government more than C$1 billion (US$1.3 billion) in 1993-1994 out of a C$11.3 billion ($15 billion) defense budget. Next month the government launches what may be the most intensive review of Canadian defense policy, including peacekeeping forces, since Canada joined NATO in 1949." (p3)

Clayton, Mark. "International: Canadians Rethink Role as International Peacekeepers." The Christian Science Monitor v86 n46, 31 Jan 1994. p3. (ISSN0882-7729).

UNITED NATIONS--ARMED FORCES--U.S. (v19)

UNITED NATIONS--CAMBODIA (v19)

"In March, 1992, the United Nations mounted its second biggest peacekeeping operation in its history--only Somalia is larger--dispatching nearly 17,000 troops and over 5,000 civilians at a cost of over $3 billion. The Cambodian peace agreement, signed in October, 1991, gave the United Nations Transitional Authority in Cambodia (UNTAC) the power not only to police a ceasefire, repatriate refugees...but also to...remove Cambodian officials from office, help manage the economy and install its own media....But two years later--although the recent elections were trumpeted abroad as a resounding UN victory--UNTAC's actual accomplishments seem lackluster and pricey....Three hundred and sixty thousand refugees were repatriated from Thailand....But UNTAC promises of land and a new life shriveled to $50 per refugee in cash or building supplies." (p16) "The corrupting effect of 22,000 peacekeepers wielding $3 billion 'UNTACed' any UN effort to reform the economy. Many UNTACers raked in $130-145 a day per diem on top of fat UN salaries in a country where the average yearly income is $140; many Third World peacekeepers joined UNTAC not out of commitment to the UN mission, but for the money." (p20)

Coburn, Judith. "Good Intentions Gone Awry: The U.N. Leaves Cambodia." APF Reporter v16 n2, 1994. p15-20. (ISSN0913-4562).

UNITED NATIONS--CIVIL RIGHTS (v19)

UNITED NATIONS--EL SALVADOR (v19)

UNITED NATIONS--PUBLIC OPINION

A March 1993 poll "sponsored by the World Federalist Association and reaching 1,200 registered voters '...supports world federalist goals to transform the UN into a global law enforcement agency responsible for international security,' said former U.S. Congressman, 1980 Independent presidential candidate, and President of the World Federalist Association John Anderson. It found: 83% of registered voters support amending the UN charter to permit trials in an International Criminal Court of national leaders accused of gross violations of human rights, including making war on ethnic groups, or causing serious damage to the global environment. 86% say giving the UN new responsibility and adequate authority is essential or helpful for practical and effective global law enforcement. 80% favor the UN having responsibility for international security. 62% support US participation in a world conference to review the UN Charter, and to propose amendments in areas where individual nations cannot solve problems alone." (p19)

"Two New Polls Find Americans Support Sending US Military...." Veterans for Peace Journal n23, Sum 1993. p19. (ISSN1063-9381).

UNITED NATIONS--U.S.

"According to a 1990 report by former U.N. officials Brian Urquhart and Erskine Childers, western European and North American nationals have held an average of 71 percent of the executive posts with authority over U.N. funds and specialized agencies. By unspoken tradition, top slots at the U.N. Development Program, the U.N. Children's Fund (Unicef) and the World Bank are reserved for men from the rich nations. By contrast, citizens of developing countries have never held more than 38 percent of the leadership posts at any time, even though these nations comprise a decisive majority in the General Assembly and in many U.N. governing bodies....Appallingly, only one woman, Nafis Sadik of Pakistan, has ever headed a U.N. organization. She supervises the New York-based U.N. Fund for Population Activities." (p3)

Dube, Siddharth. "U.N. Staff Jobs: West Hogs the Best." Toward Freedom v41 n8, Dec 1992-Jan 1993. p3,6. (ISSN0048-9898).

UNITED NATIONS--WORLD BANK

"As the world's leading development institution and agency of the United Nations, the World Bank is supposed to be helping out the world's poorer nations and not reaping whirlwind profits. Yet as the poorest nations in the world scraped together billions to service their debts, the World Bank enjoyed another record breaking year in terms of profits. According to its 1992 Annual Report, the Bank made a profit of $1.6 billion for its 1992 fiscal year, up from $1.2 billion for 1991. Out of the $9.7 billion in income the Bank earned for 1992, $7.7 billion came from interest and fees paid by developing nations....Meanwhile, the overall debt of sub-Saharan Africa continued its inexorable upward climb. According to the recently released World Debt tables, sub-Saharan Africa's debt reached $178 billion for 1991 and is estimated to reach $183 billion for 1992....For 1991 the World Bank accounted for $26.8 billion of the region's debt, up from $21 billion for 1989. Sub-Saharan African countries who are indebted to the World Bank managed to scrape together enough to ensure that the World Bank did not suffer any hardships to its balance sheets. By faithfully cutting back expenditures on health care, education, and transferring other costs onto the backs of women and the poor, sub-Saharan Africa paid out over $2.1 billion to the World Bank." (p15)

"Oxfam Calls for a Marshall Plan for Africa." NewsNotes v18 n4, Jul-Aug 1993. p15-16. (ISSN1064-1556).

UNITED NATIONS--YUGOSLAVIA (v19)

UNITED PARCEL SERVICE--U.S.

"United Parcel Service, the world's largest package distribution company, was selected as one of the 'Most Admired Corporations' in America, ranking 10th out of over 400 companies evaluated in the February 7, 1994, issue of FORTUNE magazine....UPS provides a variety of air and ground distribution services throughout the United States and in more than 185 countries. The company employs more than 280,000 people and operates one of the 10 largest airlines in the country." (pS545)

McConnell, Mitch (Sen.-Ky.). "Tribute to United Parcel Service--One of the Most Respected Companies in America," Congressional Record (1 Feb 1994). Daily ed. pS545. (ISSN0363-7239).

U.S.--ARCHIVAL RESOURCES

"The National Archives and Records Administration's operating expense budget is comprised of approximately 50 percent personnel compensation payments; 35 percent for fixed space payments, including payments to the General Services Administration for rental of space primarily for the Federal records centers, and operation and maintenance of the NARA building and Presidential libraries; 4 percent for necessary expenses such as postage, phones, accounting and payroll services, unemployment and workers compensation; and 3 percent for grants. This leaves only 8 percent for discretionary contracts, services, and other purchases. A reduction in administrative expenses will impact our ability to purchase supplies and equipment for Archives II. We must fund contracts for services to operate, maintain, and protect our facility, the cost of which continues to increase each year, so there is no other place to reduce expenses." (p141)

Mosley, Raymond A. (Acting Deputy Archivist, United States). U.S. House. Committee on Appropriations. "Treasury, Postal Service, and General Government Approp. for Fiscal Year 1994 (Part 4)." Hearing, Washington, D.C.: GPO, 1993. (ISBN0160407702). (Y4.Ap6/1:T71/994/pt.4).

U.S.--ARMED FORCES (v19)

"We [the U.S.] had 18 active Army divisions in 1990, [and] we will have only 10 by 1999. Naval ship battle forces have declined from 546...[in] 1990 to 373 today, and ultimately will go to 346. Air Force active fighter wings have already been cut nearly in half from 24 to 13. Planned bomber cuts are from 315 to 107. Active military manpower has declined by more than half a million, or 32 percent. Defense civilians are going down 330,000 or 29 percent. Even reserve forces will be 20 percent lower than they were in 1990." (pH1222)

Dicks, Norman D. (Rep.-Wash.). "Concurrent Resolution on the Budget--Fiscal Year 1995," Congressional Record (10 Mar 1994). Daily ed. pH1170-1242. (ISSN0363-7239).

"Beyond the Navy SEALs and the Army Special Forces, which make up the bulk of the Special Operations Forces, antiterrorist organizations such as Delta Force have undertaken a host of missions to protect United States interests. Many are so secret that we will never know they occurred. According to Gen. Carl W. Stiner, former commander of the Special Operations Command, 'The use of Special Operations Forces increased 35 percent last year (and) 2,924 personnel were on 146 missions in 48 countries and in 17 U.S. states (in counter-drug business).' All this effort to train our friends, or to 'keep the lid on things,' requires only 1.2 percent of the total defense budget, he said." (p33)

Feulner, Edwin, III/Messing, F. Andy, Jr. "Fair Comment: Special Forces Should Be Core of Leaner, Meaner U.S. Military." Insight v10 n8, 21 Feb 1994. p33-34. (ISSN1051-4880).

"The proportion of people in the armed services who are not minorities (that is, whites who are not of Hispanic heritage) declined over the past two decades, according to a 1991 GAO [General Accounting Office] report. In 1990, non-Hispanic whites made up 70 percent of active duty forces, a sizable drop from 84 percent in 1972. Over the same period, the proportion of blacks almost doubled from 11 percent to 21 percent. The proportion identified as of Hispanic origin rose modestly, from 3 percent to almost 5 percent. Other race and ethnic groups increased from 1 percent to 4 percent. The total number of personnel dropped from 2.7 million in 1971 (during the Vietnam War) to 2 million in 1990. With about 30 percent minorities, the armed forces in 1990 had proportionately more minorities than the civilian population which was about 24 percent minority. The 1990 civilian population, according to the Census Bureau, was 76 percent non-Hispanic white, 12 percent black, 9 percent Hispanic, and 3 percent other (Asian and Native Americans)." (p4)

Kalish, Susan. "Who's in the Army Now?" Population Today v21 n2, Feb 1993. p4-5. (ISSN0749-2448).

"Active duty separations [in the U.S.] in FY 1992 were 390,000 and are expected to decline to 345,000 in FY 1993 and to 265,000 in FY 1997. Those leaving the services will receive separation counseling, employment assistance, and may be eligible for the Voluntary Separation Incentive (VSI) or the Special Separation Bonus (SSB). These programs, made available by the 1991 National Defense Authorization Act, offer separation payments for those who leave voluntarily. In FY 1992, over 20,000 active duty members were approved for early release or early retirement and another 60,000 were approved for separation under the VSI and SSB programs....Many of those leaving the military have marketable skills which will help them to find employment. Others will continue their education. But many will join those in the unemployed labor pool which will grow by the 100,000 men and women per year who would have been recruited by the military--or by those displaced from jobs by individuals who would formerly have been recruited by the services." (p4)

"Focus: Demobilizing the Troops." Positive Alternatives v3 n3, Spr 1993. p4-5,11. (ISSN1065-0075).

"According to a survey of all [U.S.] civilian forces activated for duty, Mississippi sacrificed a greater share of its sons and daughters to the Gulf [War] than any other state in the nation. When the war started, 281 of every 100,000 Mississippians were under fire in the Middle East--almost six times higher than the national average. Blacks also shouldered more than their share of the military burden in Operation Desert Storm. Although African-Americans make up only 12 percent of the overall population, the Government Accounting Office reported that they comprised nearly 21 percent of the 'all-volunteer' army. Other reports indicated that as many as 50 percent of all front-line troops were black." (p11)

Windham, Lane. "War and Peace: Patriots for Peace." Southern Exposure v21 n1-2, Spr-Sum 1993. p11-12. (ISSN0146-809X).

U.S.--ARMED FORCES--APPROPRIATIONS AND EXPENDITURES (v19)

The U.S. "must continue to work through the sizable adjustment in military spending that has been under way since the late 1980s. From a longer-run perspective, the defense cutbacks carry the anticipation of substantial benefits for the U.S. economy. By freeing up resources that can be devoted to improving the nation's stock of productive physical and human capital, they should ultimately lead to higher living standards. In the short run, of course, lower defense spending is a depressant on economic activity, and on jobs and incomes. For industries and regions that rely heavily on military spending, the dislocations may well be sizable. In industries that depend on defense expenditures for at least 50 percent of their output, employment has fallen more than 20 percent (300,000 jobs) since 1987. And, in California, where the share of civilian employment in defense-related jobs may be almost twice the national average, the unemployment rate has risen to about 10 percent, nearly 3 percentage points above the national average." (p54)

Greenspan, Alan (Chair, Board of Governors, Federal Reserve System). U.S. Congress. Joint Economic Committee. "The 1993 Economic Report of the President." Hearing, 27 Jan 1993. Washington, D.C.: GPO, 1994. (ISBN0160440300). (Y4.Ec:Ec7/2/993/pt.1).

"According to [Les] Aspin's Bottom Up Review (BUR), released in early September, the Pentagon must be equipped for rapid intervention, anywhere in the world, against all manner of threats large and small. Notwithstanding the disappearance of the Soviet threat, the new era Defense Department will require a military structure two-thirds as large as US forces during the Cold War. Secretary Aspin's five year plan will consume more than $1.2 trillion of the nation's treasure. In 1999, ten years after the fall of the Berlin Wall, the United States will be spending approximately $240 billion on defense each year--80% as high as the Cold War average." (p15)

Conetta, Carl/others. "On Intervention: Free Reign for the Sole Superpower?" Boston Review v18 n6, Dec-Jan 1993-94. p15-16. (ISSN0734-2306).

"We [the U.S.] spent $10 billion last year just to operate our forces and maintain military installations in foreign countries, mostly in Europe. That does not include the substantial cost of paying our soldiers and buying their weapons. In fact, in fiscal year 1993, according to Department of Defense figures, our NATO allies paid less than 25 percent of the costs of maintaining troops in their countries while Japan paid more than 75 percent. If the European allies matched the Japanese contributions, the Congressional Budget Office estimates we could save the United States taxpayer $9.6 billion over 5 years." (pS4356-4357)

Lautenberg, Frank R. (Sen.-N.J.). "Valuable Infrastructure Lost," Congressional Record (14 Apr 1994). Daily ed. pS4356-4357. (ISSN0363-7239).

"According to the Congressional Budget Office, in fiscal year 1995, net interest will cost the American taxpayers $212 billion, which represents 3 percent of Gross Domestic Product. Defense spending totals $274 billion, which represents 3.9 percent of GDP. But when you look at spending trends over the next 5 years, in fiscal year 1999, net interest will cost taxpayers $261 billion, which is 3 percent of GDP. The distressing trend we are witnessing here is that interest on the debt, although it remains a constant share of GDP, rivals defense spending. Defense spending continues to fall as a share of GDP, while debt interest spirals upward. Opponents of a balanced budget amendment fear that social services and education will greatly suffer under a constitutionally mandated balanced budget. Social services would take a harder hit because in the absence of a balanced budget...these numbers also point out that domestic discretionary spending--where most education, training, and social services programs are allocated--will fall from 3.7 percent of GDP in fiscal year 1995 to 3.4 percent in fiscal year 1999." (pH1489)

Gunderson, Steve (Rep.-Wis.). "Balanced Budget Constitutional Amendment," Congressional Record (17 Mar 1994). Daily ed. pH1451-1497. (ISSN0363-7239).

"Real defense spending [in the U.S.] has declined by 35 percent since 1985 and procurement has been cut 50 percent. Defense spending is now at just 4 percent of GNP [gross national product] and 16 percent of spending, and with the Clinton cuts, it is headed to 2.8 percent of GNP and 13 percent of spending by 1998." (pE312)

Solomon, Gerald B. H. (Rep.-N.Y.). "Defense Cuts," Congressional Record (2 Mar 1994). Daily ed. pE312. (ISSN0363-7239).

The U.S. "has already spent over $32 billion on ballistic missile defense research....But the [Clinton] administration still plans to spend an additional $18 billion over the next 5 years for ballistic missile defense. For 1995, the President's budget request includes some $3.3 billion for ballistic missile defense activities, an increase of $800 million over last year's level, increasing spending on ballistic missiles defense activities by $500 million over last year's level. In testimony before the Budget Committee, the Department of Defense indicated that this increase of nearly 20 percent--when we are cutting 300 domestic discretionary programs--this increase of 20 percent makes ballistic missile defense one of the fastest growing programs in the Pentagon....We hear a lot about the growth in entitlements, but this Ballistic Missile Defense Program is growing faster than any of the entitlement programs on which so much attention is focused." (pS3423)

Sasser, Jim (Sen.-Tenn.). "Congressional Budget Concurrent Resolution," Congressional Record (22 Mar 1994). Daily ed. pS3421-3437. (ISSN0363-7239).

"In a study released last November, the General Accounting Office concluded that: For fiscal years 1990 through 1993, DOD [U.S. Dept. of Defense] allocated at least $10.4 billion to (domestic) activities. This figure, however, understates the full amount spent because data on such activities are incomplete....On March 21, the Congressional Research Service completed a study of items in the DOD budget that may not be directly related to traditional military capabilities. This study analyzed defense expenditures for fiscal year 1990-1993, the same period covered in the GAO report cited above, and the report concludes that $28.3 billion was expended during that period for items which could be defined as non-defense activities. CRS looked further at fiscal year 1994 defense appropriations and the fiscal year 1995 defense budget request, and identified another $24.3 billion in nondefense activities in these 2 years alone. All together, CRS lists $52.6 billion in defense expenditures for items not directly related to military capability." (pS3665)

McCain, John (Sen.-Ariz.). "Program," Congressional Record (24 Mar 1994). Daily ed. pS3661-3667. (ISSN0363-7239).

"The Department of Defense tells us the most likely scenario to cut the $270 billion [budget deficit] between 1996 and 2000 would require a reduction of 275,000 military people, one out of five. We would lay off 170,000 National Guard, one out of three. We would discharge 125,000 civilian workers. We would close--in addition to those we were already going to close by 1996--we would close half of the remaining 22 major bases in the United States. We would close nine logistics depots, terminate the F-18, terminate the C-17. And after the turn of the century we will have no other transport but the C-17. The 141's are wearing out, the 130's are wearing out. There is nothing left. But we would have to terminate it because it is too large an expenditure. We would have to cancel the nuclear aircraft carriers. We would have to cancel the next submarine, SSN-23, cancel the attack submarine, cancel the M-1 tank upgrades. We would have to eliminate theater missile defense. And even then, it may equal $270 billion." (pS1886-1887)

Stevens, Ted (Sen.-Alaska). "Balanced Budget Amendment," Congressional Record (25 Feb 1994). Daily ed. pS1883-1892. (ISSN0363-7239).

"Reductions in defense spending in the last 2 years have cost...California, 250,000 jobs. By 1998, estimates indicate that 650,000 jobs will be lost in the State as a result of defense downsizing....January's unemployment statistics were released, and they were amazing....California's unemployment rate soared to 10.1 percent, nearly 3 1/2 percentage points higher than the national average of 6.7 percent. Because the unemployment survey has been revised, we expected a small jump in the unemployment rate, about a half of a percentage point. But for California, the unemployment rate jumped 1.4 percentage points, compared to just three-tenths of a percent for the Nation. So the rate jumped triple what was expected by the adjustment in the methods of the accounting survey. The double-digit unemployment rate means that over 1.5 million Californians continue to seek, and are unable to find work. 200,000 more men and women are out of work this month than last month....figures indicate that California is clearly not producing enough jobs." (pS959)

Hatch, Orrin G. (Sen.-Utah). "Statements on Introduced Bills and Joint Resolutions," Congressional Record (4 Feb 1994). Daily ed. pS951-960. (ISSN0363-7239).

"There has been a total decline in [U.S.] Department of Defense funding of 34 percent since 1985 and a total procurement decline of 64 percent. But ammunition procurement has gone down almost 80 percent. So ammunition procurement has gone down more than twice the decline in the spending on the defense budget as a whole. Moreover, of course, as public spending has dropped, the private spending of the industrial base in this area has dropped as well. For example, research and development for new kinds of ammunition is off by 80 percent, similar to the decline in public funding....The stockpile is not adequate for us to fight

even one Desert Storm, much less two." (pH395)
Talent, James M. (Rep.-Mo.). "The Hollowing of U.S. Forces," Congressional Record (9 Feb 1994). Daily ed. pH394-396. (ISSN0363-7239).

"Defense spending [in the U.S.], as a percentage of the gross domestic product, has declined from its post-Vietnam high of 6.3 percent in fiscal 1986 to 4.1 percent projected for fiscal 1994 and will decline further to 3 percent in fiscal 1998." (p16)
Paige, Emmett, Jr. "Re-Engineering DOD's C3I Operations." Defense 93 n6, 1993. p15-22. (ISSN0737-1217).

"The United States will spend $31 Billion in 1994, and more than $300 Billion over the next 10 years to prepare for nuclear war. This translates into $330 per American household in 1994....The Pentagon continues to build nuclear weapons systems including: B-2 'Stealth' bombers (at $2.2 Billion per plane), Trident II submarines ($1.4 Billion each), and Trident II D-5 long-range missiles ($45 million each). These weapons were designed to defeat the Soviet Union. Now, the Pentagon can find no justification for these nuclear goliaths. According to Defense Secretary Les Aspin, the only enemies that face the United States are a few regional 'bad guys' like North Korea's Kim Il Sung and Iraq's Saddam Hussein." (p3)
"Does the United States Need Nuclear Weapons?" Defense Monitor v22 n10, 1993. p1-6. (ISSN0195-6450).

"U.S. military spending grew to record levels during the Vietnam War, fell gradually during the 1970s, then rose sharply during Ronald Reagan's two terms, reaching a peak of $355 billion (in 1993 dollars) in 1989. Spending fell somewhat during George Bush's reign, to $294 billion in his last budget, fiscal 1993. (All figures omit defense-related costs of more than $100 billion annually, such as the military's share of interests on the national debt, the Veterans Administration, and foreign military aid.)" (p42)
Breslow, Marc. "Economy in Numbers: Maintaining Military Might." Dollars and Sense n191, Jan-Feb 1994. p42-43.

"As a vocal opponent of excessive military spending, Dr....[Martin Luther King, Jr.] would be shocked to find that four years after the fall of the Berlin wall, the United States will spend $247 billion on its military. The Russians will spend less than $50 billion. Germany is united but we pay to keep more than 300,000 troops and dependents in Germany looking for something to do. Let us decide that a safe measure of our security is to spend only as much as the rest of the world combined. That would free up more than $50 billion a year to reinvest in this country. We have the money; we need a change. Dr. King would be leading the fight against a crime bill that offers more jails and more police instead of preventive measures against crime. More jail cells, more ways to kill are not the answer. It is morally wrong and cost-inefficient to cut the Housing and Urban Development budget by $4 billion while funding $100,000 new condo-style jail cells." (p10)
Jackson, Jesse L. "My Turn: What Would Dr. King Say?" Newsweek v123 n4, 24 Jan 1994. p10. (ISSN0028-9604).

"Any serious consideration of economic conversion and the reorientation of our nation's economy must take into account the enormous sums of money we spend on military research and development. In the current fiscal year, the U.S. government has allocated $43 billion to military R&D. To put this in perspective, this is over half of all government-funded scientific and technological research; the total U.S. government R&D figure is half of all R&D spending in the U.S.; U.S. spending is a little over half of all world spending on R&D. Thus, military-sponsored R&D in the United States is over 14% of the world's total R&D spending on science and technology." (p6)
Chapman, Gary. "Cover Story: 21st Century Technology: Can It Be Socially Responsible?" Positive Alternatives v3 n2, Win 1993. p6-7. (ISSN1065-0075).

"Defense spending will...be cut deeper in 1994. Inflation-adjusted defense outlays, which contracted 3.8 percent in fiscal 1993, will shrink 5.2 percent in the current fiscal year, which started October 1. That will wipe out 107,000 jobs for active-duty military personnel. These cuts could trim an additional 0.1 to 0.2 percentage point off economic growth." (p43)
Hage, David. "Predictions: Will the Economy Pick Up Steam?" U.S. News & World Report v115 n25, 27 Dec 1993. p42-43. (ISSN0041-5537).

U.S.--ARMED FORCES--ASIA (v19)

U.S.--ARMED FORCES--ASIA--EUROPE (v19)

U.S.--ARMED FORCES--EDUCATION (v19)

"In FY 1991, 97 percent of the men and women who joined the services had high school diplomas and 2.5 percent had alternative high school credentials. Fewer than .5 percent had not finished high school compared to 19 percent of all 18 to 24 year-old civilians in the United States. In FY 1991 and FY 1992, over 70 percent of new recruits scored in the top 50th percentile of the Armed Services Aptitude Battery (ASVAB), the aptitude test administered to all applicants. If the recent recruiting success continues with the services taking the highest quality youth they can attract, then we can expect that the same number of recruits will come from the top 50th percentile. This means that those who will lose the benefits of military service will be those in the 34th to 49th percentile as measured by the ASVAB. Those likely to be in this excluded group are minorities--particularly blacks. In FY 1992, 14,475--or 42 percent--of the 34,108 blacks who joined the services tested in the 34th to 49th percentile. An analysis completed by the Department of Education concludes that most of those no longer recruited will be from working class families and almost half will be from ethnic or racial minorities." (p5)
"Focus: Demobilizing the Troops." Positive Alternatives v3 n3, Spr 1993. p4-5,11. (ISSN1065-0075).

U.S.--ARMED FORCES--EUROPE (v19)

"At their peak in the late 1980s, there were 213,000 US Army troops in Europe alone. By the end of fiscal year 1993, that figure had been reduced to 98,000. By the end of FY1994, it is scheduled to fall to 75,000, according to a US Army official. In 1990, Europe was host to 25 major US Air Force bases. At the end of this year, there are scheduled to be only 11." (p18)
Grier, Peter. "As US, Europe Budgets Plummet, Are Defense Guarantees Credible?" The Christian Science Monitor v86 n35, 13 Jan 1994. p1,18. (ISSN0882-7729).

"America's role in guaranteeing European security is declining. Within two years the U.S. military presence in Europe will sink to its lowest level since the early 1950s. By 1996, just 109,000 American troops will remain on the Continent. Five years ago, there were 317,000." (p20)
Knight, Robin/others. "World Report: Is It a Wrap for NATO?" U.S. News & World Report v116 n1, 10 Jan 1994. p20-22,24. (ISSN0041-5537).

U.S.--ARMED FORCES--GAYS (v19)

U.S.--ARMED FORCES--GAYS--PUBLIC OPINION (v19)

U.S.--ARMED FORCES--MARRIAGE

"Relatively few recruits are married when they enter service for the first time. In 1992, the percentage of male recruits who had not served before and who were married ranged from 3 in the Marine Corps to 10 for both the Army and Air Force. However, by the end of their first term of service, typically four years, about 42 percent of male enlisted members have become married. Of those males who remain in service for a full career, nearly 87 percent are married, compared with 75 percent of civilians ages 40 to 44. Married members re-enlist at substantially higher rates than single members." (p6-7)

"Marriage and the First Term Family." Defense 94 n1, 1994. p6-17.

U.S.--ARMED FORCES--PUBLIC OPINION (v19)

"'Standing armies in time of peace are inconsistent with the principles of republican government, dangerous to the liberties of free people, and generally converted into destructive engines for establishing despotism.' So said the Continental Congress in 1784 as it debated the relationship of the military to democracy in America. A January 1993 Harris poll of American adults found public confidence in the military at a 27-year high. Fifty-seven per cent of those interviewed held positive opinions about the military, a total more than double that of the second most respected institution, the Supreme Court. While the 1990s are not the 1780s, this tremendous change of view suggests that large segments of our society have accepted the martial spirit as a permanent part of the American psyche. Such easy acceptance risks permanently compromising our society's fundamental values and democratic traditions." (p1)

"The Military and American Society: A Clash of Values." Defense Monitor v22 n8, 1993. p1-7. (ISSN0195-6450).

U.S.--ARMED FORCES--SALARIES, ETC. (v19)

U.S.--ARMED FORCES--SOMALIA (v19)

U.S.--ARMED FORCES--WOMEN

"Over the past two decades, gender composition [in the U.S. military] was shifting dramatically...according to a 1990 study by the Women's Research and Education Institute (WREI). Since 1973, when the male draft ended and the All Volunteer Force began, the percentage of women--previously limited to no more than 2 percent--among U.S. military personnel rose quickly to 8 percent in 1980, to 11 percent in 1989. GAO [General Accounting Office] figures show that in 1990, women made up 11 percent of active duty Army personnel, 10 percent of the Navy, 14 percent of the Air Force, and 5 percent of Marines. Overall, officers were 11 percent female in 1990. Women in the armed services were more likely than men to be minorities--39 versus 28 percent, respectively, in 1990. Among active duty military women, 31 percent were black, 4 percent Hispanic, and 4 percent other, according to GAO." (p5)

Kalish, Susan. "Who's in the Army Now?" Population Today v21 n2, Feb 1993. p4-5. (ISSN0749-2448).

U.S.--CHARITABLE CONTRIBUTIONS (v19)

"When it comes to charitable giving, people in the heartland of the United States are proving that they have hearts of gold. In a survey of the nation's largest cities, the Chronicle of Philanthropy found that 6 of the top 10 charity-giving cities are in the Midwest. Minneapolis ranks as the most generous city, followed by Columbus, Ohio; Omaha, Neb.; Cleveland; Cincinnati. Milwaukee, Atlanta, Honolulu, Hawaii, Pittsburgh, and Seattle round out the top 10." (p3)

Walters, Laurel Shaper. "From the States: Midwest Cities Rank Highest in Listing of Best Charity-Givers." The Christian Science Monitor v86 n63, 24 Feb 1994. p3. (ISSN0882-7729).

U.S.--COMMERCE (v19)

"There's no doubt that U.S. economic pressure can, at times, improve some individual rights abroad. The U.S. has pressured China to release a handful of political dissidents, and Indonesia and Mexico have promised to improve the rights of workers as well. But this casting of human rights stones can be costly. With exports accounting for 11% of GDP [gross domestic product]--twice what it was 20 years ago--and export-related jobs paying 15% to 20% more than the average, America's economic self-interest lies in opening up markets abroad, not in ceding them to rivals who have fewer scruples than does the U.S. The idealists are right to pursue their agenda of supporting individual human rights around the world. But linking that agenda to U.S. trade policy can and has hurt the American economy." (p138)

"Editorials: To Spur Human Rights, Spur Trade." Business Week n3361, 7 Mar 1994. p138. (ISSN0007-7135).

U.S.--COMMERCE--ASIA (v19)

"The Asian/Pacific market is increasingly important to the United States. United States total trade with Asian/Pacific rim nations increased 147.9 percent between 1981 and 1991. Trade with other major trading countries and blocs grew at a significantly lesser rate over this same period: With Canada, by 95 percent; with the European Community, by 91 percent, and with Latin America, by 56 percent. As a percentage of total United States trade with the world, United States total trade with the Asian/Pacific rim countries increased from 26 percent in 1981 to 36 percent in 1991." (pS16527)

Johnston, J. Bennett (Sen.-La.). "Seattle Asia Pacific Economic Cooperation Leaders Meeting," Congressional Record (19 Nov 1993). Daily ed. pS16527-16528. (ISSN0363-7239).

U.S.--COMMERCE--ASIA, SOUTHEASTERN (v19)

U.S.--COMMERCE--CANADA--MEXICO (v19)

U.S.--COMMERCE--CARIBBEAN (v19)

U.S.--COMMERCE--CHINA (v19)

U.S.--COMMERCE--DEVELOPING COUNTRIES (v19)

U.S.--COMMERCE--ECONOMIC ASPECTS (v19)

U.S.--COMMERCE--EUROPE

"The emergence of global economic competition, especially from Europe and Asia, has drawn many states--as well as cities, counties, and port authorities--into the international arena, where they have sought to promote state and local exports, attract investment, and encourage tourism. One vehicle for carrying out these activities has been to open state offices in Europe, Asia, Latin America, and elsewhere." (p43) "All of the state offices engage in trade promotion, and all but one also seek foreign direct investment. In addition, 15 engage in some tourism promotion. The average state office devotes 52 percent of its time and 55 percent of its budget to export promotion. Eighteen of the 27 office respondents said that they spend half or more of their time on state product exports....Eighteen state offices do not charge for their services to exporters; seven impose a fee for assisted trade show participation; and four have some other form of charge." (p44)

Levine, Jerry/Vandenbrande, Fabienne. "American State Offices in Europe: Activities and Connections." Intergovernmental Perspective v20 n1, Fall 1993-Win 1994. p43-46. (ISSN0362-8507).

U.S.--COMMERCE--EUROPEAN ECONOMIC COMMUNITY (v19)

U.S.--COMMERCE--FORMER SOVIET REPUBLICS

"Over the course of the 1980s, Soviet imports began to be sustained by the same US mercantile trade practices which had been applied earlier to Europe, Japan, and the third world. A high level of guarantees and bonuses, that is, subsidies, maintained Soviet purchases from the US in 1990 and 1991. As late as December 12, 1991, President Bush offered the USSR $1 billion dollars in credit guarantees for feedstuffs. Between 1987 and 1991, the US gave over $708 million in bonuses for Soviet wheat purchases. By then, subsidized sales by the US to the Soviet Union were such a large proportion of world trade that each transaction further depressed prices. Indeed, the US even revived a credit guarantee programme via the Export-Import Bank which had been defunct for sixteen years in order to offer an additional $300 million in guarantees to the Soviet Union. The former Soviet Union is on the list of twenty-eight countries to receive subsidized exports announced by President Bush in September 1992 in his campaign for re-election in farm states. Short of getting the EC [European Community] to agree to loss of major foreign and domestic markets, US policy now depends on increasing subsidized exports to cash-strapped countries whose prospects of repayment are dim." (p42)

Friedmann, Harriet. "The Political Economy of Food: A Global Crisis." New Left Review n197, Jan-Feb 1993. p29-57. (ISSN0028-6060).

U.S.--COMMERCE--JAPAN (v19)

U.S.--COMMERCE--LATIN AMERICA (v19)

U.S.--COMMERCE--MEXICO (v19)

"Mexico is currently the United States' third most important trading partner as approximately 7 percent of all U.S. exports are destined for Mexico. Currently the United States enjoys a $5.4 billion trade surplus with our southern neighbor.... Connecticut exports to Mexico have increased 143 percent to $280 million annually. This has created over 5,000 new jobs in the nutmeg State already." (p45)

Franks, Gary A. (Rep.-Conn.). U.S. House. Committee on Energy and Commerce. "NAFTA: Energy Provisions and Environmental Implications." Hearing, 22 Sep 1993. Washington, D.C.: GPO, 1994. (ISBN0160440459). (Y4.En2/3:103/70).

"The United States, Canada, and Mexico form the largest market in the world with 360 million consumers, and a total output of more than $6 trillion. Currently, liberalized trade policies in Mexico have produced tremendous job growth in the United States. Since 1986, when Mexican tariffs were lowered on U.S. goods and services, U.S. exports to Mexico have nearly tripled from $12.4 billion to $33.3 billion in 1992." (p4)

Klug, Scott L. (Rep.-Wis.). U.S. House. Committee on Energy and Commerce. "NAFTA: Energy Provisions and Environmental Implications." Hearing, 22 Sep 1993. Washington, D.C.: GPO, 1994. (ISBN0160440459). (Y4.En2/3:103/70).

"According to the International Trade Commission the U.S. exports for consumption in Mexico have increased more than 300 percent, from $8.5 billion in 1986 to nearly $31 billion in 1992. Yet...the ITC said that finished goods intended for sale in Mexico accounted for not quite $2.3 billion or less than 10 percent of our $31 billion exports to Mexico in 1992." (p73)

Collins, Cardiss (Rep.-Ill.). U.S. House. Committee on Energy and Commerce. "Telecommunications Trade." Hearing, 3 Aug 1993. Washington, D.C.: GPO, 1994. (ISBN0160435919). (Y4.En2/3:103-60).

"Since Mexico sharply reduced its tariffs in 1987, [U.S. International Trade] Commission staff estimate that U.S. exports for consumption in Mexico have grown by 224 percent by 1992, to $30.9 billion. U.S. exports to Mexico's maquila sector rose more slowly during this period, by 93 percent, to $8.7 billion. Hence, maquila-related exports as a share of total U.S. exports to Mexico fell from 32 percent in 1987 to 21 percent in 1992...." (p93)

Newquist, Don (Chair, U.S. International Trade Commission). U.S. House. Committee on Energy and Commerce. "Telecommunications Trade." Hearing, 3 Aug 1993. Washington, D.C.: GPO, 1994. (ISBN0160435919). (Y4.En2/3:103-60).

U.S.--ECONOMIC CONDITIONS (v19)

"Despite signs of modest improvement in the past few months, since the recession trough in March 1991, employment [in the U.S.] has shown essentially no net change on a payroll basis, and only a modest increase in the household series. Of course, the softness in employment in the current expansion is partly the counterpart of another development--namely, a dramatic improvement in productivity. Since the recession ended in early 1991, productivity has grown at an average annual rate of about 2.5 percent, a better than expected performance given the relatively slow pace of the economic recovery to date." (p10)

Greenspan, Alan (Chair, Board of Governors, Federal Reserve System). U.S. Congress. Joint Economic Committee. "The 1993 Economic Report of the President." Hearing, 27 Jan 1993. Washington, D.C.: GPO, 1994. (ISBN0160440300). (Y4.Ec:Ec7/2/993/pt.1).

"Growth of the capacity of the economy determines the trend of real Gross Domestic Product (GDP) over the decades, across business cycles. Potential GDP at full employment--now about 5 1/2 percent unemployment--grows...at about 2 1/2 per year. Half of that is due to the normal increase of the labor force, the other half to productivity. Productivity is growing much more slowly than before 1973, and more slowly than in other economies today....The 2 1/2 percent sustainable rate, not zero, is par for the U.S. economy. Relative to that par, we've been in recession--call it 'growth recession'--for nearly four years; although GDP change was positive in most quarters, growth was usually slower than 2 percent annual rate. That is why unemployment increased by two percentage points, about 2 1/2 million workers. As a result, GDP has by now fallen 5 or 6 percent below capacity....GDP growth averaging 4 percent will be needed to bring the unemployment rate back down to 5 1/2 percent in 1996, by creating 8 1/2 or 9 million jobs--for roughly 5 or 5 1/2 million new workers, 1 million persons re-entering the labor force, and the 2 1/2 million now unemployed." (p102)

Tobin, James (Professor of Economics, Yale University). U.S. Congress. Joint Economic Committee. "The 1993 Economic Report of the President." Hearing, 27 Jan 1993. Washington, D.C.: GPO, 1994. (ISBN0160440300). (Y4.Ec:Ec7/2/993/pt.1).

"Only 34 percent of Americans feel that the United States is in a recovery, with 35 percent believing we are still in a recession and 27 percent believing that we are in a depression....At the same time...the inflation situation now is in better shape than at any time during the past 25 years--the inflation rate was roughly 3 percent--except for 1986 when inflation was helped by a big drop in oil prices. You have to go back to 1965 to find a lower inflation rate than we had last year." (p2)

Obey, David R. (Rep.-Wis.). U.S. Congress. Joint Economic Committee. "The 1993 Economic Report of the President." Hearing, 27 Jan 1993. Washington, D.C.: GPO, 1994. (ISBN0160440300). (Y4.Ec:Ec7/2/993/pt.1).

The U.S. "has just come through three nightmare years of recession, bare-bones growth, disappearing jobs and falling income. During the recession, which began in 1990, we lost more than 2 million payroll jobs and almost 10 million people were unemployed. Since March of 1991, in technical terms, we have been in what economists technically call a recovery. But during the past six quarters, the economy has grown at an average rate of 1.9 percent, less than one third the rate of average postwar recoveries....We still have 9.3 million people unemployed. There are more people unemployed today after 21 months of recovery than there were at the worst point of every other postwar recession but one." (p1)

Obey, David R. (Rep.-Wis.). U.S. Congress. Joint Economic Committee. "The 1993 Economic Report of the President." Hearing, 27 Jan 1993. Washington, D.C.: GPO, 1994. (ISBN0160440300). (Y4.Ec:Ec7/2/993/pt.1).

"For all of last year, the Commerce Department reported that the real gross domestic product (GDP)--the total output of goods and services in the United States--advanced 2.9 percent after rising 2.6 percent in 1992. In the recession year of 1991, the GDP fell 0.7 percent." (p6)

"Economy: Economy Surges 5.9 Percent." AFL-CIO News v39 n4, 7 Feb 1994. p6. (ISSN0001-1185).

"For millions of American families, the 1990s are not the best of times. With workers' real earnings severely depreciated through much of the 1980s and early 1990s, wage earner households are scrimping to make ends meet even under the tightest of family budgets. Based on assumptions extrapolated from Bureau of Labor Statistics data, AFL-CIO economist Anne Draper has concluded that an intermediate family budget for a household of four persons in December 1993 was $36,574. The higher family budget in December was estimated at $52,698 and the lower family budget at $22,518. But data issued by BLS showed that average weekly earnings for production or nonsupervisory workers in December were $380.66. For 52 weeks on the job, that works out to $19,797.32 for the year, or $2,771 short of meeting even the lower family budget....The current federal minimum wage, which has not been raised since April 1991, is $4.25 an hour. At that rate, the minimum wage worker earns $170 a week, or $8,840 a year." (p6)

"Economy: Families Forced to Economize." AFL-CIO News v39 n3, 31 Jan 1994. p6. (ISSN0001-1185).

"Gross Domestic Product grew at a rate of 3.0 percent (when adjusted for inflation), only a slight improvement over 1992. While growth picked up dramatically in the final quarter of the year, to a 7.5 percent annual rate, that pace was not expected to be maintained in 1994. Unemployment fell from 7.1 percent in January to 6.4 percent in December, still unacceptably high. While 1 million fewer people were unemployed at year's end than at its start, 8.2 million people still were officially unemployed in December. Another 6.2 million were in part-time jobs for economic reasons and 1.1 million more had given up the search for jobs--a total of some 15.5 million trapped in partial or total unemployment. Total employment for the year grew by less than 2 million people, a rate that lagged far behind any recovery period on record. In manufacturing, the recovery truly was 'jobless,' as employment fell by 175,000 while overtime grew to record levels. Businesses continued to expand the 'contingent' work force, employing part-time, temporary and subcontracted workers. Of the new jobs created, 350,000 were in temporary service firms." (p7)

Lucore, Robert E. "Bargaining: Tough Year of Negotiation Ends on High Note." AFL-CIO News v39 n7, 21 Mar 1994. p7-10. (ISSN0001-1185).

A study by the Economic Policy Institute, "titled the 'Joyless Recovery: Deteriorating Wages and Job Quality in the 1990s,' underlines these points: The median hourly wage for male workers fell 4.9 percent from 1989 to 1993, including a 2.7 percent drop during the recovery. Blue-collar workers were hit harder by the real pay decline than white-collar and college-educated workers. Temporary-help agencies accounted for 28 percent of the jobs created during the recovery. Employment has grown only 36 percent as fast as in prior recoveries, and less than half of the new jobs were private-sector non-temporary jobs. Sixty percent of the new jobs in the first six months of 1993 were part-time positions, and half of those were filled by workers wanting full-time jobs." (p10)

Oravec, John R. "Economy: Part-Time, Temp Jobs Fuel 'Joyless' Recovery." AFL-CIO News v38 n20, 20 Sep 1993. p10. (ISSN0001-1185).

"With inflation running at 2.8 percent and employment at 6.3 percent, the 'misery index' (the combination of inflation and unemployment) is the lowest since the 1950s, [economist Edward M.] Gramlich said. The national savings rate--money that gets invested in building up America's capital stock--had been falling sharply during the 1980s, 'which was bad news for future economic growth,' he said. 'Because of President Clinton's budget bill, things look much better--probably not as healthy as the 1950s but we're doing much better than 10 to 15 years ago.' 'During the 1980s, there was a massive shift in earned income away from the bottom four-fifths of the population in favor of the top fifth,' said Gramlich. 'This was more important than the shift during the Gilded Age, more important than the shift in the '20s. This has probably been the biggest pro-rich shift in income that the U.S. has ever experienced.'" (p1 secC)

Cain, Stephen. "Local: Auto Surge Boosting State Economy--to Average, Says U-M Prof." Ann Arbor News 21 Jan 1994. p1 secC.

"Across the U.S., there's a veritable capital-spending boom going on. On Jan. 28, the Commerce Dept. announced that capital outlays soared 21% in the fourth quarter of 1993 and grew 14.7% for the entire year. The spree helped push gross domestic product up an astounding 5.9% during the December quarter and 2.8% for the year. Better yet, CS First Boston Inc. economist Rosanne M. Cahn figures that capital spending could advance an additional 15.5% this year." (p28)

Kelly, Kevin/others. "Top of the News: The Economy: Hand-over-Fist Capital Spending." Business Week n3358, 14 Feb 1994. p28-29. (ISSN0007-7135).

"For the year [1993], producer-price inflation [in the U.S.] ended up a mere 0.4%, measured from December, 1992, with core inflation at only 0.3%. Further back in the production process, commodity prices are rising, as would be expected, considering the pickup in manufacturing and housing....In manufacturing... employment rose a scant 2,000, while the factory workweek held at a record 41.7 hours. During the past year, factory output has risen by more than 5%, while jobs have fallen by 1%." (p29)

"Business Outlook: The Reich Rally May Have Some Room to Run." Business Week n3355, 24 Jan 1994. p29-30. (ISSN0007-7135).

"The Commerce Dept.'s latest [U.S.] spending survey, taken in October and November, shows that nonfarm businesses expect to spend 5.4% more on new plants and equipment in 1994, after a 7% rise in 1993. The numbers look even stronger when inflation is taken into account because Commerce expects the cost of computer equipment to keep falling. Price-adjusted capital spending is set to rise 7% in 1994 after an 8.5% surge in 1993, the strongest advance in four years....Service industries plan to boost capital spending by 6.5% in 1994, after a 10.7% jump in 1993 and a 9.1% hike in 1992. Manufacturers, however, are also set to increase their outlays. Their capital budgets will be 3.8% bigger in 1994, following a 3.1% increase in 1993. By spending more now, factories will head off possible production bottlenecks later on. The average factory operating rate has already risen 2.5 percentage points in the past year....In the past six quarters, equipment spending has accounted for nearly 40% of the growth in real gross domestic product, although that sector is less than 10% of the economy." (p35)

Cooper, James C./Madigan, Kathleen. "Business Outlook: Business Whips Out Its Checkbook, Too." Business Week n3353, 10 Jan 1994. p35-36. (ISSN0007-7135).

"Due largely to the income tax cuts that stimulated the longest peacetime economic expansion in history, Federal revenues between 1980 and 1992 increased by 100 percent. Money poured into the Treasury. It is true that Americans were paying a lower percentage of their income to taxes, but the windfall resulted because Americans were making more money--much more, a some 18 million new jobs were created and more than 4 million new businesses opened their doors. While these economic boom years cut into the budget deficit, reducing it by more than 60 percent between 1986 to 1989, from $227 to $142 billion in 1987 dollars, the economic expansion was not as effective as it should have been in addressing the long-term deficit problem. Why? The answer is simple. And it points to the second key we must use if we are to effectively cut the deficit. That key is responsible Government spending." (pS1464)

Roth, William V., Jr. (Sen.-Del.). "Statements on Introduced Bills and Joint Resolutions," Congressional Record (10 Feb

1994). Daily ed. pS1457-1487. (ISSN0363-7239).

"During the 2 1/2-year period immediately after...[the recession of the 1950s], the [U.S.] economy grew by something in excess of 10 percent. In the early 1960's, we had another recovery following a recession. During that recovery, the economy grew in a 2 1/2-year period by almost 12 percent. In 1970 we had another recovery following a recession, and the economy grew again by 10.2 percent. In 1974 we had another recovery after a recession, and the economy grew in a 2 1/2-year period by over 12 percent. That brings us to the latest recovery which we hear so much about from the other side of the aisle....Yet in the 2 1/2-year period after the 1990 recession, we have seen a recovery of a scant 6 percent." (pH1174)

Saxton, Jim (Rep.-N.J.). "Concurrent Resolution on the Budget--Fiscal Year 1995," Congressional Record (10 Mar 1994). Daily ed. pH1170-1242. (ISSN0363-7239).

"According to the Congressional Budget Office, between 1977 and 1988, the poorest 10 percent of our population had a tax increase of some 20 percent while the top 10 percent had an overall decrease of 5 percent. The very wealthiest 1 percent had a decrease of nearly 20 percent. During the same period that same very wealthiest group had a 50-percent increase in income, and the top 10 percent an increase in income of about 17 percent. On the other hand, the lowest 10 percent of families had 13-percent decline in income and the second, third, fourth, fifth, sixth, seventh, and eighth declines also had declines in income of between 2 and 8 percent." (pH10452)

Hinchey, Maurice D. (Rep.-N.Y.). "Problems in the American Economy," Congressional Record (20 Nov 1993). Daily ed. pH10451-10458. (ISSN0363-7239).

"Since 1986, real wages, measured in American dollars, are up in Mexico by 133 percent. Wages are up in the United States by 19.6 percent. And as wages rose, what happened? American investment in Mexico and world investment in Mexico grew. Mexican importation of American goods grew dramatically. Nobody disputes the fact that the increased purchase of American goods by Mexico since 1987 has created over 250,000 jobs in American export industries." (pS16607)

Gramm, Phil (Sen.-Tex.). "North American Free-Trade Agreement Implementation Act," Congressional Record (20 Nov 1993). Daily ed. pS16602-16622. (ISSN0363-7239).

"To quote Jeffrey Gates' testimony before the Senate Democratic Task Force on Defense/Economic Conversion last September: The 1980s saw the most significant rise in wealth concentration since the 1920s, with the wealthiest one percent of Americans increasing their proportional share of the nation's net worth by more than 19 percent between 1983 and 1989. Meanwhile, from 1976-1986, the share of national income flowing to the poorest 10 percent of U.S. households dropped from 1.1 percent to 0.9 percent, a drop of more than 19 percent...full-time workers living below the poverty line represented 18 percent of the U.S. workforce in 1990, up from 12.1 percent in 1979." (pS16769)

Bingaman, Jeff (Sen.-N.Mex.). "Statements on Introduced Bills and Joint Resolutions," Congressional Record (20 Nov 1993). Daily ed. pS16719-16785. (ISSN0363-7239).

"Real gross domestic product--that is the gross domestic product corrected for inflation--grew more than 3 times as fast in the first year of the Clinton Presidency than it did during the preceding 4 years. A total of almost 2 million private sector jobs, 1.901 million, to be exact, have been created since President Clinton was inaugurated. That is far more than the 1 million jobs that were added during the previous 4 years. In other words, during the first year of the Clinton administration, we created almost twice as many private sector jobs as had been created in the previous 4 years. If they continue at that rate, President Clinton will have created almost eight times more jobs in his 4-year term than were created in the preceding 4-year term of his predecessor." (pS3404)

Sasser, Jim (Sen.-Tenn.). "Congressional Budget Concurrent Resolution," Congressional Record (22 Mar 1994). Daily ed. pS3403-3415. (ISSN0363-7239).

"The low interest rates which began coming down 4 years ago and have stoked recent economic growth are creeping back up. Ten-year treasury-note interest rates--representative of long-term rates--are now at 6.4 percent, down from 8.9 percent in September 1990. This 6.4 percent is approximately equal to the 6.6-percent level reached last January when President Clinton assumed office. The administration has been quick to take credit for interest rate declines that occurred last year, but rates are not back to about the level when President Clinton took office. This increase has, according to economists, already had a dampening effect upon consumer activity. Simply stated, economic growth is not a certainty. The average peace-time expansion has lasted but 14 quarters, only 11 if one removes the exceptional 1980's expansion, the longest peace-time expansion on record. The current expansion is in its 12th quarter. The administration and the Congress must now rely on more than just the momentum of the business cycle to keep the economy strong and vibrant. We must continue to structure policies that increase net national savings for investment and growth." (pS3410)

Domenici, Pete V. (Sen.-N.Mex.). "Congressional Budget Concurrent Resolution," Congressional Record (22 Mar 1994). Daily ed. pS3403-3415. (ISSN0363-7239).

"In the 20 years following World War II, the U.S. economy grew at an average annual rate of a little less than 4 percent. According to the 1994 economic report of the President, over 40 percent of economic growth over this period was due to advancement in technology....In the last 20 years...U.S. economic growth has dropped to an annual rate of about 2.3 percent. Wage growth, productivity gains over this period have been anemic compared to previous experience with the gains made by other countries. The principal reason for this disappointing performance was not the lack of will, not the lack of worker motivation or instinct. It was the result of a dramatic decline in technology progress on the part of our country for which we are responsible." (pS2621)

Rockefeller, John D., IV (Sen.-W.Va.). "National Competitiveness Act," Congressional Record (9 Mar 1994). Daily ed. pS2614-2624. (ISSN0363-7239).

"Since the official end of the last recession in spring 1991, the U.S. economy has recorded ten consecutive quarters of positive economic growth. While this might appear to be a favorable performance, economic activity over this two-and-a-half year period has been extremely sluggish by historical standards, and terribly inconsistent. Indeed, quarterly real economic growth over the last two-and-a-half years has averaged just 2.2 percent, compared with better than 5.0 percent following the three major recessions since 1970. Moreover, four quarters of relatively healthy economic growth over this ten-quarter period were sandwiched between periods of economic activity so weak that economists were openly debating whether the economy had dipped back into recession for a second or third time." (unpaginated)

Bills, James M. "1994's Economy: A Reprise of 1993, without the Volatility." Economic Newsletter 1993. unpaginated.

"In 1987 and 1988 [in the U.S.], real GDP [gross domestic product] grew by over 4 per cent per annum and, by 1989, the rate of unemployment had fallen to below 6 per cent....In the personal sector, the sustained upturn in house prices increased mortgage debt considerably but also permitted much higher levels of borrowing (against the revalued assets)....Domestic demand buoyancy was viewed favorably by the industrial sector." (p173) "With domestic demand expanding at a higher rate than supply, overheating became evident and inflationary pressures emerged....A boom based on credit and confidence could not survive such an attack for long....High interest rates and uncertainty over the domestic market rapidly withered business confidence--investment dried up and bankruptcies of over-geared enterprises accelerated. One of the most immediate consequences of the recession was a reversal of the employment-creation trends of the mid-to-late 1980s. Between 1984 and mid-1990, almost 3 million jobs had been created, a performance superior to that of any comparable European economy. This trend was immediately reversed as industry restructured itself--between early 1990 and May 1991, 2.6 million job losses occurred." (p174)

Whynes, David K. "Economic Recession and the Welfare State." Economics and Business Education v1 n4, Win 1993. p172-177.

"America's own economic recovery is now exactly three years old. In the year to the fourth quarter of 1993, GDP [gross domestic product] grew by 3.2%, and most forecasters expect even faster growth in 1994. Inflation remains subdued, at 2.5%, but the Fed's task is to keep it low. In past expansions the Fed did not tighten policy until inflation was already rising, which was too late. This time, Alan Greenspan, its chairman, is keeping a step ahead, and is right to do so. Although there is no evidence of an imminent surge in inflation, there are good reasons to expect pressures to emerge by the end of 1994. The amount of slack in the economy is shrinking fast...and real short-term interest rates are still abnormally low." (p18)

"Leaders: Interest Rates in Bondage." Economist v330 n7856, 26 Mar 1994. p18,20. (ISSN0013-0613).

"Two deep trends in today's [U.S.] economy have converged to create an economic situation that defies simple and immediate solutions: First, the economy continues to produce new goods much faster than it produces new jobs; and second, the expansion of the economy is bringing not an increase, but a decline, in wages. Output and employment: There has never been anything quite like the recent 'jobless recovery.' Between March 1991 (the official end of the recession) and October 1993, employment grew only 36 percent as fast as its average increase in previous recoveries. Manufacturing employment actually fell 2.7 percent." (p25) "Almost three million manufacturing jobs were lost between 1979 and 1992. With last fall's cyclical upturn, new jobs are being created, but they are concentrated in lower-paying service occupations. Also, according to Lawrence Mishel and Jared Bernstein of the Economic Policy Institute, 25.9 percent of the jobs created during the recovery were part time and 27.7 percent were temporary. Even college graduates have reason to worry. Kristina Shelley of the Bureau of Labor Statistics predicts that between 1990 and 2005, 'the average annual openings in jobs requiring a (college) degree will be fewer than the opportunities available during the 1984-1990 period.'" (p26)

Judis, John B. "Clintonomics: What's the Deal?" Mother Jones v19 n2, Mar-Apr 1994. p22-32. (ISSN0362-8841).

"Consumer spending [in the U.S.] has been growing at a 3.8 percent annual rate since spring, while disposable income is expanding just 2.2 percent. These patterns have driven the national saving rate to a record low of 3.7 percent." (p43)

Hage, David. "Predictions: Will the Economy Pick Up Steam?" U.S. News & World Report v115 n25, 27 Dec 1993. p42-43. (ISSN0041-5537).

"The economy did get a booster shot in 1993--not from Clinton's fiscal stimulus, which died in Congress--but from a plunge in long-term interest rates. The stimulus to credit-sensitive sectors such as housing and business investment helped lift the economy's growth from less than 2 percent in the first half of 1993 to 2.8 percent in the third quarter and toward 4 percent in the year's final months. But the economy still faces hurdles, which will slow growth from its fourth-quarter spurt to a 2.5 to 3 percent rate in 1994." (p42)

Hage, David. "Predictions: Will the Economy Pick Up Steam?" U.S. News & World Report v115 n25, 27 Dec 1993. p42-43. (ISSN0041-5537).

U.S.--ECONOMIC CONDITIONS--PUBLIC OPINION (v19)

U.S.--EMIGRATION AND IMMIGRATION (v19)

"Most population experts tend to look at U.S. immigration as just a small piece of a much larger puzzle--the worldwide boom in human migration. The United Nations Population Fund estimates that there are 100 million international migrants (that does not include the 900 million people who migrate within their countries); at least 37 million of these are refugees or have fled violence, drought, or environmental destruction. By comparison, the United States gets a small percentage of the total. Some of the movement is attributed to the growing discrepancy in living standards between developing and developed countries. Adding to the challenge is a global population growing at 98 million people a year." (p4)

Baumgarten, Fred. Should Environmentalists Adopt an Immigration Policy?" Audubon Activist v8 n3, Nov 1993. p1,4. (ISSN0898-915X).

"While immigration is now higher than in recent decades, it is not growing as fast as some statistics suggest. Nor are the levels unprecedented compared to other periods of U.S. history. The United States granted 'green cards' (permanent resident immigrant status) to nearly 974,000 people in fiscal year 1992. This was one-third more than the annual average in the 1980s, which was itself two-thirds higher than the 1970s average....And the view is commonplace that massive illegal entry adds many hundreds of thousands more. But the legal migration figures for 1989-92 were inflated by the special amnesty of 2.6 million undocumented aliens under the 1986 Immigration Reform and Control Act (backed by then-President Ronald Reagan and then-Senator Pete Wilson). Excluding them, there were 759,000 new legal immigrants in 1992 and an average of under 600,000 per year in the 1980s...." (p8-9)

Defreitas, Gregory. "Fear of Foreigners: Immigrants as Scapegoats for Domestic Woes." Dollars and Sense n191, Jan-Feb 1994. p8-9,33-35.

U.S.--EMIGRATION AND IMMIGRATION--PUBLIC OPINION (v19)

"The Latino National Political Survey, called by the NEW YORK TIMES 'the most extensive effort to measure Hispanic attitudes to date' reveals that 'economic self-interest and a driving commitment to be a part of American society, more than a sense of ethnic identity, shape the attitudes among Hispanic groups.' Surprising to many, though not to those who follow the issue, respondents were overwhelmingly of the opinion that immigration levels are too high. From 66 to 79 percent of the various Hispanic groups agreed or strongly agreed with the statement, 'There are too many immigrants.' This is about the same proportion as the 71% of randomly sampled Americans who said immigration rates are too high in a recent WALL STREET JOURNAL/NBC poll (WSJ 12/18/92)....Currently about eight percent of all people residing in the U.S. are foreign born; in California the proportion is 22%. If current rates of immigration continue, twice as many immigrants will enter the country in the 1990s as the seven million who came in during the 1980s." (p3)

"Hot Topics: Hispanics Oppose Current High Levels of Immigration." Carrying Capacity Network Clearinghouse

Bulletin v3 n1, Jan-Feb 1993. p3. (ISSN1066-5404).

U.S.--EMPLOYMENT (v19)

"In the 34 months since the March 1991 recession low, the economy has added 2.8 million non-farm payroll jobs. By contrast, 34 months after the March 1975 recession, 8 million jobs were created; and 9.2 million jobs were added during a similar period after the 1982 recession trough." (p10)

Oravec, John R. "Jobs Picture Mixed in New Survey." AFL-CIO News v39 n5, 21 Feb 1994. p10. (ISSN0001-1185).

"While unemployment [in the U.S.] continued to edge down during 1993, more than 8.2 million workers were on the jobless rolls at the end of the year. The nation's jobless rate dropped from 7.3 percent in December 1992 to 6.4 percent in December 1993, as the number of unemployed declined by nearly 1.1 million, the Bureau of Labor Statistics reported. Over the year, payrolls grew by nearly 2 million even as a number of major corporations initiated another sequence of 'downsizing' by issuing pink slips to some 600,000 workers. Most of the job growth came in the lower-paying services sector, including 350,000 with temporary help agencies, 400,000 in retail outlets and another 300,000 in medical services." (p14)

Oravec, John R. "Economy: Creeping Recovery Shows Worrisome Jobs Trends." AFL-CIO News v39 n2, 17 Jan 1994. p14. (ISSN0001-1185).

Between 1981 and 1991, "the number of wage earners reported to the Census Bureau in the service sector grew from 18.4 million to 25.4 million--by far the largest increase both in percentage and absolute growth. During the same period the number of wage earners in manufacturing decreased from 19.4 million to 18 million, while the total number of people reporting earnings in the economy increased from 68.6 million to 80.4 million....In 1981, 28 percent of all wage earners were in manufacturing jobs, while 27 percent were employed in the service sector. Ten years later manufacturing accounted for only 22 percent of the total workforce, while service represented 32 percent." (p34)

"The Landscape: Where the Jobs Are: College Graduates and Job Prospects." Change v26 n1, Jan-Feb 1994. p33-36. (ISSN0009-1383).

"According to Department of Labor statistics, after the previous four recessions, 44 percent of workers laid off expected to be recalled once the economy improved. After this last recession, however, only 14 percent of job losers expected to be recalled to work. This is one indication that employment and the economy are not expanding as they could, or even as they have in the past....a Maine State planning office report anticipates that we will add fewer than 10,000 jobs each year, which is one-third of the growth of the past two decades. They also state that it's likely to be 1997 before Maine regains all the jobs it lost during this recession." (pH1186)

Snowe, Olympia J. (Rep.-Maine). "Concurrent Resolution on the Budget--Fiscal Year 1995," Congressional Record (10 Mar 1994). Daily ed. pH1170-1242. (ISSN0363-7239).

The U.S. has "had a steady decline in the unemployment rate, dropping from 7.7 percent in January 1993 to 6.5 percent today. From January to January, that is the fastest 1-year drop in unemployment in 6 years. And the improvement can be seen also in the total number of jobs in the private sector....If you take a look at the numbers, you see from January of 1989 to January of 1993, which happens to be the 4 years of the previous President's term, there was a total increase in jobs of one million. From January 1993 to February 1994, there has been a 1.9 million increase in the number of jobs in this country." (pH1182)

Obey, David R. (Rep.-Wis.). "Concurrent Resolution on the Budget--Fiscal Year 1995," Congressional Record (10 Mar 1994). Daily ed. pH1170-1242. (ISSN0363-7239).

"The U.S. Labor Department has warned of shortages in the labor market. Employers are having difficulty in hiring experienced, dependable workers. By the end of the decade, 1.5 million fewer workers between the ages of 16 and 24 will have entered the work force. At the same time, 5 million older Americans will be retiring." (pS2202)

McCain, John (Sen.-Ariz.). "Social Security Administration Independent Agency Act," Congressional Record (2 Mar 1994). Daily ed. pS2193-2218. (ISSN0363-7239).

"The number of people working in the United States in services in the last 20 years has skyrocketed, and the number of people working in manufacturing has plummeted. In 1952, 34 million people were working in manufacturing; today that number is 17 million people. In 1952, 59 million people were working in services; today there are 79 million people." (pS16697)

Bradley, Bill (Sen.-N.J.). "North American Free-Trade Agreement," Congressional Record (20 Nov 1993). Daily ed. pS16678-16700. (ISSN0363-7239).

"Like most unions, the miners union has been whittled down, from 400,000 members in the 1940s to 66,000 today. Since the introduction of computer-driven mine equipment, they don't need miners....Two out of every five jobs in America are either temporary or part-time. A job is not a guarantee you can feed the family when 18 percent of American workers still live in poverty. Job security may be a thing of the past, but profits are certainly not. Corporate profits are up $431.6 billion. That kind of money could feed the hungry, educate the children, house the homeless and care for the sick. But it won't be used for that and it won't create one new job either. What isn't socked back into more labor-replacing technology will be soaked up by the rich and famous." (p2)

"Editorial: Labor Day 1993: No Picnic!" People's Tribune v20 n38, 20 Sep 1993. p2.

"The politicians claim that reducing the deficit will free money that business people can then invest to create jobs. But only nine percent of 200 big business chief executive officers (CEOs) surveyed recently by FORTUNE magazine said cutting the deficit would produce jobs. And 66 percent of these CEOs said the number of employees at their companies would either decrease or remain the same during the next 12 months. As one CEO, Jack Rehm, put it, 'As business becomes more automated and productive, we need fewer bodies.' The statistics bear this out. The jobs of 40 percent of those who have been laid off in this recession have been permanently eliminated. And the number of job openings available to an unemployed worker has declined 37 percent since 1984, according to Harvard labor economist James Medoff." (p2)

"Editorial: The Rich Should Pay for the Deficit, Not the Jobless." People's Tribune v20 n33, 16 Aug 1993. p2.

"The economic development strategies that brought the so-called rural renaissance [in the U.S.]...have been achieved at a cost. Many of the same conditions and attributes that attracted branch plants also kept wages low. Despite the number of new jobs created, per capita income in the rural South was only 74 percent of that of the urban South in 1980, and the per capita income of rural blacks was less than a third of the urban South's per capita income (which was about at the national average). In mid-1985, average hourly production wages in the South were $8.07, 16 percent below the average for the non-South, $9.57." (p114)

Rosenfeld, Stuart. "Economic Development: The Divided South." Southern Exposure v21 n1-2, Spr-Sum 1993. p113-116. (ISSN0146-809X).

"Firms [in the U.S.] with 100 or fewer employees account for 67 percent of all new jobs, said economist David Birch at a recent conference on job creation. On average, though, the percentage varies widely over time. Moreover, most of this growth occurs in a small percentage of firms, the fast-growing 'gazelles,' says Dr. Birch of Cognetics, a Cambridge, Mass., consulting firm." A study "confined to one important sector, manufacturing... finds that firms with fewer than 100 employees accounted for only about one-fourth of all new jobs in the 1973-88 period....Amid all the debate over job creation, officials are not focusing enough on job retention, says business leader George Haymaker. Washington State's aluminum industry has lost almost 2,000 jobs in the last two years." (p9)

Trumbull, Mark. "Economy: Which Firms Will Be Founts of New Jobs?" The Christian Science Monitor v86 n36, 14 Jan 1994. p9. (ISSN0882-7729).

U.S.--EMPLOYMENT--FORECASTING

"The Bureau of Labor Statistics (BLS) projects annual increases in employment of 1.5 percent between 1992 and 2005, compared with 1.4 percent between 1979 and 1992. The addition of 26 million jobs could push total civilian employment to more than 147 million by 2005. Services will continue to dominate the nation's job growth, adding 24 million jobs. Growth in health and business services will be especially robust, although it will be slower than in the past. Four million additional workers should join the health-services industry, bringing employment in health services to 12.5 million in 2005. Jobs in residential care should grow faster than in any other industry sector, at 7.3 percent a year. Business services will continue to be the fastest-growing major employment sector. Between 1992 and 2005, this industry could add 3.1 million jobs. Computer and data processing services should account for 800,000 of those new jobs, growing at 5.3 percent a year." (p19)

Waldrop, Judith. "Business Reports: Labor Force: Career Opportunities to 2005." American Demographics v16 n3, Mar 1994. p19-21. (ISSN0163-4089).

U.S.--EMPLOYMENT--MANUFACTURES (v19)

U.S.--EMPLOYMENT--PUBLIC OPINION (v19)

U.S.--ENVIRONMENTAL ASPECTS

"The air [in the U.S.] is a lot cleaner than it used to be. Since 1970, lead emissions are down 97 percent; particulates (soot, smoke) have dropped 61 percent and hydrocarbons 38 percent." (p51)

Samuelson, Robert J. "Judgment Calls: Here's Some Good News, America." Newsweek v123 n5, 31 Jan 1994. p51. (ISSN0028-9604).

U.S.--ENVIRONMENTAL ASPECTS--PUBLIC OPINION

"A significant majority of Iowa producers, 80%, said too heavy reliance on purchased inputs such as fuel and fertilizer had some or a lot of influence on farm income, according to the 1993 Iowa Farm and Rural Life Poll, recently released by Iowa State University Extension. When asked about factors that somewhat or severely threaten rural America, 67% listed depletion of natural resources, and 60% listed the decline in the quality of the environment. Eighty-nine percent felt pollution of rivers, lakes, and oceans was a somewhat or very serious problem for the world, and 83% listed soil erosion, polluted land, and loss of farmland. The poll also found that 58% felt soil quality was declining worldwide; 31% felt it was declining in the United States, 21% in Iowa, 17% in their own county, and 9% on their own farm." (p3)

"Heavy Reliance on Inputs Influences Farm Income, Say Iowans in Poll." Alternative Agriculture News v11 n12, Nov 1993. p3. (ISSN8755-4941).

U.S.--HEALTH AND HYGIENE--PUBLIC OPINION (v19)

U.S.--INDUSTRIES (v19)

"America's mail-order and home-shopping industries are together worth around $80 billion a year; video rentals, $15 billion; on-line information services, $35 billion." (p10)

"Survey: Television: From Prime Time to My Time." Economist v330 n7850, 12 Feb 1994. p56(9-11). (ISSN0013-0613).

U.S.--MANUFACTURES (v19)

"Among the U.S automakers, defects per vehicle have declined from 7.3 in 1981 to only 1.5 in 1991--virtually the same rate as the Japanese. In Silicon Valley, computer chips have emerged as another quality success story. In 1980, American memory chips failed at a rate of 3,000 per billion hours of usage. Now our failure rate is comparable to that of the Japanese--at less than 100 per billion hours of computer time. In our industrial heartland, our domestic steel industry is being revitalized. Defects in steel products have dropped from 8 percent in 1982 to less than one percent today." (p662)

Franklin, Barbara Hackman (U.S. Secretary of Commerce). U.S. House. Committee on Appropriations. "Depts. of Veterans Affairs and Housing and Urban Development...Approp. for 1994 (Part 4)." Hearing, Washington, D.C.: GPO, 1993. (ISBN016040911X). (Y4.Ap6/1:V64/4/994/pt.4).

"The primary drag on the recovery seems to be the continued decline of the manufacturing sector, in which the U.S. lost roughly one million jobs between January 1991 and September 1993. Currently, U.S. manufacturing employment is at the same level as it was in 1965! According to the Office of Technology Assessment, the link between military outlays and the U.S. manufacturing sector is strong: Every dollar spent on arms procurement generates 57 cents worth of manufacturing sales. In contrast, the average dollar pumped through the U.S. economy produces only 17 cents worth of manufacturing sales. Cuts in military spending have thus played a crucial role in deindustrialization, and future trends in arms spending will certainly affect any potential reindustrialization. According to a 1993 CBO [Congressional Budget Office] report, the military-related sector is the largest single portion of the U.S. economy that has continued to contract during the current recovery. From 1987-92, this sector lost between 900,000 and 1.1 million jobs. Based on early-1993 assumptions, the CBO projected military sector layoffs of 500,000 to 800,000 (including non-manufacturing workers and Department of Defense employees) for the 1993-97 period." (p21)

Cypher, James M. "Special Section: Reversion Not Conversion." Dollars and Sense n191, Jan-Feb 1994. p20-22,37.

"In 1992, manufacturing output [in the U.S.] was 39 percent higher than in 1980 and 95 percent higher than in 1970." (p51)

Samuelson, Robert J. "Judgment Calls: Here's Some Good News, America." Newsweek v123 n5, 31 Jan 1994. p51. (ISSN0028-9604).

"Despite its superpower status, the U.S. is the only industrialized nation that saw manufacturing wages decline in the 1980s. Since 1979, we have lost 3 million manufacturing jobs. In 1990, the median income of American families was lower than in 1973. Reversing these trends will be very difficult--and made no easier by free trade. To the extent that the U.S. competes with other nations purely on cost, our wages will continue to decline. Economists call it 'factor price equalization': given mobile capital, free trade will drive the factors of production worldwide toward the same price." (p3)

"Free Trade Sets Sail: Dolphins, Wages, and NAFTA." Rocky Mountain Institute Newsletter v9 n1, Spr 1993. p1,3.

"Manufacturers account for 22 percent of the overall United States gross domestic product. Add to that already-sizable chunk of US output another dimension--the suppliers and services feeding into and off of manufacturers, such as power companies and health-care providers--and the importance of this sector grows even larger. (Experts say manufacturers pay roughly 40 percent of US health-care coverage.)" (p1)

Kaslow, Amy. "Manufacturing Outlook Appears Promising for '94." The Christian Science Monitor v86 n30, 6 Jan 1994. p1,18. (ISSN0882-7729).

"Last year, output per hour at U.S. factories increased at a record 5.1 percent pace--the largest advance since 1987. This exceptional rate of productivity growth follows a jump of 4.2 percent in 1992 and builds firmly on the upward trend that began in the 1980s. Between 1980 and 1990, manufacturing productivity rose to an average annual rate of 3.2 percent, compared with 2.2 percent in the 1970s. By producing more goods with fewer workers, American companies are able to reduce the amount of money they spend on each unit of output. This, combined with a cheap dollar and low wage growth, makes U.S. products less expensive than those of many global rivals. Says Bruce Steinberg of Merrill Lynch: 'Because of more rapidly growing productivity in the United States and labor costs that are growing less rapidly, U.S. products are more competitive in world markets.'" (p58)

Collins, Sara. "Business: America Cranks It Up." U.S. News & World Report v116 n12, 28 Mar 1994. p57-58,60. (ISSN0041-5537).

U.S.--MANUFACTURES--EMPLOYMENT (v19)

U.S.--MANUFACTURES--ENERGY CONSUMPTION

"Between 1950 and 1986, the output of the U.S. manufacturing sector, adjusted for inflation, more than tripled. But while the amount of energy used also nearly tripled and the quantity of capital increased fourfold, the number of work hours rose by only one third. In the United States, five manufacturing industries--primary metals, paper, oil refining, chemicals, and stone, clay, and glass--are notable for their high use of energy and capital on the one hand, and low labor needs on the other. These are also, by far, the biggest polluters. Among them, they account for more than 80 percent of energy use and toxics releases within the manufacturing sector--but for only 17 percent of its employment." (p6)

Renner, Michael. "Cover Story: Creating Sustainable Jobs." Positive Alternatives v3 n4, Sum 1993. p6-7. (ISSN1065-0075).

U.S.--MORTALITY

"The Centers for Disease Control and Prevention announced...that at the current rate, more Americans will lose their lives to gunshots than to automobile accidents by the year 2003. In fact, that point has already been reached in New York, the District of Columbia, and in five other States. In 1991, 43,536 people died in automobile-related accidents, as against 38,317 from gunshot wounds. Vehicle-related deaths continue to decline as a result of better safety features. Yet violent killings, often random, go on unabated. Peaks continue to attract some notice. But these are peaks above average levels that 50 years ago would have been thought epidemic. In 1943,...in East Harlem, there were exactly 44 homicides by gunshot in New York City. In 1992, there were 1,499. Among 15-24-year-olds in the United States, deaths from gunshots rose 40 percent between 1985 and 1991." (pS544)

Moynihan, Daniel Patrick (Sen.-N.Y.). "Homicides by Gunshot," Congressional Record (1 Feb 1994). Daily ed. pS544-545. (ISSN0363-7239).

"More than 200,000 people die each year in the United States, excluding homicide, suicide, and traffic accidents. Another 170,000 people die in those ways. Death, anticipated or sudden, leaves in its wake more than tears. Family, friends, fellow employees live with the lingering after effects of grief and bereavement. Some handle it well, but others suffer chronic or periodic depression, over-medication, alcohol abuse or some other dysfunctional behavior. Many of those who grieve need help; all of them would be well served by at least minimal counseling. Death, grief, and bereavement are conditions faced by hospice people every day since over 200,000 terminally ill people are cared for annually by hospices. Indeed, Medicare-certified hospices must, by law, have both social workers and clergy available for their patients and for a period after a death for the survivors to help with grief and bereavement." (pS3929)

Durenberger, Dave (Sen.-Minn.). "National Grief Teleconference," Congressional Record (25 Mar 1994). Daily ed. pS3929. (ISSN0363-7239).

"The mortality record of the United States in the twentieth century can be summarized from life tables and age-adjusted central death rates published by the Social Security Administration (Bell, Wade, and Goss, 1992) and the National Center for Health Statistics (1992). Age-adjusted central death rates for males and females in the United States in 1900 were 2,415.5 and 2,198.7 per 100,000, respectively. By 1990, these rates had declined to 1,022.3 for males (a 57.7 percent decline) and 614.0 for females (a 72.1 percent decline). For the first 90 years of the twentieth century, the annual average decline in the central death rate was 0.98 percent for males and 1.37 percent for females. At the same time, the expectation of life at birth increased for males from 46.4 to 71.6 years (a 25.2-year increase) and for females from 49.0 to 78.7 (a 29.7-year increase). The majority of the gain in life expectancy at birth in the twentieth century can be attributed to rapid and sustained declines in mortality at younger ages...." (p59)

Olshansky, S. Jay/Carnes, Bruce A. "Demographic Perspectives on Human Senescence." Population and Development Review v20 n1, Mar 1994. p57-80. (ISSN0098-7921).

"From 1960 to 1986 the inequality in mortality by education increased for both sexes." (p32) "The age-adjusted mortality rate among white men aged 25 to 64 decreased 50 percent between 1960 and 1986 for those with the highest educational attainment. These rates dropped from 5.7 per 1,000 population in 1960 to 2.8 in 1986. Among white men with the lowest educational attainment, however, the decrease was only 15 percent, dropping from 9 to 7.6 per 1,000." (p33)

Queen, Susan/others. "The Widening Gap between Socioeconomic Status and Mortality." Statistical Bulletin v75 n2, Apr-Jun 1994. p31-35. (ISSN0790-8334).

"The United States leads industrialized Western countries with the highest homicide numbers and rates. In 1991 there were 27,440 deaths from homicide and legal intervention and an additional 30,200 from suicide, producing death rates of 10.9 and 12.0 per 100,000 population, respectively. Provisional data for 1992 indicate that homicides fell by 870 deaths to 26,570 with a concomitant drop in the rate to 10.4 per 100,000 population. Suicide deaths decreased by 440 to 29,760, and the mortality rate fell to 11.7. In 1991 suicide was America's eighth leading cause of death and accounted for 1.4 percent of total deaths. Homicide and legal intervention ranked 10th and was responsible for 1.3 percent of all U.S. deaths." (p12-13)

Seltzer, Frederic. "Trend in Mortality from Violent Deaths: Suicide and Homicide, United States, 1960-1991." Statistical Bulletin v75 n2, Apr-Jun 1994. p10-18. (ISSN0790-8334).

U.S.--OFFICIALS AND EMPLOYEES (v19)

"The Executive Residence staff [at the White House] provides for the operation of the Executive Residence. A staff of 36 domestic employees accomplishes general housekeeping, prepares and serves meals, greets visitors, and provides services as required in support of official and ceremonial functions. A staff of 33 tradespersons, including plumbers, carpenters, painters, on a single shift; electricians on a double shift; and operating engineers on a 24-hour basis, maintains and makes repairs, minor modifications, and improvements to the 132 rooms and the mechanical systems and provides support for official and ceremonial functions. A staff of 12 specialized employees provides services necessary to the operation of the White House and official and ceremonial functions. This staff includes 4 florists, 4 curators and 4 calligraphers. An administrative staff consists of the Chief Usher, 4 Assistant Ushers, 1 Executive Grounds Superintendent, 1 Operating Accountant, and 1 Administrative Officer. The staff is charged with management and administrative functions of the Executive Residence. This requires coordination with the Executive Office of the President, the National Park Service, the Military, the United States Secret Service, the General Services Administration and other agencies." (p700)

Stanton, Robert G. (Regional Director, National Park Service, National Capital Region). U.S. House. Committee on Appropriations. "Treasury, Postal Service, and General Government Approp. for Fiscal Year 1994 (Part 3)." Hearing, Washington, D.C.: GPO, 1993. (Y4.Ap6/1:T71/994/pt.3).

U.S.--OFFICIALS AND EMPLOYEES--RETIREMENT

"In 1986, following years of extensive review, the Federal Employees' Retirement System Act was jointly developed by a Democratic House and a Republican Senate and signed into law by President Reagan. FERS [Federal Employees' Retirement System] is modeled on the best practices of the private sector and responsibly addresses the needs of both the Government and its employees. Costs of the system are less than 23 percent of payroll. Its enactment achieved savings of $300 million in the first year and $8.3 billion between 1987-91. All Federal employees hired after December 31, 1983, automatically became participants in FERS. Under FERS the minimum retirement age is 62 with 5 years of service, 60 with 20 years of service, and 55 to 57 after 30 years of service." (pH10739)

Clay, William (Rep.-Mo.). "Government Reform and Savings Act of 1993." Congressional Record (22 Nov 1993). Daily ed. pH10729-10893. (ISSN0363-7239).

U.S.--OFFICIALS AND EMPLOYEES--SALARIES, ETC. (v19)

"In 1990, the [U.S.] president's pay agent estimated that private employees were paid 29 percent more in wages and salaries than federal employees doing similar work. This finding was disputed by the Congressional Budget Office, which estimated that private sector workers were paid only 15 percent more in wages than federal employees doing similar work. But a study by Brent R. Moulton published in a 1990 issue of the JOURNAL OF LABOR RESEARCH found that federal employees are paid on average 3 percent more than their private counterparts. Finally, a Dartmouth study by Steven F. Venti published in PUBLIC SECTOR PAYROLLS suggested that federal employee wages could be reduced by an average of 30 percent before comparability with the private sector would be achieved." (p26)

Cox, Wendell. "Symposium: Federal Workers Benefit Heavily." Insight v10 n3, 17 Jan 1994. p25-27. (ISSN1051-4880).

U.S.--POLITICS AND GOVERNMENT (v19)

"On...[October 1, 1994], 15 years will have passed since the House and Senate unanimously authorized the establishment of Office of Inspectors General in 12 executive departments and agencies, including the Department of Transportation. During this period, the DOT OIG funded by approximately $431 million has issued more than 26,000 audit reports identifying potential savings to the American taxpayer of almost $11 billion and has secured nearly 1,400 criminal indictments and over 1,050 criminal convictions." (p423)

Schiavo, A. Mary (Inspector General, Dept. of Transportation). U.S. House. Committee on Appropriations. "Department of Transportation and Related Agencies Approp. for 1994 (Part 3)." Hearing, Washington, D.C.: GPO, 1993. (ISBN0160410649). (Y4.Ap6/1:T68/4/994/pt.3).

"The breadth and volume of CCC [Civilian Conservation Corps] work is so immense it beggars belief. [In the nine years it lasted], It included: 2 billion trees planted, 931 million acres stocked with fish, 5 million soil erosion dams, 52,000 public campgrounds, 123,000 miles of road, more than 6 million man-days spent fighting fires, and an area the size of Ohio, Iowa and Indiana drained and restored to farmland. Among its other tasks, the CCC protected grazing land, drained mosquito-infested marshes, preserved wildlife habitats, battled crop disease, cleared forest for increased growth and built firebreaks, preserved historic sites, and built hiking trails in the national parks and forests. Often the enlistees responded to natural disasters and emergencies, sometimes at peril to their lives." (p4) "At its peak in 1935-36, with 500,000 enrollees and about 100,000 staff in 2,514 camps, FDR and others wanted to make the CCC permanent. But as the economy recovered and federal funds were diverted from peace activity it became a war casualty on June 30, 1942. Nearly 3 million young men and 250,000 veterans had served their country as they served themselves and families." (p5)

Kraft, Barbara S. "The CCC: A Job Stimulus That Worked." Progressive Review n318, Jul 1993. p4-6.

"Washington commands a much larger police force of 79,000 officers who operate out of 53 federal agencies. They include the FBI, the DEA [Drug Enforcement Agency], the AFT [Bureau of Alcohol, Tobacco, and Firearms], and the US Border Patrol, among others." (p7)

Dillin, John. "National: Activists Call on Clinton for Broad Investigation of Federal Police Practices." The Christian Science Monitor v86 n34, 12 Jan 1994. p7. (ISSN0882-7729).

U.S.--POLITICS AND GOVERNMENT--APPROPRIATIONS AND EXPENDITURES (v19)

U.S.--POLITICS AND GOVERNMENT--CORRESPONDENCE

"The Administration experienced over 200,000 incoming and outgoing calls daily during its first week in office, a substantial increase over the level of traffic during previous administrations. According to AT&T estimates, the White House continues to receive upwards of 65,000 incoming calls each day. Due to the high volume of calls, it is difficult for members of the President's cabinet, other federal government employees, and even Members of Congress to reach senior White House staff. Likewise, members of the public have tremendous difficulty trying to convey their messages to the President." (p878)

U.S. House. Committee on Appropriations. "Treasury, Postal Service, and General Government Approp. for Fiscal Year 1994 (Part 3)." Hearing, Washington, D.C.: GPO, 1993. (Y4.Ap6/1:T71/994/pt.3).

"The people of America have overwhelmingly responded to the President's call to participate and become involved in their government. The volume of mail received at the White House, which continues to increase and which is greater than any President in history, will total over ten million pieces during the first year of this Presidency. In contrast, the previous White House Office received about 3.75 million pieces per year and answered about a quarter of a million. The new Administration's goal is to work toward answering in excess of six million pieces annually. To meet this dramatic increase, the following CSL increases are required: additional postage of $1,600,000, additional stationery of $360,000, and additional training for the correspondence staff of $125,000." (p514-515)

U.S. House. Committee on Appropriations. "Treasury, Postal Service, and General Government Approp. for Fiscal Year 1994 (Part 3)." Hearing, Washington, D.C.: GPO, 1993. (Y4.Ap6/1:T71/994/pt.3).

U.S.--POLITICS AND GOVERNMENT--DATA PROCESSING

"On January 15, 1993, the Executive Office of the President was served with a subpoena for data stored on the hard drives in personal computers used by certain Executive Office of the President personnel. Compliance with the subpoena required the removal and replacement of nearly three hundred personal computer hard drives between January 18-20, 1993. Total cost for the equipment alone for the White House Office is estimated at $225,000. This expense was unanticipated and unbudgeted. The Executive Office of the President had no choice but to comply with the action of the court in this matter. The expenses associated with compliance, however, represented a significant investment of funds already strained by the needs of the transition." (p826)

Thomasson, Patsy (Special Asst. of the President, Dir. of the Office of Admin.). U.S. House. Committee on Appropriations. "Treasury, Postal Service, and General Government Approp. for Fiscal Year 1994 (Part 3)." Hearing, Washington, D.C.: GPO, 1993. (Y4.Ap6/1:T71/994/pt.3).

U.S.--POLITICS AND GOVERNMENT--EMPLOYMENT (v19)

U.S.--POLITICS AND GOVERNMENT--LAW AND LEGISLATION

"There are circumstances when a conflict of interest may exist, or at least when the appearance of a conflict may arise, and the Attorney General is placed in a difficult position to effectively investigate and prosecute another high-ranking Government official. The Watergate episode certainly highlighted the potential for such conflicts. The independent counsel law has proved a useful tool on some occasions to avoid such conflicts. However, the...law has not completely fulfilled its promise or purpose. All too often it has not restored the public's confidence in Government or our legal system. Since its enactment in 1978, this law has resulted in 14 separate investigations but there has only been one final conviction of a named subject. These court-appointed prosecutors, who are accountable to absolutely nobody, have spent more than $61 million. Unfortunately, all too often there is little to show for their costly efforts." (pH378)

Fish, Hamilton, Jr. (Rep.-N.Y.). "Independent Counsel Reauthorization Act of 1993," Congressional Record (9 Feb 1994). Daily ed. pH378-389. (ISSN0363-7239).

U.S.--POLITICS AND GOVERNMENT--PUBLIC OPINION

"As the Clinton administration has demonstrated, contemporary liberalism inclines toward higher taxes and bigger government; yet the American people today, by 55-36 percent, would rather pay less in taxes and receive fewer government services than pay more taxes in return for more services....contemporary liberalism stands or falls by a faith in the efficacy of big government; but popular distrust of government is at an all-time high. In 1972, 74 percent of Americans had at least a 'fair amount' of confidence in the federal government; today, that figure has fallen to 42 percent. And in January of this year, by 69-22 percent, Americans agreed that the federal government creates more problems than it solves." (p33)

Kristol, William. "A Conservative Looks at Liberalism." Commentary v96 n3, Sep 1993. p33-36. (ISSN0010-2601).

"For two decades, more Americans have considered themselves conservative than liberal. From 1980 on, in polls taken by CBS News/NEW YORK TIMES, no more than 23 percent of the American public have identified themselves as liberals, and in January 1993 that figure stood at 18 percent. (The number identifying themselves as conservatives has averaged around 33 percent, with another 40 percent or so calling themselves moderates.) Even in the presidential race of 1992, the two non-liberal candidates received 57 percent of the vote, while Clinton, the one liberal, ran as a 'new kind of Democrat'--that is, a not-so-liberal Democrat. In 1992, moreover, over the opposition of the liberal establishment, measures limiting the terms of legislators passed in all fourteen states in which they were on the ballot." (p33)

Kristol, William. "A Conservative Looks at Liberalism." Commentary v96 n3, Sep 1993. p33-36. (ISSN0010-2601).

According to a U.S. NEWS survey "Two out of 3 Americans say the government should play a large role in solving the nation's most serious problems, and almost as many are willing to pay higher taxes to finance that effort. But the public remains deeply skeptical about the government's ability to perform well. Almost 4 out of 5 poll respondents say any additional tax money would be wasted." (p40)

Roberts, Steven V. "Special Issue: State of the Union." U.S. News & World Report v115 n25, 27 Dec 1993. p38-41. (ISSN0041-5537).

U.S.--POPULATION (v19)

"Two historic trends contribute to [the U.S.] public transit's declining percentage of the travel market. First is the continuing movement of population out of densely populated cities to suburbs or to the newer, automobile oriented cities of the South and West. The lower densities of these areas make mass transit a less economically attractive option. The second factor is the dramatic increase in accessibility to private vehicles and the resulting decrease in the transit dependent population. Only 9.2 percent of households had no vehicle available in 1990, as noted in the National Personal Transportation Survey, down from 13.5 percent in 1983. The number of total household vehicles has increased 128 percent over the last twenty years." (p68)

Pena, Federico (Secretary of Transportation). U.S. House. Committee on Appropriations. "Department of Transportation and Related Agencies Approp. for 1994 (Part 3)." Hearing, Washington, D.C.: GPO, 1993. (ISBN0160410649). (Y4.Ap6/1:T68/4/994/pt.3).

"The U.S. is now dominated and defined by its suburban communities, rather than by its rural edge. In 1990, for the first time in the country's history, over 50 percent of the population lived in metropolitan areas containing over a million people. And most of the growth that has occurred since 1950 in these urban areas has been in the suburban ring--not the inner city." (p23)

U.S. Dept. of Agriculture/Stauber, Karl N. "Rural Development: The Diversity of Rural America." Agricultural Outlook Jan-Feb 1994. p23-24.

"Environmental damage results not simply from population growth, consumption, or technology, but from all three multiplied together. On all three counts the United States scores badly. Currently, the U.S. population is growing at just over 1 percent per year--almost double the average for the developed world. This is now actually faster than many developing countries like Korea, Fiji, Uruguay, Albania, Cyprus, Mauritius, and Seychelles. Out of the 6.6 million people added to the population of the developed world every year, 2.6 million--two in every five--are added in the United States. Between now and the year 2025, the U.S. population is projected to grow by another 62 million or so. This is the rough equivalent of adding another Britain, France, or Italy to the globe." (p20)

Harrison, Paul. "The United States: Booming with Buyers--and Babies, Too." Amicus Journal v15 n45, Win 1994. p20-21. (ISSN0276-7201).

"The cost of providing worldwide universal access to family planning by the end of this decade will be $11 billion a year. It's affordable. It's just a question of priority. Currently, the U.S. spends $429 million annually on population. This will have to increase to $1.5 billion by the year 2000 if we are to continue our historic role of contributing 30 percent of the population budget. $1.5 billion? In a recession? How do we get it? From the intelligence community. At the height of the Cold War, the CIA's budget was $15 billion. Now, having utterly failed at predicting the collapse of the Soviet Union, they've been rewarded by an increase to $30 billion. We need about three percent of that to address the real threats to our national security: Waves of environmental refugees crossing our borders in hopes of food and a job, and a shrinking supply of food and water worldwide." (p24)

Fonda, Jane. "Forum: High Time for Some Population Intelligence." E Magazine v5 n1, Feb 1994. p22-24. (ISSN1046-8021).

"The fastest-growing city in America during the two-year period was Las Vegas, Nev., whose metropolitan area now extends into Arizona. It grew by 6.5 percent a year. Punta Gorda and Naples, both in Florida, and Laredo, Texas, all tied for second with a 3.9 percent growth rate. Other top growth spots included Redding, Calif., and Boise City, Idaho, (tied for fifth at 3.7 percent), and two California cities, Modesto and Bakersfield (tied for seventh at 3.4 percent). Yuma, Ariz., (3.3 percent) was ninth, and three metro areas tied for 10th--McAllen-Edinburg-Mission, Texas; Anchorage, Alaska; and Bellingham, Wash.--all at 3.2 percent." (p3)

Dillin, John. "National: Population Shifts Remake National Map." The Christian Science Monitor v86 n33, 11 Jan 1994. p3. (ISSN0882-7729).

"While the US fertility rate (number of children per woman) had dropped to 1.8 in the mid-1980s, it began to rise again and now stands at about 2.1. This seemingly small increase means the country's population (moving upward by 1.1 percent a year) could rise from 258 million today to nearly 400 million by the middle of the next century. A big portion of this annual increase is immigration--legal and illegal--which is about 1.5 million people a year." (p3)

Knickerbocker, Brad. "National: UN's Cairo Conference to Face the Social Costs of Population." The Christian Science Monitor v86 n79, 18 Mar 1994. p3. (ISSN0882-7729).

U.S.--POPULATION--ATTITUDES

"Those who believe concern about population growth remains high on the world's list of priorities should consider the contrast between Earth Day 1990 and the first such day held in 1970. On 22 April 1990, 200 million demonstrated in 136 countries, telling us of a dozen ways we are destroying our planet, of the greenhouse effect, the loss of ozone and rain forests, etc., and of a hundred ways to save our planet (reduce consumption, recycle, car pool, etc., etc.). But in the deluge of leaflets and booklets distributed by the organizing committee not one stressed the environmental threat from too many people. In contrast, on Earth Day 1970 the population bomb shared equal billing with environmental degradation....In 1970 there were more than a hundred campuses with Zero Population Growth (ZPG) chapters. Today there are none. In 1970 book stores carried several titles on population. Look now and only one is likely to be found on their shelves....In 1970, 17 major US companies worked in contraceptive research--today there is one (Hilts, 1990)....Has the population problem gone away? Hardly! In 1970, world population grew by 63 million people; in 1990 it grew by 93 million." (p56)

Paddock, William. "Our Last Chance to Win the War on Hunger." Carrying Capacity Network v4 n1, 1994. p52-65. (ISSN1066-5404).

U.S.--PUBLIC OPINION

"Harris polls in 1988 and 1993 suggest an authoritarian drift in the American public. In 1988, only 33% expressed great confidence in the military, about the same as for the Supreme Court and major educational institutions. In 1993, 57% thought highly of the military as opposed to 26% for the second place Supreme Court. Support for all other categories--such as the press, Wall Street and medicine--dropped with one exception: the White House, which was up from 17% in 1988 to 23% today." (p8)

"Weather Report: Land of the Free." Progressive Review n316, Apr 1993. p7-9.

"Consumer confidence and retail sales [in the U.S.] are up; unemployment and interest rates are down. Last August, almost half of all Americans named pocketbook issues as the main problem facing the country, but in the latest U.S. NEWS survey, only 1 in 5 identified the economy as the prime concern. Forty-six percent pick positive words--happy, satisfied, hopeful--to describe their emotions after Clinton's first year....Almost half choose negative words--uncertain, frustrated, disappointed--to sum up their feelings. The nation is facing a skills gap that threatens to divide the population along an unstable fault line: One third of all college graduates view the future with hope, but only 1 out of 10 who lack a high school diploma feels the same way. Concern about crime has shattered the nation's sense of well-being like a police siren stabbing the night: Two out of five now say it is the No. 1 problem." (p40)

Roberts, Steven V. "Special Issue: State of the Union." U.S. News & World Report v115 n25, 27 Dec 1993. p38-41. (ISSN0041-5537).

U.S.--RELIGION (v19)

"Within the last 35 years this country has experienced growing religious diversity. Since 1957, the Christian population--both Protestants and Catholics--has dropped from 92% to 81% of all persons in the U.S. while the Jewish population has shrunk from 3% to 2% of all religious observers; at the same time, other religions including Buddhism, Islam, and Hindu have grown from 1% to 6% of the population. Furthermore, only about 30% of the world population is Christian and that drops to 24% outside Northern and Latin America. Hence, a significant percentage of prospective third world immigrants will not be of white Anglo-Saxon and Christian descent. As a result, the standard sacred holidays such as Christmas and Easter will number only two among a variety of important religious days observed by employees." (p54)

Wolkinson, Benjamin/Nichol, Victor. "Religious Discrimination: Arbitrating the Grievances." Dispute Resolution Journal v48 n4, Dec 1993. 54-63.

"In answer to the National Survey of Religious Identification question 'What is your religion?,' 86 percent of respondents said they were Christians: The two largest groups were Roman Catholics, at 26 percent, and Baptists, at 19 percent. Jews represent 2 percent of the population, with Muslims, Buddhists, and Hindus numbering no more than 0.5 percent each. Of those polled, 7.5 percent said they had no religion, and 2.3 percent refused to answer. The survey found that many more Americans claim to be Catholic, Baptist, Methodist, Episcopalian, Lutheran, Presbyterian, and Unitarian-Universalist than membership figures of those denominations show." (p12)

Goodrich, Lawrence J. "Cover Story: Religion Is Alive and Diverse in US." The Christian Science Monitor v86 n32, 10 Jan 1994. p11-13. (ISSN0882-7729).

"The latest comparative figures collected on religion and sports find that money contributed to religion totaled $56.7 billion in 1992, according to the American Association of Fund-Raising Counsel. That is about 14 times the $4 billion spent on the three biggest sports--major league baseball, football, and basketball. The major sports leagues don't disclose gate receipts, but totals were obtained through league public-relations sources who asked not to be named. FINANCIAL WORLD magazine reported similar figures for 1992. Major religious organizations make public annual financial reports. In attendance, religion totaled 5.6 billion in 1993, based on annual Gallup polls. That is about 55 times greater than the 103-million total attendance reported by the three main professional sports leagues." (p19)

Cornell, George W. "Religion: News on Religion Scarce in Media." The Christian Science Monitor v86 n109, 29 Apr 1994. p19. (ISSN0882-7729).

The National Survey of Religious Identification, conducted in 1990 by the Graduate School of the City University of New York, "confirms that women tend to be more religious than men. The NSRI showed that 87 percent of American men said they are religious believers; 83 percent are Christians and 56 percent are Protestants. Among women, 92 percent identify with a religion; 89 percent are Christians, and 61 percent are Protestants. The gap is far larger among African-Americans: 52 percent of black Catholics are women, 56 percent of Episcopalians, 58 percent of Baptists, 60 percent of Methodists, all the way up to 69 percent among Holiness denominations. Among non-Christians the reverse is true: A slight majority of Jews are men; men with no religion outnumber women by a 2-to-1 margin." (p13)

Goodrich, Lawrence J. "Cover Story: Religion Is Alive and Diverse in US." The Christian Science Monitor v86 n32, 10 Jan 1994. p11-13. (ISSN0882-7729).

U.S.--RELIGION--PUBLIC OPINION

"The U.S. NEWS survey found that 30 percent of Americans believe the country as a whole is hostile to their moral or spiritual values. But when specific institutions are mentioned, the numbers climb. Television is considered hostile by 62 percent of Americans; Congress, by 47 percent, and newspapers, 46 percent. President Clinton was considered hostile by 34 percent of those surveyed presumably including those who take issue with his permissive views on abortion and gay rights. The Supreme Court is viewed as hostile by 27 percent. Yet if Americans are distressed by what they see as a rampant moral decline and a growing disdain for religion among the cultural elites, they are of no mind to coerce the country into repentance. In the U.S. NEWS poll, 91 percent agreed that individual liberty is critical to democracy, and 53 percent say that church and state must remain 'completely separate.' Seventy percent agreed that individuals must decide what's right and wrong." (p58)

Sheler, Jeffery L. "Cover Story: Spiritual America." U.S. News & World Report v116 n13, 4 Apr 1994. p48-54,56-59. (ISSN0041-5537).

"The religious tapestry of America today shows a country that by external measures is at least as religious as it has always been. About 95 percent of Americans say they believe in God or a universal spirit, and about 60 percent say they attend religious services regularly--figures that have not changed much since the 1950s. Only 9 percent of Americans profess no religion at all. More than 80 percent, including 71 percent of college graduates, believe the Bible is the inspired word of God. Studies have shown that Americans' voluntary giving to churches, synagogues and other houses of worship--an amount in the range of $38 billion annually--exceeds the gross national product of many countries. From a storefront meeting room in South Central Los Angeles to the Gothic cathedral looming within sight of the White House, there are more churches per capita in the United States than in any other nation on Earth--one for about every 900 Americans." (p50)

Sheler, Jeffery L. "Cover Story: Spiritual America." U.S. News & World Report v116 n13, 4 Apr 1994. p48-54,56-59. (ISSN0041-5537).

"The rift between private faith and secular society is perceived by many to be widening. While nearly 2 out of 3 Americans say religion is gaining influence in their personal lives, a comparable number say it is losing influence on the country in general, according to the U.S. NEWS poll. Meanwhile, almost 90 percent (including 85 percent of those who describe themselves as not very religious) say the nation is slipping deeper into moral decline." (p56) "Americans are increasingly looking to religious institutions for solutions to some of the nation's most intractable problems. In the U.S. NEWS survey, 61 percent think churches should 'take a more active and outspoken role' in solving the nation's troubles, while only 18 percent would regard such involvement negatively." (p57)

Sheler, Jeffery L. "Cover Story: Spiritual America." U.S. News & World Report v116 n13, 4 Apr 1994. p48-54,56-59. (ISSN0041-5537).

U.S.--RELIGION--SOCIAL CONDITIONS

"'From Belief to Commitment,' issued by Independent Sector (IS), shows that more than 90% of America's religious congregations are providing a multitude of health and human services to communities. Moreover, these congregations contributed $6.6 billion in 1991 directly to other organizations and individuals, more than all corporations ($6.1 billion) and almost as much as foundations ($7.7 billion)....Their largest area of involvement is human services, with almost 92% of all congregations involved to some degree. Almost as many congregations (90%) are involved in health--such as visiting the sick and working to prevent substance abuse. Other major activity areas engaged in by a large proportion of congregations include: international concerns like relief efforts (74%); programs for public benefits in such areas as civil rights and social justice (62%); education programs such as teaching adults to read (53%); art and cultural activities (50%); and environmental protection (40%)." (p3)

"90% of Religious Congregations Active in Health/Human Services." Responsive Philanthropy Sum 1993. p3-4.

U.S.--RESEARCH

The Office of Technology Assessment "surveyed Federal programs that conduct research on the toxicity of environmental pollutants, occupational toxicants, and toxic contaminants in food. It collected information through written requests for data, following up those requests with interviews of agency representatives and visits to agency laboratories." (p12) "The proportion of funds devoted to environmental health R&D [research and development] relative to health R&D declined from 6.8 to 4.9 percent in the decade from 1982 to 1991, despite expanded congressional mandates for Federal environmental responsibilities. The research being conducted is fragmented within and across at least 12 Federal agencies, resulting in the inefficient and ineffective use of resources." (p13)

Paxman, Dalton (Biological and Behavioral Sciences Program, Office of Technology Assessment). U.S. House. Committee on Science, Space, and Technology. "Risk Assessment Research." Hearing, 16 Nov 1993. Washington, D.C.: GPO, 1994. (ISBN016043615X). (Y4.Sci2:103/85).

"After several years of cutbacks, major U.S. companies spend less than 22% of R&D [research and development] on long-term projects, vs. nearly 50% by their counterparts in Japan, estimates the industry-sponsored Council on Competitiveness. This year may bring the unkindest cuts of all: In a survey by the Industrial Research Institute of 253 big R&D spenders, 41% said they would reduce total R&D in 1994, vs. 20% that plan increases. Three times as many plan to cut long-term research funding as to raise it." (p82)

Carey, John/others. "Science & Technology: Research: Could America Afford the Transistor Today?" Business Week n3361, 7 Mar 1994. p80-82,84. (ISSN0007-7135).

"Economist Edwin Mansfield at the University of Pennsylvania estimates that the U.S. industry has cut research and development by 15 percent since 1986....A recent survey by the

Industrial Research Institute shows that the number of U.S. firms that plan to cut research and development spending in 1994 is three times greater than those firms that plan to increase research and development spending in their companies in this year of 1994. IBM has cut its R&D funding from $6 billion to about $5 billion over the last 3 years and has reduced its work force by 125,000 employees...since 1987. Digital Equipment Corp. has announced its plans to reduce research and development spending in 1994 by 25 percent....AT&T Bell Labs, once regarded as the best industrial research lab in the world, has not increased R&D funding in the past 3 years and has reduced its focus on long-term R&D in response to competition." (pS2622)

Rockefeller, John D., IV (Sen.-W.Va.). "National Competitiveness Act," Congressional Record (9 Mar 1994). Daily ed. pS2614-2624. (ISSN0363-7239).

U.S.--RURAL CONDITIONS (v19)

"Large sectors of nonmetropolitan America have experienced severe economic difficulties in recent years, and these of course have had negative effects on rural education, and on the students of these schools and their families. Especially noteworthy are the following: the higher than average unemployment rates in nonmetropolitan areas for much of the past decade, which in 1991 equaled 11.5%, well above the 9.5% rate in metropolitan areas (Economic Research Service, 1991a); the higher poverty rates in nonmetropolitan areas (historically the rates have exceeded those in urbanized areas), which increased to 16.3%, compared with 12.7% in nonmetropolitan areas in 1990 (Bureau of the Census, 1990)...." (p18)

Stephens, Robert/Hunter, Bruce. "The Nation's Rural School Districts: Orphans in the School Reform Debate." Holistic Education Review v6 n1, Spr 1993. p16-24. (ISSN0898-0926).

U.S.--RURAL CONDITIONS--POPULATION

"Rural America's population is still declining....By 1990, only 25 percent of the nation's population lived in rural areas. Approximately 84 percent of the contiguous land mass of the U.S. is rural, according to definitions developed by the Office of Management and Budget. Nationally, approximately 2,300 counties are rural." (p23)

U.S. Dept. of Agriculture/Stauber, Karl N. "Rural Development: The Diversity of Rural America." Agricultural Outlook Jan-Feb 1994. p23-24.

U.S.--SEXUAL BEHAVIOR (v19)

U.S.--SOCIAL CONDITIONS (v19)

"A recent report by former Education Secretary William Bennett identifying various cultural indicators of well-being paints a disturbing picture of our culture today: There has been a 419-percent increase in illegitimate births since 1960; more than a 200-percent increase in the teenage suicide rate; and quadrupling in divorce rates; a tripling of the percentage of children living in single-parent homes; a drop of almost 80 points in SAT scores; and a 560-percent increase in violent crime, much of it by perpetrators of a younger and younger age. Another frequently cited study noted that parents today spend 40 percent less time with their children than did parents a generation ago. And all of this has occurred while total social spending by all levels of government--measured in constant 1990 dollars--has risen from $143 billion to $787 billion--more than a fivefold increase. Inflation-adjusted spending on welfare has increased by 630 percent, spending on education by 225 percent." (pH1194)

Wolf, Frank R. (Rep.-Va.). "Concurrent Resolution on the Budget--Fiscal Year 1995," Congressional Record (10 Mar 1994). Daily ed. pH1170-1242. (ISSN0363-7239).

"Over the past 30 years, the divorce rate in the United States has tripled, as has the percentage of children living in single-parent families. In 1965, the illegitimacy rate among blacks stood at 26 percent--enough for Democratic Sen. Daniel Patrick Moynihan of New York, then an assistant secretary of labor, to call the situation a crisis. Today, the rate is 68 percent and climbing, while the illegitimacy rate among whites has risen to 22 percent." (p19)

Robertson, Brian. "In Academia, New Praises for the Nuclear Family." Insight v10 n11, 14 Mar 1994. p18-20. (ISSN1051-4880).

"The revenues of the top 20 percent of...[persons in the U.S.] are 3.55 times the incomes of the lower 40 percent; our homicide rate is twice Bulgaria's; and the 426 of every 100,000 Americans who are in prison doubles Poland's proportion and is Hungary's three times over." (p33)

Kempton, Murray. "A New Year's Wish." New York Review of Books v41 n3, 3 Feb 1994. p33. (ISSN0028-7504).

"More than 70 million Americans are poor. At least 30 million are going hungry at any given time. A whole generation of our youth has been abandoned, with no education and no future. (Teen suicide was the second-greatest cause of death among people age 15 to 24 last year.) This growing mass of poor and unemployed people is a threat to the system itself; they are a revolutionary movement. The very act of trying to survive pits them against the system, since the system can't meet their needs." (p7)

Lee, R. "Moving toward a Police State: Our Rulers Exploit Fear of Crime." People's Tribune v21 n1, 27 Dec 1993. p7.

"The statistics outline an 'appalling portrait' of America's children, says Hillary Rodham Clinton, and she is right: Almost 30 percent have unmarried parents, more than half have mothers who return to work before they are a year old, almost one quarter live in poverty, 30 nations have a better record in preventing low-birth-weight babies, 16 countries do a better job of immunizing toddlers against polio. As the Carnegie Corp. concludes in a new study, this 'pattern of neglect' threatens the well-being of our 'most vulnerable' citizens, children under 3 years old. Unfortunately these children have become stuffed animals in the playpen of American politics, a source of competition, not consensus or cooperation. The left wants more government programs and regulation, the right advocates private solutions and responsibility and neither side sees much virtue in the other's arguments." (p10)

Roberts, Steven V. "Outlook: Neglecting Children--and Parents." U.S. News & World Report v116 n16, 25 Apr 1994. p10-11. (ISSN0041-5537).

U.S. ARMY (v19)

U.S. ARMY--APPROPRIATIONS AND EXPENDITURES (v19)

U.S. BORDER PATROL (v19)

U.S. COAST GUARD

"Coast Guard skills and expertise are in demand worldwide. Many developing nations use the U.S. Coast Guard as a model for their own maritime forces. In the past year, we sent 32 assistance and training teams to 24 countries, including Romania, Bulgaria, Uruguay, Honduras, and Malaysia. Our reputation as both a humanitarian agency and a law enforcement agency is a valuable tool that helps further the foreign policy objectives of the United States. Refugees seeking economic opportunity or fleeing political repression continue to sail for our shores. In fiscal year 1993, the Coast Guard intercepted 9,279 migrants. This number is down from 40,291 in fiscal year 1992. Although I recognize the folly of drawing conclusions without considering world events, I believe Coast Guard presence in the Windward Passage between Haiti and Cuba (Operation Able Manner) played a significant role in the decrease. The increasing number of illegal immigrants from China presents a new challenge." (p27)

Kime, J. William. "Change." Proceedings v119 n12, Dec 1993. p26-27. (ISSN0041-798X).

"On an average day, the [U.S.] Coast Guard: Saves 12 lives; Assists 315 boaters; Saves $2 million worth of property; Responds to 23 environmental threats; Inspects 150 commercial vessels; Investigates 17 marine accidents; Intercepts 450 pounds of contraband drugs with a street value of nearly $8 million; Interdicts more than 100 illegal immigrants; Services 150 aids to naviagation." (p36)

Kurz, Gary. "Looking for Adventure?" Proceedings v119 n12, Dec 1993. p35-37. (ISSN0041-798X).

U.S. CONGRESS (v19)

see also VOTING--U.S. CONGRESS

"As of mid-February, 21 [House] members had announced their retirements, and an additional 17 were running for another office. The total already exceeds the number of those who had made for the door at the comparable point in 1992, the cycle that eventually set the postwar record for voluntary departures from the House: 52 retirements and 13 candidacies for other offices....But the number already is well beyond the number from the last non-presidential election year (27 in 1990) and easily exceeds the average over the past couple of generations (32 since 1930)....Among the 111 House members elected in 1992 with 55 percent of the vote or less, nearly half (51) were Republicans." (p382)

Kaplan, Dave. "Special Report: House '94: Incumbents Call It Quits at Record Clip." Congressional Quarterly Weekly Report v52 n7, 19 Feb 1994. p382-386. (ISSN0010-5910).

"Vice President Gore's report ['National Performance Review'] found that, 'In fiscal year 1993, Congress required executive branch agencies to prepare 5,348 reports,' and expressed dismay that these duplicative burdens 'trapped agencies in a blizzard of paperwork.' The Congress's habit of burdening Federal agencies with unnecesssary reporting requirements is quite serious, and it is getting worse. The General Accounting Office (GAO) found that one House committee alone received over 800 reports from Federal agencies in response to mandatory reporting requirements in just the 101st Congress. Another 600 reports were sent to the same committee in the following Congress. To demonstrate just how heavy this burden can be, the Office of Management and Budget (OMB) had to submit 38 reports to one single House committee to comply with a single piece of legislation--the 1990 Budget Reconciliation Act. Furthermore, the GAO also has stated that the 'Congress imposes about 300 new requirements on Federal agencies each year. As of March 1992, there were 3,719 requirements and 3,331 communications in the 102d Congress database.'" (pS3688)

McCain, John (Sen.-Ariz.). "Statements on Introduced Bills and Joint Resolutions," Congressional Record (24 Mar 1994). Daily ed. pS3685-3745. (ISSN0363-7239).

"While [the U.S.] Congress purports to represent the entire nation, the personal experiences of its present members are far from representative. The balance is tilted heavily toward involvement in government and away from private enterprise. Of the Senate's 100 members, 54 are lawyers. Nearly 50 have served as state, city, or county officials. The Senate includes only 26 members who claim any kind of business experience, including two former bankers, three broadcast executives, and one restauranteur. There are eight ranchers and farmers, seven educators,...two journalists, a social worker, a former professional basketball player, an author, a jewelry designer, a stockbroker, an accountant, an astronaut, a minister, and two retired military officers." (p16)

Dillin, John. "Lawyers, Alert! Outsiders Line Up to Challenge Congressional Incumbents." The Christian Science Monitor v86 n36, 14 Jan 1994. p1,16. (ISSN0882-7729).

U.S. CONGRESS--PUBLIC OPINION

"A TIME/CNN poll conducted Dec. 2 found that the public was a lot less impressed with Congress' record for 1993 than the Democrats were: Only 24 percent of those surveyed said Congress had accomplished more in 1993 than in previous years; 72 percent said it had accomplished about the same or less. Just 36 percent of those surveyed thought the bills Congress passed this year would have a positive effect; 26 percent thought the effect would be negative, and 32 percent thought they would have no effect. Asked to compare this year in Congress with 1992, 43 percent of those surveyed said that 'gridlock' in government had decreased; but even more--48 percent--thought it had increased or stayed the same." (p3355)

Hook, Janet/others. "Special Report: Cover Story: Democrats Hail 'Productivity,' but Image Problems Remain." Congressional Quarterly v51 n49, 11 Dec 1993. p3355-3406.

"Half of all Americans think Congress as an institution is corrupt, according to one 1992 poll. Another survey found that 30 percent of those polled thought that most members of Congress were financially corrupt; 28 percent said about half were corrupt." (p358)

Hook, Janet. "Perspective: Everyone Loses When 'Everybody Does It.'" Congressional Quarterly v52 n6, 12 Feb 1994. p358.

"Surveys from the 1940s through the '60s consistently showed the national legislature getting good marks. When the Gallup Poll asked in 1958 whether Congress was doing a good or poor job, it found only 12 percent saying poor. In a June 1970 survey, Gallup showed its respondents a card on which there were 10 boxes, numbered from +5 (for institutions 'you like very much') down to -5 (dislike very much). Only 3 percent assigned Congress to the -4 or -5 boxes, and only 10 percent gave it a negative rating of any kind. Thirty-six percent gave it either a +4 or a +5. Things are different now. A number of survey organizations regularly ask their respondents whether they approve or disapprove of the way Congress is doing its job. The proportions bounce around, depending on the overall national mood and the latest headlines on congressional doings. But with a few brief exceptions, one of which was at the onset of the Gulf war, the proportion saying they approved Congress's performance has remained in the range of one-fourth to one-third of the public." (p22)

Ladd, Everett Carll. "Opinion/Essays: Populism Makes a Comeback in the Midst of Disillusion." The Christian Science Monitor v86 n50, 4 Feb 1994. p22. (ISSN0882-7729).

U.S. CONGRESS--SALARIES, ETC. (v19)

U.S. CONGRESS--TERM OF OFFICE

"On Election Day last November, more than 20 million voters in 14 states approved ballot measures that would cap U.S. senators' service at 12 years and representatives' at six, eight or 12. USTL [U.S. Term Limits] spokesperson Jeff Langan calls term limits the 'biggest grassroots movement ever in the United States.' But if proponents describe support for term limits as a spontaneous, populist prairie fire driven by local outrage over entrenched congressional incumbents, a COMMON CAUSE MAGAZINE analysis of campaign finance reports filed in the 14 states suggests that something else is fueling the fire: More than three-fourths of the movement's financing in 1992 came from four national groups and a relatively small number of wealthy individual donors." (p37)

Young, Amy E. "The Money behind the Movement." Common Cause Magazine v19 n2, Sum 1993. p37-39. (ISSN0271-9592).

U.S. CONGRESSIONAL BUDGET OFFICE (v19)

U.S. DEPT. OF EDUCATION (v19)

U.S. DEPT. OF ENERGY (v19)

U.S. DEPT. OF HOUSING AND URBAN DEVELOPMENT (v19)

U.S. DEPT. OF INTERIOR (v19)

U.S. DEPT. OF LABOR (v19)
U.S. DEPT. OF STATE--OFFICIALS AND EMPLOYEES (v19)
U.S. DRUG ENFORCEMENT ADMINISTRATION (v19)
U.S. ENVIRONMENTAL PROTECTION AGENCY (v19)
U.S. FEDERAL BUILDINGS FUND

"In the early days of the [U.S.] Federal Buildings Fund, limited resources were available for capital investment due to restrictions on the fund's revenues and on rental rate freezes. These caps and freezes have resulted in more than $5 billion in lost revenues, in today's dollars, to the Federal Buildings Fund. In recent years, due to the growth of the inventory and the elimination of most of those restrictions on rental rates charged by the Public Buildings Service, revenues to the Federal Buildings Fund have increased. For example, in 1992, the fund received $4 billion in rental revenues, compared to $2.3 billion in 1986. Annual appropriations for three major agencies, the Departments of Agriculture, Transportation, and the Food and Drug Administration, continue to limit their rental payments into the Federal Buildings Fund to a level below commercially equivalent rents. The lost revenues due to these limits is more than $107 million in fiscal year 1993. This is $107 million of new construction or building purchases that have been deferred or converted to leasing due to lack of resources." (p5)

Thacker, Gerald P. (Commissioner, Public Buildings Service). U.S. House. Committee on Appropriations. "Treasury, Postal Service, and General Government Approp. for Fiscal Year 1994 (Part 5)." Hearing, Washington, D.C.: GPO, 1993. (ISBN0160410053). (Y4.Ap6/1:T71/994/pt.5).

U.S. FEDERAL RESERVE

"The Federal Reserve System, including the Board of Governors and all 12 of the Reserve Banks, employs 730 economists, statisticians, and other researchers....But this vast establishment is not enough for the Fed. Since January 1991 the Fed has spent almost $3 million for 290 outside economic consultants....The American Economic Association reports that 1,020 members list their primary area as being 'domestic monetary and financial theory, and institutions.' The Federal Reserve is coincidentally paying 1,020 people to work in this and related areas. In other words, it would be fair to say that the Fed is paying more than half the economists in these areas. Amazing--does DOD [U.S. Dept. of Defense] hire half of all the mathematicians? Does Interior hire half the tree surgeons or NIH [National Institutes of Health] hire half the brain surgeons? Not on your life." (pH401)

Gonzalez, Henry B. (Rep.-Tex.). "Health Care in America," Congressional Record (9 Feb 1994). Daily ed. pH400-406. (ISSN0363-7239).

U.S. FOOD AND DRUG ADMINISTRATION

"Examples of cases where the FDA has permitted a manufacturer to knowingly market a dangerous drug or medical device are many. Between 1981 and 1986 the FDA permitted the sale of the Bjork-Shiley heart valve even though both the FDA and the manufacturer of the valve had evidence of strut fractures that led to the death of many patients. An estimated 6 million women took DES, with FDA approval, despite evidence that it caused serious reproductive harm in the offspring of women who had taken it. Most of us are aware of the problems caused by the Copper-7 IUD's, silicone breast implants, and Accutaine--all FDA sanctioned products which were not only harmful to the public but are cases in which the FDA had knowledge of the products dangers." (pS543)

Dorgan, Byron L. (Sen.-N.Dak.). "Product Liability Reform Should Not Include FDA and FAA Defense," Congressional Record (1 Feb 1994). Daily ed. pS542-543. (ISSN0363-7239).

U.S. FOREST SERVICE--ROADS (v19)
U.S. GENERAL ACCOUNTING OFFICE (v19)
U.S. INTERNAL REVENUE SERVICE

"An interesting statistic, which has only recently been developed by IRS, shows that more delinquencies are abated than collected. In fiscal year 1992, IRS abated $42.2 billion in delinquencies, while collecting only $24.2 billion. Thus, almost two-thirds of the delinquencies resolved were actually erroneous assessments that should not have been in the accounts receivable inventory." (p972)

U.S. House. Committee on Appropriations. "Treasury, Postal Service...Approp. for Fiscal Year 1994 (Part 1)." Hearing, Washington, D.C.: GPO, 1993. (Y4.Ap6/1:T71/994/pt.1).

"In reality,...IRS' gross accounts receivable balance does not mean much. Because of overstatements in the inventory and because of errors by IRS and taxpayers, much of the gross balance is invalid and does not reflect the amount of delinquent taxes actually owed. In addition, many of the valid accounts in the inventory are considered uncollectible because the delinquent taxpayers cannot pay or IRS cannot find them. After considering all of the above, IRS estimates that only about $28.1 billion of the September 30, 1992, accounts receivable balance of more than $100 billion is collectible." (p923)

Stathis, Jennie S. (Director, Tax Policy & Admin. Issues, General Gov. Div., U.S. GAO). U.S. House. Committee on Appropriations. "Treasury, Postal Service...Approp. for Fiscal Year 1994 (Part 1)." Hearing, Washington, D.C.: GPO, 1993. (Y4.Ap6/1:T71/994/pt.1).

"The [Internal Revenue] Service is a large, diverse and complex agency, administering the complex tax laws of our country. Our approximately 115,000 employees and $7 billion budget last fiscal year: collected more than $1 trillion, including $24 billion from notices and delinquent accounts; processed 204 million tax returns and more than one billion information documents; issued $100 billion in refunds to 89 million taxpayers; corresponded with more than 10 million taxpayers to adjust returns and accounts, request social security numbers, correct math errors and request signatures; completed 1.3 million examinations of tax returns and sent 5.2 million income underreporting and non-filer notices; and assisted more than 74 million taxpayers." (p776-777)

Dolan, Michael P. (Acting Commissioner, Internal Revenue Service). U.S. House. Committee on Appropriations. "Treasury, Postal Service...Approp. for Fiscal Year 1994 (Part 1)." Hearing, Washington, D.C.: GPO, 1993. (Y4.Ap6/1:T71/994/pt.1).

Some IRS rule changes are initiated to close avenues of non-compliance. "A case in point was requiring that dependent social security numbers be included on the income tax return. In 1987, the first year this requirement became effective, taxpayers claimed 69.7 million dependent exemptions--a 7 million decrease from the previous year's 76.7 million dependent exemptions. This 'miraculous disappearance' of 7 million dependents resulted in a $2.8 billion revenue increase for 1987 alone." (p788)

Dolan, Michael P. (Acting Commissioner, Internal Revenue Service). U.S. House. Committee on Appropriations. "Treasury, Postal Service...Approp. for Fiscal Year 1994 (Part 1)." Hearing, Washington, D.C.: GPO, 1993. (Y4.Ap6/1:T71/994/pt.1).

U.S. JOB CORPS (v19)
U.S. MARINE CORPS (v19)

see DIVORCE--U.S. MARINE CORPS

U.S. NATIONAL AERONAUTICS AND SPACE ADMINISTRATION

"A recent GAO [General Accounting Office] study found that 25 of the 29 projects with initial cost estimates above $200 million that NASA started between 1977 and 1991 cost more than originally estimated. The range of overruns stretched from 14 percent to over 400 percent, with a median of about 75 percent." (p13)

U.S. Congressional Budget Office. "The Risks of a Strategy of Marginal Adjustment." Reinventing NASA Mar 1994. Washington, D.C.: GPO, 1994.

"Concerns about the cost of the NASA program increased after 1990, when the Budget Enforcement Act (BEA) required a tightening of all domestic discretionary spending. As the BEA's caps on spending began to bind, the Congress significantly lowered NASA's budget from the level requested by President Bush for 1992 and 1993. In 1992, the budget request for NASA was $15.8 billion, but the Congress appropriated only $14.3 billion. In 1993, the agency's appropriation was again $14.3 billion, $700 million below the Administration's request of $15 billion." (pix)

U.S. Congressional Budget Office. "Summary." Reinventing NASA Mar 1994. Washington, D.C.: GPO, 1994.

U.S. NATIONAL ENDOWMENT FOR THE ARTS (v19)

U.S. NATIONAL PARK SERVICE (v19)

U.S. NAVY (v19)

U.S. PUBLIC BUILDING SERVICE

"The [U.S.] Public Buildings Service primarily supplies general purpose office space, but our inventory also includes some special purpose facilities, such as courthouses, border stations, laboratories and data processing centers. More than a million federal employees from all three branches of the government work in our facilities. The 258 million square feet of space in the Public Buildings Service's inventory are located in over 7,800 buildings nationwide. If the Public Buildings Service were in the private sector, it would be the largest real estate company in the country. The acquisition and operation of all of this space is financed by the Federal Buildings Fund, a revolving fund. The Federal Buildings Fund and the Public Buildings Service's rent system were established by law first in 1972. Prior to that time, the Public Buildings Service's programs were primarily funded through direct appropriations." (p4)

Thacker, Gerald P. (Commissioner, Public Buildings Service). U.S. House. Committee on Appropriations. "Treasury, Postal Service, and General Government Approp. for Fiscal Year 1994 (Part 5)." Hearing, Washington, D.C.: GPO, 1993. (ISBN0160410053). (Y4.Ap6/1:T71/994/pt.5).

U.S. RESOLUTION TRUST CORPORATION (v19)

U.S. SECURITIES AND EXCHANGE COMMISSION (v19)

U.S. SMALL BUSINESS ADMINISTRATION (v19)

U.S. SOCIAL SECURITY ADMINISTRATION (v19)

"SSA [the Social Security Administration] employs 64,000 workers in a national network of 1,300 offices. This is more than twice the number of employees at the State Department and three times the number of workers employed by the Department of Labor. And with a budget of more than $300 billion, SSA will spend more this year than the Department of Defense and nearly 10 times as much as the Department of Education. In fact, SSA's outlays this year will be larger than the combined outlays of 11 Federal departments. It simply defies common sense for an agency this large to be included under an umbrella bureaucracy." (pS16535)

Moynihan, Daniel Patrick (Sen.-N.Y.). "The Social Security Administration Independence Act of 1993," Congressional Record (19 Nov 1993). Daily ed. pS16535-16537. (ISSN0363-7239).

U.S. VETERANS' ADMINISTRATION (v19)

UNIVERSITIES AND COLLEGES--U.S.--FINANCE (v19)

UNMARRIED COUPLES--U.S. (v19)

UNTOUCHABLES--INDIA--SOCIAL CONDITIONS

"Economic deprivation is often accompanied by environmental and social discrimination. Among the groups in India to have suffered most from this trio of injustices are the low, 'scheduled' castes, called 'harijans' and 'dalits.' For centuries they have languished at the bottom of an increasingly rigid caste system. In most villages, they have least access to land, clean water and other resources. They generally do the dirtiest jobs and live in a squalid, low-lying corner of the village which is most at risk from flooding and water-borne diseases. A study of harijans in Guajarat state found they had equal access to clean water in only five out of 69 villages surveyed. In some cases, they were banned from touching water used by higher castes, but no alternative sources were provided. The influence of higher castes on development projects has resulted in new sources of clean water and other benefits being diverted away from the scheduled castes, even when the schemes were intended to help the poorest....India's scheduled tribes often suffer even more than the harijans. They tend to live in remote areas, and their territory is frequently chosen for mines, quarries, dams and tourism. The 1987-89 report of the Commissioner for Scheduled Castes and Tribes said that nearly 15% of tribal peoples had been displaced." (p20)

Dogra, Bharat. "Focus: Environmental Justice: Low Castes Languish at the Bottom of the Heap." Panoscope n37, Oct 1993. p20. (ISSN0951-8819).

URANIUM INDUSTRY--INDIANS OF NORTH AMERICA--HEALTH ASPECTS

"As multinationals and the United States government attempt to strip Indian land of its energy resources, women and children suffer. Indian women face astronomical birth defect rates as a result of uranium mining (all uranium mining in the country takes place on or nearby Indian land). In Four Corners, the Navajo face a birth defect rate 200 times higher than the national average. On the Pine Ridge reservation, the Lakota have a 60% birth defect rate." (p9)

Smith, Andrea. "American Indian Women and the Reproductive Rights Movement." Guild Practitioner v50 n1, Win 1993. p9-10. (ISSN0017-5390).

URANIUM MINES AND MINING--INDIANS OF NORTH AMERICA

"Uranium mining and aboveground nuclear-weapons tests have occurred for about 50 years on and around...[Navajo and Hopi] reservations. Since 1942, the reservation lands and the surrounding areas of the Navajo and Hopi have been mined for uranium. From 1946 to 1968, 13 million tons of uranium were mined on the Navajo Reservation. The largest underground uranium mine on Navajo and Hopi lands operated from 1979 and 1990. The worst nuclear accident happened at Uranium Mill, which is south of the Navajo Reservation. More than 1,000 open-pit and underground uranium mines on the reservation are abandoned, unreclaimed, and highly radioactive. Some 600 dwellings on Navajo tribal lands are contaminated with radiation. Former uranium mining and milling districts of the Navajo Reservation suffer from cancer and leukemia clusters and birth defects." (p29)

"State of the Peoples: Nuclear War: Uranium Mining and Nuclear Tests on Indigenous Lands." Cultural Survival Quarterly v17 n3, Fall 1993. p29-31. (ISSN0740-3291).

URBAN ECONOMICS--U.S. (v19)

"The big cities [in the U.S.] have faced massive federal disinvestment at the very moment that deindustrialization and the epidemics of the 1980s (AIDS, crack, homelessness) were imposing immense new financial burdens. In an important study, Demetrios Caraley estimates that the 64 per cent cutback in federal aid since 1980 had cost cities $26 billion per year (in constant 1990 dollars). For cities with more than 300,000 inhabitants, the average federal share of the municipal income stream has plummeted from 22 per cent in 1980 to a mere 6 per cent in 1989. Since state aid, nationally averaged, has remained constant at 16 per cent, cities have had to make up the shortfall with local resources: usually very regressive sales taxes and user fees." (p10-11)

Davis, Mike. "Who Killed LA? A Political Autopsy." New Left Review n197, Jan-Feb 1993. p3-28. (ISSN0028-6060).

URBANIZATION--KENYA

"Kenya is a country in transition from a traditional agricultural society to an urbanized society. This urbanization is occurring due to Kenyan demographics--25% of Kenyan land is arable and the population increases 4.1% yearly. The present demographic reality of the Maasai people, pastoralist dependent on their cattle, presents a microcosm of the land reality in Kenya. In 1900, the Maasai had a population of 40,000 and their cattle grazed over 150,000 square kilometers. Today, the Maasai number 360,000 people living off of 50,000 square kilometers of land. That is approximately nine times as many people living on one-third the land." (p4)

"Kenya: Land a Burning Justice Issue." NewsNotes v18 n5, Sep-Oct 1993. p4-5. (ISSN1064-1556).

URBANIZATION--SINGAPORE

"Singapore is the world's busiest container port. Roughly 700 ships are at the quays or anchorages on any given day. At least half of them take on fuel....Singapore is a leading financial services, telecommunications and information technology center for the Asia-Pacific region. The Singapore landscape has been transformed by a 25-year building boom. Along with factories, industrial estates, refineries, and shipbuilding/repair and other port facilities, Singapore has built miles of new highways, scores of commercial skyscrapers, luxury hotels and shopping centers. In addition, a new airport and a $3 billion rapid-transit system were constructed. Vast new self-contained suburban communities have been built by the government or private developers, and government apartments have been made available at low cost to nearly everyone. Today, some 87 percent of Singaporeans live in government-built apartments, and of these, 80 percent own their residences." (p7)

Wilson, Walter K. "An Esso Century in Singapore." Lamp v75 n4, Win 1993. p2-8. (ISSN0023-7418).

URINARY INCONTINENCE--U.S. (v19)

URUGUAY--ECONOMIC CONDITIONS

"The 7 percent growth rate produced in 1992 has to be put in the context of the recent history of Uruguay's growth performance. In fact, free-market policies have been pursued since 1973. According to conservative sources such as THE ECONOMIST, the policies of the dictatorship in the 1970s led to an average growth rate of 4.3 percent for 1973 to 1980. Then, as in Chile under Augusto Pinochet, in the early 1980s came the reckoning in the form of a severe downturn that reduced Gross Domestic Product (GDP) more than 16 percent. Average GDP growth for 1980 to 1991 has been a dismal 0.5 percent. The 1992 growth rate amounts to an initial burst of recovery from a decade of stagnation and negative per capita growth." (p20)

Petras, James/Vieux, Steve. "Uruguay: Free Markets and Polo Shirts." Lies of Our Times Jun 1993. p19-20. (ISSN1046-7912).

UTAH

see GANGS--UTAH; INFORMATION TECHNOLOGY--UTAH; NATIONAL PARKS AND RESERVES--UTAH; WATER CONSUMPTION--UTAH

UTAH--ECONOMIC CONDITIONS (v19)

UZBEKISTAN

see ALSO PRIVATIZATION--UZBEKISTAN

UZBEKISTAN--POPULATION

"Uzbekistan is experiencing a population explosion. It is producing children far faster than it can produce the goods needed to support them. The population, now 22 million, is increasing by about 600,000 per year. Nearly half of the population are young children. And Uzbek women, who bear five to six children on average, remain outside the workforce. Only 30 percent of the population is employed, and the load on the working population exceeds their capacities. Without sophisticated agricultural and industrial methods, it will be impossible for the workers to produce enough goods for the growing population." (p48)

"Uzbekistan: Tamerlane v. Marx." Bulletin of the Atomic Scientists v50 n1, Jan-Feb 1994. p48-51. (ISSN0096-3402).

VACATIONS--EUROPE--U.S. (v19)

VANS--U.S.

"The need for bumper standards for minivans is particularly great. Minivans have been steadily increasing in consumer popularity, especially among families looking for a safe and reliable vehicle. Yet, these vehicles are completely exempt from even the 2.5-mile-per-hour bumper standard. IIHS [Insurance Institute for Highway Safety] recently conducted 5-mile-per-hour crash tests on seven 1994 model minivans. After the tests, one model could not be driven, and six of the seven sustained some degree of damage to safety-related parts, with one sustaining such serious safety-related damage that the tailgate came unlatched and could not be closed again, presenting the risk of occupant ejection. Repair costs were extreme as well, ranging from $1,862 to $7,643." (pS1475)

Danforth, John C. (Sen.-Mo.). "Statements on Introduced Bills and Joint Resolutions," Congressional Record (10 Feb 1994). Daily ed. pS1457-1487. (ISSN0363-7239).

VASCULAR SYSTEM

see CARDIOVASCULAR SYSTEM

VEGETABLE TRADE

see also POTATO INDUSTRY; SOYBEAN INDUSTRY

VEGETABLE TRADE--JAPAN

"From 1989 to 1992, the amount of vegetables arriving at Narita Airport, by far Japan's biggest gateway for imports, grew 49% in volume, and 41% in price. This air route has become indispensable to the Japanese food industry. There are about a hundred varieties of vegetables that are airfreighted in on a regular basis, with another two hundred or so that are imported for trial marketing programs. By volume, the biggest vegetable import of 1992 was asparagus at 10,061 tonnes, a gain of 24.2% from 1991; by price, matsutake mushrooms at Y8 billion ($77 million), up 22.5%. One notable exception to the general growth was truffles, which command the highest unit price of any vegetable. Truffle imports fell 10% in 1992 to Y320 million ($3.1 million). These statistics provide a good picture of the changes that are taking place in the Japanese diet, distribution system, and business climate." (p46)

Shindo, Ushio. "Facts of Life: Imported Vegetables: Salad Days." Look Japan v39 n451, Oct 1993. p46. (ISSN0456-5339).

VEGETABLE TRADE--U.S. (v19)

VEHICLES, ELECTRIC

see ELECTRIC VEHICLES

VENEZUELA

see ALSO ANIMALS--VENEZUELA; CRIME--VENEZUELA; PRISONS--VENEZUELA

VENEZUELA--ECONOMIC CONDITIONS

"Venezuela's foreign debt stands at $35 billion and is consuming about one-quarter of the national budget. Capital flight is massive: analysts estimate that the Venezuelan oligarchy has $60 to 80 billion stashed in foreign bank accounts, and tax evasion is estimated at 70%. Oil prices have dropped from a high of $30 per barrel during the 1974-82 oil boom to $12.50 today. Critics say some $10 billion in illicit funds are laundered in Venezuela every year." (p12-13)

"Venezuela: A Daunting Task." NewsNotes v19 n2, Mar-Apr 1994. p12-13. (ISSN1064-1556).

"Venezuela's population is overwhelmingly urban--84 percent of the people live in cities and one-fifth reside in and around the capital, Caracas. Seventy percent of Venezuela's population are 'mestizo' (of mixed European and indigenous heritage), 20 percent are white, 9 percent black, and 2 percent American Indian. Venezuela's population is also very young--38 percent are under 15 years old. The country is rich in natural resources, with substantial mineral and petroleum deposits. The Venezuelan economy is dominated by the oil industry, which was nationalized in 1976. Oil accounts for 80 percent of export earnings and Venezuela is the third largest petroleum producer within the Organization of Petroleum Exporting Countries (OPEC). The country rode a wave of prosperity during the 1970s when petroleum prices were high, but was plunged into debt when prices dropped in the 1980s. Still, Venezuela boasts one of the highest per capita incomes ($2,560 per year) among South American countries, in part due to petroleum sales." (p11)

Hershey, Sharon. "Spotlight: Venezuela." Population Today v21 n3, Mar 1993. p11. (ISSN0749-2448).

VENTURE CAPITAL--JAPAN (v19)

VERMONT--POPULATION (v19)

VETERANS

see MEDICINE--U.S.--VETERANS; WOMEN VETERANS--U.S.

VETERANS--MENTAL HEALTH--U.S. (v19)

VETERANS--SERVICES FOR--U.S. (v19)

VETERANS--SERVICES FOR--U.S.--WOMEN (v19)

VETERANS--U.S. (v19)

VETERANS--U.S.--ECONOMIC CONDITIONS (v19)

VETERANS, WOMEN

see WOMEN VETERANS

VETERINARY TOXICOLOGY--U.S.

"In a recent national survey, two out of every three veterinarians [in the U.S.] said they had encountered at least one accidental pet poisoning in the past year in which antifreeze was the suspected cause. After rodenticides, antifreeze was the cause of accidental pet poisoning most frequently cited by the 310 small-animal practitioners who responded to the survey. Pesticides, human medications, chocolate, and household chemicals were among the other substances mentioned. The study was commissioned by Safe Brands Corporation, a company that manufactures a type of antifreeze/coolant that is essentially non-toxic to children and animals. Conventional antifreeze/coolant--including the leading brands Prestone, Zerex, and Peak--are made with ethylene glycol, which is appealing to pets and highly toxic. One teaspoon of undiluted, ethylene glycol-based antifreeze can kill a 7-pound cat; one and a half ounces can kill a 20-pound dog." (p11)

"Shelter Shorts: Survey Shows Antifreeze Is a Common Threat to Animals." Shelter Sense v17 n3, Mar 1994. p11. (ISSN0734-3078).

VIDEOCONFERENCING--U.S.

"The video-conferencing industry [in the U.S.] has grown from less than $200 million in revenues in 1989 to $1.3 billion in 1993, according to the North American Telecommunication Association. The group estimates that the market could reach $6.9 billion by 1997." (p6)

Heather, Rebecca Piirto. "Multimedia: Future Focus Groups." American Demographics v16 n1, Jan 1994. p6. (ISSN0163-4089).

VIETNAM

see also CAPITAL INVESTMENTS--VIETNAM; ECONOMIC ASSISTANCE, JAPANESE--VIETNAM; EDUCATION--VIETNAM; HIV INFECTIONS--VIETNAM; INVESTMENTS, FOREIGN--VIETNAM; LABOR SUPPLY--VIETNAM; MALARIA--VIETNAM; PETROLEUM INDUSTRY AND TRADE--VIETNAM

VIETNAM--ECONOMIC CONDITIONS

"The economy has improved dramatically since 1986 when Vietnam's leaders set the nation on a path toward a market economy. Economic growth reached 7.5 percent in 1993 and may reach 8 percent this year. Yet, with an average annual per-capita income of only about $200, Vietnam remains one of Asia's poorest nations." (p17)

"Vietnam: Normalization and Human Rights Concerns." NewsNotes v19 n2, Mar-Apr 1994. p17-18. (ISSN1064-1556).

"Nightmarish inflation [in Vietnam], which soared into triple digits in the mid-1980s, dropped to 6 percent last year. A once hungry Vietnam surpassed its food production targets for 1995 and now ranks as the world's third-largest exporter of rice--after the United States and Thailand. Rising oil exports have helped balance the growing bill for imports to satisfy a new breed of entrepreneurs and a new class of consumers." (p24)

"But Vietnam has not yet lived up to claims that it is the latest Asian 'tiger.' The average per capita income is still $200 to $300, or between 55 cents and 82 cents a day. Farmers and their families make up nearly 80 percent of the population, and many are suffering from low crop prices. Millions of urbanites live in blighted warrens in Hanoi and Saigon that resemble those in Calcutta; malnutrition and disease are common." (p25)

Cumming-Bruce, Nick/others. "U.S. News: Apparatchiks and Entrepreneurs." U.S. News & World Report v116 n6, 14 Feb 1994. p23-25. (ISSN0041-5537).

VIETNAM--EMIGRATION AND IMMIGRATION (v19)

VIETNAM--HEALTH AND HYGIENE (v19)

VIETNAMESE CONFLICT, 1961-1975--MISSING IN ACTION

"It has been 20 years since Americans left...[Vietnam]. Are we ever going to find out what happened to every one? No, no more so than we have for World War II, where we have almost 79,000 still unaccounted for. Out of Korea, over 8,000 are unaccounted for. In Vietnam, we can probably bring that down to a pretty good estimate, to about 1,200 that we cannot really say for sure what happened." (pS169)

Glenn, John (Sen.-Ohio). "Department of State Authorization Act," Congressional Record (26 Jan 1994). Daily ed. pS129-174. (ISSN0363-7239).

United States servicemen "missing in Vietnam have...been identified by only a few teeth or a jawbone....these cases underscore the paucity of information from Vietnam on the fate of 2,239 missing servicemen. About 1,000 of the cases remain true mysteries. According to the U.S. Army's Central Identification Laboratory Hawaii (CILHI), 584 sets of 'remains' have been turned over by Vietnam since the war's end. Of those, 284 have been identified as Americans. In the past few years, progress has been especially slow for reasons that are unclear. Last year, for instance, 67 remains were returned, but so far only three have been identified and returned to the families. About 25 more identifications are in progress....A Vietnamese emigrant, identified in classified files as 'the Mortician,' has been telling U.S. investigators since 1980 that he had been in charge of disinterring, preparing, storing and reburying the remains of U.S. servicemen during and after the war....He testified that he had worked on up to 452 sets of U.S. servicemen's remains from 1965 to 1978, about 200 of which were stored at one time in Hanoi. He passed a polygraph test." (p22)

Cary, Peter. "U.S. News: Still Searching in Vietnam: The Hunt for U.S. Servicemen." U.S. News & World Report v116 n6, 14 Feb 1994. p22. (ISSN0041-5537).

VIOLENCE

see also CONJUGAL VIOLENCE; FAMILY VIOLENCE; SCHOOL VIOLENCE

VIOLENCE--AFRO-AMERICANS--HISPANIC AMERICANS--MORTALITY

"In March 1990, Dr. Russell Sherwin, a pathologist at the U.S.C., reported that autopsies of over 100 youths, mostly Blacks and Latinos, who had died of 'non-medical' causes (that is, generally speaking, from violence, not disease), 80% had 'notable lung abnormalities;' 27% had 'severe lesions.' He described them as more severe and more prevalent than anything caused by smoking or respiratory viruses. 'These were young people and they were running out of lung.' Within 15 years, they would've been candidates for severe lung diseases, victims of the air they breathed." (p1)

"Fight Toxic Racism!" Turning the Tide v6 n2, Mar-Apr 1993. p1.

VIOLENCE--BRAZIL--WOMEN

"While Brazil has advanced from military dictatorship toward democracy, violence against women remains endemic. The first national study of the problem, in 1992, reported an average of 337 assaults on women daily. The U.S. State Department's 1993 human-rights report singles out the nation's 'high incidence of violence against women' and cites an estimate that 70 percent of it occurs in the home. 'We are the world champions in impunity to violence against women,' says Sandra Starling, who represents Sao Paulo in Brazil's legislature. In 1993, Chief [Maria] Camardella's staff of 38 handled 4,394 beatings, rapes and death threats." (p40) "In 1992, only 11 percent of 10,087 women's cases in the Rio area made it to court, and when men are convicted of murdering women, they serve an average of just four years in prison." (p41)

Robinson, Linda/Epstein, Jack. "World Report: Battered by the Myth of Machismo." U.S. News & World Report v116 n13, 4 Apr 1994. p40-41. (ISSN0041-5537).

VIOLENCE--COLOMBIA (v19)

"A Colombian sociologist recently likened the violence in his country to jungle vegetation that grows on weakened social structures. By that metaphor, their structure must be weak indeed because the violence in Colombia is staggering. Their rate of violent deaths, as documented by any number of international organizations, is among the highest in the world--and growing. In 1992, there were 28,000 murders including over 100 massacres in which four or more people were killed. The 1993 statistics have reached 30,000. The portion of these murders that is best known is related to narcotrafficking. The Medellin cartel of the late Pablo Escobar was notorious for its violent practices. Experts consider the remaining Cali cartel to be more sophisticated but let us not kid ourselves about the willingness of criminals, no matter how sophisticated, to shed blood for their greed." (pS3052)

Feingold, Russell D. (Sen.-Wis.). "Human Rights in Colombia," Congressional Record (16 Mar 1994). Daily ed. pS3051-3053. (ISSN0363-7239).

VIOLENCE--COLOMBIA--YOUTH (v19)

VIOLENCE--FLORIDA--YOUTH (v19)

VIOLENCE--GREAT BRITAIN

"Throughout the United Kingdom there are 47,000 children on child protection registers; one in three of those born in the Fifties had a criminal conviction--in a third of the cases, for violence--by the age of 31. Half of those in Britain's prisons are doing time for acts of violence. Drugs are another powerful adverse influence. They are daily more available, with some neighbourhoods awash with them." (p171)

Alton, David. "Our Video Culture." Contemporary Review v264 n1539, Apr 1994. p169-172. (ISSN0010-7565).

VIOLENCE--SOMALIA--MORTALITY

"Those of us who wish that America had bombed the rail lines to Auschwitz must acknowledge that some airmen might have been lost in the effort. And those who wish that something had been done to stop Pol Pot's mass murder of Cambodians must in theory countenance heavy American casualties. But these two cases, the most frequently-cited examples ripe for humanitarian intervention, suggest that the threshold for expending American lives must be very high. Did Somalia rise to that threshold? An argument can be made that it did. According to the International Red Cross and other reputable sources, some 300,000 Somalis had died of violence and famine by the time of the U.S. intervention, and another 1.5 million or more stood at risk out of a population estimated at around 6 million. This is a scale of death very similar to the best estimates of Cambodia's tragedy. At its higher range it even approaches the toll of Auschwitz." (p22)

Muravchik, Joshua. "Commentary: Beyond Self-Defense." Commentary v96 n6, Dec 1993. p19-24. (ISSN0010-2601).

VIOLENCE--SOUTH AFRICA (v19)

"Since Mr. [Nelson] Mandela came out of prison in 1990, there have been more than 13,000 political murders; this year 80 a week. In a country where nearly half the population has no formal job, where hatred between black and white is often rivalled by the bitterness between Mr Mandela's ANC (African National Congress) and Gatsha Buthelezi's Inkatha Freedom Party, no end to the killing is in sight." (p16)

"Leaders: Voting amid Violence." Economist v329 n7842, 18 Dec 1993. p16,18. (ISSN0013-0613).

"With the political violence has come an explosion of crime [in South Africa]. According to police statistics, 17,467 South Africans were murdered in 1993, an increase of almost 9 percent from 1992. Reported incidents of rape increased by 11 percent over the past year, although analysts say the real figure is much higher. Johannesburg, with a per capita murder rate 7.5 times New York City's, is the murder capital of the world. In many black townships and rural areas, the simplest acts of everyday life, from commuting to churchgoing to attending school, now carry the risk of random, brutal death. Pretoria's Human Sciences Research Council has identified 12 distinct types of massacres, ranging from drive-bys to 'knock knocks,' in which occupants of a household are slaughtered after opening the door." (p46)

Ransdell, Eric/Eddings, Jerelyn. "World Report: The End of the Beginning." U.S. News & World Report v116 n16, 25 Apr 1994. p44-46,59-62,64. (ISSN0041-5537).

VIOLENCE--TURKEY (v19)

VIOLENCE--U.S.

"Recent data reveal that by age 18, the average American has spent 18,000 hours in front of the television, more than is spent in a classroom, and has witnessed about 17,000 murders. A 1991 survey by the National Institute of Justice found that 22 percent of inner-city high school students owned guns, and 15 percent owned three or more guns. The most common reason for such firepower mirrored the message of the frontier: self-protection." (p5)

"The Media and Images of War: Perception versus Reality." Defense Monitor v23 n4, 1994. p1-8. (ISSN0195-6450).

"Fatal and nonfatal injuries from interpersonal violence have increased to such an extent that in 1992 violence was declared a public health emergency. The Surgeon General reports that on an average day in the United States, 65 people die and more than

6,000 are injured by interpersonal violence. Reports further indicate that violence between family members and acquaintances accounts for more than half of all homicides, that 90 percent of the time, victims and assailants are of the same race and that most violent injuries do not occur in public." (p10)

Seltzer, Frederic. "Trend in Mortality from Violent Deaths: Suicide and Homicide, United States, 1960-1991." Statistical Bulletin v75 n2, Apr-Jun 1994. p10-18. (ISSN0790-8334).

VIOLENCE--U.S.--CHILDREN

"The slow, grinding violence of poverty...takes an American child's life every 53 minutes,...the deadly, quick violence of guns...takes an American child's life every three hours and the lives of 25 children--the equivalent of a classroomful--every two days." (p182)

Weill, James D. (General Counsel, Children's Defense Fund). U.S. Congress. Joint Economic Committee. "The 1993 Economic Report of the President." Hearing, 27 Jan 1993. Washington, D.C.: GPO, 1994. (ISBN0160440300). (Y4.Ec:Ec7/2/993/pt.1).

"Children are becoming involved in violence at ever-younger ages, according to the Commission on Youth and Violence of the American Psychological Association (APA). In a study of first and second graders in Washington, DC, the commission reported that 45 percent said they had witnessed muggings, 31 percent had witnessed shootings, and 39 percent had seen dead bodies." (p2)

"Saving Youth from Violence." Carnegie Quarterly v39 n1, Win 1994. p1-5.

VIOLENCE--U.S.--PSYCHOLOGICAL ASPECTS (v19)

VIOLENCE--U.S.--WOMEN (v19)

"Continued violence against women [in the U.S.] can rapidly strike down any gains women make in the workplace, in health care reform and in Congress. The numbers do not lie. Violence occurs at least once in two-thirds of all marriages. Ninety-five percent of victims of domestic violence are women. It is estimated that 2,000 to 4,000 women are beaten to death each year. The Surgeon General says that battering 'is the single largest cause of injury to women in the United States.' Clearly, action is needed." (pH10369)

Snowe, Olympia J. (Rep.-Maine). "Violence against Women Act of 1993," Congressional Record (20 Nov 1993). Daily ed. pH10349-10370. (ISSN0363-7239).

"Abuse toward women is being recognized as a major health concern in...[the U.S.]. In 'Healthy People 2000' (1991), the Surgeon General identified violence against women as one of top 22 priority objectives for the nation's health. It has been estimated that at least three to four million women are abused each year by their husbands, boyfriends, or lovers, and 25% to 30% of all American women have experienced at least one abusive episode. Most women who are assaulted, raped, injured, or killed know their male assailant." (p56)

Greenberg, E. M. "Violence against Women: Implications for Nursing Practice." Imprint v41 n2, Feb-Mar 1994. p56-58. (ISSN0019-3038).

VIOLENCE--U.S.--YOUTH (v19)

"Although the sensational increase in violence among younger children makes the news almost daily, 18 to 20-year-olds are still the most serious problem....The murder arrest rate for 18 and 19-year-olds is higher than any other age group, according to age-specific arrest rates compiled by the U.S. Department of Justice for 1990. Moreover, looking at the distribution by age of the total arrests in 1991 for murder and nonnegligent homicide, the highest percentage of arrests for ages 21 and under are clustered in ages 18, 19, and 20. Also, in 1991, the arrest rate for 18, 19, and 20-year-olds for weapons violations was 389.9 per 100,000, roughly 4 times the rate reported for all other age groups combined (94.2 per 100,000)." (p96)

U.S. Senate. Committee on the Judiciary. "Children and Gun Violence." Hearing, 9 Jun 1993. Washington, D.C.: GPO, 1994. (ISBN0160439280). (Y4.J89/2:S.hrg.103-393).

"National Crime Survey data indicate that between 1988 and 1990 victimizations of [U.S.] youth ages 12-18 for rape, robbery, and assault increased 7.5 percent from 1,391,791 victimizations in 1988 to 1,496,416 offenses in 1990 (Bureau of Justice Statistics, 1993)....Analysis of self-reported measures of violent offending employed in the NYS [National Youth Survey] covering the period 1976 to 1980, indicates that (Elliott, 1986:483-503):...Approximately 35 percent of males were classified as serious violent offenders for at least 1 year by the age of 21, compared with 11 percent of females. On the average, serious violent offenders commit eight serious violent offenses annually. On the average, each of these individuals commit 132 delinquent offenses annually, compared with 54 for serious nonviolent offenders....Eighty-four percent of the most serious offenders had no official record." (p34)

Wilson, John J./Howell, James C. (Office of Juvenile Justice and Delinquency Prevention). U.S. House. Committee on Education and Labor. "Hearing Regarding the...Report Entitled 'A...Strategy for Serious...Juvenile Offenders.'" Hearing, 28 Oct 1993. Washington, D.C.: GPO, 1994. (ISBN0160433983). (Y4.Ed8/1:103-34).

"Youth violence [in the U.S.] has become a major quandary in today's society. Experts have called it a national health epidemic. Recent statistics show: At present rates, three of four 12-year-olds will become victims of violent crime at some time during their lives. During the 1980s over 48,000 people were murdered by youth in the 12-24 year old range. Between 1984 and 1989 homicide rates for 15-24 year olds have increased 41 percent. We must find a cure for this epidemic. Education must be part of the cure. Schools are a natural environment to begin to tackle this problem." (p78)

Newman, Jason (Co-Director, National Inst. for Citizen Education in the Law). U.S. Senate. Committee on Labor and Human Resources. "Recess from Violence: Making Our Schools Safe." Hearing, 23 Sep 1993. Washington, D.C.: GPO, 1993. (ISBN0160433096). (Y4.L11/4:S.hrg.103-313).

Delbert S. "Elliott, who is studying violence among adolescents [in the U.S.]..., says the most dramatic finding from his research is the sheer magnitude of adolescent involvement in serious offenses. Of the teenagers he interviewed, more than 35 percent of black males and 25 percent of non-Hispanic white males reported that they had, by the age of seventeen, been involved in one or more violent acts. At the peak age for girls, between ages fifteen and seventeen, more than one in five blacks and one in ten whites reported such involvement." (p2)

"Saving Youth from Violence." Carnegie Quarterly v39 n1, Win 1994. p1-5.

VIOLENCE--U.S.--YOUTH--MORTALITY

"Given the emphasis on 'teen' violence [in the media], a California Department of Justice report (8/13/93) comes as a shock: It found that 83 percent of murdered children, half of murdered teenagers and 85 percent of murdered adults are slain by adults over age 20, not by 'kids'--or, in President Clinton's stock phrase (AP, 11/14/93), '13-year-old...with automatic weapons.' In fact, FBI reports show 47-year-olds (people Clinton's age) are twice as likely to commit murder than are 13-year-olds. But while the media champion official rhetoric on violence by youth, they rarely provide similar attention to the epidemic of adult violence against youth. The National Center on Child Abuse and Neglect (5/93) reported that at least 350,000 children and teenagers are confirmed victims of sexual and other violent abuses every year by adults whose average age is 32 years. Comparison of these figures with crime reports shows that for every violent and sexual offense committed by a youth under 18, there are three such crimes committed by adults against children and teens." (p9-10)

Males, Mike. "Bashing Youth: Media Myths about Teenagers." EXTRA! v7 n2, Mar-Apr 1994. p8-11. (ISSN0895-2310).

VIOLENCE IN TELEVISION--U.S. (v19)

VIOLENCE IN TELEVISION--U.S.--CHILDREN (v19)

"When Leonard Eron surveyed every 8-year-old child in Columbia County, New York, in 1960, he found something he wasn't looking for: an astonishing, and unmistakable, correlation between the amount of violence the youngsters saw on television and the aggressiveness of their behavior." (p5) "about 500 of the now 19-year-olds from the original sample of 875 youngsters [were surveyed again]....'The correlation between violence-viewing at age 8 and how aggressive the individual was at 19 was higher than the correlation between watching violence at age 8 and behaving aggressively at age 8,' says Eron. 'There was no correlation between violence-viewing at age 19 and aggressiveness at 19. It seems there was a cumulative effect going on here.' Its persistence was documented once more in 1981, when 400 of the subjects were surveyed again, along with 80 of their offspring. The 30-year-old men who had been the most aggressive when they were 8 had more arrrests for drunk driving, more arrests for violent crime, were more abusive to their spouses...and had more aggressive children. And of the 600 subjects whose criminal justice records were reviewed, those who watched more violence on TV when they were 8 had been arrested more often for violent crimes, and self-reported more fights when consuming alcohol." (p5-6)

"Televised Violence and Kids: A Public Health Problem?" Profiles: ISR Newsletter v18 n1, Feb 1994. p5-7.

VIOLENCE IN TELEVISION--U.S.--PUBLIC OPINION (v19)

VIOLENT CRIMES--LOS ANGELES (CALIF)

"In Los Angeles between 1986 and 1989, reported violent crime, including firearm violations, occurred at an average annual rate of 67 per 1,000 people in public housing developments, compared to 22 per 1,000 citywide." (pE690)

Durbin, Richard J. (Rep.-Ill.). "Gun-Free Public Housing Zones Act of 1994," Congressional Record (18 Apr 1994). Daily ed. pE690-691. (ISSN0363-7239).

VIOLENT CRIMES--U.S. (v19)

"Since 1960 the population of the United States has risen about 40 percent. In that same period of time the rate of violent crime has shot up by 500 percent. We now have a higher crime rate than any other developed country in the world." (pH2372)

Smith, Lamar S. (Rep.-Tex.). "Crime Bill," Congressional Record (18 Apr 1994). Daily ed. pH2372. (ISSN0363-7239).

"While the population of the United States increased 44 percent since 1960, violent crime has increased by more than 500 percent. And since the early 1950's, the expected punishment for committing a serious crime in the United States has been reduced by two-thirds. Yet over that same period, the total number of serious crimes has increased sevenfold. In addition, more than half of all violent criminals are put back on the streets while awaiting trial. Of those, 20 percent escape and 16 percent commit another crime. And for every 100 serious crimes committed, only 5 criminals go to jail." (pH2603)

Dornan, Robert K. (Rep.-Calif.). "Violent Crime Control and Law Enforcement Act of 1994," Congressional Record (21 Apr 1994). Daily ed. pH2596-2613. (ISSN0363-7239).

"Five million Americans are victims of violent crime every year in this country. Sixty-five Americans are murdered and 288 are raped each and every day. A boy born in 1974 stands a greater chance of being a homicide victim than a soldier in World War II stood of dying in combat. Nine hundred and seventy-nine criminals are released early from prison every day, and approximately 6,000 convicted rapists received no prison sentence at all last year. An estimated 60,000 violent offenders will not go to prison this year, including 1,100 convicted murderers and 6,900 convicted rapists....The fact of the matter is that 6 percent of the criminals of this country are committing an average of about 70 to 80 percent of all violent crimes of this country. And they are serving only about a third of their sentences, somewhere around 37 or 38 percent." (pH1912)

McCollum, Bill (Rep.-Fla.). "Violent Crime Control and Law Enforcement Act of 1994," Congressional Record (23 Mar 1994). Daily ed. pH1905-1937. (ISSN0363-7239).

"By some measures (e.g., the FBI summary of police reports), violent crime in the nation has increased over the past decade, up 23 percent between 1980 and 1990; by other counts (the US Census survey, which asks citizens whether they have been victims of crimes), violent crimes have gone down 11 percent....In December 1993, the FBI announced that during the past year, violent crimes such as murder, rape, robbery, burglary, and arson had declined by 8 percent in the Northeast, by 6.8 percent in upstate New York, and by 5.6 percent in New York City." (p36)

Rothman, David J. "The Crime of Punishment." New York Review of Books v41 n4, 17 Feb 1994. p34-38. (ISSN0028-7504).

VIOLENT CRIMES--U.S.--PUBLIC OPINION

"There were almost 36 million American children between the ages of 5 and 14 in 1991, and only 519 of them were murdered. Actual mortality among chidlren this age has dropped steadily for decades, to less than half the 1950 rate. This is because influenza has killed more children than all the kidnappers and drive-by shootings in history. But the fear of crime is almost a separate phenomenon from the real danger it poses....The fear can be measured statistically: more than half the children (and 73 percent of the adults) questioned in a recent NEWSWEEK/Children's Defense Fund Poll said they were afraid of violent crime against them or a family member." (p44)

Adler, Jerry. "Lifestyle: Kids Growing Up Scared." Newsweek v123 n2, 10 Jan 1994. p43-49. (ISSN0028-9604).

VIOLENT CRIMES--U.S.--YOUTH (v19)

"Nearly 1 million adolescents between the ages of 12 and 19 are victims of violent crimes each year, and this has been true at least since 1985. The victimization of adolescents, particularly 12- to 15-year-olds, is growing. Teenagers are twice as likely to be assaulted as persons aged 20 and older. The rate and intensity of violence involving children and youth, moreover, has escalated dramatically, and much of it is accounted for by adolescents attacking their peers. Adolescent homicide rates have reached the highest levels in history." (pH552)

Goodling, William F. (Rep.-Pa.). "Safe Schools Act of 1994," Congressional Record (22 Feb 1994). Daily ed. pH551-553. (ISSN0363-7239).

"The Office of Juvenile Justice and Delinquency Prevention reported that arrests for violent crimes [in the U.S.] by juveniles increased 91 percent between 1970 and 1992. They also report that between 1987 and 1991, the number of violent crime arrests of juveniles increased by 50 percent--double the increase in arrests of those 18 and older. Young people are committing more crimes. In 1991, juveniles accounted for 17 percent of all violent crime arrests. The young are more often the target of crime as well. The Federal Bureau of Investigation says that children under 18 are 244 percent more likely to be killed than they were in 1986. The Office of Juvenile Justice and Delinquency Prevention records show that between 1985 and 1988, 67 out of 1,000 teenagers were victims of violent crimes compared with 26 out of 1,000 persons age 20 or older. And the Washington Post, recently reported that violence took the lives of 2,428 children in 1992, an increase of 67 percent in just 6 years." (pH1056)

Collins, Cardiss (Rep.-Ill.). "Revolving Door Justice," Congressional Record (3 Mar 1994). Daily ed. pH1055-1056. (ISSN0363-7239).

VIOLENT CRIMES--WASHINGTON (STATE)--YOUTH

"In Washington state, violent crimes by youths have doubled in numbers in the past decade despite a 3 percent reduction in the youth population. The Washington State Survey of Adolescent Health Behaviors recently found that 15 percent of 6th grade students, and 25 percent of 8th, 10th, and 12th grade students said that they had carried a weapon to school. The same survey found that students who abused drugs and alcohol were much more likely to carry weapons to school. In King County alone last year, 22 victims of homicide were children under 18. In 1992, 42 juveniles were victims of murder in Washington State, 22 of whom were child abuse victims. From 1991 to 1992, the number of gang-related homicides in the State jumped from 3 to 17. Nationally, in the last 10 years, arrests of juveniles for homicide offenses have risen 93 percent. According to the National Crime Survey, each year nearly 3 million thefts and violent crimes--one crime every 6 seconds--take place on or near school grounds. The same study suggests that 67 out of every 1,000 teenagers suffer a violent crime each year." (pS3867)

Gorton, Slade (Sen.-Wash.). "Goals 2000: Educate America Act--Conference Report," Congressional Record (25 Mar 1994). Daily ed. pS3861-3879. (ISSN0363-7239).

VIRGINIA--COMMERCE--CANADA--MEXICO (v19)

VIRUSES, COMPUTER

see COMPUTER VIRUSES

VISAS--CUBA--U.S.

The U.S. Interests Section in Havana, Cuba "has become part of city folklore over the past couple of years: here, hundreds of people can be seen standing in an endless line, waiting for a two to three-minute interview with a U.S. consular officer. This person has the final say over...petitions for visitor visas to...the United States." According to a U.S. Interests Section officer, "of some 70,000 interviews conducted in fiscal year 1993, about 60% or 42,000 were denied visas....On a busy day,...consular officers will see as many as 500 applicants; on a 'slow' day, only 300." (p1)

Reed, Gail. "U.S.-Cuba: Beware the Swinging Door." Cuba Update v15 n1, Feb 1994. p1-3. (ISSN0196-0830).

VISITORS, FOREIGN--JAPAN

see also STUDENTS, FOREIGN--JAPAN

"There were 1.28 million registered foreign residents in Japan in 1992, more than 1% of Japan's total population. Foreign residents account for about 6% of all residents living in Tokyo's Shinjuku and Toshima Wards. Between 1990 and 1993, the number of foreigners arrested for failing to leave the country when their visas expired or who worked without the necessary visa increased sharply, from 100,000 to 300,000. Local governments are most confused by these changes. Until recently they rarely had contact with foreigners. Koji Saka, President of the Japan Intercultural Academy of Municipalities (JIAM) explains, 'As visitors from many countries have come to live in Japan, we have experienced problems that we had not anticipated. It is the municipalities, not the central or prefectural governments that have to deal with these problems.'" (p10)

"What Is Internationalization?" Look Japan v39 n455, Feb 1994. p10. (ISSN0456-5339).

VITAMIN A DEFICIENCY IN CHILDREN

"Worldwide, blinding Vitamin A deficiency afflicts up to half a million children annually and is a major contributor to child mortality. At least two-thirds of the children who become blind die within a year. At any one time, 10-15 million other children show less severe forms of Vitamin A deficiency. They, too, die at excessive rates. The highest levels of Vitamin A deficiency seem to occur in south Asia, while about 20 countries in Africa, particularly in the Sahelian belt, are thought to have a significant problem." (p5)

Tapang, Hannah. "Africa: Leaves That Save Children's Lives." Panoscope n34, Jan 1993. p5-6. (ISSN0951-8819).

VITAMIN C

"With evidence growing that higher intakes of the antioxidant vitamins C and E may help protect us against cancer and heart disease, Agricultural Research and National Cancer Institute (NCI) scientists collaborated to see how well food sources stack up against supplements in raising blood levels of these vitamins. According to Gladys Block, who began the study while at NCI, about 86 percent of vitamin C in the average U.S. diet comes from fruits and vegetables. However, about 25 percent of Americans also take vitamin C supplements--alone, or in a multivitamin--according to Block, who is now at the University of California, Berkeley." (p17)

McBride, Judy. "As Vitamin Sources--Food or Supplements?" Agricultural Research v41 n12, Dec 1993. p17. (ISSN0002-161X).

VITAMIN INDUSTRY--U.S. (v19)

VITAMINS--U.S.

"The scientific evidence continues to mount supporting the importance and the necessity of vitamin supplementation. A striking example is the relationship between folic acid supplements and the reduction in neural tube birth defects. A simple multivitamin of 0.4 mg taken daily by women of childbearing age can reduce the risk of neural tube birth defects by approximately 70 percent. Neural tube birth defects now occur in about 1 of 1,600 pregnancies, resulting in the birth of 2,500 affected infants each year. Although most survive, many are in need of extensive, lifelong medical care, which can have a staggering effect on these children and our families." (pE321)

Gallegly, Elton (Rep.-Calif.). "Dietary Supplements Are Beneficial to Good Health," Congressional Record (2 Mar 1994). Daily ed. pE321-322. (ISSN0363-7239).

VOCATIONAL EDUCATION--U.S.

According to an interim report of the National Assessment of Vocational Education, between 1982 and 1990, the number of vocational credits earned by high school students decreased by 11 percent. But disabled, economically or educationally disadvantaged or students with limited English proficiency, who constitute 34 percent of high school graduates, earned 43 percent of all vocational credits. Disabled students took an average of 5.99 credits in vocational education, compared with 4.10 for all students. "The study also found that special-needs students tend to be concentrated in training for low-status occupations, such as food service, auto-body repairs, and the metalworking trades." (p1,19)

Olson, Lynn. "Enrollments in Voc. Ed. Down from '82 to '90." Education Week v13 n17, 19 Jan 1994. p1,19. (ISSN0277-4232).

VOCATIONAL REHABILITATION--U.S.--SUBSTANCE USE (v19)

VOLLEYBALL--U.S.

"Hard surface volleyball players outnumber beach volleyballers by more than two to one. But beach volleyball has sex appeal, according to Carol Campbell, group publisher of VOLLEYBALL, a magazine for both indoor and outdoor players....More than 13.2 million Americans aged 6 and older played beach volleyball in 1992, a 28 percent increase from 1989, according to the Sporting Goods Manufacturers Association in North Palm Beach, Florida. The number of frequent players has grown even faster. The number of people who played at least 25 times in 1992 was 1.4 million, almost double the number in 1989." (p4)

Waldrop, Judith. "Seasons: Beachball Bonanza." American Demographics v16 n3, Mar 1994. p4. (ISSN0163-4089).

VOLUNTARISM--U.S.--AGED

"In 1988, persons reaching age 65 [in the U.S.] had an average life expectancy of an additional 16.9 years (18.6 for females and 14.8 for males). Only 5% of those over 65 years of age reside in institutions and another 17% say they are unable to engage in their major activity; but a full 81% of the non-institutionalized 65+ population has no limitation in their activities of daily living. This healthy, active segment of the senior population represents a vast untapped resource for contributing for the betterment of America's communities. According to a 1991 U.S. Administration of Aging/Marriott Senior Living Services volunteerism survey, over 41% (15.1 million) of the 37.7 million Americans 60+ performed some form of volunteer work in the past year. An additional 37.5 percent (14 million) indicate they would volunteer if asked. In 1990 Seniors volunteered an estimated 992 million days, generating an estimated 3.6 billion hours of volunteer service, or ten times this number when considered in dollar value. The Federally supported Senior Volunteer Programs, Foster Grandparents, Senior Companions, Retired Senior Volunteer Program (RSVP) provide opportunities for volunteer service for less than one percent of senior Americans." (P38)

Butler, Frances F. (Washington Rep., National Assoc. for Senior Companion Project Directors). U.S. House. Committee on Education and Labor. "Joint Hearing on H.R. 2010, the National Service Trust Act." Hearing, 25 May 1993. Washington, D.C.: GPO, 1994. (ISBN0160433177). (Y4.Ed8/1:103-32).

"Fifteen percent of older people who volunteer their time assist education groups, and 15 percent help youth-development organizations, says a new publication from Independent Sector, a Washington-based coalition of nonprofit organizations, foundations, and corporations....Nearly half of people ages 60 to 75 volunteer an average of 4.4 hours a week. And compared with younger volunteers, they tend to remain longer." (p5)

Sommerfeld, Meg. "Partnerships." Education Week v13 n27, 30 Mar 1994. p5. (ISSN0277-4232).

VOLUNTARISM--U.S.--YOUTH (v19)

VOLUNTARY ORGANIZATIONS

see ASSOCIATIONS, INSTITUTIONS, ETC.

VOLUNTEER WORKERS IN EDUCATION--U.S. (v19)

VOLUNTEERS--U.S. (v19)

see also CAREGIVERS--U.S.

"Over half of all American adults already volunteer an average of four hours a week as it is and nearly two thirds of youths 12-17 give at least three hours--for an estimated total of 2.1 billion hours annually. According to Pacific News Service, the LA city government has more than 14,000 volunteers. The town of El Cerrito, CA, is run by 100 paid employees and nearly 500 volunteers. When Lafayette, CA got into fiscal trouble it asked for help from volunteer accountant and management consultants who came up with a plan to save about a tenth of the city's budget. So what exactly is the purpose of attempting to nationalize all this activity, converting what was formerly community service into national service?" (p6)

Smith, Sam. "Volunteering Ain't What It Used to Be." Progressive Review n319, Oct 1993. p6-7.

VOLUNTEERS--U.S.--AGED (v19)

VOTING--CANADA--U.S.

"Canadians are told that as good citizens they should vote, and 70 to 80 percent of them do, in both federal and provincial elections. But only one out of two Americans votes in presidential contests;...fewer, often around 20 to 25 percent, take part in the primaries to select presidential nominees." (p26)

Lipset, Seymour Martin. "Symposium: Why Americans Refuse to Vote." Insight v10 n6, 7 Feb 1994. p24-26. (ISSN1051-4880).

VOTING--HISPANIC AMERICANS (v19)

VOTING--LOS ANGELES (CALIF)

"One million adult Latinos--including probably half of the...manual working class [in Los Angeles]--are unnaturalized and disfranchised. Combined with the young median age of the Latino population and the obstacles to voter registration, this ensures that the city's largest ethnic group--41 per cent or 1,600,000 people--typically casts less than 50,000 votes (7-9 per cent of the total). As a result, Anglos exercise eleven times more electoral clout per capita than Latinos....Indeed, Jews alone usually mobilize twice the Latino vote, as do African-Americans (11 per cent of the population, 18 per cent of the vote). At the same time, this white-washed electorate is also a veritable gerontocracy: there are nearly twice as many over-65 voters (38.4 per cent) as under-35s (21.1 per cent). A majority of the electorate is over 50, and 70 per cent of the voting households are 'empty nests' without school-age children." (p52)

Davis, Mike. "Who Killed Los Angeles? Part Two: The Verdict Is Given." New Left Review n199, May-Jun 1993. p29-54. (ISSN0028-6060).

VOTING--SOUTH AFRICA

"An estimated 14 million black voters, including [Nelson] Mandela, will be voting for the first time in their lives. In addition, some 3 million white voters, 1.8 million mixed-race 'coloured' voters, and 650,000 Asians will vote for about 20 political parties expected to contest the election....The [Independent Electoral] Commission will...oversee the massive task of educating voters in a country where some 70 percent of the population have never voted before." (p3)

Battersby, John. "International: South Africans Gear Up for 'Liberation Day.'" The Christian Science Monitor v86 n38, 19 Jan 1994. p3. (ISSN0882-7729).

"Recent opinion polls [in South Africa] indicate support for the NP [National Party] at between 14 and 18 percent of the national vote. Of the country's 22.5 million voters, about 16.2 million are black South Africans who have never voted before. About 72 percent of blacks are expected to vote for the ANC, 5 percent for the Zulu-based Inkatha Freedom Party, 2 percent for the militant Pan-Africanist Congress (PAC), and only 1 percent for the NP." (p4)

Battersby, John. "S. Africa's National Party Courts Black Vote." The Christian Science Monitor v86 n53, 9 Feb 1994. p4. (ISSN0882-7729).

VOTING--U.S. (v19)

"Only about half of the voting age population of the United States--55 percent--voted in the last presidential election. That marked an increase from the 1988 elections, but still is deplorably low by a number of standards. To begin with, this level of turnout is still 8 percentage points below that of the 1960 election, when a 30-year decline in voter turnout began....Second, a 55 percent turnout is still about 25 percentage points below the international average....Finally, despite the participation increase in the 1992 election, turnout in the last three presidential elections averaged only a little less than 53 percent. By way of comparison, the three elections of 1952, 1956, and 1960 averaged a little more than 61 percent." (p27)

Teixeira, Ruy A. "Symposium: Make Voting Easy, More Interesting." Insight v10 n6, 7 Feb 1994. p27-29. (ISSN1051-4880).

VOTING--U.S.--CATHOLICS

"While Catholic members of Congress were somewhat less pro-choice than average during the 1970s and 1980s, since 1980 they have moved in a pro-choice direction. In 1993, over 60 percent of the Catholics in Congress supported President Clinton's removal of the gag rule, opposed parental-notification requirements, and favored fetal-tissue research. In the 1992 presidential election, Catholics voted for Clinton 44 percent to 36 percent over Bush, with 20 percent choosing Perot. In contrast, white Protestants favored Bush 46 percent to 33 percent, with 21 percent for Perot. Evangelical and fundamentalist Protestants gave Bush 59 percent, Clinton 25 percent, and Perot 16 percent. Without the Catholic vote, Clinton may not have won or would have just barely squeaked through to victory." (p19-20)

Menedez, Albert J. "The Political Power of the Catholic Church: American Catholics: A Social and Political Portrait." Humanist v53 n5, Sep-Oct 1993. p17-20. (ISSN0018-7399).

VOTING--U.S. CONGRESS

"Missing a vote has become a relatively rare event in Congress. Despite an avalanche of votes, members voted 96.2 percent of the time in 1993. That is the highest level of voting participation for Congress since CONGRESSIONAL QUARTERLY began tracking recorded votes in 1953. Thomas E. Mann, director of governmental studies at the Brookings Institution, says the fresh blood in Congress probably helped raise the scores....House members voted 96 percent of the time, and senators, 97.6 percent of the time. (The preponderance of House votes kept the overall percentage closer to the House total.) In each chamber, participation increased by 3 percentage points over the previous year. The overall score was nearly 3 percentage points higher than in 1992. The previous record of 95 percent was found in 1989, 1990 and 1991. Members managed to achieve these high scores in spite of large increases in the numbers of votes in both chambers. In 1993, House members voted on 597 issues. (Including quorum calls--not counted in the study--the House took 615 votes, 127 more than the previous year and the most since 1980.) The Senate took 395 roll call votes, 125 more than in 1992." (p3439)

Thomas, Jennifer S. "Vote Studies: Voting Participation: Freshmen Help Spur Congress to a Record Voting Rate." Congressional Quarterly v51 n50, 18 Dec 1993. p3439-3440.

WAGES

see also EMPLOYEE FRINGE BENEFITS

WAGES--AFRO-AMERICAN MEN (v19)

WAGES--AFRO-AMERICANS

"Because black workers [in the U.S.] tend to be stuck at the bottom of the occupational and skill ladder, when the value of the minimum wage was allowed to be eroded by inflation in the 1980s, black workers were disproportionately hurt. A report released by Economic Policy Institute in 1991 showed that between 1979 and 1989, wages fell for the bottom 80 percent of the workforce, but the sharpest declines were among those with the lowest wages at the beginning of the decade. In 1973, 56.5 percent of black workers earned at least 200 percent of the poverty level for a family of four; by 1991, only 42.6 percent of black workers earned this much. The decline in wages has hit black workers and households especially hard." (p149)

McFate, Katherine (Joint Center for Political and Economic Studies). U.S. House. Committee on Ways and Means. "Historical Trends in Poverty and Family Income." Hearing, 26 Oct 1993. Washington, D.C.: GPO, 1994. (ISBN0160435765). (Y4.W36:103-42).

"The relative earnings position of young black males with little education deteriorated substantially [in the U.S.]. In 1970, for every dollar that a white male under 25 years of age who had not graduated from high school earned, similarly situated black males earned $1.11. By 1988, this advantage disappeared completely. For every dollar young, uneducated white males earned, blacks earned only 35 cents. Overall, however, the ratio of wage and salary earnings of black males to the wage and salary earnings of white males improved from 1970 to 1988. It was .62 in 1970 and .63 in 1988. Thus, the experiences of young black males diverged from those of black males generally. In particular, the ratios of black to white earnings for males 25 to 40 years of age and for those over 40 both showed stable movements over the span of the 1970s and 1980s. The widening of the racial earnings gap between young black and white males was not uniform across all educational levels among men under the age of 25. There were sharp drops in the ratio for high school dropouts. There were dramatic increases in the ratio for college graduates." (p124)

Myers, Samuel L., Jr. (Hubert H. Humphrey Inst. of Public Affairs, Univ. of Minnesota). U.S. House. Committee on Ways and Means. "Historical Trends in Poverty and Family Income." Hearing, 26 Oct 1993. Washington, D.C.: GPO, 1994. (ISBN0160435765). (Y4.W36:103-42).

WAGES--COLLEGE GRADUATES--U.S. (v19)

WAGES--EUROPE--U.S. (v19)

WAGES--GEORGIA (REPUBLIC)

"The average salary in Georgia is 35,000 coupons per month, which is the equivalent of about $3.50. The average wage in Georgia is about 10 times less than in Russia, which is also going through very difficult times. Many people want to move somewhere else, at least to Russia or Ukraine. From January to October 1993, about 800,000 people left the country. And it is the most talented professional people who are leaving, those who have a chance to build a new life in a new place." (p23)

Urigashvili, Besik. "Georgia: 'Damn This War....'" Bulletin of the Atomic Scientists v50 n1, Jan-Feb 1994. p20-24. (ISSN0096-3402).

WAGES--GREAT BRITAIN (v19)

WAGES--INDONESIA

"The components of the American dream are manufactured in small towns such as Serang in west Java. Warehouse-like factories, dotted among the rice fields, churn out fashionable athletic shoes for joggers and tennis players in the West. At P.T. Eltri, a South Korean-owned firm which manufactures for Nike, LA Gear and Adidas, hundreds of women crouch over sewing machines and half-formed basketball shoes. On the walls, stickers bearing the Nike slogan jauntily urge them, 'Just Do It'. The women need all the encouragement they can get. Even after a recent 40% rise, most are paid less than $10 for a five-day week. With 2.5m new entrants to the labour force each year, there is no shortage of Indonesians willing to work for so little....The Indonesian government wants to keep costs down, but is also keen to contain labour unrest and meet the rising expectations of workers....It recently increased the minimum wage in west Java to 3,800 rupiah ($1.80) a day and is threatening to prosecute factory owners who fail to meet their new obligations." (p35)

"Asia: Indonesia: Doing It, Earning It." Economist v330 n7852, 26 Feb 1994. p35-36. (ISSN0013-0613).

WAGES--KOREA (SOUTH) (v19)

WAGES--MEXICO (v19)

"There is a large amount of testimony already in Congressional records that Mexican labor is not free. Wages and working conditions are completely controlled by the government with cooperation of compliant trade unions. The result is an hourly wage of approximately $1.25 in Mexican refineries compared to the prevailing average hourly wage of nearly $18.15 in U.S.

refineries. This wage differential can worsen at any time should the Mexican peso be further depreciated with respect to the U.S. dollar. The peso has declined from 12.5 to the dollar in 1977 to 3100 at the end of 1992. During this period, real wages have declined." (p120)

Hancock, Nolan W. (Citizenship-Legislative Dir., Oil, Chemical and Atomic Workers International Union). U.S. House. Committee on Energy and Commerce. "NAFTA: Energy Provisions and Environmental Implications." Hearing, 22 Sep 1993. Washington, D.C.: GPO, 1994. (ISBN0160440459). (Y4.En2/3:103/70).

WAGES--MEXICO--U.S. (v19)

"For years, Mexican and American researchers had been compiling data showing that the single most important contributing factor to immigration--illegal or not--was the wage differential....As long as the wage differential between the United States and Mexico, for example, averaged nearly eight to one, young enterprising Mexicans of all social strata were going to continue their trek north. In 1990, the Mexican minimum wage was 55 cents an hour; its counterpart in California--where fully half of all undocumented Mexican immigrants make their home--was about $4.50 an hour. Similarly, a tenured university professor in Mexico, Brazil, or Argentina, with a Ph.D. and recognized publications, received between $250 and $800 a month in the early nineties, yet could often make three to four thousand dollars per month, after taxes, at a major American university." (p52)

Castaneda, Jorge G. "Latin America and the End of the Cold War." Transition v3 n1, 1993. p45-64. (ISSN0041-1191).

WAGES--MICHIGAN

"A typical manufacturing job in Michigan...paid an average annual salary of $39,000 in 1992, while the average retail job paid just $13,000. The average health services job paid $28,000, and the average business services job paid $26,000." (p1 secF)

Muller, Joann. "Business: Open to Change." Detroit Free Press 16 Mar 1994. p1 secF.

WAGES--MIMINUM WAGE--DOMINICAN REPUBLIC

"American insistence that free trade must be accompanied by fair labour practices in poor countries will soon face a practical test. The United States trade representative, Mickey Kantor, is to rule on a petition from the AFL-CIO, America's labour federation, to deny preferential access to products from the Dominican Republic. For the 160,000 workers in the Dominican Republic's free-trade zones and for the companies that employ them to assemble goods for the American market, much rides on the decision. For the country too: a large proportion of its exports goes to the United States, and nearly 30% of that total enters free or at reduced duties, either under the rich countries' 'generalised system of preferences' or under the United States' Caribbean Basin Initiative....the legal minimum wage is $96 a month, for a 44-hour working week--about 51 cents an hour, though many workers in the zones add to their earnings with overtime." (p50,52)

"International: Labour and Trade: Freedom." Economist v331 n7861, 30 Apr 1994. p50,52. (ISSN0013-0613).

WAGES--MINIMUM WAGE--FRANCE--U.S.

"In France, the minimum wage rose from around 40% of the average wage in the early 1970s to 50% by the mid-1980s. The jobless rate among those aged 24 or under rose from 4% to more than 20%. America's federal minimum wage, in contrast, fell from 40% to 30% of the average wage in the 1980s; its youth unemployment rate is barely half that in France." (p70)

"Schools Brief: A Bad Case of Arthritis." Economist v330 n7852, 26 Feb 1994. p70-71. (ISSN0013-0613).

WAGES--MINIMUM WAGE--MONGOLIA

"The minimum wage in Mongolia was calculated on the basis of basic consumption requirements of a household of five members with two full-time earners. The minimum wage multiplied by two was taken to be the poverty line for households. The minimum wage was set at 700 tughriks per month in September 1991. However, the consumer price index had risen by at least 150 per cent by September 1992, so the minimum wage should have been 1,750 tughriks per month if its real purchasing power were to have been maintained. The average monthly earnings of employees in the civil service and state budget organizations (1,900 tughriks per month) was only slightly above the required minimum." (p629)

Lee, Eddy. "Initiating Transition in a Low-Income Dualistic Economy: The Case of Mongolia." International Labour Review v132 n5-6, 1993. p623-638. (ISSN0020-7780).

WAGES--MINIMUM WAGE--U.S.

"While the minimum wage was...raised recently, it fared far less well than the EIC [Earned Income Tax Credit] during the 1980s. The minimum wage remained at $3.35 an hour from January 1981 through March 1990; during this period, the cost of living rose 48 percent. Legislation enacted in 1989 raised the wage floor in two steps--in April 1990 and April 1991--to its current level of $4.25 an hour. These increases made up less than half of the ground lost to inflation during the 1980s....As a result, the value of the minimum wage remains well below its historic level. The minimum wage is below its traditional level of purchasing power. Currently, the minimum wage is 22 percent lower than its average during the 1970s, after adjusting for inflation. If the value of the minimum wage were to have the same purchasing power in 1993 as it averaged in the 1970s, it would need to be $5.42 an hour." (p185)

Shapiro, Isaac (Exec. Director, Center for Budget and Policy Priorities). U.S. Congress. Joint Economic Committee. "The 1993 Economic Report of the President." Hearing, 27 Jan 1993. Washington, D.C.: GPO, 1994. (ISBN0160440300). (Y4.Ec:Ec7/2/993/pt.1).

WAGES--TRADE-UNIONS--U.S.

"Median weekly earnings of wage and salary workers increased to $575 for union members last year [1993], $149 more than the $426 weekly pay for non-union workers. Over the year, weekly pay for union workers rose $28, more than double the $13 raise for non-union workers. On an annual basis, the $149 per week difference in median earnings works out to a $7,750 advantage for the union worker, the BLS [Bureau of Labor Statistics] survey of U.S. households showed." (p10)

Oravec, John R. "Membership and Union Advantage Moving Ahead." AFL-CIO News v39 n5, 21 Feb 1994. p1,10. (ISSN0001-1185).

WAGES--U.S. (v19)

"The Labor Department's Employment Cost Index for all workers, measuring changes in total compensation including both benefits and wages, increased by 3.5 percent during 1993. Union workers had a clear advantage, as their total compensation rose by 4.3 percent. Looking only at wages and salaries, union and non-union workers experienced almost identical increases. Private-sector union workers received 3 percent raises, compared to 3.1 percent for non-union employees." (p7-8)

Lucore, Robert E. "Bargaining: Tough Year of Negotiation Ends on High Note." AFL-CIO News v39 n7, 21 Mar 1994. p7-10. (ISSN0001-1185).

"Pay rates in manufacturing are often higher than in services....The average hourly pay of an American manufacturing worker in 1993 was $11.75; workers in retail trade got a paltry $7.29. But workers in finance ($11.32) and in wholesale trade ($11.71) came closer to their metal-bashing brethren. And service industries are catching up: pay increases in wholesaling and finance have outstripped those in manufacturing over the past decade." (p92)

"Schools Brief: The Manufacturing Myth." Economist v330 n7855, 19 Mar 1994. p91-92. (ISSN0013-0613).

"Perhaps the best measure [of real wages] is average employee compensation (which includes non-wage benefits). This rose by a paltry 5% in real terms between 1973 and 1992. What is certain is that the gap between the wages of skilled and unskilled workers has widened. In manufacturing, the average wages of white-collar workers rose by 10% more than those of blue-collar workers in the 1980s. Many low-skilled workers suffered a cut in real pay. The bottom 10% of wage-earners saw their real wages fall by 13% between 1979 and 1989." (p73)

"Business: Economics Focus: First among Unequals." Economist v330 n7846, 15 Jan 1994. p73. (ISSN0013-0613).

"When the [U.S.] public was asked by the Roper Organization in 1981 whether the government was 'efficient and well run,' 74 percent said no. In a 1986 Market Opinion Research survey, 69 percent had only some or hardly any confidence in the federal government. Yet, most career public officials are outstanding at what they do--and they are not paid nearly enough for it. White-collar entry positions range from a $12,406 annual salary for the simplest office work to $69,427 for highly qualified administrators....Federal employees were last given their full scheduled pay increases in October 1977. Since then, pay disparity has grown steadily worse. The 1993 National Wage Survey conducted by the Bureau of Labor Statistics found an average pay gap of 30.24 percent between federal workers and their private sector counterparts. A 1991 General Accounting Office report revealed that when comparing 22 white-collar occupations in the federal and private sectors, the pay was higher for those in the private sector in all 22 categories. The study included accountants, computer operators, file clerks and typists, among others, in 22 metropolitan statistical areas with at least 10,000 white-collar federal employees" (p22-24)

Shaw, G. Jerry. "Symposium: Wage Gap Cured with Locality Pay." Insight v10 n3, 17 Jan 1994. p22-24. (ISSN1051-4880).

According to a report from the U.S. Commerce Department's Census Bureau, "The median earnings of women, aged 25 and older, who worked year-round full time was $18,648 for high school graduates in 1992; $24,849 for those with a two-year associate's degree; $29,284 for those with a four-year bachelor's degree; and $35,018 for those with a master's degree. Comparable figures for men were $26,766, $32,349, $40,381, and $47,260." (p9)

Leach, Susan Llewelyn. "Economic Reports: Census Says Americans Learn More, Earn Less." The Christian Science Monitor v86 n71, 8 Mar 1994. p9. (ISSN0882-7729).

WAGES--U.S.--EFFECT OF EDUCATION ON (v19)

WAGES--U.S.--IMMIGRANTS (v19)

WAGES--U.S.--WOMEN (v19)

"In the United States...in 1988, women in their early 20s earned 90% of the hourly pay of men of the same age. Women aged 45 and over were paid, on average, only 45% of the hourly wage for men of the same age." (p81)

"Schools Brief: The War between the Sexes." Economist v330 n7853, 5 Mar 1994. p80-81. (ISSN0013-0613).

"At the end of the 1970s, 6.8 per cent of all full-time women workers were earning over $30,000. By 1986 10.3 per cent (2.9 million women) earned more than $30,000, adjusted for inflation. (For the workforce as a whole, 25 per cent earned over $30,000.) At the other end of the spectrum, almost 18 per cent of women working full time earned less than $10,000--about the same proportion as at the end of the 1970s. In addition, 28 per cent of employed women worked part time, and earned even less--about one-third of full-time women workers' pay. The reciprocal of increased opportunity for highly-educated women over the 1980s is the rapid growth of contingent work (part-time, temporary and contract employment without benefits) primarily in retail and service industries. Following a historic pattern, women of colour are over-represented among the low-paid workers who fill the service and retail sales jobs which have expanded in the 1980s to meet new needs generated by women's increased participation in paid labour (e.g. supermarkets and department stores open seven nights a week, fast-food outlets, childcare, nursing homes)." (p115)

Brenner, Johanna. "The Best of Times, the Worst of Times: US Feminism Today." New Left Review n200, Jul-Aug 1993. p101-159. (ISSN0028-6060).

"A recent survey by MS. magazine found equal pay and job discrimination the top concerns of American women. More women are working: They do so in industrial nations at 77 percent of the men's rate in 1991, up from 59 percent 20 years earlier. But women's pay still averages two thirds of men's, mainly because women are clustered in low-wage 'women's jobs.' In the United States, year-round full-time working women earned 71 percent of the male wage in 1992, up from 62 percent a decade earlier. But women high school graduates earn slightly less than do men who dropped out of school before ninth grade." (p48)

MacFarquhar, Emily/others. "World Report: The War against Women." U.S. News & World Report v116 n12, 28 Mar 1994. p42-45,48. (ISSN0041-5537).

WAR (v19)

see ANGOLA--HISTORY--CIVIL WAR, 1975-; BURUNDI--HISTORY--CIVIL WAR; CROATIA--WARS--SERBIA; IRELAND--HISTORY--CIVIL WAR; LEBANON--HISTORY--CIVIL WAR, 1975-; SUDAN--HISTORY--CIVIL WAR; TAJIKISTAN--HISTORY--CIVIL WAR

WASHINGTON, D.C.

"Opponents argue that the State of New Columbia would be at a financial disadvantage without Federal payments. However, for the past 30 years, the Federal payment has never exceeded 20 percent of the city's budget. Moreover, Washington, DC's economy enables it to meet the costs of self-government. The business services are competitive with the rest of the United States. Legal services rank higher than 41 States, and finance, insurance, and real estate rank higher than 14 States. With 20 million tourists visiting the District each year, tourism is also a great source of revenue." (pH10443)

Stokes, Louis (Rep.-Ohio). "New Columbia Admission Act," Congressional Record (20 Nov 1993). Daily ed. pH10421-10445. (ISSN0363-7239).

"Our Founders created the District of Columbia to be a separate, 100-mile region under the exclusive control of Congress as the seat of the Federal Government for a good reason--they realized that the Federal Government must not be dependent upon, nor subject to, the influence of any single State. In 1990, the Federal Government spent $28,592 per capita in the District, more than seven times the total U.S. spending per capita. In addition, the District receives $4.72 in Federal funds for every $1 paid in Federal taxes. Connecticut, with the highest per capita tax burden, receives only 67 cents for every $1 paid in Federal taxes. Residents of the city of Washington, DC, have but one grievance that matters: They have no vote in Congress." (pH10401)

Smith, Lamars (Rep.-Tex.). "Providing for Consideration of H.R. 51, New Columbia Admission Act," Congressional Record (20 Nov 1993). Daily ed. pH10393-10404. (ISSN0363-7239).

WASHINGTON, D.C.--POPULATION

"In 1970, the District [of Columbia] ranked ahead of 10 States in terms of population. But since then, the District has declined by 168,000 people or more than 22 percent of its population. The District now ranks ahead of just three States and will likely be passed by at least one of those by the end of this year. If the trend of the past three decades continues, the District's population will be less than 500,000 by the year 2010, not merely making it the smallest State, but also shrinking it below the size of a congressional district and threatening its economic life." (pH10424)

Ballenger, Cass (Rep.-N.C.). "New Columbia Admission Act," Congressional Record (20 Nov 1993). Daily ed. pH10421-10445. (ISSN0363-7239).

WASHINGTON (D.C.)

see CRIME--NEW YORK (NY)--WASHINGTON (D.C.); HOMICIDE--WASHINGTON (D.C.); POLICIE--WASHINGTON (D.C.)

WASHINGTON (STATE)

see AUTOMOBILE TRAVEL--WASHINGTON (STATE); CHILDREN--WASHINGTON (STATE)--SOCIAL CONDITIONS; HAZARDOUS WASTE SITES--WASHINGTON (STATE); NUCLEAR POWER PLANTS--WASHINGTON (STATE); TROUT--WASHINGTON (STATE); VIOLENT CRIMES--WASHINGTON (STATE)--YOUTH

WASHINGTON (STATE)--COMMERCE (v19)

WASHINGTON (STATE)--ECONOMIC CONDITIONS (v19)

WASTE PAPER--U.S.

"Even if the top 130 newsstand titles sell six out of 10 of their newsstand copies, they're still shredding an average of 52 million magazines per month, or nearly four billion pages. A year's worth of unsold newsstand copies nationwide adds up to about 600,000 tons, according to the Magazine Publishers of America (MPA). That's a considerable chunk of the four million tons of coated paper used each year to print magazines. And the waste continues to build. Magazine sell-through has been dropping for years and shows no sign of improving. The best of the single-copy sellers, like checkout standards COSMOPOLITAN and TV GUIDE, once sold eight or nine of every 10 copies on the newsstand. They now sell just six to eight. For TV GUIDE alone, which sells about eight million newsstand copies of each issue, the difference between a 70 and 80 percent sell-through is about a million copies per week. As for the rest of the 3,000 or so titles on 180,000 newsstands nationwide, sell-through is three to five out of 10 copies, hitting bigger only with the occassional Charles-and-Di, swimsuit or '10 Best' cover hype." (p40)

Cyr, Diane. "The Magazine Racket." E Magazine v4 n6, Dec 1993. p38-43. (ISSN1046-8021).

In the U.S. "a whopping 3.8 million tons of third-class (namely junk) mail was sent in 1990, 95 percent of which landed in the landfill. And of the 14 pieces the average American gets a week, 12 pieces are catalogues or other bulk-mail items." (p8)

"Econotes: The U.S. (Junk) Mail." Environmental Action v25 n4, Win 1994. p7-8. (ISSN0013-922X).

WASTE PAPER--U.S.--POLITICS AND GOVERNMENT

"The U.S. Senate must put an end to the practice of wasting paper. The Office of the Secretary of the Senate estimates that nearly 42 million sheets of copier-grade paper are used by the Senate during a calendar year. Using double-sided rather than one-sided copies would reduce the quantity of paper used in the conduct of Senate business by as much as 50 percent. According to the Congressional Research Service, this practice alone could save over 1,700 trees annually. Urging witnesses to submit testimony on double-sided paper could save even more trees. In addition, using figures, provided by the Secretary of the Senate, I estimate that double-sided copying in Senate offices would save the American taxpayer almost $100,000 a year just in copier paper procurement costs. Moreover, while there occasionally are legitimate reasons for using a double-spaced format--such as drafting legislation--printing documents single-spaced as a general rule would further reduce the quantity of paper needed to produce documents and the expenditure for procuring copy paper." (pS2018)

Lautenberg, Frank R. (Sen.-N.J.). "Senate Use of Double-Sided Paper," Congressional Record (28 Feb 1994). Daily ed. pS2017-2019. (ISSN0363-7239).

WASTE PAPER--U.S.--RECYCLING (v19)

WASTES, RADIOACTIVE

see RADIOACTIVE WASTES

WATER--FLUORIDATION

"Research in the United States and Canada convincingly demonstrated that water fluoridation is an effective and very cheap means of lowering the prevalence of caries. In the early 1950s, this method was called 'mass prevention of dental caries'. This description is accurate: 120 million of the 250 million population of the USA (1989) benefited from this measure, 25 million in Australia, Canada, Ireland and the United Kingdom, and many millions more in other countries." (p7)

Marthaler, T. M. "Fluoridation at Community Level." World Health n1, Jan-Feb 1994. p7-9. (ISSN0043-8502).

WATER--FLUORIDATION--BRAZIL

"Imagine a country which produces its own edible salt from natural resources at, say, three sites. The bigger the country the better, because it is naturally more cost-effective to build three fluoridation units for a population of 30 million rather than for only three million. Brazil is such a country. North of 20S latitude there is an immense 'Amazonian' area having a population of some 70 million. Through the salt consumed there, every individual in an area measuring about 3600 km east-west and 1800 km north-south can be provided with the desired small amount of fluroide--a supplement of 1-2 mg of fluoride per day--at practically no cost. For the 70 million inhabitants, 300 tons of a soluble fluoride compound per year need to be added to some 160 000 tons of edible salt; the supply of the fluoride compound is easily dispatched in a few small shiploads." (p8)

Marthaler, T. M. "Fluoridation at Community Level." World Health n1, Jan-Feb 1994. p7-9. (ISSN0043-8502).

WATER--POLLUTION

"A...troublesome threat to water quality is the paints used on boat bottoms: Tributyltin (TBT), a tin compound used in marine bottom paints, caused alarm in the late 1970s in France, where Pacific oysters were being found with gruesome deformities. Later on, in Britain, researchers discovered female dog whelk snails with penises. Both problems were directly linked to TBT in the sediment near marinas and boat repair facilities. 'Such a graphic correlation is virtually unheard of in environmental science,' notes Mike Rexrode of the U.S. Environmental Protection Agency (EPA). 'These deformities are caused by very tiny amounts of TBT--just .02 parts per billion in the case of the Pacific oyster, and .7 parts per trillion in the case of the dog whelk snail.' In 1981, France banned the use of TBT paints for all boats under 25 meters long." (p20)

Knight, Katherine. "Currents: Gently Down the Stream?" E Magazine v4 n5, Sep-Oct 1993. p20-21. (ISSN1046-8021).

"A surprising proportion of the pollutants entering coastal waters originates not from the adjacent coastal land but from more distant sources. Of the polluting nutrients, about half come from inland. In the eastern United States, for instance, the Chesapeake Bay has been overwhelmed by nutrients from inland sources. Farms contribute one-third and air pollution another one-quarter of the nitrogen pollution that has caused eutrophication, algal blooms, and oxygen depletion in this estuary--once one of the most productive in the world. The oyster catch in the Chesapeake has fallen from 20,000 tons in the 1950s to under 3,000 tons in the late 1980s, at least partly as a result of this pollution." (p23)

Weber, Peter. "It Comes Down to the Coasts." World Watch v7 n2, Mar-Apr 1994. p20-29. (ISSN0896-0615).

WATER--POLLUTION--CASPIAN SEA--VOLGA RIVER

"The Caspian Sea, the largest landlocked sea in the world, has historically been the major source of sturgeon and caviar. In point of fact, its annual sturgeon catch constituted 90 to 95 percent of all world commercial landings. Starting in the early 1950s the Soviet government used forced labor to dam the Volga River and other tributaries for reservoirs and hydroelectric plants, and by the late 1960s, the decrease in freshwater flow to the Caspian disrupted fish spawning and survival. In an attempt to save the fishery, the government built dozens of hatcheries and began stocking up to 100 million juvenile sturgeon a year. At the same time, however, pollution began increasing at almost an exponential rate. Between 1980 and 1992, copper content in the Volga increased 11.5 times, zinc 9.8 times, lead 5.6 times and cadmium 4.9 times. By 1989, concentrations of petroleum products in the northern Caspian exceeded the maximum permissible concentration by nine times, and there were also considerable concentrations of phenols, surface-active agents, and pesticides." (p26)

Boyle, Robert H. "The Cost of Caviar." Amicus Journal v16 n1, Spr 1994. p22-28. (ISSN0276-7201).

WATER--POLLUTION--GREAT LAKES (v19)

WATER--POLLUTION--NEPAL (v19)

WATER--POLLUTION--OREGON

"Over 1,750,000 residents of Oregon receive domestic water from systems that utilize forested watersheds as their source of supply. According to the Oregon Department of Forestry, over 290,000 acres of western Oregon forest land received permits for herbicide application in 1992. Because of inadequate testing of many of the chemicals being used, people and animals have been placed at risk." (p15)

Eisler, David/Kutcher, Gary. "Labor Intensive Forestry: Oregonians Taking the Initiative: Banning Clear-Cutting and Forestry Pesticides." Journal of Pesticide Reform v14 n1, Spr 1994. p14-15. (ISSN0893-357X).

WATER--POLLUTION--RUSSIA

"The Neva River feeds the Neva Bay, flowing through the city of St. Petersburg. Over 2500 industrial enterprises situated on the banks of the Neva release untreated industrial waste directly into the river. Within St. Petersburg's city limits, 250 outlets release untreated sewage--industrial, household and agricultural--directly into the Neva. Looking into the river from one of Petersburg's many bridges, one sees streams of different colors welling up from deeper river waters. These are discharges from the city sewer system that have made it through the city's treatment plants. Over half of all liquid wastes received by the city's sewer system pass through them. Over 1000 tons of iron, petroleum products and aluminum, and over 500 tons of heavy metal compounds enter the sewer system together with liquid wastes every year....Lake Ladoga, which is intricately linked with the Neva, is surrounded by pulp and paper factories and huge livestock farms. All of these enterprises dump harmful and untreated substances into the lake including fertilizers and pesticides. By 1988, two million tons of toxic wastes had already accumulated in Lake Ladoga and more than 7000 tons of phosphorous were dumped into the lake in that year alone." (p23)

"Toxic Nightmare: Mendeleyev's Table Frolics in Petersburg's Drinking Water." Surviving Together v11 n4, Win 1993. p23. (ISSN0859-6286).

WATER--POLLUTION--TENNESSEE

"The 305(b) [or The Status of Water Quality in Tennessee] report indicates that 63% of all Tennessee stream sections and 80% of all lakes fully support all designated activities: swimming, fishing, domestic water supply, irrigation, navigation, and industrial use. Stream sections and lakes that only partially support these uses number 26% and 11%, respectively. Approximately 11% of all stream sections and 9% of all lakes were in the nonsupporting category, meaning that at least one of their uses was severely restricted....Of the 804 waterbodies in Tennessee, 53 were posted against a specific public use. This included 15 sections that had potential toxic contamination; 13 of which were caused by seepage from dumps and industrial sites and were labeled for possible contamination of fish. The other two sites were posted against human contact: one due to contamination from Oak Ridge and the other from solid waste and sewage near Chattanooga. The remainder of the 53 sites were posted against human contact due to potential bacterial contamination, usually resulting from municipal discharges but also due to failure of domestic waste treatment systems (septic systems)." (p10)

Yoder, Daniel C./others. "Tennessee's Water Quality: Status, Concerns, and Solutions." Tennessee Farm and Home Science n169, Win 1994. p6-14.

WATER--POLLUTION--U.S. (v19)

"Controlling point-source discharges is about as far as the...[U.S.] has gotten in meeting the goals of the Clean Water Act. Under the deadlines set out in 1972, by 1983 all of the nation's waters were to be fishable and swimmable. And by 1985, the discharge of any pollutant into U.S. waters was to have been eliminated. According to EPA's 1990 Water Quality Inventory, 37 percent of rivers and streams assessed did not meet fishing and swimming standards. The figure could be higher, since only 36 percent of the nation's 1.8 million river miles were monitored. And industrial releases of toxic substances into American waters still average 360 million pounds a year." (p32)

McGivney, Annette. "Troubled Waters." E Magazine v4 n5, Sep-Oct 1993. p30-37. (ISSN1046-8021).

"The most recent biennial reports to EPA on water quality [in the U.S.] show that nontraditional sources of pollution are clearly the leading reason for impairment in surface waters with runoff from agricultural lands being the leading source. For rivers 35 percent of the impaired river miles are impaired by siltation and 25 percent by nutrients, two pollutants normally associated with runoff. Furthermore, by state accounts, nearly 50 percent of the impaired river miles are adversely impacted by agricultural sources, more than double the next highest ranking source category." (p263)

Wayland, Robert. "What Progress in Improving Water Quality?" Journal of Soil and Water Conservation v48 n4, Jul-Aug 1993. p261-266. (ISSN0022-4561).

"The EPA (1990) published the 'National Pesticide Survey', a comprehensive look at water from 1349 wells across the...[U.S.]. As the name implies, this study looked specifically for pesticide contamination of well water. Each sample was analyzed for 126 different pesticides or pesticide breakdown by-products. In addition, each sample was analyzed for nitrates....The EPA study looked at two different types of wells: those serving 15 or more households (community wells) and those serving less than 15 households (domestic rural wells). The results showed that none of the community wells and 0.6% of the domestic rural wells contained at least one pesticide at unsafe levels, while 0.2% of the community wells and 2.4% of the domestic rural wells contained unsafe nitrate levels. Of the 126 pesticide compounds measured, 114 were not found at all--not in any of the samples at any detectable level. Also, the pesticide most often found at unsafe levels was the herbicide DCPA, commonly used as a lawn herbicide." (p11)

Yoder, Daniel C./others. "Tennessee's Water Quality: Status, Concerns, and Solutions." Tennessee Farm and Home Science n169, Win 1994. p6-14.

"The findings of the latest EPA report, the 'National Water Quality Inventory,' show that since 1992, almost 40 percent of the nation's rivers, lakes, and streams have become too polluted to use for fishing, swimming, boating, or other recreational uses. Agricultural runoff--which affects 72 percent of impaired rivers--and municipal and urban runoff were cited as the leading sources of water-pollution problems in the United States." (p5)

Couloumbis, Angela E. "Environment: New Bid to Clean Up Anacostia." The Christian Science Monitor v86 n108, 28 Apr 1994. p5. (ISSN0882-7729).

"'Recent state assessments show 30 percent of rivers, 42 percent of lakes, and 32 percent of estuaries surveyed continue to be degraded, mainly by silt and nutrients from farm and urban runoff, combined sewer overflows, and municipal sewage....Seven hundred forty million pounds of toxic chemicals pour into waterways and municipal sewers each year.'...The NRDC [National Resources Defense Council] finds that urban and agricultural runoff (nonpoint source pollution) continues to impair more than 125,000 miles of rivers, nearly 2 million acres of lakes, about 1.2 million acres of coastal waters, and some 5,000 square miles of estuaries." (p3)

Knickerbocker, Brad. "Refining the Clean Water Act May Not Be Easy for Clinton." The Christian Science Monitor v86 n52, 8 Feb 1994. p3. (ISSN0882-7729).

WATER--U.S.--PURIFICATION--CHLORINATION

"Drinking chlorinated water may be associated with more than 1,000 cases of rectal and bladder cancer in the United States annually, according to a study published last year in the AMERICAN JOURNAL OF PUBLIC HEALTH. Since chlorination is neither fail-safe nor without health risks of its own, most systems, particularly those that depend on water from sources of poor or variable quality, must also filter their water to eliminate microorganisms. Filtration is an end-of-the-pipe solution that allows water suppliers to remove physically much of the particulate matter that causes turbidity. Without filtration, health officials feel that people run a much higher risk from pathogens. In fact, from 1971 to 1990, communities that relied only on disinfection experienced eight times the rate of waterborne disease outbreaks as communities that both filtered and disinfected their water, according to figures compiled by the U.S. Centers for Disease Control and Prevention (CDC) and the EPA." (p25)

King, Jonathan. "Something in the Water." Amicus Journal v15 n3, Fall 1993. p20-25,27-28. (ISSN0276-7201).

WATER, UNDERGROUND--POLLUTION--U.S. (v19)

WATER, UNDERGROUND--U.S. (v19)

WATER CONSUMPTION--UTAH

"Utah residents use more than twice as much water as other Americans, according to a 1990 study just released by the U.S. Geological Survey. Living in the second driest state in the nation, each Utahn uses an average of 218 gallons of water for domestic needs every day. Watering--and overwatering--of lawns and gardens during the summer months accounts for half of all annual domestic water use, according to the survey. Utah water officials say the high consumption is due in part to low water prices, a lack of meters and old attitudes from 150 years of building dams and reservoirs, reports the SALT LAKE TRIBUNE." (p5)

"Hotline: In Utah, Water Grows on Trees." High Country News v25 n18, 4 Oct 1993. p5. (ISSN0191-5657).

WATER-POWER--CHINA

"China has the largest untapped hydroelectric potential in the world, with an exploitable capacity of 436 (GW) [gigawatt], but only five percent has been developed. Hydropower will grow from 40 GW in 1990 to 80 by 2000. Bulldozers have already begun moving earth on preliminary work for the Three Gorges Dam on the Yangtze, described as the most important construction in China since the Great Wall. The power from the Three Gorges dam would be a tremendous asset in fueling China's industrial revolution; its generation would vastly reduce air pollution and its damaging effects on lungs. The 17-18-year project has been discussed for more than 70 years and was formally approved in 1992. It is not the highest dam in the world nor would it contain the world's largest reservoir, but its projected hydroelectric output of 17.7 GW is exceeded only by a dam in the former Soviet Union, Turukhansk, with a planned capacity of 20.0 GW." (p5)

Wilson, Nancy C. "China Faces Hard Energy Choices: Booming Economy, Soaring Emissions." Climate Alert v6 n3, May-Jun 1993. p1,4-7.

WATER-POWER--QUEBEC

Hydro Quebec projects place at "stake...much of northern Quebec, a land where Innu, Inuit and Cree have lived thousands of years. For only two decades has there been either electricity or a single Hydro-electric official. James Bay Phase I has already flooded 4,425 square miles of land. The project, the size of Connecticut, is comprised of nine dams, 206 dikes, five major reservoirs, and a diversion of four rivers, all without an environmental assessment prior to construction. Phase II would consist of 21 dams and 200 dikes. It promises the diversion of four more rivers. Underwater would be an area the size of Lake Erie. This sequel is on the rocks, so to speak. Pressure and litigation from environmentalists and Natives has not only caused the cancellation of the largest contract, the New York Power Authority to the tune of $21 billion, but forced an environmental review of the project." (p14)

LaDuke, Winona. "Hydro Quebec Fears Cree Activists." Earth First! v13 n7, 1 Aug 1993. p14.

WATER-POWER--RUSSIA

In Russia "Small scale hydropower engineering has an economic potential of about 100 million tons of standard fuel. Small hydroelectric stations have a capacity of up to 30 megawatts. Until the 60s the USSR had several thousand small hydroelectric stations which were made unnecesssary by big-scale power engineering. All attempts to restore them were unsuccessful because of the disadvantageous correlation of prices: one kilowatt of a small hydroelectric station costs 1,200 rubles, a thermal power station 400 rubles, an atomic power station 700 rubles (1990 prices). Still, small hydroelectric stations can be quite useful in many regions, especially in rural areas." (p51)

Medvedev, Yuri. "Energy: Alternative Prospects for Power: Considering the Options for Russia." Surviving Together v11 n4, Win 1993. p50-51. (ISSN0859-6286).

WATER QUALITY MANAGEMENT--COASTAL STATES (v19)

WATER QUALITY MANAGEMENT--U.S.

"In general, water quality concerns affecting human health focus on six general types of contaminants....The concerns associated with these may take several forms, but the U.S. Environmental Protection Agency (EPA) generally classifies their hazards in terms of a maximum contaminant level (MCL) or health advisory level (HAL). These levels reflect the maximum levels of a contaminant that can be consumed over an average human lifetime without causing adverse health effects; they are determined from epidemiological and laboratory studies (EPA 1990). The HAL for many pesticides is in the range of 1 to 10 parts per billion (ppb)--one ppb is equivalent to...one small drop of contaminant in 13,000 gallons of water, which would fill two semi-tanker trucks or one good-sized backyard swimming pool. Despite some debate as to the danger associated with nitrates, the HAL is 10 parts per million (ppm) of nitrate-nitrogen, which would be the concentration resulting from dumping 6 pounds of fertilizer into that swimming pool." (p8)

Yoder, Daniel C./others. "Tennessee's Water Quality: Status, Concerns, and Solutions." Tennessee Farm and Home Science n169, Win 1994. p6-14.

WATER REUSE--U.S.--PUBLIC OPINION

"In the United States, public opinion surveys conducted since 1965 show the degree of resistance [to wastewater reuse] increases gradually as water reuse approaches bodily contact and reaches maximum at the drinking level. Approximately 60 per cent of the people surveyed were not in favor of drinking water reclaimed from sewage while about 30 per cent were not opposed. Although information about attitudes toward drinking reclaimed water for people outside the United States is not available, sewage reuse for non-drinking purpose is widely practiced in other nations." (p8 secA)

NKuchia, John M. "No Reason to Be Squeamish about Reusing Wastewater." Ann Arbor News 5 Jan 1994. p8 secA.

WATER SKIING--U.S.

"Waterskiing was a demonstration sport in 1972 and 1988. The sport is popular in the US, with 15 million recreational skiers. Of the 30,000 members of the Winterhaven, Fla.-based American Water Ski Association (AWSA), 70 percent compete in tournaments. Last year, the AWSA sanctioned 700 tournaments, up from 650 in 1992." (p17)

Scherer, Ron. "Sports: Tug of War with a Boat Isn't Easy." The Christian Science Monitor v86 n36, 14 Jan 1994. p17. (ISSN0882-7729).

WATER-SUPPLY (v19)

"Between 1955 and 1990 the number of people living in countries with less than 1,000 cubic meters of renewable fresh water per person per year--a key hydrological measure of water scarcity--ballooned from 3.7 million to 131 million. Based on United Nations projections of population growth, the number of people living in such countries will expand still further by 2025 to something between 817 million and 1.079 billion. This is roughly an eighth of the projected 2025 world population. And when countries in water stress--a category defined as having available between 1,000 and roughly 1,700 cubic meters of annual per capita renewable water--are included, it appears that one in three human beings will live in countries with critical water shortages by 2025. Most of this scarcity will be found in the expected regions, the Middle East and northern and eastern Africa, but water-short countries will be scattered across the globe." (p2)

Engelman, Robert. "Guest Column: Finite Water, Growing Population, Uncertain Climate?" Climate Alert v6 n6, Nov-Dec 1993. p2-3.

"Ninety-seven percent of all water on our planet is saline, and 2 percent is frozen. We depend on that last 1 percent to sustain all human life and economic activity on Earth....World population is 10 times today what it was 300 years ago, and we are now doubling the population every 40 years. Yet we have no more fresh water on this planet than we had when our ancestors still lived in caves." (pE353)

Mineta, Norman Y. (Rep.-Calif.). "The Water Quality Act of 1994," Congressional Record (7 Mar 1994). Daily ed. pE353-354. (ISSN0363-7239).

"More than a billion people lack adequate and safe water supplies. Contaminated water causes more than 80% of the diseases in the developing world, and the death of 4 to 5 million children a year from diarrhea....Wetlands, waterfowl, and fisheries are declining rapidly, with more than half of some habitats already lost in Europe, Latin America, and the U.S. Global warming is expected to worsen many of these problems. Seizing an opportunity to combat these crises, EDF [Environmental Defense Fund], the International Rivers Network, and other non-governmental organizations (NGO's) are urging reforms at the World Bank, which is developing a new Water Resources Policy that could guide its future water loans. The Bank is the largest single source of funds for water projects worldwide. Unfortunately, World Bank loans for irrigation, water supply, hydropower and other water-related projects--totaling over $40 billion--have often made the problems worse, not better. Agricultural productivity actually declined in 43% of 21 Bank-funded irrigation projects reviewed in 1989; and 44% of 129 water supply and sewerage loans were judged to be unsatisfactory because of cost overruns or unacceptably low economic returns. Many large-scale dam projects also displace hundreds of thousands of people, often sending them deeper into poverty." (p1)

"EDF Seeks Solutions to Global Water Scarcity, Pollution." EDF Letter v24 n3, May 1993. p1,5. (ISSN0163-2566).

WATER-SUPPLY--AFRICA

"Of the nearly 500 million people living in Sub-Saharan Africa in 1990, it was estimated (by WHO [World Health Organization] and UNICEF) that 265 million lacked safe drinking water and 344 million lived without adequate sanitation facilities....In some of the worst drought-affected countries, renewable fresh water per person has dropped by more than 65% over the past 40 years." (p1) "Africa currently receives less water supply and sanitation investments than any other region. It is estimated that between 1981 and 1990, only 10% of global water supply and sanitation investments were made in African countries." (p2)

News release. "WHO Calls for New International Partnership on Water and Sanitation in Africa." WHO Press 21 Mar 1994. p1-2.

WATER-SUPPLY--CALIFORNIA (v19)

"As of 1991, California farmers controlled 83 percent of the 34 million acre-feet of water captured by federal and state projects, notes Marc Reisner, an expert in water marketing. Nearly 20,000 farmers pay from $2.50 to more than $19 per acre-foot for irrigation water, while Southern California's Metropolitan Water District pays as much as $230 per acre-foot for residential water. Reisner also points out that four agricultural industries--cotton, rice, alfalfa and irrigated pasture--used one-third of California's captured water in 1986 while contributing only $1.7 billion to the state's $60 billion gross domestic product." (p18)

Hanson, Gayle. "Can a River Run through the Open Market?" Insight v10 n12, 21 Mar 1994. p18-20. (ISSN1051-4880).

WATER-SUPPLY--CHINA

"Chinese water specialists warn of a mass exodus from Beijing early next century unless the authorities take drastic steps to quench the capital's thirst. There are fears that the forest of high-rise buildings and swanky hotels which sprang up in Beijing in the 1980s could one day be standing in the world's biggest ghost town....The water shortage is not confined to Beijing. According to a survey published in a 1989 book, THE CRISIS IN THE SOURCE OF LIFE, 40 Chinese cities are in the throes of a crisis and another 143 have a serious problem, with total supply falling short of demand by about 20 million cubic metres a day. Beijing is in north China's semi-drought region, and the per capita water resources available are only 4% of the global average. The metropolitan area, which covers 10 counties and includes much farmland, gets about 600 millimetres of rain a year. But nearly all of this falls in short sharp bursts in the summer, and quicky runs off." (p10)

Yong, Wang/Chengshi, Xu. "Beijing Scrapes the Bottom of Its Water Barrel." Panoscope n34, Jan 1993. p10-11. (ISSN0951-8819).

WATER-SUPPLY--DEVELOPING COUNTRIES

"Many people assume that public money is the only way to bring water to the poor. In fact, as the World Bank pointed out in Noordwijk, private enterprise has seized upon this job. In Jakarta, for example, some 800,000 households have installed their own septic tanks; about 32% of the city's 8m people buy their water from street vendors and another 54% rely on private wells. In one Nigerian province street water-sellers are used mainly by the poor, who therefore spend more of their income on water than do the rich. In Lima, for example, a poor family uses only one-sixth as much water as a rich one, but its monthly water bill is three times as big. The sad truth is that, in many poor countries, a sizeable public investment in water and sewerage has mainly benefited the rich. Some of the rich work for water bureaucracies, which care more about providing jobs than water. So in Manila 58% of water distributed is unaccounted for; most Latin American utilities employ between ten and 20 people for every 1,000 water connections, compared with between two and three people in the region's best-run water services. In Mexico less than 10% of sewage-treatment plants work properly. Yet water utilities rely on subsidies for a large and rising share of their income." (p17)

"Leaders: Of Wets and Water." Economist v330 n7856, 26 Mar 1994. p17. (ISSN0013-0613).

WATER-SUPPLY--EGYPT--SUDAN

"Under a 1959 agreement with Sudan, Egypt is entitled to 55.5 billion cubic meters (bcm) of Nile water each year; Sudan is allotted 18.5 bcm. To meet its needs, Egypt supplements Nile water with small amounts of groundwater, agricultural drainage water, and treated municipal wastewater. In all, Egypt had 63.5 bcm available in 1990. Unfortunately, even modest projections show Egypt's demand rising to 69.4 bcm by the end of the decade--about 9 percent more water than is available now." (p12)

Postel, Sandra. "The Politics of Water." World Watch v6 n4, Jul-Aug 1993. p10-18. (ISSN0896-0615).

WATER-SUPPLY--ISRAEL--JORDAN

"Water scarcity is most acute in the Jordan River basin, which is shared by Israel, Jordan, the occupied West Bank, and part of Syria....Israel's annual water use already exceeds its renewable supply (the amount of water that nature makes available each year) by some 15 percent, meaning that in a typical year Israel has to overdraw its groundwater account to meet its needs. With an expected influx of up to a million immigrants from former Soviet states, Israel's yearly water deficit will only worsen. The Jordanians use less than half as much water as the Israelis on a per capita basis. But their demands are also bumping up against supply limits, even as the country's population rises by 3.4 percent a year, one of the highest growth rates in the world. With the nation's water use projected to increase by 40 percent during this decade, competition grows keener each year. King Hussein declared in 1990 that water was the only issue that could take him to war with Israel." (p11)

Postel, Sandra. "The Politics of Water." World Watch v6 n4, Jul-Aug 1993. p10-18. (ISSN0896-0615).

WATER-SUPPLY--NEVADA

"Nevada's Colorado River Commission recently revealed that it had reached a secret 'gentleman's agreement' with Chevron Shale Oil Co. and Getty Oil Exploration Co. Under the agreement, Nevada would negotiate for the temporary use of 175,000 acre-feet of Colorado River water a year--enough for around 700,000 new people in Las Vegas. Under the plan, Nevada would lease the water for about $8.75 million a year for at least 30 to 50 years, while the rapidly growing southern part of the state seeks a permanent supply, the LAS VEGAS REVIEW-JOURNAL reported The water would be delivered to the Las Vegas area via Lake Mead. In exchange, Nevada would build a $200 million reservoir on Roan Creek, near DeBeque, 30 miles northeast of Grand Junction, Colo. At around $200 an acre-foot, the water would be cheap, commission representatives said, compared to the projected $900 to $1,200 an acre-foot cost of importing ground water from central Nevada or $1,500 to $2,000 an acre-foot to desalt ocean water, two other options the area is pursuing to supply future residents. Water planners claim the Las Vegas area will tap out its current Colorado River allotment within 13 years." (p2)

Christensen, Jon. "Las Vegas Moves on Western Colorado's Water." High Country News v25 n4, 8 Mar 1993. p2. (ISSN0191-5657).

WATER-SUPPLY--OHIO

"The forthcoming report of the Ohio Governor's Task Force on Water Quality will show that 72 percent of the funding for wastewater treatment in the state in 1975 came from the federal government; in 1992, the federal payment covered 29 percent. Even more amazing, 71 percent of all of the money for wastewater treatment in 1975 was grants; in 1992, only 17 percent was grants. We have switched from a system of predominantly federal grants to one of predominantly state loans, with local revenues meeting 82 percent of the costs." (p28)

Pompili, Michael J. "Views from State, Local, and Private Organizations." Intergovernmental Perspective v20 n1, Fall 1993-Win 1994. p27-31. (ISSN0362-8507).

WATER-SUPPLY--TEXAS

"The Edwards Aquifer encompasses roughly 8,000 square miles in central and south Texas, supplying high-quality water to 1.5 million people for municipal, agricultural, industrial, and recreational purposes. The principal springs that seep from the aquifer provide exclusive habitat for several endangered or threatened fish, plants amphibians, and invertebrates; its upland watersheds contain essential habitat for two endangered songbirds. Increased pumping to supply a rapidly growing population is already 'overdrawing' the aquifer (withdrawing more water than is naturally replenished). Continued depletion would threaten the region's environment and economic prosperity." (p3)

"EDF Plan Can Protect Texas Aquifer." EDF Letter v24 n3, May 1993. p3. (ISSN0163-2566).

WATER-SUPPLY--THAILAND

"Thailand had sparse rains last year, but, even if nature is kinder next time, water shortages could soon become a chronic national problem. Over the past 20 years urbanisation and the decision to encourage rice farmers to grow a second crop during the dry season have driven up demand for water. Meanwhile, the supply of water has fallen. Half of Thailand's forests have been chopped down over the past 30 years, and forests are crucial for the retention of rainfall. Since 1975 the flow of water from the Ping River, in northern Thailand, into the Bhumibol dam, which supplies Bangkok, has fallen by more than half....Domestic consumers account for only about 4% of water used in Thailand. Agriculture guzzles about 90% and industry takes the rest." (p35)

"Asia: Thailand: Drying Out." Economist v330 n7850, 12 Feb 1994. p35-36. (ISSN0013-0613).

WATER-SUPPLY--U.S. (v19)

"Fresh, clean water may be the most limiting natural resource in the immediate future of our food production system. Only about one-fourth of the 1.4 trillion gallons per day of the U.S. renewable supply is actually withdrawn for use--there is plenty of water in the aggregate. But available supply at the right place and right time is another matter....RCA [Resource Conservation Act] analysts project, however, that only under the 'high stress' demand scenario will irrigated acres increase, from 50 million in 1990 to 68 million acres in 2030, and a net reduction is more likely as cropland needs decline. Local shortages will still be a problem. Salinity problems and competition have forced some irrigated land out of production in the West....It is unlikely that past subsidies or inattention to water quality impacts of large irrigation projects will continue." (p292)

Libby, Lawrence W. "The Natural Resource Limits of U.S. Agriculture." Journal of Soil and Water Conservation v48 n4, Jul-Aug 1993. p289-294. (ISSN0022-4561).

"Americans use more fresh water than any other country in the world--112 cubic miles total per year. That's more than the entire population of China, which is more than four times larger than that of the U.S." (p20)

Hren, Ben/Bartolomeo, Nick. "Special Report: Carrying Capacity Project: Our Unquenchable Thirst." Outdoor America v59 n1, Win 1994. p15-22.

WATER SYSTEMS--U.S. (v19)

WEALTH

"Consider this: global distribution of wealth has become increasingly concentrated in the past 30 years, in spite of significant world-wide economic growth. In 1960, those nations making up the wealthiest 20% of the world's population accounted for 70% of the annual gross world profit (GWP). In 1989, the concentration of GWP in the wealthiest nations had grown to 83%--five times greater than the total GWP of the remaining 80% of the world." (p413)

Brown, George E., Jr. "Viewpoint: The Mother of Necessity: Technology Policy and Social Equity." Science and Public Policy v20 n6, Dec 1993. p411-416.

WEALTH--GREAT BRITAIN (v19)

WEALTH--U.S.

"According to a 1992 Federal Reserve study, the wealthiest 1 percent of our population now owns 37 percent of the wealth....While the bottom 90 percent owns only 31 percent of the wealth. That means that the wealthiest 1 percent of our population own more wealth than the bottom 90 percent. That, my friends, is what oligarchy is all about." (pH10454)

Sanders, Bernard (Rep.-Vt.). "Problems in the American Economy," Congressional Record (20 Nov 1993). Daily ed. pH10451-10458. (ISSN0363-7239).

WEAPONS

see also FIREARMS; MILITARY WEAPONS

WEAPONS--CAMBODIA

"On December 8, 1993, a massive cache of arms was discovered along the Thai-Cambodia border. Thai police seized 1,500 tons of Chinese-made weapons, including antitank mines, rockets, grenades, machine guns, over a dozen artillery pieces, and more than 1 million rounds of ammunition. Contrary to Thai military claims that the weapons seized are a remnant from the days of the Cambodian civil war, there is substantial evidence that the arms cache was part of a continuing effort to assist the Khmer Rouge. The most incriminating of this evidence involves the circumstances of the seizure. It was the interception of a shipment of arms from the storage site to Khmer Rouge-controlled areas of Cambodia that led police to the guarded compound. Further testament to Thai-Khmer Rouge cooperation, Khmer Rouge soldiers, apparently guarding the site, were apprehended in the raid of December 8, 1993." (pS489)

McCain, John (Sen.-Ariz.). "Foreign Relations Authorization Act," Congressional Record (1 Feb 1994). Daily ed. pS478-490. (ISSN0363-7239).

WEAPONS--MIDDLE EAST (v19)

WEAPONS--RESEARCH--FINANCE (v19)

WEAPONS--U.S. (v19)

WEAPONS INDUSTRY

see also FIREARMS INDUSTRY AND TRADE

"Estimating the size of the trade in covert arms--everything from rifles to rockets--is by definition a tricky business. Guesses range from $1 billion-2 billion for the average year's skulduggery (mostly by governments that do not want their neighbours to know what weapons they are buying or selling), to $5 billion-10 billion if there is a good war or two to drive demand. Complementing that, SIPRI [Stockholm International Peace Research Institute] estimates that $18.5 billion was spent worldwide in 1992 on more official imports of the bigger conventional weapons such as tanks, artillery or aircraft, down from a 1987 peak of $46.5 billion. Like the overt weapons trade, the covert sort has its lean and fat years. But recently, clandestine sales have been holding up nicely." (p21)

"The Covert Arms Trade." Economist v330 n7850, 12 Feb 1994. p21-23. (ISSN0013-0613).

"Denial by Western states could boost production in the dozen developing states with military-industrial bases--though the market for weapons produced in India, Israel, Brazil, South Korea, South Africa and Taiwan is currently falling. In the realm of weapons of mass destruction, around 14 states have been developing chemical weapons programmes while 11 states are developing biological weapons programmes. Some 20 states are also developing ballistic or cruise missile capabilities (with the potential for acquiring technologically advanced systems), though some experts doubt the feasibility or military value of chemical/biological systems." (p26)

Pugh, Michael. "Combatting the Arms Proliferation Problem." NATO Review v42 n1, Feb 1994. p24-27. (ISSN0255-3813).

WEAPONS INDUSTRY--BRAZIL

"In the second half of the 80s Middle Eastern demand for arms [made by Brazil] decreased as a result of the depressed oil price and a considerable excess stock of military equipment. The end of the Iran-Iraq war--Iraq being the main buyer of Brazilian arms--represented a 'coup de grace' for the Brazilian arms industry. The turning point was 1988: exports in that year fell to 200 million dollars, equalling their 1982 value, prior to the beginning of sales derived from the conflict....It was alleged by the military and entrepreneurs that arms exports reached billions of dollars. However, this was not the case. At their peak, in 1987, exports never surpassed 570 million dollars (averaging 1975-88, US$186 million). This represented 2% of Brazilian total exports in that year." (p391)

Dagnino, Renato. "Brazilian S&T: To the Barracks or into the Labs? Military Programmes and Brazilian S&T Policy." Science and Public Policy v20 n6, Dec 1993. p389-395.

WEAPONS INDUSTRY--DEVELOPING COUNTRIES--U.S.

"According to a Congressional Research Service report on 'Conventional Arms Transfers to the Third World', 1992 was the third year in a row that the U.S. ranked first in the value of arms transfer agreements and actual arms transfers to the Third World. In 1992, U.S. arms transfer agreements with Third World countries were valued at $13.6 billion and totaled 57% of the world market, up from 49% in 1991. France was second with agreements valued at only $3.8 billion. In fact, the value of U.S. arms transfer agreements was more than the total of the next nine leading suppliers combined! The value of actual U.S. arms deliveries to the Third World was $7.6 billion, amounting to 60% of the market and some $3.1 billion more than the next seven leading suppliers." (p24)

"Arms Proliferation: Proposal to Subsidize Overseas Arms Sales." NewsNotes v18 n5, Sep-Oct 1993. p24.

(ISSN1064-1556).

WEAPONS INDUSTRY--MIDDLE EAST--U.S.

"The arms trade hits hardest on the developing world: 70% of the arms sold in the 1980s were bought by developing countries, and in the last 30 years, virtually all of the 100 wars and 15 million war-related deaths (nearly two-thirds of them civilian) were in the developing world. During the Cold War, the USSR, US and China flooded Third World countries with arms, and although the superpower competition is over, these weapons continue to fuel wars and internal violence. After the Persian Gulf War, many leaders called for action to restrict the spread of conventional weapons--especially to the volatile Middle East. However, as of 1993, no binding multilateral limits have been imposed on the flow of conventional weapons. Since the end of the Gulf War, the US has agreed to sell $46 billion worth of arms to the Third World, including $26 billion worth to the Middle East." (p20)

"Beyond Yugoslavia: Conventional Arms Proliferation." Veterans for Peace Journal n23, Sum 1993. p20. (ISSN1063-9381).

WEAPONS INDUSTRY--U.S.

"Weapons that kill people are rampant in the world, despite the so-called end to the Cold War. Of 180 nations, the United States regularly sells weapons to 142 of them, according to the Center for Defense Information. During 1991, the U.S. licensed military weapons valued at $63-billion, 40% of which--some $26.2-billion--went to 59 authoritarian governments. Six of the Third World's top ten weapons recipients got supplies from the USA. Are some of these weapons used to strike at our own troops serving overseas?" (p5)

"Weapons Sales May Be a Dangerous Boomerang." Human Quest v207 n2, Mar-Apr 1993. p5. (ISSN0897-8786).

"The Center for Defense Information reported in 1992 that the U.S. was currently providing weapons to fifty-nine authoritarian governments, including Saudi Arabia, Indonesia, Morocco, Thailand and Guatemala. It reported that U.S. weapons manufacturers promote the sale of their products to foreign nations irrespective of human rights abuses, type of government or aggression against neighboring states. The ten leading Third World arms buyers in 1992 were Taiwan, Saudi Arabia, Indonesia, Kuwait, Malaysia, Egypt, Israel, Singapore, Thailand and the United Arab Emirates." (p24)

"Arms Proliferation: Proposal to Subsidize Overseas Arms Sales." NewsNotes v18 n5, Sep-Oct 1993. p24. (ISSN1064-1556).

"In its annual report on arms sales to developing nations, the Congressional Research Service said the U.S. leads the world in weapons export agreements for the third year in a row. Although worldwide sales fell by 16% in 1992, the U.S. 'remained the undisputed leader in arms sales to the Third World,' the study said. The report does not include commercial sales figures. U.S. arms agreements last year totaled $13.6 billion making the U.S. the 'predominant arms supplier...since the Cold War's end.' Since that time the U.S. has sold over $47 billion in weapons. Other top suppliers last year were France, U.K., Russia and Germany which has bumped China to sixth place. The report lists two primary reasons for the commanding U.S. lead: the performance of U.S. weaponry during the Gulf War, and a reduction in Pentagon purchases which has prompted U.S. manufacturers to market their products overseas." (p13)

"U.S. #1 in Arms Sales for Third Consecutive Year." Veterans for Peace Journal n24, Fall 1993. p13. (ISSN1063-9381).

WELFARE, PUBLIC

see PUBLIC WELFARE

WELFARE RECIPIENTS--U.S.--SUBSTANCE USE

"A recent investigation conducted by my minority staff on the Senate Special Committee on Aging and the GAO [General Accounting Office] found that the SSI [Supplemental Security Income] and SSDI [Social Security Disability Insurance] programs are out of control and are, in effect, subsidizing drug and alcohol abuse, with little enforcement of treatment requirements. Out of the estimated 250,000 addicts on the rolls through either heroin, alcohol, or other drugs, however, only 78,000, are required to seek treatment. Of that 78,000, only approximately 9 percent seek treatment. So the calculations are that out of the total of 250,000 that we know are addicted, only about 3 percent get any kind of treatment at all. Similarly, only a portion of the estimated 250,000 drug addicts and alcoholics now on the disability rolls have their checks go to a representative payee." (pS2197)

Cohen, William S. (Sen.-Maine). "Social Security Administration Independent Agency Act," Congressional Record (2 Mar 1994). Daily ed. pS2193-2218. (ISSN0363-7239).

WEST (U.S.)--ECONOMIC CONDITIONS (v19)

WEST VIRGINIA--ECONOMIC CONDITIONS

"'Montani Semper Liberi' is the motto of West Virginia: 'Mountain Men are Always Free.' But not as free as all that. Between 1980 and 1990 West Virginia lost 8% of its population, more than any other state. Yet many, homesick, creep back; and, despite an unemployment rate of 12%, the country's highest, and an income per head of around $14,000 a year, the country's lowest, an extraordinary number stick it out, unbudging....West Virginia remains America's leading deep-mine coal producer, producing as much, 150m tonnes a year, as it did in the 1940s. It accounts for half of the country's coal exports. But one mechanical shearer, working the seam, now digs out as much in six weeks as the old pick-and-auger miners could manage in a year. In 1948, more than 125,000 men worked in West Virginia's mines. Now 22,000 do. They make a king's wage, taking home about $700 a week; but their colleagues who are laid off stay, for the most part, on welfare." (p30-31)

"American Survey: West Virginia: The Company Store." Economist v330 n7852, 26 Feb 1994. p30-31. (ISSN0013-0613).

WESTERN FANS (v19)

WETLANDS

"Wetlands, which are breeding, resting, and feeding grounds for waterbirds ranging from pelicans to sandpipers, are being drained all over the world....The United States Fish and Wildlife Service (USFWS), for example, estimates that 53 percent of the country's wetlands remain--a statistic that is grimly reflected in the steady decline of waterfowl dependent on these areas. USFWS surveys show a 30 percent drop in the populations of North America's 10 most common duck species, from 37 million in 1955 to 26 million in 1992." (p12)

Youth, Howard. "Flying into Trouble." World Watch v7 n1, Jan 1994. p10-19. (ISSN0896-0615).

WETLANDS--CALIFORNIA

"As 94 percent of California's wetlands disappeared over the past century, so did the birds that depended on them. Fifty years ago, 15 million waterfowl wintered in California's Central Valley. By the mid-1970s, however, that had dropped to 12 million, and its' since fallen to 4 million. According to biologists, seasonal flooding of ricelands could reverse this decline. 'It's a wonderful opportunity,' says the Nature Conservancy's Harvey Carlson. 'Not only are these precisely the lands that used to be wetlands, but they're all set up to be flooded. You have the pumps, the canals, the levees, the trained managers to operate the system.'" (p4)

"Bed & Breakfast for Ducks: Farmers and Conservationists

Join Forces." Rocky Mountain Institute Newsletter v9 n3, Fall-Win 1993. p4.

WETLANDS--GUATEMALA

"Despite the potential environmental damage, in 1992 Guatemala's Ministry of Energy and Mines awarded huge concessions in the Peten to two companies: Basic Petroleum International, a French firm; and Pentagon Petroleum of Baton Rouge, Louisiana. The concessions allow exploration throughout the Laguna del Tigre, the largest freshwater wetland in Central America and an important stopover for North American migratory birds. This area lies within the boundaries of the recently created 1.5 million hectare (3.7 million acre) Maya Biosphere Reserve which, according to Guatemalan law, is supposed to be off limits to logging and mining. But with an estimated 200 million barrels of oil waiting to be extracted, Guatemala has put economic development ahead of the environment." (p11)

Bryce, Robert. "In Brief: Guatemala: Trading the Rainforest for Oil?" E Magazine v5 n1, Feb 1994. p10-11. (ISSN1046-8021).

WETLANDS--MIDDLE WEST (v19)

WETLANDS--U.S. (v19)

"Agricultural run-off alone continues to damage 100,000 miles of rivers and streams every year, according to the EPA. Poorly maintained or antiquated municipal sewer systems also contribute heavily to continued water pollution, as does airborne pollution. Although the Clean Water Act has brought about an overall improvement in water quality, an estimated 30 percent of American rivers and streams remain too polluted for fishing and drinking. In this context, the role of wetlands is crucial. In addition to providing havens for wildlife and nurseries for fish, wetlands help trap and filter pollution and control flooding. Despite Section 404 [of the Clean Water Act] the nation is still losing about 290,000 acres of wetlands a year." (p1,4)

Garrett, Daniel/Baumgarten, Fred. "Contentious Issues Flood Clean Water Debate." Audubon Activist v8 n2, Oct 1993. p1,4. (ISSN0898-915X).

"An estimated 104 million acres of wetlands cover the lower 48 states, in addition to 170 million acres in Alaska. A critical habitat for wildlife, wetlands are also used to control floods and maintain water quality. Over the years, farmers and developers have sparred with environmentalists over preserving the nation's wetlands. In the mid-1980s wetlands were disappearing at a rate of nearly 300,000 acres annually." (p3382)

Hook, Janet/others. "Special Report: Cover Story: Democrats Hail 'Productivity,' but Image Problems Remain." Congressional Quarterly v51 n49, 11 Dec 1993. p3355-3406.

WETLANDS--VALUATION--CALIFORNIA (v19)

WHALES (v19)

"Despite the widely held opinion that humpbacks have recovered, their current global population may be only 10 to 20 percent of their historical peak. During the era of modern whaling, some 140,000 humpbacks were taken from the waters of the Southern Hemisphere, leaving only a remnant population. Bowheads have been reduced by as much as three-quarters of their original stock, and right whales have been reduced by as much as 98 percent. According to the Center for Marine Conservation, fin whale populations have shrunk by 85 percent." (p26)

Walters, Mark Jerome. "Special Report: Whales: Have They Been Saved?" Animals v126 n5, Sep-Oct 1993. p22-26. (ISSN0030-6835).

"While it is true that humans have never driven any species of whale to extinction, several species have been pushed to the brink. As few as 0.5 percent of the original population of blue whales remains, despite gains in California coastal waters. A quarter of a million once churned through the Antarctic Ocean; today only a few thousand may survive. Recovery--if it occurs at all--could take centuries....the status of whale stocks, not least of all those of the blue whale, are subject to drastic reassessments. For example, at the 1989 IWC [International Whaling Commission] meeting in San Diego, California, the commission released a report on a decade-long survey of whales in the Southern Hemisphere. Where they had expected to find at least 4,000 blue whales (expectations based partly upon earlier work), they spotted a mere tenth of that number. The survey found only 2,000 fin whales in the Southern Hemisphere instead of the expected 100,000, and 3,000 sperm whales rather than the nearly 1 million anticipated." (p25)

Walters, Mark Jerome. "Special Report: Whales: Have They Been Saved?" Animals v126 n5, Sep-Oct 1993. p22-26. (ISSN0030-6835).

WHALING (v19)

"Last May in Kyoto, Japan, the International Whaling Commission (IWC) resumed its annual battle over the future of whaling. The United States, Great Britain, and most other member nations of the IWC--an international body that regulates whale harvests--vowed to maintain the 1986 global ban against commercial whaling, while Japan and Norway vehemently argued against it. By the time the rancorous gathering adjourned, the moratorium had been upheld. So far, Japan has abided by the decision. But Norwegian whalers promptly took to the seas, vowing to kill hundreds of minkes during the coming year. Indeed, the only group that seemed able to agree on the whaling issue was one that disagrees about everything else: in a symbolic gesture, the U.S. Congress voted 382 to 0 last year to continue the moratorium." (p22)

Walters, Mark Jerome. "Special Report: Whales: Have They Been Saved?" Animals v126 n5, Sep-Oct 1993. p22-26. (ISSN0030-6835).

The May 1993 "meetings of the International Whaling Commission (IWC) in Kyoto culminated a ten-year effort by Japan, Norway and Iceland to scuttle the IWC ban on commercial whaling that was first enacted in 1982. The CHRISTIAN SCIENCE MONITOR reported that Japan spent $80 million over the past year to influence Japanese public opinion in favor of commercial whaling. This public relations campaign continued right through the conference week and included special 'whale meat eating' days and an IWC banquet featuring whale steaks and whale-meat soup. The TOKYO SHIMBUN reported that Japan offered $234 million this year in economic aid to various countries to secure IWC votes in favor of whaling. But the effort came up far short, as IWC members voted 18 to six against adopting a revised management plan that would have led to a resumption of commercial whaling. In addition to Japan, five votes in favor of whaling came from a group of small Caribbean nations receiving large Japanese aid grants." (p6)

Phillips, David. "Marine Mammal Project: Whaling Rejected at IWC Meeting." Earth Island Journal v8 n3, Sum 1993. p6. (ISSN1041-0406).

WHALING--NORWAY (v19)

WHEAT TRADE (v19)

WHEAT TRADE--CANADA

"Since the CFTA [the Canadian Free Trade Agreement] was implemented, Canadian wheat has flooded into the U.S. market. Imports of durum have increased from nothing in 1985-86 to 15 million bushels in each of the last 2 years. Imports of hard red spring wheat last year--a record 35 million bushels--were five times the average in the 5-year period prior to implementation of the CFTA. This has happened not because Canadian wheat farmers are more efficient or more competitive than U.S. producers, but because the CFTA put in place a system of unfair competition. For example, the CFTA allows Canada to use transportation subsidies on wheat and barley shipments into the United States. And it does nothing to curb the secretive, anticompetitive pricing practices of the Canadian Wheat Board." (pS16682-16683)

Conrad, Kent (Sen.-N.Dak.). "North American Free-Trade Agreement," Congressional Record (20 Nov 1993). Daily ed. pS16678-16700. (ISSN0363-7239).

WHEAT TRADE--CANADA--CHINA--U.S. (v19)

WHEAT TRADE--CHINA (v19)

WHEAT TRADE--CHINA--U.S. (v19)

WHEAT TRADE--EUROPEAN ECONOMIC COMMUNITY (v19)

WHEAT TRADE--MEXICO--U.S. (v19)

WHEAT TRADE--U.S. (v19)

U.S. "Wheat exports rose 5 percent to 36.1 million tons, the largest since FY 1989. Larger shipments and slightly higher prices boosted the export value to $4.7 billion. Gains to Latin America, South Asia, and Africa overcame a 50-percent reduction in wheat shipments to China and the FSU [former Soviet Union]." (p2)

U.S. Dept. of Agriculture/Greene, Joel. "Exports Rose Slightly in FY 1993." Foreign Agricultural Trade of the United States Nov-Dec 1993. p2-3.

WILD TURKEYS--U.S. (v19)

WILDERNESS AREAS--IDAHO (v19)

WILDERNESS AREAS--U.S.

"Formerly called the Jersey Jack Roadless Area, Cove/Mallard links the Gospel Hump Wilderness and the Frank Church River of No Return Wilderness areas, forming the largest roadless complex in the lower 48. The Forest Service began the construction of 145 miles of roads into Cove/Mallard last summer. The roads are planned as part of numerous timber sales totalling 82 million board feet. The sales contain more than 200 cutting units, mostly in lodgepole and Ponderosa pine forest above 5,000 feet elevation. The low-value timber will be cut at an estimated $6 million deficit, to be paid by taxpayers." (p4)

Neuman, Margaret E. "Updates: Concentrating on Cove/Mallard in Wild Idaho." Northwest Conservation Sum 1993. p4.

"In the lower 48 states, very few greater ecosystems remain which much resemble their natural condition. But in today's GNCE [Greater North Cascades Ecosystem] still reside every (known) species that was here before white settlement. Moreover there is, arguably, enough habitat for this 'dance of all partners' to persist. We can compare it to the Northern Continental Divide Ecosystem of northwest Montana, which many people consider among the wildest places in the States. Including all U.S. and adjacent Canadian lands (both ecosystems cross the international border), each has some 1.1 million acres in protected national park and wilderness areas. In total publicly owned land, the Northern Continental Divide contains some 3.2 million acres, the North Cascades slightly more. Had the North Cross-State Highway (Washington 20) not been constructed through the heart of this ecosystem, the GNCE would boast the largest contiguous roadless area in the lower United States. Incidentally, for six months of the year the highway is closed by snow." (p21)

Friedman, Mitch. "From the Bookshelf to the Battlefront with Cascadia Wild." Northwest Conservation Fall 1993. p21.

"Of the nearly 34 million acres of designated wilderness on the national forests at the end of 1991, there existed 450,000 acres of non-federal lands [in the U.S.]. The largest single agglomeration of inholdings lies in the Boundary Waters Canoe Area Wilderness (BWCAW) in northern Minnesota. Here, 288,000 acres within the million acres of designated wilderness are owned by entities other than the federal government. The situation is moderated substantially by the fact that more than 100,000 acres of these non-federal inholdings are owned by the state, which can manage them as state wilderness if it desires, and much of the remainder consists of innumerable lake beds; under Minnesota law, these lake beds are the property of the state and are thus counted as non-federal lands." (p23)

Pearson, Mark. "The Private Parts of Paradise." Wilderness v56 n200, Spr 1993. p20-27. (ISSN0736-6477).

WILDLIFE

see ANIMALS

WILDLIFE CONSERVATION--CALIFORNIA

"The California Desert Protection Act was first introduced in 1985. After more than 8 years of effort, the Senate vote today clears the way for establishment of the largest wilderness area ever created in the lower 48 States. The act will protect 6.4 million of the 25 million acres of the southern California desert as wilderness and national park areas. The desert teems with more than 760 species of wildlife, including bighorn sheep and the endangered desert tortoise. The topography of the desert includes giant dunes, extinct volcanoes, and more than 100,000 archeological sites. The desert is also home to a vast array of plant life, including the oldest Joshua tree forest in the country." (pS4193)

Biden, Joseph R., Jr. (Sen.-Del.). "California Desert Protection Act of 1993," Congressional Record (13 Apr 1994). Daily ed. pS4190-4210. (ISSN0363-7239).

WILDLIFE CONSERVATION--U.S. (v19)

"Since 1955, the Fish and Wildlife Service has carried out eight major surveys about Americans' interactions with birds and animals. It defines 'consumptive' behavior as fishing and hunting. 'Nonconsumptive' activities include watching, photographing, and feeding animals and birds. In 1991, 40 million Americans age 16 or older consumed wild creatures--26 million went fishing, 4 million went hunting, and 10 million did both. Even more (76 million) participated in nonconsumptive activities, but they formed a smaller consumer market. Consumptive activities accounted for $41 billion of the $59 billion spent on wildlife." (p34)

Crispell, Diane. "Targeting Hunters." American Demographics v16 n1, Jan 1994. p34-38,40. (ISSN0163-4089).

"The CRP [Conservation Reserve Program] authorized in 1985 and continued in 1990, is America's first major effort at reversing declining wildlife habitat on farmlands since the soil bank program of the 1950s. Approximately 36 million acres have been enrolled in CRP, 330,000 of them in Michigan. Ten-year CRP contracts begin to expire in 1995 with the bulk of them expiring in 1997....CRP payments for the 10 years of the program total about $17.4 billion. From that, deduct the $4.4 billion that would have been paid in price-support payments for the crops that would have been grown on CRP land. That puts the actual cost at around $13 billion....The U.S. Department of Agriculture estimates that small game hunting on CRP land generates somewhere in the vicinity of $3.8 billion to $5 billion in economic activity. Add waterfowl and big-game hunting, fishing and other recreational uses and that figure is closer to $10 billion, according to CRP proponents. In addition, there are economic benefits associated with reduced soil erosion (more than $2 billion) and increased water quality ($3.6 billion). Added together, the CRP produces more wildlife and environmental benefits than it costs." (p1 secC)

Gwizdz, Bob. "Budget Axe May Threaten Program That Helps Wildlife." Ann Arbor News 29 Jan 1994. p1 secC.

WILDLIFE MANAGEMENT--U.S. (v19)

WILDLIFE REFUGES--NEW MEXICO

"The world's largest private land-conservation group, The Nature Conservancy...spent $18 million to buy New Mexico's immense and biologically exquisite Gray Ranch. The Conservancy's purchase of the 502-square-mile property, about 200 miles west of El Paso and east of Tucson on the Mexico border, enthralled biologists; within its boundaries are believed to be 718 species of plants, an estimated 75 species and subspecies of mammals, and 52 kinds of reptiles and amphibians, including three on the federal list of endangered species. Some 150 types of birds breed here, and more than 70 plants are rare or endangered. Bill Waldman, director of the Conservancy's New Mexico office, said at the time: 'More separate species and subspecies of mammals are found on the Gray Ranch than on any existing national wildlife refuge or national park in the continental United States.'" (p1)

Selcraig, Bruce. "The Continuing Saga of New Mexico's Gray Ranch." High Country News v25 n3, 22 Feb 1993. p1,10-11. (ISSN0191-5657).

WILDLIFE REFUGES--U.S.

"In 1992 the U.S. Federal government authorized the creation of Monterey Bay National Marine Sanctuary, which covers 5,312 square miles of California coastal waters and is the largest of the country's national parks. It contains a spectacular submarine canyon that is deeper than the Grand Canyon. Oil, gas, and mineral exploration is banned from the sanctuary, and the discharge of pollutants is strictly limited to protect the bay's water quality and amazing array of sea life. A 94-square-mile 'hole' west of San Francisco, however, has been excluded from reserve controls. This area is where dredges deposit their loads and the city dumps untreated sewage." (p34)

"Sequoia Forest Beneath the Sea: Editor's Note." Wildlife Conservation v96 n4, Jul-Aug 1993. p34. (ISSN1048-4949).

WILDLIFE REHABILITATORS

"Whether a sick or injured animal belongs to an endangered or common species, wildlife rehabilitators strive to nurse it back to health and, hopefully, release it back to the wild. Those patients that can't make it on their own are often kept as education animals, accompanying rehabilitators on lectures. There is a network of...wildlife healers that crisscrosses the nation, and it is rapidly expanding. 'Nobody knows how many rehabbers are out there,' says Jan White, president of the International Wildlife Rehabilitation Council (IWRC), a Suisun, California-based organization founded in 1972. Its 1500 members reside mostly in the United States, Canada, and Great Britian. Last year IWRC, which runs the only wildlife-rehabilitator-certification program in the country, granted credentials to 700 rehabbers. Many more, however, are out there than are registered with the IWRC--White estimates roughly 5,000 rehabbers nationwide." (p20-21)

Ten Eyck, Laura. "Special Report: To Heal a Mockingbird." Animals v126 n6, Nov-Dec 1993. p20-23. (ISSN0030-6835).

WIND POWER--GREAT BRITAIN

"Wales is home to eight of Britain's 19 wind farms. Two more are being built and another 20 are planned. So far there are 400 wind turbines dotted along the country's elevated skylines. The biggest concentration is a 30m [pounds sterling] facility at Llandinam in Powys, which provides enough power for 21,000 homes. The Department of Trade and Industry estimates that, eventually, wind power could provide up to 10% of Britain's energy needs. But to achieve that would require building 38,000 windmills across 4,000 square kilometres of land, or 1.7% of Britain's landscape." (p60)

"Britain: A New Way to Rape the Countryside." Economist v330 n7847, 22 Jan 1994. p60. (ISSN0013-0613).

WIND POWER--U.S.

"Wind 'farms,' which arrange individual turbines in rows like crops, harvest their 'fuel' only when it is available in sufficient quantity. In California, that's about 30 percent of the time, mostly in the summer when utilities need extra energy to run air conditioners. The vast majority of existing wind power development--75 percent of the world's total--is in California. But according to the U.S. Department of Energy, 36 other states also have sufficient wind fuel to supply well over 20 percent of the nation's need for electricity....Wind farms offer significant air quality benefits. According to the American Wind Energy Association (AWEA), California's wind farms offset more than 2.7 billion pounds of carbon dioxide, the primary culprit in global warming. Other pollutants avoided, including nitrous oxides and particulates that contribute to smog and acid rain, total another 16 million pounds." (p18)

Asmus, Peter. "Currents: Who Owns the Wind?" E Magazine v4 n3, May-Jun 1993. p18-20. (ISSN1046-8021).

WINE INDUSTRY (v19)

WISCONSIN

see PUBLIC WELFARE--WISCONSIN

WOLVES--BRITISH COLUMBIA

The British Columbia "government has an ongoing poisoning program to reduce the number of wolves in the province. Using a substance called Compound 1080 (sodium monofluoroacetate), the Environment Ministry's Wildlife Branch lays poisoned bait near sites where ranchers have complained of predators harassing livestock....Compound 1080 is classified as a 'super' toxic poison, and was banned in the US by the Environmental Protection Agency in 1989. It is toxic to all life, especially canines. There is no known antidote. Here are some facts: 48 milligrams or less than 1/500 ounce will kill a 150-pound person, and 25% of this amount will kill a 35-pound child. One teaspoon is sufficient to kill between 30 and 100 people each weighing 150 pounds. One ounce can kill 20,000 canines. Death can result from cardiac failure, progressive failure of the central nervous system, or respiratory arrest following severe prolonged convulsions. Contrary to BC Environment public relations, it is not a 'humane' way of 'managing' wildlife." (p11)

"Killing Wolves in 'Super, Natural' British Columbia." Earth First! v14 n1, 1 Nov 1993. p11.

WOLVES--CANADA--U.S. (v19)

WOLVES--EUROPE

"Many European countries that still have wolves are implementing reimbursement programs for farmers suffering livestock depredation. But it remains to be seen whether such programs will placate European farmers. Though currently unprotected and formerly the target of massive eradication efforts, wolves in Eastern Europe remain the continent's healthiest population. In the 1980s, the former Soviet government killed tens of thousands of wolves in a predator-control program involving bounties, poison, and hunting from aircraft and snowmobiles. In 1990 alone, the same government purchased 20,000 wolf skins. Somehow, the wolves held on, suffering only short-term population fluctuations. Current political disarray leaves the region's wolves in question, but they remain the continent's last best hope for repopulation elsewhere. That reality has made educating Eastern Europeans about wolf conservation a top priority for the European Wolf Network." (p13)

Ten Eyck, Laura. "Endangered in Europe: The Big, 'Bad' Wolf." Animals v127 n1, Jan-Feb 1994. p8-13. (ISSN0030-6835).

WOMEN

see also ABUSED WOMEN--U.S.; ADVERTISING--CIGARETTE INDUSTRY--U.S.--WOMEN; AFRO-AMERICAN WOMEN HEADS OF HOUSEHOLDS; AFRO-AMERICAN WOMEN--EMPLOYMENT; AIDS (DISEASE)--WOMEN; CARDIOVASCULAR SYSTEM--DISEASES--U.S.--WOMEN; EXERCISE FOR WOMEN--U.S.; HIV INFECTIONS--SOUTH AFRICA--WOMEN; HOUSEHOLDS--U.S.--WOMEN; INCOME--U.S.--WOMEN; LABOR SUPPLY--AFRICA--WOMEN; LABOR SUPPLY--WOMEN; LIFE EXPECTANCY--U.S.--WOMEN;

LITERACY--WOMEN; MYOCARDIAL INFARCTION--U.S.--WOMEN; NORTH AMERICAN FREE TRDE AGREEMENT--WOMEN; PREGNANT WOMEN--U.S.--TOBACCO USE; SEXUAL HARASSMENT OF WOMEN--U.S.; TRADE-UNIONS--CANADA--U.S.--WOMEN; U.S.--ARMED FORCES--WOMEN; UNEMPLOYMENT--EUROPE, EASTERN--WOMEN; VIOLENCE--BRAZIL--WOMEN; VIOLENCE--U.S.--WOMEN; WAGES--U.S.--WOMEN; WOMEN EXECUTIVES--U.S.; WOMEN IN BUSINESS--U.S.--PUBLIC OPINION; WOMEN IN POLITICS; WOMEN IN SPORTS--U.S.; WOMEN VETERANS--U.S.; WOMEN, INFANTS, AND CHILDREN PROGRAM; WOMEN--CHICAGO (ILL)--SOCIAL CONDITIONS; WOMEN--CHINA; WOMEN--ECONOMIC CONDITIONS; WOMEN--EDUCATION (HIGHER)--U.S.; WOMEN--EDUCATION--U.S.; WOMEN--EMPLOYMENT

WOMEN--CHICAGO (ILL)--SOCIAL CONDITIONS

"The statistics in a recent report by Chicago Women in Philanthropy (CWIP)...[go] beyond the numbers to focus on why women and girls are getting such crumbs from the philanthropic table. Grantmakers' 'stunning short-sightedness is exposed' by the CWIP data, according to 'Shortsighted,' CWIP's November 1992 report. Organizations that help women and girls in need received only 1.4% of the $300 million awarded in Chicago by foundations and corporations in 1990. That's $4.1 million or about 1.4 cents per dollar....With women and children comprising more than 75% of all people living in poverty, says the report, grantmakers are shortsighted if they think we can effectively address the problem of poverty without viewing it through a 'gender lens.'" (p8)

"Grantors' 'Stunning Shortsightedness' towards Women Analyzed in Chicago." Responsive Philanthropy Sum 1993. p8-9.

WOMEN--CHINA

"The number of women in China in their 20s peaked in 1992 and is now declining. This is a milestone for the demographic giant, since it is in the 20s that women are most likely to bear children. Based on the 1990 Census of China, there are now about 123.2 million women ages 20 to 29 in China. Projections from CHINA POPULATION TODAY indicate that the number will decline all through the decade and will be at 102 million by the year 2000, a drop of 17 percent since 1992." (p5)

Kalish, Susan. "In China, the Peak Childbearing Years Have Peaked." Population Today v21 n1, Jan 1993. p5. (ISSN0749-2448).

WOMEN--ECONOMIC CONDITIONS

"Poverty...plagues women in much greater degree than it does men. Three out of 5 single mothers, whose ranks increased from 5.8 million in 1980 to 7.7 million in 1990, live in or near poverty, according to a study released last month by Washington, D.C.-based Women Work!, a training and advocacy organization for displaced homemakers and single mothers. Their median annual personal income: $9,353. 'The perception is that there's been dramatic change for women,' says Women Work! Executive Director Jill Miller. 'The troubling thing about the survey is that it shows it's not really that way.'" (p50)

Guttman, Monika/others. "World Report: Separating the Sisters." U.S. News & World Report v116 n12, 28 Mar 1994. p49-50. (ISSN0041-5537).

WOMEN--EDUCATION--INDIA--PAKISTAN (v19)

WOMEN--EDUCATION--U.S.

"The term equity describes a concept whereby students make career choices based on inherent talents and abilities rather than on stereotypes or biased expectations. Equitable education is a vehicle that allows students equal access to the curriculum in order to encourage a broader range of career choices." (p69)

"Females are indoctrinated to believe that their three life choices are to become a homemaker, a career person, or one who integrates family and career....It has long been known that females have traditionally received lower salaries than their male counterparts. However, the future impact may be greater due to an increase in divorce rates, female-headed families, and the birthrate of unmarried women. Of today's three-year-olds, 60 percent will be raised by a single parent at some time before they are eighteen, and more than half of them will live in poverty. In 1987, approximately 20 percent of all families with children were headed by women, and over 50 percent of these families with dependents under eighteen lived below the poverty level. When considering that 90 percent of American females will work outside the home during their lives and that three out of four wives are presently employed, it is imperative that vocational programs provide equitable educational opportunities for all students." (p70)

Foldesy, Eunice M./Foldesy, George. "Occupational Education: Equity Issues." Clearing House v67 n2, Nov-Dec 1993. p69-70. (ISSN0009-8655).

WOMEN--EDUCATION (HIGHER)--U.S.

"At the University of Michigan's School of Business Administration, just about one in four MBA applicants are women so far this spring, down from nearly one in three a year ago. Other major business schools, such as Columbia and Harvard, have about 30 percent female MBA students. Stanford and Massachusetts Institute of Technology MBA programs come in at 26 percent women. In contrast, the medical field is more equally split between the sexes. Women consistently make up about 40 percent of all medical school applicants in the United States, including at the U-M. And, the number of female applicants--now at about two out of five--is on the rise." (p1 secC)

Moilanen, Kathy Ann. "More Women Shun MBA Path." Ann Arbor News 18 May 1994. p1 secC.

"Women now account for 55 percent of all college students and 59 percent of those in master's programs. For Ph.D.'s, law degrees and medical degrees, the proportion of women is at or near 40 percent, a huge rise in a single generation and still climbing. A new survey of college freshmen showed--for the first time--that more women than men plan to go for advanced degrees." (p23)

Leo, John. "On Society: When 'Subtle Sexism' Is a Con." U.S. News & World Report v116 n5, 7 Feb 1994. p23. (ISSN0041-5537).

WOMEN--EMPLOYMENT

"In the past couple of decades, every country in the OECD [Organization for Economic Cooperation and Development] has seen a rise in the proportion of women who enter the workforce....Since 1980 the number of women with paid jobs has increased by an average of 2% a year. At the same time the proportion of men in work has fallen in most countries--partly because younger men have stayed in education for longer, while older men have been taking earlier retirement. As a result, women accounted for 46% of America's workforce last year, up from only 17% a century ago....On present trends, the typical worker in some rich countries will be a woman by the early 21st century." (p80)

"Schools Brief: The War between the Sexes." Economist v330 n7853, 5 Mar 1994. p80-81. (ISSN0013-0613).

WOMEN--EMPLOYMENT--GREAT BRITAIN

"In 1977 women part-timers in non-manual jobs [in Great Britain] earned 83% of the hourly rate paid to women full-timers in such jobs. In 1992 they earned only 73%. This suggests that the increased supply of women wanting to work part-time put downward pressure on wages." (p81)

"Schools Brief: The War between the Sexes." Economist v330 n7853, 5 Mar 1994. p80-81. (ISSN0013-0613).

WOMEN--EMPLOYMENT--RUSSIA

"Since the 1930s, the USSR State Committee of Labor was producing Lists of Jobs Banned for Women, yet approximately one-third of women employed in industry work in hazardous conditions legally closed to them. More than 4 million Soviet women worked in conditions that did not meet safety standards. Unskilled manual work, which is generally performed by men throughout the rest of the world, is a 'female prerogative' in Russia. In 1989, the share of women performing manual work in industry was 43 percent (compared to 26 percent for men); in construction, 79 percent (compared to 44 percent for men); and in agriculture, 79 percent (compared to 55 percent for men)." (p45)

Mirovitskaya, Natalia. "Women: Women and the Post-Socialist Reversion to Patriarchy." Surviving Together v11 n2, Sum 1993. p44-46. (ISSN0859-6286).

"The total labor pool in Russia is comprised of 86.7 million people. The workforce is 48 percent female and employs almost the entire pool of working age women. Women are found in virtually all occupations except mining and heavy transport. About 46.5 percent of working women are concentrated in industry, construction and transportation, and 13 percent are in trade and public catering. As the result of a distinct trend towards alternative employment in the past two decades, 33 percent of women now work in the social sphere (health, education, arts and culture, and science). The proportion of women in agriculture has declined for several decades and is now only 7.6 percent....From 1979 to 1989, the level of women's labor participation in the former Soviet Union decreased from 84 to 80 percent, while their share of the total labor force declined from 51.2 to 48 percent." (p44)

Mirovitskaya, Natalia. "Women: Women and the Post-Socialist Reversion to Patriarchy." Surviving Together v11 n2, Sum 1993. p44-46. (ISSN0859-6286).

WOMEN--EMPLOYMENT--SOUTH AFRICA

"Domestic work remains the largest occupation for black women in South Africa: More than 900,000 maids earn an average of 250 rand a month, a little more than $80. Often, a maid's job comes with 'accommodation,' a small room in back of the main house, which is supposed to be a benefit but also means the maid is always on call. There is no minimum wage for maids and no job security." (p53)

Eddings, Jerelyn. "World Report: Fighting the Next Battle." U.S. News & World Report v116 n12, 28 Mar 1994. p53-54. (ISSN0041-5537).

WOMEN--EMPLOYMENT--SPAIN (v19)

WOMEN--EMPLOYMENT--U.S. (v19)

"Female high school seniors [in the U.S.] were much more ambitious about their educational and career goals in 1992 than they were 20 years earlier, a recent study shows. Data for the study by the National Center for Education Statistics came from two surveys: the National Longitudinal Survey of 1972 and a 1992 follow-up to the National Education Longitudinal Study of 1988....Female seniors in 1992 were nearly four times more likely than their 1972 peers to expect to attend graduate or professional school--35.4 percent, compared with 9.1 percent. And about half as many girls in 1992 were planning to attend vocational, trade, or business school after high school as had in 1972....The type of work young women anticipate doing has changed markedly. In 1972, 25.5 percent of female seniors expected to be in clerical work--an occupation that attracted only 5.7 percent of the next generation of girls." (p7)

Lawton, Millicent. "Female Seniors in 1992 More Ambitious than in '72, Study Finds." Education Week v13 n24, 9 Mar 1994. p7. (ISSN0277-4232).

"Barely half of the women [in the U.S.] between the ages of 25 and 44 were working in 1970, a figure which climbed to 70 percent by 1986 and is expected to top 80 percent by 1995, according to the newsletter FUTURESCAN. By comparison, more than 90 percent of men in that age bracket work." (p21)

Miniter, Richard. "Women's Successes Smash Business Myths." Insight v10 n8, 21 Feb 1994. p20-23. (ISSN1051-4880).

"In 1991, for the first time this century, the percentage of women in the work force dropped, according to the Bureau of Labor Statistics. During the last half of 1990 and into the first quarter of 1991, 74 percent of women aged 20 to 44 participated in the labor force, down 0.5 percent from the year before. While women's work force participation jumped back in 1992, data show that the rate of increase in the 20 to 39 age group is slowing, acccording to bureau economist Howard Hayghe." (p16-17)

Neuman, Elena. "More Moms Are Homeward Bound." Insight v10 n2, 10 Jan 1994. p16-19. (ISSN1051-4880).

"Women still represent only 2 percent of top-level management [in the U.S.]. And as recently as 1992, only 1 percent of women who worked at full-time jobs--a mere 368,000 nationwide--earned more than $75,000--compared with the 3.2 million men who exceeded that level. The sticky floor is equally real. More than two-thirds of the nation's 54 million working women are clustered in clerical, food service, or sales positions, or in nursing, teaching, or child care. Most are in low-paying slots, with little chance of upward mobility. Eighty percent of all women workers (and 40 percent of full-time women workers) earn less than $25,000. Women are more likely to be among the working poor. More than 4 million families headed by women struggle to survive below the poverty line." (p19)

Nussbaum, Karen. "Opinion/Essays: Removing Barriers for Working Women." The Christian Science Monitor v86 n83, 24 Mar 1994. p19. (ISSN0882-7729).

"The progress women in America have made has been uneven. Women now fill some professional schools--40 percent of medical school students and almost half of law students are now women--and are advancing in many other fields as well. But like men, women without skills, training or advanced degrees are getting left behind in an increasingly knowledge-based economy. On top of that, many women workers are still crowded into traditional 'women's occupations,' including secretary, schoolteacher, cashier and nurse. In 1984, 21 percent of all women workers held jobs in six low-salaried fields; last year, the figure was 22 percent, according to U.S. Department of Labor statistics." (p49-50)

Guttman, Monika/others. "World Report: Separating the Sisters." U.S. News & World Report v116 n12, 28 Mar 1994. p49-50. (ISSN0041-5537).

WOMEN--EMPLOYMENT--U.S.--PUBLIC OPINION

"If most women [in the U.S.] support a 'women's movement' and the majority do not want to return to the traditional family, they are ambivalent about the changes that have taken place. Almost half of the women interviewed in...[an August 21, 1989] NEW YORK TIMES poll felt that 'women have had to give up too much in order to gain better jobs and more opportunities than twenty years ago.' Working women feel extremely pressed, especially when they work full time and have children. Sixty-eight per cent of wives who work full time and 84 per cent of those with children under eighteen said they did not have enough time for themselves. A large majority of these women said they, not their husbands, did most of the housework and childcare and 42 per cent felt their husbands did less than their fair share of chores." (p111)

Brenner, Johanna. "The Best of Times, the Worst of Times: US Feminism Today." New Left Review n200, Jul-Aug 1993. p101-159. (ISSN0028-6060).

"Public-opinion surveys seem to demonstrate strong support not only for feminist ideas but for women's self-organization. In 1985 the majority of women [in the U.S.] felt they did not have an equal chance with men in becoming business executives or entering prestige professions. More women felt that they were excluded from leadership responsibilities (46 per cent) in 1985 than in 1970 (31 per cent). In 1974 64 per cent of women had agreed that being taken care of by a loving husband was more important than making it on one's own, compared to 48 per cent of women in 1985. Although most women are working to support themselves and their families, the majority (66 per cent) would continue to work even if they didn't have to. A marriage where husband and wife share responsibilities is preferred to the male-breadwinner family by 57 per cent of all women. But many women are also conscious of men's resistance to this idea: more than half agreed that 'men are willing to let women get ahead, but only if women still do all the housework at home.'" (p110)

Brenner, Johanna. "The Best of Times, the Worst of Times: US Feminism Today." New Left Review i200, Jul-Aug 1993. p101-159. (ISSN0028-6060).

WOMEN--HEALTH AND HYGIENE--U.S. (v19)

see also EXERCISE FOR WOMEN--U.S.

"According to a 1993 Gallup poll, women are more likely to have had a physical examination within the last 2 years from an ob-gyn [obstetrician/gynecologist] than from any other type of doctor--72 percent versus 57 percent--and the majority of these women, 52 percent, consider their ob-gyn to be their primary care physician. Many of us already recognize the important role that ob-gyns play in providing reproductive health services....We know that ob-gyns administer critical preventive health services such as pap smears and mammograms which can save countless lives. But, we may be less familiar with the primary care services they provide such as blood pressure checks, cholesterol screenings, and identification of domestic violence. According to data from the National Center for Health Statistics, a general medical exam was the second most frequently cited purpose of patient visits to ob-gyns in 1989 and 1990, accounting for 7 million visits each year. A 1992 survey of ob-gyns by the American College of Obstetricians and Gynecologists for the Department of Health and Human Services' Office of Disease Prevention and Health Promotion, found that 71 percent routinely asked about smoking, 55 percent about alcohol use, 51 percent about diet, 48 percent about exercise, and 40 percent about emotional health." (pS16844-16845)

Boxer, Barbara (Sen.-Calif.). "Obstetrician-Gynecologists as Primary Care Providers--S. Res. 170," Congressional Record (20 Nov 1993). Daily ed. pS16844-16845. (ISSN0363-7239).

WOMEN--MEDICAL CARE--U.S. (v19)

WOMEN--SOCIAL CONDITIONS

"Twenty-five years ago, a band of militant women picketed the Miss America Pageant in Atlantic City, tossed bras, girdles and other 'boob-girlie symbols' into the trash and added an epithet (bra burners) and a rallying cry (women's liberation) to the English language. A quarter of a century later, few countries are without a women's movement; few governments are immune to women's demands. Traditional notions of a woman's place are eroding, and gender gaps are narrowing. Yet much of the world is still waging war against women. In 1980, the United Nations summed up the burden of inequality: Women, half the world's population, did two thirds of the world's work, earned one tenth of the word's income and owned one hundredth of the world's property. Fourteen years later, despite the fall of repressive regimes, a decade of high growth, the spread of market economics and the rise of female prime ministers and CEOs, women remain victims of abuse and discrimination just about everywhere. The 1993 U.N. Human Development Report found that there still is no country that treats its women as well as its men." (p42,44)

MacFarquhar, Emily/others. "World Report: The War against Women." U.S. News & World Report v116 n12, 28 Mar 1994. p42-45,48. (ISSN0041-5537).

"As a result of poverty, but also of discriminatory feeding practices in childhood, 56% of pregnant women in developing countries are anaemic, a figure rising to 88% in India." (p1)

"Only 27% of couples use contraception. Each year, 140 million women in developing countries become pregnant although they did not want a child....At least two million girls a year suffer female circumcision. An estimated 85 to 114 million girls and women in the world are genitally mutilated. In some countries, domestic violence is the leading cause of injury among women of reproductive age; between 22% and 35% of women who visit emergency rooms are there for that reason....Certain health conditions, such as chronic bronchitis and back pain, are particularly linked with women's traditional roles. These include burning of biomass fuels in cooking and heating homes, the carrying of heavy loads of water and fuel wood, and the use of household chemicals." (p2)

News release. "Women's Right to Health." WHO Press 13 Apr 1994. p1-2.

WOMEN--U.S.--ALCOHOL USE

"A recent news release from The American Council for Drug Education states that surprising numbers of women are abusing alcohol, and with alarming results. Of the 15.1 million people in the United States with alcohol problems, nearly one third are women. Statistics like these have prompted scientific research into gender-based health issues....New studies show that women who consume an equal amount of alcohol as men undergo a 'quicker and stronger physiological reaction than men, even if their weight is the same.' The reasons have not been fully explained, but it appears that women absorb more alcohol in a more concentrated form than men do." (p22)

"Women Alcoholics Out of the Closet?" Women & Recovery Fall 1993. p22.

WOMEN--U.S.--SEXUAL BEHAVIOR (v19)

WOMEN, INFANTS, AND CHILDREN PROGRAM (v19)

"The United States ranks below 20 western countries in infant mortality. The richest, most powerful nation on earth ranks 74th in percentage of low birthweight infants. A WIC [Women, Infants, and Children] program capable of helping every eligible American family will dramatically...[reverse] this shameful statistic. A General Accounting Office report showed that WIC reduced the incidence of very low birth weight by 44 percent. A study released by the Secretary of Agriculture last year showed dollar savings in reduced Medicaid costs ranged from $2.3 million in Florida to $4.5 million in North Carolina. GAO calculated that the government investment paid for itself within a year--and averted $1 billion more in medical expenses through the age of 18." (pS3747)

Leahy, Patrick J. (Sen.-Vt.). "Senate Concurrent Resolution 65--Relating to Children in Poverty," Congressional Record (24 Mar 1994). Daily ed. pS3747-3748. (ISSN0363-7239).

The Special Supplemental Food Program for Women, Infants and Children's "effectiveness is remarkable. WIC decreases the incidence of very low birthweight by 44 percent. It lowers the incidence of late fetal deaths by up to one-third and increases the head size of infants whose mothers participated in WIC during pregnancy. Head size normally reflects brain growth during pregnancy. But WIC's benefits reach far beyond infancy. Children who participate in WIC appear to be better prepared for school. The 4- and 5-year-olds whose mothers participated in WIC during pregnancy were found to have higher vocabulary test scores. In addition, children who participated in WIC after their first birthday scored higher on memory tests....Not only is support for WIC morally right, it is fiscally right. Every

$1 spent on a pregnant woman under WIC saves between $1.92 and $4.21 in Medicaid costs for newborns and mothers and from $2.98 to $4.75 for newborns alone. A 1993 study conducted by the Department of Agriculture found that the savings in Medicaid resulting from a reduction in the incidence of low birthweight was $4.5 million in North Carolina in 1987." (pE578)

Kildee, Dale E. (Rep.-Mich.). "Introduction of 'A Child Is Wasting' Resolution," Congressional Record (24 Mar 1994). Daily ed. pE577-578. (ISSN0363-7239).

WOMEN ASTRONAUTS (v19)

WOMEN EXECUTIVES--U.S. (v19)

"Among companies with more than 100 employees, white male managers outnumber white female managers by a ratio of 3-to-1, according to a 1990 Equal Employment Opportunity Commission study. But surveys of this kind mask the substantial gains female managers have made at smaller firms. Companies with fewer than 100 employees often offer the best opportunities for ambitious middle managers. A woman who resigns as vice president of a large corporation to run a smaller company has clearly gained, but from the perspective of the EEOC, the economy has lost one female executive--because the study doesn't count companies with fewer than 100 employees." (p22)

Miniter, Richard. "Women's Successes Smash Business Myths." Insight v10 n8, 21 Feb 1994. p20-23. (ISSN1051-4880).

"There are some encouraging signs for female executives scaling the heights of American business. Gilbert Tweed Associates, a New York-based executive search company, reports that 14 percent of 1991 searches were dedicated to finding women and minority candidates, up from 7 percent in 1987. The number of corporate boards selecting women reached a new high of 60 percent in 1992, according to a study by Korn-Ferry International, a recruiting agency. 'Women have been managers in significant numbers only since the mid-1970s,' [Roger] Selbert writes. Indeed, the statistics are impressive considering it takes 25 years of job experience to become president of a major corporation and 30 years to make chairman." (p22)

Miniter, Richard. "Women's Successes Smash Business Myths." Insight v10 n8, 21 Feb 1994. p20-23. (ISSN1051-4880).

WOMEN IN BUSINESS--U.S. (v19)

WOMEN IN BUSINESS--U.S.--PUBLIC OPINION

"Overall, a profound pro-business cultural shift is under way among women [in the U.S.], although some in the feminist movement have been slow to acknowledge it. A recent poll documents the change in the zeitgeist. Of 1,000 women between the ages of 18 and 25 polled by ESQUIRE magazine in December, more than 66 percent say they would rather teach their daughters to start a business than to find and keep Mr. Right. As for the famous argument made by Pulitzer Prize-winning journalist Susan Faludi in her 1991 book, BACKLASH: THE UNDECLARED WAR AGAINST WOMEN, that women have lost ground in recent years, the young women polled by ESQUIRE don't buy it. Eighty-two percent 'disagree that the status of women has gone down in the past decade.' And many young careerists see improvements for women in the business sector." (p21)

Miniter, Richard. "Women's Successes Smash Business Myths." Insight v10 n8, 21 Feb 1994. p20-23. (ISSN1051-4880).

WOMEN IN POLITICS

"Even where female politicians have made gains, women's rights have not always followed. Twenty-five years ago, only three women had run a modern country: India's Indira Gandhi, Israel's Golda Meir and Sri Lanka's Sirimavo Bandaranaike. Since then, 25 more women have been elected head of state or government. Six women prime ministers and three presidents hold office today, as do 300 women ministers in 142 countries. But until recently, when Pakistan's Benazir Bhutto jumped on their small bandwagon, only Prime Minister Gro Harlem Brundtland of Norway and President Mary Robinson of Ireland had strongly pushed women's causes or candidacies. Bhutto, the first woman to lead a Muslim country, was criticized in her first term for failing women. Back in power, she has a women's agenda, including separate women's police stations and courts, a 10 percent quota for government jobs and the expansion of education for girls. But a litmus test will be whether she challenges an Islamic ordinance that allows rape victims to be charged with adultery; some 2,000 women languish in Pakistani jails under the law." (p45)

MacFarquhar, Emily/others. "World Report: The War against Women." U.S. News & World Report v116 n12, 28 Mar 1994. p42-45,48. (ISSN0041-5537).

WOMEN IN POLITICS--EUROPE, EASTERN

"That the democratization of Eastern Europe should be tantamount to the selective political empowerment of men is evidenced by the outcomes of the democratic elections which have been held in the former Soviet bloc. These had the immediate effect of making all of the East-European parliaments far more exclusively male institutions than had been the case previously....The greatest change in this respect has been witnessed in Romania. There, the 1990 elections saw a decrease in the percentage of female members of parliament from about one-third to 3.5 per cent. In the Czech and Slovak Federal Republic, there was a corresponding fall from 29.5 to 6 per cent; in Bulgaria the drop was from 21 to 8.5 per cent, in Hungary from 20.9 to 7 per cent and in the ex-GDR [German Democratic Republic] from 32.2 to 20.5 per cent. Following the 1991 election in Poland, 44 out of a total of 460 members of parliament are women, roughly half the level of representation during state socialism. The government formed after this election sacked the only two women ministers in post, as well as a number of female vice-ministers, leading one observer of the Polish Sejm to comment: 'the liberal, European and modern Congress is reminiscent of an English club where only men are allowed to enter.'" (p72)

Watson, Peggy. "The Rise of Masculinism in Eastern Europe." New Left Review n198, Mar-Apr 1993. p71-82. (ISSN0028-6060).

WOMEN IN POLITICS--U.S. (v19)

"Over the 1980s the number of women running for and being elected to state and local office increased steadily. By 1991, women were 18 per cent of state legislators compared to 4.8 per cent in 1971, and 17.1 per cent of the mayors of cities larger than thirty thousand compared to 1 per cent in 1971. In 1990, a record eighty-five women received major party nomination for statewide office and fifty of them won election, bringing the number of women holding statewide offices to a new high of fifty-nine. Thus, by 1992, many more women were poised to challenge for national office. Contrary to the image of the 1992 women candidates as 'outsiders,' most were experienced activists with political credentials and party connections. On the other hand, 1992 opened unusual opportunities for women candidates: the retirement of many incumbents, redistricting, and a surge of contributions from many women who previously had not donated to electoral campaigns, increased the women's chances to win in both primaries and the general election. In 1992, a record 108 women ran for Congress; 47 were elected to the House (an increase of 19 seats), five to the Senate (an increase from two to six seats). Of course, women are still grossly under-represented in Congress (6 per cent of the Senate, 11 per cent of the House)." (p127-128)

Brenner, Johanna. "The Best of Times, the Worst of Times: US Feminism Today." New Left Review n200, Jul-Aug 1993. p101-159. (ISSN0028-6060).

WOMEN IN SCIENCE--U.S. (v19)

WOMEN IN SPORTS--U.S.

"In 1970, less than one out of every 25 [U.S.] high school girls was an athlete. By 1990, nearly 1 out of every 3 was a girl. The number of female high school athletes has grown by 1.7 million in the last 20 years. As a result, 35 percent of all high school athletes are now girls compared to a mere 7 percent 20 years ago. This is good. This shows improvement. But continued sex discrimination remains a factor in keeping this percentage below 50 percent, which represents the enrollment percentage." (p45)

Collins, Cardiss (Rep.-Ill.). U.S. House. Committee on Energy and Commerce. "Intercollegiate Sports." Hearing, 23 Jun 1993. Washington, D.C.: GPO, 1994. (ISBN0160435307). (Y4.En2/3:103-58).

"The physical, psychological and sociological benefits of sports participation [in the U.S.] are extremely important. We know, for example: Girls who play sports are 92% less likely to use drugs; They are three times more likely to graduate; They are 80% less likely to have unwanted pregnancies; Teenage girls who participate in as little as two hours of exercise a week reduce the risk of breast cancer; Women who exercise throughout their lives stimulate bone growth and maintenance; the fact that osteoporosis is far more prevalent among women than men is partially explained by the discrepancies between sport participation. Eighty-two percent of the top women executives in the FORTUNE 500 companies report that they were tomboys during their school days. This is consistent with what we've been told by Barbara Palmer, former women's athletic director at Florida State University. She said that as her women's teams became more competitive on a national basis, she received regular calls from the headhunters in business and industry. These recruiters have learned that the competencies and attitudes learned in athletic participation are the ones most desired of business leaders." (p132)

Benda, Nancy (Director, Equal Education Opportunity Program, Florida Dept. of Education). U.S. House. Committee on Energy and Commerce. "Intercollegiate Sports." Hearing, 23 Jun 1993. Washington, D.C.: GPO, 1994. (ISBN0160435307). (Y4.En2/3:103-58).

WOMEN LAWYERS--SALARIES, ETC.--U.S. (v19)

WOMEN-OWNED BUSINESS ENTERPRISES--U.S. (v19)

"Affirmative action cannot explain...the explosive growth of female-owned businesses, which grew sixfold from 1972 to 1987, according to Joline Godfrey, author of OUR WILDEST DREAMS: WOMEN ENTERPRENEURS MAKING MONEY, HAVING FUN, DOING GOOD, a book on female entrepreneurs. For female capitalists, 1992 was a turning point. In that year, female-owned businesses for the first time employed more of the U.S. population than the FORTUNE 500 companies. U.S. Census data pinpoint 49 metropolitan areas where female-owned businesses made sales in excess of $1 billion, and the data confirm that the growth of women's share of the national economic pie is continuing. In 1980, women owned 26 percent of the nation's businesses and by 1990 they owned more than 32 percent. The federal Small Business Administration projects that women will own half of all the businesses in the United States by the end of the decade." (p20)

Miniter, Richard. "Women's Successes Smash Business Myths." Insight v10 n8, 21 Feb 1994. p20-23. (ISSN1051-4880).

WOMEN PRISONERS--U.S. (v19)

"The NEW YORK TIMES recently reported that '...the number of women sent to prison [in the U.S.] rose to 2,264 in 1989, from 337 in 1982, an increase of more than 500 percent.' In addition, the report stated, 'it is estimated that women now in prison left 167,000 children behind'--85 percent of women in prison are mothers, mothers who experience real grief at the painful loss of their children." (p10)

White, Karen Marie. "Smashing the Myth of the Gilded Cage." New Directions for Women v22 n5, Sep-Oct 1993. p10. (ISSN0160-1075).

WOMEN SOLDIERS--U.S. (v19)

WOMEN SOLDIERS--U.S.--MINORITIES (v19)

WOMEN VETERANS--MEDICAL CARE--U.S. (v19)

WOMEN VETERANS--U.S. (v19)

"Of...[the] total veterans population [in the U.S.] of 27 million, 1.2 million are women who volunteered for military service....Today, there are over 200,000 women on active duty. They represent more than 11 percent of our total active force. Another 143,000 women serve in the reserve components. While the male veteran population is declining, the number of women veterans is increasing." (p15)

Montgomery, G. V. 'Sonny'. "Vet News: To Serve Her Country." Rollin' Times Jan 1994. p15.

WOMEN'S COLLEGES--U.S. (v19)

WOOL INDUSTRY

"The most recent estimate of world sheep population was 1.12 billion in September 1992, down 3.6 percent from a year earlier. It was the smallest number in 6 years and 4.2 percent below the recent peak 2 years earlier. Of the decline in world sheep numbers from the previous year, three-fourths, 42 million, occurred in Australia and the former Soviet Union. The latest data on world wool production in the 1992/93 season indicates that 3.66 billion pounds, clean (6.35 billion, greasy), were produced, down 3.8 percent from the previous season and 14.5 percent below the all-time record high 3 years earlier. About 70 percent of the decline from 1991/92 occurred in New Zealand and the former Soviet Union. New Zealand had a harsh winter in 1992, while economic and political turmoil continued in the former Soviet Union. The 1992/93 world clip was divided as follows: merino, 45 percent; crossbred, 24 percent; and other (mostly carpet) 31 percent." (p15)

U.S. Dept. of Agriculture. "Foreign Wool Situation and Outlook." Cotton and Wool Situation and Outlook Report Nov 1993. p15-16.

WOOL INDUSTRY--AUSTRALIA (v19)

"Australia's wool industry nose-dived in 1989-90 with the fall in commodity prices. The $6 billion (Australian; US$4.2 billion) export industry fell to $3.4 billion last year. And a government plan to buy up wool from farmers at a guaranteed high floor price backfired when wool prices collapsed and stayed down. A 3.7 million-bale stockpile of wool was left." (p9)

Foster, Catherine. "Economic Reports: Nothing Sheepish about Australia's Wool Industry." The Christian Science Monitor v86 n88, 31 Mar 1994. p9. (ISSN0882-7729).

WOOL INDUSTRY--U.S. (v19)

"In the third quarter of 1993, raw wool mill consumption was 37.1 million pounds, clean, almost 7 percent below the second quarter and almost 1 percent above a year earlier....Worsted-system mill consumption was 18.8 million pounds, slightly above the second quarter, but down 3 percent from a year earlier. The woolen system used 15.6 million pounds, 7 percent less than the second quarter, but 10 percent more than a year ago. The strength of the woolen system in the first 9 months of 1993 has resulted from the currently popular 'soft' look and light-weight fabrics such as flannel in suits, slacks, and jackets, in contrast to the 'hard' look of worsted fabrics. The woolen system's mill use of raw wool during January-September 1993 was 8 percent above last year and 12 percent more than in 1991. In contrast, the worsted system use of raw wool during January-September 1993 was 6 percent below the comparable 1992 period and 5 percent below 1991. Carpet mill use was 2.7 million pounds, 16 percent below a year earlier." (p13-14)

U.S. Dept. of Agriculture. "U.S. Wool Situation and

Outlook." Cotton and Wool Situation and Outlook Report Nov 1993. p12-14.

"Raw wool exports [from the U.S.] in the third quarter [of 1993] were 564,000 pounds, 72 percent of the second quarter and 51 percent of a year earlier....These raw wool exports have resulted from strong promotional efforts overseas by domestic trade associations, wholesalers, and others. Overseas shipments of shorn wool amounted to 385,000 pounds, about 71 percent went to Germany, and 10 percent to Japan. Exports of raw wool not shorn (pulled) were 98,000 pounds. About 40 percent went to both the United Kingdom and Canada. Exports of carbonized wool were 81,000 pounds, about 52 percent went to the United Kingdom and 48 percent to Italy." (p14)

U.S. Dept. of Agriculture. "U.S. Wool Situation and Outlook." Cotton and Wool Situation and Outlook Report Nov 1993. p12-14.

WORK EXPERIENCE

see APPRENTICES

WORKERS

see EMPLOYEES

WORKERS' COMPENSATION--U.S.

"As late as 1985, the average [Worker's Compensation] claim paid $11,500--$3,500 for medical expenses and $8,000 for lost wages. Today, the average claimant gets nearly $23,000--$7,800 in medical expenses and $15,000 in wage indemnities." (p16)

Tucker, William. "Worker's Comp Near a Breakdown." Insight v10 n1, 3 Jan 1994. p16-19. (ISSN1051-4880).

WORKING MOTHERS--MIDDLE WEST (v19)

WORKING MOTHERS--SIOUX FALLS (SD) (v19)

WORKING MOTHERS--U.S. (v19)

"Twenty percent of the preschoolers [in the U.S.] whose mothers worked in 1992 have fathers at home as the primary care giver, and this is up from 15 percent of the preschoolers being cared for by their fathers in 1988. The statistics in 1992 show 16 percent are cared for by their grandparents and 8 percent by other relatives. Thirty-one percent of recent mothers who had a child in 1992 had...less than a high school education as compared to 72 percent that had graduate degrees, and so we see a changing situation among the working mothers. In 1993...the Census Bureau advises that 80 percent of Americans 25 years and older completed high school." (pH1311)

Mink, Patsy T. (Rep.-Hawaii). "Welfare Reform; The Gender Issue," Congressional Record (11 Mar 1994). Daily ed. pH1310-1314. (ISSN0363-7239).

WORKING MOTHERS--U.S.--PUBLIC OPINION

"A 1991 WASHINGTON POST poll found that 55 percent of Americans believed a child is likely to suffer if his mother works outside the home, up from 48 percent in 1989. A 1990 Gallup Poll for the LOS ANGELES TIMES showed that 73 percent of the public believed child fare best when they have a mother at home. And a 1990 Times-Mirror poll found that 73 percent of respondents believed too many children are being raised in day care, up from 68 percent in 1987." (p17-18)

Neuman, Elena. "More Moms Are Homeward Bound." Insight v10 n2, 10 Jan 1994. p16-19. (ISSN1051-4880).

"In particular, women's attitudes toward their work and family have changed....For 20 years, about 30 percent of women surveyed said they would quit their jobs to care for their children if they didn't need the money. In 1989, the number grew to 38 percent. By 1991, it had jumped to 56 percent." (p18)

Neuman, Elena. "More Moms Are Homeward Bound." Insight v10 n2, 10 Jan 1994. p16-19. (ISSN1051-4880).

WORLD BANK

"The report accompanying the Senate Foreign Operations, Export Financing, and Related Programs Appropriations Bill contains the following critique of the World Bank: 'An internal review of the World Bank's loan portfolio concluded that the number of projects judged unsatisfactory at completion increased from 15 percent in fiscal 1981 to 37.5 percent in fiscal 1991. It also determined that borrowers' compliance with loan conditions, particularly financial conditions, was only 25 percent. It found that the role of Bank staff has evolved from independent evaluators of country-proposed projects to advocates of projects to move money and gain promotions, with a resulting decline in project quality.'" (pH10837)

Kasich, John R. (Rep.-Ohio). "Government Reform and Savings Act of 1993." Congressional Record (22 Nov 1993). Daily ed. pH10729-10893. (ISSN0363-7239).

WORMS--NORTH AMERICA (v19)

WOUNDS AND INJURIES--U.S. (v19)

YEN, JAPANESE--EVALUATION

"Japanese exporters, who saw their market share and profits eroded by the rising yen, are hoping that the recent decline of Japan's currency against the dollar will provide some relief in 1994. The yen soared nearly 20 percent from the end of 1992 to a peak of nearly 100 to the dollar in August. But the yen has now declined to about 109 to the dollar, and most economists figure it will weaken further. The reason: Imports of cheap manufactured goods have started to rise at a fast pace, while the volume of exports has declined. This means that Japan's soaring trade surplus is beginning to decline in both dollar and yen terms, an encouraging sign." (p71)

Butler, Steven. "Predictions: Will Japan Inc. Boom Again in '94?" U.S. News & World Report v115 n25, 27 Dec 1993. p71. (ISSN0041-5537).

YOUTH

see also ADVERTISING--CIGARETTE INDUSTRY--CALIFORNIA--YOUTH; AFRO-AMERICAN YOUTH--SOCIAL CONDITIONS--PUBLIC OPINION; AIDS (DISEASE)--YOUTH; ANABOLIC STEROIDS--U.S.--YOUTH; CIGARETTE HABIT--U.S.--YOUTH; FIREARMS--NEW YORK (NY)--YOUTH; FIREARMS--U.S.--YOUTH; GAMBLING--U.S.--YOUTH; GAYS--U.S.--YOUTH; JUVENILE DELINQUENTS; MARIHUANA--U.S.--YOUTH; MURDER--U.S.--YOUTH; RACISM--GERMANY--YOUTH--PUBLIC OPINION; TRAFFIC ACCIDENTS--MISSOURI--YOUTH; TRAFFIC ACCIDENTS--U.S.--YOUTH; VIOLENCE--U.S.--YOUTH; VIOLENT CRIMES--U.S.--YOUTH; VIOLENT CRIMES-WASHINGTON (STATE)--YOUTH

YOUTH--CANADA--U.S.

"The PHYSICIANS FINANCIAL NEWS (Sept. 13, 1993) reports that according to the Centers for Disease Control in Atlanta, Georgia, suicide and homicide rates among [U.S.] children as young as 10 are sky-rocketing. Suicides are up 7.9%, to 9.6 per 100,000; homicides are up 6.7%, to 11.2 per 100,000. In Canada violence among young people is surging. In 1982 young offenders (under 18 years) were responsible for less than 10,000 acts of violence, by 1992 that number had more than doubled to 20,033." (p3)

Lamont, Mary. "What's Been Happening to the Family?" ProLife News v19 n3, Mar 1994. p3,10.

YOUTH--EMPLOYMENT--U.S.

"In 1988, the William T. Grant Foundation Commission on Work, Family and Citizenship issued a report that vividly documented the plight of the 20 million [U.S.] youth between the ages of 16 and 24 who were unlikely to ever attend college. Described in the report as the 'Forgotten Half,' these 20 million young men and women faced a job market in which the chance of finding a good job with decent wages, that provided the opportunity to master new skills and earn promotions, was rapidly shrinking. In constant dollars the earnings of 20- to 24-year-old male high school graduates had fallen nearly 30 percent from their 1973 level, and the teenage unemployment rate was 15.8 percent. For these youth, the report stated, 'their lives as adults start in the economic limbo of unemployment, part-time jobs, and poverty wages. Many of them never break free.'" (pS4684)

Kennedy, Edward M. (Sen.-Mass.). "School-to-Work Opportunities Act of 1993--Conference Report," Congressional Record (21 Apr 1994). Daily ed. pS4683-4691. (ISSN0363-7239).

YOUTH--FRANCE--QUEBEC--SUICIDAL BEHAVIOR (v19)

YOUTH--MICHIGAN--SEXUAL BEHAVIOR

"About one-fifth of Ann Arbor high-school students questioned in a 1993 Ann Arbor News poll said they had a friend with an STD [sexually transmitted disease]. Sixty-three percent of Michigan high-school students have had sexual intercourse, and 26 percent have had it with four or more partners. Of those, only slightly more than one-third used condoms the last time they had intercourse, according to the 1992 Michigan Youth Risk Behavior Survey in Michigan high schools....About one-quarter of the 177 AIDS cases in Washtenaw County have been in the 20-29 age group. Experts believe most of these people probably were infected as teen-agers. Nationally, the number of AIDS-infected teens is growing faster than any other age group, according to the Centers for Disease Control and Prevention (CDC)." (p1 secD)

Martino, Anne V. "At Risk." Ann Arbor News 21 Apr 1994. p1 secD.

YOUTH--NEW MEXICO--MORTALITY (v19)

YOUTH--QUEBEC--SUICIDAL BEHAVIOR (v19)

YOUTH--SOUTH AFRICA--SOCIAL CONDITIONS (v19)

YOUTH--U.S.--ALCOHOL USE (v19)

"Alcohol remains the No. 1 drug problem among America's youth....More and more we read about kids in school drinking alcohol. Statistics tell part of the sad story. About 4.6 million 14- to 17-year-olds in 1985 experienced negative consequences, such as arrests for involvement in an accident as a result of alcohol use. In 1988, more than 800 children up to the age of 14 and more than 8,000 15- to 24-year-olds died in alcohol-related highway accidents. Drivers 16 to 24 years of age represent approximately 17 percent of our licensed drivers but are involved in about 36 percent of all fatal, alcohol-related crashes. Nearly a third of high school seniors believe there is no great risk in having four or five drinks almost everyday....According to a nationwide survey 88 percent of the 790 high school coaches polled said that alcohol poses the greatest drug threat to high school athletes...." (pS889)

Byrd, Robert C. (Sen.-W.Va.). "Unanimous Consent Agreement," Congressional Record (4 Feb 1994). Daily ed. pS879-891. (ISSN0363-7239).

"Drug use among American young people has been making a clear comeback in the past two years. That is the conclusion of University of Michigan research scientists Lloyd Johnston, Patrick O'Malley, and Jerald Bachman, all at the University's Institute for Social Research." (p1) "Two-thirds of the eighth-graders and nearly nine-tenths of the 12th-graders have tried alcohol, while a quarter of the eighth-graders and half of the 12th-graders have used in the month prior to the survey....Asked if they had five or more drinks in a row on at least one occasion in the prior two weeks, 14 percent of eighth-graders, 23 percent of 10th-graders, and 28 percent of 12th graders said they had." (p4)

News release. "Drug Survey." University of Michigan News and Information Services 27 Jan 1994. p1-6.

YOUTH--U.S.--DRUG USE (v19)

"Illicit drug use--led by an upsurge in marijuana smoking by eighth, 10th and 12th graders--is making a clear and frightening comeback among American school children, according to a new national survey. Marijuana use among the eighth graders, for example, increased by nearly 50 percent in the past two years. 'Obviously we must do something different or risk the resurgence of a full-blown epidemic,' warned Lloyd Johnston of the University of Michigan's Institute for Social Research, who has headed the government-sponsored study since its inception in 1975." (p1 secA) "In addition to what Johnston calls the 'fairly sharp turnaround in illicit drug use at all grade levels,' the researcher said he is even more worried about an attitude adjustment among eighth, 10th and 12th graders that has resulted in less disapproval of drug use and a decline in the perception of various drugs' dangerousness....For example, 47 percent of the eighth graders and 30.5 percent of the 12th graders do not now believe that there is a 'great risk' associated with smoking a pack-a-day of cigarettes. Consequently, smoking is increasing among the young people...." (p10 secA)

Cain, Stephen. "Drug Study Finds National Relapse." Ann Arbor News 31 Jan 1994. p1,10 secA.

"In April 1993, the Kercher Center for Social Research at Western Michigan University conducted a drug use survey of Michigan schools. Their report, the 'Michigan Alcohol and Other Drugs School Survey: Report on the Ann Arbor Public Schools,' has recently become available. Some of the more striking findings from the national survey and comparison with the survey report on the Ann Arbor Public Schools are: Marijuana: Nationally, 26 percent of seniors smoked marijuana during the previous year, a 16 percent increase from the year before. In Ann Arbor, 33.2 percent of seniors smoked marijuana during the previous year. LSD: Nationally, 6.2 percent of 10th graders have tried LSD. In Ann Arbor, 8.6 percent of 10th graders have tried LSD. Inhalants: Nationally, 19.4 percent of eighth graders have sniffed glue or similar compounds, an 11 percent increase. In Ann Arbor, 21.8 percent of eighth graders have sniffed glue or similar compounds. Stimulants: Nationally, 11.8 percent of eighth graders have used amphetamines or similar uppers. In Ann Arbor, 12.8 percent of eighth graders have used amphetamines or similar uppers." (p8 secA)

Chaffin, Barbara A. "Other Voices: Ann Arbor Youths Top National Averages in Illegal Drug Use." Ann Arbor News 14 Feb 1994. p8 secA.

"Fewer teenagers these days think drugs are dangerous....An annual survey of 50,000 junior high and high school students in more than 400 schools across the...[U.S.] found that, in 1993, 42.9 percent of high school seniors said they had used an illicit drug at least once by the time they graduated from high school. The study done by University of Michigan researchers also found that 8 percent of eighth-graders, 14 percent of 10th-graders, and 19 percent of seniors said they smoked cigarettes daily--up from 1992 by almost 2 percent....Only 36 percent of eighth-graders, 30 percent of the 10th-graders, and 22 percent of the 12th-graders perceive risk in trying marijuana once or twice, said Lee Brown at the Office of National Drug Control Policy." (p2)

Couloumbis, Angela E. "National: After Years of Decline, Drug Use by Youth Again on the Rise." The Christian Science Monitor v86 n49, 3 Feb 1994. p2. (ISSN0882-7729).

"Drug use among American young people has been making a clear comeback in the past two years. That is the conclusion of University of Michigan research scientists Lloyd Johnston, Patrick O'Malley, and Jerald Backman, all at the University's Institute for Social Research." (p1) Eleven "percent of the eighth-graders (one in every nine) reported using an inhalant in the previous year, compared with 8 percent of the 10th-graders and 7 percent of the 12th-graders. Among 12th-graders, inhalant use has risen fairly steadily from the mid-70s to the late-80s." (p3)

News release. "Drug Survey." University of Michigan News and Information Services 27 Jan 1994. p1-6.

YOUTH--U.S.--ETHICS

"The Josephson Institute for Ethics, founded by Michael Josephson in Marina del Rey, California, revealed recently that lying and cheating among our youth is commonplace. 'We're setting up a kind of backward society where cheaters prosper and honesty is not always the best policy,' says Josephson after a survey of nearly 7,000 high school and college students. Even so, some 71% of college students wish to teach 'firm ethical values' to their children." (p5)

"Optimism Is Dominant in This Journal's 189th Year." Human Quest v207 n1, Jan-Feb 1993. p5. (ISSN0897-8786).

YOUTH--U.S.--RELIGION (v19)

YOUTH--U.S.--SEXUAL BEHAVIOR (v19)

"In 1988, 79% of males (Sonenstein, Pleck, & Ku, 1991) and 53.2% of females (Forrest & Singh, 1990) in the U.S. aged 15 to 19 had experienced sexual intercourse. Sexual activity may have serious negative health impact on adolescents. Unwanted teen pregnancy continues...in 1988, women 19 years of age and younger gave birth to 488,940 infants (National Center for Health Statistics: Advance Report of Final Natality Statistics, 1984; 1990.) Further, sexually active adolescents have remarkably high rates of sexually transmitted diseases; the Division of STD/HIV Prevention (1991) reported that two-thirds of all cases of sexually transmitted diseases occur in individuals 24 years of age and under." (p14)

Wilson, Michele D./others. "Attitudes, Knowledge, and Behavior Regarding Condom Use in Urban Black Adolescent Males." Adolescence v29 n113, Spr 1994. p13-26. (ISSN0001-8449).

"The sexual revolution of the 1960s, characterized by more permissive attitudes toward sexual relations (Hamburg, 1986), resulted in a substantial increase in sexual activity in adolescents (Chilman, 1986). The percentage of sexually active adolescents increased from 10 to 20% in the early 1960s to approximately 50 to 60% by the end of the decade and has remained at this level (Brooks-Gunn & Furstenburg, 1989; Centers for Disease Control, 1992; King et al., 1989; Sante Quebec, 1991)." (p37)

Nguyet, Nguyen T. Minh/others. "Sexual Behaviors and Condom Use: A Study of Suburban Male Adolescents." Adolescence v29 n113, Spr 1994. p37-48. (ISSN0001-8449).

"Age is the single most important predictor of sexual initiation, with 39.6 percent of ninth graders, 47.6 of tenth graders, 57.3 percent of eleventh graders, and 71.9 percent of twelfth graders reporting past sexual intercourse. Moreover, while the median age of reported first sexual intercourse for male and female students was 16.1 and 16.9 years respectively, 33.5 percent of male and 20 percent of female students engaged in sexual intercourse prior to age fifteen (Centers for Disease Control 1992a, 1992b)." (p229-230)

Robenstine, Clark. "HIV/AIDS Education for Adolescents: School Policy and Practice." Clearing House v67 n4, Mar-Apr 1994. p229-232. (ISSN0009-8655).

YOUTH--U.S.--SEXUAL BEHAVIOR--PUBLIC OPINION

"In 1940 teachers named the top problems in [U.S.] public schools as talking out of turn, chewing gum, making noise, and running in halls. In 1990 teachers named the top problems as drug abuse, alcohol abuse, pregnancy, suicide, and rape. A recent Roper Starch Worldwide poll amongst 12- to 17-year-olds and parents found that pressure to have sex at too young an age tops the list of issues that both see as a threat to children. The pollsters found that 46 percent of the parents and 44 percent of the children ranked pressure for early sex as somewhat or extremely threatening to young people. AIDS was ranked as the next biggest threat to young people." (pH1807)

Doolittle, John T. (Rep.-Calif.). "Improving America's Schools Act of 1994," Congressional Record (22 Mar 1994). Daily ed. pH1794-1809. (ISSN0363-7239).

YOUTH--U.S.--SOCIAL CONDITIONS (v19)

"The economic and social well-being of disadvantaged American youths and young adults--those with limited education or skills, from poor families and impoverished neighborhoods, and from minority backgrounds--has deteriorated substantially over the last twenty years....Approximately 50 percent of out-of-school young Americans (those age 16 to 24 years) without a high school degree are currently not employed. And more than 70 percent of young black high school dropouts are currently not employed....Almost 700,000 young men from 16 to 34 years of age were incarcerated in 1989. Richard Freeman of Harvard estimates that approximately 50 percent of 18-34 year old, black male, high school dropouts had criminal records in the late 1980s....A smaller proportion of young disadvantaged Americans are marrying and forming families. Those that do are increasingly poor, as are their children." (p23)

Katz, Lawrence F. (Chief Economist, U.S. Dept. of Labor). U.S. House. Committee on Ways and Means. "Children and Families at Risk in Deteriorating Communities." Hearing, 7 Dec 1993. Washington, D.C.: GPO, 1994. (ISBN0160436567). (Y4.W36:103-43).

"Statistics for the United States show that 24 million children live in poverty, 14 million are being raised in single-parent families, 2 million suffer from abuse each year, and 3 million are victims of crime annually (McWhirter, McWhirter, McWhirter, and McWhirter 1993). Other data point to challenges faced by students and teachers today. For example, 25 percent of adolescents will be infected by sexually transmitted diseases by the time they graduate, 10 percent of adolescent females become pregnant each year, 37 percent of seniors engage in heavy drinking and 37 percent use illicit drugs, and 25 percent of adolescents drop out of school each year (Johnston, O'Malley, and Bachman 1988; Liontos 1991; McWhirter et al. 1993; National Center for Health Statistics 1988)." (p207)

Miller, Darcy. "Using Literature to Build Self-Esteem in Adolescents with Learning and Behavior Problems." Clearing House v67 n4, Mar-Apr 1994. p207-211. (ISSN0009-8655).

YOUTH--U.S.--SUBSTANCE USE (v19)

YOUTH--U.S.--SUICIDAL BEHAVIOR (v19)

YOUTH--U.S.--TOBACCO USE (v19)

"According to a new report to the U.S. surgeon general, nearly 20 percent of high school males use smokeless tobacco; some 67 percent began before age 12. About 28 percent were age five or younger. Use among some Native American youth--including females--exceeds 50 percent. In Sioux County, N.D., a startling 91 percent of the 7th-grade boys dip. Children aren't just casual users; on average, they dip six times daily and consume 3.5 cans a week. 'Nearly 75 percent of our 1992 users admit they are addicted,' the report says. 'Forty-two percent have tried to quit, many two or three times.'" (p23)

Denny, Jeffrey. "Little Dippers." Common Cause Magazine v19 n2, Sum 1993. p23. (ISSN0271-9592).

In the U.S., "some 2.5 million out of 10 million smokeless tobacco users are under 21, according to a 1991 government survey. Close to one-fifth of all high-school males have used it and on average began at age 9....Dubbed the 'stealth tobacco addiction' by one health advocate, snuff dipping is easy to hide from parents, coaches and teachers. Low excise taxes also help make it cheaper than smoking. Teen snuff dipping helps explain why snuff use has increased 24 percent since 1986 even while cigarette smoking in America has sharply declined. But many health advocates say that snuff dipping is as bad or worse than smoking because of exposure to high levels of nicotine and chemicals linked to cancer; dippers quadruple their chances for mouth cancer and are 50 times more likely than nonusers to develop throat cancer. Last year there were more than 30,000 new cases of oral cancer, 75 percent of which are linked to smoking or smokeless tobacco." (p21)

Denny, Jeffrey. "The Kings of Snuff." Common Cause Magazine v19 n2, Sum 1993. p20-22,24-27. (ISSN0271-9592).

The U.S. Surgeon General, Joycelyn Elders, has issued a report on smoking among the nation's youth which "says that by age 18, about two-thirds of young people have tried cigarettes and that more than three million adolescents smoke regularly....To encourage schools to join anti-smoking efforts, Dr. Elders and the U.S. Centers for Disease Control and Prevention have released guidelines for school health programs designed to discourage tobacco use among students....Cheryl L. Perry, a University of Minnesota professor and senior scientific editor of the C.D.C. report, estimates that only 3 percent to 5 percent of schools use the kind of life-skills-training program she and other researchers believe works." (p3)

Sklaroff, Sara. "Across the Nation: Advocates Seek to Increase Anti-Smoking Efforts in Schools." Education Week v13 n24, 9 Mar 1994. p3. (ISSN0277-4232).

"Tobacco sales to minors in New York state in 1991 are estimated to have yielded $39.5 million to the tobacco industry, according to an article in the December, 1992 NEW YORK STATE JOURNAL OF MEDICINE. The authors concluded that approximately 135,700 teens smoked an average of 1.3 million cigarettes a day in the state. They estimated that 60,100 packs of cigarettes are sold illegally to minors every day, or about 21.9 million packs a year in the entire state. Figuring an average pack cost $1.80, this means that illegal sales produce $39.5 million a year. The authors, using the DiFranza and Tye estimate that 31% of total sales price minus taxes equal the tobacco industry's profit, concluded that the tobacco industry makes about $8.3 million a year from sales of cigarettes to minors in New York state." (p8)

"State News: Illegal Tobacco Sales in New York total $39.5 Million." Tobacco-Free Youth Reporter v5 n1, Spr 1993. p8-9.

ZAIRE--ECONOMIC CONDITIONS (v19)

ZAIRE--HEALTH AND HYGIENE

"Political turmoil, economic chaos and widespread armed forces' violence have left over 800,000 people destitute in Zaire. Malnutrition is worsening, particularly among children, who account for some 60 per cent of the displaced....Around 470,000 of the displaced come from Shaba in the Kasai region. Another 135,000, still concentrated in sites in Likasi and Kolwezi, are living in appalling conditions under constant threat of violence." (p4)

"Emergencies Pose Continuing Challenges: Zaire." Africa Recovery v7 n3-4, Dec 1993-Mar 1994. p4.

ZAMBIA

see also HAZARDOUS WASTES--ZAMBIA

ZAMBIA--EMPLOYMENT

"Cuts in the copper mines and civil service, and the enforced closure of state-owned companies, means Zambia's mainstream employment has shrunk from 500,000 10 years ago to 300,000 today. International Monetary Fund (IMF) structural adjustment will eliminate another 100,000 jobs in the next two years, economists predict. As a result, more than 3 million people depend on the fringe economy to survive." (p16)

Nyakutemba, Elias. "Focus: The Informal Sector: Destroying Forests to Make a Living." Panoscope n38, Jan 1994. p16. (ISSN0951-8819).

ZIMBABWE

see also AIDS (DISEASE)--ZIMBABWE; CORN INDUSTRY--ZIMBABWE; PEDIATRIC TOXICOLOGY--ZIMBABWE; PESTICIDES--ZIMBABWE; POISONING--ZIMBABWE; RHINOCEROSES--ZIMBABWE

ZIMBABWE--ECONOMIC CONDITIONS

"In spite of very modest growth in 1991 and 1992, inflation [in Zimbabwe] rose sharply: from 16.1 per cent in 1990 to 23.3 per cent in 1991 and 42.1 per cent in 1992, mainly as a result of devaluation. A massive 40 per cent devaluation in the second half of 1991 was followed by smaller ones in 1992 and 1993. In 1991 the Zimbabwe dollar had to be devalued: exports were virtually stagnant whereas imports had grown by about 25 per cent a year....For lower income urban households the inflation rate was 47 per cent in 1992, against 35.9 for higher income urban households. Between 1991 and 1992 food prices for lower income urban households rose 53.4 per cent against 47 per cent for all items." (p568-569)

"News Features: Zimbabwe: Falling Wages and Rising Unemployment: The Negative Side of Structural Adjustment." International Labour Review v132 n5-6, 1993. p567-571. (ISSN0020-7780).